"No other guide ha[...] a pleasure to read.[...]"

". . . Excellently organized for the casual traveler who is looking for a mix of recreation and cultural insight."
Washington Post

★ ★ ★ ★ ★ (5-star rating) "Crisply written and remarkably personable. Cleverly organized so you can pluck out the minutest fact in a moment. Satisfyingly thorough."
Réalités

"The information they offer is up-to-date, crisply presented but far from exhaustive, the judgments knowledgeable but not opinionated."
New York Times

"The individual volumes are compact, the prose succinct, and the coverage up-to-date and knowledgeable . . . The format is portable and the index admirably detailed."
John Barkham Syndicate

". . . An abundance of excellent directions, diversions, and facts, including perspectives and getting-ready-to-go advice — succinct, detailed, and well organized in an easy-to-follow style."
Los Angeles Times

"They contain an amount of information that is truly staggering, besides being surprisingly current."
Detroit News

"These guides address themselves to the needs of the modern traveler demanding precise, qualitative information . . . Upbeat, slick, and well put together."
Dallas Morning News

". . . Attractive to look at, refreshingly easy to read, and generously packed with information." *Miami Herald*

"These guides are as good as any published, and much better than most." *Louisville* (Kentucky) *Times*

The Stephen Birnbaum Travel Guides

Canada
Caribbean, Bermuda, and the Bahamas
Disneyland
Europe
Europe for Business Travelers
Florida for Free
France
Great Britain
Hawaii
Ireland
Italy
Mexico
South America
Spain and Portugal
United States
USA for Business Travelers
Walt Disney World

CONTRIBUTING EDITORS

Susan Heller Anderson	Rebecca Day	Jill Newman
Lynn Angell	Vicky Elliott	Marilyn Newton
Barbara Bell	John Foy	Carol Offen
Janet Bennett	Carol Frankel	Rosemary Perkins
Colette Boulard	Carolyn Friday	Sam Perkins
Frederick H. Brengelman	Alice Garrard	Michael Perreca
Rebecca Brite	Edward Guiliano	H. W. Rochefort
Bernard Cartier	Mireille Guiliano	Margery Safir
Kevin Causey	Kathy Gunst	Nancy Solomon
Ron Clason	Jeffrey C. Haight	Marcie Stamper
Roger Collis	Ben Harte	David Stevens
Charles Cupic	Amy Hollowell	Nick Stout
Karen Cure	David Howley	Phoebe Tait
Stephanie Curtis	Catherine Lauge	Catherine Temerson
Les Daly	Harriet Leins	Pat Wells
Diane Darrow	Will MacAdam	David Wickers
Jeff Davidson	Maguy Macario	John Yohalem
Linda Davidson	Carole Martin	Kristin Zimmerman

COVER	MAPS	SYMBOLS
Robert Anthony	Victoria Wong	Gloria McKeown
		Victoria Wong

A Stephen Birnbaum Travel Guide

Birnbaum's
FRANCE
1991

Stephen Birnbaum
Alexandra Mayes Birnbaum
EDITORS

Lois Spritzer
EXECUTIVE EDITOR

Laura L. Brengelman
Managing Editor

Kristin Moehlmann
Senior Editor

Ann-Rebecca Laschever
Julie Quick
Beth Schlau
Associate Editors

Julie Hassinger Marks
Assistant Editor

HOUGHTON MIFFLIN COMPANY / BOSTON   1990

ISBN: 0-395-55736-4
ISSN: 0749-2561 (Stephen Birnbaum Travel Guides)
ISSN: 0749-2553

Printed in the United States of America

WP 10 9 8 7 6 5 4 3 2 1

Contents

GETTING READY TO GO

All the practical travel data you need to plan your vacation down to the final detail.

When and How to Go

Preparing

On the Road

PERSPECTIVES

A cultural and historical survey of France's past and present, its people, politics, and heritage.

THE CITIES

Thorough, qualitative guides to each of the 16 cities most often visited by vacationers and businesspeople. Each section, a comprehensive report of the city's most appealing attractions and amenities, is designed to be used on the spot. Directions and recommendations are immediately accessible because each guide is presented in a consistent form.

DIVERSIONS

A selective guide to 20 active and cerebral vacations, including the places to pursue them where your quality of experience is likely to be highest.

For the Experience

For the Body

For the Mind

DIRECTIONS

The most spectacular routes and roads, most arresting natural wonders, and most magnificent châteaux, manor houses, and gardens—all organized into 18 specific driving tours.

A Word from the Editor

To tell the truth, it sometimes seems easier to deal with France as just a chapter in a guidebook that deals with all of Europe than to try to treat this extraordinary country adequately all by itself. In a more general guidebook, it's possible to maintain the fiction that France is a truly homogeneous nation, with a single face and similar sensitivities in every corner of the country.

But the fact is that the diversity that flourishes across the Gallic landscape is extraordinarily broad, and in trying to provide a guide to each separate region it sometimes feels as if there are at least a dozen different countries demanding attention, rather than several areas of a single sovereign nation. Trying somehow to connect the dour visages found along the Brittany coast with the exuberant Mediterranean mentality of Marseilles is quite a task; no less irreconcilable is the Teutonic temperament of Alsatians when compared to the gentle demeanor of the denizens of the Dordogne.

In very practical terms, it's these very broad differences that provide the most compelling reason for the creation of this detailed guide to French life and landscape. Where travelers once routinely visited only Paris and said they'd seen France, there's a far broader recognition nowadays that Paris is no more a mirror of France than New York is an accurate image of the many faces of the United States. Just one tangible manifestation that travel suppliers are finally acknowledging this fact is the host of new transatlantic flights that head directly to such regional centers as Nice, Nantes, Marseilles, Bordeaux, Strasbourg, and others, ignoring Paris entirely. This newly revised guide to France continues our own recognition of the increasing need to treat the world's most popular travel destinations in considerably greater depth.

Such treatment only reflects the growing desire among travelers to return to treasured foreign travel spots again and again. Once upon a time, even the most dedicated travelers would visit distant parts of the world no more than once in a lifetime — usually as part of that fabled Grand Tour. But greater numbers of would-be travelers are now availing themselves of the increasingly easy opportunity to visit favored parts of the world over and over again.

So where once it was routine to say you'd "seen" a particular country after a very superficial, once-over-lightly encounter, the more perceptive travelers of today recognize that it's entirely possible to have only skimmed the surface of a specific travel destination even after having visited that place more than a dozen times. Similarly, repeated visits to a single site permit true exploration of special interests, whether they be sporting, artistic, or intellectual. Multiple visits also allow an ongoing relationship with foreign citizens sharing similar interests and an opportunity to discover and appreciate different perspectives on a single field of endeavor.

For those of us who spent the dozen years working out the special system under which we present information in this series, the luxury of being able to devote nearly as much space as we'd like to just a single country is as close to guidebook heaven as any of us expects to come. But clearly this is not the first guide to the glories of France — one suspects that guides of one sort or another have existed at least since Caesar's legions began their exercise in tripartite division. Guides to France have existed literally for centuries, so a traveler might logically ask why a new one is necessary at this particular moment.

Our answer is that the nature of travel to France, and even the travelers who now routinely make the trip, have changed dramatically of late. For the past 2,000 years or so, travel to and through France was an extremely elaborate undertaking, one that required extensive advance planning. Even as recently as the 1950s, a person who had actually been to Paris, Lyons, Marseilles, or Nice could dine out on his or her experiences for years, since such adventures were quite extraordinary and usually the province of the privileged alone.

With the advent of jet air travel in the late 1950s, however, and of increased-capacity, wide-body aircraft during the 1960s, travel to and around once distant lands became extremely common. In fact, in 2½ decades of nearly unending inflation, air fares may be the only commodity in the world that have actually gone down in price. And as a result, international travel is now well within the budgets of mere middle class mortals.

Attitudes as well as costs have also changed significantly in the last couple of decades. Beginning with the so-called flower children and hippies of the 1960s, international travel lost much of its aura of mystery. Whereas their parents might have chosen a superficial sampling of Paris and Versailles, these young people, motivated as much by wildly inexpensive "youth fares" as by the inclination to see the world, simply picked up and settled in various parts of Europe for an indefinite stay. While living as inexpensively as possible, they usually adopted the local lifestyle with great gusto and generally immersed themselves in things European.

Thus began an explosion of travel to and through France. And over the years, the development of inexpensive charter flights and economical packages fueled and sharpened the new American interest in and appetite for more extensive exploration.

Now, as we are into the 1990s, those same flower children have undeniably aged. While it may be impolite to point out that they are probably well into their untrustworthy thirties and forties (and most firmly entrenched in Establishment activities), their original zeal for travel remains unabated. For them, it's hardly news that the way to get to the Côte d'Azur is to head toward the Mediterranean, make a left, and then wait for the pebbled beachfronts to appear. Such experienced and knowledgeable travelers have decided precisely where they want to go and are more often searching for ideas and insights to expand their already sophisticated travel consciousnesses. And — reverting to former youthful instincts and habits — they are after a deeper understanding and fuller assimilation of French consciousness. Typically, they visit single countries (or even cities) several times, and may actually do so more than once in a single year. Expansion of the routes of France's high-speed *TGV* trains have made their roamings around the French countryside far easier and more efficient, and broadly increased transatlantic gateways within France mean a much easier time mapping regional itineraries

Obviously, any new guidebook to France must keep pace with and answer the real needs of today's travelers. That's why we've tried to create a guide that's specifically organized, written, and edited for this more demanding modern audience, travelers for whom qualitative information is infinitely more desirable than mere quantities of unappraised data. We think that this book — and the other guides in our series — represent a new generation of travel guides, one that is especially responsive to contemporary needs and interests.

For years, dating back as far as Herr Baedeker, travel guides have tended to be encyclopedic, seemingly much more concerned with demonstrating expertise in geography and history than in any analysis of the sorts of things that more often concern a typical modern tourist. But today, when it is hardly necessary to tell a traveler where Paris is, it is hard to justify devoting endless pages to historical perspectives. As suggested earlier, it's not impossible that the guidebook reader may have been to France nearly as often as the guide-book editor, so it becomes the responsibility of that editor to provide new perceptions and to suggest new directions in order to make the guide genu-inely valuable.

That's exactly what we've tried to do in this series. I think you'll notice a different, more contemporary tone to the text, as well as an organization and focus that are distinctive and more functional. And even a random reading of what follows will demonstrate a substantial departure from the standard guidebook orientation, for we've not only attempted to provide information of a more compelling sort, but we also have tried to present the data in a format that makes it particularly accessible.

Needless to say, it's difficult to decide just what to include in a guidebook of this size — and what to omit. Early on, we realized that giving up the encyclopedic approach precluded the inclusion of every single route and restaurant, a realization that helped define our overall editorial focus. Simi-larly, when we discussed the possibility of presenting certain information in other than strict geographic order, we found that the new format enabled us to arrange data in a way we feel best answers the questions travelers typically ask.

Large numbers of specific questions have provided the real editorial skele-ton for this book. The volume of mail I regularly receive seems to emphasize that modern travelers want very precise information, so we've tried to orga-nize our material in the most responsive way possible. Readers who want to know the best restaurants around Lyons or the best places to find inexpensive couturier fashions in Paris will have no trouble extracting that data from this guide.

Travel guides are, above all, reflections of personal taste, and putting one's name on a title page obviously puts one's preferences on the line. But I think I ought to amplify just what "personal" means. I don't believe in the sort of personal guidebook that's a palpable misrepresentation on its face. It is, for example, hardly possible for any single travel writer to visit thousands of restaurants (and nearly that number of hotels) in any given year and provide accurate appraisals of each one. And even if it *were* possible for one human being to survive such an itinerary, it would of necessity have to be done at a dead sprint and the perceptions derived therefrom would probably be less valid than those of any other intelligent individual visiting the same establishments. It is, therefore, impossible (especially in a large, annually revised guidebook *series* such as we offer) to have only one person provide all the data on the entire world.

I also happen to think that such individual orientation is of substantially less value to readers. Visiting a single hotel for just one night or eating one hasty meal in a random restaurant, hardly equips anyone to provide appraisals that are of more than passing interest. No amount of doggedly alliterative or oppressively onomatopoeic text can camouflage a technique that is essentially specious on its face. We have, therefore, chosen what I like to describe as the "thee and me" approach to restaurant and hotel evaluation and, to a somewhat more limited degree, to the sites and sights we have included in the other sections of our text. What this really reflects is a personal sampling tempered by intelligent counsel from informed local sources; these additional friends-of-the-editor are almost always residents of the city and/or area about which they have been consulted.

Despite the presence of several editors, writers, researchers, and local contributors, very precise editing and tailoring keep our text fiercely subjective. So what follows is the gospel according to the Birnbaums, and it represents as much of our own taste and instincts as we can manage. It is probable, therefore, that if you like your cities stylish and your mountainsides uncrowded, prefer small hotels with personality to huge high-rise anonymities, and recognize chocolate as the real reason for remaining alive, we're likely to have a long and meaningful relationship. Readers with dissimilar tastes may be less enraptured.

I also should point out something about the person to whom this guidebook is directed. Above all, he or she is a "visitor." This means that such elements as restaurants have been specifically picked to provide the visitor with a representative, illuminating, stimulating, and above all, pleasant experience. Since so many extraneous considerations can affect the reception and service accorded a regular restaurant patron, our choices can in no way be construed as an exhaustive guide to resident dining. We think we've listed all the best places in various price ranges, but they were chosen with a visitor's perspective in mind.

Other evidence of how we've tried to tailor our text to reflect modern travel habits is most apparent in the section we call DIVERSIONS. Where once it was common for travelers to spend a foreign visit nailed to a single spot, the emphasis today is more likely to be directed toward pursuing some athletic enterprise or special interest while seeing the surrounding countryside. So we've selected every activity we could reasonably evaluate and organized the material in a way that is especially accessible to activists of either an athletic or cerebral bent. It is no longer necessary, therefore, to wade through a pound or two of extraneous prose just to find the very best crafts shop or the quaintest country inn within a reasonable radius of your destination.

If there is a single thing that best characterizes the revolution in and evolution of current holiday habits, it is that most travelers now consider travel a right rather than a privilege. Travel today translates as the enthusiastic desire to sample all of the world's opportunities, to find that elusive quality of experience that is not only enriching but comfortable. For that reason, we've tried to make what follows not only helpful and enlightening but also the sort of welcome companion of which every traveler dreams.

I also should point out that every good travel guide is a living enterprise; that is, no part of this text is carved in stone. In our annual revisions, we refine, expand, and further hone all our material to serve your travel needs even better. To this end, no contribution is of greater value to us than your personal reaction to what we have written, as well as information reflecting your own experiences while using our book. We earnestly and enthusiastically solicit your comments about this book *and* your opinions and perceptions about places you have recently visited. In this way, we will be able to provide the most current information — including the actual experiences of recent travelers — and to make those experiences more readily available to others. Please write to us at 60 E. 42nd St., New York, NY 10165.

We sincerely hope to hear from you.

STEPHEN BIRNBAUM

How to Use This Guide

A great deal of care has gone into the organization of this guidebook, and we believe it represents a real breakthrough in the presentation of travel information. Our aim is to create a new, more modern generation of travel books and to make this guide the most useful and practical travel tool available today.

Our text is divided into five basic sections in order to present information in the most useful way on every possible aspect of a French vacation. This organization itself should alert you to the vast and varied opportunities available, as well as indicate all the specific data necessary to plan a successful trip. You won't find much of the conventional "swaying palms and shimmering sand" text in this guide; we've chosen instead to deliver more useful and practical information. Prospective French itineraries tend to speak for themselves, and with so many diverse travel opportunities, we feel our main job is to highlight them and to provide basic details — how, when, where, how much, and what's best — to assist you in making the most intelligent possible choices.

Here is a brief summary of the five basic sections and what you can expect to find in each. We believe that you will find both your travel planning and en-route enjoyment enhanced by having this book at your side.

GETTING READY TO GO

This mini-encyclopedia of practical travel facts is a sort of know-it-all companion with all the precise information necessary to help create a successful journey through France. There are entries on more than 30 separate topics, including how to travel, what preparations to make before leaving, what to expect in the different regions of France, what your trip is likely to cost, and how to avoid prospective problems. The individual entries are specific, realistic, and where appropriate, cost-oriented.

We expect you to use this section most in the course of planning your trip, for its ideas and suggestions are intended to simplify this often confusing period. Entries are intentionally concise, in an effort to get to the meat of the matter with the least extraneous prose. These entries are augmented by extensive lists of specific sources from which to obtain even more detailed information, plus some suggestions for obtaining travel information on your own.

PERSPECTIVES

Any visit to an unfamiliar destination is enhanced and enriched by understanding the cultural and historical heritage of that area. We have, therefore, provided just such an introduction to France, its past and present, people, architecture, literature, and food and drink.

THE CITIES

Individual reports are presented on the 16 cities most visited by travelers, prepared with the aid of researchers, contributors, professional journalists, and other experts on the spot. Each report offers a short-stay guide within a consistent format: An essay introduces the city as a contemporary place to live and visit; *At-a-Glance,* material is actually a site-by-site survey of the most important, interesting, and sometimes most eclectic sights to see and things to do; *Sources and Resources* is a concise listing of pertinent tourist information, meant to answer a broad range of potentially pressing questions as they arise — from simple things like the address of the local tourist office, how to get around, which sightseeing tours to take, and when special events occur to something more difficult like where to find the best nightspot or hail a taxi, which are the chic places to shop, and where the best skiing, golf, tennis, fishing, and swimming are to be found. *Best in Town* is our collection of cost-and-quality choices of the best places to eat and sleep on a variety of budgets.

DIVERSIONS

This section is designed to help travelers find the very best locations at which to pursue a wide range of athletic and cerebral activities, without having to wade through endless pages of unrelated text. With a list of more than 20 specific special interests, DIVERSIONS provides a guide to the special places in France where the quality of experience is likely to be highest. Whether you seek golf courses or tennis courts, want to go fishing or bicycling, or are searching for romantic château hotels or inspiring cooking schools, each category is the equivalent of a comprehensive checklist of the absolute best in France.

DIRECTIONS

Here are 18 itineraries that range all across France, along the most beautiful routes and roads, past the most spectacular natural wonders, through the most historic cities and countryside. DIRECTIONS is the only section of this book that is organized geographically, and its itineraries cover highlights of France in short, independent segments that each describe journeys of five to seven days' duration. Itineraries can be connected for longer trips, or used individually for short, intensive explorations.

Although each of the book's sections has a distinct format and a special function, they have been designed to be used together to provide a complete inventory of travel information. To use this book to full advantage, take a few minutes to read the table of contents and random entries in each section to get a firsthand feel of how it all fits together.

Pick and choose needed information from different sections. Assume, for example, that you have always wanted to take that typically French vacation, an eating tour of the country's temples of gastronomy — but you never really knew how to organize it or where to go. Turn first to the chapter entitled

Food and Drink in the PERSPECTIVES section, where you will find a discussion of the food specialties and wines of the various regions, a glossary of food terms, and advice on French menus, manners, and methods. Next, choose specific restaurants from the selections offered in each city chapter in THE CITIES, in each tour route in DIRECTIONS, and in the roundup of the best in the country called *Haute Gastronomie* in the DIVERSIONS section. Then, refer to *Useful Words and Phrases,* GETTING READY TO GO, to help you with everything from making reservations to deciphering the menu. We've even provided instructions on how to write a letter requesting reservations (an important prelude to visiting many of France's great restaurants, which are often booked weeks — or months — in advance), as well as a discussion of special food and wine tours and some of their suppliers.

In other words, the sections of this book are building blocks designed to help you put together the best possible trip to France. Use them selectively as tools, sources of ideas, a reference work for accurate facts, and a guidebook to the best buys, the most exciting sites and sights, the most pleasant accommodations, the tastiest food — *the best travel experiences* that you can possibly have.

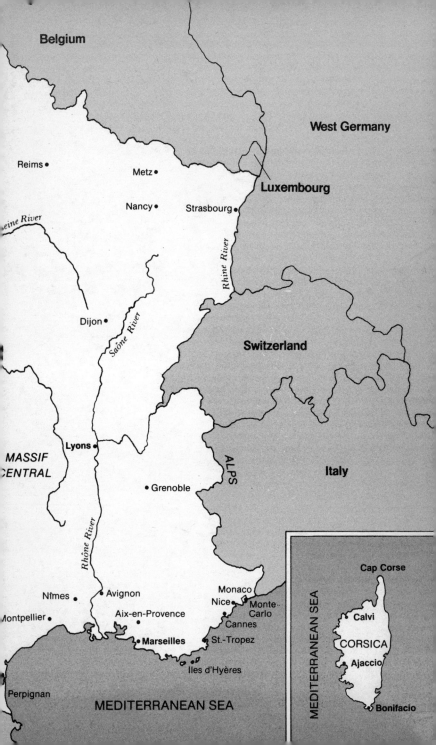

GETTING READY TO GO

When and How to Go

When to Go

 The decision of exactly when to travel may be imposed by the requirements of a rigid schedule; more likely there will be some choice, and the decision will be made on the basis of precisely what you want to see and do, the activities in which you'd like to participate, or events you'd like to attend, and what suits your mood.

There really isn't a "best" time to visit France. For North Americans as well as Europeans, the period from mid-May to mid-September has long been — and remains — the peak travel period, traditionally the most popular vacation time. As far as weather is concerned, France also is at its best then, warmer than Great Britain or Ireland, but more comfortable than many destinations farther south on the Continent, where heat waves are inevitable.

It is important to emphasize that France is hardly a single-season destination; more and more travelers who have a choice are enjoying the substantial advantages of off-season travel; that is, late September through early May. Though many lesser tourist attractions may close for the winter — from around November through *Easter* — the major ones stay open and are far less crowded, as is the country in general. During the off-season, French life proceeds at its most natural pace, and a lively social and cultural calendar flourishes. What's more, travel generally is less expensive.

For some, the most convincing argument in favor of off-season travel is the economic one. Airfares drop and hotel rates go down in the fall, winter, and early spring. Relatively inexpensive package tours become available, and the independent traveler can go farther on less, too. Europe is not like the Caribbean, where high season and low season are precisely defined and rates drop automatically on a particular date. But many French hotels reduce rates during the off-season, and on the Riviera and at other seaside resorts savings can be as much as 30%. Although many smaller guesthouses and inns may close off-season in response to reduced demand, there are still plenty of alternatives, and cut-rate "mini-break" packages — for stays of more than 1 night, especially over a weekend (when business travelers traditionally go home) — are more common.

There are, however, some notable exceptions to this rule. The general tourism off-season is high season for skiers in the Alps, meaning higher prices and crowds everywhere there is snow. And spring and fall are favored times for major international trade fairs — Bordeaux, Dijon, Lille, Lyons, Marseilles, Metz, Nancy, Nantes, Nice, Rennes, Strasbourg, and Toulouse, as well as Paris, all have several each year. Particularly in the larger cities, such major trade shows or conferences held at the time of your visit are sure to affect the availability not only of discounts, but even of a place to stay.

It should be noted that what the travel industry refers to as shoulder seasons — the months immediately before and after the peak summer months — often are sought out because they offer reasonably good weather and smaller crowds. But be aware that near high-season prices still can prevail for many popular destinations during these periods.

CLIMATE: Most people want to visit when the weather is likely to be best, and the most common concern about off-season travel has to do with temperature and rain. Even though the northern French city of Calais is at approximately the same latitude as Vancouver, Canada, and the southern city of Perpignan is at approximately the same latitude as Detroit, France has a relatively mild climate most of the year, generally fair and warm in the summertime and not too cold in winter. But there's more to it than that; the climate of so large a country is hardly uniform. *Please note that although temperatures usually are recorded on the Celsius scale in France, for purposes of clarity we shall discuss climate and temperature using the more familiar Fahrenheit scale.*

To the west, the influences of the Atlantic Ocean soften extremes of temperature and create a pattern of precipitation characterized by a high percentage of days year-round with at least some drizzle. This tempering is most pronounced near Cherbourg at Cap de la Hague, the northern tip of Normandy's Cotentin Peninsula, which projects into the English Channel and which, because of the Gulf Stream, often has winter temperatures as warm as those in Nice. Moving east, the climate becomes more and more of the traditional continental type, with colder winters, hotter summers, and rain tending to fall more distinctly in an alternation of definitely wet and definitely dry days. In the Mediterranean zone of the south, where there generally is less rain, what precipitation there is occurs mostly in the spring and fall. There is more sun, too, making winters milder and summers hotter than anywhere else in France — but less humid.

Mountains further contribute to variations in the climate. There are snow-covered peaks all year in the Pyrénées and the Alps, and parts of the Massif Central remain snow-covered until late in the spring. Mountains also affect the weather in surrounding regions. The Alps shelter the nearby Côte d'Azur, reinforcing the effects of the Mediterranean and giving the area a distinct southern exposure. The Vosges Mountains accentuate the continental climate of Alsace, making it penetratingly cold in winter and comfortably warm to stiflingly hot in summer.

Paris has about the same weather as the Middle Atlantic states in the US, though it's usually not warmer than the middle to upper 70s F in summer or colder than 30F in winter. The weather is most pleasant late spring through early fall (May through September or October), but since there are a nearly infinite number of reasons to go to Paris — the majority of them totally independent of any considerations about weather — it is probable that quite a few travelers will visit at other times. During the winter, when France is warm compared to North American cities in the same latitude, it frequently is overcast or actually raining (there is precipitation during about 15 days of each winter month). Central heating is widely available, but be forewarned that thermostats usually are set too low to effectively warm up drafty and damp historic buildings. Most travelers will find it damp and chilly not only in the dead of winter but also in the early spring and late fall. The lyricist of "April in Paris" clearly hadn't spent many early spring days under the consistently leaden Parisian skies. At other times of the year, a raincoat and folding umbrella still are very handy; even in summer, the city averages 12 or 13 days of rain per month.

Lyons, in central France, is at once a northern city and the gateway to both the Alps and the Mediterranean. It can be colder than Paris in the winter, though temperatures rarely drop below freezing for long and it is less damp than Paris. In summer, temperatures do not rise much above the high 70s F. Spring and fall can be rainy, and thick fogs are an occasional late fall and winter phenomenon.

The Mediterranean climate at Marseilles is dry and joyously sunny almost 300 days a year, with summer days in the mid-80s F and winter days that rarely go below 40F. It rains in the spring and fall in brief but heavy downpours. Marseilles, along with the rest of Provence, can be windy when the capricious *mistral* (a cold, dry wind from the north) whips down the Rhône — fall, winter, or spring — at up to 65 miles an hour, for anywhere from a few hours to a few days. Farther east along the coast, on the Côte d'Azur, Nice is a bit warmer in winter and slightly cooler in summer, and has approximately the same number of days of sunshine (though tourist officials would have you believe it has a lot less rain than it does). It, too, is subject to sudden visitations by the *mistral.* In general, you can go swimming on the Côte d'Azur from May (and sometimes from April) through September, and those who live there often begin sunbathing on their terraces, or in other sheltered spots, as early as February.

The chart below lists average low and high temperatures for specific cities at different times of the year to help in planning. (For information on packing a basic wardrobe, see *How to Pack,* in this section.)

Now travelers can get current readings and 3-day Accu-Weather forecasts through *American Express Travel Related Services'* Worldwide Weather Report number. By dialing 900-WEATHER and punching in either the area code for any city in the US or an access code for any one of 225 major travel destinations around the world, an up-to-date recording will provide current temperature, sky conditions, wind speed and direction, heat index, relative humidity, local time, beach and boating reports, and highway reports. For locations in France, punch in the first three letters of the city (service includes Bordeaux, Cannes, Grenoble, Lourdes, Lyon, Marseilles, Nice, Paris, and Val D'Isère). For instance, by entering PAR, you will hear the weather report for Paris. This 24-hour service can be accessed from any Touch-Tone phone in the US and costs 75¢ per minute. The charge will show up on your phone bill. For a free list of the cities covered, send a self-addressed, stamped envelope to *1-900-WEATHER,* 261 Central Ave., Farmingdale, NY 11735.

AVERAGE TEMPERATURES (in F)

	January	April	July	October
Aix-en-Provence	34–50	44–64	62–83	49–67
Ajaccio	37–55	45–64	61–81	52–72
Avignon	34–49	45–67	61–87	49–68
Biarritz	39–52	46–61	61–73	52–66
Bordeaux	36–48	43–63	57–77	46–64
Cannes	37–54	46–63	63–81	52–68
Chartres	33–43	39–56	53–72	44–59
Cognac	35–47	43–62	58–78	47–64
Dijon	28–39	41–61	57–77	43–59
Grenoble	27–43	41–61	57–79	45–61
Limoges	30–45	39–61	54–77	43–63
Lyons	30–41	43–61	59–81	45–61
Marseilles	36–50	46–64	63–84	50–68
Monte Carlo	46–54	54–61	72–79	61–68
Montpellier	34–52	46–64	61–84	50–68
Nancy	28–39	39–59	55–75	41–59
Nantes	36–46	43–59	57–75	46–61
Nice	39–55	48–63	64–81	54–70
Paris	34–43	43–61	59–77	46–61
Perpignan	39–54	50–66	66–84	54–68
Reims	30–41	39–59	55–75	43–59
Rouen	32–43	39–59	54–73	45–59
Strasbourg	28–37	41–61	55–77	43–57
Toulouse	34–48	43–63	59–81	46–64

SPECIAL EVENTS: Many travelers may want to schedule a visit to France to coincide with some special event. The highlight of a sports lover's trip may be attending the French championships of a favorite game. For a music lover, a concert in a great cathedral may be particularly thrilling and much more memorable than seeing the same church in the course of a conventional sightseeing itinerary. A folklore festival can bring nearly forgotten traditions alive or underscore their continuing significance in modern life.

In France, the calendar of such events is a busy one from spring through fall, with the notable exception of August, when most of the country is on vacation. In winter, too, a great deal is happening. In Paris, the cultural season proceeds at a pace few other cities can match. Museums and galleries mount special exhibitions; opera, ballet, and musical comedy take place at the *Opéra,* the new *Opéra Bastille,* the *Salle Favart– Opéra Comique,* the *Théâtre de la Ville,* and the *Théâtre Musical de Paris Châtelet*; concerts are held at the *Salle Pleyel,* the *Salle Gaveau,* the *Théâtre des Champs-Elysées,* and the *Palais des Congrès*; and there is theater everywhere, from the *Comédie-Fran- çaise* to cabarets and *cafés-théâtres.* Other cities and towns of all sizes promote their own smaller cultural programs.

The events noted below are the major ones, but they are only a sampling. Among the many *not* mentioned are flower shows in the spring, numerous additional music festivals that proliferate as spring progresses into summer, midsummer festivities, and more. Most towns with St.-Jean in their names celebrate the feast day of John the Baptist on or near June 24. Some regions are known for their own kinds of festivals — for instance, in Brittany, where every town or village has a day of religious observance and pilgrimage known as a *pardon.* Some of the more colorful *pardons* — which date back to the days when penitents received indulgences on saints' days and *Ascension Thursday,* and which may be the only occasions left for visitors to see the characteristic Breton costumes in large numbers — are the *Pardon de St. Yves* (the first Sunday after May 19) in Tréguier, the *Pardon de St. Anne* (the last Sunday in August) in Ste.-Anne-La-Palud, and the *Troménie* (the second Sunday in July) in Locronan, where every 6 years (next in 1995) a *Grande Troménie* takes place.

A further cause for celebration not exhausted by the list below is the harvesting of the grape. Almost every district that makes wine also makes merry about it, and while two of the most important wine festivals are mentioned (in Burgundy, in September and November), there are many more — sometimes in the most unexpected places. Even Paris has one, the *Fête des Vendanges à Montmartre*, early in October, to celebrate the harvest in the city's last remaining vineyard on Montmartre. The events in the following list are arranged by month. Since there can be some variation from year to year, check with the French Government Tourist Office for the exact date of anything you don't want to miss.

January
Monte Carlo Rallye: The dean of European motor rallies. Monaco has been the finish line since the first competitors made it to the principality in 1911. Monaco.

February
Carnival: Torchlight processions, parades of floats, flower battles, masked balls, and other revelry begin 3 weekends before *Lent* and end when King Carnival is burned in effigy on *Shrove Tuesday.* Nice.

International Circus Festival: Several nights of competition among the best acts from the best big tops in the world. February 2–6. Monaco.

March
Prix du Président de la République: Horse race at *Auteuil Racecourse*, usually held on *Easter* Sunday. Paris.

Lyons International Fair: A major European trade fair for 2 weeks that continues a business tradition with origins in the 15th century. Lyons.

April

International Tennis Championships: The big event at the *Monte Carlo Country Club*. Monaco.

May

Son et Lumière: Sound and light shows and costumed pageantry illuminate the châteaux of the Loire and their history. May through September at some castles; from June through August, the season is in full swing. Loire Valley.

Festival of the Guardians: Celebration by the cowboy-herdsmen of the Camargue, with parades and blessing of horses. First week in May. Arles.

Joan of Arc Commemorations: Pageants and processions in honor of the most beloved of French saints. Among the cities celebrating is the one she led to victory against the English on May 7 and 8, 1429; the one to which she accompanied the dauphin to be crowned as Charles VII; and the one that remembers her on the weekend nearest May 30, the anniversary of the day she was burned at the stake there in 1430. Orléans, Reims, Rouen.

International Film Festival: The world's most famous film festival. Two weeks of starlets splashing, photographers flashing, nonstop screenings, business dealing, and the awarding of the Golden Palm. Cannes.

Paris Marathon: A mid-month opportunity to see 42 kilometers of the French capital — on the run. Paris.

Musical May: Two weeks of opera, symphony, chamber concerts, and solo recitals in theaters, churches, and country châteaux. Bordeaux.

Grande Bravade: Religious procession and folkloric frolic from May 16 to 19 in honor of St. Tropez. The *Bravade des Espagnoles* a month later celebrates a victory over the Spanish and is less rowdy. St.-Tropez.

Gypsies' Pilgrimage: A gathering of Gypsies from all over Europe to honor their patron saint, Sarah, and others. The celebration in a Camargue village begins on May 23 with a candlelight vigil and ends on May 25 with a procession to the sea. Repeats in October and December are not as showy. Ste.-Marie-de-la-Mer.

Monaco Grand Prix: A major Formula I motor race in late May or early June. Run since 1929 right through the streets of Monaco.

Feria de la Pentecôte: Five days of bullfights, bull races, folk dancing, and flamenco in an ancient southern town. Late May or early June. Nímes.

Lyons International Festival: Three weeks or so of classical music, jazz, theater, and dance, from late May into June, in many locations, including a Roman amphitheater. Lyons.

French Open Tennis Championships: The first of the *Grand Slam* tournaments, bridging the months of May and June at *Roland Garros Stadium*. Paris.

June

Paris International Air Show: Aviation fair held only in odd-numbered years at Le Bourget Airport. Paris.

Strasbourg International Music Festival: Two weeks of first-rate music, some of it soaring in the city's superb Gothic cathedral. Strasbourg.

Festival du Paris: Music, dance, opera. Each year the culture of a different foreign country is highlighted. Mid-May to the end of June. Paris.

Grand Steeplechase de Paris: Major horse race and opening event of the *Grande Semaine* (Big Week). Next to last Sunday of the month at *Auteuil Racecourse*. Paris.

Grand Prix de Paris: The original grand prix — a horse race, not a motor race — first run in 1863. Part of the *Grande Semaine,* this classic test for 3-year-olds takes place the last Sunday of the month at *Longchamp Racecourse.* Paris.

The 24 Hours of Le Mans: A grueling 2-day tear around one of the most famous motor racing circuits in the world. Le Mans.

July

Grand Prix de France de Formule I: Motor racing at Le Castellet in early July.

Grand Jazz Parade: A 10-day (and night) jazz festival–jam session attracting top performers from the US and the Continent. Nice.

Bastille Day: July 14, the anniversary of the storming of the Bastille prison in 1789; France's national holiday. Celebrated everywhere with parades, fireworks, and dancing in the streets, but nowhere more colorfully than in Paris, where it all began, or in the medieval town of Carcassonne, which goes up in mock flames. Nationwide.

Tour de France: Arrival on the Champs-Elysées of the most famous bicycle race of them all, some 3 weeks (starts late June to early July) and 2,000-plus miles from the starting point. All Paris turns out for the late July finish. Paris.

Festival d'Avignon: France's theater festival par excellence, presenting the classic, the contemporary, the French, and the foreign in an early July to early August wrap-up of the state of the stage art. Avignon.

International Festival of Lyric Art and Music: About 3 weeks of high-caliber music making, especially by the vocal cords, from mid-July to early August. Aix-en-Provence.

Chorégies d'Orange: A 3-week festival of opera and choral works. Three or four productions are staged beautifully each year. Mid-July to early August. Orange.

International Fireworks Festival: Several nights of spectacular displays by the world's most skilled pyrotechnists. Mid-July to early August. Monaco.

Festival Estival: Concerts of classical music, from antique to very modern, in churches, museums, concert halls, and in great quantity, filling the mid-July to late-September gap between the capital's *Festival du Paris* and the *Festival d'Automne* to come. Paris.

August

Basque Folk Festival: A week of singing, dancing, *pelote* games, and bullfights, which bridges the end of July and the beginning of August in Bayonne, the chief town of French Basque country.

Red Cross Gala: An elegant and expensive dinner-dance at the *Monte Carlo Sporting Club* to benefit the Monégasque Red Cross. Monaco.

September

Music Festival of Besançon and Franche-Comté: Almost a month of classical, particularly chamber, music, highlighted by a contest for young conductors. Besançon, Doubs.

Fête de la Vigne–Fête Folklorique Internationale: A grape harvest–cum–folklore festival that sings (in a medley of tongues), dances, and tastes its way along a Burgundy wine route. Dijon, Côte d'Or.

Festival Berlioz: A 10-day celebration of the composer's music in his hometown and in a city where he performed. La Côte St.-André, Lyons.

Festival d'Automne: Music, dance, and theater festival, stressing the contemporary in these arts. Mid-September to December. Paris.

October

Prix de l'Arc de Triomphe: Horse race at *Longchamp Racecourse* run since 1920; the stakes are high. First Sunday of the month. Paris.

November

International Food and Wine Fair: A major trade fair showcasing the finest food and wine from all over the world. Dijon.

Les Trois Glorieuses: Three glorious days of wine-related merrymaking including the most important wine auction of the year. The third Saturday, Sunday, and Monday of the month at three sites in Burgundy. Clos-de-Vougeot, Beaune, Meursault.

December

Santons Fair: Christmas crib figures on display in crèches and for sale in the main streets of this Mediterranean port city, the last Sunday in November through *Epiphany.* Marseilles.

Shepherd's Festival: A centuries-old tradition at *Christmas:* midnight mass in a tiny hilltop village in Provence. Les-Baux-de-Provence.

Traveling by Plane

Flying is the most efficient way to get to France, and it is the quickest, most convenient means of travel between different parts of the country once you are there. Although touring by car, bus, or train is certainly the most scenic way to see the countryside, and the distances between major destinations are not all that great, most travelers only have time to explore one area. Cruise ships generally function as hotels for passengers cruising European waters rather than as efficient transportation to a single country. Air travel is far faster and more direct — the less time spent in transit, the more time spent at your destinations in France.

The air space between North America and Europe is the most heavily trafficked in the world. It is served by dozens of airlines, almost all of which sell seats at a variety of prices under widely different terms. Since you probably will spend more for your airfare than for any other single item in your travel budget, try to take advantage of the lowest fare offered by either scheduled or charter companies. You should know what kinds of flights are available, the rules and regulations pertaining to air travel, and all the special package options.

SCHEDULED FLIGHTS: Among the dozens of airlines serving Europe from the United States, those offering regularly scheduled flights to France, many on a daily basis, are *Air France, American, British Airways, Continental, Delta, Egypt Air, Lufthansa, Northwest, Pakistan International, Pan American, SAS (Scandinavian Air Systems), SwissAir, TWA, United,* and *UTA (Union of Transport Air).*

Gateways – At present, nonstop flights to France depart from Anchorage, Atlanta, Boston, Chicago, Dallas/Fort Worth, Houston, Los Angeles, Miami, New York, Newark, Raleigh, St. Louis, San Francisco, and Washington, DC. Additional direct flights (meaning, usually, that there is no change of flight number between the originating and terminating cities, though there may be one or more stops en route and perhaps a change of plane) depart from some of the above cities and a few others as well.

Nonstop or direct, the majority of these flights land in Paris, either at Charles de Gaulle or Orly airports. A number of carriers, however, have expanded their routes to include other destinations in France. *American* flies nonstop to Lyons; *Air France* flies nonstop to Lille, Lyons, Nice, and Strasbourg; *Pan American* flies to Nice; and *UTA* offers nonstop flights to Bordeaux, Nantes, and Toulouse, and additional nonstop or direct flights to Marseilles and Montpellier.

Tickets – When traveling on one of the many regularly scheduled flights, a full-fare ticket provides maximum travel flexibility (although at considerable expense), because tickets are sold on an open reservation system. This means that there are no advance booking requirements: A prospective passenger can buy a ticket for a flight right up to the minute of takeoff — if a seat is available. If your ticket is for a round trip, you can make the return reservation any time you wish — months before you leave or the day before you return. Assuming any paperwork required for stays in France of longer than 3 months is in order, you can remain at your destination for as long as you like. (Tickets generally are good for a year and can be renewed if not used.) You also can cancel your flight at any time without penalty. However, while it is true that this category of ticket can be purchased at the last minute, it is advisable to reserve well in advance during popular travel periods and around holiday times.

No matter what kind of ticket you buy, it is wise to reconfirm that you will be using your return reservations. For instance, if you do not call the airline to let them know you will be using the return leg of your reservation, they (or their computer) may assume you are not coming and automatically cancel your seat. For further information, see "Reservations," below.

Fares – Airfares continue to change so rapidly that even experts find it difficult to keep up with them. This ever-changing situation is due to a number of factors, including airline deregulation, volatile labor and fuel costs, and vastly increased competition. Before the Airline Deregulation Act of 1978, US airlines had no choice but to set their rates and routes within the guidelines of the Civil Aeronautics Board (CAB), and they could compete for passengers only by offering better service than their competitors. With the loosening of controls (and the elimination of the CAB), airlines are now engaged in a far more intense competition relating to prices and schedules, which has opened the door to a wide range of discount fares and promotional offers. Intensifying the competitive atmosphere has been the creation of several new carriers offering fewer frills and far lower prices. These carriers seem to appear and disappear with dismaying regularity. They have, however, served to drive down fares from time to time and make the older, more entrenched carriers aware that they are in a genuine competition for travelers' dollars. As Europe, too, moves closer to the deregulation of airline fares, the price of intra-European and other international travel is expected to lessen as well.

Perhaps the most common misconception about fares on scheduled airlines is that the cost of the ticket determines how much service will be provided on the flight. This is true only to a certain extent. A far more realistic rule of thumb is that the less you pay for your ticket, the more restrictions and qualifications are likely to come into play before you board the plane (as well as after you get off). These qualifying aspects relate to the months during which you must travel, how far in advance you must purchase your ticket, the minimum and maximum amount of time you may or must remain abroad, your willingness to make up your mind concerning a return date at the time of booking — and your ability to stick to that decision. It is not uncommon for passengers sitting side by side on the same wide-body jet to have paid fares varying by hundreds of dollars, and all too often the traveler paying more would have been equally willing to accept the terms regulating the far less expensive ticket. The ticket you buy will fall into one of several fare categories currently being offered by scheduled carriers flying between the US and France.

In general, the great variety of fares between the US and France can be reduced to four basic categories, including first class, coach (also called economy or tourist class), and excursion or discount fares. The fourth category, called business class (an intermediate between first class and coach, with many of the amenities of first class and more legroom than coach), has been added by many airlines in recent years. In addition, Advance Purchase Excursion (APEX) and "Eurosaver" fares offer savings under certain conditions.

In a class by itself is the *Concorde,* the supersonic jet developed jointly by France and Great Britain that cruises at speeds of 1,350 miles an hour (twice the speed of sound) and makes transatlantic crossings in half the time of conventional, subsonic jets. *Air France* offers *Concorde* service to Paris from New York; *British Airways* flies from Miami, Washington, DC, and New York to London. Additionally, *British Airways* has an arrangement with *Enterprise Airlines* for connecting flights between Boston and New York for the *Concorde* service; those taking a *British Airways'* *Concorde* flight from New York to London can buy the ticket in conjunction with a business class ticket to Paris (on a regular, subsonic jet). Service is "single" class (with champagne and caviar all the way) and the fare is expensive, about 20% more than a first class ticket on a subsonic aircraft. Some discounts have been offered, but time is the real gift of the *Concorde:* It makes a New York to Paris run in 3¾ hours.

A first class ticket is your admission to the special section of the aircraft with larger seats, more legroom, sleeperette seating on some wide-body aircraft, better (or at least more elaborately served) food, free drinks, free headsets for movies and music channels, and above all, personal attention. First class fares are about double those of full-fare economy, although both first class passengers and people paying economy fares are entitled to reserve seats and are sold tickets on an open reservation system. An additional advantage of a first class ticket is that if you're planning to visit several cities within France or elsewhere in Europe, you may include any number of stops en route to your most distant destination, provided that certain set, but generous, maximum permitted mileage limits are respected.

Not too long ago, there were only two classes of air travel, first class and all the rest, usually called economy or tourist. But because passengers paying full economy fares traveled in the same compartment as those flying for considerably less on various promotional or discount fares, the airlines introduced special services to compensate those paying the full price. Thus, business class came into being — one of the most successful of recent airline innovations. At first, business class passengers were merely curtained off from the other economy passengers. Now a separate cabin or cabins — usually toward the front of the plane — is the norm. While standards of comfort and service are not as high as in first class, they represent a considerable improvement over conditions in the rear of the plane, with roomier seats, more legroom and shoulder space between passengers, and fewer seats abreast. Free liquor and headphones, a choice of meal entrées, and a separate counter for speedier check-in are other inducements. As in first class, a business class passenger may travel on any scheduled flight he or she wishes, may buy a one-way or round-trip ticket, and have the ticket remain valid for a year. There are no minimum or maximum stay requirements, no advance booking requirements, and no cancellation penalties, and the fare allows the same free stopover privileges as first class. Airlines often have their own names for their business class service — such as Le Club on *Air France,* Clipper Class on *Pan American,* and Ambassador Class on *TWA.*

The terms of the coach or economy fare may vary slightly from airline to airline, and, in fact, from time to time airlines may be selling more than one type of economy fare. Economy fares sell for substantially less than business fares, the savings effected by limited frills and stopovers. Coach or economy passengers sit more snugly, as many as 10 in a single row on a wide-body jet, behind the first class and business class sections, and receive standard meal service. Alcoholic drinks are not free, nor are the headsets (except on *British Airways,* which does offer these services free of charge). If there are two economy fares on the books, one (often called "regular economy") may still offer unlimited stopovers. The other, less expensive fare (often called "special economy") may limit stopovers to one or two, with a charge (typically $25) for each one. Like first class passengers, however, passengers paying the full coach fare are subject to none of the restrictions that usually are attached to less expensive discount fares. There are no advance booking requirements, no minimum stay requirements, and no cancellation penalties. Tickets are sold on an open reservation system: They can be bought for a flight up to the minute of takeoff (if seats are available), and if the ticket is round-trip, the return reservation can be made any time you wish — months before you leave or the day before you return. Both first class and coach tickets generally are good for a year, after which they can be renewed if not used, and if you ultimately decide not to fly at all, your money will be refunded. The cost of economy and business class tickets does not vary much in the course of the year between the US and France, though on some transatlantic routes they vary in price from a basic (low-season) price in effect most of the year to a peak (high-season) price during the summer.

Excursions and other discount fares are the airlines' equivalent of a special sale, and usually apply to round-trip bookings. These fares generally differ according to the season and the number of travel days permitted. They are only a bit less flexible than full-fare economy tickets and are, therefore, useful for both business travelers and tourists. Most round-trip excursion tickets include strict minimum and maximum stay requirements and reservations can be changed only within the prescribed time limits. So don't count on extending a ticket beyond the established time of return or staying less time than required. Different airlines may have different regulations concerning the number of stopovers permitted, and sometimes excursion fares are less expensive during midweek. Needless to say, these reduced-rate seats are most limited at busy times such as holidays, when full-fare coach seats sell more quickly than usual. Passengers fortunate enough to get a discount or excursion fare ticket sit with the coach passengers, and, for all intents and purposes, are indistinguishable from them. They receive all the same basic services, even though they have paid anywhere between 30% and 55% less for the trip. Obviously, it's wise to make plans early enough to qualify for this less expensive transportation.

These discount or excursion fares may masquerade under a variety of names, they may vary from city to city (from the East Coast to the West Coast, especially), but they invariably have strings attached. A common requirement is that the ticket be purchased a certain number of days — usually no fewer than 7 or 14 days — in advance of departure, though it may be booked weeks or months in advance (it has to be "ticketed," or paid for, shortly after booking, however). The return reservation usually has to be made at the time of the original ticketing and cannot be changed later than a certain number of days (again, usually 7 or 14 days) before the return flight. If events force a passenger to change the return reservation after the date allowed, the difference between the round-trip excursion rate and the round-trip coach rate probably will have to be paid, though most airlines allow passengers to use their discounted fares by standing by for an empty seat, even if they don't otherwise have standby fares. Another common condition is a minimum and maximum stay requirement; for example, 6 to 14 days or 1 to 6 days, but including at least a Saturday night. Last, cancellation penalties of up to 50% of the full price of the ticket have been assessed — check the specific penalty in effect when you purchase your discount/excursion ticket — so careful planning is imperative.

Of even greater risk — and bearing the lowest price of all the current discount fares — is the ticket where no change at all in departure and/or return flights is permitted, and where the ticket price is totally nonrefundable. If you do buy a nonrefundable ticket, you should be aware of a new policy followed by many airlines, regarding international flights, that may make it easier to change your plans if necessary. For a fee — set by each airline and payable at the airport when checking in — you *may* be able to change the time or date of a return flight on a nonrefundable ticket. However, if the nonrefundable ticket price for the replacement flight is higher than that of the original (as generally is the case when trading in a weekday for a weekend flight), you will have to pay the difference. Any such change must be made a certain number of days in advance — in some cases as little as 2 days — of either the original or the replacement flight, whichever is earlier; restrictions are set by the individual carrier.

In the past, some excursion fares offered to France came unencumbered by advance booking requirements and cancellation penalties, permitted one stopover (but not a free one) in each direction, and had "open jaws," meaning that you could fly to one city and depart from another, arranging and paying for your own transportation between the two. Excursion fares of this type do not, at present, exist on flights between the US and France, but a newer and less expensive type of excursion, the APEX, or advance purchase excursion, does.

As with traditional excursion fares, passengers paying an APEX fare sit with and receive the same basic services as any other coach or economy passengers, even though they may have paid up to 50% less for their seats. In return, they are subject to certain restrictions. The ticket usually is good for a minimum of 7 days abroad and a maximum, currently, in the case of tickets to France, of 6 months; and as its name implies, it must be "ticketed" or paid for in its entirety a certain period of time before departure — usually 21 days. The drawback to an APEX fare is that it penalizes travelers who change their minds — and travel plans. The return reservation must be made at the time of the original ticketing, and if for some reason you change your schedule while abroad, you pay a penalty of $100 or 10% of the ticket value, whichever is greater, as long as you travel within the validity period of your ticket. But if you change your return to a date less than the minimum stay or more than the maximum stay, the difference between the round-trip APEX fare and the full round-trip coach rate will have to be paid. There also is a penalty of $125 or more for canceling or changing a reservation *before* travel begins — check the specific penalty in effect when you purchase your ticket. No stopovers are allowed on an APEX ticket, but it is possible to create an open-jaw effect by buying an APEX on a split-ticket basis; i.e., flying to Paris and returning from Nice (or some other city). The total price would be half the price of an APEX to Paris plus half the price of an APEX to Nice. APEX tickets to France are sold at basic and peak rates (peak season is around May through September) and may include surcharges for weekend flights.

There also is a Winter or Super APEX, which may go under different names for different carriers (*Air France* calls it "Eurosaver", for example). Similar to the regular APEX fare, it costs slightly less, but is more restrictive. It is available only for off-peak winter travel and is limited to a stay of between 7 and 21 days. Advance purchase still is required (currently, 30 days prior to travel), and ticketing must be completed within 48 hours of reservation. The fare is nonrefundable except in cases of hospitalization or death.

Another type of fare that sometimes is available is the youth fare. At present, most airlines flying to France are using a form of APEX fare as a youth fare for those through age 25. The maximum stay is extended to a year, and the return booking must be left open. Seats can be reserved no more than 3 days before departure, and tickets must be purchased when the reservation is made. The return is booked from France in the same manner, no more than 3 days before flight time. There is no cancellation penalty, but the fare is subject to availability, so it may be difficult to book a return during peak travel periods.

Standby fares, at one time the rock-bottom price at which a traveler could fly to Europe, have become rather elusive. At the time of this writing, most major scheduled airlines did not regularly offer standby fares on direct flights to France. Because airline fares and their conditions constantly change, however, bargain hunters should not hesitate to ask if such a fare exists at the time they plan to travel.

While the definition of standby varies somewhat from airline to airline, it generally means that you make yourself available to buy a ticket for a flight (usually no sooner than the day of departure), then literally stand by on the chance that a seat will be empty. Once aboard, however, a standby passenger has the same meal service and frills (or lack of them) enjoyed by others in the economy class compartment.

Something else to check is the possibility of qualifying for a GIT (group inclusive travel) fare, which requires that a specific dollar amount of ground arrangements be purchased, in advance, along with the ticket. The requirements vary as to number of travel days and stopovers permitted, and the number of passengers required for a group. (The last can be as few as two full fares.) The actual fares also vary, but the cost will be spelled out in brochures distributed by the tour operators handling the ground arrangements. In the past, GIT fares typically were among the least expensive in the fare schedules of the established carriers. But although very attractive group fares still may appear from time to time, the advent of discount fares has caused group fares to all but disappear from some air routes, or their price tags become the equivalent of the other discount fares. Travelers reading brochures on group package tours to France will find that, in almost all cases, the applicable airfare given as a sample (to be added to the price of the land package to obtain the total tour price) is an APEX fare, the same discount fare available to the independent traveler.

The major airlines serving France from the US sometimes also offer individual fare excursion rates similar to GIT fares, which are sold in conjunction with ground accommodation packages. Previously called ITX, these fares generally are offered as part of "air/hotel/car/transfer packages," and can reduce the cost of an economy fare by more than a third. The packages are booked for a specific amount of time, with return dates specified; rescheduling and cancellation restrictions and penalties vary from carrier to carrier. These fares are offered to Bordeaux, Cannes, and Paris, as well as to other popular destinations in France. At the time of this writing, this type of fare was offered by *American, Pan American, Northwest,* and *TWA,* but only *Pan American*'s offer represented a substantial savings over the standard economy fare. (For further information on package options, see *Package Tours,* in this section.)

Finally, travelers looking for the least expensive possible airfares should scan the pages of their local newspapers for announcements of special promotional fares. Most major airlines traditionally have offered their most attractive special fares to encourage travel during slow seasons and to inaugurate and publicize new routes. Even if none of these conditions apply, prospective passengers can be fairly sure that the number of discount seats per flight at the lowest price is strictly limited, or that the fare offering includes a set expiration date — which means it's absolutely necessary to move fast to obtain the lowest possible price. Unfortunately, special fare offers can come and go quickly, and may not be available precisely when you want to travel.

Among other special airline promotional deals for which you should be on the lookout are discount or upgrade coupons, sometimes offered by the major carriers and found in mail order merchandise catalogues. For instance, *Pan American* recently issued coupons which cost $25 each and were good for a 25% discount or an upgrade on an international airline ticket — including flights to France. The only requirement beyond the $25 fee was that a coupon purchaser was required to buy at least one item from the catalogue. There usually are some minimum airfare restrictions before the coupon is redeemable, but in general these are worthwhile offers. Restrictions often include certain blackout days (when the coupon cannot be used at all) during peak travel periods. These coupons are particularly valuable to business travelers who tend to buy full-fare tickets, and while the coupons are issued in the buyer's name, they can be used by others who are traveling on the same itinerary.

Given the frequency with which the airfare picture changes, it is more than possible that by the time you are ready to fly, the foregoing discussion may be somewhat out of date. That's why it is always wise to comparison shop, and that requires reading the business and travel sections of your newspaper regularly, and calls to all the airlines that serve your destination from your most convenient gateway. The potential savings are well worth the effort.

Ask about discount or promotional fares and about any conditions that might restrict booking, payment, cancellation, and changes in plans. Check the prices from other cities. A special rate may be offered in a nearby city but not in yours, and it may be enough of a bargain to warrant your leaving from that city. If you have a flexible schedule, investigate standby fares. But remember that, depending on your departure point, they may not work out to be the rock-bottom price. (And if standing by on connecting flights, beware of the likelihood of having to stand by a second time.) Ask if there is a difference in price for midweek versus weekend travel, or if there is a further discount for traveling early in the morning or late at night. Also be sure to investigate package deals, which are offered by virtually every airline. These may include a car rental, accommodations, and dining and/or sightseeing features, in addition to the basic airfare, and the combined cost of packaged elements usually is considerably less than the cost of the exact same elements when purchased separately.

If in your research you come across a deal that seems too good to be true, keep in mind that logic may not be a component of deeply discounted airfares — there's not always any sane relationship between miles to be flown and the price to get there. More often than not, the level of competition on a given route dictates the degree of discount, and don't be dissuaded from accepting an offer that sounds irresistible just because it also sounds illogical. Better to buy that inexpensive fare while it's being offered and worry about the sense — or absence thereof — while you're flying to your desired destination.

When you're satisfied that you've found the lowest possible price for which you can conveniently qualify (you may have to call the airline more than once, because different clerks have been known to quote different prices), make your booking. Then, to protect yourself against fare increases, purchase and pay for your ticket as soon as possible after you've received a confirmed reservation. Airlines generally will honor their tickets, even if the operative price at the time of your flight is higher than the price you paid; however, if fares go up between the time you *reserve* a flight and the time you *pay* for it, you likely will be out of luck. Finally, with excursion or discount fares, it is important to remember that when a reservation clerk says that you must purchase a ticket by a specific date, this is an absolute deadline. Miss the deadline and the airline automatically may cancel your reservation without telling you.

■ **Note:** Another wrinkle in the airfare scene is that if the fares go *down* after you purchase your ticket, you *may* be entitled to a refund of the difference. However, this is only possible in certain situations — availability and advance purchase restrictions pertaining to the lower rate are set by the airline. If you suspect that you may be able to qualify for such a refund, check with your travel agent or the airline (although some airline clerks may not be aware of this policy).

Frequent Flyers – Most of the leading US carriers serving France — including *American, Continental, Delta, Northwest, Pan American, United,* and *TWA* — now also offer a bonus system to frequent travelers. After the first 10,000 miles, for example, a passenger might be eligible for a first class seat for the coach fare; after another 10,000 miles, he or she might receive a discount on his or her next ticket purchase. The value of the bonuses continues to increase as more miles are logged.

Bonus miles also may be earned by patronizing affiliated car rental companies or hotel chains, or by using one of the credit cards that now offers this reward. In deciding whether to accept one of the many offers of a credit card from one of the issuing organizations that tempt you by offering frequent flyer mileage bonuses on a specific airline, first determine whether the interest rate charged on the unpaid balance is the same as (or less than) possible alternate credit cards, and whether the annual "membership" fee also is equal or lower. If these charges are slightly higher than those of competing cards, weigh the difference against the potential value in airfare savings. Also ask about any bonus miles awarded just for signing up — 1,000 is common, 5,000 generally the maximum. (For further information on credit cards, see *Credit and Currency*, in this section.)

For the most up-to-date information on frequent flyer bonus options, you may want to send for the monthly *Frequent* newsletter. Issued by Frequent Publications, it provides current information about frequent flyer plans in general, as well as specific data about promotions, awards, and combination deals to help you keep track of the profusion — and confusion — of current and upcoming availabilities. For a year's subscription, send $28 to Frequent Publications, 4715-C Town Center Dr., Colorado Springs, CO 80916 (phone: 800-333-5937).

There also is a monthly magazine called *Frequent Flyer*, but unlike the newsletter mentioned above, its focus is primarily on newsy articles of interest to business travelers and other frequent flyers. Published by Official Airline Guides (PO Box 58543, Boulder, CO 80322-8543; phone: 800-323-3537), *Frequent Flyer* is available for $24 for a 1-year subscription.

Low-Fare Airlines – In today's economic climate, the stimulus for special fares increasingly is the appearance of airlines associated with bargain rates. These tend to be smaller carriers that can offer more for less because of lower overhead, uncomplicated route networks, and other limitations in their service. On these airlines, all seats on any given flight generally sell for the same price, which is somewhat below the lowest discount fare offered by the larger, more established airlines — even after they cut their fares in response. This gap, too, may disappear in the future, but it is important to note that tickets offered by the smaller airlines specializing in low-cost travel frequently are not subject to the same restrictions as the lowest-priced ticket offered by the more established carriers. They may not require advance purchase or minimum and maximum stays, may involve no cancellation penalties, may be available one-way or round-trip, and may, for all intents and purposes, resemble the competition's high-priced full-fare coach. But never assume this until you know it's so. A disadvantage to low-fare airlines, however, is that when something goes wrong, such as delayed baggage or a flight cancellation due to equipment breakdown, their smaller fleets and fewer flights mean that passengers may have to wait longer for a solution than they would on one of the major carriers.

At press time, the only airline offering a relatively low fare to France was *Virgin Atlantic* (phone: 212-242-1330 in New York City; 800-862-8621 elsewhere in the US), which flies from Los Angeles and New York (JFK and Newark) to Paris daily year-round and from Miami to Paris at least four times a week. The airline sells tickets in several fare categories, including business or "upper" class, economy, APEX, and nonrefundable variations on standby (which, in the case of flights to Paris, must be purchased within 3 days prior to departure). At the time of this writing, their round-trip fare from New York to Paris was $499. Fares from Los Angeles are somewhat higher.

In a class by itself is *Icelandair*, which always has been a scheduled airline but has long been known as a good source of low-cost flights to Europe. *Icelandair* flies from New York and Orlando to Luxembourg (just across the border from the Lorraine region in northeastern France and less than an hour by train from Metz, about 2½ hours from Strasbourg, or an average of 4 hours from Paris). In addition, the airline increases the options for its passengers by offering "thru-fares" on connecting flights from Luxembourg to various European cities, including Paris and Nice. The price of the intra-European flights (aboard Luxembourg's *Luxair*) is included in the price *Icelandair* quotes for the transatlantic portion of the travel. The airline sells tickets in a variety of categories, from unrestricted economy fares to a sort of standby "3-days-before" fare (which functions just like the youth fares described above but has no age requirement). Travelers should be aware, however, that most *Icelandair* flights stop in Reykjavík for 45 minutes en route to and from Luxembourg — a minor delay for most, but one that further prolongs the trip for passengers who will wait again in Luxembourg to.board connecting flights to their ultimate destinations. For reservations and tickets, contact a travel agent or *Icelandair* (phone: 212-967-8888 in New York City; 800-223-5500 elsewhere in the US).

Intra-European Fares – The cost of the round trip across the Atlantic is not the only expense to be considered. Flights between European cities, when booked in Europe, can be quite expensive.

Recent Common Market moves toward airline deregulation are expected to lead gradually to a greater number of budget fares. In the meantime, however, the high cost of European fares can be avoided by careful use of stopover rights on the higher-priced transatlantic tickets — first class, business class, and full-fare economy. If your ticket doesn't allow stopovers, ask about excursion fares such as PEX, Super PEX — the same as APEX and Super APEX, but without the advance purchase rules and, therefore, more expensive — APEX for round trips, and Eurobudget for one-way trips. If the restrictions that govern them allow you to use them (frequently the minimum stay requirement means staying over for at least one Saturday night), you may save as much as 35% to 50% off full-fare economy. Note that these fares, which once could be bought only after arrival in Europe, are now sold in the US and can be bought before departure.

Discounts currently are available on routes between some European countries and do exist for air travel within France. *Air Inter,* the country's major domestic airline, offers reduced rates to families, married couples, senior citizens, students, youths, and children of various ages — all of which are available to French citizens as well as foreign visitors buying their tickets after arrival in France. In addition, for foreigners only, the airline offers discounted "Visit France" fares, which must be bought in the US in conjunction with a transatlantic ticket to France (both the international flight, which can be aboard any carrier, and the intra-France flight must be issued on the same ticket). *Air Inter* also offers a discount pass, the France Pass, which permits unlimited travel for any 7-day period within a given month. The pass can be used on all of the airline's routes with the exception of certain peak-hour flights (the "red flights" used mostly by business travelers). Further information on ticketing for *Air Inter*'s current airfare packages is available from *Air France* (*Air Inter*'s general sales agent in the US) or from *Jet Vacations* (phone: 800-JET-0999 or 212-247-0999).

It is not easy to inform yourself about stopover possibilities by talking to most airline reservations clerks. More than likely, an inquiry concerning any projected trip will prompt the reply that a particular route is nonstop aboard the carrier in question, thereby precluding stopovers completely, or that the carrier does not fly to all the places you want to visit. It may take additional inquiries, perhaps with the aid of a travel agent, to determine the full range of options regarding stopover privileges. Travelers might be able to squeeze in visits to Lisbon and Madrid on a first class ticket to Nice, for instance; Amsterdam and Brussels can be visited on a ticket to Paris; and Paris might only be the first of many free European stopovers possible on a one-way or round-trip ticket to Eastern Europe or points beyond. The airline that flies you on the first leg of your trip across the Atlantic issues the ticket, though you may have to use several different airlines in order to complete your journey. First class tickets are valid for a full year, so there's no rush.

Taxes and Other Fees – Travelers who have shopped for the best possible flight at the lowest possible price should be warned that a number of extras will be added to that price and collected by the airline or travel agent who issues the ticket. In addition to the $6 International Air Transportation Tax — a departure tax paid by all passengers flying from the US to a foreign destination — there is now a $10 US Federal Inspection Fee levied on all air and cruise passengers who arrive in the US from outside North America (those arriving from Canada, Mexico, the Caribbean, and US territories are exempt). Payable at the time a round-trip or incoming ticket is purchased, it combines a $5 customs inspection fee and a $5 immigration inspection fee, both instituted in 1986 to finance additional inspectors to reduce delays at gateways.

Still another fee is charged by some airlines to cover more stringent security procedures, prompted by recent terrorist incidents. The 8% Federal US Transportation Tax, which applies to travel within the US or US territories, already is included in advertised fares and in the prices quoted by reservations clerks. It does not apply to passengers flying between US cities en route to a foreign destination, unless the trip includes a stopover of more than 12 hours at a US point. Someone flying from Los Angeles to New York and stopping in New York for more than 12 hours before boarding a flight to Europe, for instance, would pay the 8% tax on the domestic portion of the trip.

Reservations – For those who don't have the time and patience to investigate personally all possible air departures and connections for a proposed trip, a travel agent can be of inestimable help. A good agent should have all the information on which flights go where and when, and which categories of tickets are available on each. Most have computerized reservation links with the major carriers, so that a seat can be reserved and confirmed in minutes. An increasing number of agents also possess fare-comparison computer programs, so they often are very reliable sources of detailed competitive price data. (For more information, see *How to Use a Travel Agent,* in this section.)

When making reservations through a travel agent, ask the agent to give the airline your home phone number, as well as your daytime business phone number. All too often the agent uses the agency number as the official contact for changes in flight plans. Especially during the winter, weather conditions hundreds or even thousands of miles away can wreak havoc with flight schedules. Aircraft are constantly in use, and a plane delayed in the Orient or on the West Coast can miss its scheduled flight from the East Coast the next morning. The airlines are fairly reliable about getting this sort of information to passengers if they can reach them; diligence does little good at 10 PM if the airline has only the agency or an office number.

Reconfirmation is strongly recommended for all international flights (though generally it is not required on domestic flights). Some (though increasingly fewer) reservations to and from international destinations are automatically canceled after a required reconfirmation period (typically 72 hours) has passed — even if you have a confirmed, fully paid ticket in hand. It always is a good idea to call ahead to make sure that the airline did not slip up in entering your original reservation, or in registering any changes you may have made since, and that it has your seat reservation request in the computer. Although policies vary from carrier to carrier, some recommend that you reconfirm your return flight 48 to 72 hours in advance. If you look at the back of your ticket, you'll see the airline's reconfirmation policy stated explicitly. If in doubt — call.

Every travel agent or airline ticket office should give each passenger a reminder to reconfirm flights, but this seldom happens, so the responsibility rests with the traveler. Don't be lulled into a false sense of security by the "OK" on your ticket next to the number and time of the flight. That only means that a reservation has been entered; a reconfirmation still may be necessary.

If you plan not to take a flight on which you hold a confirmed reservation, by all means inform the airline. Because the problem of "no-shows" is a constant expense for airlines, they are allowed to overbook flights, a practice that often contributes to the threat of denied boarding for a certain number of passengers (see "Getting Bumped," below). Let the airline know you're not coming and you'll spare everyone some inconvenience and confusion. Bear in mind that only certain kinds of tickets allow the luxury of last-minute changes in flight plans: Those sold on an open reservation system (first class and full-fare coach) do, while excursions and other discount fares often are restricted in some way. Even first class and coach passengers should remember that if they do not show up for a flight that is the first of several connecting ones, the airline will very likely cancel all of their ongoing reservations unless informed not to do so.

Seating – For most types of tickets, airline seats usually are assigned on a first-come, first-served basis at check-in, although some airlines make it possible to reserve a seat at the time of ticket purchase. Always check in early for your flight, even with advance seat assignments. A good rule of thumb for international flights is to arrive at the airport *at least* 2 hours before the scheduled departure to give yourself plenty of time in case there are long lines.

Most airlines furnish seating charts, which make choosing a seat much easier, but there are a few basics to consider. You must decide whether you prefer a window, aisle, or middle seat. On flights where smoking is permitted, you also should specify if you prefer the smoking or nonsmoking section.

The amount of legroom provided (as well as chest room, especially when the seat in front of you is in a reclining position) is determined by something called "pitch," a measure of the distance between the back of the seat in front of you and the front of the back of your seat. The amount of pitch is a matter of airline policy, not the type of plane you fly. First class and business class seats have the greatest pitch, a fact that figures prominently in airline advertising. In economy class or coach, the standard pitch ranges from 33 to as little as 31 inches — downright cramped. The number of seats abreast, another factor determining comfort, depends on a combination of airline policy and airplane dimensions. First and business classes have the fewest seats per row. Economy generally has 9 seats per row on a DC-10 or an L-1011, making either one slightly more comfortable than a 747, on which there are normally 10 seats per row. Charter flights on DC-10s and L-1011s, however, often have 10 seats per row and can be noticeably more cramped than 747 charters, on which the seating normally remains at 10 per row.

Airline representatives claim that most aircraft are more stable toward the front and midsections, while seats farthest away from the engines are quietest. Passengers who have long legs and are traveling on a wide-body aircraft might request a seat directly behind a door or emergency exit, since these seats often have greater than average pitch, or a seat in the first row of a given section, since these seats have extra legroom. It is often impossible, however, to see the movie from these seats, which are directly behind the plane's exits. Be aware that the first row of the economy section (called a "bulkhead" seat) on a conventional aircraft (not a wide-body) does *not* offer extra legroom, since the fixed partition will not permit passengers to slide their feet under it, and that watching a movie from this first row seat can be difficult and uncomfortable. A window seat protects you from aisle traffic and clumsy serving carts, and also allows you a view, while an aisle seat enables you to get up and stretch your legs without disturbing your fellow travelers. Middle seats are the least desirable, and seats in the last row are the worst of all, since they seldom recline fully. If you wish to avoid children on your flight or if you find that you are sitting in an especially noisy section, you usually are free to move to any unoccupied seat — if there is one.

If you are overweight, you may face the prospect of a long flight with special trepidation. Center seats in the alignments of wide-body 747s, L-1011s, and DC-10s are about 1½ inches wider than those on either side, so larger travelers tend to be more comfortable there.

Despite all these rules of thumb, finding out which specific rows are near emergency exits or at the front of a wide-body cabin can be difficult because seating arrangements on two otherwise exact same planes vary from airline to airline. There is, however, a quarterly publication called *Airline Seating Guide* that publishes seating charts for most major US airlines and many foreign carriers as well. Your travel agent should have copies, or you can buy the US edition for $39.95 per year and the overseas edition for $44.95. Order from Carlson Publishing Co., Box 888, Los Alamitos, CA 90720 (phone: 213-493-4877).

Simply reserving an airline seat in advance, however, actually may guarantee very little. Most airlines require that passengers arrive at the departure gate at least 45 minutes (sometimes more) ahead of time to hold a seat reservation. *Pan American,* for example, may cancel seat assignments and may not honor reservations of passengers who have not checked in some period of time — usually around 45 minutes, depending on the airport — before the scheduled departure time, and they *ask* travelers to check in at least 1 hour before all domestic flights and 2 hours before international flights. As this is only one airline's policy, it pays to read the fine print on the back of your ticket carefully and plan ahead.

A far better strategy is to visit an airline ticket office (or one of a select group of travel agents) to secure an actual boarding pass for your specific flight. Once this has been issued, airline computers show you as checked in, and you effectively own the seat you have selected (although some carriers may not honor boarding passes of passengers arriving at the gate less than 10 minutes before departure). This also is good — but not foolproof — insurance against getting bumped from an overbooked flight and is, therefore, an especially valuable tactic at peak travel times.

Smoking – One decision regarding choosing a seat has been taken out of the hands of many travelers who smoke. Effective February 25, 1990, the US government adopted a restrictive airline smoking ban that prohibits smoking on all flights scheduled for 6 hours or less within the US and its territories. The new regulation applies to both domestic and international carriers serving these routes.

In the case of flights to France, these rules do not apply to nonstop flights flying directly from the US to Europe or those flying with a continuous flight time of over 6 hours between stops in the US or its territories. Smoking is not permitted on segments of international flights where the flight time between US landings is under 6 hours — for instance, flights that include a stopover (even with no change of plane) or connecting flights. To further complicate the situation, several individual carriers are banning smoking altogether on certain routes. (As we went to press, this ban had not yet extended to flights to France.)

On those flights that do permit smoking, the US Department of Transportation has determined that nonsmoking sections must be enlarged to accommodate all passengers who wish to sit in a nonsmoking section. The airline does not, however, have to shift seating to accommodate nonsmokers who arrive late for a flight or for travelers flying standby, and in general not all airlines can guarantee a seat in the nonsmoking section on international flights. Cigar and pipe smoking are prohibited on all flights, even in the smoking sections.

For a wallet-size guide, which notes in detail the rights of nonsmokers according to these new regulations, send a self-addressed, stamped envelope to ASH (Action on Smoking and Health), Airline Card, 2013 H St. NW, Washington, DC 20006 (phone: 202-659-4310).

Flying with Children – On longer flights, the bulkhead seats usually are reserved for families traveling with small children. As a general rule, an infant under 2 years of age (and not occupying a seat) flies to Europe at 10% of whatever fare the accompanying adult is paying. A second infant without a second adult pays the fare applicable to children ages 2 through 11. In most cases this amounts to 50% of an adult economy fare and two thirds of an adult APEX fare.

Although airlines will, on request, supply bassinets for infants, most carriers encourage parents to bring on board their own infant safety seat, which then is strapped into the airline seat with a regular seat belt. This is much safer — and certainly more comfortable — than holding the child in your lap. If you do not purchase a seat for your baby, you have the option of bringing the infant restraint along on the off-chance that there might be an empty seat next to yours — in which case many airlines will let you have that seat free for your baby and infant seat. However, if there is no empty seat available, the infant seat no doubt will have to be checked as baggage (and most likely you will have to pay an additional charge), since it generally does not fit under the seat or in the overhead racks.

The safest bet is to pay for a seat — this usually will be the same as fares applicable to children ages 2 through 11. You might have to do some number-juggling to determine the cheapest fare for the infant. Excursion fares, which usually are the least expensive, do not have children's rates, whereas the higher priced fares usually are the ones that offer discounts for children.

Be forewarned: Some safety seats designed primarily for use in cars do not fit properly into plane seats. Although nearly all seats manufactured since 1985 carry labels indicating whether they meet federal standards for use aboard planes, actual seat sizes may vary from carrier to carrier. At the time of this writing, the FAA was in the process of reviewing and revising airline policies with regard to infant travel and safety devices — it was still to be determined if children should be *required* to sit in safety seats and whether the airlines will have to provide them.

When checking in, and using either a bassinet or infant seat, request a bulkhead or other seat that has enough room in front to use it. On some planes, bassinets hook into a bulkhead wall; on others it is placed on the floor in front of you. Even if you do use a bassinet, babies must be held during takeoff and landing.

The entire subject of flying with children — including a discussion of car seats — is covered in a special supplementary issue of a newsletter called *Family Travel Times,* published by *Travel With Your Children* (*TWYCH*). An annual subscription (10 issues) is $35, and the "Airline Guide" supplement is available separately for $10, or it will be included free with a subscription. Contact *TWYCH* at 80 Eighth Ave., New York, NY 10011 (phone: 212-206-0688). (For more information on flying with children, see *Hints for Traveling with Children,* in this section.)

Meals – If you have specific diet requirements, be sure to let the airline know well before departure time. The available meals include vegetarian, seafood, kosher, Muslim, Hindu, high protein, low calorie, low cholesterol, low fat, low sodium, diabetic, bland, and children's menus. There is no extra charge for this option. It usually is necessary to request special meals when you make your reservations — check-in time is too late. It's also wise to reconfirm that your request for a special meal has made its way into the airline's computer — the time to do this is 24 hours before departure. (Note that special meals generally are not available on intra-European flights on small local carriers. If this poses a problem, try to eat before you board, or bring food with you.)

Baggage – Travelers from the US face two different kinds of rules. When you fly in on a US airline or on a major international carrier, US baggage regulations will be in effect. Though airline baggage allowances vary slightly, in general all passengers are allowed to carry on board, without charge, one piece of luggage that will fit easily under a seat of the plane or in an overhead bin and whose combined dimensions (length, width, and depth) do not exceed 45 inches. (If you prefer not to carry it with you, most airlines will allow you to check this bag in the hold.) A reasonable amount of reading material, camera equipment, and a handbag also are allowed. In addition all passengers are allowed to check two bags in the cargo hold: one usually not to exceed 62 inches in combined dimensions, the other not to exceed 55 inches. No single bag may weigh more than 70 pounds. Note, however, that this weight restriction may vary on some European airlines, ranging from as much as 88 pounds permitted for first class passengers to as little as 50 pounds for economy class — so check with the specific carrier in advance. (For instance, *Air France* permits 88 pounds in first class, 66 pounds in business class, and 50 pounds in economy class.)

On European local or trunk carriers, in general, baggage allowances follow the same guidelines as major carriers. However, especially on regional and local airlines, luggage may be subject to the old weight determination, under which each economy or discount passenger is allowed only a total of 44 pounds of luggage without additional charge. First class or business passengers are allowed a total of 66 pounds. (If you are flying from the US to Europe and connecting to a domestic flight, you generally will be allowed the same amount of baggage as on the international flight. If you break your trip and then take a domestic flight, the local carrier's weight restrictions will apply.)

Charges for additional, oversize, or overweight bags usually are made at a flat rate; the actual dollar amount varies from carrier to carrier. If you plan to travel with a bike, skis, golf clubs, or other sports gear, be sure to check with the airline beforehand. Most have procedures for handling such baggage, but you probably will have to pay for transport regardless of how much other baggage you have checked.

Airlines' policies regarding baggage allowances for children vary and usually are based on the percentage of full adult fare paid. Children paying 50% or more of an adult fare on most US carriers are entitled to the same baggage allowance as a full-fare passenger, whereas infants traveling at 10% of an adult fare are entitled to only one piece of baggage, the combined dimensions of which may not exceed 45 inches — 39 inches on *TWA*. Particularly for international carriers, it's wise to check ahead. Often there is no luggage allowance for a child traveling on an adult's lap or in a bassinet. For instance, *Air France*'s policy is that children not occupying a seat are allowed no luggage. (For more information, see "Flying with Children," above.)

To reduce the chances of your luggage going astray, remove all airline tags from previous trips, and label each bag inside and out — with your business address rather than your home address on the outside, to prevent thieves from knowing whose house might be unguarded. Lock everything and double-check the tag that the airline attaches to make sure that it is correctly coded for your destination: CDG for Charles de Gaulle, OLY for Orly in Paris, or NCE for Nice, for instance.

If your bags are not in the baggage claim area after your flight, or if they're damaged, report the problem to airline personnel immediately. Keep in mind that policies regarding the specific time limit in which you have to make your claim vary from carrier to carrier. Fill out a report form on your lost or damaged luggage and keep a copy of it and your original baggage claim check. If you must surrender the check to claim a damaged bag, get a receipt for it to prove that you did, indeed, check your baggage on the flight. If luggage is missing, be sure to give the airline your destination and/or a telephone number where you can be reached. Also take the name and number of the person in charge of recovering lost luggage.

Most airlines have emergency funds for passengers stranded away from home without their luggage, but if it turns out your bags are truly lost and not simply delayed, do not then and there sign any paper indicating you'll accept an offered settlement. Since the airline is responsible for the value of your bags within certain statutory limits ($1,250 per passenger for lost baggage on a US domestic flight; $9.07 per pound or $20 per kilo for checked baggage, and up to $400 per passenger for unchecked baggage, on an international flight), you should take some time to assess the extent of your loss (see *Insurance,* in this section). It's a good idea to keep records indicating the value of the contents of your luggage. A wise alternative is to take a Polaroid picture of the most valuable of your packed items just after putting them in your suitcase.

Considering the increased incidence of damage to baggage, it's now more than ever a good idea to keep the sales slips that confirm how much you paid for your bags. These are invaluable in establishing the value of damaged baggage and eliminate any arguments. A better way to protect your precious baggage from the luggage eating conveyers is to try to carry your gear on board wherever possible.

Be aware that airport security increasingly is an issue all over Europe, and the French take it very seriously. Heavily armed police patrol the airports and unattended luggage of any description may be confiscated and quickly destroyed. Passengers checking in at Charles de Gaulle and other French airports may undergo at least two separate inspections of their tickets, passports, and luggage by courteous but serious airline personnel — who ask passengers if their baggage has been out of their possession between packing and the airport, or if they have been given gifts or other items to transport — before checked items are accepted.

Airline Clubs – US carriers often have clubs for travelers who pay for membership. These are not solely for first class passengers, although a first class ticket *may* entitle a passenger to lounge privileges. Membership (which, by law, now requires a fee) entitles the traveler to use the private lounges at airports along their route, to refreshments served in those lounges, and to check-cashing privileges at most of their counters. Extras include special telephone numbers for individual reservations, embossed luggage tags, and a membership card for identification. Two airlines that fly to France and offer membership in such clubs are *Pan American* — the *Clipper Club,* single yearly membership $150, spouse an additional $45; 3-year and lifetime memberships also available — and *TWA* — the *Ambassador Club,* single yearly membership $150, spouse an additional $25; lifetime memberships also available. However, such companies do not have club facilities in all airports; other airlines also offer a variety of special services in many airports.

Getting Bumped – A special air travel problem is the possibility that an airline will accept more reservations (and sell more tickets) than there are seats on a given flight. This is entirely legal and is done to make up for "no-shows," passengers who don't show up for a flight for which they have made reservations and bought tickets. If the airline has oversold the flight and everyone does show up, there simply aren't enough seats. When this happens, the airline is subject to stringent rules designed to protect travelers.

In such cases, the airline first seeks ticketholders willing to give up their seats voluntarily in return for a negotiable sum of money, or some other inducement such as an offer of upgraded seating on the next flight or a voucher for a free trip at some other time. If there are not enough volunteers, the airline may bump passengers against their wishes.

Anyone inconvenienced in this way, however, is entitled to an explanation of the criteria used to determine who does and does not get on the flight, as well as compensation if the resulting delay exceeds certain limits. If the airline can put the bumped passengers on an alternate flight that is *scheduled to arrive* at their original destination within 1 hour of their originally scheduled arrival time, no compensation is owed. If the delay is more than an hour but less than 2 hours on a domestic US flight or less than 4 hours on an international flight, they must be paid denied-boarding compensation equivalent to the one-way fare to their destination (but not more than $200). If the delay is more than 2 hours beyond the original arrival time on a domestic flight or more than 4 hours on an international flight, the compensation must be doubled (but not more than $400). The airline also may offer bumped travelers a voucher for a free flight instead of the denied-boarding compensation. The passenger can choose either the money or the voucher, the dollar value of which may be no less than the monetary compensation to which the passenger would be entitled. The voucher is not a substitute for the bumped passenger's original ticket; the airline continues to honor that as well. Keep in mind that the above regulations and policies are for flights leaving the US only, and do *not* apply to charters or to inbound flights originating abroad, even on US carriers.

In France, each airline is free to determine what compensation it will pay to passengers who are bumped because of overbooking. However, they are required to spell out their policies on the airline ticket. *Air France*'s policy, for example, is similar to US policy. Passengers involuntarily bumped are paid twice the price of a one-way ticket (up to $400) if they reach their destination 4 or more hours late. Keep in mind that this is one airline's policy only. Don't assume every carrier will be as generous.

To protect yourself as best you can against getting bumped, arrive at the airport early, allowing plenty of time to check in and get to the gate. If the flight is oversold, ask immediately for the written statement explaining the airline's policy on denied-boarding compensation and its boarding priorities. If the airline refuses to give you this information, or if you feel they have not handled the situation properly, file a complaint with both the airline and the appropriate government agency (see "Consumer Protection," below).

Delays and Cancellations – The above compensation rules also do not apply if the flight is canceled or delayed, or if a smaller aircraft is substituted due to mechanical problems. Each airline has its own policy for assisting passengers whose flights are delayed or canceled or who must wait for another flight because their original one was overbooked. Most airline personnel will make new travel arrangements if necessary. If the delay is longer than 4 hours, the airline may pay for a phone call or telegram, a meal, and, in some cases, a hotel room and transportation to it.

■ **Caution:** If you are bumped or miss a flight, be sure to ask the airline to notify other airlines on which you have reservations or connecting flights. When your name is taken off the passenger list of your initial flight, the computer usually cancels all of your reservations automatically, unless *you* take steps to preserve them.

CHARTER FLIGHTS: By booking a block of seats on a specially arranged flight, charter operators offer travelers air transportation, often coupled with a hotel room, meals, and other travel services, for a substantial reduction over the full coach or economy fare.

Charters once were the best bargain around, but this is no longer necessarily the case. As a result, charter flights have been discontinued in many areas, but they can still be a good buy to some popular travel destinations, including France. Charters are especially attractive to people living in smaller cities or out-of-the-way places, because they frequently take off from nearby airports, saving travelers the inconvenience and expense of getting to a major gateway to begin their European trip.

Where demand persists, charter operators will continue to rent planes or seats from scheduled airlines (or from special charter airlines) and offer flights to the public directly through advertisements or travel agents. You buy the ticket from the operator or the agent, not from the airline owning the plane. With the advent of APEX and various promotional fares on the major airlines and the appearance of low-fare airlines, however, charter flights lost some of their budget-conscious clientele and suffered some lean years, especially on highly competitive routes with a choice of other bargains. At the same time, many of the larger companies running charter programs began to offer both charter flights and discounted scheduled flights (see below). Nevertheless, among the current offerings, charter flights to European cities are common, a sign that they still represent a good value.

Charter travel once required that an individual be a member of a club or other "affinity" group whose main purpose was not travel. But since the approval of "public charters" years ago, operators have had some of the flexibility of scheduled airlines, making charters more competitive. Public charters are open to anyone, whether belonging to a group or not, and have no advance booking requirements or minimum stay requirements. Operators can offer air-only charters, selling transportation alone, or they can offer charter packages — the flight plus a combination of land arrangements such as accommodations, meals, tours, or car rental.

Though charters almost always are round-trip, and it is unlikely that you would be sold a one-way seat on a round-trip flight, on rare occasions one-way tickets on charters are offered. Although it may be possible to book a one-way charter in the US, giving you more flexibility in scheduling your return, note that US regulations pertaining to charters may be more permissive than the charter laws of other countries. For example, if you want to book a one-way foreign charter back to the US, you may find advance booking rules in force.

From the consumer's standpoint, charters differ from scheduled airlines in two main respects: You generally need to book and pay in advance, and you can't change the itinerary or the departure and return dates once you've booked the flight. In practice, however, these restrictions don't always apply. Today, although most charters still require advance reservations, some permit last-minute bookings (when there are unsold seats available), and some even offer seats on a standby basis.

Some things to keep in mind about the charter game:

1. It cannot be repeated often enough that if you are forced to cancel your trip, you can lose much (and possibly all) of your money unless you have cancellation insurance, which is a *must* (see *Insurance,* in this section). Frequently, if the cancellation is made sufficiently far in advance (often 6 weeks or more), you may forfeit only a $25 or $50 penalty. If you cancel only 2 or 3 weeks before the flight, there may be no refund at all unless you or the operator can provide a substitute passenger.
2. Charter flights may be canceled by the operator up to 10 days before departure for any reason, usually underbooking. Your money is returned in this event, but there may be too little time to make new arrangements.
3. Most charters have little of the flexibility of regularly scheduled flights regarding refunds and the changing of flight dates; if you book a return flight, you must be on it or lose your money.
4. Charter operators are permitted to assess a surcharge, if fuel or other costs warrant it, of up to 10% of the airfare up to 10 days before departure.
5. Because of the economics of charter flights, your plane almost always will be full, so you will be crowded, though not necessarily uncomfortable.

The savings provided by charters varies, depending on their point of departure in the US and on the countries to which they are headed (some governments do not allow charters to land at all; others allow them to undercut scheduled fares by a wide margin). As a rule, a charter to any given destination can cost anywhere from $50 to $200 less than an economy fare on a major carrier, with East Coast charters realizing a greater saving than those on the West Coast.

Bookings – If you do fly on a charter, read the contract's fine print carefully and pay particular attention to the following:

1. Instructions concerning the payment of the deposit and its balance and to whom the check is to be made payable. Ordinarily, checks are made out to an escrow account, which means the charter company can't spend your money until your flight has safely returned. This provides some protection for you. To ensure the safe handling of your money, make out your check to the escrow account, the number of which must appear by law on the brochure, though all too often it is on the back in fine print. Write the details of the charter, including the destination and dates, on the face of the check; on the back, print "For Deposit Only." Your travel agent may prefer that you make out your check to the agency, saying that it will then pay the tour operator the fee minus commission. It is perfectly legal to write the check as we suggest, however, and if your agent objects too vociferously (he or she should trust the tour operator to send the proper commission), consider taking your business elsewhere. If you don't make your check out to the escrow account, you lose the protection of that escrow should the trip be canceled. Furthermore, recent bankruptcies in the travel industry have served to point out

that even the protection of escrow may not be enough to safeguard a traveler's investment. More and more, insurance is becoming a necessity (see *Insurance,* in this section). The charter company should be bonded (usually by an insurance company), and if you want to file a claim against it, the claim should be sent to the bonding agent. The contract will set a time limit within which a claim must be filed.

2. Specific stipulations and penalties for cancellations. Most charters allow you to cancel up to 45 days in advance without major penalty, but some cancellation dates are 50 to 60 days before departure.

3. Stipulations regarding cancellation and major changes made by the charterer. US rules say that charter flights may not be canceled within 10 days of departure except when circumstances — such as natural disasters or political upheavals — make it physically impossible to fly. Charterers may make "major changes," however — such as in the date or place of departure or return — but you are entitled to cancel and receive a full refund if you don't accept these changes. A price increase of more than 10% at any time up to 10 days before departure is considered a major change; no price increase is allowed during the 10 days immediately before departure.

Among the charter operators serving France is *Air France*'s subsidiary, *Air Charter,* which offers spring and summer service between New York and France (to both Paris and Nice). The booking agent is *Jet Vacations* (888 7th Ave., New York, NY 10106; phone: 800-JET-0999 or 212-247-0999).

DISCOUNTS ON SCHEDULED FLIGHTS: The APEX fare is an example of a promotional fare offered on regularly scheduled transatlantic flights by most major airlines. Promotional fares often are called discount fares because they cost less than what used to be the standard airline fare — full-fare economy. Nevertheless, they cost the traveler the same whether they are bought through a travel agent or directly from the airline. Tickets that cost less if bought from some outlet other than the airline do exist, however. While it is likely that the vast majority of travelers flying to Europe in the near future will be doing so on a promotional fare or charter rather than on a "discount" air ticket of this sort, it still is a good idea for cost-conscious consumers to be aware of the latest developments in the budget airfare scene. Note that the following discussion makes clear-cut distinctions among the types of discounts available based on how they reach the consumer; in actual practice, the distinctions are not nearly so precise. One organization may operate part of its business in one fashion and the remainder in another; a second organization may operate all of its business in the same fashion, but outsiders — and sometimes the organization itself — would have difficulty classifying it.

Courier Travel – There was a time when traveling as a courier was a sort of underground way to save money and visit otherwise unaffordable destinations, but more and more, the once exotic idea of traveling as a courier is becoming a very "establishment" exercise. Courier means no more than a traveler who accompanies freight of one sort or another, and typically that freight replaces the traveler's right to check baggage. Be prepared, therefore, to carry all your own personal travel gear in a bag that fits under the seat in front of you. In addition, the so-called courier usually pays only a portion of the total airfare — the freight company pays the remainder — and the courier also may be assessed a small registration fee.

There are over 4 dozen courier companies operating actively around the globe and there are at least two travel newsletters that have sprung up for the purpose of publishing courier opportunities. One of these, called *Travel Secrets* (PO Box 2325, New York, NY 10108) lists more than 20 US and Canadian courier companies. The other, *Travel*

Unlimited (PO Box 1058, Allston, MA 02135) lists 30 to 40 courier companies and agents worldwide. In addition, courier companies are listed in the yellow pages and, in general, are best used by folks with a *very* flexible travel schedule.

Net Fare Sources – The newest notion for reducing the costs of travel services comes from travel agents who offer individual travelers "net" fares. Defined simply, a net fare is the bare minimum amount at which an airline or tour operator will carry a prospective traveler. It doesn't include the amount that normally would be paid to the travel agent as a commission. Traditionally, such commissions amount to about 10% on domestic fares and from 8% to 20% on international tickets — not counting significant additions to these commission levels that are payable retroactively when agents sell more than a specific volume of tickets or trips for a single supplier. At press time, at least one travel agency in the US was offering travelers the opportunity to purchase tickets and/or tours for a net price. Instead of making their income from individual commissions, this agency assesses a fixed fee that may or may not provide a bargain for travelers; it requires a little arithmetic to determine whether to use the services of a net travel agent or those of one who accepts conventional commissions. One of the potential drawbacks of buying from agencies selling travel services at net fares is that some airlines may refuse to do business with them, thus limiting your options.

Travel Avenue (formerly *McTravel Travel Services*) is a formula fee–based agency that rebates its ordinary agency commission to the customer. For domestic flights, an agent will find the lowest retail fare, then rebate from 8% to 11%, depending on the airline selected, of that price minus an $8 ticket writing charge. The rebate percentage for international flights varies from 8% to 25%, again depending on the airline, and the ticket writing fee is $20. The ticket-writing charge is imposed per ticket; if the ticket includes more than eight separate flights, an additional $8 or $20 fee is added.

Travel Avenue will rebate on all tickets, including Max Savers, Super Savers, and senior citizen passes; if the customer is using a free flight coupon, an additional $5 coupon processing fee also is added. Available 7 days a week, reservations should be made far enough in advance to allow the tickets to be sent by first class mail, since extra charges accrue for special handling. It's possible to economize further by making your own airline reservation, then asking *Travel Avenue* only to write/issue your ticket. For travelers who live outside the Chicago area, business may be transacted by phone, and purchases may be charged to a credit card.

And for travelers to Europe seeking discounts on other travel services, *Travel Avenue* offers a similar net cost service, through which travelers can collect rebates on the cost of hotel accommodations and car rentals if the booking is made through *Travel Avenue*. Upon return home, you simply send *Travel Avenue* a copy of your receipt and they will send you a check for 5% of the total bill — returning part of their agency commission to the consumer. For further information, contact *Travel Avenue* at 641 W. Lake, Suite 201, Chicago, IL 60606-1012 (phone: 312-876-1116 in Illinois; 800-333-3335 elsewhere in the US).

Consolidators and Bucket Shops – Other vendors of travel services can afford to sell tickets to their customers at an even greater discount because the airline has sold the tickets to them at a substantial discount, a practice in which many airlines indulge, albeit discreetly, preferring that the general public not know they are undercutting their own "list" prices. Airlines anticipating a slow period on a particular route sometimes sell off a certain portion of their capacity at a very great discount to a wholesaler, or consolidator. The wholesaler sometimes is a charter operator who resells the seats to the public as though they were charter seats, which is why prospective travelers perusing the brochures of charter operators with large programs frequently see a number of flights designated as "scheduled service." As often as not, however, the consolidator, in turn, sells seats to or through a travel agency specializing in discounting. Airlines also can sell seats directly to such an agency, which thus acts as its own consolidator. The airline offers the seats either at a net wholesale price, but without the volume-purchase requirement that would be difficult for a retail travel agency to fulfill, or at the standard price, but with a commission override large enough (as high as 50%) to allow both a profit and a price reduction to the public.

Travel agencies specializing in discounting once were known as "bucket shops," a term fraught with connotations of unreliability. But in today's highly competitive travel marketplace, more and more conventional travel agencies are selling consolidator-supplied tickets, and the old bucket shops are becoming more respectable, too. Agencies that specialize in discounted tickets are located in most large cities and can be found by studying the smaller ads in the travel sections of the Sunday newspapers. They deal largely in transatlantic and other international tickets, and on the whole, do not offer notable reductions on domestic travel (if they sell domestic tickets at all).

Before buying a discounted ticket, whether from a bucket shop or a conventional, full-service travel agency, keep the following considerations in mind: To be in a position to judge the amount of money you'll be saving, first find out the "list" prices of tickets to your destination by calling the major airlines serving the route. Then do some comparison shopping among agencies, always bearing in mind that the lowest-priced ticket may not provide the most convenient or most comfortable flight (bargain prices usually are available on an airline's least popular routes, so your routing might be roundabout or you may be required to endure a long layover along the way). Also bear in mind that a ticket that may not differ much in price from that available directly from the airline may, however, allow the circumvention of booking restrictions such as the advance-purchase requirement. If your plans are less than final, be sure to find out about any other restrictions such as penalties for canceling a flight or changing a reservation. Most discount tickets are non-endorsable, meaning they can be used only on the airline that issued them, and they usually are marked "nonrefundable" to prevent their being cashed in for a list price refund. (A refund of the price paid for the ticket often is possible, but it is obtained through the outlet from which it was purchased rather than from the airline.)

A great many bucket shops are small businesses operating on a thin margin, so it's a good idea to check the local Better Business Bureau for any complaints registered against the one with which you're dealing — before parting with any money. If you still do not feel reassured, consider buying discounted tickets only through a conventional travel agency, which can be expected to have found its own reliable source of consolidator tickets — some of the largest consolidators, in fact, sell only to travel agencies.

A few bucket shops require payment in cash or by certified check or money order, but if credit cards are accepted, use that option, which allows purchasers to refuse to pay charges for services they haven't received. Note, however, if buying from a charter operator selling seats for both scheduled and charter flights, that the scheduled seats are not protected by the regulations — including the use of escrow accounts — governing the charter seats. Well-established charter operators, nevertheless, may extend the same protections to their scheduled flights, and when this is the case consumers should be sure that the payment option selected directs their money into the escrow account.

■ **Note:** Although rebating and discounting are becoming increasingly common, there is some legal ambiguity concerning them. Strictly speaking, it is legal to discount domestic tickets but not international tickets. On the other hand, the law that prohibits discounting, the Federal Aviation Act of 1958, is consistently ignored these days, in part because consumers benefit from the practice and in part because many illegal arrangements are indistinguishable from legal ones. Since the line separating the two is so fine that even the authorities can't always tell the difference, it is unlikely that most consumers would be able to do so, and in fact it is not illegal to *buy* a discounted ticket. If the issue of legality bothers you, ask the agency whether any ticket you're about to buy would be permissible under the above-mentioned act.

OTHER DISCOUNT TRAVEL SOURCES: An excellent source of information on economical travel opportunities is the *Consumer Reports Travel Letter,* published monthly by Consumers Union. It keeps abreast of the scene on a wide variety of fronts, including package tours, rental cars, insurance, and more, but it is especially helpful for its comprehensive coverage of airfares, offering guidance on all the options from scheduled flights on major or low-fare airlines to charters and discount sources. For a year's subscription send $37 to *Consumer Reports Travel Letter,* PO Box 2886, Boulder, CO 80322 (phone: 800-525-0643). Another source is *Travel Smart,* a monthly newsletter offering information on a wide variety of trips with additional discount travel services available to subscribers. For a year's subscription, send $37 to Communications House, 40 Beechdale Rd., Dobbs Ferry, NY 10522 (phone: 914-693-8300 in New York; 800-327-3633 elsewhere in the US).

Still another way to take advantage of bargain airfares is open to those who have a flexible schedule. A number of organizations, usually set up as last-minute travel clubs and functioning on a membership basis, routinely keep in touch with travel suppliers to help them dispose of unsold inventory at discounts of between 15% and 60%. A great deal of the inventory consists of complete tour packages and cruises, but some clubs offer air-only charter seats and, occasionally, seats on scheduled flights. Members pay an annual fee and get a toll-free hot line number to call for information on imminent trips. In some cases, they also receive periodic mailings with information on bargain travel opportunities for which there is more advance notice. Despite the suggestive names of the clubs providing these services, last-minute travel does not necessarily mean that you cannot make plans until literally the last minute. Trips can be announced as little as a few days or as much as 2 months before departure, but the average is from 1 to 4 weeks' notice. It does mean that your choice at any given time is limited to what is offered and if your heart is set on a particular destination, you might not find what you want, no matter how attractive the bargains. Among these organizations are the following:

Discount Club of America, 61-33 Woodhaven Blvd., Rego Park, NY, 11374; (phone: 718-335-9612 or 800-321-9587). Annual fee: $39.

Discount Travel International, Ives Building, 114 Forrest Ave., Suite 205, Narberth, PA 19072 (phone: 800-334-9294). Annual fee: $45 per household.

Encore Short Notice, 4501 Forbes Blvd., Lanham, MD 20706 (phone: 301-459-8020 or 800-638-0930 for customer service). Annual fee: $48 per family.

Last-Minute Travel Club, 132 Brookline Ave., Boston, MA 02215 (phone: 617-267-9800 or 800-LAST-MIN). As of this year, no fee.

Moment's Notice, 425 Madison Ave., New York, NY 10017 (phone: 212-486-0503). Annual fee: $45 per family.

Spur-of-the-Moment Tours and Cruises, 10780 Jefferson Blvd., Culver City, CA 90230 (phone: 213-839-2418 in California; 800-343-1991 elsewhere in the US). No fee.

Traveler's Advantage, 3033 S. Parker Rd., Suite 1000, Aurora, CO 80014 (phone: 800-548-1116). Annual fee: $49 per family.

Worldwide Discount Travel Club, 1674 Meridian Ave., Miami Beach, FL 33139 (phone: 305-534-2082). Annual fee: $40 per person; $50 per family.

Generic Air Travel – Organizations that apply the same flexible-schedule idea to air travel only and sell tickets at literally the last minute also exist. The service they provide sometimes is known as "generic" air travel, and it operates somewhat like an ordinary airline standby service except that the organizations running it offer seats on not one but several scheduled and charter airlines.

One pioneer of generic flights is *Airhitch* (2901 Broadway, Suite 100, New York, NY 10025; phone: 212-864-2000), which arranges flights to Europe from various US cities at very low prices. Prospective travelers register by paying a fee (applicable toward the fare) and stipulate a range of acceptable departure dates and their desired destination, along with alternate choices. The week before the date range begins, they are notified of at least two flights that will be available during the time period, agree on one, and remit the balance of the fare to the company. If they do not accept any of the suggested flights, they lose their deposit; if, through no fault of their own, they do not ultimately get on any agreed-on flight, all of their money is refunded. Return flights are arranged the same way. *Airhitch* cautions that, given the number of variables attached to the flights, they are suitable only for travelers willing to accept approximate destinations, although the time period will be the one specified and, for a majority of travelers, the place of arrival, too. At the time of this writing, fares to France ranged from $160 or less one way from the East Coast, $269 or less from the West Coast, and $229 or less from other points in the US. Another of the company's programs, the Target program, offers greater certainty regarding destinations.

Bartered Travel Sources – Say a company buys advertising space for a hotel in a newspaper. As payment, the hotel gives the publishing company the use of a number of hotel rooms in lieu of cash. This is barter, a common means of exchange among hotels, airlines, car rental companies, cruise lines, tour operators, restaurants, and other travel service companies. When a bartering company finds itself with excess hotel rooms (or empty airline seats or cruise ship cabin space, and so on) and offers them to the public, considerable savings can be enjoyed.

Bartered-travel clubs can often offer discounts of up to 50% to members, who pay an annual fee (approximately $50 at press time) that entitles them to select the flights, cruises, or hotels which the company obtained by barter. Members usually present a voucher, club credit card, or scrip (a dollar-denomination voucher negotiable only for the bartered product) to the hotel, which in turn subtracts the dollar amount from the bartering company's account.

Selling bartered travel is a perfectly legitimate means of retailing. One advantage to club members is that they don't have to wait until the last minute to obtain room or flight reservations. However, hotel rooms and airline seats usually are offered to members on a space-available basis. Ticket vouchers are good only for a particular hotel and cannot be used at other hotels. The same goes for car rentals, cruises, package tours, and restaurants. The following clubs offer bartered travel at a discount to members:

IGT (In Good Taste) Services, 1111 Lincoln Rd., 4th Floor, Miami Beach, FL 33139 (phone: 800-444-8872 or 305-534-7900). Annual membership fee is $48 per person.

The Travel Guild, 18210 Redmond Way, Redmond, WA 98052 (phone: 206-885-1213). Annual membership fee is $48 per family.

Travel World Leisure Club, 225 W. 34th St., Suite 2203, New York, NY 10122 (phone: 212-239-4855 or 800-444-TWLC). Annual membership fee is $50 per family.

CONSUMER PROTECTION: Consumers who feel that they have not been dealt with fairly by an airline should make their complaints known. Begin with the customer service representative at the airport where the problem occurs. If he or she cannot resolve your complaint to your satisfaction, write to the airline's consumer office. In a businesslike, typed letter, explain what reservations you held, what happened, the names of the employees involved, and how you expect the airline to remedy the situation. Send copies (never the originals) of the tickets, receipts, and other documents that back your claims. Ideally, all correspondence should be sent via certified mail, return receipt requested. This provides proof that your complaint was received.

If you still receive no satisfaction and your complaint is against a US carrier contact the US Department of Transportation. Passengers with consumer complaints — lost baggage, compensation for getting bumped, smoking and nonsmoking rules, deceptive practices by an airline, charter regulations — should write to the Consumer Affairs Division, Room 10405, US Department of Transportation, 400 Seventh St. SW, Washington, DC 20590, or call the office at 202-366-2220. DOT personnel stress, however, that consumers initially should direct their complaints to the airline that provoked them.

Travelers with an unresolved complaint involving a French airline also can contact the US Department of Transportation. DOT personnel will do what they can to help resolve all such complaints, although their influence may be limited.

A more effective direction for your complaint may be the *Direction Départmentale de la Concurrences, de la Consommation et la Repression des Frauds* (8 Rue Froissart, Paris 75003; phone: 1-42-71-23-10). Consumers with complaints against French airlines or other travel-related services can write to this agency, in French, outlining the specifics in as much detail as possible (keep in mind that if a translator is required for this correspondence it could get expensive). They will try to resolve the complaint or, if it is out of their jurisdiction, will refer the matter to the proper authorities, and will notify you in writing (in French) as to the result of their inquires and/or any action taken.

The deregulation of US airlines has meant that the traveler must find out for himself or herself what he or she is entitled to receive. The Department of Transportation's informative consumer booklet *Fly Rights* is a good place to start. To receive a copy, send $1 to the Superintendent of Documents, US Government Printing Office, Washington, DC 20402-9325 (phone: 202-783-3238). Specify its stock number, 050-000-000513-5, and allow 3 to 4 weeks for delivery.

To avoid more serious problems, *always* choose charter flights and tour packages with care. When you consider a charter, ask your travel agent who runs it and carefully check out the company. The Better Business Bureau in the company's home city can report on how many complaints, if any, have been lodged against it in the past. As emphasized above, protect yourself with trip cancellation and interruption insurance, which can help safeguard your investment if you or a traveling companion is unable to make the trip and must cancel too late to receive a full refund from the company providing your travel services. (This is advisable whether you're buying a charter flight alone or a tour package for which the airfare is provided by charter or scheduled flight.) Some travel insurance policies have an additional feature, covering the possibility of default or bankruptcy on the part of the tour operator or airline, charter or scheduled.

Should this type of coverage not be available to you (state insurance regulations vary, there is a wide difference in price, and so on), your best bet is to pay for airline tickets and tour packages with a credit card. The federal Fair Credit Billing Act permits purchasers to refuse payment for credit card changes where services have not been delivered, so the onus of dealing with the receiver for a bankrupt airline falls on the credit card company. Do not rely on another airline to honor the ticket you're holding, since the days when virtually all major carriers subscribed to a default protection program that bound them to do so are long gone. Some airlines may voluntarily step forward to accommodate the stranded passengers of a fellow carrier, but this is now an entirely altruistic act.

Traveling by Ship

 There was a time when traveling by ship was extraordinarily expensive, time consuming, utterly elegant, and utilized almost exclusively for getting from one point to another. Times have changed in many ways for ship travel; after a period when the very idea of seaborne transportation was almost completely sunk by the coming of swift, inexpensive jets, cruising has floated to very near the top of leisure travel options.

Alas, the days when steamships reigned as the primary means of transatlantic transportation are gone, when Italy, France, Sweden, Germany, Norway, the Netherlands, and England — and the US — had fleets of passenger liners that offered week-plus trips across the North Atlantic. Only one ship (*Cunard*'s *Queen Elizabeth 2*) continues to offer this kind of service between the US and Europe with any degree of regularity; others make the trip at most a few times a year. At the same time, the possibility of booking passage to Europe on a cargo ship is becoming less practical. Fewer and fewer travelers, therefore, first set foot on French soil with sea legs developed during an ocean voyage.

Although fewer travelers to Europe are choosing sea travel as a means of transport to a specific destination, more and more people are cruising around Europe. No longer primarily pure transportation, ocean cruising is currently riding a wave of popularity as a leisure activity in its own right, and the host of new ships (and dozens of rebuilt old ones) testifies dramatically to the attraction of vacationing on the high seas. And due to the growing popularity of travel along coastal and inland waterways, more and more travelers — particularly repeat travelers — are climbing aboard some kind of waterborne conveyance once they've arrived in France and are seeing the country from its western coastal waters, from the banks of a river, or the towpath of a canal.

The only thing that's lacking from the cruising scene today is any of that old elegance, though modern-day passengers don't seem to notice. Cruise ships seem much more like motels-at-sea than the classic liners of a couple of generations ago, but they are consistently comfortable and passengers are determinedly pampered. Prices are reasonable, and cruises focusing on French ports rarely last more than 2 weeks. What's more, since the single cruise price covers all the major items in a typical vacation — transportation, accommodations, all meals, entertainment, a full range of social activities, and sports and recreation — a traveler need not fear any unexpected assaults on the family travel budget.

When selecting a cruise, your basic criteria should be where you want to go, the time you have available, how much you want to spend, and the kind of environment that best suits your style and taste (in which case price is an important determinant). Rely on the suggestions of a travel agent — preferably one specializing in cruises (see "A final note on picking a cruise," below) — but be honest with the agent (and with yourself) in describing the type of atmosphere you're seeking. Ask suggestions from friends who have been on cruises; if you trust their judgment, they should be able to suggest a ship on which you'll feel comfortable.

There are a number of moments in the cruise-planning process when discounts are available from the major cruise lines, so it may be possible to enjoy some diminution of the list price almost anytime you book passage on a cruise ship. For those willing to commit early — say 4 to 6 months before sailing — most of the major cruise lines routinely offer a 10% reduction off posted prices, in addition to the widest selection of cabins from which to choose. For those who decide to sail rather late in the game

— say, 4 to 6 weeks before departure — savings often are even greater — an average of 20% — as steamship lines try to fill up their ships. The only negative aspect is that the range of cabin choice tends to be limited, although it is possible that a fare upgrade will be offered to make this limited cabin selection more palatable. In addition, there's the option of buying from a discount travel club or a travel agency that specializes in last-minute bargains; these discounters and other discount travel sources are discussed at the end of *Traveling by Plane,* above.

Most of the time, the inclusion of air transportation in the cruise package costs significantly less than if you were to buy the cruise separately and arrange your own air transportation to the port. If you do decide on one of these economical air/sea packages, be forewarned that it is not unusual for the prearranged flight arrangements to be less than convenient. The problems often arrive with the receipt of your cruise ticket, which also includes the airline ticket for the flight to get you to and from the ship dock. This is normally the first time you see the flights on which you have been booked and can appraise the convenience of the departure and arrival times. The cruise ship lines generally are not very forthcoming about altering flight schedules, and your own travel agent also may have difficulty in rearranging flight times or carriers. That means that the only remaining alternative is to ask the line to forget about making your flight arrangements and to pay for them separately by yourself. This may be more costly, but it's more likely to give you an arrival and departure schedule that will best conform to the sailing and docking times of the ship on which you will be cruising.

Prospective cruise ship passengers will find that the variety of cruises is tremendous, and the quality, while generally high, varies depending on shipboard services, the tone of shipboard life, the cost of the cruise, and operative itineraries. Although there are less expensive ways to see France and other European countries, the romance of a sea voyage remains irresistible for many, so a few points should be considered by such sojourners before they sign on for a seagoing vacation (after all, it's hard to get off in mid-ocean). Herewith, a rundown on what to expect from a cruise, a few suggestions on what to look for and arrange when purchasing passage on one, and some representative prices for different sailings.

CABINS: The most important factor in determining the price of a cruise is the cabin. Cabin prices are set according to size and location. The size can vary considerably on older ships, less so on newer or more recently modernized ones, and may be entirely uniform on the very newest vessels.

Shipboard accommodations have the same pricing pattern as hotels. Suites, which consist of a sitting room–bedroom combination and occasionally a private small deck that could be compared to a patio, cost the most. Prices for other cabins (interchangeably called staterooms) usually are more expensive on the upper passenger decks, less expensive on lower decks; if the cabin has a bathtub instead of a shower, the price probably will be higher. The outside cabins with portholes facing the water cost more than inside cabins without views and generally are preferred — although many experienced cruise passengers eschew more expensive accommodations for they know they will spend very few waking hours in their cabins. As in all forms of travel, accommodations are more expensive for single travelers. If you are traveling on your own but want to share a double cabin to reduce the cost, some ship lines will attempt to find someone of the same sex willing to share quarters (see *Hints for Single Travelers,* in this section).

FACILITIES AND ACTIVITIES: You may not use your cabin very much. Organized shipboard activities are geared to keep you busy. A standard schedule might consist of swimming, sunbathing, and numerous other outdoor recreations. Evenings are devoted to leisurely dining, lounge shows or movies, bingo and other organized games, gambling, dancing, and a midnight buffet. Your cruise fare includes all of these activities — except the cost of drinks.

All cruise ships have at least one major social lounge, a main dining room, several bars, an entertainment room that may double as a discotheque for late dancing, an exercise room, indoor games facilities, at least one pool, and shopping facilities that can range from a single boutique to an arcade. Still others have gambling casinos and/or slot machines, card rooms, libraries, children's recreation centers, indoor pools (as well as one or more on open decks), separate movie theaters, and private meeting rooms. Open deck space should be ample, because this is where most passengers spend their days at sea.

Usually there is a social director and staff to organize and coordinate activities. Evening entertainment is provided by professionals. Movies are mostly first run and drinks are moderate in price (or should be) because a ship is exempt from local taxes when at sea.

To prepare for possible illnesses, travelers should get a prescription from their doctors for pills, patches, or stomach pacifiers to counteract motion sickness. All ships with more than 12 passengers have a doctor on board, plus facilities for handling sickness or medical emergencies.

Shore Excursions – These side trips almost always are optional and available at extra cost. Before you leave, do a little basic research about the ports you'll be visiting and decide what sights will interest you. If several of the most compelling of these are some distance from the pier where your ship docks, chances are that paying for a shore excursion will be worth the money.

Shore excursions usually can be booked through your travel agent at the same time you make your cruise booking, but this is worthwhile only if you can get complete details on the nature of each excursion being offered. If you can't get these details, better opt to purchase your shore arrangements after you're on board. The fact is that your enthusiasm for an excursion may be higher once you are on board because you will have met other passengers with whom to share the excitement of "shore leave." And depending on your time in port, you may decide to forget about the guided tour and venture out on your own.

Meals – All meals on board almost always are included in the basic price of a cruise and generally the meals are abundant and quite palatable. Evening meals are taken in the main dining room, where tables are assigned according to the passengers' preferences. Tables usually accommodate from 2 to 10; specify your preference when you book your cruise. If there are two sittings, you also can specify which one you want at the time you book or, at latest, when you board the ship. Later sittings usually are more leisurely. Breakfast frequently is available in your cabin, as well as in the main dining room. For lunch, many passengers prefer the buffet offered on deck, usually at or near the pool, but again, the main dining room is available.

DRESS: Most people pack too much for a cruise on the assumption that daytime wear should be chic and every night is a big event. Comfort is a more realistic criterion.

Daytime wear on most ships is decidedly casual. For warm-weather cruises, women can wear a cover-up over a bathing suit through breakfast, swimming, sunbathing, deck activities, lunch, and early cocktails without any change; for men, shorts (with swim trunks underneath) and a casual shirt will be appropriate on deck or in any public room. (Bare feet and swimsuits are usually inappropriate in the dining room.) For travel in cooler seasons, casual, comfortable clothes, including a variety of layers to adjust for changes in the weather, are appropriate for all daytime activities. Also bring along a comfortable pair of rubber-sole, low-heel shoes or sneakers, as sloping gangways and wet decks can be slippery. (For further information on choosing and packing a basic wardrobe, see *How to Pack,* in this section.)

Evening wear for most cruises is dressy-casual. Formal wear probably is not necessary on 1-week cruises, optional on longer ones. There aren't many nights when it's expected. Most ships have a captain's cocktail party the first or second night out and a farewell dinner near the end of the cruise. Women should feel comfortable in hostess gowns, cocktail dresses, or stylish slacks. (To feel completely secure, you may want to pack one very dressy item.) Jackets and ties always are preferred for men in the evening, but a long-sleeve, open-neck shirt with ascot or scarf usually is an acceptable substitute.

TIPS: Tips are a strictly personal expense, and you *are* expected to tip — in particular your cabin and dining room stewards. The general rule of thumb (or palm) is to expect to pay from 10% to 20% or your total cruise budget for gratuities — the actual amount within this range is based on the length of the cruise and the extent of personalized service provided. Allow $2 to $5 a day for each cabin and dining room steward (more if you wish), and additional sums for very good service. (*Note:* Tips should be paid by and for each individual in a cabin, whether there are one, two, or more.) Others who may merit tips are the deck steward who sets up your chair at the pool or elsewhere, the wine steward in the dining room, porters who handle your luggage (tip them individually at the time they assist you), and any others who provide personal service. On some ships you can charge your bar tab to your cabin; throw in the tip when you pay it at the end of the cruise. Smart travelers tip twice during the trip: about midway through the cruise and at the end; even wiser travelers tip a bit at the start of the trip to ensure better service throughout.

Although some cruise lines do have a no-tipping policy and you are not penalized by the crew for not tipping, naturally you aren't penalized for tipping either. If you can restrain yourself, it is better not to tip on those few ships that discourage it. However, never make the mistake of not tipping on the majority of ships, where it is a common, expected practice. (For further information on calculating gratuities, see *Tipping,* in this section.)

SHIP SANITATION: The US Public Health Service (PHS) currently inspects all passenger vessels calling at US ports, so very precise information is available on which ships meet the Public Health Service requirements and which do not. The further requirement that ships immediately report illness that occurs on board adds to the available data.

So the problem for a prospective cruise passengers is to determine whether the ship on which he or she plans to sail has met the official sanitary standard. US regulations require the PHS to publish actual grades for the ships inspected (rather than the old pass or fail designation) so it's now easy to determine any cruise ship's sanitary status. Nearly 4,000 travel agents, public health organizations, and doctors receive a copy of each monthly ship sanitation summary, but be aware that not all agents fully understand what this ship inspection program is all about. Again, the best advice is to deal with a travel agent who specializes in cruise ships and cruise bookings, for he or she is most likely to have the latest information on the sanitary conditions of all cruise ships (see "A final note on picking a cruise," below). To receive a copy of the most recent summary or a particular inspection report, write to Chief, Vessel Sanitation Program, Public Health Service, 1015 N. America Way, Room 107, Miami, FL 33132, or call 305-536-4307.

TRANSATLANTIC CROSSINGS: For seagoing enthusiasts, *Cunard*'s *Queen Elizabeth 2* is one of the largest and most comfortable vessels afloat, having undergone a complete overhaul and refurbishing, from a replacement of its engines to a redecoration of passenger quarters. Each year, in addition to a full calendar of Caribbean and European cruises, plus a round-the-world cruise, the *QE2* schedules approximately a dozen round-trip transatlantic crossings between June and, usually, December.

The *QE2* normally sets its course from New York to Southampton, England (a 5-day trip) and then directly back to the US, although on a few of the crossings it proceeds from Southampton to Cherbourg, France, or to other European ports before turning back across the Atlantic. Passengers whose ultimate destination is France wait several hours as Southampton-bound passengers disembark and US-bound passengers board, then continue on to Cherbourg; those returning to the US from France embark in

Cherbourg and sail directly home. (Similarly, on some crossings, the ship calls at various East Coast US ports in addition to New York, thus giving passengers a choice of where to embark or disembark.) For France-bound travelers on crossings *not* scheduled to call at Cherbourg, *British Airways* (in conjunction with *Cunard*) offers travelers the option of paying a supplement for air transportation from Southampton to Paris; contact *British Airways* for details. Another alternative is to take the *Sealink* ferry from Southampton to Le Havre (see "Ferries," below).

Transatlantic crossings, however, do not come at bargain prices. Last year, the one-way, per-person cost of passage from New York to either Southampton or Cherbourg ranged from around $1,400 (for the least expensive, two-per-cabin, transatlantic class accommodations at the end of the season) to $8,925 (for one of the grandest travel experiences imaginable). *Cunard* brings a voyage aboard a luxury liner within reach of the less affluent traveler, however, by offering an air/sea package in conjunction with *British Airways.* The one-way ticket to Europe by sea includes an allowance toward return economy class airfare from London to any of 57 North American cities — a free flight home, in essence, provided certain length-of-stay restrictions are respected. The allowance can be applied to an upgraded air ticket if desired, and if you want to splurge, you can even fly home on a specially reserved *British Airways'* supersonic *Concorde,* provided you make up the difference between the allowance and the *Concorde* fare (the shortfall at press time was $995).

Cunard also offers various European tour packages applicable to the basic air/sea offer. Among the tours offered in 1990 were combination Paris/London packages, including 3 days and 2 nights in each city; a 14-day Alpine Splendor package featuring a stop in Paris and other European cities; and a Best of Europe package, including a trip on the famed *Venice Simplon–Orient Express* train. (For further information on this luxury train and a connecting cruise aboard the *Orient Express* ship — yes, of rail fame — see *Package Tours,* in this section.)

Cunard is now also offering a particularly economical round-trip air/sea option for travelers with a flexible schedule. Special "standby" fares are available on some transatlantic crossings between the US and London (20 sailings were offered between April and December 1990) and include airfare on *British Airways* to a number of US gateways. The package cost (at press time, $1,195 to $1,950 — depending on dates of travel) includes a berth in a double-occupancy "minimum" room on the *QE2* and a one-way *British Airways* economy class ticket to or from London and New York, Boston, Philadelphia, Miami, Chicago, Detroit, or Washington, DC. For an additional $100, passengers may fly to or from other *British Airways* US gateways including Anchorage, Atlanta, Houston, Los Angeles, Pittsburgh, San Diego, San Francisco, and Seattle. Although this fare is offered strictly on a space-available basis, confirmations are provided 3 weeks prior to sailing. To qualify for this fare, travelers must submit a written application and a $100 deposit to a travel agent or *Cunard*; full payment is due upon confirmation. For information, check with your travel agent or contact *Cunard,* 555 Fifth Ave., New York, NY 10017 (phone: 212-880-7500, 800-221-4770, or 800-5-CUNARD).

Another interesting transatlantic crossing possibility for those who have the time is what the industry calls a positioning cruise. This is the sailing of a US- or Caribbean-based vessel from its winter berth to the city in Europe from which it will be offering summer cruise programs. Eastbound positioning cruises take place in the spring; westbound cruises return in the fall. Since ships do not make the return trip until they need to position themselves for the next cruise season, most lines offering positioning cruises have some air/sea arrangement that allows passengers to fly home economically — though the cruises themselves are not inexpensive.

Among the ships that have been offering positioning cruises for a number of years are *Cunard*'s *Vistafjord* and ships of the *Royal Viking Line* and *Royal Cruise Line.*

Itineraries and ports of call vary from year to year. Typically, the ships set sail from Florida or from San Juan, Puerto Rico, and cross the Atlantic to any one of a number of European ports where the trip may be broken — Lisbon, Málaga, Barcelona, Genoa, Venice, Piraeus, Cherbourg, Le Havre, Southampton — before proceeding to cruise European waters (i.e., the Mediterranean, the Baltic Sea, the Black Sea, through the Norwegian fjords). Passengers can elect to stay aboard for the basic transatlantic segment alone or for both the crossing and the subsequent European cruise.

Those interested in including a cruise to other European waters before, during, or after their trip to France will find that a number of European cruises depart from French ports — primarily Le Havre and Nice. In May, the *Royal Cruise Line*'s *Crown Odyssey* will make a 12-day cruise called "Great Capitals of Europe," which includes a stop in Paris. Also offered by *Royal Cruise Lines* is a "Best of Italy, France, and the Greek Isles," which includes stops in Nice and Monte Carlo aboard the *Golden Odyssey.*

Paquet French Cruises operates a 14-day cruise to some of the world's most famous archeological sites. Cruises depart from Toulon in France, and ports of call include Athens and Rhodes (Greece), Syracuse (Sicily), Tartus (Syria), and Mersin (Turkey). Fares range from $1,995 to $5,980. For information, contact *Paquet French Cruises,* 240 S. Country Rd., Palm Beach, FL 33480 (phone: 800-999-0555).

In summer, the coastal waters of Europe are busy with ships offering cruises of varying lengths, and the French city of Nice (or Monaco) in particular is frequently included as a port of call on the Mediterranean cruises. But while many cruises out of continental ports include at least one stop in France and many begin or end in a French port, few regularly devote a significant portion of the cruise to exploring French territory.

For these and other offerings, book well in advance in order to qualify for substantial "early bird" discounts. For information ask your travel agent or contact the following cruise lines directly: *Cunard,* 555 Fifth Ave., New York, NY 10017 (phone: 212-880-7500, 800-221-4770, or 800-5-CUNARD); *Royal Viking Line,* 95 Merrick, Coral Gables, FL 33134 (phone: 305-447-9660 in Miami; 800-634-8000 elsewhere in the US); and *Royal Cruise Line,* One Maritime Plaza, Suite 1400, San Francisco, CA 94111 (phone: 800-792-2992 or 415-956-7200 in California; 800-227-0925 or 800-227-4534 elsewhere in the US).

FREIGHTERS: An alternative to conventional cruise ships is travel by freighter. These are cargo ships that also take a limited number of passengers (usually about 12) in reasonably comfortable accommodations. The idea of traveling by freighter has long appealed to romantic souls, but there are a number of drawbacks to keep in mind before casting off. Once upon a time, a major advantage of freighter travel was its low cost, but this is no longer the case. Though freighters usually are less expensive than cruise ships, the difference is not as great as it once was, and excursion airfares are certainly even less expensive. Accommodations and recreational facilities vary, but freighters were not designed to amuse passengers, so it is important to appreciate the idea of freighter travel itself. Schedules are erratic, and travelers must fit their timetable to that of the ship. Passengers have found themselves waiting as long as a month for a promised sailing, and because freighters follow their cargo commitments, it is possible that a scheduled port could be omitted at the last minute or a new one added.

Anyone contemplating taking a freighter from a US port across the Atlantic should be aware that at press time, only a few freighter lines were carrying passengers on such transatlantic crossings. Once a week, *Polish Ocean Lines*' freighters accommodate 6 passengers in 3 double cabins on voyages approximately 8 to 10 days in length from Port Newark, New Jersey, to Le Havre (France), Rotterdam (Holland), and Bremerhaven (West Germany). The one-way fare from Newark ranged from $1,010 to $1,105 per person in 1990, and passengers also could board in Baltimore, Maryland, or

Wilmington, North Carolina, for an additional $150; round-trip fares were simply double the one-way fares. For information, contact *Gdynia America Line,* the general agent for *Polish Ocean Lines,* at 39 Broadway, 14th Floor, New York, NY 10006 (phone: 212-952-1280).

Container Ships Reederi departs approximately every 2 weeks and, with a capacity of 6 passengers, sails from Long Beach, California, via the Panama Canal to Felixstowe (Great Britain), Le Havre (France), and Rotterdam (Holland), taking 23 to 24 days to make the trip. The one-way, per-person fare ranges from $1,975 to $2,315. For information, contact the line's general agent, *Freighter World Cruises* (address below). Another line, *Lykes Lines,* sails to Felixstowe, Le Havre, and Rotterdam from New Orleans, with a capacity of up to 8 passengers. The trip lasts 12 to 13 days, and ships leave every 8 days year-round; a one-way ticket costs $1,400 for a cabin, $1,500 for a suite. Contact *Lykes Lines,* 300 Poydras, New Orleans, LA 70130 (phone: 800-535-1861 or 504-523-6611).

Last, *Mediterranean Shipping Co.* sails from Baltimore, Boston, New York, and Newport News (Rhode Island) to Antwerp (Belgium), Bremen and Hamburg (West Germany), Felixstowe (Great Britain), and Le Havre (France), taking 18 to 19 days for the trip. The ships can carry 12 passengers and leave weekly year-round. Prices vary, based on departure point and destination, but on average the one-way fare runs between $1,900 and $2,100. Contact *Mediterranean Shipping*'s representative, *Sea the Difference,* 96 Morton St., New York, NY 10014 (phone 800-666-9333 or 212-691-3760).

Specialists dealing only (or largely) in freighter travel exist to help prospective passengers arrange trips. They provide information, schedules, and, when you're ready to sail, booking services. Among these agencies are the following:

> *Freighter World Cruises:* A freighter travel agency that acts as general agent for several freighter lines. Publishes the twice-monthly *Freighter Space Advisory,* listing space available on sailings worldwide. A subscription costs $27 a year, $25 of which can be credited toward the cost of a cruise. 180 S. Lake Ave., Suite 335, Pasadena, CA 91101 (phone: 818-449-3106).
>
> *Pearl's Travel Tips:* Run by Ilse Hoffman, who finds sailings for her customers and sends them off with all kinds of valuable information and advice. 333 E. 79th St., Penthouse S., New York, NY 10021 (phone: 212-734-6327).
>
> *TravLTips Cruise and Freighter Travel Association:* A freighter travel agency and club ($15 a year or $25 for 2 years) whose members receive the bi-monthly *TravLTips* magazine of cruise and freighter travel. PO Box 188, Flushing, NY 11358 (phone: 718-939-2400 in New York; 800-872-8584 elsewhere in the US).

INLAND WATERWAYS: Cruising the canals and rivers of Europe is becoming more and more popular, probably in reaction to the speed of jet travel and the normal rush to do as much as possible in as little time as possible. A cabin cruiser or converted barge averages only about 5 miles an hour, covering in a week of slow floating the same distance a car would travel in a few hours of determined driving. Passengers see only a small section of countryside, but they see it in depth and with an intimacy simply impossible any other way.

France's 25,000 miles of rivers are connected and paralleled by 3,000 miles of canals, making the country ideal for inland cruising. One choice area is Burgundy, where the network of rivers and canals happens to be especially dense. Here the rivers of the north and west of France — the Seine, the Loire, and the Marne — are connected to the rivers of the south and east — the Saône, the Rhône, and eventually the Rhine and even the Garonne — and cruising possibilities are limited only by time. The Canal de Briare, begun in the early 17th century and one of the oldest in France; the 19th-century Canal

Latéral à la Loire, running along the middle section of the Loire; the Canal du Nivernais, the Canal du Centre, and the Canal de Bourgogne, in the heart of Burgundy; as well as the Canal de la Marne à la Saône and the Saône itself all provide wonderfully tranquil vantage points from which to view rural France. Waterside scenes range from cattle grazing in fertile pastures, to forests, orchards, and vineyards, not to mention old abbeys and châteaux (though the most famous châteaux of the Loire are to the west of this nexus of waterways) and such historic and picturesque towns as Sancerre, Nevers, Auxerre, Langres, and Dijon, once the capital of the Dukes of Burgundy.

Another choice area for inland waterway cruising is in the south of France, especially along the Canal du Midi, the technical tour de force of a 17th-century tax collector and amateur engineer, Pierre-Paul Riquet. The canal, which opened in 1681 to create a link between the Atlantic and the Mediterranean, runs an especially scenic 160-mile course across the Languedoc region, beginning at Toulouse on the Garonne River and climbing to a high point near Castelnaudary, then descending toward its Mediterranean terminal at Sète. En route, it passes the medieval walled city of Carcassonne, the equally ancient city of Béziers, and such marvels of 17th-century engineering as the world's oldest canal tunnel and the lock staircase of Fontséranes, which carries the canal down a level of 80 feet in a distance of 350 yards. Adjacent canals include the Canal Latéral à la Garonne, running alongside the Garonne west of Toulouse and extending into the wine region of Bordeaux, and the Canal du Rhône à Sète, skirting the wild, marshy expanse of the Camargue from Sète to the Rhône River.

A third, less frequented cruising area is in northern France — in Brittany, where the rivers Vilaine and Erdre, the Canal d'Ille et Rance, and the Canal de Nantes à Brest cut through the peaceful Breton countryside and connect such old towns as Rennes, the historic capital of the duchy of Brittany, Dinan, and Josselin, the site of a magnificent, turreted castle right at the water's edge. A fourth area, no less picturesque, is in the northeast corner of the country, on the Grand Canal d'Alsace, which weaves in and out of the Rhine and runs along the Alsatian wine route south of Strasbourg, and on adjoining canals such as the Canal de la Marne au Rhin, which leads from Strasbourg into Lorraine, and the Canal du Rhône au Rhin, which crosses the region of Franche-Comté on its way to Burgundy.

There are two ways to cruise the inland waterways: by renting your own self-drive boat or by booking aboard a hotel boat. If you choose to skipper your own diesel-powered cruiser, you will be shown how to handle the craft and told whom to call if you break down. But once you cast off, you and your party — the boats sleep from 2 to 10 people — will be on your own. You help lockkeepers (*éclusiers*) operate the gates and do your own cooking (in addition to village markets, the lockkeepers themselves often have fresh provisions) or eat at cafés and restaurants along the way. The cost of the rental can vary considerably depending on the size of the boat, the season, and the area. A boat sleeping two comfortably can cost from $600 to $700 per week in spring or fall and jump to $1,100 to $1,800 and up per week at the height of the summer; an 8-berth boat can range anywhere from $1,000 to $8,000 per week. The average rental, however, sleeping four, works out to about $175 per person per week during the low season and $300 per person per week in the high season. Fuel is not included.

The alternative is to cruise on a hotel boat — often a converted barge, or *péniche*. In France, these carry anywhere from 6 to 24 guests, occasionally even more, as well as the crew. You can charter the boat and have it all to yourself or join other guests aboard. Cruises usually last from 3 days to a week; accommodations can be simple or quite luxurious, and most meals usually are included. When reading the brochure, note the boat's facilities (most cabins have private washbasins, showers, and toilets, but bathrooms also can be separate and shared), as well as the itinerary and any special features, such as sightseeing excursions, that may be offered. Many of the French cruises have a special emphasis such as French food and include wine tasting excursions to vineyards and wine cellars; others make a point of visiting historic spots. Prices can range from $500 per person, double occupancy, to over $1,750.

The travel firms listed below, including the operators of hotel-boat cruises and representatives of self-drive boat suppliers, can provide information or arrange your whole holiday afloat in France.

Abercrombie & Kent/Continental Waterways: Runs hotel-boat cruises in Burgundy. 1420 Kensington Rd. Suite 103, Oak Brook, IL 60521 (phone: 708-954-2944 in Illinois; 800-323-7308 elsewhere).

Bargain Boating, Morgantown Travel Service: Books self-skippered boats in Alsace and Lorraine, Brittany, Burgundy, the Cognac area of Poitou-Charentes, and the south of France. PO Box 757, Morgantown, WV 26507-0757 (phone: 800-637-0782 or 304-292-8471).

Blakes Vacations: Books self-skippered boats in Alsace, Brittany, Burgundy, Charente, and on the Lot River. 4939 Dempster St., Skokie, IL 60077 (phone: 312-539-1010 in Illinois; 800-628-8118 elsewhere in the US).

Esplanade Tours: Books hotel-boat cruises in Alsace, Burgundy, and the Franche-Comté, as well as along the Canal du Midi and elsewhere in the south of France. 581 Boylston St., Boston, MA 02116 (phone: 800-628-4893 or 617-266-7465).

Etoile de Champagne: Offers luxury chartered hotel-boat cruises thoughout the inland waterways of France. 50 Congress St., Boston, MA 02109 (phone: 800-356-8846 or 617-227-3000).

Floating Through Europe: Operates hotel-boat cruises in Alsace and Lorraine, Burgundy, Champagne, and the south of France. 271 Madison Ave., New York, NY 10016 (phone: 800-221-3140 or 212-685-5600).

French Country Waterways, Ltd.: Books hotel-boat cruises that traverse the Rhine river and nearby canals in the Alsace area. Included in the 7-day, 6-night trips are all meals and table wines, all side tours and excursions, and even bicycles. Available but at an additional cost are hot-air balloon rides on a number of the trips. PO Box 2195, Duxbury, MA 02331 (phone: 617-934-2454 or 800-222-1236 throughout the continental US).

French Experience: Books self-drive boats in Alsace and Lorraine, the Aquitaine, Brittany, Burgundy, the Camargue, the Midi, Nivernais, and the Upper Loire. 370 Lexington Avenue, Suite 812, New York, NY 10017 (phone: 800-28-FRANCE or 212-986-3800).

Skipper Travel Services: Books self-drive boats in Alsace, Brittany, Burgundy, the Loire, and the south of France. Also offers hotel-boat cruises in some of these regions, as well as in Charante. 210 California Ave., Palo Alto, CA 94306 (phone: 415-321-5658).

French Cruise Lines (FCL) also offers inland cruises on the Rhône, Saône, and Seine rivers aboard two 100-passenger ships, the *Arlène* and the *Normandy.* Ports of call include Paris, Rouen, and Villequier. Round-trip fares for the 6- and 7-night river cruises range from $1,350 to $1,550 and include all meals, but not wine — only the finest French vintages are served. For information, contact *French Cruise Lines,* 701 Lee St., Des Plaines, IL 60016 (phone: 800-222-8664).

■ **A final note on picking a cruise:** A "cruise-only" travel agency can best help you choose a cruise ship and itinerary. Cruise-only agents also are best equipped to tell you about a particular ship's "personality," the kind of person with whom you'll likely be traveling on a particular ship, what dress is acceptable (it varies from ship to ship), and much more. Travel agencies that specialize in booking cruises usually are members of an association called the *National Association of*

Cruise Only Agencies (NACOA). For a listing of the agencies in your area (requests are limited to three states), send a self-addressed, stamped envelope to *NACOA*, PO Box 7209, Freeport, NY 11520, or call 516-378-8006.

FERRIES: Numerous ferries link France with its largest island, Corsica, and with Great Britain and Ireland and other countries. Nearly all of them carry both passengers and cars — you simply drive on and drive off in most cases — and most of the routes are in service year-round. Some operators offer reduced rates for round-trip excursions, midweek travel, or off-season travel. Space for cars should be booked as early as possible, especially for July and August crossings, even though most lines schedule more frequent departures during the summer. Note that long journeys, of 8 to 10 hours or more, tend to be scheduled overnight.

The shipping line *Société Nationale Maritime Corse-Méditerranée (SNCM)* operates passenger and car carrying ferries between Marseilles, Nice, and Toulon on the French mainland and the Corsican ports of Bastia, Ile-Rousse, and Calvi (northern Corsica) and Ajaccio and Propriano (southwestern Corsica). Sailings vary from almost daily to two or three times a week or less, depending on the route and the season, with some of the routes served in summer only. The crossing takes from 5 to 6 hours (Nice to Calvi or Ile-Rousse, the shortest routes) up to 10 or 12 hours (Marseilles to Bastia, the longest route), and there are day as well as night ferries, the latter with cabins or *couchettes* available. *SNCM* also operates international sailings between Marseilles and Tunis (Tunisia) every sixth or seventh day depending on the season, and between Toulon and Porto Torres, Sardinia, about once a week, also depending on the season. Reservations can be made in the US by contacting *French Line* (2 World Trade Center, Suite 2164, New York, NY 10048; phone: 212-524-0996) or through *SNCM* offices in Paris, Marseilles, Nice, Toulon, and other French cities. Anyone planning to transport a car by ferry in high season should make the reservation well in advance — as early as February if possible.

Ferries between France and Great Britain include the fleet of *Sealink* ships connecting Calais with Dover, Boulogne with Folkestone, Dieppe with Newhaven, and Cherbourg with Weymouth (no winter service). For information write or call the central office, *Sealink British Ferries Limited* (Southern House, Lord Warden Square, Dover, Kent, CT179DH England; phone: 011-44-304-203-203). *P&O European Ferries* (Channel House, Channel View Rd., Dover, Kent, CP179TJ England; phone: 011-44-304-203-388) also operates ferry services to Great Britain, from Calais and Boulogne to Dover, and from Le Havre and Cherbourg to Portsmouth. Other service is available from Le Havre to Southampton, St.-Malo to Portsmouth and the Channel Islands, and from Roscoff to Plymouth. Ferries to Ireland leave from Le Havre and Cherbourg en route to Rosslare Harbour and from Le Havre and Roscoff en route to Cork.

Hoverspeed Hovercraft carry both cars and passengers on a cushion of air across the English Channel between Calais and Boulogne and Dover. Since *Hovercraft* travel a few feet above the water, they can be affected by waves and are grounded when the Channel is rough. When the weather is good, however, they make the trip in an average of 35 minutes (compared to the ferry's 1¼ to 1¾ hours).

Most ferry arrivals and departures are well served by connecting passenger trains or buses, and passengers can buy through train tickets between Paris and London that include the sea portion of the trip. The Paris to London route on through services by train/*Hovercraft*/train, for example, takes an average 5½ hours; from Paris to London on through services by train/ferry/train can take from 7 to 9 hours by day, depending on the route, or about 9½ to 10½ hours overnight.

There also are ferry links between France and Morocco, Algeria, and Tunisia. Corsica also can be reached by ferry from the Italian mainland and from the island of Sardinia.

Traveling by Train

Perhaps the most economical, and often the most pleasant, way to see a lot of a foreign country in a relatively short time is by rail. It certainly is the quickest way to travel between two cities up to 300 miles apart (beyond that, a flight normally would be quicker, even counting the time it takes to get to and from the airport). But time isn't always the only consideration. Traveling by train is a way to keep moving and seeing at the same time, and with the special discounts available to visitors, it can be an almost irresistible bargain. You only need to get to a station on time; after that, put your watch in your pocket and relax. You may not get to your destination exactly at the appointed hour (although French trains are quite punctual for the most part), but you'll have a marvelous time looking out the window and enjoying the ride.

TRAINS: While North Americans have been raised to depend on their cars, Europeans have long been able to depend on public transporation. The government-owned and -operated *Société Nationale des Chemins de Fer Français (SNCF)* — known to the English-speaking world as *FrenchRail Inc.* — is one of the world's most extensive railway systems. It also is one of the world's most modern systems — so modern, in fact, that anyone whose knowledge of French trains was acquired before September 27, 1981, cannot be said to be truly *au courant.* On that day, the opening of the first section of a new high-speed rail line between Paris and Lyons ushered in a new railway era in France, making possible the inauguration of passenger service aboard the world's fastest train, the *TGV (Train à Grande Vitesse).* Though *TGV*s are capable of speeds of up to 317 mph (or 511 kmh) — per the world record set by a *TGV* train on May 9, 1990 — their maximum speed in commercial operation is limited to 186 mph. Yet even at that relative snail's pace, the *TGV* in one fell swoop cut the travel time between France's two largest cities from 4 hours to 2 hours and 40 minutes, and when a second section of new track opened in 1983, the time dropped again to a mere 2 hours.

At present, travelers who want to experience *TGV* service can choose from numerous daily departures from Paris to Lyons or vice versa. But because the trains are capable of running on conventional track, as well as on their own special track, it is not necessary to be traveling strictly between Paris and Lyons in order to ride them. If you're bound from Paris to Dijon, Besançon, Lausanne, or Bern (or vice versa), to Chambéry, Geneva, or Grenoble, to Avignon, Nîmes, Montpellier, Marseilles, Toulon, or Nice — as well as a number of other cities en route — you can travel via *TGV*, riding at top speed along one or both portions of the special track and then proceeding more slowly along the old track toward your final destination. It also is possible to board a *TGV* train at an intermediate stop and ride it a short way, say from Avignon to Marseilles, though in this case you will experience *TGV*'s rolling stock but not its top speed.

The new *TGV* line to the Atlantic Coast is scheduled to be completed early this year. This *TGV* service will extend to points south and west of Paris, including Bordeaux, Nantes, Quimper, Rennes, Tours, and the Spanish border. The effect that these additional high-speed trains will have on travel to western cities will be added convenience for wide-ranging day trips — traveling through the Gallic countryside will be easier than ever.

As a matter of policy — the French refer to it as the *démocratisation de la vitesse* — *TGV* trains carry both first and second class passengers, and a trip between any two cities by *TGV* costs no more than a trip between the same two cities by conventional train and track. In practice, however, a supplement is charged for traveling at rush hours and on peak days, and these departures account for a good portion of the *TGV* schedule. In addition, reservations are obligatory. On the Paris–Lyons line, each train carries 275 second class passengers and 111 first class passengers, with no standees allowed. The new Atlantic line will carry 369 in second class and 116 in first class.

Reservations can be made following the same procedures as for any other train or, provided you already have a ticket to your destination, by using the last-minute *TGV* Réservation Rapide machines in the station. These will reserve a seat (if one is available) on any *TGV* departing within 1½ hours of a request. You cannot specify a smoking or nonsmoking car or an aisle or a window seat by machine, and meals cannot be reserved this way either, but the machine can be instructed to restrict its search to only those trains not requiring payment of a supplement. Otherwise, the necessary surcharge must be dropped into the machine in coin.

Besides the *TGV*, other categories of trains the visitor is likely to encounter in France include the *Euro City (EC)* trains, *Intercité (IC)* trains, *rapides,* and expresses. The first of these, as their name implies, are largely international trains operated by several of Europe's national railway companies, including *FrenchRail Inc.* The *EC* network, introduced in May 1987, has by now all but replaced the *Trans-Europe Express (TEE)*, which has provided the European Economic Community with efficient, luxurious train service since the 1950s.

While it is the *TGV* system that represents the state of the art in train technology, *EC* trains are the prestige trains of Europe. They use modern, air conditioned coaches and travel at a minimum speed of 54 miles per hour (the average includes time for station stops). With the exception of some first class-only Paris–Brussels trains, the *EC*s generally offer both first and second class service and require payment of a supplement for all departures. The supplement includes the price of a reserved seat. *Intercité (IC)* trains are similar to *EC* trains in that they provide a high standard of service, have both first and second class cars, and require supplements.

A *rapide* is a fast train making limited stops. More and more, this category is becoming synonymous with the type of equipment used on the routes: *Turbotrains* and *Corail* trains. Both are examples of the latest in French railway technology, both were developed to run at speeds up to 125 mph, and both provide such amenities as air conditioned, soundproofed coaches, and the announcement of stations over a public address system. No supplement is required and seat reservations are optional. Express trains, the next category, make many more intermediate stops along main lines than do *rapides,* though they can be the fastest trains on secondary or transverse routes where *rapides* are rare and where slower trains — in the direct or omnibus categories — abound. In fact, the French railway system resembles something of a giant spider web or a wheel, with most of the main lines radiating like spokes from Paris at the center. Service between provincial cities on the same spoke is fast and frequent, but in the case of towns on different spokes, it is sometimes faster and easier to get from one to the other by going the long way around — via Paris.

A word about the many train stations in Paris: There are six main ones, each the starting point for trains to a particular region. The Gare de l'Est, simply enough, is the departure point for eastbound trains to Alsace in France; Austria, Luxembourg, southern Germany, and Switzerland. The Gare du Nord, equally clear, is the departure point for northbound trains to Boulogne, Calais, and Lille in France; Belgium, the Netherlands, and northern Germany. Trains to the west depart from the Gare St.-Lazare — to Cherbourg, Dieppe, Le Havre, and the rest of Normandy — and from the Gare Montparnasse — to Brittany, Chartres, Le Mans, and Nantes. The Gare d'Austerlitz serves the southwest, including Bordeaux and Toulouse, and Spain. The Gare de Lyon serves the southeast, including the Côte d'Azur, Grenoble, Lyons, Marseilles; Italy and Switzerland.

The stations are anywhere from ½ mile to 4 miles apart, but they are connected by an interstation shuttle bus or by the Paris métro (subway), which usually is faster. If you are taking a trip that requires a transfer from station to station with little time to spare, be sure to find out beforehand exactly how to make the connection and how long it will take. Note, also, that Paris is not the only city in France with more than one railroad station.

RESERVATIONS, DINING AND SLEEPING CARS, OTHER SERVICES: Both first and second class seats on most better trains can be reserved in advance, either before you leave home or after your arrival in France. Reservations reduce flexibility, but they are advisable during the summer on popular routes, particularly those leading to the Atlantic or Mediterranean coasts and onward into Spain or Italy. They also are advisable at any time of the year if it is imperative that you be on a particular train. In France, seats can be reserved as much as 6 months in advance by mail, 2 months in advance in person, or 9 days in advance by phone, with the reservation period closing anywhere from the night before to 2 or 3 hours before the departure of the train (the obligatory *TGV* reservation can be made up to a few minutes before departure). In the US, the reservation period usually runs from 2 months to 15 days before departure. The reservation fee is a flat amount per seat ($6 including communications charges if made in the US).

Dining facilities on French trains vary. On *EC* trains, passengers still can take meals in the traditional way, in a separate dining car. On *TGV* trains, meals in first class are served airline-style, at the passenger's seat, but each train also carries a bar car selling sandwiches, cold plates, and other simple meals to both classes. *Corail* trains and *Turbotrains* tend to offer the same possibilities as the *TGV*, while other trains may have a self-service *Gril Express* cafeteria car or no more than an ambulatory vendor dispensing sandwiches and beverages from a cart. If you're sure you will want to eat en route, it's a good idea to inquire beforehand exactly what meal service is offered on the train you'll be taking. Reservations for the dining car and for meals served at your seat should be made at the same time you make your seat reservation.

Sleeping accommodations are found on overnight trains going long distances, such as between Paris and Biarritz, Bordeaux, Grenoble, and Toulouse, and points along the Mediterranean. Two types of arrangements are possible: *couchettes* and sleepers.

Couchettes, available in both first and second class versions, basically are the coach seats of a compartment converted to sleeping berths, with pillows, sheets, and blankets. First class compartments contain four *couchettes* (an upper and a lower on each side of the aisle); second class compartments contain six (an upper, middle, and lower on each side). Since *couchettes* cost only a standard supplement per person (about $17 in either class at present if reserved in the US) above the first or second class fare, they are a relatively inexpensive way to get a night's rest aboard the train. However, they provide privacy only for those traveling with a family or other group that can use the whole compartment; individual travelers are mixed with strangers of either sex.

Sleepers are actual bedroom compartments providing one to three beds with a mattress, pillow, sheets, and blanket, plus a washbasin with hot and cold water. Several kinds of compartments are available, though not always on every train. Singles, specials, and doubles are all first class accommodations. The special is the least expensive, and is a slightly smaller individual compartment than the single; the double is for two people who have booked it together. Tourist compartments (T2 and T3) are second class compartments for two and three people traveling together or for strangers, though unlike *couchette* accommodations, strangers of the opposite sex are segregated. Sleeper accommodations, in France, require payment of the basic first or second class fare plus a supplement that varies with the type of compartment (and beyond French borders, with the type of compartment and the distance traveled). From the least to the most expensive, sleeper arrangements can cost anywhere from twice the price of a *couchette* to as much as eight times more.

Naturally, it is best to travel light. More and more modern trains (such as *TGV* and *Corail*) are equipped with a place to put luggage just inside the doors, but otherwise you will have to hoist your suitcase up onto the overhead rack. If you have too much luggage to handle yourself, it can be sent as registered baggage, which is limited to three pieces per person, up to 30 kilos (approximately 66 pounds) each, for a set fee per piece. But do not expect registered baggage to travel on the same train as you do, because this possibility is limited to only a few trains. In many stations, you'll find self-service luggage carts at your disposal, and most stations have either a baggage checkroom (*consigne*) or 24-hour luggage lockers (*consigne automatique*) where you can temporarily free yourself of surplus bags.

Drivers should be aware of a variety of *SNCF* services. One of particular interest to foreign visitors is *Train + Auto,* a car-rental service available in more than 230 French cities. Using *Train + Auto,* passengers can reserve a car 24 hours in advance and find it waiting for them at their destination station. Car carrying trains, called *Trains Autos-Couchettes (TAC)* or *Motorail,* are another convenience. These operate principally between northern points of entry (i.e., Boulogne, Calais, Strasbourg) and the Atlantic and Mediterranean, as well as between Paris and numerous points southeast to southwest (from the Alps to the Riviera, across the Pyrénées to the Atlantic, and into neighboring countries). This service allows car owners to take to the rails for long distances while their car travels with them on the same train. Bookings should be made well in advance, especially in summer. *SNCF* also provides parking lots at reasonable prices in the vicinity of stations throughout France. To find them, look for the "Parco-train" signs.

Similar services exist for bicyclists. Some 280 stations in cities throughout France offer *Train + Vélo,* through which traditional or 10-speed bikes can be rented by the half-day, the day, or longer. Travelers with their own bicycles can ship them as registered baggage for a fee (bicycle and owner do not necessarily ride the same train), but there are many short- and medium-distance trains on which bicycles are accepted as free baggage provided their owners load them onto and take them off the baggage car themselves. (For further information on renting and transporting bicycles, see *Camping and RVs, Hiking and Biking* in this section.)

SNCF also has introduced special, summer-only tourist trains — including, in conjunction with *Provence Railways* (see below), the *Alpazur* from Grenoble to Nice — which make scenic runs with multilingual commentary (verify that this is still operative beforehand), and offers live entertainment en route. Among other seasonal trains are the *Bocage* (Paris to Normandy), the *Cevenol* (Paris to Marseilles), the *Trouvère* (Paris to Calais), and the *Valentré* (Paris to Toulouse). For information on these and other routes, inquire about *Loisirail* trains at any of the *FrenchRail Inc.* offices in the US, or at rail stations in France.

Other combination sightseeing ventures are afternoon outings or excursions of one or a few days aboard *Services de Tourisme SNCF* buses. These operate out of some 250 French cities, but as they are designed mainly for the local traveler, they are conducted in French. *Franceshrinkers,* on the other hand, is strictly for English-speaking visitors. This program consists of a number of day-trip itineraries from Paris, including Burgundy, Chartres and Versailles, Giverny and Versailles, the Loire Valley, and Le-Mont-St.-Michel.

Sealink ships, operated by *SNCF* with British partners, cross the Channel to Great Britain from the French ports of Calais, Boulogne, Cherbourg, St.-Malo, Dunkerque, and Dieppe. Travelers can buy through train tickets from Paris to London, with no need to make separate arrangements for the sea portion of the journey. Travel is by rail to the water, where the ship waits, equipped or not with sleeping cabins depending on the length of the trip. Passengers walk to the ship and, on the other shore, board a waiting train to complete the journey. *Hoverspeed Hovercraft,* also run jointly by *SNCF* and British partners, skim across the surface of the water with their cargo of passengers and autos, crossing the Channel from Boulogne or Calais to Dover in about 35 minutes. (For additional information on current rail/ship/rail connections between France and Great Britain, see *Traveling by Ship,* in this section.)

The next step in the development of this network is a link across the English Channel. The Eurotunnel (also referred to as the "Chunnel") is currently under construction; the official scheduled completion date is 1992 — the popular current estimate is late 1993 to 1994. This addition will connect the French railway (and other continental service) with that of the British; the underwater portion of the trip will take approximately 35 minutes.

TICKETS AND FARES: French train fares are based on a combination of the distance traveled and the quality of accommodations chosen. Most trains have both first and second class cars, with a ticket in first class costing 50% more than a ticket in second class. Because of this, first class generally is less crowded. It also is more spacious. On *TGV, Corail* trains, and *Turbotrains,* for instance, second class passengers sit four in a row — two abreast on either side of the aisle — while first class passengers sit three in a row. Anyone electing to travel second class, however — as most of the French do — probably will find it perfectly satisfactory, with service that can be compared favorably to that found anywhere in North America.

A round-trip ticket between any two points, as a rule, simply costs double the price of a one-way ticket. The exception is the *billet séjour,* which allows a reduction of 25% for round trips or circle trips (which do not have to return to the point of origin) of at least 1,000 kilometers (620 miles) total distance with a stay of at least 5 days before the return portion is begun. The *billet séjour,* which can be bought only in France, is one of several ways the French economize on train travel. Other methods include the Couple Card and the Family Card, both technically open to foreigners though not easily used by the short-term visitor (a *livret de famille* or *certificat de concubinage* — also available through *FrenchRail Inc.* — must be presented to apply for them). Another card, the Carte Vermeil, provides 60% discounts on tickets for off-peak travel (either first or second class) for senior citizens, and is more easily obtained. (This card is available at railway stations throughout France; the only restriction is that the tickets must be bought in France for the discount to be applied.) Most visitors who plan to do a lot of train travel, however, will find that a rail pass (see below) is an equally good bargain. Passes generally are meant for foreigners only, and often must be bought in the US (or some other foreign location) prior to arrival in France.

Tickets can be bought at train stations, at auxiliary *SNCF* offices where they exist, at travel agencies displaying the *SNCF* sign, and, if necessary, aboard the train, though they'll cost more that way. They also can be bought at *FrenchRail Inc.* offices in the US (addresses below), where, given fluctuations in exchange rates, they may cost a bit more or less than they would if bought in France. (The *French and European Fares* booklet, issued annually by *FrenchRail Inc.,* gives the price charged in US dollars for certain trips, both within France and between France and its neighbors.) Tickets bought in France are valid for any train, any day — pending the payment of supplements and reservations fees necessary for some trains; the period of validity is 2 months or, in the case of a ticket bought with a reservation, for 2 months counted from the day of the intended trip. Tickets bought in North America are valid for 6 months and include fees for supplements.

Tickets purchased in Europe cannot be used until they are stamped with a date, and reminders to this effect — *compostez votre billet* — are posted in stations throughout France. Before proceeding to the platform, look for the bright orange ticket stamping machine (*composteur*) usually found just at the gate and insert your ticket until a click is heard. Failure to do so can be an expensive mistake, because the presentation of an unstamped ticket aboard the train will cost its bearer a 20% fine. A ticket stamped with any date but the date of departure will be considered null and void, costing the bearer a fine plus the price of a new ticket. The penalties are so severe because tickets on French trains are merely spot-checked; an unstamped ticket is no different from an unused ticket, for which you may request a refund. Only rail passes bought outside France — which must be validated by an information clerk (see below) — are exempt from this requirement. Round-trip tickets must be stamped both for the departure and the return, and if any trip is interrupted en route, the ticket must be stamped again before resuming travel if the stopover has been overnight.

OTHER RAILROADS: A few trains in France have nothing to do with *SNCF*. Minor railways include the privately owned, narrow-gauge *Chemins de Fer de Provence*, or *Provence Railways*, which operates over a scenic route between Nice and Digne. The limited system of *Corsican Railways* connects Bastia to Ajaccio, with an offshoot to Ile-Rousse and Calvi.

The *Orient Express* also passes through France. The legendary *Orient Express* of old, the luxury hotel on wheels that carried tourists and tycoons, kings and conspirators, from London and Paris via Eastern Europe to Istanbul, made its final run in 1977 but has since been revived as the *Venice Simplon–Orient Express*. It leaves London for Paris and Venice weekly from mid-February to September and twice weekly from September to mid-November, giving passengers a nostalgic taste of the golden age of rail aboard sumptuously restored carriages of the 1920s. Information on these deluxe trips, which can be taken all the way or in part in either direction, is available from *Venice Simplon–Orient Express*, Suite 2565, One World Trade Center, New York, NY 10048 (phone: 212-938-6830 in New York State; 800-524-2420 elsewhere).

PASSES: Rail passes are offered by the national railroad companies of most European countries. They allow unlimited train travel within a set period, frequently include connecting service via other forms of transportation, and can save a considerable amount of money, as well as time. The only requirement is validation of the pass by an information clerk on the day of your first rail trip; for subsequent trips, there is no need to stand in line — and lines can be very long during peak travel seasons. Designed primarily for foreign visitors, these passes generally must be bought in advance in the US. Although these passes are among the best bargains around, when considering your options be sure you look into the comparable cost of individual train tickets which — depending on the number of days you plan to travel — may work out to be more economical.

France's own pass, the France Railpass, offers unlimited train travel on the *SNCF* network throughout the country. Flexibility and economy are the primary advantages of the Railpass, which can be purchased for either first or second class and for periods of 4 or 9 days. The 4-day pass can be used for any 4 days within a 15-day period; the longer-term pass is good for any 9 days within a period of 30 days. These passes also include a free round trip by rail between Orly or Charles de Gaulle airports and downtown Paris, unlimited travel on the Paris métro and bus systems for 1 day, discounts on entry to museums and regional tourist attractions, a discount ride on the privately owned *Chemins de Fer de Provence* railway, discounts on *SNCF*'s *Train + Auto* car rental service, and a 10% reduction on sightseeing excursions by *SNCF* bus. Passholders should contact the regional tourist offices in the areas they plan to visit to receive a booklet entitling them to additional local discounts.

At the time of this writing, the France Railpass cost from $175 (first class) to $99 (second class) for the 4-day version, and from $249 (first class) to $149 (second class) for the 9-day version. Children ages 4 through 11 are entitled to their own passes at a bit more than half the adult price (children under 4 travel free on French trains provided they do not occupy a seat). Holders of the pass are exempt from paying the supplements required on certain fast trains such as *TGV*s, *IC*s, and *EC*s (although those with a second class pass still have to pay the difference between classes to ride the first class *EC*). The France Railpass is meant for nonresidents of France only and, therefore, must be bought before going abroad either from a travel agent or through *FrenchRail Inc.* offices.

The France Rail 'N Drive Pass combines rail travel and car rental through *Avis*. Designed for in-depth tourism, it provides 4 days of unlimited train travel, plus 3 days of car rental (including unlimited mileage, taxes, insurance, and drop-off charges). The total 7 days' transportation may be used during a 15-day period. As we went to press, prices (based on two people traveling together) started at $149 per person for a second class pass; an upgrade to a first class ticket cost an additional $20. The *Avis* network includes 450 locations throughout France, more than 200 of them in railway stations. Reservations from the US should be made at least 7 days in advance by calling France Rail 'N Drive (a division of *Avis*) at 800-331-1084; cars also may be reserved in France 24 hours in advance by contacting any *Avis* office. The France Rail 'N Drive Pass can be upgraded with 1 day air travel within France on *Air-Inter,* the French domestic airline, for $50. This program is called *Fly, Rail & Drive*.

The Eurailpass, the first and best known of all rail passes, also is valid in France, as well as in 16 other European countries. It entitles holders to 15 or 21 days or 1, 2, or 3 months of unlimited first class travel plus many extras, including free travel or substantial reductions on Danube and Rhine river trips, lake steamers, ferry crossings, and transportation by bus and private railroads. Since the Eurailpass is a first class pass, Eurail travelers can ride *EC* trains and any others as they wish, and as with France Railpass–holders, they are exempt from all supplements. At the time of this writing, the prices for first class Eurailpasses were as follows: a 15-day pass cost $340; a 21-day pass cost $440; a 1-month pass cost $550; a 2-month pass cost $750; and a 3-month pass cost $930. A Eurailpass for children under 12 is half the adult price but includes the same features, whereas the Eurail Youthpass, for travelers under 26 years of age, is slightly different. The Youthpass is valid for travel in second class only. As we went to press, it was available in a 1-month version for $380 and a 2-month version for $500.

The Eurail Saverpass resembles the basic Eurailpass, except that it provides 15 days of unlimited first class travel for three people traveling together during peak season; two people traveling together qualify if travel takes place entirely between October 1 and March 31. Under these restrictions, each 15-day ticket costs $100 less than the 15-day Eurailpass.

Another option is the Eurail Flexipass, which can be used for first class travel for any 5 days within a 15-day period ($198), 9 days within a 21-day period ($360), or 14 days within a 30-day period ($458). All of these passes must be bought before you go, either from travel agents or from the US offices of the various European national railway companies.

As with the France Rail 'N Drive Pass, both the 7-day Eurailpass and the 9-day Eurail Flexipass can be combined with 3 to 8 days of car rental through *Hertz.* The program, marketed under the name *Hertz* EurailDrive Escape, starts at $229 per person (based on two people traveling together), and the car rental includes unlimited mileage, basic insurance, and taxes, as well as some drop-off options within most of the countries of rental. Reservations must be made in the US at least 7 days in advance by calling *Hertz* at 800-654-3001.

For those planning to travel throughout both Great Britain and France, however, there is a new pass covering train travel in just these two countries. (The Eurailpass is not valid in Great Britain.) Called the BritFrance Railpass, it comes in two versions, a 5-day pass that is valid for travel during any 5 days out of 15 consecutive days, and a 10-day pass, valid for any 10 days out of any 30-day period. The BritFrance Railpass includes a round-trip ticket aboard the *Hoverspeed Hovercraft* across the English channel, plus certain supplements aboard *FrenchRail Inc.* trains, including the high-speed *TGV* trains and peak-hour travel. As we went to press, the cost of the 5-day pass ranged from $199 (economy class) to $269 (first class); the 10-day pass cost from $299 (economy class) to $399 (first class). The passes are available either from any *BritRail* or *FrenchRail* offices in the US.

FURTHER INFORMATION: *FrenchRail Inc.* offices in the US make reservations, sell tickets and rail passes, and provide information on all *SNCF* services. They distribute the yearly *French and European Fares* booklet, which, along with brochures on the France Railpass and the Eurailpass, provides a good start in adding up the fares of trips you think you might take, in order to judge whether a rail pass would be worth your while. Addresses are 610 Fifth Ave., New York, NY 10020 (phone: 800-848-7245 or 212-582-2816); 2121 Ponce de Leon Blvd., Coral Gables, FL 33134 (phone: 305-445-8648); 11 E. Adams St., Chicago, IL 60603 (phone: 312-427-8691); 9465 Wilshire Blvd., Beverly Hills, CA 90212 (phone: 213-451-5150); and 360 Post St., San Francisco, CA 94108 (phone: 415-982-1993).

FrenchRail also distributes the *Eurail* booklet *Through Europe by Train,* which gives timetables of the main rail services between cities all over Europe as well as between the most important cities in France. Another booklet, *Trains d'Affaires,* gives the schedules of selected trains within France. A summary of *TGV* schedules also is available.

If these extracts are not enough to help you plan a rough itinerary, you may want to buy the *Thomas Cook European Timetable* ($19.95), a weighty and detailed compendium of European international and national rail services that is the most revered and accurate railway reference in existence. The *Timetable* comes out monthly, but because most European countries, France included, switch to summer schedules at the end of May (and back to winter schedules at the end of September), the June edition offers the first complete summer schedule (and October the first complete winter schedule). The February through May editions, however, contain increasingly more definitive supplements on upcoming summer schedules that can be used to plan a trip in advance. The *Thomas Cook European Timetable* is sold by some travel bookstores and by the *Forsyth Travel Library* (PO Box 2975, Shawnee Mission, KS 66201-1375; add $3 for airmail postage; Kansas residents add 5½% sales tax). You can order by phone and pay by credit card by calling 800-367-7984 or 913-384-0496.

Some other books you may want to consult before embarking on an extensive rail trip in Europe include the *Eurail Guide* ($14.95) by Kathryn Saltzman Turpin and Marvin Saltzman; available in most travel bookstores, it also can be ordered from Eurail Guide Annual (27540 Pacific Coast Hwy., Malibu, CA 90265; add $2.05 per book for postage and handling); and *Europe by Eurail* ($12.95) by George Wright Ferguson; available from Globe Pequot Press (PO Box Q, Chester, CT 06412; phone: 203-526-9571). Both guides discuss train travel in general, contain information on France in addition to information on other countries included in the Eurail network (the Saltzman book also discusses Eastern Europe and the rest of the world), and suggest numerous sightseeing excursions by rail from various base cities.

In France, there is no dearth of information sources, beginning with the information desk found in main stations. The myriad blue and orange, nearly wallet-size, city-to-city timetables — *fiches-horaires* — that can be picked up from the display racks in most stations are particularly handy and extremely portable. Also very useful — if you read French — is the *Guide Pratique du Voyageur,* a booklet explaining everything you need to know about French trains from how to travel with *petits animaux* (they must have a ticket) to how to find your *voiture.* Its companion *Guide du Voyageur TGV* explains the new high-speed trains. An English-language version of the latter, *The Traveller's Guide to TGV,* is available from *FrenchRail Inc.* offices in the US.

Finally, although any travel agent can assist you in making arrangements to tour France by rail, you may want to consult a train travel specialist, such as *Accent on Travel* (1030 Curtis St., Suite 201, Menlo Park, CA 94025; phone: 415-326-7330 in California; 800-347-0645 elsewhere in the US).

Traveling by Car

 Driving certainly is the most flexible way to explore out-of-the-way regions of France. Trains whiz much too fast past too many enticing landscapes, pass between France's hills and mountains rather than climb up and around them for a better view, frequently deposit passengers in an unappealing part of town, and don't permit many spur-of-the-moment stops and starts. In a car you go where you want when you want, and can stop along the way as often as you like for a meal, a photograph, or a particularly appealing view.

France is the largest country in Western Europe, yet it is still small enough to be an ideal area to cover by car. The distance from Calais in the north to Nice in the southeast is approximately 760 miles (1,216 km); from Strasbourg in the northeast to Biarritz in the southwest is roughly the same. Within these extremes, distances between points of interest are reasonably short, and the historical and cultural density is such that the flexibility of a car can be used to maximum advantage. A visitor can cover large amounts of territory, visiting major cities and sites, or spend the same amount of time motoring from village to village. (See DIRECTIONS for our choices of the most interesting driving routes.) Travelers who wish to cover the country from end to end can count on a good system of highways to help them make time, while those choosing to explore only one region will find that the secondary and even lesser roads generally are well surfaced and in good condition. Either way, there is plenty of satisfying scenery en route, because — except for some predictably unlovely spots in the industrial north — *la belle France* is just that.

But driving isn't an inexpensive way to travel. Gas prices are far higher in Europe than in North America, and car rentals seldom are available at bargain rates. Keep in mind, however, that driving becomes more economical with more passengers. Because the price of getting wheels abroad will be more than an incidental expense, it is important to investigate every alternative before making a final choice. Many travelers find this expense amply justified when considering that rather than just the means to an end, a well-planned driving route can be an important part of the adventure.

Before setting out, make certain that everything you need is in order. Read about the places you intend to visit and study relevant maps. If at all possible, discuss your intended trip with someone who already has driven the route to find out about road conditions and available services. If you can't speak to someone personally, try to read about others' experiences. Automobile clubs (see below) and French Government Tourist Offices in the US (see *Tourist Information,* in this section, for addresses) can be good sources of driving information, although when requesting brochures and maps be sure to specify the areas you are planning to visit. (Also see "Maps," below.)

DRIVING: A US citizen driving in France must have a valid driver's license from his or her state of residence. Proof of liability insurance also is required and is a standard part of any car rental contract. (To be sure of having the appropriate coverage, let the rental staff know in advance about the national borders you plan to cross.) If buying a car and using it abroad, the driver must carry an International Insurance Certificate, known as a Green Card. Your insurance agent or carrier at home can arrange for a special policy to cover you in Europe, and will automatically issue your Green Card.

The French drive on the right, like Americans, and obey somewhat similar traffic rules. For the most part, the basic rule of the road in France is *priorité à droite* (priority to the right), which means that unless there is some indication to the contrary, the car coming from the right has the right of way, even if coming from a minor side street or if entering a traffic circle from an approach road. However, *priorité à gauche* (priority to the left) has been introduced at selected traffic circles. These are marked by a sign showing arrows going around in a circle, meaning that cars already in those circles have priority over cars entering. In built-up areas, priority to the right is the norm with few exceptions; in rural areas, most principal roads have the right of way, the priority indicated by a sign reading *passage protégé* or by a sign with a yellow square (standing on one of its angles, like a diamond). When the yellow square appears with a black bar, the road loses its priority and the right of way reverts to those coming from the right. This usually is the case at the entrance to a town, but not always, so keep an eye on the signs.

Seat belts are compulsory for the driver and front seat passenger. In addition, children under 10 must travel in the back seat — and, again, seat belts always are recommended. Use the horn sparingly — only in emergencies and when approaching blind mountain curves. In Paris and some other cities, honking is forbidden; at night, flash your headlights instead.

As in the rest of continental Europe, distances are measured in kilometers (1 mile equals 1.6 kilometers; 1 kilometer equals .62 mile) and are registered as kilometers per hour (kmh) on the speedometer. French speed limits are 130 kmh (81 mph) on toll autoroutes (superhighways), 110 kmh (68 mph) on dual carriageways (4-lane highways) and free autoroutes, and 90 kmh (56 mph) on other roads outside built-up areas. In towns, unless otherwise indicated, the speed limit is 60 kmh (37 mph); on the *périphériques* around Paris the speed limit is 80 kmh (48 mph).

Keep in mind, when touring along France's scenic roadways, that it is all too easy to inch up over the speed limit. And use alcohol sparingly prior to getting behind the wheel. Europeans are most zealous in prosecuting offenders of driving laws, especially in the matter of drinking and driving, and — despite their casual attitude and lack of restrictions regarding the sale of wine and liquor — the French are no exception. The Breathalyzer test has made its appearance in France, and drivers caught with more than the permitted level of alcohol can be subject to a heavy fine, payable in cash on the spot, or may even face a jail sentence. If you've been drinking, do as the natives do and walk home, take a cab, or make sure that a licensed member in your party sticks strictly to soft drinks. (For further information, see *Drinking and Drugs,* in this section.) Police also have the power to impose on-the-spot fines for other infractions such as speeding, failure to stop at a red light, and failure to wear a seat belt.

Pictorial direction signs are standardized according to the International Roadsign System and their meanings are indicated by their shapes — triangular signs mean danger; circular signs give instructions; and rectangular signs are informative. Driving in French and other European cities can be a tricky proposition, since many of them do not have street signs posted at convenient corners, but instead identify their byways with plaques attached to the walls of corner buildings. These often are difficult to spot until you've passed them, and since most streets don't run parallel to one another, taking the next turn can lead you astray. Fortunately most European cities and towns post numerous signs pointing the way to the center of the city, and plotting a course to your destination from there may be far easier. Look for the signs that read CENTRE VILLE.

Except for stretches of free autoroutes in the vicinity of cities, most of the autoroutes (designated by A) in France are *autoroutes à péage,* or toll roads, and they are fairly expensive. They save time, gas, and wear and tear on the car, but they are obviously not the roads to take if you want to browse and linger along the way. The other main roads, the *routes nationales* (designated by N), and the secondary, or regional, *routes départementales* (designated by D) are free, well maintained, and much more picturesque; and undesignated minor roads may offer the most charming scenery of all.

Be aware that in recent years, numerous changes have been taking place in the numbering of French roads. Many N roads have become D roads, some merely changing their prefix from N to D, some changing numbers as well. Another recent development is a new, Europe-wide road-numbering system. The European designations, prefaced by an E, appear together with the individual country's road numbers, so, for example, autoroute A1 in France also could be called E5, but Germany's A1 would have a different E number. Both designations appear on Michelin's newest maps, but expect discrepancies between the old and new numbers to appear in maps, guidebooks, and brochures for some time to come.

Traffic congestion is at its worst on main roads (particularly those radiating from Paris and other major cities) on the days before and after public holidays, on the first and last days of July and August, and, above all, on the days surrounding August 15 (*Assumption Day*), the date on which every French family that has not already done so sets out on vacation. At these times, look for signs pointing out detours or alternative routes to popular holiday destinations. Service stations, information points, and tourist offices distribute free maps of the alternate routes, which, although technically longer, will probably get you to your goal faster in the end by bypassing the bottlenecks.

■ **Note:** Pay particular attention to parking signs in large French cities, especially those indicating "control zones," where an unattended parked car presents a serious security risk. If you park in a restricted zone, unlike in the US (where you chance only a ticket or being towed), you may return to find that the trunk and doors have been blown off by overly cautious security forces. More likely, however, you'll return to find one of the car's wheels "clamped," a procedure that renders your car inoperable and involves a tedious (and costly) process to get it freed.

Automobile Clubs – Many European automobile clubs offer emergency assistance to any breakdown victim, whether a club member or not; however, only members of these clubs or affiliated clubs may have access to certain information services and receive discounts on or are entitled to reimbursements for towing and repair services.

Members of the *American Automobile Association (AAA)* are often automatically entitled to a number of services from foreign clubs. With over 31 million members in chapters throughout the US and Canada, the *AAA* is the largest automobile club in North America. *AAA* affiliates throughout the US provide a variety of travel services to members, including a travel agency, trip planning, free travelers' checks at some locations, and reimbursement for foreign roadside assistance. They will help plan an itinerary, will send a map with clear routing directions, and will even make hotel reservations; these services apply to traveling in both the US and France. Although *AAA* members receive maps, brochures, and other publications for no charge or at a discount (depending on the publication and branch), non-members also can order from an extensive selection of highway and topographical maps. You can join the *AAA* through local chapters (listed in the telephone book under *AAA*) or contact the national office at 1000 AAA Dr., Heathrow, FL 32746-5063 (phone: 407-444-8544).

Although reciprocal service arrangements between US and French automobile clubs are less common than in other countries, the *Association Française des Auto Clubs* (9 Rue Anatole de la Forge, 75017 Paris; phone: 42-27-82-00) will provide travel information to members of US auto clubs such as the *AAA*. The main French automobile club is the *Automobile Club de France* (6-8 Pl. de la Concorde, Paris 75008; phone: 42-65-34-70). However, this club is more of an automobile enthusiasts association rather than the American type of "on the road assistance" organization. Motorists may not find it particularly helpful in an emergency.

MAPS: The most comprehensive and up-to-date road maps of France are published by Michelin, the French tire company (one of whose founders also was a cartographer). Besides all the other information pertinent to motorists that they contain, Michelin maps also plot (in yellow) a network of alternate *routes de dégagement* selected to bypass major cities and avoid congestion (mostly D roads paralleling N roads), while especially scenic stretches are further highlighted in green. These are often the choicest travel routes in the country. Michelin's red map 989 covers the entire country in considerable detail (the scale is 1:1,000,000; 1 cm equals 10 km) and should be sufficient for the needs of most motorists, but for those traveling extensively in one region, Michelin also publishes a series of 17 regional maps and a series of about 40 "detailed" or sectional maps (the scale of both series is 1:200,000; 1 cm equals 2 km). Michelin maps are readily available all over France, in bookstores and map shops around the US, and also can be ordered from the company's US headquarters, Michelin Guides and Maps (PO Box 3305, Spartanburg, SC 29304-3305; phone: 803-599-0850 in South Carolina; 800-423-0485 elsewhere in the US). A new edition of each map appears every year; if you're not buying directly from the publisher, make sure that the edition you buy is no more than 2 years old by opening one fold and checking the publication date, given just under the black circle with the map number.

The Rand McNally Road Atlas of France is another good source of information for travelers choosing to make their way through France by car. Like their American counterparts, these maps provide regional maps of the country that include both major and secondary roads, with information on emergency assistance and highway laws and regulations. They are available in any *Rand McNally Map and Travel Bookstore,* or can be ordered through their main warehouse (phone: 800-627-2897) for $16.95 plus $5 shipping with either a credit card or pre-paid check.

The *Automobile Association of America (AAA)* also provides several useful reference sources, including a map of France, the 600-page *Travel Guide to Europe* (price varies from branch to branch), and the 64-page *Motoring Europe* ($6.95). All are available through local *AAA* offices. Another invaluable guide, *Euroad: The Complete Guide to Motoring in Europe,* is available for $8.80, including postage and handling, from VLE Limited, PO Box 547, Tenafly, NJ 07670 (phone: 201-567-5536).

GASOLINE: Called *essence* in France, gasoline is sold by the liter. A liter is slightly more than 1 quart; 3.8 liters equal a US gallon. Gas is available in the following grades: *ordinaire* and *super* (two grades of regular, leaded gas), *diesel,* and *sans plomb* (unleaded).

At the time of this writing, *ordinaire* (regular leaded) averaged about 5.99F or $1.05 US per liter ($4.20 per gallon) in Paris; *super* (super leaded) and *sans plomb* (unleaded) about 6.10F or $1.07 per liter ($4.28 per gallon); *diesel* about 4.56F or 80¢ per liter (about $3.20 per gallon). Note that these prices may be somewhat lower in the provinces. However, gas prices everywhere rise and fall depending on the worldwide price of oil, and an American traveling overseas is further affected by the prevailing rate of exchange, so it is difficult to say exactly how much fuel will cost when you travel. It is not difficult to predict, however, that fuel will cost substantially more than in the US, so check the current price just before you go and budget accordingly.

Remember that, depending on where you're driving, unleaded fuel may be difficult — if not impossible — to find, as it has only recently been introduced in France. At least until all European gas stations sell unleaded, your best bet is to rent a car that takes leaded (regular) gasoline.

Particularly when traveling in rural areas, fill up whenever you come to a gas station. It may be a long way to the next open station. (Even in more populated areas, it may be difficult to find an open station on Sundays or holidays.) You don't want to get stranded on an isolated stretch — so it is a good idea to bring along an extra few gallons in a steel container. (Plastic containers tend to break when a car is bouncing over rocky roads. This, in turn, creates the danger of fire should the gasoline ignite from a static electricity spark. Plastic containers also may burst at high altitudes.)

Considering the cost of gas in Europe relative to US prices at the time of this writing, gas economy is of particular concern. The prudent traveler should begin by doing some preliminary research, planning an itinerary, and making as many reservations as possible in advance, in order to not waste gas figuring out where to go, stay, or eat. Drive early in the day, when there is less traffic. Then leave your car at the hotel and use local transportation whenever possible after you arrive at your destination.

Although it may be as dangerous to drive at a speed much below the posted limit as it is to drive above it (particularly on toll autoroutes — superhighways where the speed limit is 130 kmh or 81 mph), at 89 kmh (55 mph) a car gets 25% better mileage than at 112 kmh (70 mph). The number of miles per liter or gallon also is increased by driving smoothly. Accelerate gently, anticipate stops, get into high gear quickly, and maintain a steady speed.

Breakdowns – If you break down on the road, immediate emergency procedure is to get the car off the road. Some roads may have narrower shoulders than you're used to, so make sure you get all the way off, even if you have to hang off the shoulder a bit. To signal for help, raise the hood, and tie a white rag to the door handle or radio antenna. Don't leave the car unattended, and don't try any major repairs on the road.

Motor patrols usually drive small cars painted a uniform color. Orange emergency phones are located along major autoroutes for stranded travelers to dial for roadside assistance. On secondary roads, emergency phones often are posted with phone numbers of local garages providing towing and basic repair services. Bear in mind that on very rural routes, these boxes may be few and far between.

Aside from these options, a driver in distress will have to contact the nearest service center by pay phone. Car rental companies also provide emergency service and breakdown assistance; ask for a number to call when you pick up the vehicle.

RENTING A CAR: Although there are other options, such as leasing or outright purchase, most people who want to drive in Europe simply rent a car. Travelers to France can reserve a rental car through a travel agent or international rental firm before they leave home, or from a local company once they are in Europe. Another possibility, also arranged before departure, is to rent the car as part of a larger travel package (see "Fly/Drive," below, as well as *Package Tours,* in this section).

Renting is not inexpensive, but it is possible to economize by determining your own needs and then shopping around among car rental companies until you find the best deal. As you comparison-shop, keep in mind that rates vary considerably, not only from city to city, but also from location to location within the same city. It might be less expensive to rent a car in the center of a city rather than at the airport. Ask about special rates or promotional deals, such as weekend or weekly rates, bonus coupons for airline tickets, or 24-hour rates that include gas and unlimited mileage.

Rental car companies operating in France can be divided into three basic categories: large international companies; national or regional companies; and local companies. *Avis, Budget, Hertz,* and other international firms maintain offices in most major French cities. Because of aggressive local competition, the cost of renting a car can be less expensive once a traveler arrives in France, as compared to the prices quoted from the US. Local companies usually are less expensive than the international giants.

Given this situation, it's tempting to wait until arriving to scout out the lowest priced rental from the company located the farthest from the airport high-rent district and offering no pick-up services. But if your arrival coincides with a holiday or coincides with a peak travel period, you may be disappointed to find that even the most expensive car in town was spoken for months ago. Whenever possible, it is best to reserve in advance, anywhere from a few days in slack periods to a month or more during the busier seasons.

If you do decide to wait until after you arrive and let your fingers do the walking through the local phone books, you'll often find a surprising number of small companies listed — particularly in the larger metropolitan areas. You'll also find that many of these companies have representatives at the airport, so you may want to begin your search there and not wait until arriving at your hotel. (Even when renting a car from the middle to the end of your stay, you may want to return to the airport rental counters, as you will have the best chance of being able to drop off the car there just before departure.) The best guide to sorting through the options may be to contact the local tourist board, which usually can provide recommendations and a list of reputable firms.

Renting from the US – Travel agents can arrange foreign rentals for clients, but it is just as easy to do it yourself by calling the international divisions of such familiar car rental firms as *Avis* (phone: 800-331-1084), *Budget* (phone: 800-527-0700), *Dollar Rent a Car* (known in Europe as *EuroDollar;* phone: 800-421-6868), *Hertz* (phone: 800-654-3001), or *National* (phone: 800-CAR-EUROPE).

All of these companies publish directories listing their foreign locations, and all quote weekly flat rates based on unlimited mileage with the renter paying for gas. Some also offer time and mileage rates (i.e., a basic per-day or per-week charge, plus a charge for each mile, or kilometer, driven), which generally are only to the advantage of those who plan to do very little driving — the basic time and mileage charge for a given period of time is lower than the unlimited mileage charge for a comparable period, but the kilometers add up more quickly than most people expect.

It also is possible to rent a car before you go by contacting any of a number of smaller or less well-known US companies that do not operate worldwide but specialize in European auto travel, including leasing and car purchase in addition to car rental, or are actually tour operators with a well-established European car rental program. These firms, whose names and addresses are listed below, act as agents for a variety of European suppliers, offer unlimited mileage almost exclusively, and frequently manage to undersell their larger competitors by a significant margin.

Comparison shopping always is advisable, however, because the company that has the least expensive rentals in one country may not have the least expensive in another, and even the international giants offer discount plans whose conditions are easy for most travelers to fulfill. For instance, *Budget* and *National* offer discounts of anywhere from 15% to 30% off their usual rates (according to the size and length of the car), provided that the car is reserved a certain number of days before departure (usually 7, but it can be less), is rented for a minimum period (5 days or, more often, a week), and in most cases, is returned to the same location that supplied it or to another in the same country. Similar discount plans include *Hertz*'s Affordable Europe and *Avis*'s Supervalue Rates Europe.

Note: Avis also offers two helpful free services for its customers: the "Know Before You Go" US hot line (212-876-AVIS) and an "On Call Service" for customers calling once in Europe. Both provide travelers with tourist information on Belgium, France, Germany, Great Britain, Holland, Italy, and Switzerland. Topics may range from questions about driving (distances, gasoline prices, and license requirements) to queries about currency, customs, tipping, and weather. (Callers to the US number then receive a personal letter confirming the information discussed.) For the European service, there is a different toll-free number in each country; the numbers are given to you when you rent from *Avis*. In France, call 19-05-90-83-85 (the *Avis* personnel at this number all speak English).

There are legitimate bargains in car rentals provided you shop for them. Call all the familiar car rental names whose toll-free numbers are given at the beginning of this section (don't forget to ask about their special discount plans), and then call the smaller companies listed below. In the recent past, the latter have tended to offer significantly lower rates, but it always pays to compare. Begin your shopping early, because the best deals may be booked to capacity quickly and may require payment 14 to 21 days or more before picking up the car.

> *Auto Europe,* PO Box 1097, Camden, ME 04843 (phone: 207-236-8235; 800-223-5555 throughout the US; 800-458-9503 in Canada).
>
> *Cortell International,* 17310 Red Hill Ave., Suite 360, Irvine, CA 92714 (phone: 800-228-2535 or 714-724-1003).
>
> *Europe by Car,* One Rockefeller Plaza, New York, NY 10020 (phone: 212-581-3040 in New York State; 800-223-1516 elsewhere in the US), or 9000 Sunset Blvd., Los Angeles, CA 90069 (phone: 800-252-9401 or 213-272-0424).
>
> *Foremost Euro-Car,* 5430 Van Nuys Blvd., Suite 306, Van Nuys, CA 91401 (phone: 818-786-1960 or 800-272-3299 in California; 800-423-3111 elsewhere in the US).
>
> *Kemwel Group,* 106 Calvert St., Harrison, NY 10528 (phone: 800-678-0678 or 914-835-5555).

One of the ways to keep the cost of car rentals down is to deal with a car rental consolidator, such as *Connex International* (983 Main St., Peekskill, NY 10566; phone: 800-333-3949 or 914-739-0066). *Connex*'s main business is negotiating with virtually all of the major car rental agencies for the lowest possible prices for its customers. For example, at the time of this writing, a subcompact car in France was available for $149 (plus 25% tax) a week with unlimited mileage — comparable deals available from other major car rental companies run substantially higher. (*Connex* also can offer significant numbers of other travel services, varying from hotel accommodations to sightseeing programs.)

Local Rentals – It has long been common wisdom that the least expensive way to rent a car is to make arrangements in Europe. This is less true today than it used to be. Many medium to large European car rental companies have become the overseas suppliers of stateside companies such as those mentioned previously, and often the stateside agency, by dint of sheer volume, has been able to negotiate more favorable rates for its US customers than the European firm offers its own. Still, lower rates may be found by searching out small, strictly local rental companies overseas, whether at less than prime addresses in major cities or in more remote areas. But to find them you must be willing to invest a sufficient amount of vacation time comparing prices on the scene. You also must be prepared to return the car to the location that rented it; drop-off possibilities are likely to be limited.

The brochures of some of the smaller car rental companies, available from French Government Tourist Offices in the US, can serve as a useful basis for comparison. Overseas, the local phone book (if you can read French) is a good place to begin. (For further information on local rental companies, see the individual city reports in THE CITIES.)

Travelers intending to rent a car only occasionally, relying mainly on other means of transportation, should be aware of *Citer, Dergi Cie Location,* and *Mattei,* three French chains represented in many cities. Also bear in mind that *FrenchRail Inc. (SNCF)* offers a car rental service in conjunction with *Avis* at more than 230 locations throughout France. The car is reserved at least 24 hours in advance, is available by the day or longer, and is waiting for you at the station of your destination. Note that the rates are comparable to those charged by *Avis* for cars reserved in France: That is, if you know beforehand that you will want the car for more than a few days (for 5 days, for example, the minimum rental period on *Avis*'s discount plan), you will do better to reserve it before leaving the US. France Rail 'N Drive Pass is another joint offering of *Avis* and *French Rail.* The pass provides for 7 days of travel — 4 days by train (second class, though you can pay for an upgrade to first) and 3 days by rental car — to be used at any time during a 15-day period of validity. (A longer pass provides for 9 days of train travel and 6 days of car rental to be used within 1 month's time.) The pass must be bought in the US, however, even though, when in France, passholders are free to reserve cars with only 24 hours' notice. A similar rail-and-drive program offered by *Hertz,* EurailDrive Escape, is valid in France and in all the other countries of the Eurail network. (For further information on these and other economical rail options, see *Traveling by Train,* in this section.)

Requirements – Whether you decide to rent a car in advance from a large international rental company with French branches or wait to rent from a local company, you should know that renting a car is rarely as simple as signing on the dotted line and roaring off into the night. If you are renting for personal use, you must have a valid drivers license and will have to convince the renting agency that (1) you are personally creditworthy, and (2) you will bring the car back at the stated time. This will be easy if you have a major credit card; most rental companies accept credit cards in lieu of a cash deposit, as well as for payment of your final bill. If you prefer to pay in cash, leave your credit card imprint as a "deposit," then pay your bill in cash when you return the car.

If you don't have a major credit card, renting a car for personal use becomes more complicated. If you are planning to rent from an international agency with an office near your home, the best thing to do is to call the company several days in advance and give them your name, home address, and information on your business or employer; the agency then runs its own credit check on you. This can be time consuming, so you should try to have it done before you leave home. If you are paying in cash and are planning to rent a car in France, it is best to make arrangements in advance — otherwise you must bring along a letter of employment and go to the agency during business hours (don't forget to take the time difference into account) so that it can call your employer for verification.

In addition to paying the rental fee up front, you also will have to leave a hefty deposit when you pick up the car — either a substantial flat fee or a percentage of the total rental cost. (Each company has a different deposit policy; look around for the best deal.) If you return the car on time, the full deposit will be refunded; otherwise, additional charges will be deducted and any unused portion of the deposit will be returned.

If you are planning to rent a car once in France, *Avis, Hertz,* and other US rental companies usually *will* rent to travelers paying in cash and leaving either a credit card imprint or a substantial amount of cash as a deposit. This is not necessarily standard policy, however, as *Budget,* some of the other international chains, and many French companies *will not* rent to an individual who doesn't have a valid credit card. In this case, you may have to call around to find a company that accepts cash.

Also keep in mind that although the minimum age to drive a car in France is 18 years, the minimum age to rent a car varies with the company supplying it. Many firms have a minimum age requirement of 21 years, some raise that to 23 or 25 years, and for some models of cars it rises to 30 years. The upper age limit at many companies is between 69 and 75; others have no upper limit or may make drivers above a certain age subject to special conditions.

Costs – Given all the competition, the price charged for a rental car changes continuously, rising and falling according to the level of tourist traffic. The rate your friend paid last December may have been higher than the one you'll pay in May, and a super-bargain rate may be withdrawn as soon as the advertiser moves some cars off the lot and onto the road again. Nevertheless, there are some constants governing pricing in the international car rental market.

Finding the most economical car rental will require some telephone shopping on your part. As a *general* rule, expect to hear lower prices quoted by the smaller, strictly local companies than by the well-known international names, with those of the national French companies falling somewhere between the two.

If you are driving short distances for only a day or two, the best deal may be a per-day, per-mile (or per-kilometer) rate: You pay a flat fee for each day you keep the car (which can be as low as $25), plus a per-mile charge of 12¢ to 40¢ — or 7¢ to 25¢ per kilometer — or more. An increasingly common alternative is to be granted a certain number of free miles or kilometers each day and then be charged on a per-mile or per-kilometer basis over that number. Flat weekly rates also are available, and some flat monthly rates that represent a further saving over the daily rate — however, even these longer term rentals still will not be inexpensive.

A better alternative for touring the countryside may be a flat per-day rate with unlimited free mileage; this is certainly the most economical rate if you plan to drive over 100 miles (160 kilometers) a day. (Note: When renting a car in France, the term "mileage" may refer either to miles or kilometers.) Make sure that the low, flat daily rate that catches your eye, however, is indeed a per-day rate: Often the lowest price advertised by a company turns out to be available only with a minimum 3-day rental — fine if you want the car that long, but not the bargain it appears if you really intend to use it no more than 24 hours for in-city driving.

Other factors influencing cost include the type of car you rent. Rentals are based on a tiered price system, with different sizes of cars — variations of budget, economy, regular, and luxury — often listed as A (the smallest and least expensive) through F, G, or H, and sometimes even higher. The typical A car available in France is a two-door subcompact or compact, often a hatchback, seating two or three adults (such as a small Fiat, Ford, Peugeot, or Renault), while the typical F, G, or H luxury car is a four-door sedan seating four or five adults (such as a BMW or Mercedes). The larger the car, the more it costs to rent in the first place and the more gas it consumes, but for some people the greater comfort and extra luggage space of a larger car (in which bags can be safely locked out of sight) may make it worth the additional expense, especially on a long trip. Be warned, too, that relatively few European cars have automatic transmissions, and those that do are more likely to be in the F group than the A group. Cars with automatic shift must be specifically requested at the time of booking, and, again, they cost more (anywhere from $5 to $10 a day more than the same model with standard shift) and consume more gas.

Electing to pay for collision damage waiver (CDW) protection will add considerably to the cost of renting a car. The renter may be responsible for the *full value* of the vehicle being rented, but you can dispense with the possible obligation by buying the offered waiver at a cost of about $13 a day. Before making any decisions about optional collision damage waivers, check with your own insurance agent and determine whether your personal automobile insurance policy covers rented vehicles; if it does you probably won't need to pay for the waiver. Be aware, too, that increasing numbers of credit cards automatically provide CDW coverage if the car rental is charged to the appropriate credit card. However, the specific terms of such coverage differ sharply among individual credit card companies, so check with the credit card company for information on the nature and amount of coverage provided (also see *Credit and Currency*, in this section). Considering that repair costs for a rental car have become a real headache of late, and car rental companies are getting away with steep fees (up to the full retail price of the car) for damage to their property, if you are not otherwise covered it is wise to pay for the insurance offered by the car rental company rather than risk traveling without any coverage.

Overseas, the amount renters may be liable for should damage occur has not risen to the heights it has in the US. In addition, some French car rental companies' agreements include collision damage coverage. In this case, the CDW supplement frees the renter from liability for the *deductible* amount — as opposed to the standard CDW coverage, described above, which releases the driver from liability for the full value of the car. In France, this deductible typically ranges from $2,000 to $2,500 at present, but can be more for some luxury car groups. As with the full liability waiver, the cost of waiving this liability — generally $18 to $25 a day — is far from negligible, however. As mentioned above, drivers who rent cars in the US often are able to decline the CDW because many personal car insurance policies (subject to their own deductibles) extend to rental cars, unfortunately, such coverage usually does not extend to cars rented outside the US and Canada. Similarly, CDW coverage provided by some credit cards if the rental is charged to the card may be limited to cars rented in the US or Canada.

When inquiring about CDW coverage and costs, you should be aware that a number of the major international car rental companies now are automatically including the cost of this waiver in their quoted prices. This does not mean that they are absorbing this cost and you are receiving free coverage — total rental prices have increased to include the former CDW charge. The disadvantage of this inclusion is that you probably will not have the option to refuse this coverage, and will end up paying the added charge — even if you already are adequately covered by your own insurance policy or through a credit card company.

Additional costs to be added to the price tag include drop-off charges or one-way service fees. The lowest price quoted by any given company may apply only to a car that is returned to the same location from which it was rented. A slightly higher rate may be charged if the car is to be returned to a different city within the same country, and a considerably higher rate may prevail if the rental begins in one country and ends in another.

A further consideration: Don't forget that all car rentals are subject to a Value Added Tax (VAT). This tax rarely is included in the rental price that's advertised or quoted, but it always must be paid — whether you pay in advance in the US or pay it when you drop off the car. In France, the VAT rate on car rentals currently is 28% — less than the 33.33% it used to be, but still the highest in Europe. In general, the tax on one-way rentals is determined by the country in which the car has been rented, so even if you intend to visit only France, you still might consider a nearby country as the pickup point — the tax rate in Belgium is 25% (no great bargain), but in Germany it is 14%; in Spain and Luxembourg, 12%; and in Switzerland, no tax is charged. For a tourer planning to explore Alsace and/or Burgundy, Lyons, and Provence, therefore, there's a strong financial incentive to pick up his or her rental car in Switzerland and then drive across the nearby French border (at a 28% car rental cost saving!). Some rental agencies that do not maintain their own fleets use a contractor, whose country of registration determines the rate of taxation. An example is the *Kemwel Group,* whose one-way rentals from all countries except Germany, Italy, and Sweden are taxed at the Danish rate of 22%.

Kemwel Group's special programs offer savings to the client and allow travel agents to earn commissions on CDW fees and on the VAT. The new SuperSaver Plus and UniSaver Plus tariffs offer inclusive rentals in 24 countries throughout Europe and the Middle East. These programs offer full insurance coverage (with a $100 deductible) and all European VAT, plus unlimited mileage. Rates range from $79 up and are available in some 35 cities across Europe. Bookings must be reserved and paid for at least 7 days before delivery of the car, and the vehicle must be returned to the *Kemwel* station from which it was originally rented. For further information, contact *Kemwel Group Inc.,* 106 Calvert St., Harrison, NY 10528 (phone: 800-678-0678 or 914-835-5555).

Rental cars usually are delivered with a full tank of gas. (This is not always the case, however, so check the gas gauge when picking up the car, and have the amount of gas noted on your rental agreement if the tank is not full.) Remember to fill the tank before you return the car or you will have to pay to refill it, and gasoline at the car rental company's pump is always much more expensive than at a service station. This policy may vary for smaller, regional companies; ask when picking up the vehicle. (For further information on gasoline economy, see "Gasoline," above.)

Finally, currency fluctuation is another factor to consider. Most brochures quote rental prices in dollars, but these dollar amounts are frequently only guides; that is, they represent the prevailing rate of exchange at the time the brochure was printed. The rate may be very different when you call to make a reservation and different again when the time comes to pay the bill (when the amount owed may be paid in cash in foreign currency, or as a charge to a credit card, which is recalculated at still a later date's rate of exchange). Some companies guarantee rates in dollars (often for a slight surcharge), but this is an advantage only when the value of the dollar is steadily declining overseas. If the dollar is growing stronger overseas, you may be better off with rates in the local currency.

Before you leave the lot, check to be sure the rental car has a spare tire and jack in the trunk. In addition, particularly for extensive touring, you may want to pick up the following equipment: a first-aid kit; a flashlight with an extra set of batteries; a white towel (useful for signaling for help, as well as for wiping the car windows); jumper cables; flares and/or reflectors; a container of water or coolant for the radiator; and a steel container for extra gasoline (see "Gasoline," above).

Fly/Drive – Airlines, charter companies, car rental companies, and tour operators have been offering fly/drive packages for years, and even though the basic components of the package have changed somewhat — return airfare, a car waiting at the airport, and perhaps a night's lodging in the gateway city all for one inclusive price used to be the rule — the idea remains the same. You rent a car *here* for use *there* by booking it along with other arrangements for the trip. These days, the very minimum arrangement possible is the result of a tie-in between a car rental company and an airline, which entitles customers to a rental car for less than the company's usual rates, provided they show proof of having booked a flight on that airline.

Slightly more elaborate fly/drive packages can be found listed under various names (go-as-you-please, self-drive, or, simply, car tours) in the independent vacations sections of tour catalogues. Their most common ingredients are the rental car plus some sort of hotel voucher plan, with the applicable airfare listed separately. You set off on your trip with a block of prepaid accommodations vouchers, a list of hotels that accept them (usually members of a hotel chain or association), and a reservation for the first night's stay, after which the staff of each hotel books the next one for you or you make your own reservations. Naturally, the greater the number of establishments participating in the scheme, the more freedom you have to range at will during the day's driving and still be near a place to stay for the night. The cost of these combination packages generally vary according to the size of the car and the quality of the hotels; there usually is a drop-off charge if the car is picked up in one city and dropped off in another. Most packages are offered at several different price levels, ranging from a standard plan covering stays in hotels to a budget plan using accommodations such as small inns or farmhouses. Airlines also have special rental car rates available when you book their flights, often with a flexible hotel voucher program. For further information on available packages, check with the airline or your travel agent.

Less flexible car tours provide a rental car, a hotel plan, and a set itinerary that permits no deviation because the hotels all are reserved in advance. The deluxe car tours packaged by *AutoVenture* (425 Pike St., Suite 502, Seattle, WA 98101; phone: 800-426-7502 or 206-624-6033), whose tours come in either self-drive or chauffeured versions and feature some or many of the overnight stays in châteaux-hotels and inns belonging to France's first-rate *Relais & Châteaux* association, are of this type. The *French Experience* also offers packaged self-drive tours featuring château accommodations in various regions of France, including Brittany, Alsace, and the Wine Country. For information, contact the *French Experience, Inc.,* 370 Lexington Ave., Suite 812, New York, NY 10017 (phone: 212-986-3800). *Avis* offers less deluxe car tours with its Personally Yours program. You must book at least 2 weeks in advance to receive this planned itinerary service. For information on other packagers of car tours, see *Package Tours,* in this section.

LEASING: Anyone planning to be in Europe for 3 weeks or more should compare the cost of renting a car with the cost of leasing one for the same period. While the money saved by leasing — rather than renting for a 23-day (the minimum) or 30-day period — may not be great, the savings on a long-term lease — 45, 60, 90 days, or more — amounts to hundreds, even thousands, of dollars. Part of the saving is due to the fact that leased cars are exempt from the stiff taxes applicable to rental cars. In addition, leasing plans provide for collision insurance with no deductible amount, so there is no need to add the daily cost of collision damage waiver protection, an option offered by rental companies (see above). A further advantage of a car lease — actually a financed purchase/repurchase plan — is that you reserve your car by specific make and model rather than by group only, and it is delivered to you fresh from the factory.

Leasing as described above is offered only in Belgium and France, and the savings it permits can be realized to the fullest only if cars are picked up and returned in these countries. Even in France, pick-up and drop-off locations are likely to be limited, and the charge for delivery to another location can be high, and on top of this must be added an identical return charge. If you don't intend to keep the car very long, the two charges can nullify the amount saved by leasing rather than renting, so you will have to do some arithmetic.

One of the major car leasing companies is *Renault,* offering leases of new cars for 23 days to 6 months. The cars are exempt from tax, all insurance is included, and there is no mileage charge. There is no pickup or drop-off charge for most major cities in France — the car usually is picked up and returned at the airport. Charges for other locations in France and elsewhere in Europe range from $85 to $350 and up (each way). For further information and reservations, ask your travel agent or contact *Renault USA,* 650 First Ave., New York, NY 10016 (phone: 212-532-1221 in New York State; 800-221-1052 elsewhere in the US).

Peugeot also offers a similar leasing arrangement, called the "Peugeot Vacation Plan." In acccordance with the standard type of financed purchase/repurchase leasing plan, travelers buy a new car in France, drive it for anywhere between 22 to 175 days, then sell it back to *Peugeot* for a guaranteed price (the original price minus the actual charge for usage). The tax-free "purchase" includes unlimited mileage, factory warranty, full collision damage waiver coverage (no deductible), and 24-hour towing and roadside assistance. Pick-up and drop-off locations and charges are similar to *Renault's. Peugeot's* "European Delivery" program is a full-purchase program, including shipment of the car to the US, as discussed below. For further information, contact *Peugeot Motors of America,* 1 Peugeot Plaza, Lyndhurst, NJ 07071 (phone: 201-935-8400). Some of the car rental firms listed above — *Auto-Europe, Europe by Car, Foremost Euro-Car,* and *Kemwel* — also arrange European car leases.

BUYING A CAR: If your plans include both buying a new car of European make and a driving tour of Europe, it's possible to combine the two ventures and save some money on each. By buying the car abroad and using it during your vacation, you pay quite a bit less for it than the US dealer would charge and at the same time avoid the expense of renting a car. There are two basic ways to achieve this desired end, but one, factory delivery, is far simpler than the other, direct import.

Factory delivery means that you place an order for a car in the US, then pick it up in Europe, often literally at the factory gate. It also means that your new car is built to American specifications, complying with all US emission and safety standards. Because of this, only cars made by manufacturers who have established a formal program for such sales to American customers may be bought at the factory. At present, the list includes Audi, BMW, Jaguar, Mercedes, Peugeot, Porsche, Saab, Volkswagen, and Volvo, among others (whose manufacturers generally restrict their offerings to those models they ordinarily export to the US). The factory delivery price, in US dollars, usually runs about 5% to 15% below the sticker price of the same model at a US dealership and includes the cost of shipping the car home. All contracts except BMW's include US customs duty, but the cost of the incidentals, and the insurance necessary for driving the car around Europe, is extra, again except for BMW's plan.

One of the few disadvantages of factory delivery is that car manufacturers make only a limited number of models available each year, and for certain popular models you may have to get in line early in the season. Another is that you must take your trip when the car is ready, not when you are, although you usually will have 8 to 10 weeks' notice. The actual place of delivery can vary; it is more economical to pick up the car at the factory, but arrangements can be made to have it delivered elsewhere for an extra charge.

Cars for factory delivery usually can be ordered either through one of the manufacturer's authorized US dealers or through companies — among them *Europe by Car, Foremost Euro-Car,* and *Kemwel* (see above for contact information) — that specialize in such transactions. (Note that *Foremost Euro-Car* services all of the US for rentals and leasing, but they only arrange *sales* for California residents.) For example, Jaguars must be ordered through a US dealer and picked up at the factory in Coventry, England, although they can be dropped off for shipment home in any number of European cities. For information, write to *Jaguar Cars,* 600 Willow Tree Rd., Leonia, NJ 07605 (phone: 201-592-5200).

Occasionally an auto manufacturer offers a free or discounted airfare in connection with a European delivery program. Mercedes-Benz has a 1991 program including discounted round-trip airfare ($500 for two economy fare seats or one business class seat) from any US gateway served by *Lufthansa, Pan American,* or *TWA,* to Stuttgart (where the buyer picks up the car), plus a 1-night stay at the local *Ramada* or *Hilton* hotel, and 15 days' free comprehensive road insurance. For details, contact *Mercedes-Benz of North America,* 1 Mercedes Dr., Montvale, NJ 07645 (phone: 800-458-8202).

The other way to buy a car abroad, direct import, is sometimes referred to as "gray market" buying. It is perfectly legal, but not totally hassle-free. Direct import means that you buy abroad a car that was meant for use abroad, not one built according to US specifications. It can be new or used, and may even include — in Great Britain — a steering wheel on the right side. The main drawback to direct import is that the process of modification to bring the car into compliance with US standards is expensive and time-consuming; it typically costs from $5,000 to $7,000 in parts and labor and takes from 2 to 6 months. In addition, the same shipping, insurance, and miscellaneous expenses (another $2,000 to $5,000, according to estimates) that would be included in the factory-delivery price must be added to the purchase price of the car, and the considerable burden of shepherding it on its journey from showroom to backyard garage usually is borne by the purchaser. Direct import dealers do exist (they are not the same as your local, factory-authorized foreign car dealer, with whom you are now in competition), but even if you use one, you still need to do a great deal of paperwork yourself.

Once upon a time, the main advantage of the direct import method — besides the fact that it can be used for makes and models not available on factory delivery programs — was that much more money could be saved importing an expensive car. Given today's exchange rates, however, the method's potential greater gain is harder to realize and must be weighed against its greater difficulties. Still, if direct importing interests you, you can obtain a list of those makes and models approved for conversion in this country, and of the converters licensed to bring them up to US standards, by contacting the Environmental Protection Agency, Manufacturers' Operations Division, EN-340-F, Investigations/Imports Section, 401 M Street SW, Washington, DC 20460 (phone: 202-382-2479).

If you have special problems getting your car into the US, you might consider contacting a specialist in vehicle importation, such as Daniel Kokal, a regulatory consultant with *Techlaw* (14500 Avion Pkwy., Suite 300, Chantilly, VA 22021; phone: 703-818-1000).

Package Tours

If the mere thought of buying a package for travel to and through France conjures up visions of a race through ten cities in as many days in lockstep with a horde of frazzled fellow travelers, remember that packages have come a long way. For one thing, not all packages necessarily are escorted tours, and the one you buy does not have to include any organized touring at all — nor will it necessarily include traveling companions. If it does, however, you'll find that people of all sorts — many just like yourself — are taking advantage of packages today because they are economical and convenient, save you an immense amount of planning time, and exist in such variety that it's virtually impossible not to find one that fits at least the majority of your travel preferences. Given the high cost of travel these days, packages have emerged as a particularly wise buy.

Aside from the cost-saving advantages of package arrangements, France itself is ideally suited to package travel. The reason is that, essentially, France is a roam-and-do destination as distinct from, say, the Caribbean, where most visitors go to a single island for a week or two and unpack everything until they're ready to return home. To be sure, many visitors do seek out a single city or area for a concentrated visit, booking themselves into a hotel, apartment, home, country inn, or farm that serves as a base from which they make regional tours and visits. But the bulk of North American travelers want to explore as much of France as possible within the restrictions of time and travel funds available. Hence the popularity — and practicality — of package arrangements.

There are hundreds of package programs on the market today. In the US, numerous packages to France are offered by tour operators or wholesalers, some retail travel agencies, airlines, charter companies, hotels, and even special-interest organizations, and what goes into them depends on who is organizing them. The most common type, assembled by tour wholesalers and sold through travel agents, runs the gamut from deluxe everything to simple tourist class amenities or even bare necessities. Fly/drive and fly/cruise packages usually are the joint planning efforts of airlines and, respectively, car rental companies and cruise line operators. Charter flight programs may range from little more than airfare and a minimum of ground arrangements to full-scale escorted tours or special-interest vacations. There also are hotel packages organized by hotel chains or associations of independent hotels and applicable to stays at any combination of member establishments; resort packages covering arrangements at a specific hotel; and special-interest tours, which can be once-only programs organized by particular groups through a retail agency or regular offerings packaged by a tour operator. They can feature food, music or theater festivals, a particular sporting activity or event, a commemorative occasion, even nature study or scientific exploration.

In essence, a package is an amalgam of travel services that can be purchased in a single transaction. A package tour to and through France may include any or all of the following: round-trip transatlantic transportation, local transportation (and/or car rentals), accommodations, some or all meals, sightseeing, entertainment, transfers to and from the hotel at each destination, taxes, tips, escort service, and a variety of incidental features that might be offered as options at additional cost. In other words, a package can be any combination of travel elements from a fully escorted tour offered at an all-inclusive price to a simple fly/drive booking allowing you to move about totally on your own. Its principal advantage is that it saves money: The cost of the combined arrangements invariably is well below the price of all of the same elements if bought separately, and particularly if transportation is provided by charter or discount flight, it could be even less than just a round-trip economy airline ticket on a regularly scheduled flight. A package tour provides more than economy and convenience: It releases the traveler from having to make individual arrangements for each separate element of a trip.

Lower prices are provided by package travel as a result of high-volume purchasing. The tour packager negotiates for services in wholesale quantities — blocks of airline seats or hotel rooms, group meals, dozens of rental cars, busloads of ground transport, and so on — and they are made available at a lower per-person price because of the large quantities purchased for use during a given time period. Most packages, however, are subject to restrictions governing the duration of the trip and require total payment by a given time before departure.

Tour programs generally can be divided into two categories — escorted (or locally hosted) and independent — depending on arrangements offered. An escorted tour means that a guide will accompany the group from the beginning of the tour through to return; a locally hosted tour means that the group will be met upon arrival in each city by a different local host. On independent tours, you generally have a choice of hotels, meal plans, and sightseeing trips in each city, as well as a variety of special excursions. The independent plan is for people who do not want a set itinerary, but who prefer confirmed reservations. Whether you choose an escorted or independent tour, always bring along complete contact information for your tour operator in case problems arise, although US tour operators often have French affiliates who are available to give additional assistance or make other arrangements on the spot.

To determine whether a package — or more specifically, which package — fits your travel plans, start by evaluating your interests and needs, deciding how much and what you want to spend, see, and do. Gather whatever package tour information is available for your schedule. Be sure that you take the time to read the brochure *carefully* to determine precisely what is included. Keep in mind that travel brochures are written to entice you into signing up for a package tour. Often the language is deceptive and devious. For example, a brochure may quote the lowest prices for a package tour based on facilities that are unavailable during the off-season, undesirable at any season, or just plain nonexistent. Information such as "breakfast included" (as it often is in packages to France) or "plus tax" (which can add up) should be taken into account. Note, too, that the prices quoted almost always are based on double occupancy: The rate listed is for each of two people sharing a double room, and if you travel alone, the supplement for single accommodations can raise the price considerably (see *Hints for Single Travelers*).

In this age of rapidly rising airfares, the brochure most often will *not* include the price of an airline ticket in the price of the package, though sample applicable fares from various gateway cities usually will be listed separately as extras to be added to the price of the ground arrangements. Before doing this, check the latest fares with the airline, because the samples invariably are out of date by the time you read them. If the brochure gives more than one category of sample fares per gateway city — such as an individual tour-basing fare, a group fare, an excursion or other discount ticket, or, in the case of flights to France, an APEX, winter APEX, or super APEX, PEX, or Super PEX — your travel agent or airline tour desk will be able to tell you which one applies to the package you choose, depending on when you travel, how far in advance you book, and other factors. (An individual tour-basing fare is a fare computed as part of a package that includes land arrangements, thereby entitling a carrier to reduce the air portion almost to the absolute minimum. Though it always represents a saving over full-fare coach or economy, lately it has not been as inexpensive as the excursion and other discount fares that also are available to individuals. The group fare usually is the least expensive fare, and it is the tour operator, not you, who makes up the group.) When the brochure does include round-trip transportation in the package price, don't forget to add the round-trip transportation cost from your home to the departure city to come up with the total cost of the package.

Finally, read the general information regarding terms and conditions and the responsibility clause (usually in fine print at the end of the descriptive literature) to determine the precise elements for which the tour operator is — and is not — liable. Here the tour operator frequently expresses the right to change services or schedules as long as equivalent arrangements are offered. This clause also absolves the operator of responsibility for consequences beyond human control, such as floods or avalanches, or injury to you or your property. In reading, ask the following questions:

1. Does the tour include airfare or other transportation, sightseeing, meals, transfers, taxes, baggage handling, tips, or any other services? Do you want all these services?
2. If the brochure indicates that "some meals" are included, does this mean a welcoming and farewell dinner, two breakfasts, or every evening meal?
3. What classes of hotels are offered? If you will be traveling alone, what is the single supplement?
4. Does the tour itinerary or price vary according to the season?
5. Are the prices guaranteed; that is, if costs increase between the time you book and the time you depart, can surcharges unilaterally be added?
6. Do you get a full refund if you cancel? If not, be sure to obtain cancellation insurance.
7. Can the operator cancel if too few people join? At what point?

One of the consumer's biggest problems is finding enough information to judge the reliability of a tour packager, since individual travelers seldom have direct contact with the firm putting the package together. Usually, a retail travel agent is interposed between customer and tour operator, and much depends on his or her candor and cooperation. So ask a number of questions about the tour you are considering. For example: Has the agent ever used the package provided by this tour operator? How long has the tour operator been in business? Is the tour operator a member of the *United States Tour Operators Association* (*USTOA*)? (The *USTOA* will provide a list of its members upon request; it also offers a useful brochure, *How to Select a Package Tour.* Contact the *USTOA,* 211 E. 51st St., Suite 12B, New York, NY 10022; phone: 212-944-5727. Also check the Better Business Bureau in your area to see if any complaints have been filed against the operator.) Which and how many companies are involved in the package? If air travel is by charter flight, is there an escrow account in which deposits will be held; if so, what is the name of the bank?

This last question is very important. US law requires that tour operators deposit every charter passenger's deposit and subsequent payment in a proper escrow account. Money paid into such an account cannot legally be used except to pay for the costs of a particular package or as a refund if the trip is canceled. To ensure the safe handling of your money, make your check payable to the escrow account — by law, the name of the depository bank must appear in the operator-participant contract, and usually is found in that mass of minuscule type on the back of the brochure. Write the details of the charter, including the destination and dates, on the face of the check; on the back, print "For Deposit Only." Your travel agent may prefer that you make your check out to the agency, saying that it will then pay the tour operator the fee minus commission. But it is perfectly legal to write your check as we suggest, and if your agent objects too strongly (the agent should have sufficient faith in the tour operator to trust him or her to send the proper commission), consider taking your business elsewhere. If you don't make your check out to the escrow account, you lose the protection of that escrow should the trip be canceled or the tour operator or travel agent fail. Furthermore, recent bankruptcies in the travel industry have served to point out that even the protection of escrow may not be enough to safeguard your investment. Increasingly, insurance is becoming a necessity (see *Insurance,* in this section), and payment by credit card has become popular since it offers some additional safeguards if the tour operator defaults.

■ **A word of advice:** Purchasers of vacation packages who feel they're not getting their money's worth are more likely to get a refund if they complain in writing to the operator — and bail out of the whole package immediately. Alert the tour operator or resort manager to the fact that you are dissatisfied, that you will be leaving for home as soon as transportation can be arranged, and that you expect a refund. They may have forms to fill out detailing your complaint; otherwise, state your case in a letter. Even if the availability of transportation home detains you, your dated, written complaint should help in procuring a refund from the operator.

SAMPLE PACKAGES TO FRANCE: There are so many packages available to France today that it's probably safe to say that just about any arrangement anyone might want is available for as long as it is wanted, whether it's to hit the highlights from Le Mont St.-Michel to Monte-Carlo, to explore a selected region in depth, or to visit only Paris. The keynote is flexibility. Nevertheless, those seeking the maximum in structure will find that the classic sightseeing tour by motorcoach, fully escorted and all-inclusive (or nearly), has withstood the test of time and still is well represented among the programs of the major tour operators. Typically, these tours begin in Paris and take 2 to 3 weeks — or more — to trace a rough loop westward through Normandy and Brittany, south to the Loire Valley, the Dordogne, the Bordeaux region, and the Pyrénées, then east across Languedoc to Provence and the French Riviera, with excursions to Monaco possible from the final stopping place at Nice. Tours that trace the half circle in reverse, beginning in Nice and finishing in Paris, are equally common. Longer programs may make a full circle around the whole of France, adding the Alps, the Burgundy wine region, Alsace, Lorraine, and more to the itinerary. Shorter programs — some as short as 1 week — tend to explore a selected region — for instance, the château country — in depth.

Hotel accommodations in these packages usually are characterized as first class or better, with private baths or showers in all rooms, although more than a few tour packagers offer less expensive alternatives by providing more modest lodgings. Breakfast daily almost always is included, whereas the number of lunches and dinners may vary considerably, and meals include wine (or other alcoholic beverages) only when the tour literature clearly states so. Also included are transfers between airport and hotel, baggage handling, tips to maids and waiters, local transportation, and sightseeing excursions and admission fees, as well as any featured evening entertainment, personal expenses for laundry, incidentals and souvenirs, and tips to the motorcoach driver and to the tour escort, who remains with the group from beginning to end — almost everything, in fact, except round-trip airfare between the US and France (which generally is shown separately).

Among these types of escorted, highly structured package tours of France are those offered by *Globus-Gateway,* which send more travelers from the US to Europe than any other tour operator. This company offers two programs: a 12-day tour and the 15-day La France tour. Breakfasts are included daily, as are dinners except in Paris and Nice. For information, contact *Globus-Gateway,* 150 S. Los Robles Ave., Suite 860, Pasadena, CA 91101 (phone: 818-449-2019 in California or abroad; 800-556-5454 elsewhere in the US).

Maupintours's (PO Box 807, Lawrence, KS 66044; phone: 913-843-1211 in Kansas or abroad; 800-255-4266 elsewhere in the US) 12-day France Highlights tour begins in Paris and continues around France to the Loire Valley, Mont St.-Michel, and Normandy, and then returns to Paris. Ten breakfasts, eight lunches, and six dinners are included. *Travcoa* (PO Box 2630, Newport Beach, CA 92658; phone: 818-449-0919 in California; 800-992-2003 elsewhere in the US) offers a lineup of packages, for 17, 19, or 30 days, that includes all meals. *Olson Travel World*'s 21-day Treasures of France tour makes a full circle around the country and includes all meals except two lunches and three dinners at the conclusion of the trip in Paris (where packagers of even the most inclusive tours assume participants prefer to have a greater amount of free time and choices). For information, contact *Olson Travel World*, 100 N. Sepulveda Blvd., Suite 1010, El Segundo, CA 90245 (phone: 213-615-0711 in California or abroad; 800-421-5785 in California; 800-421-2255 elsewhere in the US).

An equally common type of package to France is the car tour or fly/drive arrangement, often described in brochures as a self-drive or go-as-you-please tour. These are independent vacations, geared to travelers who want to cover as much ground as they might on an escorted group sightseeing tour but who prefer to do it on their own. The most flexible plans include no more than a map of France, a rental car, and a block of as many prepaid hotel vouchers needed for the length of the stay (the packages are typically 4 or 7 days long, extendable by individual extra days or additional package segments), along with a list of participating hotels at which vouchers are accepted. In most cases, only the first night's accommodation is reserved; from then on, travelers book their rooms one stop ahead as they drive from place to place. When the hotels are members of a chain or association — which they usually are — the staff of the last hotel can reserve the next one for you. In other cases, there may be a choice of reserving all accommodations before departure — usually for a fee. Operators offering these packages usually sell vouchers in more than one price category; travelers may have the option of upgrading accommodations by paying a supplement directly to more expensive establishments.

Another type of fly/drive arrangement is more restrictive in that the tour packager supplies an itinerary that must be followed day by day, with a specific hotel to be reached each night. Often these plans are more deluxe as well. The car tours packaged by *AutoVenture* (425 Pike Street, Suite 502, Seattle, WA 98101; phone: 206-624-6033 in Washington or abroad; 800-426-7502 elsewhere in the US) feature overnight stays in hotels that are elegant converted castles or manor houses or old and distinctive country inns, most of them members of the prestigious *Relais & Châteaux* association, known for its overall high standards. Any of *AutoVenture*'s six French itineraries, 6 to 14 days in length, can be bought in either a self-drive or a chauffeured version. A similar level of luxury is available on shorter self-drive or chauffeured tours offered by *David B. Mitchell & Company, Relais & Châteaux*'s US representative. Recent itineraries included 7- to 11-day tours of central France and along the Riviera. For information, contact *David B. Mitchell & Company* (200 Madison Ave., New York, NY 10016; phone: 800-372-1323 or 212-889-4822). *Abercrombie & Kent International* (1420 Kensington Rd., Oak Brook, IL 60521; phone: 708-954-2944 in Illinois; 800-323-7308 elsewhere in the US) also features 7-day to 11-day self-drive itineraries in France, including stays in hotels that are converted manor houses, castles, and other stately homes.

A further possibility for independent travelers is a "stay put" package in France. Not surprisingly, since Paris alone is of such great interest to visitors, the Paris city package is the most popular. Basically, the city package — no matter what the city — includes transfers between airport and hotel, a choice of accommodations (with continental breakfast) in several price ranges, plus any of a number of other features you may not need or want but would lose valuable time arranging if you did. Common features are

1 or 2 half-day guided tours of the city; in Paris, a boat cruise on the Seine; passes for unlimited travel by métro (subway) or bus; discount cards for shops, museums, and restaurants; temporary membership in and admission to clubs, casinos, and discotheques; and car rental for some or all of your stay. Other features may be anything from a souvenir travel bag to a wine tasting, dinner and a show. The packages usually are a week in length — although 4-day and even 14-day packages are available, amd most packages can be extended by extra days — and are sometimes hosted; that is, a representative of the tour company may be available at a local office or even in the hotel to answer questions, handle problems, and assist in arranging activities and optional excursions.

Jet Vacations (1775 Broadway, New York, NY 10019; phone: 212-247-0999 or 800-JET-0999), a tour operator affiliated with *Air France* specializing in travel to France, has Paris packages with a wide range of hotel choices among its tour programs. After Paris, the Riviera is the most popular place to spend a block of time in France, and *Jet Vacations* bases its "stay put" packages in this area in Cannes, La Napoule, Monte Carlo, or Nice. *American Express*'s travel agency also offers Paris city packages. Call 800-YES-AMEX or contact the nearest office of *American Express Travel* for information.

The World of Oz offers a 7-day, 6-night independent holiday package including accommodations at private châteaux and a rental car (self-drive or chauffeured). You can spend time at one château or travel to a different one each day, choosing among a network of 60 privately owned châteaux. Contact *World of Oz,* 211 E. 43rd Street, New York, NY 10017 (phone: 212-661-0580 or 800-248-0234). Another company that offers accommodations packages at private châteaux is *Châteaux Accueil.* Owners are in residence, often functioning as hosts, and in many cases English is spoken. For information, contact *Châteaux Acccueil*'s US representative, *DMI Tours* (14340 Memorial Dr., Houston, TX 77079; phone: 800-553-5090).

Such packages often are offered by the package travel divisions of major airlines. *TWA Getaway Tours* (phone: 800-GETAWAY) offers a 7-day, 6-night Paris Rendezvous package, as well as a 15-day escorted tour of France and Monaco. *British Airways Holidays* (phone: 800-AIRWAYS) also offers a combination London/Paris city package, including 3 nights in each city.

Special interest tours are a growing sector of the travel industry, and programs focusing on food and wine are prominent among the packages of this sort put together for visitors to France. One thing to note is that they tend to be quite structured arrangements rather than independent ones, and they rarely are created with the budget traveler in mind. Also note that inclusive as they may be, few food and wine tours include *all* meals in the package price. This is not necessarily a cost cutting technique on the part of the packager; rather, because of the lavishness of some of the meals, others may be left to the discretion of the participants, not only to allow time for leisure, but also to allow for differing rates of metabolism. Similarly, even on wine tours that spend entire days in practically full-time tasting, unlimited table wine at meals may not always be included in the package price. The brochures usually are clear about what comes with the package and when.

Among the various food and wine tours, groups on *Bacchants' Pilgrimages'* annual 3-week Southern France Classic tour visit châteaux, vineyards, and wine cellars from the Loire Valley to Cognac, Bordeaux, the Côtes du Rhône, Burgundy, Champagne, and Paris, tasting all the way. Included are winery-hosted luncheons, picnics, two dinners in three-star restaurants, and other luncheons and dinners in restaurants of lesser fame. Bookings are through travel agents or *Bacchants' Pilgrimages,* 345 California St., Suite 2570, San Francisco, CA 94104 (phone: 415-981-8518).

For groups of 10 or more travelers, *Travel Concepts* offers a variety of custom-designed food and wine tours throughout France. For information, contact *Travel Concepts,* 62 Commonwealth Ave., Suite 3, Boston, MA 02116 (phone: 617-266-8450).

Inland waterway trips on canal or river barges outfitted as hotels are another type of special interest package in France. Because the pace is slow, these trips frequently appeal to second-time visitors as a way to see a very small section of the country in depth. Hotel barges can carry as few as 6 to 8 or as many as 24 passengers in addition to crews of 3 to 8 people, and while the atmosphere and dress aboard are casual, the accommodations (most have cabins with private bathrooms) and attention paid to food (all meals usually are included, with unlimited table wine common) make many of the cruises quite luxurious. Packages usually are by the week, though shorter and longer ones exist.

Floating through Europe (271 Madison Ave., New York, NY 10016; phone: 212-685-5600 in New York State; 800-221-3140 elsewhere) packages week-long cruise itineraries in Alsace, Burgundy, Champagne, Lorraine, and on the Canal du Midi in southern France. *Esplanade Tours* (581 Boylston St., Boston, MA 02116; phone: 617-266-7465 in Massachusetts; 800-426-5492 elsewhere) also offers week-long cruises along the Canal du Midi, as well as elsewhere in the south of France and in Burgundy, Alsace, and Franche-Comté. Both *Abercrombie & Kent/Continental Waterways* (1420 Kensington Rd., Oakbrook, IL 60521; phone: 708-954-2944 in Illinois; 800-323-7308 elsewhere) and *French Country Waterways* (PO Box 215, Duxbury, MA 02331; phone: 800-222-1236 or 617-934-2454) offer cruises in Burgundy: the former, with packages that vary in length from 3 to 9 days; the latter, with a week-long Wine Cruise or a Gourmet Cruise that features shore excursions to Michelin-starred restaurants. (The various French waterways, as well as other companies offering inland cruises are discussed in *Traveling by Ship.*)

Ski packages are foremost among the sports-related packages. The foundation of the package usually is a week or two of hotel or condominium accommodations at a ski resort (Avoriaz, Chamonix, Courchevel, Les Menuires, Tignes, and Val d'Isère are the common destinations), and for those choosing the hotel rather than the apartment, the price often includes a meal plan of breakfast and dinner daily. The other features of a ski vacation — round-trip bus, train, or rental car transportation between the airport and the resort, ski passes, baggage handling, taxes, and tips — are included in varying combinations according to the packager. If transatlantic transportation is by charter flight (not unusual on ski packages), airfare, too, will be included in the price.

Besides *Jet Vacations* (address above), which offers 1-week ski vacations primarily to French resorts, other ski-trip packagers with a number of European destinations, including France, are *Alpine Skiing and Travel* (534 New State Hwy., Raynham, MA 02767; phone: 508-823-7707; 800-551-8822 in Massachusetts; 800-343-9676 elsewhere in the US); *Adventures on Skis* (815 North Rd., Westfield, MA 01085; phone: 413-568-2855, 800-447-1144 in Massachusetts; 800-628-9655 elsewhere); and *Steve Lohr's Skiworld and Travel* (206 Central Ave., Jersey City, NJ, 07307; phone: 201-798-3900 in New Jersey; 800-223-1306 elsewhere). All offer a good selection of resorts. *Club Med,* which operates its own resort villages around the world, has club hotels in several French ski resorts; vacation packages there include lessons at the club's private ski schools. For information, contact *Club Med* (40 W 57th St., New York, NY 10019; phone: 800-CLUB MED).

Special-interest tours for practitioners and spectators of other sports include many bicycle and hiking tours of varying levels of difficulty. For the names and addresses of their organizers, see *Camping and RVs, Hiking and Biking,* in this section. Horseback riding holidays (for accomplished riders) in France — in the regions of Alsace, Beaujolais, the Dordogne, the Loire, Provence, and Souillac for 1 or 2 weeks — are arranged by *FITS Equestrian* (2011 Alamo Pintado, Solvang, CA 93463; phone: 805-688-9494).

Golf packages are offered by *InterGolf* (1980 Sherbrooke St. W., Suite 210, Montreal H3H 1E8, Canada; phone: 800-363-6273) and *Marsans Intercontinental* (19 W. 34th St., New York, NY 10001; phone: 212-239-3880 in New York State; 800-223-6114 elsewhere in the US). Tennis and golf tours operated in conjunction with canal cruises are organized by *McKinley Wilson International* (PO Box 1623, La Quinta, CA 92253; phone: 619-564-5443). The latest additions to their programs are three Tennis Experience tours. The first, from the last week of May through mid-June, includes center court seats to the *French Open International Tennis Championship* in Paris; the second is the week-long Luxury Canal Barging and Tennis tour in July, with daily stops at private tennis clubs; and, third, Château Tennis, a week-long program, run several times between May and October, includes stays at three different châteaux (2 nights at each). *Jet Vacations* (address above) takes groups to the *French Open* via the *Concorde.*

Fisherfolk might enjoy the opportunity to fish private waterways along the Rilse River offered by *Fishing International* (Hilltop Estate, 4010 Montecito Ave., Santa Rosa CA 95404; phone: 800-950-4242 or 707-542-4242). These week-long packages include accommodations in a small country inn and breakfast daily, and the opportunity to exchange fish stories about the Gallic one that got away with fellow enthusiasts.

Other special-interest packages cater to travelers attracted to the arts. Tours for music and opera lovers, offered by *Dailey-Thorp,* 315 W. 57th St., New York, NY 10019 (phone: 212-307-1555), visit various French musical events, including the *Aix-en-Provence International Festival of Lyric Art and Music,* the *Orange Festival,* and the *Berlioz Festival* in Lyons. Tours also visit Paris many times each year to enjoy the cultural attractions of the French capital.

For art enthusiasts, *Prospect Art Tours* offers 5- to 10-day tours visiting key museums and private galleries and art collections throughout France. All tours depart from London. For information contact *Prospect Art Tours* (454-458 Chiswick High Rd., London W45TT; phone: 81-995-2151 or 81-995-2163) or their US agent, *The British Connection* (2490 Black Rock Turnpike, Suite 240, Fairfield, CT 06430; phone: 203-254-7221).

Artwork of France's earliest inhabitants can be explored through *Past Time Tours'* Cave Art of France excursions. The 14-day tour includes educational lectures and a look at some of the world's most intriguing prehistoric ritual art and symbols. Leaving from Paris, the tour begins in Toulouse and continues on to Foix and Les Eyzies. For information, contact *Past Time Tours,* 800 Larch La., Sacramento, CA 95864-5042 (phone: 916-485-8140).

And for those who want to go antiquing through France's Auvergne region, *Far Horizons* (PO Box 1529, 16 Fern La., San Anselmo, CA 94960; phone: 415-457-4575) offers a 13-day trip, highlighted by visits to numerous antiques shops, flea markets, and country fairs, as well as stops at local museums. The group is limited to 12 shoppers, and accommodations are in the Châteaux de Jayet, home of trip leaders Reine and Ken Salter.

The *Bombard Society* (6727 Curran St., McLean, VA 22101; phone: 703-448-9407 or 800-862-8537) offers aerial tours of the French countryside. Great Balloon Adventure, offered in 1-week or shorter programs in Burgundy and the Loire Valley from spring through fall, includes daily flights via hot-air balloon (flown by pilots, not tour participants), sightseeing, hotel accommodations, and meals, many of which are candlelit buffets served after the day's flight.

For travelers interested in touring by rail, the plush *Venice Simplon–Orient Express* includes a stop in Paris on it's deluxe excursions. Although it spends only a brief time on French soil, it provides a fine add-on to either the beginning or end of a Paris stay. *Venice Simplon–Orient Express* now also offers passengers the opportunity to connect to a special cruise aboard its ship the *Orient Express,* which makes week-long cruises between Venice and Istanbul. For information, contact *Venice Simplon–Orient Express,* Suite 2565, One World Trade Center, New York, NY 10048 (phone: 212-938-6830 in New York State; 800-524-2420 elsewhere in the US). For further information, see *Traveling by Train,* in this section.

Camping and RVs, Hiking and Biking

 CAMPING: France welcomes campers, whether they come alone or with a group, with tents or in recreational vehicles. Camping is probably the best way to enjoy the French countryside. And fortunately, campgrounds in France are plentiful — there are over 8,500 of them.

Where to Camp – Campers are not restricted to the official sites. Using private property, however, means first obtaining permission of the landowner or tenant — as well as assuming the responsibility of leaving the land exactly as it was found in return for the hospitality. When in difficulty, remember that tourist information offices throughout France can direct visitors to sites in the areas they serve.

Most French campgrounds are well marked and rates usually are posted at the entrance. Still, it's best to have a map or check the information available in one of the guidebooks listed below. It's also not always easy to find camping facilities open before June or after September, so a guide that gives this information comes in particularly handy off-season. (Michelin's *Camping et Caravaning France* is published in French only, but contains detailed information on these facilities.)

Directors of campgrounds often have a great deal of information about their region, and some even will arrange local tours or recommend the best restaurants, shops, beaches, or attractions in the area. Campgrounds also provide the atmosphere and opportunity to meet other travelers and exchange useful information. Too much so, sometimes — the popularity of the French campgrounds causes them to be quite crowded during the summer, and campsites are frequently so close together that any attempt at privacy or getting away from it all is sabotaged. Campgrounds fill quickly at the height of the summer season, and the more isolated sites always go first. It's a good idea to arrive early in the day and reserve your chosen spot — which leaves you free to explore the area for the rest of the day.

The following organizations and publications will help in planning camping excursions in France:

> *Association Camping Club de France,* 218 Boulevard St.-Germain, Paris 75008 (phone: 1-45-48-30-03). Provides specific information on member campgrounds.
>
> *Association Camping Qualité France,* 105 Rue Lafayette, Paris 75010 (phone: 1-48-78-13-77). Publishes a guide rating campgrounds by stars.
>
> *L'Astrolabe,* 46 Rue de Provence, Paris 75009 (phone: 1-42-85-42-95). A travel bookshop in Paris with a comprehensive collection of maps and other useful information.
>
> *Camping et Caravaning France* ($12.95), one of Michelin's comprehensive guides, covers more than 2,000 campgrounds throughout France. Readily available in bookstores throughout France and in some travel bookstores and French-language bookstores in the US, it also can be ordered from Michelin Guides and Maps (PO Box 3305, Spartanburg, SC 29304-3305; phone: 803-599-0850 in South Carolina; 800-423-0485 elsewhere in the US).
>
> *Fédération Française de Camping et de Caravaning,* 78 Rue de Rivoli, Paris 75004 (phone: 1-42-72-84-08). A national federation of campgrounds which will provide a list of its members upon request.
>
> *Fédération Nationale des Gîtes Ruraux de France,* 35 Rue Godot-de-Mauroy, Paris 75009 (phone: 1-47-42-25-43). Issues a list of farms where camping is permitted.

French for Travellers published by Berlitz ($6.95), is a pocket-size guide which devotes five pages to camping vocabulary, including *Pouvons-nous camper dans votre champ?* (May we camp in your field?)

Union Nationale des Associations de Tourisme, an organization of tourism-related service associations, will direct you to the appropriate resource for general tourist information, including data on campgrounds. 8 Rue César Franck, Paris 75015 (phone: 1-43-06-88-21).

The *American Automobile Association (AAA)* can provide its members with a 600-page *Travel Guide to Europe* and 64-page *Motoring Europe.* Contact the nearest branch of *AAA.* In addition, the *Automobile Association of Great Britain (AA)* publishes a comprehensive guide, *Camping and Caravanning in Europe* ($12.95), listing over 4,000 sites throughout Europe. To order, contact AA Publishing, Fonum House, Basingstoke, Hampshire RG21 2EA, England (phone: 44-256-20123). Another source of information on campgrounds are local tourist offices, almost all of which provide brochures about camping in their respective areas.

The French international camping organization *Fédération Internationale de Camping et Caravaning* issues a pass, called a *carnet.* Available in the US from the *National Campers and Hikers Association* (4804 Transit Rd., Bldg. 2, Depew, NY 14043; phone: 716-668-6242), for $23, which includes membership in the organization, it entitles the bearer to information on and modest discounts at many campgrounds in France (and elsewhere in Europe).

For those campers flying to Paris who need a piece of ground immediately on which to pitch their tent, nearby possibilities include *Camping du Bois de Boulogne, Allée du Bord de l'Eau,* beside the Seine near the Suresnes Bridge (phone: 45-24-30-00). In Versailles, try *Camping Municipal* (31 Rue Berthelot in Porchefontaine; phone: 39-51-23-61); it's just 5 minutes on foot from the train station. As with any accommodations in or around Paris, it's wisest to call ahead.

Horseback riding enthusiasts should contact the *Association Nationale pour le Tourisme Equestre (ANTE)/Délégation Nationale au Tourisme Equestre de la Fédération Française d'Equitation,* Ile St.-Germain, 170 Quai de Stalingrad, Parc Intercommunale de Hauts-de-Seine, Issy les Moulineaux 92130.

Those who want to combine camping and caravanning with a little trout fishing need permission to do so (see *Gone Fishing,* DIVERSIONS). To learn how to get clearance to slap some big ones on the griddle, write to the *Conseil Supérieur de la Pêche,* 134 Avenue Malakoff, Paris 75016 (phone: 1-45-01-20-20).

Necessities – For outdoor camping, necessities include a tent with flyscreens (the lighter and easier to carry and assemble the better), a sleeping bag, a foam pad or air mattress (or one of the new combination self-inflating air mattresses), a rain poncho (which, in a pinch, can double as a ground cloth), first-aid kit (including sunscreen and insect repellent), sewing and toilet kits, a small backpacking cookstove (building fires is prohibited in many areas, especially during dry periods), fuel for the stove, matches, nested cooking pots and utensils, a canteen, three-quarter ax (well sharpened and sheath-protected), jackknife, and flashlight with an extra set of batteries.

Keep food simple. Unless backpacking deep into the wilderness — there *is* wilderness in France, but you can't get *too* many days away from civilization — you probably will be close enough to a store to stock up on perishables; staples such as sugar, coffee, and powdered milk can be carried along. Dehydrated food has become quite popular among both hikers and campers, but it can be quite expensive. An economical option for the more enterprising camper is to dry a variety of food at home; camping supply stores and bookstores carry cookbooks covering this simple process. Keep in mind, particularly in wilderness areas, that accessible food will lure scavenging wildlife that may invade tents and vehicles.

Recreational Vehicles – Recreational vehicles (RVs, known in France as "camping-cars") will appeal most to the kind of person who prefers the flexibility of accommodations — there are numerous campgrounds throughout France, and many provide RV hookups — and enjoys camping with a little extra comfort.

An RV undoubtedly saves a traveler a great deal of money on accommodations, and if cooking appliances are part of the unit, on food as well. However, it is important to remember that renting an RV is a major expense; also, any kind of RV increases gas consumption considerably.

Although the term recreational vehicle is applied to all manner of camping vehicles, whether towed or self-propelled, generally the models available for rent in France are motorized RVs, either converted vans or larger, fully equipped homes on wheels. Although most models are equipped with standard shift, occasionally automatic shift vehicles may be available for an additional charge. Towed vehicles can be hired overseas, but usually are not offered by US companies.

When camping with a recreational vehicle, it is essential to have some idea of the terrain you'll be encountering. Not only are numerous mountain passes closed in winter, but grades are often too steep for certain vehicles to negotiate. Car tunnels or piggyback services on trains can help bypass the orneriest summits, but they also impose dimensions limitations and often charge high fees. Local tourist offices should have information about existing conditions and whether or not a particular pass is closed.

Those who plan to camp all over Europe should make sure that whatever vehicle they drive is equipped to deal with the electrical and gas standards of all the countries on their itinerary. There are differences, for instance, between the bottled gas supplied in Great Britain and France (and elsewhere on the Continent). You should have either a sufficient supply of the type the camper requires or equipment that can use either. When towing a camper, note that nothing towed is automatically covered by the liability insurance of the primary vehicle, and the driver must carry a specific endorsement for the towed vehicle.

Among the companies offering RV rentals in France or in neighboring countries (which can be driven into France) are the following:

Avis Car Away, 60 Rue de Caen, Paris 92400 (phone: 1-43-34-15-81). Affiliated with *Avis* car rentals, this company rents motor homes for two to six people. Prices vary according to term of rental and time of year — high season is most expensive, longer rentals are less expensive per week — and include linens, dishes, and other amenities. Pickup and drop-off locations include Brest, Nice, and Paris; one-way rentals are available for an additional charge.

Connex International, 983 Main St., Peekskill, NY 10566 (phone: 800-333-3949 or 914-739-0066). Rents motorized RVs in Germany.

Europe by Car, One Rockefeller Plaza, New York, NY 10020 (phone: 212-581-3040 in New York State; 800-223-1516 elsewhere in the US), or 9000 Sunset Blvd., Los Angeles, CA 90069 (phone: 800-252-9401 or 213-272-0424). Rents motorized RVs in Belgium, Germany, and Holland.

Foremost Euro-Car, 5430 Van Nuys Blvd., Suite 306, Van Nuys, CA 91401 (phone: 818-786-1960 or 800-272-3299 in California; 800-423-3111 elsewhere in the US). Rents motorized RVs in Frankfurt, Germany.

FCI Location, Zone Industrielle de Sant-Brendan, Quentin 22800 (phone: 96-74-08-36). Rents motorized recreational vehicles on an unlimited mileage basis; rates vary according to season, and include insurance, linens, and other frills.

Trois Soleils, Maison Trois Soleils, 2 Route de Paris, 67117 Ittenheim (phone: 88-69-17-17 for reservations; 30-69-06-60 for the Paris branch). Rents motorized RVs as well as some basic campers; pickup and drop-off locations include Paris, Bordeaux, Strasbourg, and Montpellier.

The general policy with the above agencies is to make reservations far enough in advance to receive a voucher required to pick up the vehicle at the designated location in Europe. RV rentals also may be arranged on arrival from a number of other European companies. Among them is *Autotours* (address below). For other rental sources, ask at local car rental companies and national tourist board offices.

The French-language magazine for RV enthusiasts, *Le Monde du Camping Car,* includes recommendations on routes and campgrounds, itineraries, feature articles, and other general RV information, including local sales and rental companies. A 1-year subscription of 10 issues costs 210F (approximately $37); this must be paid in francs by international money order, available at US banks and post offices. To subscribe, write to Monique Deregard, *Le Monde du Camping-Car,* 15/17 Quai de l'Oise, Paris 75019 (phone: 1-40-34-22-07).

For information on how to operate, choose, and use a recreational vehicle, see *Living on Wheels* by Richard A. Wholters (Dutton; currently out of print; check your library or bookstore). You also might want to subscribe to *Trailer Life,* published by *TL Enterprises* (29901 Agoura Rd., Agoura, CA 91301; phone: 800-234-3450 or 818-991-4980). A 1-year subscription costs $12; $9 for members of the Good Sam Club, which provides discounts on a variety of services for RV owners and which also is run by *TL Enterprises.*

Another useful resource is the complimentary package of information on RVs offered by the *Recreational Vehicle Industry Association (RVIA).* It includes a catalogue of RV sources and consumer information; write to the *Recreational Vehicle Industry Association,* Dept. RK, PO Box 2999, Reston, VA 22090 (phone: 703-620-6003). The *Recreational Vehicle Rental Association (RVRA),* an RV dealers group, publishes an annual rental directory *Who's Who in RV Rentals;* send $5 to the *Recreational Vehicle Rental Association,* 3251 Old Lee Highway, Suite 500, Fairfax, VA 22030 (phone: 703-591-7130).

Finally, you may want to subscribe to the recreational vehicle and motorhome magazine, *Trailblazer.* A year's subscription costs $24; write to *Trailblazer,* 1000 124th Ave. NE, Bellevue, WA 98005.

Organized Camping Trips – A packaged camping tour abroad is a good way to have your cake and eat it, too. The problems of advance planning and day-to-day organizing are left to someone else, yet you still reap the benefits that shoestring travel affords. Be aware, however, that these packages usually are geared to the young, with ages 18 to 35 as common limits. Transfer from place to place is by bus or van (as on other sightseeing tours), overnights are in tents, and meal arrangements vary. Often there is a food fund that covers meals in restaurants or in the camps; sometimes there is a chef, and sometimes the cooking is done by the participants themselves.

The *Specialty Travel Index* is a directory to special-interest travel and is an invaluable resource. Listings include tour operators specializing in camping, not to mention myriad other interests that combine nicely with a camping trip, such as biking, ballooning, diving, horseback riding, canoeing, motorcycling, and river rafting. It costs $5 per copy, $8 for a year's subscription of two issues. Write to *Specialty Travel Index,* 305 San Anselmo Ave., San Anselmo, CA 94960 (phone: 415-459-4900).

Among such packages are the European camping tours offered by *Autotours* (20 Craven Terrace, London W2, England; phone: 44-71-258-0272), which range from 3 to 10 weeks. France is included in all their itineraries, which start and end in London. *Himalayan Travel* (PO Box 481, Greenwich, CT 06836; phone: 800-225-2380) also offers a variety of camping tours, including four just in France.

A French agency that specializes in adventure travel–hiking and canoe/kayak trips, as well as sailing, diving, and horseback riding vacations–which, for the most part, leave from Paris for locations outside France and include camping, is *Nouvelles Frontières* (87 Boulevard de Grenelle, Paris 75015; phone: 1-42-73-05-68). Their New York office (at 12 E. 33rd St., 11th Floor, New York, NY 10016; phone: 212-779-0600) will make flight and car rental arrangements for you in France, and also can book other *Nouvelles Frontières* trips. In addition, a number of packagers listed below under "Hiking" and "Biking" also may offer these pursuits in combination with camping — it pays to call and ask when planning your trip.

HIKING: If you would rather eliminate all the gear and planning and take to the outdoors unencumbered, park the car and go for a day's hike. Trails abound in France — 18,600 miles of them — as does specific information on how to find them.

Mountaineering and hiking clubs are a particularly good source of trail information for the average hiker and for those who are hiking on their own, without benefit of a guide or group, for a map of the trail is a must. Information about France's vast trail network, as well as maps and guidebooks for specific regions, are available (mostly in French) from the *Fédération Française de la Randonnée Pédestre* (*FFRP;* 9 Av. Georges-V, Paris 75008; phone: 1-47-23-62-32). A British company that specializes in maps and other publications for hikers and climbers, and that publishes English translations of the *Topo-Guides* of the *FFRP,* is the *Robertson MacCarta Shop* (122 King's Cross Rd., London WC1X 9DS, England; phone: 1-278-8278).

Those whose hiking enters the realm of mountain climbing can get information from *Club Alpin Français, Commission de Randonnées* (9 Rue la Boétie, Paris 75008; phone: 1-47-42-38-46). Serious hikers may want to check at their library for the very comprehensive but out-of-print *On Foot through Europe: A Trail Guide to France & the Benelux Nations* by Craig Evans. More than 200 pages are devoted to France alone, including information about guides and guidebooks, weather, lodgings, equipment, useful addresses, long-distance footpaths, cross-country skiing possibilities, national and regional parks, and 20 individual provinces and the resources specific to each.

Other books devoted to hiking in France are *Walking in France* by Rob Hunter (Oxford Illustrated Press paperback; $9.95) and *Long Walks in France* by Adam Nicolson (Harmony Books; out of print but check your library). Both feature a variety of walks of various intensities in areas throughout the countryside and are helpful in pointing out other resources for hikers. A useful set of guidebooks is the *Walking Through* series, which covers ten European cities (including Paris), and is available from VLE Limited (PO Box 444, Ft. Lee, NJ 07024; phone: 201-585-5080) for $3; these guides also may be found at select bookstores.

To make outings safe and pleasant, find out in advance about the trails you plan to hike and be realistic about your own physical limitations. Particularly in the French Alps, it is easy to underestimate the challenge of the grade combined with the thinner air of the high altitudes. Choose an easy route if you are out of shape. Stick to defined trails unless you are an experience hiker or know the area well. Whether heading out for a short jaunt or a longer trek, particularly in more remote areas, let someone know where you are going and when you expect to be back. If the hike is impromptu, leave a note on your car.

All you need to set out are a pair of sturdy shoes and socks; jeans or long pants to protect your legs; a canteen of water; a hat to protect you from the sun; and, if you like, a picnic lunch. It is a good idea to dress in layers, so that you can add or remove clothing according to the elevation and weather. Make sure, too, to wear clothes with pockets or bring a pack to keep your hands free. Some useful and important pocket or pack stuffers include trail mix, a jackknife, first-aid kit, map, compass, and sunglasses. You also may want to tuck in a lightweight waterproof poncho (available in camping supply stores) in case of unexpected showers. In areas where snakes are common, include a snakebite kit.

Organized Hiking Trips – Those who prefer to travel as part of an organized group should refer to the January/February issue of *Sierra* magazine for the *Sierra Club*'s annual list of foreign outings. Some trips are backpacking trips, moving to a new camp each day; others make day hikes from a base camp. Overnights can be in small hotels, inns, farmhouses, guesthouses, or campgrounds. Although destinations change each year, among recent itineraries offered in France were hikes to such places as the Basque country and to the French Alps, and a trip to Paris to explore the Parisian ecology: where the city's water and power come from and how Paris deals with air pollution and mass transit. For information, contact the *Sierra Club*, Outing Department, 730 Polk St., San Francisco, CA 94109 (phone: 415-776-2211).

American Youth Hostels also sponsors foreign hiking trips, though fewer than its foreign biking trips. As with the *Sierra Club,* the itineraries offered vary from year to year, usually ranging from around 15 to 52 days. France has been included among the destinations offered in recent years. For information on upcoming offerings, contact the *American Youth Hostels* (address below; see *Hints for Single Travelers,* in this section, for membership information).

Mountain Travel, a company specializing in adventure trips around the world, offers a great variety of trips ranging from easy walks that can be undertaken by anyone in good health to those that require basic or advance mountaineering experience. Three itineraries in France are offered: an intermediate climb in the Alps; the classic *tour du Mont Blanc* (a 12-day trek); and a moderate-to-strenuous sojourn called "Hiking the Haute Route." Note that *Mountain Travel* also designs special itineraries for independent travelers. Contact *Mountain Travel,* 6420 Fairmount Ave., El Cerrito, CA 94530 (phone: 415-527-8100 in California; 800-227-2384 elsewhere in the US).

Other companies offer hiking tours in France include the following:

Alternative Travel Groups, 1-3 George St., Oxford, England 0X1 2AZ (phone: 800-527-5997). The motto of this company is that "The best way to see a country is on foot." Among its numerous itineraries worldwide, they offer walking tours in the Dordogne and Provence.

Baumeler Tours, 10 Grand Ave., Rockville Centre, New York, NY 11570-9861 (phone: 516-766-6160, collect, in New York State; 800-6-ABROAD elsewhere in the US). Offers hiking trips in the Loire Valley and Provence. (Also see "Biking," below.)

Butterfield & Robinson, 70 Bond St., Suite 300, Toronto, Ontario M5B 1X3 (Canada; phone: 800-387-1147 or 416-864-1354). This company offers several hiking tours — although fewer than its biking tours (see below) — including the finest in French food and accommodations.

Distant Journeys, PO Box 1211, Camden, ME 04843 (phone: 207-781-5339 from June 1 to October 15; 207-236-9788 during the rest of the year). Offers a 12-day hiking tour of Mont-Blanc, the highest peak in the Alps.

Europeds, 883 Sinex Ave., Pacific Grove, CA 93950 (phone: 408-372-1173). Offers a 9-day inn-to-inn walking tour in the Dordogne. (Also see "Biking," below.)

Forum Travel International, 91 Gregory, #21, Pleasant Hill, CA 94523 (phone: 415-671-2900). Offers 20 enticing itineraries throughout the countryside, in four grades of difficulty — the most energetic grade covering as many as 20 miles (32 km) a day, and geared to those already accustomed to hard mountain walking. (Also see "Biking," below.)

Himalayan Travel, PO Box 481, Greenwich, CT 06836 (phone: 800-225-2380). Among the itineraries offered throughout France are 4 hiking and camping trips and 12 hotel-to-hotel tours afoot.

Wilderness Travel, 801 Allston Way, Berkeley, CA 94710 (phone: 415-548-0420 in California or abroad; 800-247-6700 elsewhere in the US). Offers trips in the French Alps, similar to those packaged by *Mountain Travel* above. (Also see "Biking," below.)

Yamnuska, Inc., PO Box 1920, Canmore, Alberta, Canada T0L 0M0 (phone: 403-678-4164). Offers a 12-day Mont-Blanc tour in the French Alps.

An alternative to dealing directly with the above companies is to contact *All Adventure Travel,* a specialist in hiking and biking trips worldwide. This company, which acts as a representative for numerous special tour packagers offering such outdoor adventures, can provide a wealth of detailed information about each packager and programs offered. They also will help you design and arrange all aspects of a personalized itinerary. This company operates much like a travel agency, collecting commissions from the packagers. Therefore, there is no additional charge for these services. For information, contact *All Adventure Travel,* PO Box 4307, Boulder, CO 80306 (phone: 800-537-4025 or 303-939-8885).

BIKING: For young or energetic travelers, a bicycle offers a marvelous way of seeing France, especially in those regions conducive to easy cycling, such as Normandy, the Loire Valley, or the Médoc wine region north of Bordeaux. The French, from ages 8 to 85, have long depended on bicycles for transportation, and they typically respect foreigners who arrive in their communities *à vélo.* Besides being a viable way to get around France — and to burn calories to make room for unlimited portions of fabulous French food — biking is a great way to meet people. Remember, however, that most country folk do not speak English, so pack a copy of a good French-English phrase book if your French is not up to par. (For information on pronunciation and a list of basic terms you're likely to use en route, see *Useful Words and Phrases,* in this section.)

Road Safety – While the car may be the bane of cyclists, cyclists who do not follow the rules of the road strike terror into the hearts of drivers. Follow the same rules and regulations as motor vehicle drivers. Stay to the right side of the road. Ride no more than two abreast — single file where traffic is heavy. Keep three bicycle lengths behind the cycle in front of you. Stay alert to sand, gravel, potholes, and wet or oily surfaces, all of which can make you lose control. Wear bright clothes and use lights or wear reflective material at dusk or at night, and, above all, even though French cyclists often don't, always wear a helmet.

Choosing, Renting, and Buying a Bike – Although many bicycling enthusiasts choose to take along their own bikes, bicycles are available for rent throughout France, although, particularly in rural areas, it may pay to check ahead.

As an alternative to renting, you might consider buying a bicycle in France, often for less than you might pay in the US. However, the bicycle may take some getting used to — seats especially need breaking in at first — and if you bring it home, it will be subject to an import duty by US Customs if its price (or the total of purchases in France) exceeds $400. When evaluating this cost, take into account additional charges for shipping. Those planning to buy a bicycle, be it in the US or France, should consider a good-quality, lightweight touring bike that has the all-important low gears for hill climbing and riding against the wind. A European bicycle purchased in the US should have proof-of-purchase papers to avoid potential customs problems.

Bike shops in Paris that rent bicycles and sometimes sell used ones include *Bicyclub de France* (8 Pl. de la Porte Champerret, Paris 75017; phone: 47-66-55-92) and *Paris-Vélo* (2 Rue du Fer à Moulin, Paris 75905; phone: 43-37-59-22). For further details on bicycle rental shops in French cities, see *Sources and Resources* in the individual city reports of THE CITIES.

A bicycle is the correct size for you if you can straddle its center bar with feet flat on the ground and still have an inch or so between your crotch and the bar. (Nowadays, because women's old-fashioned, barless bikes are not as strong as men's, most women use men's bicycles.) The seat height is right if your leg is just short of completely extended when you push the pedal to the bottom of its arc.

To be completely comfortable, divide your weight; put about 50% on your saddle and about 25% each on your arms and legs. To stop sliding in your seat and for better support, set your saddle level. A firm saddle is better than a soft springy one for a long ride. Experienced cyclists keep the tires fully inflated (pressure requirements vary widely, but are always imprinted on the side of the tire; stay within 5 pounds of the recommended pressure). Do not use top, or tenth, gear all the way; for most riding the middle gears are best. On long rides remember that until you are very fit, short efforts with rests in between are better than one long haul, and pedal at an even pace.

The happiest biker in a foreign country is the one who arrives best prepared. Bring saddlebags (*paniers*), a handlebar bag, a tool kit that contains a bike wrench, screwdriver, pliers, tire repair kit, cycle oil, and work gloves, a bike repair book, a helmet (a rarity among French cyclists), a rain suit, a water bottle, a flashlight with an extra set of batteries, a small first aid kit, and muscles that have been limbered up in advance.

Even the smallest towns usually have a bike shop, so it's not difficult to replace or add to gear; however, because tires and tubes are sized to metric dimensions in France, when riding your own bike, bring extras from home. Good maps infinitely improve a bike trip, and Michelin and IGN topographical maps, available throughout France, provide detailed and clear road references. Seasoned bikers swear that the second day of any trip is always the worst, so keep this in mind and be ready to meet the mental and physical challenges ahead.

Airlines going from the US (or elsewhere) to France generally allow bicycles to be checked as baggage and require that the pedals be removed, handlebars be turned sideways, and the bike be in a shipping carton, which some airlines provide, subject to availability — call ahead to make sure. If buying a shipping carton from a bicycle shop, check the airline's specifications and also ask about storing the carton at the destination airport so that you can use it again for the return flight. Although some airlines charge only a nominal fee, if the traveler has already checked two pieces of baggage, there may be an excess baggage charge of $70 to $80 for the bicycle. As regulations vary from carrier to carrier, be sure to call well before departure to find out your airline's specific regulations.

When the going gets rough, remember that arduous parts of the journey can be avoided by loading your bicycle on the luggage van of a train. Travelers can check their bicycles as baggage for a fee or carry them on and off the train as hand baggage on a short- or medium-length journey. In some instances, the bicycle can be checked on a train independently of its owner and can be picked up at the station upon arrival there; a number of stations provide a plastic or cardboard cover for the bicycle for a nominal fee, and a few will actually pick it up at or deliver it to a designated address. Bicycle insurance also is available — and advisable.

FrenchRail Inc. (SNCF) also offers a *Train + Vélo* special, whereby in some 280 French cities bicycles with ten or fewer speeds can be rented right in the train station for as little as half a day and as many as 10 or more. Rates start at about $6.50 a day and decrease with the number of days; group rates are negotiable. Those travelers who show a credit card need not pay a returnable deposit. The bicycle may be returned to the same station or to another that also rents bikes; ask at the ticket window for the *Guide du Train et du Vélo,* a brochure listing participating stations.

A good book to help you plan a trip is *Bicycle Touring in Europe,* by Karen and Gary Hawkins (Pantheon Books; $8.95); it offers information on buying and equipping a touring bike, useful clothing and supplies, and helpful techniques for the long-distance biker. Another good general book is *Europe by Bike,* by Karen and Terry Whitehall (Mountaineers Books; $10.95). *Bicycling in France* is an excellent reference which focuses specifically on touring in France; published by Haynes, it's out of print, but check your library. The *International Youth Hostel Handbook, Volume One: Europe and the Mediterranean* ($8.95 plus $2 for postage) is a guide to all the hostels of Europe to which members of *AYH* have access; a map of their locations is included. (For information on joining *American Youth Hostels*, see *Hints for Single Travelers*, in this section.)

A list of suggested itineraries also may be obtained on request from the French Government Tourist Office, or locally from the Syndicats d'Initiative. The Comité Régional de Tourisme des Pays de la Loire is particularly good at this. Contact them at Maison du Tourisme, Place du Commerce, Nantes 44000 (phone: 40-48-15-45).

Biking Tours – A number of organizations offer bike tours in France. Linking up with a bike tour is more expensive than traveling alone, but with experienced leaders an organized tour often becomes an educational as well as a very social experience that may lead to long-term friendships.

One of the attractions of a bike tour is that the shipping of equipment — your bike — is handled by organizers, and the shipping fee is included in the total tour package. Travelers simply deliver the bike to the airport, already disassembled and boxed; shipping cartons can be obtained from most bicycle shops with little difficulty. Independent bikers must make their own arrangements with the airline, and there are no standard procedures (see above). Although some tour organizers will rent bikes, most prefer that participants bring a bike with which they are already familiar. Another attraction of *some* tours is the existence of a "sag wagon" which carries extra luggage, fatigued cyclists, and their bikes, too, when pedaling another mile is impossible.

Most bike tours are scheduled from May to October, last 1 or 2 weeks, are limited to 20 or 25 people, and provide lodging in inns or hotels, though some use hostels or even tents. Tours vary considerably in style and ambience, so request brochures from several operators in order to make the best decision. When contacting groups, be sure to ask about the maximum number of people on the trip, the maximum number of miles to be traveled each day, and the degree of difficulty of the biking; these details should determine which tour you join and can greatly affect your enjoyment of the experience. Planning ahead is essential because trips often fill up 6 months or more in advance.

Among the companies offering biking tours in France are the following:

Backroads Bicycle Touring, 1516 Fifth St., Berkeley, CA 94710-1713 (phone: 415-527-1555 in California; 800-533-2573 elsewhere in the US). Offers superior food and accommodations on its 8-day Loire Valley tour. Geared to beginning and intermediate riders, it features stays in châteaux.

Baumeler Tours, 10 Grand Ave., Rockville Centre, NY 11570-9861 (phone: 516-766-6160, collect, in New York State; 800-6-ABROAD elsewhere in the US). Specializing in bicycling tours, both individual and escorted, this company offers four 9-day trips in the Loire Valley and Provence. (Also see "Hiking," above.)

Country Cycling Tours, 140 W. 83rd St., New York, NY 10024 (phone: 212-874-5151), which offered 21 departures of its four 10- to 14-day itineraries to France in 1990 (one to the Loire Valley, one to Périgord and the Dordogne, one to Brittany and Normandy, and the fourth to the wine country of Alsace).

Earth Ventures, 2625 N. Meridien St., Suite 612, Indianapolis, IN 46208-7705 (phone: 317-926-0453). Itineraries to France include four 8- to 10-day biking tours, which include a combination of either ballooning, canoeing, or sailing, in Burgundy, the Loire Valley, Provence, and the Riviera.

Eurobike, PO Box 40, DeKalb, IL 60115 (phone: 815-758-8851). Offers three tours in France: one in Bordeaux, one in Burgundy, and a tour of Brittany and the Loire Valley.

Europeds, 883 Sinex Ave., Pacific Grove, CA 93950 (phone: 408-372-1173). Offers ten 6- to 18-day biking tours throughout France. (Also see "Hiking," above.)

Forum Travel International, 91 Gregory, #21, Pleasant Hill, CA 94523 (phone: 415-671-2900). Offers a variety of biking itineraries, each with a specific theme, including Gourment Biking in Alsace; Food, Art & Wine: Biking in Burgundy;

Wine Country & Castles: Champagne, Burgundy & the Loire. (Also see "Hiking," above.)

Gerhard's Bicycle Odysseys, PO Box 757, Portland, OR 97207 (phone: 503-223-2402). Offers 2-week trips to Europe and usually has an itinerary that visits France.

Peregrine Adventures, PO Box 3838, Park City, UT 84060 (phone: 801-649-0460). Offers 8- to 10-day biking tours in Burgundy, Châteaux de la Loire, Côte d'Azur, and Provence.

Progressive Travel Ltd., 1932 First Ave., Seattle, WA 98101 (phone: 800-245-2229). Their three 5- to 9-day inn-to-inn itineraries cover Burgundy, the Dordogne, and Provence.

Rocky Mountain Cycling Tours, PO Box 1978, Canmore, Alberta, Canada T0L 0M0 (phone: 403-678-6770). Organizes four bike and barge trips along France's extensive canal system.

Travent International, PO Box 305, Waterbury Center, VT 05677 (phone: 800-325-3009 or 802-244-5420). Offers seven inn-to-inn bicycling tours in Alsace, Burgundy, the Dordogne, the Loire Valley, Normandy, and Provence.

Wilderness Travel, 801 Allston Way, Berkeley, CA 94710 (phone: 415-548-0420 in California or abroad; 800-247-6700 elsewhere in the US). Offers biking trips in Burgundy, the Loire valley, and Provence, with an emphasis on regional food and wine. (Also see "Hiking," above.)

For those seeking a deluxe tour package, *Butterfield & Robinson* (70 Bond St., Suite 300, Toronto, Ontario M5B 1X3, Canada; phone: 800-387-1147 or 416-864-1354) offers a number of first class, sophisticated 9-day bike trips to France each year, with many meals taken in Michelin-starred restaurants and overnights frequently spent in prestigious *Relais & Châteaux* hotels. Last year, groups went to Alsace, the Loire Valley, Normandy, Provence, and Savoy and on wine tasting trips through the vineyards of Bordeaux and Burgundy; another offering is a Tour de France. Bikes are provided, though you can take your own, and there are many departure dates for each itinerary. Trips are open to anyone aged 18 or older; biking tours are rated at three levels of difficulty. (Also see "Hiking," above.)

Hundreds of other organizations sponsoring biking tours have sprung up in response to an explosion of interest.

The *American Youth Hostels (AYH)* and its local chapters, or councils also sponsors a variety of biking tours to Europe each year. You don't have to be a youngster to take an *AYH* trip; membership is open to all ages, and the catalogue includes a group of trips for adults only. *AYH* tours are for small groups of 9 or 10 participants and tend to be longer than average (up to 5 weeks). Departures are geared to various age groups and levels of skill, and frequently feature accommodations in hostels — along with hotels for adult groups and campgrounds for younger groups.

The *Metropolitan New York Council of American Youth Hostels,* an *AYH* affiliate with a particularly broad tour program, recently offered a 4-week national trip called La Belle France, as well as several tours combining France with other countries. Last summer, among the itineraries offered by the organization were one tour exclusively in France and two European trips passing through France, including a 22-day tour of France, Belgium, and England. For information on current offerings, contact your local council, the national organization (PO Box 37613, Washington, DC 20013-7613; phone: 202-783-6161), or the *Metropolitan New York Council of American Youth Hostels* (891 Amsterdam Ave., New York, NY 10025; phone 212-932-2300).

The *International Bicycle Touring Society (IBTS)* is another nonprofit organization that regularly sponsors low-cost bicycle tours overseas led by member volunteers. Participants must be over 21. A sag wagon accompanies the group, accommodations are in inns and hotels, and breakfast is included. For information, send $2 plus a self-addressed, stamped envelope to *IBTS*, PO Box 6979, San Diego, CA 92106-0979 (phone: 619-226-TOUR). The *Sierra Club* also occasionally includes a bike tour in its group of European offerings. For news about upcoming free-wheeling events, contact the club's Outing Department (address above).

You also may want to investigate the tours of the Continent offered by the *Cyclists' Touring Club (CTC)*, Britain's largest cycling association. In addition to offering organized tours, *CTC* also has a number of planned routes available in pamphlet form for bikers on their own and helps members plan their own tours. The club also publishes a yearly handbook, as well as magazines. For information, contact the *CTC* at Cotterell House, 69 Meadrow, Godalming, Surrey GU7 3HS, England (phone: 4868-7217).

The *League of American Wheelmen* (6707 Whitestone Rd., Suite 209, Baltimore, MD 21207; phone: 301-944-3399) publishes *Tourfinder*, a list of organizations, non-profit and commercial, that sponsor bicycle tours of the US and abroad; the list is free with membership ($25 individual, $30 family) and can be obtained by non-members who send $5. The *League* also can put you in touch with biking groups in your area.

Preparing

Calculating Costs

$ After years of living relatively high on the hog, travel from North America to Europe dropped off precipitously in 1987 in response, among other considerations, to the relative weakness of the US dollar on the Continent. Many Americans who had enjoyed bargain prices in Europe found that the recent disadvantageous exchange rates really put a crimp in their travel planning. But although the halcyon days of dollar domination seem over for the present, discount fares and the availability of charter flights can greatly reduce the cost of a European vacation; package tours can even further reduce the price. France always has been one of the most popular European countries for both the first-time and the seasoned traveler, and while it has never been one of Europe's less expensive destinations, it is certainly one where the competition for American visitors works to inspire surprisingly affordable travel opportunities. Nevertheless, most travelers still have to plan carefully and manage their travel funds prudently.

In France, estimating travel expenses depends on the mode of transportation you choose, the part or parts of the country you plan to visit, how long you will stay, the level of luxury to which you aspire, and in some cases, what time of year you plan to travel. In addition to the basics of transportation, hotels, meals, and sightseeing, you have to take into account seasonal price changes that apply on certain air routings and at popular vacation destinations, as well as inflation, price fluctuations, and the vagaries of currency exchange. So, while the guidelines in this book will remain useful, costs for both facilities and services may have changed somewhat in the months since publication.

DETERMINING A BUDGET: A realistic appraisal of your travel expenses is the most crucial bit of planning you will undertake before any trip. It also is, unfortunately, one for which it is most difficult to give precise, practical advice. Travel styles are intensely personal, and personal taste determines cost to a great extent. Will you stay in a hotel every night and eat every meal in a restaurant, or are you planning to camp or picnic amidst France's picturesque and peaceful countryside, thus reducing your daily expenditures? Base your calculations on your own travel style, and make estimates of expenses from that. If published figures on the cost of travel always were taken as gospel, many trips would not be taken. But in reality, it's possible to economize. On the other hand, don't be lulled into feeling that it is not necessary to do some arithmetic before you go. No matter how generous your travel budget, without careful planning beforehand — and strict accounting along the way — you will spend more than you anticipated.

When calculating costs, start with the basics, the major expenses being transportation, accommodations, and food. However, don't forget such extras as local transportation, shopping, and such miscellaneous items as laundry and tips. The reasonable cost of these items usually is a positive surprise to your budget; such extras as drinks served with imported liquors and airport departure taxes are definite negatives.

Package programs can reduce the price of a vacation in France, because the group rates obtained by the tour packager usually are lower than the tariffs for someone traveling on a freelance basis; that is, paying for each element — airfare, hotel, meals, car rental — separately. And keep in mind, particularly when calculating the major expenses, that costs vary according to fluctuations in the exchange rate — that is, how much of a given foreign currency a dollar will buy.

Other expenses, such as the cost of local sightseeing tours or excursions, will vary from city to city. Tourist information offices are plentiful throughout France, and most of the better hotels will have someone at the front desk to provide a rundown on the cost of local tours and full-day excursions in and out of the city. Travel agents also can provide this information. Special discount passes that provide tourists with unlimited travel by the day or the week on regular city transportation are available in many large cities. The French Government Tourist Office and *Air France* — both well aware that they need to entice cost-conscious Americans to consider a French vacation these days — offer a free brochure filled with special offers, at rates guaranteed in dollars. Last year it was called *France '90, A Great Value.* It will be updated as the need arises, and is available from either *Air France* or from one of the French Government Tourist Offices listed in *Tourist Information,* in this section. Entries in the individual city reports in THE CITIES also give specific information on these activities.

For purposes of a rough estimate — if you spend every night in a moderately priced hotel and eat every meal in a moderately priced restaurant, you can expect to spend around $200 to $300 for two people per day. This figure does not include transportation costs, but it does include accommodations (based on two people sharing a room), three meals, some sightseeing, and other modest entertainment costs. The accommodations take into consideration the differences between relatively inexpensive lodgings in rural areas (about $50 to $60 per night for two) and moderate hotels in urban areas (about $75 to $100 per night for two). With the exception of major cities such as Paris, these averages should be about right for a room for two throughout France. You can find places that are much less expensive or places at which you spend more for a commensurate increase in quality of service and comfort.

Meals are all calculated for inexpensive to moderate restaurants. The entertainment calculated in this daily expense figure includes one sightseeing tour and admission to one museum or historic site and/or one recreation — such as greens fees for a round of golf or renting a mount for an afternoon ride about the countryside.

As noted in *When to Go,* slightly lower hotel rates can be expected in France during the off-season — January through March. Many hotels offer "mini-break" packages, that is, a discount for a stay of 2 or more nights, usually over a weekend; though these discounts may be in effect any time of the year, they are most common when demand is lowest. In large cities, seasonal price variations may be negligible — with the exception of a dramatic rise in the cost of accommodations and services during *Christmas* and other holidays. During the shoulder season months in spring (April through May) and fall (September through October), prices generally are somewhat more reasonable even for luxury hotels — although, again, high season prices may prevail in large cities and popular tourist areas.

You should be able to use these averages to forecast a reasonably accurate picture of your daily travel costs, based on exactly how you want to travel. Savings on the daily allowance can occur while motoring in rural areas; budget-minded families also can take advantage of inexpensive accommodations along the Atlantic Coast, as well as some of the more economical accommodations options to be found in France. Campgrounds are particularly inexpensive, and they are located throughout the country (see *Camping and RVs, Hiking and Biking,* in this section). For information on other economical accommodations alternatives, such as renting an apartment, house, or cottage, home exchanges, and bed and breakfast establishments, see the discussions of accommodations in *On the Road,* in this section.

Picnicking is another excellent way to cut costs, and France abounds with well groomed parks and idyllic pastoral settings. A stop at a local market can provide a feast of fine cheeses and meats, crusty *baguettes,* fresh fruit, and perhaps a bottle of wine, at a surprisingly economical price — especially when compared to the cost of a restaurant lunch.

In planning any travel budget, it also is wise to allow a realistic amount for both entertainment and recreation. Are you planning to spend time sightseeing and going to local museums? Do you intend to spend your days skiing at a popular resort? Is daily tennis a part of your plan? Will your children be disappointed if they don't take a *bateau-mouche* on the Seine? If so, charges for these attractions and recreations must be taken into account. General guidelines on the costs of these and other activities can be found in our DIVERSIONS chapters, as well as in the *Sources and Resources* sections of the individual city reports in THE CITIES. Finally, don't forget that if haunting discotheques or music halls every night is an essential part of your vacation, or you feel that one performance of the *Orchestre de Paris* at the *Salle Pleyel* may not be enough, allow for the extra cost of nightlife. This one item alone can add a great deal to your daily expenditures, particularly in the large cities and major tourist and resort areas.

If at any point in the planning process it appears impossible to estimate expenses, consider this suggestion: The easiest way to put a ceiling on the price of all these elements is to buy a package tour. A totally planned and escorted one, with almost all transportation, rooms, meals, sightseeing, local travel, tips, and a dinner show or two included and prepaid, provides an exact total of what the trip will cost beforehand, and the only surprise will be the one you spring on yourself by succumbing to some irresistible, expensive souvenir.

The various types of packages available are discussed in *Package Tours,* in this section, but a few points bear repeating here. Not all packages are package *tours.* They often are no more than loosely organized arrangements that include transatlantic transportation, a stay at a hotel, transfers between hotel and airport, baggage handling, taxes, and tips, which leave the entire matter of how you spend your time and where you eat your meals — and with whom — up to you. Equally common are the hotel-plus-car packages, which take care of accommodations and local transportation. On such independent or hosted "tours," there may be a tour company representative or affiliated French travel agent available at a nearby office to answer questions, or a host may be stationed at a desk in the hotel to arrange optional excursions, but you will never have to travel in a group unless you wish to.

More and more, even experienced travelers are being won over by the idea of package travel, not only for the convenience and the planning time saved, but above all for the money that can be saved. Whatever elements you include in your package, the organizer has gotten them for you wholesale — and they are paid for in advance, thus eliminating the dismal prospect of returning to your hotel each night to subtract the day's disbursements from your remaining cash, when you should be enjoying a glass of wine in peace at a sidewalk café.

The possibility of prepaying certain elements of your trip is an important point to consider even if you intend to be strictly independent — with arrangements entirely of your own making, all bought separately. You may not be able to match the price of the wholesale tour package, but at least you will have introduced an element of predictability into your accounting, thus reducing the risk that some budget-busting expense along the way might put a damper on the rest of your plans.

Those who want to travel independently — but also want to eliminate the element of surprise from their accommodations budget — can take advantage of the hotel voucher schemes that frequently come as part of a fly/drive package. Travelers receive a block of prepaid vouchers and a list of hotels that accept them as total payment for a night's stay, and for those who may want to upgrade their lodgings from time to time, there is often another set of hotels that accepts the same vouchers with payment of a supplement.

With the independent traveler in mind, what follows are some suggestions on how to pin down the cost of a trip beforehand. But there are two more variables that will influence the cost of your holiday whether you buy a package or do it all yourself. One is timing. If you are willing to travel during the less trafficked, off-season months, when airfares are at their lowest levels, you'll find many hotels' rates lower also. Keep in mind those periods between the traditional high and low seasons, generally referred to as the shoulder months (approximately late March to mid-May and late September to mid-November). Although costs are only a little lower than in high season and the weather may not be as predictable, you won't be bucking the crowds that in peak months can force a traveler without a hotel reservation into the most expensive hostelry in town. Don't forget, however, to find out what is going on in any place where you plan to spend a good deal of your vacation. The availability and possible economy gained by off-season travel often are negated if a major conference or other special event is scheduled to take place at the time you plan to visit. For instance, because of trade shows and conventions, September is one of the busiest months of the year in Paris, and because of the *International Film Festival*, Cannes is already in high gear by mid-May.

Another factor influencing the cost of a French trip is whether you will be traveling alone or as a couple. The prices quoted for package tours almost always are based on double occupancy of hotel rooms, and the surcharge — or single supplement — for a room by yourself can be quite hefty. When shopping for a hotel room, you'll find that there are many more double rooms than singles. Don't expect a discount if you occupy a double room as a single, and don't expect single rooms to cost less than two-thirds the price of doubles.

■ **Note:** The volatility of exchange rates may mean that between the time you originally make your hotel reservations and the day you arrive, the price in US dollars may vary substantially from the price originally quoted. To avoid paying more than you expected, it's wise to confirm rates by writing directly to hotels or by calling their representatives in the US. Remember that you also must determine whether it's more economical to pay for services in dollars before departure or in local currency once in France. (For further information on exchange rates and getting the most out of your travel dollars, see *Credit and Currency,* in this section.)

TRANSPORTATION COSTS: In earlier sections of GETTING READY TO GO we have discussed the comparative costs of different modes of transportation and the myriad special rates available through package tours, charter flights, train passes, car rental packages, and other budget deals. See each of the relevant sections for specific information. Transportation is likely to represent the largest item in your travel budget (cumulatively, only food and accommodations are likely to be higher), but the encouraging aspect of this is that you will be able to determine most of these costs before you leave. Most fares will have to be paid in advance, particularly if you take advantage of charter air travel or other special offerings.

Airfare is really the easiest cost to pin down, though the range and variety of flights available may be confusing initially. The possibilities are outlined fully in *Traveling by Plane,* in this section. Essentially, you can choose from various types of tickets on scheduled flights, ranging in expense from the luxury of the *Concorde* and first class fares to APEX and discount tickets or charters.

Fares for regularly scheduled flights do drop during the winter. Charter fares, most often built into a total package plan, usually are the lowest air transportation possibilities available, and midweek travel generally costs less than weekend travel. Excursion fares mean savings if you can fit your travel plans into a given time frame; these and reduced tour-basing fares (for which you qualify by booking a package or ground arrangements of a set value) mean savings on travel to the most popular destinations. But since airline deregulation in the US virtually eliminated the rule book, special promotional fares can be offered almost anytime. So check each airline serving your destination (ask specifically about excursion and tour-basing prices), and to guard against human and computer error, *triple* check the price quoted by the airline you pick before making a final booking. (For information on these and other special deals, see *Traveling by Plane,* in this section.)

The most important factors in determining which mode of transportation to choose in traveling about France are the amount of traveling you plan to do and the length of time you will be abroad. If you intend to move about a great deal among cities, a pass allowing unlimited train travel is likely to be the most economical approach. The France Railpass is valid for travel in France only; the BritFrance Railpass is valid for travel in France and Great Britain; and the Eurailpass is valid for France and much of the rest of Europe. All three must be purchased before you leave home, and are attractively priced, but if you are traveling strictly in France, the France Railpass, which costs less and is available in first and second class versions for periods of 4 or 9 days, is the one to buy. For more information on economical rail options, see *Traveling by Train,* in this section.

Although driving provides maximum flexibility, renting a car anywhere in Europe is a substantial expense. Car rental costs do vary from city to city, as well as according to season (but don't expect rates to be as low as the deeply discounted bargain rates so often found in the US), the type of car you choose, and whether the car is rented independently or as part of a package deal.

If you want to drive through the countryside, you should look carefully into fly/drive arrangements versus straight rentals, and also compare the rates offered by some of the smaller firms specializing in car travel in Europe with the rates offered by the larger, more familiar car rental companies. (For specific information on car rental availability and rates, see *Sources and Resources* in the individual THE CITIES chapters.) The latter all have discount plans, provided the car is booked a certain number of days before pickup and the rental is for a minimum period of time. Look for a flat rate that also offers unlimited mileage — usually the best deal. Also, when estimating driving costs, don't forget that the price of gas in Europe averages more than twice the price you're accustomed to paying in the US, so be sure to take this substantial expense into account. This cost also provides a significant incentive to rent a car that delivers the highest possible mileage per gallon — or liter — of gas. (For further information, see *Traveling by Car,* in this secion.)

FOOD: Meals are a more difficult expense to estimate. If you rent an apartment, house, or cottage, or are camping out, you will be able to prepare some meals yourself. Depending on where you're staying, groceries can be more expensive than they are at home, but they certainly will be less expensive than eating out. Restaurant dining — particularly in the better establishments of major cities and in prime tourist areas — is going to hit your purse, wallet, or credit card hardest.

Independent travelers eating all of their meals in restaurants should allow roughly $60 to $80 a day for food. This amount includes breakfast (the price of the standard continental breakfast of *café au lait,* rolls or croissants, butter, and jam — sometimes optional, sometimes obligatory — usually is posted separately from the price of the room in French hotels), lunch, and an average dinner. The estimate for dinner is based on a fixed menu (at a fixed price) in moderate, neither-scrimp-nor-splurge restaurants, which at least can include a tasty and occasionally imaginative food selection, but no cocktails before dinner. This also should cover taxes and gratuities and perhaps a carafe of French wine at dinner — but you won't be splurging. If ordering an à la carte dinner and the pick of the wine list in one of the major cities, be prepared for the tab to rise much higher, and if you're addicted to *haute gastronomie,* the sky is the limit.

All of this is no reason to forgo your trip, however — remember, it's *dining* that is going to hit your wallet hard. If you're up to a steady diet of pizza, *steak frites* (a thin slice of steak and French fries), and café snacks of *croque-monsieur* (a toasted cheese sandwich with ham) and *croque-madame* (toasted cheese with ham and egg), you will do very well indeed. And there is some relief out in the countryside, where the breakfast that comes with the bed in *auberges* (inns), *logis* (small, family-run hotels), and *gîte-chambre-d'hôte* (a type of bed and breakfast establishment) can still be a filling one, apt to hold most folks through midday (though even travelers on a tight budget are advised not to skip lunch). If you stick to picnic lunches and finish off the day with a carefully chosen meal in a bistro or country inn, you will sacrifice nothing in experience and still hold down costs. Our restaurant selections, chosen to give the best value for money — whether expensive or dirt cheap — are listed in the *Best in Town* sections of THE CITIES and in the *Eating Out* sections of each tour route in DIRECTIONS.

ACCOMMODATIONS: There is a wide range of choice and a substantial difference in degrees of luxury provided among the expensive, moderate, and inexpensive French hotels. Although room costs in France cover a very broad spectrum, for purposes of making an estimate, expect to pay slightly more in France than you would pay in a major American city for equivalent accommodations. Figure on the high side, however, if you're visiting major resort areas or tourism centers during high season. Slightly lower rates can be expected off-season.

Most expensive — as high as $300 to $500 for a double room — will be the "palace" hotels of Paris and the Riviera. Rates at international hotels with a full complement of business services also tend toward the top of the scale. Generally, the member hotels of international chains in any given city are priced roughly equally. In the larger cities (such as Paris and Nice), this ranges from around $125 and up, although similar hotels elsewhere range from about $60 to $80 for a double. There is a big step down from these international class hotels to those in the moderate category in the same cities, and prices generally will be about $20 to as much as $50 less per night.

There is no sacred edict stating that travelers must stay at deluxe hotels, and, in fact, you might be missing a good deal of the European experience by insisting on international standards and skipping over the great small hotels. In the more inexpensive range are one- and two-star hotels (according to the government's official classification system) that many will find perfectly adequate, if not usually full of charm. In rural areas, there are *logis* (one- and two-star family-run hotels) and *auberges* (inns, usually not rated) and a type of bed and breakfast establishment (the *gîte-chambre-d'hôte*) that is being used more and more by tourists. In the last of these, you can spend the night in surroundings that may be homey or Spartan but almost always are clean, and the prices are low. Budget accommodations designed to offer basic (but acceptable) lodgings at especially economical prices — a double room may cost as little as $30 to $40, even in some central cities — do exist and, recognizing the need, travel agents, tour packagers, airlines, and tourist offices are doing what they can to make their whereabouts known.

There are other options for less expensive accommodations for anyone staying in one place for an extended period of time. One is renting an apartment, called a "self-catering holiday" in Europe. These are available in most cities and often can be arranged through travel agents. The other is a home exchange, in which you and a French family exchange houses for an agreed-upon period of time. (For further information, see the discussion of accommodations in *On the Road,* in this section.)

Should you require more advance information on hotels, contact a branch of the French Government Tourist Office, which distributes regional versions of the annual *Guide des Hôtels de France,* a publication with ratings of all hotels considered tourist accommodations according to the government's star classification system, listings of US representatives handling reservations for French hotels, and a wealth of other useful information. For a list of French Government Tourist Offices, see *Tourist Information,* in this section.

LOCAL TAXES AND SERVICE CHARGES: A sales tax or VAT (value added tax) is added to both goods and services in many European countries. In France, the tax rate ranges from lows of 5.5% and 7% on food to a high of 33.33% on luxury articles. The VAT is buried in the prices charged for hotel rooms and restaurant meals, so you won't even notice it. It also is included in the amount shown on the price tag of purchased goods. There is no escaping the tax on services, but for foreigners, the tax on purchases, typically 18.6%, can frequently be reimbursed. For a full discussion of VAT refunds, see *Shopping,* in this section.

A service charge, usually of 12% to 15%, is almost universal on restaurant and hotel bills in France. Nevertheless, there still are many situations not covered by the service charge or where an additional gratuity is appropriate. For more on these, see *Tipping,* in this section.

■**A note on our hotel/restaurant cost categories:** There are a great many moderate and inexpensive hotels and restaurants which we have not included in this book. Our *Checking In* and *Eating Out* listings include only those places we think are best in their price range. We have rated our listings by general price categories: expensive, moderate, and inexpensive. The introductory paragraph of each listing explains just what those categories mean within the context of local prices.

Planning a Trip

123
Travelers fall into two categories: those who make lists and those who do not. Some people prefer to plot the course of their trip to the finest detail, with contingency plans and alternatives at the ready. For others, the joy of a voyage is its spontaneity; exhaustive planning only lessens the thrill of anticipation and the sense of freedom.

For most travelers, however, any week-plus trip to France can be too expensive for an "I'll take my chances" type of travel. Even perennial gypsies and anarchistic wanderers have to take into account the time-consuming logistics of getting around, and even with minimal baggage, they need to think about packing. Hence, at least some planning is crucial. This is not to suggest that you work out every hour of your itinerary in minute detail before you go, but you still have to decide certain basics at the very start: where to go, what to do, and how much to spend. These decisions require a certain amount of consideration. So before rigorously planning specific details, you might want to establish your general travel objectives:

1. How much time will you have for the entire trip, and how much of it are you willing to spend getting where you're going?
2. What interests and/or activities do you want to pursue while on vacation? Do you want to visit one, a few, or several different places?
3. At what time of year do you want to go?
4. What kind of topography or climate would you prefer?
5. Do you want peace and privacy or lots of action and company?
6. How much money can you spend for the entire vacation?

Obviously, your answers will be determined by your personal tastes and lifestyle. These will dictate the degree of comfort you require; whether you select a tour or opt for total independence; and how much responsibility you want to take for your own arrangements (or whether you want everything arranged for you, with the kinds of services provided in a comprehensive package trip).

With firm answers to these major questions, start reviewing literature on the areas in which you're most interested. Good sources of information are airlines, hotel representatives, and travel agents who specialize in planning and arranging trips (see *How to Use a Travel Agent,* in this section). Also consult general travel sources such as reliable, annually updated guidebooks and maps. Motor clubs (see *Traveling by Car,* in this section) often can be a good source for brochures on France. There also are good little city guides available at newsstands and bookstores throughout Europe.

Government departments and private clubs focusing on outdoor activities, such as golf, fishing, hunting, boating, mountain climbing, hiking, biking, nature study, and other special interests also may be able to provide information on these sports. For information on wilderness trips, hiking, and biking, see *Camping and RVs, Hiking and Biking,* in this section, and for information on these and other activities, see the various sections of DIVERSIONS, as well as the individual city reports in THE CITIES.

The French Government Tourist Office has five locations in the US and the Monaco Government Tourist and Convention Bureau is located in New York (see *Tourist Information* for addresses). Stop in or write to any of these branches — all are ready sources for brochures, maps, and other information on the French cities and countryside.

Up-to-date travel information on France is plentiful, and you should be able to accumulate everything you want to know, not only about the places you plan to visit, but also about the relevant tour and package options (see *Package Tours,* in this section). And if you're visiting France for the first time, make a special effort to read about your destination's food, history, and culture. A good place to start is the section in this guide called PERSPECTIVES, but if you're planning an extended stay in a particular city or region, you'll probably want to do even more extensive reading.

You now can make almost all of your own travel arrangements if you have time to follow through with hotels, airlines, tour operators, and so on. But you'll probably save considerable time and energy if you have a travel agent make the reservations and arrangements for you. The agent also should be able to advise you of alternative arrangements of which you may not be aware. Only rarely will a travel agent's services cost a traveler any money, and they may even save you some (see *How to Use a Travel Agent,* in this section). Well before departure (depending on how far in advance you make your reservations), the agent will deliver a packet that includes all your tickets and hotel confirmations and often a day-by-day outline of where you'll be when, along with a detailed list of your flights.

If it applies to your schedule and destination, pay particular attention to the dates when off-season rates go into effect. In major tourism areas, accommodations costs may be lower during the off-season (and the weather often is equally fair at this time). Off-season rates frequently are lower for other facilities, too, although don't expect to save much on car rental costs during any season. In general, it is a good idea to beware of holiday weeks, as rates at hotels generally are higher during these periods and rooms are heavily booked. (In addition, service is apt to be under par unless more staff people are employed for the holidays, since the regular bellhops, maids, dining room personnel, and others will be trying to cope with a full house instead of being able to provide personal attention to individual guests.)

Make plans early. During the summer season and on American holidays, make hotel reservations at least a month in advance in all major cities. If you are flying at these times, and want to benefit from savings offered through discount fares or charter programs, purchase tickets as far ahead as possible. The more specific your requirements, the earlier you should book. Many hotels require deposits before they will guarantee reservations, and this most often is the case during peak travel periods. (Be sure to request a receipt for any deposit, or, better yet, charge the deposit to a credit card.) *Holy Week (Easter)* and most national holidays also are times requiring reservations well in advance in France.

Before your departure, find out what the weather will be like at your destination. Consult *When to Go* for information on climatic variations and a chart of average temperatures in various French cities, as well as for a list of special events that may occur during your stay. See *How to Pack* for further details on the weather and what clothes to take. See THE CITIES for information on special events that may occur during your stay, as well as for other essential information on local resources, transportation, and so on.

While arranging a vacation is fun and exciting, don't forget to prepare for your absence from home. Before you leave, attend to these household matters:

1. Arrange for your mail to be forwarded, held by the post office until you return, or picked up daily at your house. Someone should check your door occasionally to pick up any unexpected deliveries. Piles of mail or packages announce to thieves that no one is home.
2. Cancel all deliveries (newspapers, milk, and so on).
3. Arrange for the lawn to be mowed and plants watered at regular intervals.
4. Arrange for the care of pets.
5. Etch your social security number in a prominent place on all appliances (television sets, radios, cameras, kitchen appliances). This considerably reduces their appeal to thieves and facilitates identification.
6. Leave a house key and your itinerary with a relative or friend. Notify the police, the building manager, or a neighbor that you are leaving, and tell them who has your key and itinerary.
7. Empty the refrigerator and lower the thermostat.
8. If you use a computer with a hard disk, back up all your files onto diskettes and store them in a safe place away from the equipment.
9. Immediately before leaving, check that all doors, windows, and garage doors are securely locked.

To discourage thieves further, it is wise to set up several variable timers around the house so that lights and even the television set or a radio go on and off several times in different rooms each night.

Make a list of any valuable items you are carrying with you, including credit card numbers and the serial numbers of your traveler's checks. Put copies in your purse or pocket, and leave other copies at home. Put a label with your name and home address on the inside of your luggage to facilitate identification in case of loss. Put your name and business address — *but never your home address* — on a label on the outside of your luggage.

Review your travel documents. If you are traveling by air, check to see that your ticket has been filled in correctly. The left side of the ticket should have a list of each stop you will make (even if you are only stopping to change planes), beginning with your departure point. Be sure that the list is correct, and count the number of carbons to see that you have one for each plane you will take. If you have confirmed reservations, be sure that the column marked "status" says "OK" beside each flight. Have in hand vouchers or proof of payment for any reservation for which you've paid in advance; this includes hotels, transfers to and from the airport, sightseeing tours, car rentals, and tickets to special events.

Reconfirmation of reservations is strongly recommended for all international flights. Although policies vary from carrier to carrier, you should call to reconfirm your flight 48 to 72 hours before departure, both going and returning. However, this will not prevent you from getting bumped in case the flight is overbooked. Reconfirmation is particularly recommended for point-to-point flights within Europe. (For further information, see *Traveling by Plane,* in this section.)

If you will be driving while in France, bring your driver's license and any other necessary identification, proof of insurance (if applicable), maps, guidebooks, a flashlight with an extra set of batteries, and sunglasses; a small first-aid kit also is a good idea. If driving about for more than a day, upon arrival you may want to pick up emergency flashers, a container of water or coolant for the radiator, and a steel container for extra gas. For more information on driving in France, see *Traveling by Car,* in this section.

Finally, you always should bear in mind that despite the most careful plans, things do not always occur on schedule. If you maintain a flexible attitude at all times, and shrug as cheerfully as possible in the face of postponements and cancellations, you will enjoy yourself a lot more.

How to Use a Travel Agent

 A reliable travel agent remains your best source of service and information for planning a trip abroad, whether you have a specific itinerary and require an agent only to make reservations, or need extensive help in sorting through the maze of airfares, tour offerings, hotel packages, and the scores of other arrangements that may be involved in a trip to France.

You should know what you want from a travel agent so that you can evaluate what you are getting. It is perfectly reasonable to expect your travel agent to be a thoroughly knowledgeable travel specialist, with information about your destination and, even more crucial, a command of current airfares, ground arrangements, and other wrinkles in the travel scene. Most travel agents work through computer reservations systems (CRS) to assess the availability and rates of flights, hotels, and car rentals, and they can book reservations through the CRS. Despite reports of "computer bias," in which a computer may favor one airline over another, the CRS should provide agents with the entire spectrum of flights available to a given destination and the complete range of fares in considerably less time than it takes to telephone the airlines individually — and at no extra charge to the client.

To make the most intelligent use of a travel agent's time and expertise, you should know something of the economics of the industry. As a client, traditionally you pay nothing for the agent's services; with few exceptions, it's all free, from hotel bookings to advice on package tours. Any money the travel agent makes on the time spent arranging your itinerary — booking hotels or flights, or suggesting activities — comes from commissions paid by the suppliers of these services — the airlines, hotels, and so on. These commissions generally run from 8% to 20% of the total cost of the service, although suppliers often reward agencies that sell their services in volume with an increased commission called an override.

Among the few exceptions to the general rule of free service by a travel agent are the agencies beginning to practice *net pricing*. In essence, such agencies return all of their commissions and overrides to their customers and make their income by charging a flat fee per transaction instead (thus adding a charge after the reduction for commissions has been made). Sometimes, the rebate from the agent arrives later, in the form of a check. For further information, see "Net Fare Sources," in *Traveling by Plane,* in this section.

Net fares and fees are a very recent and not widespread practice, but even a conventional travel agent sometimes may charge a fee for such special services as long-distance telephone or cable costs incurred in making a booking, for reserving a room in a place that does not pay a commission (such as a small, out-of-the-way hotel), or for special attention such as planning a highly personalized itinerary. A fee also may be assessed in instances of deeply discounted airfares. In most instances, however, you'll find that travel agents make their time and experience available to you at no charge, and you do not pay more for an airline ticket, package tour, or other product bought from a travel agent than you would for the same product bought directly from the supplier.

This commission system implies two things about your relationship with an agent:

1. You will get better service if you arrive at the agent's desk with your basic itinerary already planned. Know roughly where you want to go, what you want to do, and how much you want to spend. Use the agent to make bookings (which pay commissions) and to advise you on facilities, activities, and alternatives within the limits of your itinerary. You get the best service when you are requesting commissionable items. Since there are few commissions on camping or driving/camping tours, an agent is unlikely to be very enthusiastic about helping to plan one. (If you have this type of trip in mind, see *Camping and RVs, Hiking and Biking* for other sources of information on campgrounds throughout France.) The more vague your plans, the less direction you can expect from most agents. If you walk into an agency and say, "I have 2 weeks in June; what shall I do?" you most likely will walk out with nothing more than a handful of brochures. So do a little preliminary homework.

2. Be wary. There is always the danger that an incompetent or unethical agent will send you to a place offering the best commissions rather than the best facilities for your enjoyment. The only way to be sure you are getting the best service is to pick a good, reliable travel agent, one who knows where to go for information if he or she is unfamiliar with an area — although most agents are familiar with major destinations throughout France.

You should choose a travel agent with the same care with which you would choose a doctor or lawyer. You will be spending a good deal of money on the basis of the agent's judgment, so you have a right to expect that judgment to be mature, informed, and interested. At the moment, unfortunately, there aren't many standards within the travel agent industry to help you gauge competence, and the quality of individual agents varies enormously.

At present, only nine states have registration, licensing, or other forms of travel agent–related legislation on their books. Rhode Island licenses travel agents; Florida, Hawaii, Iowa, and Ohio register them; and California, Illinois, Oregon, and Washington have laws governing the sale of transportation or related services. While state licensing of agents cannot absolutely guarantee competence, it can at least ensure that an agent has met some minimum requirements.

Perhaps the best-prepared agents are those who have completed the CTC Travel Management program offered by the *Institute of Certified Travel Agents* and carry the initials CTC (Certified Travel Counselor) after their names. This indicates a relatively high level of expertise. For a free list of CTCs in your area, send a self-addressed, stamped, #10 envelope to *ICTA,* 148 Linden St., Box 82-56, Wellesley, MA 02181 (phone: 617-237-0280 in Massachusetts; 800-542-4282 elsewhere in the US).

An agent's membership in the *American Society of Travel Agents (ASTA)* can be a useful guideline in selecting a travel agent. But keep in mind that *ASTA* is an industry organization, requiring only that its members be licensed in those states where required; be accredited to represent the suppliers whose products they sell, including airline and cruise tickets; and adhere to its Principles of Professional Conduct and Ethics code. *ASTA* does not guarantee the competence, ethics, or financial soundness of its members, but it does offer some recourse if you feel you have been dealt with unfairly. Complaints may be registered with *ASTA,* Consumer Affairs Department, PO Box 23992, Washington, DC 20026-3992 (phone: 703-739-2782). First try to resolve the complaint directly with the supplier. For a list of *ASTA* members in your area, send a self-addressed, stamped, #10 envelope to *ASTA,* Public Relations Dept., at the address above.

There also is the *Association of Retail Travel Agents (ARTA),* a smaller but highly respected trade organization similar to *ASTA.* Its member agencies and agents similarly agree to abide by a code of ethics, and complaints about a member can be made to *ARTA*'s Grievance Committee, 1745 Jeff Davis Hwy., Arlington, VA 22202-3402 (phone: 800-969-6069 or 703-553-7777).

Agencies that are members of the *National Association of Cruise Only Agencies (NACOA)* have demonstrated professionalism in the selling of cruises. For a list of cruise-only agencies in your area (requests are limited to three states), send a self-addressed, stamped envelope to *NACOA,* PO Box 7209, Freeport, NY 11520 or call 516-378-8006. Agencies that belong to a travel consortium, such as *Travel Trust International* (phone: 800-522-2700 in New York; 800-223-8953 elsewhere in the US), have access to preferred rates, as do the huge networks of *American Express* (phone: 800-YES-AMEX) and *Carlson Travel Network* (formerly *Ask Mr. Foster;* phone: 818-788-4118) travel agencies.

A number of banks own travel agencies, too. These provide the same services as other accredited commercial travel bureaus. Anyone can become a client, not only the bank's customers. You can find out more about these agencies, which belong to the *Association of Bank Travel Bureaus,* by inquiring at your bank or looking in the yellow pages.

Perhaps the best way to find a travel agent is by word of mouth. If the agent (or agency) has done a good job for your friends over a period of time, it probably indicates a certain level of commitment and competence. Always ask not only for the name of the company, but for the name of the specific agent with whom your friends dealt, for it is that individual who will serve you, and quality can vary widely within a single agency. There are some superb travel agents in the business, and they can facilitate vacation or business arrangements.

Once you've made an initial selection, be entirely frank and candid with the agent. Budget considerations rank at the top of the candor list, and there's no sense in wasting the agent's (or your) time poring over itineraries that you know you can't afford. Similarly, if you like a fair degree of comfort, that fact should not be kept secret from your travel agent, who may assume that you wish to travel on a tight budget even when that's not the case.

Entry Requirements and Documents

US citizens no longer need a visa to enter France or Monaco. A current US passport is the only document required, and that same passport also is needed to reenter the US. However, immigration officers in French airports *may* want to see that you have sufficient funds for your trip (for example, traveler's checks, credit cards, etc.) and a return ticket to the US. For US resident aliens, the requirements are determined by their country of origin, and they should inquire at the nearest French consulate or embassy to find out what documents are needed to enter and remain in either France or Monaco (there is no frontier between the two countries, and French regulations pertain).

Vaccination certificates are required only if the traveler is entering from an area of contagion as defined by the World Health Organization and, as the US is considered an area "free from contagion," an international vaccination certificate is no longer required for entering France for a short period of time. Because smallpox is considered eradicated from the world, only a few countries continue to require visitors to have a smallpox vaccination certificate. You will certainly not need one to travel to France or Monaco or to return to the US.

VISAS: As a general rule, possession of a US passport entitles the bearer to remain in either France or Monaco as a tourist for up to 90 days. Visas for study, residency, work, or stays of more than 3 months are still required as before and US citizens should address themselves to the French consulate.

Issuing tourist visas is a routine service provided by the consulates, though it is a good idea to apply well in advance. This is particularly important for travelers who live some distance from the nearest French consulate and are applying by mail. Two items are necessary to apply for a visa: a valid passport and a completed visa form. (These forms may be obtained through your travel agent or by sending a self-addressed, stamped envelope to the nearest French consulate with a written request.) The processing charge is $9 for a 3-month visa that permits multiple reentries of up to 90 days total, and $15 for a 5-year, multiple-reentry visa. Cash, money order, or certified check may be used for payment if applying in person; money order or certified check if applying by mail. Application must be made at the French consulate within your jurisdiction (see *Tourist Information* for addresses). Visas normally are issued on the spot; however, if there is a backlog, you may have to return to pick it up a few days later. To avoid frustration and wasted time, it is a good idea to call ahead to check during what hours and days visa requests are accepted.

PASSPORTS: While traveling in France, carry your passport with you at all times. If you lose your passport while abroad, report the loss to the nearest US consulate or embassy immediately. You can get a 3-month temporary passport directly from the consulate, but you must fill out a "loss of passport" form and follow the same application procedure — and pay the same fees — as you did for the original (see below). It's likely to speed things up if you have a record of your passport number and the place and date of its issue; keep a record of this information separate from your passport — you might want to give it to a traveling companion to hold. (For a complete list of US consulates and embassies in France, see *Medical and Legal Aid and Consular Services,* in this section.)

US passports are now valid for 10 years from the date of issue (5 years for those under age 16). The expired passport itself is not renewable, but must be turned in along with your application for a new and valid one (you will get it back, voided, when you receive the new one). Delivery can take as little as 2 weeks or as long as a month, and anyone applying for a passport for the first time should allow at least 4 weeks for delivery — even 6 weeks during the busiest season, from approximately mid-March to mid-September.

Normal passports contain 24 pages, but frequent travelers can request a 48-page passport at no extra cost. Every individual, regardless of age, must have his or her own passport. Family passports are no longer issued.

Passport renewal can be done by mail, but anyone applying for the first time or anyone under 16 renewing a passport must do so in person at one of the following places:

1. The State Department passport agencies in Boston, Chicago, Honolulu, Houston, Los Angeles, Miami, New Orleans, New York City, Philadelphia, San Francisco, Seattle, Stamford, CT, and Washington, DC.
2. A federal or state courthouse.
3. Any of the 1,000 post offices across the country with designated acceptance facilities.

Application blanks are available at all these offices and must be presented with the following:

1. Proof of US citizenship. This can be a previous passport or one in which you were included. If you are applying for your first passport and you were born in the United States, an original or certified birth certificate is the required proof. If you were born abroad, a Certificate of Naturalization, a Certificate of Citizenship, a

Report of Birth Abroad of a Citizen of the United States, or a Certification of Birth is necessary.

2. Two 2-by-2-inch, front-view photographs in color or black and white, with a light, plain background, taken within the previous 6 months. These must be taken by a photographer rather than by a machine.

3. A $42 passport fee ($27 for travelers under 16), which includes a $7 execution fee. *Note:* Your best bet is to bring the exact amount in cash (no change is given), or a separate check or money order for each passport.

4. Proof of identity. Again, this can be a previous passport, a Certificate of Naturalization or of Citizenship, a driver's license, or a government ID card with a physical description or a photograph. Failing any of these, you should be accompanied by a blood relative or a friend of at least 2 years' standing who will testify to your identity. Credit cards or social security cards do not suffice as proof of identity — but note that since 1988, US citizens *must* supply their social security numbers.

Passports can be renewed by mail with forms obtained at designated locations only if the expired passport was issued no more than 12 years before the date of application for renewal and if it was not issued before the applicant's 16th birthday. Send the completed form with the expired passport, two photos, and $35 (no execution fee required) to the nea. :st passport agency office.

As getting a passport — or international visa — through the mail can mean waiting as much as 6 weeks or more, a new mini-industry has cropped up in those cities where there is a US passport office. The yellow pages currently list quite a few organizations willing to wait in line to expedite obtaining a visa or passport renewal; there's even one alternative for those who live nowhere near the cities mentioned above. In the nation's capital there's an organization called the *Washington Passport and Visa Service.* It may be the answer for folks in need of special rapid action, since this organization can get a passport application or renewal turned around in a single day. What's more, their proximity to an embassy or consulate of every foreign country represented in the US helps to speed the processing of visa applications as well. *Washington Passport and Visa*'s fee for a 3- to 5-day turnaround is $25; for next-day service the charge is $50; for same-day service they charge $75. For information, application forms, and other prices, call 800-272-7776.

If you need an emergency passport, it also is possible to be issued a passport in a matter of hours by going directly to your nearest passport office (there is no way, however, to avoid waiting in line). Explain the nature of the emergency, usually as serious as a death in the family; a ticket in hand for a flight the following day also will suffice. Should the emergency occur outside of business hours, all is not lost. There's a 24-hour telephone number in Washington, DC (phone: 202-634-3600) that can put you in touch with a State Department duty officer who may be able to expedite your application.

DUTY AND CUSTOMS: As a general rule, the requirements for bringing the majority of items into France is that they must be in quantities small enough not to imply commercial import.

No duty is imposed on quantities up to 2 liters of wine, 2 liters of alcohol under 38.8 proof, 1 liter above 38.8 proof, 200 cigarettes, 50 cigars, 250 grams of loose tobacco, 50 grams of perfume, a quarter of a liter of cologne, 500 grams of coffee, 40 grams of tea, and on items designated as gifts valued at less than 300F (or approximately $50 per item).

If you are bringing along a computer or any other electronic equipment for your own use that you will be taking back to the US, you should register the item with the US Customs Service in order to avoid being asked to pay duties both entering and returning from France. (Also see *Customs and Returning to the US,* in this section.) For information on this procedure, as well as for a variety of informative pamphlets on US customs regulations, contact the local office of the US Customs Service or the central office, PO Box 7407, Washington, DC 20044 (phone: 202-566-8195). Additional information regarding French customs regulations is available from the French Government Tourist Office; see *Tourist Information* in this section for addresses of offices in the US.

■**One rule to follow:** When passing through customs, it is illegal not to declare dutiable items — penalties range from stiff fines and seizure of the goods to prison terms — so don't try to sneak anything through, it just isn't worth it.

Insurance

 It is unfortunate that most decisions to buy travel insurance are impulsive and usually are made without any real consideration of the traveler's existing policies. Too often the result is the purchase of needlessly expensive, short-term policies that duplicate existing coverage and reinforce the tendency to buy coverage on a trip-by-trip basis rather than to work out a total and continuing travel insurance package that might well be more effective and economical.

Therefore, the first person with whom you should discuss travel insurance is your own insurance broker, not a travel agent or the clerk behind the airport insurance counter. You may discover that the insurance you already carry — homeowner's policies and/or accident, health, and life insurance — protects you adequately while you travel and that your real needs are in the more mundane areas of excess value insurance for baggage or trip cancellation insurance.

TYPES OF INSURANCE: To make insurance decisions intelligently, however, you should first understand the basic categories of travel insurance and what they cover. Then you can decide what you should have in the broader context of your personal insurance needs, and you can choose the most economical way of getting the desired protection: through riders on existing policies; with one-time short-term policies; through a special program put together for the frequent traveler; through coverage that's part of a travel club's benefits; or with a combination policy sold by insurance companies through brokers, automobile clubs, tour operators, and travel agents.

There are seven basic categories of travel insurance:

1. Baggage and personal effects insurance
2. Personal accident and sickness insurance
3. Trip cancellation and interruption insurance
4. Default and/or bankruptcy insurance
5. Flight insurance (to cover injury or death)
6. Automobile insurance (for driving your own or a rented car)
7. Combination policies

Baggage and Personal Effects Insurance – Ask your agent if baggage and personal effects are included in your current homeowner's policy, or if you will need a special rider to cover you for the duration of a trip. The object is to protect your bags and their contents in case of damage or theft at any time during your travels, not just while you're in flight and covered by the airline's policy. Furthermore, only limited protection is provided by the airline. Baggage liability varies from carrier to carrier, but generally speaking, for domestic flights, luggage usually is insured to $1,250 — that's per passenger, not per bag. For most international flights, including domestic portions of international flights, the airline's liability limit is approximately $9.07 per pound or $20 per kilo (which comes to about $360 per 40-pound suitcase) for checked baggage and up to $400 per passenger for unchecked baggage. These limits should be specified on your airline ticket, but to be awarded the specified amount, you'll have to provide an itemized list of lost property, and if you're including new and/or expensive items, be prepared for a request that you back up your claim with sales receipts or other proof of purchase.

If you are carrying goods worth more than the maximum protection offered by the airline, bus, or train company, you should consider excess value insurance. Additional coverage is available from airlines at an average, currently, of $1 per $100 worth of coverage, up to a maximum value of $5,000. This insurance can be purchased at the airline counter when you check in, though you should arrive early to fill out the necessary forms and to avoid holding up other passengers. Major credit card companies, including American Express and Diners Club, also provide coverage for lost or delayed baggage. In some cases, you must enroll in advance to qualify. Check your membership brochure or contact the credit card company for details (see phone numbers listed in *Credit and Currency*). Excess value insurance also is included in certain of the combination travel insurance policies discussed below.

■ **A note of warning:** Be sure to read the fine print of any excess value insurance policy; there are often specific exclusions, such as cash, tickets, furs, gold and silver objects, art, and antiques. And remember that insurance companies ordinarily will pay only the depreciated value of the goods rather than their replacement value. The best way to protect the items you're carrying in your luggage is to take photos of your valuables, and keep a record of the serial numbers of such items as cameras, typewriters, radios, and so on. This will establish that you do, indeed, own the objects. If your luggage disappears en route or is damaged, deal with the situation immediately. If an airline loses your luggage, you will be asked to fill out a Property Irregularity Report before you leave the airport. If your property disappears at other transportation centers, tell the local company, but also report it to the police (since the insurance company will check with the police when processing the claim). When traveling by train, if you are sending excess luggage as registered baggage, remember that some trains may not have provisions for extra cargo; if your baggage does not arrive when you do, it may not be lost, just on the next train!

Personal Accident and Sickness Insurance – This covers you in case of illness during your trip or death in an accident. Most policies insure you for hospital and doctors' expenses, lost income, and so on. In most cases, it is a standard part of existing health insurance policies, though you should check with your broker to be sure that your policy will pay for any medical expenses incurred abroad. If not, take out a separate vacation accident policy or an entire vacation insurance policy that includes health and life coverage.

Trip Cancellation and Interruption Insurance – Although modern public charters have eliminated many of the old advance booking requirements, most charter and package tour passengers still pay for their travel well before departure. The disappointment of having to miss a vacation because of illness or any other reason pales before the awful prospect that not all (and sometimes none) of the money paid in advance might be returned. So cancellation insurance for any package tour is a must. Although cancellation penalties vary (they are listed in the fine print in every tour brochure, and before you purchase a package tour you should know exactly what they are), rarely will a passenger get more than 50% of this money back if forced to cancel within a few weeks of leaving. Therefore, if you book a package tour or charter flight, you should have trip cancellation insurance to guarantee full reimbursement or refund should you, a traveling companion, or a member of your immediate family get sick, forcing you to cancel your trip or *return home early*. The key here is *not* to buy just enough insurance to guarantee full reimbursement for the cost of the package or charter in case of cancellation. The proper amount of coverage should be sufficient to reimburse you for the cost of having to catch up with a tour after its departure or having to travel home at the full economy airfare if you have to forgo the return flight of your charter. There usually is quite a discrepancy between a charter airfare and the amount necessary to travel the same distance on a regularly scheduled flight at full economy fare.

Trip cancellation insurance is available from travel agents and tour operators in two forms: as part of a short-term, all-purpose travel insurance package (sold by the travel agent); or as specific cancellation insurance designed by the tour operator for a specific charter tour. Generally, tour operators' policies are less expensive, but also less inclusive. Cancellation insurance also is available directly from insurance companies or their agents as part of a short-term, all-inclusive travel insurance policy.

Before you decide on a policy, read each one carefully. (Either type can be purchased from a travel agent when you book the charter or package tour.) Be certain that your policy includes enough coverage to pay your fare from the farthest destination on your itinerary should you have to miss the charter flight. Also, be sure to check the fine print for stipulations concerning "family members" and "pre-existing medical conditions," as well as allowance for living expenses if you must delay your return due to bodily injury or illness.

Default and/or Bankruptcy Insurance – Although trip cancellation insurance usually protects you if *you* are unable to complete — or begin — your trip, a fairly recent innovation is coverage in the event of default and/or bankruptcy on the part of the tour operator, airline, or other travel supplier. In some travel insurance packages, this contingency is included in the trip cancellation portion of the coverage; in others, it is a separate feature. Either way, it is becoming increasingly important. Whereas sophisticated travelers have long known to beware of the possibility of default or bankruptcy when buying a charter flight or tour package, in recent years more than a few respected scheduled airlines have unexpectedly revealed their shaky financial condition, sometimes leaving hordes of stranded ticketholders in their wake. Moreover, the value of escrow protection of a charter passenger's funds has been unreliable lately. While default/bankruptcy insurance will not ordinarily result in reimbursement in time to pay for new arrangements, it can ensure that you will eventually get your money back, and even independent travelers buying no more than an airplane ticket may want to consider it.

Should this type of coverage be unavailable to you (state insurance regulations vary, there is a wide variation in price, and so on), the best bet is to pay for airline tickets and tour packages with a credit card. The federal Fair Credit Billing Act permits purchasers to refuse payment for credit card charges where services have not been delivered, so the potential onus of dealing with a receiver for a bankrupt airline falls on the credit card company. You must, however, make your claim within 60 days of receiving your bill from the credit card company. What's more, do not assume that another airline automatically will honor the ticket you're holding on a bankrupt airline, since the days when virtually all major carriers subscribed to a default protection program are long gone. Some airlines may voluntarily step forward to accommodate stranded passengers, but this is now an entirely altruistic act.

Flight Insurance – US and French airlines have carefully established limits of liability for the death or injury of passengers. For international flights, they are printed right on the ticket: a maximum of $75,000 in case of death or injury. Although these limitations once were established by state law for domestic flights, each case currently is decided in court on its own merits — this means potentially unlimited liability. But remember, these limits of liability are not the same thing as insurance policies; every penny that an airline must pay in the case of death or injury will be subject to a legal battle.

This may make you feel that you are not adequately protected, but before you buy last-minute flight insurance from an airport vending machine, consider the purchase in light of your total existing insurance coverage. A careful review of your current policies may reveal that you are already amply covered for accidental death, sometimes up to three times the amount provided for by the flight insurance you're buying in the airport.

Be aware that airport insurance, the kind typically bought at a counter or from a vending machine, is among the most expensive forms of life insurance coverage, and that even within a single airport, rates for approximately the same coverage vary widely. Often policies sold in vending machines are more expensive than those sold over the counter, even when they are with the same national company.

If you buy your plane ticket with an American Express, Carte Blanche, or Diners Club credit card, you are automatically issued life and accident insurance at no extra cost. American Express automatically provides $100,000 to its Green and Gold cardholders, and $500,000 to Platinum cardholders in insurance, Carte Blanche provides $150,000, and Diners Club provides $350,000. Additional coverage can be obtained at extremely reasonable prices, but a cardholder must sign up for it in advance. With American Express, $4 per ticket buys an additional $250,000 worth of flight insurance; $7.50 buys $500,000 worth; and $14 provides an added $1 million worth of coverage. (Rates vary slightly for New York residents.) Both Carte Blanche and Diners Club also offer an additional $250,000 worth of insurance for $4; $500,000 for $6.50. Both also provide $1,250 free insurance — over and above what the airline will pay — for checked baggage that's lost or damaged. American Express provides $500 coverage for checked baggage, $500 for carry-on baggage, and $250 for valuables, such as cameras and jewelry.

Automobile Insurance – Public liability and property damage (third-party) insurance is compulsory in Europe, and whether you drive your own car or a rental you must carry insurance. Car rentals in France usually include public liability, property damage, fire, and theft coverage and, sometimes (depending on the rental company), collision damage coverage with a deductible. In your car rental contract, you'll see that for about $13 a day, you may buy optional collision damage waiver (CDW) protection. If partial coverage with a deductible is included in the rental contract, CDW will cover the deductible in the event of an accident. If the contract does not include collision damage coverage, you may be liable for as much as the full retail value of the car, and CDW relieves you of all responsibility for any damage to the rental car. Before agreeing to this coverage, however, check your own auto insurance policy with your own broker. It may very well cover your entire liability exposure without any additional cost, or you may automatically be covered by the credit card company (American Express, or premium cards from Visa or MasterCard) to which you are charging the cost of your rental.

You also should know that an increasing number of the major international car rental companies are automatically including the cost of the CDW in their basic rates. Car rental prices have increased to include this coverage, although rental company ad campaigns may promote this as a new, improved rental package "benefit." The disadvantage of this inclusion is that you may not have the option to turn down the CDW — even if you are already adequately covered by your own insurance policy or through a credit card company. For more information on this confusing issue, see *Traveling by Car,* in this section.

Your rental contract (with the appropriate insurance box ticked off) as well as proof of your personal insurance policy, if applicable, are required as proof of insurance. If you will be driving your own car in Europe, you must carry an International Insurance

Certificate (called a Green Card), available through insurance brokers in the US, or take out an *assistance frontiére* policy at customs as you enter the country.

Combination Packages – Short-term insurance policies, which may include any combination or all of the types of insurance discussed above, are available through retail insurance agencies, automobile clubs, and many travel agents. These combination policies are designed to cover you for the duration of a single trip.

Two examples of standard combination policies, providing comprehensive coverage for travelers, are offered by *Wallach & Co.* The first, *HealthCare Global,* is available to men and women up to age 84. The medical insurance, which may be purchased for periods of 10 to 180 days, provides $25,000 medical insurance and $50,000 accidental-death benefit. The cost for 10 days is $25; for 76 days and over, it is $1.50 a day. Combination policies may include additional accidental death coverage and baggage and trip cancellation insurance options. For $3 per day (minimum 10 days, maximum 90 days), another program, *HealthCare Abroad,* offers significantly better coverage in terms of dollar limits, although the age limit is 75. Its basic policy includes $100,000 medical insurance and $25,000 accidental-death benefit. As in the first policy, trip cancellation and baggage insurance also are available. For further information, write to *Wallach & Co.*, 243 Church St. NW, Suite 100D, Vienna, VA 22180 (phone: 703-281-9500 in Virginia; 800-237-6615 elsewhere in the US).

Other policies of this type include the following:

Access America International: A subsidiary of the Blue Cross/Blue Shield plans of New York and Washington, DC, now available nationwide. Contact *Access America,* 600 Third Ave., PO Box 807, New York, NY 10163 (phone: 800-284-8300 or 212-490-5345).

Carefree: Underwritten by The Hartford. Contact *Carefree Travel Insurance,* Arm Coverage, PO Box 310, Mineola, NY 11501 (phone: 800-645-2424 or 516-294-0220).

NEAR Services: Part of a benefits package offered by a travel service organization. An added feature is coverage for lost or stolen airline tickets. Contact *NEAR Services,* 450 Prairie Ave., Calumet City, IL 60409 (phone: 800-654-6700 or 708-868-6700).

Tele-Trip: Underwritten by the Mutual of Omaha Companies. Contact *Tele-Trip Co.,* PO Box 31685, 3201 Farnam St., Omaha, NE 68131 (phone: 402-345-2400 in Nebraska; 800-228-9792 elsewhere in the US).

Travel Assistance International: Provided by Europ Assistance Worldwide Services, and underwritten by Transamerica Occidental Life Insurance. Contact *Travel Assistance International,* 1333 15th St. NW, Suite 400, Washington, DC 20005 (phone: 202-347-2025 in Washington, DC; 800-821-2828 elsewhere in the US).

Travel Guard International: Underwritten by the Insurance Company of North America, it is available through authorized travel agents; or contact *Travel Guard International,* 1145 Clark St., Stevens Point, WI 54481 (phone: 715-345-0505 in Wisconsin; 800-826-1300 elsewhere in the US).

Travel Insurance PAK: Underwritten by The Travelers. Contact *The Travelers Companies,* Ticket and Travel Plans, One Tower Sq., Hartford, CT 06183-5040 (phone: 203-277-2319 in Connecticut; 800-243-3174 elsewhere in the US).

WorldCare Travel Assistance Association: This organization offers insurance packages underwritten by Transamerica Premier Insurance Company and Transamerica Occidental Life Insurance. Contact *WorldCare Travel Assistance Association,* 605 Market St., Suite 1300, San Francisco, CA 94105 (phone: 800-666-4993 or 415-541-4991).

How to Pack

No one can provide a completely foolproof list of precisely what to pack, so it's best to let common sense, space, and comfort guide you. Keep one maxim in mind: Less is more. You simply won't need as much clothing as you think, and though there is nothing more frustrating than arriving at your destination without just the item that in its absence becomes crucial, you are far more likely to need a forgotten accessory — or a needle and thread or scissors — than a particular piece of clothing.

As with almost anything relating to travel, a little planning can go a long way. There are specific things to consider before you open the first drawer or fold the first pair of underwear:

1. Where are you going — city, country, or both?
2. How many total days will you be gone?
3. What's the average temperature likely to be during your stay?

The goal is to remain perfectly comfortable, neat, clean, and adequately fashionable wherever you go, but actually to pack as little as possible. The main obstacle to achieving this end is habit: Most of us wake up each morning with an entire wardrobe in our closets, and we assume that our suitcase should offer the same variety and selection. Not so — only our anxiety about being caught short makes us treat a suitcase like a mobile closet. This worry can be eliminated by learning to travel light and by following two firm packing principles:

1. Organize your travel wardrobe around a single color — blue or brown, for example — that allows you to mix, match, and layer clothes. Holding firm to one color scheme will make it easy to eliminate items of clothing that don't harmonize; and by picking clothes for their adaptability and compatibility with your basic color, you will put together the widest selection with the fewest pieces of clothing.
2. Use laundries to renew your wardrobe. Never overpack to ensure a supply of fresh clothing — shirts, blouses, underwear — for each day of a long trip. Businesspeople routinely use hotel laundries to wash and clean clothes. If these are too expensive, there are local, self-service laundries, called *blanchisseries automatiques,* in most towns of any size.

CLIMATE AND CLOTHES: Exactly what you pack on your trip will be a function of where you are going and when, and the kinds of things you intend to do. A few degrees can make all the difference between being comfortably attired and very real suffering, so your initial step should be to find out what the general weather conditions — temperature, rainfall, seasonal variations — are likely to be in the areas you will visit.

Although most of France is farther north than the US — Paris, sitting astride latitude 48°52', is about even with Quebec's Gaspé Peninsula — the climate generally is milder. Residents of the Middle Atlantic states will find that the same wardrobe they would be wearing at home will, with a few adjustments, also be appropriate for most parts of France in the same season. Anyone going to France from the late fall through the early spring should take into account that while central heating is prevalent in French hotels, interiors often are not heated to the same degree they would be in the US. Thus, although there is no need to prepare for subzero winters outdoors, most people will probably feel more comfortable wearing heavier clothing indoors than they might at home: for instance, sweaters rather than lightweight shirts and blouses.

Another adjustment to be made concerns winter travel in the south of France. There the average coastal temperature in January is a balmy 48F, but at the same time that the temperature might be rising to the mid-50s along the coast, the hills above the coast will be cold and possibly covered with snow. In addition, even on the warmest day on the Riviera, the thermometer drops considerably after sunset. Thus, warm clothes, including some kind of topcoat, are still needed in the south of France in winter, but weather requiring lighter clothing also must be anticipated. The key to meeting such a challenge and still traveling light is to dress in layers (see below).

More information about the climate in France, along with a chart of average low and high temperatures for specific cities, is given in *When to Go* in this section; other sources of information are airlines and travel agents.

Keeping temperature and climate in mind, consider the problem of luggage. Plan on one suitcase per person (and in a pinch, remember that it's always easier to carry two small suitcases than to schlepp one roughly the size of the *QE2*). Standard 26- to 28-inch suitcases can be made to work for 1 week or 1 month, and unless you are going for no more than a weekend, never cram wardrobes for two people into one suitcase.

FASHION: On the whole, France is no more formal than North America, but the celebrated French sense of style — a subject apart from the question of formality versus informality — is a genuine thing. This knack for knowing almost intuitively what is smart is most evident in Paris and in the more glamorous resorts of the Côte d'Azur. But since chic as the Parisians possess it is something one either has or has not, and, in the latter case, is acquired slowly rather than on the eve of a trip, the best rule to follow in choosing a travel wardrobe is to be guided by your own taste. On the Left Bank in Paris, anything goes; on the Right Bank, wear what you would in any cosmopolitan American city.

Although the French do enjoy dressing up, attire more formal than a cocktail dress or evening pants for women and something as formal as black tie for men is necessary only for the most elegant occasions — such as Friday dinner at *Maxim's,* a ball, or an *Opéra* opening night. A blazer or sports jacket, trousers, and tie will get a man into the finest restaurants in Paris (or anywhere else), and sometimes even the tie is not *de rigueur.* For women, a dress or a suit will do in the same situations. Other diners may be more formally dressed, but you won't be turned away or made to feel self-conscious if you do not match them. By the same token, you won't feel you've overdone it if you choose to turn an evening at an elegant restaurant into something special and dress accordingly. If you're planning a number of more formal evenings during your trip, bring two or three changes of clothes. Bear in mind that coordinates also are a good way of providing a number of dressier options without adding to your luggage content.

The advice to follow your own taste and wear what you would in similar situations at home also applies to the Côte d'Azur, the other part of France that is very sensitive to the dictates of fashion. To attempt to live up to the chic of St.-Tropez, for instance, can be difficult, because St.-Tropez to some extent sets the style for summer fashions all over Europe. If you wish to try, the advice might be to be stylishly casual by day and anything from stylishly casual to dressy to *outré* at night, depending on the resort.

Women should figure on a maximum of five daytime and three late afternoon–evening changes. Whether you are going to be gone for a week or a month, this number should be enough. For daytime activities, women might pack jeans or light slacks, blouses, one or two swimsuits (depending on where you're going), and a pair of comfortable shoes or sneakers. In warmer weather, include T-shirts, a pair of shorts; skirts and summer dresses are a cool choice for touring. Also pack lightweight sandals for beach and evening wear. As the weather can be damp and chilly even during the summer, also include a lightweight sweater or jacket. In colder weather, corduroy or wool slacks, and a longer skirt which can be worn with turtlenecks, blouses, and sweaters, and a pair of boots will provide a number of comfortable alternatives. Low-heel pumps are appropriate for both dressier daytime and evening wear. Again, before packing, lay out every piece of clothing you think you might want to take. Select clothing on the basis of what can serve several functions and accessorize everything beforehand so you know exactly what you will be wearing with what. Eliminate items that don't mix, match, or interchange within your chosen color scheme. If you can't wear it in at least two distinct incarnations, leave it home.

Men also will find that color coordination is crucial. Solid colors coordinate best, and a sport jacket that goes with a pair of pants from a suit and several pairs of slacks provides added options. For travel in warmer weather, lightweight cotton shirts and a coordinating cotton sweater paired with casual slacks or chinos (and the sport jacket on damp, chilly days) will suffice for many occasions; also bring along shorts and one or two bathing suits (again, depending on your destination). Include several shirts that can be used for both daytime and evening wear, and sneakers and/or loafers (include at least one pair of double-duty shoes that go with both casual and dressier attire). For touring in colder weather, bring heavier slacks or corduroys, long-sleeve shirts or turtlenecks, a wool sweater, and a warm jacket or coat. Hanging bags are best for packing suits and jackets.

For both men and women, layering is the key to comfort — particularly when touring in parts of the countryside where mornings and evenings can be chilly even when the days are mild. No matter where you are traveling in France, however, layering is a good way to prepare for atypical temperatures or changes in the weather. For unexpectedly cold days or for outings in the countryside, a recommended basic is a lightweight wool or heavy cotton turtleneck, which can be worn under a shirt and perhaps a third layer, such as a pullover sweater, jacket, or windbreaker. In warmer weather, substitute a T-shirt and lightweight cotton shirts or sweaters for the turtleneck and wool layers. As the weather changes, you can add or remove clothes as required, and layering adapts well to the ruling principle of dressing according to a single color scheme. Individual items in layers can mix and match, be used together or independently.

If you are planning to be on the move — either in a car, bus, train, plane, or aboard a boat — consider loose-fitting clothes that do not wrinkle, although the recent trend toward fabrics with a wrinkled look is a boon to travelers. Despite the tendency of designers to use more and more 100% natural fabrics, synthetics — particularly the new washable rayon blends — are immensely practical for a trip, and they have improved immeasurably in appearance lately. As a general rule, clothes in pure cotton and linen are perishable and hard to keep up and should be left behind. Lightweight wools, manmade fabrics — such as jerseys and knits, and drip-dry fabrics that can be rinsed in Woolite or a similar cold-water detergent — travel best (although in very hot weather cotton clothing may be the most comfortable), and prints look fresher longer than solids.

Pack clothes that have a lot of pockets for traveler's checks, documents, and tickets. Then, if your bag gets lost or stolen, you will retain possession of the essentials. Men who prefer to keep their pockets free of coins, papers, and keys might consider a shoulder bag, useful for carrying camera equipment, as well as daily necessities.

An umbrella — a telescoping model is best — or raincoat is needed in most parts of the country at most times of the year. Particularly when traveling from fall through spring, a raincoat with a zip-out lining — and maybe even a hood — is a versatile choice. The removable lining allows you to adapt to temperature changes, and the hood is better suited (and less cumbersome) than an umbrella for fine, misty rain, although a practical alternative is a rain hat that can be rolled up in a pocket or carry-on bag.

Other useful apparel is a warm wool sweater or jacket, even in summer. This will not be needed to take the chill off overly air conditioned rooms (air conditioning is not the rule in France), but even in a heat wave it will be welcome for exploring caves in the Dordogne or champagne cellars in Epernay. And finally — since the best touring of castles, churches, and countryside is done on foot — pack a comfortable pair of walking shoes.

Your carry-on luggage should contain a survival kit with the basic things you will need in case your luggage gets lost or stolen: a toothbrush, toothpaste, all medications, a sweater, nightclothes, and a change of underwear. With these essential items at hand, you will be prepared for any unexpected occurrence that separates you from your suitcase. If you have many 1- or 2-night stops, you can live out of your survival case without having to unpack completely at each hotel.

Other items you might consider packing are a flashlight with extra batteries, small sewing and first-aid kits (including insect repellent), binoculars, and a camera or camcorder (see *Cameras and Equipment,* in this section).

Sundries – If you are traveling in the heat of summer and will be spending a lot of time outdoors, pack special items so you won't spend your entire vacation horizontal in a hotel room (or hospital) because of sunburn. Be sure to take a sun hat (to protect hair as well as skin), sunscreen, and tanning lotion, which is available in graduated degrees of sunblock corresponding to the level of your skin's sensitivity. (The quantity of sunscreen is indicated by number: the higher the number, the greater the protection.) A good moisturizer is necessary to help keep your skin from drying out and peeling. The best advice is to take the sun's rays in small doses — no more than 20 minutes at a stretch — increasing your sunbathing time as your vacation progresses. Also, if you are heading for a vacation on skis, do not underestimate the effect of the sun's glare off snowy slopes, especially in higher altitudes — the exposed areas of your face and neck are particularly susceptible to a painful burn.

PACKING: The basic idea of packing is to get everything into the suitcase and out again with as few wrinkles as possible. Simple, casual clothes — shirts, jeans and slacks, permanent press skirts — can be rolled into neat, tight sausages that keep other packed items in place and leave the clothes themselves amazingly unwrinkled. The rolled clothes can be retrieved, shaken out, and hung up at your destination. However, for items that are too bulky or too delicate for even careful rolling, a suitcase should be packed with the heaviest items on the bottom, toward the hinges, so that they will not wrinkle more perishable clothes. Candidates for the bottom layer include shoes (stuff them with small items to save space), a toilet kit, handbags (stuff them to help keep their shape), and an alarm clock. Fill out this layer with things that will not wrinkle or will not matter if they do, such as sweaters, socks, a bathing suit, gloves, and underwear.

If you get this first, heavy layer as smooth as possible with the fill-ins, you will have a shelf for the next layer — the most easily wrinkled items, like slacks, jackets, shirts, dresses, and skirts. These should be buttoned and zipped and laid along the whole length of the suitcase with as little folding as possible. When you do need to make a fold, do it on a crease (as with pants), along a seam in the fabric, or where it will not show (such as shirttails). Alternate each piece of clothing, using one side of the suitcase, then the other, to make the layers as flat as possible. Make the layers even and the total contents of your bag as full and firm as possible to keep things from shifting around during transit. On the top layer put the things you will want at once: nightclothes, an umbrella or raincoat, a sweater.

With men's two-suiter suitcases, follow the same procedure. Then place jackets on hangers, straighten them out, and leave them unbuttoned. If they are too wide for the suitcase, fold them lengthwise down the middle, straighten the shoulders, and fold the sleeves in along the seam.

While packing, it is a good idea to separate each layer of clothes with plastic cleaning bags, which will help preserve pressed clothes while they are in the suitcase. Unpack your bags as soon as you get to your hotel. Nothing so thoroughly destroys freshly cleaned and pressed clothes as sitting for days in a suitcase. Finally, if something is badly wrinkled and can't be professionally pressed before you must wear it, hang it overnight in a bathroom where the bathtub has been filled with very hot water; keep the bathroom door closed so the room becomes something of a steamroom. It really works miracles.

LUGGAGE: If you already own serviceable luggage, do not feel compelled to buy new bags. If, however, you have been looking for an excuse to throw out that old suitcase that saw you through 4 years of college and innumerable weekends, this trip to France can be the perfect occasion.

Luggage falls into three categories — hard, soft-sided, and soft — and each has advantages and disadvantages. Hard suitcases have a rigid frame and sides. They provide the most protection from the depredations of rough handling, but they also are the heaviest. Wheels and pull straps are available to rectify this problem, but they should be removed before the luggage is turned over at check-in or they may be wrenched off in transit. In addition, hard bags will sometimes pop open, even when locked, so a strap around the suitcase is advised.

Soft-sided suitcases have a rigid frame that has been covered with leather, fabric, or a synthetic material. The weight of the suitcase is greatly reduced, but many of the materials used as coverings (except leather, which also is heavy) are vulnerable to rips and tears from conveyor machinery. Not surprisingly, the materials that wear best generally are found on more expensive luggage.

The third category, seen more and more frequently, is soft luggage. Lacking any rigid structural element, it comes in a wide variety of shapes and sizes and is easy to carry, especially since it often has a shoulder strap. Most carry-on bags are of this type because they can be squeezed under the plane seat. They are even more vulnerable to damage on conveyor equipment than soft-sided bags, and as the weak point on these bags is the zipper, be sure to tie some cord or put several straps around the bag for extra insurance. Also be prepared to find a brand-new set of wrinkles pressed into everything that was carefully ironed before packing.

Whatever type of luggage you choose, remember that it should last for many years. Shop carefully, but be prepared to make a sizable investment. In fact, you might consider putting off the purchase of new luggage until you get to Paris, where some of the world's most impeccably designed and carefully crafted leather goods can be found.

It always is a good idea to add an empty, flattened airline bag or similar piece of luggage to your suitcase; you'll find it indispensable as a beach bag or to carry a few items for a day's outing. Keep in mind, too, that you're likely to do some shopping, so save room for those items. If you're planning on any extensive shopping, you might consider packing one of those soft, parachute-cloth suitcases that fold into a small envelope when not in use.

For more information on packing and luggage, send your request with a self-addressed, stamped, #10 envelope to *Samsonite Travel Advisory Service* (PO Box 39609, Dept. 80, Denver, CO 80239) for its free booklet, *Lightening the Travel Load: Travel Tips & Tricks.*

SOME FINAL PACKING HINTS: Apart from the items you pack as carry-on luggage (see above), always keep all necessary medicine, valuable jewelry, and travel or business documents in your purse, briefcase, or carry-on bag, not in the luggage you will check. Tuck a bathing suit into your handbag or briefcase, too; in the case of lost baggage, it's frustrating to be without one. And whether in your overnight bag or checked luggage, cosmetics and any liquids should be packed in plastic bottles or at least wrapped in plastic bags and tied.

Golf clubs and skis may be checked through as luggage (most airlines are accustomed to handling them), but tennis rackets should be carried onto the plane. Some airlines require that bicycles be partially dismantled and packaged (see *Camping and RVs, Hiking and Biking,* in this section). Check with the airline before departure to see if there is a specific regulation regarding any special equipment or sporting gear you plan to take.

Hints for Handicapped Travelers

 From 35 to 50 million people in the US alone have some sort of disability, and at least half this number are physically handicapped. Like everyone else today, they — and the uncounted disabled millions around the world — are on the move. More than ever before, they are demanding facilities they can use comfortably, and they are being heard. The disabled traveler will find that services for the handicapped have improved considerably over the last few years, both in the US and abroad, and though accessibility is far from universal, it is being brought up to more acceptable standards every day.

PLANNING: Good planning is essential: Collect as much information as you can about your specific disability and facilities for the disabled in the area you're visiting, make your travel arrangements well in advance, and specify to all services involved the exact nature of your condition or restricted mobility, as your trip will be much more comfortable if you know that there are accommodations and facilities to suit your needs. The best way to find out if your intended destination can accommodate a handicapped traveler is to write or phone the local tourist association or hotel and ask specific questions. If you require a corridor of a certain width to maneuver a wheelchair or if you need handles on the bathroom wall for support, ask the hotel manager. A travel agent or the local chapter or national office of the organization that deals with your particular disability — for example, the *American Foundation for the Blind* or the *American Heart Association* — will supply the most up-to-date information on the subject. The following sources offer general information on access:

Access to the World, by Louise Weiss, offers sound tips for the disabled traveler abroad. Published by Facts on File (460 Park Ave. S., New York, NY 10016; phone: 212-683-2244), it costs $16.95. Check with your local bookstore; it also can be ordered by phone with a credit card.

Access Travel: A Guide to the Accessibility of Airport Terminals, published by the Airport Operators Council International, provides information on more than 500 airports worldwide — including the major airports in France — with ratings according to 70 features, including accessibility to bathrooms, corridor width, and parking spaces. For a free copy, write to the Consumer Information Center, Access America, Dept. 563W, Pueblo, CO 81009, or call 202-293-8500 and ask for "Item 563W — Access Travel." To help travel agents plan trips for the handicapped, this material is reprinted with additional information on tourist boards, city information offices, and tour operators specializing in travel for the handicapped (see "Tours," below) in the *Worldwide Edition* of the *Official Airline Guides Travel Planner,* issued quarterly by Official Airline Guides, 2000 Clearwater Dr., Oak Brook, IL 60521 (phone: 708-574-6000).

Air Transportation of Handicapped Persons is a booklet published by the US Department of Transportation, and will be sent at no charge upon written request. Ask for "Free Advisory Circular #AC-120-32" from the Distribution Unit, US Dept. of Transportation, Publications Section, M-443-2, Washington, DC 20590.

Comité National Français de Liaison pour la Réadaptation des Handicapes (CNFLRH), a French organization affiliated with *Mobility International/USA* (see listing below), is a central source of information to contact both before and during your trip (if you visit in person, call beforehand for an appointment). The *CNFLRH* also publishes, in French, *Touristes Quand Même!,* a city-by-city listing of local services accessible to the handicapped such as banks, churches, pharmacies, and pools, as well as some tourist sites, medical specialists for the physically disabled — physical therapists, orthopedists, and so on — and sources of wheelchair rental and repair. Last updated in 1987, it has recently been augmented by a third volume covering Paris alone. To obtain a copy, contact a branch of the French Government Tourist Office, or contact *CNFLRH,* 38 Bd. Raspail, Paris 75007 (phone: 1-45-48-90-13).

Handicapped Travel Newsletter is regarded as one of the finest sources of information for the disabled traveler. It is edited by wheelchair-bound Vietnam veteran Michael Quigley, who, undaunted, has traveled to 93 countries around the world and writes regular columns for travel magazines. Issued every 2 months (plus special issues), a subscription is $10 per year. Write to *Handicapped Travel Newsletter,* PO Box 269, Athens, TX 75751 (phone: 214-677-1260).

Information Center for Individuals with Disabilities (ICID), Fort Point Pl., 1st Floor, 27-43 Wormwood St., Boston, MA 02210 (phone: 617-727-5540/1 or 800-462-5015 in Massachusetts only); both numbers offer voice and TDD (telecommunications device for the deaf) service. *ICID* provides information and referral services on disability-related issues and will help you research your trip. The center publishes fact sheets on vacation planning, tour operators, travel agents, and travel resources.

The Itinerary is a travel magazine for people with disabilities. Published bimonthly, it includes information on accessibility, listings of tours, news of adaptive devices, travel aids, and special services, as well as numerous general travel hints. A subscription is $10 a year; write to *The Itinerary,* PO Box 2012, Bayonne, NJ 07002-2012 (phone: 201-858-3400).

Mobility International/USA (MIUSA), the US branch of *Mobility International,* a nonprofit British organization with affiliates in some 35 countries, offers advice and assistance to disabled travelers — including information on accommodations, access guides, and study tours. Among its publications are a quarterly newsletter and a comprehensive sourcebook, *World of Options, A Guide to International Education Exchange, Community Service, and Travel for Persons with Disabilities.* Individual membership is $20 a year; subscription to the newsletter alone is $10 annually. For more information, contact *MIUSA,* PO Box 3551, Eugene, OR 97403; phone: 503-343-1284, both voice and TDD (telecommunications device for the deaf).

National Rehabilitation Information Center, 8455 Colesville Rd., Suite 935, Silver Spring, MD 20910 (phone: 301-588-9284). A general information, resource, research, and referral service.

Paralyzed Veterans of America (PVA) is a national veterans service organization. Its members are all veterans who have suffered spinal cord injuries, but it offers advocacy services and information to all persons with a disability. *PVA* also sponsors *Access to the Skies,* a program that coordinates the efforts of the national and international air travel industry in providing airport and airplane access for the disabled. Members receive several helpful publications, as well as regular notification of conferences on subjects of interest to the disabled traveler. For information, contact *PVA/ATTS Program,* 801 18th St. NW, Washington, DC 20006 (phone: 202-USA-1300).

Royal Association for Disability and Rehabilitation (RADAR; 25 Mortimer St., London W1N 8AB, England; phone: 81-637-5400) offers a number of publications for the handicapped, including a comprehensive guide, *Holidays and Travel Abroad for the Disabled,* which provides helpful advice to the disabled traveler abroad. Available by writing to *RADAR,* the price, including airmail postage, is £3 (about $4.80); *RADAR* requires payment in pounds sterling, so this should be sent via an international money order (available at the post office).

Society for the Advancement of Travel for the Handicapped (SATH), 26 Court St., Penthouse, Brooklyn, NY 11242 (phone: 718-858-5483). To keep abreast of developments in travel for the handicapped as they occur, you may want to join *SATH,* a nonprofit organization whose members include travel agents, tour operators, and other travel suppliers, as well as consumers. Membership costs $40 ($25 for students and travelers who are 65 and older) and the fee is tax deductible. *SATH* publishes a quarterly newsletter, an excellent booklet, *Travel Tips for the Handicapped,* and provides information on travel agents or tour operators who have experience (or an interest) in travel for the handicapped. *SATH* also offers a free 48-page guide, *The United States Welcomes Handicapped Visitors,* that covers domestic transportation and accommodations, as well as travel insurance and other useful hints for the handicapped traveler abroad. Send a self-addressed, #10 envelope to *SATH* at the address above, and include $1 for postage.

TravelAbility, by Lois Reamy, is a vast database with information on locating tours for the handicapped, coping with public transport, and finding accommodations, special equipment, and travel agents, and includes a helpful step-by-step planning guide. Although geared mainly to travel in the US, it is full of information useful to handicapped travelers anywhere. Previously published by Macmillan, *TravelAbility* is currently out of print, but may be available at your library.

Travel Information Service at Moss Rehabilitation Hospital is a service designed to help physically handicapped people plan trips. It cannot make travel arrangements, but it will supply information on travel accessibility for a nominal fee. Contact the *Travel Information Service,* Moss Rehabilitation Hospital, 12th St. and Tabor Rd., Philadelphia, PA 19141 (phone: 215-456-9600).

The *Canadian Rehabilitation Council for the Disabled* publishes a useful book by Cinnie Noble, *Handi-Travel: A Resource Book for Disabled and Elderly Travelers* ($12.95, $2 for shipping and handling, 50¢ each additional copy). This comprehensive travel guide is full of practical tips for those with disabilities affecting mobility, hearing, or sight. To order this book and for other useful information, contact the *Canadian Rehabilitation Council for the Disabled,* 45 Sheppard Ave. E., Suite 801, Toronto, Ontario M2N 5W9, Canada (phone: 416-250-7490).

A few more basic resources to look for are *Travel for the Disabled,* by Helen Hecker ($9.95), and by the same author, *The Directory of Travel Agencies for the Disabled* ($12.95). *Wheelchair Vagabond,* by John G. Nelson, is another useful guide for travelers confined to a wheelchair (softcover, $9.95; hardcover, $14.95). All three are published by Twin Peaks Press (PO Box 129, Vancouver, WA 98666); to order call 800-637-CALM. Additionally, *The Physically Disabled Traveler's Guide,* by Rod W. Durgin and Norene Lindsay, is helpful and informative. It is available from Resource Directories (3361 Executive Pkwy., Suite 302, Toledo, OH 43606; phone: 419-536-5353) for $9.95, plus $2 for postage and handling.

Also check the library for Mary Meister Walzer's *A Travel Guide for the Disabled: Western Europe* (Van Nostrand Reinhold), which dedicates a chapter to travel in France and gives access ratings to a fair number of hotels — mostly in Paris and on the Côte d'Azur — along with information on the accessibility of some sightseeing attractions, restaurants, theaters, stores, and more.

The annually revised red *Michelin Guide to France* (Michelin; $17.95), which lists the better hotels and restaurants of the country and rates them according to the quality of their accommodations, food, service, and so on, uses the international symbol of access to point out hotels with rooms suitable for wheelchair-bound guests, as do the regional hotel guides distributed by the French Government Tourist Office. For more information on the Michelin books and to place an order, contact Michelin Guides and Maps, PO Box 3305, Spartanburg, SC 29304-3305 (phone: 803-599-0850). See the discussion of accommodations in *On the Road,* in this section.

It should be noted that almost all of the material published with disabled travelers in mind deals with the wheelchair-bound traveler, for whom architectural barriers are of prime concern. For travelers with diabetes, a pamphlet entitled *Ticket to Safe Travel* is available for 50¢ from the New York chapter of the *American Diabetes Association* (505 Eighth Ave., 21st Floor, New York, NY 10018; phone: 212-947-9707). For those with heart-related ailments, *Travel for the Patient with Chronic Obstructive Pulmonary Disease,* is available for $2 from Dr. Harold Silver, 1601 18th St. NW, Washington, DC 20009 (phone: 202-667-0134); the *American Heart Association* (7320 Greenville Ave., Dallas, TX 75231; phone: 214-373-6300) also provides a number of useful publications. For blind travelers, a wealth of additional information is available from the *American Foundation for the Blind* (15 W. 16th St., New York, NY 10011; phone: 212-620-2147 in New York State; 800-232-5463 elsewhere in the US).

Travelers who depend on Seeing Eye dogs should check with the airline they plan to fly and the authorities of the countries they plan to visit well before they leave. France requires that dogs and cats over 3 months of age have veterinary certificates dated within 5 days prior to arrival. These pets also must be inoculated against rabies 1 month to 1 year prior to arrival.

For further information, *Seeing Eye Dogs as Air Travelers* can be obtained free from *Seeing Eye* (Box 375, Morristown, NJ 07963-0375; phone: 201-539-4425). *The American Society for the Prevention of Cruelty to Animals (ASPCA)* also offers a very useful book, *Traveling With Your Pet,* which includes inoculation requirements by country and territory. It is available for $5 (which includes postage and handling). Send check or money order to the *ASPCA,* Education Dept., 441 E. 92nd St., New York, NY 10128 (phone: 212-876-7700).

PLANE: Advise the airline that you are handicapped when you book your flight. The Federal Aviation Administration (FAA) has ruled that US airlines must accept disabled and handicapped passengers as long as the airline has advance notice and the passenger represents no potentially insurmountable problem in the event emergency evacuation procedures must be followed. As a matter of course, US airlines were pretty good about helping handicapped passengers even before the ruling, although each airline has somewhat different procedures. French airlines also generally are good about accommodating the disabled traveler, but again, policies vary from carrier to carrier. Ask for specifics when you book your flight.

Disabled passengers always should make reservations well in advance, and should provide the airline with all relevant details of their condition at that time. These details include information on mobility, toilet and special oxygen needs, and requirements for equipment that must be supplied by the airline, such as a wheelchair or portable oxygen. Be sure that the person to whom you speak understands fully the degree of your disability — the more details provided, the more effective the help the airline can give you. On the day before the flight, call back to make sure that all arrangements have been prepared, and arrive early on the day of the flight so that you can board before the rest of the passengers. Carry a medical certificate with you, stating your specific disability or the need to carry particular medicine. (Some airlines require the certificate; you should find out the regulations of the airline you'll be flying well beforehand.)

Because most airports have jetways (corridors connecting the terminal with the door of the plane), a disabled passenger usually can be taken as far as the plane, and sometimes right onto it, in a wheelchair. If not, a narrow boarding chair may be used to take you to your seat. Your own wheelchair, which will be folded and put in the baggage compartment, should be tagged as escort luggage to assure that it's available at planeside upon landing rather than in the baggage claim area. Travel is not quite as simple if your wheelchair is battery-operated: Unless it has non-spillable batteries, it might not be accepted on board, and you will have to check with the airline ahead of time to find out how the batteries and the chair should be packaged for the flight. Usually people in wheelchairs are asked to wait until other passengers have disembarked. If you are making a tight connection, be sure to tell the attendant.

Passengers who use oxygen may not use their personal supply in the cabin, though it may be carried on the plane as cargo when properly packed and labeled. If you will need oxygen during the flight, the airline will supply it to you (there is a charge) provided you have given advance notice — 24 hours to a few days, depending on the carrier.

Useful information on every stage of air travel, from planning to arrival, is provided in the booklet *Incapacitated Passengers Air Travel Guide.* To receive a free copy, write to Senior Manager, Passenger Services, International Air Transport Association, 2000 Peel St., Montreal, Quebec H3A 2R4, Canada (phone: 514-844-6311).

For an access guide to hundreds of airports worldwide, write for *Access Travel: A Guide to the Accessibility of Airport Terminals,* a free publication of the *Airport Operators Council International,* which includes detailed information on airports in Lyons, Marseilles, Nice, Paris, and Toulouse. The US Department of Transportation's *Air Transportation of Handicapped Persons* explains the general guidelines that govern air carrier policies. It is available free when requested in writing. For information on obtaining both of these publications, see the source list above.

The following airlines have TDD toll-free lines in the US for the hearing-impaired: *American* (phone: 800-582-1573 in Ohio; 800-543-1586 elsewhere in the US); *Continental* (phone: 800-343-9195 from 8 AM to 1 AM, Eastern Standard Time); *Pan American* (phone: 800-722-3323); *TWA* (phone: 800-252-0622 in California; 800-421-8480 elsewhere in the US); and *United* (phone: 800-942-8819 in Illinois; 800-323-0170 elsewhere in the US).

SHIP: Cunard's *Queen Elizabeth 2* is considered the best-equipped ship for the handicapped — all but the top deck is accessible. The *QE2* crosses the Atlantic regularly from April through December between New York and and its home port of Southampton, England, sometimes calling at Cherbourg, France, and other European ports. Handicapped travelers are advised to book reservations at least 90 days in advance to reserve specialized cabins. For further information on the *QE2*, see *Traveling by Ship,* in this section.

GROUND TRANSPORTATION: Perhaps the simplest solution to getting around is to travel with an able-bodied companion who can drive. If you are accustomed to driving your own hand-controlled car and determined to rent one, you may have to do some extensive research, as it is difficult in Europe to find rental cars fitted with hand controls. If agencies do provide hand-control cars, they are apt to be few and in high demand. The best course is to contact the major car rental agencies listed in *Traveling by Car* well in advance of your departure, but be forewarned, you still may be out of luck.

The *American Automobile Association* (*AAA*) publishes the booklet *The Handicapped Driver's Mobility Guide,* available free to members and for $3 to non-members. Contact your local *AAA* office, or send a self-addressed, stamped, 6-by-9-inch envelope to *AAA* Traffic Safety Department, 1000 AAA Dr., Heathrow, FL 32746-5063.

Another quite expensive option is to hire a chauffeured auto. Other alternatives include taking taxis or using local public transportation, however, your mobility may be limited in rural areas.

BUS AND TRAIN: Bus travel, which is limited in France with the exception of metropolitan areas, is not recommended for travelers who are totally wheelchair-bound unless they have someone along who can lift them on and off or they are members of a group tour designed for the handicapped that is using a specially outfitted bus. If you have some mobility, however, you'll find local personnel usually quite happy to help you board and exit.

Train travel for the wheelchair-bound is well organized in France and becoming more so every day. All *TGV* trains — France's very high speed trains, which happen to be the fastest trains in the world — have doors at platform level so that passengers can roll on and off, and spaces have been set aside where they can travel in their own wheelchairs. It is possible to take the *TGV* from Paris to Lyons, Dijon, Avignon, Nîmes, Montpellier, Marseilles, and other cities as well. Later this year, an Atlantic *TGV* line will sweep through Tours, Nantes, Quimper, and Bordeaux. (For detailed information, see *Traveling by Train.*) Other trains in France are not as well adapted to wheelchairs, but timetables for each route specify which departures are accessible. A booklet describing *Société Nationale des Chemins de Fer Français (SNCF),* or *FrenchRail Inc.* services for the handicapped can be picked up in major railroad stations in France, primarily those in Paris. Unfortunately, it is issued in French only. Ask for *Le Supplément au Guide Pratique du Voyageur à l'Attention des Personnes à Mobilité Réduite.* Another useful booklet is the *Guide des Transports à l'Usage des Personnes à Mobilité Réduite,* available from the *Comité National Français de Liaison pour la Réadaptation des Handicapés (CNFLRH),* 38 Bd. Raspail, Paris 75007 (phone: 1-45-48-90-13).

TOURS: Programs designed for the physically impaired are run by specialists who have researched hotels, restaurants, and places of interest to be sure they present no insurmountable obstacles. The following travel agencies and tour operators specialize in making group and individual arrangements for travelers with physical or other disabilities. All of them have experience in travel to Europe and many of them have specific experience in travel to France. Because of the requirements of handicapped travel, however, the same packages may not be offered regularly.

Access: The Foundation for Accessibility by the Disabled, PO Box 356, Malvern, NY 11565 (phone: 516-887-5798). Travelers referral service that acts as an intermediary with tour operators and agents worldwide and provides information on accessibility at various locations. The firm also offers access to its audio/video travel library.

Accessible Tours/Directions Unlimited, 720 N. Bedford Rd., Bedford Hills, NY 10507 (phone: 914-241-1700 in New York state; 800-533-5343 elsewhere in the US). Arranges group or individual tours for disabled persons traveling in the company of able-bodied friends or family members. Accepts the unaccompanied traveler if completely self-sufficient.

Evergreen Travel Service/Wings on Wheels Tours, 19505L 44th Ave. W., Lynnwood, WA 98036-5658 (phone: 206-776-1184; 800-435-2288 throughout the US). The oldest company in the world offering worldwide tours and cruises for the disabled (Wings on Wheels) and sight impaired/blind (White Cane Tours). Most programs are first class or deluxe, and include a trained escort. *Evergreen* also is offering a service called Evergreen Flying Fingers, for the deaf.

Flying Wheels Travel, 143 W. Bridge St., Box 382, Owatonna, MN 55060 (phone: 507-451-5005 or 800-535-6790 throughout the US). Handles both tours and individual arrangements.

The Guided Tour, 555 Ashbourne Rd., Elkins Park, PA 19117 (phone: 215-782-1370). Arranges tours for people with developmental and learning disabilities and sponsors separate tours for members of the same population who also are physically disabled or who simply need a slower pace.

Sprout, 893 Amsterdam Ave., New York, NY 10025 (phone: 212-222-9575). Arranges travel programs for mildly and moderately disabled teens and adults.

Travel Horizons Unlimited, 11 E. 44th St., New York, NY 10017 (phone: 212-687-5121 in New York; 800-343-5032 elsewhere in the US). Travel agent and registered nurse Mary Ann Hamm designs trips for individual travelers requiring all types of kidney dialysis and handles arrangements for the dialysis.

Whole Person Tours, PO Box 1084, Bayonne, NJ 07002-1084 (phone: 800-462-2237 or 201-858-3400). Handicapped owner Bob Zywicki travels the world with his wheelchair and offers a lineup of escorted tours (many by himself) for the disabled. Send a self-addressed, stamped envelope for a general tour brochure of foreign and domestic programs. *Whole Person Tours* also publishes *The Itinerary,* a bimonthly newsletter for disabled travelers (a 1-year subscription costs $10).

Hints for Single Travelers

Just about the last trip in human history on which the participants were neatly paired was the voyage of Noah's Ark. Ever since, passenger lists and tour groups have reflected the same kind of asymmetry that occurs in real life, as countless individuals set forth to see the world unaccompanied (or unencumbered, depending on your outlook) by spouse, lover, friend, or relative.

There are some things to be said for traveling alone. There is the pleasure of privacy, though a solitary traveler must be self-reliant, independent, and responsible. Unfortunately, traveling alone also can turn a traveler into a second class citizen.

The truth is that the travel industry is not very fair to people who vacation by themselves. People traveling alone almost invariably end up paying more than individuals traveling in pairs. Most travel bargains, including package tours, accommodations, resort packages, and cruises, are based on *double occupancy* rates. This means that the per-person price is offered on the basis of two people traveling together and sharing a double room (which means they will each spend a good deal more on meals and extras). The single traveler will have to pay a surcharge, called a single supplement, for exactly the same package. In extreme cases, this can add as much as 30% to 55% to the basic per-person rate. As far as the travel industry is concerned, single travel has not yet come into its own.

Don't despair, however. Throughout France, there are scores of smaller hotels and other hostelries where, in addition to a cozier atmosphere, prices are still quite reasonable for the single traveler. There are, after all, countless thousands of individuals who *do* travel alone. Inevitably, their greatest obstacle is the single supplement charge, which prevents them from cashing in on travel bargains available to anyone traveling as part of a pair.

The obvious, most effective alternative is to find a traveling companion. Even special "singles' tours" that promise no supplements usually are based on people sharing double rooms. Perhaps the most recent innovation along these lines is the creation of organizations that "introduce" the single traveler to other single travelers, somewhat like a dating service. If you are interested in finding another single traveler to help share the cost, consider contacting the agencies listed below. Some charge fees, others are free, but the basic service offered by all is the same: to match the unattached person with a compatible travel mate. Among the better established of these agencies are the following:

Classic Singles Network: Offers tours catering to the mature single client — the majority of its members are over 45 years old. For information, contact *Classic Singles Network,* 100 N. Sepulveda Blvd., Suite 1010, El Segundo, CA 90245 (phone: 800-421-5785 in California; 800-421-2255 elsewhere in the US).

Contiki Holidays: Specializes in vacations for 18- to 35-year-olds. Packages to France are frequently offered. For information, contact *Contiki Holidays,* 1432 E. Katella Ave., Anaheim, CA 92805 (phone: 714-937-0611; 800-624-0611 in California; 800-626-0611 elsewhere in the continental US).

Cosmos: This agency, specializing in budget motorcoach tours of Europe, offers a guaranteed-share plan whereby singles who wish to share rooms (and avoid paying the single supplement) are matched by the tour escort with like-minded individuals of the same sex and charged the basic double-occupancy tour price. Contact the firm at one of its three North American branches: 95-25 Queens Blvd., Rego Park, NY 11374 (phone: 800-221-0090 from the eastern US); 150 S. Los Robles Ave., Pasadena, CA 91101 (phone 818-449-0919; 800-556-5454 from the western US); and 1801 Eglinton Ave. W., Suite 104, Toronto, Ontario M6E 2H8, Canada (phone: 416-787-1281).

Grand Circle Travel: Arranges extended vacations, escorted tours, and cruises for retired Americans, including singles. Membership, which is automatic when you book a trip through *Grand Circle,* includes discount certificates on future trips and other extras. Contact *Grand Circle Travel,* 347 Congress St., Boston, MA 02210 (phone: 800-248-3737 or 617-350-7500).

Insight International Tours: Offers a matching service for single travelers. Several tours are geared for travelers in the 18 to 35 age group. Contact *Insight International Tours,* 745 Atlantic Ave., Boston MA 02111 (phone: 800-582-8380 or 617-482-2000).

Jane's International: This service puts potential traveling companions in touch with one another. No age limit, no fee. Contact *Jane's International,* 2603 Bath Ave., Brooklyn, NY 11214 (phone: 718-266-2045).

STI: Offers multi-country escorted tours ranging from 2 weeks to 52 days, including itineraries throughout Europe. Contact *STI,* 8619 Reseda Blvd., Suite 103, Northridge, CA 91324 (phone: 800-525-0525).

Saga International Holidays: A subsidiary of a British company specializing in older travelers, many of them single, *Saga* offers a broad selection of escorted coach tours, cruises, and apartment-stay holidays, including packages, for people age 60 and over or those 50 to 59 traveling with someone 60 or older. Members of the *Saga Holiday Club* receive the club magazine, which contains a column aimed at helping lone travelers find suitable traveling companions. A 1-year club membership costs $5. Contact *Saga International Holidays,* 120 Boylston St., Boston MA 02116 (phone: 800-343-0273 or 617-451-6808).

Singleworld, which organizes its own packages and also books singles on the cruises and tours of other operators, arranges shared accommodations if requested, charging a one-time surcharge that is much less than the single supplement would be. *Singleworld* actually is a club joined through travel agents for a yearly fee of $20, paid at the time of booking. About two-thirds of this agency's clientele are under 35, and about half this number are women. *Singleworld* organizes tours and cruises with departures categorized by age group. Contact *Singleworld,* 401 Theodore Fremd Ave., Rye, NY 10580 (phone: 914-967-3334 or 800-223-6490 in the continental US).

Travel Companion Exchange: Every 8 weeks, this group publishes a directory of singles looking for travel companions and provides members with full-page profiles of likely partners. Members fill out a lengthy questionnaire to establish a personal profile and write a small listing, much like an ad in a personals column. This listing is circulated to other members who can request a copy of the complete questionnaire and then go on to make contact to plan a joint vacation. It is wise to join as far ahead of your scheduled vacation as possible so that there's enough time to determine the suitability of prospective traveling companions. Membership fees range from $6 to $11 per month (with a 6-month minimum enrollment), depending on the level of service required. The membership package includes a travel newsletter for singles. A sample issue costs $4. Contact *Travel Companion Exchange,* PO Box 833, Amityville, NY 11701 (phone: 516-454-0880).

A special guidebook for solo travelers, prepared by Eleanor Adams Baxel, offers information on how to avoid paying supplementary charges, how to pick the right travel agent, how to calculate costs, and much more. Entitled *A Guide for Solo Travel Abroad* (Berkshire Traveller Press), it's out of print, so check your library. A new book for single travelers is *Traveling on Your Own* by Eleanor Berman; available in bookstores, it also can be ordered by sending $12.95, plus $2 postage and handling (per book), to Random House, Customer Service Dept., 400 Hahn Rd., Westminster, MD 21157 (phone: 800-726-0600).

The single traveler who is particularly interested in getting to know Europeans better than chance encounters in train stations would allow may be interested in two very different possibilities. One is *Club Med,* an organization that heartily welcomes singles. Of its more than 100 activity-oriented resorts in countries around the world, 11 are in France — and more than 90% of the guests at its French resorts are European. Though the clientele often is under 30, there is a considerable age mix: the average age is 37. For details, contact *Club Med* (3 E. 54th St., New York, NY 10022; phone: 800-CLUB-MED) or call one of the two *Club Med* Boutiques: in San Francisco, 415-982-4200; in New York, 212-750-1687.

The other possibility is the United States Servas Committee, which maintains a list of hosts around the world (some 480 in France) who are willing to take visitors into their homes as guests for a 2-night stay. Servas will send an application form and a list of some 200 interviewers around the US for you to contact. After the interview, if you are accepted as a Servas traveler, you'll receive a certificate making you eligible to become a member. The membership fee is $45 for an individual, with a $15 deposit to receive the host list, refunded upon its return. For more information, contact The United States Servas Committee, 11 John St., Room 706, New York, NY 10038 (phone: 212-267-0252).

WOMEN AND STUDENTS: Two specific groups of single travelers deserve special mention: women and students. Countless women travel by themselves in Europe, and such an adventure need not be feared. You generally will find people courteous and welcoming, but remember that crime is a worldwide problem (although most French cities are generally regarded as safer than American cities — for everyone, including single women.) Keep a careful eye on your belongings while on the beach, lounging in a park, or traveling on a bus or train; lock your car and hotel doors; deposit your valuables in the hotel's safe; and never hitchhike.

One lingering inhibition many female travelers still harbor is that of eating alone in public places. The trick here is to relax and enjoy your meal and surroundings; while you may run across the occasional unenlightened waiter, dining solo is no longer uncommon. A book offering lively, helpful advice on female solo travel is *The Traveling Woman*, by Dena Kaye. Though out of print, it may be found in your local library.

Studying Abroad – A large number of single travelers, needless to say, are students. Travel *is* education. Travel broadens a person's knowledge and deepens his or her perception of the world in a way no media or "armchair" experience ever could. In addition, to study a country's language, art, culture, or history in one of its own schools is to enjoy the highest form of liberal education.

There are many benefits for students abroad, and the way to begin to discover them is to consult the *Council on International Educational Exchange (CIEE)*. This organization, which runs a variety of work, study, and travel programs for students, is the US sponsor of the International Student Identity Card (ISIC). Reductions on trains, airfare, and entry fees to most museums and other exhibitions are only some of the advantages of the card. To apply for it, write to *CIEE* at one of the following addresses: 205 E. 42nd St., New York, NY 10017 (phone: 212-661-1414); 312 Sutter St., San Francisco, CA 94108 (phone: 415-421-3473), and 919 Irving St., San Francisco, CA 94122 (phone: 415-566-6222). Mark the letter "Attn. Student ID." Application requires a $10 fee, a passport-size photograph, and proof that you are a matriculating student (this means either a transcript or a letter or bill from your school registrar with the school's official seal; high school and junior high school students can use their report cards). There is no maximum age limit, but participants must be at least 12 years old. The *ID Discount Guide,* which gives details of the discounts country by country, is free with membership. Another free publication of *CIEE* is the informative, annual, 64-page *Student Travel Catalog,* which covers all aspects of youth-travel abroad for vacation trips, jobs, or study programs, and also includes a list of other helpful publications. You can order the catalogue from Dept. ISS — #15 at the New York address given above.

Another card of value in France, and also available through *CIEE,* is the Federation of International Youth Travel Organizations (FIYTO) card. This provides many of the benefits of the ISIC card and will facilitate entry to certain "youth hotels" throughout France. In this case, cardholders need not be students, merely under age 26. To apply, send $10 with a passport-size photo and proof of birth date to *CIEE* at one of the addresses above.

CIEE also sponsors charter flights to Europe that are open to students and non-students of any age. Flights between New York and Paris (with budget-priced add-ons available from Boston, Chicago, Denver, El Paso, Los Angeles, Las Vegas, Minneapolis, St. Louis, Salt Lake City, San Diego, San Francisco, Seattle, and several other US cities) arrive and depart daily from Kennedy (JFK) or Newark airports during the high season. Regularly scheduled direct flights also are offered from Boston to Brussels.

Youth fares on transatlantic flights currently are offered by most of the scheduled airlines flying to Europe. Although the situation may change in the future, at press time, the youth fare was almost the same as the standard APEX fare, and there may be substantial drawbacks: a 7- or 14-day minimum stay, no stopovers, notification of availability and payment in full 1 to 3 days before the flight, and the return may only be left open if this is arranged before the trip, and again may be subject to 24-hour notice of availability. This space available restriction means that if you really must be home by a certain date, you are better off opting for a different type of ticket. Discount fares vary from carrier to carrier. To find out about current discounts, contact the individual airlines. Also see *Traveling by Plane,* in this section, for more information on economical flight alternatives.

Students and singles in general should keep in mind that youth hostels exist in many cities throughout France. They are always inexpensive, generally clean and well situated, and they are a sure place to meet other people traveling alone. Hostels are run by the hosteling associations of some 60-plus countries that make up the *International Youth Hostel Federation (IYHF)*; membership in one of the national associations affords access to the hostels of the rest. To join the American affiliate, *American Youth Hostels (AYH)*, write to the national office at PO Box 37613, Washington, DC 20013-7613 (phone: 202-783-6161), or contact the local *AYH* council nearest you. As we went to press, new membership rules and rates were in effect: Membership in *AYH* currently costs $25 for people between the ages of 18 and 54; $10 for youths under 18, $15 for seniors, and $35 for family membership. The *AYH Handbook,* which lists hostels in the US, comes with your *AYH* card (non-members can purchase the handbook for $5 plus $2 postage and handling); the *International Youth Hostel Handbooks,* which list hostels worldwide, must be purchased ($10.95 each, plus $2 for postage). In addition, the French national organization of youth hostels, *Ligue Française pour les Auberges de la Jeunesse* (38 Bd. Raspail, Paris 75007; phone: 1-45-48-69-84) provides a list of hostels offering low-cost lodging, open to travelers of all ages. Tourist boards also publish information sheets on hostels and on hosteling package holidays.

FrenchRail Inc. also offers discounts to students and youths. While the France Railpass, good for unlimited travel on the *FrenchRail (SNCF)* network, is sold only in adult and children's (ages 4 to 12) versions, there is a version of the Eurailpass restricted to travelers (including non-students) under 26 years of age. The Eurail Youthpass entitles the bearer to either 1 or 2 months of unlimited second class rail travel in 17 countries, including France. In addition, it is honored on many European steamers and ferries (including ferry crossings between Ireland and France on the *Irish Continental Line*) and on railroad connections between the airport and the center of town in various cities (including Paris). The pass also entitles the bearer to reduced rates on some bus lines in several countries, France among them. The Eurail Youthpass can be purchased only by those living outside Europe or North Africa, and it must be purchased before departure. Contact a travel agent, the national railway office of one of the countries in the Eurail network, or *FrenchRail Inc.* (For addresses of the latter in the US, see *Traveling by Train,* in this section).

Opportunities for study in France range from summer or academic-year courses in the French language and civilization designed specifically for foreigners (including those whose school days are well behind them) to long-term university attendance by those intending to take a French degree. The Cultural Services of the French Embassy provides information on university study in France and is responsible for distributing and reviewing application forms for those wishing to take a degree in France. It also can supply a list of the large number of summer and academic-year language and civilization courses given by universities and other cultural institutions. Contact the French Cultural Services at one of the following locations:

Boston: 126 Mt. Auburn St., Cambridge, MA 02138 (phone: 617-354-3464)
Chicago: 1170 Olympic Center, 737 N. Michigan Ave., Chicago, IL 60611 (phone: 312-664-3525)
Houston: 2727 Allen Pkwy., Suite 951, Houston, TX 77019 (phone: 713-528-2231)
Los Angeles: 8350 Wilshire Blvd., Suite 306, Beverly Hills, CA 90211 (phone: 213-651-0601)
Miami: 1 Biscayne Tower, Suite 1710, 2 S. Biscayne Blvd., Miami, FL 33131 (phone: 305-372-1376)
New Orleans: 3305 St. Charles Ave., New Orleans, LA 70115 (phone: 504-897-6385)
New York: 972 Fifth Ave., New York, NY 10021 (phone: 212-439-1400)
San Francisco: 540 Bush St., San Francisco, CA 94108 (phone: 415-397-4330)
Washington, DC: 4101 Reservoir Rd. NW, Washington, DC 20007 (phone: 202-944-6000)

Some language schools of particular interest should be noted here, among them, those of the *Alliance Française.* Exams at this venerable institution dedicated to the diffusion of French culture are a universal standard of French proficiency. The school in Paris is in the heart of the student quarter, but there also are schools in Bordeaux, Lyons, Marseilles, Nancy, Nice, Rouen, and Toulouse. The *Alliance Française* offers year-round courses of various duration and at varying levels, from elementary to highly advanced and for special needs (commercial French, translation, corrective phonetics). For information and application forms, write to the main headquarters: *Alliance Française de Paris,* 101 Bd. Raspail, Paris 75006 (phone: 1-45-44-38-28). The *Institut Catholique de Paris* (21 Rue d'Assas, Paris 75006; phone: 1-42-22-41-80) also has courses at all levels in French language and civilization, with considerable use of audiovisual methods.

Eurocentres (13 Passage Dauphine, Paris 75006; phone: 1-43-25-81-40) is an international foundation with headquarters in Zürich and schools of language and civilization in several European countries. Classes at the Paris branch, open year-round, take place in a classical building equipped with the latest in multimedia learning aides; in summer, classes also are offered at centers in Amboise and La Rochelle.

The *Chambre de Commerce et d'Industrie de Paris* sponsors programs and exams in commercial French (not for beginners), with emphasis on understanding the French business world. For details and a list of schools that give preparatory courses for the tests, contact the *Chambre de Commerce et d'Industrie de Paris,* Service des Examens, 42 Rue du Louvre, Paris 75001 (phone: 1-45-08-35-00).

Then there's the *Sorbonne.* The University of Paris offers a variety of courses in French language and civilization during both the summer and the academic year. The *Cours de Civilisation Française de la Sorbonne* — a potpourri of grammar, literature, history, and fine arts — is a model for courses at a number of other French universities that offer special programs for foreigners. Since the program's creation in 1919, it has been the vehicle through which more than 100,000 students the world over have come to know France and its most illustrious universities. The course is offered for any level of proficiency. Classes run October through January; February through May; and for sessions of several different lengths over the summer. For information write or call *Cours de Civilisation Française de la Sorbonne,* 47 Rue des Ecoles, Paris 75005 (phone: 1-40-46-22-11, Ext. 2664). Another very popular source of year-round courses in language and civilization is the *l'Université d'Eté pour les Etudiants Etrangers* at the University of Provence. The courses take place in Aix-en-Provence, one of the most gracious towns in the south of France. University-age students tend to dominate, and the town is one large, animated campus. Contact the *Office Universitaire des Relations Extérieures,* Cours d'Eté, 29 Av. Robert-Schuman, Aix-en-Provence 13621 (phone: 1-42-59-99-30, Ext. 317; or 1-42-59-22-71).

Another organization specializing in travel as an educational experience is the *American Institute for Foreign Study (AIFS).* Although it does not specialize in travel to France, approximately a third of the participants in its hundred-some programs around the world — tours, academic year, and summer programs — choose to study in France. The programs at the University of Paris, the University of Grenoble, and the *Collège International de Cannes* are, naturally, most favored by those studying French. At the *Sorbonne,* the European Studies Program is the major course offering; in Grenoble, courses include Modern French Theater and International Relations; in Cannes, Computer Science, Business Administration, Acting, French Cuisine, and Landscape Drawing are included in the prospectus. Again, *AIFS* caters primarily to bona fide high school or college students, but its non-credit international learning and continuing education programs are open to independent travelers of all ages. (Approximately 30% of *AIFS* students are over 25.) Contact *AIFS,* 102 Greenwich Ave., Greenwich, CT 06830 (phone: 800-727-AIFS, 203-869-9090, or 203-863-6087 for summer programs; 203-863-6095 for programs in French).

Complete details on more than 1,700 available courses and suggestions on how to apply are contained in two books published by the *Institute of International Education* (IIE Books, 809 UN Plaza, New York, NY 10017; phone 212-883-8200): *Vacation*

Study Abroad, \$24.95; and *Academic Year Abroad,* \$29.95. A third book, *Teaching Abroad,* costs \$21.95. All prices include book rate postage; first class postage is \$4 extra. IIE Books also offers a free pamphlet, called *Basic Facts on Study Abroad.*

AFS Intercultural Programs sets up exchanges between US and foreign high school students on an individual basis for a whole academic year or a semester. For more information, contact *AFS Intercultural Programs,* 313 E. 43rd St., New York, NY 10017 (phone 800-AFS-INFO or 212-949-4242).

Work, Study, Travel Abroad: The Whole World Handbook, issued by the *Council on International Educational Exchange (CIEE),* is an informative, chatty guide on study programs, work opportunities, and travel hints. To obtain it, send \$10.95 plus postage (\$1 for book rate; \$2.50 first class) to *CIEE,* 205 E. 42nd St., New York, NY 10017 (phone 212-661-1414).

Elderhostel is a network of schools, colleges, and universities that sponsors weeklong study programs for people over 60 years of age on campuses throughout Europe, including France. Some of its programs are offered in cooperation with the *Experiment in International Living* (below) and involve home stays. Contact *Elderhostel,* 80 Boylston St., Suite 400, Boston, MA 02116 (phone: 617-426-7788 or 617-426-8056). An informational videotape describing *Elderhostel's* programs is available for \$5.

The University of New Hampshire, the original sponsor of *Elderhostel,* has its own program for travelers over 50; contact *Interhostel,* University of New Hampshire, Division of Continuing Education, 6 Garrison Ave., Durham, NH 03824 (phone: 603-862-1147 weekdays, 1:30-4 PM Eastern Standard Time). For more details about both programs, see *Hints for Older Travelers.*

If you are interested in a home-stay travel program, in which you learn about French culture by living with a family, contact the *Experiment in International Living* (PO Box 676, Brattleboro, VT 05302-0676; phone: 802-257-7751 in Vermont, or 800-345-2929 elsewhere in the US), which sponsors home-stay educational travel. The organization aims its programs at high school or college students, but it also can arrange home stays of 1 to 4 weeks for adults in more than 40 countries. It is possible, after participating in the programs, to join supplemental travel/activities programs and tour France.

National Association of Secondary School Principals (NASSP), an association of administrators, teachers, and state education officials. It sponsors *School Partnership International,* a program in which secondary schools in the US are linked with partner schools abroad for an annual short-term exchange of students and faculty. 1904 Association Dr., Reston, VA 22091 (phone: 703-860-0200).

Those interested in campus stays should know about the *U.S. and Worldwide Travel Accommodations Guide,* which lists several hundred colleges and universities in Europe — including France — that offer simple, but comfortable, accommodations in their residence halls, primarily during the summer season. The accommodations vary from single and double rooms to full apartments and suites with kitchens, and the rooms can be booked by the day, week, or month. Prices range from \$12 to \$24 per night, with an average of about \$18. An added bonus of this type of arrangement is that visitors usually are free to utilize various campus sport and recreation facilities. For a copy of the guide, which describes services and facilities in detail, send \$11.95 to *Campus Travel Service,* PO Box 5007, Laguna Beach, CA 92652 (phone: 714-497-3044).

WORKING ABROAD: Jobs for foreigners in France are not easy to come by and in general do not pay well enough to cover all the expenses of a trip. They do provide an invaluable learning experience, however, while helping to make a trip more affordable. Work permits can be obtained through the *Council on International Exchange* (address above) only by students over 18 who are enrolled and working toward a degree in a US college or university and who have 2 years of college French or its equivalent to their credit. The permit allows them to work for 3 months at any time of year, but the students must find their own jobs, although *CIEE*'s Paris office is available to help them in the search. (Jobs as bilingual hotel, restaurant, and office workers are among those most commonly found.)

Hints for Older Travelers

Special package deals and more free time are just two factors that have given Americans over age 65 a chance to see the world at affordable prices. Senior citizens make up an ever-growing segment of the travel population, and the trend among them is to travel more frequently and for longer periods of time. No longer limited by 3-week vacations or the business week, older travelers can take advantage of off-season, off-peak travel that is both less expensive and more pleasant than traveling at prime time in high season. In addition, overseas, as in the US, discounts are frequently available.

PLANNING: When planning a vacation, prepare your itinerary with one eye on your own physical condition and the other on a topographical map. Keep in mind variations in climate, terrain, and altitudes, which may pose some danger for anyone with heart or breathing problems.

An excellent book to read before embarking on any trip, domestic or foreign, is Rosalind Massow's *Travel Easy: The Practical Guide for People Over 50*, available for $6.50 to members of the *American Association of Retired Persons (AARP)*, $8.95 for non-members (add $1.75 postage and handling per order, not per book). Order from AARP Books, c/o Scott, Foresman, 1865 Miner St., Des Plaines, IL 60016 (phone: 800-238-2300). It discusses a host of subjects, from choosing a destination to getting set for departure, with chapters on transportation options, tours, cruises, avoiding health problems, and handling dental emergencies en route. Another book, *The International Health Guide for Senior Citizens,* covers such topics as trip preparations, food and water precautions, adjusting to weather and climate conditions, finding a doctor, motion sickness, and jet lag. The book also discusses specific health and travel problems, and includes a list of resource organizations that provide medical assistance for travelers; it is available for $4.95 postpaid from Pilot Books, 103 Cooper St., Babylon, NY 11702 (phone: 516-422-2225). A third book on health for older travelers, Rosalind Massow's excellent *Now It's Your Turn to Travel* (Collier Books), has a chapter on medical problems; it is now out of print but may be available in your library. (Also, see *Staying Healthy*, in this section.) *Travel Tips for Senior Citizens* (State Department publication 8970), a useful booklet with general advice, also is currently out of print but may be found in libraries.

An excellent book for budget-conscious older travelers is *The Discount Guide for Travelers Over 55* by Caroline and Walter Weintz (Dutton; $7.95). You also may want to send for *101 Tips for the Mature Traveler*, a free publication available from *Grand Circle Travel* (347 Congress St., Suite 3A, Boston, MA 02210; phone: 617-350-7500, 800-221-2610, or 800-831-8880).

If you are traveling in the fall, winter, or spring, bear in mind that you often will not find central heating in public places in France and that even if your hotel has it, it may not warm your room up to the temperatures you're accustomed to at home. Bear in mind also that even in summer you will need something warm for the evening in many areas of the country, and rainwear year-round is a good idea, too. However, remember that one secret to happy traveling is to *pack lightly.* (For further hints on what to bring, see *How to Pack,* in this section.)

HEALTH: Health facilities in France generally are excellent, and a number of organizations exist to help travelers avoid or deal with a medical emergency overseas. For further information on these services, see *Medical and Legal Aid and Consular Services,* in this section.

Pre-trip medical and dental checkups are strongly recommended, particularly for older travelers. In addition, be sure to take along any prescription medication you need, enough to last *without a new prescription* for the duration of your trip; pack all medications with a note from your doctor for the benefit of airport authorities. It also is wise to bring a few common non-prescription over-the-counter medications with you: Aspirin or a non-aspirin pain reliever and something for stomach upset may come in handy. If you have specific medical problems, bring duplicate prescriptions and a "medical file" composed of the following:

1. A summary of your medical history and current diagnosis.
2. A list of drugs to which you are allergic.
3. Your most recent electrocardiogram, if you have heart problems.
4. Your doctor's name, address, and telephone number.

■ **A word of caution:** Don't overdo it. Allow time for some relaxation each day to refresh yourself for the next scheduled sightseeing event. Traveling across time zones can be exhausting, and adjusting to major climatic changes can make you feel dizzy and drained. Plan on spending at least 1 full day resting before you start touring. If you're part of a group tour, be sure to check the planned itinerary thoroughly. Some package deals sound wonderful because they include all the places you've ever dreamed of visiting. In fact, visiting all of them can become so hectic and tiring that you'll be reaching for a pillow instead of a camera.

DISCOUNTS AND PACKAGES: The Carte Vermeil entitles anyone over 60 to a variety of discounts, including a 60% discount on rail fares in France during off-peak hours. (This doesn't restrict you to night trains only; rather, you travel during "blue periods" — from Saturday noon to Sunday at 3 PM and from Monday noon to Friday at 3 PM, excluding holidays.) The card, which is available only in France, can be obtained by filling out a form at a major railroad station and presenting it, along with one's passport, to the designated official at the station. The cost in 1990 was 125F (about $22) and the card is good for a year; discounts are applicable to tickets bought in France only.

The Carte Vermeil or other proof of age (such as a passport) will enable older travelers to take advantage of other senior citizen discounts in France — entrance fees to monuments, museums, some concerts, movies, theaters, and so on. Keep an eye out for the phrases *tarif réduit* (reduced rate) and *troisième âge* ("third age," the French version of our "senior citizen" or "golden age"). Wherever you go and whatever you do, remember to ask if there are special rates for senior citizens. The answer will frequently be yes.

Many US hotel and motel chains, airlines, car rental companies, bus lines, and other travel suppliers offer discounts to older travelers. For instance, *Air Inter,* the national French domestic airline, offers special rates for senior citizens on selected flights within France, including potential savings of up to 60%.

Some discounts, however, are extended only to bona fide members of certain senior citizens organizations. Because the same organizations frequently offer package tours to both domestic and international destinations, the benefits of membership are twofold: Those who join can take advantage of discounts as individual travelers and also reap the savings that group travel affords. In addition, because the age requirements for some of these organizations are quite low (or nonexistent), the benefits can begin to accrue early. Among the organizations dedicated to helping you see the world are the following:

American Association of Retired Persons (*AARP*): The largest and best known of these organizations. Membership is open to anyone 50 or over, whether retired or not. *AARP* offers travel programs, designed exclusively for senior citizens, that cover the globe; they include a broad range of escorted tours, hosted tours, and cruises, including tours and resort packages. Dues are $5 per year or $12.50 for 3 years, and include spouse. For membership information, contact *AARP Travel Service,* 100 N. Sepulveda Blvd., Suite 1010, El Segundo, CA 90245 (phone: 800-227-7737 or 213-322-7323).

Mature Outlook: Through its *Travel Alert,* last-minute tours, cruises, and other vacation packages are available to members at special savings. Hotel and car rental discounts and travel accident insurance also are available. Membership is open to anyone 50 years of age or older, costs $9.95 a year, and includes its bimonthly newsletter and magazine as well as information on package tours. Contact the Customer Service Center, 6001 N. Clark St., Chicago, IL 60660 (phone: 800-336-6330).

National Council of Senior Citizens: Here, too, the emphasis is always on keeping costs low. This group offers a different roster of tours each year, and its travel service also will book individual tours for members. Although most members are over 50, membership is open to anyone, regardless of age, for an annual fee of $12 per person or $16 per couple. Lifetime membership costs $150. For information, contact the *National Council for Senior Citizens,* 925 15th St. NW, Washington, DC 20005 (phone: 202-347-8800).

Certain travel agencies and tour operators specialize in group travel for older travelers, among them the following:

Grand Circle Travel: Caters exclusively to the over-50 traveler and packages a large variety of escorted tours, cruises, and extended vacations. Packages to London are featured regularly. *Grand Circle* also publishes a quarterly magazine (with a column for the single traveler) and a helpful free booklet, *101 Tips for the Mature Traveler Abroad.* Contact *Grand Circle Travel*, 347 Congress St., Suite 3A, Boston, MA 02210 (phone: 617-350-7500 or 800-221-2610 and 800-831-8880 throughout the US).

Grandtravel: An agency that specializes in trips for grandparents and their grandchildren (aunts and uncles are welcome, too), bringing the generations together through travel. Several itineraries coincide with school vacations and emphasize historic and natural sites. Transportation, accommodations, and activities are thoughtfully arranged to meet the needs of the young and the young-at-heart. Contact *Grandtravel,* 6900 Wisconsin Ave., Suite 706, Chevy Chase, MD 20815 (phone: 301-986-0790 in Maryland; 800-247-7651 elsewhere in the US).

Insight International Tours: Offers a matching service for single travelers. Several tours are geared for mature travelers. Contact *Insight International Tours,* 745 Atlantic Ave., Boston, MA 02111 (phone: 617-482-2000 or 800-582-8380 throughout the US).

Saga International Holidays: A subsidiary of a British company specializing in the older traveler, *Saga* offers a broad selection of escorted coach tours, cruises, and apartment-stay holidays, including packages, for people age 60 and over or those 50 to 59 traveling with someone 60 or older. Members of the Saga Holiday Club receive the club magazine, which contains a column aimed at helping lone travelers find suitable traveling companions (see *Hints for Single Travelers*). A 1-year club membership costs $5. Contact *Saga International Holidays,* 120 Boylston St., Boston MA 02116 (phone: 800-343-0273 or 617-451-6808).

Many travel agencies, particularly the larger ones, are delighted to make presentations to help a group select destinations. A local chamber of commerce should be able to provide the names of such agencies. Once a time and place are determined, an organization member or travel agent can obtain group quotations for transportation, accommodations, meal plans, and sightseeing. Groups of 40 or more usually get the best breaks.

Another choice open to older travelers is a trip that includes an educational element. *Elderhostel* is a network of schools, colleges, and universities that sponsors weeklong study programs for people over 60 years of age on campuses throughout Europe, including France. An informational videotape describing *Elderhostel*'s programs is available for $5. Accommodations are in residence halls, and meals are taken in student cafeterias. Travel to the programs usually is by designated scheduled flights, and participants can arrange to extend their stay at the end of the program. Elderhostelers must be at least 60 years old (younger if a spouse or companion qualifies), in good health, and not in need of special diets. For information, contact *Elderhostel,* 80 Boylston St., Suite 400, Boston, MA 02116 (phone: 617-426-7788 or 617-426-8056).

Interhostel, a program sponsored by the Division of Continuing Education of the University of New Hampshire, sends travelers back to school at cooperating institutions in 33 countries on 4 continents, including — usually — France. Participants attend lectures on the history, economy, politics, and cultural life of the country they are visiting, go on field trips to pertinent points of interest, and take part in activities meant to introduce them to their foreign contemporaries. Trips are for 2 weeks; accommodations are on campus in university residence halls or off campus in modest hotels (double occupancy). Groups are limited to 35 to 40 participants who are at least 50 years old (or at least 40 if a participating spouse is at least 50), physically active, and not in need of special diets. For further information or to receive the three free seasonal catalogues, contact *Interhostel,* UNH Division of Continuing Education, 6 Garrison Ave., Durham, NH 03824 (phone: 603-862-1147 weekdays, 1:30 to 4 PM Eastern Standard Time).

Hints for Traveling with Children

 What better way to be receptive to the experiences you will encounter than to take along the young, wide-eyed members of your family? Their company does not have to be a burden or their presence an excessive expense. The current generation of discounts for children and family package deals can make a trip together quite reasonable.

A family trip will be an investment in your children's future, making geography and history come alive to them and leaving a sure memory that will be among the fondest you will share with them someday. Their insights will be refreshing to you; their impulses may take you to unexpected places with unexpected dividends. The experience will be invaluable to them at any age.

PLANNING: It is necessary to take some extra time beforehand to prepare children for travel. Here are several hints for making a trip with them easy and fun.

1. Children, like everyone else, will derive more pleasure from a trip if they know something about the country before they arrive. Begin their education about a month before you leave. Using maps, travel magazines, and travel books, give children a clear idea of where you are going and how far away it is. Part of the excitement of the journey will be associating the tiny dots on the map with the very real places they will visit a few weeks later. You can show them pictures of streets and scenes in which they will stand within a month. Don't shirk history lessons, but don't burden them with dates. Make history light, anecdotal, pertinent, but

most of all, fun. If you simply make materials available and keep France and your travel plans a topic of everyday conversation, your children will absorb more than you realize.

2. Children should help to plan the itinerary, and where you go and what you do should reflect some of their ideas. If they know something about the sites they'll visit beforehand, they will have the excitement of recognition when they arrive and the illumination of seeing how something is or is not the way they expected it to be.

3. Learn the language with your children — a few basics like *bonjour* ("good morning"), *au revoir* ("good-bye"), and *merci bien* ("thanks a lot"). You need no other motive than a perfectly selfish one: Thus armed, your children will delight the French and help break the ice wherever you go.

4. Give children specific responsibilities: The job of carrying their own flight bags and looking after their personal things, along with some other light travel chores, will give them a stake in the journey. Tell them how they can be helpful when you are checking in or out of hotels.

5. Give each child a travel diary or scrapbook to take along. Filling these with impressions, observations, and mementos will pass the time on trains and planes and help to assimilate their experiences.

6. Familiarize the children with francs (see *Credit and Currency,* in this section). Give them an allowance for the trip, and be sure they understand just how far it will or won't go.

One useful resource to which you may want to refer is the *Berlitz Jr.* instructional series for children, which includes a French edition. The series combines an illustrated storybook with a lively 60-minute audiocassette. Each book features a character, Teddy, who goes to school and learns to count and spell and speak French phrases. The book/cassette package is available from the Aladdin Books division of Macmillan Publishing Company for $19.95, plus shipping and handling. To order, contact Aladdin Books, Front and Brown Sts., Riverside, NJ 08075 (phone: 800-257-5755).

No matter what the reading level of your children, there are books to stimulate their interest in a trip to France. Young children en route to Paris may already be familiar with the adventures of Babar the elephant and so may particularly enjoy *Babar Loses His Crown* ($7.99 plus $1 for postage; available through Random House, Westminster, MD 21157, or call 800-733-3000 to order by credit card) in which Babar, too, sightsees in the capital. Also of note is *Babar's French Lessons* ($10.95; also from Random House). Both these books by Laurent De Brunhoff are appropriate for children from kindergarten to grade 3. Albert Lamorisse's *The Red Balloon* (Doubleday; $6.95; grades 3 to 6), a French classic about a young boy befriended by a balloon, is illustrated with photos from the film of the same name that show typical Paris street scenes. Piero Ventura's beautifully illustrated *Great Painters* (Putnam; $20.95) is an excellent introduction to painting for older children (ages 12 and up); it discusses Italian, Flemish, and English painting, then focuses on French painting from the Romantic movement through Impressionism, Fauvism, and Cubism. David Macaulay's *Cathedral: The Story of Its Construction* (Houghton Mifflin; $14.95, or $6.95 paperback; kindergarten to grade 5), in which line drawings explain the process to children who cannot read the text, is particularly suited to preparing children for a visit to a country famous for its cathedrals. *Castle,* by the same author and at the same price, uses the same technique. For good readers interested in history or spy stories, there's *The French Resistance,* by Don Lawson (Silver Burdett & Ginn; $8.95). Especially recommended as a guidebook for families visiting any part of France is the tiny, encyclopedic *Welcome to France*

(Passport Books, National Textbook Company; $4.95 in bookstores or call 800-323-4900), which can be read by children in grades 4 or 5 and up, and is informative for adults as well. It points out all sorts of unfamiliar things that will likely be seen on the trip, from tall vineyard tractors and tiled roofs to *baguettes* and *boules* (there's a box to check when each thing has been spotted). It also suggests what to do in Paris, tells what to look for in churches and châteaux, talks about food, wine, and festivals, and even includes a license plate game.

And for parents, *Travel With Your Children* publishes a newsletter, *Family Travel Times,* that focuses on the child traveler and offers helpful hints. Membership is $35 a year. For a sample copy of the newsletter, send $1 to *Travel With Your Children,* 80 Eighth Ave., New York, NY 10011 (phone: 212-206-0688).

PACKING: Choose your children's clothes much as you would your own. Select a basic color (perhaps different for each child) and coordinate everything with it. Plan their wardrobes with layering in mind — shirts and sweaters that can be taken off and put back on as the temperature varies. Take only drip-dry, wrinkle-resistant items that they can manage themselves and comfortable shoes — sneakers and sandals. Younger children will need more changes, but keep it to a minimum. No one likes to carry added luggage. (Remember that *you* will have to manage most of it!)

Take as many handy snacks as you can squeeze into the corners of your suitcases — things like dried fruit and nut mixes, hard candies, peanut butter, and crackers — and moist towelettes for cleaning. Don't worry if your supply of nibbles is quickly depleted. Airports and train stations are well stocked with such items.

Pack a special medical kit with children's aspirin or acetaminophen, an antihistamine or decongestant, and medication for motion sickness and diarrhea. Do not feel you must pack a vacation's worth of Pampers. Disposable diapers (*les couches*) are available in every *pharmacie* (drugstore) and *supermarché* (supermarket). A selection of baby foods also is available in most *supermarchés,* but in the event that you may not be able to find the instant formula to which your child is accustomed, bring along a supply in the 8-ounce "ready-to-feed" cans. Disposable nursers are expensive but handy. If you breast-feed your baby, there is no reason you can't enjoy your trip; just be sure you get enough rest and liquids.

Good toys to take for infants are the same sorts of things they like at home — well-made, bright huggables and chewables; for small children, a favorite doll or stuffed animal for comfort, spelling and counting games, and tying, braiding, and lacing activities; for older children, playing cards, travel board games with magnetic pieces, and hand-held electronic games. Softcover books and art materials (crayons, markers, paper, scissors, glue sticks, and stickers) ward off boredom for children of most ages, as do radio-cassette players with headphones. Take along a variety of musical and storytelling cassettes, extra batteries, and maybe even an extra set of headphones so two children can listen. *Advice:* Avoid toys that are noisy, breakable, or spillable, those that require a large play area, and those that have lots of little pieces that can be scattered and lost. When traveling, coordinate activities with attention spans; dole out playthings one at a time so you don't run out of diversions before you get where you're going. Children become restless during long waiting periods, and a game plus a small snack — such as a box of raisins or crackers — will help keep them quiet. It also is a good idea to carry tissues, Band-Aids, a pocket medicine kit (described above), and pre-moistened washcloths.

GETTING THERE AND GETTING AROUND: Begin early to investigate all available discount and charter flights, as well as any package deals and special rates offered by the major airlines. Booking sometimes is required up to 2 months in advance. You may well find that charter plans offer no reductions for children, or not enough to offset the risk of last-minute delays or other inconveniences to which charters are subject. The major scheduled airlines, on the other hand, almost invariably provide hefty discounts for children (for specific information on fares and in-flight accommodations for children, also see *Traveling by Plane*, in this section).

PLANE: When you make your reservations, tell the airline that you are traveling with a child. As a general rule, children under 2 travel free in a plane if they sit on an adult's lap — although on some carriers you will have to pay 10% of the adult fare. But it's much safer — and certainly more comfortable — to purchase an adjacent seat for the baby and bring an infant restraint which is then strapped into the airline seat with a regular seat belt. (The airlines do not provide infant seats, so you will have to bring your own. If you do not purchase a seat for your baby and bring the infant restraint along on the off chance that there will be an empty seat next to yours, if an additional seat is not available, you will have to pay to check it as baggage.) There is no special fare for an infant, although discounts for children sometimes are in effect, and you can inquire about this when making a reservation — between the ages of 2 and 12, children generally travel at half or two-thirds of the adult fare.

If using one of these infant restraints, you should try to get bulkhead seats which will provide extra room to care for your child during the flight. You also should request a bulkhead seat when using a bassinet (some airlines do provide bassinets) — again, this is not as safe as strapping the child in. On some planes, bassinets may hook into a bulkhead wall; on others it is placed on the floor in front of you. Even if you do use a bassinet, babies must be held during takeoff and landing. Request seats on the aisle if you have a toddler or if you think you will need to use the bathroom frequently. (Try to discourage children from being in the aisle when meals are served.)

Carry onto the plane all you will need to care for and occupy your children during the flight — formula, diapers, a sweater, books, favorite stuffed animals, and so on. (Never check as baggage any item essential to a child's well-being, such as prescription medicine.) Dress your baby simply, with a minimum of buttons and snaps, because the only place you may have to change a diaper is at your seat. The flight attendant can warm a bottle for you.

Just as you would request a vegetarian or kosher meal, you are entitled to ask for a hot dog or hamburger instead of the airline's regular dinner if you give at least 24 hours' notice. Some, but not all, airlines have baby food aboard. While you should bring along toys from home, you also can ask about children's diversions. Some carriers, such as *Pan American*, have terrific free packages of games, coloring books, and puzzles.

When the plane takes off and lands, make sure your baby is nursing or has a bottle, pacifier, or thumb in its mouth. This sucking will make the child swallow and help to clear stopped ears. A piece of hard candy will do the same thing for an older child.

Avoid night flights. Since you probably won't sleep nearly as well as your kids, you risk an impossible first day at your destination, groggily taking care of your rested, energetic children. Nap time is, however, a good time to travel, especially for babies, and try to travel during off-hours, when there are apt to be extra seats. If you do have to take a long night flight, keep in mind that when you disembark, you probably will be tired and not really ready for sightseeing. The best thing to do is to head for your hotel, shower, have a snack, and take a nap. If your children are too excited to sleep, give them some toys to play with while you rest.

■**Note:** Newborn babies, whose lungs may not be able to adjust to the altitude, should not be taken aboard an airplane. And some airlines may refuse to allow a pregnant woman in her 8th or 9th month aboard, for fear that something could go wrong with an in-flight birth. Check with the airline well ahead of departure and carry a letter from your doctor stating that you are fit to travel — and indicating the estimated date of birth.

SHIP AND TRAIN: By ship, children through age 12 usually travel at a considerably reduced fare. If you plan to travel by train when abroad, note that on *FrenchRail Inc. (SNCF),* children under 4 travel free provided they do not occupy a seat; children under 4 occupying a seat and from 4 through 11 travel at a lower fare. For yourself, you might consider buying a France Railpass, which offers unlimited travel on French trains for a set period of time at a reduced rate (see *Traveling by Train*). A similar pass, the Eurailpass, is good for unlimited train travel throughout France and the neighboring countries of Europe. Both passes must be bought in the US, so plan before you leave. Note that on buses and subways in France, children under 4 ride free, those aged 4 to 10 for half fare.

CAR: Without a doubt, a car is the most flexible means of transportation. Driving allows you complete independence in arranging your schedule and itinerary. Keep your car supplied with dried fruits, crackers, candy bars, bottled water, and facial tissue and/or toilet paper. You may even want to pick up a cooler so that you can picnic along the way. There's nothing lovelier than stopping at a beautiful site and eating lunch as you look out on the surroundings. There are plenty of places to pull over and have a meal.

ACCOMMODATIONS AND MEALS: Often a cot will be placed in a hotel room at little or no extra charge. If you wish to sleep in separate rooms, special rates are sometimes available for families in adjoining rooms; some places do not charge for children under a certain age. In many of the larger chain hotels, the staff are more used to noisy or slightly misbehaving children. These hotels also are likely to have swimming pools or gamerooms — both popular with most young travelers. Write the hotel in advance to discuss how old your children are and how long you plan to stay, and to ask for suggestions on sleeping arrangements.

You might want to look into accommodations along the way that will add to the color of your trip. For instance, hotels in the *Relais du Silence* group — an association of moderately priced independent hotels, mostly in the country — include old manor houses, châteaux, and inns that your children will love. (If you do stay at one of these *relais,* be sure to discuss the fact that they will have to be particularly well-behaved — as the name suggests, the emphasis is on peace and quiet.) Other types of accommodations to investigate include *logis,* simple, small, family-run hotels in towns and villages; *auberges,* very simple inns in rural areas; and *gîtes,* a heading that covers several types of lodgings — a *gîte* can be a room in a private house, much like a bed and breakfast, but it also can be a self-catering accommodation in a country cottage or on a farm. (See the discussion of accommodations in *On the Road,* in this section, for a fuller discussion of places to stay in France.) Camping facilities, which range from merely adequate to truly outstanding, are often in beautiful, out-of-the-way spots. They usually are well equipped and less expensive than any hotel you will come across. (See *Camping and RVs, Hiking and Biking,* in this section.)

THINGS TO REMEMBER: If you are spending your vacation traveling, rather than visiting one spot or engaging in one activity, pace the days with children in mind: Break the trip into half-day segments, with running around or "doing" time built in; keep travel time on the road to a maximum of 4 or 5 hours a day. First and foremost, don't forget that a child's attention span is far shorter than an adult's. Children don't have to see every museum or all of any museum to learn something from their trip; watching, playing with, and talking to other children can be equally enlightening experiences. Also, remember the places that children the world over love to visit: zoos, country fairs and small amusement parks, beaches and nature trails. And France, the home of the puppet Guignol, is rife with Punch and Judy shows and other lively entertainments. Let your children lead the way sometimes — their perspective is different from yours, and they may lead you to things you would never have noticed on your own.

Staying Healthy

The surest way to return home in good health is to be prepared for medical problems that might occur on vacation. Below we've outlined some things you need to think about before you go.

Obviously, your state of health is crucial to the success of a vacation. There's nothing like an injury or illness, whether serious or relatively minor, to dampen or destroy a holiday. And health problems always seem more debilitating when you are away. However, most problems can be prevented or greatly alleviated with intelligent foresight and attention to precautionary details.

Older travelers or anyone suffering from a chronic medical condition, such as diabetes, high blood pressure, cardiopulmonary disease, asthma, or ear, eye, or sinus trouble, should consult a physician before leaving home. A checkup is advisable. A pre-trip dental checkup is not a bad idea, either.

People with conditions requiring special consideration when traveling should consider seeing, in addition to their regular physician, a specialist in travel medicine. For a referral in a particular community, contact the nearest medical school or ask a local doctor to recommend such a specialist. The *American Society of Tropical Medicine and Hygiene* publishes a directory of more than 70 travel doctors across the country. Send a 9-by-12-inch self-addressed, stamped envelope ($1.05 postage) to Dr. Leonard Marcus, Tufts University, 200 W. Boro Rd., North Grafton, MA 01536.

No matter where you travel, you should carry an all-purpose identification card listing your name, home address, social security number, blood type, drug allergies, chronic health problems, health insurance information, and whom to contact in case of emergency. When you register at a hotel, it's not a bad idea to include your home address; this will facilitate the process of notifying friends, relatives, or your own doctor in case of an emergency.

FIRST AID: Put together a compact, personal medical kit including Band-Aids; first-aid cream; antiseptic; nose drops; insect repellent; aspirin; an extra pair of prescription glasses or contact lenses (and a copy of your prescription for glasses or lenses); sunglasses; over-the-counter remedies for diarrhea, indigestion, and motion sickness; a thermometer; and a supply of those prescription medicines you take regularly. In a corner of your kit, keep a list of all the drugs you have brought and their purpose, as well as duplicate copies of your doctor's prescriptions (or a note from your doctor). These copies could come in handy if you are ever questioned by police or airport authorities about any drugs you are carrying, and also will be necessary to refill any prescriptions in the event of loss. Considering the essential contents of this kit, keep it with you, rather than in your luggage.

SUNBURN: Depending on when and where you're traveling, the burning power of the sun can be phenomenal (particularly along the coast) and can quickly cause severe sunburn or sunstroke. To protect yourself against these ills, wear sunglasses, take along a broad-brimmed hat and cover-up, and use a sunscreen lotion. When choosing a sunscreen, look for one that has a PABA (para-amino-benzoic acid) base. PABA blocks out most of the harmful ultraviolet rays of the sun.

Some tips on tanning:

1. Allow only 20 minutes or so the first day; increase your exposure gradually.
2. You are most likely to get a painful burn when the sun is the strongest, between 10 AM and 2 PM.

3. When judging if you've had enough sun, remember that time in the water (in terms of exposure to ultraviolet rays) is the same as time lying on the beach.
4. A beach umbrella or other cover doesn't keep all the rays of the sun from reaching you. If you are sensitive to light, be especially careful.
5. As many ultraviolet rays reach you on cloudy days as on sunny days. And the sun is particularly strong when reflected off snowy slopes — as in the Alps. Even if you don't feel hot, you still are exposed to rays.

If, despite these precautions, you find yourself with a painful sunburn, take a cooling bath, apply a first aid spray or the liquid of an aloe plant, and stay out of the sun. If you develop a more serious burn and experience chills, fever, nausea, headaches, or dizziness, consult a doctor at once.

WATER SAFETY: France is famous for the rocky beaches of the Côte d'Azur and the sandy beaches of Brittany are, by some standards, even finer, but it's important to remember that the sea, especially the wild Atlantic, also can be treacherous. A few precautions are necessary. Beware of the undertow, that current of water running back down the beach after a wave has washed ashore; it can knock you off your feet and into the surf. Even more dangerous is the riptide, a strong current of water running against the tide that can pull you out toward sea. If this happens, don't panic or try to fight the current, because it will only exhaust you; instead, ride it out while waiting for it to subside, which usually happens not too far from shore, or try swimming away parallel to the beach.

INSECTS AND OTHER PESTS: Mosquitoes and other biting insects can be trouble-some. We recommend using some form of repellent against bug bites, especially for campers. Vitamin B-1 or thiamine tablets will alter your body chemistry to help repel mosquitos — a terrific nuisance in some rural areas. If you are at all susceptible to mosquito bites, you will be amazed at how quickly the vitamins work — although they do not work for everyone. It still is *always* a good idea to use some form of topical insect repellent. As many of the stronger, effective insect repellents have a pungent odor, you may want to try a relatively new discovery, Skin-So-Soft hand lotion, made by Avon. This orderless skin softener actually has been approved by the FDA as an effective insect repellent. Burning mosquito coils containing pyrethrin or citronella candles is another effective precaution.

If you do get bitten, the itching can be relieved with baking soda or antihistamine tablets. Should a bite become infected, which is common in the tropics, treat it with a disinfectant or antibiotic cream. *Note:* Antihistamines should not be combined with alcohol or cortisone cream, or taken when driving.

Though rarer than insect bites, bites from venomous snakes, spiders, poisonous centipedes, or sea creatures such as jellyfish can be serious. If possible, always try to catch the villain for identification purposes. In most cases, particularly if spasms, numbness, convulsions, or hemorrhaging occurs, consult a doctor at once. The best course of action may be to head directly to the nearest emergency ward or outpatient clinic of a hospital. Cockroaches and termites thrive in warm climates, but pose no serious health threat.

FOOD AND WATER: Water is clean and potable throughout France. If you are at all unsure, ask if water is meant for drinking — if it isn't, it should be marked *eau non potable*. Still, travelers may want to do as the French do and drink bottled water, at least at the beginning of the trip. This is not because there is something wrong with the water as far as the residents are concerned, but new microbes in the digestive tract to which you have not become accustomed may cause mild stomach or intestinal upsets. Particularly in rural areas, the water supply may not be thoroughly purified; local residents either have developed immunities to the natural bacteria or boil it for drinking. You also should avoid drinking water from streams or freshwater pools. In campgrounds water usually is indicated as drinkable or for washing only — again, if you're not sure, ask.

Milk is pasteurized throughout France, and milk products (cheese, yogurt, ice cream, and so on) are safe to eat, as are fresh produce, meat, poultry, and fish. Because of Mediterranean pollution, however, fish and shellfish should be eaten cooked.

Following all these precautions will not guarantee an illness-free trip, but it should minimize the risk. As a final hedge against economic if not physical problems, make sure your health insurance will cover all eventualities while you are away. If not, there are policies designed specifically for travel. Many are worth investigating. As with all insurance, they seem like a waste of money until you need them. For further information, also see *Insurance* and *Medical and Legal Aid and Consular Services,* both in this section.

HELPFUL PUBLICATIONS: Practically every phase of health care — before, during, and after a trip — is covered in *The New Traveler's Health Guide* by Drs. Patrick J. Doyle and James E. Banta. It is available for $4.95, plus $2 postage and handling, from Acropolis Books Ltd., 80 S. Early, Alexandria, VA 22304 (phone: 800-451-7771 or 703-709-0006).

The *Traveling Healthy Newsletter*, which is published six times a year, also is brimming with healthful travel tips. For a subscription, which costs $24, contact Dr. Karl Neumann, MD, 108-48 70th Rd., Forest Hills, NY 11375 (phone: 718-268-7290).

For more information regarding preventive health care for travelers contact the *International Association for Medical Assistance to Travelers (IMAT),* at 417 Center St., Lewiston, NY 14092 (phone: 716-754-4883) or write to the US Government Printing Office, Washington, DC 20402, for the US Public Health Service's booklet *Health Information for International Travel* (HEW Publication CDC-86-8280; enclose a check or money order for $4.75 payable to the Superintendent of Documents).

On the Road

Credit and Currency

 It may seem hard to believe, but one of the greatest (and least understood) costs of travel is money itself. If that sounds simplistic, consider that you can lose as much as 30% of your travel dollars' value simply by changing money at the wrong place or in the wrong form. So your one single objective in relation to the care and retention of your travel funds is to make them stretch as far as possible. When you do spend money, it should be on things that expand and enhance your travel experience, with no buying power lost due to carelessness or lack of knowledge. This requires more than merely ferreting out the best airfare or the most charming budget hotel. It means being canny about the management of money itself. Herewith, a primer on making money go as far as possible overseas.

CURRENCY: The basic unit of currency in France is the French franc, which is divided into 100 centimes. The French franc also is the basic unit of currency in Monaco, although Monégasque coins with the same face value as French coins are in circulation there (and are fully convertible in France). The franc is distributed in coin denominations of 10F, 5F, 2F, 1F, and ½F, and 20 centimes, 10 centimes, and 5 centimes. Paper money is distributed in denominations of 500F, 200F, 100F, 50F, and 20F.

A brief word about the French way of expressing numbers: In essence, the French use a comma where Americans use a decimal point and vice versa. Thus five thousand francs, which we express as 5,000F, will be written in France as F5.000, Ff5.000, or 5.000F (or "Fr."); fifty centimes, which we write as 50 centimes (there is no abbreviation for "centimes"), is expressed as a decimal (hundredths of a franc) and appears in France as 0,50 (often without an accompanying "F," "Ff," or "Fr."); and four francs, fifty centimes appears as F4,50, Ff4,50, or 4,50F. (Note that throughout this book we use the American decimal style.)

Like all foreign currency, the value of French currency in relation to the US dollar fluctuates daily, affected by a wide variety of phenomena. As we went to press, the exchange rate for French francs was 5.7F to $1 US, or approximately 18¢ US to 1F.

Although US dollars may be accepted in France (particularly at points of entry), you certainly will lose a percentage of your dollar's buying power if you do not take the time to convert it into French francs. By paying for goods and services in the local currency, you save money by not negotiating invariably unfavorable exchange rates for every small purchase, and avoid difficulty where US currency is not readily — or happily — accepted. *Throughout this book, unless specifically stated otherwise, prices are given in US dollars.*

FOREIGN EXCHANGE: Because of the volatility of exchange rates, be sure to check the current value of the French franc before finalizing any travel budget. And before you actually depart on your trip, shop around carefully for the most advantageous exchange rate offered by various financial institutions — US banks, US currency exchange firms, or French banks. Almost invariably, the best exchange rates for US dollars will be found in French banks.

For the best sense of current trends follow the rates posted in such international newspapers as the *International Herald Tribune,* check with your own bank, or check with *Deak International Ltd.* (for the nearest location, call 800-972-2192 in Illinois; 800-621-0666 elsewhere in the US). *Harold Reuter and Company,* a currency exchange service in New York City (200 Park Ave., Suite 332 E., New York, NY 10166; phone: 212-661-0826) also is particularly helpful in determining current trends in exchange rates. *Ruesch International* also offers up-to-date foreign currency information and currency-related services (such as converting French franc VAT refund checks into US dollars; see *Shopping,* in this section). *Ruesch* also offers a pocket-sized *Foreign Currency Guide* (good for estimating general equivalents while planning) and a helpful brochure *6 Foreign Exchange Tips for the Traveler*. Contact *Ruesch International* at one of the following addresses: 3 First National Plaza, Suite 2020, Chicago, IL 60602 (phone: 312-332-5900); 1925 Century Park E., Suite 240, Los Angeles, CA 90067 (phone: 213-277-7800); 608 Fifth Ave., "Swiss Center," New York, NY 10020 (phone: 212-977-2700); or 1350 Eye St. NW, 10th Floor and street level, Washington, DC 20005 (phone: 800-424-2923 or 202-408-1200).

In France, you will find the official rate of exchange posted in banks, airports, and hotels. In some places, the difference between exchange rates offered in banks and in hotels is not as extreme as in other foreign countries — although generally you will get more local currency for your US dollar at banks than at any other commercial establishment. The convenience of exchanging money in your hotel (sometimes on a 24-hour basis) *may* make up for some of the difference in the exchange rate. Don't try to bargain in banks or hotels — no one will alter the rates for you.

That said, however, the following rules of thumb are worth remembering.

Rule number one is as simple as it is inflexible: Never (repeat: *never*) exchange dollars for foreign currency at hotels, restaurants, or retail shops, where you are sure to lose a significant amount of your dollar's buying power. If you do come across a storefront exchange counter offering what appears to be an incredible bargain, there's just too much counterfeit specie in circulation to take the chance (see Rule number three, below).

Rule number two: Estimate your needs carefully; if you overbuy, you lose twice — buying and selling back. Every time you exchange money, someone is making a profit, and rest assured it isn't you. Use up foreign notes before leaving, saving just enough for last-minute incidentals and tips.

Rule number three: Don't buy money on the black market. The exchange rate may be better, but it is a common practice to pass off counterfeit bills to unsuspecting foreigners who aren't familiar with the local currency. It's usually a sucker's game, and you are almost always the sucker; it also can land you in jail.

Rule number four: Learn the local currency quickly and keep abreast of daily fluctuations in the exchange rate. These are listed in the English-language *International Herald Tribune* daily for the preceding day, as well as in every major newspaper in France. Banks post their daily exchange rates, which might vary by only a few tenths of a centime from bank to bank. Rates change to some degree every day. For rough calculations, it is quick and safe to use round figures, but for purchases and actual currency exchanges, carry a small pocket calculator that helps you compute the exact rate. Inexpensive calculators specifically designed to quickly convert currency amounts for travelers are widely available.

When changing money, don't be afraid to ask how much commission you're being charged, and the exact amount of the going rate. In fact, in any exchange of money for goods or services, you should work out the rate before making any payment.

TIP PACKS: It's not a bad idea to buy a *small* amount of French coins and banknotes before your departure. But note the emphasis on the word "small," because, for the most part, you are better off carrying the bulk of your travel funds abroad in US dollar traveler's checks (see below). Still, the advantages of tip packs are threefold: You become familiar with the currency (really the only way to guard against making mistakes or being cheated during your first few hours in a new country); you are guaranteed some money should you arrive when a bank or exchange counter isn't open or available; and you don't have to depend on hotel desks, porters, or taxi drivers to change your money. A "tip pack" is the only French currency you should buy before you leave.

If you do run short upon arrival, dollars often are accepted at points of arrival. In other areas, they either *may* be accepted, or someone may accommodate you by changing a small amount — though invariably at a less than advantageous rate.

TRAVELER'S CHECKS: It's wise to carry traveler's checks on the road instead of (or in addition to) cash, since it's possible to replace traveler's checks if they are stolen or lost; travelers usually can receive partial or full replacement funds the same day if they have their purchase receipt and proper identification. Issued in various denominations and available in both US dollars and French francs, when presented with adequate proof of identification (credit cards, driver's license, passport) traveler's checks are as good as cash in most hotels, restaurants, stores, and banks.

You will be able to cash traveler's checks fairly easily in France, but don't expect to meander into a small village and be able to get instant cash. Also, even in metropolitan areas, don't assume that restaurants, small shops, and other establishments are going to be able to change checks of large denominations. Worldwide, more and more establishments are beginning to restrict the amount of traveler's checks they will accept or cash, so it is wise to purchase at least some of your checks in small denominations — say, $10 and $20 or the current equivalent in francs. Also, don't expect to change them into US currency except at banks and international airports.

When deciding whether to buy your travel funds in US or French denomination traveler's checks, keep in mind that the exchange rates offered by the issuing companies in the US generally are far less favorable than those available from banks both in the US and abroad. Therefore, it usually is better to carry the bulk of your travel funds abroad in US dollar traveler's checks.

Every type of traveler's check is legal tender in banks around the world and each company guarantees full replacement if checks are lost or stolen. After that the similarity ends. Some charge a fee for purchase, others are free; you can buy traveler's checks at almost any bank, and some are available by mail. Most important, each traveler's check issuer differs slightly in its refund policy — the amount refunded immediately, the accessibility of refund locations, the availability of a 24-hour refund service, and the time it will take for you to receive replacement checks. For instance, American Express offers a 3-hour replacement of lost or stolen traveler's checks at any American Express office — other companies may not be as prompt. (Note that American Express's 3-hour policy is based on the traveler's being able to provide the serial numbers of the lost checks — without these numbers, refunds can take up to 3 business days.)

We cannot overemphasize the importance of knowing how to replace lost or stolen checks. All of the traveler's check companies have agents around the world, both in their own name and at associated agencies (usually, but not necessarily, banks), where refunds can be obtained during business hours. Most of them also have 24-hour toll-free telephone lines, and some will even provide emergency funds to tide you over on a Sunday.

Be sure to make a photocopy of the refund instructions that will be given to you by the issuing institution at the time of purchase. To avoid complications should you need to redeem lost checks (and to speed up the replacement process), keep the purchase receipt and an accurate list, by serial number, of the checks that have been spent or cashed. You may want to incorporate this information in an "emergency packet," also including your passport number and date of issue, the numbers of the credit cards you are carrying, and any other bits of information you can't bear to be without. Always keep these records separate from the checks and original records themselves (you may want to give them to a traveling companion to hold).

Although most people understand the desirability of carrying travel funds in the form of traveler's checks as protection against loss or theft, an equally good reason is that US dollar traveler's checks invariably get a better rate of exchange than cash does — usually by at least 1% (although this discrepancy has been known to be substantially higher). The reasons for this are technical, but it is a fact of travel life that should not be ignored.

That 1% won't do you much good, however, if you already have spent it buying your traveler's checks. Several of the major traveler's check companies charge 1% for the privilege of using their checks; others don't — but the issuing institution (i.e., the particular bank at which you purchase them) may itself charge a fee. Thomas Cook checks issued in US currency are free if you make your travel arrangements through its travel agency, for example; and if you purchase traveler's checks at a bank in which you or your company maintain significant accounts (especially commercial accounts of some size), you also might find that the bank will absorb the 1% fee as a courtesy. American Express traveler's checks are available without charge to members of the *Automobile Association of America (AAA)* at some *AAA* offices in the US (the policy varies from state to state).

American Express, Citicorp, Thomas Cook, MasterCard, and Visa all offer traveler's checks, but not at all locations. Call the service numbers listed below to find a participating branch near you. Here is a list of the major companies issuing traveler's checks that are accepted in France and the numbers to call in the event that loss or theft makes replacement necessary:

American Express: To report lost or stolen checks in the US, call 800-221-7282. From France, American Express advises travelers to call the following toll-free number: 19-05-90-86-00, which will connect them to the American Express office in Brighton, England; another (slower) option is to call 801-968-8300, collect; or contact the nearest American Express office.

Bank of America: To report lost or stolen checks in the US, call 800-227-3460. In France, call the following toll-free number: 19-05-90-21-22. Travelers also can call 19-01-6297466, collect, to reach the Bank of America office in London; or 415-624-5400, collect, for their US office.

Citicorp: To report lost or stolen checks in the US, call 800-645-6556. From France and elsewhere worldwide, call 813-623-1709, collect.

MasterCard: To report lost or stolen checks in the US, call 800-223-9920. In France, call the New York office, 212-974-5696, collect, which will direct you to the nearest branch of MasterCard or *Wagons-Lits,* its European agent.

Thomas Cook MasterCard: To report lost or stolen checks in the US, call 800-223-7373. In France, call the US office, 609-987-7300, collect, which will direct you to the nearest branch of Thomas Cook or *Wagons-Lits,* its European agent.

Visa: To report lost or stolen checks in the continental US, call 800-227-6811; 415-574-7111, collect, worldwide. From France and elsewhere in Europe, you also can call this London number collect: 71-937-8091.

CREDIT CARDS: There are two different kinds of credit cards available to consumers in the US, and travelers must decide which kind best serves their needs — although many travelers elect to carry both types. "Convenience" or "charge" or "travel and entertainment" cards — American Express, Diners Club, and Carte Blanche — are widely accepted. They cost the cardholder a basic annual membership fee ($40 to $65 is typical for these three), but put no strict limit on the amount that may be charged on the card in any month. However, the entire amount charged must be paid in full at the end of each billing period (usually a month), so the cardholder is not actually extended any long-term credit.

"Bank cards" also are rarely issued free these days (with the exception of Sears Discover Card), and certain services they provide (check cashing, for example) can carry extra cost. But this category comprises *real* credit cards, in the sense that the cardholder has the privilege of paying a small amount (1/36 is typical) of the total outstanding balance in each billing period. For this privilege, the cardholder is charged a high annual interest rate (currently three to four times the going bank passbook savings rate) on the balance owed. Many banks now charge interest from the purchase date, not from the first billing date (as they used to do); consider this when you are calculating the actual cost of a purchase. In addition, a maximum is set on the total amount the cardholder can charge, which represents the limit of credit the card company is willing to extend. The major bank cards are Visa and MasterCard, with Discover growing rapidly.

Unless you have established a firm credit history, getting any credit card will involve a fairly extensive credit check. To pass, you will need a job (at which you have worked for at least a year), a minimum salary, and a good credit rating.

Note that some establishments you may encounter during the course of your travels may not honor any credit cards and some may not honor all cards, so there is a practical reason to carry more than one. Also keep in mind that some major US credit cards may be issued under a different name in Europe. For instance, in Europe, MasterCard may go under the name Access or Eurocard; Visa often is called Carte Bleue — wherever these equivalents are accepted, MasterCard and Visa may be used. The following is a list of credit cards that enjoy wide domestic and international acceptance:

> *American Express:* Emergency personal check cashing at American Express or representatives' offices (up to $500 in cash for all cardholders: traveler's check limits depend on the type of card: up to $500 for Green cardholders; up to $1,000 for Optima cardholders; up to $4,500 for Gold cardholders; and up to $9,500 for Platinum cardholders); emergency personal check cashing for guests at participating hotels (up to $100); and, for holders of airline tickets, at participating airlines (up to $50). Extended payment plan for cruises, tours, and railway and airline tickets, as well as other prepaid travel arrangements. $100,-000 free travel accident insurance on plane, train, bus, and ship if ticket was charged to card; up to $1 million additional low-cost flight insurance available. Contact *American Express,* PO Box 39, Church St. Station, New York, NY 10008 (phone: 212-477-5700 in New York; 800-528-4800 elsewhere in the US; 801-964-6665 abroad, cardholders may call collect).
>
> *Carte Blanche:* Extended payment plan for air travel (from $2,000 to $5,000, depending on credit line). $350,000 free travel accident insurance on plane, train, and ship if ticket was charged to card, plus $1,250 checked or carry-on baggage insurance and $25,000 rental car insurance. Medical, legal, and travel assistance available worldwide (phone: 800-356-3448 in the US; 214-680-6480, collect, from abroad). Contact *Carte Blanche,* PO Box 17326, Denver, CO 80217 (phone: 800-525-9135 in the US; 303-790-2433 abroad, cardholders may call collect).
>
> *Diners Club:* Emergency personal check cashing for guests at participating hotels and motels (up to $250 per stay). Qualified card members are eligible for extended payment plan. $350,000 free travel accident insurance on plane, train, and ship if ticket was charged to your card, plus $1,250 checked and carry-on baggage insurance and $25,000 rental car insurance. Medical, legal, and travel assistance available worldwide (phone: 800-356-3448 in the US; 214-680-6480,

collect, from abroad). Contact *Diners Club,* PO Box 17326, Denver, CO 80217 (phone: 800-525-9135 throughout the US for customer service; for lost or stolen cards, call one of the following 24-hour service numbers: 800-525-9341 in the US; 303-790-2433, collect, from abroad).

Discover Card: Created by Sears, Roebuck and Co., it provides the holder with cash advances at more than 500 locations in the US, and offers a revolving credit line for purchases at a wide range of service establishments. Other deposit, lending, and investment services also are available. For information, call 800-858-5588 in the US (if you can't reach this number by dialing directly, dial for an operator, who will be able to place the call).

MasterCard: Cash advances are available at participating banks worldwide, and a revolving credit line can be set up for purchases at a wide range of service establishments. Interest charges on unpaid balance and other details are set by issuing bank. Check with your bank for information. MasterCard also offers a 24-hour emergency lost card service; call 800-336-8472 in the US; 314-275-6690, collect, from abroad.

Visa: Cash advances are available at participating banks worldwide, and a revolving credit line can be set up for purchases at a wide range of service establishments provided by issuer. Interest charges on unpaid balance and other details are set by issuing bank. Check with your bank for information. Visa also offers a 24-hour emergency lost card service; call 800-336-8472 in the US; 415-574-7700, collect, from abroad.

In addition to the credit card services discussed above, a number of other details are set by the issuing institutions. For instance, a number of credit cards now offer the added incentive of "bonus" programs. Each time the card is used, the cardholder gathers either points with a monetary equivalent, which can be applied toward the total cost of selected purchases or travel arrangements, or a credit with a specific travel supplier such as frequent flyer mileage bonuses with an airline. (For more information on frequent flyer bonuses, see *Traveling by Plane,* in this section.) When deciding on whether one of these cards provides the best deal, you should compare the potential value of these and other special programs with the variations in interest rates charged on unpaid balances and annual membership fees.

One of the thorniest problems relating to the use of credit cards abroad concerns the rate of exchange at which a purchase is charged. Be aware that the exchange rate in effect on the date that you make a foreign purchase or pay for a foreign service has nothing at all to do with the rate of exchange at which your purchase is billed to you when you get the invoice (sometimes months later) in the US. The amount American Express (and other convenience cards) charges is ultimately a function of the exchange rate in effect on the day your charge is received at an American Express service center, and there is a 1-year limit on the time a shop or hotel can take to forward its charge slips. The rate at which Visa and other bank cards process an item is a function of the rate at which the hotel's or shop's bank processed it.

The principle at work in this credit card–exchange rate roulette is simple, but very hard to predict. You make a purchase at a particular dollar versus local currency exchange rate. If the dollar gets stronger in the time between purchase and billing, your purchase actually costs you less than you anticipated. If the dollar drops in value during the interim, you pay more than you thought you would. There isn't much you can do about these vagaries except to follow one very broad, very clumsy rule of thumb: If the dollar is doing well at the time of purchase, its value increasing against the local currency, use your credit card on the assumption it will still be doing well when billing takes place. If the dollar is doing badly, assume it will continue to do badly and pay with traveler's checks or cash. If you get too badly stuck, the best recourse is to complain, loudly. Be aware, too, that most credit card companies charge an unannounced, un-itemized 1% fee for converting foreign currency charges to US dollars.

No matter what you are using — traveler's checks, credit cards, or cash — plan ahead. That way you won't live through the nightmare of arriving in a small town on a Friday afternoon without any local currency. If you do get caught in this situation, you may have to settle for a poor exchange rate at a hotel or a restaurant. In this case, change just enough dollars to get you through the weekend.

Also, carry your travel funds carefully. You might consider carrying your money (cash and traveler's checks) in more than one place. Never put money in a back pocket or an open purse. Money should be kept in a buttoned front pocket, in a money purse pinned inside your shirt or blouse, or in one of the convenient money belts or leg pouches sold by many travel shops. It may be quaint and old-fashioned, but it's safe.

SENDING MONEY ABROAD: If you have used up your traveler's checks, cashed as many emergency personal checks as your credit card allows, drawn on your cash advance line to the fullest extent, and still need money, have it sent abroad via the *Western Union Telegraph Company.* A friend or relative can go, cash in hand, to any of *Western Union*'s 9,000 offices in the US, where, for a *minimum* charge of $12 (it rises with the amount of the transaction) plus a $22 international bank fee, the funds will be transferred to the *Crédit Commercial de France* (*Western Union*'s correspondent French bank) in major French cities. When the money arrives in France, you will not be notified — you must go to the bank to inquire. The transfer will take anywhere from 2 to 5 business days. The funds will be turned over in local currency (French francs) based on the rate of exchange in effect on the day of receipt. For a higher fee, the US party to this transaction may use his or her MasterCard or Visa card to send up to $2,000 by phone by dialing *Western Union*'s toll-free number (800-325-4176) anywhere in the US.

American Express offers a similar service in France called "Moneygram," completing money transfers in as little as 10 minutes. The sender — who must be an American Express cardholder — must go to an American Express office in the US and can use cash, a personal check, money order, or an American Express Optima, Gold, or Platinum card for the transfer. Optima cardholders also can arrange for this transfer over the phone. The minimum transfer charge is $25, which rises with the amount of the transaction; the sender can forward funds of up to $10,000 (credit card users are limited to the amount of pre-established credit line). To collect at the other end the receiver must go to an American Express office in France (there are 12 in France, 3 in Paris alone) and present a passport as proof of identification. For further information on this service, call 800-543-4080.

If you are literally down to your last centime, the nearest US consulate (see *Medical and Legal Aid and Consular Services*) will let you call home to set these matters in motion.

Accommodations

From elegant, centuries-old châteaux to modern, functional high-rises and modest, inexpensive inns, it's easy to be comfortable and well cared for on almost any budget in France. Paris and the Riviera are admittedly full of deluxe establishments providing expensive services to people with money to burn, but more affordable alternatives always have been available, particularly in the countryside.

On the whole, deluxe and first class accommodations in France, especially in the large metropolitan centers (Paris and Lyons, for instance), are somewhat more expensive than the same types of accommodations in the US (see *Calculating Costs,* in this section). When the dollar is strong, such top-of-the-line establishments are within the range of a great number of travelers who otherwise are not able to afford them. But lately, the generally unfavorable rate of exchange has rendered princely accommodations very pricey. Once upon a time, such things as the superiority of New World plumbing made many of the numerous less expensive alternatives unacceptable for North Americans. Today, the gap has closed considerably, and the majority of hostelries catering to the tourist trade are likely to be at least adequate in their basic facilities. When shopping around, also keep in mind that although prices quoted for all accommodations in France must include the minimum 11% Value Added Tax (VAT), an additional service charge, usually of 10%, 12½%, or 15%, often is added to hotel and guesthouse bills.

Our accommodations choices are included in the *Best in Town* sections of THE CITIES and in the *Checking In* sections of each tour route in DIRECTIONS. They have been selected for a variety of travel budgets, but the lists are not comprehensive; with some diligent searching, before you leave and en route, you can turn up an equal number of "special places" that are uniquely yours.

Also consult the brochures and booklets cited in the descriptions below, most of which are available free from the US offices of the French Government Tourist Office (for addresses, see *Tourist Information,* in this section). Other publications can be purchased from the travel bookstores listed in *Books and Magazines,* also in this section.

HOTELS AND INNS: Hotels may be large or small, part of a chain or independent, new and of the "international standard" type or well established and traditional. There are built-for-the-purposes premises and converted stately homes and villas, resort hotels offering plenty of opportunities for recreation, and smaller tourist hotels offering virtually none.

The annual *Guide des Hôtels de France,* issued by the French ministry in charge of tourism, doesn't list all the hotels in the country, but it does list all those (more than 18,000) that are considered tourist hotels and that are officially graded according to the government's star system of classification. The highest rating is four stars plus L, indicating, to use the official definition, a luxury hotel. Four stars means a top hotel; three stars a very comfortable hotel; two stars, a good average hotel; and one star or *HRT* (for *Hôtels Rattachés Tourisme;* literally, hotels linked to tourism), a plain but fairly comfortable hotel. The guide, which comes out in early spring, is too extensive to be distributed to the general public, but regional versions with the same information are available by writing to the French Government Tourist Office nearest you and specifying the area of the country in which you are interested (for instance, *Paris–Ile-de-France* and *Riviera–Côte d'Azur* are two of the titles). The listing for each hotel includes its address and telephone number, number of rooms, amenities, star category, and minimum and maximum room prices; though the latter inevitably are somewhat out of date by the time of publication, they include service charges and applicable taxes and certainly serve as a valid estimate. The French Government Tourist Office also distributes a list of US representatives handling reservations for French hotels, as well as a special list of selected Paris hotels, with their ratings and the names of the US representatives.

Even without any of the above guides in hand, it is not difficult for visitors in France to figure out where a particular hotel fits in the scheme of things. A dark blue, octagonal "Commissariat Général au Tourisme" sign on the front of any hotel that has been classified clearly reveals the number of stars attained. Inside, a detailed rendering of prices appears by law near the reception desk. A good many hotels, in fact, actually display minimum and maximum prices on the front door, where they are easily legible from the street. The posted prices include service and, except in a few cases, all taxes, so that receiving the bill at the end of a stay is rarely a cause for shock. The prices also usually are for double rooms (since in France, as elsewhere, there are more double than single rooms), and the price of a double usually holds whether it's occupied by one or two people. The price of breakfast — which may be obligatory or optional — also must be posted by the reception desk.

Note that while French hotels do not observe well-defined high and low seasons as far as room rates are concerned, visitors can expect to pay a premium for travel during the peak summer months and to encounter more advantageous terms the rest of the year. This is especially true along the Riviera and in other coastal resorts, where off-season rates can be up to 30% lower than midsummer rates; elsewhere, less significant reductions may be found off-season. Special offers — such as a discount for stays of 3 nights or longer (particularly over weekends, when business travelers traditionally go home) — also are more common during the off-season, though they may be found at any time of year. For Paris hotels dependent on convention and trade show business, for instance, July and August are the slack months, when rates are reduced to help fill the house.

Hotels earn their stars according to a variety of criteria, among them the percentage of rooms with private bathrooms. All rooms in a four-star L hotel and 90% of the rooms in a four-star hotel must have them; the required proportion drops to 30% in a two-star; and there is no requirement for one-star hotels. There may be, therefore, a number of room types in any given hotel, especially in two- and three-star establishments, where the most expensive rooms will have private bathrooms containing a tub or a shower (usually slightly less expensive) and the least expensive rooms will have only a *cabinet de toilette* (that is, a washbasin with hot and cold water and a bidet) or, simply, a washbasin. (Guests in rooms with a *cabinet de toilette* or less have access to the public bathroom in the hall.) Central heating is universal in classified tourist hotels (though it may not always be adequate by American standards), and the type of breakfast provided is nearly universal: continental, which consists of coffee, tea, or hot chocolate with bread, rolls, or croissants, butter, and jam. Also nearly universal is the bolster pillow found on a French bed; for those who prefer it, the more familiar kind of pillow usually is stashed in the closet (if not, ask for one).

As in other countries, a great many hotels in France are members of chains or hotel associations. Among the well-known, international names with properties in France, particularly in the capital, are the following:

Best Western: Has 135 properties in France. Call 800-528-1234.
Hilton International: Has 3 properties in France. Call 800-445-8667.
Holiday Inn: Has 12 properties in France. Call 800-465-4329.
Inter-Continental: Has 3 properties in France. Call 800-327-0200.
Marriott: Has 1 property in France (in Paris). Call 800-228-9290.
Minotels Europe: Has 141 properties in France. Call 800-336-4668.
Trusthouse Forte: Has 4 properties in France. Call 800-225-5843.

Among the larger French chains — whose names may be less familiar but many of whom nevertheless have a US office that will provide information and take reservations — are the *Pullman International* group of approximately 90 hotels subdivided into *Pullman* four-star hotels, the *Altéa* business hotels (still considered first class, but located in secondary cities), the *Arcade* two-star hotels, and the *Primo* budget hotels. For information and reservations, contact *Pullman International* (c/o *Mondotels,* 1500 Broadway, New York, NY 10036; phone: 800-223-9862 or 212-719-9363) or *Utell International* (10606 Burt Circle, Omaha, NE 68114; phone: 800-44-UTELL).

Other French hotel chains include *Ibis* and *Novotel*, which together have almost 500 properties throughout France, and *Sofitel,* with about 30 properties in France. All three are represented by *Resinter Reservations* (2 Overhill Rd., Scarsdale, NY 10583; phone:

800-221-4542). Another well-established French hotel group is *Minotels Accueil* (phone: 1-45-84-58-00), with 168 member establishments in France.

Relais & Châteaux – A very special case among French hotel associations is one that, though native to France, has grown to include establishments in many other countries. Three groups of members — *Relais de Campagne, Châteaux-Hôtels,* and *Relais Gourmands* — belong to the *Relais & Châteaux* association, including approximately 150 establishments throughout France.

The first two groups are of particular interest to travelers who wish lodgings reflecting the ambience, style, and, frequently, the history of the places they are visiting. Some of the properties actually are ancient castles (several dating back to the 13th century) that have been converted into hotels. Others are old inns (*relais* means a posthouse or inn), manor houses, and even converted mills, convents, and monasteries. A few well-known city establishments are included, such as the *Crillon* and the *Residence du Bois* in Paris, but most are in quiet surroundings in the countryside, and frequently are graced with parklands, ponds, and flowering gardens.

For all their charm, members of the *Relais & Châteaux* group are not necessarily prohibitively expensive. At the rate of exchange at the time of this writing, the least expensive double room cost $150 per night — although prices ranged anywhere up to $500 for the most elegant establishments. (Prices include service and tax; some include breakfast and dinner, but if meals are not included they can add to the cost considerably, since all *Relais & Châteaux* properties have good — but expensive — restaurants.) Accommodations and service from one *relais* or château to another can range from simple but comfortable to elegantly deluxe (they are rated three-star, four-star, and four-star L by the government, and the association has its own color-coded rating system as well), but they all maintain very high standards in order to retain their memberships, as they are reviewed annually.

The third group of members, *Relais Gourmands,* is composed of exceptionally fine restaurants. These establishments also may have rooms for rent, but the establishments are *not* rated on the basis of their accommodations, so they may not match (or even come close to) the standards of room quality maintained by the others. An illustrated catalogue of all the *Relais & Châteaux* properties is published annually and is available for $5 from *Relais & Châteaux* (2200 Lazy Hollow, Suite 152D, Houston, TX 77063) or from *David B. Mitchell & Company* (200 Madison Ave., New York, NY 10016; phone: 212-696-1323 or 800-372-1323); reservations can be made through these companies or through a travel agent.

Relais du Silence, Logis, Auberges, Gîtes – Several other French hotel associations merit consideration. One, *Relais du Silence,* is similar to the *Relais & Châteaux* group but on a more modest scale. Hotels in this group, too, are mainly former manor houses, rustic wayside inns, châteaux, and other characteristic properties in picturesque country settings or at the edges of small, quiet villages (as the name implies, a premium is placed on peaceful surroundings). Most of the *Relais du Silence* — there are more than 100 in France — correspond to two- and three-star hotels in the government classification system, though a few four-star establishments also are included, and $40 to $80 will buy a good double room at most — at least three-quarters — of them. The annual *Relais du Silence* booklet, also illustrated, is available from the French Government Tourist Office.

Another group well worth knowing about is the *Fédération Nationale des Logis et Auberges de France,* whose approximately 5,000 members make it by far the largest in the country. The very great majority are *logis* (literally, lodging, dwelling, or home), which are small — anywhere from 10 to 20 rooms is the average — family-run hotels at the one-star level scattered in towns and villages throughout the countryside. The remainder are *auberges* (inns), establishments that usually are too simple to be classified in the government's star system and always are found in rural locations (they used to be known as *auberges rurales*). Each group adheres to its own quality charter, which places great store in friendly service, stresses home cooking with regional specialties on the menu, and regulates such things as the amenities provided (all rooms in both the *logis* and *auberges* have a sink with hot and cold running water). Room prices, single or double, usually are not more than $30 a night and can be a good deal less. The annual guide *Logis et Auberges de France* (in French), listing 5,000 hotels and inns, is available from the *Fédération Nationale des Logis et Auberges de France* in France, can be ordered from the *Tattered Cover* (2955 East 1st Ave., Denver, CO 80206 (phone: 800-833-9327 or 303-322-7727) for $11.95 plus shipping and handling, and may be found in some travel bookstores.

Finally, a last organization, the *Fédération Nationale des Gîtes Ruraux de France,* may be of interest. This is an association of the owners of several types of holiday accommodations, the majority of which are grouped under the heading *Gîte de France* (literally, lodging or stopping place) and offer self-catering country rentals by the week or longer. (These are discussed in "Apartments, Houses, Cottages" below.)

Hotels in Monaco – Information on hotels in the Principality of Monaco is available from *SBM* (450 Park Ave., New York, NY 10022; phone: 212-688-9890) or the Monaco Government Tourist and Convention Bureau (845 Third Ave., New York, NY 10022; phone: 212-759-5227). As in France, levels of comfort and price range from the prime four-star deluxe category down to the very economical one-star. The top hotels, including such diverse specimens as the opulent 19th-century landmark *Hôtel de Paris* and the gleaming modern sprawl of *Loews,* are resort hotels in the worldly social center of Monte Carlo, on or off the beach, but usually complete with a swimming pool and at least one of the country's most gala restaurants. Budget accommodations tend to cluster not far away in the vicinity of the train station. Monaco's hoteliers frequently offer reduced rates to travelers who stay a specified length of time during the off-season.

BED AND BREAKFAST AND OTHER ACCOMMODATIONS: Across the English Channel, where they are a staple of the low-cost lodging scene, bed and breakfast establishments are found wherever there are extra rooms to let in a private home and a host or hostess willing to attend to the details of hospitality. They are not yet so commonplace in France or on the rest of the Continent, but they do exist, and not only in rural locations.

A smaller French group than those discussed above offers overnight accommodations under the heading *Gîte de France–Chambre d'Hôte*. The *gîte chambre d'hôte,* actually a room in a private house or on a farm, is the nearest French equivalent to the bed and breakfast establishments of Great Britain. At latest count, there were about 6,000 of them; many are in the countryside. The rooms provided are very modest, but their owners — like the owners of other types of *gîtes* — are governed by a charter spelling out minimum standards of comfort.

A *gîte chambre d'hôte,* or bed and breakfast establishment (commonly known as a B&B), provides precisely what the name implies. Though any hotel or inn does the same, it is unusual for a bed and breakfast establishment to offer the extra services found in the other hostelries, and consequently the bed and breakfast route often is the least expensive way to go.

Beyond these two fundamentals, nothing else is predictable about going the bed and breakfast route. The bed may be in an extra room in a family home, in an apartment with a separate entrance, or in a free-standing cottage elsewhere on the host's property. You may have a patio, garden, or pool at your door or only the bare necessities; in European B&Bs, private baths are the exception rather than the rule. The breakfast probably will be a version of the standard continental breakfast: fruit plus juice, croissant, toast, roll, or homemade bread, with jam or marmalade, and coffee or tea. Although, particularly in rural areas, the breakfast may be a heartier one, and as often as not (language barrier aside), served along with some helpful tips on what to see and do and a bit of family history to add to the local lore. Occasionally a kitchenette will be included, in which case, you may be furnished with the makings of a breakfast you'll have to prepare for yourself.

Bed and breakfast establishments range from private homes and lovely mansions to small inns and guesthouses; prices average from $15 to $35 per person per night, breakfast included — with establishments offering luxurious surroundings running somewhat higher. Despite their name, some B&Bs offer an evening meal as well — by prior arrangement and at extra cost, naturally.

The best rule of thumb is to find out as much as you can before you book to avoid disappointment. The French Government Tourist Office distributes a *Gîtes Ruraux de France* brochure explaining the overall system, and a selection of about 200 *gîtes chambres d'hôte* is included in the *French Farm and Village Holiday Guide* (see below).

Regional and departmental guides to *gîtes* can be obtained in France from the *Fédération Nationale des Gîtes Ruraux de France* (35 Rue Godot-de-Mauroy, Paris 75009; phone: 1-47-42-25-43). This guide also includes two other types of *gîtes* — *gîtes camping-caravaning à la ferme* (campsites) and *gîtes d'étape* (stopovers for back-packers, cyclists, and horseback riders). With the appropriate guide in tow, those traveling by car and with a modicum of French can book rooms from *gîte* to *gîte* as they drive through France, deciding early in the morning or as late as lunch where they want to stay and calling ahead.

In addition to consulting the above-mentioned organizations and publications, travelers interested in B&B accommodations should contact *The French Experience* (370 Lexington Ave., New York, NY 10017; phone: 212-986-1115), which represents the *Café Couette* bed and breakfast association of France. These accommodations are available throughout France, and rates begin at about $24 per person per night; with private bath, at $37 per person per night. This company also handles rental properties in France (see below).

Another useful source of information on bed and breakfast establishments overseas is the *Bed & Breakfast Reservations Services Worldwide, Inc.* (a trade association), which provides a listing of its members for $3. To order the most recent edition, contact them at PO Box 39000, Washington, DC 20016 (phone: 800-842-1486).

Farmhouses – In the country, city people rediscover the sounds of songbirds and the smell of grass. Suburbanites get the chance to poke around an area where the nearest neighbor lives miles away. Parents can say to their children, "No, milk does not originate in a cardboard carton," and prove it. Youngsters can meet people who live differently, think differently, and have different values. But even if there were no lessons to be learned, a stay at a farm would be a decidedly pleasant way to pass some time, so it's no wonder that throughout France there are numerous farms which welcome guests.

Farm families often put up guests on a bed-and-breakfast basis — for a night or two or by the week, with weekly half-board plans available. Two good sources of information on farm stays (as well as rentals) are the *Fédération Nationale des Gîtes Ruraux de France* and *French Farm and Village Holiday Guide* (see below). If the peace and quiet and the coziness of the welcome are appealing, a farmhouse can be an ideal base from which to explore a region by car or by foot and an especially good idea for those traveling with children.

Apartments, Houses, Cottages – Another alternative to hotels for the visitor content to stay in one spot for a week or more is to rent a house or an apartment (usually called a "flat" overseas). Known to Europeans as a "holiday let" or a "self-catering holiday," a vacation in a furnished rental has both the advantages and disadvantages of living "at home" abroad. It certainly is less expensive than staying in a first class hotel for the same period of time, although very luxurious and expensive rentals are available, too. It has the comforts of home, including a kitchen, which can mean savings on food costs. Furthermore, it gives a sense of the country that a large hotel often cannot. On the other hand, a certain amount of housework is involved because if you don't eat out, you have to cook, and though some holiday lets (especially the luxury ones) come with a cleaning person, most don't. (Although if the rental doesn't include domestic help, arrangements often can be made with a nearby service.)

For those who wish to arrange a rental themselves, write or call the French Government Tourist Office (for locations in the US, see *Tourist Information,* in this section), or contact the *Fédération Nationale des Agents Immobiliers* (129 Rue du Faubourg-St.-Honoré, Paris 75001) for a list of real estate agencies handling seasonal rentals throughout France, including many seaside resorts.

The *Fédération Nationale des Gîtes Ruraux de France,* an association of, among others, the owners of 35,000 *Gîtes de France* — country cottages, farmhouses, and apartments for rent by the week or longer — is a source of strictly rural rentals. Selected *gîtes* are listed in the *French Farm and Village Holiday Guide,* available from travel bookstores for $12.95. The listings are arranged *département* by *département* (very roughly, county by county) throughout France, and each entry is accompanied by a black-and-white photo, details of the accommodations, and the price. For more comprehensive listings of the *gîtes* in any particular *département,* however, it is necessary to write to the appropriate *relais départemental* (departmental headquarters) of the federation, each of which publishes a yearly guide (some free, some for a small fee) to the properties in its area. All of the *relais départemental* addresses are in the *Gîtes Ruraux de France* brochure available from the French Government Tourist Office. Once a *gîte* is chosen, the prospective renter books it with the proprietor directly or, where it exists, through a departmental booking service.

Many tour operators regularly include a few rental packages among their more conventional offerings; these generally are available through a travel agent. In addition, certain companies in the US specialize in rentals of apartments, houses, cottages, and other properties. They handle the booking and confirmation paperwork, generally for a fee included in the rental price, and can be expected to provide more information about the properties they handle than that which might ordinarily be gleaned from a listing in an accommodations guide. Among such agencies that represent properties in France are the following:

At Home Abroad: Mostly villas along the Riviera, in the Dordogne region, and in the hill towns of Provence, as well as apartments and châteaux in other areas. The minimum rental period usually is 2 weeks or 1 month. Photographs of properties and a newsletter are available for a $50 registration fee. 405 E. 56th St., Apt. 6H, New York, NY 10022 (phone: 212-421-9165).

B & D De Vogue Travel Services (Paris Accueil/Paris Sejour Reservations): Apartment rentals in Paris are the specialty; minimum rental period is 7 nights, with weekly maid service included. PO Box 4712, New Windsor, NY 12550 (phone: 914-565-6951); or *Paris Séjour Réservations,* 90 Av. des Champs Elysées, Paris 75008 (phone: 1-42-56-30-00).

Blake's Vacations: Rents country homes throughout inland France. 49-39 Dempster St., Skokie, IL 60077 (phone: 800-628-8118)

Castles, Cottages, and Flats: The name says it all. French properties are located in Brittany and on the Riviera. PO Box 261, Westwood, MA 02090 (phone: 617-329-4680).

Chez Vous: Offers country homes and villas in the Dordogne, Lot, and Garonne river valleys. 220 Redwood Highway, Suite 129E, Mill Valley, CA 94941 (phone: 415-331-2535).

Coast to Coast Resorts: Handles country homes and villas in the Aquitaine, Brittany, the Dordogne, and Normandy. 860 Solar Building, 1000 16th St. NW, Washington, DC 20036 (phone: 800-368-5721 or 202-293-8000).

Eastone Overseas Accommodations: Handles apartments, castles, and villas throughout France. 198 Southampton Dr., Jupiter, FL 33458 (phone: 407-575-6991/2) or 20000 Horizon Way, Suite 110, Mount Laurel, NJ 08054 (phone: 609-722-1010).

Europa-Let, Inc.: Offers apartments, cottages, and villas in Paris, on the Riviera, and in southwest France. PO Box 3537, Ashland, OR 97520 (phone: 800-462-4486 or 503-482-5806).

The French Experience: Rents apartments throughout France. 370 Lexington Ave., New York, NY 10017 (phone: 212-986-1115).

Hideaways International: Rents private homes and villas throughout France. 15 Goldsmith St., PO Box 1270, Littleton, MA 01460 (phone: 800-843-4433 or 508-486-8955).

Home Tours International: Handles apartments in Paris. 1170 Broadway, New York, 10001 (phone: 800-367-4668 or 212-689-0851).

Rent A Vacation Everywhere (RAVE): Moderate to luxurious villas and apartments throughout Europe, but particularly in France and Italy. Minimum rental is 1 week. 328 Main St. E., Suite 526, Rochester, NY 14604 (phone: 716-454-6440).

Vacances en Campagne: Over 400 properties in France. Minimum rental period is 2 weeks in July and August, 1 week the rest of the year. A catalogue is available for $5. PO Box 297, Falls Village, CT 06031 (phone: 203-824-5155 in Connecticut; 800-533-5405 elsewhere).

VHR Worldwide: Rents apartments, country homes, and villas throughout France. 235 Kensington Ave., Norwood, NJ 07648 (phone: 201-767-9393, locally; 800-NEED-A-VILLA elsewhere in the US).

Villas International (formerly *Interchange*): Some 5,000 rentals include apartments in Paris; chalets in the Alps; country lodgings in Brittany, Burgundy, the Dordogne, the Loire Valley, and Provence; and villas and apartments on the Atlantic Coast and the Riviera. The minimum rental is 1 week. 71 W. 23rd St., New York, NY 10010 (phone: 212-929-7585 in New York State; 800-221-2260 elsewhere in the US).

And for further information, including a general discussion of all forms of vacation rentals, evaluating costs, and information on rental opportunities in France, see *A Traveler's Guide to Vacation Rentals in Europe.* Available in general bookstores, it also can be ordered from Penguin USA (120 Woodbine St., Bergenfield, NJ 07621; phone: 800-331-4624 and ask for cash sales) for $11.95 plus $2 for postage and handling.

HOME EXCHANGES: Still another alternative for travelers who are content to stay in one place during their vacation is a home exchange: The Smith family from Chicago moves into the home of the Chabrol family in Paris, while the Chabrols enjoy a stay in the Smiths' home. The home exchange is an exceptionally inexpensive way to ensure comfortable, reasonable living quarters with amenities that no hotel possibly could offer; often the trade includes a car. Moreover, it allows you to live in a new community in a way that few tourists ever do: For a little while, at least, you will become something of a local resident.

Several companies publish directories of individuals and families willing to trade homes with others for a specific period of time. In some cases, you must be willing to list your own home in the directory; in others, you can subscribe without appearing in it. Most listings are for straight exchanges only, but each of the directories also has a number of listings placed by people interested in either exchanging or renting (for instance, if they own a second home). Other types of arrangements include exchanges of hospitality while owners are in residence, or youth exchanges, where your teenager is put up as a guest in return for your putting up their teenager at a later date. A few

house-sitting opportunities also are available. In most cases, arrangements for the
actual exchange take place directly between the you and the foreign host. There is no
guarantee that you will find a listing in the area in which you are interested, but each
of the organizations given below includes French homes among its hundreds or even
thousands of foreign listings.

Home Base Holidays: For $42 a year, subscribers receive four listings, with an
option to list in all four. 7 Park Ave., London N13 5PG (phone: 81-886-8752).

International Home Exchange Service/Intervac US: The $35 fee includes copies
of the three directories published yearly and an option to list your home in one
of them; a black-and-white photo may be included with the listing for an
additional $8.50. A 10% discount is given to travelers over 65. Box 190070, San
Francisco, CA 94119 (phone: 415-435-3497).

InterService Home Exchange: An affiliate of *Intervac International,* this service
publishes three directories annually that include more than 7,000 exchanges in
over 30 countries worldwide. For $35, interested home-swappers are listed in
and receive a copy of the February, March, and May directories; a black-and-
white photo of your home may be included with the listing for an additional $10.
Box 387, Glen Echo, MD 20812 (phone: 301-229-7567).

Loan-A-Home: Specializes in long-term (4 months or more, excluding July and
August) housing arrangements worldwide for students and professors, businesspeople, and retirees, although its two annual directories (with supplements)
carry a small listing of short-term rentals and/or exchanges. $35 for one direc-
tory and one supplement; $45 for a copy of two directories and two supplements.
2 Park La., Apt. 6E, Mt. Vernon, NY 10552 (phone: 914-664-7640).

Vacation Exchange Club: Some 6,000 listings, including several hundred in
France. For $24.70 a year, the subscriber receives two directories — one in late
winter and one in the spring — and is listed in one of them. For $16, subscribers
receive both directories but no listing. 12006 111th Ave., Suite 12, Youngtown,
AZ 85363 (phone: 602-972-2186).

World Wide Exchange: The $45 annual membership fee includes one listing (for
house, yacht, or motorhome) and three guides. 1344 Pacific Ave., Suite 103,
Santa Cruz, CA 95060 (phone: 408-476-4206).

Worldwide Home Exchange Club: Handles over 1,000 listings a year worldwide.
For $20 a year, you will receive two listings yearly, as well as supplements. 45
Hans Place, London SW1X OJZ, England (phone: 71-589-6055).

Home Exchange International (HEI), with offices in New York, Los Angeles, London, Paris, and Milan, functions in a different manner in that it publishes no directory
and shepherds the exchange process most of the way. Interested parties supply *HEI*
with photographs of themselves and their homes, information on the type of home they
want and where, and a registration fee of $50. The company then works with its other
offices to propose a few possibilities, and only when a match is made do the parties
exchange names, addresses, and phone numbers. For this service, *HEI* charges a
closing fee, which ranges from $150 to $450 for domestic or international switches from
2 weeks to 3 months in duration, and from $275 to $525 for switches longer than 3
months. Contact *Home Exchange International,* 185 Park Row, PO Box 878, New
York, NY 10038-0272 (phone: 212-349-5340), or 22458 Ventura Blvd., Woodland
Hills, CA 91364 (phone: 818-992-8990).

HOME STAYS: France does not offer a formal "meet the French" program, but those
attracted by the idea of actually staying in a private home as the guest of a foreign family
should check with the United States Servas Committee, which maintains a list of hosts
throughout the world willing to throw open their doors to foreigners, entirely free of
charge. The aim of this nonprofit cultural program is to promote international under-

standing and peace, and every effort is made to discourage freeloaders. Servas will send you an application form and the name of the nearest of some 200 interviewers around the US for you to contact. After the interview, if you're approved, you'll receive documentation certifying you as a Servas traveler. There is a membership fee of $45 for an individual and there also is a deposit of $15 to receive the host list, refunded on its return. The list gives the name, address, age, occupation, and other particulars of each host, including languages spoken. From then on, it is up to you to write them directly, and Servas makes no guarantee that you will be accommodated. If you are, you'll normally stay 2 nights.

Servas stresses that you should choose only people you really want to meet and that for this brief period you should be interested mainly in your hosts, not in sightseeing. It also suggests that one way to show your appreciation once you've returned home is to become a host yourself. The minimum age of a Servas traveler is 18 (however, children under 18 may accompany their parents), and though quite a few are young people who have just finished college, there are travelers (and hosts) in all age ranges and occupations. Contact Servas at 11 John St., Room 706, New York, NY 10038 (phone: 212-267-0252).

Another organization offering home stays with French families is *Friends in France*. Travelers can choose from over 40 homes, ranging from simple country homes to stately châteaux. Prices range from about $40 to $125 per night for a double room, including a continental breakfast. In this sense these resemble bed and breakfast accommodations rather than the traditional home stay arrangement, however, the host families are from a diverse spectrum of backgrounds and occupations, and their participation in the program generally is indicative of an interest in people and an eagerness to share their own little corner of France with their visitors. Through a detailed questionnaire, plus follow-up contact, *Friends in France* helps select the most suitable home or homes for your stay. There is a minimum stay of 3 nights and a maximum of 2 weeks with any one family; you can visit one or several homes during the course of your stay. About half the host families have an English-speaking member and the visitor's knowledge of French is taken into account when selecting the host family. A free brochure describing the program and a brochure for $5 describing the participating properties are available from *Friends in France* (PO Box 1044, Rocky Hill, CT 06067; phone: 203-563-0195).

You also might be interested in a publication called *International Meet-the-People Directory*, published by the *International Vistor Information Service*. It lists several agencies in a number of foreign countries that arrange home visits for Americans, either for dinner or overnight stays. To order a copy, send $4.95 to the *International Visitor Information Service*, 733 15th St. NW, Suite 300, Washington DC 20005 (phone: 202-783-6540)

RESERVATIONS: To the extent that you are able to settle on a precise itinerary beforehand, it is best to make advance reservations for accommodations in any major French city or resort area, even if you are traveling during the off-season. To be sure of finding space in the hotel of your choice, several months before arrival is not too soon to make the booking. Hotel rooms in the larger provincial cities also should be reserved in advance year-round. Because many of them also are important meeting centers, even off-season travelers may find hotel space scarce and *complet* (full) signs all over town if a large convention is being hosted. Also keep in mind that larger hotels are the ones most frequently booked as 2- and 3-day stopover centers for thousands of tour groups. For instance, February, June, and September are the busiest months in Paris due to the simultaneous presence of business and convention travelers and tourists.

During the peak travel season — May to October — visitors should expect to pay a premium for traveling in Europe. However, not even a willingness to pay for top accommodations will guarantee a room if you don't have reservations. It is wise to make reservations as far in advance as possible for popular tourist areas throughout France, including Monaco, as well as for hotel, farm, and other accommodations near major summer destinations like St.-Tropez and Côte d'Azur, where the number of rooms and limited facilities, not the price, is likely to be the qualifying factor. This advice becomes particularly compelling during July and August, when the French themselves take to the road, packing vacation spots and coastal resorts from Normandy to the Côte d'Azur. And even though July and August (and December) are traditionally the slowest months of the year for Paris hotels, advance reservations still are highly recommended.

The simplest way to make a reservation is to leave it all to a travel agent, who will provide this service at no charge if the hotel or guesthouse in question pays agents a commission. The regional hotel guides distributed by the French Government Tourist Office use a symbol to show which establishments pay such a commission — the larger and more expensive ones invariably do, and more and more budget hotels are beginning to follow suit. If the one selected doesn't, the travel agent may charge a fee to cover costs or you may have to make the reservation yourself.

Reserving a room yourself is not difficult if you intend to stay mainly in hotels that are members of chains or associations, whether French ones with US representatives or American ones with hotels overseas. Most international hotel chains list their toll-free (800) reservation numbers in the white pages of the telephone directory, and any hotel in a chain can secure reservations for you at sister facilities. Naturally, the more links in the chain, the more likely that an entire stay can be booked with a minimum number of letters or phone calls to one central reservations system. If booking with primarily French establishments, either a travel agent or the French and Monaco government tourist offices will be able to tell you who in the US represents the chain or a particular hotel. (The US phone numbers of some of these chains and associations operating in France are given in the discussion of hotels above.)

Hotels that are not represented in the US will have to be contacted directly. All the hotel entries in the *Best in Town* sections of THE CITIES chapters include phone numbers for reservations; where they exist, phone numbers also are included in the *Best en Route* sections of DIRECTIONS. If you choose to write rather than telephone, it's a good idea to enclose at least two International Reply Coupons (sold at post offices and banks) to facilitate a response, and to leave *plenty* of time for the answer. Give full details of your requirements and several alternate dates, if possible. You will probably be asked to send a deposit for at least 1 night's lodging, payable by check or credit card; in return, be sure to get written confirmation of your reservation and a receipt for any deposit. (For a sample reservation letter in French, see *Useful Words and Phrases,* in this section.)

Nevertheless, if the hotel you want to visit has no rooms available on your chosen dates, take heart. The advice to make reservations early always is woven into every travel article; making a *late* reservation may be almost as good advice. It's not at all unusual for hotel rooms, totally unavailable as far as 6 months ahead, suddenly to become available a week to a day before your arrival. Cancellations tend to occur closer to, rather than farther from, a designated date. One possible strategy is to make reservations at another hotel so you won't be left high and dry, find out what the cancellation restrictions are, and check back with your first choice closer to your date of arrival. It also is true that hotels that report SRO status to travel agents may remarkably discover a room if you call (FAX is even better) directly close to your proposed arrival date.

There also is reason to believe that hotels increasingly are offering one rate to travelers working through travel agents and less expensive rates to vacationers and commercial clients who book directly. Even if you do use a travel agent, it sounds like a prudent course to double check hotel rates if saving money is one of your prime travel concerns.

Reservation Services in France – Though not all travelers would face the prospect of arriving in a strange city without a reservation with equal sangfroid, in France there are services that help book empty rooms for those who risk it. To begin with, the hotel reservation board at Charles de Gaulle Airport's terminal building No. 1 provides information on more than 300 Paris hotels, showing vacancies in green (or a full house in red) at the push of a button; using the phone provided, a confirmed reservation can be made on the spot.

In addition, the tourist offices of 35 French cities (and in several of the larger airports and railway stations as well) provide an *Accueil de France* service that will reserve a room in the area for a small fee. In Paris, the service is available at the main Office de Tourisme de Paris (127 Av. des Champs-Elysées; for information, call 47-23-61-72), open daily year-round, and at branch offices in the Gare d'Austerlitz, Gare de l'Est, Gare de Lyon, and Gare du Nord train stations.

The same system also can be used by those who prefer to give full rein to their wanderlust unhampered by hotel reservations made too far in advance but who still appreciate the security of knowing where they will spend the next night. Any *Accueil de France* service can book a room ahead for you, provided the area you're going to also has an *Accueil* service. The reservation is made via telex to the *Accueil* office in the destination city; you pay a service charge plus a deposit (usually half of 1 night's stay) and receive in return a check for this amount to present to the hotel, where the sum will be deducted from your bill. The annually revised *Michelin Red Guide to France* ($17.95) lists the addresses of all the *Accueil* offices in the system. To order, contact Michelin Guides and Maps (PO Box 3305, Spartanburg, SC 29304-3305; phone: 803-599-0850).

OVERBOOKING: Although the problem is not unique to France, the worldwide travel boom has brought with it some abuses that are pretty much standard operating procedure in any industry facing a demand that frequently outstrips the supply. Anticipating a certain percentage of no-shows, hotels routinely overbook rooms. When cancellations don't occur and everybody with a confirmed reservation arrives as promised, it's not impossible to find yourself with a valid reservation for which no room exists.

There's no sure way to avoid all the pitfalls of overbooking, but you can minimize the risks. Always carry evidence of your confirmed reservation. This should be a direct communication from the hotel — to you or your travel agent — and should specify the exact dates and duration of your accommodations and the price. The weakest form of confirmation is the voucher slip a travel agent routinely issues, since it carries no official indication that the hotel itself has verified your reservation.

Even better is the increasing opportunity to guarantee hotel reservations by giving the hotel (or its reservation system) your credit card number and agreeing that the hotel is authorized to charge you for that room no matter what. It's still possible to cancel if you do so before 6 PM of the day of your arrival (before 4 PM in some areas), but when you do cancel under this arrangement, make sure you get a cancellation number to protect you from being billed erroneously.

If all these precautions fail and you are left standing at the reservation desk with a reservation the hotel clerk won't honor, you have a last resort: Complain as long and as loudly as necessary to get satisfaction! The person who makes the most noise usually gets the last room in the house. It might as well be you.

What if you can't get reservations in the first place? This is a problem that often confronts businesspeople who can't plan months ahead. The word from savvy travelers is that a bit of currency (perhaps attached discreetly to a business card) often increases your chances with recalcitrant desk clerks. There are less venal ways of improving your odds, however. If you are traveling on business, ask an associate at your destination to make reservations for you.

There is a good reason to do this above and beyond the very real point that a resident has the broadest knowledge of local hotels. Often a hotel will appear sold out on its computer when in fact a few rooms are available. The proliferation of computerized reservations has made it unwise for a hotel to indicate that it suddenly has five rooms available (from cancellations) when there might be 30 or 40 travel agents lined up in the computer waiting for them. That small a number of vacancies is much more likely to be held by the hotel for its own sale, so a local associate is an invaluable conduit to these otherwise inaccessible rooms. Another efficient alternative is communication with the hotel via a FAX machine, which can prove useful in arranging and confirming reservations.

Time Zones, Business Hours, and Public Holidays

TIME ZONES: The countries of Europe fall into three time zones. Greenwich Mean Time — measured from Greenwich, England, at longitude 0°0′ — is the base from which all other time zones are measured. Areas in zones west of Greenwich have earlier times and are called Greenwich Minus; those to the east have later times and are called Greenwich Plus. For example, New York City (Greenwich Minus 5) is 5 hours earlier than Greenwich, England; when it is noon in Greenwich, it is 7 AM in New York. France and Monaco both fall into the same Greenwich Plus 1 time zone, so that when it is noon in Paris and Monte Carlo, it is 6 AM in New York and Washington (5 AM in Chicago and Houston, 4 AM in Denver and Phoenix, and 3 AM on the West Coast).

Like most Western European nations, France (and Monaco) moves its clocks ahead an hour in the spring and back an hour in the fall. France goes on daylight saving time the last Sunday in March, whereas the US does so on the first Sunday in April. Similarly, France goes off daylight saving time the last Sunday in September, while the US changes its clocks on the last Sunday in October. Therefore, during a bit of April there is a 7-hour time difference between the East Coast (and a 10-hour difference between the West Coast) and France, and for most of October there is a 5-hour difference from the East Coast (and 8 hours from the West Coast).

French and other European timetables use a 24-hour clock to denote arrival and departure times, which means that hours are expressed sequentially from 1 AM. By this method, 9 AM is recorded as 0900, noon as 1200, 1 PM as 1300, 6 PM as 1800, midnight as 2400, and so on. For example, the departure of a train at 7 AM will be announced as "0700"; one leaving at 7 PM will be announced as "1900."

PUBLIC HOLIDAYS: France shuts down even more thoroughly than the US does on public holidays. Banks, offices, stores, museums, and public monuments — even most gas stations — are closed tight, and banks and some offices also close at *noon* the day before a holiday. The French national holidays are as follows: *New Year's Day, Easter Monday, Labor Day* (May 1), *V-E Day* (May 8), *Pentecost Monday* (May 20, this year), *Ascension Thursday* (40 days after *Easter*), *Whitmonday* (the second Monday after the Ascension), *Bastille Day* (July 14), the *Feast of the Assumption* (August 15), *All Saints' Day* (November 1), *Armistice Day* (November 11), and *Christmas Day.* Monaco celebrates most of the same holidays and adds a few of its own, including the *Feast Day of St.-Dévoté,* patron saint of the principality (January 27), and *National Day* (November 19).

BUSINESS HOURS: Travelers who are used to the American workday may be surprised to find that the French, like many other Europeans, follow a more eccentric schedule. Business (office) hours are from 9 AM to 6 PM, traditionally with a generous

2½-hour lunch break (although the current trend is toward shorter, closer to 1-hour, breaks) starting at 12:30 or 1 PM. Banks generally are open on weekdays from 9 or 9:30 AM to 4:30 PM; in addition, in the countryside, banks may close between noon and 2 PM for lunch.

Department stores and other large emporia generally are open from about 9:30 AM to 6:30 PM (including Saturdays); they usually have 1 or 2 days when they are open until 9 or 10 PM. Many are closed on Monday mornings. Fashion boutiques, perfume shops, and similar retail establishments, usually are open Tuesdays through Saturdays from 10 AM to noon, and from 2 to 6:30 or 7 PM. Small food stores such as butcher shops and bakeries may open at 9 AM, close for lunch around 12:30 or 1 PM, reopen at 3:30 or 4 PM, and close between 7 and 8 PM. They and other small shops close on Monday mornings and sometimes for the whole day, but if open Sunday, close by 1 or 2PM.

Mail, Telephone, and Electricity

 MAIL: Before you leave home, fill in a "change of address card" (available at post offices) which is the form you need to get the post office to hold your mail until your return. If you are planning an extended stay in France, you can have your first class mail forwarded to your vacation address. There generally is no charge for this service. (Note that many post offices will need 2 to 3 weeks' notice to put this change of address into effect.)

There are several places that will receive and hold mail for travelers in France. Mail sent to you at a hotel and clearly marked "tourist mail, hold for arrival" is one safe approach. Post offices also will extend this service to you if the mail is addressed to the French equivalent of US general delivery, called *Poste Restante*. This probably is the best way for travelers to have mail sent if they do not have a definite address. The central or main post office in each city or town handles *Poste Restante*, so make sure you call at the correct office when inquiring about your mail.

In Paris, the main post office, open 24 hours a day, is at 52 Rue du Louvre (Paris 75001). If your mail is addressed to you, simply, "Poste Restante, Paris," this is where it will be delivered. But in Paris (and other large cities), mail marked "Poste Restante" can be directed to a post office closer to where you will be staying by having the sender add the correct *arrondissement* number — or full postal code (see below) — in addition to the name of the city. In this case, your mail will go to the main post office in the appropriate district, not to one clear across town. There is a small charge for picking up your mail. And don't forget to take your passport with you when you go to collect it; the post office requires formal identification before it will release anything. The Ministry of Posts, Telecommunications, and Telediffusion distributes a brochure in several languages, entitled *Bienvenue*. Ask for it at the post office.

If you are an American Express customer (a cardholder, a carrier of American Express traveler's checks, or traveling on an *American Express Travel Service* tour) you can have mail sent to their offices in cities on your route; letters are held free of charge — registered mail and packages are not accepted. You must be able to show an American Express card, traveler's checks, or a voucher proving you are on one of the company's tours to avoid paying for mail privileges. Those who aren't clients must pay a nominal fee each time they inquire about if they have received mail, whether or not they actually have a letter. There also is a forwarding fee, for clients and non-clients alike. Mail should be addressed to you, care of American Express, and should be marked "Client Mail Service." The Paris office is at 11 Rue Scribe, Paris 75009. Additional information on its mail service and addresses of other American Express offices in France are contained in the pamphlet *Services and Offices,* available from the nearest US branch of American Express.

US embassies and consulates abroad do not accept mail for tourists. They will, however, help out in emergencies — if you need to receive important business documents or personal papers, for example. It is best to inform them either by separate letter or cable, or by phone (particularly if you are in the country already) that you will be using their address for this purpose.

The post office in France is indicated by a sign with the letters "PTT" (which stands for "Postes, Télécommunications, et Télédiffusion," and is pronounced *Pay-Tay-Tay*) or by a sign with a blue bird (looking something like an arrow) on a white disk. Stamps can be bought both there, at *tabacs* (tobbacco shops), or at coin-operated vending machines painted yellow. Letter boxes also are yellow. Note that there no longer is such a thing as a *lettre pneumatique* in Paris. The old system, by which a letter (a *pneu,* for short) could be whooshed through a tube of compressed air from one end of the tube to the other in a matter of hours, was shut down in 1984 after more than a century of service.

The French postal code consists of a 5-digit number. The first 2 digits indicate in which of the country's 95 *départements* the address is located and the remaining numbers indicate the town, city, or, more specifically, the district. For instance, all addresses in the city of Paris (a *département* unto itself), begin with 75; a postal code number of 75001 or 75002 means that the address is in the first or second of the city's 20 *arrondissements.* The postal code always should be specified. Sometimes this will merely speed delivery, but sometimes — because many small towns in France have the same name — delivery of a letter may depend on it. (If you do not have the correct postal code, call a French consulate or embassy and ask them to look it up.)

Letters sent from France to the US always should be sent via air mail — otherwise they may end up going the *long* way by boat. Although letters have been known to arrive in as short a time as 5 days, it is a good idea to allow at least 10 days for delivery in either direction. If your correspondence is important, you may want to send it via one of the special courier services: Federal Express, DHL, and other international services are available throughout France. The cost is considerably higher than sending something via the postal service — but the assurance of its timely arrival sometimes is worth it.

TELEPHONE: If you are planning to be away for more than a month, you may be able to save money by asking the telephone company to temporarily suspend your home telephone service. You also can arrange to have your calls transferred to another number.

The French telephone system is not too different from our own. The French have direct dialing, operator-assisted calls, collect calls, reduced rates for certain times of the day and days of the week, and so on.

The number of French subscribers has grown by leaps and bounds in the last few decades — from 2 million in 1955 to 23 million in 1985 — consequently, in 1986 the country completely rehauled its telephone system. All French telephone numbers now have 8 digits, the new number composed of the old 6- or 7-digit number prefaced by the 1- or 2-digit prefix (area code). An exception occurs in Paris and its suburbs, where the prefix was 1. These numbers are now prefaced by a 4, creating an 8-digit number, and the 1 is used as the city code. Ile-de-France numbers, where the prefix was 3 or 6, also follow the rule — for instance, the former number 9-51-95-36 has become new number 39-51-95-36 or 69-51-95-36, prefaced by 1 for the city code.

The procedure for calling most areas of France from the US is as follows: dial 011 (the international access code) + 33 (the country code) + the local 8-digit number (which includes the city code). For example, to place a call from anywhere in the US to Lyons, dial 011 + 33 + the local 8-digit number. The only exception to this rule is when calling the Paris/Ile-de-France area: You must add a 1 (the city code) before the local 8-digit number. For instance, to make a call from the US to Paris, dial 011 + 33 (the country code) + 1 (the city code) + the local 8-digit number.

Direct dialing within the country, between nations, and overseas is possible throughout France. The procedure for making a station-to-station call to the US from France is as follows: dial 19 (wait for a dial tone) + 1 (the US country code) + the area code + the local number. For instance to call directly to New York from anywhere in France, dial 19 + 1 + 212 + the local number. For an operator-assisted call to the US, dial 19, wait for a dial tone, then dial 3311.

France is divided into essentially two zones: Paris/Ile-de-France and all the rest, that is, the provinces. The procedure for dialing within France is as follows:

To call within Paris and the Ile-de-France area: Dial the local 8-digit number (beginning with 4, 3, or 6).

To call from the Paris/Ile-de-France area to the provinces: Dial 16 (wait for a dial tone) + the local 8-digit number.

To call from the provinces to the Paris/Ile-de-France area: Dial 16 (wait for a dial tone) + 1 + the local 8-digit number.

To call between provinces: Dial the local 8-digit number.

For an operator-assisted call within France, dial 10. Because this operator may not speak English, be aware that to call collect, you must specify *en PCV* (pronounced *Pay-Say-Vay*), and to make an international person-to-person call, you must specify *en PER* (*Pay-Uh-Air*), for *communication personnelle*. To call person-to-person within France, specify *avec préavis* (pronounced *pray*-ah-vee). You can make collect calls from France to the US (or to any other country where they are accepted), but you cannot call collect within France. If you need a French number and can speak a minimum of French, dial 12 for directory assistance.

For emergency assistance throughout France, you can dial the following numbers (much as you would dial 911 in the US): 17 for the police (who can arrange for other emergency assistance); 18 for the fire department. An alternative may be to dial 12 for a local operator who can connect you to emergency service. If you do not speak French, ask the local operator to connect you to an international operator ("Operateur international, s'il vous plait."); otherwise, ask someone to make the call for you. For further information on what to do in the event of an emergency, see *Medical and Legal Aid and Consular Services,* in this section.

Public pay phones are found in post offices, cafés, and in booths on the street. Though some still take coins (inserted before dialing), most pay phones in major cities now use plastic phone cards, *télécartes,* which may be purchased at post offices, train stations and other transportation centers, and tobacco shops or newsstands. The *télécarte* may be purchased in three denominations: 40, 50, and 120 units — for 30.80F (about $5.40), 38.50F (about $6.75), and 92.40F (about $16.21), respectively. The units, like message units in US phone parlance, are a combination of time and distance. To use the card, you insert it into a slot in the phone and dial the number you wish to reach. A display gradually will count down the value (in francs) that remains on your card. When you run out of units on your card, you can insert another card.

In some cafés, you may have to purchase a *jeton* (token) from the cashier to use the phone. The inserted token doesn't drop until you push the button on the front of the phone, and this should be done only after your party answers.

Phone booths from which you can direct-dial long-distance calls within France, as well as international calls to most European countries and the United States, are now found in even the smallest French towns. Instructions on their use usually are in the booth. Simply put, a fistful of coins is dropped into the phone before you begin. When your call is connected, the coins begin to drop automatically and you can continue to feed coins as you talk. Any unused coins are returned after your call is completed.

If you have trouble placing a call from a phone booth or if you cannot gather a sufficient amount of change, remember that long-distance and international calls also can be made at post offices in France. In fact, this may be the simplest way to place such a call. Go to the telephone counter and explain what kind of call you want to make. You may be assigned a *cabine* (booth) from which to direct-dial the call yourself, or the clerk may put the call through for you, telling you which *cabine* to go to when he or she is about to connect the call. In either case, after you have hung up, return to the counter and pay the clerk for the call. There is no extra charge for phone calls made at the post office with or without the assistance of the attendant (surcharges for operator-assisted calls such as collect and person-to-person still apply, naturally); the only drawback to using the post office is that there frequently is a line of people already waiting for an empty booth.

A third way to place calls is through your hotel switchboard. In the case of international calls, it also is the most expensive way. One of the most unpleasant surprises travelers encounter in many foreign countries is the amount they find tacked onto their hotel bill for telephone calls, because foreign hotels routinely add on astronomical surcharges. A practice initially begun to cover the expense of installing phone equipment and maintaining multilingual personnel to run it around the clock, it now is firmly entrenched as a profit making operation for many hotels, and the French — according to the number of customer complaints received by *AT&T* — are among the worst offenders.

Until recently, the only recourse against this unconscionable overcharging was to call collect from abroad or or use a telephone credit card, available through a simple procedure from any local US phone company. (Note, however, that even if you use a telephone credit card, some hotels still may charge a fee for line usage.) Now, *American Telephone and Telegraph (AT&T)* offers USA Direct, a service that connects users, via a toll-free number, with an *AT&T* operator in the US, who will then put the call through at the standard international rate. In France, you simply dial 19, wait for a dial tone, then dial 0011. A new feature of this service is that travelers abroad can reach US toll-free (800) numbers by calling a USA Direct operator, who will connect them. Charges for all calls made through USA Direct appear on the caller's regular US phone bill. For a brochure and wallet card listing toll-free numbers by country, contact International Information Service, *AT&T Communications* (635 Grant St., Pittsburgh, PA 15219; phone: 800-874-4000).

AT&T also has put together Teleplan, an agreement among certain hoteliers that sets a limit on surcharges for calls made by guests from their rooms. Teleplan currently is in effect in selected hotels in France. Teleplan agreements stipulate a flat amount for credit card or collect calls (currently between $1 and $10), and a flat percentage (between 20% and 100%) on calls paid for at the hotel. For further information, contact *AT&T*'s International Information Service (address above).

Until Teleplan becomes universal, it's wise to ask the surcharge rate *before* calling from a hotel. If the rate is high, it's best to use a telephone credit card or one of the direct-dial services listed above, make a collect call, or place the call and ask the party to call right back. If none of these choices is possible, make international calls from the local post office or special telephone center to avoid surcharges.

When to Call – There are a lot of digits involved once you start dialing outside the national borders, but avoiding operator-assisted calls can cut costs considerably and bring rates into a reasonable range. As in the US, phone rates in France vary with the time of day. Reductions range from 30% to 65% and the rates tend to change every few hours, so it's best to check the schedule in the brochure *Bienvenue* issued by the Ministry of Posts, Telecommunications, and Telediffusion and available at French post offices.

For long-distance calls *within* France, a 50% reduction in rates is in effect weekdays from 7:30 PM until 8 the following morning. On Saturdays, the reduced rate goes into effect at 4 PM and continues all day Sunday until 8 AM Monday. (This reduction also is in effect all day on national holidays.) For calls to the US, the reduction in rates, approximately 15%, is not nearly so dramatic, but it is in effect for longer hours. Regular rates prevail daily from 2 PM to 8 PM; reduced rates are in effect the remaining hours and on Sundays. (Don't forget the time difference when placing your call; see *Time Zones, Business Hours, and Public Holidays,* above.)

Making connections in Europe sometimes can be hit or miss — all exchanges are not always in operation on the same day. If the number dialed does not go through, try later or the next day. So be warned: Those who have to make an important call — to make a hotel reservation in another city, for instance — should start to do so a few days ahead.

■ **Note:** For quick reference, you might want to get a copy of a helpful pamphlet, *The Phone Booklet,* which lists the nationwide, toll-free (800) numbers of travel information sources and suppliers — such as major airlines, hotel and motel chains, car rental companies, and tourist information offices. Send $2 for postage and handling to *Scott American Corporation,* Box 88, West Redding, CT 06896.

ELECTRICITY: The US runs on 110-volt, 60-cycle alternating current. France runs on 220-volt, 50-cycle alternating current (110-volt current still exists in a few parts of France), as does the rest of Europe, although 240-volt also may be used. The large difference between US and European voltage means that without a converter, the motor of a US appliance used overseas would run at twice the speed it's meant to and would quickly burn out.

Travelers can solve the problem by buying a lightweight converter to transform foreign voltage into the US domestic kind (there are two types of converters, depending on the wattage of the appliance) or by buying dual-voltage appliances that convert from one to the other at the flick of a switch (hair dryers of this sort are common). The difference between the 50-cycle and 60-cycle currents will cause no problem — the appliance will simply run more slowly — but it still will be necessary to deal with differing socket configurations before plugging in. To be fully prepared, bring along an extension cord (in older or rural establishments the electrical outlet may be farther from the sink than the cord on your razor or hair dryer can reach), and a wall socket adapter with a full set of plugs to ensure that you'll be able to plug in anywhere. (A standard European plug of two long, round prongs is required in most of France.)

One good source for sets of plugs and adapters for use worldwide is the *Franzus Company* (PO Box 142, Beacon Falls, CT 06403; phone: 203-723-6664). *Franzus* also publishes a useful brochure, *Foreign Electricity Is No Deep Dark Secret,* which provides information about converters and adapter plugs for electric appliances to be used abroad but manufactured for use in the US. To obtain a free copy, send a self-addressed, stamped envelope to *Franzus* at the above address; a catalogue of other travel accessories is available on request.

Medical and Legal Aid and Consular Services

MEDICAL AID ABROAD: Nothing ruins a vacation or business trip more effectively than sudden injury or illness. You will discover, in the event of an emergency, that most tourist facilities — transportation companies, hotels, and resorts — are equipped to handle the situation quickly and efficiently. Most French towns and cities of any size have a public hospital and even the

the tiniest village has a medical clinic or private physician nearby. The level of medical care available in France generally is excellent, providing the same basic specialities and services that are available in the US. All hospitals are prepared for emergency cases, and many hospitals also have walk-in clinics to serve people who do not really need emergency service, but who have no place to go for immediate medical attention.

Before you go, be sure to check with your insurance company about the applicability of your policy while you're abroad; many policies do not apply, and others are not accepted in Europe. Older travelers should know that Medicare does not make payments for medical services provided outside the US. If your medical policy does not protect you while you're traveling, there are comprehensive combination policies specifically designed to fill the gap. (For a discussion of medical insurance and a list of inclusive combination policies, see *Insurance,* in this section.)

French hospitals fall into three categories, with the CHRU (Centre Hôpital Régional et Universitaire, or Central Regional University Hospital), a large, full-service hospital associated with a major medical university, at the top of the list. Others are the CHR, which designates a full-service regional hospital; and the CH, which means that the hospital is the central one in its town or city (and probably has 24-hour emergency service).

If a bona fide emergency occurs, an inability to speak French can pose a serious problem, not in receiving treatment at a large teaching hospital such as a CHRU, where many doctors — *médecins* in France — and other staff members will speak English, but in getting help elsewhere or in getting to the place where help is available. The fastest way to receive attention may be to go directly to the emergency room of the nearest hospital.

In every city, an emergency number for *SAMU* (*service d'aide médicale urgente,* "medical help for serious emergencies") is listed in the front of the telephone directory along with other emergency numbers. *SAMU* sends out well-equipped and well-staffed ambulances, but because the dispatcher is not likely to speak English, and will be unable to determine the nature of the emergency, what equipment will be needed, or even where to send the ambulance, travelers with little or no French language ability should try to get someone else to make the call. If the situation is desperate and no bilingual speaker can be found, the international operator may be able to make the call to *SAMU* and stay on the line as interpreter.

Another alternative also requiring a basic command of French is to dial 17 for the police (who can connect you to other emergency services) or to dial 18 for the fire department. (These numbers both are valid nationwide.) To reach the international operator, dial 12 for a local operator, and ask to be connected to an international operator ("Operateur international, s'il vous plait.") to whom you can explain the situation.

If a doctor is needed for something less than an emergency, there are several ways to find one. Ask at your hotel; the local *SAMU* emergency number also may be of help (again, if you can speak French). Callers often will be given the name of a general practitioner, since private doctors (usually specialists) see patients upon referral only. If you are already at the hospital, you may see the specialist there, or you may make an appointment to be seen at his or her office.

In addition, though general practitioners deliver primary care, there is no violation of protocol in approaching a specialist directly. Call the appropriate department of a teaching hospital (such as a CHRU) or the nearest US consulate or embassy (see *Medical and Legal Aid and Consular Services,* below), which also maintain a list of doctors. Remember that if you are hospitalized you will have to pay, even in an emergency.

If you are staying in a hotel or motel, ask for help in reaching a doctor or other emergency services, or for the house physician, who may visit you in your room or ask you to visit an office. Travelers staying at a hotel of any size probably will find that the doctor on call speaks credible English — if not, request one who does. (This service is apt to be expensive, especially if the doctor makes a "house" call to your room.) When you register at a hotel, it's not a bad idea to include your home address and telephone number; this will facilitate the process of notifying friends, relatives, or your own doctor in case of an emergency.

Emergency dental care also is available throughout France (see the front page of the local telephone directory), although travelers are strongly advised to have a dental checkup some weeks before the trip to allow time for any necessary dental work to be done. Again, any US consul also can provide a list of English-speaking dentists in the area the consulate serves.

French drugstores, *pharmacies,* are identified by a green cross out front. There should be no problem finding a 24-hour drugstore in any major French city — for one thing, pharmacists who close are required to give the addresses of the nearest all-night drugstores in the window. In small towns, where none may be open after normal business hours, you may be able to have one open in an emergency situation — such as a diabetic needing insulin — although you may be charged a fee for this off-hour service.

Bring along a copy of any prescription you may have from your doctor in case you should need a refill. In the case of minor complaints, French pharmacists may do some prescribing, and some are not averse to filling a foreign prescription; however, do not count on this — you may have to have a local doctor write a prescription. Even in an emergency, a traveler will more than likely be given only enough of a drug to last until a local doctor can write a prescription. As "brand" names vary in different countries, it's a good idea to ask your doctor for the generic names of any drugs you use so that you can ask for their equivalents should you need a refill. Americans also will notice that some drugs sold only by prescription in the US are sold over the counter in France (and vice versa). Though this can be very handy, be aware that common cold medicines and aspirin that contain codeine or other controlled substances will not be allowed back into the US.

Emergency assistance also is available from the various medical programs designed for travelers who have chronic ailments or whose illness requires them to return home. The *Medic Alert Foundation* sells identification emblems which specify that the wearer has a health condition that may not be readily apparent to a casual observer. A heart condition, diabetes, epilepsy, and severe allergy are the sorts of things that these emblems were developed to communicate, conditions that can result in tragic errors if not recognized when emergency treatment is necessary and when you may be unable to speak for yourself. In addition to the identification emblems, the foundation maintains a computerized central file from which your complete medical history is available 24 hours a day by telephone (the phone number is clearly inscribed on the ID badge). The one-time membership fee, between $25 and $45, is tax deductible, and is based on the type of metal from which the emblem is made — the choices ranging from stainless steel to 10K gold-filled. For information, contact the *Medic Alert Foundation,* Turlock, CA 95381-1009 (phone: 209-668-3333 or 800-ID-ALERT).

International SOS Assistance also offers a program to cover medical emergencies while traveling. Members are provided with telephone access — 24 hours a day, 365 days a year — to a worldwide, monitored, multilingual network of medical centers. A phone call brings assistance ranging from a telephone consultation to transportation home by ambulance or aircraft, and in some cases transportation of a family member to wherever you are hospitalized. The service can be purchased for 2 weeks ($25), 2 weeks plus additional days ($25, plus $2.50 for each additional day), 1 month ($50), or 1 year ($195). These rates are for individual travelers; couple and family rates also are available. For information, contact *International SOS Assistance,* PO Box 11568, Philadelphia, PA 19116 (phone: 215-244-1500 or 800-523-8930).

The *International Association of Medical Assistance to Travellers (IAMAT)* provides its members with a directory of affiliated medical centers in over 140 countries (500 cities, including 23 in France) to call for a list of participating English-speaking doctors. Participants agree to adhere to a basic charge of around $30 to see a patient referred by *IAMAT*. To join, simply write to *IAMAT;* in about 3 weeks you will receive a membership card, the booklet of members, and an inoculation chart. A nonprofit organization, *IAMAT* appreciates donations; with a donation of $25 or more, you will receive a set of worldwide climate charts detailing weather and sanitary conditions. Delivery of this material can take up to 5 weeks, so plan ahead. Contact *IAMAT,* 417 Center St., Lewiston, NY 14092 (phone: 716-754-4883).

The *International Health Care Service* provides information about health conditions in various foreign countries, as well as a variety of travel-related health services. A pre-travel counseling and immunization package costs $185 for the first family member and $165 for each additional member; a post-travel screening is $75 to $135, plus lab work. Appointments are required for all services. Contact the *International Health Care Service,* New York Hospital–Cornell Medical Center, 440 E. 69th St., New York, NY 10021 (phone: 212-472-4284). *The International Health Care Travelers Guide,* a compendium of facts and advice on health care and diseases around the world, can be obtained by sending $4.50 and a self-addressed, stamped envelope to PO Box 210 at the address above.

Those who return home ill with a condition they suspect is travel related and beyond the experience of their regular physician should consider seeing a specialist in travel medicine. For information on finding such a specialist in your area, see *Staying Healthy,* in this section.

For a thorough description of the medical services in 19 of France's larger cities and in Monaco, see *Traveling Healthy,* by Sheilah M. Hillman and Robert S. Hillman, MD. Unfortunately out of print, it may be found in the library.

Practically every phase of health care — before, during, and after a trip — is covered in *The New Traveler's Health Guide* by Drs. Patrick J. Doyle and James E. Banta. It is available for $4.95, plus $2.50 postage and handling, from Acropolis Books Ltd., 80 S. Early St., Alexandria, VA 22304 (phone: 800-451-7771 or 703-709-0006).

LEGAL AID AND CONSULAR SERVICES: There is one crucial place to keep in mind when outside the US, namely, the American Services section of the US Consulate. If you are injured or become seriously ill, the consulate will direct you to medical assistance and notify your relatives. If, while abroad, you become involved in a dispute that could lead to legal action, the consulate, once again, is the place to turn.

It usually is far more alarming to be arrested abroad than at home. Not only are you alone among strangers, but the punishment can be worse. Granted, the US consulate can advise you of your rights and provide a list of lawyers (a number of leading US firms maintain offices in Paris), but it cannot interfere with local legal process. Except for minor infractions of the local traffic codes, there is no reason for any law-abiding traveler to run afoul of immigration, customs, or any other law enforcement authority.

The best advice is to be honest and law abiding. If you get a traffic ticket, pay it. If you are approached by drug hawkers, ignore them. The penalties for possession of hashish, marijuana, cocaine, and other narcotics are even more severe abroad than in the US. (If you are picked up for any drug-related offense, do not expect US foreign service officials to be sympathetic. Chances are they will notify a lawyer and your family and that's about all. See "Drugs," below.)

In the case of minor traffic accidents, it often is most expedient to settle the matter before the police get involved. If, however, you are involved in a serious accident, where an injury or fatality results, the first step is to contact the nearest US consulate (addresses below) and ask the consul to locate a lawyer to assist you. If you have a traveling companion, ask him or her to call the consulate (unless either of you has a local contact who can help you quickly). Competent lawyers practice throughout France, and it is possible to obtain good legal counsel on short notice.

The US Department of State in Washington, DC, insists that any American citizen who is arrested abroad has the right to contact the US embassy or consulate "immediately," but it may be a while before you are given permission to use a phone. Do not labor under the illusion, however, that in a scrape with foreign officialdom, the consulate can act as an arbitrator or ombudsman on an American citizen's behalf. Nothing could be farther from the truth. Consuls have no power, authorized or otherwise, to subvert, alter, or contravene the legal processes, however unfair, of the foreign country in which they serve. Nor can a consul oil the machinery of a foreign bureaucracy or provide legal advice. The consul's responsibilities do encompass "welfare duties" including providing a list of lawyers and information on local sources of legal aid, informing relatives in the US, and organizing and administrating any defense monies sent from home. If a case is tried unfairly or the punishment seems unusually severe, the consul can make a formal complaint to the authorities. For questions about Americans arrested abroad, how to get money to them, and other useful information, call the *Citizens Emergency Center* of the Office of Special Consular Services in Washington, DC: phone: 202-647-5225. (For further information about this invaluable hot line, see below.)

Other welfare duties, not involving legal hassles, cover cases of both illness and destitution. If you should get sick, the US consul can provide names of doctors and dentists as well as the names of all local hospitals and clinics; the consul also will contact family members in the US and help arrange special ambulance service for a flight home. In a situation involving "legitimate and proven poverty" — of an American stranded abroad without funds — the consul will contact sources of money (such as family or friends in the US), apply for aid to agencies in foreign countries, and in a last resort — which is *rarely* — arrange for repatriation at government expense, although this is a loan that must be repaid. And in case of natural disasters or civil unrest, consulates around the world handle the evacuation of US citizens if it becomes necessary.

The consulate is not occupied solely with emergencies and is certainly not there to aid in trivial situations, such as canceled reservations or lost baggage, no matter how important these matters may seem to the victimized tourist. The main duties of any consulate are administrating statutory services, such as the issuance of passports and visas; providing notarial services; the distribution of VA, social security, and civil service benefits to resident Americans; depositions; extradition cases; and reporting to Washington the births, deaths, and marriages of US citizens living within the consulate's domain.

We hope that none of the information in this section will be necessary during your stay in France. If you can avoid legal hassles altogether, you will have a much more pleasant trip. If you become involved in an imbroglio, the local authorities may spare you legal complications if you make clear your tourist status. And if you run into a confrontation that might lead to legal complications developing with a French citizen or with local authorities, the best tactic is to apologize and try to leave as gracefully as possible. Do not get into fights with residents, no matter how belligerent or provocative they are in a given situation.

The US embassies and consulates in France are at the following locations:

Bordeaux: Consulate General: 22 Cour du Maréchal Foch, Bordeaux 33080 (phone: 56-52-65-95)

Lyons: Consulate General: 7 Quai du Général Sarrail, Lyons 69454, (phone: 78-24-68-49)

Marseilles: Consulate General: 12 Bd. Paul Paytral, Marseilles 13286 (phone: 91-54-92-00)

Nice: Consulate: 31 Rue du Maréchal-Joffre, Nice 06000 (phone: 93-88-89-55)

Paris: Embassy: 2 Ave. Gabriel, Paris 75001 (phone: 1-42-96-12-02 or 1-42-61-80-

75); Consulate: 2 Rue St.-Florentin, Paris 75001 (same phone numbers as Embassy).

Strasbourg: Consulate General: 15 Av. d'Alsace, Strasbourg 67082 (phone: 88-35-31-04)

You also can obtain a booklet with addresses of most US embassies and consulates around the world by writing the Superintendent of Documents, US Government Printing Office, Washington, DC 20402, and asking for publication #78-77, *Key Offices of Foreign Service Posts.*

As mentioned above, the US State Department operates a *Citizens Emergency Center,* which offers a number of services to American travelers abroad and their families at home. In addition to giving callers up-to-date information on trouble spots, the center will contact authorities abroad in an attempt to locate a traveler or deliver an urgent message. In case of death, illness, arrest, destitution, or repatriation of an American citizen on foreign soil, it will relay information to relatives at home if the consulate is unable to do so. Travel advisory information is available 24 hours a day to people with Touch-Tone phones (phone: 202-647-5225). Callers with rotary phones can get travel advisory information at this number from 8:15 AM to 10 PM on weekdays; 9 AM to 3 PM Saturdays. For emergency calls, from 8:15 AM to 10 PM weekdays, and 9 AM to 3 PM Saturdays, call 202-647-5225. For emergency calls only, at all other times, call 202-634-3600 and ask for the Duty Officer.

Drinking and Drugs

DRINKING: The French are well known for their production and enjoyment of fine wines and liqueurs, and many would not contemplate a dinner — or even lunch — unaccompanied by a glass of wine. The consumption of wine, beer, and other alcohol is viewed more casually in France than in the US, and alcoholic beverages can be bought at corner cafés, supermarkets, and small grocery stores, as well as from special shops featuring vintage wines and liqueurs.

There are fewer restrictions on the sale of wine and liquor in France than in the US. The legal drinking age is 16 for purchasing or ordering alcohol, but persons under the age of 16 can be served in a bar or restaurant if accompanied by a parent or guardian. Wine and liquor can be sold 7 days a week, 365 days a year, although on holidays you may have trouble finding a store open for business.

Cafés, the inexpensive streetside establishments that serve liquor in addition to coffee and simple fare, generally open in the morning, sometimes as early as 5 or 6 AM, and close at around 1 to 3 AM. Specific hours are determined by local regulations, but some cafés can and do receive permission to stay open 24 hours. Bars — more expensive establishments — and nightclubs have no mandated closing times: Some may close as early as 11 or 12 PM, while others may stay open through dawn, depending on the proprietor. There is no "last call" in France — if an establishment is open, drinks are served, although the proprietor does reserve the right to refuse service to anyone who appears drunk.

Although there is no restriction against having an open container of liquor in your car, the French have passed and rigorously enforce strict laws concerning drinking and driving. The Breathalyzer test is used across the country and a person is considered legally drunk with level of .8 grams of alcohol per liter of blood — stricter than average blood alcohol levels set by US state laws of approximately 1 gram per liter. If a person is arrested while driving intoxicated, a fine ranging from 500F to 8,000F (about $90 to $1,400) and up and a prison term anywhere from 1 months to over 1 year may be imposed. If a person driving in this condition causes an accident resulting in bodily injury, the penalties are substantially more severe. When setting off for an evening on the town, visitors should leave their cars behind and make alternate plans for transportation back to the hotel; otherwise choose a "designated driver" in your party who will stick strictly to soft drinks.

Every visitor to France may import up to 2 liters of wine, 2 liters of alcohol under 38.8 proof, and 1 liter above 38.8 proof. Anything in excess of this amount is subject to duties and taxes. Also be aware that neighboring countries also may impose duties or have other restrictions on those entering with large amounts of alcohol, so it pays to check these restrictions in advance. If you plan to take any quantity over the allowed 1 liter (such as a case of wine) back into the US, you will have to pay duties (see *Customs and Returning to the US* in this section).

DRUGS: Illegal narcotics are not as prevalent in France as in the US, and the moderate legal and social acceptance that marijuana has won in the US has no counterpart in France. Due to the international war on drugs, enforcement of drug laws is becoming increasingly strict throughout the world. Local narcotics officers and customs officials are renowned for their absence of understanding and lack of a sense of humor.

Opiates and barbiturates, and other increasingly popular drugs — "white powder" substances like heroin and cocaine — are a problem throughout Europe as in the US. The main drawback to buying any illegal drug (besides the health hazards) is the inherent risk of getting locked up. France has toughened its laws regarding illegal drugs and narcotics and these laws do not distinguish between types of drugs — possession of marijuana, cocaine, heroin, and other narcotics are treated with equal severity.

Don't assume that you're safe in carrying even small amounts of controlled substances for "personal use" — particularly for foreigners, the maximum penalties may be imposed for possessing even *traces* of illegal drugs. If you are charged with possession or sale of personal use amounts, you face a fine of 5,000 to 50,000 francs (about $900 to $9,000) and from 1 to 5 years imprisonment *for a first offense.* First-time offenders convicted of possession for the purpose of trafficking face fines ranging from 5,000 to 50 million francs (as much as $8,000,000!) *in addition to* a minimum 10-year prison term; second-time offenders face double that fine and a minimum 20-year prison term. These fines are strictly enforced and a prison term will be increased by up to 2 years if the offender cannot pay the imposed fine. There is a high conviction rate in these cases and bail for foreigners is rare.

The best advice we can offer is: Don't carry, use, buy, or sell illegal drugs. The dangers are clear enough when indulging in your own home; if taking drugs while traveling, you may endanger not only your own life but also put your fellow travelers in jeopardy. And if you get caught, you may end up spending your hard-earned vacation funds on bail and attorney's fees — and wind up in jail. There isn't much that the American consulate can do for drug offenders beyond providing a list of lawyers. Having broken a local law, an offender puts his or her fate in the hands of the local authorities.

Those who carry medicines that contain a controlled drug should be sure to have a current doctor's prescription with them. Ironically, travelers can get into almost as much trouble coming through US customs with over-the-counter drugs picked up abroad that contain substances that are controlled in the US. Cold medicines, pain relievers, and the like often have codeine or codeine derivatives that are illegal except by prescription in the US. Throw them out before leaving for home.

■**Be forewarned:** US narcotics agents warn travelers of the increasingly common ploy of drug dealers asking travelers to transport a "gift" or other package back to the US. Don't be fooled into thinking that the protection of US law applies abroad — accused of illegal drug trafficking, you will be considered guilty until you prove your innocence. In other words, do not, under any circumstances, agree to take anything across the border for a stranger.

Tipping

Throughout France (and most of Europe), a service charge — generally 12% to 15% — almost always is added to basic hotel and restaurant bills. This can confuse Americans not familiar with the custom. On the one hand, many a traveler, unaware of this policy, has left many a superfluous *pourboire*. On the other hand, travelers aware of the policy have made the mistake of assuming that it takes care of everything. It doesn't. While "service included" in theory eliminates any question about how much and whom to tip, in practice there still are occasions when on-the-spot tips are appropriate. Among these are tips to show appreciation for special services, as in the case of a fairly large tip — as much as 30 to 50F (about $5.25 to $8.75) — to the hotel doorman who has gotten taxis for you over the course of your stay, as well as tips meant to say "thank you" for services rendered.

In restaurants, the service charge may appear in either of two ways. If you see *service compris* (s.c.) in the fine print at the bottom of the menu, the service charge already is calculated in the prices listed. If you see *service 12% en sus,* it means that a charge of 12% will be added to the final bill. (If you are at all unsure if the service charge already has been added, you should feel no embarrassment about asking a waiter when the bill is presented.) Unlike a tip in the US, this service charge is rarely optional. What is optional is the decision to do as the French might and leave the waiter several extra coins (around 10F) if you liked the service. On those few occasions where a service charge hasn't been added, a 15% tip — just as in the US — usually is a safe figure, although one should never hesitate to penalize poor service or reward excellent and efficient attention by leaving less or more.

Although it's not necessary to tip the maître d' of most restaurants — unless he has been especially helpful in arranging a special party or providing a table (slipping him something in a crowded restaurant *may* get you seated sooner) — when tipping is appropriate, the lowest amount should be 25F (about $4.40). The sommelier is not tipped for simply serving the wine, although if he has selected the wine for you, it is customary to leave him 10% of the price of the bottle. In the finest restaurants, where a multiplicity of servers are present, plan to tip 5% to the captain in addition to the standard tip for the waiter. Tipping in bars and cafés is similar to tipping in restaurants: Service usually is included, but you may wish to leave a few extra francs on the table.

In allocating gratuities at a restaurant, pay particular attention to what has become the standard credit card charge form, which now includes separate places for indicating gratuities for waiters and/or captains. If these separate boxes do not appear on the charge slip presented, simply ask the waiter or captain how these separate tips should be indicated. Be aware, too, of the increasingly common, devious practice of placing the amount of an entire restaurant bill (in which service already has been included) in the top box of a charge slip, leaving the "tip" and "total" boxes ominously empty. Don't be intimidated: Leave the "tip" box blank and just repeat the total amount next to "total" before signing. Whenever possible, tips should be left in cash, not charged on a credit card; this is because tips indicated on credit card receipts often are not given to the help for whom they were intended.

As in restaurants, visitors usually will find a service charge of 10% to 15% included in their final bill at most French hotels. No additional gratuities are required — or expected — beyond this billed service charge. It is unlikely, however, that a service charge will be added to bills in small guesthouses or modest bed and breakfast establishments. In these cases, guests should let their instincts be their guide; no tipping is expected by members of the family who own the house, but it is a nice gesture to leave something for others — such as a dining room waiter or a maid — who may have been helpful. A gratuity of around 10F (about $1.75) per night is adequate in these cases.

If a hotel does not automatically add a service charge, it is perfectly proper for guests to ask to have an extra 10% to 15% added to their bill, to be distributed among those who served them. This may be an especially convenient solution in a large hotel, where it's difficult to determine just who out of a horde of attendants actually performed particular services. For those who prefer to distribute tips themselves, a chambermaid generally is tipped at the rate of 10F (about $1.75) per person per night, or 45F to 50F (around $8 to $9) per week (even when service has been included, you might want to leave an additional small tip). Tip the concierge for specific services only, with the amount of such gratuities dependent on the level of service provided. (Remember, if he has obtained theater or concert tickets for you, he has included a service charge in the price, although you may want to tip him in advance to encourage him to use his influence in obtaining hard-to-get tickets.) If you leave your shoes outside the room at night for a shine, give the hall porter 5F to 10F when you next see him. If you order from room service, 10F to the waiter for each delivery is sufficient. For other special services, such as personal deliveries, 10F generally is sufficient.

Bellhops, doormen, and porters at hotels and transportation centers, generally are tipped at the rate of 5F to 10F (about 90¢ to $1.75) per bag for carrying luggage, along with a small additional amount if a doorman helps with a cab or car. Taxi drivers are rarely tipped by their French customers, but since *your* taxi driver knows you are a foreigner (and an American to boot), something is expected. Fortunately, 15% of the fare is considered quite adequate. If you arrive without any French currency, go ahead and tip in US currency. (When in doubt, it is preferable to tip — in any denomination or currency — than not to tip.)

In France, ushers in a movie house, theater, or concert hall are tipped 2 to 5F. Tour guides also should be tipped. If you are traveling in a group, decide together what you feel like giving and present it from the group at the end of the tour (5 francs per person is a reasonable tip). If you have been individually escorted, the amount will depend on your degree of satisfaction, but it should not be less than 10% and could easily be as high as 50% of the total tour fee. Museum and monument guides also usually are tipped, and it is a nice touch to tip a caretaker who unlocks a country church for viewing.

In barbershops and beauty salons, tips also are expected, but the percentages vary according to the type of establishment. Since the prices usually are quite a bit higher in expensive salons (particularly in Paris), no more than 10% is common; in less expensive establishments, a 15% or 20% tip is in order. (As a general rule the woman who washes your hair should get an additional 5F or 10F). The washroom attendant in these places, or wherever you see one, should get a franc or two.

Tipping always is a matter of personal preference. In the situations covered above, as well as in any others that arise where you feel a tip is expected or due, feel free to express your pleasure or displeasure. Again, never hesitate to reward excellent and efficient attention and to penalize poor service. If you didn't like the service — or the attitude — don't tip.

Shopping

Browsing through the department stores (*grands magasins*), boutiques, street markets (*marchés*), and craft studios (*ateliers*) of France will undoubtedly be one of the highlights of your trip. Visitors from the US may not be quite as enthusiastic about prices as they might have been a few years ago, as prices in France, as in the rest of Europe, have risen dramatically. But there still is plenty of value left for the money and enough quality and craftsmanship to make many an item irresistible. To help steer you toward the best, several sections of this book are devoted to shopping. In THE CITIES, individual city reports include a list of specific shops and markets, as well as descriptions of special shopping streets where they exist. And in DIVERSIONS, there is a roundup of where to buy the best of what France has to offer.

WHAT TO BUY: Food and wine, lingerie and perfume, the highest of high fashion and the chicest of ready-to-wear, shoes and accessories, leather goods, kitchenware worthy of the greatest French chefs from Escoffier to Paul Bocuse, china and crystal — all are products for which the French are famous. Paris is, without a doubt, the shopping capital of France. It has the haute couture salons of designers famed around the world, some of the world's grandest purveyors of *joaillerie* (jewelry, but what jewelry!), expensive and less expensive boutiques, art galleries, antiques shops, as well as branches of *Galeries Lafayette* and *Au Printemps,* the country's leading department store chains, and other, less expensive chains. It's safe to say that whatever you want to bring home from France could be found in Paris. But if you made all your purchases in Paris, you'd miss the pleasure of shopping for regional specialties at the source — of visiting a *parfumerie* in Grasse or a porcelain factory in Limoges, of buying crystal in Baccarat, mustard in Dijon, faïence in Quimper, truffles in the Périgord region, or herbs in Provence, also the home of lovely printed cottons. Unlike the US, where discounts at factory outlets can be considerable, the price at the source usually will be the same as elsewhere in France, and in the rare instance where there is some sort of discount, it probably will be truly minimal, perhaps only 5%. But the potential discount would not be the reason to go to the source. Rather, the chance to sniff, to taste, to watch the artisan at work, and to see, for example, an entire town in Normandy dedicated to the production of copperware and named after the frying pans it produces are reason enough.

Budget travelers need not feel cheated by the limits of their purse. There are other shopping experiences beyond the Vuittons and Laliques and the luxury goods of Paris that are uniquely French and possibly more enjoyable. Flea markets (*marchés aux puces*) and *brocanteurs* (dealers in used goods) abound to delight the poor, the thrifty, the just plain stingy, and the *amateur* of bric-a-brac. Food shopping in itself can be an experience you never will forget. Shop as the French do: Take a string bag and wander from the *boulangerie* (bakery) for a still-warm *baguette* to the *charcuterie* (delicatessen) for ham and sausages and all sorts of already-prepared temptations from cold salads to pâté. Stop in at a *crèmerie* and a *fromagerie* for dairy products and a bewildering variety of cheeses, at the *primeur* for fruits and vegetables of a quality and freshness not often seen at home, and at the *pâtisserie* for pastry. The *épicerie*, something like our corner grocery shop, sells everything from packaged meats and cheeses to fruits and vegetables and wine, including assorted odds and ends you may have just run out of, such as detergent.

If you are in a position to indulge in a proper shopping spree, however, do it sensibly. Quality goods are not necessarily less expensive in a fashionable French boutique than the same goods would be in an equally fashionable US store. To be sure, do some homework before you go, and arrive prepared with a list of the things you want — as specific as possible, with brands or labels — and the cost of each in the US. In many cases, you will find it less expensive to buy abroad, but frequently you will find it is not, and knowing the difference is crucial to a successful shopping trip. Once you've arrived, it is still necessary to comparison shop as much as time permits, bearing in mind that the price tags you see will include a sales tax known in France as the TVA, which can be as high as 33.33% on luxury items. In some but not all cases, foreign residents are eligible for a refund.

VALUE ADDED TAX: Commonly abbreviated as VAT (Value Added Tax), this is a tax levied by various European countries and added to the purchase price of most merchandise. In France, it is known as the *taxe à la valeur ajoutée* (TVA), and it ranges from a low of 5.5% to 7% on food (depending on the degree of processing) to a high of 33.33% on such things as cameras, furs, jewelry, and luggage. Typically, the rate is 18.6%, as on most clothing, for instance. The tax is meant to apply only to residents of France, but visitors are required to pay it, too. Having done so, visitors are then entitled to a refund (except on purchases of antiques and works of art worth over 30,000F, gold, food, wine, medicine, and tobacco), provided the total value of purchases in a single store amounts to 1,200F or more (European Economic Community residents have a higher minimum than do residents of other countries) and provided the articles in question leave France with them. (Articles shipped out of the country can escape the tax.) A further proviso is that the store agrees to participate in the tax-refund scheme — paperwork is involved and no store is obliged to do it. They also are not required to refund the total amount of the tax if they can prove to authorities that offering the service raises their operating costs. If they post a sign indicating that they do provide the refund, however, they are required to follow through with this policy.

To claim the refund, shoppers must ask the store clerk for an export sales form, a document that will be given to them in triplicate along with a stamped envelope addressed to the store. Proof of eligibility (such as a passport) must be shown, and the form must be signed in the store. At departure time, this same document must be presented with the merchandise (do not pack it in the bottom of your suitcase), with the envelope, and by the same person who signed it in the store, to the French customs *détaxe* (tax refund) booth in the airport (or at the railroad station if departure from France is by train). This must be done before going through passport control, and since there are frequently lines of other travelers waiting to go through the same formalities, early arrival at the airport or station is recommended. The customs official returns one copy of the form, countersigned, to the buyer, to be saved until reimbursement is received. Tax-refund forms for purchases made in Monaco also are handled by French customs.

When and how the refund is received varies. Certain of the large department stores in Paris — *Galeries Lafayette* and *Au Printemps,* for example — have an arrangement that allows immediate payment at an airport bank window before travelers proceed through the remaining departure formalities. In most other cases, however, customs returns a copy of the export document to the store, which then mails a refund check, in French francs, to your home address. The drawback to this method is that it can take months before you receive the refund, and if the refund is less than a significant amount, conversion charges imposed by local banks — which can run as high as $15 or more — could make the whole exercise hardly worth your while.

Far less costly is sending your foreign currency check (after endorsing it) to *Ruesch International,* which will convert it to a check in US dollars for a $2 fee (deducted from the dollar check). Contact *Ruesch International* at one of the following addresses: 3 First National Plaza, Suite 2020, Chicago, IL 60602 (phone: 312-332-5900); 1925 Century Park E., Suite 240, Los Angeles, CA 90067 (phone: 213-277-7800); 608 Fifth Ave., "Swiss Center," New York, NY 10020 (phone: 212-977-2700); or 1350 Eye St. NW, 10th Floor and street level, Washington, DC 20005 (phone: 800-424-2923 or 202-408-1200).

Two other methods of reimbursement are possible if the purchases in France are made by credit card. The preferable one is that the store will agree to make two credit card charges, one for the price of the goods, the other for the amount of the tax. Then, when the stamped copy of the form arrives from customs, the store simply tears up the charge slip for the sales tax and the amount never appears on your account. The other possibility is that, upon receipt of the stamped form, the store requests the international billing center to credit your account with the amount of the sales tax.

DUTY-FREE SHOPS: If common sense says that it always is less expensive to buy goods in an airport duty-free shop than to buy them at home or in the streets of a foreign city, travelers should be aware of some basic facts. Duty-free, first of all, does not mean that the goods travelers buy will be free of duty when they return to the US. Rather it means that the shop has paid no import tax acquiring goods of foreign make because the goods are not to be used in the country where the shop is located. This is why duty-free goods are available in the restricted, passengers-only area of international airports or are delivered to departing passengers on the plane. In duty-free stores, travelers save money only on goods of foreign make because they are the only items on which an import tax would be charged in any other store. There usually is no saving on locally made items, but in countries that impose VAT taxes (see above) that are refundable to foreigners, the prices in airport duty-free shops also are minus this tax, sparing travelers the often cumbersome procedures they would otherwise have to follow to obtain a VAT refund.

Beyond this, there is little reason to delay buying locally made souvenirs until reaching the airport. In fact, because airport duty-free shops usually pay high rents, the locally made goods sold in them may be more expensive than they would be in a downtown store. The real bargains are foreign goods, but — let the buyer beware — not all foreign goods are automatically less expensive in an airport duty-free shop. You can get a good deal on even small amounts of perfume, costing less than the usually required minimum purchase, tax free. Other fairly standard bargains include cameras, clothing, watches, chocolate and other foods and luxury times — but first be sure to know what these items cost elsewhere. Terrific savings do exist (they are the reason for such shops, after all), but so do overpriced items that an unwary shopper might find equally tempting. In addition, if you wait to do your shopping at airport duty-free shops, you will be taking the chance that the desired item is out of stock or unavailable. Among the airports with duty-free shops in France are Bordeaux, Lille, Lyons, Marseilles, Montpellier, Nantes, Nice, Paris (both Charles de Gaulle and Orly), and Strasbourg.

In France, there are many shops *not* at the airport that call themselves duty-free shops. This can be confusing, because they are subject to the same rules as other shops but you must show a foreign (not French) passport to shop there. Foreign goods, if any, sold there have not escaped the import tax, and no purchases, French or foreign, become free of value added taxes until you buy enough to fulfill the minimum (see explanation above). You still are required to turn in export forms at the *détaxe* booth on departure in order to receive the refund. A few shops pay the refund on the spot, but they are trusting that you won't forget to turn in the forms. If you do forget or simply don't bother, they are out of pocket: They must pay to the government the tax they already have refunded to you.

What "tax-free" means in the case of shops such as these is something of an advertising strategy. They are announcing loud and clear that they do, indeed, offer the VAT refund service. Because they handle such sales in volume, these shops frequently have streamlined the paperwork. But because they have had to hire extra personnel to do so, they are less likely than other shops to refund the entire amount of the VAT, retaining some of it as reimbursement for their higher overhead.

Religion on the Road

 France is a Catholic country by and large, and every town, right down to the most isolated village, has its own church. And in larger, more heavily populated areas, some amount of religious variety is reflected in the numerous Protestant churches, Jewish synagogues, and the occasional mosque or temple.

The surest source of information on religious services in an unfamiliar country is the desk clerk of the hotel or guesthouse in which you are staying; the local tourist information office, an American consul, or a church of another religious affiliation also can provide this information. Throughout France, travelers will have the choice of attending services at numerous churches and other places of worship — and in larger towns and cities, morning, afternoon, and evening services may be scheduled daily. If you aren't in an area with services held in your own denomination, you might find it interesting to attend the service of another religion. You also might enjoy attending a service in French — even if you don't understand all the words. Some of the most beautiful cathedrals in the world are found in France, and few things are more inspiring than a high mass set amidst medieval arches and stained glass.

Customs and Returning to the US

 Whether you return to the United States by air or sea, you must declare to the US customs official at the point of entry everything you have bought or acquired while in Europe. The customs check can go smoothly, lasting only a few minutes, or can take hours, depending on the officer's instinct. To speed up the process, keep all your receipts handy and try to pack your purchases together in an accessible part of your suitcase. It might save you from unpacking all your belongings.

DUTY-FREE ARTICLES: In general, the duty-free allowance for US citizens returning from abroad is $400, provided your purchases accompany you and are for personal use. This limit includes items used or worn while abroad, souvenirs for friends, and gifts received during the trip. A flat 10% duty based on the "fair retail value in country of acquisition" is assessed on the next $1,000 worth of merchandise brought in for personal use or gifts. Amounts over $1,400 are dutiable at a variety of rates. The average rate for typical tourist purchases is about 12%, but you can find out rates on specific items by consulting *Tariff Schedules of the United States* in a library or any US Customs Service office.

Families traveling together may make a joint declaration to customs, a procedure that permits one member to exceed his or her duty-free exemption to the extent that another falls short. Families also may pool purchases dutiable under the flat rate. A family of three, for example, would be eligible for up to a total of $3,000 at the 10% flat duty rate (after each member had used up his or her $400 duty-free exemption) rather than three separate $1,000 allowances. This grouping of purchases is extremely useful when considering the duty on a high-tariff item, such as jewelry or a fur coat.

There are certain articles, however, that are duty-free only up to certain limits. Individuals are allowed 1 carton of cigarettes (200), 100 cigars, and 1 liter of liquor or wine if over 21. Alcohol above this allowance is liable for both duty and an Internal Revenue Service tax. Antiques, if they are 100 or more years old and you have proof from the seller of that fact, are duty free, as are paintings and drawings if done entirely by hand. To avoid paying duty twice, register the serial numbers of foreign-made watches and electronic equipment with the nearest US Customs bureau before departure; receipts of insurance policies also should be carried for other foreign-made items. (Also see the note at the end of *Entry Requirements and Documents*, in this section.)

Gold, gold medals, bullion, and up to $10,000 in currency or negotiable instruments may be brought into the US without being declared. Sums over $10,000 must be declared in writing.

Personal exemptions can be used once every 30 days; in order to be eligible, an individual must have been out of the country for more than 48 hours. If any portion of the exemption has been used once within any 30-day period or if your trip is less than 48 hours long, the duty-free allowance is cut to $25.

The allotment for individual "unsolicited" gifts mailed from abroad (no more than one per day per recipient) has been raised to $50 retail value per gift. These gifts do not have to be declared and are not included in your duty-free exemption (see below). Although you should include a receipt for purchases with each package, the examiner is empowered to impose a duty based on his or her assessment of the value of the goods. The duty owed is collected by the US Postal Service when the package is delivered (also see below). More information on mailing packages home from abroad is contained in the US Custom Service pamphlet *International Mail Imports* (see below for where to write for this and other useful brochures).

CLEARING CUSTOMS: This is a simple procedure. Forms are distributed by airline or ship personnel before arrival. (Note that a $5 per-person service charge — called a user fee — is collected by airlines and cruise lines to help cover the cost of customs checks, but this is included in the ticket price.) If your purchases total no more than the duty-free $400 limit, you need only fill out the identification part of the form and make an oral declaration to the customs inspector. If entering with more than $400 worth of goods, you must submit a written declaration.

Customs agents are businesslike, efficient, and not unkind. During the peak season, clearance can take time, but this generally is because of the strain imposed by a number of jumbo jets discharging their passengers at the same time, not because of unwarranted zealousness on the part of the customs people. Efforts to streamline procedures include the Citizens' Bypass Program, which allows Americans whose purchases are under $400 to go to the "green line," where they simply show their passports to the customs inspector. This, in effect, completely eliminates the old obligatory inspection, although inspectors still retain the right to search any luggage they choose, so don't do anything foolish and illegal.

It is illegal not to declare dutiable items; not to do so, in fact, constitutes smuggling, and the penalty can be anything from stiff fines and seizure of the goods to prison sentences. It simply isn't worth doing. Nor should you go along with the suggestions of foreign merchants who offer to help you secure a bargain by deceiving customs officials in any way. Such transactions frequently are a setup, using the foreign merchant as an agent of US customs. Another agent of US customs is TECS, the Treasury Enforcement Communications System, a computer that stores all kinds of pertinent information on returning citizens. There is a basic rule to buying goods abroad, and it should never be broken: *If you can't afford the duty on something, don't buy it.* Your list or verbal declaration should include all items purchased abroad, as well as gifts received abroad, purchases made at the behest of others, the value of repairs, and anything brought in for resale in the US.

Do not include in the list items that do not accompany you, i.e., purchases that you have mailed or had shipped home. As mentioned above, these are dutiable in any case, even if for your own use and even if the items that accompany your return from the same trip do not exhaust your $400 duty-free exemption. It is a good idea, if you have accumulated too much while abroad, to mail home any personal effects (made and bought in the US) that you no longer need rather than your foreign purchases. These personal effects pass through customs as "American goods returned" and are not subject to duty.

If you cannot avoid shipping home your foreign purchases, however, the US Customs Service suggests that the package be clearly marked "Not for Sale" and that a copy of the bill of sale be included. The customs examiner usually will accept this as indicative of the article's fair retail value, but if he or she believes it to be falsified or feels the goods have been seriously undervalued, a higher retail value may be assigned.

FORBIDDEN ITEMS: Narcotics, most plants, and many types of food are not allowed into the United States. Drugs are totally illegal, with the exception of medication prescribed by a physician. It's a good idea not to travel with too large a quantity of any given prescription drug (although, in the event that a pharmacy is not open when you need it, bring along several extra doses) and to have the prescription on hand in case any question arises either abroad or when reentering the US.

Any authentic archaeological find or other artifacts considered by the Ministre de L'Education Nationale to be a "national treasure" cannot be exported from France. They will be confiscated at the French border, and the violator runs the risk of being fined or imprisoned. People interested in anything that might qualify as such an item should check with French customs.

Tourists have long been forbidden to bring into the US foreign-made US trade-marked articles purchased abroad (if the trademark is recorded with customs) without written permission. It's now possible to enter with one such item in your possession as long as it's for personal use.

Customs implements the rigorous Department of Agriculture regulations concerning the importation of vegetable matter, seeds, bulbs, and the like. Living vegetable matter may not be imported without a permit, and everything must be inspected, permit or not.The exceptions include dried bamboo, beads made of most seeds, mushrooms, nuts, seeds, seashells, shamrocks, spices, straw articles, canned or processed vegetables, some plants, and truffles — a specialty of Périgord in southwest France.

Other processed foods and baked goods usually are okay. Regulations on meat products generally depend on the country of origin and manner of processing. As a rule, commercially canned meat, hermetically sealed and cooked in the can so that it can be stored without refrigeration, is permitted, but not all canned meat fulfills this requirement. Be careful in buying pâté, for instance. Goose liver pâté in itself is acceptable, but the pork fat that often is part of it, either as an ingredient or a rind, is not. Even canned pâtés may not be admitted for this reason. (The imported ones you see in US stores have been prepared and packaged according to US regulations.)

Customs also enforces federal laws that prohibit the entry of articles made from the furs or hides of animals on the endangered species list. Beware of shoes, bags, and belts made of crocodile and certain kinds of lizard, and anything made of tortoise-shell. And if you're shopping for big-ticket items, beware of fur coats made from the skins of spotted cats. They are sold in Europe, but they will be confiscated upon your return to the US and there will be no refund. For information about animals on the endangered species list, contact the Department of the Interior, US Fish and Wildlife Service, Office of Management Authority, PO Box 27329, Washington, DC 20038-7329 (phone: 202-343-5634), and ask for the free publication *Facts About Federal Wildlife Laws.*

For information about transporting plants or wildlife, write to *Quarantines,* US Department of Agriculture, Federal Bldg., Hyattsville, MD 20782, or get in touch with the Animal and Plant Health Inspection Service office nearest your home (check under the US Department of Agriculture listings in your telephone book).

The US Customs Service publishes a series of free pamphlets with customs information. It includes *Know Before You Go,* a basic discussion of customs requirements pertaining to all travelers; *International Mail Imports; Travelers' Tips on Bringing Food, Plant, and Animal Products into the United States; Importing a Car; GSP and the Traveler; Pocket Hints; Currency Reporting; Pets, Wildlife, US Customs; Customs Hints for Visitors (Nonresidents);* and *Trademark Information for Travelers.* For the entire series or individual pamphlets, write the US Customs Service, PO Box 7407, Washington, DC 20044, or contact any of the seven regional offices, in Boston, Chicago, Houston, Los Angeles, Miami, New Orleans, and New York. The Customs

Service has a tape-recorded message whereby callers using Touch-Tone phones can get more information on various topics; the number is 202-566-8195. These pamphlets provide great briefing material, but if you still have questions after you're in France, you can contact the US customs representative at the US Embassy in Paris, at 2 Rue St.-Florentin, Paris 75001 (phone: 1-42-96-12-02 or 1-42-61-80-75).

Sources and Resources

Tourist Information

The French Government Tourist Office has introduced a telephone information service for US travelers. Called "France On Call," it provides details on all of the historical and geographical provinces of France, including schedules of cultural and special events, a variety of travel services (airlines, car rentals, package tours, and so on), current weather conditions, currency exchange rates, and visa and passport requirements. To reach this service, dial 900-420-2003. Note that there is a 50¢ per minute charge for all calls; this charge will appear on your telephone bill. When calling this number, you also may want to request a copy of the French Government Tourist Office's 72-page, *France Discovery Guide,* which features information on sightseeing, current discount travel offers, and detailed itineraries for planning your trip. Other than the per-minute call cost, there is no charge for this publication.

Another information service for traveler's in France, is *minitel*, a computerized information system that is available at some hotels. Hotel guests will find a computer terminal located in the lobby that will provide a variety of information for a number of regions (there is a "menu" specifying selections). For instance, by entering 3615-BORDEAUX, travelers will be given information on facilities, tourist attractions, etc. in the province of Bordeaux.

Below is a list of the French and Monégasque government tourist offices in the US. They offer a wide variety of useful travel information, and most publications are free for the asking. When requesting brochures and maps, state the regions you plan to visit, as well as your particular areas of interest: accommodations (châteaux-hotels, resorts, the type of country rental or guesthouse known as a *gîte,* and so on), restaurants, special events, tourist attractions, guided tours, and facilities for specific sports and activities. Because most of the material you receive will be oversize brochures, there is little point in sending a self-addressed, stamped evelope with your request, unless this request is specified. Offices generally are open on weekdays, during normal business hours.

French Government Tourist Offices

Chicago: 645 N. Michigan Ave., Suite 630, Chicago, IL 60611-2836 (phone: 312-337-6301)

Dallas: 2305 Cedar Springs Rd., Suite 205, Dallas, TX 75201 (phone: 214-720-4010)

Los Angeles: 9454 Wilshire Blvd., Suite 303, Beverly Hills, CA 90212-2967 (phone: 213-271-6665)

New York: 610 Fifth Ave., New York, NY 10020-2452 (requests by mail only); walk-in office on street level: 628 Fifth Ave., New York, NY 10020 (phone: 212-757-1125).

Monaco Government Tourist and Convention Bureau

542 S. Dearborn St., Suite 550, Chicago, IL 60605 (phone: 312-939-7863)

New York: 845 Third Ave., 19th Floor, New York, NY 10022 (phone: 212-759-5227)

Information on the major cities of France may be requested from the tourist offices cited (with address and phone number) in the *Sources and Resources* section of the relevant chapter in THE CITIES section. In addition, nearly every town and village in France has its own Syndicat d'Initiative, which serves as a tourist information center. These are too numerous to mention, but since most Americans arrive in France via Paris, listed below are the Paris offices of the Maisons de Province — the central sources of tourist information for each region. (Note that the numbers listed below include the city code, 1, for Paris; if calling within the city, do not use the initial 1.)

Maison des Alpes Dauphiné, 2 Pl. André Malraux, Paris 75001 (phone: 1-42-96-08-43 or 1-42-96-08-56)

Maison de l'Alsace, 39 Av. des Champs-Elysées, Paris 75008 (phone: 1-42-25-93-42 or 1-42-56-15-94)

Maison de l'Auvergne, 194 bis Rue de Rivoli, Paris 75001 (phone: 1-42-61-82-38)

Maison de Bretagne, 17 Rue de l'Arrivée, Paris 75015 (phone: 1-45-38-73-15)

Maison de la Drôme, 14 Bd. Haussmann, Paris 75009 (phone: 1-42-46-66-67)

Maison du Gers et de l'Armagnac, 16-18 Bd. Haussmann, Paris 75009 (phone: 1-47-70-39-61)

Maison des Hautes Alpes, 4 Av. de l'Opéra, Paris 75001 (phone:1-42-96-05-08; or 1-47-03-91-18 for a recording in French on snow and other weather conditions)

Maison du Limousin, 18 Bd. Haussmann, Paris 75009 (phone: 1-47-70-32-63)

Maison du Lot-et-Garonne, 15-17 Passage Choiseul, Paris 75002 (phone: 1-42-96-51-43 or 1-42-97-51-43)

Maison de la Région Nord–Pas de Calais, 18 Bd. Haussmann, Paris 75009 (phone: 1-47-70-59-62)

Maison du Périgord, 30 Rue Louis-le-Grand, Paris 75002 (phone: 1-47-42-09-15)

Maison du Poitou-Charentes, 68 Rue de Cherche-Midi, Paris 75006 (phone: 1-42-22-83-74)

Maison des Pyrénées, 15 Rue St.-Augustin, Paris 75002 (phone: 1-42-61-58-18)

Maison de la Savoie et de la Haut-Savoie, 31 Av. de l'Opera, Paris 75001 (phone: 1-42-61-74-73)

Office de Tourisme de la Principauté de Monaco, 9 Rue de la Paix, Paris 75002 (phone: 1-42-96-12-23)

The French government maintains a number of consulates in the US. Where required, the consulates are empowered to sign official documents, such as those required for study, work, or an extended stay of over 3 months in France. (For entry information, see *Entry Requirements and Documents,* and for the addresses of the US embassy and consulates in France, see *Medical and Legal Aid and Consular Services* — both in this section.) Consulates also are empowered to notarize copies or translations of American documents, which is necessary for those papers to be considered legal in France.

Listed below are the Monegasque consulate and French consulates in the US. (Note that French consulates also often handle consular matters for Monaco.) In general, these offices are open 9 AM to 1 PM, Mondays through Fridays — call ahead to be sure.

Monegasque Consulate in the US

Consulat Général de Monaco, 845 Third Ave., New York, NY 10022 (phone: 212-759-5227)

French Consulates in the US

Boston: Visa Dept.: 20 Park Plaza (in the Statler Office Bldg.), Suite 620, Boston, MA 02116 (phone: 617-451-6755/6); other business: 3 Commonwealth Ave., Boston, MA 02116 (phone: 617-266-1680)

Chicago: Olympia Center, 737 N. Michigan Ave., Suite 2020, Chicago, IL 60611 (phone: 312-787-5359, -5360, or -5361; recorded visa information: 312-787-7889)

Detroit: 100 Renaissance Ctr., Suite 1550, Detroit, MI 48243 (phone: 313-568-0990)

Houston: 2727 Allen Pkwy., Suite 976, Houston, TX 77019 (phone: 713-528-2181)

Los Angeles: Wilshire Tower, 8350 Wilshire Blvd., Suite 310, Beverly Hills, CA 90211 (phone: 213-653-3120)

Miami: 1 Biscayne Tower, Suite 3300, 2 S. Biscayne Blvd., Miami, FL 33131 (phone: 305-372-9798)

New Orleans: 3305 St. Charles Ave., New Orleans, LA 70115 (phone: 504-897-6381/2)

New York: Main office and to apply by mail for a visa: 934 Fifth Ave., New York, NY 10021 (phone: 212-606-3688; recorded visa information: 212-606-3680)

San Francisco: 540 Bush St., San Francisco, CA 94108 (phone: 415-397-4330)

Washington, DC: 4101 Reservoir Rd. NW, Washington, DC 20007-2176 (phone: 202-944-6000)

Theater and Special Event Tickets

The French Government Tourist Office can supply information on the many special events and festivals that take place in France, though they cannot in all cases provide the actual program or detailed information on ticket prices. In more than one section of this book you will read about events that spark your interest — everything from music festivals and special theater seasons to sporting championships — along with telephone numbers and addresses to which to write for descriptive brochures, reservations, or tickets. Since many of these occasions often are fully booked well in advance, you should think about having your reservation in hand before you go. If you do write, remember that any request from the US should be accompanied by an International Reply Coupon to ensure a response (send two of them for an airmail response). Actual tickets usually can be paid for by an international money order or by foreign draft. These international coupons, money orders, and drafts are available at US post offices and banks.

Books and Magazines

Throughout GETTING READY TO GO, numerous books and brochures have been recommended as good sources of further information on a variety of topics. In many cases, these are publications of the French Government Tourist Office and are available at any of their US offices. Others are published by other French and US government agencies, specialty clubs and organizations, tour operators, and other travel service suppliers, and are available directly from these sources or found in the travel section of any good general bookstore. If you still can't find something, the following bookstores and/or mail order houses specialize in travel, but not to any particular country or continent. They offer books on France along with guides to the rest of the world and, in some cases, even an old Baedeker guide or two.

Book Passage, 51 Tamal Vista Dr., Corte Madera, CA 94925 (phone: 415-927-0960 in California; 800-321-9785 elsewhere in the US). Travel guides and maps to all areas of the world. A free catalogue is available.

Complete Traveller, 199 Madison Ave., New York, NY 10016 (phone: 212-685-9007). Travel guides and maps. A catalogue is available for $2.

Forsyth Travel Library, PO Box 2975, Shawnee Mission, KS 66201-1375 (phone: 800-367-7984 or 913-384-0496). Travel guides and maps, old and new, to all parts of the world. Ask for the "Worldwide Travel Books and Maps" catalogue.

Gourmet Guides, 2801 Leavenworth St., San Francisco, CA 94133 (phone: 415-771-3671). Travel guides and maps, along with cookbooks. Mail order lists available on request.

Phileas Fogg's Books and Maps, Stanford Shopping Center, Palo Alto, CA 94304 (phone: 415-327-1754). Travel guides, maps, and language aids.

Tattered Cover, 2955 East 1st Ave., Denver, CO 80206 (phone: 800-833-9327 or 303-322-7727). The travel department alone of this enormous bookstore carries over 7,000 books, as well as maps and atlases. No catalogue is offered (the list is too extensive), but a newsletter, issued three times a year, is available on request.

Thomas Brothers Maps & Travel Books, 603 W. Seventh Street, Los Angeles, CA 90017 (phone: 213-627-4018). Maps (including road atlases, street guides, and wall maps), guidebooks, and travel accessories.

Traveller's Bookstore, 22 W. 52nd St. (lobby), New York, NY 10019 (phone: 212-664-0995). Travel guides, maps, literature, and accessories. A catalogue is available for $2.

Travel Suppliers, 16735 Lake Forest La., Yorba Linda, CA 93686 (phone: 714-528-2502). Mail order suppliers of books, maps, language aids, and travel paraphernalia from money belts and pouches to voltage and currency converters. A catalogue is available.

In addition, the *Librairie de France/Libreria Hispanica* (French and Spanish Book Corporation), which specializes in language dictionaries and French and Spanish fiction and nonfiction, carries some French-language guidebooks published in France. Of the company's two locations in New York, the store at 610 Fifth Ave., New York, NY 10020 (phone: 212-581-8810), has the greater selection of travel material; the other store is at 115 Fifth Ave., New York, NY 10003 (212-673-7400).

Before or after your trip, you may want to subscribe to a publication devoted exclusively to France. *La Belle France: The Sophisticated Guide to France,* an 8-page monthly newsletter, contains hotel and restaurant reviews, as well as shopping information for Paris and other cities, and often includes short articles spotlighting a luxury destination. Subscriptions are available from Travel Guide (414 E. Water St., Charlottesville, VA 22901; phone: 804-295-1200) for $56 a year. *France Today,* another monthly newsletter, focuses on French politics, business, and culture, as well as travel and events. Subscriptions are available from *France Today* (1051 Divisadero St., San Francisco, CA 94115; phone: 415-921-5100) for $25 (12 issues per year).

The New York Times, Wall Street Journal, USA Today, Los Angeles Times, and other US newspapers can be bought in many of the larger cities and resort areas, at hotels, airports, and newsstands. Note that some papers may cost more than in the US, and some may be available a day or two after publication.

A subscription to the *International Herald Tribune* also is a good idea for dedicated travelers. This English-language newspaper is written and edited mostly in Paris, and is *the* newspaper read regularly and avidly by Americans abroad to keep up with world news, US news, sports, the stock market (US and foreign), fluctuations in exchange rates, and an assortment of help-wanted ads, real estate listings, and personals, worldwide in scope. Published 6 days a week, it is available at newsstands throughout the US and in cities worldwide, including major cities throughout Europe. To subscribe, write or call the Subscription Manager, *International Herald Tribune,* 850 Third Ave., 10th Floor, New York, NY 10022 (phone: 800-882-2884 or 212-752-3890). (Note that you also can have your subscription transferred to an address in France.)

The French are well known for their fine food and sampling the regional fare is likely to be one of the highlights of any visit. You will find reading about local edibles worthwhile either before you go or after you return. *Gourmet,* a magazine specializing in food, frequently features mouthwatering articles on the foods of France (particularly Paris), although its scope is much broader than France alone. It is available at newsstands throughout the US for $2.50 or for $18 a year from *Gourmet,* PO Box 2886, Boulder, CO 80322-2886.

The Food of France (Random House; $10.95), by the foreign correspondent and food writer Waverley Root, has been described by Craig Claiborne (former food columnist of *The New York Times*) as "the most lucid and definitive book ever written in English" on French cuisine. Recipes are one strong point of *French Regional Cooking* (William Morrow; out of print but available in libraries) by Anne Willan, founder of La Varenne (a well-known cooking school in France); others are the introductions to the 12 regions covered and the short features on particular ingredients and techniques. Paula Wolfert's *The Cooking of South West France* (Harper & Row; $10.95), all recipes, traditional and new, from the Périgord to the Pyrénées, is a highly regarded cookbook with plenty of explanatory notes and plenty of personal anecdotes. Though not wholly devoted to food and with no recipes, *Two Towns in Provence* (Vintage Books; $9.95), by the very fine essayist M.F.K. Fisher, offers great pleasure to the literary taste buds in memories of time spent (and meals eaten) in Aix-en-Provence and Marseilles. Finally, *Menu French: The A to Z of French Food,* is a bilingual glossary of just about any term (or delicacy) you're likely to come across during your gastronomic exploration of France; it can be ordered from the publisher, Editions Scribo (37 Rue du Chemin Vert, Paris 75527; phone: 1-43-38-26-00) for 122F (about $21.40), including shipping and handling.

Gourmet's France is too large to be tucked into a suitcase, but its well-written text describing drives through France from region to region and restaurant to restaurant makes wonderful reading, and there are recipes at the back. Patricia Wells's *Food Lover's Guide to Paris* is a guide not only to eating places in the capital but also to such spots as the best cafés and tea salons, markets, bakeries, cheese shops, chocolate shops, kitchenware shops, and book shops specializing in the art of cooking. Both currently are out of print but should be available in libraries.

The oenophile will love the late *Alexis Lichine's Guide to the Wines and Vineyards of France.* The writer, who was a vineyard owner and wine maker, includes driving itineraries and information on hotels and restaurants along the wine routes in addition to solid information on wine. Although out of print (look in your local library), also by the same author is *Alexis Lichine's Guide New Encyclopedia of Wine and Spirit* (Knopf; $45).

Still, the most famous guide to the hotels and especially the restaurants of France is the compendious *Michelin Red Guide to France* ($17.95), which annually rates the worthy establishments city by city across the country. Serious bon vivants would not unfold a napkin without the recommendation of this bible, while restaurants cling to any lucky stars they have been fortunate enough to earn. (Three is the maximum; and when our paths converge, our restaurant selections in the *Best in Town* sections of THE CITIES and the *Eating Out* sections of DIRECTIONS note which ones have been so honored.) The Michelin guide is only a listing, however, and in French; the English introduction explaining the symbols that accompany each entry is must reading for this 1,000-plus-page tome to be of use. For more information on the Michelin books and to place an order, contact Michelin Guides and Maps, PO Box 3305, Spartanburg, SC 29304-3305 (phone: 800-423-0485 or 803-599-0850).

Another hotel and restaurant guide, by Henri Gault and Christian Millau, is almost as famous in France and much more forthcoming in justifying its opinions. The English translation of this candid and irreverent guide, *The Best of France* (Simon & Schuster; $16.95), makes a delightful supplement to Michelin.

For yet more sources of reading material, here are some bookstores in Paris with a selection of books in English:

L'Astrolabe, 46 Rue de Provence (phone: 1-42-85-42-95)
Brentano's, 37 Av. de l'Opéra (phone: 1-42-61-52-50)
Galignani, 224 Rue de Rivoli (phone: 1-42-60-76-07)
Itinéraires, 60 Rue St.-Honoré (phone: 1-42-33-92-00)
W. H. Smith, 248 Rue de Rivoli (phone: 1-42-60-37-97)
Ulysse I, 35 Rue St.-Louis-en-l'Ile (phone: 1-43-25-17-35); specializing in international travel books.
Ulysse II, 26 Rue St.-Louis-en-l'Ile (phone: 1-43-29-52-10); specializing in travel books on France.

Weights and Measures

 When you are traveling in France, you'll find that just about every quantity, whether it is length, weight, or capacity, will be expressed in unfamiliar terms. In fact, this is true for travel almost everywhere in the world, since the US is one of the last countries to make its way to the metric system. It may happen soon in the US, and your trip to France may serve to familiarize you with what one day may be the weights and measures at your grocery store.

There are some specific things to keep in mind during your trip. Fruits and vegetables at a market are recorded in kilos (kilograms), as is your luggage at the airport and your body weight. The latter is particularly pleasing to people of significant size, who instead of weighing 220 pounds hit the scales at a mere 100 kilos. (A kilo equals 2.2 pounds and 1 pound is .45 kilos.)

Body temperature is measured in degrees Centigrade or Celsius rather than on the Fahrenheit scale, so that a normal body temperature is expressed as 37C, not 98.6F, and freezing is 0 degrees C rather than 32F. Gasoline is sold by the liter (approximately 4 to 1 gallon), and tire pressure gauges are in kilograms per square centimeter rather than pounds per square inch. Highway signs are written in kilometers rather than miles (1 mile equals 1.6 kilometers; 1 kilometer equals .62 mile). And speed limits are in kilometers per hour, so think twice before hitting the gas when you see a speed limit of 100. That means 62 miles per hour.

The tables and conversion factors listed below should give you all the information you will need to understand any transaction, road sign, or map you encounter on your travels.

CONVERSION TABLES
METRIC TO US MEASUREMENTS

Multiply:	by:	to convert to:
LENGTH		
millimeters	.04	inches
meters	3.3	feet
meters	1.1	yards
kilometers	.6	miles
CAPACITY		
liters	2.11	pints (liquid)
liters	1.06	quarts (liquid)
liters	.26	gallons (liquid)
WEIGHT		
grams	.04	ounces (avoir.)
kilograms	2.2	pounds (avoir.)

US TO METRIC MEASUREMENTS

LENGTH		
inches	25.	millimeters
feet	.3	meters
yards	.9	meters
miles	1.6	kilometers
CAPACITY		
pints	.47	liters
quarts	.95	liters
gallons	3.8	liters
WEIGHT		
ounces	28.	grams
pounds	.45	kilograms

TEMPERATURE

$$°F = (°C \times 9/5) + 32 \qquad °C = (°F - 32) \times 5/9$$

APPROXIMATE EQUIVALENTS		
Metric Unit	**Abbreviation**	**US Equivalent**
LENGTH		
meter	m	39.37 inches
kilometer	km	.62 mile
millimeter	mm	.04 inch
CAPACITY		
liter	l	1.057 quarts
WEIGHT		
gram	g	.035 ounce
kilogram	kg	2.2 pounds
metric ton	MT	1.1 ton
ENERGY		
kilowatt	kw	1.34 horsepower

Cameras and Equipment

Vacations are everybody's favorite time for taking pictures and home movies. After all, most of us want to remember the places we visit — and show them off to others. Here are a few suggestions to help you get the best results from your travel photography or videography.

BEFORE THE TRIP

If you're taking your camera or camcorder out after a long period in mothballs — or have just bought a new one — check it thoroughly before you leave to prevent unexpected breakdowns or disappointing pictures.

STILL CAMERAS

1. Shoot at least one test roll, using the kind of film you plan to take along with you. Use all the shutter speeds and f-stops on the camera, and vary the focus to make sure everything is in order. Do this well before your departure so there will be time to have the film developed and to make repairs, if necessary. If you're in a rush, most large cities have shops that can process film in as little as an hour. Repairs, unfortunately, take longer.

2. Clean your camera thoroughly, inside and out. Dust and dirt can jam mechanisms, scratch film, and mar photographs. Remove surface dust from lenses and camera body with a soft camel's hair brush. Next, use at least two layers of crumpled lens tissue and your breath to clean lenses and filters, but as they are easily scratched, don't rub hard and don't use water, saliva, or compressed air. Persistent stains can be removed by using a cotton swab moistened with liquid lens cleaner. Anything that doesn't come off easily needs professional attention; a periodic professional cleaning is also advisable. Once your lenses are clean, protect them from dirt and damage with skylight or ultraviolet filters.

3. Check the lithium batteries for your camera's light meter, and take along extras just in case yours wear out during the trip.

VIDEO CAMCORDERS

1. If you haven't used your camcorder lately, use a "practice" videocassette to reacquaint yourself with the various shooting techniques — such as panning, zooming, and segueing (that is, transitioning without pause) from one scene to another. Practice fully before you leave; don't save it for the plane.

2. Clean and maintain your camcorder lenses with a soft, dry cloth. Don't use solvents such as paint thinner or chemically treated cloths. Once your camcorder lenses are clean, protect them from dirt and damage with inexpensive skylight or ultraviolet filters. If your camcorder's heads need cleaning, a recorded tape will tell you. A "snowy" tape is a sign that a head cleaning is needed. If a head cleaning doesn't improve the picture, the problem may lie elsewhere. In that case, take the camcorder to a professional for a check-up. Check the operation of each component on your camcorder, making sure that each feature performs correctly. If there's an internal problem, don't try to fix it yourself. You could void the manufacturer's warranty or, even worse, cause further damage. Even if all appears well at home, take a head cleaner along on your trip to make sure your videos remain clear and sharp.

3. Check the lithium batteries for your camcorder's light indicators, and take along extras just in case yours wear out during the trip. If you took along all your camcorder accessories, your carrying bag would get heavy and cumbersome, but there are a few "musts." Take extra nickel-cadmium (Ni-Cd) batteries so that you always have one or two power sources ready while another is recharging back at the hotel. You never know when a once-in-a-lifetime opportunity will present itself, and if you just used up your 45-minute allotment of power on a local festival, you'll have none left to shoot anything else. Remember that the more features you use, including reviewing what you've taped in the electronic viewfinder, the more battery power you will consume.

EQUIPMENT TO TAKE ALONG

Keep your gear light and compact. Items that are too heavy or bulky to be carried comfortably on a full-day excursion will likely remain in your hotel room, so leave them home.

1. Invest in a broad camera or camcorder strap if you now have a thin one. It will make carrying the camera much more comfortable.

2. A sturdy canvas or leather camera or camcorder bag, preferably with padded pockets (not an airline bag), will keep your equipment organized and easy to find.

3. For cleaning, bring along a camel's hair brush that retracts into a rubber squeeze bulb. Also take plenty of lens tissue, soft cloths, and plastic bags to protect equipment from dust and moisture.

STILL CAMERAS: Lenses and Other Equipment – Most single-lens-reflex (SLR) cameras come with a 50mm, or "normal," lens — a general-purpose lens that frames subjects within an approximately average angle of view. This is good for street scenes taken at a distance of 25 feet or more, and for full-length portraits shot at 8 to 12 feet.

Any lens from 35mm on down offers wide-angle capabilities, which in effect pull segments of the peripheral scene into the picture, and are especially handy for panoramas and landscapes. A wide-angle lens in the 20–28mm range is perfect for French gardens. Where the normal perspective of a 50mm lens provides only a partial view of Le Mont St.-Michel, a 20mm incorporates these majestic spires and the surrounding seas in one flowing scene. While a 50mm lens only provides a partial view of Notre Dame, taken from the proper perspective a 20mm lens can frame the whole structure above the waters of the Seine. The wide-angle lens is also excellent for linking people with their surroundings because of its great depth of field — that is, sharp focus from foreground to background — that can focus pictures between 3½ feet and infinity. And it also can be valuable when there's very little space between you and your subject.

Wide-angle lenses are especially handy for panoramas, for cityscapes, and for large buildings or statuary from which you can't step back. For extreme closeups, a macro lens is best, but a screw-on magnifying lens is an inexpensive alternative. Keep in mind that wide-angle lenses have a tendency to distort when used very close to a subject, or when dealing with vertical lines. Tall trees or a high-rise hotel may seem to converge toward the top of the frame, for example. Once you're aware of these effects, you can use them to creative advantage.

Where a wide-angle lens extends normal perspective, a telephoto lens focuses on a portion of the overview, providing perspective in detail. Telephoto lenses, 125mm to 1,000mm, are good for shooting details from a distance and permit dramatic silhouettes of sailboats against a setting sun, detailed portraits, floral design, and candids — although when choosing a lens, keep in mind that the weight of the higher ranges may prove difficult to support without a tripod (see below).

In addition to individual telephotos, a number of telephoto zoom lenses have become popular with travel photographers. Zooms offer the most versatility as they incorporate a range of focal lengths. A typical telephoto zoom — ranging from 70mm to 210mm, for example — allows you to frame a picture as you want it by choosing the most appropriate lens setting for the situation. That means carrying one lens with millimeter-to-millimeter variations from 70mm to 210mm. Also try a 35mm to 80mm. In general, beware of inexpensive models which can result in poor photographs.

The drawbacks of a zoom lens are its weight and a potential loss of clarity when compared with individual telephotos. This is less of a problem with the better lenses; and both problems are being eliminated by technological advances.

A 2X Teleconverter is a simple addition to a camera kit. Lightweight and easy to carry, the 2X doubles the focal length of various lenses, converting a 20mm into a 40mm, a 50mm into a 100mm, a 70mm to 210 zoom into a 140mm to 420mm, and so forth. Though there is again a potential loss of clarity, and in low-lighting situations focusing may be somewhat more difficult due to the extra thickness of lens glass, the 2X is a versatile accessory that's easy to use.

While it may seem excessive, a small, lightweight tripod is a real asset in assuring picture quality. This is particularly true when the heavier telephoto lenses are used, or in situations where the available light is limited and shots will be made at speeds slower than 1/60 of a second. For sharp detail, closeups, night, or limited-light pictures while in France, a tripod is a must.

A small battery-powered electronic flash unit, or "strobe," is handy for very dim light or night use, but only if the subject is at a distance of 15 feet or less. Flash units cannot illuminate an entire scene (they're only effective up to about a dozen feet), and many museums and other establishments do not permit flash photography, so take such a unit only if you know you will need — and be able to use — it. (If you do violate these rules and take a picture in such a restricted area your film, and even your camera, may be confiscated.)

Subjects as varied as the interiors of cathedrals, châteaux, and wine cellars all become photographable with a flash. It also can provide frontal light for a backlit subject and additional light in a variety of dim situations, as it is often overcast in France. If your camera does not have a hot-shoe, you will need a PC cord to synchronize the flash with your shutter. Be sure to take along extra batteries for the flash.

Film – Travel photographs are normally best in color. Good slide films are Koda-chrome 64 and Fujichrome 50, both moderate- to slow-speed films that provide satu-rated colors and work well in most outdoor light. For very bright conditions, try slower film, like Kodachrome 25. If the weather is cloudy, or you're indoors with only natural light, use a faster film, such as Kodachrome 200 or 400. There are now even faster films on the market for low-light situations. The result may be pictures with whiter, colder tones and a grainier image, but high-speed films open up picture possibilities that slower films cannot.

Films tend to render color in slightly different ways. For instance, while Kodachrome results in "warmer" tones and brings out reds and oranges, Ektachrome, a similar film, is "colder" and produces crisp, clear colors — particularly blues and greens. (It is also worth noting that Ektachrome generally can be processed at more photolabs than Kodachrome.) Fujichrome is noted for its yellows, greens, and whites. You might test films as you test your camera (see above) to determine your preference.

If you prefer film that develops into prints rather than slides, try Kodacolor 100 or 400 for most lighting situations. Vericolor is a professional film which comes in speeds of 160 and 400 and gives excellent results, especially for skin tones, but is particularly sensitive to temperature extremes which may cause color alteration. Bring it along for taking shots of people *if* you're sure you can protect it from extreme heat and cold. A newer all-purpose film with similar properties to Vericolor in terms of quality results is Ektar. It is not as sensitive to temperature changes as Vericolor, and comes in three speeds: 25, 125, and 1000. All lens and filter information applies equally to print and slide films.

If you are concerned about airport security X-rays damaging undeveloped film (X-rays do not affect processed film), store it in one of the lead-lined bags sold in camera shops. This possibility is not as much of a threat as it used to be, however. In the US, incidents of X-ray damage to unprocessed film (exposed or unexposed) are few because low-dosage X-ray equipment is used virtually everywhere. However, when crossing international borders, travelers may find that foreign X-ray equipment may deliver higher levels of radiation and damage film.

As a rule of thumb, photo industry sources say that film with speeds up to ASA 400 can go through security machinery in the US five times without any noticeable effect. Nevertheless, if you're traveling without a protective bag, ask to have your photo equipment inspected by hand. (Naturally, this is possible only if you're carrying your film and camera on board with you — a good idea, because it helps to preclude loss or theft or the possibility at some airports that checked baggage will be X-rayed with equipment more powerful than normally used for hand baggage.)

In the US, Federal Aviation Administration regulations require that if you request a hand inspection, you get it, but overseas the response may depend on the humor of the inspector. One type of film that should never be subjected to X-rays is the new, very high-speed ASA 1000 film; there are lead-lined bags made especially for it — and, in the event that you are refused a hand inspection, this is the only way to save your film. Finally, the walk-through metal detector devices at airports do not affect film, though film cartridges may set them off.

How much film should you take? If you are serious about photography, pack at least one roll of film (36 exposures) for each day of your trip. Film is especially expensive abroad, and any extra can be bartered away or brought home and safely stored in your refrigerator. (Processing is also more expensive abroad and not as safe as at home.) Nevertheless, if you don't bring enough, you should have no trouble getting any standard film in most places in France; it's sold everywhere.

VIDEO CAMCORDERS: In general, camcorders are self-contained, automated, point-and-shoot devices, though for the more ambitious film-making traveler, 8mm video or movie cameras allow the operator a greater degree of control over the images recorded and superior image quality. What follows is a brief roundup of tips and suggestions for the beginning home moviemaker, and those travelers who need to brush up on their videotaping technique.

Your camcorder has some type of zoom feature, whether it's 4:1, 6:1, or all the way up to 12:1. For most people, that's enough. Although some models have a fixed lens, others, like 8mm video, provide you the option of adding a telephoto for close-up shooting or a wide-angle lens if you often find yourself not being able to fit all of what you want to shoot into the viewfinder. If you do decide to add a lens, check that the one you buy will fit your camcorder. You may be able to double up on your filters, though. As long as it's the same size, your camera filter should be able to fit on your camcorder lens. (See the discussion of filters below.)

Although the lux ratings of camcorders now are low enough to achieve some impressive videos in low light situations, for good clarity and color saturation, you should have an additional light (10 watts or higher) to brighten indoor shooting. Generally, the lights can be easily attached to the camcorder and come with the necessary accessories such as battery charger, battery pack, and light diffuser. All that can get fairly heavy, however, so you might want to leave your light at home. Most museums and churches prohibit the use of video lights — both for security reasons and because they can be harmful to paintings and stained glass, not to mention annoying to other visitors.

In general, Europe operates on 220 volt 50 Hz electric current, as opposed to the 110 volt 60 Hz current that is the standard in the United States. To compensate for the difference, you'll need to make sure that the battery charger that comes with your camcorder is compatible with the current in the countries you're touring. Most chargers are compatible, but owner's manuals don't always spell this out. So if it's unclear, be sure to call the company and ask. If the charger is incompatible, you'll have to get a voltage converter. Even if your camcorder's charger is compatible with the current and voltage ratings in other countries, you'll need a plug adaptor kit to cope with the variations in plug configurations found in France. Voltage converters and adapter plug kits are available from some of the companies listed above specializing in travel paraphenalia; also see *Mail, Telephone, and Electricity,* in this section, for further information and sources.

You'll also be in for a shock if you try to play back your tape through a European TV set or VCR. Whereas the United States and Canada use the NTSC television standard, most European countries operate on the PAL standard. Still other European countries use the SECAM standard, so the chance of your playing back your video movies through a TV set in another country is unlikely. Because the various systems use a different number of lines-per-frame and frames-per-second, they are incompatible with each other. (For the same reason, if you send a tape of your sister's wedding to your brother in France, he won't be able to view it.) In order to review what you've taped, you'll either have to use the electronic viewfinder on your camcorder, or have to take along a small portable NTSC TV to which you could connect your camcorder. For the same incompatibility reasons, however, you won't be able to view European telecasts with your portable. Although there are a few multiple-standard TV sets available, don't count on there being one in your hotel room.

Tapes – It usually is best to buy tapes before leaving home, as they probably will be lots more expensive near major tourist and resort areas. It also will be less confusing, since different countries have their own ways of labeling tape. Although the variations in recording and playback standards won't affect your ability to use the tape, they will affect how quickly you record. Because the tape moves slower in a PAL camcorder than in an NTSC camcorder, you will get less recording time from a European tape than is indicated on the label. So if you buy a E-160 tape designed for a PAL camcorder, you will really have only about 2 hours of recording time (T-120) on your NTSC camcorder.

If you do run out of tape while on your trip, you shouldn't have a hard time finding what you need. Most of the major tape brands — TDK, Sony, Memorex, Maxell, BASF, Fuji, and Scotch — are available throughout the US, but when buying tapes abroad, you're bound to run into some unfamiliar names. Stick to what you know, if possible. When choosing, especially among unfamiliar brands, be sure that it is indeed the correct tape format — 8mm, VHS, Super-VHS, Beta, and so on — for your camcorder.

Also, if an unknown brand is priced substantially below the rest, there's probably a reason. First of all, the image quality may be poor. Secondly, the few dollars you save in buying the least expensive videocassettes will mean nothing a few years from now when the tape is showing signs of wear. You also should be aware of the potential problem of low-quality tapes damaging the heads of camcorders.

Because you'll want to keep your accessories to a manageable number — especially if you're using a full-size camcorder — you should use the longest-length tape possible for recording your trip. Depending on the tape speed of your equipment, the longest 8mm and VHS tapes generally run for 2 hours and VHS-C cassettes run for 20 minutes. VHS and VHS-C cassettes can record in the extended-play mode for 6-hour and 60-minute recordings, respectively, but extending the recording time reduces the picture quality substantially. It's best to record in the standard-play mode, because you'll get the best picture quality.

With the wide variety of grades and types of videocassettes on the market, it's easy to get confused about what kind of tape to buy for a particular application. Certain camcorders can record in stereo, so for those you'll want a hi-fi videocassette for better sound quality. If you have a Super VHS, Super VHS-C, or Hi Band 8mm camcorder, you'll want to buy the corresponding tapes for those high-end machines to achieve the best possible picture quality. A Super VHS-C videocassette will not improve your regular VHS-C video picture, however. Get a high-grade or professional quality tape for the once-in-a-lifetime videos that you plan to watch a lot. Before loading up on videocassettes for your trip, think about how much time you'll actually spend shooting, and about how many tapes you'll really want to view later. Plan on a tape for every other day of your vacation, or, if you intend to use your camcorder heavily, a tape for each day. Remember that you always can edit a tape, and even reuse it if you decide you don't want to keep it.

Your videocassettes generally are safe from the X-rays in airport detector devices, but the electromagnetic fields generated by those devices could cause dropouts in your tapes, which are recorded by an electromagnetic process. The lead-lined bags that protect against X-rays unfortunately don't protect against an electromagnetic field, so your best bet is to take your tapes along for a hand inspection. Because cassettes have been favorite carriers for terrorist explosives over the years, however, airport officials may insist that you put everything through the X-ray machine. If you don't have a choice, put them through and hope for the best.

FILTERS: For both Camcorders and SLR cameras, filters are important considerations. Take a skylight filter (1A or 1B) for each lens. There's no need to remove it, except to replace it with a different filter. Not only will it provide the filtration needed to combat atmospheric haze and ultraviolet light, but it also will protect the lens surface.

A polarizering filter goes one step beyond the skylight variety, cutting out reflections from non-metallic surfaces (water and glass, for instance) and penetrating haze for extra clarity and rich color saturation. It will also add impact to greens and blues in a landscape. While its effects are dramatic, it can be a difficult filter to use as it cuts back on light (it's a dark filter) and creates deep shadows. It will work well only under certain lighting conditions. In spite of these drawbacks, it remains an excellent filter for certain effects.

Unless you plan to experiment with the increasingly diverse range of specialty filters now available (diffraction, multiple image, and closeup, for instance), skylights and a polarizer are just about all you'll need. Stick to the medium- to high-priced glass filters (Hoya, Tiffen, or Vivitar, for example) to assure picture quality.

SOME FINAL TIPS

Get organized. A small, lightweight canvas camera bag with cushioning and Velcro dividers is perfect for carrying lenses, lens tissue, filters, rolls of film or tapes, and a strobe. It's amazing how compact camera equipment is when packed properly. For better pictures, remember the following pointers:

1. Get close. Move in to get your subject to fill the frame.
2. Vary your angle. Shoot from above or below; look for unusual perspectives.
3. Pay attention to backgrounds. Keep it simple or blur it out.
4. Look for details: not just a whole building, but a decorative element; not an entire street scene, but a single remarkable face.
5. Don't be lazy. Always carry your camera gear with you, loaded and ready for unexpected opportunities.

For Better Videos – Try to plan your movie with an introduction, a development, and a conclusion. Sometimes you can't help but get a video collage, but shoot with an eye — and an ear — toward how it's going to look and sound on a TV set. You're not just capturing a moment, as you do with still photography; you're telling a story.

1. To divide the tapes by country or region, use the camcorder's titling feature, if it has one, or shoot museum signs or some other kind of marker that indicates where you are. Use your fade in/fade out feature to provide smooth transitions.
2. Suppress your impulse to point and shoot and then find another object to shoot. Your viewers will need several seconds to focus on a subject and orient themselves to what they're seeing. Stay on each subject for at least 5 or 6 seconds — longer if the situation warrants.
3. Try not to shoot directly into strong, bright light as this may damage your camcorder. Your subject is also likely to appear as a silhouette because the camcorder will adjust for the brightest source. Some camcorders, however, do have backlight compensating features.
4. Vary your shooting techniques. Using the various buttons available at your fingertips, zoom in and out and pan from side to side to view your subject. If your subject is stationary, walk around (but hold the camera steady) to get a different angle. Your objective should be to create a smooth flow.
5. Your camcorder won't be welcome everywhere, although as they become more popular, they are increasingly accepted. In any event, before lugging your gear with you, check with the places you plan to visit.
■ **A note about courtesy and caution:** When photographing in France (and anywhere else in the world), ask first. It's common courtesy. Furthermore, some governments have security regulations regarding the use of cameras and will not permit the photographing of certain subjects, such as some government and military installations. When in doubt, ask.

Useful Words and Phrases

The French as a nation have a reputation for being snobbish and brusque to tourists, and, unfortunately, many Americans have allowed this stereotype to dissuade them from visiting France. The more experienced traveler, however, knows that on an individual basis, the French people are usually cordial and helpful, especially if you speak a few words of their language. Don't be afraid of misplaced accents or misconjugated verbs — in most cases you will be understood (and possibly corrected) and then advised on the menu or pointed in the right direction. Below is a basic guide to pronunciation, as well as a selection of commonly used words and phrases to speed you on your way.

French words are stressed on the vowel preceding the last consonant in the word except that a final accented *e* (*è*) is stressed. Final consonants are pronounced only if they precede words beginning with vowels. Vowels preceding nasals (*m*, *n*) are nasalized (i.e., pronounced with emission of air through the nose) and the *m* or *n* is not pronounced.

French consonants are pronounced almost as in English with these exceptions:

> *ch* is pronounced like *sh* in *push*
> *c* before *e*, *i*, or *y* is pronounced *s*; otherwise as *k*
> *s* is pronounced as *z* between vowels
> *gn* is pronounced like *ny* in canyon
> *g* before *e*,*i*, or *y* is pronounced like *si* in vision; otherwise like *g* in *go*
> *j* is pronounced like *si* in vision
> *ll* following *i* is pronounced like *y* in year
> *qu* is pronounced as *k* (not *kw*)
> *h* is silent

French vowels are different from those in English, but usually can be pronounced intelligibly following these rules:

> Final unaccented *e* is silent; it signals that a preceding consonant is pronounced.
> *è* is pronounced like the *a* in *late*
> *e* is pronounced as in *met*
> *i* is pronounced as in *machine*
> *o* is pronounced like *ou* in *ought*
> *u* is pronounced like *i* in *bit* but with the lips rounded
> *an* and *en* are pronounced like the *a* in *father* but nasalized
> *in* is pronounced with the vowel of *met* but nasalized
> *ai* is pronounced like *e* in *met*
> *au* is pronounced like *o* in *cold*
> *oi* and *oy* are pronounced *wa*
> *ou* is pronounced as in *youth*
> *eu* is pronounced like the *e* of *men* but with the lips rounded
> Final *er* is pronounced like the *ay* of *delay*

Greetings and Everyday Expressions

Good morning! (Hello!)	*Bonjour!*
Good afternoon, good evening!	*Bonsoir!*
How are you?	*Comment allez-vous?*
Pleased to meet you!	*Enchanté!*
Good-bye!	*Au revoir!*
See you soon!	*A bientôt!*
Good night!	*Bonne nuit!*
Yes!	*Oui!*
No!	*Non!*
Please!	*S'il vous plaît!*
Thank you!	*Merci!*
You're welcome!	*De rien!*
Excuse me!	*Excusez-moi* or *pardonnez-moi!*
It doesn't matter.	*Ca m'est ègal.*
I don't speak French.	*Je ne parle pas français.*
Do you speak English?	*Parlez-vous anglais?*

Please repeat.	*Répétez, s'il vous plaît.*
I don't understand.	*Je ne comprends pas.*
Do you understand?	*Vous comprendez?*
My name is . . .	*Je m'appelle . . .*
What is your name?	*Comment vous appelez-vous?*
miss	*mademoiselle*
madame	*madame*
mister/sir	*monsieur*

open	*ouvert*
closed	*fermé*
entrance	*l'entrée*
exit	*la sortie*
push	*poussez*
pull	*tirez*
today	*aujourd'hui*
tomorrow	*demain*
yesterday	*hier*

Help!	*Au secours!*
ambulance	*l'ambulance*
Get a doctor!	*Appelez le médecin!*

Checking In

I have (don't have) a reservation.	*J'ai une (Je n'ai pas de) réservation.*
I would like . . .	*Je voudrais . . .*
a single room	*une chambre pour une personne*
a double room	*une chambre pour deux*
a quiet room	*une chambre tranquille*
with bath	*avec salle de bains*
with shower	*avec douche*
with a sea view	*avec une vue sur la mer*
with air conditioning	*une chambre climatisée*
with balcony	*avec balcon*
overnight only	*pour une nuit seulement*
a few days	*quelques jours*
a week	*une semaine (au moins)*
with full board	*avec pension complète*
with half board	*avec demi-pension*
Does that price include breakfast?	*Est-ce-que le petit dejeuner est inclus?*
Are taxes included?	*Est-ce-que les taxes sont compris?*
Do you accept traveler's checks?	*Acceptez-vous les chèques de voyage?*
Do you accept credit cards?	*Acceptez-vous les cartes de crédit?*

Eating Out

ashtray	*un cendrier*
bottle	*une bouteille*
(extra) chair	*une chaise (en sus)*
cup	*une tasse*
fork	*une fourchette*
knife	*un couteau*
spoon	*une cuillère*

napkin	*une serviette*
plate	*une assiette*
table	*une table*
beer	*bière*
coffee	*café*
black coffee	*café noir*
coffee with milk	*café au lait*
cream	*crème*
fruit juice	*jus de fruit*
lemonade	*citron pressé*
milk	*lait*
mineral water	
(non-carbonated)	*l'eau minérale*
mineral water (carbonated)	*gazeuse*
orangeade	*orange pressé*
port	*vin de porto*
sherry	*vin de Xérès*
red wine	*vin rouge*
white wine	*vin blanc*
rosé	*rosé*
tea	*thé*
water	*eau*
cold	*froid*
hot	*chaud*
sweet	*doux*
(very) dry	*(très) sec*
bacon	*bacon*
bread	*pain*
butter	*beurre*
eggs	*oeufs*
soft boiled	*à la coque*
hard boiled eggs	*oeuf dur*
fried	*sur le plat*
scrambled	*brouillé*
poached	*poché*
ham	*jambon*
honey	*miel*
sugar	*sucre*
jam	*confiture*
juice	*jus*
orange	*jus d'orange*
tomato	*jus de tomate*
omelet	*omelette*
pepper	*poivre*
salt	*sel*
Waiter!	*Garçon!*
Waitress!	*Mademoiselle!*
I would like	*Je voudrais*
a glass of	*un verre de*

a bottle of	*une bouteille de*
a half bottle of	*une demie-bouteille*
a liter of	*un litre de*
a carafe of	*une carafe de*

The check, please.	*L'addition, s'il vous plaît.*
Is the service charge included?	*Le service, est-il compris?*
I think there is a mistake in the bill.	*Je crois qu'il y a une erreur dans l'addition.*

See also the glossary of food terms in *Food and Drink*, PERSPECTIVES.

Shopping

bakery	*boulangerie*
bookstore	*librairie*
butcher store	*boucherie*
camera shop	*magasin de photographie*
clothing store	*magasin de vêtements*
delicatessen	*charcuterie*
department store	*grand magasin*
drugstore (for medicine)	*pharmacie*
grocery	*épicerie*
jewelry store	*bijouterie*
newsstand	*kiosque à journaux*
notions (sewing supplies) shop	*mercerie*
pastry shop	*pâtisserie*
perfume (and cosmetics) store	*parfumerie*
pharmacy/drugstore	*pharmacie*
shoestore	*magasin de chaussures*
supermarket	*supermarché*
tobacconist	*bureau de tabac*

cheap	*bon marché*
expensive	*cher*

large	*grand*
larger	*plus grand*
too large	*trop grand*
small	*petit*
smaller	*plus petit*
too small	*trop petit*

long	*long*
short	*court*
old	*vieux*
new	*nouveau*
used	*d'occasion*
handmade	*fabriqué à la main*

Is it machine washable?	*Est-ce-que c'est lavable à la machine?*
How much does this cost?	*Quel est le prix?/Combien?*

What is it made of?	*De quoi est-il fait?*
camel's hair	*poil de chameau*
cotton	*coton*
corduroy	*velours côtelé*
filigree	*filigrane*
lace	*dentelle*
leather	*cuir*
linen	*lin*
silk	*soie*
suede	*suède*
synthetic	*synthètique*
wool	*laine*
brass	*cuivre jaune*
copper	*cuivre*
gold (plated)	*or (plaqué)*
silver (plated)	*argent (plaqué)*
wood	*bois*
May I have a sales tax rebate form?	*Puis-je avoir la forme pour la détaxe?*
May I pay with this credit card?	*Puis-je payer par cette carte de crédit?*
May I pay with a traveler's check?	*Puis-je payer par chèques de voyage?*

Getting around

north	*le nord*
south	*le sud*
east	*l'est*
west	*l'ouest*
right	*droite*
left	*gauche*
Go straight ahead	*tout droit*
far	*loin*
near	*proche*
airport	*l'aéroport*
bus stop	*l'arrêt de bus*
gas station	*station service*
train station	*la gare*
subway	*le métro*
map	*carte*
one-way ticket	*aller simple*
round-trip ticket	*un billet aller et retour*
gate	*porte*
track	*voie*
in first class	*en première*
in second class	*en deuxième*
no smoking	*défense de fumer*

Does this subway/bus go to . . . ?	*Est-ce que ce métro/bus va à . . . ?*
What time does it leave?	*A quelle heure part-il?*
gas	*essence*
regular (leaded)	*ordinaire*
super (leaded)	*super*
unleaded	*sans plomb*
diesel	*diesel*
Fill it up, please.	*De plein, s'il vous plaît.*
the tires	*pneus*
the oil	*huile*
Danger	*Danger*
Caution	*Attention*
Detour	*Détour*
Dead End	*Cul-de-sac*
Do Not Enter	*Défense d'entrer*
No Parking	*Défense de garer*
No Passing	*Défense de dépasser*
No U-turn	*Défense de faire demi-tour*
One way	*Sans interdit*
Pay toll	*Péage*
Pedestrian Zone	*Zone piètone*
Reduce Speed	*Ralentissez*
Steep Incline	*Côte à forte inclination*
Stop	*Stop; Arrêt*
Use Headlights	*Allumez les phrases*
Yield	*Cédez*
Where is the . . . ?	*Où se trouve . . . ?*
How many kilometers are we from . . . ?	*A combien de kilomètres sommes nous de . . . ?*

Personal Items and Services

aspirin	*aspirine*
Band-Aids	*pensements*
barbershop	*coiffeur pour hommes*
bath	*bain*
bathroom	*salle de bain*
beauty shop	*salon de coiffeur*
condom	*préservatif*
dentist	*dentist*
disposable diapers	*couches*
dry cleaner	*nettoyage à sec* or *teinturerie*
hairdresser	*coiffeur pour dames*
laundromat	*laundrette* or *blanchisserie automatique*
post office	*bureau de poste*
postage stamps (air mail)	*timbres (par avion)*
razor	*rasoir*
sanitary napkins	*serviettes hygiéniques*
shampoo	*shampooing*
shaving cream	*crème à raser*

shower	*douche*
soap	*savon*
tampons	*tampons*
tissues	*tissus*
toilet	*toilette* or *WC*
toilet paper	*papier hygiénique*
toothbrush	*brosse à dents*
toothpaste	*pâte dentifrice*

Where is the men's/ladies' room?	*Où est la toilette?*

Days of the Week

Monday	*lundi*
Tuesday	*mardi*
Wednesday	*mercredi*
Thursday	*jeudi*
Friday	*vendredi*
Saturday	*samedi*
Sunday	*dimanche*

Months

January	*janvier*
February	*février*
March	*mars*
April	*avril*
May	*mai*
June	*juin*
July	*juillet*
August	*août*
September	*septembre*
October	*octobre*
November	*novembre*
December	*décembre*

Numbers

zero	*zéro*
one	*un*
two	*deux*
three	*trois*
four	*quatre*
five	*cinq*
six	*six*
seven	*sept*
eight	*huit*
nine	*neuf*
ten	*dix*
eleven	*onze*
twelve	*douze*
thirteen	*treize*
fourteen	*quatorze*
fifteen	*quinze*
sixteen	*seize*
seventeen	*dix-sept*
eighteen	*dix-huit*

nineteen	*dix-neuf*
twenty	*vingt*
twenty-one	*vingt-et-un*
thirty	*trente*
forty	*quarante*
fifty	*cinquante*
sixty	*soixante*
seventy	*soixante-dix*
eighty	*quatre-vingts*
ninety	*quatre-vingt-dix*
one hundred	*cent*

Colors

black	*noir*
blue	*bleu*
brown	*brun*
gray	*gris*
green	*vert*
orange	*orange*
pink	*rose*
purple	*violet*
red	*rouge*
yellow	*jaune*
white	*blanc*

Writing Reservations Letters

Restaurant
Street Address
Postal Code, City
France

Dear Sir:

   I would like to reserve a table for (number of) persons for lunch/dinner on (day and month), 199?, at (hour) o'clock.

or

   I would like to reserve a room for (number of) people for (number of) nights.

   Would you be so kind as to confirm the reservation as soon as possible?

   I am very much looking forward to meeting you. (The French usually include a pleasantry such as this.)

   With my thanks,
(Signature, followed by your typed name and address)

Monsieur:

   Je voudrais réserver une table pour (number) personnes pour le déjeuner/dîner du (day and month) 199?, à (time using the 24-hour clock) heures.

or

   Je voudrais réserver une chambre à (number) personne(s) pour (number) nuits.

   Auriez-vous la bonté de bien vouloir me confirmer cette réservation dès que possible?

   J'attends avec impatience la chance de faire votre connaissance.

   Avec tous remerciements,

PERSPECTIVES

Food and Drink

 France is the gastronomic capital of the world; it's no accident that so many food-related words — cuisine, gourmet, menu, sauté — come from the French language. So it's only natural that the French are very serious about food and drink. They fuss over the quality of ingredients, prepare each dish with great care and style, and eat with even greater enthusiasm. As a result, dining in France can be the most memorable aspect of any visit — or the most uncomfortable. French dining customs are just enough like ours to make the differences hard to notice, but those differences count for a lot in a nation preoccupied with gastronomy. Fortunately, it's not hard to pick up the French manner and tempo of eating if you look about you and notice what's going on.

THE FRENCH DINING EXPERIENCE

Start with breakfast, which in France generally consists of coffee and rolls. The coffee is strong, usually mixed half and half with hot milk (*café au lait*), although you also can have it black (*café noir*) or take tea (*thé*) or hot chocolate (*chocolat*) instead. Rolls — plain crusty French bread rolls; flaky, buttery croissants; or somewhat sweeter, doughy *brioches* — are served with butter and jam. The French don't much care for the fruit juice, eggs, bacon, cereal, and pancakes of the staple American or English breakfast. If you insist, you can get them, but in all but the most tourist-oriented hotels they will bear little relationship to what you know. And in any case you'll pay preposterous prices for disappointing examples, since the French think of them as exotic — and charge accordingly.

Lunch has its special customs, too. Most French restaurants traditionally serve a full dinner at midday: at least three courses, accompanied by wine. However, if you can't handle a major meal at noon or if you're saving yourself for a three-star extravaganza at dinner, you may prefer something light. Don't go to an elaborate restaurant for a quick bite; you will almost certainly wind up with more food — and a higher bill — than you intended, and the meal likely will last a couple of hours. Try a bistro or brasserie instead, one which serves simple meals; a pizzeria (now common almost everywhere in France and often quite good); or a snack bar (found in abundance around the universities and other gathering places of the young). At any of these you can find an omelette or a slice of quiche.

Or try a sandwich. In France this usually means a length of crisp French bread covered by a very thin layer of good ham or cheese — period. It's basic, but very satisfying. The *croque-monsieur,* a toasted (French toast, natch) ham and cheese sandwich, (or a *croque-madame*; the feminine form sports a fried egg on top), also is delicious and inexpensive, as is *steak frites.* In the latter, the piece of meat will be small and nearly paper thin, but it will be competently grilled and very tasty — even pink inside if you so request. And it's served with lots of those fine *frites;* after all, this is the home of the original French fry.

Perhaps the very best option at lunchtime is to hunt out the local public market or food shopping street. Every town and neighborhood has one, since the French shop for their food a day (sometimes a meal) at a time, bringing home whatever appeals to them for that afternoon or evening. Tiny butcher stores, fishmongers, greengrocers, pastry shops, and bread bakers form a cluster of tempting sights and scents. Best of all are the *charcuteries* and *traiteurs,* shops that sell everything from simple salads, pâté, ham, cheese, and sausage to whole geese in *galantine,* sparkling with aspic, lapped in creamy *chaud-froid* sauce, and garlanded with cut-vegetable "flowers." You can go from shop to shop and, for remarkably little money, acquire two or three slices of pâté or *saucisson* (salami), a chunk of cheese, a quarter-pound of olives, some vegetables in vinaigrette, a crusty *baguette* of bread, and a small bottle of wine or mineral water — then go sit in a nearby park or by a scenic river for a glorious *picnique* (the French invented that, too). For the more timid traveler, all this can be accomplished, with far less stress, and a minimal knowledge of the language, by going to a local *supermarché* (supermarket). In addition to the conventional variety, you can find them in the *sous sol* (basement) of any major department store. Be prepared to be dazzled — these places bear little resemblance to your neighborhood *A&P.* You also can find a wide choice of wines and spirits, at prices far lower than at formal wine shops.

But there's no reason to pass up a full-course restaurant meal at lunch (traditionally served only between 12 and 2 PM) and another at dinner (served between 7 and 9 PM) if your waistline, appetite, and schedule can stand it. Travelers will find that almost every city or region has too many interesting restaurants to be sampled during the course of the average visit. For the best dining experience, it pays to select both your restaurant and your meal carefully.

First, choose a restaurant based on your budget and the sort of meal you'd most like to sample. In general, there are three basic types of restaurants in France: the temples of haute cuisine, the bistro serving *cuisine bourgeoise,* and the neighborhood brasserie or hangout. The dining experience in each is dramatically different.

The temples of haute cuisine are supremely elegant and quite formal. Their menus are diverse, though they bear a family resemblance to those in the more ambitious French restaurants in major American cities. The taste of similar dishes will be subtly better in France, however, because the ingredients are more likely to have been raised *sans* additives and also usually are fresher. In this type of restaurant you'll find the perennially aristocratic appetizers — caviar, oysters, smoked salmon, pâté, and terrine; noble meat and game dishes such as venison, wild boar, grouse, and pheasant; severely simple roasts with luscious, complex sauces; exquisite sautés of veal and chicken with cream and wild mushrooms; an enormous spectrum of fish (many with unfamiliar names) prepared in a dazzling variety of ways; perfect vegetables lavishly set forth as courses in themselves; a cheese selection seemingly without end; and dessert carts laden with finely sculptured fantasies executed in pastry, whipped cream, and meringue. These are the makings of magnificent meals, though hardly the sort of feast one would want every day; even the French don't eat this way all the time. Our advice, therefore, is to plan just a few of these glorious dinners and space them out for the most dramatic gastronomical memories.

At the opposite end of the spectrum are the unpretentious neighborhood brasseries, where the food is relatively quick and simple. It's easy to enjoy a full meal at this kind of place as long as you stay within the limits of the kitchen's power. That means that if someone has been so misguided as to put pheasant Souvaroff with truffles and foie gras on the menu at the equivalent of $6 a portion, don't order it. It won't be the dish it should be. Order instead such dependable dishes as onion soup gratinée, grilled or sautéed cutlets, chops, sausages, roast chicken, or the hearty stew or fricassee of the day. For an appetizer, try freshly made vegetable soup or fresh asparagus if they happen to be in season; for dessert, a slice of apple tart, some chocolate mousse, or caramel custard. These are dishes that the humblest restaurants in France can do well. But once again, it would be a pity to eat *only* in places of this kind, because you'll miss most of the truly interesting dishes France has to offer.

Perhaps the most fun of all is the third type of restaurant, the medium-priced establishment that serves *cuisine bourgeoise,* the traditional cooking of a particular region. There are at least half a dozen distinct styles of regional French cooking, ranging from the steamy *choucroutes* of Alsace to the spicy sauces of Provence. The chefs at these little bistros and family-run eateries take classic dishes, add their personal interpretations, and produce food that is both strongly individual and thoroughly representative of their area. They use the best ingredients from the markets — meat, fish, fruits, vegetables, and dairy products. Even the traveler who knows little about either France or food will enjoy the marvelous diversity of most *cuisine bourgeoise.*

So much for the restaurants; the next step is to figure out the menu. At first glance, a French menu can inspire culture shock, for it's often handwritten in indecipherable script. Do not be stampeded into ordering the first items you recognize. Let the waiter help, but don't let him rush you. Take your time; remember, the table is yours for as long as you want it. Also remember that many restaurants post menus outside, so you might combine an afternoon's sightseeing with a little menu reading before dinner.

Most French menus are divided into à la carte offerings and prix fixe (fixed price) meals, called *menus*, which offer good value for the money. There may be several different *menus,* ranging from the economical *menu touristique,* which usually offers the most pedestrian dishes, to the more expensive *menu gastronomique* or *menu de dégustation,* which may run to five or nine or more small courses and feature regional specialties, seasonal delicacies, and the dishes of which the chef is most proud. The latter can be a wonderful way to taste a bit of everything that's best in the local cuisine, wherever in France you may be.

The sequence of courses in France is fairly similar to that in the US, but a few differences are worth noting. For example, appetizers in France are served at almost every lunch and dinner, but are called *entrées*. Also, unless otherwise specified, *salade* means only lettuce — good flavorful greens — tossed with a simple vinaigrette dressing. Salad is never eaten early in a meal — although you can order crudités (an assortment of fresh raw vegetables) as an *entrée* — and it isn't served automatically. Rather, it's presented as an abundant, separate course, after the main dish and before cheese or dessert; the idea is that its astringency clears the palate to prepare for fuller enjoyment of what follows.

Cheese also plays a more prominent role in a French dinner than in the American equivalent. It's customary to drink wine at dinner, and ordering some cheese "with which to finish the wine" is a pleasant part of that custom. The better the restaurant, the more pride it will take in a full and varied cheese tray — offering as many as forty varieties at a time. This can be intimidating if you don't recognize more than one or two of them, but just ask the waiter to name what's unfamiliar and explain whether they are strong, sharp, soft, runny, creamy, or crumbly. You may request small portions of two or three different cheeses or a substantial piece of the one that looks most appealing. Cheese typically is accompanied by bread and sometimes butter, especially if one of the selections is hard or dry.

Finally, there is the matter of drink. The American custom of starting a meal in a restaurant with a cocktail comprised of hard liquor very seldom is duplicated in France. A French "drink" is far more apt to be a house apéritif — perhaps a glass of champagne with a dash of raspberry liqueur — or a glass of wine. You can ask to see the wine list right away or simply request a carafe of the house's red, white, or rosé to sip while reading the menu. (Carafe wine is relatively inexpensive and can be undistinguished, but almost always is potable.) Alternatively, mineral water (with or without gas) is a common initial request, especially since glasses of cold water seldom appear on a French table as a matter of course. Mineral water also is a common beverage (along with wine) during a meal. Coffee never is served during a meal, but rather at the very end, in small cups; it's a strong, dark brew into which the French often stir great quantities of sugar, but no milk. The French also brew first-rate decaffeinated coffee (*décaféinée*) that is far better than the watery equivalent most often served in American restaurants. A beverage called "American coffee" is served in many places, but usually it's awful, so beware.

France also produces some of the world's best wines, and every visitor should try them. Bordeaux, Burgundy, and Champagne are widely known for their fine wines, although almost every corner of France has its own. When ordering wine, remember that the local wine usually marries well with the local cuisine. It's also wise to remember that no one is as familiar with a restaurant's wine list as that restaurant's own staff, especially when the list has a heavy bias of wines from an unfamiliar region, including wines from small producers. So when ordering wine, as with food, don't hesitate to ask questions and take advice. Below is a region-by-region discussion and description of the foods and wines for which France is famous.

REGIONAL SPECIALTIES

BRITTANY: In this seafaring province, concentrate on the seafare: Brittany is renowned for its wonderful variety of Atlantic ocean fish, including bass, cod, herring, mackerel, sardines, sole, tuna, and turbot. Equally good are the crustaceans: clams, lobsters, mussels, oysters, scallops, sea urchins, winkles, and whelks. A tasty mussel dish called *moules marinières* is served everywhere along the coast, and the famous Bélon oysters, known for their delicate and characteristic flavor, are enjoyed throughout the world. Two other popular Breton seafood dishes are *assiette de fruits de mer,* a large platter of mixed shellfish, and *cotriade,* a chowder of fish and mussels, potatoes, cream, and sorrel. Confirmed meat eaters should try the region's famous *pré-salé* lamb, derived from animals grazed in salt marshes so that the flesh acquires an intriguing tang. The bounty of Brittany also extends to myriad fresh fruits and vegetables — strawberries (especially from Plougastel), blueberries, blackberries, artichokes, peas, potatoes, cabbage, cauliflower, and beans. Finally, for dessert or a snack anytime, have a *galette* (the Breton name for crêpe), a paper-thin pancake that can be eaten either dusted with powdered sugar or filled with cheese, fruit, jam, eggs, or ham.

Brittany is one of the very few French provinces without its own vineyards. The nearby Loire Valley, however, provides a ready selection of wines, including muscadet, a popular fruity white wine that goes beautifully with fish and seafood. Although most of the wine drunk in Britanny is white — and drunk young — a chilled beaujolais or light red sometimes is served, especially if the fish is accompanied with a red wine sauce. With oysters, chablis, blanc de blancs, and champagne are time-honored dinner partners.

As an alternative to wine, sparkling or still cider is served in *crêperies* as well as in many other restaurants. Two varieties are offered: one is dry and "hard;" the other is sweet, more like apple juice. You may order a bottle or a *bol* (the bowl usually used in French homes for *café au lait*).

NORMANDY: Another seacoast province, Normandy also is known for many of the same fish and seafoods as Brittany; particularly prized here are turbot and Dover sole. Be sure to try this region's famous *sole normande,* garnished with mussels, shrimp, and mushrooms, *moules à la crème* (mussels in cream sauce), as well as the fish stew called *matelote à la normande,* a tasty mixture of shellfish, fin fish, cream, and cider. These last two ingredients suggest Normandy's other great specialties, dairy products and apples. The area's lush, green pastures and ubiquitous brown and white cattle yield a wonderful, thick, nutty, ivory cream; rich butter; and extraordinary cheeses (for example, camembert, pont-l'évêque, and livarot). The several varieties of apples produced by Normandy's acres of orchards are used widely in local cookery: in main dishes along with fish or meat, as well as in pies, turnovers, fritters, cakes, and jams. Apples also are pressed into a strong, dry cider and a fiery apple brandy called calvados, both of which are used in many dishes.

Since Normandy produces no wine of its own, many wine lists include a good selection of Loire wines: sancerre and muscadet are reliable white wines with fish and seafood; the rosés and soft reds of Chinon and Bourgeuil are versatile. The spectacular cheese trays call for a medium- to full-bodied red bordeaux, burgundy, or côte du Rhône. As in Brittany, cider is an alternative to wine, especially with simple meals or in dishes prepared with cider. Calvados can be poured during a pause in the middle of an elaborate meal, known as "Le Trou Normand."

CHAMPAGNE AND THE NORTH: More famous for its wines than for its cuisine, the Champagne region nevertheless offers several specialties worth noting. For example, the *charcuterie* is excellent, particularly the *andouillettes de Troyes* (chitterling sausages) and *pieds de porc Ste.-Menehould* (breaded and grilled pigs' feet). Fish from the area's rivers and streams are prepared in a number of ways — sautéed or braised and served with champagne sauce or *à la nage* (in a light, buttery, brothy sauce). Herring from the English Channel is salted, smoked, or marinated. The cornucopia of vegetables harvested from Champagne's broad, fertile fields — artichokes, asparagus, beans, cabbage, carrots, cauliflower, leeks, peas, and potatoes — has inspired several hearty regional dishes: *parmentier,* a leek and potato soup; *flamiche,* a leek quiche; and *potée champenoise,* a pork, cabbage, and potato soup. The verdant northern flat lands also produce many flavorful cheeses, among them brie and coulommiers (soft), boursin (creamy), and maroilles (strong).

Champagne, the sparkling wine that derived its name from the region, makes up 60% to 80% of the region's wine lists. Who could wish for or imagine anything else? Champagne is safe to order since it goes well with almost everything — except spicy dishes — and certainly with the fish and seafood that are most often prepared with a champagne sauce. If you wish to indulge in a few bottles at the source — where prices for the bubbly are as low as they get — start with a light champagne such as a *blanc de blancs* or a *crémant* or even a glass of the white *côteaux champenois* (still wine), and with the main dish move to a fuller type of champagne, which might even be a rare vintage. Champagne will go well with a mild cheese; otherwise, accompany the local cheeses with a red *côteaux champenois* such as bouzy, cumières, or ambonnay, which are similar to beaujolais but have more fragrance. For a final touch, consider a glass of *marc de Champagne,* the local brandy.

ALSACE-LORRAINE: Here, on the border of France and Germany, look for dishes with a German influence, cooked with a French flair, such as dumplings, *spaetzle,* noodles, and that big dish of mixed meats (pork, sausage, goose) and spicy sauerkraut called *choucroute garnie.* Ham, smoked bacon, many kinds of sausages, pâtés, and terrines make up this region's delicious *charcuterie;* particularly famous are the *saucisse de Strasbourg,* a kind of knackwurst, and the *boudin noir* (black pudding) of Nancy. Alsace is perhaps best known for its foie gras, a lush pâté made from the livers of specially fattened geese; geese and duck feature very prominently on menus in both areas and are served in a number of succulent ways — roasted, braised, or preserved in a *confit.* Chefs make skillful use of the salmon, trout, and other freshwater fish caught in the region's icy streams, as well as of the wild mushrooms and game taken from its forests. Several dishes associated solely with Lorraine are *potée lorraine,* a pork, cabbage, and potato soup; *tourte à la lorraine,* a pie containing pork, veal, and egg custard; and that classic, *quiche lorraine,* a tart made with bacon, eggs, and cream. For dessert in Alsace, try the *kugelhopf,* a sweet coffee cake made with almonds and raisins; in Lorraine, macaroons or *madeleines* (finger-size sponge cakes); or in both areas, a tart made from luscious native fruits.

The wine in Alsace, one of France's most abundant wine producing areas, can be outstanding. The spicy, dry, and fragrant area wines are all white and drunk young except for the "reserve" bottlings, which benefit from some bottle age and can be surprisingly long-lived. Alsatian wines are known by the name of the variety of grape from which they are made. Riesling, gewürz-traminer, sylvaner, and pinot gris (or tokay d'Alsace) are the best, and they offer a range of tastes to complement the region's diversity of dishes. Sylvaner, the region's most plentiful wine, is a fresh and fruity dry wine of moderate distinction that is served as an apéritif or as an accompaniment to some of the traditional, earthy dishes such as brain salad, pigs' feet, onion pie, or platters of *choucroute.* For fish, seafood, and poultry, Riesling is a fine choice — dry and elegant, crisp and fruity. Tokay d'Alsace is a good alternative for fowl or white meat; it has the fullest body of the wines of Alsace, broader than the others. Gewürztraminer is a dry, fruity, spicy wine with an unmistakable zing that helps it stand up to powerfully flavored dishes. It goes well with the stronger regional cheeses and the renowned foie gras. In Lorraine, the wines of Alsace are preferred, and there is the local *vin gris* of the Côtes de Toul, pale beige and rosé in color and as unpretentious as the food of the region. Both provinces make superb fruit brandies, often served chilled, that are well worth contemplating at the close of a meal. Known as *eaux-de-vie* or *alcools blancs,* they are colorless and made from a broad range of fragrant fruits: *kirsch* (cherry), *framboise* (raspberry), *mirabelle* (small yellow plum), *quetsch* (purple plum), and *poire* Williams (pear).

BURGUNDY AND THE NORTHERN RHÔNE: For the most part, Burgundian cuisine is not subtle or sophisticated but hearty and lusty — the perfect foil for the big, complex red and white wines of the region. Typically very satisfy-ing, several Burgundy dishes will be familiar to many Americans, for exam-ple, that classic *escargots à la bourguignonne,* snails in their shells, stuffed with shallot-and-parsley-seasoned garlic butter. Three other fine Burgundian specialties, which are all enhanced by the same rich, red wine sauce made with bacon, tiny white onions, and mushroom caps, are *boeuf bourguignon, coq au vin,* and *oeufs en meurette;* the first is based on beef, the second on chicken, the third on poached eggs. One item that Americans may find disappointing, however, is the much-prized Charolais beef: Those brought up on prime Black Angus often find this French beef unimpressive. Its texture tends to be softer than the American equivalent, though it is quite tasty. Instead, try the chicken from Bresse, renowned for its flavor and distinguished by a numbered tag on each bird (also by its blue feet), or ham from the Morvan hills, particularly when served cold in parsleyed aspic as a first course, called *jambon persillé*. From the Dijon area, two food items not to be missed are the mustard — creamy or whole grain, plain or flavored — and *pain d'épice,* a strong, delicious gingerbread.

The favorite apéritif taken before a meal in Burgundy is kir, dry white wine with black currant liqueur (cassis). During a meal, red wines generally are enjoyed with red meats, game, or cheeses, and white wines with hors d'o-euvres, oysters, fish, shellfish, and white meats. In choosing Burgundies, look for the name of the town rather than a château: Beaune, Chambertin, Clos de Vougeot, Corton, Musigny, Nuits-St.-Georges, Pommard, and Vosne Ro-manée are famous for their red wines; Chablis, Corton, Meursault, and Mon-trachet for their whites. The name of the producer is an important clue to quality, and restaurateurs should be able to point out local wines produced in very limited quantities that are good values. Complex, quality burgundies need some bottle age to reach their peak. For reds, good recent vintages are 1981, 1978, 1976, 1972, and 1971; for whites, 1982, 1981, 1979, 1978, and 1976.

The most popular red wine in Burgundy is beaujolais, a versatile and reliable wine that comes in four grades of increasing quality: Beaujolais, Beaujolais Supérieur, Beaujolais-Villages, and Cru Beaujolais, the latter bear-ing the name of one of nine villages. The most popular white wine is chablis, which is dry and flinty (slightly metallic) and which also comes in four categories of increasing quality: Petit Chablis, Chablis, Chablis Premier Cru, and Chablis Grand Cru, the latter bearing one of seven small vineyard names. Delicate pouilly-fuissé and refreshing mâcon are two other white wines widely available and moderately priced.

The wines of the Rhône Valley are mostly red and robust. The southern vineyards produce the area's most celebrated red, the dark, full-bodied Châteauneuf-du-Pape, as well as gigondas, which goes well with red meat and cheeses. In the northern area, the best wines are the rich, strong côte Rôtie and hermitage and the more delicate St.-Joseph. Côtes du Rhône and côtes du Rhône Villages are generally soft, flavorful table wines that are fine values. The Rhône also produces France's best rosé wine, the fruity tavel, which is a possible accompaniment to spicy, Mediterranean dishes.

THE ALPS: The cuisine of these provinces, like the landscape, is remarkable yet basic, drawing upon the many lakes, streams, forests, fields, and pastures for a wide variety of fresh ingredients. Regional menus include many kinds of fish, such as grayling, trout, perch, and pike (the latter is best when formed into dumplings called *quenelles* and served *à la Nantua,* with a sauce made of puréed crayfish and cream — a great local favorite). Meat dishes range from wild game — venison, boar, hare — to *charcuterie* — ham, pâté, and sausage. Wild mushrooms often are used in sautés, stews, and fricassees; look especially for the distinctive, wrinkled, black *morilles* (morels) in cream sauce or pastry. Another Alpine specialty is the local dairy produce, and visitors will delight in the wonderful cheeses made from the milk of high-pasture herds (gruyère, comté, reblochon, tomme de Savoie, vacherin, beaumont, morbier) and also enjoy the savory and imaginative use of cheese in fondues and gratins.

In the Alps, most of the local wine is very dry, light, and white. Seyssel, the local sparkling wine, is probably the area's best and makes a good apéritif and accompaniment to fish dishes. The reds of the neighboring Côtes du Rhône are well stocked and marry splendidly with the hearty regional cuisine. For a cordial, try chartreuse, the famous green or yellow liqueur made from assorted herbs and aromatic plants.

PROVENCE: Provençal food epitomizes Mediterranean-style cooking in France. Many dishes are fragrant with such herbs as fennel, thyme, rosemary, and bay leaf; others are composed of tomatoes, garlic, olive oil, and olives. In fact, olives of every conceivable size and color, cured with herbs or salt or flavored oil, feature prominently in the cuisine. For example, *tapenade,* a popular appetizer, is a lively spread of minced black olives, garlic, and anchovies served on crackers, bread, or raw vegetables. Also typically Mediterranean is the extensive use of seafood (clams, cockles, crabs, mussels, sea anemones, sea urchins) and fish (bass, red mullet, sardines), either grilled or combined in chunky, spicy soups. The most famous of the latter is the bouillabaisse of Marseilles, a soup based on Mediterranean rockfish seasoned with saffron, cayenne, garlic, tomatoes, and herbs and served with a fiery mayonnaise known as rouille, made of garlic, red pepper, bread crumbs, olive oil, and fish broth. It is said that only Mediterranean bouillabaisse is authentic, for it is only here that the essential fish ingredient called *rouget* is found. (Elsewhere in the region, similar fish soups usually are called bourrides or *soupes de poisson.*) The ties to Italian cuisine are very close in Provence, as seen in the frequent appearance of *pistou,* a paste of basil, cheese, garlic, and olive oil that's stirred into soups or used as a sauce for fish or gnocchi or pasta (like its Italian cousin, pesto). And Nice has its version of the pizza in its *pissaladière niçoise,* a thin base of bread or pastry baked with a topping of succulently braised onions, olive oil, anchovies, and black olives. Nice also is famous for its *salade niçoise* — tuna, tomatoes, black olives, capers, potatoes, string beans, and hard-boiled eggs. Its sandwich form, *pan bagnat,* is available at every local snack bar. A well-kept secret (by the locals) is *socca,* ground chick peas spread in a pizza pan and baked in a brick oven until it rises to a light, fluffy pancake. Consumed with generous sprinklings of coarse ground pepper, and washed down with numerous glasses of ice-cold rosé, this indulgence is a 4 PM ritual for beachgoers fleeing the hot afternoon sun to go to the cool back alleys of Nice's Vieille Ville (Old City).

The celebrated apéritif along the Mediterranean coast is *pastis* (essence of aniseed), which is high in alcohol and is usually served diluted with ice water. The local wines are uncomplicated but perfect with the well-seasoned food and the ambience: eating outdoors overlooking the sea calls for a nice, refreshing, fruity wine, and côtes de Provence, mostly dry rosés, are just that. Or try a bottle of bandol *rouge* (red), b*lanc de Provence* (white), or bellet (red or white).

LANGUEDOC: Although allied with Provence to the east and Gascony to the west, this area has a cuisine all its own. For example, the popular and well-known dish called cassoulet, a rich ragout of white beans, lamb, pork, sausage, and (usually) preserved goose or duck, is a great specialty and source of regional pride; in fact, you'll find slightly different and very personal versions of cassoulet offered by almost every restaurant chef in Toulouse, Carcassonne, and Castelnaudary. Try to sample it late in the week, when it's had a chance to age in the pot for a few days. Also indigenous is *brandade de morue,* a purée of olive oil, milk, garlic, and cod (usually dried salt cod that has been reconstituted by long soaking, an amazingly successful process). Once again, the area's *charcuterie* — ham, pâté, sausage — is superior, and pork and lamb often appear in flavorful *fricassées à la languedocienne;* that is, stewed with tomatoes, eggplant, garlic, and wild mushrooms. Finally, Languedoc is the home of Roquefort, the world-famous blue cheese that's ripened in the mountain caves of the Rouergue area.

Languedoc-Roussillon is the largest wine producing area in France, yet most of the wine is only mediocre and is distributed as *vin ordinaire.* The local food requires full-bodied reds, and only the area's best reds — corbières, minervois, and fitou — are worthwhile, as is clairette du Languedoc, a full-bodied white wine. With roquefort, try one of the sweet white wines such as banyuls or muscat de Frontignan or perhaps a sauternes or barsac from not-too-distant Bordeaux.

GASCONY AND THE PYRÉNÉES: The cuisine in this southwestern corner of France is strongly influenced by Basque cookery. An example is the sauce called *pipérade,* a mixture of red and green sweet peppers, onions, and tomatoes, to which eggs or ham may be added. It is particularly tasty when served with the region's fish — sardines, tuna, swordfish, and fresh anchovies. Bayonne ham, uncooked and spicily dry-cured in salt and red pepper, also is typically Basque and is eaten alone or included in a variety of dishes. Geese and duck are widely bred in these provinces and commonly prepared in two ways: *confit,* in which the meat is cooked and preserved in its own fat, and *magret,* in which the boneless breast is sliced into fillets and grilled. Goose livers become foie gras, and goose necks (*cous d'oie*) are stuffed with various ingredients — pork, foie gras, truffles — and served rather like a sausage. The wild mushrooms known as *cèpes* are much prized here; when stewed in goose fat with garlic and shallots, they make a side dish sometimes richer than the main one.

Most wine lists in these areas include a nice selection from neighboring Bordeaux that will stand up to the hearty food. So will the local full-bodied reds from Madiran, which also go well with the various duck and goose preparations. Another possibility is the white wine made in the Jurançon region of the Pyrénées; it's a deep gold, with a flowery bouquet and often a heavy, sweet taste. Not to be missed after a meal is an aged armagnac, the region's fiery brandy that is similar in character and quality to cognac.

BORDEAUX: Perhaps best known for its great vineyards and fine wines, Bordeaux also produces some superb cooking. Two kinds of oysters highly prized in France — *claires* and *portugaises* — are gathered from the estuaries of the Gironde River (although Americans familiar with fresh bluepoints and chincoteagues may not find these so extraordinary). Another delicacy is caviar derived from the sturgeon that swim up the Gironde to spawn. Since this is prime wine country, it's not surprising that many dishes — mussels, crayfish, chicken, *cèpes* — are rendered *à la bordelaise;* that is, with a rich red or white wine sauce. A particular favorite of the town of St.-Emilion, *lamproie à la bordelaise,* is lamprey eel (once again, from the Gironde) cooked in a dense, spicy sauce of red wine, leek, garlic, and the eel's own blood. Another specialty, *entrecôte à la bordelaise,* is filet of beef prepared with a sauce of red wine, shallots, and beef marrow. Delicious fruits from neighboring areas — for example, the Charentais melon (similar to a tiny canteloupe) and prunes from Agen — often are used in fine cakes and pastries.

In Bordeaux do as the Bordelais do: drink bordeaux. It is hard to go wrong, and besides, most wine lists will offer very few wines from other regions except champagne. Although good dry white wines are produced in Graves and lighter and fruitier whites in Entre-Deux-Mers, it is the reds for which Bordeaux is famous, and the Bordelais even drink a light red wth their fish. The rich, full-bodied, and long-lived reds of the various Bordeaux *communes* (villages) are perfect with red meats, game, and cheeses.

Hundreds of château-bottled wines are available; thus the choices can be overwhelming, but any waiter in a reliable restaurant should be helpful. Look for some bottle age in quality reds, though there are lesser "Cru Bourgeois" reds that are good and ready to drink young. Recent vintages of merit are 1982, 1981, 1979, 1978, 1976, 1975, and 1970. In 1855, the wines of the Médoc were classified in an attempt to distinguish their relative quality. The so-called first growths — Château Lafite-Rothschild, Château Latour, Château Margaux, Château Mouton-Rothschild (added later), and Château Haut-Brion — are unquestionably the greatest wines of Bordeaux, along with four other Bordeaux wines from outside the classified area: Château Pétrus in Pomerol, Château Ausone and Château Cheval-Blanc in St.-Emilion, and Château d'Yquem (a sweet white dessert wine) from Sauternes. These wines of undisputed quality bear a price to prove it. The 1855 classification included second-, third-, fourth-, and fifth-growth wines as well, but with the varying fortunes of the châteaux over the years, the classifications are somewhat unreliable today beyond the first growths. Some wines from the lesser growths have, in fact, risen almost to the quality of the first growths without bringing the corresponding high prices and are often excellent values.

Perhaps the most fitting conclusion to a fine meal in Bordeaux would be the famous *digestif* produced in nearby Cognac.

DORDOGNE, PÉRIGORD, AND QUERCY: These ancient provinces are the home of the black truffle, and the regional cuisine makes liberal use of that exotic underground mushroom. Fresh truffles (incomparably better than canned) enliven omelettes, pâtés, sauces, and sautés. Any dish labeled *périgourdine* or *quercynoise* inevitably will contain an abundance of truffles and often foie gras as well. Walnuts and walnut oil also are regional specialties and are used in many dishes. To accompany the hearty portions of this area, try the full-bodied deep reds from Cahors, the reds from Bergerac (especially from Pécharmant), or those from nearby Bordeaux. A plate of fresh foie gras is complemented nicely by a glass of sweet white wine — for example, a montbazillac, made in Périgord — or perhaps a sauternes or barsac, both truly fine wines from Bordeaux.

LOIRE VALLEY: The cuisine of this region makes extensive use of fish from that great river, the Loire: pike and shad, prepared with *beurre blanc,* a rich white butter sauce; and salmon and mullet, grilled and served with *beurre à la maître d'hôtel* (parsley butter). Another favorite is *petite friture,* a platter of tiny fish (2 to 3 inches long), lightly floured and crisply deep-fried. Sometimes featured as a first course, the *charcuterie* is rich and varied, including pâtés and terrines, a delicate white sausage called *boudin blanc,* pungent *andouillettes* (sausages made from hog chitterlings), and succulent potted pork in the form of *rillettes* (shredded) or *rillons* (chunked). The fertile Loire Valley also yields some very fine fruits and vegetables — apples, apricots, cherries, melons, peaches, pears, plums, and strawberries; the Vineuil asparagus is especially prized. Small, piquant cheeses are also a Loire specialty; look for valençay, pyramide, crottin, and St.-Maure. For dessert, don't miss the luscious *gâteau Pithiviers,* buttery puff pastry filled with almond cream.

The wine regions of the Loire produce a wealth of good white wines to go with the wonderful fish. Dry, light, flinty sancerre and pouilly-fumé are interesting and reliable alternatives to muscadet, the dry, soft, inexpensive wine that goes so well with fish. The ever-popular muscadet comes in three designations of increasing quality: Muscadet, Muscadet des Côteaux de la Loire, and Muscadet de Sèvre-et-Maine. This diverse wine region also produces two slightly sweet sparkling white wines, saumur and vouvray, and sweet white and rosé wines from Anjou. The latter sometimes marry well with *charcuterie,* pâtés, and pork dishes, as do the pleasant local reds, especially chinon and bourgeuil. All of the wines of the Loire are best when drunk young.

FOOD TERMINOLOGY

agneau: lamb

aïoli: garlic mayonnaise

américaine, à l': (usually lobster), sautéed in olive oil with garlic and tomatoes

anchois: anchovy

andouillette: chitterling sausage

aneth: dill

anis: aniseed

apéritif: before-dinner drink

asperge: asparagus

assiette de . . . : plate of . . .

aubergine: eggplant

avocat: avocado

baguette: long, thin loaf of bread

ballottine: roll of boned, stuffed meat or fish

bar: sea bass

barbue: brill

basilic: basil

béarnaise, à la: Béarn style, with a rich sauce made of egg yolks, vinegar, shallots, tarragon, white wine, and butter

béchamel: white sauce made with milk, flour, and butter

beignet: fritter

beurre: butter

beurre à la maître d'hôtel: parsley butter

bifteck: steak

bigorneaux: winkles

billy by: cream of mussel soup

blanc de volaille: white meat of chicken

blanquette de veau: veal stew in white cream sauce

boeuf: beef

bordelaise, à la: Bordeaux or bordelaise style, with a sauce of red wine, shallots, and bone marrow

boudin: black pudding

bouillabaisse: fish stew

bourguignonne, à la: Burgundy style, with a red wine sauce of onions, mushrooms, and bacon

bourride: fish stew

brandade de morue: purée of salt cod made with oil, garlic, and cream

brioche: sweet roll

brochet: pike

brochette de . . . : meat or fish grilled on a skewer

café au lait: coffee mixed with hot milk

café crème: coffee served with cream or warm milk

café noir: black coffee

Calvados: apple cider brandy

canard: duck

carbonnade: beef braised in beer and onions

carré d'agneau: rack of lamb

cassoulet: casserole made of white beans and pork

cèpe: wild mushroom

cerise: cherry

champignon: mushroom

chantilly: whipped cream

charcuterie: pork products such as hams, sausages, pâtés, and terrines

chaud: hot

chevreau: kid

chevreuil: venison

chiffonnade: thin strips, usually of vegetables

chou: cabbage

choucroute: sauerkraut

choucroute garnie: platter of mixed meats such as pork, sausage, and goose served with sauerkraut

chou-fleur: cauliflower

ciboulette: chives

cidre: cider

citron: lemon

civet: rich stew

concombre: cucumber

confiture: jam

coq: cock, also used to indicate hen or chicken

coques: cockles

coquillages: shellfish

coquilles St.-Jacques: scallops

côte: rib, chop

côtelette: cutlet, usually of lamb or mutton

crème: cream

crème brûlée: custard topped with carmelized brown sugar crust

crème fouettée: whipped cream

crème fraîche: slightly soured cream

crêpe: thin pancake

cresson: watercress

crevette: shrimp, prawn

croque-monsieur: toasted cheese sandwich with ham

croûte, en: in a pastry crust

daurade: sea bream

dijonnaise, à la: Dijon style, with mustard sauce

dinde, dindon, dindonneau: turkey

eau minérale: mineral water

eaux-de-vie: colorless fruit brandies

échalote: shallot

écrevisse: crayfish

entrecôte: rib steak

entrée: main dish

épices: spices

épinard: spinach

escargots: snails

estragon: tarragon

faisan: pheasant

farci: stuffed

fenouil: fennel

feuilleté: flaky or puff pastry

fines herbes: mixture of herbs, including parsley, chives, tarragon, and chervil

flan: custard tart

foie gras: goose liver, usually cooked, seasoned, and served as a pâté

fondue (de fromage): melted cheese

frais/fraîche: fresh

fraise: strawberry

framboise: raspberry

frappé: iced, frozen

fricassée: stew

frites: French fries

friture: small fried fish

froid: cold

fromage: cheese

fruits de mer: seafood

fumé: smoked

galantine: boned meat, fish, or poultry served in aspic

galette: pancake filled with cheese, jam, ham, or egg

garbure: thick bean and vegetable soup

gâteau: cake

gelée: aspic

gigot: leg, usually of lamb or mutton

glace: ice cream

gratin: dish with toasted cheese on top

grenouille: frog; usually refers to frogs' legs

grillade: food that has been grilled

grive: thrush

haricot: bean

homard: lobster

huile: oil

huître: oyster

jambon: ham

jardinière, à la: garden style, with mixed fresh vegetables

julienne: vegetables cut in thin strips

jus d'orange: orange juice

lait: milk

lamproie: lamprey eel

langouste: spiny lobster

langue: tongue

lapin: rabbit

légumes: vegetables

madeleines: small sponge cakes

magret: filet of duck breast

maître d'hôtel: head waiter

maquereau: mackerel

marron: chestnut

matelote: fish and seafood stew

merlan: whiting

meunière, à la: fish dusted with flour and fried in butter, parsley, and lemon

meurette: red wine sauce made with mushrooms, onions, bacon, and carrots

morille: morel

mornay sauce: white sauce made with milk, flour, butter, and cheese

morue: salt cod

moule: mussel

mousse: dessert of sweetened cream that's been flavored (for example, with chocolate) and whipped to a froth

moutarde: mustard

mouton: mutton

myrtille: blueberry

nantua, à la: Nantes style cream sauce made with puréed crayfish

niçoise, à la: in the style of Nice, made with tomatoes, onions, anchovies, and olives

nouilles: noodles

oeuf: egg

oie: goose

oignon: onion

oseille: sorrel

oursin: sea urchin

pain: bread

pâté: a rich spread of minced meat or fish seasoned with herbs, baked, and usually served cold

pâtisserie: pastry shop

pêche: peach

persil: parsley

persillade: a mixture of parsley and garlic or shallot

petit pain: roll

pied: foot, usually of pig or sheep

pipérade: a mixture of red and green sweet peppers, onions, and tomatoes, often stirred into eggs or an omelette and served with ham

piquant: spicy

pistou: basil, cheese, garlic, and olive oil paste, sometimes stirred into soups

Pithiviers: puff pastry filled with almond cream

plat du jour: specialty of the day

poire: pear

poireau: leek

pois: peas

poisson: fish

poivre: pepper

poivre vert: green peppercorns

pomme: apple

pomme de terre: potato

porc: pork

potage: soup

pot-au-feu: beef boiled with vegetables

potée: pork, cabbage, and potato soup

poularde, poule, poulet: chicken

poussin: very young chicken

praire: clam

provençale, à la: in the style of Provence, with tomatoes, onions, olives, and garlic

prune: plum

pruneau: prune

quenelle: light dumpling made of fish or chicken

quiche lorraine: tart made with eggs, cream, and bacon

ragoût: stew

raisin: grape

ratatouille: vegetable casserole made of eggplant, tomatoes, onion, pepper, and olives

rillettes: shredded, cooked pork

rillons: chunked, cooked pork

ris: sweetbreads

riz: rice

rognon: kidney

rôti: roast meat

roulade: rolled and stuffed meat or fish

salade verte: green salad

saucisse, saucisson: sausage, salami

saumon: salmon

sauté: fried lightly

sel: salt

serviette: napkin

sorbet: sherbet

sucre: sugar

suprême de . . . : boneless fillet, usually chicken or fish

terrine: baked minced meat or fish seasoned with herbs and served cold

thé: tea

thon: tuna

tournedos: fillet of beef

truffe: truffle

truite: trout

vapeur: steamed

veau: veal

velouté: creamy white sauce

vichyssoise: potato and leek soup, usually served cold

vin: wine

vinaigre: vinegar

vinaigrette: salad dressing made of oil, vinegar, herbs, and mustard

volaille: chicken

vol-au-vent: puff pastry shell

History

The history of France is the history of an ancient, brilliant, powerful, and learned society. It is the history of a country without whose aid the American Revolution would not have succeeded. It also is the history of division, for the absence of an internal national consensus has been a constant. Early on, there were fraternal and dynastic battles, struggles between feudal lords and the central monarchy; later there were religious wars, then revolution, and still more divisions — monarchists battling republicans, Nazi collaborators battling French *résistants,* and today the strong ideological right vies with the equally strong ideological left for power. In so many ways a model for Western civilization, France nonetheless differs from Anglo-Saxon nations in one critical respect: It remains splintered on the basic question of precisely which form of government its people desire, a stubborn legacy of divisiveness handed down through the centuries.

THE GAULS AND THE ROMANS

The history of the region today known as France begins well before the history of the people known as French. It begins with cavemen in the paleolithic and neolithic eras, first hunters and then farmers. And it begins with art, for these cavemen left magnificent drawings in the caves of Lascaux. But the history of a clearly identified, distinctive people begins only around the 5th century BC with the Celts, Germanic tribes who occupied the area in successive waves. The Celts became known as Gauls; their empire, extending west to Portugal, rivaled that of Rome in size. Primarily a rural people, with superior agricultural tools and prodigious metallurgical skills, the Gauls possessed a common language and a power structure based on warriors, nobles, and priests. And their character included traits not wholly foreign to their eventual descendants: a passion for luxurious fashion, pride, and a distinct dislike for centralized authority. Yet the Gauls implanted a civilization, not a state, and this was the weakness of their empire. Gaul's wealth was great, its internal power struggles greater still, and the combination inevitably made it a tempting prize for potential conquerors.

Of these, the Romans were the most powerful. In the 2nd century BC, the Romans conquered Provence, which lay on the road to Spain. The rest of Gaul fell in 52 BC, when Julius Caesar defeated the Gallic chief Vercingétorix. Caesar took all of Gaul, dividing it (as he wrote) into three parts and instituting a Roman rule that brought two crucial innovations, roads and urban centers, and the development of a Gallo-Roman civilization. The Gauls' Indo-European language blended with Latin, customs blended, and religions blended, too, and when the Roman emperor Constantine converted to Christianity in the 4th century AD, Gaul also became Christian.

During 5 centuries of Roman rule, Gaul became again the richest territory n Western Europe; it was once more a most tempting jewel for invaders — whose course was hardly checked by a series of ineffectual emperors and the empire's consequent internal decline. The new invaders — mostly Germanic tribes, but also the Mongolian Huns — came at first to pillage, their continuous incursions further weakening the empire. Then, in the 5th century, one of these Germanic groups, the Franks, came not just to pillage but to stay — men, women, and children crossing the Rhine in a massive migration. By AD 476, the date that traditionally marks the fall of the Roman Empire in the West, they had gained a foothold in Gaul, and in 486, under their chieftain Clovis I, they threw out the last Roman governor.

THE EARLY DYNASTIES

Clovis was the first of the Merovingian dynasty of Frankish kings. He converted to Christianity, enlarged the domain of the Frankish kingdom, made Paris his capital, and achieved the territorial unification of most of the realm. But when he died in 511 he divided the kingdom among his sons in accordance with Frankish tradition, and the result was disastrous. Family quarrels ensued, independent areas and small kingdoms resurfaced. The Merovingian monarchy came to rule only in name, the real power passing to "palace mayors" such as Pepin of Herstal in 687 and then to his son, Charles Martel, celebrated for defending southern France against Arab invaders in 732.

Then, a second dynasty was established. Martel's son, Pepin the Short (Pépin le Bref), imposed himself over the last of the Merovingians and became King of the Franks in 751. The first of the Carolingian dynasty, he left two crucial legacies. The first was the institution of the *sacre* (practiced in 754 by Pope Boniface himself), a religious ritual that proclaimed the divine right of the king to rule. The second was a son, Charles. Crowned king in 768, Charles defended the faith, attacked the Muslims in Spain, conquered the Lombards in Italy and the Bavarians and Saxons to the east, led a cultural and scientific renaissance, and became master of most of the European continent. In 800, he was crowned emperor of the West by Pope Leo III; he was known to the world as Charlemagne.

But in 814 Charlemagne, too, died, and his empire and his dynasty would in time follow. His son Louis the Pious (Louis le Pieux) ruled it all, but *his* sons stopped at nothing, including civil war, in their scramble for territory. In 870, the Treaty of Mersen divided Charlemagne's empire into a "French" West Frankish kingdom, a Germanic East Frankish kingdom, and a kingdom of Italy.

A third dynasty eventually emerged in the West Frankish kingdom that would develop into modern France. Its founder was Hugh Capet, named king in 987. He succeeded, where others before him had failed, in at last establishing the principle of primogeniture — the eldest son would get everything. With the cry "The King is dead, long live the King," the central flaw of all the preceding dynasties was effaced, an orderly succession of power finally assured. But the king did not have a great deal left over which to reign — a small area around Paris, in the case of the first Capetian —

because the disorder of the times had, in the meantime, fostered the development of the feudal system, in which royal land was given to a noble class of feudal lords in return for their services — military and other — to the king. Frequently, these vassals became richer and more powerful than the king, as happened with the Dukes of Burgundy, Brittany, and Aquitaine, the Counts of Flanders, Champagne, and Anjou, and, above all, with William the Conqueror, Duke of Normandy, who conquered England in 1066 and sat on its throne.

But the Church called the faithful to the Crusades. Powerful lords departed to fight in distant lands, and in their absence the French monarchy had its first real opportunity to regain its lands and consolidate its influence. Well known to readers of Shakespeare, Philip Augustus (Philippe-Auguste; 1180–1223), the Capetian king, was the principal actor in this power play. He ascended the throne to find his rule precarious: a mixture of marriage, acquisition, and annexation had placed the greater part of his realm in the hands of the great-grandson of William the Conqueror, Henry Plantagenet, who was not only King Henry II of England but also the Duke of Normandy and Lord of Brittany, Anjou, and Aquitaine as well. In short, Henry, a vassal of the King of France, presided over French possessions about six times larger than those ruled by the King of France himself.

Philip set about to change this embarrassing state of affairs by plotting with Henry's son, Richard the Lion-Hearted (Coeur de Lion). Henry died in battle in France. Richard became king. Philip plotted against Richard. Richard died in battle in France. Philip fought with Richard's successor, John. Before it was over, Philip had won back almost all of the Plantagenet's French possessions, except for southern France, and annexed his conquests to his kingdom. Philip Augustus died in 1223, but his dynasty continued; among the Capetians who followed him were two other famed kings. One was Louis IX (1226–70). As Louis the Iron-Gloved, he dominated his vassals and further strengthened his central authority, encouraged the terror of the Inquisition, and put yellow badges on the Jewish citizens of his realm; as St.-Louis, he was known as a just, generous, charitable man, a patron of the arts and learning. The other renowned Capetian was Philip the Fair (Philippe le Bel; 1285–1314), who provoked the Papal Schism and saw Pope Clement V install his court in Avignon (1305); and it was the complexities of his succession that led to a catastrophe, a war that raged for an entire century.

THE HUNDRED YEARS WAR

From the very first, French history and English history were inextricably intertwined. The Iron Age Celts who had settled France later moved on to settle England, and already Frenchmen had sat, simultaneously and contradictorily, as vassals owing allegiance to the French king and as sovereigns of England. The Hundred Years War was born of the continuing dynastic quarrels between these two sibling peoples: Philip the Fair's sons produced no male heirs; the Capetian dynasty in France thus passed to the Valois family, with Philip VI of Valois named king (1328–50). But King Edward III of England was a Capetian — his mother was a daughter of Philip the Fair

— and he claimed the French throne for himself. In 1337, Edward and Philip went to war. France relied on the traditional use of knights; England, in a military innovation, introduced archers, foot soldiers with long bows, for whom the saddled knights became sitting ducks. In 1346, the English decimated the French cavalry at the battle of Crécy; 10 years later, the English won again at Poitiers and took as prisoner King John II of France. All the while the Black Death raged. The first round of the war ended in 1360 with the Treaty of Brétigny, which freed John in exchange for a ransom and granted to the English a significant expanse of French territory.

Another round of the war took place under King Charles V of France (1364–80), who by the time of Edward III's death in 1377 had managed to recapture almost all of the French territory in England's possession. Then Charles VI (1380–1422) became the French king; during his reign the military situation again became dramatic. In 1415 the English attacked France and won the decisive battle of Agincourt, with great slaughter of French knights. By now, the powerful Dukes of Burgundy were allied with the English against the French crown, and in 1420 the three parties concluded the fateful Treaty of Troyes in an attempt to end the hostilities. By its terms, Henry V of England was named "heir to France"; that is, Charles VI would rule until his death and then be succeeded by the English king, thereby disinheriting his own son, the dauphin (later Charles VII).

France was thus about to cease its existence as an independent nation when a small woman stepped in and changed the course of history. Joan of Arc's mission was to see the dauphin crowned king. Though the young Charles repudiated the treaty signed by his father and undertook to rule at his father's death in 1422, he was a weak and vacillating king and his realm was small. The English already controlled most of France north of the Loire at that point, and his attempts to oppose their advance southward were halfhearted. Joan rallied the French troops and led them to a crucial victory over the English at Orléans in 1429. She then accompanied Charles to Reims — where French kings traditionally were crowned — for his coronation as Charles VII (1422–61) in the cathedral. The next year she was captured by the Burgundians, turned over to the English, and delivered to a court of clergymen at Rouen. She was burned as a witch in 1431, but in the meantime she had given Charles the impetus he needed to carry on alone. By 1453 only Calais remained English, and Louis XI (1461–83) finished his father's work. The Hundred Years War was over; France was at last French again.

A SOCIETY IN FLUX

The second half of the 15th century was largely a time of reconstruction and economic development. France became rich and powerful, and Lyons became one of the great financial and trading capitals of Europe. The French kings, free from the English menace, now had powerful dreams. Charles VIII (1483–98) and Louis XII (1498–1515) were "chivalry kings," with knightly visions of adventure and glory. Their object was Italy, to which France held some dynastic claims. Charles invaded, so did Louis; sometimes the French ruled parts of Italy, at other times they were pushed back to their own borders. The next king, Francis I (1515–47), ended the campaign. The enduring result of the Italian wars was not geopolitical but cultural. They brought the French into contact with the art, architecture, and literature of the Italian Renaissance and spread it to and through France. Leonardo da Vinci, Benvenuto Cellini, and Andrea del Sarto worked at the court of Francis I, a patron of the arts and letters, whose reign was marked by the greatest flowering of the French Renaissance.

Society began to change. The period of transition from the Middle Ages to the Renaissance also was a period of transition from the old feudal society to a "modern" bourgeois society. New ideas were propagated by Erasmus, Rabelais, and Montaigne. Church reform was preached by the German Martin Luther and John Calvin, a Frenchman. A good portion of Catholic France converted to Protestantism. Oddly, the monarchy, a beneficiary of the Catholic *sacre,* showed tolerance toward the new Protestants — or Huguenots, as they were known in France — and advocated limited religious freedom for all. But radicals on both sides soon made tolerance impossible, and the two religious movements quickly became political.

A series of civil and religious wars (the Wars of Religion, or the Huguenot Wars) broke out in France in 1562. In 1572, thousands of leading Huguenots were killed in Paris (the St. Bartholomew's Eve Massacre) and thousands more were slaughtered in the provinces; later, fanatical Catholic leaders were killed in a plot orchestrated by the French monarchy itself. Then a new crisis came in 1589, when the last Valois king was killed and the French throne was empty. Religious fervor reached a new peak. The new dynasty was the Bourbon family; the presumed new king, Henri of Navarre. But Henri was a Protestant, and the Catholic factions quickly rejected his claim, supporting a Catholic Bourbon instead. War came again, now with all the European powers taking sides.

Henri of Navarre won the military battle for France, but Paris remained staunchly Catholic. Perched at the gates of the capital and faced with a hostile population, the victorious Henri made a decision summed up by his alleged remark: "Paris is well worth a mass." He ruled as Henri IV, a Catholic king and a great king, who accorded the Protestants limited religious freedoms once again in the Edict of Nantes (1598). Thus, 36 years of civil and religious war came to an end. Agriculture, trade, and commerce prospered under Henri's chief minister, Sully. But his reign ended abruptly when a madman assassinated him in 1610.

Louis XIII was a minor at the time of his father's death. During most of his reign, real power rested with a remarkable, worldly, and very determined churchman, Cardinal Richelieu, whose goal was to establish an absolute monarchy. His plan and his power, however, aroused opposition and provoked numerous conspiracies. Nevertheless, Richelieu went a long way toward realizing his goal before his death in 1642. A year later Louis XIII died, too. Again the heir was a minor, and again power fell to a churchman, Richelieu's disciple, Cardinal Mazarin. This cardinal also survived plots, a revolt (the Fronde), and even exile, but he educated the heir to the French throne in a fashion true to Richelieu's dream. And when Mazarin died in 1661, the young French king personally assumed all power.

ABSOLUTISM: LOUIS XIV

Mazarin's avid pupil was Louis XIV (1643–1715). "L'état c'est moi," he proclaimed ("I am the state"), and this absolutism would be the model, not only for 17th-century France, but for most other European countries throughout the 18th century. Louis XIV in effect created the modern state. He monopolized the administration of justice and the use of armed force. His finance minister, Colbert, put the French economy in order, applying Richelieu's mercantilist philosophy to expand trade, promote industry, create strict quality controls, institute protective tariffs, and to grant subsidies to build a merchant marine. The king took the *sacre,* establishing his domination over the Church as well as rule by divine right over his subjects. And Louis XIV dominated the nobility. He brought the nobility to himself and smothered it. He built the enormous palace of Versailles, more magnificent than anything Europe had ever known, and created rituals wherein it was an honor to attend the king's person, to be present at his arising, his meals, his preparation for bed. He patronized the arts, letters, and sciences, attracting the most brilliant of their practitioners to his court. All revolved around Louis, the sun whose light shone on the favored. So Louis XIV was dubbed the Sun King; the country he ruled over was the France of the Illumination. Its population was three times that of England. The French were laying claim to Canada, exploring the Great Lakes and the Mississippi, building plantations in the West Indies, and constructing the most imposing navy in Europe. Nicolas Poussin and Claude Lorrain painted; Corneille, Racine, Molière, Descartes, and Pascal wrote. French culture, architecture, and engineering were emulated everywhere; the French language became the mark of the civilized man. Under Louis XIV, France was the splendor of Europe.

But the Sun King lived too long and would see the eclipse. Influenced by the Counter Reformation, he revoked the Edict of Nantes. The result was not only the end of France's religious tolerance (unique in Europe at the time) but also the costly emigration of skilled and industrious Huguenot merchants and artisans. Louis's extravagant spending finally alienated his subjects. But above all, his grandiose wars undid him. Louis XIV fought the War of Devolution, the Dutch Wars, the War of the League of Augsburg, and the War of the Spanish Succession. Territory was gained — Louis's grandson sat on the throne of Spain — but the wars devastated the French economy and united Louis's foreign enemies against him. Disastrous harvests followed at home, then famine. The nobility grew restless. In 1715, Louis XIV died. As heir to his rule of 7 decades, he left a 5-year-old child.

THE FRENCH REVOLUTION: ITS ADVENT AND PHASES

The new king, Louis XV, would occupy the throne just short of 60 years. A regent was appointed to rule during his minority, which lasted until 1723, and for 2 decades after that his early reign was guided by his chief adviser, Cardinal Fleury. The nobility took heart, and some power. The philosophers of the Enlightenment — Montesquieu, Voltaire, and Rousseau among them

— were popularizing ideas of justice quite incompatible with an absolute monarchy. But Louis XV, too, engaged in ruinous wars, first the War of the Austrian Succession and then the Seven Years War, which cost France its Canadian possessions. The country was living through a financial crisis, which was not new, only newly acute. And it was paradoxical, because though France was a wealthy country, most of its rich were exempt from taxes, a holdover of privilege from feudal times. The poor were burdened unjustly and resentful; the government was poor to the verge of bankruptcy. Louis XIV had attempted reform toward the end of his reign, but the effect had been negligible. Louis XV was unable to institute remedies.

The reign of Louis XVI, who came to the throne in 1774, was dominated by the financial crisis. The king's ministers, one after another, sought reforms that would make the privileged classes — clergy and nobles — pay their fair shares of the burden, but the fearful king failed to provide strong support. The crisis deepened, aggravated by the expense of French help in the American Revolution. Further attempts to impose taxation on the privileged were blocked by the Assembly of Notables and the Parlement of Paris, both of them referring to the ancient consultative institution, the Estates-General, as the only body with the power to approve new taxes.

The Estates-General dated from feudal times but, in fact, had not met since 1614. It recognized representation from three social castes: the clergy (First Estate), the nobles (Second Estate), and "everyone else" (Third Estate) — a formula that effectively ignored the emergence of an important new class, the bourgeoisie. Thus, any meeting of the Estates-General in 18th-century France invited an almost inevitable clash between the aristocracy and the new bourgeoisie, the former seeking to recoup power lost to the absolute monarchy, the latter, creditors of the state, making a bid for recognition and influence equal to its economic contribution. Convening the Estates-General posed still another threat. Despite its divisive potential and its obsolescence, it was a national institution. The French monarchy had succeeded in unifying a nation, and now general discontent in France could be expressed on a national level far more easily than in other countries of the era.

As a last resort, the king called a meeting of the Estates-General to discuss fiscal reform. Lists of grievances were ordered to be drawn up in the provinces. Though they were intended merely to stimulate discussion, they raised expectations, and by the time the assembly met at Versailles in May 1789, the Third Estate and the less conservative nobles and clergy saw it as a true embodiment of the will of the people, a forum for initiating sweeping general reforms.

The struggle for control of the Estates-General came to a head immediately in the question of voting procedure. If tradition were respected, voting would be by order, and the first two estates always would outnumber the third; if voting were by head count, the Third Estate, which had more delegates, always would outnumber the first two. Louis wavered, and on June 17, 1789, the Third Estate broke away and declared itself a National Assembly. On June 27, 1789, Louis recognized the fait accompli, but some of his actions gave rise to rumors that he meant to suppress the assembly. On July 14, an angry mob took its first collective steps and stormed a prison in Paris, the

Bastille, a symbol of the *ancien régime.* Then the *grande peur* (great fear) began, fed by alarm over food shortages and economic depression. The peasants revolted in the countryside; labor problems ignited the cities. The French Revolution was under way.

The outbreak of revolution in France had a far greater impact than the earlier outbreak of revolution in America, a distant, new land. At the time of the storming of the Bastille, France, for all its internal problems, was still the power center of Europe, the leader in intellectual thought, the most populous country under a single government, the model for most of the Western world. Against the background of the 18th century, the French Revolution was the most momentous revolutionary movement in history, and its repercussions were not to be equaled until the Bolshevik Revolution of 1917 in Russia.

The National Assembly at Versailles took control and set about changing French society. The nobles and clergy were forced to relinquish their traditional privileges, and the feudal system was swept from the land. Legal equality was established in "The Declaration of the Rights of Man and Citizen." The revolution remade France in a bourgeois and secular mold. Economic controls and restrictive labor unions were abolished; all trades were opened up to all men. Church property was confiscated, religious orders suppressed. All previous administrative structures were erased; a system of departments, similar to states, came into being. And in 1791 a constitution was proclaimed, reducing the absolute monarchy to a constitutional monarchy.

This was the point at which the revolution's moderates would like to have stopped, but once again, the moderate cause was not advanced by the king's actions. Louis and his queen, Marie-Antoinette, attempted to flee to join counter-revolutionary émigré groups abroad. They were arrested at Varennes, brought back to Paris, and forced to accept the constitution. The monarchy thus discredited, the advantage in the National Assembly passed to the republicans. Royalist émigré circles, in the meantime, rallied kings, nobles, and clergy in the rest of Europe to unite in restoring the monarch to his former authority. Austria took the lead, and in April 1792 France responded to the threat by declaring war. The military emergency gave more voice to radical forces. The Jacobins, initially a middle-of-the-road group, gained leadership; then, led by Danton, Marat, and Robespierre, they adopted ever more extreme positions. In August 1792, the royal family was imprisoned. An insurrectionary government, the Commune of Paris, was set up, and there were massacres and general hysteria.

This was the second, or radical, phase of the French Revolution. The Commune forced the National Assembly to order elections for a National Convention, which would draw up a new constitution. At its first meeting, on September 21, 1792, the convention abolished the monarchy and proclaimed the First French Republic (a French revolutionary calendar would later count time from its birth). The republic continued to wage war and for a while was victorious, occupying Savoie and Belgium and crossing the Rhine. But Louis XVI and Marie-Antoinette had been accused of treason for collusion with the Austrian enemy. After Louis was guillotined on January 21,

1793, the enemies of the new republic found allies, and France was soon at war with all of Europe.

This emergency gave rise to the Reign of Terror. The new constitution drawn up by the National Convention finally was finished, but it never was put into effect. Instead, in April 1793, the Committee of Public Safety came into being, essentially a dictatorship to defend the Revolution from enemies within and without, and to pull France back from the edge of anarchy. Robespierre emerged as its leader. Denounced by some as a bloodthirsty fanatic, praised by others as an idealistic patriot, Robespierre was not controversial only in terms of his personal honesty and true revolutionary commitment. He repressed counter-revolutionary strife with a vengeance. Before the Reign of Terror was over, nearly 40,000 had died, many by the guillotine, including Marie-Antoinette ("The people have no bread? Let them eat cake!"), many by mass drowning. Improvement of France's military fortunes allowed public reaction to set in, just as more repressive measures aroused fears in the National Convention that the Reign of Terror would turn on its own members. Robespierre was arrested and sent to the guillotine in July 1794. After a period of White Terror, when many former terrorists lost their lives, the radical phase of the Revolution was over.

Still another new government, the Directory, was formed in 1795. It was reactionary and not a solution. In March 1797, elections were held. The constitutional monarchists won, but the Directory annulled most of the election results. Revolts came, more annulled elections followed, and purges took place on all sides of the political spectrum. The Directory was now in effect a dictatorship. All the classic reasons for a coup d'état again existed; it came on November 9, 1799. Its leader was a popular and victorious young general who proclaimed a new system of government for the republic, a Consulate, and designated himself first consul. His name was Napoleon Bonaparte.

THE EMPIRE

Once more a strong, controversial leader was in charge of France, and also a brilliant one. With Talleyrand as his foreign minister, Bonaparte quickly restored peace, concluding treaties with Austria and Great Britain. A concordat with the papacy recognized Roman Catholicism as the religion of most of the French in return for recognition of the republic by the Vatican and its acceptance of the French principle of religious tolerance. The major advances of the Revolution were institutionalized and the modern state began to take clear form. Bonaparte reorganized the government and the educational system, ended tax privileges, developed a sound currency and public credit, and founded the Bank of France. He reformed the legal system, codifying French laws for the first time in the Napoleonic Code (1804), and made justice in France uniform, assuring all citizens equal civil rights. Commercial and criminal codes followed.

Immensely popular, Bonaparte was elected first consul for life in 1802. Then, 2 years later, he turned the Consulate into an Empire and had himself made Emperor Napoleon I. What had been a welcome stabilization took on more authoritarian tones — it is a common distinction of the French to admire Bonaparte while expressing doubts about Napoleon — and France soon was deeply involved in a resumption of foreign wars. Only a brief peace in 1801 and 1802 had separated what history calls the French Revolutionary Wars from what it calls the Napoleonic Wars. Similarly, there are no clear turning points to mark the transitions from early warfare to protect the Revolution from foreign interference, warfare to extend it to other countries, and wars of pure conquest.

Napoleon had little trouble exporting the Revolution. United at home, the French were unstoppable beyond their borders. The emperor came closer than anyone in history to imposing real political unity on the European continent, and it was not always by force alone. In the early stages of the Empire, progressives welcomed the ideas of the French Revolution; it was the conservative governments, afraid of the reforms that came with the emperor's armies, that organized alliances against him. By 1810, Napoleon's territorial influence covered the entire European mainland with the exception of the Balkan peninsula. His brothers sat as Kings of Spain, Holland, and West-phalia; his sister as Queen of Naples; he himself as King of Lombardy, Venetia, and the former papal states. Having had his childless marriage with Josephine annulled, he married Marie-Louise, the daughter of the Emperor of Austria. Napoleon was supreme. Historians refer to him as "an enlightened despot." The reforms he carried to all of Europe explain the adjective, his means explain the noun.

But Napoleon's downfall finally came. From 1803, France had been at war with Great Britain. Victorious on land, the emperor was defeated at sea in the Battle of Trafalgar (1805), so he decided to wage economic warfare. In 1806, he launched the Continental System, a boycott that forbade trade with the British by France or any of her European allies. The Continental System, however, ruined continental shippers and exporters, and resentment grew among the merchant classes. In the meantime, the progressives who had hailed Napoleon's reforms now had the reforms and no longer needed Napoleon; strong nationalist movements were beginning to develop. Yet until an ally changed camps, no one could challenge Napoleon's army. The ally who bolted was Alexander I, Czar of Russia. Dissatisfied with the meager fruits of his alliance with the emperor, Alexander withdrew from the Continental System. Napoleon determined to crush him.

The story, a military nightmare, is well known. Intending a short, flash war, Napoleon entered Russia in June 1812 with a huge army and very few supplies. After a battle at Borodino, which resulted in severe loss of life on both sides, the Russian forces changed tactics and refused to fight again, retreating into the heart of Russia and devastating the land as they went. Napoleon pursued them into Moscow in September; the city burst into flames, leaving the emperor and his Grand Army camping in a ruin. Without hope of replenishing supplies from the devastated countryside and far from his own supply line, he attempted to negotiate. The czar refused. Napoleon ordered a retreat in mid-October, not wanting to be in Moscow with his army in the winter. But in 1812, winter came unusually early and with unusual severity. By late November, the Grand Army had been decimated.

The forces against Napoleon now converged; his allies deserted him. Finally, the Quadruple Alliance — Russia, Prussia, Austria, and Great Britain — attacked; their combined armies entered Paris. In April 1814, the emperor abdicated and was sent into exile on Elba. He regained power for 100 days, but after his defeat at Waterloo in June 1815, the Napoleonic Empire was ended definitively. The Congress of Vienna remade the map of Europe, shrinking France to its borders of 1790. The former emperor was exiled to the island of St.-Helena, leaving behind him an immense legend and institutional transformations that remain throughout Europe to this day.

THE NINETEENTH CENTURY

The collapse of the Empire was followed by the Restoration, a return to the monarchy. From 1815 to 1830, the Bourbon family — Louis XVIII and Charles X — again ruled, but it ruled over a new France, one that permitted no return to the old, prerevolutionary order. France was a bourgeois country now, with a prosperous middle class. So when an ultra-royalist movement developed and seemed poised to reinstate the *ancien régime,* it was the middle class that reacted, throwing out Charles X in the July revolution of 1830 and bringing to power a king with liberal, bourgeois leanings. The king was Louis-Philippe, of the house of Bourbon-Orléans; his reign is known as the July Monarchy. For nearly 2 decades he ruled over a country primarily concerned with developing industry and modern transportation systems, in the process largely ignoring parliamentary reform and social legislation. Hence he became increasingly unpopular, satisfying neither monarchists nor the lower classes. The result was the fall of the monarchy anew, in 1848.

The July Monarchy immediately was replaced by the Second Republic, destined to last only 4 years. Its president was none other than Louis-Napoleon Bonaparte, the nephew of the deposed emperor, elected both by virtue of his apparent liberalism and the country's nostalgia for Bonapartism. Louis began to consolidate his authority, and the fact that reactionary forces in France still were strong and republicanism still a revolutionary idea did not work against him. When a workers' revolt broke out, followed by social unrest and economic crisis, republicanism became synonymous with disorder. Louis was ready. In December 1851, he pulled off a coup d'état, giving himself dictatorial powers. In November 1852, he made the Second Republic the Second Empire and himself France's second emperor, Napoleon III. Plebiscites approved both moves.

In many respects, his reign was brilliant. The Industrial Revolution advanced, the bourgeoisie grew in strength, a modern infrastructure for the country developed, construction boomed. But Napoleon III was unsuccessful in his attempts to found an empire in Mexico, although he acquired other colonial possessions, and in the end he was brought down by a foreign war, the Franco-Prussian War of 1870–71. Napoleon had underestimated the force of German unity fostered by Otto von Bismarck. The Prussians marched through a Paris magnificently rebuilt by Baron Haussmann; France lost Alsace and Lorraine; and the Second Empire collapsed.

France's Third Republic dates from 1870, when Napoleon III was captured by the Prussians and effectively deposed, but a few years went by before the form of the new government was sure. The Germans needed a properly constituted French government to sign peace terms. An election was held for a National Assembly, its expressed duties to ratify Bismarck's harsh treaty and to write a new constitution. The monarchists came to power in the elections, prepared to bow to Bismarck's humiliating terms. But the republicans of Paris revolted and set up, once again, a revolutionary Commune of Paris. The Commune of 1871 was short-lived: Civil war broke out between it and the National Assembly at Versailles; government troops besieged the city, and the Communards took to the barricades. Before it was crushed, however, the fighting exceeded that of any of the French Revolution.

France might have become a monarchy again had the monarchist camp not soon split between supporters of the Bourbon family and of the Orléans family. This division allowed the adoption, in 1875, of a republican constitution and preserved the Third Republic. Contemporary France began to emerge. The establishment of secular, compulsory public education, the expansion of the railroads, the recognition of labor unions, and the separation of church and state all came in this period. The country's acquisitions abroad developed into a veritable colonial empire. The arts at home glittered spectacularly.

Yet there still was no universal agreement on a form of government. The monarchists still held some power, and much of the Third Republic's energy was spent simply fighting the enemies of the republican system. And there was the Dreyfus Affair, an ugly incident in which a Jewish army officer was falsely accused and convicted of treason. The celebrated author Emile Zola wrote an explosive letter, "J'Accuse," demanding a new trial. The affair shook the country and caused an international furor. Finally, in 1899, Dreyfus was pardoned and in 1906 fully exonerated.

THE WORLD WARS

The Third Republic nonetheless endured. While ministerial instability was chronic, continuity of policy was sustained, and in time republicanism became a credible form of government in France. The country was relatively comfortable. Then, in 1914, the Great War, World War I, broke out.

Much of the war — the battle of the Ardennes, the first battle of the Marne, the battle of Verdun, the battle of the Somme, the second battle of the Marne — was fought on French soil. Joffre, later Nivelle (eventually removed for incompetence), then Pétain (who came out of the war a hero) and Foch (who was made supreme commander of the French, British, and American armies) were the military leaders; Premier Clemenceau maintained morale and led the French delegation to the Paris Peace Conference in 1919. The war was one of attrition, at times of useless carnage in defense of positions more symbolic than strategic, of horrifying trench fighting, of poison gas. Nearly 2 million Frenchmen died; a sixth of the nation's revenue was lost. As one of the victors, France was rewarded with the return of Alsace and Lorraine, but the price had been deadly. Afterward, the French sought only recovery and reconstruction.

In the early postwar years the country was run by a series of conservative coalitions; then, in the mid-1920s, by the Radical Socialists, a center-left party committed to private enterprise but advocating progressive social legislation. In the meantime, politics on both sides was becoming polarized. On the left, the Communists broke off from the more moderate Socialists; on the right, Action Française, an extremist group with royalist tendencies, began to agitate. France's economic recovery, dependent on war reparations from Germany, collapsed when Germany failed to pay. The Great Depression arrived. And France had other problems: While its own government changed hands continually, Adolf Hitler came to power in neighboring Germany.

In 1934, a political and financial scandal, the Stavisky Affair, rocked the country, discrediting the Radical Socialist party and provoking fascist riots. Faced with the threat, the left closed ranks; Radical Socialists, Socialists, and Communists formed the Popular Front. In 1936, the Front won a decisive electoral victory. Premier Léon Blum put through a vast program of social reform, including the 40-hour work week, paid vacations, and collective bargaining laws. Steps were taken to put strategic industries under government control, to curtail private influence over the Bank of France, and to provide price supports for farmers. The Popular Front was a French New Deal, more radical only in its proclamations. Nonetheless, the French right saw it as a revolution and noisily protested that Catholic France had fallen into the hands of a leftist, a Socialist, a Jew.

In truth, the Popular Front was the right government at the wrong time. The 40-hour work week was long overdue in France, but it came into being just as Germany was working day and night to manufacture arms. The German effort obliged the French to do the same, and the simultaneous imposition of emergency rearmament and reform labor laws was an economic impossibility. In 1937, the Blum government fell, brought down by a Senate that refused to grant it emergency financial powers.

The new government was formed by the Radical Socialists. Abandoning its allies on the left, it took a conservative turn. Edouard Daladier became premier. He quickly proved incapable of dominating France's internal problems, weaker still in facing the ever-growing threat from Germany. It was Daladier's France that appeased Nazi Germany at Munich.

But war with Germany came nonetheless. On September 3, 1939, 2 days after the German invasion of Poland, France and Great Britain declared war. In May 1940, Germany entered France. Surprised by the attack route, lacking armored divisions and air force resources, divided as a nation, and governed by a small group of defeatist politicians, France fell. On June 13, 1940, Paris was occupied by Nazi soldiers. On June 16, Premier Paul Reynaud resigned rather than agree to surrender, and an 84-year-old man, Marshal Pétain, the same gentleman who had commanded so nobly in World War I, succeeded him. On June 22, France signed an armistice with Nazi Germany. The world was stunned. The country was divided into two zones: the occupied zone north of the Loire, including Paris; and, south of the Loire, the so-called free zone, meaning only that for a time German soldiers did not physically occupy the soil. In July, Pétain moved the government south from occupied Paris to Vichy, the Third Republic was voted out of existence, and the Government of Unoccupied France came into being, with Pétain as "chief of state." That he was remembered as a war hero was unfortunate, confusing a large portion of the French population, who followed him blindly.

In fact, the Vichy government was a national disgrace. Behind the aged Pétain stood Pierre Laval, a cynical, dishonorable man who openly proclaimed his hopes for a Nazi victory. The slogan "Liberty, Equality, Fraternity," born in France, was banned from official use as Pétain and Laval led their country into its most ignominious period. The Vichy government was not passive; it embraced the Nazis, it collaborated actively, it went beyond even German demands in enthusiastically delivering French Jews to Nazi concentration camps. Later, the French militia under Joseph Darnand would show more viciousness than even the German SS.

There was another France as well: that of Charles de Gaulle, Jean Moulin, Pierre Mendès-France, André Malraux, and men and women of all political colors who refused to collaborate and who together formed the *Résistance*. Some, like de Gaulle, went into exile, establishing a Free French movement in London; others remained on French soil, fighting at enormous risk as an effective anti-Nazi underground. After the German invasion of Russia, French Communists joined en masse. The French Résistance was a genuinely heroic movement, but it included only a shamefully small fraction of the French population. By an overwhelming majority, the French people were collaborators, active or passive. And this division — collaborator versus *résistant* — virtually was a moral civil war, far outlasting the division of French territory by the occupying army.

The territorial division ended in 1942 as a result of the Allied invasion of North Africa, and the Germans occupied all of France. In one act of national courage, the French fleet at Toulon scuttled itself rather than fall into German hands, a sacrifice that destroyed French naval power. Two years later the occupation ended. On June 6, 1944, British and American forces began the liberation of France by invading Europe via the beaches of Normandy. In August, Paris was liberated, and de Gaulle, the symbol of Free France, entered the city as head of a provisional government. (A story sworn to by all Frenchmen is that Paris, which had been mined by the Germans, still was standing because of the man who until the last moment had subjugated it. The Nazi general in Paris was an art lover and he knew the Nazi cause was lost. When headquarters gave the order to blow the city up, he refused.) By the end of 1944, all of France had been liberated. Spontaneous reprisals against collaborators took an ugly turn in many parts of the country. Laval and Pétain both were tried for treason. Laval was shot in 1945. Pétain's death sentence was commuted to life imprisonment by de Gaulle.

POSTWAR FRANCE

The provisional government ruled only until a new republic, the Fourth Republic, was proclaimed in 1946. The new constitution, much like that of the Third Republic, did not provide for as strong an executive as de Gaulle would have liked, and he retired from the scene. The government again became an affair of shaky coalitions, which nevertheless undertook to rebuild the economy with the aid of the US Marshall Plan. The nationalization of the banks and major industries took place. The French statesmen Jean Monnet and Robert Schuman were instrumental in setting Europe on the course of economic and political cooperation that in time resulted in the European Community. But inflation was rising and there were colonial problems. Ho Chi Minh declared Vietnam an independent republic in 1945; French troops arrived to fight the insurgents the following year. Cambodia was granted its independence in 1949, Laos in 1950. In 1954, the fall of Dien Bien Phu effectively brought an end to French power in Indochina. In North Africa, Morocco and Tunisia became independent in 1956. And there was war in Algeria.

The Algerian independence movement violently divided the French people, for administratively Algeria was not a *colony* but a *département* of France. Ultra-nationalists and major portions of the army considered the independence movement a war of secession and intended to keep Algeria French at all costs. More liberal factions saw the justice of the Algerian National Liberation Front's cause. At the height of the hostilities, there were approximately 500,000 French troops and some 1,000,000 European colonists in Algeria. In 1958, extremists of both groups, fearing that the French government would come to terms with the Algerians, threatened a military and civilian revolt that brought the situation to a head. An appeal was made to the only person thought strong enough to bring France through the emergency.

Charles de Gaulle responded to the appeal and the Fourth Republic was replaced by the Fifth Republic. De Gaulle designed a new constitution that allowed for a bicameral legislature but invested immense power in the presidency, perhaps the unavoidable compromise for a nation traditionally torn between the reign of a king and the democratic process. In January 1959, de Gaulle became president, his urgent task the resolution of the Algerian crisis in the midst of increasing violence. Demonstrations by colonists and the army in Algeria gave way to the terrorist campaign of the violent, dangerous, and deadly efficient OAS (Secret Army Organization), an extreme right-wing group agitating against any accord with the Algerians. There were assassination conspiracies everywhere.

De Gaulle overrode all threats. Courageous, and above all realistic, he accepted the inevitable and granted Algeria's independence. The hostilities ended in 1962, though the loss of Algeria remained for years a bitter issue for the country's right wing and ultra-nationalists. As for the Algerians, not until 1983 — and then only out of consideration for the new French Socialist government — did an Algerian head of state visit France.

After Algeria, de Gaulle devoted himself to realizing his vision of France as the leader of Europe. He saw to the development of nuclear weapons and asserted an independent foreign policy, recognizing the People's Republic of China, withdrawing from the military wing of NATO, blocking Britain's entry into the Common Market, and boycotting meetings while still believing in a Europe strong enough to act as a third force between Russia and the United States. De Gaulle was again, for many Frenchmen, the symbol of a free France, in both physical stature and national legend a figure larger than life. But he had a consistent attitude of arrogant grandeur and, in time, while his personal integrity was unquestioned, some saw him assuming the posture of a monarch more than that of a president.

The nation grew restless once more. Labor unions protested inflation and a lack of housing, students protested government expenditures on arms as well as an obsolete educational system, and opposition leaders protested the government's control over the mass media. In May 1968, these forces came together in an explosion whose force has often been underestimated outside France. Students demonstrated by the hundreds of thousands and 10 million workers went out on strike; the country was paralyzed, the government close to being overthrown. Only by securing the support of the army and by promising reforms was de Gaulle able to survive. Then an equally strong counterreaction set in, and in the next general election the Gaullists won a major victory.

But in April 1969 de Gaulle planted the seeds of his own political demise by proposing a national referendum on a complex series of constitutional reforms, announcing that he would consider the results a vote of confidence on himself. The reforms were defeated by a small margin. August, austere, always a symbol, de Gaulle was true to his word. He retired to his country home, where he died a year later. For most Frenchmen, he remains a figure of sincere admiration.

The Fifth Republic went on. In 1969, Georges Pompidou, a Gaullist, became president and served until his death in 1974. Then Valéry Giscard d'Estaing, a conservative (but not a member of the Gaullist party), was elected president in a close race that had the country split nearly evenly at the polls between right and left. In the next elections, in May 1981, the almost even split went the other way, and François Mitterrand, a Socialist, became president.

To the relief of some and the disappointment of others, socialism has not really changed the face of France very much. Some industries have been nationalized, but other industries and most banks had already been run by the state under previous governments. Civil liberties have been assured in a more typically American fashion than before. The death penalty has been abolished. On questions of foreign policy, such as relations with the Soviets, the Middle East, cooperation with NATO, and missile deployment, France under the Socialists moved closer to American positions; only Central America, energy, and international monetary policy remain real differences.

Domestically, however, France has been plagued by severe economic problems — high unemployment, inflation, a heavy burden of social services, a relatively weak currency, and a balance of payments deficit. Insoluble labor problems were avoided only because of the unions' ideological support of the government, though economic reality forced severe (and unpopular) austerity measures.

So unpopular were these Socialist edicts that the Socialists lost control of the French legislature to a coalition of centrists and conservatives in March 1986, and the neo-Gaullist Mayor of Paris, Jacques Chirac, became prime minister. When Mitterand ran against Chirac in the presidential elections of mid-1988, however, Mitterand won a second term as president. His victory was by such a decisive margin that he called for early parliamentary elections, hoping to win back a Socialist majority in the 577-seat National Assembly and end 2 years of "cohabitation."

But the predicted landslide did not materialize. Although the Socialists won a bloc of 276 seats, they fell short of a majority, as did the center-right alliance, which emerged from the voting with 271 seats. On the far right, the voters rejected the xenophobic rhetoric of the National Front of Jean-Marie Le Pen, who blamed most of France's problems on its immigrant population, thereby cutting its parliamentary representation from 32 seats to 1 seat. This result was due as much to a recent change in the voting system, which made it difficult for small parties to win seats, as to a defection by supporters. On the left, the Communists salvaged 27 of their 35 seats.

Over the last couple of years, France's Fifth Republic has been neither extremely right wing nor markedly left of center, and the right-left political division remains strong with no real national consensus of government direction. Since 1988, French voters have gravitated toward the middle of a winding road, and social and political life seems to have become more reactive than purposeful. Cabinet dissension and strikes among public workers occur regularly, though neither seriously seems to impede the course of day-to-day life.

The impending unification of Germany has stirred newly animated concern among those with long memories, while at the same time, overt anti-Semitic acts seem to be on the rise. France, alone among the NATO allies, has been willing to negotiate for the release of French hostages with Middle Eastern terrorists, and France seems to be just about the only western nation to have created a nuclear energy policy that's still growing with the blessing of the majority of French citizens.

Thus the mosaic of French life in the 1990s can be described accurately as varied and often contradictory. Prime Minister Mitterand occupies a position that's more "grandfather" rather than vital leader, but the quality of life for French citizens doesn't seem to be hampered much by the absence of a visionary leader. For the most part, France remains a prosperous place perched on the beginning of a new century.

Literature

In France, the life of the mind always has flourished right along with the life of the senses. So the same country that can boast of offering the world's hautest cuisine, greatest wines, and most elegant fashions (not to mention many of Europe's greatest artistic and architectural masterpieces) also can legitimately claim to have produced some of the world's greatest literature.

The early Middle Ages produced a great military epic, the "Chanson de Roland" (Song of Roland; ca. 1100), which made Charlemagne's defeat at Roncevaux, in 778, into a heroic legend. The medieval era also was one of chivalry and courtly love, as reflected in the verse tales of Chrétien de Troyes (ca. 1135–1183), in the poetry of the southern troubadours, and in the 13th-century philosophical allegory *Roman de la Rose* (Romance of the Rose). In 1431, the year Joan of Arc was burned at the stake, France's greatest poet of the Middle Ages was born: François Villon. Though educated at the Sorbonne, he often associated with thieves and criminals and, in 1462 or 1463, was sentenced to be hanged for the murder of a priest. The sentence was commuted, but he left Paris and disappeared without a trace. His poetry reflects a graphic preoccupation with death and a poignant regret for his deeds.

By the 16th century, Pierre de Ronsard (1524–85), the most successful poet of his day, was writing charming love poems in which the transience of youth and the inevitability of death are arguments for enjoying the here and now. He and the six other poets of the Pléiade group used Latin, Greek, and Italian examples to set new formal standards for French verse and to enrich the French language to enable it to develop a literature to rival the models.

François Rabelais (ca. 1494–1553), a monk who gave up the religious life to practice medicine in Lyons (a lively intellectual center at the time), usually is regarded as the first French prose writer to reflect the spirit of Renaissance humanism, and he did it with a bang. With an avid interest in all the forms of learning, he celebrated the pleasures of both the mind and the body, unabashedly mixing scatology and scholarship, erudition and hedonism. His satirical novels about two giants, *Pantagruel* (1532) and *Gargantua* (1534), were lusty, witty, coarse, and irreverent, and they were condemned as sacrilegious and obscene by the theologians at the Sorbonne. Rabelais mocked religious dogma and medieval asceticism. The philosophy that emerges from his writings is progressive and optimistic, rooted in a spirited love of life and faith in the goodness of human nature.

While Rabelais gave his name to a singular style of humor, Michel Eyquem de Montaigne (1533–92), the other towering figure of the age, invented the short form of expository writing known as the essay. He spent years of his life cloistered in the tower library of his château in the Périgord (while the religious wars raged nearby), writing his engaging *Essais,* meaning "attempts"; two books appeared in 1580, a third in 1588. In his loose, casual style, he set out to study in depth a most fascinating subject — himself — and in so doing he entertained his reader by discussing nearly every topic of interest to mankind. Montaigne was a skeptic, and his views are surprisingly modern. He was repelled by dogmatic opinion and constantly stressed the relativity of all customs and beliefs. In addition, he favored the acquisition of judgment and wisdom over bookishness for its own sake, preferring "a well-made head rather than a well-filled one."

Montaigne's outlook paved the way for the 17th-century classical ideal of the *honnête homme* — a cultured and harmonious being, innately refined, elegant, and poised. This paragon of good taste and civilized virtues — measured, thoughtful, discreet, gallant, and brave — probably still lurks as a model of behavior somewhere in the French collective unconscious, lodged there by the insistent drilling of the works of the country's great classical writers into the head of every schoolchild.

Two events traditionally are regarded as having ushered in the golden age of classicism. The first was the founding of the Académie Française by Cardinal Richelieu after writers had begun meeting secretly to discuss literary matters. The Academy was recognized by Louis XIII in 1635 and still is a powerful institution (housed, since 1805, in one of the most beautiful buildings in Paris, the 17th-century Institut de France). From the beginning, its function was to purify the language, establish linguistic standards and grammatical rules, and pass judgment on literary works; the opportunity to exercise this last function came almost immediately, with the appearance in 1636 of the second event to launch the golden age, a fiery play by Pierre Corneille (1606–84).

Corneille's *Le Cid* was an immense popular success ("beautiful as *Le Cid*" became a common catch phrase), but it was criticized by the Academy for its insufficient adherence to the classical rule of the three unities. This rule required that for the sake of verisimilitude (presumably), a play's action had to unfold within 24 hours, in a single setting, and without extraneous subplots or changes in mood (violent events or deaths were not permitted to occur onstage, either). The Academy's criticism of *Le Cid* probably was instigated by Cardinal Richelieu (himself a writer) out of jealousy, yet this extreme concern for fixed rules, correctness, order, and regularity is characteristic of the period. Oddly enough, in spite of these restrictions — or perhaps thanks to them — the classical movement engendered masterpieces of stylized, polished perfection that helped set the tone for the long and absolutist reign of Louis XIV, who ascended to the throne at the age of 5 in 1643 and reigned from 1661 to 1715. Under the Sun King, French letters truly reached their zenith. As Louis's splendid court radiated brilliance from Versailles, as French artists and writers responded to the encouragement of royal patronage, and as aristocratic salons proliferated in Paris, French literature and art came to dominate Europe, and French became the common language of its educated classes.

The degree to which it respected the unities notwithstanding, *Le Cid* was the first masterpiece of French classical tragedy. It dealt inspiringly with the noble conflict between love and honor, a theme Corneille so exploited in all his tragedies that it became known as a *situation cornélienne*. His heroes always are well born, ardent souls who dominate their unruly passions and weaknesses through reason and will power. This optimistic, rational view of human psychology foreshadowed the *Treatise on Passions* (1649) by René Descartes (1596–1650), the great mathematician and creator of analytic geometry, whose *Discours de la Méthode* (Discourse on Method; 1637) — "I think, therefore I am" — laid the foundations of modern philosophy. In contrast, the tragedies of Corneille's younger rival, Jean Racine (1639–99), are emotional and pessimistic in the extreme, bearing the mark of his austere upbringing according to the doctrines of Jansenism, a Roman Catholic reform movement to which a belief in predestination was fundamental.

While some critics feel that the tighter tragedies Corneille wrote after *Le Cid* are his true masterpieces (*Horace* and *Cinna* in 1640, *Polyeuctus* in 1643), others speculate that if he had not been obliged to fetter his baroque genius and conform to the rule of the three unities, he might have been as great as Shakespeare. This issue doesn't arise in the case of Racine; the three unities suited him perfectly. Like the proverbial chef who can whip up an unforgettable meal out of nothing, Racine required few ingredients to create moving, sublime tragedies. A master stylist, his plays *Andromache* (1667) and *Phaedra* (1677) are both "fire under ice," the action hinging entirely on the violent psychological reactions of his characters. His heroes and heroines are the obsessive, helpless victims of their emotions — unrequited love, jealousy, ambition, pride, hatred, and cruelty — a spectrum with which Racine probably was intimately acquainted, for he was a particularly odious man, disloyal and ruthlessly selfish (he even was accused of poisoning his mistress, a celebrated actress).

On the other hand, the man who launched Racine's career (and whom Racine promptly double-crossed) is very fondly remembered. Molière (the pseudonym of Jean-Baptiste Poquelin, 1622–73) was a native Parisian (his parents lived near *Les Halles,* at 96 Rue St.-Honoré) who rebelled against his prosperous bourgeois background to found a theatrical company. After touring the provinces for 12 years, the troupe returned to Paris in 1658 and won the Sun King's enduring patronage. An inscription at the corner of Rue de Valois and Rue St.-Honoré marks the spot where Molière's *Palais-Royal* used to stand (it burned down in 1781). This was the theater in which he produced most of his own plays and where, just hours before his death, he struggled through his last comic performance, ironically in the title role of the hypochondriac in *La Malade Imaginaire* (The Imaginary Invalid).

Molière used a whole gamut of comic devices, from slapstick farce to refined verbal satire, to expose a wide range of human failings, including pretension, affectation, pedantry, and misguided aspirations. As a result, he created a hilarious but thought-provoking form of comedy based on the portrayal of contemporary mores and universal character types: *Le Bourgeois Gentilhomme* (The Would-Be Gentleman) and *Les Femmes Savantes* (The Learned Women). He was not a social reformer, but the wickedness and hypocrisy that he exposed in his two most heartfelt comedies, *Tartuffe* and *Le Misanthrope,* provide a rather bleak view of mankind and society. Perhaps this was inevitable. In the beginning of his career, Molière obstinately had tried to produce tragedies (the "nobler" genre); by the end of his life, he had succeeded in elevating comedy to the level of tragedy.

There were other important 17th-century literary figures. The posthumously published *Pensées* (Thoughts) of Blaise Pascal (1623–62), a mathematical prodigy and Jansenism's deepest thinker, anticipated modern Existentialism. Jean de La Fontaine (1621–95), a worldly, amused observer of human nature and social behavior, is best remembered for his witty and vivid verse *Fables*. François de La Rochefoucauld (1613–80), on the other hand, produced his *Maximes* (Maxims), the darkest book of observations the world has ever known, pithily demonstrating that all our noblest sentiments really are dictated by self-love and self-interest. Meanwhile, his great friend Madame de La Fayette (1634–92) wrote the first French psychological novel, *La Princesse de Clèves*, a concise analysis of the inner workings of love and jealousy. Finally, Madame de Sévigné (1626–96), their common friend and fellow aristocrat, has gone down in history for her extraordinarily lively letters, mostly to her beloved daughter, describing the literary, political, and cultural events of the capital. From 1677 to her death, she lived in the magnificent mansion in Paris that now is the *Musée Carnavalet*.

The absolute monarchy of Louis XIV left the kingdom bankrupt. In the 18th century, as the monarchy continued to decline under Louis XV and Louis XVI, the court ceased to be the center of cultural and artistic life and became a target of intellectual criticism. In Parisian salons and the new cafés (like *Le Procope*, which still stands on Rue de l'Ancienne-Comédie), the *philosophes* of the Enlightenment (when they weren't in jail or exile for their writings) and other brilliant conversationalists mixed with disciples, artists, scientists, or eminent foreigners to reappraise absolutism and challenge all existing institutions and values. The democratic reforms these thinkers advocated, their belief in progress and the perfectibility of man, eventually cleared the way for momentous events such as the American and French Revolutions. In the meantime, they helped make Paris, which already was Europe's capital of refinement and elegance, into an exciting cosmopolitan center bristling with wit, daring, and intellectual ferment.

Six years after Louis XIV's death, the critical disposition of the new century was made tangible by Charles Louis de Secondat de Montesquieu (1689–1755) in his immensely successful *Lettres Persanes* (Persian Letters; 1721), in which contemporary French customs and institutions were seen through the "naive" eyes of visiting Persians. Anglophilia soon was in the air, as well as a growing admiration for the works of English philosophers and scientists. Montesquieu spent almost 2 years in England and came away commending the democratic features of its constitutional monarchy. The same was true of François-Marie Arouet, known as Voltaire (1694–1778). After 3 years of political exile across the Channel, he presented his observations and praise in a book entitled *Lettres Philosophiques* (Philosophical Letters on the English; 1733), an implicit attack on the bigotry, intolerance, and despotism of the French regime that caused enough of a furor to be banned. He is best known for his much later work, *Candide* (1759), a masterful tale that ironically refutes simplistic optimism and passivity and is written in his characteristically witty, clear, and simple prose style. As a polemicist, playwright, poet, novelist, historian, critic, and letter writer, Voltaire's literary output was staggering; in addition, he was a very clever financier and landowner, a guest at the "enlightened" courts of Europe, and, at the end of his long life, a revered patriarchal figure (Benjamin Franklin, for one, made a point of taking his grandson to visit him). For all these reasons, it is not surprising that the 18th century is sometimes called the Age of Voltaire.

However, it is customary to regard Voltaire as the last representative of the classical era and his younger, even more influential contemporary, the Swiss Jean-Jacques Rousseau (1712–78), as the herald of the new era of Romanticism. Rousseau opposed Voltaire and the other *philosophes* by challenging the values imposed by so-called progress and civilization and by viewing with contempt the conformist ideal of the *honnête homme.* He first drew the spotlight to himself in 1750 by winning an essay contest with his negative response to the question of whether progress in the arts and sciences contributed to the improvement of human nature. His discourse on inequality (1754) was more outspoken, and by the time *The Social Contract* appeared in 1762, opening with the ringing "Man is born free, and is everywhere in chains" — and further denouncing the corrupting influence of society and the evils of property, social inequality, and tyranny — Rousseau was a hero to some, a heretic to others. That same year, in *Emile,* he advocated an educational approach that would allow human potential to develop freely, an approach that formed the basis of all subsequent theories of progressive education. As a philosopher and political thinker, Rousseau directly inspired the French Revolution. At the same time, his nonconformity, his feeling for nature, his concern for sincerity, and his overt *sensibilité* — qualities that permeate such works as the epistolary novel *La Nouvelle Héloise* (The New Heloise; 1761) and the autobiographical *Confessions* (published posthumously) — touched off the Romantic movement.

Rousseau was such a controversial, indeed pivotal, figure that he tends to eclipse that other "emotional" *philosophe,* his sometime friend Denis Diderot (1713–84). Novelist, playwright, essayist, art critic, and protégé of Catherine the Great of Russia, Diderot struggled for many years, in spite of political opposition, to edit the 17 volumes of his monumental *Encyclopédie* (1751–65), one of the great liberal achievements of the period.

By the time Louis XVI came to the throne in 1774, indignation at the abuses and privileges of the hereditary aristocracy was running high. Pierre-Augustin Caron, called Beaumarchais (1732–99), a noble by marriage rather than birth, voiced this pre-Revolutionary discontent in his widely acclaimed comedies *The Barber of Seville* (1775) and *The Marriage of Figaro* (1784), which later inspired the famous operas by Rossini and Mozart.

The years of the French Revolution and of the Napoleonic regime, from 1789 to 1815, were years of upheaval and of limited literary output. The best writer publishing at the time (while many of his fellow aristocrats were being guillotined) was François-René de Chateaubriand (1768–1848), a founder of the Romantic movement in French literature. A 5-month stay in America in 1791–92 inspired him to write lush but inaccurate descriptions of the American wilderness (and of Niagara Falls) in tales that promoted an idealized, drawing room view of the American Indian. He exploited all the future Romantic themes and, above all, elaborated on a new persona, the sensitive genius with uncommon vision, who, ever since Rousseau, had begun to appear in fiction as in life. His restless, introspective hero, René, suffered from the insatiable, melancholic longings that became typical of the Romantic personality.

Even so, Romanticism came into full flower in France only as a result of foreign exposure. As the works of German and English authors became known, a new vitality was injected into the literary climate and young writers began rebelling against the strictures of their classical heritage. The four major Romantic poets were Alphonse de Lamartine (1790–1869), Alfred de Vigny (1797–1863), Victor Hugo (1802–85), and Alfred de Musset (1810–57), who also was an excellent playwright. The dominating figure was Hugo. A poet of great power, scope, and technical virtuosity, he dealt with every possible lyrical theme and also wrote gripping, melodramatic novels, of which the most famous remain *The Hunchback of Notre-Dame* (1831) and *Les Misérables* (1862). In 1830, the first performance of his Romantic drama, *Hernani,* was such a radical departure from the conventional theater that it prompted a riot between the classicists and Hugo's young Romantic supporters, the classicists objecting to Hugo's violation of the rules, the Romantics ultimately prevailing. For Hugo, Romanticism included political liberalism; he actively sympathized with the downtrodden and fought against social injustice, with the result that his opposition to Napoleon III sent him into exile for 20 years in the Channel Islands. He returned to France at the proclamation of the Third Republic in 1870 and was idolized as a leftist and champion of the people. The house he lived in from 1838 to 1843, at 6 Place des Vosges, now is a museum.

The growing influence of science during the 19th century led writers to try to depict people objectively, in their specific social milieus. In fiction, Romanticism gradually gave way to Realism, while at the end of the century, Realism gave way to Symbolism, particularly in poetry.

No writer better portrayed the social changes wrought by industrialization or the transformation of the rich bourgeoisie into the new ruling class than Honoré de Balzac (1799–1850). In close to 100 novels and short stories, grouped under the general title of *La Comédie Humaine* (The Human Comedy), he created a vast fresco of urban and rural France from 1815 to 1848. Despite the breadth of the undertaking, his characters are not simply social types but also highly individual flesh-and-blood human beings, with overriding passions and gripping personal dramas. Money is a major theme in Balzac's work, as it was in his own life. He wrote night and day in order to repay the debts he had incurred from disastrous business ventures. In fact, the coffeepot that provided the necessary stimulant to his effervescent imagination can be seen at the *Musée Balzac,* his home from 1842 to 1848, at 47 Rue Raynouard, a street that also briefly housed Jean-Jacques Rousseau and Benjamin Franklin.

Balzac was one of the rare contemporaries to fully appreciate the genius of Henri Beyle, known as Stendhal (1783–1842). In his own day, Stendhal wrote, as he said, "for the happy few"; today his masterpieces, *Le Rouge et le Noir* (The Red and the Black; 1831) and *La Chartreuse de Parme* (The Charterhouse of Parma; 1839), are widely admired for their psychological insight, political liberalism, and sober, ironic style.

While Stendhal wrote *La Chartreuse de Parme* in a record-breaking 7 weeks, Gustave Flaubert (1821–80) labored for nearly 5 years to produce that cool and scathing indictment of bourgeois provinciality, *Madame Bovary* (1857). The same painstaking care went into his other novels, including *L'Education Sentimentale* (The Sentimental Education; 1869). A meticulous researcher and perfectionist, he read each sentence of his impersonal prose out loud and rewrote paragraphs over and over again until he had found exactly the right words and rhythms.

It would seem that no novelist could have had a clearer or more pessimistic view of the contrast between our exalted romantic illusions and the actual platitude, or uneventfulness, of our lives than Flaubert. Yet his disciple Guy de Maupassant (1850–93), the master of the short story (who also produced some first-rate novels), was even more pessimistic. Though he, too, was a superb craftsman, he did not share Flaubert's religious devotion to the cause of art. For him, no pursuit or conviction could give a larger meaning to human life, which he portrayed in his fiction, with the sparsest means and seeming impartiality, as absurd, brutal, or pitiful.

Emile Zola (1840–1902), a friend and admirer of Flaubert and de Maupassant, went beyond Realism and forsook their economical, selective style to become the leader of the Naturalist School. Sheer weight characterizes his writing. Starting where Balzac left off, he produced the 20 heavily documented "slice of life" novels of the Rougon-Macquart series (1871–93), tracing the "natural and social history of a family under the Second Empire" (1852–70). The series covers almost every possible occupation and shows the grimmest aspects of lower class life, all with the scientist's aim of illustrating how heredity, biology, and the environment determine human behavior. A reformer and a socialist, in 1898 Zola wrote his famous open letter to the president of France, "J'Accuse," in defense of Captain Alfred Dreyfus, the Jewish army officer whom he believed wrongly convicted of treason.

One of Zola's supporters in this courageous stand was the novelist, poet, playwright, and critic Jacques-Anatole Thibault, or Anatole France (1844–1924), whose first full-length novel, *La Crime de Sylvestre Bonnard* (1881), had been a great success. As a result of the Dreyfus Affair, which he made the subject of four novels, France's work became increasingly devoted to political satire. His *Les Dieux Ont Soif* (The Gods Are Thirsty; 1912), a novel about the French Revolution and a searingly ironical indictment of political fanaticism, is considered his masterpiece. After a long career, France was awarded the Nobel Prize for literature in 1921.

Some of the other popular 19th-century writers still are read today. Alexandre Dumas (1802–70), for example, is remembered for *Les Trois Mousquetaires* (The Three Musketeers) and *Le Comte de Monte Cristo* (The Count of Monte Cristo); his son, Alexandre Dumas *fils* (1824–95), wrote the autobiographical novel and stage play *La Dame aux Camélias,* which inspired Verdi's *La Traviata* (not to mention 23 motion pictures, including *Camille* with Greta Garbo). Jules Verne (1828–1905), the author of *Vingt Mille Lieues sous les Mers* (Twenty Thousand Leagues under the Sea) and *La Tour du Monde en Quatre-Vingt Jours* (Around the World in Eighty Days), is regarded as the grandfather of contemporary science fiction.

French poets of the latter half of the 19th century reacted against the vague emotion of Romanticism on the one hand and the Realism of contemporary prose on the other. The Symbolists — Verlaine, Rimbaud, and Mallarmé — sought to go beyond transient, sensory reality to suggest the inner, eternal absolute. Symbolism's precursor was Charles Baudelaire (1821–67), whose *Les Fleurs du Mal* (Flowers of Evil; 1857) influenced not only the French but also English-language poets such as Swinburne, T. S. Eliot, Pound, and Yeats. He himself had found a kindred spirit in Edgar Allan Poe and worked for years on a translation of Poe's tales. Baudelaire was a dandy and a decadent; he drank to excess, he experimented with opium and hashish, and he spent the last years of his life in physical and mental torment. His poems have been described as "suggestive magic," yet they are unflinchingly honest about depravation, misery, and his personal sense of despair.

In contrast, Paul Verlaine (1844–96), who lived just as dissolute a life as Baudelaire, wrote poetry that is gentle and melancholic, candid and poignant. His notorious 2-year relationship with the rebellious, visionary boy genius Arthur Rimbaud (1854–91) ended disastrously. During one of their drunken arguments, Verlaine shot and wounded Rimbaud and, as a result, spent 2 years in prison for attempted murder. Rimbaud, on the other hand, after having completely revolutionized poetry with his hallucinatory imagery, complex rhythms, and free verse, gave up writing at the age of 19. He traveled widely and finally settled into the trade of coffee, arms, and slaves in Abyssinia.

Stéphane Mallarmé (1842–98) led the quiet life of an English teacher ascetically devoted to his art. Only when he began to be known in the mid-1880s did young writers and admirers flock to the Tuesday evening gatherings at his tranquil apartment on Rue de Rome to listen to his theories of poetry. His work is extremely complex and elusive, built on the suggestive music of words, and one of his longer poems, "L'Après-midi d'un Faune" (The Afternoon of a Faun; 1867), inspired Debussy's orchestral "Prélude" (1887).

Paris at the turn of the century was a lively, high-spirited city. The Belle Epoque flourished, with its great expositions, its literary cabarets and cafés (one of the most famous, the *Lapin Agile* in Montmartre, still exists), controversial art exhibitions, theaters, vaudeville shows, music halls, literary reviews, and the first movie projections. There was increasing interaction among the various arts, as painters, writers, musicians, and actors stimulated, supported, and opposed one another. Out of this exchange arose an unprecedented number of schools, cliques, and movements.

The Romantics and some of the Symbolist poets already had rejected tradition, defied convention, and scandalized public opinion. The avant-garde followed boldly in their wake. Today, we almost expect to be bewildered by new trends in art, and the nonconformist writer or artist is practically a cliché. It is hard for us to imagine, for example, the effect produced by Alfred Jarry (1873–1907) when he appeared at Mallarmé's funeral dressed like a bicycle racer, with bright yellow shoes. A forerunner of the Dadaist and Surrealist movements as well as of the later Theater of the Absurd represented by Samuel Beckett (1906–89), Eugène Ionesco (b. 1912), and Jean Genet (1910–86), Jarry's grotesque farce, *Ubu-Roi,* caused a scandal on its opening night in 1896 comparable to the one caused by Victor Hugo's *Hernani* in 1830.

Meanwhile, just as Baudelaire, as an art critic, had shown unerring taste in defending the controversial painters of his time (Delacroix, Corot, Manet, Daumier), the poet Guillaume Apollinaire (1880–1918) promoted the works of the innovative painters of his day: Vlaminck, Derain, Chagall, Duchamp, Modigliani, Rousseau, De Chirico, Picabia, Delaunay, Léger, Picasso, Braque, and Gris. He dominated the avant-garde from 1913 to his death, and his poetic innovations opened the path to Surrealism, a term credited to him. The Surrealist movement, which thrived between the two world wars, drew inspiration from Freud and tried to unleash the forces of the unconscious through automatic writing and free association.

The discovery of the unconscious also dominated the fiction of this period. Many good French novelists turned out excellent sagas in the tradition of Balzac and Zola — notably the Nobel Prize winners Romain Rolland (1866–1944) and Roger Martin du Gard (1881–1958) as well as Georges Duhamel (1884–1966) and Jules Romains (1885–1972). But all these works pale next to the beauty and complexity of Marcel Proust's monumental cycle novel, *Remembrance of Things Past* (the French title is *A la Recherche du Temps Perdu;* In Search of Lost Time, "lost" implying both "gone" and "wasted"). Like Stendhal, Proust (1871–1922) is admired more today than he was by his contemporaries, though he owes part of his fame to the conditions under which he wrote. A social butterfly in his youth, severe asthma and total dedication to his artistic mission turned him into a recluse working in bed in a darkened, cork-lined room. The first volume of this masterpiece was rejected by several publishers so Proust had it printed at his own expense. Yet it now is clear that he wrote one of the greatest novels ever. Living up to Mallarmé's remark that "the world was made to end up in a beautiful book," he put all his energy and experience of life into his work. Thanks to pitiless self-analysis, he reached beyond the traditional, static views of human psychology and created a richly textured social universe activated by the forces of love, jealousy, death, memory, and time.

The only contemporary novelist comparable to Proust in intensity may be James Joyce, who lived from time to time in Paris and serves to recall another important feature of the city before World War II: It was the home of so many Irish, English, and American writers. "Paris was where the 20th century was," said Gertrude Stein, who entertained America's "lost generation" of writers (as well as painters like Cézanne and Picasso) at 27 Rue de Fleurus. Beginning with Oscar Wilde, who spent his last days at *L'Hôtel* on Rue des Beaux-Arts in 1900, the list of expatriates who lived and worked in Paris is impressive: Ernest Hemingway, F. Scott Fitzgerald, Sherwood Anderson, John Dos Passos, Jean Rhys, Ford Madox Ford, D. H. Lawrence, Henry Miller, Anaïs Nin, George Orwell, James Joyce, Samuel Beckett. Others, like Ezra Pound, T. S. Eliot, and Thornton Wilder, often passed through. Though they frequented all the cafés of Montparnasse — *Le Dôme, Le Sélect, La*

Rotonde, La Coupole, La Closerie des Lilas — their great haunt was *Shakespeare & Company,* the bookshop owned by Sylvia Beach, an American, at 12 Rue de l'Odéon (it no longer exists; the bookshop of the same name on the *quai* is not the original). Sylvia Beach also published Joyce's *Ulysses* (1922), a work that encountered monumental publication and censorship difficulties elsewhere because of charges of obscenity.

At the same time, many important French writers emerged: Colette (1873–1954), for example, who began by ghostwriting for her first husband, Willy, and whose *Gigi* was made into a Hollywood movie; the great poet and essayist Paul Valéry (1871–1945); Catholic novelists and playwright-poets such as Nobel Prize winner François Mauriac (1885–1970), Georges Bernanos (1888–1948), Paul Claudel (1868–1955), and Charles Péguy (1873–1914); novelists of adventure and heroism like André Malraux (1901–76), who became minister of culture under de Gaulle, and Antoine de St.-Exupéry (1900–44); the historical novelist Marguerite Yourcenar (b. 1903), the first woman to be elected to the French Academy, in 1982; the Belgian-born detective story writer Georges Simenon (1903–89), famous for his Inspector Maigret series; and André Gide (1869–1951), winner of the Nobel Prize for literature in 1947. Gide's writings raised moral issues that foreshadowed the philosophical school of Existentialism. He also made formal innovations, such as in his novel *Les Faux-Monnayeurs* (The Counterfeiters; 1926), that prepared the way for the *nouveau roman* (new novel) of the 1950s and 60s.

World War II brought the Existentialists to the forefront. Jean-Paul Sartre (1905–80) and Simone de Beauvoir (1908–86), as well as their friend, the Algerian-born Albert Camus (1913–60), who actually evolved his own philosophy of the absurd, grew increasingly influential in France and abroad, and by now a whole generation has been bred on their philosophy of free will, moral responsibility, and political commitment. In postwar Paris, Sartre and Simone de Beauvoir also helped make the *Café Flore* and *Les Deux Magots,* on Boulevard St.-Germain, into fashionable intellectual watering holes. Camus — novelist, playwright, essayist — received the Nobel Prize in 1957, while Sartre — philosopher, novelist, playwright, literary critic, and Marxist — turned it down in 1964.

Parallel to these writers, who used fiction and drama as their vehicles, there arose the technical experiments of the new novelists, or anti-novelists, including Nathalie Sarraute (b. 1902), Claude Simon (b. 1913), Alain Robbe-Grillet (b. 1922), and Michel Butor (b. 1926), all of whom still are writing today; Simon won the Nobel Prize in 1985. In a complete departure from the traditional novel, they proceeded to "decompose" reality by dispensing with chronology, plot, character, and meaning — either by magnifying the ephemeral and contradictory elements of life, by jumbling chronology and plot, or by concentrating on the description of the flat surface of things (leading some readers to feel that human psychology has been unfairly replaced by the legs of chairs).

Marguerite Duras (b. 1914) and the late Samuel Beckett (who wrote in both French and English) do not properly belong to this school, yet they, too, rejected the conventional novel. Both also have written excellent plays, while Duras and Robbe-Grillet have put their talent into films as well. French cinema always has had a literary bent (as exemplified in the 1940s by the collaboration between the poet Jacques Prévert and the director Marcel Carné, and by the experimental films of Jean Cocteau) and one of the most exciting artistic developments of the 1960s was the New Wave cinema of directors led by Alain Resnais, Claude Chabrol, Eric Rohmer, Jean Eustache, Jean-Luc Godard, and the late François Truffaut.

French intellectual life today is as lively as ever, particularly in the social sciences. The study of linguistics and the work of the anthropologist Claude Lévi-Strauss (b. 1908) engendered a method of analysis called Structuralism, which focuses on the patterns of relationships within systems of communications. A lively school of New Criticism, headed by Roland Barthes (1915–80), attacked the orthodox, academic approach to literary criticism and opened the door to every kind of interpretation — structural, linguistic, psychoanalytic, Marxist. Sociologists, philosophers, and historians also are producing interesting work, while the difficult, pun-filled writings of France's leading psychoanalyst, Jacques Lacan (1901–81), are the subject of heated debate. Because most poets, novelists, and playwrights draw inspiration from these recent trends, cut-and-dried distinctions between imaginative and scholarly writing are hard to make. But one thing is certain: French writers today know they are part of one of the world's oldest, most distinguished literary traditions.

Painting

Compared to the history of Italian or Flemish art, the history of French painting begins relatively late. To be sure, there was painting in France from the earliest times. Witness the cave drawings at Lascaux: mysterious dots, bars, and bison-like images thought to represent hunting scenes or symbolic rituals. But the development of a great and characteristically French school of painting did not really begin until the 17th century. Before that, the creative genius that eventually made French painting dominant in the world of art found expression in other forms, and where painting did appear, its style usually was borrowed, in no way particularly French. The Celts, who settled France before the Christian era, and the Franks, who came in the 5th century, made gold and silver objects and splendid jewelry. Architecture and sculpture were the preeminent arts of the Romanesque period, and the Gothic period added the glorious art of stained glass, which reached its height in the cathedral at Chartres.

Painting in the form of manuscript illumination flourished in various centers throughout the Middle Ages. In the early 15th century, the Duke of Berry employed a distinguished group of miniaturists at his court, including the Franco-Flemish Limbourg brothers, whose *Très Riches Heures du Duc de Berry* (*Book of Hours;* 1415) is a masterpiece of refined elegance in the International Gothic style. Painting in other forms appeared sporadically; one of the earliest examples was a medieval panel portrait of King John the Good (1360–64). During the 14th and 15th centuries, a flowering of the arts took place in the south of France, first around the papal court in Avignon, then at the court of Good King René in Aix-en-Provence. The frescoes on the walls of the Palace of the Popes (the religious cycles were done by an Italian, Matteo Giovanetti, but the secular hunting, fishing, and landscape scenes are thought to be the work of French artists) belong to the mid-14th century. And two panel paintings — the *Pietà* of Villeneuve-les-Avignon, attributed to Enguerrand Charonton, and the *Aix Annonciation,* by the Master of the Annunciation of Aix — are masterpieces of Provençal painting in the mid-15th century.

Nor were other areas of France lacking in painters in the 15th century. Jean Fouquet (ca. 1420–80), a native of Tours and a leading illuminator as well as *peintre du roi* (court painter) to Louis XI, is remembered not only for the illuminations in his *Book of Hours of Etienne Chevalier* (ca. 1450–55) but also for his panel portraits, *Charles VII* and *Guillaume Juvénal des Ursins.* The *Moulins Triptych* (1498–99), by the Master of Moulins, is an outstanding example of late-15th-century portraiture. Nevertheless, painting in France at this time was neither a first art nor, since strongly suggestive of its Flemish and Italian sources, an original one.

Painting did play a notable role in the French Renaissance, but its style still was imported, the result of contact with the Italian Renaissance through the

Italian Wars begun by Charles VIII in 1494. And what was imported was not the High Renaissance but the post-Renaissance, or Mannerism, an exaggerated, self-conscious, luxurious, elitist style. The two most prominent French painters of the early 16th century were Jean Bourdichon (1457–1521) and Jean Perréal (ca. 1455–1530), about whom almost nothing is known. What is known is that when Francis I, whose reign is considered the height of the French Renaissance, became king in 1515, he set about bringing the greatest painters in Italy to his court. Leonardo da Vinci came in 1516; during the 1530s, Il Rosso and Francesco Primaticcio arrived to direct the decoration of the Galerie François I at the Fontainebleau palace. Thus the School of Fontainebleau was born. French artists began working beside the Italian masters, and the new Mannerist style of painting — along with a taste for elaborate stucco work — took hold in the country, to remain in vogue for the rest of the century. But it still was not a French style, and there still was no painting that could legitimately be called French.

THE SEVENTEENTH-CENTURY BEGINNINGS

It was during the baroque period (1600–1750) that the history of French painting really began. The masters of the early French baroque were Georges de La Tour (1593–1652) and the Le Nain brothers, Antoine (1588–1648) and Mathieu (1607–77). Influenced by Caravaggio, La Tour explored *chiaroscuro,* painting nocturnal scenes in the main and mastering the effects of lighting from hidden or revealed sources (*Magdalen with the Night Light*). The Le Nain brothers concentrated instead on the effects of daylight. But the three shared one innovation: Their scenes gave an importance to daily life, not just to historical, allegorical, or religious themes. The Le Nains in particular were the first of the great baroque painters to portray unsentimentalized scenes of peasants, and their work later influenced the 19th-century painters Courbet and Manet.

It was also in the 17th century that there first appeared French painters whose names are readily recognized today. Claude Gellée, known as Claude Lorrain (1600–82), and Nicolas Poussin (1594–1665), both of whom worked in Italy, were masters of baroque landscape painting. They drew their inspiration from the Italian countryside and painted primarily for an Italian elite, but both remained profoundly French as painters. Together they represented the polarity within the baroque movement as a whole. Poussin was a model of classical reason and restraint, using Italian landscapes as a background for monumental figure paintings based on classical texts and exploiting classical references for their narrative value (*Arcadian Shepherds,* 1650). Lorrain was the model of unrestrained romanticism, of the irrational and magical, using the Roman countryside as a nostalgic backdrop for minute, at times inconsequential, figures, and exploiting symbols from the past for their emotive value (*Landscape with a Rustic Dance,* 1639).

While Poussin and Lorrain were working in Italy, Philippe de Champaigne (1602–74) was working in Paris. His stunning portrait of his daughter, a nun, and her prioress in their cell (*Ex-Voto,* 1662) is unusual in its directness and psychological perspective. But the most influential painter working in Paris was Simon Vouet (1590–1649), court painter to Louis XIII. Vouet, too, had been to Rome, and it was Poussin's classicism that prevailed in his work; his style tempered the exuberance of the late Mannerists to the taste of the French monarchy, and he was a master of pictorial decoration. Vouet was the artistic arbiter of the first half of the 17th century, the head of a large *atelier* (studio), yet he is remembered chiefly for one student, Charles Le Brun (1619–90), the man who ruled artistic tastes in the second half of the century.

As court painter to Louis XIV, Le Brun was the interior decorator of Versailles. He decorated the Grands Apartements; he painted the ceiling of the Galerie des Glaces (Hall of Mirrors) in allegories to Louis's glory. He married the classical spirit to the flamboyance of the baroque and dedicated the union to serve the Sun King's visions of grandeur, thereby giving lavish visual form to the ideology behind the absolute monarchy and making its setting the marvel of Europe.

Le Brun, in essence, created the Louis XIV style, an accomplishment made possible also because he was the director of the Gobelins tapestry manufactory and the chancellor of the Académie Royale de Peinture et de Sculpture of Paris. The former had been bought by Louis in the 1660s and had been turned into a workshop of the decorative arts, producing everything from jewelry to furniture. The latter, an association of artists founded in 1648, had grown under royal patronage into a powerful palace school of art, dictating aesthetic rules for painting and sculpture just as the French Academy dictated grammar and style for language and literature.

THE EIGHTEENTH CENTURY

Because Louis XV was only 5 years old when Louis XIV died, a regent ruled France from 1715 to 1723. This period of transition, appropriately known as the Regency, was a time of general relaxation from the rigid ceremonial and public lifestyles imposed by the Sun King. For a while Paris, not Versailles, was the center of society and artistic activity. This change in atmosphere marked art, as did architectural changes. Townhouses became the focus of the artist's attention, architectural proportions were reduced, and smaller, more intimate genre paintings now were required for decoration. Regular salons came into being, offering a showcase for artists not trained at the Academy. Antoine Watteau (1684–1721), who studied with a painter of theatrical scenes and with a decorative painter, was one such artist. He showed his works of fashionable people amusing themselves under the heading of "*fêtes galantes.*" These scenes of love and gallantry, influenced by earlier Venetian styles, took place outdoors, where lovers in shimmering silk finery met beneath flesh-like statues in otherworldly parks. They differed in every way from the state portraits and massive allegorical themes that had dominated painting style for more than a century, just as their poignant evocation of mystery, their suggestion of the transitoriness of love and life, set them apart from the *fêtes* of artists still to come. Watteau also introduced characters from the Italian and French comedy into his work, thus beginning a tradition in French painting — the theater as material for pictorial art — that lasted until the end of the 19th century.

But Watteau was the important exception. The mainstream of official French art passed through a lesser artist, François Le Moyne (1688–1737). Le Moyne's classicism, his large scale, and his use of allegory were 17th-century baroque, but his lightness, elegance, and clear colors were of the 18th century, representing the transition to the new style, rococo. And Le Moyne had an important pupil, François Boucher (1703–70), who became court painter to Louis XV and a favorite of the king's favorite, Madame de Pompadour (for whom he created Boucher blue). If Le Brun had captured the spirit of the Sun King's *grand siècle*, Boucher captured the lightheartedness and frivolity of the rococo period. He employed sweet pastel colors, pinks and blues that evoked a fairy-tale tone, and he was versatile. Along with large, mythological schemes, he painted landscapes, portraits, erotic scenes, and "keyhole" paintings, glimpses into the intrigues of a leisure class the painter knew well.

Jean-Honoré Fragonard (1732–1806) carried on in Boucher's tradition during the reigns of both Louis XV and Louis XVI. He was a specialist in small boudoir scenes and airy, graceful *fêtes galantes*, set in Italianate or frankly artificial decors. Paintings such as *The Swing* (1766) or the large *Progress of Love* panels (1771) painted for the house of Madame du Barry captured all the empty gaiety and beauty of the 18th century. Fragonard's use of paint, applied with direct, impromptu strokes (*Inspiration*, 1769), recalls the spontaneity of Rubens from Flanders, while his ease and grace reflect the influence of the Italian Tiepolo.

Fragonard, however, fell out of step with the times, as a reaction to the fashionably meaningless set in. Art critics, including the renowned Diderot, criticized the frivolity at court and the works of Boucher and Fragonard associated with it. They championed simpler paintings, such as still lifes and domestic scenes with humble subjects whose moral overtones were in keeping with the ideas of the Enlightenment philosophers — paintings by the likes of Jean-Baptiste Oudry (1686–1755), Jean-Baptiste-Siméon Chardin (1699–1779), and Jean-Baptiste Greuze (1725–1805).

Of the three, Chardin was the master. In ideological terms, his depictions of the family life of the Parisian middle classes, done in straightforward, muted colors, were seen as the healthy antithesis to court art and the life it reflected. In technical terms, his still lifes are extraordinarily executed (*The Rayfish*, 1727) and show a deep reverence for the everyday objects of the "common man." His genre scenes recall those of the Le Nains, yet rival those of Vermeer as among the finest ever painted (*The Morning Toilet*, 1740). Their technical purity, subtle color harmonies, and quality of composition would be later recognized by, among others, Paul Cézanne.

THE NINETEENTH CENTURY

The 19th century in French art was, quite simply, spectacular. The history of modern Europe often is dated from the French Revolution, and the beginning of modern art often is dated from one French painter, Jacques-Louis David (1748–1825), who was, initially, court painter to Louis XVI. David became the spokesman for the enormous artistic changes that corresponded to the political and philosophical changes taking place in late 18th-century France, and his oeuvre constitutes a bridge to the 19th century. A reaction against the frivolities of rococo and an interest in archaeological excavations came together at this time in a new appreciation for classical standards of excellence. Simultaneously, revolutionary ideas were leading steadily to the conclusion that the moment was heroic.

Joseph-Marie Vien (1716–1809) already had shown a willingness to move toward the neo-classical, and David had been his pupil. Now, having studied in Rome, David began to produce large canvases, based on ancient legends, that visually communicated a libertarian message. His monumental *Oath of the Horatii* (1784), a celebration of the stoic virtues of family and national honor, was shown at the Salon (the official art exhibition held by the Academy since 1737 and at this point open only to Academy members) and won for David dual recognition as the interpreter of the republican spirit and the apostle of neo-classicism. Baroque compositional methods were abandoned. Instead, David strove for the neo-classic ideals of precision and clarity of space and forms, rejecting clutter. Also remarkable is his strong use of sharply focused light, derived from Caravaggio. David became the "official" artist of the Revolution; he even designed festivals and processions as propaganda for the cause. Then, when Napoleon came to power, he became the official recorder of the Napoleonic epic. He was, in addition, a magnificent portrait painter (*Madame Récamier,* 1800), and although he was criticized for his rigid adherence to neo-classical theory in his later years, he dictated standards of academic teaching in France for a generation.

But neo-classicism was short-lived as a school, and for the most part it soon degenerated into mediocre pastiches of antiquity. There were two exceptions, both students of David: Baron Antoine Gros (1771–1835), a painter of battle scenes glorifying Napoleon, and Jean-Auguste-Dominique Ingres (1780–1867), who clearly wanted to break from his teacher. Ingres was both the last great neo-classicist and an experimenter. He distorted nature for dramatic effect, used sensuous color schemes, and frequently chose themes that were more exotic than classical, but, in the tradition of Poussin, his draftsmanship was fastidious, his work the epitome of cool, finished clarity. Ingres was a master of portraiture, attaining an astounding unity of precise observation and psychological perception. He stood on the road between neo-classicism and the movement that followed, Romanticism.

Romanticism had its precursors in the landscape painter Hubert Robert (1733–1808) and the marine painter Claude-Joseph Vernet (1714–89). There were also David's "opponent," Pierre-Paul Prud'hon (1758–1823), who interpreted reality more than reproducing it, and Théodore Géricault (1791–1824), who explored the extremes of human sentiment and experience.

But one man soon came to embody all that was Romanticism in France. Eugène Delacroix (1798–1863) was the Romantic temperament itself; he sought liberty, change, and emotions for their own sake. He visited North Africa and thereafter frequently chose exotic subjects; he filled his work with movement and excitement. He was at the same time the last great decorative painter in the French style (he painted the library of the Palais-Bourbon and the ceiling of the Galerie d'Apollon in the *Louvre*, among other projects) and the man who liberated draftsmanship, composition, and, above all, color, from neo-classical restraint. His influence on the Impressionists, the post-Impressionists, and even on the early Modernist painters who used color to express emotion was substantial.

Meanwhile, other painters worked as well. Honoré Daumier (1808–79), the caricaturist and social satirist, often has been compared to Rembrandt because of the boldness of his acute observation (*Chess Players,* 1863). Théodore Chassériau (1819–56) was renowned for his paintings of Arab subjects; Georges Michel (1763–1843) painted simple landscapes in the environs of Paris. The Barbizon School, an informal group of landscape painters active from roughly the 1830s to the 1870s, was at work in the town of Barbizon, near the Fontainebleau forest, continuing a study of the effects of light on landscape that had begun in the 17th century. Led by Théodore Rousseau (1812–67) and including such painters as Jules Dupré (1812–89) and Charles-François Daubigny (1817–78), they painted sunrises and sunsets that at times verged on the sentimental, but at their best the Barbizon painters showed a perception of natural phenomena that linked them to the later Impressionists.

Both Camille Corot (1796–1875) and Jean-François Millet (1814–75) painted with the Barbizon group, but they evolved in different directions. Corot's early works were strikingly simple and direct, even though he is best known for his Arcadian landscapes — Italian and French countrysides bathed in silvery light and populated with dancing nymphs and shepherds. Millet concentrated on the real people who inhabited the landscapes, producing large-scale figure paintings of peasants that elevated their lives and work to almost spiritual levels (*The Sower,* 1848). While his subject matter again recalled the Le Nains, his treatment marked the transition from Romanticism to Realism.

Realism in France had a standard bearer in Gustave Courbet (1819–77), an admirer of Millet and a professed socialist (he eventually was exiled). Several of his works had already either been banned from the Salon (which in this period was opened to all, not just Academy artists, although the Academy approved the exhibitions) or had scandalized public and critics alike. Then, having been refused admission to the *Paris World Exhibition of 1855,* Courbet held his own "anti-establishment" exhibition, posting at the entrance just one word: "Realism." According to Courbet, art should reflect the customs, ideas, and appearances of its time as perceived by the artist, but his honest portrayal of these elements was not without controversy. Unlike Millet, he did not elevate nature with dignified peasants, and because of both his naturalistic style and his subject matter — everything from scenes of daily life, nudes, and landscapes to a peasant funeral and drunken priests — Courbet's works were at times accused of the most terrible offense: ugliness.

In breaking with what was considered appropriate subject matter, Courbet flouted academic convention, and this was crucial. It led to the work of perhaps the most important figure of the 19th century, Edouard Manet (1832–83). In 1863, Manet's *Luncheon on the Grass* was rejected by the jury of the official Salon and even shocked the audience at the Salon des Refusés, a special show organized to display the works of the by now numerous painters who had incurred Academy disfavor. The painting had an "outrageous" subject, a nude (the artist's model and mistress) sitting with two fully clothed gentlemen while another woman prepared to dip into a shallow pool in the background. That Manet had borrowed the subject from 16th-century Italian masters was lost in the general outcry, which seemed more moral than aesthetic in motivation.

Yet Manet indeed was making an aesthetic statement. The surprising juxtaposition of nude and clothed figures in a landscape — unbelievable subject matter, devoid of any historical or allegorical significance — was his way of declaring his independence from the requirement that a painting have literal, storytelling content. He chose to combine or select any elements for the sake of artistic unity and made color balance and composition the prime pictorial concerns. Emotional and symbolic content is eliminated; technique is emphasized. In Manet's paintings there is no illusion of space, no modeling to create depth. The painting is no longer a "window on the world" but a two-dimensional surface that is given significant form by strictly visual elements. This has been called "pure painting" or "art for art's sake," and it became of fundamental importance to painting in the 20th century.

Manet was a pivotal figure in the course of French painting, the point of departure for the technical and stylistic development of the next half century, when one school of art would become the most celebrated, the most easily accessible, the most coveted internationally, and perhaps the most universally appreciated of any in the history of painting: Impressionism. The Impressionists included Claude Monet (1840–1926), Alfred Sisley (1839–99), Camille Pissarro (1830–1903), Pierre-Auguste Renoir (1841–1919), and others who, after their rejection by the Salon of 1873, organized an independent exhibition in 1874, the first of eight Impressionist exhibitions during the 1870s and 1880s. Direct descendants of the Barbizon painters and their *plein air* studies, the Impressionists also were primarily concerned with landscapes, French landscapes. Of them, Monet was the Impressionist par excellence. It was his painting of 1872, *Impression — Sunrise,* that had given the group its name, and it was his focus on light — its effects on objects and colors as the essence of the painting — that defined the group. He and the other Impressionists translated this sensation of light and color to their canvases in freely applied brushstrokes.

Monet and Renoir are the most famous of this group today, yet they did not follow the same path. Monet sought to carry naturalism to its optical ultimate, to portray the constant changes of the landscape bathed in constantly changing light. Form dissolves into shimmering color; objects seem weightless (as in his series pictures, *Poplars, Haystacks, Rouen Cathedral,* and *Water-Lilies*). Renoir began as an Impressionist, but his fascination with chic, gay society and his sheer delight in the warmth and sensuality of the female figure refused to be limited by the Impressionists' stricter study of the visual effects of light. He is best known for his luminous, porcelain-like portraits of women — shopgirls, laundresses, upper class women and children. He revived the spirit of Boucher and Fragonard, and, in a mix of realism and idealism, he blended Impressionistic color and spontaneity with a recollection of the 18th century.

Another internationally recognized painter also took part in the first Impressionist exhibition but never fully adapted to the Impressionist style. Edgar Degas (1834–1917) adhered more closely than the Impressionists to the 19th-century tradition of figure painting, draftsmanship, and strong composition. Like Manet, Degas was a member of the most social and cultivated Parisian circles. For him, no sunlit landscapes; his interest was less in light than in gesture, and his "landscapes" were of city life, theater, cafés, and concert halls. A detached and aloof observer of women, Degas did not portray the "feminine charm" of voluptuous, idealized women as Renoir did; his women are performers, and their beauty is expressive and active.

By the mid-1880s, Impressionism was no longer new. If not unanimously accepted, it certainly was well established, and an assortment of styles grouped under the general heading of post-Impressionism began to emerge. Henri de Toulouse-Lautrec (1864–1901) was indebted to the innovations of the Impressionists, although his main source of inspiration was Degas. Lautrec, too, painted dancers, but of a different sort: cabaret dancers. A member of an ancient noble family, he arrived in Paris in 1881 and began painting posters spotlighting the dancers of the Moulin Rouge. Though his career was relatively brief, Lautrec produced more than 360 lithographs, pastels, and highly animated line drawings of subjects in dance halls, cafés, circuses, and brothels, testimonials to the life he led around his Montmartre studio.

Paul Cézanne (1839–1906), Georges Seurat (1859–91), Paul Gauguin (1848–1903), and Vincent Van Gogh (1853–90) all had their roots in the Impressionist style, yet they all felt the need to go beyond the mere study of light and color and its momentary effects. Cézanne and Seurat explored the architectonic elements of form and color, striving to attain harmony and balance in their compositions. Seurat sought a more scientific method with which to reproduce the special quality of light in nature, and by studying contemporary theories of color and vision and applying them to his work methodically, he arrived at Divisionism, a technique using pigments of pure color systematically applied to the canvas like a mosaic, to be blended by the eye of the viewer and fused by the optical response alone. The technique, also known as Pointillism, distinguished the neo-Impressionists, as Seurat and his followers — including Paul Signac (1863–1935) — were known. Seurat's greatest work, *Sunday Afternoon on the Island of La Grande Jatte* (1886), while Impressionistic in color, is a carefully designed composition of geometrically divided space, and it had a major impact on avant-garde movements in Europe at the end of the century. Nonetheless, it was Cézanne who was the truly revolutionary figure, certainly one of the most important painters of the century.

Cézanne had been one of the original artists at the Impressionist exhibition of 1874, but he was unable to reconcile the transitory quality and lack of clarity of the Impressionist images with his admiration for the old masters, especially Poussin. He felt they had achieved a balance, harmony, and monumentality in their work that had yet to be surpassed, even though their traditional approach now was seen as academic, not the result of direct observation, and thus unfaithful to nature. Cézanne wanted to "make of Impressionism something solid and durable, like the art of the museums," while still respecting the actual appearance of nature. The search for structure and balance led him to simplify forms and to use color to model fundamental shapes. His patches of pigment and parallel and regular brushstrokes explore and define the basic structure of his subjects. If necessary, he was not averse to distortion to enhance their essence. "We must seek the cylinder," he said, "the sphere, and the cone in nature." As a result, his landscapes, while vibrant with color, had a new solidity and strength. This formal discipline and analysis of space and composition became a key source for the 20th-century Cubists.

Gauguin and Van Gogh had different ambitions. For them, nature was only the starting point. They found the extreme objectivity of the Impressionists stifling, and they searched for meaning in subject matter and color. Gauguin wrote that the Impressionists painted what was in front of their eyes, rather than what lay in the "mysterious center of thought." He fostered a Synthetist school of thought based on the use of symbols to convey descriptive or emotive power. Inspired by medieval stained glass and folk art, he sought more primitive sources for his work, and his search for the unspoiled life finally led him to Tahiti, where he settled for the rest of his life. His canvases from the South Seas seemed barbaric, not only in their exotic subjects, but also in their broad areas of brilliant, "unnatural" color, which had nothing of Cézanne's structural modeling. His bold compositions aimed at conveying the simplicity and directness of primitive society; they stood as a powerful rejection of the civilization he had left behind as well as of its art.

The story of Van Gogh's life and the intermittent insanity that caused him to cut off his ear and eventually kill himself is the stuff of legend. He absorbed the lessons of the Impressionists and for a time was Gauguin's painting companion, but he was closest to his brother, Théo, to whom he wrote that he painted to make life "bearable . . . Really, we can speak only through our paintings." Most of the paintings for which he is remembered were done during a period of only 3 years in the South of France. Van Gogh simplified forms, heightened color, applied pigment thickly in vigorous strokes, and often resorted to distortion to express his feelings. The swirling *Starry Night* (1889), with its startling, violent, blazing blue and yellow bands of color, is a prime example; it was painted in an asylum a year before his death. Another example is his dramatic *Portrait of Dr. Gauchet,* painted only months before the artist took his own life. (It is the consummate irony that this canvas recently sold for $82.5 million — the highest price ever paid for a painting — as Van Gogh earned not one centime from his work during his lifetime.) His paintings display a passion and intensity that reflect his torment and go well beyond a naturalistic representation of reality.

While Van Gogh's work influenced the later Fauves in France and the German Expressionists, Gauguin's already had given rise, in the 1890s, to a series of artistic currents referred to as Symbolism. Gustave Moreau (1826–98) and Odilon Redon (1840–1916), both rooted in the Romantic tradition, made use of the works of literary Symbolists (Baudelaire, Mallarmé) to paint often strange, dreamlike visions. Followers of Gauguin — Paul Sérusier (1864–1927), Maurice Denis (1870–1943), Pierre Bonnard (1867–1947), and Edouard Vuillard (1868–1940) — merged in the Nabi group (from the Hebrew word for "prophet"). The latter two often are called Intimists because they later applied Impressionist technique to the painting of domestic interiors rather than landscapes. Their work is abstract and decorative, almost Oriental in feeling, emphasizing the flat painting surface, brushwork, and radiant color. Also working at this time was Henri Rousseau (1844–1910), a folk artist of genius whose magical paintings of enchanted forests and animals achieve the directness and innocence that Gauguin left France to pursue.

THE TWENTIETH CENTURY

The first of the avant-garde "isms" to develop in the 20th century was Fauvism, which carried on the legacy of both Van Gogh and Gauguin. It took its name — *fauves* means "wild beasts" — from critical reaction to the distorted forms and the exuberant, violent colors, used for their expressive qualities, in the paintings exhibited by a group of artists in 1905. Henri Matisse (1869–1954), the foremost of the Fauves, was influenced by North African and Near Eastern art, and their effect can be seen in his transformation of reality into large surfaces of pure color and brilliantly colored decorative patterns. Maurice Vlaminck (1876–1958) and André Derain (1880–1954) were also Fauves, though the group was loosely constituted otherwise. Raoul Dufy (1877–1953) was influenced by them; Georges Rouault (1871–1958), who had exhibited with the group initially, and Georges Braque (1882–1963), who had shown with it subsequently, both went their own ways. By the end of the decade, the group no longer existed, but it had during its brief life announced the definitive end of the 19th-century concept of realism.

And in the meantime another movement, much more cerebral, was making its appearance on the Parisian art scene: Cubism. It was heralded in 1907 by a startling Salon entry, *Les Demoiselles d'Avignon,* by Pablo Picasso (1881–1973). Picasso's inspiration was Cézanne rather than the post-Impressionist strains that were tending to the dissolution of nature into color and light. Cézanne's analysis of space and composition, his emphasis on structure, concurred with Picasso's interest in primitive art and its simplification of form, becoming, together, the source of his abstraction. He began dissecting objects to reveal several views of them simultaneously, fragments of the three-dimensional subject appearing in various shallow, or flat, planes in the two-dimensional picture.

Picasso's collaborator in this novel approach to the problem of depth versus surface was Braque, who simultaneously began emphasizing flat planes, rigid geometric forms, and subdued colors. Taken together, their work constitutes the first, or analytical, phase of Cubism, which gave way, after 1912, to a synthetic phase, in the development of which Juan Gris (1887–1927) played a role. This later phase, characterized by a brighter palette and by the use of collage (which Braque had invented by the inclusion of typographical letters in his pictures), continued into World War I. Collage Cubism, by using cut and pasted scraps of recognizable material such as newspaper, finally totally eliminated the illusion of space and was a revolutionary development in the history of painting. The Cubists were the most significant of all the early-20th-century art movements. Their point of departure — to show an object not as it was, but in its totality as the mind's eye perceived it — both suggested and complemented the abstract movements begun by artists outside France. Cubism was the seminal moment in the evolution of modern abstract and nonobjective art.

Inevitably their experiments were reinterpreted by other artists. Robert Delaunay (1855–1941) led the Orphist group, combining the Cubists' faceting of the object with the Fauvists' color concerns and the Italian Futurists' emphasis on frenetic modern rhythms. Later, Delaunay became clearly abstract. Fernand Léger (1881–1955), meanwhile, used large humanized machine forms, painted with brilliant metallic primary colors, to "mechanize" his interpretations of pre- and postwar Europe. He, in turn, influenced still another group, the Purists, who criticized Cubism as overly decorative and celebrated the machine as a form devoid of unnecessary detail. Amédée Ozenfant (1886–1966) and Le Corbusier (Charles Edouard Jeanneret; 1887–1965) formulated Purism, which, more than in painting, was of consequence in the field of architecture.

Before the 19th century was over, Paris had become the center of the art world, and even before World War I there was a large group of expatriate painters living and working in the French capital. Not only Picasso and Gris, but Amedeo Modigliani (1884–1920) and Chaim Soutine (1894–1943) were here. Marc Chagall (1887–1985), who combined a Cubist influence with personal fantasy, came before the war and returned after it. The School of Paris — those artists based in the city between the two world wars — was thus a fully international company. And during the 1920s, it produced another art movement of spectacular importance: Surrealism.

Surrealism grew out of and was tied closely to Dada, a nihilistic "anti-art" movement that mocked the solemnity of aesthetic doctrines. Dadaism's major French exponents were Marcel Duchamp (1887–1968) and Francis Picabia (1879–1953). While the origin of its name — *dada* means "hobbyhorse" in French — is controversial, it is thought to have been chosen at random, as though to underscore the movement's preoccupation with absurdity and chance. Dada died quickly, but its concerns became part of the premise of Surrealism, which further explored the possibilities of chance, the depth of the unconscious as revealed by Freud, and the Symbolism of painters such as Redon. All came together in the Surrealists' dedication to an expression of thought, or of the imagination, free of the conscious control of reason and free of any aesthetic convention or moral constraint.

Surrealists painting in Paris included Max Ernst (1891–1976), Jean Arp (1887–1966), Yves Tanguy (1900–55), Salvador Dali (1904–1989), André Masson (b. 1896), Joan Miró (1893–1983), and Roberto Matta (b. 1911). Some, such as Tanguy and Dali, depicted dream images, distortions of familiar objects, hallucinatory "versions" of reality. Ernst, too, worked in this vein and also invented the technique of *frottage* (in a word, rubbings). Others, such as Miró and Masson, moved toward a personal set of symbols, a kind of calligraphy that was the pictorial response to the "automatic writing" of the literary Surrealists André Breton and Louis Aragon. But even though their work developed in more than one direction, the impact of the Surrealist movement was great. Picasso's *Guernica* (1937) would certainly not have taken the same form without it, and Jackson Pollock's Abstract Expressionism owed its origins to Surrealist automatic writing.

Surrealism marked a decisive moment in the history of French painting. It was the last major international art movement to originate and be centered in Paris. During World War II, Paris was occupied by the Nazis, and many of the leading Surrealists fled to the United States, shifting the center of their activity to New York. Nevertheless, while the war put an end to certain aspects of Parisian artistic life, it was not the end of French painting.

In France, Maurice Estève (b. 1904), Edouard Pignon (b. 1905), and Jean Bazaine (b. 1904) carried on in the mostly nonfigurative style of the School of Paris. A diluted version of American Abstract Expressionism, *art informel,* also grew up, exemplified by Georges Mathieu (b. 1921) and Pierre Soulages (b. 1919). Nicolas de Staël (1914–55) produced works that read either as a representation of reality or as a series of abstract forms and colors. Other painters, such as Balthus (Balthasar Klossowski de Rola; b. 1908) and Alberto Giacometti (1901–66), returned to the figurative tradition. The former created realistic paintings rich in erotic evocations. Giacometti's figures have an elongated, gnawed appearance, as if the images were about to disappear in space. Jean Dubuffet (1901–85), recognized as a master artist with roots in the Dada-Surrealist tradition, became known for his *art brut.* The work of the mentally insane and children were among his sources. Even his working materials, such as sand mixed with paint, were unconventional.

No one cohesive style has emerged in contemporary France. There have been Op and Pop movements. New Realism was practiced by Arman (b. 1928) and especially by the wildly eccentric Yves Klein (1928–62), who used women for paintbrushes and created huge monochromatic blue and gold canvases, enigmatic in their simplicity. Kinetic art was explored by Victor Vasarely (b. 1908), whose geometric optical forms largely erase the boundary between painting and sculpture. And no one movement is any longer exclusively French.

Communication among capitals, among artists through travel, exhibitions, and the media, has to a large extent decentralized art styles in the postwar period; there are no clear-cut textbook divisions, and Paris no longer is the uncontested center of organized art movements. Still, few countries can rival France in the history of painting. And the largest population of artists in Europe still is found in one single shining city: Paris.

Architecture

The architecture of France — as much as the landscape, the food, and the wine — is to be seen and savored. More than 2,000 years of history remain very much alive here, and almost every building style found in the Western world is present in some form. The French architectural panorama includes the religious — churches, monasteries, and abbeys; military — castles built during the Middle Ages and fortifications such as those of the Marquis de Vauban, a 17th-century military engineer; domestic — châteaux, manor houses, and palaces; and commercial — coaching inns, water mills, town halls, and so on. Some of these buildings were constructed over a period of time — sometimes several centuries — and may reflect several different architectural styles; they also may have been adapted to new tastes and needs over time. The transition from one style to another never is clear-cut, and regional variations of any given style persist.

Most cities, even those with a restored old section, contain this mixture of architecture. Although many people are shocked today at the proximity of the brazenly modern *Centre Georges Pompidou* (often referred to simply as "the Beaubourg") to beautiful old Parisian houses, it actually is quite common throughout France to find ornate 19th-century structures next to simple 16th-century dwellings. Such contrasts are inevitable, and sometimes can be appealing. Unfortunately, I.M. Pei's futuristic glass pyramids, which are set smack in the center of the historic museum's courtyard and serve as the new entrance to the *Louvre,* is not a case in point and is the subject of heated controversy.

The caves of La Madeleine, close to Sarlat in the Dordogne region, contain three different architectural layers, one on top of the other: the first, 10,000 years old, from the Magdalenian (or upper paleolithic) period; the second, a troglodyte village, where primitive cave dwellers lived; and finally, the ruins of a feudal castle. In effect, the caves provide an abbreviated account of history. (The Dordogne, it should be noted, is famous for its prehistoric sites — close to 200 have been discovered — such as Celtic tombstones and graves, from which ornamental collars, bracelets, and helmets have been extracted.)

The Romans, who appeared in France during the 1st century BC, also left striking reminders of their stay. Designers of roads, aqueducts, amphitheaters, and other public places, they extended their civilization to every land they conquered. Nímes retains some especially outstanding Roman vestiges: the Pont du Gard aqueduct (19 BC); the Maison Carrée, or Square House (1 BC); and the amphitheater (AD 50). The 3rd century marked the beginning of the end of the Roman Empire, and during the next 600 years continual fighting and turmoil reaped much more destruction than construction; the creation of the feudal system in the 9th and 10th centuries brought a semblance of order once again. Although very little remains today from this turbulent time, some interesting monuments and graves from the Merovingian and Carolingian periods (the 6th through the 9th centuries) can be found, often deeply hidden in the crypts of early churches, as in St. Peter's in Vienne and the tomb of St. Martin in Tours.

From the mid-11th to the mid-12th century, Romanesque architecture thrived in France. It derived its inspiration from Rome, not only the source of style for the Holy Roman Empire, but also the seat of papal authority, and it was affected as well by Byzantine and Islamic influences (mosaics and pointed arches, for example). In France, Romanesque buildings were characterized by solidity and massive size, heavy walls, barrel vaults, rounded arches, and flattened columns, or pilasters; structures were imposing and the space within them clearly defined. This was an age of great economic prosperity closely tied to technological development and a strong religious fervor, as seen in the number of Romanesque churches remaining today. Churches, abbeys, and castles had sparse decoration. Outstanding examples of existing Romanesque architecture include St. Front Cathedral in Périgueux in the Dordogne, Autin Cathedral in Burgundy, and the château of La Cité in Carcassonne.

The Gothic period in France began in the middle of the 12th century and lasted until the Renaissance, at the end of the 15th century. It was characterized by the pointed arch, flying buttresses (which reinforced the walls and enabled great stained glass windows to be set in them), rose windows (large, round, stained glass windows that resemble an open rose) over the center portal of the west front of the church or at one or both transept ends, ribbed vaulting, and often heavily decorated portals. This style gave the impression of lightness and soaring spaces.

Early, primitive Gothic architecture in the late 12th and the 13th centuries gave way to a style known as Rayonnant in the 14th century, which moved from solid walls to a skeletal masonry frame interspersed with stained glass unmatched today for its beauty and craftsmanship; Ste.-Chapelle in Paris, with walls seemingly made entirely of glass, is the most striking example of this. Late, Flamboyant Gothic architecture, which dominated the 15th century, was ornamented more elaborately. Over 3 centuries the Gothic designs became increasingly more vertical, especially in comparison to the Romanesque box shape; religious sculpture became more realistic, and flowers and plants began to serve as subject matter for reliefs. Notre-Dame of Paris, built between 1163 and 1330, is one of the finest examples of Gothic architecture; others include the cathedrals of Chartres and Strasbourg and the house of Jacques Coeur in Bourges.

The Renaissance period flourished in France in the 16th and 17th centuries, heralding a return to classic (Greek and Roman) architecture. The Roman arch, vault, dome, and the Corinthian column reappeared; stairs were straight; and buildings, which were harmonious and symmetrical with traditional proportions, often had several stories, an upper floor mirroring the ones below it. Renaissance buildings focused inward, with their center — usually under the dome — as their focal point. Francis I, a prolific builder who was impressed with the art and architecture of Italy, encouraged its classical form in his own country; he built Chambord and Fontainebleau as well as a wing of the lovely château at Blois. The château at Chenonceaux also was constructed during this period, as were other magnificent estates along the Loire, Seine, and Marne rivers.

The baroque style was popular in France during the 17th and 18th centuries; though still classical in form, it differed from the Renaissance in that its structures expanded outward instead of inward. Massive, elegant, and theatrical, they employed opulent, sculptured decoration and curving stairs. During this period, grand planning that included the integration of buildings and landscapes became very important, as witnessed by the work of André Le Nôtre, a third-generation landscape architect, in the Tuileries Gardens and the gardens of Versailles.

François Mansart built the Château Maisons, now known as Maisons-Lafitte, near Paris; the gardens and park that surrounded the château no longer exist, but the interior remains almost the same as when it was built in the mid-1600s. It was Mansart who designed and popularized the sloping roof that became known as the mansard roof. Other striking examples of the French baroque style include the Place des Vosges, the Colonnade (east front) of the *Louvre*, and the Luxembourg Palace in Paris as well as many of the houses in the old section of Bordeaux. The use of double columns to line the fronts of buildings was seen for the first time during this period; prominent examples include the palace of Versailles and the *Louvre*.

By the end of the 18th century, rococo — a style similar to baroque but lighter in character and execution — had become popular in French architecture, especially in and around Paris. The geometrical forms used in the baroque style became more complex in rococo; buildings were asymmetrical; naves of churches were longer; arches displayed abundant ornamentation; and white interiors with gold gilding were popular. A rococo building appears more sculpture than structure, like a gigantic wedding cake. Shells, scrolls, flowers, and plants monopolize motifs; in fact, the term most likely comes from the French *roc* and *coquille,* "rock" and "shell." At this time, people demanded comfort above showiness, and rococo designs emphasized intimacy rather than grandeur, with rooms that, while still opulent, were also playful. The Petit Trianon at Versailles, built as a retreat from formal palace life for Mme. du Barry and later enjoyed by Marie-Antoinette — exemplifies the rococo style.

The curtain fell on this exuberant period of almost 300 years of power, prestige, and wealth — all reflected in 16th-, 17th-, and 18th-century French architecture — with the beginning of the French Revolution in 1789.

Neo-classicism was highly espoused by the prestigious Ecole des Beaux-Arts (School of Fine Arts) in Paris in the 19th century. Though classical in design, it was looser and more natural in execution. (*Neo* means "in the style of" an earlier period, though usually employing different materials and technology.) Neo-classical buildings often were constructed in the shape of an H or a U, with wings that opened out to their environments rather than closing off from it and directing the focus inward, as was common during the Renaissance. Examples of this style include the Madeleine (Church of St. Mary Magdalen) and the Arc de Triomphe in Paris.

The Industrial Revolution brought inevitable changes after 1830. Architects and engineers, working with iron — and soon steel and reinforced concrete — conceived new designs for bridges, train stations, and other public spaces and structures. Arches and columns of metal became commonplace, and buildings stretched to greater heights; the combination of glass and metal created walls and roofs that were seemingly transparent. A striking symbol of this period is the Eiffel Tower, built for the *Paris Exhibition of 1889*.

Art Nouveau emerged briefly in the late 19th and early 20th centuries. Important because it fostered a complete break with tradition and paved the way for new thinking about architecture, it was characterized by highly decorative, elongated ornamentation — long, sinuous, intertwining curves — based on vegetable images. Façades often were asymmetrical, with a lot of metalwork and glasswork in free-flowing, three-dimensional designs. Hector Guimard's wrought-iron entrances to the Paris métro are outstanding reminders of this brief period in French architectural history.

Modernism followed closely on the heels of Art Nouveau during the early 20th century; it rejected previous styles and emphasized simplicity and purity of line. The destruction during the two world wars forced massive reconstruction, and the growing need for housing led to innovations in technology and architecture, and to more sophisticated and rational structures to fit emerging lifestyles. Le Corbusier, a creative renegade who became the father of modern French architecture, designed *unités d'habitation* ("housing units") in accordance with a communal vision of society. His Unité d'Habitation in Marseilles incorporates shops, services (including a gymnasium, swimming pool, and nursery), a small hotel, and 2-level apartments for 1,600 residents. His Villa Savoye, in Poissy, has a glass-enclosed living area on the ground floor, continuing windows around the second, and a rooftop garden and solarium. In the words of the architect, who died in 1965, these various creations were *machines à habiter* ("machines to live in"), a functionalist's vision of life and a response to the political anarchy that had prevailed for the past century. Le Corbusier also built the concrete Notre-Dame du Haut pilgrimage chapel at Ronchamp, modeled on a nun's pointed headdress, with an outdoor pulpit and altar, a small indoor chapel, irregular, wedge-shape stained glass windows, and a jaunty roof slightly raised to permit a strip of daylight to enter.

French architecture gradually has developed an international style during the 20th century, and numerous French architects have succeeded in building interesting, sometimes controversial structures. Among them: Emile Aillaud, who designed the headquarters of the Communist party in Paris; Paul Chemetov and Henri Cireani, whose reinforced-concrete housing projects (in Illkirsch, in the Bas-Rhin; in the St.-Denis suburb of Paris; and in nearby Marne-La-Vallée) are livable and visually appealing; and François Rodier, who uses traditional brick in very modern ways in northern France. The revival of interest in rehabilitating France's city centers has encouraged contemporary French architects to approach urban housing with renewed interest, including restoring existing structures, be they old factories or historic landmarks. The wealth of architectural riches in this one country is enormous. French architecture, whether it attracts, inspires, or intimidates, constantly makes its presence felt. The traveler who appreciates it is bound to come away with a fuller sense of the country, its history, its joie de vivre.

THE CITIES

THE CITIES

AIX-EN-PROVENCE

Paris may be a typical American's dream of the best place to live in France, but Parisians frequently dream of living in Aix-en-Provence. Aix is the provincial city that most French admire, according to recent polls, and the reasons are entirely understandable. There's the matter of size, for one thing. With 125,000 residents and a significant university population, the city is large — and sophisticated — enough to have its share of good restaurants, smart shops, art galleries, serious libraries and bookstores, cafés and nightclubs, theater and music, and other urban amenities. Yet it's still small enough that almost everything is within easy walking distance, little of interest is ever more than 20 minutes away, and — miraculous in this age of urban sprawl — the countryside starts at the end of the bus lines (except if you're headed toward Marseilles).

Aix often *feels* small, too. Perhaps because of its Mediterranean character, daily life still proceeds at a comparatively slow, human pace, although this is changing. And despite the construction accompanying its recent rapid growth, most of its buildings still have comfortable proportions that are easily dwarfed by the limestone massif — the Mont Ste.-Victoire — that the talent of native son Paul Cézanne transformed into the most famous monument of the nearby landscape. Sadly, however, almost half of the lush pine trees on the lower slopes of Ste.-Victoire have burned during forest fires in the last few years. Ste.-Victoire gets its name from a battle that was fought at the bottom of the mountain by Marius, the popular Roman general who defeated the invading Teutonic tribes, killing more than 100,000 Teutons and taking as many prisoners in the process. To this day, many sons of the region still are named Marius.

Even the city's location strikes the perfect balance. It's close to the Mediterranean beaches, but aloof from the noise and the crowds. It's near the hills and valleys of rustic Provence but far enough away to escape the torpor of the backcountry. Once the capital of Provence, it's off the main rail lines today, though still a crossroads. But people don't only pass *through* Aix; they come *to* Aix.

Ever since Roman times, they've come for Aix's warm thermal springs, which were well known to the ancient world. Before the arrival of the Romans, the area had been occupied for centuries by a Celto-Ligurian tribe whose capital, Entremont, was on a plateau north of the present Aix and whose faith in the local water extended to a belief that it assured fertility. The Roman consul Caius Sextius destroyed Entremont in 123 BC and the following year established a fortified camp near the springs, calling it Aquae Sextius (Waters of Sextius). The boulevards circling Aix today (its modern name is a contraction of the Latin name) follow the line of the old ramparts, and a huge 18th-century spa, including the *Hôtel des Thermes,* stands on the Cours

Sextius, near the site of the original Roman baths. Aix's thermal springs continue to be noted for their purity and nearly sodium-free quality, good for circulatory ailments, and people continue to come to drink the water, immerse themselves in it, and otherwise submit to the 3-week "cure."

Others come during the summer for the *International Festival of Lyric Art and Music.* One of Europe's better-known music festivals and possibly France's best, it features first-rate singers, instrumentalists, and ensembles in concerts and fully staged operas in historic settings around town. Hotels are booked months in advance, the tempo of the Provençal lifestyle accelerates in anticipation, and for the 3 weeks of the festival, the city is filled with action.

Aix's cultural traditions predate its festival by some 800 years. In the 12th century, the Counts of Provence made the town their capital, and their court soon became known for its love of music and poetry. This was the age of the troubadors, the poet-musicians who traveled from court to court singing their ballads in the Provençal tongue and spreading ideals of chivalry and romantic love throughout Europe. The town's most civilized era, however, was the 15th century. In 1409, both the university and "Good King René" (1409–80) were born. Called "the last of the troubadors," René held the title of Count of Provence among others (he was also Duke of Anjou and titular King of Naples) and proved to be in all respects a remarkable example of the culture of his time. He was a patron of the arts as well as a poet, musician, and painter himself; he was a student of classical languages, mathematics, and law, yet at the same time an unaffected man of the people who organized popular festivals, tilled the soil, and introduced the muscatel grape to the region. The people were not happy, however, when René levied heavy taxes and printed worthless money to finance his cultural projects.

Provence was added to the kingdom of France a few years after the death of René, though Aix remained important as the seat of the provincial *parlement,* or court of justice, from 1501 to 1790. It flourished during the 17th and 18th centuries in particular, when wealthy and noble magistrates built many of the elegant *hôtels,* or townhouses, that give the city its characteristic look today. The period also is remembered in Aix's main thoroughfare, named for Count Mirabeau, a prominent resident of the latter part of the 18th century. Before achieving the eminence that brought him immortality in the Cours Mirabeau, the count had achieved some notoriety by tricking a rich heiress of Aix into marriage and then running up debts large enough to bring about his imprisonment. Even jail did not teach him a lesson, however, and he continued to pursue women for their money and be sent back to prison for his philanderings. Nevertheless, he remained popular with the masses (if not with his fellow nobles), and when Louis XVI summoned the States-General of 1789 — a meeting that proved to be the first step toward ending the monarchy — Mirabeau was elected to represent the third estate for Aix-en-Provence. He went on to become the leading statesman of the first years of the French Revolution. A statue of Mirabeau is in St.-Cannat, about 20 miles (32 km) north of Aix; true to life, the skin on the statue is pockmarked, the result of Mirabeau's bout with smallpox.

The Revolution swept away the *ancien régime* and the provincial *parle-*

ments along with it, and in the 19th century, as Marseilles grew, Aix went into a period of decline from which it began to rise only in the mid-20th century, but with a vengeance. Its recent growth has been astronomical, in fact (the population in 1950 was a mere 50,000, less than half of what it is today), and one reason Aix thrives again — besides the music festival and the thermal cure — is successful light industry: clothing and, notably, candy. Many of the remarkably sweet Provençal almonds go into *calissons d'Aix,* diamond-shaped candies that are protected and controlled, like fine wines, as an *appellation d'origine* item. This delicious trademark, a mixture of almonds and melon preserves, has a history to equal its status. In the 17th century, *calissons* were blessed by the bishop and distributed to the faithful in an annual ceremony commemorating the end of the plague of 1630. Only in the mid-19th century, however, did the making of them become an actual industry, and now the rich candies are exported worldwide.

Critics say that after the music festival, Aix goes back to being a sleepy university town. They complain that there's more theater in nearby Avignon, more excitement in even closer Marseilles. But visitors come even when there's no festival, gravitating to the Cours Mirabeau, again the perfect balance. It has something of the grandeur of the Champs-Elysées, a bit of the chic of the Boulevard St.-Germain, and a touch of the boisterousness of the Boulevard St.-Michel — but with its arch of plane trees, it's almost intimate, especially since it can be walked in just a few minutes. It is a meeting place, as well as a place to be seen. Settling in at a sidewalk café, visitors and natives alike linger over a *pastis* or a cool beer — or an ice cream sundae. (Coffee machines tend to be shut off in midafternoon to encourage customers to order more expensive drinks.) Eventually they may stroll over to one of the nearby outdoor markets to breathe the distinctive Provençal scents of rosemary, thyme, and basil and to enjoy the visual barrage of pulpy red tomatoes, dark green *courgettes* (zucchini), luscious melons, bins of variously colored and flavored olives, and tables strewn with garlic tresses and other produce.

Natives and long-term residents complain that these scenes are becoming more and more scarce as the city grows and fast-food establishments mar the landscape along the Cours Mirabeau. They wistfully recall when Aix was just a big village and the major roads that lead out of it today were truly country lanes. Those living in Petit Rocquefavour, at the edge of town, remember hearing the tinkle of sheep bells at night, as flocks were led around the town to their summer pasture in the Alps. Today, they are more likely to hear the blare of traffic as exasperated drivers search in vain for a parking place, or the sound of an automobile alarm going off as someone tries to break into a car.

Even so, when one needs a refuge from modern sounds and pressures, there's always the silence of the charming cloister of the Cathédrale St.-Sauveur or the immense cathedral itself. And when one becomes weary after roaming through the inviting maze of Old Aix's pedestrian zones, benches seem to beckon everywhere. And you still can turn down almost any street — on foot — to find one of the city's ever-present fountains, whose sounds quickly soothe the nerves. Massive or tiny, traditional or original, they are pretty places to sit, read, or meet people, and they're among Aix's most endearing features. Along with the festival, the thermal cure, and the diet-smashing *calissons,* they make clear what matters most to this delightful city, which, despite staggering growth, rarely puts progress ahead of *douceur de vivre.*

AIX AT-A-GLANCE

SEEING THE CITY: The town itself is so flat and its skyline, happily, so low, that a panoramic view is hard to find. Outside the city, the best vista is from the excavations of the pre-Roman settlement on the Plateau d'Entremont, 2 miles (3 km) miles north of Aix by the road to Puyricard (open from 9 AM to noon and 2 to 5 PM daily except Tuesdays; a bus leaves every half hour, or every hour on Sundays, from the *Bar Corona,* Bd. de la République). You'll have a striking view of the Montagne Ste.-Victoire, too, which dominates Aix to the east. To get there, take a minibus from Gare Routière; buses run from 9 AM to 8 PM. Also recommended is the tourist bureau's tour of private dwellings.

SPECIAL PLACES: Most of the sights in Aix are within the circle of boulevards that follow the outline of the city's ancient walls. North of the Cours Mirabeau — the café-filled main thoroughfare, which cuts across the circle in an east-west direction — is Vieil Aix (Old Aix), a zone of old squares and narrow streets, many of them pedestrian islands. South of the Cours is the newer Quartier Mazarin, a neighborhood of 17th- and 18th-century *hôtels* (town-houses), which looks like a grid on the map; it was planned by Michael Mazarin, an Archbishop of Aix and a brother of Cardinal Mazarin. The whole of the area north and south of the Cours can be walked easily, and you probably will be tempted to explore more of it than is required to visit the specific sites listed below. On your way to Place St.-Jean-de-Malte in the Quartier Mazarin, for instance, you may want to detour ever so slightly to see the Fontaine des Quatre-Dauphins, whose four delightful dolphins have graced the pretty square of the same name since 1667. On the other side of the Cours, just off Rue Espariat in Vieil Aix, Place d'Albertas is a cobblestone square with a fountain in the middle and no modern intrusion to mar its 18th-century serenity. A bit farther north, around the corner from the Hôtel de Ville, Place des Cardeurs is a long, open space where people come to sit. It's paved with brick and stone, surrounded by old buildings in varying stages of restoration, and outfitted with plenty of benches. An antiques fair takes place here in summer.

Cours Mirabeau – Four rows of shady plane trees distinguish this lovely wide avenue that's been the focal point of Aix since the 17th century (though it takes its name from a statesman and revolutionary of the 18th century). One of France's most appealing boulevards, it combines the elegance of the Champs-Elysées with its own intimacy — it's so short it can be walked in barely 10 minutes. The stately 17th- and 18th-century *hôtels* that line it have become, on one side, mostly banks (note the giant male caryatids holding up a wrought-iron balcony at No. 38, now a university building). On the other side are mostly bookshops, restaurants, and lively cafés. At each end is a 19th-century fountain: a large one topped by three female figures in the center of the circular Place de la Libération (popularly called La Rotonde), where the Cours begins, and a smaller one of Good King René holding a bunch of grapes where it runs into the Hôtel de Poët and ends. Two other fountains are along the way: the 17th-century Fontaine des Neuf-Canons and the Fontaine d'Eau-Chaude, the latter no more than a large moss-covered rock from which warm (well, tepid — and non-potable) water still springs, just as it did for the Romans 2,000 years ago. (The pipes transporting the water have rusted, though, and it no longer tastes as good as it once did.) The cafés are the main attraction of the Cours, however, and each has its own personality. Stake out a sidewalk table at apéritif time and, especially when the university is in session and the weather is warm, more people than Aix possibly could hold seem to pass in review, most on foot, but enough aboard cars and motorbikes to set the roadway buzzing.

VIEIL AIX

Cathédrale St.-Sauveur – A curious blend of architectural styles, spanning 15 centuries, makes this massive cathedral interesting. The baptistry, off to the far right (southern) side as you enter, is the oldest part, dating to the 4th and 5th centuries; its eight Roman columns are a stark contrast to the gilt 16th-century Renaissance cupola they support. From right to left, then, the church grows progressively younger. The southernmost aisle, Romanesque, was the nave of a 12th-century church. To its left is a Gothic nave, built from the 13th to the 15th centuries, and to the left of that is a newer, baroque aisle from the 17th century. One of the treasures of the church, the 15th-century *Triptyque du Buisson Ardent* (Triptych of the Burning Bush), is on the wall of the Gothic nave and usually is closed, showing only two panels in grisaille depicting the Virgin and a praying angel, but ask the caretaker to open it and you will see the brilliance of its colors (predominantly red) fairly gleam in the interior dimness. Done by Nicolas Froment, court painter to King René, it shows the Virgin and Child in the center, with the king and his wife, Queen Jeanne, kneeling in the side panels. Upon request, the caretaker also will uncover the 16th-century sculptured wooden doors on the exterior of the Gothic nave, another of the church's treasures. Unfortunately, few of the 16th-century Flemish tapestries of the life of the Virgin, originally woven for Canterbury Cathedral and later owned by St.-Sauveur, are likely to be on view. Some were sold centuries ago, while others were stolen just a few years ago. Concerts are given here in July. Pl. de l'Université (phone: 42-23-45-65). Information about the concerts also can be obtained at the tourist office (2 Pl. du Général-de-Gaulle; phone: 42-26-02-93).

Cloître St.-Sauveur – This delightful small Romanesque (12th-century) cloister is reached through a doorway on the right aisle of the cathedral or from the street. It's a favorite spot of Aix residents, who come to sit and chat or read a newspaper under its arches, which rest on pairs of delicate columns, some plain and some carved, with carved capitals. Pl. des Martyrs-de-la-Résistance.

Musée des Tapisseries – In the former archbishop's palace adjoining the cloister and cathedral, this small, now renovated museum contains some very rare Beauvais tapestries, including a series on the life of Don Quixote dating from the 17th and 18th centuries. A few pieces of furniture from the same period also are on display. The interior courtyard is the focal point of Aix's music festival in July and August, when it turns into an elaborate outdoor opera house. Closed Tuesdays the month of January, and from 12:30 to 2:30 PM. Admission charge. Palais de l'Ancien Archevêché (stairway on the left), 28 Pl. des Martyrs-de-la-Résistance (phone: 42-23-09-91).

Musée d'Histoire Naturelle – Don't miss the dinosaur egg exhibit. Also pay particular attention to the painted wood panels from the 17th century. Closed mornings and Sundays. Hôtel Boyer d'Equilles. 6 Rue Espariat (phone: 42-26-23-67).

Place de l'Hôtel de Ville – The 16th-century clock tower at one corner of this square catches the eye first. On high, it is ornate with wrought-iron trim, including an ironwork Provençal bell cage at the very top. Farther down and less prominent is a mechanical statue representing the season, one of four that rotate and make their appearance during the course of the year. The 17th-century building with the Italianate façade next to the clock tower is the Hôtel de Ville (Town Hall). Built by Parisian architect Pierre Pavillon, it is notable for its sculpted wooden doors and a beautiful wrought-iron balcony and archway in the interior courtyard; the building is notable, too, for its outstanding 300,000-volume library, the Bibliothèque Méjanes (open Tuesday and Friday afternoons), named for the Marquis de Méjanes, who founded it in the 18th century. On the south side of the square the old grain market, an 18th-century building decorated with carvings by Chastel, an Aix sculptor of the period, now houses a branch of the post office. The square itself, surrounded by plane trees and with another of Aix's many fountains at its center, is the site of a colorful flower market. When the vendors move off, the cafés put out their tables.

Eglise Ste.-Marie-Madeleine – Its west front was redone in the mid-19th century, though the church dates from the 17th century. Inside are some interesting artworks, including a very large painting (in the aisle left of the altar) that's alternately been attributed to Rubens and to Rembrandt, and the center panel of a highly original 15th-century triptych of the Annunciation, with inexplicable diabolical figures. There is a marble Virgin by Chastel from the 18th century, who's also credited with the Preacher's Fountain out front. Pl. des Prêcheurs (phone: 42-38-02-81).

Outdoor Produce Market – A Provençal market is a market par excellence, and the one that takes place in Aix on Tuesday, Thursday, and Saturday mornings is the *crème de la crème.* There's everything here to stock a larder or supply a memorable picnic: ripe fruit, vegetables, cheese, ham, sausage, pâté, herbs and spices, dozens of varieties of olives, huge crusty country bread. The crowded, sprawling marketplace, alas, is a favorite with pickpockets. Pl. des Prêcheurs. (A smaller market takes place daily on Pl. Richelme.)

Chapelle du Sacré-Coeur – A replica of the one in the palace at Versailles, this beautiful 17th-century Jesuit chapel was known to the public for 300 years by its ornate façade alone. Since the summer of 1983, however, its striking cream-colored architecture — with vaulted ceilings and stone columns — has been an inviting setting for art exhibits. Reopened at the initiative of two art lovers, its restoration is being financed by proceeds from the activities. It's also a pleasant, refreshingly cool place to stroll. Open during exhibitions only; schedules are posted on the door and listed in a brochure available at the tourist office. 20 Rue Lacépède.

QUARTIER MAZARIN

Musée Granet – Aix's museum of fine arts and archaeology was founded in the late 18th century and eventually took its name from the early-19th-century Aixois painter François-Marius Granet, a major donor (many of his own works are displayed, and there is a portrait of him by Ingres). Today, the museum is considered among the finest in Provence. In a 17th-century building, the former priory of the Knights of Malta, it contains eight paintings by Cézanne — a recent donation and all that there is in Aix of its native son's work — and a very good collection of Provençal, Flemish, and Italian paintings from the 16th to the 19th century. There also are pieces from 20th-century masters such as Martung, Léger, and Matisse and works of contemporary artists and, in summer, some avant-garde paintings. Also exhibited are archaeological finds from the pre-Roman settlement at Entremont — such things as death masks, warriors' torsos, and other examples of Celto-Ligurian statuary — and exhibits of Egyptian, Greek, and Roman origin. Closed Tuesdays and some holidays. Open daily during the summer. Admission charge. Pl. St.-Jean-de-Malte and 13 Rue Granet (phone: 42-38-14-70).

Eglise St.-Jean-de-Malte – This 13th-century church is next door to the *Musée Granet,* once the chapel of the Knights of Malta priory. The church was the first Gothic building in Provence, and though the tarnished façade has been sorely neglected, its interior is worth a visit. There are lovely stained glass windows to the front and back, and the motif of the Maltese cross is repeated on pillars and windows throughout. Pl. St.-Jean-de-Malte (phone: 42-38-25-70).

ELSEWHERE

Pavillon de Vendôme – This elegant 17th-century mansion, just beyond the Old Town, originally was built as the provincial residence of the Cardinal de Vendôme. It has some fine 17th- and 18th-century furnishings and paintings, but its attraction lies particularly in its overall architecture and lovely grounds, which include a rose garden, a playground, and various semiprivate nooks in addition to the main formal garden of velvety green lawn dotted with boxwood carved into swirling shapes, like the tops of mad ice cream cones. All of this is hidden from the bustle of the town by a high wall, and the Aixois who retreat here to push prams, read, or knit on the park benches seem oblivious to the suffering of the two striking male figures holding up the balcony of the building, visibly groaning from the weight of it on their heads. Closed Tuesdays; admission charge. 32 Rue Celony (phone: 42-21-05-78).

Atelier de Cézanne (Cézanne's Studio) – The 2-story, brown-shuttered house that the artist built in 1897 (and used until his death in 1906) is a bit of a walk uphill at the edge of the city, but the intimate glimpse of his working conditions that it provides makes the effort worthwhile. Only the actual studio — one high-ceilinged room with a huge northern window and other windows overlooking the treetops to the south — can be visited, but it is preserved as he left it, with his cap and cape on a wall hook, a coal stove, a few pieces of furniture, some sketches, letters, and books, and a profusion of vases, bottles, pitchers, dried flowers, and fresh and dried fruit (they're changed from time to time) — the subjects of numerous still lifes. The garden surrounding the house is quietly pleasant. Closed Tuesdays; admission charge. 9 Av. Paul-Cézanne (phone: 42-21-06-53).

Fondation Vasarely – This huge building decorated with alternating black and white circles is hard to miss in the hilly suburb west of town. Devoted to the oeuvre of the Hungarian geometric artist Victor Vasarely, the largely glass structure consists of eight hexagonal main rooms, pleasantly lit with natural light from skylights. The giant floor-to-ceiling works include the artist's vibrantly colored wall murals, Aubusson tapestries, and multidimensional works, including a revolving sculpture. In an upstairs gallery, you can learn all about Vasarely and get a glimpse from overhead at some of his massive creations. Open from 9:30 AM to 12:30 PM and 2 to 5:30 PM; closed Tuesdays. Admission charge. Take bus No. 12 from La Rotonde. 1 Av. Marcel-Pagnol, Jas-de-Bouffan (phone: 42-20-01-09).

■**EXTRA SPECIAL:** The landscape surrounding Aix, with the stark white Montagne Ste.-Victoire jutting dramatically above it, is still much as it appears in so many of Cézanne's canvases. Route D17 leading east toward the village of Le Tholonet was enough of a favorite of the painter to be called now the Route de Cézanne, and to follow in his footsteps, whether by car, bicycle, or with your own footsteps, is a memorable part of a stay in Aix. From the top of the Cours, take Rue Maréchal-Joffre and follow it as it becomes Boulevard des Poilus, then Avenue des Ecoles-Militaires-St.-Cyr-et-St.-Maixent, and eventually D17. It's 3½ miles (6 km) to Le Tholonet, where you can sit down for a sip before turning back or proceeding to the mountain, which has paths for hikers (at various levels of proficiency). These paths look deceptively simple, so be careful if you are not fit. Alternatively, go on one of the guided visits (in French) to sites associated with Cézanne organized by the Aix Tourist Office on Fridays, April through November, for a modest fee. During the summer, an English version is offered.

SOURCES AND RESOURCES

 TOURIST INFORMATION: The Office de Tourisme (2 Pl. du Général-de-Gaulle; phone: 42-26-02-93) is just off La Rotonde and has an English-speaking staff. Open daily from 8 AM to 10 PM in summer and from 8 AM to 7 PM the rest of the year (hours are shorter on Sundays and holidays), it stocks the usual brochures listing hotels, restaurants, sights, sports facilities, villas and flats for rent, and other pertinent information. It also distributes free, large maps, organizes guided tours of the city and surrounding area (some in English during summer months), exchanges currency, and publishes an inexpensive monthly brochure, *Le Mois à Aix,* listing events.

Local Coverage – *Le Provençal* and *Le Méridional* are two regional dailies with Aix editions. *La Semaine d'Aix* is a free weekly that can be picked up in a number of places; it gives mostly movie schedules and reviews. *L'Aixois* is an exhaustive guide to everything from health food stores and hairdressers to fencing clubs and all-night gas stations. They all are in French. *Paradox* (2 Rue Reine-Jeanne; phone: 42-26-47-99) is a good English-language bookstore with material on the region.

 TELEPHONE: The city code for Aix-en-Provence is 42, which is incorporated into all local 8-digit numbers. When calling a number in Aix from the Paris region (including the Ile-de-France), dial 16, wait for a dial tone, then dial the 8-digit number. When calling a number from outside Paris, dial only the 8-digit number. When calling from the US, dial 33 (which is the country code), followed by the 8-digit number.

 GETTING AROUND: Incontestably the best way to see Aix is on foot. It's a walker's paradise, manageable in size and brimming with pedestrian islands. Conversely, it's a driver's nightmare, with narrow streets and few parking spots. Illegally parked cars are swiftly towed away, especially if they have out-of-region plates.

Bicycle – Bikes can be rented at *Cycles Nadeo* (Montée d'Avignon; phone: 42-21-06-93) and at *Avis* (11 Cours Gambetta; phone: 42-21-64-16). Bicycles also can be rented at the train station.

Bus – About a dozen main lines serve the city, most of them departing from La Rotonde or the Gare Routière, and there's also a limited minibus system. Tickets are sold individually on the bus or in economical *carnets* (packets) of ten. Most lines stop before 8 PM, and weekend service is skimpy. The tourist office has schedules. The Gare Routière on Rue Lapierre is the depot for intercity bus service. There are regular buses to Arles, Avignon, Marseilles, and other points in Provence and along the coast as far as Nice. *TRPA* buses run frequently between Gare Routière and Marignane Airport (for schedule information, phone 42-27-17-91).

Car Rental – *Hertz* is at 43 Av. Victor-Hugo (phone: 42-27-91-32) and *Avis* at 11 Cours Gambetta (phone: 42-21-64-16). Other major international and European firms also are represented.

Taxi – There are stands at the train and bus stations and around the city, and cabs also can be hailed on the street. To phone for one, call, among others, *Taxi Mirabeau* (phone: 42-21-21-61) or *Les Artisans* (phone: 42-26-29-30 day and night). Radio taxi service is very reliable (phone: 42-27-71-11), as is the cab service at the train station (phone: 42-27-62-12) and at Gare Routière (phone: 42-27-20-92).

Train – The train station (Gare SNCF) is at the end of Av. Victor-Hugo (phone: 42-27-51-63), but Aix is not very well connected to its neighbors by rail. In most cases, you'll have to change at Marseilles or take the bus (see above).

SPECIAL EVENTS: Aix's *Festival International d'Art Lyrique et de Musique* (International Festival of Lyric Art and Music), an annual event since 1948, is one of the most famous in Europe. Though almost any kind of classical music can be heard, the emphasis is on vocal music. In fact, three operas are staged each year — anything from Rameau to Britten, but almost always something by Mozart, after whom the festival originally was named — and the singers are internationally known. The *Théâtre de l'Archevêché* — the outdoor courtyard of the archbishop's palace — usually is the setting for the operas, while the settings for the concerts include the Cathédrale St.-Sauveur, where symphonies, oratorios, and even solo recitals take place, and the adjoining Cloître St.-Sauveur, where more intimate works are presented. The festival goes on for approximately 3 weeks, from mid-July to early August, and tickets sell out fast, even though they're pricey — as high as 450F ($80). Programs are available at French tourist offices abroad and throughout France; you can write for information and reservations directly to the festival office at the Palais de l'Ancien Archevêché (13100 Aix-en-Provence; phone: 42-23-37-81; for reservations, 42-23-11-20). Bookings by mail can be made 3 months in advance; reservations are advisable, especially for the Mozart operas. Other events in Aix include the *International Painting Festival* in the second half of June; *Aix en Musique,* 2 weeks of primarily classical — but also jazz and ethnic — music in late June or early July, mostly for free; and *Danse à Aix,* 10 days of modern dance and ballet in early July. For details, see *Le Mois à Aix* or consult the tourist office.

MUSEUMS: In addition to those mentioned in *Special Places,* other museums of interest include the following:

   Musée du Vieil Aix – Honors Aix's glorious past with old Carnival puppets and *santons,* hand-painted clay figures of religious or Provençal characters. Closed Mondays and the month of October. 17 Rue Gaston-de-Saporta (phone: 42-21-43-55).

   Musée Paul-Arbaud – A large collection of old Provençal ceramics, paintings, and books on Provence. Open afternoons; closed Sundays. 2 Rue du Quatre-Septembre (phone: 42-38-38-95).

SHOPPING: Some of the best-known souvenirs of Aix are ultra-rich sweets (surely not part of the thermal cure): the traditional almond paste *calissons d'Aix,* the hazelnut-flavored nougat *victorines,* and unforgettable fresh chocolates from the nearby Puyricard chocolatiers, among France's best. Less caloric treats are the Côtes de Provence wines and the fragrant herbs of Provence. Colorful and distinctive Provençal cotton fabrics, antiques, and designer clothes are among other treasures to be found in the lovely shops on pedestrian streets such as the Rue Fabrot, Rue Marius-Reinaud, and Rue des Cordeliers. The Place de Verdun crafts and flea market, on Tuesday, Thursday, and Saturday mornings (it's actually an extension of the Place des Prêcheurs food market), is a good place to browse (since everything is overpriced) for interesting old postcards, maps, jewelry, and furniture. During the summer Place des Cardeurs has a flea market on Saturdays. Note that some shops are open on Sunday mornings, but many are closed on Mondays.

   Bacchus – A great wine cellar in which to find out about any kind of alcoholic beverage — and bottled water, too — but the proprietors speak very broken English. 27 Rue d'Italie (phone: 42-38-07-41).

Bechard – The best pastry shop in Aix. 12 Cours Mirabeau (phone: 42-26-06-78).

Calissons du Roi René – A *calissons d'Aix* maker with very reasonable prices. 7 Rue Papassaudi (phone: 42-26-67-86).

Chocolaterie de Puyricard – An outlet of the nearby factory. 7 Rue Rifle-Rafle (phone: 42-21-13-26).

Galerie Manuel – Art gallery featuring Aixois painters, with four exhibits each year. 4 Rue Manuel (phone: 42-27-59-40).

Les Olivades – Provençal prints by the yard and in bags, eyeglass cases, bedspreads, and other articles, plus painted furniture. 5 Rue des Chaundronniers (phone: 42-23-57-47).

Leonard Parli – Established in 1874, it's among the oldest makers of *calissons d'Aix*. 33 Av. Victor-Hugo (phone: 42-26-05-71).

Souleiado – Beautiful Provençal prints — yard goods, ready-to-wear, and gift items. Pl. des Tanneurs (phone: 42-26-12-90).

SPORTS AND FITNESS: Golf – There is a course at *Golf Club Aix-Marseille* (Domaine de Riquetti; phone: 42-24-20-41).

    Horseback Riding – The tourist office has a list of riding clubs, some of which offer daily rates.

Jogging – A good course stretches along the Arc River at Pont de l'Arc under the trees.

Swimming – The *Piscine Municipale* (Rte. du Tholonet; phone: 42-21-41-08) is not too far from the center and is open daily year-round — covered in winter, uncovered in summer. Another pool, the *Piscine du Jas-de-Bouffan,* is in suburban Jas-de-Bouffan (on Av. Marcel-Pagnol; phone: 42-20-00-78).

Tennis – There are hard-surface public courts at the municipal stadium (on Rte. du Tholonet; phone: 42-21-41-08) and in Jas-de-Bouffan (Av. Marcel-Pagnol; no phone).

THEATER: For mainstream productions, go to the *Théâtre Municipal* (on Rue de l'Opéra; phone: 42-38-44-71). It hosts the French classics and foreign ones in translation and other types of *spectacles,* including dance and numerous musical events from recitals to operettas and opera. The *Rex* (48 Cours Mirabeau; phone: 42-38-12-25) books variety acts and personal appearances by *chansonniers* and other musical and theatrical luminaries as well as the occasional dance group or musical comedy not playing at the *Théâtre Municipal.* Though the *Rex* is not itself an outstanding theater, the entertainment there can be excellent. Mime, songs, and poetry are the province of *La Fontaine d'Argent,* a popular café-théâtre — with a *crêperie* open before the show (5 Rue Fontaine d'Argent; phone: 42-38-43-80). For other French theaters, see *Le Mois à Aix. Ciné Mazarin* (6 Rue Laroque; phone: 42-26-99-85) comprises three theaters that feature films in their original languages — often English — with French subtitles, as well as debates and appearances by guest stars; free movie gazette available. *Studio 24* (24 Cours Sextius; phone: 42-27-63-22) and *Buster Keaton* (45 Rue Manuel; phone: 42-26-86-11) also show films in English.

MUSIC: Aix is not completely silent after the summer festival season is over. Its churches and cloisters continue to be the austere settings for concerts of classical music. Several operas and operettas can be heard each year, most of them at the *Théâtre Municipal,* a few of the lighter ones at the *Rex* (see addresses above). The former also is the scene of classical concerts, whereas the music heard at the latter is likely to be in a more popular vein — *chansons,* jazz, and rock. A jazz pianist plays at the *Blue Note* restaurant (see *Eating Out*). In December, a *Foire aux Santons* (a figurine fair) is held next to the tourist office. Consult *Le Mois à Aix* and *Le Provençal,* both local papers, then check posters for last-minute events.

NIGHTCLUBS AND NIGHTLIFE: On weekends, the *Casino Municipal*'s restaurant, *Le Vendôme* (Pl. du Général-de-Gaulle; phone: 42-26-01-00), is a popular, traditional dinner-and-dance-to-an-orchestra spot with moderate to expensive prices. A fashionable (but younger) disco-oriented crowd heads slightly out of town to the *Rétro 25* (Rte. N8, Pont de Luynes; phone: 42-24-01-00), an "in" club enlivened with video films and fashion shows; the older crowd goes dancing and sometimes listens to excellent live jazz at *Le Hot Brass* (Rte. d'Equilles, Celony; phone: 42-21-05-57). *Le Richelme* (Rue de la Verrerie; phone: 42-23-49-29) is for the young disco set. A popular nightspot is *Oxydium* (Farm Le Fangas on the road to Les Milles; phone: 42-27-92-16). Most clubs open at 10 PM and are closed Mondays. Gamblers can indulge in their favorite vice every day from 3 PM until 2 AM (3 AM on Saturdays) in the elegant *Casino Municipal* (2 bis Av. Napoléon-Bonaparte; phone: 42-26-30-33). There's baccarat, roulette, *trente-et-quarante,* and *boule. Note:* No jacket-and-tie requirement, but jeans and sneakers (for men or women) are *interdit.*

BEST IN TOWN

CHECKING IN: Aix has many hotels, but rooms seem to vanish during the festival, having been spoken for months in advance. Note that most hotel rates do not include breakfast (a pleasant alternative is taking a fresh crois-sant and *café au lait* at a sidewalk café on the Cours Mirabeau). Expect to pay $85 to $130 for a double room at hotels listed as expensive; from $40 to $80 for those listed as moderate; and less than $40 for hotels we call inexpensive (usually starting at $15).

Les Augustins – Converted from an old convent built in the 12th century, this small place has been beautifully restored. Just off the Cours Mirabeau, it has 32 rooms with vaulted ceilings. Reserve in advance; ask for one of the two rooms (each has a terrace) overlooking the 15th-century Campanile des Augustins. No restaurant. 3 Rue de la Masse (phone: 42-27-28-59). Expensive.

Mercure Paul Cézanne – This delightful hostelry excels not only in its decor — all 44 rooms are done tastefully, usually with fine antiques — but also in its atmosphere and service. Near the train station, it has one drawback: an occasional problem with street noise. Ask for an air conditioned room. No restaurant. 40 Av. Victor-Hugo (phone: 42-26-34-73). Expensive.

Le Pigonnet – Tucked amid shady chestnut trees and lovely flowered grounds near the outskirts of the city, this is more a typical Provençal mansion. The 50 carefully decorated rooms, some of which are air conditioned, fulfill the promise of their bucolic setting. There's a pool, too, and a fine restaurant, *Le Patio* (see *Eating Out*). 5 Av. du Pigonnet (phone: 42-59-02-90). Expensive.

Le Domaine de Tournon – Not centrally located, but the countryside here is worth the detour. A luxury hotel, it has comfortable rooms (all with color TV sets), a swimming pool, tennis courts, and a restaurant that serves duck dishes and *pieds paquets,* a local lamb specialty. On D63C toward Les Pinchinats; take the Péri-phérique to Place Bellegarde and turn right on the Ancienne Route des Alpes (phone: 42-21-22-05). Expensive to moderate.

Le Manoir – A converted 14th-century cloister with 43 rooms and period furnish-ings. The public rooms have exposed beams and French Provincial furniture, and there's a pretty, shaded terrace on a gravel courtyard off the street — an exceed-ingly quiet street though quite centrally located. No restaurant. Closed mid-January to mid-February. 8 Rue d'Entrecasteaux (phone: 42-26-27-20). Moderate.

Mas d'Entremont – Comfort and charm are appealingly combined in this *mas,* or large, Provençal farmhouse. Its 14 rooms and bungalows (with kitchenette) are beautifully furnished and the pine- and cypress-filled grounds overlooking Aix are an enchanting setting. It has a fine restaurant featuring seafood and other light dishes. Closed from November to *Easter.* Montée d'Avignon, 2 miles (3 km) north of Aix on N7 (phone: 42-23-45-32). Moderate.

Le Nègre-Coste – In the oldest 18th-century *hôtel* on the Cours Mirabeau, this is a favorite among traveling theater and journalists. Its 37 renovated and sound-proof rooms have retained their period character and furnishings. No restaurant. 33 Cours Mirabeau (phone: 42-27-74-22). Moderate.

Quatre-Dauphins – This unpretentious family place primarily has economy and a lovely neighborhood to recommend it. The rooms are small, and none has a private toilet, although they all have phones. 54 Rue Roux-Alphéran (phone: 42-38-16-39). Moderate.

Le Moulin – Beyond the railroad station, in the vicinity of Parc Joseph-Jourdan and the new university (not the most central location) the 37 simple, white rooms do have kitchenettes and private baths. Parking on the premises. Closed December 15 to January 6. 1 Av. Robert-Schuman (phone: 42-59-41-68). Moderate to inexpensive.

Cardinal – Small, extremely pleasant, and near the *Musée Granet,* this is perhaps the best buy for the money in Aix. Its 30 simple rooms are comfortable and thoughtfully decorated and nearly all of them have a private bathroom. The two top-floor rooms have a lovely rooftop view. Most of the staff speak English. 24 Rue Cardinale (phone: 42-38-32-30). Inexpensive.

 EATING OUT: Though Aix has only a handful of truly fine restaurants, it does offer a choice of cuisines — Provençal, traditional, regional, and foreign. Provençal cooking draws inspiration from the celebrated local aromatic herbs and also makes good use of olive oil, garlic, tomatoes, and onions. Since this is the south, the accent is on light dishes, and seafood is common. Pizza parlors abound, serving far better than what passes for the species in Paris. Other types of snack shops — even fast-food outlets on Cours Mirabeau — also can be found. Note that service often is unbearably slow, and most restaurants take their last orders before 9:30 or 10 PM. Expect to pay $80 and up for a three-course dinner à la carte for two including wine and service in restaurants listed as expensive, $50 to $80 in the moderate ones, and less than $30 in the inexpensive ones.

Le Clos de la Violette – By far the best dining room in Aix, and the only one with a Michelin star. Cooking is Provençal, with most of the herbs and some of the vegetables coming from the owner's garden. Reserve well in advance. Closed Sundays, Mondays for lunch, and 2 weeks in winter and 2 weeks in spring. Reservations necessary. 10 Av. Violette (phone: 42-23-30-71). Expensive.

Le Patio – Framed by the varied hues of green on the beautiful grounds of the *Pigonnet* hotel, this terrace restaurant looks like a Renoir painting. Try the *noisette d'agneau au basilic,* one of the delicious specialties, and delight in the refuge from city life provided by the setting. Closed Sunday evenings and from the end of September to *Easter.* Reservations unnecessary. 5 Av. du Pigonnet (phone: 42-59-02-90). Expensive.

Le Picotin – This small spot, decorated in a simple country style, specializes in southwestern French and Basque cooking. Duck dishes are prominent, desserts are excellent, and the friendly owner attentive. Closed Sunday evenings, Monday lunch, and December 24 to January 10 (except for *New Year's Eve*). Reservations necessary. 16 Rue de la Paix (phone: 42-27-95-44). Expensive to moderate.

Relais Ste.-Victoire – A small (there are 4 rooms and 6 suites) stopover for travelers, located outside town in beautiful Cézanne country. The menu of sumptuous Provençal specialties changes with the seasons. Closed Sundays and Mondays and during school vacation in November and February. Reservations necessary. Beaurecueil (phone: 42-66-91-34 or 42-66-94-98). Expensive to moderate.

L'Abbaye des Cordeliers – Outdoor dining in the shade of lime trees is one of the pleasures of summer at this former cloister. Indoors is a pretty room with exposed beams. Traditional dishes, especially grilled meats, are the mainstays, and they're served in generous portions. Reservations are essential as seating is limited. Closed Sunday evenings, Mondays, and the month of October. 21 Rue Lieutaud (phone: 42-27-29-47). Moderate.

La Brocherie – Attractively rustic with a pleasant courtyard, it, too, specializes in meats grilled over a wood fire. With good service, this is an excellent buy. Closed Sundays, Mondays, and a week each in November, February, and June. Reservations are essential for the courtyard. 5 Rue Fernand-Dol (phone: 42-38-33-21). Moderate.

Cay Tam – Good Vietnamese and Chinese cooking. Try the spring rolls and the lacquered pork. Open evenings only; closed Mondays for lunch. No reservations. 29 Rue de la Verrerie (phone: 42-27-28-11). Moderate.

Chez Jo (Le Bar des Augustins) – One of Aix's best pizzerias, it also serves traditional dishes. Very informal, with tightly packed tables inside as well as out, it's a late favorite with the fashionable crowd. Closed Sundays. Reservations advised. 59 Rue Espariat (phone: 42-26-12-47). Moderate.

Le Vieux Lyon – Excellent regional food and burgundy wines. English is spoken. Closed Sundays. No reservations. 17 Rue du Petit Saint Esprit (phone: 42-26-49-49). Moderate.

Al Dente – Only pasta is served here, but it's fresh, light, and well prepared. Closed Sundays for lunch. No reservations. 14 Rue Constantin (phone: 42-96-41-03). Inexpensive.

Bar à Thé – Besides a half-dozen teas, the fare here consists of excellent vegetable *tartes,* salads, and homemade cakes (expecially the chocolate cake). This is a tiny dollhouse of a place, but the decor is tasteful rather than cute. It's become one of Aix's more fashionable spots, a pleasant place to linger — especially at the tables outside on the quiet square (just off the main *place*) — from noon to 11 PM. Closed Sundays, Mondays, and from early August to early September. No reservations. 66 Pl. Richelme (phone: 42-23-51-99). Inexpensive.

Blue Note – Hidden on a side street, Aix's *restaurant américain* is informal, with old American posters and a dartboard decorating the exposed brick walls. Its burgers, ribs, corn on the cob (a rarity in France), and especially its cheesecake please many more than homesick Americans. Open till midnight, there's a jazz pianist on Tuesdays and Fridays. Closed Mondays and August 1 to 15. No reservations. 10 Rue de la Fonderie (phone: 42-38-06-23). Inexpensive.

Croque-Mitoufle – The specialties of this charming tearoom next to Aix's beautiful music conservatory include spinach and endive *tartes,* homemade ice cream, and a wide variety of teas. Open daily for lunch and tea only; closed Sundays in summer, Sundays and Mondays in winter, and the whole month of August. No reservations. Rue Joseph-Cabassol (phone: 42-26-25-42). Inexpensive.

 BARS AND CAFÉS: Aix's premier sidewalk café, without any doubt, is *Les Deux Garçons* (55 Cours Mirabeau), so named for the two waiters who bought it. Whether outside in the shade of the plane trees or inside in the midst of its lovely rococo decor, it has been *the* place for people watching since 1793. It's open till 1 or 2 AM daily, and it also serves a full menu. It also is one of the few places where you still can order only coffee or tea any time of the day or night. Many bars no longer offer customers these drinks because of the low profit margin. Opposite the *Casino Municipal, Le Cintra* (14 Pl. Jeanne-d'Arc) has a pleasant terrace and offers a choice of 115 international beers (plus Alsatian specialties such as *choucroute*) with which to while away the hours up to the 3 AM closing time. *Le Petit Verdot* (7 Rue Entrecasteaux) is a wine bar that serves food; it is open for lunch and dinner daily except Sundays and Monday noon. *Le Grimaldier,* a nicely renovated café-restaurant (1 Av. des Belges), attracts a cosmopolitan crowd for drinks or ice cream until 1 AM. The "in" place in Aix for the young university crowd is *Bistro Aixois* (37 Cours Sextius).

AVIGNON

Avignon grew up in a strategic spot just north of the intersection of the Rhône and Durance rivers. On the traditional route from Paris to the Mediterranean, it always has had the vibrant style of a crossroads town. But Avignon also is a monument to one crucial period of glory, and to appreciate the city it's best to get right to the point, which is the history of the papacy in the 14th century.

Very early in that century, a pope was elected who refused — largely because of continuous internecine violence in Italy — to take up residence in Rome. Why he decided to live in a relatively anonymous town in Provence instead was not exactly a quirk of fate. Pope Clement V was a Frenchman by birth and somewhat beholden to Philip the Fair, then King of France, for his election. Avignon, though not a part of the French kingdom (it belonged to the Counts of Provence), was close enough to be within the king's sphere of influence. In addition, it had a strategic riverside location and was also next to a papal possession, the Comtat Venaissin. Clement V arrived in Avignon in 1309, and while he preferred to live (for the most part) in the peaceful countryside of the neighboring papal territory, his official presence instantly transformed the relatively unknown town into a capital of the Christian world.

The Avignon Captivity had begun. For almost 70 years thereafter, a total of seven popes, all French, reigned from here. Clement V's successor, John XXII (who had been a bishop in Avignon before becoming pope), was the first to establish his permanent residence in Avignon proper; he moved into the episcopal palace, found it too small, and enlarged it. Pope Benedict XII, who succeeded John XXII in 1334, found it still wanting, and the next year began to demolish it to make way for his own palace, a structure that left no doubt of his intention to remain in Avignon. Nor was there any doubt in the mind of his successor, Clement VI, pope from 1342 to 1352, who bought the city from the Countess of Provence and spent the duration of his papacy completing what Benedict XII had begun, doing it so zealously, in fact, that his additions amounted to an entirely new palace attached to the older one.

By the time Innocent VI succeeded Clement VI in 1352, Avignon's main tourist attraction — the massive and staunch Palace of the Popes — was essentially the same size and shape it is today. Innocent VI added reinforcements to the structure, including two towers, and Urban V, his successor in 1362, added little more than a gallery in the garden, no longer extant. Urban V did, however, make an attempt to restore the papacy to Rome, leaving Avignon in 1367, but returned (after finding the Eternal City still too prone to violence and another French king too vehemently opposed to the move) a few months short of his death in 1370. The next pope, Gregory XI, accomplished the return to Rome in 1377, just before his death in 1378.

The Avignon Captivity also has gone down in history as the "second Babylonian Captivity" because of charges that Avignon was Babylon, a "scarlet whore heralding the world's end." This wasn't entirely exaggeration, for the holy site had become a place of exceeding worldliness, of which the flagrantly luxurious palace was a telling symbol. And across the river in Villeneuve-lès-Avignon, the sumptuous homes of the cardinals almost rivaled that of the popes. Throughout this period, the city also was the banking and commercial center of southern Europe.

With so much money flowing from the Church's coffers, the arts flourished — the Sienese painter Simone Martini worked here from 1339 to 1344, painting frescoes on the porch of the cathedral, and he was followed by other Italian artists who worked in the palace. The great Italian poet Petrarch spent many years in Avignon, and it was here that he met Laura, who inspired his famous love lyrics. Petrarch was a regular at the court of Clement VI (and in his later years an active champion of the return of the papacy to Rome). Troubadours and mountebanks came to Avignon, as well as processions of penitents, religious minorities seeking the pope's protection, and every kind of thief and evildoer seeking refuge within the boundaries of the papal enclave. A spirit of tolerance prevailed; crime and prostitution prospered — Petrarch called the city "a sink of vice."

When Gregory XI moved the papacy back to Rome, Avignon's tenure as the capital of Christianity was over, but it did not exactly fade into immediate obscurity. No sooner had a new pope, Urban VI, replaced Gregory XI than his attempt to introduce reforms caused the College of Cardinals to declare his election null and void and choose a second pope, Clement VII, who returned to Avignon. During the resulting Great Schism, the Christian world had two popes reigning simultaneously, one in Rome and one in Avignon — each excommunicated the other one — and there was even a third pope during the later years. All but those of the Roman line were declared antipopes after the healing of the schism by the Council of Constance in 1415, but before that happened, two popes of the Avignon line managed to prolong the city's period of glory past the turn of the century: Clement VII lived in the palace from 1378 to 1394; Benedict XIII, from 1394 to 1409. At the height of the papacy in Avignon, the city had 35 monasteries and 60 churches, whose bells rang so often that the French writer François Rabelais named it "La Ville Sonnant," the bell-ringing city.

When the schism ended, Avignon became merely an important provincial city, with merchants manufacturing silk and smuggling salt and tobacco. The palace housed the papal legates who ruled it until it became part of French territory, along with the Comtat Venaissin, in 1791. For a time the palace served as a prison, a barracks, and an archive before restoration began in the early 20th century. Today, it still dominates the city, just as its reason for being dominates the city's history, but it would be a mistake to think it is the only reminder of the past in Avignon.

In fact, from the moment you step inside the city walls — also built by the popes and still intact — testaments of many other periods of Avignon's past surround you, though they may be less conspicuous than the remnants of the 14th century. Retreat north from the barren stone of the palace to the calm greenery of the Rocher des Doms (Doms' Rock) park and consider that ducks swim, pigeons roost, and children giggle down the slide on the very spot that was the cradle of Avignon, inhabited some 4,000 years before Christ. Go to the lookout point for a breath of cool river air and there beneath you, in splendid incompleteness, is the 12th-century Pont St.-Bénézet, the bridge better known everywhere as "le Pont d'Avignon" celebrated in the children's song. Across the Rhône, at what was once the bridge's western end, is the square fortress built by Philip the Fair in the last decade of the 13th century. If you visit the upper class Balance quarter west of the palace to admire its beautiful, restored 17th-century townhouses, be aware that 1st-century pottery and other Gallo-Roman relics were unearthed here during the neighborhood's renewal in the 1960s. This was the site of Roman arcades, or "fusteries," as is evident from street names in the vicinity. Some relics are on display in the neighborhood. Nearby, the central Place de l'Horloge was the site of the Roman forum.

All in all, today's town of nearly 100,000 people (fewer than 20% of whom live within the familiar ramparts) contains nearly 100 national historic monuments. Like the walls, often lined by open-air vegetable markets (or by parked cars when the markets are closed) and encircled by busy, six-lane streets, or the Palace of the Popes, with its modern convention center, most of them are the sites of contemporary cultural events, part of a living, thriving present. In recent decades, in fact, Avignon, which once answered a religious call, seems to be responding more and more to a clearly cultural vocation. This is evident in the number of artists living on and enlivening the beautiful Rue des Teinturiers, in the number of art cinemas, galleries, and experimental theaters populating the inner city. But it is much more evident in the annual international *Festival d'Avignon,* one of France's liveliest arts gatherings and its most important theater festival.

Each summer, professional and amateur artists and spectators, serious and less serious, descend on the city in droves; café prices soar (though not so high as along the Riviera), and Place de l'Horloge seems taken over by all the flower children who've survived from the 1960s — among other tourists. Between the official festival events and those along its fringes, more than 100 different *spectacles* take place every day for a month. Divine intervention also still seems to be present in Avignon — a few years ago, during a performance of Shakespeare's *The Tempest,* there was a half-minute windstorm, occurring at the precise moment that it came up in the text. While an avant-garde dance performance or a controversial drama enjoys the spotlight in the courtyard of the palace, a mime or a fire-eater holds court out front in the palace square, which always is filled with people looking for a "show." Something of the lust for life of former times is well in evidence then, and 5 centuries after the departure of the popes, Avignon once again stands out as one of the remarkable cities of Provence.

AVIGNON AT-A-GLANCE

SEEING THE CITY: On the far bank of the Rhône, directly opposite "le Pont d'Avignon" and at the entrance to the unspoiled medieval town of Villeneuve-lès-Avignon, is the Tour Philippe-le-Bel (Philip the Fair Tower). From the top of this late-13th-century edifice there is a striking 180° view of Avignon, with the vast Palace of the Popes in the foreground, the city's densely packed rooftops beyond, and Mount Ventoux in the distance. The tower is open daily except Tuesdays and the month of February. Admission charge. Montée de la Tour Philippe-le-Bel, Villeneuve-lès-Avignon (phone: 90-25-42-03, ext. 160).

SPECIAL PLACES: The sights of Avignon are arranged conveniently. If you're coming from the station, you'll have a good view of a stretch of city wall as you enter the historic center at Porte de la République. Then it's straight ahead along tree-lined Cours Jean-Jaurès and Rue de la République to Place de l'Horloge, which is not only Avignon's main square but also only a few steps from Place du Palais, where the immense medieval papal palace as well as the city's cathedral, its main museum, and the lovely public park are all located. Across Place du Palais from the palace, signs point down a side street and steps to the famous bridge. Place de l'Horloge also gives access to a pedestrian shopping zone around Rue de la Bonneterie, which eventually leads to Rue des Teinturiers, perhaps the street that best provides a feeling of old Avignon unadorned. All the sights below are within walking distance of each other except Villeneuve-lès-Avignon, which is 2 miles across the Rhône. As in other towns in southern France, museums and churches generally are closed between noon and 2 PM.

CITY CENTER

Palais des Papes (Palace of the Popes) – This imposing fortress-residence was the home of five of the seven popes of the Babylonian Captivity and of two of the antipopes of the Great Schism. If you face it, you will see that it's actually two palaces, with a total area of more than 150,000 square feet, whose differing styles reflect less the passage of time than the differing personalities of the popes who commissioned them. The austere Romanesque "old palace" on the left was built from 1335 to 1342 under the ascetic Benedict XII, while the "new palace" on the right, in the more ornate Flamboyant Gothic style, was built from 1342 to 1352 under the more worldly Clement VI. Unfortunately, both parts of the palace now are mostly bare. A fire in 1413 devastated paintings and ceilings in the two huge halls (Consistory and Grand Tinel, or Banquet Hall), looting and vandalism during the French Revolution destroyed furniture and statuary, and when the palace later served as a barracks and prison, frescoes were literally cut up and removed. In recent years, centuries-old tapestries have been added throughout and new wooden ceilings have replaced lost ones in a few rooms (including the Consistory and Grand Tinel), but the highlights of the hour-long tour are the rooms where the original decoration remains. Among these are St. John's Chapel, with frescoes attributed to Matteo Giovanetti, and St. Martial's Chapel, with frescoes definitely by Giovanetti and remarkable for the predominant, vivid lapis lazuli blue. (The quaint graffiti here date from the 15th century.) The walls of the Pope's Bedchamber, covered with a pattern of oak and grape foliage on a dark blue ground, may reflect the taste of either Benedict XII or Clement VI, who both used the room; the colorful glazed tiles of the recently redone floor are copies of 14th-century designs. The Chambre du Cerf (Deer Room), Clement VI's study, is outstanding. Its painted wooden ceiling, protected by a false one in the 18th century, is in its original state, and the walls are full of surprisingly secular hunting, fishing, and bird trapping frescoes.

The palace is open daily year-round, with guided tours leaving hourly or half-hourly depending on the season. In summer, there are two tours a day in English, but unguided visits are permitted; off-season, guided tours are obligatory and in French. Admission charge. Pl. du Palais (phone: 90-86-03-32).

Cathédrale de Notre-Dame des Doms – Next up the hill from the palace is Avignon's cathedral. It dates from the 12th century, was partly rebuilt from the 14th to the 17th century, and was topped by a tall gilded statue of the Virgin — which towers over the area — in the 19th century. Inside are the tombs of Popes John XXII and Benedict XII; outside on the porch are sketches of two frescoes by Simone Martini (the upper layers have been removed and are on display in the palace). Pl. du Palais (phone: 90-82-36-55).

Rocher des Doms – This rocky promontory overlooking the Rhône is a short climb uphill from the cathedral. The highest point in the city, it was inhabited in prehistoric times, but today it is a delightful public park. With sloping lawns, lovely trees and flowerbeds, a duck pond and a grotto for swans, a shaded playground for children and a shaded café for their elders, it is also something of a rarity among French parks, meant to be enjoyed rather than simply admired. There is an immense esplanade from which you'll have a wonderful, broad view across the river to the vast green fields of Villeneuve-lès-Avignon (a viewing table at one corner explains what is what as far as the eye can see) or, looking back, over the red roofs of the city. Follow the esplanade around to the left and you'll look right down upon the Pont St.-Bénézet. North of the cathedral; a toylike mini-train leaves regularly in season from Place du Palais, a boon if you're too tired to walk.

Musée du Petit Palais – The "little palace" was built shortly after the arrival of the papacy in Avignon and became the official archbishop's palace when the "big palace" was built across the square for the popes. Remodeling in the 15th century gave the medieval building a Renaissance finish, and today, with its striking white stone and graceful archways, it superbly suits its role as a museum (which it has been since 1976). On display are paintings and sculpture of the Avignon School from the 12th to the 16th century and Italian paintings from the 13th to the 16th century. Some 300 of the paintings are a minuscule part of an enormous horde put together by a rich 19th-century Roman, Gian Pietro Campana. Campana's passion for art exhausted his own finances, depleted the coffers of the bank of which he was director, and ended with his imprisonment for misappropriation of funds, but not before he had acquired approximately 15,000 objets d'art, including 1,100 paintings (so many that he ran his own restoration workshops, not always with felicitous results). Napoleon III eventually bought the collection with a view to opening a museum. Instead, it was divided among the *Louvre* and a hundred or so provincial museums, and only recently have some of the paintings been reassembled here. Particularly rich in Italian and Provençal painting from the Middle Ages and the Renaisance, the selection is representative, ranging from a Virgin and Child by the Sienese Taddeo di Bartolo to a Holy Conversation by the Venetian Carpaccio, and includes an early Botticelli madonna. In addition to the art, pay attention to the views of the Rhône River and Villeneuve-lès-Avignon. Closed Tuesdays and holidays. Admission charge. Pl. du Palais (phone: 90-86-44-58).

Pont St.-Bénézet – According to legend, France's most famous bridge, "le Pont d'Avignon," immortalized in a song known by children everywhere, was built as a result of the divine vision of a young shepherd named Bénézet. When it was completed in 1185, an engineering miracle, it was 1,000 yards long and had 22 arches across the Rhône. Only four remain now, the rest destroyed by the Rhône's high waters in the middle of the 18th century, and the bridge stops tantalizingly short of the Ile de la Barthelasse, which divides the river into two branches at this point. It was actually on the island and *under* the bridge rather than *on* it — *sous le pont* rather than *sur le pont* — that everyone danced in circles. Still standing on the narrow cobblestone span is the 2-story St. Nicholas Chapel, bare but for modern graffiti, in which St. Bénézet is said to be buried. The entrance to the bridge is somewhat obscure: If you're coming from the Porte du Rhône, turn right, pass under the bridge, and go into the postcard shop just beyond it. Open daily in summer; closed December 25 through January 2. Admission charge. Quai de la Ligne (phone: 90-85-60-16).

Place de l'Horloge (Clock Tower Square) – This large bustling 15th-century square is the center of Avignon and you'll undoubtedly pass through it en route to the

Palais des Papes. It's brimming with sidewalk cafés and assorted street performers, and in summer the "show" goes on until the wee hours. On your immediate left coming from the train station is the stately Hôtel de Ville (enter to see its massive columns), built in the mid-19th century around the old Gothic belfry that gives the square its name. Next door is the elegant *Théâtre Municipal* from the same decade. The square is on the site of a Roman forum, many of whose assorted 1st-century vestiges have been removed to a nearby street corner (Rues St.-Etienne and Racine).

Rue des Teinturiers – A charming cobblestone street, it's lined on one side by a narrow canal whose brush-like waterwheels rise above a stone wall. The waters once served the cloth dyers for whom the street is named. On the other side of the street are old-fashioned upholstery, photography, and antiques shops as well as restaurants and café-theaters. In the southeast quarter of the city, within the walls.

City Walls – The 3 miles of turreted and battlemented stone ramparts encircling the historic center of Avignon were built in the 14th century as the popes' first line of defense against marauders and foreign armies. If today they don't seem high enough for defensive purposes, it's because the moat that originally surrounded them has not been excavated. The area is now a huge parking lot. Originally, also, there were only seven *portes* (gates) leading into the city; the other openings were added in the 19th century when the walls were restored by the architect Viollet-le-Duc.

ENVIRONS

Villeneuve-lès-Avignon – This area first was occupied by Gaul–Romans. After Ste.-Cesarie's death in the 6th century, the place became a site of devotion, where Benedictine monks later built a small monastery and started a settlement. Philip the Fair, the French king, founded the "new town by Avignon" as a stronghold in the late 13th century, when Avignon belonged to the Counts of Provence and the territory on this side of the river belonged to France. He began by constructing the square keep of the Tour Philippe-le-Bel in 1293, to which an upper story and watchtower were added in the 14th century. Later 14th-century kings built the Fort St.-André, whose crenellated walls completely enclose the top of a nearby hill and end in twin round towers defending a massive gateway. But the development of the "new city" really was due to the arrival of the papacy, when it was named Villeneuve (New City). Because 14th-century Avignon was too crowded to accommodate all the papal court, this is where cardinals built their grand residences, thus turning Villeneuve into a wealthy residential suburb that witnessed a brilliant ecclesiastical life until the French Revolution.

Today, besides Tour Philippe-le-Bel (see *Seeing the City*) and Fort St.-André, from which there is also a remarkable view, there are several other places to visit in this quiet medieval town. The ruined Chartreuse du Val-de-Bénédiction (Val de Bénédiction Charterhouse), on Rue de la République, was once the largest and most important Carthusian monastery in France and a small part is now being restored. It was founded in 1356 by Pope Innocent VI, whose white marble tomb is in a chapel of the church. Open daily (phone: 90-25-05-46). The *Musée Municipal,* in a 17th-century building on Rue de l'Hôpital, contains many items from the charterhouse and a notable 15th-century painting, Enguerrand Charonton's *Coronation of the Virgin,* considered a masterpiece of the Avignon School. The parish church of Notre-Dame (Pl. J.-Meissonier), founded as the collegiate church in the 14th century, holds another of Villeneuve's treasures: a small ivory Virgin and Child following the curve of the elephant's tusk from which it was carved. A festival of music and dance, held here every summer, is a perfect complement to the *Festival d'Avignon* (see below). Villeneuve-lès-Avignon is 2 miles (3 km) northwest of Avignon and can be reached by bus No. 20 from the Avignon train station. (The bus takes you to, but not *into,* Villeneuve; ask where to get off.)

■**EXTRA SPECIAL:** The *Festival d'Avignon,* begun shortly after World War II, is France's foremost theater festival — though to call it that alone is to fail to communicate its scope, because it's also an international festival of dance, film, music, and every other possible manifestation of the performing arts. Still, its core is theater. From early July to early August, almost any French troupe of any note will make an appearance here. Similarly, the audience is full of Parisian playgoers taking their measure and trying to discern which way the French theater is heading, since a good number of the French productions are premières of plays by living playwrights of international reputation. These are interspersed with performances of Racine and other French classics and with productions by foreign companies of their ancients and moderns, including, occasionally, productions in English. The main stage is the courtyard — Cour d'Honneur — of the Palais des Papes, but the list of parallel "Off Avignon" activities is by now so long that all of the city becomes a stage at this time, with concerts, debates, café-theater, and street theater going on in theaters, churches, cloisters, and squares throughout. For details, contact the tourist office or the *Festival d'Avignon* (41 Cours Jean-Jaurès; phone: 90-82-65-11).

SOURCES AND RESOURCES

TOURIST INFORMATION: Avignon's Office de Tourisme (41 Cours Jean-Jaurès; phone: 90-82-65-11) is open daily from mid-June to mid-August and closed Sundays the rest of the year. It handles information and currency exchange and — through the *Accueil de France* accommodations service — will book you a room for a fee. Just outside the train station, the hotel-run *VTH* reservation center, which books rooms in and around Avignon and the Vaucluse region, also is open to change money on weekends (phone: 90-82-05-81). The tourist office distributes a free brochure with map, *Avignon Pratique,* listing useful data on hotels, restaurants, and sights. A free monthly brochure on cultural events is published in the off-season only, since the festival calendar dominates the summer months.

Local Coverage – The regional dailies *Le Provençal, Vaucluse Matin, Gazette Provençale,* and *Le Méridional* all have Avignon editions (in French, naturally). The *Maison de la Presse,* the stationery store opposite the tourist office, carries books and maps on Avignon and the region in English.

TELEPHONE: The city code for Avignon is 90, which is incorporated into all local 8-digit numbers. When calling a number in Avignon from the Paris region (including the Ile-de-France), dial 16, wait for a dial tone, then dial the 8-digit number. When calling a number from outside Paris, dial only the 8-digit number. When calling from the US, dial 33 (which is the country code), followed by the 8-digit number.

GETTING AROUND: The ramparts and one-way streets make driving in Avignon difficult and slow. Almost everything within the walls can be seen easily — and best — on foot. For the rest of the city or across the Rhône, there are alternatives.

Bicycle – Rental bikes are available at the train station, Gare *SNCF,* Services Bagages (phone: 90-82-62-92); at *Dopieralski* (84 Rue Guillome Puy; phone: 90-86-32-49); and at *Cycles Peugot* (Place Pie; phone: 90-82-32-19).

Boat – Cruise boats leave Avignon for 2-day trips to Lyons on Tuesdays and

Wednesdays and for a 7-hour trip to Aigues-Mortes, in the Camargue region, on Mondays and Fridays. For more information, contact *SNCM* (3 Rue Président-Carnot, Lyons; phone: 78-42-22-70). For information about other boat trips on the Rhône, contact *Le Cygne* in Beaucaire (phone: 66-59-35-62 or 66-59-45-08); *EuropaBoat* in Arles (phone: 90-93-74-34) and in Avignon, (phone: 90-82-51-75); and *Grand Bateaux de Province* in Avignon (phone: 90-85-62-25).

Bus – Tickets can be bought individually on the bus or, before boarding, in economical packets of ten from booths in Place Pie or at Porte de la République. Obtain schedules there, too. There's no evening service, and weekend service is skimpy.

Car Rental – All the major firms are here, plus *SNCF*'s own *Train + Auto* rental plan at the station (phone: 90-82-20-89).

Taxi – There are stands at the train station and scattered around Avignon, or call *Radio Taxis* (phone: 90-82-20-20).

Train – The train station (Gare *SNCF*) is just outside Porte de la République at the foot of Cours Jean-Jaurès. Avignon is well served by trains en route between Paris and Nice. The *SNCF* has extended its high-speed *TGV* (*train à grand vitesse*) network southeast from Paris to Marseilles via Avignon. For information, call 90-82-50-50.

SPECIAL EVENTS: Besides the summer drama festival (see *Extra Special*), there's a month-long dance festival in February. Two secondhand dealers' fairs take place yearly by the river on Les Allées des Oulles, one in spring during *Pentecost* weekend and one in early September; there is an artisans' fair also by the river each July. The flea market is held every Sunday at Pl. des Charmes. On July 14, *Bastille Day,* there are extraordinary fireworks off the Pont St.-Bénézet, with dancing on the bridge into the night. In mid-November, young Côte de Rhône wine is baptized during the *Wine Festival*.

MUSEUMS: In addition to those mentioned in *Special Places,* the following museums are of interest:

Musée Calvet – A diverse art collection (including David, Daumier, Delacroix, Soutine, Vlaminck, Dufy, and the 18th-century Avignon painter Joseph Vernet), archaeological artifacts, and a collection of wrought-iron hardware from the 15th to the 19th century are housed in a classic 18th-century mansion with exceptional grounds. Long closed for restoration, the museum is due to reopen this summer. 65 Rue Joseph-Vernet (phone: 90-86-33-84).

Musée Lapidaire – Gallo-Roman objects displayed in a former Jesuit chapel. Some of the major works from the *Musée Calvet* (above) are on display here while that museum is closed. 27 Rue de la République (phone: 90-86-33-84).

SHOPPING: The side streets off Rue de la République — notably the pedestrian zone dominated by Rue de la Bonneterie — are filled with quality shops, particularly for clothing and Provençal antiques. The parallel Rue Joseph-Vernet is another elegant shopping street, featuring well-known Parisian names. Local specialties include excellent *eaux de vie* and liqueurs made from peaches and pears by the Manguin family on the Ile de la Barthelasse and the tasty, liquor-filled chocolate candies called (naturally enough in this city of the popes) *papalines*. Also available are regional items such as the colorful Provençal cottons and aromatic *herbes de Provence*–scented products.

Avidis – Wines and spirits. 101 Route de Lyons.

Cristallerie des Papes – Unique handcrafted and hand-blown glass. At Fontaine de Vaucluse, 15 miles (25 km) south of Avignon.

Librairie Roumanille – A publishing house and bookstore selling rare books and manuscripts about Provence and also old prints. 19 Rue St.-Agricol.

Olivades – Fabric and gifts of Provence. Rue des Marchands.

Salle d'Exposition, Espace St.-Bénézet – A group of artisans sell items ranging from almond cookies to herbal products to hand-painted scarves. Entrance on Rue Ferruce or on Quai de la Ligne, next to the bridge.

Souleiado – Marvelous Provençal fabric, fashions, and gift items. 3 Rue Joseph-Vernet.

La Taste – Provençal goods — wine, soap, honey, and more. 5 Rue de la Balance.

 SPORTS AND FITNESS: BASKETBALL – Avignon boasts a basketball team, *Entente Sportif Avignonese (ESA)*, in the top national league. The caliber of play is equal to the better American college squads, and the season runs from September to May. *ESA* plays at Cosec St. Chaman's (Av. Elsa Trilet; phone: 90-87-13-00).

Mountain Climbing – Scale the slopes at Les Dentelles de Montmirail and around Fontaine de Vaucluse. For information, contact *Club Alpin Français* (68 Rue Joseph-Vernet, 84000 Avignon; phone: 90-82-59-15). The club is open only on Thursday afternoons.

Swimming – One Olympic-size pool (phone: 90-82-54-25) is on the Ile de la Barthelasse, open May 15 to early September; another, the *Piscine Municipale* (phone: 90-87-00-90), is on Av. Pierre-Sémard, part of the Route de Marseille.

Tennis – Reserve in advance for the municipal courts at the *Parc des Sports* (Av. Pierre de Coubertin; phone: 90-88-53-59 or 90-87-45-51), next to the municipal swimming pool on the Route de Marseille. Among the private courts are those at the *Tennis Club de la Duplessis* (Ile de la Barthelasse; phone: 90-86-17-56).

 THEATER: Drama is alive and well year-round, but except when it's absolutely kicking during the *Festival d'Avignon,* it is rarely in English. The *Amis du Théâtre Populaire* (17 Pl. du Palais; phone: 90-83-59-24) would know of any productions in English in the area. The *Théâtre Municipal* (Pl. de l'Horloge; phone: 90-82-23-44) stages a wide range of established theatrical works as well as opera, operettas, and ballet, whereas important new works often originate at the *Théâtre du Chêne Noir* (8 bis Rue Ste.-Catherine; phone: 90-86-58-11). The *Théâtre des Halles* (4 Rue N.-A.-Biret; phone: 90-85-52-57) is a new company staging the works of contemporary playwrights. There's amateur theater at *La Tarasque* (5 Rue de Taulignan; phone: 90-85-43-91). There's also much exciting café-theater, notably at the *Théâtre du Chien Qui Fume* (75 Rue des Teinturiers; phone: 90-85-25-87), with various performances daily from morning till night (closed Mondays), and at *La Tache d'Encre* (22 Rue des Teinturiers; phone: 90-85-46-03), a pleasant restaurant with weekend performances in its tiny back room.

The *Utopia* cinema complex, at Rue Galante and Rue République, features films in original languages, many in English. It also has a cafeteria, a bulletin board, and its own free French newspaper.

 MUSIC: For classical, contemporary, or jazz, the eclectic *Théâtre Municipal* (see above) is still the place, as is the *Chapelle des Pénitents Blancs* (Pl. Principale; phone: 90-86-58-80), which often has art exhibits as well. There's frequently jazz, folk, or rock at *La Tache d'Encre* (address above). Major rock acts perform at the *Palais des Expositions* on the Route de Marseille. For information on jazz concerts, contact the *A.J.M.* — part of the *Théâtre du Chêne Noir* (8 bis Ste.-Catherine; phone: 90-86-58-11).

 NIGHTCLUBS AND NIGHTLIFE: Seven miles (11 km) out of town, at Rochefort-du-Gard, is *Sholmes* (phone: 90-31-73-43), a splashy, upper class nightclub complete with pool, restaurant with Moroccan specialties, and dance floor (no jeans or sneakers here).

BEST IN TOWN

CHECKING IN: Avignon has a large inventory of hotels, particularly when you include the 20 or so just across the river in Villeneuve-lès-Avignon, but there are never enough during the peak festival period. If you're driving, consider the numerous two-star (for example, *Ibis* and *Climat*) and three-star (*Mercure* and *Novotel*) chain hotels on the roads leading into town, none more than a 10-minute ride away. There also are many country hotels in villages on both sides of the Rhône, all the way to Arles. Note that most hotel rates don't include breakfast. Expect to pay $65 and up for a double room at hotels listed as expensive, from $30 to $55 for those listed as moderate, and less than $30 for the inexpensive ones.

Les Frênes – Three miles (5 km) from Avignon, it has an imposing garden with roses and century-old trees, antiques-filled guestrooms, and a swimming pool. Its restaurant boasts a Michelin star. Closed December 31 to March 1 (restaurant opens April 1). Av. Vertes Rives, Montfavet (phone: 90-31-17-93). Expensive.

La Magnaneraie – A 15th-century residence with 20th-century comforts, offering peace and quiet in a pine forest setting. The restaurant serves traditional French and Provençal fare and has a very good selection of wines. 37 Rue Camp de Bataille, Villeneuve-lès-Avignon (phone: 90-25-11-11). Expensive.

Mercure Palais des Papes – Although in the heart of the city — midway between the Pont St.-Bénézet and the Palace of the Popes — this was designed around a courtyard and is a remarkably quiet enclave. The building is tastefully modern, its sandstone color blending harmoniously with the restored town houses in the surrounding La Balance quarter. The 85 soundproof rooms have all the amenities of a classic luxury hotel. Rue Ferruce (phone: 90-85-91-23). Expensive.

Le Prieuré – This distinguished *hostellerie* was built in the 14th century as a residence for a cardinal, then became a priory. Now renovated (with no sacrifice of its period charm) and supplemented by a modern wing, it's *the* luxury hotel of the area and reason enough to cross the Rhône. It's removed from the sounds of the city, yet has a fine view, and it's set in shady grounds that have room for a large swimming pool and tennis courts. The modern annex, by the pool, has larger rooms (with better views) than those in the original building, but both sections are equally refined and all 35 rooms are exquisitely furnished. Another plus is a restaurant where diners can eat indoors or on the outdoor terrace. Closed from early November to mid-March. 7 Pl. du Chapitre, Villeneuve-lès-Avignon (phone: 90-25-18-20). Expensive.

Le Rocher Pointu – In the hamlet of Aramon, 7½ miles (12 km) outside Avignon, this bed and breakfast establishment in a farmhouse on 7 isolated acres has 4 guestrooms, each with private bath. Kitchen, barbecue, and a lounge are at patrons' disposal. Plan-de-Dève, Aramon (phone: 66-57-41-87). Expensive to moderate.

Angleterre – Modest, but very clean and pleasant, and just a short walk from the train station in a quiet neighborhood. All rooms have direct-dial phones and some look out onto a large terrace. The majority have a private bathroom, making it an exceptionally good buy. Closed December 15 to January 20. 29 Bd. Raspail (phone: 90-86-34-31). Moderate.

Cité des Papes – Literally down the street from the papal palace and just off Place de l'Horloge, this shiny modern hotel has an unbeatable, if noisy, location. Fortunately, its 63 pretty rooms are soundproofed and well furnished, though occasionally quite small. Closed from mid-December to mid-January. 1 Rue Jean-Vilar (phone: 90-86-22-45). Moderate.

Europe – This former 16th-century palace, the best hotel in the city, has a graceful elegance. Aubusson tapestries decorate the high walls in the antiques-furnished public rooms, and the 47 bedrooms, with beamed ceilings of dark wood, are richly appointed. In summer its pleasant restaurant, *La Vieille Fontaine,* serves meals in the lovely courtyard amid huge plants, a stone sundial over the doorway, and, of course, the old fountain. The restaurant is closed Sundays. 12 Pl. Crillon (phone: 90-82-66-92). Moderate.

La Ferme Jamet – A true 16th-century Provençal farm, with 4 bedrooms, 3 bungalows, and 4 apartments with kitchenette and living room. There's also a private garden, tennis court, and swimming pool; fruit, vegetables, and wine are for sale. Closed November through February. About 3 miles (5 km) from Avignon on Ile de la Barthelasse (phone: 90-86-16-74). Moderate.

Mignon – Translated it means cute, and it really is. Set 200 yards from the Palais de Papes, it has 15 rooms tastefully decorated and soundproofed. 12 Rue J.-Vernet (phone: 90-82-17-30). Moderate.

Régina – A very conveniently situated budget hotel just off Place de l'Horloge on the main street leading from the train station. Ask for a quieter room in the back during the festival. Nothing fancy here (only the lobby is air conditioned), but it's clean and comfortable and almost all rooms have a toilet. 6 Rue de la République (phone: 90-86-49-45). Inexpensive.

EATING OUT: Ever since the popes arrived, there's been a tradition of good eating in Avignon. Besides the dining "palaces," there are many topnotch restaurants charging moderate prices and serving a wide range of foods from Provençal (heavy on olive oil, tomatoes, and local herbs) to Oriental. Pizzerias are particularly plentiful and frequently quite good. Note that many restaurants take their last orders as early as 9 PM. Expect to pay $55 and up for a meal for two without wine in restaurants listed as expensive, from $30 to $55 in those listed as moderate, and from $15 to $30 in the inexpensive ones. A service charge usually is included in the price.

Brunel – The two young Brunel cousins have a solid reputation for inventive cooking and perfectly fresh products, and have earned themselves one Michelin star. Their specialties include hot oysters with curry, a warm pâté of duck and gigondas wine, and a luscious strawberry mousse. The prix fixe menu, available at lunch only, is an excellent bargain. Reservations necessary. Closed Sundays, Mondays (except in June and July), 2 weeks in late February, and August 1–15. 46 Rue de la Balance (phone: 90-85-24-83). Expensive.

Hiely-Lucullus – From its simple façade and unprepossessing location upstairs on a commercial street, you wouldn't suspect the exquisite dining reigning at Avignon's best — and one of France's finest — restaurants, nor that it rates two Michelin stars. There is only a prix fixe menu here (no à la carte), but the choice for each course is wide, cheese and dessert are included, and the value is extraordinary (the best for the money in Avignon). The emphasis is regional, with such specialties as *pieds et paquets provençale* (mutton, tripe, and feet in a stew) and grilled Alpilles lamb. There are fine local wines from the Côtes du Rhône, including good carafes, and the service is gracious and professional. Reservations necessary. Closed Mondays (except in summer) and Tuesdays. 5 Rue de la République (phone: 90-86-17-07). Expensive to moderate.

Les Trois Clefs – This small, pretty place has a young chef with big ideas and the menu reflects his very personal style. Specialties include delicious veal kidneys with a honey sauce and eggs poached *à la cantadine.* The warm decor is highlighted by mounted photos of old Avignon, ca. 1900; service is similarly warm. Reservations necessary. Closed Sundays and during school vacation in November and February. 26 Rue des Trois Faucons (phone: 90-86-51-53). Expensive to moderate.

La Fourchette II – Long a popular favorite for quality dining at low prices and for its decor. The menu includes delicious terrines, grilled sea bass with ratatouille, and homemade sherbets. Reservations necessary. Closed Saturdays and Sundays. 17 Rue Racine (phone: 90-85-20-93). Moderate.

L'Isle Sonnante – After working in many restaurants throughout France, Mr. and Mrs. Gradassi chose to open their own place in what used to be *La Fourchette I*. They have adapted their background in preparing traditional French fare to Provençal dishes. All wines come from nearby vineyards. Reservations necessary. Closed Sundays and Mondays. 7 Rue Racine (phone: 90-82-56-01). Moderate.

Le Vernet – Nice touches such as tasty hors d'oeuvres brought before you order and chewy sweets brought with your coffee add to the atmosphere here, which is equally pleasurable whether you dine inside the stately 18th-century building or amid the statuary behind a high wall in the courtyard. Also pleasurable is the food; try the deliciously light asparagus flan and the roast young rabbit with garlic. Reservations unnecessary. Closed Saturday dinner, Sundays (except in summer), and February. 58 Rue Joseph-Vernet (phone: 90-86-64-53). Moderate.

Au Pied de Boeuf – The orange awning and large potted plants of this friendly and informal place stand out on a dreary stretch of storefronts beyond the ramparts but within walking distance of the center. The couple who run it serve a meal of top value made up of such things as a variety of filling salads, grilled *magrets* (breast of duck) with mustard, and good strawberry *tartes*. Reservations unnecessary. Closed Sundays. 49 Av. Pierre-Sémard (phone: 90-82-16-52). Moderate to inexpensive.

Cafeteria Flunch – For delicious ice cream sundaes (though the salads and hot dishes merely are acceptable), try this simple place. No reservations. Open daily except *Christmas*. 11 Bd. Raspail (phone: 90-86-06-23). Inexpensive.

Crêperie du Cloître – Open for lunch and dinner, it has a large choice of crêpes and salads, as well as live entertainment on Friday nights during the summer. No reservations. Closed Sundays in off-season. 9 Pl. du Cloître, St. Pierre (phone: 90-85-34-63). Inexpensive.

Pain Bis – At this vegetarian eatery, even the wine is organic. The food is well prepared, tasty, and varied, with daily menu changes, and the atmosphere is warm and friendly. No reservations. Closed Sundays. 6 Rue Armand de Pontmartin (phone: 90-86-46-77). Inexpensive.

Simple Simon's – For meat loaf Indian style or just tea and scones, this authentic English restaurant and tearoom can't be beat. The decor and service are charming. No reservations. Open till midnight in July (orders taken only until 7 PM the rest of the year); closed Sundays and Mondays except during festivals, and all of August. 26 Rue Petite-Fusterie (phone: 90-86-62-70). Inexpensive.

BARS AND CAFÉS: For a late drink, the lively Place de l'Horloge is always a good bet, though prices often are higher here. One of the picks on this street is *Bar la Civette*, seedy and cool, where the artists meet after the show. Elsewhere, there's *Le Pezet* (Cours Jean-Jaurès), a comfortable bar.

BIARRITZ

The premier resort city on France's Atlantic coast is well down in the south-west corner of the country on the Bay of Biscay, at the edge of Basque country, about 20 miles (32 km) from the Spanish border. It is modern in comparison to many French cities, for most of its fanciful pastel structures were built in the last 100 years or so. Not too much before that — before the Second Empire (1852–70) of Napoleon III — it was little more than a fishing village, but when a stroke of luck caused Napoleon and Empress Eugénie to spend their summers here, Biarritz quickly became not only a notable French resort town, but one of the most fashionable seaside watering spots in the world. Until well into the 20th century it was "the Beach of Kings and the Queen of Beaches," and today it remains a very popular and busy summer place, though its days of glory are long gone.

Once before in its history Biarritz experienced a similar change of fortune. As markings on the cliffs around Pointe St.-Martin seem to attest, the site is believed to have been inhabited during various prehistoric periods. However, it wasn't until approximately the 12th century that it gradually began to be known as a fishing village and small whaling port. Whaling was lucrative and the village grew prosperous, thanks in large part to nearby Bayonne, the major market for its catch and by-products. A church — Eglise St.-Martin — was built, one of the few vestiges today of this early prosperity. Then the whales left the Bay of Biscay and a grave crisis hit the city. From the beginning of the 16th century to the beginning of the 19th, Biarritz was a fairly sleepy place, though not without some notable activity, such as the restoration of the church in 1541 and the construction of the first lighthouse.

Gradually, the inhabitants of Bayonne began to come here to enjoy the beauty of the coast and to bathe in the sea, a new activity that caught on quickly. They were followed by the Spanish nobility, especially many exiles from the Carlist wars who were unable to set foot in nearby San Sebastián, in their native Spain. Most fateful for Biarritz was the arrival of the Countess de Montijo, who came here regularly after 1838 with her two beautiful daughters, one of whom, Eugénie, was destined to marry Napoleon III in 1853. Remembering her summers in Biarritz, Eugénie persuaded Napoleon to accompany her in 1854 and he was charmed enough by the sight to begin immediately to build an extravagant villa-palace, the Villa Eugénie, in which the couple spent their summers until 1868. Forthwith, Biarritz became the summer capital of France.

By the fall of the empire, the cachet of the city was well established, so that even after Eugénie sold the villa from her exile in England (it became the Palais-Biarritz, then the *Hôtel du Palais*), royalty came to call. The Avenues Reine-Victoria, Edouard-VII, and Alphonse-XIII are named after only a few of the European kings and queens who wintered or summered here. So many

Grand Dukes and Princes of Russia regularly vacationed here that they even built their own church. Through the Belle Epoque and the Roaring Twenties — until the Great Depression — Spanish and French aristocracy, English gentry, and American millionaires mixed at the gaming tables and at the balls, played golf, tennis, and water polo, strolled the promenades, and tooled about town in their Bugattis, Hispano-Suizas, and Rolls-Royces. Shortly, they were sharing their playground with the masses.

The city's star began to fade a bit during the 1950s, when the spotlight turned to the Mediterranean's Côte d'Azur and chic spots such as St.-Tropez, which was unknown before Brigitte Bardot. For a time, Biarritz seemed like a fading dowager, obliged to content itself with the memory of a glorious past. Of late, though, as the Côte d'Azur becomes more and more crowded and expensive and less and less friendly, a gradual shift back to the Atlantic coast seems to have begun. Visitors who've sampled life on both coasts find the residents of Biarritz approachable and sincere, even humble, in comparison. Often, a fruit seller or a waiter or a woman in a butcher shop is happy just to chat, to talk about the region. Their patience may be thinner during July and August — high tourist season — but they have not yet become so bored with their returning popularity that they are offhand and condescending.

In recent decades, Biarritz also has gained a reputation among the international surfing set as the scene of some of the world's best waves. In addition, almost every imaginable sport can be pursued here, from golf — at the *Centre International d'Entraînement au Golf,* Europe's most extensive golf training center (see *Sports and Fitness*) — to horseback riding to people watching. The grand promenade takes place nightly on Place Clemenceau, Place Ste.-Eugénie, and on the pathways that wind above the shore from one end of town to the other, laid out to take advantage of the city's splendid natural beauty. Otherwise, Biarritz, with a population of approximately 30,000 people, is refreshingly free of obligatory tourist sights. The main ones still are the wide sandy beaches, framed by rocky cliffs and green hills blooming with blue and mauve hydrangeas. In this setting, the pale Victorian buildings — tawdry turn-of-the-century marvels that look like giant bits of confectionery — add a touch of fantasy that gives the city a special appeal.

BIARRITZ AT-A-GLANCE

 SEEING THE CITY: The most outstanding of a number of panoramic vistas in Biarritz is the one from Pointe St.-Martin, a high plateau at the northern tip of the city. It can be reached by taking the narrow paths that twist precariously through the Pointe St.-Martin gardens along the tops of cliffs dropping straight down to the shore. From the point, even without climbing the lighthouse, the eye can take in most of the Biarritz waterfront: wide sweeps of sandy beach, sharply rising cliffs that serve as dramatic pedestals for frivolous Victorian villas, a blue and white casino, rocks, and a tiny port in the distance. The St.-Martin headland marks the dividing line between the Landes region north of Biarritz, characterized by sand dunes and forests, and the wild, rugged terrain of the Côte Basque south of it, and the contrast between the two is visible. While you're here, note the lighthouse. It was built in 1834, is 240 feet high, and can be climbed in summer. It also is possible to climb down a few steps below the lighthouse to a cave, La Grotte de la Chambre d'Amour. According to legend, this was the secret meeting place of the son of a wealthy landowner and the daughter of a poor peasant family, forbidden by their parents to marry. One night the couple met in the cave as the tide was rising, and a sudden swell swept them to their deaths — whether accident or suicide is not known.

SPECIAL PLACES: Biarritz's seafront and the promenade — *promenade du bord de mer* — that accompanies much of it are the resort's primary attractions. The promenade consists of sinuous paths that have been carved by man along the plateaus and into the cliffsides, turning the fern- and flower-carpeted rocks into a magnificent public park. From the Pointe St.-Martin gardens, instead of following the sidewalks of Avenue de l'Impératrice, go down the staircase marked "Descente de l'Océan," which takes you to Allée Winston-Churchill, a paved walkway running along the Plage Miramar. After passing the stately *Palais* hotel, the path widens into the Quai de la Grande Plage. This is the main promenade, which continues to the opposite end of the city and a final viewpoint overlooking the southernmost stretch of beach. At a leisurely pace, the walk requires about 3 hours; it takes you past most of the points of interest listed below and several magnificent seascapes.

SEAFRONT

Hôtel du Palais – Unquestionably the most arresting manmade sight in Biarritz is this large red brick building with white trim and a gray roof, fronted by ample green lawn and set in a commanding spot on the Grande Plage, the resort's most popular beach. Napoleon III built it in the 1850s as a summer palace for himself and Empress Eugénie, who had summered in Biarritz as a girl. Known then as the Villa Eugénie (and dubbed by some "Eugénie's Basque folly"), it saw its share of eminent personages when Eugénie was in residence; today, as a luxury hotel, it maintains its regal bearing. Even if you're not a guest, you can glimpse some of the palatial trappings in the public rooms or dine in style in the rotunda restaurant. 1 Av. de l'Impératrice (phone: 59-24-09-40).

Eglise Orthodoxe Russe – A Byzantine Russian church across Avenue de l'Impératrice from the hotel, built in 1892 by the colony of Russian notables who wintered here. It has a striking, sky blue dome. 1 Rue de Russie.

Grande Plage – One of the town's four main beaches. In the city's heyday around the turn of the century, it was the site of leisurely promenades by ladies with long, billowing skirts, wide-brimmed hats, and lacy parasols to protect them from the sun. Today, the scene is a lot less *habillé* — few of the female bathers bother to wear bathing-suit tops — and the beach is one of the two most favored by surfers, though the surf here is not as rough as that of the Plage de la Côte des Basques. Sprawled along the Grande Plage like an albino whale is the *Casino Municipal,* likely to be either renovated or razed and replaced in the near future. The resort's other casino, the *Casino Bellevue,* the giant blue and white wedding cake on the hill above the southern end of the beach, offers glamorous gaming and a nightclub (phone: 59-24-11-22). The Grande Plage is extended north to Pointe St.-Martin by the Plage Miramar.

Place Ste.-Eugénie – From the southern edge of the Grande Plage, steps and a path lead past the Rocher du Basta to this gracious open *place* lined with hotels and their terraced restaurants, one of the gathering places of the resort. The Eglise Ste.-Eugénie, at one end of the square, is relatively modern. From the Place Ste.-Eugénie, Rue Mazagran — full of pedestrians browsing through charming shops — climbs gradually to the Place Clemenceau, the city's main shopping area.

Port des Pêcheurs – This small fishing port below Place Ste.-Eugénie is one of the most picturesque places in Biarritz. It is crowded with boats, slight wooden houses and shacks backed up against a small cliff, huge piles of lobster traps, driftwood, rope, and other scattered fishing paraphernalia. There's also a collection of small harborside restaurants and cafés from which to choose. The little harbor is protected from the surf by a system of manmade breakwaters and concrete walls; in order to reach open water, the boats pass through several canals and compartments and then navigate between dangerous-looking rocks that jut out beyond the walls.

Rocher de la Vierge – The rocky Plateau de l'Atalaye forms one side of the Port des Pêcheurs. Walk through the tunnel Napoleon III had carved through the plateau to reach an esplanade from which a metal footbridge leads several hundred feet out into the sea to a magnificent rock islet. This, the Virgin's Rock, is named for the statue of the Virgin crowning it, whose duty it has been since 1865 to protect the sailors and fishermen of the Bay of Biscay. The metal footbridge, built during the 1880s by craftsmen of the famous engineer Eiffel, replaces an earlier wooden one that was meant to be part of a large port Napoleon intended to build. The bridge allows visitors to walk all the way out to the terraced edge of the rock, a dramatic spot high above the crashing surf, for classic views of the sea, the coastline, or, simply, down. Esplanade de la Vierge.

Musée de la Mer – The same esplanade that gives access to the Rocher de la Vierge also holds a simple but touching monument to the city's casualties during the two World Wars as well as this museum, dedicated to the sea and its inhabitants. It currently is undergoing a much needed renovation which will include a new aquarium. Founded in 1933, it has 3 floors of marine exhibits, maps of the ocean floor, and remnants of Biarritz's past whaling culture, including the impressive skull of a colossal whale. The museum's roof tank, home of three species of seals, also is being expanded and modernized. If you can, catch the seals at feeding time — 10:30 AM and at 5 PM each day. Open daily from 9 AM to 6 PM (future plans include evening hours once the renovation is completed). Admission charge. Esplanade de la Vierge, 14 Plateau Atalaye (phone: 59-24-02-59).

Plage du Port-Vieux – This small horseshoe beach is along the pathway on the other side of the Atalaye plateau. It's well protected by rocks, and the shallow, calm waters are favored by families with children. The *Port Vieux Club*, a restaurant with a terrace and a small disco, is tucked into the rocks at the back of the beach.

La Perspective – From Port Vieux, the path leads up to yet another plateau, where the flower-lined promenade offers tremendous views north over the distance already covered and south over the vast and rocky Plage de la Côte des Basques as far as the mountains of Spain. Paved, switchback paths lined with benches and stone balustrades crisscross the steep incline that drops from La Perspective to the beach, which is the wildest and most exposed in Biarritz and the one most highly regarded by surfers. At high tide, however, the entire stretch of the Plage de la Côte des Basques is forbidding, with breakers crashing at the base of the cliffs and splashing onto Boulevard du Prince-de-Galles only feet away from the seawall. In the cliff face over the boulevard are the remains of bunkers from World War II.

Musée de l'Automobile Miniature – The newest addition to Biarritz's museums, this one houses a collection of over 6,000 miniature models of cars, fire trucks, and other vehicles. There's an audiovisual presentation of the history of the automobile. Open daily from 10 AM to noon and 3 to 7 PM (until 9 PM on Fridays) during the summer; daily except Tuesdays from 1 to 6 PM weekdays, and 10 AM to noon and 3 to 6 PM on weekends during the winter. 13 Plateau Atalaye (phone: 59-24-52-50).

ELSEWHERE

Eglise St.-Martin – Biarritz's only old religious monument is up the hill and away from the beaches and the town center. Probably begun in the 12th century, it was restored in 1541 and has a Flamboyant Gothic chancel. Rue St.-Martin.

Musée Historique de Biarritz – Paintings, costumes, objets d'art, and documents illustrate the two principal activities of this port — fishing and agriculture. There also are exhibits showing life during Biarritz's golden era, when it was known as the "Beach of Kings," during and after the reign of Napoleon III. Closed Thursdays and Sundays. Open 3 to 6 PM. Salle Saint Andrew's, Rue Broquedis (phone: 59-24-86-28).

ENVIRONS

Musée Basque – An excellent museum of Basque culture, one of the best regional museums in France, is 5 miles (8 km) away in Bayonne. It has everything from traditional costumes, furniture, typical Basque interiors, and the tools of various local trades to theater, dance, and local history. A museum within the museum is devoted to the Basque game of *pelote,* with examples of the balls, gloves, rackets, bats, and baskets used, plus models of frontons. At press time, the museum was closed for renovations and scheduled to reopen early this year. Corner of Rue Marengo and Quai des Corsaires, Bayonne (phone: 59-59-08-98).

Musée Bonnat – This stately museum, also in Bayonne, was built at the end of the 19th century to house the works of art bequeathed to the city by a native son, the 19th-century painter and collector Léon Bonnat. Certainly one of the country's outstanding art galleries, its collection includes works from the 13th century to the Impressionists. Among them are — in addition to Bonnat's own paintings — some lovely Aragonese primitives, paintings by such Old Masters as Rubens and Rembrandt as well as such later masters as Goya, Ingres, Delacroix, and Degas, an archaeological collection, and a huge lode of drawings by Flemish, Dutch, Italian, French, and German artists from the Renaissance to the 19th century, which are displayed in changing exhibitions. Closed Tuesdays and holidays; admission charge. 5 Rue Jacques-Laffitte, Bayonne (phone: 59-59-08-52).

■**EXTRA SPECIAL:** One of the main reasons to make a day trip south along the Côte Basque is to visit St.-Jean-de-Luz, 9 miles (14 km) away. If Biarritz is "the Queen of Beaches," then this delightful resort, about half its size but with a broad scallop of safe and sandy beach on a well-protected bay, is at least a crown prince or princess. Like Biarritz, St.-Jean is a former whaling port turned fishing village, but in the process of becoming a resort, it has retained more of its Basque character than its neighbor and has not put its seafaring past entirely behind it. It remains an important fishing port, though the catch these days is largely tuna — in fact, an annual tuna festival is one of the town's summer celebrations (others are the weekly bullfights and a festival in honor of the Basque fish soup *ttoro*). The picturesque port and the maze of streets behind it are among the sightseeing attractions, as is the house in which Louis XIV lived in 1660 when he came here to marry Marie-Thérèse, the Infanta of Spain, as well as the interesting, typically Basque church where the ceremony took place. After a stop in St.-Jean-de-Luz (for restaurants or hotels, see the *Pyrénées* tour, DIRECTIONS), you can continue along the coastal road — Corniche Basque — to Hendaye, another popular resort, about 9 miles (14 km) away at the Spanish border. The views are magnificent en route, and some people consider the beaches of Hendaye the best on the coast.

SOURCES AND RESOURCES

TOURIST INFORMATION: Biarritz's Tourist Information Office, the Comité de Tourisme et des Fêtes (phone: 59-24-20-24), has its administrative headquarters centrally located in a suitably grand edifice — the Javalquinto Palace, former residence of the Dukes of Osuna — on Square d'Ixelles, near the corner of Av. Joseph-Petit and Rue Louis-Barthou. It is open daily except Sundays year-round and on Sunday mornings in season. The friendly, efficient staff, most of whom speak fluent English, will provide maps, hotel and restaurant listings, and any other information you might need, at no charge, and will assist in choosing a hotel or making reservations. A small pamphlet listing pertinent information about the city's amenities and essential services is available for a few francs. Though the tourist office does not operate regular sightseeing tours, it does furnish guides for larger groups and supplies information about a number of local companies operating excursion buses to the Pays Basque and other neighboring regions.

Local Coverage – The daily newspaper is *Sud-Ouest.* Many bookstores and other shops in the heart of town carry newspapers and magazines in English.

TELEPHONE: The city code for the Biarritz area (including Anglet, Bayonne, and St.-Jean-de-Luz) is 59, which is incorporated into all local 8-digit numbers. When calling a number in the Biarritz area from the Paris region (including the Ile-de-France), dial 16, wait for a dial tone, then dial the 8-digit number. When calling a number from outside Paris, dial only the 8-digit number. When calling from the US, dial 33 (which is the country code), followed by the 8-digit number.

GETTING AROUND: The most practical way to get around the center of town is to walk.

Bicycle – *Caron* (10 Av. de la Marne; phone: 59-24-06-31) and *Capdeboscq* (16 Av. Jaulerry; phone: 59-24-13-64) both rent bikes.

Bus – Public buses do not operate within Biarritz, but there is service (every half hour) between the center and the train station, and there are regular connections between Biarritz and neighboring communities. Call *STAB* (phone: 59-24-26-53) for information on buses to Anglet and Bayonne, *ATCRB* for information on buses to St.-Jean-de-Luz (phone: 59-24-36-72), and *TPR* (phone: 59-27-45-98) for information on buses to Pau.

Car Rentals – The major companies represented here include *Avis* (25 Av. Edouard-VII; phone: 59-24-33-44); *Budget* (32 Av. de Bayonne; phone: 59-63-11-77); *Europcar* (Rte. de Cazalis, near the airport; phone: 59-23-82-82); and *Hertz* (17 Av. Foch; phone: 59-24-02-01 or 59-03-65-53; 59-23-67-94 on Sundays and holidays).

Taxi – Though taxis don't generally cruise the winding streets in the heart of town, there's a station on Av. de Verdun (phone: 59-24-16-13) and there are radio taxi services, including *B.A.B. Radio Taxi* (phone: 59-63-17-17).

Train – The Biarritz–La Négresse train station is almost 2 miles (3 km) southeast of the center of town, about 10 minutes by bus. Along with Bayonne and St.-Jean-de-Luz, the resort is a regular stop for trains en route from Paris and Bordeaux to points in Spain. The trip from Biarritz to Bayonne takes approximately 10 minutes by train; to St.-Jean-de-Luz, about 15 minutes. For train information, call 59-23-58-97 or 59-55-50-50.

SPECIAL EVENTS: Biarritz's ambitious tourist authorities have worked hard over the past few years to enhance the city's appeal with creative and lively events, such as the week-long *Semaine de l'Amitié* (Week of Friendship) devoted to a different country and an aspect of its culture each July (a recent year featured jazz in Louisiana; the focus in 1990 will be the state of Georgia). Other events include annual golf tournaments during the summer and the *Festival du Film d'Entreprise* (Industrial Film Festival) in June. The city's *Bastille Day* fireworks, July 14, are stunning. The *Concours Hippique International,* a jumping championship in which equestrians from a dozen or more nations compete, falls in August. On August 15, *Nuit Féerique* (roughly translated, "magic" or "fairy" night), a grand fireworks display lights up the Grande Plage and the cliffs along the seafront. The following Sunday, for the traditional *Fête de la Mer* (Sea Festival), a helicopter drops flowers on the Rocher de la Vierge in memory of Biarritz's sailors, and there is a naval parade in late August, followed by the *Imperial Ball,* a relatively new Biarritz tradition with much sparkle and magic. September brings the *Festival International de Bridge,* the *Biarritz Arena Surf Masters* (the world championship of professional surfing), and the *Festival de Cinéma et de Télévision Ibérique et Latino Américain de Biarritz,* a Spanish- and Portuguese-language film and television festival. A music festival, predominantly classical, is held every fall. Two golf tournaments also take place in the fall: The *Pro-Am de Bulles Laurent Perrier,* which draws as many as 800 participants annually, takes place the last week of September or the first week of October; the annual *AGF Biarritz Ladies Open* is in late October.

 SHOPPING: The best shopping streets are Avenue Victor-Hugo, Rue Maza-gran, and Avenue Maréchal-Foch, all of which converge on Place Clemen-ceau, the heart of town. Such well-known names as *Cartier, Hermès, Cacharel,* and *Kenzo* are represented here by boutiques, even though, for the most part, the activity on the beaches is more important than that in the shops. Particularly noteworthy are a handful of shops specializing in household linen and other articles made of the colorful cotton and wool of the nearby Pays Basque. (You may pay more for them here than you would in the small towns in the Pyrénées, but the shops in Biarritz offer a wider selection and many will accept credit cards.) There also are several shops selling the gastronomic delicacies of the neighboring Landes and Gers regions — foie gras (goose liver), *confit d'oie* and *confit de canard* (flavorful preserved goose and duck), and Armagnac, to name just a few.

Arostéguy Maison – An *épicerie* carrying everything from Petrossian caviar to canned cassoulet. 5 Av. Victor-Hugo (phone: 59-24-00-52).

Bakara – Interesting antiques, old dolls, curiosities. 23 Rue Mazagran (phone: 59-22-08-95).

Boutique Fancy – A small ladies' specialty shop with a lovely, albeit expensive, selection of casual wear. 20 Pl. Clemenceau (phone: 59-24-22-75). A second shop, specializing in shoes, is at 2 Av. Maréchal-Foch.

Cannelle – Another women's boutique, with *prêt-à-porter* for summer and winter. 12 Rue Mazagran (phone: 59-24-51-47).

Daranatz – One of the best chocolate shops in Biarritz. 12 Av. Maréchal-Foch (phone: 59-24-21-91).

Dodin – The chocolate sold here is devastatingly tempting. 9 Pl. Clemenceau (phone: 59-24-16-37) and 7 Rue Gambetta (phone: 59-24-16-37).

Galérie des Arceaux – One of several local antiques shops, this one specializes in 19th-century furniture and porcelain. 14 Av. Edouard-VII (phone: 59-22-08-00).

Henriet – Chocolates, made with oranges, pistachios, and almonds. The *"rocher de Biarritz"* is a specialty. Pl. Clemenceau (phone: 59-24-24-15).

Hermès – For those who didn't have time to visit the Paris shop, this one offers much the same merchandise, with an emphasis on beachwear. Av. Edouard-VII (phone: 59-24-00-64).

Mille et Un Fromages – Cheese, wine, and other fixings for a picnic or a snack. 8 Av. Victor-Hugo (phone: 59-24-67-88).

Nouvelles Galéries-Biarritz Bonheur – The town's major department store, with everything from bikinis to bicycles and a supermarket in the basement. 17 Pl. Clemen-ceau (phone: 59-24-45-25).

Parfumerie Royale – The best names in perfume: Yves Saint Laurent, Guerlain, Shiseido, and many others. 1 Rue Mazagran (phone: 59-24-00-17).

Paries – A place for chocoholics. 27 Pl. Clemenceau (phone: 59-22-07-52).

Saint Léon – One of the most extensive collections of Basque linen. 18 Av. Victor-Hugo (phone: 59-24-19-81).

 SPORTS AND FITNESS: Not surprisingly, one of the city's strongest points is the wide range of sporting activities possible — on the water, on land, and at the well-equipped *Parc des Sports d'Aguiléra* complex east of town. The most popular spectator sport is the exceedingly fast *cesta punta,* one of the many varieties of the Basque ball game known as *pelote* (and very similar to the form of the game known in the United States as jai alai). Frequent *cesta punta* games are played at the *Euskal-Jaï* (phone: 59-23-91-09) fronton at the Aguiléra sports complex. Other forms of *pelote* are played at the open-air fronton at *Parc Mazon* (Av. Maréchal-Joffre); at the fronton at Plazi-Berri (Av. Maréchal-Foch; phone: 59-23-06-86); and at the *Trinquet St.-Martin* (Av. Pasteur; phone: 59-23-11-23).

Bowling – *Silver Bowling* is at the *Casino Municipal* and is open every day year-round from 3 PM to 2 AM. Enter from the Grande Plage (phone: 59-24-12-12).

Fishing – Surf casting and fishing from the rocks are popular. Contact the tourist office for information.

Golf – The city is justifiably proud of its elaborate *Centre International d'Entraîne-ment au Golf* (Golf Training Center; 10 Rte. National; phone: 59-23-74-65). And for practicing newly acquired skills, there are six topnotch golf courses within 15 miles (24 km) of the city. The two closest are *Golf du Biarritz* (Av. Edith-Cavell; phone: 59-03-71-80) and *Chiberta* (104 Bd. des Plages, in Anglet; phone: 59-63-83-20). Visitors are welcome.

Horseback Riding – To hire a horse, go to *Centre Equestre* (Allée Gabrielle-Dorziat; phone: 59-23-73-00), which also organizes group rides along the beach and offers instruction.

Sailing – *Monsieur Hontebeyrie,* at Port des Pêcheurs, rents Hobie Cats. The *International Sailing School* (phone: 59-47-06-32 or 59-02-38-06), in operation from mid-June to mid-September in nearby Socoa, next to St.-Jean-de-Luz, offers courses for all age groups at reasonable prices. *Haizean* (phone: 59-47-05-05) organizes day or week-end cruises.

Scuba Diving – The ocean floor, at depths of 15 feet and more, can be very beautiful when the weather is good. For information about equipment, lessons, and clubs, contact the tourist office.

Spas – Biarritz is a saltwater spa town: The *Centre de Thalassothérapie Louison Bobet* (Av. de l'Impératrice; phone: 59-24-20-80) and *Thermes Marins* (80 Rue de Madrid; phone: 59-23-01-22) both offer a variety of spa therapies. In early 1989, the latter moved into modern, sun-flooded quarters overlooking the sea, with state-of-the-art equipment and facilities.

Squash – *Milady Squash* (phone: 59-23-27-29) is at 86 Rue de Simonnet.

Surfing – Introduced in 1958 and one of Biarritz's big draws. The most intrepid surfers head for the Plage de la Côte des Basques; the Grande Plage is somewhat less exposed. *Ecole de Surf Plums* (5 Pl. Clemenceau; phone: 59-24-08-04) offers group and individual lessons. *Moraitz* surf shop (25 Rue Mazagran; phone: 59-24-22-09) offers classes, and sells and rents boards, as does the *Freedom Surf Shop* (2 Av. Reine Victoria; phone: 50-01-26-02).

Swimming – The safest beach is the *Plage du Port-Vieux.* In addition to that and all the other beaches, there are swimming pools. The *Piscine Municipale* (phone: 59-24-05-83), an indoor pool of heated seawater at the *Casino Municipal,* and the outdoor pool at the *Palais* hotel (phone: 59-24-09-40), also heated seawater, can both be used for a fee.

Tennis – There are 12 tennis courts (2 cement, 10 clay; 2 lighted) at the *Parc des*

Sports d'Aguiléra (phone: 59-24-25-96 or 59-23-93-24), and professionals are available for lessons. *Biarritz Olympique Tennis* (phone: 59-41-20-80) has 14 courts (4 are covered). Or reserve a court at the *Côte Basque Country Club* (phone: 59-52-22-55), just outside Biarritz along N10.

Windsurfing – Lessons and boards are available at *Yacht Club de Socoa* (phone: 59-47-13-31) or at *Quai 34* in nearby Guéthary (phone: 59-54-83-19).

THEATER AND MUSIC: Performances of Basque music and dancing take place frequently during the summer season. Two or three times a week, at either Parc Mazon or Plaza Berri, you'll be able to see a *pelote* match and a folklore exhibition. Much less frequently, the highly respected *Groupe Oldarra* presents its own Basque song and dance *spectacle,* also usually at Parc Mazon. In addition to the annual fall music festival, concerts by visiting and local individuals and ensembles take place year-round in venues such as the Eglise Ste.-Eugénie, the *Palais* hotel, and the *Casino Bellevue.*

NIGHTCLUBS AND NIGHTLIFE: About a dozen establishments in Biarritz call themselves nightclubs. Among the more sophisticated and popular of the lot are the chic *Copacabana* (22 Av. Edouard-VII; phone: 59-24-65-39); the *Play Boy* (Pl. Clemenceau; phone: 59-24-38-46), an old if now slightly fading favorite where the music is recorded and shifts in mood with the mood of the disk jockey; and *Scala* (Bd. Général-de-Gaulle; phone: 59-24-74-90), where the recorded music varies — rock, new wave, etc. — and the crowd is young. Dress is casual in all four. The *Casino Bellevue* (Pl. Bellevue; phone: 59-24-11-22) is open daily in season from about 4 PM. General entry is free, but you pay a small sum to enter the room where baccarat, roulette, and blackjack are played. It has a nightclub, *La Plantation*.

BEST IN TOWN

CHECKING IN: At last count, Biarritz's hotel inventory numbered nearly 1,000 rooms, their comforts ranging from the super luxe of the *Palais* to the simplicity of various small budget hotels that are nevertheless near the beaches and in the path of refreshing sea breezes. A healthy number of rooms in all categories have ocean views, and about 60% of the hotels are open year-round. During high season — July through September — some of the hotels operate on a full-pension system, charging a flat rate per person for room and board, including continental breakfast, lunch, and dinner. Reserving in advance is recommended highly if you want a room during July or August, but the tourist office will try to assist travelers who need help finding rooms. There also are a number of hotels in the neighboring beach communities of Bidart and Anglet, both rapidly becoming important resorts in their own right. In the hotels listed below, expect to pay $80 and up for a double room in high season (without full pension) in the expensive category, from $50 to $80 in the moderate category, and under $50 in the inexpensive category.

Château de Brindos – A charming Italianate villa hidden in a thick grove of trees at the edge of a lake filled with water lilies and some swans. The lovely surroundings, the grand interiors, the highly rated restaurant (see *Eating Out*), and the availability of only 13 rooms make it a perfect choice for those who prefer tranquillity to proximity to the beach (though the hotel does have a heated swimming pool as well as a tennis court). The restaurant is closed from early January to March. Lac de Brindos, approximately 3 miles (5 km) southeast of Biarritz, off N10 (phone: 59-23-17-68). Expensive.

Miramar – One of the most modern properties in Europe. Unfortunately, the building itself looks like a nuclear-age command center, but the 126 rooms and suites are undeniably comfortable, the service is excellent, and the restaurant has earned a Michelin star. It also has a lobby bar, boutiques, gym, sauna, heated seawater swimming pool (outdoor), and the *Centre de Thalassothérapie Louison Bobet* (a saltwater spa). 11 Av. de l'Impératrice (phone: 59-41-30-00). Expensive.

Palais – This imposing imperial villa dominating the Grande Plage still looks much as it did when Eugénie and Napoleon spent their summers here in the 19th century. In its reincarnation as a 140-room hotel, it offers a renovated version of the Old World grandeur to which its original owners were accustomed: public rooms still rife with marble floors, columns, chandeliers, and draperies; guestrooms done with period furnishings; attentive service. The heated seawater swimming pool on a terrace by the beach has cabanas and a casual poolside restaurant that draws the lunch crowd, and there are two more formal restaurants, *La Rotonde* and the *Grand Siècle* (see *Eating Out* for both). Closed from November to *Easter*. 1 Av. de l'Impératrice (phone: 59-24-09-40). Expensive.

Régina et Golf – A luxury hostelry that offers old-fashioned grandeur on a small scale. It's set majestically above the city on a plateau near the lighthouse, public gardens, and golf course, and many of its 70 rooms, most of them recently remodeled, have breathtaking views. There also is a restaurant specializing in seafood. Closed from November through April. 52 Av. de l'Impératrice (phone: 59-41-33-00). Expensive.

Plaza – Fairly modern and unpretentious, this 60-room place has a gracious air and a prime location overlooking the beaches and the center of Biarritz. The rooms are spacious and well furnished, and most have balconies commanding an ocean view. The bar is a rich, elegant room; the staff understands some English; there are parking facilities. Actually, you get more than you pay for here. Open year-round. Av. Edouard-VII (phone: 59-24-74-00). Expensive to moderate.

Président – A typical "French modern" property that might seem more at home in a business center than a resort. Nonetheless, its 64 rooms are comfortable, and it's handy for the beach, restaurants, and shopping. No restaurant. Open year-round. Pl. Clemenceau (phone: 59-24-66-40). Expensive to moderate.

Le Château du Clair de Lune – Just 10 minutes from Biarritz, this is an exquisite miniature château set well back from the road and surrounded by gardens and woods. A treasure of simple refinement, it has 7 individually decorated rooms and the ambience of a private home. 48 Av. Alan Seeger, Rte. d'Arbonne (phone: 59-23-45-96). Moderate.

Windsor – The oceanside door of this 37-room hostelry is just a frog's leap from the Grande Plage. The welcome is friendly, and the rooms, many with views, are simply decorated and comfortable. Closed from mid-November to mid-March. 11 Av. Edouard-VII, Grande Plage (phone: 59-24-08-52). Moderate.

Le Petit Hôtel – One of the best bargains in town, on a tiny street in the heart of Biarritz. It has a fresh, pretty lobby and 12 cheerful rooms. The owners, Mme. and M. Puig, are charming people. 11 Rue Garderes (phone: 59-24-87-00). Moderate to inexpensive.

Edouard-VII – Simple, with 15 rooms and up the hill from the beaches and town center. The jovial proprietor is a gem; his rooms are clean (though not fancy), his restaurant serves good home-style food, and there is a delightful dining terrace. Closed from October through February. 21 Av. Carnot (phone: 59-24-07-20). Inexpensive.

Palacito – Though the welcome here can be curt, this 26-room hotel is conveniently located, clean, reasonably priced, and open all year except for 2 weeks in January. No restaurant. Sq. Gambetta (phone: 59-24-04-89). Inexpensive.

EATING OUT: From a gastronomic point of view, Biarritz is ideally situated. A rich fishing center with all manner of fresh fish and seafood, it also benefits from its proximity to the Landes and Gers regions, rich in foie gras, and to the Basque country, famous for air-dried ham, fish soups (such as the peppery *ttoro*), and Basque cakes. The resort's restaurants, therefore, are impressive in their number and variety, and the quality is, for the most part, high, while the prices remain reasonable. (A definite trend is the proliferation of ample, inexpensive fixed-price menus in places that would otherwise be considered very pricey.) Dinner for two in an expensive restaurant will cost $85 and up, not including wine (service usually is included); in a restaurant listed as moderate, between $50 and $85; and in an inexpensive eatery, less than $50. With your meal, try the Madiran and Jurançon wines of the region.

Café de Paris – An airy, garden-like spot in the shadow of the *Casino Bellevue,* considered by some to be the best dining establishment on France's Atlantic coast. Pierre Laporte, son of the founder of this Biarritz landmark, opened in 1927, directs the kitchen and generally lives up to his reputation, which merits one Michelin star. There is a special fixed-price menu for two. Closed from November to mid-March and Mondays in low season. Reservations advised. 5 Pl. Bellevue (phone: 59-24-19-53). Expensive.

Château de Brindos – It's worth a visit to this tranquil villa-hotel if only to enjoy a meal in its beautifully appointed dining room overlooking the lake. The food won't let you down, however; Basque specialties and dishes such as *mousseline* of turbot encased in puff pastry rate one Michelin star. Closed from early January to March. Reservations advised. About 3 miles (5 km) southeast of Biarritz, just off N10 (phone: 59-23-17-68). Expensive.

La Rotonde – Though the ornate chandeliers, marble columns, and other Belle Epoque touches of the *Palais*'s panoramic round dining room set you up for the rather dusty old clichés of hotel food, there have been some well-received shifts to lighter, more modern specialties lately. (Also worth trying is the hotel's newer "gastronomic" restaurant, *Le Grand Siècle,* with chef Gregoire Sein at the stove.) Closed from mid-October to May. Reservations advised. *Hôtel du Palais,* 1 Av. de l'Impératrice (phone: 59-24-09-40). Expensive.

Galion – Ocean views, a marine motif, and nouvelle cuisine featuring fresh seafood are the attractions of this local favorite. Closed Sundays, Monday dinner, and during February. Reservations advised. 17 Av. Général-de-Gaulle (phone: 59-24-20-32). Expensive to moderate.

La Gascogne – A staid, conservative, yet comfortable sort of place, where people talk in whispers above their china dinner plates. Its fixed-price menus are a comparative bargain. For lunch, they feature such things as *salade basquaise* and *poulet basquaise;* at dinnertime, one of the recommended combinations includes fresh, giant oysters followed by a three-layered fish pâté and a chicken dish served with a delicious tarragon and cream sauce. Closed from mid-December to mid-February. Reservations advised. 11 Av. du Maréchal-Foch (phone: 59-24-20-12). Expensive to moderate.

L'Alambic – A slick, modern grill room, this is Pierre Laporte's second dining spot, less expensive and more casual than his elegant *Café de Paris* next door. The diverse, buffet-style hors d'oeuvres, the prime ribs, steaks, and the paella are among the things to try. Closed November to March and on Mondays off-season. Reservations advised. 3 Pl. Bellevue (phone: 59-24-53-41). Moderate.

La Belle Epoque – The entrance to this genteel dining room is through a crystal and silver boutique. The decor is true to the name, with handsome wood and a central dining court with palm trees. The food, however, is up to date and creative. The *ragoût du pêcheur* (fish stew) contains everything that swims. Closed for 2 weeks in January and on Mondays off-season. Reservations advised. 10 Av. Victor-Hugo (phone: 59-24-66-06). Moderate.

Chez Albert – The largest and best known of a handful of delightful, casual seafood eateries tucked away in the old Port des Pêcheurs, below Place Eugénie. Dinner comes with entertainment in the form of Albert, your flamboyant host. Closed Wednesdays and from December to April. Reservations advised. Port des Pêcheurs (phone: 59-24-43-84). Moderate.

Le Comptoir – Sleek and contemporary, this brasserie near the center of town looks onto a beautiful garden and offers good quality at a resonable price. Reservations advised on weekends. On the corner of Rue Monhaut (phone: 59-24-46-46). Moderate.

Les 3 Salsas – For those homesick for south-of-the-border fare, this casual, popular spot specializes in Mexican dishes. Closed off-season. Reservations unnecessary. 5 Rue Harispe (phone: 59-23-04-53). Moderate.

Le Vaudeville – A trendy addition to the city's dining scene, where residents and well-informed visitors enjoy fine food at reasonable prices. Closed Monday and Tuesday lunch, 10 days in February, and 10 days in June. Reservations advised. 5 Rue du Centre (phone: 59-24-34-66). Moderate.

Auberge de la Négresse – Bright, active, and near the train station, it's off the beaten beach track, a bit tricky to find but worth the search. The simple, traditional specialties that keep it crowded include foie gras, grilled *louvine* (sea bass, or *loup,* in local parlance), and roast milk-fed lamb. The head cook also is a butcher and does wonders with meat dishes. Closed Mondays and October. Reservations unnecessary. 10 Av. de l'Aérodrome, under the viaduct (phone: 59-23-15-83). Moderate to inexpensive.

Les Flots Bleus – Perched on the cliffs overlooking Plage de la Côte des Basques, this wonderful family place is far from the commotion of the town center. You can order anything from Italian food to Moroccan couscous to *crêpes à la provençale,* though the specialties are seafood dishes of the region, including a fresh fish soup that could feed a boatload of people. If you're lucky, you'll be served by Madame Casagrande, originally from Venice, who has customers returning from as near as Bordeaux and as far as the Jersey shore and San Diego. When you meet her, you'll understand why. Open year-round. Reservations unnecessary. 41 Perspective Côte Basques (phone: 59-24-10-03). Moderate to inexpensive.

BARS AND CAFÉS: A popular spot with locals and visitors alike is *Les Colonnes* (4 Av. Edouard-VII). It has a perfectly coordinated wood, leather, brass, and bamboo interior, a terrace in front with tables and chairs set under a portico, and a view of the ocean and beach beyond. *Le Choucas,* a lively, sleek, but not overbearing café on Place Clemenceau, is perfect for people watching. Also on Place Clemenceau is the newly renovated *La Coupole* (phone: 59-24-09-96) and the café/bar *Le Royalty* (phone: 59-24-01-34). Recorded pop/rock plays continually and a live band performs several nights a week and on weekends (from 10 PM until customers feel like going home). Snacks are served at any hour. *Le Corsaire,* on the tiny waterfront of Port des Pêcheurs, used to be a highly regarded seafood restaurant. Now it is an intimate bar, small and cozy inside, with stucco walls, brass lamps, and pop/disco playing softly from the speakers. Another alternative: *Bar Le Mazagran,* a homey, friendly café and *salon de thé* on Rue Mazagran at the head of Pl. Ste.-Eugénie; its ice cream sundaes are recommended.

BORDEAUX

The people of Bordeaux pronounce the name of their city slowly, with great import. They roll the syllables on their tongues as if each vowel were a fine wine to be savored and appreciated. Bordeaux, originally the Latin *Burdigal,* was founded on the bank of the Garonne River where it suddenly diverts from its meandering path to take the shape of a gigantic crescent moon. A quick glance at a map will show how the city also has taken this shape, as have the two major roads that loop around it. It's only fitting that the symbol of Bordeaux, then, is a crescent moon.

Originally a village of Gallic tribes, Bordeaux prospered as a military headquarters for the colonizing Romans, who introduced grape growing to the region. The town withstood assaults by successive waves of Visigoths, Arabs, and Normans, and first began to achieve mercantile fame as an English city. It was part of the dowry of the colorful Eleanor (Alienor), daughter of the ruling Duke of Aquitaine and Count of Poitiers, on her marriage, at age 15, to the future Louis VII of France. In 1152, after 15 years and two daughters, Louis sued for annulment and, in his eagerness to be rid of his high-spirited wife, tossed back the riches she had brought to the ill-fated union. Eleanor, then 30 years old, packed up and left "the monk in a crown," as her circle contemptuously referred to him, and to the amazement of all married the teenage Henry Plantagenet, Duke of Normandy and Count of Anjou, 2 months later. The gilded couple's combined territories in France equaled those of the French sovereign, and when Henry inherited the crown of England in 1154, a long struggle for the possession of the Aquitaine began between the English and French.

Throughout the Anglo-French wars of the next 3 centuries, the Bordelais considered themselves more English than French and were content to remain under the rule of England. The laissez-faire policies of the English crown granted a privileged independence to the shippers and traders of the city, and the English taste for claret, as the English alone called the red wines of Bordeaux, allowed the wine growers to increase their production many times over. By the middle of the 14th century, the equivalent of a million modern cases of wine was leaving the port of Bordeaux yearly, much of it for the thirsty market across the English Channel.

Bordeaux, along with the rest of the province of Aquitaine, reverted to France at the conclusion of the Hundred Years War in 1453. Although the English influence then waned, the long arm of the Parisian government did not make itself felt in any consistent way until the 18th century, when Louis XV ascended the throne. An economic boom, begun during the reign of Louis XIV, was well under way in Bordeaux. The city was shipping wine, foodstuffs, and textiles as far away as the expanding colonial markets in America and the West Indies, and wine, armaments, hardware, and manufactured goods to Africa. Foreign ships brought fine wood, tobacco, rum, sugar, coffee, and raw materials into its port.

This enormously profitable mercantile operation enriched both private and public purses, and provided a steady flow of cash for the vast program of public works that transformed Bordeaux into one of the most handsome provincial cities in France. The king, aware of Bordeaux's commercial and strategic importance, appointed governors (*intendants*) to oversee the city during this period, and it is to them that it owes its modern face. Each *intendant* in turn tried to outdo his predecessor in clearing away slums, crowded alleyways, and swampy marshland to create broad quays, public parks, and boulevards lined with splendid *hôtels particuliers.* Many of these mansions still stand today as townhouses for the wealthiest shippers and wine growers. Public buildings dating from this era include the 18th-century architectural ensemble of Place de la Bourse, with the Hôtel des Douanes (Customs House) and the Hôtel de la Bourse (Stock Exchange), the Hôtel de Ville (originally the Palais Rohan) with its beautifully landscaped mayoral garden, and the *Grand Théâtre.* Other striking samples of this heritage can be seen around Place de la Comédie, Place Gambetta, and Place Tourny and the streets connecting them — Cours Clemenceau, Cours de l'Intendance, and Allées de Tourny.

During the late 19th century, Bordeaux suffered a disastrous and bewildering upheaval brought about by the invasion of the American vine louse *Phylloxera vastatrix,* which ate the roots of the source of "red gold" in the surrounding vineyards. The cost to France was incalculable, but one estimate puts it at more than that of the Franco-Prussian War of 1870–71. Finally, the roots of native American species, which were immune to the parasite, were grafted onto the French vine stocks, and eventually business resumed and Bordeaux recovered its economic balance. Even with the foreign roots, the growers assert that the vineyards reach deep into French soil and the wine produced is purely French.

The life, livelihood, and lure of Bordeaux do not rest solely on the reputation of the wine produced almost in its backyard, as the Bordelais are the first to tell you. The city also is well known for its interest in architectural revival, particularly of buildings dating from the 18th century. Everywhere in the city, restoration and rehabilitation are in progress, but nowhere is this resurgence more obvious and exciting than in the old part of town by the river, Vieux Bordeaux. Recently the restoration work has extended into the adjacent St.-Michel quarter. Along many of the cobbled streets of these old quarters, workers are busily scraping away dingy façades and exposing amber stone, drawing deserved attention to ancient doorways, window trims, and gracefully curving stairways. Everywhere, too, the eye is entertained by fine examples of the ornamental ironwork and hardware — lacy balcony railings, handsome door knockers and hinges — with which Bordeaux's buildings, particularly those of the 18th century, are so admirably adorned.

Bordeaux is also a cultural and trade center, holding important industrial conferences at a complex called Le Lac. And it is a vacation spot as well, because in every direction, and in each case no more than an hour away, lie places to go for a day, a weekend, or a week or more of relaxation, exercise, or cultural diversion. Due east lies the picturesque medieval village and wine producing area of St.-Emilion; due south, the serene forests of Les Landes, with tiny villages and extensive bicycle and horse trails; to the southwest, the Arcachon Basin and the old resort town from which it takes its name; and west and northwest lie miles of beaches backed by forest and two large lakes perfect for swimming, fishing, and boating. And almost due north lies the Médoc, acres of the most noble vineyards in France. Nestled in a bend of the Garonne River, Bordeaux beckons travelers not only to a vital urban center, the home of almost 600,000 people and filled with attractions to look at, stroll through, buy, and admire, but also to an entire region of abiding richness and beauty.

BORDEAUX AT-A-GLANCE

SEEING THE CITY: Bordeaux is a flat city that boasts no skyscraper or revolving rooftop restaurant from which to view the pleasing network of wide boulevards, smaller streets, and winding passageways. The tower of Eglise St.-Michel, the tallest structure in the city, unfortunately is not open to the public. You can get a marvelous view, especially in the evening, by crossing over to the east bank of the Garonne on the Pont de Pierre and heading north until you are opposite the Place de la Bourse and Porte Cailhau; from here you see the impressive buildings along the quays and the entry to the old city. In the center, marvelous squares — Place de la Comédie, Place Gambetta, Place du Parlement, Place Tourny, for instance — with streets branching off them in every direction open up to give the effect of looking at different parts of the city through a wide-angle lens.

SPECIAL PLACES: Bordeaux is best seen on foot. The downtown area, for example, is traversed easily beginning at the Place de la Comédie, the heart of town. Wander up Cours de l'Intendance as far as Place Gambetta, stopping at Eglise Notre-Dame on Place du Chapelet (Rue Martignac leads there). At Place Gambetta, you can sip coffee at the outdoor café, *Le Régent,* study a map, and people watch. From Porte Dijeaux — an early corruption of Porte des Juifs — follow Rue Bouffard to its end, where you will find Cathédrale St.-André on your left and the Hôtel de Ville (Town Hall), backed by the *Musée des Beaux-Arts,* on your right; flip a coin to see which to visit first. Then follow the pedestrian Rue des Trois Conils along the modern St.-Christoly commercial center toward the river as far as Place St.-Projet, the oldest town square in the city and once a source of fresh water from underground springs for the community. Turn left onto Rue Ste.-Catherine, another pedestrian street (but don't be surprised when motorcycles, even cars, whiz by) that will take you back to the Place de la Comédie. If you have a little energy left, stroll along Allées de Tourny, surely one of the loveliest thoroughfares in Bordeaux, named after the governor who perhaps did the most to beautify the city. Another area, the most exciting these days because of the burgeoning restoration movement and the proliferation of small restaurants, shops, and galleries, is Vieux Bordeaux (Old Bordeaux). This section twists and turns from the river at Porte Cailhau, and almost every street leads to a pleasant discovery of one kind or another. It's the kind of place that encourages you to get happily and irrevocably lost, though in your meanderings be sure to find Rue des Argentiers and Rue des Bahutiers — silversmiths' and chestmakers' streets — named for the merchants who used to work along them. Finally, there are the special places that require a bit of a hike, a drive, a bus ride, or perhaps a boat ride, but are their own reward for the effort it takes to get there.

DOWNTOWN

Grand Théâtre – Designed by the architect Victor Louis (who also designed the famous arcades of the Palais-Royal in Paris) and completed in 1780, this theater, with its 12 Corinthian pillars, has been the inspiration for theaters around the world, including *L'Opéra* in Paris. The 12 statues of muses and goddess-patrons of the arts, posed regally on the front balcony, extend an open invitation to enjoy a theatrical, operatic, or philharmonic event. The interior is richly decorated and the acoustics are practically perfect. Pl. de la Comédie (phone: 56-90-91-60; for reservations, 56-48-58-54).

Maison du Vin – This striking, flatiron-shaped building is a source of information about wine, wine making, and châteaux in the region that are open for tours and tastings. Changing exhibits, as well as blind tastings in the handsome, remodeled ground-floor center, make it all the more interesting. Closed Saturday afternoons and Sundays. 1 Cours du 30-Juillet (phone: 56-00-22-66).

Eglise Notre-Dame – An Italian Revival church of the late 17th and early 18th century, completely restored inside and out. Tucked away on Place du Chapelet at the end of Rue Martignac, just off Cours de l'Intendance.

Musée des Beaux-Arts (Fine Arts Museum) – In existence since the early 19th century, this small museum was created at the behest of Napoleon Bonaparte when he was premier consul of France. It houses an important collection of paintings and sculpture, with the emphasis on French works (Delacroix, Redon, Corot, Matisse, Seurat, Renoir, and Rodin), although Italian and Flemish painters also are well represented. Open 10 AM to noon and 2 to 6 PM; closed Tuesdays. Guided visits by appointment. Entrance in the garden of the Hôtel de Ville, Cours d'Albret. The *Galerie des Beaux-Arts,* cater-cornered to the museum and entered from Pl. du Colonel-Raynal, is open only for special exhibitions (phone: 56-90-91-60).

Musée d'Aquitaine – Bordeaux's oldest museum (1781) is in a restored and modernized 1885 building. It houses permanent collections and temporary exhibitions covering the Bordeaux area from prehistoric times to the present — though only those rooms covering the years from 1715 (half the total) were open last year; the remainder were expected to reopen as we went to press. The history, agriculture, aquaculture, viticulture, commerce, art, and daily life of the province are well illustrated, in almost an acre of rooms, through artworks, tools, documents, and more. Also displayed are some of the books of Nobel Prize winner François Mauriac, one of France's most famous contemporary writers (d. 1970). A Bordeaux native, Mauriac drew much inspiration for his work from the area. The museum is open from 10 AM to 6 PM; closed Tuesdays; no admission charge on Wednesdays. 20 Cours Pasteur at the corner of Cours Victor-Hugo (phone: 56-90-91-60).

Hôtel de Ville (Town Hall) – Formerly the Palais Rohan, it was built in the 18th century for the prince-archbishop, later cardinal, de Rohan, who declared, when he insisted on the lavish dwelling, "I am not a king, I wouldn't consider being a prince, I am a Rohan!" Features of the original decoration include finely carved wainscoting, the grand staircase, and the monotone mural paintings (grisailles) by the Bordelais painter Lacour in the grand dining room. The interior now consists mainly of offices and state rooms, which are closed to all except groups (ask at the tourist office or the Town Hall), but the exterior is worth a look for its simple, striking lines. The lintels of the windows in the side sections are decorated with garlands of fruit; the interior wainscoting is the work of the Bordeaux sculptor Cabirol. Guided visits on Wednesdays at 2:30 PM are open to the public. The garden, flanked on one side by the *Musée des Beaux-Arts,* closes at 6:30 PM, except 8:30 or 9 PM in summer. Pl. Pey-Berland.

Cathédrale St.-André – The original cathedral was built during the 11th and 12th centuries and portions were added during the boom period of British rule; when the funds ran out, the building-in-progress stopped. To an amateur's eye, at least, the existing hodgepodge, complete with flying buttresses, appears all of a piece, if not downright winsome, in its gracefully landscaped setting. Inside, the cathedral is surprisingly light and airy, and a magnificent organ fills the back of it. Through its impressive 13th-century Porte Royale have passed the lowly and the great. Viollet-le-Duc made moldings of some of the statues of the door to use in his restoration of Notre-Dame in Paris. The representations of the Apostles, Last Judgment, Resurrection, and Divine Court are particularly beautiful. Pl. Pey-Berland.

Centre National Jean Moulin – The center is named for the writer, artist, and Resistance hero who was murdered by Klaus Barbie's Gestapo headquartered at Lyons. Only a few years old, it houses an extensive collection related to the events of World War II, including important documents and photographs detailing the history and achievements of the Resistance. Don't overlook the powerful paintings by Jean-Jacques Morvan on the second floor and the reproduction of Moulin's clandestine office on the third floor. Open weekdays from 2 to 6 PM; closed weekends and holidays. Pl. Jean Moulin (phone: 56-90-91-60).

VIEUX BORDEAUX (OLD BORDEAUX)

Porte Cailhau – This is one of the entries to the old city, dating from 1495. Although it now stands alone, it's possible to see where the ramparts once were attached. Just north of Pont de Pierre at Quai de la Douane.

Eglise St.-Pierre – A small Romanesque church built from the 15th to the 19th century. On Thursday mornings, the food market in the square facing the church is a good place for lunch. Pl. St.-Pierre.

Place du Parlement – Constructed primarily around 1760, this is one of the quietest, sunniest, and most tranquil of Bordeaux's lovely *places*. Any of the small streets branching from it inevitably lead to restaurant or a tiny shop full of treasures. Due east is the Place de la Bourse.

Place de la Bourse (former Stock Exchange) – This square was laid out and built from 1730 to 1755. The beautiful grouping of warm, gold-tinged stone laced with elegant wrought iron is a fitting symbol of the wealth and taste of the age. Quai de la Douane, north of Pont de Pierre.

Les Quais – Walk along the quays from St. Michael's Church to Place de la Bourse — braving the noise and car fumes — to appreciate the backdrop of 18th-century buildings. Most notable are the faces carved over doorways and in walls; called *mascarons,* they represent the people of Bordeaux at that time, from shipper to slave, as well as mythology and fantasy. Supposedly there are a couple of hundred *mascarons,* no two of them alike. Quais des Salinières, Quai Richelieu, Quai de la Douane.

Pont de Pierre – It's impossible not to notice this graceful, low-slung, and recently restored bridge with its 17 arches looping the Garonne. Remarkably, it was Bordeaux's only bridge from the time it was built, in 1822, until the completion of Pont St.-Jean in 1965. It's most beautiful at dusk. Opposite Pl. de Bir-Hakeim.

Eglise St.-Michel – The basilica of St. Michael's was badly damaged during World War II, but the modern stained glass windows over the high altar work well in their 15th-century setting. Two original windows from the 16th century remain in the transept. The bell tower, built separately, at 375 feet is the tallest in the south of France. Pl. St.-Michel at Rue des Faures.

La Grosse Cloche (The Great Bell) – Along busy Cours Victor-Hugo, lined with 18th- and 19th-century buildings, this 13th- to 16th-century clock tower looks oddly out of place. The bell used to signal the beginning of the grape harvest but now chimes only on days of national rejoicing. Beside the tower is the tiny Eglise St.-Eloi, which was built into the wall of the old city. There is a movement afoot to restore this church, named after the patron saint of ironworkers; it is not now open to the public. Rue St.-James, just off Cours Victor-Hugo.

Maison des Montaigne – Built in the 16th century, the family home of the philosopher Michel de Montaigne still stands, though it is privately owned and not open to the public. (The Château de Montaigne, where he was born and died, is about 30 miles/48 km east of Bordeaux.) 23-25 Rue de la Rousselle.

Cité Internationale des Vins – This ambitious project, currently under construction and targeted for completion in 1992, will be a 5-acre trade and cultural center dedicated to the wine industry. It is in the Chartrons district, where for centuries the majority of the wine activity of the region was carried on. The area will include restored *chais,* an international *maison des vins* and market, a wine museum, a research center, shops, pedestrian walks, and restaurants. There also will be a 150-room, four-star hotel on a ship docked at Quai des Chartrons. Between Cours Xavier Arnozan (where many of the elite of Bordeaux have their mansions), Cours de Verdun, and Quai des Chartrons.

Casa de Goya and Espace Goya – Two institutions in the house where the painter lived and died in exile. They include a permanent exhibition of Goya's life in Bordeaux and replicas of his rooms, and a Spanish cultural center offering occasional movies, concerts, lectures, and exhibitions. Open weekdays from 1:30 to 6 PM and also Wednesday mornings from 9 to noon; closed on weekends. There are guided tours the first Friday of the month at 2:30 PM for a small fee. 57 Cours de l'Intendance (phone: 56-52-79-37).

ELSEWHERE

Musée d'Art Contemporain/L'Entrepôt Lainé – During the 1800s and early 1900s this was the storehouse for the coffee, rum, wood, and spices shipped to Bordeaux from its colonies. Today it is a storehouse for talent, the up-and-coming modern arts center in southwest France. In 1973 the city saved the building from demolition and completely remodeled it inside to accommodate art exhibits and to house the *Musée d'Art Contemporain,* incorporating the *Centre d'Art Plastique Contemporain (CAPC).* From its beginning as a center with temporary exhibits, the *CAPC* has blossomed into an increasingly important museum. Closed Mondays. The museum café is pleasant and inexpensive. Near Quai des Chartrons and the Esplanade des Quinconces. 3 Rue Ferrère at Rue Foy (phone: 56-44-16-35).

Jardin Public – A 5-minute walk from the Place Tourny or Esplanade des Quinconces, this idyllic spot, surrounded by 19th-century townhouses, is the place to see the Bordelais at rest and at play — young children, with a parent or two in tow, and retired friends knitting, reading, or chatting on park benches. The tiny pond is put to good use by swans, ducks, and by children going for a joy ride in a small boat called *Le Petit Mousse.* Also here is an old and charming botanical garden and a bust by the sculptor Zadkine of 20th-century writer François Mauriac, a native son of Bordeaux and a Nobel Prize winner. Open until 8 PM, and an hour later in summer. Cours de Verdun.

Palais Gallien (Roman Palace) – A relic of Bordeaux's distant past, this 3rd-century Roman amphitheater could accommodate 15,000 spectators. The ruins are blocked from public access, but it is possible to get a couple of worthwhile views of them. Just follow Rue du Palais Gallien to its end, in the direction of the traffic.

Eglise St.-Seurin – In the middle of a busy commercial and residential neighborhood, this appears to be an edifice that time forgot. Residents walk their dogs and chat in the church grounds, while a hundred feet away lies an 11th-century crypt with 6th-century tombs, discovered only in the 1960s. Guided tours of the crypt are offered by the tourist office, and an audiovisual show about the archaeological findings is presented from April through October on Tuesday and Saturday afternoons at 2 and 6 PM. Painters often congregate in the garden here the first Saturday afternoon of each month. Pl. des Martyrs-de-la-Résistance (phone: 56-48-22-08).

Quartier Mériadeck – Although this modern complex of chrome, concrete, and steel buildings is almost right across the street from the *Fine Arts Museum,* it's easy to miss if you don't know it's here. Not only interesting as a modern center for living, working, and shopping in what is essentially an 18th-century city, its plaza and the varied styles of its buildings deserve a look. While you're here, drop by the 5-story *Centre Commercial de Mériadeck* with 100 boutiques. Between Rues Jean-Fleuret and Claude-Bonnier, opposite the garden of the Hôtel de Ville.

Cimetière de la Chartreuse – Graveyard lovers should wend their way a few blocks west of Mériadeck to this very old cemetery, with its interesting tombs, at St. Bruno's Church; both church and cemetery date from the 18th century. The church has a painting by Philippe de Champaigne and a statue by Bernini; the cemetery has a monument marking the spot where Goya was temporarily buried. Open 8 AM to 6 PM. Corner of Rue François-de-Sourdis and Rue Georges-Bonnac (phone: 56-93-17-20).

Le Lac – North of downtown Bordeaux — and a car, bus, or taxi ride away — this is a conference and exposition center with a lake for sailing, a golf course, as well as a stadium and a rose garden. In June, *Le Lac* is the site of a well-known wine exposition. It also is the site of several comfortable hotels (see *Checking In*). The drawbacks of Bordeaux-le-Lac are that it is out of the way in a not very attractive area, and as one Bordelais summed it up, "The lake is artificial, but the mosquitoes are real." West of the Pont d'Aquitaine.

ENVIRONS

Blaye – This small walled city, built in 1688–89, is on the right bank of the Gironde about 30 miles (48 km) north of Bordeaux. It can be reached by boat, and of the several boat trips possible from Bordeaux, this one is most highly recommended. Excursion days — which begin at 9:30 AM and end at 6 PM — are posted in the tourist office, where tickets can be purchased. Pack a picnic or eat at *La Citadelle* (phone: 57-42-17-10), in the citadel in Blaye; it's good if expensive. To reach Blaye by land, drive to Lamarque and take the ferry across the Gironde or go by way of St.-André-de-Cubzac, following the scenic route along the Dordogne and stopping to admire the view from the terrace of the Château de Bourg. From May to mid-October, the tourist office (phone: 57-42-12-09) offers bus excursions to different vineyards in the area. Buses leave the tourist office daily at 1:30 PM for the 1½-hour trip.

Château de Labrède – The birthplace and home of Montesquieu from 1689 to 1775, this castle-like château was built from the 13th to the 15th century. Surrounded by a large moat, the impressive dwelling is open weekend afternoons in season; closed winter to *Easter.* Admission charge. About 12 miles (19 km) south of Bordeaux via N113 and D108 (phone: 56-20-20-49). The Bordeaux Tourist Office has the best information (phone: 56-44-28-41).

Château Haut-Brion – In 1855, the wines of 60 or so of the 100 châteaux in the Médoc were classified according to excellence. The famous red wine produced here, only a few miles southwest of the center of Bordeaux, was the only one outside the Médoc to be included in the classification, and this is the perfect place for visitors who want to visit a vineyard but have no time, or perhaps transportation, to go to the Médoc. The château is now owned by the US ambassador to France under Dwight D. Eisenhower, Douglas Dillon, and most of its wine is sold to the United States. Tours take place mornings and afternoons, but reservations are necessary. Closed weekends and in August. In Pessac, via N650, or take a bus from Quai Richelieu in Bordeaux (phone: 56-98-28-17 or 56-98-33-73).

■**EXTRA SPECIAL:** St.-Emilion is one of the most picturesque wine villages of France, and it is only a 45-minute drive east from Bordeaux. Follow N89 and signs to Libourne/Périgueux, and from Libourne those toward La Réole and Bergerac on D17E until you come to the steep hills, narrow, winding cobblestone streets, small ocher stone houses with red tile roofs, and the bustling square of this minuscule town. During the 12th century, this was the stopping place for pilgrims on their way to Santiago de Compostela in Spain, and pilgrims of one sort or other have been passing through ever since.

Park at the top of the hill (and the town) near the Eglise Collégiale or behind the museum and walk to the Place du Clocher for a sweeping view of the Dordogne Valley and the town. The tourist office, at Place de Créneaux (phone 57-24-72-03), has maps of St.-Emilion (sometimes) and a list of the châteaux and vineyards open to the public (English is spoken at châteaux Ausone, Figeac, Cheval-Blanc, Beauséjour, and at Haut-Sarpe, where there also is a village). The Maison du Vin de St.-Emilion is at Place Pierre-Meyrat (phone: 57-74-42-42); open daily from 9:30 AM to 12:30 PM and 2 to 6 PM, except *Christmas* and *New Year's.*

The Eglise Monolithe is almost unique in Europe — a subterranean church hewn into the side of a limestone cliff. Begun in the 9th century and consistently enlarged through the 12th century, probably by chipping away at existing grottoes, cracks, and crevices, it stands on top of catacombs dating from the 8th or 9th century, discovered when a citizen tried to enlarge his wine cellar. The eerie, cobweb-strewn church is used only twice a year, once for the celebration of the beginning of the grape harvest, famous throughout Europe. Wine producers, called the *jurade* and garbed in bright red robes and caps and white capes, parade through the town, hold a torchlit initiation ceremony in the church, and, at day's end, climb the steep steps to the top of the early-13th-century Tour du Roi to proclaim the *ban des vendanges,* sending the people of St.-Emilion into the vineyards according to a tradition that dates back to Richard the Lion-Hearted. If you plan to attend — it's always on the Sunday closest to September 20 — arrive by midmorning and stand near the door of the church to ensure a good view. There also are exhibitions, lectures, and very good concerts in St.-Emilion, especially during the *Grandes Heures de St.-Emilion,* when music is performed in an ancient church or perhaps a private castle.

Be sure to visit the Cordelier Cloisters, on Rue des Cordeliers, a 14th-to-15th-century convent and cloister that is now an arresting, overgrown shell of stone walls, stairways, and columns. Of the town's two hotels, the better is the *Hostellerie de Plaisance,* which has 12 large, comfortable, expensive bedrooms, and a moderately priced restaurant (Place du Clocher; phone: 57-24-72-32). Of the town's ten restaurants, the rustic, moderately priced *Logis de la Cadène* (Place de Marche au Bois; phone: 57-24-71-40) is open for lunch and dinner in season, lunch only in the off-season. And don't leave town without sampling the *truffes au vin,* chocolate truffles filled with St.-Emilion wine.

Just south of St.-Emilion lies the charming region known as Entre-Deux-Mers, a patchwork of green hills, windmills, water mills, small vineyards, abbeys, castles, and villages nestled between the Garonne and the Dordogne rivers. Visit the picturesque village of La Réole, the medieval towns of St.-Macaire and Castelmoron-d'Albret, the *bastides* (medieval fortified cities) of Créon and Sauveterre-de-Guyenne, and the nearby Labarthe mill on the Gamage River. St.-Ferme, the beautiful ruins of Blasimon with its carved doorway, and La Sauve-Majeure are ancient abbeys. Among the castles to be explored are La Benauge, Cadillac, Duras, and Rauzan. Just a water farther south lies the renowned Sauternes region and châteaux Yquem, Filhot, and de Malle. Only a little farther still is Bazas, with its 17th-to-19th-century houses and 13th-to-14th-century cathedral. Nearby are Roquetaillade Castle and the villages of Villandraut and

Uzeste. A music festival is held in Uzeste every summer. Discovering and exploring these special, tucked-away parts of the region is one of the greatest pleasures of a visit to the area.

SOURCES AND RESOURCES

TOURIST INFORMATION: The Office de Tourisme de Bordeaux (12 Cours du 30-Juillet; phone: 56-44-28-41) can provide maps and information as well as set up tours in and around the city and, through its Accueil de France accommodations service, reserve hotel rooms. There also are branch tourist offices at the Gare Saint-Jean (phone: 56-91-64-70) and at the airport (phone: 56-34-39-39). They also sell a ticket permitting entry to ten Bordeaux museums. The office often is crowded, and you may feel pressured to ask your questions in a hurry and move along; sometimes it's simpler to ask to see the book of information about museums and activities. Perhaps more useful, especially for sports and cultural activities, is the Centre d'Information Jeunesse Aquitaine, a block south of Cathédrale St.-André (5 Rue Duffour-Dubergier; phone: 56-48-55-50). Officially an information center for cultural and sports events, the center, which with its bright red exterior looks like an arcade from outside, has a helpful staff that offers maps and information to anyone who enters. Check the bulletin boards for announcements of concerts, movies, and lectures. Tourist information in English is available in season by calling 56-48-04-61. For information about regional wines and which châteaux are open for tours and tastings, visit the Maison du Vin (phone: 56-00-22-66), across from the tourist office.

Local Coverage – The French daily *Sud-Ouest* is published in Bordeaux and distributed all over the southwest. *Bordeaux Journal Municipal d'Information,* published monthly by the mayor's office, is packed with news about sports, expositions, and cultural events. It is available free at the office of l'Entrepôt Lainé (3 Rue Ferrère; phone: 56-90-91-60), or at the Town Hall (Hôtel de Ville). The tourist office publishes a free quarterly newsletter, *Euro-Tourist,* which lists upcoming performances, cultural and sports events, expositions, and so on. Tourist information also is obtainable through *Minitel,* France's computerized information system that is available at some hotels. To access the information, dial 3615-BORDEAUX. The weekly *Applaudir,* sold in bookstores, is filled with information on theater, music, special exhibits, cinema, restaurants, bars, and more. The annual, student-produced *Le Bordeluche* is a guide to restaurants, entertainment, sports facilities, city services, and such things as babysitters, private detectives, and 24-hour gas stations. All of these are in French.

Bradley's Bookshop, Bordeaux's only English-language bookstore (32 Pl. Gambetta; phone: 56-52-10-57), stocks phrase books, maps, guidebooks, and dictionaries, as well as best sellers and classics. Even if you don't read French, drop by *Mollat* (9-15 Rue Vital-Carles; phone: 56-44-84-87), a revered and lovely bookstore in an early-19th-century building on the spot where Montesquieu's last home once stood. The selection of books on Bordeaux is outstanding. Closed Monday mornings.

English newspapers and other international publications are sold at the newsstand in front of the *Grand Hotel de Bordeaux* (2 Pl. de la Comédie), *Toute La Presse* (68 Rue St.-Rémi, just below Rue Ste.-Catherine), and *Le Temps de Vivre* (63-65 Rue Ste.-Catherine).

TELEPHONE: The city code for Bordeaux is 56, which is incorporated into all local 8-digit numbers. When calling a number in Bordeaux from the Paris region (including the Ile-de-France), dial 16, wait for a dial tone, then dial the 8-digit number. When calling a number from outside Paris, dial only the

8-digit number. When calling from the US, dial 33 (which is the country code), followed by the 8-digit number.

GETTING AROUND: Airport – The Airport International de Bordeaux-Merignac is France's fifth largest airport, routing over 2 million passengers a year. To reach the center of Bordeaux from the airport, take bus No. 73 (about a 30-minute ride), the *CCI* shuttle, or a taxi. For airport information, call 56-34-84-84.

Boat – Guided boat tours are given of the Bordeaux harbor. Information and tickets are available on Wharf des Quinconces (or Wharf des Queyries on the other side of the river) as well as at the tourist office.

Bus – The city bus system, *CGTFE,* serves Bordeaux and some of the suburbs. A single ticket, which must be stamped when you enter the bus, is good for only one ride. Buy a *carnet* of 10 tickets; they not only are less expensive, but each one can be used for four rides within an hour. Free maps and schedules can be obtained from major terminals such as those at Gare St.-Jean or Place Gambetta, near Place Tourny, at 10 Cours de Verdun, or easily located Place Jean-Jaurès, near the quais. Long-distance buses to the coast, the Arcachon Basin, and points inland are provided by *CITRAM* (14 Rue Fondaudège; phone: 56-81-39-80).

Car Rental – Major companies, including *Avis* (phone: 56-92-85-87), *Budget* (phone: 56-47-84-22), *Europcar* (phone: 56-91-83-83), and *Hertz* (phone: 59-91-01-71), are represented, as are a number of local firms. They are all within a block or two of the train station and are easy to spot. Ask about special rates; the weekend rate — from midnight Friday until midnight Monday — is often the best buy.

Taxi – Cabs come in all shapes, sizes, and colors, and can be distinguished by a small sign on top of the vehicle. Taxi stands are designated by a triangular sign with a "T". Two centrally located ones are at the Place Gambetta end of Cours Clemenceau and at the corner of Rue Esprit-des-Lois and the *Grand Théâtre;* there's also one at the train station. To call a cab day or night, dial 56-96-00-34, 56-80-70-37, or 56-31-61-07.

Train – Gare St.-Jean, Bordeaux's main train station, is south of the center, just inland from the river and Pont St.-Jean. For information, call 56-92-50-50; for reservations, call 56-92-76-56.

SPECIAL EVENTS: Bordeaux is charged with creative energy, and calendars fill up quicker than usual in May and November. The *Mai Musical* is nearly a month-long music extravaganza, when performers from solo pianists to massed choirs to jazz groups take up residence at the *Grand Théâtre* (Pl. de la Comédie; phone: 56-90-91-60), the cathedral, and at various châteaux within easy reach of the city. Information about performers, dates, and locations may be obtained from the tourist office. In November, the spotlight is on dance, when the annual *SIGMA* festival lures well-known international soloists and groups to Bordeaux for 2 weeks. For information, contact the tourist office (phone: 56-44-28-41). In June, and sometimes in September, the *Nuit du Vieux Bordeaux* fills the streets of the St.-Pierre quarter with music, crowds, and a holiday atmosphere. To give inanimate objects their share of attention, the city holds a *foire à la brocante,* or flea market, in May and November at Place des Quinconces. Antiques fairs, *foires aux antiquaires,* are held at *L'Entrepôt Lainé* or *Le Lac* in the fall and winter. The *Semaine Mondiale de Vins,* one of Europe's most important wine fairs, is held here during June.

MUSEUMS: Noteworthy museums not mentioned in *Special Places* include the following:

Maison des Metiers de l'Imprimerie – Dedicated to the art of printing, this small museum includes a dozen or so old presses displayed in an old factory. Open from 2 to 6 PM Mondays and Wednesdays, and from 9 AM to 1 PM Saturdays. 10 Rue Ft.-Louis (phone: 56-92-61-17).

Musée des Arts Décoratifs – In the former Hôtel Lalande, this museum — one of Bordeaux's loveliest — displays ceramics, glassware, ironwork, furniture, and other *objets,* much of it from 18th-century Bordeaux. There also are changing exhibitions. Open afternoons except Tuesdays from 2 to 6 PM; no admission charge Wednesdays. 39 Rue Bouffard (phone: 56-90-91-60).

Musée des Douanes – A well-restored floor of one of the 18th-century Place de la Bourse buildings is dedicated to customs' history. Open daily except Mondays from 10 AM to noon and 1 to 5 PM (6 PM in summer). 1 Pl. de la Bourse (phone: 56-52-45-47).

Musée d'Histoire Naturelle – Tucked away in the back of the Jardin Public, this small, well-maintained museum in the late-18th-century Hôtel de Lisleferme has simple but well-executed exhibitions. Be sure to see the butterflies on the third floor and the photographs that show how the museum's stuffed elephant was mounted and carried through the streets of Bordeaux to its present home in the lobby. Open afternoons except Tuesdays. 5 Pl. Bardineau; enter through the gate of the garden or Rue Emile-Zola (phone: 56-48-29-86).

Musée des Chartons – Devoted to wine making, this semi-private museum exhibits collections of old bottles, labels, tools. Open Mondays through Fridays by appointment only. 41 Rue Borie (phone: 56-44-27-77).

SHOPPING: When it comes to buying gifts and souvenirs, Bordeaux is a gold mine for the unique to the utilitarian. If it's clothes you want, traverse the "golden triangle," whose angles are Place Gambetta, Place Tourny, and Place de la Comédie and whose sides are Cours de l'Intendance, Cours Clemenceau, and Allées de Tourny, where the well-heeled citizens of Bordeaux shop. Place du Parlement has become popular for clothing, shoes, and accessories for a young clientele. If you prefer riding escalators to walking, head to the shopping center at Mériadeck and its 100 boutiques. If it's antiques you're after, the best bets are Rue Bouffard, Rue des Remparts, and Rue Notre-Dame, but you also can snoop along the small streets around St. Michael's Church. Don't overlook *Village Notre-Dame,* an old covered market filled with shops, near the church on the outskirts of Les Chartrons. Occasionally, an object of real interest and value (although usually in need of restoration) turns up among the run-of-the-mill wares at the flea market in front of the church on Sunday mornings.

The Bordelais swear that the best cheese comes from *Jean d'Alos* (4 Rue Montesquieu; phone: 56-44-29-66); they also swear by the fresh, homemade products at *Cerruti* (21 Rue Voltaire; phone: 56-44-24-51), a deluxe grocery with a certain snob appeal. By contrast, the Thursday-morning market in front of St. Peter's Church, bright tents and umbrellas and all, looks like an encampment of Gypsies. In fact, they are farmers and vendors of organically grown produce, homemade bread, quiches, tarts, and pies, and homemade wines made from organically grown grapes. Get here early to buy the best produce or go for an informal lunch (wine can be purchased by the glass). If you find yourself reconnoitering Rue Ste.-Catherine at lunchtime, you might want to pick up a sandwich of *jambon de Bayonne,* a ham similar to the famous Parma ham, from the stand called *Laurent Petricorena* (33 Rue Ste.-Catherine, near Rue Porte-Dijeaux).

Wine connoisseurs have many choices for browsing, gleaning information, and buying (1985 and 1986 vintages are very good and still reasonably priced, but will benefit from additional years before being opened). The best-known, and purportedly the best, wine stores in Bordeaux are *Badie* (Place Tourny; phone: 56-52-23-72), and *La Vinothèque,* near the tourist office (Cours du 30-Juillet; phone: 56-52-32-05). Also near the tourist office are two other excellent wine shops: *Bordeaux Magnum* (3 Rue Gobineau; phone: 56-48-00-06) and *L'Intendant* (2 Allées de Tourny; 56-48-01-29), a striking new shop with a dramatic spiral staircase leading to 4 levels of wine. For a more intimate experience, visit a *cave* (cellar), generally a fresh, dark, somewhat old shop where Bordelais buy simple wines (but good and very good wines also can be found here). Another interesting alternative is to buy from a local wine maker, such as Pierre Roubin, who sells on Thursdays at the organic market at St. Peter's or on the weekends from his home in Bellefond, near Rauzan (phone: 56-23-93-71).

Boutique des Girondins – If you are a soccer fan or want to surprise one back home, this is the place for T-shirts, caps, and other memorabilia of Bordeaux's beloved team, *Les Girondins.* 16-18 Allées de Tourny (phone: 56-81-07-62).

Cadiot Badie – Excellent bonbons in pretty tin boxes. 26 Allées de Tourny (phone: 56-44-24-22).

La Comtesse du Barry – A wide choice of regional and national food specialties, some made from the recipes of well-known French chefs. They will send goods by mail. 2 Pl. Tourny (phone: 56-44-81-15).

Jacqueline Dourthe – Original creations by the well-known Bordeaux dress designer. 18 Rue Lafaurie de Monbadon (phone: 56-52-35-78).

Galerie Présidence – The work of up-and-coming French artists, displayed in impressively restored gallery space. 20 Rue du Parlement St.-Pierre (phone: 56-52-29-57).

Interchasse – Men's and women's fashion, hats, jewelry, and gift items in an interesting atmosphere. 19 Rue des Remparts (phone: 56-44-56-83).

M. Mazuque – A small gift shop in Vieux Bordeaux that specializes in engraving glass and crystal. Items are for sale at reasonable prices and can be mailed home. 10 Rue des Bahutiers (phone: 56-52-94-14).

Pictures – Movie posters of French, English, and American films. In front of the *Musée d'Aquitaine,* at 25 Cours Pasteur (phone: 56-44-50-88).

La Soierie – Silk and leatherware for *les dames*. Closed at lunchtime and Mondays in winter. 27 Rue du Parlement St.-Pierre (phone: 56-51-23-75).

Summer Time – Charming, eclectic collection of gifts and items for the home; heady potpourri, scented candles, lamps, painted screens, and white piqué bed linen. Place du Parlement (phone: 56-48-26-67).

 SPORTS AND FITNESS: If you're inclined to get lots of exercise on vacation — or to watch professionals do so — Bordeaux has ample opportunities. It is within an hour of the Arcachon Basin and the Côte d'Argent, where golf, tennis, swimming, biking, and horseback riding can be enjoyed. Information of particular interest to handicapped sports enthusiasts is available from Mr. Dachary at the *Amicale Sportive des Handicapés Physiques d'Aquitaine* (phone: 56-50-31-12).

Bowling – A new addition to the Mériadeck sports complex is a 24-lane bowling alley. Terrace Général-Koenig, Rue Corps Franc de Pommiers (phone: 56-93-05-85).

Golf – Two 18-hole municipal courses are just north of *Le Lac* (Av. de Pernon; phone: 56-48-26-67); clubs can be rented; closed Tuesdays. There also is an 18-hole course at *Golf Bordelais* (Av. d'Eysines; phone: 56-28-56-04).

Horse Racing – Every Sunday in spring and summer races are run at the *Hippodrome,* northwest of the downtown area, and the "Derby of the South" is held here each year (phone: 56-28-24-73).

Ice Skating – A large *patinoire* (rink) is at Mériadeck, 100 Cours du Maréchal-Juin (phone: 56-98-38-37). The space also is used for concerts, hockey competitions, boxing matches, and even the circus. Closed in summer. Call ahead for exact days and hours. For diehards who like to ice skate in summer, there's a rink open in nearby Arcachon (Allée de Mimosa; phone: 56-83-24-56).

Rugby – For information about upcoming games, call 56-85-94-01 or check the newspapers.

Soccer – The popular local team, *Les Girondins de Bordeaux,* plays at the *Stade Municipal.* Pl. Johnston (phone: 56-98-49-34).

Squash – For a refreshing break from sightseeing, stop by *Squash de Bordeaux,* where exercise combines readily with lunch, dinner, or a drink at the bar. You bring your own athletic shoes and clothes; they provide rackets, 3 courts, saunas — and a pleasant restaurant for *après* sport. Sometimes closed 1 month in summer. 369 Av. de Verdun, Merignac (phone: 56-97-51-12).

Swimming – Enclosed and outdoor municipal pools are at 116 Rue Judaïque (phone: 56-96-65-30). Another municipal pool (covered) is in the Grand Parc (Rue des Généraux-Duché; phone: 56-50-31-97); it is accessible to handicapped swimmers.

Tennis – Several clubs in the area have courts available to visitors. For information, contact the *Ligue de Guyenne* (53 Rue de Colonel-Moll, 33400 Talence; phone: 56-37-02-90). The indoor courts at Mériadeck are open daily and can be rented by the hour. Terrace Général-Koenig, Rue Corps Franc de Pommiers (phone: 56-96-21-39).

 THEATER: The major theaters in town are the *Grand Théâtre* (Pl. de la Comédie; phone: 56-90-91-60), where operas and ballets are performed; a few blocks away, at *Théâtre Fémina* — not a feminist theater as its name might imply (Rue de Grassi; phone: 56-52-45-19) — classical and contemporary plays are performed regularly. The *Théâtre du Port de la Lune* (Pl. Renaudel; phone: 56-91-98-00), opened in 1987, hosts classic and modern plays. A new room, when complete, will more than double the theater's present seating capacity. The *Théâtre de Poche de Saint-Michel* (48 Rue Carpenteyre; phone: 56-92-25-06) is a small café-theater mounting a wide variety of pieces.

To find out what's happening at these and other theaters, pick up the latest free copy of the *Bordeaux Journal Municipal d'Information* (phone: 56-90-91-60), or even better (but not free), *Applaudir.*

 MUSIC: The Bordelais love music and have numerous opportunities to listen to it. The *Orchestre National Bordeaux-Aquitaine,* the *Orchestre de la Musique Municipale,* the *Jeunesses Musicales de France,* and chamber music groups perform, most often at the *Grand Théâtre* (Pl. de la Comédie), the *Théâtre Fémina* (Rue de Grassi), the modern *Centre André-Malraux–Conservatoire National de Region* (22 Quai St.-Croix), the *Palais des Sports* (Rue Ravez, off Cours d'Alsace et Lorraine), in the *patinoire* at Mériadeck (be forewarned that the acoustics are bad at the highest, and least expensive, tier of seating), and in the cathedral or various churches in the city. Churches, most notably Notre-Dame and St.-Seurin, also sponsor musical events.

 NIGHTCLUBS AND NIGHTLIFE: Bordeaux is much livelier during the day than in the evening, and a big night out for residents appears to be dinner and a movie. If you decide to follow suit, see *Eating Out* and take in a classic or second-run avant-garde film at *Théâtre Trianon–Jean Vigo* (6 Rue Franklin; phone: 56-44-35-17); first-run films, primarily French and American, are shown at the *Gaumont, Marivaux, Ariel,* and *Français* cinemas, all near Place Gambetta.

The following discos are popular, though most are off the beaten track: the equally chic *Studio 21* (21 Rue Mably; phone: 56-44-35-22) and *Sénéchal* (57 Quai de Paludate; phone: 56-85-54-80); *Performance* (at the corner of Rue Ramonet and Quai des Chartrons; phone: 56-81-68-92) with video screens, electronic games, and a young crowd; *Le St.-Germain,* a piano bar in the *Sofitel-Aquitania* hotel (Bordeaux-le-Lac; phone: 56-36-66-30); *Macumba* (Rte. du Cap-Ferret, Mérignac; phone: 56-34-05-48); and *Pacha* (Rte. d'Arcachon, toward Pessac l'Alouette; phone: 56-36-66-30). For cocktails, go to *L'Orchidée Noire* (2 Pl. Pey-Berland; phone: 56-44-40-04); for cocktails plus rock 'n' roll and video entertainment, to *Babylone* (67 Rue de la Rousselle; phone: 56-44-35-

78). An increasingly good place to try is *Le Salon Jaune* (32 Rue Cornac; phone: 56-44-47-67), a bar-restaurant with videos and cinema. For jazz, drop in at *La Taverne des Argentiers* on Saturday nights — no cover (7 Rue Teulère) — or *Black Jack,* a piano bar (35 Pl. Gambetta; phone: 56-81-71-38). Café-theaters include *L'Onyx* (11 Rue Fernand-Philippart; phone: 56-44-26-12) and the *Théâtre de Poche de Saint-Michel* (49 Rue Carpenteyre; phone: 56-92-25-06). For rock and jazz, go to *Le Café Carabosse* (Rue de Bègles between the railway station and the *Capucins Market;* phone: 56-91-43-27); the *White Spirit* (15 Rue Notre-Dame; phone 56-52-37-82); and *Le Comptoir des Iles,* an exotic place, perfect for the last drink of the evening (Pl. du Gen.-Sarrail, at Rue Ste.-Catherine near Pl. de la Victoire; phone: 56-94-50-71). For music with a Latin beat, try *Tupac Amaru* (23 Rue des Argentiers; phone: 56-44-21-80), and *Le Chaski,* in a 12th-century room (at 8 Rue de Mérignac; phone: 56-44-78-12). Whenever possible, call ahead to verify days and times that clubs are open.

BEST IN TOWN

CHECKING IN: Bordeaux is full of hotels within walking distance of almost anything a visitor might want to do or see. Expect to pay more than $100 for a double room at a very expensive hotel; $60 to $100 at an expensive one; between $50 and $60 for moderate lodging; and under $50 in the inexpensive range.

Aquitania-Sofitel – If you plan to spend a lot of time in Le Lac (for, perhaps, a conference or an exposition), this is a comfortable, freshly modernized place to which to return at the end of the day. It has 212 rooms and a swimming pool. Bordeaux-le-Lac (phone: 56-50-83-80). Very expensive.

Grand Bordeaux – A jewel of a building (built as a mansion for the Count de Rolly), it has been a hotel since 1850 and is the perfect counterpoint to the *Grand Théâtre* across the street. Yet the 95 rooms and 3 suites on the inside have been completely remodeled and are quiet and comfortable (but a bit of a letdown if you want to feel as if you were going back in time by staying there). One reception room, however, retains a marble hall dating from the time of Napoleon III. No restaurant, but self-service continental breakfast is available. 2 Pl. de la Comédie (phone: 56-90-93-44). Very expensive to expensive.

Pullman-Mériadeck – Modern and bustling, this hotel in the Quartier Mériadeck has 196 rooms, the elegant, highly touted *Le Mériadeck* restaurant, and a bar. 5 Rue Robert-Lateulade (phone: 56-56-43-43). Very expensive to expensive.

Burdigala – This classic old edifice in the Mériadeck section has been transformed into an elegant establishment. Its 71 rooms and 7 duplex suites offer modern comforts. 115 Rue Georges-Bonnac (phone: 56-90-16-16). Expensive.

Mercure Pont d'Aquitaine – A 100-room property near the *Aquitania-Sofitel,* with a heated swimming pool and a tennis court. Rue Grand Barrail, Bordeaux-le-Lac (phone: 56-50-90-14). Expensive.

Grand Hôtel Français – Totally renovated in 1990, this old standby has risen to new heights of comfort and elegance. A grand stairway and gracious sitting rooms recall Vieux Bordeaux. There's an excellent room service menu with food provided by a well-respected local caterer. 12 Rue du Temple (phone: 56-48-10-35). Expensive to moderate.

Sainte-Catherine – Warm golden stones and wrought iron give this deluxe hostelry in the heart of Old Bordeaux a special charm. The 91 rooms are large and comfortable. There's a restaurant and piano bar. 27 Rue du Parlement Ste.-Catherine (phone: 56-81-95-12). Expensive to moderate.

Albion – Formerly part of the Campaville chain, it's in the center of town in a restored 18th-century building. The 45 rooms are quite charming, especially those on the top floor, which have beamed ceilings and a beautiful view. Decor is all beige and pink and there are phones, TV sets, air conditioning, and private baths throughout; self-service continental breakfast is offered. Pl. Gambetta and 4 Cours Clemenceau (phone: 56-52-98-98). Moderate.

Arcade – Across from the railroad station and a short bus ride from the center of town, this modern, efficient 140-room hotel is a good value, though not in the classiest part of town. 60 Rue Eugène-Le-Roy (phone: 56-91-40-40). Moderate.

Gambetta – An old hotel on a pedestrian street that has been renovated inside (not out); its 33 rooms, though small, are comfortable, with TV sets, private bath, and mini-bar. There's also a lounge, elevator, and friendly management. Breakfast is available. Dogs welcome, too. 66 Rue Porte-Dijeaux (phone: 56-51-21-83). Moderate.

Hôtel du Théâtre – The welcome is warm and the rooms pleasant at this 18th-century structure in the heart of Bordeaux. There's also a bar, a small meeting room, a sauna, and solarium. 10 Rue Maison-Daurade (phone: 56-79-05-26). Moderate.

Normandie – A classic hotel with a refurbished stone façade, it has 98 rooms and a bar. In front of the tourist office, at 7 Cours du 30-Juillet (phone: 56-52-16-80). Moderate.

Royal Médoc – Charming and just a few blocks from the Place de la Comédie, this place offers 45 modern, tastefully decorated rooms and also has a bar. 3-5 Rue de Sèze (phone: 56-81-72-42). Moderate.

Bayonne – Quiet and comfortable, it's conveniently near the *Grand Théâtre.* Credit cards are accepted. 4 Rue Martignac (phone: 56-48-00-88). Moderate to inexpensive.

Continental – This old hotel with its floor-to-ceiling windows and stately armoires retains its share of elegance. Just off Place Gambetta, it has 50 rooms. 10 Rue Montesquieu (phone: 56-52-66-00). Moderate to inexpensive.

Saint Clair – Though not classy, it's pleasant and just a block from the *Grand Théâtre.* The hallways are a little dreary, but the spiral staircase that leads to the 14 rooms is light and airy. Near Rue Ste.-Catherine, at 18 Rue des Piliers de Tutelle (phone: 56-48-51-03). Moderate to inexpensive.

Vieux Bordeaux – Mme. Ortenzi gives guests a warm welcome in this neat 18th-century house in Quartier St.-Pierre, then sends them up to one of the 11 simple, clean rooms — ask for one on the street side. A couple of blocks from both Pl. du Parlement and Pl. St.-Pierre. 22 Rue du Cancéra (phone: 56-48-07-27). Inexpensive.

 EATING OUT: The food of southwest France has come into its own as a distinct cuisine to be appreciated and enjoyed, and Bordeaux's vast array of restaurants gives ample opportunities to do so. Regional delights include foie gras (fattened goose or duck liver), *confit* (preserved fattened goose or duck), *cèpes* (dark wild mushrooms, usually sautéed in oil with garlic), *entrecôte* (steaks grilled over the coals of dried grapevine prunings and garnished with shallots), and seafood such as *lamproie* (eel), *huítres* (oysters, served with whole wheat bread in these parts), and *alose,* a fish that usually is grilled, then presented in elegant and exciting ways. The fact that many restaurants are in beautifully restored buildings only enhances the pleasures of eating out here. Expect to pay $100 or more for a meal for two at restaurants listed as very expensive; between $80 and $100 at restaurants listed as expensive; between $60 and $80 in the moderate range; and under $60 at those listed as inexpensive. A service charge usually is included. These prices do not include wine, which can cost as little as $10 or $15 a bottle or as much as you're willing to pay. In a few restaurants you can buy regional wines by the glass, which provides an opportunity to try different varieties and vintages with each course. Although it's easy to think of Bordeaux wines as primarily red, like those of the Médoc and St.-Emilion, don't overlook the whites of Graves and Sauternes (a classic with *foie gras*).

St.-James – Regal interpretations of local delicacies, as well as an exhaustive wine list, have earned this place two Michelin stars. Its set menu, which includes the price of wine and service, is an astonishingly good value; dishes include *saumon frais à la crème au caviar* (fresh salmon in caviar cream), *civet de canard à la cuillere* (duck stew), and *crème au miel et au safran* (honey and saffron custard). Open daily. Across the Garonne and well away from the center, in suburban Bouliac at 3 Pl. Camille-Hostein (phone: 56-20-52-19). Very expensive to expensive.

Le Clavel Barnabet – Tasty variations on regional specialties, such as *lapereau à la royale* (rabbit stuffed with foie gras) and *lamproie à la bordelaise* (eel in red wine sauce), are served in a historic 19th-century structure with rock-work decorations. There also is a 5,000-bottle wine cellar. Closed Sundays and Mondays. 44 Rue Charles Domercq (phone: 56-92-91-52). Expensive.

Jean Ramet – This simple, well-loved place has friendly service, an intimate atmosphere, and well-prepared food. Popular entrées include *salade tiede de homard* (lobster salad), and *pigeonneau de Madame Raymonde* (squab). Try the *délice glacé au pralin* for dessert. Prices on the lunch menu (weekdays only) are agreeably lower. Open Mondays through Fridays for lunch and dinner. Near Pl. de la Bourse, at 7 Pl. Jean-Jaurès (phone: 56-44-12-51). Expensive.

Le Cailhau – From the cheery awning and cobblestone sidewalk in front to the beamed ceilings and dozens of tables with candelabra and fresh flowers inside, this is an inviting, romantic place. Linger over your meal, then stroll along the streets of Vieux Bordeaux. Especially tasty is the *homard au citron* (lobster in lemon). Closed Saturdays at lunch, Sundays, and August. Beside Porte Cailhau, at 3 Pl. du Palais (phone: 56-81-79-91). Expensive to moderate.

La Tupina – The classic and very good cooking of southwest France is the strength of this friendly restaurant. It is becoming more and more known, yet it's still the sort of place where if you ask to see the kitchen, they'll show it to you. Lunch and dinner daily except holidays. 6 Rue Porte-de-la-Monnaie (phone: 56-91-56-37). Expensive to moderate.

Le Bistrot de Bordeaux – Cozy and busy, this place serves up tasty bistro fare; skate salad and *filet mignon de canard au cidre et aux pommes* (duck filet with cider and apples), a well-known house specialty, get top billing. Local wine is sold by the glass, and there is a wine boutique on the second floor for heftier purchases. Closed Saturday lunch and Sundays. 10 Rue des Piliers-de-Tutelle (phone: 56-81-35-94). Moderate.

Le Mousquetaire – In a charming 2-story house near the *Grand Théâtre,* this place serves seafood, salads, and regional specialties. With its cheerful black and white tile floor, wooden stairs, and lace-curtained windows that look out onto the busy street, it has the feel of country in the city. Closed Sundays. 4 Rue des Piliers-de-Tutelle (phone: 56-48-00-39). Moderate.

La Ténarèze – On one of Bordeaux's loveliest, quietest squares – sit outdoors in summer and enjoy some of the tasty dishes of southwest France, especially from Armagnac and Gers. Closed Sundays in summer and Sunday evenings in winter. 18 Pl. du Parlement (phone: 56-44-43-29). Moderate.

Le Vieux Bordeaux – You'll appreciate the refined cooking and the elegant surroundings. Highlights on the menu include *saumon frais à la piperade* (fresh salmon with vegetables), *pigeon rôti aux gousses d'ail et ses pommes croustillantes* (roast squab with garlic and crisp potatoes), and creative desserts, such as *nougat* *glacé au coulis de framboises* (iced nougat with raspberry relish). Closed Saturday lunch, Sundays, and August. 27 Rue Buhan (phone: 56-52-94-36). Moderate.

La Cage aux Pommes – Specializes in original and classical regional recipes based on liver, duck, and fish — with a different menu for each season. Closed all day Saturdays and Sundays at lunch. 8 Rue de la Vieille-Tour (phone: 56-81-64-97). Moderate to inexpensive.

Le Chalut – Well-prepared seafood dishes at reasonable prices. Treat yourself to the fish *rillettes* and the fish soup. Closed Sundays and Monday lunch. 59 Rue du Palais-Gallien (phone: 56-81-43-51). Moderate to inexpensive.

L'Ombrière – A typical brasserie that's a local favorite for good, simple food and its open terrace on the Place du Parlement. Closed Sundays and Mondays. 14 Pl. du Parlement (phone: 56-44-82-69). Moderate to inexpensive.

Darricau – The crème de la crème of *pâtisseries/salons de thé*. Sit in the upstairs salon if it's open (it has windows that look out onto the pleasant little square), and take a minute to admire the mirrored Art Deco doors (leading to *les toilettes*) on the landing. Open daily. 7 Pl. Gambetta (phone: 56-44-21-49). Inexpensive.

Jegher – Dating from 1856, it offers out-of-this-world pastries, chocolates, and ice cream in an Old World setting across from the Jardin Public. Closed Sundays in summer. 36 Cours de Verdun (phone: 56-52-15-28). Inexpensive.

Le Morne Rouge – A cozy, semi-exotic spot where the Bordelais go when they are tired of French cooking. The menu features specialties from the French island of Martinique in the West Indies. Closed Sundays, Mondays, and August. 48 Rue du Hâ (phone: 56-81-39-26). Inexpensive.

 BARS AND CAFÉS: Step through the door at *Le Lug* (5 Rue des Faussets; phone: 56-81-04-87), and you suddenly go from Vieux Bordeaux to Greenwich Village — at least that's the way it feels in this little coffeehouse filled with parsons tables and benches, original works by local artists, and a sideboard laden with cheeses, breads, and desserts. Coffee beans are ground right on the premises and exotic teas are sold as well. Come here for lunch or an evening snack; and when the weather chills, sit on the couch in front of the fire and sip your coffee. It's open daily except Sundays until 1 AM. For beer, the widest selection is at *A l'Entracte* bar, also an inexpensive snack bar, near Pl. Gambetta (17 Rue du Palais Gallien; phone: 56-44-92-14). A popular coffee bar is *Brûlerie Gama* (just off Pl. Gambetta; 109-111 Rue Porte-Dijeaux), where you can rub elbows with the Bordelais as you stand at the counter and have a quick cup of coffee or cappuccino. It's open during business hours only.

CANNES

Some towns are important as centers of political power, commerce, or industry, others as focuses of artistic creativity or religious pilgrimage. Cannes is nothing more and never anything less than a playground — its raison d'être is pleasure. Over the past decade, the growth of convention business has brought professionals from all over the world, particularly in the spheres of film, television, music, and advertising. They arrive, pale and earnest, with impressive-looking attaché cases. But in each one, under the files and computer printouts, is a swimsuit. When they leave Cannes, tanned and relaxed, whatever business has been done has for the most part been done over a shrimp salad at a beachside restaurant or an apéritif on the terrace of one of the great seafront hotels. The majority of the 73,000 people who live in Cannes work in the service industry, and even they manage to make their labors their pleasures. In fact, work in Cannes is a delightful joke and there's no attempt to hide it — they call the conventions here "festivals."

It would be difficult to have it otherwise along La Croisette, the splendid promenade of palms and plane trees that curves gently around the bay from the Vieux Port to the *Palm Beach Casino.* On one side of the street are the dazzling white hotels — "palaces," the French call them — and condominiums; on the other, the tempting gravelly sands of the well-kept beaches. The whole is framed by the Esterel plateau, its deep red, even purple, rocky soil thickly overgrown with pines, cork oaks, and lavender. The air is sweet with the roses, mimosa, and begonias of the town's gardens. In the port, only a few diligent fishing boats bob up and down among the motor launches and yachts of the idle rich.

For centuries even the French didn't realize the pleasurable possibilities of that exquisite bay. Since the Middle Ages, Cannes — named after the cane reeds of its old marshlands — had been nothing but a fishing port with a tower and fortifications, built by abbots from the nearby Iles de Lérins to protect the villagers against Saracen pirates. In 1834, an English lord led a benevolent invasion. Turned back at the Italian frontier because of the fear of a cholera epidemic spreading from Provence, Lord Brougham (pronounced *Broom*) was obliged to spend the night in Cannes. The bouillabaisse he was served for dinner that evening and his walk along the seafront the next morning persuaded him that here was a place where a man might comfortably escape the winter chills of the north. After a distinguished political career, during which he spearheaded the movement to abolish slavery in England, Lord Brougham built a home in Cannes and was followed, not only by the fashionable aristocracy of England, but also by their cousins and fellow nobles from Russia, Germany, and Switzerland. They built grandiose villas, a yacht club, and a casino, and the French gradually tumbled to the idea that in Cannes they might have a gold mine.

The French contingent was led by the writer Prosper Mérimée, best known for the story of *Carmen* that inspired Bizet's opera. He had come on an official inspection of historic monuments in the region and stayed to cure his asthma; he died here in 1870. Other notables included Guy de Maupassant, who sailed in Cannes Bay for many years, and Frédéric Mistral, who wrote poems about the city. In those days, many rheumatics believed that to lie on the beach mummified in the Cannes sand (rather than the nastier pebbles of Nice) was enough to cure what ailed them. Europe's upper crust was soon convinced that Cannes was a good place to live and a good place to die.

During the fabled years of the Belle Epoque at the turn of the century, Cannes was clearly established as one of the major poles of attraction for a sparkling society of princes, archdukes, successful artists, and their plethora of mistresses. Before he became King Edward VII, the Prince of Wales liked to sail his yacht *Britannia* into the harbor and dally with one of his ladies at the old *Gray d'Albion* hotel. (His not so clandestine visits are commemorated on the port's Albert Edouard Jetty, and his bronze bust stands in the gardens of La Croisette.) It was in a Cannes restaurant that the prince first tasted some flambéed crêpes, which he named after his dinner companion, Suzette. One of his favorite ladies was the actress "the Belle Otéro," whose breasts are said to have been the model for the domes at either end of the great *Carlton* hotel.

This preposterous, glorious wedding cake of an edifice, one of those legendary places that people visit whether they're staying there or not, was built just before World War I. It served first as a hospital for the wounded, but came into its own as the very symbol of Cannes's hedonism in the 1920s. In other towns, the monuments are cathedrals and castles. In Cannes, the monuments are the great hotels. People will argue forever over the relative merits of the *Majestic-Croisette,* the *Grand,* the *Martinez,* the *Gray d'Albion* — or the *Carlton* — and though their budgets may not be able to afford the price of a room, they'll at least check out the bar on the terrace and, for a half hour or so, join the Cannes elite.

This "elite" doesn't actually live in Cannes — it's a transient group of shooting stars that flash through from season to season. They come as long as the sun shines, often expense-accounted on one of those convention junkets, but their most glittering moment is the *International Film Festival.* This glamorous institution has placed Cannes second only to Hollywood as a focus for the world's movie industry, though it certainly got off to a false start when its opening took place on the day Hitler invaded Poland, September 1, 1939. It then was launched with proper honors in 1946, when Ray Milland won the Best Actor award for *Lost Weekend.* Each merry month of May since, the festival cleverly has combined the tinsel of cavorting topless starlets with nobler claims to cinematic art in the person of a Fellini, a Bergman, a Coppola, or a Scorsese, each evening ending in a gala made glittering by an ocean of stunning dresses and dinner jackets. This spicy mixture of the gaudy and the sophisticated has come to epitomize the very spirit of Cannes. The locals love to complain about the flashy interlopers, but they also love to gather at the *Palais des Festivals* to watch the stars arrive. In Cannes, glamour and luxury have always been condemned and indulged with equal enthusiasm.

Whereas the population of other towns along the coast is solidly Provençal, the Cannois are a colorful mixture of retired Parisians, affluent one-time refugees from Eastern Europe and North Africa, and since the 1970s, a considerable contingent of wealthy transplants from the oil kingdoms of the Persian Gulf and war-torn Lebanon (you'll notice that the signs in many banks and jewelry shops are posted in French, English, and Arabic). Close to 100 newspapers, in almost as many languages, are sold on Cannes newsstands. Much of the cosmopolitan populace lives in seafront condominiums and in the grand villas on the eastern heights of town, La Californie. But the true natives are by no means submerged. Their domain is north and west of the Vieux Port, and in the cool of the day you'll see the men lobbing their *boules* in the sandy gravel among the plane trees of the Allées de la Liberté. In the Old Harbor itself, the seamen putter about in their boats with ropes and sails and paint and varnish, as in any other Mediterranean port, just a few yards — but a whole world — away from the gaudy glitter of La Croisette.

CANNES AT-A-GLANCE

SEEING THE CITY: Cannes is very proud of the panorama of its bay and the surrounding countryside, and to show it off to best advantage it has built an observatory, unashamedly called Super-Cannes, high on a hill above the eastern edge of town, about 2½ miles (4 km) from the center. An elevator takes you up to a deck some 1,000 feet above sea level, from which the view really is spectacular — all the way over to the Côte d'Azur, including Nice and Monte Carlo, to the Italian Riviera, and, on the many clear days, south to Corsica and northeast to the snow-capped Alps. By car, drive north on Boulevard de la République, east on Avenue de Vallauris, and turn right onto Boulevard Beausoleil. At press time, the observatory was closed. Also recommended is the romantic nighttime view of the city lights from the tower and ramparts up on Le Suquet at the western edge of town. When it comes to sensational views, Cannes offers something for everyone. Those who spend nights on the town can enjoy glorious sunrises, while those who retire early can admire the spectacular sunsets.

SPECIAL PLACES: Roughly speaking, there are two sides to Cannes, with the Vieux Port as the dividing line. West (and north) of it is the "old town," topped by the hill of Le Suquet. East of it is the more modern resort, strung along the tree-lined promenade that traces the curve of the bay. Both of these areas can and should be seen on foot, but to visit La Californie, the hill north and east of the center, and Super-Cannes at its top, a car or taxi or the bus is desirable.

La Croisette – Rarely has a town been so dominated by one street as Cannes is by the Boulevard de la Croisette. Named after a little cross that once adorned the point at its eastern end, this seafront promenade provides an indispensable introduction to the town's glossy elegance. A walk of a mile and a half along the palm trees will take you from the Old Harbor (Vieux Port) at its western end past cafés, antiques shops, art galleries, boutiques, and the great hotels — beware of Rolls-Royces gliding silently from the driveways — to the quieter residential neighborhood of the condominiums. The best time for people watching — Cannes's main sightseeing activity — is between 11 AM and noon, when the late risers are looking for a salad-brunch on the beach, and at the end of the afternoon, when the beautiful people are out admiring each other's suntan and new casual wear. In the gardens of the more sedate condominium stretch of La Croisette, take a look at the marvelous profusion (according to season) of primroses, cyclamens, snapdragons, and begonias amid the pink and white blossoming tamarisks, and red and purple bougainvillea hanging from balconies or climbing walls. The best public displays are the 14,000 roses of the Parc de la Roseraie, just north of the Port Pierre-Canto. Like La Croisette itself, this riot of flowers owes its beginnings to the English, who, in a perennially mild climate, were finally able to realize their green-thumbed dreams outside the hothouse.

Pointe de la Croisette – This promontory at the far eastern end of Boulevard de la Croisette closes the bay of Cannes and embraces the town's second harbor, the new Port Pierre-Canto, which has become the favorite mooring for some of the Mediterranean's most luxurious yachts. Conveniently nearby is the gleaming white *Palm Beach Casino,* founded with typical Cannes insouciance in 1929, the year of the great Wall Street crash. The *Palm Beach*'s own little harbor is the home of the ultra-swank *Yacht Club*.

Beaches – These spotless golden strands are the town's pride and joy, swept and sifted daily and reinforced with new sand at the slightest hint of erosion. They are divided into three areas: two stretches of mainly public beach — the Plages du Midi beyond the Old Harbor on the west side of town and the Plage Gazagnaire around Pointe de la Croisette on the east side of town — plus the mainly private beaches along La Croisette, attached to the big hotels or beachfront restaurant concessions. You can picnic and bathe for free on the public beaches — Gazagnaire is good for morning sun, the Plages du Midi better for the afternoon. But the more chic Croisette beaches are the heart of Cannes's resort life and, even though private, are open to anybody willing to rent a beach mattress and/or umbrella (about $10 each for a half day). Waiters will serve you drinks, snacks, and desserts right there by your mattress. Pedal boats can be rented on beaches, too.

Palais des Festivals – At the western end of La Croisette, overlooking the Old Harbor, this sprawling 5-tiered beige and white convention hall is the home of the *International Film Festival* and other shows throughout the year. (Though it's been open since 1982, many still refer to it as the "new" *Palais* to distinguish it from the still-standing "old" *Palais*.) Many find its north front — the film crowd calls it the "bunker" — a little forbidding, but the formal gardens at the rear with a small amphitheater, fountains, and reflecting pools offer a pleasant refuge from the madding crowd. If you have business inside the *Palais* — equipped with every imaginable audiovisual device — the idea is to make it as quickly as you can to one of the upper terraces for a lovely view of the bay.

Vieux Port – The Old Harbor is a great place to browse in the early morning, when the town's fishermen and few remaining "old salts" are fixing up their boats. They pick up their tackle and equipment at the ship chandlers tucked in among the restaurants and pizzerias on the Quai St.-Pierre, which forms the western arm of the port. Opposite, on the Jetée Albert-Edouard, which forms the eastern arm, is the Gare Maritime, from which you can take bay cruises to the Iles de Lérins just offshore (see *The Côte d'Azur,* DIRECTIONS). Moored at the far end of the Quai Laubeuf in the Vieux Port is a three-masted galleon. The *Neptune,* built for a phenomenal $8.2 million, was featured in Roman Polanski's 1986 *Cannes Film Festival* entry, *Pirates* (a phenomenal flop!). Note the figurehead and abundant wood carvings. It's open to the public daily from 10 AM to sunset; there is a nominal admission charge.

Rue Meynadier – Before Cannes became a resort town, this was Main Street (it links the old and new parts of the city) — its original name was Rue Grande. You can still see some splendid carved doors on the 18th-century houses of the town's wealthier merchants (a particularly fine specimen is No. 18). Today, it's a lively pedestrian zone, with boutiques and excellent cheese and specialty food shops leading to the covered market, *Marché Forville,* on the site of the old *Halles* at the western end of the street.

Allées de la Liberté – Running east of the Mairie (City Hall) in front of the harbor, these delightful avenues of plane trees shelter a flower market every morning except Monday, *boules* players in the afternoon, and a flea market all day Saturday. Just north of the Allées, in the little Square Brougham, is a statue of the English lord who "created" modern Cannes.

Le Suquet – This is the little fortified hill, also known as Mont-Chevalier or La Castre (The Fortress), to which old Cannes clung in medieval days under the very nominal protection of the abbots of the Iles de Lérins. Narrow streets, some of them just a series of spiraling steps, wind their way up around the hill to leave the modern resort far below. Rue Louis-Perrissol takes you to the ramparts and square tower, Tour de Mont-Chevalier, erected at the top in 1080 as a lookout against invading pirates. The late Gothic church nearby, Notre-Dame-d'Espérance, was completed in the 17th century and has a madonna to which miraculous powers were attributed. Just south of the church and built from rock carved out of the hillside is the 12th-century Romanesque Chapelle Ste.-Anne, no longer used for worship. Many shops and restaurants are under the medieval arches of Suquet, and a market is held here every morning except Sundays.

Musée de la Castre – In the remains of the abbots' old fortress, also at the top of Le Suquet, the museum draws on the wide-ranging archaeological collections donated to the town in the 19th century by the Dutch Baron Lycklama. Pride of place is given to sculpture, ceramics, and artifacts of the Mediterranean (Egyptian, Greek, Roman, Etruscan, and North African) and the Middle East (Babylonian and Persian). But there also are some fine pre-Columbian sculpture and weavings from Mexico, some important Oriental exhibits — Chinese porcelain and sculpture, Japanese military uniforms, and sculpture from Thailand and Laos — and last but not least, a fine collection of regional paintings. Closed Tuesdays and holidays; admission charge (phone: 93-38-55-26).

La Californie – This luxury residential area rises on the northeast side of town with its pinnacle at Super-Cannes. If it's at all reminiscent of California, it's because of the rugged terrain and wild vegetation, which recall the Hollywood Hills overlooking Los Angeles. A half-hour's drive around its winding roads — Avenue Fiesole, Boulevard des Pins, Boulevard Alexandre-Lacour — will give you a glimpse of the grand villas built by the old European aristocracy and the new Persian Gulf plutocracy who underwrite the city's tax base.

■**EXTRA SPECIAL:** The terrace of the *Carlton* hotel bar is perhaps the best-known spot in Cannes, yet many people steer clear of it, motivated either by a process of inverted snobbery (by which they refuse to be seen in such a place) or by fear of the price of a drink. They are wrong, for the terrace is without a doubt the absolute quintessence of Cannes's mystique, a stage for whatever is magic or merely gloriously vulgar about the town. Think of the exorbitant cocktail as the price of a ticket to one of the great shows of European razzmatazz. Curtain time is around 9 PM, and the show goes on, on balmy nights, into the wee small hours of the morning. 58 La Croisette.

SOURCES AND RESOURCES

TOURIST INFORMATION: The Cannes Office de Tourisme, Palais des Festivals (1 La Croisette; phone: 93-39-24-53 or 93-39-01-01), is open daily except Sundays year-round. It provides brochures, maps, assistance with guided tours of the surrounding countryside, and an *Accueil de France*

service, which books hotel rooms in the vicinity for a fee. Be sure to pick up the indispensable, free booklet *The Month in Cannes,* which is packed with information on what's happening and useful addresses. The tourist office also has *7 Jours et 7 Nuits,* a free weekly guide (in French). There's a branch of the tourist office at the train station (phone: 93-99-19-77 or 93-39-24-53).

Local Coverage – The principal daily newspaper of the Côte d'Azur, *Nice-Matin,* has a regional edition for Cannes and Grasse worth consulting for information about movies, concerts, and other events. *Paris–Côte d'Azur* is a bimonthly magazine covering cultural and social events in Cannes. The monthly *Gault Millau* magazine publishes a detailed Cannes restaurant guide in its May issue to coincide with the film festival. (Both magazines are in French.) Bookstores often stock back numbers if you're here later in the summer. *Semaine des Spectacles de la Côte d'Azur,* in French, is a weekly guide on sale at bookstores. The *Cannes English Bookstore* (11 Rue Bivouac Napoléon; phone: 93-99-40-08) has English-language books, but no newspapers.

TELEPHONE: The city code for Cannes is 93, which is incorporated into all local 8-digit numbers. When calling a number in Cannes from the Paris region (including the Ile-de-France), dial 16, wait for a dial tone, then dial the 8-digit number. When calling a number from outside Paris, dial only the 8-digit number. When calling from the US, dial 33 (which is the country code), followed by the 8-digit number.

GETTING AROUND: Bicycle – The best way to see the surrounding countryside. Bicycles (and motorcycles) can be rented at *France Rent* (54 Rue Georges Clémenceau; phone: 93-39-33-60) or *Cannes Location Rent* (5 Rue Allieis; phone: 93-39-46-15).

Bus – The terminus of the *Société des Transports Urbains de Cannes* (*STUC*) is at Place de l'Hôtel-de-Ville (phone: 93-39-18-71). Seven main routes operate in town and minibus No. 8 runs along La Croisette to Palm Beach. Buses for the Nice airport also leave from the Hôtel de Ville terminus (phone: 93-39-11-39) and from Square Mérimée (phone: 93-72-30-83).

Car Rental – All the major international companies are represented: *Avis* (69 La Croisette; phone: 93-94-15-86); *Budget* (3 Rue André-Chaude; phone: 93-99-44-04); *Europcar* (3 Rue du Commandant-Vidal; phone: 93-39-75-20); *Hertz* (147 Rue d'Antibes; phone: 93-99-04-20).

Taxi – Meter rates operate inside town; set rates are used for excursions beyond the city limits. Besides the Place de l'Hôtel-de-Ville (phone: 93-39-60-80) and the train station (phone: 93-38-30-79), cab stands are outside the main hotels, most conveniently at the *Majestic* (phone: 93-99-52-10) and the *Carlton* (phone: 93-38-09-76).

Train – Most trains running along the coast between Marseilles and Nice also stop in Cannes. Gare *SNCF* is on Rue Jean-Jaurès, a few blocks back from La Croisette. Call 93-99-50-50 for information.

Boat – Boats leave daily from the port, at Jetée Albert-Edouard, for day trips to the Lérin Islands. At St.-Honorat, monks guide visitors through the monastery where Lerina liquor is made. Call Gare Maritime des Iles (phone: 93-39-11-82).

SPECIAL EVENTS: The old tradition of folkloric flower battles and mimosa festivals has given way to stylish conventions and sporting events. In January, *MIDEM* (*Marché International du Disque et de l'Edition Musicale*) draws professionals of the classical and popular music recording and publishing industry. *Carneval de Cannes* takes place on the last Sunday of March. The prestigious *International Film Festival* runs for 2 weeks in May. (If you're not assured of accreditation as a professional, it's unlikely you'll get a hotel room. You probably won't get tickets for the main festival screenings, either, though screenings of many,

many films that are not part of the competition take place at the same time and you will be able to see a movie or two.) Also in May, there's an international horse show, *Concours Hippique,* at the *Stade des Hespérides;* in August, an *International Fireworks Festival* lights up the bay. The *Yacht Club* stages a *Regatta* in September, and in October *Vidcom* brings the video industry to town (the tourist office can tell you how to get in to see the latest gadgetry).

SHOPPING: Many of the most fashionable boutiques of Paris have well-stocked branches down here, particularly those that specialize in casual and beach wear. Those who, like Holly Golightly, can afford only "breakfast" at *Tiffany's* might like at least to munch a croissant outside the eye-boggling windows of the jewelry shops along La Croisette. La Croisette is the prime focus of the town's most elegant shops, but many also are found inside the great hotels. The shopping center of the *Gray d'Albion* (17 La Croisette) is perhaps the most opulent on the Côte d'Azur.

The second main shopping street, running parallel to the seafront, is the Rue d'Antibes, with a more democratic mix of prices from the expensive down to the moderate. There seems to be nothing really inexpensive in Cannes, and the best bet for a bargain is at the *Marché aux Puces* (Flea Market), held on the Allées de la Liberté on Saturdays from 9 AM to about 7 PM. The Rue Meynadier pedestrian zone is devoted mainly to high class food shops, but these provide excellent gifts — the better shops package wines and food delicacies for shipment abroad. This area is also popular among the attractive young Cannois for the great bargains to be had in the trendy, open-air boutiques that overflow into the street. If you're buying food for a picnic or other immediate consumption, don't forget the *Marché Forville,* the covered market for vegetables, fruit, and fish. This is *not* a good town for buying art and antiques, though there are plenty of both.

Alexandra – High class women's wear — carrying the major younger French and Italian labels — Chloé, Jean-Louis Scherrer, Giorgio Armani, and Christian Lacroix. Boutiques are located at Rond-Point Duboys-d'Angers and at 47 La Croisette (phone: 93-38-41-29).

Cannolive – A 100-year-old shop featuring olive oil, Provençal liqueurs, and orange wine (a local apéritif). 16 Rue Vénizelos (phone: 93-39-08-19).

Cartier – Home of the ultimate in jewelry and leather goods. 57 La Croisette (phone: 93-99-58-73).

Christofle – Classic and modern chinaware and silver. 109 Rue d'Antibes (phone: 93-38-54-06).

Ernest – A first class delicatessen — ham, sausage, but especially exquisite pâté in cans, earthenware, or airtight glass containers. Its pastry shop is across the street. 52 Rue Meynadier (phone: 93-39-25-96; pastries, 93-39-19-07).

La Ferme Savoyarde – Great for cheese. 22 Rue Meynadier (phone: 93-39-63-68).

Gérard – Jewelry designs with a touch of fantasy. 14 La Croisette (phone: 93-99-10-12).

Hermès – Quite apart from the classic leathers and silks, they make the world's greatest beach towels. Gray d'Albion, 17 La Croisette (phone: 93-39-08-90).

Il Etait Une Fois – Interesting antiques. If you're not a professional or experienced amateur, take one with you for pricing. 3 Rue Dr.-Monod (phone: 93-39-86-57).

Maiffret – The venerable manufacturer of sinfully good chocolates and candy, particularly the local specialty, candied figs, apricots, strawberries, pears, plums, and melon. Watch them being made in the mezzanine "lab." 31 Rue d'Antibes (phone: 93-39-08-29).

Sadya – The sexiest lingerie in town. 19 Rue du Commandant André (phone: 93-39-09-58).

Van Cleef & Arpels – Exquisite gold jewelry and gems. 61 La Croisette (phone: 93-94-15-08).

 SPORTS AND FITNESS: For any information about sports, call the Office Municipal de la Jeunesse (2 Quai St.-Pierre; phone: 93-38-21-16). The most relaxing spectator sport in town — and free — is *boules* at the *Boulodrome de la Pantiero* on Allées de la Liberté.

Fishing – Deep-sea fishing is organized by the *Club de Pêche Sportive de Cannes* at the *Sofitel-Méditerranée* hotel (Bd. Jean-Hibert; phone: 93-63-73-67), and the *Fishing Club de Cannes-Mandelieu* (phone: 93-49-83-94). Fishing equipment is available at *Félix, Pêche Marine* (4 Bd. La Source; phone: 93-43-07-25), and at *Atrizzi Serge* (5 Rue Felix Faure; phone: 93-39-10-41).

Golf – Your hotel can advise you about access to the *Golf Club de Cannes-Mandelieu* (phone: 93-49-55-39), the *Golf Country Club de Cannes-Mougins* (phone: 93-75-79-13), or *Golf de Valbonne* (phone: 93-42-00-08 or 93-42-05-29 for the pro shop).

Sailing and Windsurfing – As with scuba diving (see below), these sports are organized by the *Centre Nautique Municipal* (2 Quai St.-Pierre; phone: 93-38-21-16). Equipment can be rented at the *Base du Mouré Rouge* (9 Rue Esprit-Violet; phone: 93-43-83-48). Sailboats (and motorboats) are also for rent at *New Boat* (Port de la Napoule; phone: 93-93-12-34).

Scuba Diving – Contact the *Centre Nautique Municipal* (address and phone above).

Swimming – The public beaches are the Plages du Midi and Plage Gazagnaire; private beaches are along La Croisette. Pool fanciers can try *Piscine Municipale* (Av. Pierre de Coubertin; phone: 93-47-12-94), or the swimming pools at the *Palm Beach Casino* (phone: 93-43-91-12), or — if you're a guest — at the *Pullman Beach, Majestic, Montfleury, Sofitel-Méditerranée, Beau Séjour,* or *Cannes Palace* hotels.

Tennis – Your hotel can help you get one of the many courts at the *Complexe Sportif Montfleury* (Av. Beauséjour; phone: 93-38-75-78); *Gallia Tennis Club* (Bd. de Strasbourg; phone: 93-38-75-78); or *Tennis-Club* (Municipal de l'Aérodrome, Av. Francis Tonner; phone: 93-47-05-82). Lessons are available at the *Cannes Tennis Club* (1 Rue Lacour; phone: 93-43-58-85).

 MUSIC: The *Orchestre Cannes–Provence–Côte d'Azur* gives classical music concerts in the *Salle Claude Debussy* of the new *Palais des Festivals*. Chamber music recitals can be heard at Notre-Dame-d'Espérance on Le Suquet.

 NIGHTCLUBS AND NIGHTLIFE: The smartest discos — don't go before midnight — are the *Jackpot* (at the *Palm Beach Casino;* phone: 93-43-91-12), *Jane's* (in the *Gray d'Albion;* phone: 93-68-54-54), and the *Galaxy* (at the casino of the *Palais des Festivals;* phone: 93-38-12-11). The younger, wilder crowd hangs out at the *Studio Circus,* a converted movie house at (48 Bd. de la République; phone: 93-38-32-98); gays and celebrities dance under laser beams at *Whiskey-a-Gogo* (115 Av. de Lérins; phone: 93-43-20-63). For jazz, try *Le Ragtime* (opposite the *Palais des Festivals,* La Croisette; phone: 93-48-47-10); and for an English pub atmosphere, complete with dart games — as well as *Rolling Stones* music — join the young clientele at *The Swan* (4 Rue Clemenceau; phone: 93-39-05-57).

The other action in town is gambling — from 5 PM daily November through May at the *Casino Croisette* of the *Palais des Festivals* (phone: 93-38-12-11); from 7 PM daily June through October at the much more elegant *Palm Beach Casino* on Pointe de la Croisette (phone: 93-43-91-12). There's an entrance fee and you'll need your passport; jackets, but not formal wear, are required for men. The games include roulette, baccarat, and blackjack (no craps). The *boule* room at the *Palais des Festivals* offers a proletarian form of low-stakes roulette in which a golf-size ball teeters around a tableful of numbers. It won't break you or make you rich, but you get a nice high watching the ball.

BEST IN TOWN

CHECKING IN: Before even thinking of checking into a Cannes hostelry, consider that it's neither possible nor desirable to do this town on the cheap. It's not like one of the major European capitals, where there's so much going on in the theaters, museums, and concert halls that it doesn't really matter what kind of hotel you choose — or where it's situated. This is an expensive resort town where the Mediterranean is the whole story, and it's just no fun being in a third-rate hotel far from the sea. Even if they're not on La Croisette, the hotels near the water are hardly inexpensive. You'll find a few that are conveniently located and reasonably priced, but nothing under $60 for double occupancy — and you'll have to book several months in advance to get those prices. Prices go up in May during the film festival and hotels always are booked; be prepared to reserve possibly years in advance. Hotels in the expensive category — the so-called palaces — run from $150 and way up for a double room with continental breakfast. Moderate hotels range from $75 to $100, and inexpensive ones, for the most part out in the boondocks, under $75.

Carlton Inter-Continental – Numero uno in terms of old-fashioned prestige and glamour, the decor has retained its Belle Epoque charm, and renovations — by new Japanese owners — of the 295 rooms and 30 suites (complete with air conditioning, color TV sets, and more) have modernized the traditional comforts. The bathrooms alone are monumental enough to justify a good part of the price, and the view of La Croisette and the sea undoubtedly is the best in town. Its 13-room Imperial Suite offers all the comforts at $6,000 a day. The service (outside film festival time) is efficient without being obsequious. In addition to the famous big bar and terrace, there's a delightful, intimate, smaller bar off the lobby. The food at *La Côté* restaurant (see *Eating Out*) has won it a Michelin star. No swimming pool, but a private beach. 58 Bd. La Croisette (phone: 93-68-91-68). Expensive.

Grand – The most discreet of the "palaces," set back at the end of an avenue of palms winding among tailored lawns and flowerbeds, this is the place to get away from the mob in perfect comfort. Service and amenities in the 76 rooms have an appropriate refinement. Swingers may find the bar *too* quiet. 45 La Croisette (phone: 93-38-15-45). Expensive.

Gray d'Albion – The most modern of Cannes's properties is part of a huge luxury shopping and apartment complex. The 186 rooms and 14 suites boast all the most up-to-date comforts, including phones in the bathrooms and VCRs in the suites. Set away from the sea, the eighth and ninth floors have a Mediterranean view. The hotel has its own discotheque, *Jane,* a private beach, and a great restaurant, *Royal Gray* (see *Eating Out*). 38 Rue des Serbes (phone: 93-68-54-54). Expensive.

Majestic – Many connoisseurs insist this is really the best of the "palaces," more sophisticated than its more celebrated rival, the *Carlton.* Certainly the 248 rooms and 13 suites and their amenities are impeccable, and the service is very good, if sometimes a little overconfident. Its great asset is the lovely swimming pool in tree-shaded grounds that set the hotel quietly back from the bustling Croisette. Its restaurant is slowly gaining a reputation as one of Cannes's better eating places. The bar and terrace are a joy. Open year-round. 6 La Croisette (phone: 93-68-91-00). Expensive.

Novotel Montfleury – In the middle of a park looking down a hill to the sea, this is the luxury spot for the sporting crowd. The *Complexe Sportif Montfleury* shares the location, and hotel guests can avail themselves of heated swimming pools, tennis courts, a volleyball court, and other facilities, including a skating rink in winter. It's perhaps the one place in Cannes where you won't mind not being near La Croisette. The 180 rooms, many with spacious balconies, and Presidential Suite are very modern and superbly furnished. 25 Av. Beauséjour (phone: 93-68-91-50 or 93-38-75-78). Expensive.

Splendid – By a stroke of luck, this modest but well-run and comfortable place near the Old Harbor hit the jackpot when the *Palais des Festivals* was built just across the street. This, combined with a ringside view of the *boules* games on the Allées de la Liberté, gives it one of the best locations in town. There is no restaurant, but breakfast service is fine, and the 64 rooms come with a kitchenette for those who want to take advantage of the nearby food market. 4-6 Rue Félix-Faure (phone: 93-99-53-11). Expensive to moderate.

Beau Séjour – Very well equipped, with 46 rooms, it is 300 yards from the beach and has its own swimming pool and garden. The service is efficient and the restaurant, less pretentious than those of the "palaces," is a pleasant surprise. Closed from the end of October to mid-December. 5 Rue des Fauvettes (phone: 93-39-63-00). Moderate.

Canberra – The 62 rooms are simply but nicely done, with air conditioning and television sets. There is a small bar and a quiet little garden, and it's in the shopping district. 120 Rue d'Antibes (phone: 93-38-20-70). Moderate.

Century – This modern hotel has only 35 rooms, but they're big and have air conditioning, TV sets, and — important in this busy shopping area — good sound-proofing. Closed December 1 to January 7. 133 Rue d'Antibes (phone: 93-99-37-64). Moderate.

Palma – By the rose garden at the east end of La Croisette, this hostelry has 52 small, bright, cozy rooms, most with ocean views. Those that don't face the sea, however, offer the best summer rates in town. The service is without a doubt the friendliest on La Croisette. 77 La Croisette (phone: 93-94-22-16). Moderate.

Corona – Modest, clean rooms, air conditioned and soundproof, and only a short walk from La Croisette and the railroad station. What you save on the hotel bill you can spend at the *Gray d'Albion* shopping center across the street. Closed in November. 55 Rue d'Antibes (phone: 93-39-69-85). Inexpensive.

EATING OUT: Cannes's fancy touch has been more successful in creating great hotels than great cuisine, though things are getting better, particularly at the upper end of the price scale, and only a few miles away in Mougins, one of the most famous restaurants in France continues to satisfy (and satiate) the most stringent of critics. In the more modest bistros, however, it's best to choose simpler fare — straightforward seafood dishes, for instance — rather than the attempts at something more elaborate. Note that the local cooking is not especially Provençal, no more so than the resident population. But the fruit and vegetables season is longer than in other parts of France, and fresh fish is in abundance; therefore, you can be assured of eating light and quickly prepared dishes. For ice cream lovers, however, Cannes is a paradise. Beside the traditional chocolate, coffee, and nut flavors, there are licorice, ginger, and honey ices, cream cheese sherbets, and even *croque-monsieur* ice cream, a type of ice cream sandwich. As with hotel prices, restaurant prices must be seen in a specifically Cannes context: At the expensive restaurants listed, expect to pay at least $100 and up for a meal for two; moderate means $50 to $100; while $50 or as little as $25 for two is considered inexpensive. Prices do not include drinks or wine; usually a service charge is included.

Le Moulin de Mougins – One of the best dining rooms in all of France is just outside the charming market town of Mougins, a 15-minute drive from Cannes. Roger Vergé, the owner and master chef, offers a warm welcome to the converted 16th-century mill where he won the coveted three Michelin stars only 5 years after opening. Among his specialties are *salade Mikado,* a creation of mushrooms, avocado, tomato, and truffles; violet asparagus with truffles; artichokes, scallops, and smoked salmon in lime sauce; *aiguillettes de canard de Challons au sang*, strips of duck breast followed by the grilled legs; and, for dessert, *soufflé glacé aux fraises des bois*, cold wild strawberry soufflé. Reservations are essential, as are coat and tie. Organic products, made by the master chef himself, are sold in the adjacent boutique. Closed Mondays and Thursdays at lunchtime and from January 29 to April 5. On D3 at Notre-Dame-de-Vie, about 4 miles (6 km) north of Cannes (phone: 93-75-78-24). Expensive.

Le Festival – One of the best of the swank spots on La Croisette, though for those who come here to be seen, a good meal is quite secondary. Best bet is the fish, especially salmon *à la menthe* (mint), and nearly everything on the pastry trolley is lethally good. Closed Sundays for dinner, Mondays from January to *Easter,* and November 19 to December 27. Reservations necessary. 52 La Croisette (phone: 93-38-04-81). Expensive.

La Palme d'Or – Provençal fare par excellence, served in an Art Deco room hung with photos of Hollywood stars. It won a Michelin star in 1990. A meal here must end with the beautiful cheese selection or a superb dessert — or both! Prix fixe meals are available. Closed Mondays and Tuesday afternoons, and mid-November to mid-January. Reservations necessary. 73 La Croisette (phone: 92-98-30-18). Expensive.

Royal Gray – On the first floor of the *Gray d'Albion,* this is a marvelously imaginative exception to the disappointments that the restaurants of many large hotels can be (not just in Cannes), and it has justifiably been given two Michelin stars. Conceding nothing in the elegance of its pink and violet decor, it manages to give courteous, efficient, and unpompous service, for one thing. For another, the cooking of Chef Jacques Chiboisit is inventive rather than flashy (a salad of fresh salmon marinated in ginger on a bed of green vegetables), or straightforward without being dull (sea perch with truffles and squash, or sliced duck *aiguillettes* in burgundy with spring turnips). The sweet-toothed would die rather than miss the apple *mille-feuille* pastry in caramel sauce or the hot walnut cake. And the terrace is famous in its own right. Closed Sundays (except in summer), Mondays, and February 1 through March 6. Reservations necessary. 38 Rue des Serbes (phone: 93-99-04-59). Expensive.

La Côte – One of the most beautiful dining rooms in the south of France, offering fine, light food. Try the fresh pasta with seafood or any fish dish. Open year-round. Reservations necessary. 58 La Croisette (phone: 93-58-91-68). Expensive to moderate.

Villa Dionysos – A small, Italian-style palace, where a woman chef makes some of the simplest and purest food on the entire Riviera. Two excellent fixed-price menus make this restaurant irresistable. Open year-round. Reservations necessary. 7 Rue Marceau (phone: 93-38-79-73). Expensive to moderate.

Chez Astoux – Great trays of oysters, clams, mussels, sea urchins, winkles, crabs, and shrimp that will keep you busy all evening are one reason not to overlook this seafood bistro close to the Old Harbor. The scrumptious chocolate profiteroles are another. The atmosphere is noisy, lively, and very friendly. Open daily. Reservations advised. 43 Rue Félix-Faure (phone: 93-39-06-22). Moderate.

Au Mal Assis – Nicely situated on the Old Harbor, and you're much better seated than the name implies. The fish is first class, the service amiable. Closed mid-October to late December. Reservations unnecessary. 15 Quai St.-Pierre (phone: 93-39-05-35 or 93-39-13-38). Moderate.

Le Maschou – This place stands out for its good charcoal-grilled steaks and its candlelit setting, where the plain look pretty and the pretty stunning. It's a favorite with the *jeunesse dorée*. Dinner only. Closed Sundays and November to mid-December. Reservations necessary. 17 Rue St.-Antoine (phone: 93-39-62-21). Moderate.

La Mère Besson – This is that rarity in Cannes, an authentic Provençal restaurant. It's very fashionable, always crowded, and everybody table-hops. Try the fragrant beef stew, *daube provençale*. Closed Sundays, and for lunch, September through June, and 1 week in February. Reservations necessary. 13 Rue des Frères-Pradignac (phone: 93-39-59-24 or 93-38-94-01). Moderate.

Les Santons de Provence – A classic Provençal bistro that is a favorite of the locals. Closed Mondays off-season, November 25 to December 22, and February 6 to March 21. Reservations advised. 6 Rue du M. Joffre (phone: 93-39-44-51). Moderate to inexpensive.

Au Bec Fin – Fine, straightforward cooking prevails here. The excellent steaks are served thick, the plain grilled fish — local *daurade* (sea bream), *rascasse* (hogfish), or sea bass — graced with perhaps a touch of fennel, and the salads are the best in town. Closed Saturday nights and Sundays. Reservations necessary. Near the railroad station; 12 Rue du 24-Août (phone: 93-38-31-33). Inexpensive.

Beach Restaurants – These establishments defy classification. Strung along La Croisette, some of them are connected to the big hotels, all of them are relatively expensive, but they're still a delightful way to enjoy the beach at lunchtime. Your best bet is to have the prix fixe menu of the day or one of the very good salads — *niçoise*, shrimp, or crabmeat — plus a small carafe of wine or mineral water, and maybe some strawberries. Service is slow, but nobody's in a hurry on the beach. The best people watching locations — make a reservation — are the *Maschou Beach* (phone: 93-39-37-37), *Hawaii Beach* (phone: 93-38-17-47), *Lido Plage* (phone: 93-38-25-44), *Plage Club des Sports,* where volleyballers go (phone: 93-38-59-72), and the *Plage Sportive* (phone: 93-38-63-73). Also excellent are *L'Ondine,* with some of the best cooking on the beach at the best prices (phone: 93-94-23-15), and *Le Goéland* (phone: 93-38-22-05), where the mattress comes with the beach's admission price, and lots of fresh vegetables garnish the fish dishes.

 BARS AND CAFÉS: The *Petit Carlton* — no relation (93 Rue d'Antibes; phone: 99-39-27-25) — is a rather scruffy tavern staked out at festival time by movie buffs who can't or don't want to afford the "grand" *Carlton*. It serves merely edible meals and retains its counterculture ambience the rest of the year. The traditional wicker chairs of the redecorated *Blue Bar* (48 Bd. Croisette; phone: 93-39-03-04), next to the "old" *Palais des Festivals,* are still the stalwarts' favorite rendezvous: It's the best of the sidewalk cafés on La Croisette, a good spot for breakfast, lunch, or dinner, and the service is fast — besides which, sooner or later everybody in Cannes passes by. *Le Ragtime* is a fashionable piano bar decked out in smart 1920s decor (phone: 93-68-47-10). Strategically opposite the "new" *Palais des Festivals* at La Croisette, it functions as a tearoom in the afternoon, an expensive restaurant at night, and as a bar all day. (At night, the restaurant musicians are piped down to the bar on a video screen.) At the risk of tiresome repetition, the best hotel bars remain the *Carlton* terrace and the *Majestic,* the latter with superior potato chips.

CHARTRES

There are places in the world where the center seems to hold, and Chartres is one of them. An enduring gift of the Middle Ages, the town wraps itself around the treasure casket of an incomparable cathedral and its unrivaled collection of stained glass and sculpture. To the traveler scaling the steep, winding streets and wandering along the banks of the river Eure, with its reedy waters and stone bridges, there are no jarring notes.

Since 1963, the municipality has been carefully restoring the town, shoring up timbers and gables and respecting the integrity of the original houses, but this city is not a museum. Though Chartres no longer is the bustling crossroads that supported the extravagant building projects of the 13th century, it still is a prosperous market town, sitting at the center of some of France's richest arable land. On Saturdays, when the gardeners of the Beauce region are out in force for the *Marché des Fleurs* and farmers stack their produce under the arches of the covered market, crowds of shoppers mill around well-kept stores in the pedestrian zones. In the back streets, matronly neighbors in blue aprons gossip from their windows, and inviting courtyards offer glimpses of ancient iron pumps and greenery within. And on the feast days that draw pilgrims with their backpacks to special services at the cathedral, there may be a lean and tousle-headed ascetic pacing the cobbles and wrangling with himself, a shade of the many pilgrims who have passed this way.

Recent excavations have shown that a settlement flourished here under the Romans, who first called it Autricum and then "the town of the Carnutes" — after the Gallic tribe of the area — and built a forum, an amphitheater, and a temple on the banks of the Eure. Until the Romans and Christianity took hold, Chartres was an important center of the Druid religion in Gaul; in fact, the Roman temple and, in the 4th century, the first Christian church seem to have risen on the same spot already hallowed by the Druids. Then, after 876, when Charles the Bald, the French king, gave the city the Sancta Camisia (the robe Mary is said to have worn when she gave birth to Christ), Chartres became an important center of the cult of the Virgin Mary.

By the end of the 10th century, under the leadership of counts such as Thibaut the Cheat, whose domain extended as far as Blois in the Loire Valley, Chartres had become one of medieval Europe's most exciting cities. It was a center of learning, the home of scholars such as its Bishop Fulbert, who set about building a predecessor of Chartres's cathedral after an earlier church had been destroyed by fire in 1020; of Bernard of Chartres, who preached the Crusades here in the 12th century; and John of Salisbury, the secretary of Thomas à Becket. All the while, pilgrims flocked in, bringing offerings to Mary's shrine.

In 1194, a fire razed the flourishing town, leaving only the crypt, parts of the façade, and a steeple of the cathedral. But the holy relic miraculously escaped damage, fueling enthusiasm for the construction of a new building on the old foundations. The main body of the cathedral that stands today was completed between 1194 and 1225, financed by gifts from the crowned heads of Europe and the well-heeled merchants of the city. Chartres's status as a spiritual center persisted into the 14th century, when the county became a dependency of the Kings of France, many of whom became its benefactors, and in 1594 Henri IV of Navarre had himself crowned here, one of the few exceptions to the rule that French kings be crowned in Reims Cathedral.

Some residents of Chartres complain that interest focuses so heavily on the medieval city that history here seems to stop in the 18th century. In fact, Chartres contributed several important figures to the French Revolution, including the revolutionary theorist Abbé Sieyès, who lived in Chartres and wrote his treatise on the third estate here. When the Revolution broke out, the cathedral was declared a Temple of Reason; there was talk of pulling the place to the ground and its treasure was plundered, but its statuary and stained glass escaped the excesses of vandalism.

By the 19th century, although Chartres had lost its political importance, the beauty of the town attracted writers and artists (the musical tradition surrounding the cathedral had always been strong). The writer Théophile Gautier frequently stayed in the area, as did Anatole France and Alfred de Musset, who wrote a novella here. Corot painted a fine canvas of the cathedral, now in the *Louvre,* showing its former dark lead roof, which was replaced with today's blue-green copper one after a fire in 1836. Much later, the Lithuanian painter Chaim Soutine translated the landscapes of the Eure Valley into swirling canvases during the Nazi occupation, which he spent in hiding nearby because he was a Jew. The town's World War II hero and one of the architects of the French Resistance was Jean Moulin, who was prefect of the Eure-et-Loir *département* at the beginning of the war.

More recent town leaders have worked to ensure the city's continued evolution. Ambitious projects such as the recently opened multi-purpose exhibition hall, *Chartrexpo* (capacity 7,000), should help this medieval city ease into the 21st century.

Yet, despite all the evidence of its continuing vitality through the centuries, Chartres *is* its cathedral. It is in its picture of medieval life that Chartres lives most intensely: in the clear gaze of its statues and the intense colors of its stained glass, undimmed by time.

CHARTRES AT-A-GLANCE

SEEING THE CITY: Nobody forgets seeing Chartres cathedral for the first time across the Beauce plain, its two spires like the masts of a sailing ship afloat on a sea of grain. Because it sits on a spur of elevated ground, it looms onto the horizon whether you arrive by road, on the A10 past Versailles from Paris or on N154 from Rouen and Normandy, or by rail (there are trains roughly every hour from the Gare Montparnasse in Paris). As you approach, the layers of the city peel off: sprawling 20th century, sturdy bourgeois 19th century, then the unspoiled medieval core. It all can be seen from the highly decorated turrets of the cathedral's North Tower, a winding walk up narrow stairs (entrance inside the North Door); from April through September, 9:30 to 11:30 AM and 2 to 5:30 PM (shorter hours in low season); closed Sunday mornings and the month of January. Admission charge.

The stone bridges on the river Eure along the Rue de la Foulerie-Frou and the Rue de la Tannerie in the Basse Ville (Lower Town) also give an unforgettable view of the city. Flanked by sober medieval buildings, the narrow stream flows past tree-lined banks, carrying the eye up to the cathedral, and low walls provide a comfortable resting place for contemplation. Two other good views: a profile of the town's major churches from the Pont de la Courtille at the extreme southeast of the Old Town, and from the well-mown terraced lawns of the Bishop's Garden, immediately behind the cathedral, a panorama over to the rich countryside on which Chartres's prosperity was based.

For easy sightseeing of the charming old quarters along the banks of the river Eure, take a ride on *Le Petit Train de Chartres*. This open-air trolley, run by the local tourist office, travels a 35-minute route, with commentary in English. Hourly departures from 10 AM to 7 PM *Easter* to November; admission charge. For information, inquire at the tourist office (Pl. de la Cathédrale; phone: 37-21-54-03).

SPECIAL PLACES: All the sights below, with the exception of the last one, Eglise St.-Martin-au-Val, are in the Old Town, the hub of which is the cathedral and which has upper and lower levels. The Haute Ville (Upper Town) takes in the cathedral as well as the area south and west of it, including the commercial center around Place des Epars and such streets as Rue Noël-Ballay and Rue du Cygne. The Basse Ville (Lower Town) is east of the cathedral, running along the river. All of this is easily walked; even St.-Martin-au-Val, which actually is beyond the limits of the Old Town, is no more than a 15-minute walk from Notre-Dame. On your way back, be sure to wander along Rue aux Herbes, Rue de la Petite Cordonnerie, and the Place de la Poissonnerie, where curious old houses give one a sense of the medieval city come alive.

CHARTRES CATHEDRAL

If the Parthenon sums up Greek civilization and St. Peter's in Rome stands for the Renaissance, Notre-Dame de Chartres is the last word in Gothic architecture. The cathedral of today is probably the fifth church to be built on the spot — fires and sword destroyed its previous incarnations — and because most of it was constructed within a period of 30 years (1194–1225), it has an unusual architectural homogeneity. Its two spires, which do not match and give it a lopsided look, are from completely different eras. The South Tower to the right (called the Clocher Vieux, or Old Tower) is in the Romanesque style, elegantly sober and unadorned to the tip of its steeple; it was finished in about 1160 for the previous cathedral and survived the fire of 1194. The North Tower to the left (the Clocher Neuf, or New Tower) is, at least at its base, which also survived the fire of 1194, older than the Old Tower, but its steeple in the convoluted Flamboyant style of the early 16th century was built by Jean Texier, or Jehan de Beauce, to replace a wooden one that burned in 1506. The 12th- and 13th-century statuary surrounding the cathedral's three main doorways — the Royal Portal in the western façade and the porches of the northern and southern transepts — is a gold mine of information on the life and thought of the people of the Middle Ages, and its stained glass windows are considered the most beautiful in France, a country where exquisite stained glass has been preserved in remarkable quantity.

■ **Note:** Authorities recently decided to restrict tourists from entering the cathedral during its most important masses. Therefore, visitors not attending mass will not be permitted to go into the nave from Saturday at 7:45 PM until Sunday at noon.

Nave – The size of the building staggers even the blasé modern observer; there can be few structures, one feels, that enclose as much space. The nave is broader than any other in France. The ogival arches rise to 122 feet; and the walls, opened up by flying buttresses that carry the weight of the vaults, are studded with 27,000 square feet of mostly medieval stained glass, the most complete collection anywhere in the world. Brilliant reds, yellows, and greens puncture the deep aquamarine background that has come to be known as Chartres blue, telling the familiar Bible stories over and over again. It's best to come armed with binoculars (available at the *Optique des Changes*, 9 Rue des Changes; and at *La Crypt*, 18 Cloître Notre Dame) to appreciate, frame by frame, the detail of these luminous texts. Most prized are the three 12th-century lancet windows under the spire of the west front, retrieved, like the famous Blue Virgin window by the choir (Notre-Dame de la Belle Verrière), from the earlier Romanesque cathedral. They show the Tree of Jesse (on the right), scenes from the life of Christ (middle) and the Passion (left). It's well worth unraveling it all with the help of the detailed brochures available in English.

Choir – Like the massive baroque altarpiece, which is a little out of place here but striking in its sweep and movement, the ornate stone tableaux of the choir screen were an afterthought, embellishments on the Gothic. Begun by Jehan de Beauce in 1516 and finally completed in 1716, they show scenes in the lives of Christ and the Virgin, but are more eloquent about the courtiers and seamstresses of the Renaissance.

Chapelle de St.-Piat – The cathedral's treasure house, behind the choir, displays the famous relic of the Virgin's robe as well as embroidered vestments and other precious objects given to the church. Closed during lunch, Sunday mornings, and January.

Crypt – The third largest in the world (after those of Canterbury Cathedral in England and St. Peter's in Rome), the U-shaped crypt houses some interesting 12th-century murals, statues rescued from the Royal Portal, and a carved Madonna that is a replica of one burned during the French Revolution. The crypt is the oldest part of the cathedral, most of it dating back to Fulbert's time in the 11th century, but it contains an even earlier crypt (that of a 9th-century church) and parts of Gallo-Roman origin. Guided tours (the only way the crypt can be visited and for which there is a charge) leave several times daily from the Maison des Clercs, 18 Cloître Notre-Dame, just across from the cathedral.

Royal Portal – The sculpted triple doors that make up the entrance in the western façade survive from the earlier cathedral and are considered among the finest examples of French Romanesque art. They present the stern and ethereal mid-12th-century vision of Christ in majesty, the figures elongated, the lines pure.

North Porch – The three arches here, carved in the 13th century, concentrate on the Old Testament and the prophecies of Christ's coming, with, in parentheses, the story of the Creation and a fascinating series showing the months, the arts, and the virtues as seen through medieval eyes.

South Porch – Also 13th century, the sculpture of the southern doorway (Portail du Midi) focuses on Christ, who is seen presiding at a vividly depicted Last Judgment, complete with sinners and demons, and surrounded by phalanxes of martyrs and confessors of the Church. The grisly end awaiting martyrs and sinners makes compulsive viewing, and there are some exquisite visions of the ideal courtly knight (watch for St. George and St. Maurice, outermost figures flanking the entrance).

AROUND THE TOWN

Musée des Beaux-Arts – Behind the cathedral are the former Bishop's Palace, built during the 17th and 18th centuries, and the Bishop's Garden, which falls in terraces toward the river and provides a view over the Lower Town and beyond. The palace, now a fine arts museum, contains tapestries, furniture, and enamels as well as an exceptional collection of ten paintings by the Fauvist Maurice Vlaminck, together with part of his collection of African sculpture. Closed Sunday mornings in winter and Tuesdays year-round; admission charge. 29 Cloître Notre-Dame (phone: 37-36-41-39).

Enclos de Loëns/Centre International du Vitrail – The fine ogival arches of this 13th-century cellar, down a small side street north of the cathedral, were built, unusually, for a secular purpose: Wine was stored here by the priests. The spacious beamed attic houses the *Centre International du Vitrail* (International Stained Glass Center), which features displays of ancient and contemporary stained glass and permanent exhibitions that detail the history and techniques of stained glass making. The art continues to flourish in workshops around town. There also are frequent temporary exhibitions. Closed Mondays and lunchtime. 5 Rue Cardenal-Pie (phone: 37-21-65-72).

Tertre St.-Nicolas – These stone steps — built during the 14th century — descend precipitously from the *Musée des Beaux-Arts* to Place St.-André and the river and afford a lovely view of the city.

Eglise St.-André – This 12th-century Romanesque church, deconsecrated since the Revolution, gave its name to Chartres's *St. Andrew's Fair,* held in November (see *Special Events*). The back wall carries the stump of a bridge, now covered with greenery, that used to reach over the river Eure. Rue de la Brèche, just beyond Pl. St.-André.

Porte Guillaume – From the ruins of the city's last remaining 14th-century gate, fortified in the Hundred Years War and bombed by the Nazis, there are some bucolic views of the river. On the banks of the Eure, at Rue du Bourg–Porte Guillaume.

Eglise St.-Pierre – If Chartres ever lost its cathedral, it would still be remembered for this late-13th-century church, once the church of a Benedictine abbey. The graceful ribs of its flying buttresses, each finished with a fearsome gargoyle, leave room inside for wall-to-wall stained glass (13th to 16th century) and a unique impression of light and air. Pl. St.-Pierre.

Eglise St.-Aignan – Less elegant, and balanced on a single flying buttress, this 16th-century structure has an interesting sculpted doorway and exquisite Renaissance stained glass windows, including one that shows the life and resurrection of the Virgin (the fourth along from the entry). The highly decorative and colorful polychrome interior is a change from Gothic sobriety. Pl. St.-Aignan, off Rue des Grenets.

Escalier de la Reine Berthe – At the junction of Rue du Bourg and Rue des Ecuyers, is a house with an unusual timbered spiral staircase from the 16th century decorated with weatherbeaten wooden sculptures. The name recalls the wife of a 10th-century Count of Chartres who went on to marry a King of France. 35 Rue des Ecuyers.

Eglise St.-Martin-au-Val – This church includes a fine crypt, some of whose pillars date from just before Charlemagne, and the tombs of 6th-century bishops. Pl. St.-Martin-au-Val, off Rue St.-Brice.

■**EXTRA SPECIAL:** Malcolm Miller, the well-tailored Englishman who conducts tours of the cathedral from *Easter* through November, has become something of an institution among English-speaking visitors here. Miller has made the cathedral his life's work, and his descriptions of the stained glass and sculpture have set audiences alight from Chartres to Kalamazoo. If he's not off lecturing somewhere else, try to catch him holding court during his 12:15 and 2:45 PM tours — imaginatively explaining the principles of medieval architecture by getting his audience to impersonate flying buttresses. Miller has been training a young man to take over when he's away, so even if you land here in January or February, a good English tour should be available. Private tours can be arranged in advance by contacting Miller in his superb medieval home (26 Rue des Ecuyers; phone: 37-28-15-58).

SOURCES AND RESOURCES

 TOURIST INFORMATION: Chartres's Tourist Office, or Syndicat d'Initiative, recently took up residence in sparkling new quarters (Pl. de la Cathédrale; phone: 37-21-54-03) just to the left of the square in front of the cathedral — very close to its old location. Maps, pamphlets, and information are dispensed from 9:30 AM to 12:30 PM and 2 to 6:30 PM daily from May to October; closed Sundays and holidays off-season. From *Easter* through October, a currency exchange booth stays open from 9:30 AM to 7:30 PM daily, including Sundays and holidays, on the square in front of the cathedral. The tourist office also keeps tabs on Malcolm Miller's whereabouts. Off-season, call the tourist office ahead of time to be absolutely certain of an English-speaking guide. There are, alternatively, French tours at 10:30 AM and 3 PM, except January and February. For self-guided tours of the Old Town, the tourist office also rents an hour-long cassette tape (in English, French, or German); it comes complete with a tape player and a map.

Local Coverage – Two daily newspapers, *L'Echo Républicain* and *La République du Centre,* are published in Chartres and carry movie listings. Books about Chartres and its cathedral can be purchased in the cathedral shop and at local bookstores. Malcolm Miller's books, in English, are excellent. *Le Guide de Chartres* by Jean Villette is good for those who read French. A pamphlet on Chartres and its main attractions, in English, is available for a small charge at the tourist office.

 TELEPHONE: The city code for Chartres is 37, which is incorporated into all local 8-digit numbers. When calling a number in Chartres from the Paris region (including the Ile-de-France), dial 16, wait for a dial tone, then dial the 8-digit number. When calling a number from outside Paris, dial only the 8-digit number. When calling from the US, dial 33 (which is the country code), followed by the 8-digit number.

GETTING AROUND: Like any medieval city, Chartres is best appreciated on foot. A good pair of legs is the best vehicle to negotiate the steep and winding streets of the Old Town, and pedestrian zones have recently been instituted in the commercial center. The town's area is easily manageable, and all the major sights can be fit into a day, though the fare is rich and is worth a longer visit.

Bicycle – These can be rented by the half-day, the day, or longer at the train station (phone: 37-36-18-56).

Bus – A good network of local buses serves the immediate neighborhood; information can be obtained from *STAC,* in suburban Lucé, 57 Rue de la Beauce (phone: 37-35-68-02).

Car Rental – Perhaps the best-situated company is *Avis,* which has an office off the main hall of the train station (its main office is at 36 Av. du Maréchal-Leclerc in Lucé; phone: 37-28-37-37). *Europcar* also is represented (16 Av. Jehan-de-Beauce; phone: 37-21-49-39), as is *Hertz* (3 Rue du Grand Faubourg; phone: 37-21-90-90).

Taxi – Taxis congregate outside the train station, or call 37-36-00-00. For a lightning visit of a few hours, and with a couple of other people, it would be feasible to rent a cab for the 55-mile (88-km) ride from Paris.

Train – The train station, at Pl. Pierre-Sémard, is west of the cathedral and within walking distance (the cathedral is plainly visible from the station). For train information, call 37-28-50-50; for reservations, call 37-28-42-61. The trip between Chartres and Paris's Gare Montparnasse takes about an hour, and service is frequent.

SPECIAL EVENTS: On Sundays in late April and May, student pilgrims crowd into Chartres after their 25-mile hike through the forest of Rambouillet. The pilgrimages are a tradition started early in this century by the Catholic poet Charles Péguy, who originally made the trip on foot from Paris when his son fell dangerously ill (the child survived). Contact l'Abbé Hercouët (phone: 37-21-32-33). The *Chartres Organ Festival,* attracting performers from all over the world, takes place in July and August in the cathedral; and the *Concours International d'Orgue,* one of the world's most important organ competitions, takes place in Chartres in mid-September of even-numbered years. The *Samedis Musicaux* (Musical Saturdays) series, featuring chamber and choral music, takes place periodically during the year in a variety of historic buildings. An antiques fair takes place every October at the Collegiate Church of St. Andrew, and a flea market on the fourth Sunday of each month at the Place St.-Pierre. *St. Andrew's Fair* — a lot of bumper cars and candy apples with little trace of its historic origins — comes in late November or early December. The winding streets of Chartres's Old Town provide the perfect setting for a superb *Medieval Festival.* Held annually in mid-June, it attracts groups, dressed in colorful, Gothic-style garb, from all over the world.

MUSEUMS: The *Musée des Beaux-Arts* is described in *Special Places.* Prehistoric remains found locally are in the *Museum of Natural Sciences* (Square Noël-Ballay, Bd. de la Courtille; phone: 37-28-36-09). *La Maison Picassiette* (22 Rue du Repos; phone: 37-34-10-78), east of town, features an unorthodox naif art form: murals made from pieces of broken plates. It is open from *Easter* through September. There's also the *Musée de l'Ecole* (1 Rue du 14 Juillet; phone: 37-28-57-90), with a classroom from the days of the Third Republic and a remarkable collection of authentic furniture and equipment; open Wednesdays during the school year and by appointment. *Le COMPA (Conservatoire du Machinisme et des Pratiques Agricoles),* Chartres's newest museum, is devoted to the history and future of agrarian societies. The emphasis is on agricultural techniques and the equipment of "La Planete Agricole" (Agricultural Planet). Closed Mondays. Open 10 AM to 6 PM (7 PM on weekends). 1 Rue de la République (phone: 37-36-11-30).

SHOPPING: For a town of its size, Chartres's shopping facilities are impressive. There is a branch of the *Au Printemps* department store on Rue Marceau and a *Monoprix* supermarket on Rue Noël-Ballay, together with a healthy overspill of Paris fashions. *Galerie de France* is a horseshoe-shaped mini-mall in the main shopping area just off Place des Epars on Rue Noël-Ballay. Its dozen or so shops include *Rodier, Maison de la Presse, 18ème Parallele,* and more.

The town's good burghers evidently are fond of their food, to judge by the appetizing terrines (Chartres's pâtés are a specialty) sold at local *charcuteries.* Another local specialty, the attractive, glazed pottery, *poterie du marais,* can be purchased at the source, the kilns of St. George sur Eure (6 miles/10 km from town; phone: 37-26-74-11). Other shops of note include the following:

Ariane – Original hand-knit sweaters, antique lace, linen, and children's wear, some made by the friendly proprietress Annich Laillet. 39 Rue des Changes (phone: 37-21-20-68).

Le Collectionneur – Beautiful old leatherbound books, as well as prints and a variety of gift items. 3C Cloître Notre-Dame (phone: 37-21-90-89).

Darreau Charcuterie des Epars – A variety of sausage, salami, and pâté. 6 Rue Delacroix.

Ferme Sainte-Suzanne – More than 150 farm-fresh cheeses. 7 Rue de la Pie (phone: 37-21-88-24).

La Galerie du Cloître – Located in a beamed stone loft, it features a wide variety of art forms — painting, sculpture, glasswork, tapestry — made mainly by local artists. 8 Cloître Notre-Dame (phone: 37-36-30-37).

Galerie DB – Displays and sells the work of contemporary artists, in the dramatic setting of an old priory. 12 Rue Porte Cendreuse (phone: 37-30-99-22).

La Galerie du Vitrail – Old and new stained glass pieces are on exhibit and for sale. There also are audiovisual presentations on the subject. 17 Cloître Notre-Dame (near the cathedral; phone: 37-36-10-03).

Tartine & Trottinette – Charmingly cluttered toy and crafts shop with some very unusual items. 38 Rue des Changes (phone: 37-36-03-38).

SPORTS AND FITNESS: Chartres has public swimming pools and tennis courts, and there are several riding schools in the area (ask at the tourist office for information). In the leafy setting of the Eure at the Pont de la Courtille, the friendly man at *La Petite Venise* rents flat blue rowboats that seat four or five, from *Easter* to the end of October. During less temperate seasons, *sportifs* can try *Chartres Bowling* (Barjouville-Rocade; phone: 37-35-82-82), or enjoy a game of squash. There are also frequent horse races at the *Hippodrome* (Av. Jean Mermoz; phone: 37-34-93-73).

THEATER: Fast trains and Chartres's proximity to the capital haven't done much for the performing arts; however, artists occasionally give pre-premiere performances before opening in Paris. The *Forum de la Madeleine* (1 Mail Jean-de-Dunois; phone: 37-35-08-83) puts on frequent performances, predominantly *chanson française* and comedies, but the *Théâtre Municipal* (Bd. Chasles; phone: 37-21-57-29) is a shadow of what it was 100 years ago. While there are regular programs of music and modern dance as well as occasional plays from September to June, determined playgoers make the trek into Paris.

MUSIC: Fine organ music adds another dimension to the beauty of Notre-Dame de Chartres, and though concerts are held throughout the year, the height of musical activity comes in July and August with the free Sunday concerts of the *Chartres Organ Festival,* a chance to hear internationally known musicians play one of France's great organs in this magnificently resonant space. The classical concerts of the *Samedis Musicaux* (Musical Saturdays) take place periodically in a variety of historic buildings. Tickets are available at the tourist office. Programs of jazz and rock are part of the fare at the *Théâtre Municipal* (see above); opera fans follow the playgoers to Paris.

NIGHTCLUBS AND NIGHTLIFE: Hardly a Chartres specialty, but the fearless may like to try the *Lido-Club* (Av. Marcel-Proust; phone: 37-34-41-41). There's even a roller disco off the RN10 at *Le Bois Paris.* An addition to the area's nighttime scene is a disco called *The Palladium,* open Friday and Saturday nights (1 Rue de la République; phone: 37-22-22-67) in St.-Prest, about 4 miles (6 km) from Chartres. For just hanging out, there are some comfortable piano bars: *L'Escalier* (1 Rue du Bourg; phone: 37-28-11-25) is open late and frequently features live music, guitar or piano, as does *Le Moulin* (see *Bars and Cafés*).

BEST IN TOWN

 CHECKING IN: Chartres is a cosmopolitan rendezvous from mid-April through mid-November, and since there are few hotels, it's important to book ahead for this period. Perhaps because most of the 3 million or so annual visitors come only for the day, Chartres's hotels are disappointing for a tourism center of this importance and, with one or two exceptions, are only for the most intrepid. None is in the heart of the medieval town. *Chartrexpo,* a vast exhibition center on the eastern outskirts of town, has stimulated the development of new hotels: most of them of characterless modern chains, however. The tourist office can supply names of a few friendly families in the Old Town who offer bed and breakfast in their homes. It is said that the best view of the cathedral is from the youth hostel. A double room listed here as expensive will cost from $60 to $80; the moderate category ranges from roughly $35 to $60; and inexpensive, less than $35.

Château d'Esclimont – One of France's most elegant château hostelries, this 48-room Renaissance palace is flanked by four round towers and surrounded by a tranquil park; only a few miles from Chartres. A member of the prestigious Relais & Châteaux group, it boasts both *grand* comfort and luxury. There also is a restaurant. Saint Symphoriem le Château (phone: 37-31-15-15). Expensive.

Grand Monarque – The town's most imposing establishment has an impressive façade on the central Place des Epars, a good (if expensive) restaurant offering a mix of classic and nouvelle cuisine, and a popular bar with its own attempt at stained glass. In the 19th century, the building was two grand townhouses, with room for a coach and horses to pass in the space now occupied by the *réception.* Recent renovations have spiffed up the lobby and restaurant and added a conference room, a winter garden, and 15 new rooms with wood-beamed ceilings and modern marble baths. The 42 older rooms are individually decorated, and most look onto the courtyard where horses once were stabled. 22 Pl. des Epars (phone: 37-21-00-72). Expensive.

Le Manoir du Palomino – This elegant hostelry, only 4 miles (6 km) from Chartres, offers not only good food but a wide range of fitness facilities, with golf, a sauna, a gym, and a bodybuilding center. Some rooms are more deluxe (and more expensive) than others; ask for the best and book well in advance. 28300 St.-Prèst (phone: 37-22-27-27). Expensive.

Mercure Chartres-Châtelet – Part of the nationwide chain, this 48-room hotel opened a decade ago with a mock medieval lobby and a modern wing that the architect cleverly angled toward the cathedral. A majority of the functional, well-equipped rooms look over an uncluttered space to the great landmark, making up for the lack of inspiration within. It is on the leafy avenue leading down to the train station and is associated with a nearby restaurant, *Le Rempart.* 6-8 Av. Jehan-de-Beauce (phone: 37-21-78-00). Expensive.

Boeuf Couronné – Half of the 26 spotless rooms here, at the top of the avenue leading to the train station, look out to the cathedral. There are a bar and outside terraces, and a restaurant that serves local specialties with a reasonably priced menu. 15 Pl. du Châtelet (phone: 37-21-11-26). Moderate.

De la Poste – Few of the 60 rooms look onto the cathedral, but most do overlook a courtyard. A relatively peaceful night is guaranteed. The restaurant has three copious, reasonably priced menus. 3 Rue du Général-Koening (phone: 37-21-04-27). Moderate.

Ibis – A member of the nationwide chain, what this motel lacks in Old World charm it makes up for in such practicalities as meeting rooms, easy parking, and an inexpensive restaurant with fast service. Set beside the river, with 15 rooms overlooking the cathedral. Pl. de la Porte-Drouaise (phone: 37-36-06-36). Moderate.

Saint-Jean – One of Chartres's better bargains, this 19th-century bourgeois house near the train station offers simple, clean rooms and renovated baths (with or without WC). 6 Rue de Faubourg Saint-Jean (phone: 37-21-35-69). Inexpensive.

 EATING OUT: Chartres's restaurants, all in all, don't live up to the promise of the shopfronts of its butchers and bakers, but one or two illustrious names have come to nest here. At the lower end of the market is a cosmopolitan selection of Vietnamese and Algerian restaurants and pizza parlors, but variety may not make up for an absence of overall quality. Don't miss the local specialty, *marsauceux,* a soft-crusted cheese wrapped in chestnut leaves. Meals at the established and expensive restaurants cost $75 to $100 (and up) for two, with service usually included; at restaurants in the moderate range, $50 to $75; and in inexpensive restaurants, $25 to $50.

Henri IV – Jacques Corbonnois, trained by Maurice Cazalis, who was the doyen of Chartres's chefs, carries on his master's good work. The paneled dining room specializes in a creation of duck liver with apples; there also are good sweetbreads, fish, and duck, and the pâtés and bread are made on the premises. The bill will be hefty and service can be a little flustered. Closed Monday evenings, Tuesdays, and the month of February. Reservations advised. 31 Rue Soleil-d'Or (phone: 37-36-01-55). Expensive.

La Vieille Maison – Elegant dining in an old house near the cathedral. Bernard Roger, the unassuming chef, uses the freshest produce to create a varied menu; his favorites are poultry from nearby Brou, game, and a sweetbread dish cooked with foie gras and homemade noodles. Closed Sunday evenings and Mondays. Reservations advised. 5 Rue au Lait (phone: 37-34-10-67). Expensive.

Le Bistrot de la Cathédrale – This restaurant–wine bar has a fine location facing the cathedral. Comfortably rustic decor, a tile floor, and an open, uncluttered atmosphere supply the backdrop for some imaginative country food and some good Loire wines. Closed Sunday evenings and Mondays. Reservations unnecessary. 1 Cloître Notre-Dame (phone: 37-36-59-60). Moderate.

Blanquette – Owned by the same management as *La Vieille Maison,* this sleek, modern spot serves sophisticated but reasonably priced fare, including the trout with leeks house specialty and a popular cauliflower mousse with Roquefort sauce appetizer. A good selection of wine can be ordered by the glass. Reservations advised. 45 Rue des Changes (phone: 37-21-99-36). Moderate.

Café Serpente – The proprietor has his hands on a prime location: the former post office building, classified as a monument and facing the cathedral. The place is done up as a turn-of-the-century bistro, with a moderately priced fixed menu. It also caters to the tourist in a hurry with a selection of fast food. Closed the first 2 weeks of January. Reservations unnecessary. 2 Cloître Notre-Dame (phone: 37-21-68-81). Moderate to inexpensive.

Le Tripot – The chic local crowd eats here. Bunches of dried flowers hang from the rafters, an open fire burns in the winter, and the attempt to make rustic elegant succeeds. Straightforward country food is appetizingly presented, with multicolored pickle jars and lots of salad greens, and there is a pleasing selection of good Loire Valley wines. Open daily. Reservations unnecessary. 11 Pl. Jean-Moulin (phone: 37-36-60-11). Moderate to inexpensive.

Le Biniou – An unpretentious Breton *crêperie* that serves everything on a pancake, using such ingredients as fried onions, scrambled eggs, and fresh cream for the savory versions, and Calvados and apple compote for dessert. Bowls of Breton cider help wash it all down. Cassette tapes alternate with an occasional group that plays live music, showing off the sounds of the Breton bagpipe that gives the restaurant its name. Closed Tuesdays and Wednesdays. Reservations unnecessary. 7 Rue Serpente (phone: 37-21-53-12). Inexpensive.

Le Buisson Ardent – One of those fancy places that are a bit too heavy on the decor for comfort, it offers two fixed menus and both a cocktail bar and a tearoom. Closed Sunday evenings, Tuesday evenings, and Wednesdays. Reservations advised. 10 Rue au Lait (phone: 37-34-04-66). Inexpensive.

Tartine Show – Fast food French-style, this high-tech eatery with a bright, open kitchen serves up everything imaginable on a "raft" of good, country-style bread. In addition to these open-face sandwiches (called *tartines* in French), there are traditional sandwiches, plus salads, pastries, and drinks. Located just across from the cathedral. Dinner daily; lunch Tuesdays through Saturdays. No reservations. 1 Rue Fulbert (phone: 37-36-28-07). Inexpensive.

Le Trois Lys – Another *crêperie,* this one nestled cozily in a crooked old half-timbered house by the river, in one of the oldest parts of Chartres. Pleasant atmosphere, affordable prices, and scenic surroundings make it worth the short walk down to the river and the Basse Ville. Closed Sundays and Mondays. Reservations unnecessary. 3 Rue Porte Guillaume (phone: 37-28-42-02). Inexpensive.

 BARS AND CAFÉS: The river Eure flows slowly by at *Le Moulin* (21 Rue de la Tannerie; phone: 37-35-87-87), an idyllic spot for a long cocktail. In winter, there is a log fire and comfort; in summer, a wooden patio over the water. Snacks and a cocktail or an exotic punch are not cheap, but the setting is impeccable. Closed Sunday evenings.

DIJON

Arriving at the Dijon train station, a traveler has little sense of the enchanting medieval city just a few blocks away. The streets on the outskirts of town are very much a part of the 20th century: Dijon's skyline is mostly marked by high-rises and industrial plants. But walk into the center of town and you're immediately transported into an earlier time and place, where the routines of the 20th century fit unobtrusively into the older fabric of the city. Here is Dijon's most dazzling architectural sight, the Palace of the Dukes of Burgundy, and around it are narrow cobblestone streets, one leading into the next, lined with old houses, mansions, and cathedrals.

Dijon dates back to Roman times. But it was relatively unknown until 1015, when Robert I, the first Duke of Burgundy of the Capetian line, chose it as the capital of his duchy. It still was nothing more than that in 1364, when Philip the Bold became the first Duke of Burgundy of the Valois line. Then, in slightly more than 100 years, the four Valois dukes — Philip the Bold, John the Fearless, Philip the Good, and Charles the Bold — transformed Dijon into a fit setting for their increasingly princely reign. The borders of the duchy quickly expanded to include other parts of France and even parts of today's Belgium, the Netherlands, and Luxembourg, and the power of the dukes came to equal that of the French king — or of any other ruler of Christendom, for that matter. So rich and splendid was the court at Dijon that the Valois Dukes of Burgundy shortly became known as the Grand Dukes of the Occident.

As patrons of the arts, the dukes, especially the two Philips, attracted the greatest masters of the time to Dijon and left the city with an outstanding architectural and artistic heritage. Philip the Bold, who ruled for 40 years, embarked on the construction of the ducal palace and of a mausoleum in the 14th century; Philip the Good, who ruled for 48 years, greatly enlarged the palace in the 15th century (adding, among other things, the kitchen seen today; it was at the legendary banquets of the dukes that many of the city's great culinary traditions began).

All along, the dukes were a powerful force in European politics. Both John the Fearless and Philip the Good allied themselves with the English against the French during the Hundred Years War; it was Philip the Good, in fact, who captured and sold Joan of Arc to her English enemies after her string of victories for Charles VII, the French king. But Charles the Bold's conniving with the English against Louis XI led to the end of the duchy of Burgundy. In 1477, after a reign of only 10 years, Charles was defeated and killed in battle, and Louis XI seized the duchy for the French crown.

Dijon's most glorious age was over, though the city did not fade completely into obscurity. It remained the capital of the province of Burgundy, and substantial townhouses continued to be built. At the end of the 17th century, the States-General of Burgundy, a regional assembly of nobles, clergy, and the third estate that met once every 3 years, voted to add to the palace in order to accommodate their gatherings and their permanent bureaucracy. The man chosen for the project was Jules Hardouin-Mansart, the architect and town planner of Louis XIV. Mansart was responsible not only for the design of the new section but also for the redesign of older sections and of the square in front of the palace — a much larger conception that, when finished in the 18th century, unified these disparate elements into a classical whole.

The 18th century also brought Dijon its university and the Canal de Bourgogne, a romantic body of water that weaves its way through the city and eventually flows into the river Saône (pronounced *Sown*). The 19th century was marked by the coming of the railroad, an event of definite consequence in Dijon's fortunes. The city became one of France's major transportation crossroads, and its population grew from 20,000 in 1850 to approximately 150,000 today (250,000 including the surrounding areas). Dijon also developed as an important industrial and commercial center known especially for its gastronomic specialties — above all, mustard.

Although mustard seeds date back to prehistoric times, local legend has it that it was the great Dukes of Burgundy who first gave mustard its name during their lengthy and elaborate banquets. In the early 1500s it was difficult to preserve meat, so the dukes had their chefs create a sauce that would disguise the meat's often rancid smell and taste. *Moult ma tarde,* meaning "a long time I delay my meal," was the term given to this spicy condiment; later, the phrase was shortened to *moutarde* ("mustard").

But mustard is hardly Dijon's only gastronomic contribution. Classic Burgundian dishes such as *escargots* (snails) in garlic butter, *coq au vin,* and the famed *boeuf bourguignon* are featured in the city's bistros, cafés, and fine restaurants, many of them housed in historic buildings with huge stone fireplaces and decorated with period furniture. The best are the old family-run restaurants, where third- and in some cases fourth-generation sons and daughters are maintaining the culinary traditions created by their fathers, grandfathers, and great-grandfathers. These are places to linger in, for it is here that the Dijonnais are truly in their element.

Because Dijon is the capital of Burgundy, set at the northern tip of the Côte d'Or, the region's "golden slope" (or its gold coast!) wine area, it is not surprising that its restaurants offer some of the finest wines in France, if not the world. Within an hour's drive are the vineyards that produce beaujolais, pouilly-fuissé, romanée-conti, and a wide variety of other, equally exquisite red and white burgundies. Dijon also is the home of cassis, a sweet, burgundy-colored liqueur made from fresh black currants. (The trendy drink kir, a combination of *aligoté* — a dry white wine — and cassis, is named for a much beloved Dijon mayor, Canon Kir.)

Travelers often use Dijon as a starting point for a tour of the vineyards of Burgundy, traveling by waterway or taking the famed Route des Grands Crus (the national highway that links the major wine producing communes of the Côte d'Or). While it's certainly true that the landscape around Dijon is quite lovely, don't make the mistake that many do and head directly out of town. The Dijonnais have spent a lot of time and energy preserving their heritage.

Many of the old streets and buildings have been restored with loving care, and a walking tour through the center of the city takes you past some of the most impressive medieval mansions and Gothic cathedrals in France. Dijon is a beautiful city that deserves attention.

DIJON AT-A-GLANCE

SEEING THE CITY: Toward the middle of the 15th century, Philip the Good, the reigning Duke of Burgundy, added a tall tower to his palace so that he would always be able to keep watch against invaders. Today that tower, Tour Philippe-le-Bon, offers the city's most spectacular views. Once you've climbed the 316 steps to the top, you'll be greeted by the beauty of Dijon's colorful rooftops, its dramatic church steeples, and the tranquil surrounding valleys. From this vantage point, the late afternoon light gives Dijon a magical glow. (For more information on hours, ask at the Town Hall — Hôtel de Ville — in the palace. There is a small admission charge.)

SPECIAL PLACES: The Palais des Ducs et des Etats de Bourgogne (known as the Palais des Ducs for the sake of brevity) is the focal point of Dijon. Except for two of them, all the sights listed below are within walking distance of this monument. The Chartreuse de Champmol and Lake Kir are farther out, beyond the railroad station to the west of central Dijon.

Palais des Ducs et des Etats de Bourgogne (Palace of the Dukes and of the States-General of Burgundy) – This huge, highly ornate set of buildings gives a good sense of the power of the Dukes of Burgundy and of the continuing importance of the city even after the duchy had been annexed to the French crown. Its construction spanned 5 centuries. Begun by Philip the Bold in the 14th century, it grew substantially under Philip the Good in the 15th century, continued to expand despite the dukes' downfall, and was completed in the 19th century. A great transformation came during the 17th and 18th centuries, when additions were built for the Etats de Bourgogne, a regional assembly, and the medieval ducal quarters gained a classic veneer designed by Jules Hardouin-Mansart, the architect of Versailles.

Today, part of the palace houses Dijon's Hôtel de Ville (Town Hall) and as such is open to the public (you may have to ask to see specific rooms, however), and part of it houses the *Musée des Beaux-Arts* (see below). Throughout, there are impressive architectural details such as grand marble staircases and giant banquet halls — ask to see the extravagantly decorated fireplace in the Salon de la Renommée in the Hôtel de Ville section — though one of the most interesting rooms, the kitchen built by Philip the Good, requires some imagination to make it come alive. What was once the finest kitchen in all of Burgundy is bare today, but its six fireplaces, each with its own chimney, are enormous. The huge glass window, made from the bottoms of wine bottles, is noteworthy, too; the well directly outside the kitchen in the courtyard was once the site of the palace bakery. The most famous room in the palace, also dating back to Philip the Good, is the Salle des Gardes (Guard Room), entered through the museum. It contains the marble and alabaster tombs of Philip the Bold and John the Fearless, both originally in the Chartreuse de Champmol, the Carthusian monastery founded by Philip toward the end of the 14th century to use as a ducal mausoleum. His tomb, built between 1385 and 1410, is one of the masterpieces of the Flemish sculptor Claus Sluter, who was assisted by his nephew and student, Claus de Werve. Pl. de la Libération.

Musée des Beaux-Arts – This museum's eclectic collection is considered one of the most impressive in France, surpassed only by the *Louvre* in Paris. Installed largely in one of the newer sections of the palace, it contains an assortment of paintings and sculptures ranging from early French and Flemish masters to more contemporary artists such as Picasso, Matisse, and Rodin. The museum has a variety of other art objects including Byzantine enamelwork, Renaissance furniture, and primitive masks and sculptures from Africa. Some of the palace's original furnishings, dating back to the 1500s, also are on view. Be sure to visit the wing housing the modern art collection, too. Particularly interesting here is the way in which the art is displayed — thematically rather than by period or artist. Closed Tuesdays. Admission charge. Pl. de la Ste.-Chapelle (phone: 80-30-31-11).

Place de la Libération – Across the street from the palace, this late-17th-century square and the Louis XIV houses that line it also came off the drawing board of Hardouin-Mansart. The palace façade, the square (actually a semicircle), and the houses create one harmonious classical ensemble.

Eglise Notre-Dame – Built in the 13th century, this church is considered the finest surviving example of Gothic architecture in Burgundy. For the most dramatic view of its unusual exterior, walk around the corner from the Rue de la Chouette and look directly up at the gargoyles that sit in three rows on the upper half of the façade and seem to take on a life of their own. One of the church towers houses the famous Flemish mechanical clock, Jacquemart, which Philip the Bold brought back from Courtrai as a war trophy in 1383. At that time, there was only the little iron blacksmith, who hit the bell every hour on the hour. At the beginning of the 17th century the people of Dijon, thinking the blacksmith might be lonely, gave him a wife, Jacqueline. In the early 18th century, they produced a son, Jacquelinet, and a daughter, Jacquelinette, followed in 1881. Along the Rue de la Chouette (Owl Street), you'll see a small stone owl set into the church's exterior. It is said that if you place your left hand on the owl, it will bring good luck. Inside the church, the 11th-century Vierge Noire (Black Virgin), in a chapel to the right of the choir, is one of the oldest wooden statues in France and an object of veneration. Pl. Notre-Dame.

Eglise St.-Michel – A second major church in Dijon, St. Michael's is a fascinating mixture of styles. It was begun at the end of the 15th century in the Gothic style (note the Flamboyant Gothic side doors) and all but finished in the 16th century with a full Renaissance façade. The towers came later. Pl. St.-Michel.

Cathédrale St.-Bénigne – This Gothic cathedral has been rebuilt four times since the 6th century. The most interesting part of the present structure, which rose between 1280 and 1314 on the site of a Romanesque basilica, is what remains of the basilica: the 10th-century crypt with the tomb of St. Bénigne. The cathedral's 18th-century organ is outstanding. Frequent recitals take place here; check with the tourist office for further information. Pl. St.-Bénigne.

Historic Homes – Dijon has a wealth of beautifully preserved townhouses and other buildings dating back to the 15th to 18th century. The historical society has designated many of these as landmarks and provided each one with a plaque giving its date, original use, and outstanding architectural feature. Further information is contained in a brochure (ask the tourist office for *Maisons et Hôtels Particuliers du XVe au XVIIIe Siècle à Dijon*), which traces an architectural walking tour through downtown Dijon. Be sure to see the buildings along Rue de la Chouette, Rue des Forges, and Rue Berbisey and note the Hôtel Chambellan at 34 Rue des Forges and the Hôtel de Vogüé at 8 Rue de la Chouette. The 15th-century Hôtel Chambellan, with its beautifully carved staircase and balcony in the courtyard, is considered a very fine example of Flamboyant Gothic architecture, and the Hôtel de Vogüé, built in the early 17th century, sports an eye-catching patterned tile roof typical of Burgundian architecture.

Les Halles Centrales (Central Market) – Every Tuesday, Friday, and Saturday, the streets surrounding *Les Halles* fill with vendors and merchants selling everything from fresh braids of garlic from the south of France to antique kitchenware and books. The market itself — a huge, open building — is a wonderful place to gather picnic makings or simply to gaze at the glories of French food. There also are little coffee counters where you can grab an espresso and a croissant. Rue Quentin.

Jardin de l'Arquebuse et Jardin Botanique – Described in the brochure as "an island of calm, green, and flowers in the heart of the city," these idyllic gardens are precisely that. There are virtually acres to explore, scattered with elaborate flower beds and herb gardens. The unusual name comes from the Compagnie de l'Arquebuse, which installed itself here in the 16th century and used the area for archery and *harquebus* (a gun of the times) practice. The *harquebusiers* barracks now houses the *Musée de l'Histoire Naturelle* (see *Museums*) and a large flower, herb, and botany library. Rue de l'Arquebuse.

Chartreuse de Champmol (Champmol Charterhouse) – In 1383, Philip the Bold founded a Carthusian monastery and set about establishing a necropolis for the dukes within its confines. Though the monastery was destroyed in 1793 and the site is now occupied by a psychiatric hospital, two important works of sculpture by Claus Sluter can still be seen: a chapel doorway and the Puits de Moïse (Well of Moses), actually the hexagonal pedestal of a former calvary group. Sluter was the greatest of the artists in service to Philip the Bold, and the six powerful figures of prophets on the well are notable as milestones in the development of realism in medieval sculpture. They rank as one of the Flemish artist's two masterpieces, along with the tomb of Philip made for Champmol and now in the *Museum of Fine Arts.* Open to visitors during office hours. About a 30-minute walk west of the center; entrance from Bd. Chanoine-Kir.

Lac Kir – Named for Dijon's popular mayor, the late Canon Kir, this manmade lake is about a 15-minute drive from downtown. Though it is surrounded by some of Dijon's more modern buildings and can get crowded in the summer, it is a pleasant spot for water sports and an afternoon picnic. Reachable by bus No. 18 or via the N5 toward Paris.

■ **EXTRA SPECIAL:** A good mustard should be hot enough to "tweak" your nose, but not so hot that it's unenjoyable. That's how the people of Dijon describe their legendary condiment. One of the best places to visit to get a "taste" of the pungent spread is the *Grey Poupon* shop (32 Rue de la Liberté; phone: 80-30-41-02). It has been selling mustard since 1777, and residents still bring in empty crocks and jars to be filled with the golden paste. Be sure to see the collection of antique mustard jars belonging to the Grey and Poupon families; they are unusually beautiful. Assorted mustards, vinegars, and other condiments produced by Maille, one of the better Dijon brands, are on sale, as are replicas of the old china crocks; they'll even fill them with mustard and pack them for traveling.

SOURCES AND RESOURCES

TOURIST INFORMATION: The Dijon Office de Tourisme is in the center of town (Pl. Darcy; phone: 80-43-42-12), and there also is a branch in the old part of the city (34 Rue des Forges; phone: 80-30-35-39). Both are open daily from 9 AM to 9 PM in summer; 9 AM to 6 PM in winter (closed during lunchtime). They stock a wide variety of maps, brochures, and guidebooks on all aspects of the city, many of them in English, and are well supplied with information about touring the surrounding wine country of Burgundy. The offices also distribute lists of hotels and restaurants in the city and its environs, and will try to help book rooms locally. (For those late arrivals without accommodations, there is a lighted bulletin board outside the main tourist office that lists room availability in Dijon.) The tourist office's *Accueil de France* accommodations service can book rooms anywhere in France for a small fee. It also has a currency exchange and visitors can get the Dijon Passions card (no charge), which entitles the holder to local bonuses and discounts, including half-price entry to local museums. The card is valid for 1 year. Another bulletin board announces concerts, university events, sporting events, and festivals. Guided walking tours of the city (in French) leave here at 3 PM daily during the summer, from early July through September. There is a small charge.

If you are still in the early planning stages of a tour of Burgundy and are interested in wine (and in purchasing local wine), contact the tourist office in Beaune or the *Comité Interprofessionnel de la Côte d'Or et de l'Yonne pour les Vins d'Appellation Contrôlée de Bourgogne* (Rue Henri-Dunant, 21200 Beaune; phone: 80-22-21-35), which puts out pamphlets on the wine growers.

Local Coverage – Consult *Le Bien Public* or *Les Dépêches*. The *Maison de la Presse* (26 Rue de la Liberté; phone: 80-30-45-62) is a good place to buy French magazines and newspapers as well as English and American newspapers and stationery items.

TELEPHONE: The city code for Dijon is 80, which is incorporated into all local 8-digit numbers. When calling a number in Dijon from the Paris region (including the Ile-de-France), dial 16, wait for a dial tone, then dial the 8-digit number. When calling a number from outside Paris, dial only the 8-digit number. When calling from the US, dial 33 (which is the country code), followed by the 8-digit number.

GETTING AROUND: Central Dijon is compact. By far, the easiest and most pleasant way to see the city is on foot.

Bicycle – Biking is fairly common and it is not terribly hazardous. It is an ideal way to reach Lake Kir and other surrounding sites. Bikes are rented by *Cycles Pouilly* (3 Rue de Tivoli and 3 Pl. Wilson; phone: 80-66-61-75).

Bus – City bus service is provided by *STRD* (*Société des Transports Routiers Dijonnais*), which operates an easily used network throughout Dijon and its environs. Bus maps are available from the tourist office or from the central bus station (Pl. Grangier; phone: 80-30-60-90). In addition to individual tickets, there are unlimited-travel tickets, sold on a weekly basis for a very good price. Buses stop running at 8:30 PM.

Car Rental – All the major firms are represented. Near the train station are *ADA* (20 bis Av. Foch; phone: 80-45-35-50) and *Hertz* (18 Av. Foch; phone: 80-43-55-22). *Europcar* also has an office (47 Rue Guillaume Tell; phone: 80-43-28-44).

Taxi – Taxis are available 24 hours a day at the train station and at the post office on Pl. Grangier. You also can call *Taxi Radio* (phone: 80-41-41-12) directly. Prices are reasonable, but fares double after 8 PM. Dijon taxis also offer city tours, narrated in English on cassette, and various itineraries for excursions outside of town — to the vineyards of Burgundy, for example. For reservations or additional information, call *Central Radio Taxi Dijon* (phone: 80-41-41-12), or ask the tourist office for a brochure about this service.

Train – The Gare de Dijon-Ville is at the opposite end of Av. du Maréchal-Foch from Pl. Darcy (phone: 80-41-50-50 for information, 80-43-52-56 for reservations).

SPECIAL EVENTS: Every 3 or 4 years in March (the last one was in 1989), the city hosts *Florissimo*, a major floral exhibition showcasing the exotic blooms of five continents (at the *Palais des Congrès*, just outside the center of town at 3 Bd. de Champagne; phone: 80-71-44-34). The huge *Antiques*

Fair of mid-May and the *Dijon Flea Market* of early September both take place in the *Forum,* Rue Général Delaborde. The *Eté Musical,* when local artists present classical concerts at many of Dijon's most beautiful monuments, occurs during the month of July. Late August is the time for the traditional *Fête de la Vigne* (Grape Harvest Festival) which is celebrated along with the *Fête Folklorique Internationale* (International Folk Dance and Song Festival). For true food and wine lovers, and for those whose business it is, however, the above is simply an appetizer for the *Foire Internationale et Gastronomique* (International Food and Wines Fair), held the first 2 weeks of November. This is one of the country's major trade fairs, a showcase for the very finest edibles and potables from all over France and the world, and an opportunity for some magnificent tasting. It takes place at the *Palais des Congrès* (phone: 80-71-44-34).

MUSEUMS: The city offers a special entry card, good for a year, that allows visitors to enter all of its museums for one very reasonable fee. In addition to those mentioned in *Special Places,* museums of interest (all are closed on Tuesdays) include the following:

Espace Grevin – The newest of Dijon's museums, opened in June 1990, is a franchise of Paris's wax museum. It houses an exhibit portraying the history of the Burgundy region through Grevin's famous wax figures (M. Grevin was considered the Mme. Toussaud of Paris). There's a wine tasting facility next door (see *Eating Out*). 13 Av. Albert 1er; phone: 80-42-03-03).

Musée Archéologique – In the dormitory of the former Benedictine Abbey of St. Bénigne, this small museum has an impressive collection of Gallo-Roman and medieval artifacts and a famous bust of Christ by Claus Sluter. Next to the Cathédrale St.-Bénigne, at 5 Rue Dr.-Maret (phone: 80-30-88-54).

Musée d'Art Sacré – Ever-changing exhibits of religious art from churches of the region. Many works currently are being housed here while the churches they belong to undergo repair or restoration. Open 9 AM to noon and from 2 to 6 PM; closed holidays. 15 Rue Ste.-Anne (phone: 80-30-06-44).

Musée d'Histoire Naturelle – Geological and zoological specimens of the Dijon region are displayed in the old barracks of the *harquebusiers* (see *Special Places*). 1 Av. Albert 1er, Jardin de l'Arquebuse (phone: 80-41-61-08).

Musée Magnin – Housed in the Hôtel Lantin, a gorgeous 17th-century mansion bequeathed to the city by Maurice Magnin, this collection documents elegant 17th-century life with period furniture and paintings. 4 Rue des Bons-Enfants, off Pl. de la Libération (phone: 80-67-11-10).

Musée Rude – A local favorite dedicated to the works of the 19th-century sculptor François Rude, set up in the transept of a deconsecrated church. Formerly open by appointment only, it now is open to the public from 10 AM to noon and from 2 to 5:45 PM.. 8 Rue Vaillant (phone: 80-66-87-95).

Musée de la Vie Bourguignonne (Museum of Burgundian Life) – This museum occupies two rooms of a 15th-century building attached to *CBDO,* one of the city's most charming restaurants (see *Eating Out*). One room is filled with heraldry and authentically costumed models of medieval Burgundian knights and the other is devoted to wine — antique wine presses, corkscrews, bottles, labels, tools, and other wine making equipment. 17 Rue Ste.-Anne (phone: 80-30-65-91).

SHOPPING: The city's best shopping is along the Rue de la Liberté, and food and wine are among the best buys. Look for such regional specialties as mustard, cassis (black currant liqueur), *pain d'épice* (gingerbread), and burgundy wines. Dijon also is a good town for antiques. You'll come across a number of tempting shops in the vicinity of Notre-Dame, particularly along the Rue Verrerie.

Laura Ashley – Her standard designs by the yard in ready-to-wear clothing, and home decorating items. 18/20 Rue Piron (phone: 80-30-04-44).

Escargots de Bourgogne – Fresh, canned, or in sealed glass jars — nothing but escargots in this crowded little shop operated by savvy, friendly Mme. Verdier. 14 Rue Bannelier (phone: 80-30-22-15).

Mulot et Petitjean – A good place for gifts: regional foods and wines including *pain d'épice* in a variety of shapes — a wine bottle or a snail. 1 Pl. Notre-Dame; also at 16 Rue de la Liberté and 13 Pl. Bossuet (phone: 80-30-07-10).

Nouvelles Galeries – Everything from clothing and cosmetics to sewing equipment and fabrics at a moderately priced department store. The food and wine department downstairs is an ideal place for preparing a picnic. 41-49 Rue de la Liberté (phone: 80-30-49-25).

Au Pain d'Autrefois – Behind a recently fancified façade hides the heart and soul of this bread maker — an old bread oven. Pick up some interesting breads to accompany your wine and cheese purchases. 47 Rue du Bourg (phone: 80-37-47-92).

Simone Porcheret – A dream of a cheese shop with some of the most wonderful and aged cheeses likely to be found anywhere. Ask for *citeaux* made by local monks. 18 Rue Bannerlier (phone: 80-30-21-05).

Rafael – Chic boutique near the Palais des Ducs, with elegant women's clothing by Armani, Celine, and others. 10 Rue Piron (phone: 80-30-97-07).

Udebert Nouveautés – Dijon's most established women's specialty shop. Everything from accessories to undergarments. 62-68 Rue de la Liberté. (phone: 80-30-44-56).

Au Vieux Dijon – Interesting antiques. 36 Rue Verrerie (phone: 80-31-89-08).

 SPORTS AND FITNESS: Ballooning – Hardly the do-it-yourself version of the sport, and expensive. Nevertheless, a trip over the Burgundy vineyards in a hot-air balloon can be thrilling on a clear day. You'll be picked up at a major Dijon hotel; all flights end with a bottle of burgundy wine. Contact *Air Escargot* (Remigny, 71150 Chagny-France; phone: 85-87-12-30) or *Air Aventure* (6727 Curran St., McLean, VA 22101-3804; phone: 800-862-8537 in the US, 80-26-63-30 in Dijon).

Boating – *Navigation et Technique* offers 2-hour cruises on the canal during the summer and rents houseboats for longer stays (Port du Canal, Plombières-les-Dijon; phone: 80-45-44-60). Motorboats for a day of cruising through the dams can be rented from *Locadif* (Gissey-sur-Ouche, Pont de Pany; phone: 80-49-04-76).

Golf – The 18-hole *Golf de Bourgogne* course (Norges-la-Ville; phone: 80-35-71-10) is 6 miles/10 km from Dijon, but there is no equipment for rent. *Golf de Beaune à Levernois*, a public course (in Levernois, 1½ miles/2 km from Beaune toward Verdun-sur-le-Doubs; phone: 80-24-10-29), is another option.

Jogging – A number of parks throughout town are ideal for jogging. The most accessible is probably Place Darcy, a small park in the center. The Parc de la Colombière (dating from Louis XIV) has 80 acres to roam somewhat south of the center. In addition, there is Lake Kir, the artificial lake west of the center, and the beautiful Parc de la Combe à la Serpent, also west of town.

Sailing and Windsurfing – Equipment for these can be rented at Lake Kir. Take N5 out of Dijon toward Paris.

Swimming – Swimming is forbidden at Lake Kir because of pollution, but indoor pools open to the public are *Piscine du Carrousel* (Cours du Parc; phone: 80-67-20-12); *Piscine de la Fontaine d'Ouche* (Fontaine d'Ouche, Av. du Lac; phone: 80-43-38-19); and *Piscine des Grésilles* (Bd. Champollion; phone: 80-71-37-35).

Tennis – The *Parc des Sports* (Pl. Gaston Gerard; phone: 80-71-29-43) has 17 outdoor courts open to the public, and there also are courts at Lake Kir (phone: 80-41-69-66).

THEATER AND MUSIC: The very elegant *Théâtre Municipal,* set off to one side of the ducal palace at Pl. du Théâtre (phone: 80-67-23-23), is Dijon's oldest theater and its main site for a full range of theatrical activity including plays, operettas, opera, ballet, and classical concerts. The city's avant-garde theater, *Théâtre du Parvis St.-Jean* (Rue Danton; phone: 80-30-12-12), puts on a wide variety of experimental productions as well as music and dance. Dijon University also holds a number of noteworthy theater, dance, and musical events (call 80-66-64-13 for information), while various churches — especially St.-Michel and St.-Bénigne — are used for organ recitals and choral and orchestral concerts. The *Eldorado* (21 Rue Alfred de Musset; phone: 80-66-12-34 or 80-66-51-89) is an old movie house specializing in "art films," frequently in English. The *Bistro de la Scène* (203 Rue d'Auxonne; phone: 80-67-87-39), a relatively new café/theater, presents plays, jazz, and concerts.

NIGHTCLUBS AND NIGHTLIFE: Dijon is not noted for a wild nightlife. What most people do for an evening's entertainment is eat and drink, often stretching dinner out to 10 or 11 PM and then lingering at the bar with a snifter of cognac or Burgundian *marc* (grape brandy). But because this is a university town, nightclubs and discos do exist. These include *La Jamaique* (14 Pl. de la République; phone: 80-73-52-19), a popular meeting spot serving exotic cocktails, and playing a West Indian beat.

BEST IN TOWN

CHECKING IN: Compared to those in Paris, the prices in Dijon are extremely reasonable. Accommodations here in a very plush first class hotel can cost as little as $75 — roughly a third of the tariff for similar digs in the capital. But many of the best bets around town are the old family hotels, some now being run by the fourth generation. A double room below in the expensive category will cost from $50 to $90, $35 to $50 in moderate, and under $35 in inexpensive — where you may end up sharing a toilet down the hall. Breakfast, unless otherwise noted, is not included.

Altéa – About a 15-minute walk from the center of town and convenient to the *Palais des Congrès,* this sleek, modern hotel is part of the national chain. The 123 rooms are very comfortable, with extremely large bathrooms. Rear rooms all have views of the center. Restaurant, *Le Château-Bourgogne* (see *Eating Out*), and bar. 22 Bd. de la Marne (phone: 80-72-31-13). Expensive.

Le Chapeau Rouge – A small, well-respected place next to the St. Bénigne Cathedral, it has been run by the same family since 1922. A few of the 33 rooms have beautiful 18th-century furniture; the rest are tastefully decorated with a good balance of old and new. The front rooms have double-paned windows for protection from noise in this central location, and a few of the side rooms have dramatic views of the cathedral. Over half of its rooms recently were renovated and some now include a saltwater Jacuzzi. There is a restaurant (see *Eating Out*) and a bar. 5 Rue Michelet (phone: 80-30-28-10). Expensive.

La Cloche – The building dates back to 1424, but all that remains of the original structure are the exterior walls, including the façade. Following a complete renovation, it now ranks as Dijon's most elegant hostelry, with 80 attractively furnished rooms and suites enhanced by wonderful views of the Place Darcy park and the hotel's own peaceful little garden. A tea and coffee shop overlooks the garden; there's an excellent restaurant, *Jean-Pierre Billoux* (see *Eating Out*), a bar, and a boutique. Phones are in the rooms, and in many of the bathrooms as well. 14 Pl. Darcy (phone: 80-30-12-32). Expensive.

Wilson – Ceiling beams, warm stone hearths, and a central courtyard, all relics of the 17th-century coaching inn, within whose frame this recently opened 3-star hotel was constructed, make this a charming place to stay. 1 Rue de Longvic (phone: 80-66-82-50). Expensive.

Jura – A friendly place with a lovely private garden. The rooms are comfortable with modern decorations, and those that face the street — the main thoroughfare between Place Darcy and the railroad station — have soundproof windows. Bar; no restaurant. Closed *Christmas* to mid-January. 14 Av. du Maréchal-Foch (phone: 80-41-61-12). Moderate.

Nord – Run by the same family for four generations, this charmer feels more like a country inn than a city hotel. The 26 rooms are clean and quiet with large baths and fluffy down comforters on every bed, and there's a wine bar in the cellar where you can try out the tastes of Burgundy. Restaurant. Closed *Christmas* through mid-January. 2 Rue de la Liberté (phone: 80-30-58-58). Moderate.

Du Palais – In the heart of the city's historic quarter, this fine old building is just down the street from the Palais de Justice. Many of the 17 rooms have antique furnishings and often are frequented by visiting lawyers. 23 Rue du Palais (phone: 80-67-16-26). Moderate to inexpensive.

Terminus et Grande Taverne – Small and family-run, it has been in business for more than a century. The rooms are quiet, with simple, old-fashioned decor. Convenient to the train station. Bar and restaurant. 24 Av. du Maréchal-Foch (phone: 80-43-53-78). Moderate to inexpensive.

Thurot – Down a quiet side street just a few minutes' walk from the train station, it's run by two friendly elderly women. A bit like a motel, though the rooms are clean and comfortable, and while there is no restaurant, the little bar downstairs dispenses drinks and coffee. 4 Passage Thurot (phone: 80-43-57-46). Inexpensive.

 EATING OUT: Dijon is considered one of the capitals of French haute cuisine and is a wonderful place to sample traditional Burgundian food and wine at very reasonable prices. Specialties to look for include kir and kir royal (apéritifs made of cassis — black currant liqueur — mixed with *aligoté,* a dry white wine or champagne), served at virtually every bar and restaurant in town; *escargots à la bourguignonne* (snails in garlic butter); *jambon persillé* (ham in parslied aspic); *oeufs pochés en meurette* (eggs poached in red wine with mushrooms and ham); *rognon de veau à la dijonnaise* (veal kidney in a Dijon mustard sauce); *coq au vin* (chicken in wine); and the famed *boeuf bourguignon* (beef stewed in wine). Burgundian food tends to be hearty and satisfying, though a number of chefs in town are producing lighter food, in the nouvelle style, with good results. Burgundy's vineyards also yield some of the best wines of France, if not the world, and Dijon's restaurants and bistros offer these, too, at extremely reasonable prices. Beaujolais nouveau often goes for as little as $5 a bottle. Expect to pay from $100 and up for dinner for two at restaurants listed below as expensive; between $50 and $90 at those listed as moderate; and under $50 at the inexpensive ones. Prices do not include wine; usually a service charge is included.

Jean-Pierre Billoux – Considered by many to be Dijon's best chef, Monsieur Billoux garnered two Michelin stars for refined and original fare that includes dishes such as *suprème de pintade au foie de canard et aux câpres* (guinea hen with duck liver and capers). An elegant room, it's in the old *caves* (wine cellars) of the renovated 15th-century *Hôtel de la Cloche.* Closed January. Reservations necessary. 14 Pl. Darcy (phone: 80-30-11-00). Expensive.

Le Chapeau Rouge – In the *hostellerie* of the same name, this candlelit dining room serves excellent regional and nouvelle cuisine that has won it a Michelin star. Start with *croustade d'escargots à la crème de basilic,* and then move on to the *rognon de veau à la dijonnaise* (veal kidney in mustard sauce) or *pigeonneau farci* (stuffed baby pigeon). The pastry cart is impressive, as is the plate of petits fours served at the end of every meal. Excellent wine list. Reservations necessary. 5 Rue Michelet (phone: 80-30-28-10). Expensive.

Le Château-Bourgogne – Not the old-fashioned setting its name suggests, but a spare, contemporary dining room in the *Altéa* hotel. The Burgundian chef who runs the well-respected kitchen received his training from the famed Troisgros brothers. The menu is primarily nouvelle, although you'll also find classic dishes such as fresh duck foie gras and grilled lamb with fresh thyme. Quite a good wine list. Open daily. Reservations necessary. 22 Bd. de la Marne (phone: 80-72-31-13). Expensive.

La Chouette – This small, medieval dining room down the street from the Eglise Notre-Dame serves some of the best food in town and has earned a Michelin star. Try the delicate (and very fresh) *lotte aux raisins* (monkfish with raisins in a Mercurey wine sauce), fresh crayfish in a *beurre blanc, pigeon de Bresse rôti aux morilles farci au foie gras* (pigeon stuffed with goose liver and roasted with wild mushrooms), and any of the exquisite desserts. Closed Monday evenings and Tuesdays. Reservations necessary. 1 Rue de la Chouette (phone: 80-30-18-10). Expensive.

CBDO La Toison d'Or (Restaurant de la Compagnie Bourguignonne des Oenophiles) – Dining here is an experience that should not be missed. It's a 17th-century mansion, where the original beams, huge stone fireplaces, and a decoration of tapestries and period furniture give it the feel of an elegant country inn. The food is a mixture of hearty Burgundian specialties — rabbit *en gelée* and *coq au vin* — and lighter, nouvelle dishes such as salmon, turbot, and spinach terrine and thinly sliced breast of duck with grapes. A good wine list, though not an outstanding one considering the restaurant's affiliation, and the *compagnie* stocks its own wine for sale direct from growers. After dinner, be sure to ask for a tour of the adjoining 15th-century courtyard and museum (see "Museums," *Sources and Resources*). Closed Saturdays at lunch, holidays, and the first 3 weeks of August. Reservations necessary. 18 Rue Ste.-Anne (phone: 80-30-73-52). Expensive to moderate.

Thibert – Sophisticated decor and refined cooking have won Jean-Paul Thibert a Michelin star. A favorite with locals, this place also is situated on one of Dijon's most beautiful squares. Closed Sunday dinner, Monday lunch, 3 weeks in January, and 2 weeks in August. Reservations necessary. 10 Pl. Wilson (phone: 80-67-74-64). Expensive to moderate.

Le Chabrot – Christian Bouy, the jovial, mustachioed owner, supplies a warm welcome and a menu prepared by his young chef, Joel Guillaud, who is particularly talented with fish — the salmon menu has 15 versions of that *poisson* alone. In addition to the main dining room, there's a wine bar and a 12th-century *cave*. Reservations advised. 36 Rue Monge (phone: 80-30-69-61). Moderate.

La Porte Guillaume – This fourth-generation establishment is one of the most charming — and moderately priced — dining rooms in town. Don't be surprised by the abundance of mustachioed waiters here; it's a tradition that's been observed for more than a century (take a look at the old family photo on the wall above the fireplace and you'll see). The food, too, is traditional, and it is delicious. The escargots are loaded with garlic, the *coq au vin* and *boeuf bourguignon* can't be beat, and there are about 25 varieties of cheese on the cheese tray. Both the *menu dégustation* and the *menu bourguignon* are worth the price. Reservations advised. 2 Rue de la Liberté, at Pl. Darcy (phone: 80-30-58-58). Moderate.

L'Amandier – Cozy, with ancient stone walls, elegant tableware, and burgundy-colored linen, it represents one of Dijon's best dining values: A three-course, fixed-price meal runs less than $18. Ordering from the regular menu will cost more, but the quality and service justify the extra expense. Closed Sundays and Monday evenings. Reservations advised. 23 Rue Crebillon (phone: 80-30-36-00). Moderate to inexpensive.

Brasserie du Théâtre – A popular university hangout known for its good, inexpensive food. In the summer, there is outdoor dining on the terrace. Closed Tuesday evenings and Wednesdays. Reservations unnecessary. Pl. du Théâtre (phone: 80-67-13-59). Moderate to inexpensive.

Hostellerie de l'Etoile – An ancient façade and a warm, wood-paneled dining room on one side contrast with a modern exterior and eating area on the other side of this restaurant, which occupies an entire block (there's an entrance on each side). Despite the large number of diners served daily, the quality is high and prices reasonable. Try *oeufs pochés en meurette* (poached eggs in red wine with mushrooms and ham), the Dijon specialty that is prepared perfectly here. Ask for a table in the old room when you reserve if you're partial to "La Vieille France." Closed Sundays and Monday lunch. Reservations advised. 1 Rue Marceau (phone: 80-73-20-72). Moderate to inexpensive.

Le Dôme – A favorite gathering spot after the Saturday market at *Les Halles.* Good home cooking. Closed Sundays. Reservations unnecessary. 16 bis Rue Quentin (phone: 80-30-58-92). Inexpensive.

BARS AND CAFÉS: The *Concorde* (2 Pl. Darcy) is a turn-of-the-century brasserie (recently renovated) and a favorite local hangout. A full menu is offered at lunch and dinner (with specialties like *choucroute garnie* and *pot-au-feu*), but most people congregate here for a carafe of wine, a cold mug of imported or Alsatian beer, or a demitasse of excellent coffee. Another place to people watch on Place Darcy is the recently redecorated *Le Glacier,* a popular brasserie and café with a nice selection of wine and beer and a limited menu. Sit by the window and you'll be mesmerized for hours. The *Brighton* (33 Rue Auguste-Comte) is an agreeable "English-style" pub, and *Messire* (3 Rue Jules-Mercier) is another popular bar with a good selection of wine and beer.

■ **Note:** There are a growing number of wine bars and tasting rooms offering visitors the opportunity to sample some of Burgundy's fine wines by the glass. *Le Caveau de la Porte Guillaume* (Pl. Darcy; phone: 80-30-61-26) has tastings from noon to 3 AM. Choose from among some 20 wines — cost of sampling is about $7. *La Cave du Clos* (3 Rue Jeannin; phone: 80-67-64-62) has a newly renovated wine bar/tasting boutique where a glass of Santenay Premier Cru, for example, can be tasted for $2 or less. They also operate a restaurant, *Le Clos des Capucines,* and a newly inaugurated *Ecole du Vin,* headed by oenologist Yves Nicot, where groups can take short wine courses (length of course geared to groups' needs). *Les Caves de l'Espace Grevin* (13 Av. Albert 1er; phone: 80-42-03-03) opened in June 1990. This tasting center next to Dijon's new museum (*Espace Grevin*) has three vaulted ceiling *caves* where tasters can choose from among 150 Burgundy wines. Admission charge is about $10 per person; a *tastevin* (a souvenir tasting cup) is included. *L'Etape Burgonde* (3 Rue de Montigny; phone: 80-30-20-17) offers samplings of Burgundy wines and regional cheese and meat specialties from 10 AM to 9 PM. Tasters also can purchase bottles or cases to take home (they will ship anywhere).

LYONS

Lyons is something of an enigma, a city of contradictions, which may have something to do with its geography. It's essentially a northern city that faces south, so that a whiff of the Mediterranean coming up from Marseilles is often mixed with a chilly blast from the Alps. It has been a border city, at various times in its history the Roman headquarters of Gaul, part of the Holy Roman Empire, and for a long time only tenuously under the French crown, as well as a crossroads, where foreign traffic and trade have always been heavy. A city in the midst of plenty, it has a magnificent site at the confluence of the Rhône and Saône rivers, within easy reach of the Bresse, Charolais, Beaujolais, Burgundy, Forez, Jura, Dauphiné, and other regions, all producers of good things to eat and drink. "Lyons is washed by three rivers," goes one saying, "the Rhône, the Saône, and the Beaujolais," and it certainly is true that the best beaujolais gets only as far as Lyons and stops there.

Until Michel Noir was elected mayor of Lyons in 1989, only three people had held that office since 1905 — solid evidence, one would think, of conservatism — if not outright passivity. Yet the city's mayor from 1905 to 1957 was Edouard Herriot, a stormy, anti-clerical Radical Socialist who was Premier of France more than once during those many years. And during the German occupation of France in World War II — while Herriot was a Nazi prisoner — Lyons was the capital of the French Resistance; its *traboules,* the secret passages in the old sections that connect street to street by cutting through the buildings, served as passageways for daring patriots. Today, Lyons probably is the most dynamic and forward-looking city in France. It already has decided that the Lyons of the 21st century will be across the Rhône, east of the peninsula that has been its center for more than 2 centuries, and it already has built a new center to match.

Today, Lyons has a population of more than 400,000 in the city proper and 1.12 million in the greater urban area, making it the second largest city in France. At least twice in its history, it outstripped Paris in importance. It celebrated its 2,000th anniversary a quarter of a century ago, taking the date from October 10, 43 BC, when a former lieutenant of Julius Caesar, Lucius Munatius Plancus, founded a colony named Lugdunum on one of the hills of Lyons — Fourvière. There are various versions of the origin of the name; *dunum* means "hill," and *Lug* seems to have referred to an early deity of the Celts, who were established at the confluence of the two rivers at least 6 centuries before the Romans.

Lugdunum became the capital from which the Romans administered the three provinces of Gaul, and their emperors made it into a substantial city. Between 16 and 14 BC, Augustus built a 4,500-seat theater on Fourvière, which was enlarged in Hadrian's time to hold 10,000 people. Nearby, a smaller theater was built for music and speeches. The town also had a circus for chariot races, since gone, and in a settlement called Condate across the Saône on the slope of another hill, the Croix-Rousse, the Amphithéâtre des Trois-Gaules, discovered in 1958. This appears to have been the periodic gathering place of delegates of the 60 Gallic tribes into which the Romans had further divided the three provinces, and the site, in the 2nd century, of the martyrdom of early Christians. Another area, on what was then an island in the Rhône (but is now the peninsula that holds the heart of the city), was a commercial zone of warehouses and workshops and a wealthy residential district.

As the Roman Empire declined, so, too, did the influence of Lyons, though it remained a city of religious consequence, gaining in churches and abbeys and ruled by its archbishops until the 14th century, when it was added to the French kingdom. Then, with the Renaissance, came its second great period of history. Already a crossroads of trade and commerce, Lyons now became the center of banking, printing, and the silk trade in France. Charles VII virtually secured the city's economic future by authorizing its first trade fairs in 1420, two per year at first (later extended to four), events that continue today after occasional interruptions over the centuries. Merchants flocked from all over Europe, bankers arrived from Italy in the late 15th century, and, when François I granted the Lyonnais the privilege of manufacturing silk free of taxes (just as they had earlier been granted a monopoly in the sale of silk), silk weavers arrived from Genoa in the first part of the 16th century.

Lyons soon was the foremost silk producer of Europe, richer and more populous during this period than Paris. Merchants and bankers built impressive *hôtels,* or townhouses, in the new center of the city, the area between Fourvière and the Saône, now known as Vieux Lyon. But the city also was a renowned intellectual center. German printers had come in the late 15th century and printing shops flourished, attracting scholars and writers, among them Rabelais, who practiced medicine in Lyons and published two volumes of his *Gargantua and Pantagruel* here on the occasion of trade fairs in 1532 and 1534.

Lyons was then and still is a working city. Strikes by journeyman printers around 1540 were among the first real labor disputes in history. The silk industry was subject to repeated boom-and-bust cycles, and the brutally repressed uprisings of the silk workers, called *canuts,* of the Croix-Rousse in the 1830s are landmarks in the history of the labor movement. Eventually, the introduction of the power loom during the 1870s put an end to the clacking of tens of thousands of hand looms in the *ateliers* of Lyonnais *canuts,* and though today the city is the center of a vast industrial agglomeration in which the manufacture of textiles (silk and synthetics) is still important, the metallurgical and petrochemical industries are no less vital.

Lyons and the Lyonnais have something of a reputation for secrecy, so it is perhaps the city's place in the history of printing that explains why such an ostensibly reticent place should produce so many books about itself — its cooking, its history and geography, its dialect and argot (a rich subject going back to Greco-Roman origins), its humor (self-deprecatory, except where food is concerned). And if these days Lyons is making an effort to be more open toward visitors, it hardly can be described as ready to surrender itself on first acquaintance. As in many similar mercantile cities, you are welcome but left pretty much on your own. "The outsider who disembarks at Lyons immediately feels more of an outsider than anywhere else," the writer Frédéric Dard, a Lyonnais himself, has written. "Everyone understands that he has just arrived in a forbidden city having nothing to offer but its work and its cooking."

Even discounting the exaggeration, that is not a bad start, because Lyons is, more or less by common consent, the gastronomic capital of France. For many a traveler, food is just about the *only* reason to stop here en route to the Côte d'Azur or Italy. For many a Frenchman, that — besides business — may be the reason, too, but enough of one to make a special trip. Indeed, the institution of the 2-hour high-speed *TGV* train between Paris and Lyons has made it possible — and by no means unheard of — for a Parisian to visit Lyons for lunch and be back home in time for dinner.

The Lyonnais pride themselves as connoisseurs of the art of *bien manger,* and their patronage of the art supports a reported 700 to 800 restaurants, with presumably not a bad one in the lot. In fact, cooks who open a new restaurant in Lyons need nerves of steel and good financial backing to tide them over the initial period of skepticism, but there is ample potential reward. A restaurant that does good business in Lyons is the closest thing to a sinecure that life can offer.

One reason for the city's high culinary standards is its location in the midst of a region of agricultural abundance, producing the finest of raw ingredients. Another may be something in the genes or the genealogy of the Lyonnais that has by now set a precedent for producing the finest of cooks. Superchefs of such worldwide fame as Paul Bocuse, Alain Chapel, George Blanc, and Pierre Troisgros (along with the late Jean, one of the two legendary Troisgros *frères*), though not working in Lyons, are all local boys, descendants of local chefs, practicing their trade in the Lyonnais region, 7, 12, 41, and 53 miles (11, 19, 66, 85 km) away, respectively. The restaurant of Fernand Point, *La Pyramide* (sold in 1987 to a Parisian real estate company following the death of M. Point's widow), where they all studied, is now reopened and is only 18 miles (29 km) away. But behind the great male chefs is a tradition of female restaurateurs, the great *mères* or *cuisinières lyonnaises,* whose interpretations of home cooking gave rise to some of the classic specialties of Lyons. That tradition goes back at least to the 18th century, when Mère Guy de la Mulatière opened a restaurant that still exists in Lyons (under the name *Roger Roucou;* see *Eating Out*), and was brought into the 20th century by Mère Filloux, long since gone, who taught Mère Brazier, now also gone. One of the last of the line, Léa Bidault of *Chez Léa,* now is retired.

It's safe to say, then, that the average Lyonnais takes cooking very seriously, as seriously as the average Frenchman takes love, and that in the heart of the Lyonnais love and food are equally sacrosanct. Among food fanciers in the know, one fable that combines the two has become the stuff of legend in Lyons. It's said that in 1847, Mme. Célestine Blanchard opened the *Restaurant du Cercle.* One day her chef, Jacques Rousselot, feeling especially inventive, whipped up a new chicken dish for her that he dubbed *poulet Célestine.* The dish was so marvelous that Célestine fell in love with Jacques —

and consummated the affair by marriage. Only in Lyons could it have happened — or would people believe it might have happened — that cuisine would be the catalyst for *amour.*

LYONS AT-A-GLANCE

SEEING THE CITY: There are two natural vantage points for a panoramic view. One is from the slopes or the top of Fourvière, on the right bank of the Saône, and more particularly from the *observatoire* of the basilica at the top of the hill, open daily from March through October and on Saturdays and Sundays the rest of the year. Pending payment of the admission charge and a climb of almost 300 steps, you'll have a splendid view of the city and the surrounding countryside. The other is from the height of Croix-Rousse, between the two rivers a bit north of the center. From here you can descend toward the flat ground of the peninsula by several routes that offer excellent, sometimes unexpected views. (Head down via Rue des Pierres-Plantées and the Montée de la Grande-Côte, for instance, or via Place Bellevue and Rue des Fantasques. On the west, Place Rouville has a view of Fourvière and the bend in the Saône.) A manmade height is the Crédit Lyonnais tower in the Part-Dieu quarter on the flat left bank of the Rhône. The *Pullman Part-Dieu* hotel, its restaurant, and *Panache Bar* occupy the 31st to 41st floors of the tower, with views toward the city or the Alps, depending on which side of the cylindrical building you find yourself.

SPECIAL PLACES: Overall, Lyons covers a large area, but for sightseeing purposes it can be broken down into distinct, compact areas defined by the two rivers that meet in the city. The Saône flows into the city from the north, curving first around Croix-Rousse and then Fourvière. The Rhône flows in from the northeast, and the two run nearly parallel for a short distance, creating between them a narrow peninsula of a few miles before they meet and flow south as one. The heart of the city is on the peninsula, or *presqu'île.* To the west, on the right bank of the Saône, is the old quarter, Vieux Lyon, at the foot of Fourvière. To the east is the left bank of the Rhône, where the main attractions for visitors are a park and the new urban complex, La Part-Dieu. Sightseeing can be managed by foot, with an occasional shortcut by public transport.

FOURVIÈRE AND VIEUX LYON

Vieux Lyon – Stretched out for about half a mile and squeezed between the slope of Fourvière and the Saône River, this is the most extensive and homogeneous urban Renaissance ensemble in France. Its three *quartiers* of St.-Paul, St.-Jean, and St.-Georges include some 200 buildings dating from the end of the Gothic period to the 17th century when this was the center of town. In poor condition at the end of World War II, the area has been extensively renovated (under the auspices of the Comité pour la Renaissance du Vieux-Lyon, 5 Pl. de la Baleine; phone: 78-37-16-04), and it now is a lively and animated quarter day and night. To explore it, walk along such streets as Rue St.-Jean (the main street), Rue Lainerie, Rue Juiverie, and Rue du Boeuf, and if possible, poke into courtyards and cut through the *traboules* (see *Extra Special*) that lead through buildings from one street to another. If you are interested in a detailed visit and read a minimum of French, a booklet called *Miniguide du Vieux-Lyon,* available at most bookstores and some newsstands, will greatly enhance a walking tour.

Cathédrale St.-Jean – One of the prime reference points of Vieux Lyon. Begun in the 12th century with an apse in the Romanesque style, it was completed in 1420 in Flamboyant Gothic. Despite the mixture of styles, it forms a harmonious mass whose four relatively short towers give it a powerful, rather low-slung look. It is richly decorated and has interesting stained glass windows, the earliest of which are from the 13th century. The cathedral was the site of two church councils in the 13th century, of the consecration of Pope John XXII in the 14th century, of the marriage of Henri IV and Marie de Médicis in 1600, and of Richelieu's receiving his cardinal's hat in 1622. A curiosity is the astronomical clock in the transept, which strikes the hours from noon to 3 PM accompanied by the crowing of a mechanical rooster and a procession of figures representing the Annunciation. Pl. St.-Jean.

Hôtel de Gadagne – The most imposing Renaissance mansion in Vieux Lyon was built in the early 16th century for two brothers, each of whom had a wing; it then was purchased by a rich Italian banking family, from which it gets its name. Two museums are housed behind its façade: the city's historical museum and one devoted to marionettes (see *Museums*). Open 10:45 AM to 6 PM. Closed Tuesdays. Pl. de Petit-Collège (phone: 78-42-03-61).

Place du Change – This square is framed principally by two buildings. The Loge du Change (on the uphill side), now a church, formerly housed money changers. It owes its present aspect to the 18th-century architect Jacques Soufflot (he designed the Panthéon in Paris), but it incorporates parts of an older commercial exchange building. Opposite, at No. 2, is the Maison Thomassin, from the 14th and 15th centuries. Its Gothic façade and courtyard make it probably the finest pre-Renaissance house in Vieux Lyon.

La Tour Rose – This building with the splendid Florentine façade takes its name from the circular stair tower in the courtyard. Typical of many buildings in this quarter, the hill behind is so steep that every floor was in effect a ground floor, with terraces and a hanging garden. It was said not jokingly of such houses that the people lived downstairs and stabled their horses on the fourth floor. 16 Rue du Boeuf.

Nouveau Guignol de Lyon – At the end of the 18th century, an unemployed silkworker, Laurent Mourguet, invented the puppet named Guignol, the principal character — along with his wife, Madelon, and his friend, Gnafron (whose nose is the color of beaujolais) — in countless comedies. There are Guignol theaters all over France and several in Lyons, and there always has been a Mourguet descendant involved in this theater, now in the basement of the Palais du Conservatoire. The characters are spiritual ancestors of every Lyonnais, and their language is full of the almost forgotten local argot. Even Guignol's costume, with its pigtail and tight black hat, is that of a Lyons silkworker of the period. Performance times vary, so check ahead. Entrance on Rue Louis-Carrand (phone: 78-28-92-57 or 78-37-31-79). Note to Guignol fans: Related addresses in the neighborhood are 2 Pl. St.-Paul, the house where Mourguet lived and first gave performances; 53 Rue St.-Georges, the home of *Le Petit Bouif* (the Cercle Laurent Mourguet), which also gives performances and can claim direct descent — phone 78-37-31-79 for information; and 2 Montée du Gourguillon, the *Maison de Guignol,* a kind of museum of original Guignol sets and costumes.

Théâtres Romains de Fourvière (Roman Theaters) – Uncovered by archaeological digs in the 1930s, the two theaters, halfway up Fourvière from Vieux Lyon, are the most important visible remnants of Gallo-Roman Lugdunum. The large theater, the oldest in France and the same size as the more famous ones in Orange and Arles, once held as many as 10,000 spectators. A smaller theater, or *odéon,* similar in layout to the large theater but seating only 3,000, is nearby, as are the ruins of a Temple of Cybèle and ongoing archaeological explorations. Open daily 9 AM to sundown. No admission charge. You can reach the site from Vieux Lyon by walking up the Montée de Gourguillon or by taking the funicular. 8 Rue de l'Antiquaille (phone: 78-25-94-68).

Musée Gallo-Romain – Adjacent to the two Roman theaters, this splendid museum, laid out in an assembly of spiral ramps, is a comprehensive presentation of the history of Lugdunum from prehistoric through Roman times. Two inscriptions on bronze — the Gallic calendar from Coligny and the Claudian table — are among the most interesting exhibits: The text of the former is the longest inscription in the Gallic language still extant, and that of the latter is a speech delivered before the Roman Senate by the Emperor Claudius in AD 48. Also interesting are several mosaic floors, including the beautiful mosaic of *Cupid and Pan Fighting,* as well as the huge one with a recurring swastika motif, in which some versions of the motif are clearly defined and others somewhat deformed and harder to find. The museum also has models of the two Roman theaters as they were in ancient times set up near floor-to-ceiling windows looking out onto the ruins as they are now. No admission charge. Open Wednesdays through Sundays from 9:30 AM to noon and 2 to 6 PM. 17 Rue Cléberg (phone: 78-25-94-68).

Basilique Notre-Dame de Fourvière – The top of Fourvière had already been a place of pilgrimage for centuries when, in 1870, the Archbishop of Lyons invoked the aid of the Virgin in keeping Prussian troops out of Lyons during the Franco-Prussian War and vowed, in return, to build a church worthy of the miracle. The resulting edifice, built during the last 3 decades of the 19th century, is a curious mixture of all possible styles, visible from almost everywhere, and, with its four ungainly towers, it has been likened to an elephant on its back. Inside are mosaic murals and stained glass windows; the rest of the church, inside and out, is elaborately carved stone. The 12th-to-18th-century chapel to the right of the church, the place of pilgrimage proper, contains the miracle working statue of the Virgin. The esplanade to the left affords a view of the city stretching to and beyond the Rhône, with the façade of St.-Jean directly below and Place Bellecour behind it. The observatory (admission charge) in one of the towers affords a more circular view. Pl. de Fourvière.

PRESQU'ILE (PENINSULA)

Basilique St.-Martin-d'Ainay – All that remains of an important ensemble of religious buildings belonging to a Benedictine abbey on what used to be an island in the Rhône. Consecrated by Pope Pascal II in 1107, it is, despite later additions, considered a fine illustration of the Carolingian style. 5 Rue de l'Abbaye-d'Ainay.

Place Bellecour – This square was laid out in the last years of the reign of Louis XIV (1710–14) on what was then open land belonging to the Ainay abbey. The buildings that originally surrounded it were torn down during the Revolution; these, in Louis XVI style, were put up when Napoleon came to power. The vast rectangular open space measures more than 200 by 300 yards and includes an equestrian statue of the Sun King, also a replacement of one torn down during the Revolution, and the pavilion of the Lyons Tourist Office, in the southeast corner by the florists' kiosks.

Musée Historique des Tissus (Museum of Textile History) – In the former Hôtel de Villeroy (1730), this is perhaps the finest fabric museum anywhere and a reminder of Lyons's past importance as a silk center. Its 28 rooms house a collection of European, Near Eastern, and Far Eastern fabrics ranging from ancient ones made before Christ to modern ones designed by Raoul Dufy and Sonia Delaunay. The French collection is dominated by the work of the 18th-century designer of Lyonnais silks, Philippe de Lasalle, including creations made for Marie-Antoinette and Catherine the Great of Russia. Open 10 AM to noon and 2 to 5:30 PM. Guided tours are given Tuesdays through Sundays at 2:30 PM. Closed Mondays and holidays; admission charge includes entrance to the adjoining *Musée des Arts Décoratifs.* 34 Rue de la Charité (phone: 78-37-15-05).

Musée des Arts Décoratifs – Next door to and a logical extension of the textile museum, its collection covers furniture, *boiseries* (woodwork), tapestries, silver, porcelain, clocks, and the like, all installed in the former Hôtel de Lacroix-Laval. Hours are the same as those above; tickets for one are valid for the other. 30 Rue de la Charité (phone: 78-37-15-05).

Rue Mercière – The Via Mercatoria (Merchants' Street) of Roman times was an outright slum about a decade ago, but, along with the parallel Quai St.-Antoine, it has undergone a dramatic revival and now is a center of small restaurants and boutiques and Lyonnais nightlife. In the morning, the Quai St.-Antoine is the scene of one of France's most abundant and colorful street markets for food and flowers, worth a visit even if you're not buying.

Eglise St.-Nizier – This church stands on the presumed site of an early Christian sanctuary that may have been Lyons's cathedral until the 6th century. The present church is largely from the 15th century, as is one of its towers; the contrasting one is from the 19th century. The interior is Flamboyant Gothic. The church gained a certain notoriety some years ago when it was occupied by the city's prostitutes protesting police harassment. Rue de Brest at Pl. St.-Nizier.

Place des Terreaux – Roughly speaking, this is where, in the city's early history, the Rhône and Saône met — *terreaux* refers to the alluvial soil carried by the Rhône that made this area into terra firma. It lies at the foot of Croix-Rousse and is bordered on the south by the Palais St.-Pierre and on the east by the Hôtel de Ville. At the western end is a monumental fountain by Bartholdi (of Statue of Liberty fame) of a team of galloping horses representing "the rivers flowing to the sea." The city of Bordeaux, for which it was made, refused it, and the city fathers of Lyons apparently decided it could just as well represent Lyons's Rhône and Saône as Bordeaux's Garonne and Dordogne.

Hôtel de Ville – One of the handsomest Town Halls in France, according to some. It was built in the mid-17th century by the Lyonnais architect Simon Maupin, partly destroyed by fire in 1674, and restored by the noted architects Jules Hardouin-Mansart and Robert de Cotte. It consists of an imposing rectangle of buildings around a central courtyard on two levels, separated by a peristyle, and includes several magnificently decorated ceremonial rooms. Pl. des Terreaux.

Musée des Beaux-Arts – The Palais St.-Pierre, built in the 17th century as an abbey for the Benedictine Dames de St.-Pierre, now serves as a museum, and one of the principal pleasures of a visit is entering the arcaded cloister with its statues, among them works by Rodin and Bourdelle. The comprehensive collection includes ancient and more modern sculpture and paintings by Veronese, Tintoretto, Rubens, El Greco, Cranach, Lyonnais artists of various periods, Impressionists, and other 19th-century artists. No admission charge. Open Wednesdays through Sundays from 10:30 AM to 6 PM. Closed holidays. Pl. des Terreaux (phone: 78-28-07-66).

Amphithéâtre des Trois-Gaules – The ruins of this amphitheater on the slope of the Croix-Rousse came to light in 1958. It apparently was the site of combats between animals and gladiators, public executions, and the martyrdom of early Christians as well as the site of annual meetings of delegates from the 60 Gallic nations into which the Romans had subdivided the three provinces of Gaul. Entrance from 1 Rue Lucien-Sportisse.

THE LEFT BANK OF THE RHÔNE

Parc de la Tête d'Or – Covering more than 250 acres, this park was created at a bend of the Rhône in 1856 and it contains a large lake, a zoo, botanical gardens, and a Guignol theater. The 100,000-plant rose garden is heaven in June. The main entrance is from Pl. du Général-Leclerc.

La Part-Dieu – The name of this modern urban complex derives from the earlier *quartier* where, during the early 1960s, the city decided to create a new city center before the fact, anticipating and encouraging Lyons's push to the east. It lies on the flat plain on the left bank of the Rhône, unhemmed by nature as are the peninsula (by the Rhône and Saône) and Vieux Lyon (by Fourvière and the Saône). One of the first buildings to open was the central food market, *Les Halles* (1971), at 102 Cours Lafayette on the northern edge of the complex; another was the Maison de la Radio-Télévision (1972). Now this administrative, commercial, and cultural city of concrete, steel, plastic, and glass includes a railroad station (where the high-speed *TGV* trains stop 2 hours after leaving Paris), the 41-story Crédit Lyonnais–*Pullman Part-Dieu* hotel tower, the 2,000-seat *Auditorium Maurice Ravel* (mainly for concerts, but also for opera and ballet), a municipal library of more than 2 million volumes, numerous government buildings, and the *Centre Commercial,* billed as the largest shopping center in Europe. There is parking for 10,000 cars and the city's métro (new in the last decade and still growing) also provides easy access.

■ **EXTRA SPECIAL:** Unique to Lyons are its *traboules,* corridors that link one street to another by passing through two or more buildings. The word comes from the Latin *trans ambulare,* "to walk through"; there is even a verb, *trabouler.* They are found in two neighborhoods — Vieux Lyon and the Croix-Rousse slope — both once centers of the silk industry. In Vieux Lyon they are of architectural interest, with vaulted Gothic ceilings; in Croix-Rousse, where they were the scene of bloody uprisings of the silkworkers in 1831 and 1834, they are part of a partly abandoned working class area, filthy but evocative. The *traboules* probably were created originally to conserve land in cramped areas, but they lend themselves easily to the Lyonnais penchant for secrecy and privacy. In Croix-Rousse, a businessman could always appear to be going to or coming from some business appointment while in fact ducking through to an adjacent street of ill repute. They were practical ways, too, of moving a roll of silk from one place to another in the rain without getting it wet. It is possible to go from the top of Croix-Rousse to Place des Terreaux at the bottom by using *traboules* and their interior staircases for the descent, emerging into each street only long enough to cross it. And you cannot really explore Vieux Lyon without going into its *traboules.* Neither can be done without extraordinary patience and determination, however, unless you have a map such as the ones in the Michelin *Vallée du Rhône* guide, the *Miniguide du Vieux-Lyon,* and other guidebooks. Go into any substantial-looking bookstore and make your desire to *trabouler* known.

SOURCES AND RESOURCES

TOURIST INFORMATION: The city and regional tourist office (Office de Tourisme de Lyon/Communauté–Syndicat d'Initiative) has two locations. The Pavillon du Tourisme (Pl. Bellecour; phone: 78-42-25-75) is the more central. It dispenses general information, maps, and brochures, and houses an *Accueil de France* accommodations service, which can book rooms anywhere in France (for a nominal fee). Open daily 10 AM to 6 PM from June 15 to September 15; closed Sundays the rest of the year. The other location is the Centre d'Echanges de Perrache (at the Perrache railroad station; phone: 78-42-22-07), also closed Sundays. Walking tours to various parts of the city — Vieux Lyon by day or night, *Musée Gallo-Romain* and the Roman theaters, the Croix-Rousse *traboules* — and a general city tour by bus also are organized by the tourist office, with varying frequency in varying languages depending on the season. *Lyon Ballade* offers daily city tours by minibus; commentary in English is provided on audio tape (8 Rue Perrod; phone: 78-27-08-42).

Local Coverage – A little rudimentary French will come in handy in Lyons, where foreign-language tourist guides hardly exist. The principal daily newspaper is *Le Progrès*, which carries information on entertainment and other events. There also is *Lyon Matin*, and Lyons editions of two Paris dailies, *Liberation* and *Le Figaro*, are available. The most useful guide to entertainment, theater, music, and the like, is the weekly *Lyon Poche*, available at all newsstands. A virtually indispensable guide to restaurants in Lyons and environs is *Lyon Gourmand*, a booklet published annually and available (until it sells out) at bookstores and newsstands; its commentary is in French, but a system of symbols makes it easy to tell what to expect. (*Lyon Gourmand* is, in fact, one of a series of miniguides issued by the same publisher — to different aspects of Lyons history, to surrounding regions, and so on — that readers of French will find useful. Each costs only a few dollars.) Another guide, *Le Petit Futé*, is for long-term visitors; it lists such things as beauty shops, dance schools, and libraries as well as restaurants, bars, and nightclubs. The Lyons map and street guide of the *Plan Guide Blay* series (there is one for every French city of any size) is useful for finding out-of-the-way *rues;* it also contains a map of the métro system. Lyons is prolific in books about itself, anything from coffee table picture volumes to obscure histories and multivolume works on the Lyonnais dialect and slang. Some large bookstores, such as *Flammarion* (19 Pl. Bellecour, across from the Pavillon du Tourisme), group them all in one section for easy perusal. The Lyons Tourist Office also publishes a monthly listing of local cultural events; it is available free at their offices.

 TELEPHONE: The city code for Lyons is 78, which is incorporated into all local 8-digit numbers. When calling a number in Lyons from the Paris region (including the Ile de France), dial 16, wait for a dial tone, then dial the 8-digit number. When calling a number from outside Paris, dial only the 8-digit number. When calling from the US, dial 33 (which is the country code), followed by the 8-digit number.

 GETTING AROUND: Air – Lyons's Satolas International Airport is served by direct *Air France* flights twice a week from New York's JFK Airport, as well as by daily flights from Paris and other European cities.

Bicycle – Bicycles can be rented at *Loca Sport* (62 Rue Colombier; phone: 78-61-11-01).

Boat – For information on daily sightseeing boat rides on Lyons's two rivers, contact *Navig'Inter* (13 bis Quai Rambaud; phone: 78-42-96-81) or *A. F. T.* (76 Rue de la République; phone: 78-42-00-17). Boats leave every afternoon from April to November from the left bank of the Quai des Célestins. Lunch and dinner cruises aboard *L'Hermès* depart from Quai Claude Bernard (phone: 78-42-96-81).

Bus – Lyons's public transport system, *TCL*, operates 90 bus lines in the city and suburbs; 3 métro, or subway, lines (these are being extended and a fourth line is under construction and scheduled for completion in 1993); and 2 funiculars. The same tickets are good for all three modes of transport (and combinations thereof) and can be used for 1 hour after validation, but not for return trips. Tickets may be purchased singly or in books of six (for a 20% discount) from bus drivers and at *TCL* kiosks around the city, but the simplest method is to use the automatic coin machines in métro stations. The tickets must be validated in the ticket-stamping machines on the buses and at the gates to métro trains and funiculars before boarding. Of particular interest to the short-term visitor is the *ticket liberté*, 2- or 3-day unlimited-travel tickets costing, respectively, seven and ten times the price of a single ticket — the 48 (and 72) hours begin from the time the ticket is first validated. These tickets can be purchased at the Perrache bus-métro station, at the *TCL* office (43 Rue de la République) and at *TCL* kiosks. Maps of the system are available in the same places. The métro and most bus lines run from 5 AM to midnight. For information, call *TCL* at 78-71-70-00.

Car Rental – All the major firms are represented at Satolas Airport and in the city, and *SNCF*'s *Train + Auto* plan is available at Lyons's railroad stations. But while a car can be useful for excursions in the region or for the greater distances on the left bank of the Rhône, Vieux Lyon and the center of the city between the two rivers are much better negotiated on foot and by public transportation.

Funicular – Known locally as the *ficelle.* The two lines both leave from Gare St.-Jean, at the end of Avenue Adolphe-Max near the Cathédrale St.-Jean. One goes to the top of Fourvière, depositing passengers in front of Notre-Dame de Fourvière; the other climbs the St.-Just hill, making an intermediate stop at the Minimes station, near the Théâtres Romains de Fourvière. Bus-métro tickets are valid for the *ficelle,* but you also can buy a discounted round-trip ticket valid for a day. Service on the St.-Just line stops at 9 PM and on the Fourvière line at 9:30 PM.

Métro – The three-line subway system is very easy to use provided you have a map showing where to transfer from one line to another. *Line A,* the backbone of the system, runs north from Gare de Perrache to, among others, Place Bellecour and the Hôtel de Ville (switch here to *Line C* for Place de la Croix-Rousse), then goes to the left bank of the Rhône and runs to the eastern fringes of the city. Switch to *Line B* at the Charpennes station for Gare des Brotteaux and Part-Dieu. (See the discussion of bus lines above.)

Taxi – Lyons is amply served by taxis. They generally can be flagged on principal thoroughfares, and there are cab stands at main squares and intersections. In general, it does not take long for a hotel concièrge or a restaurant employee to call one by phone.

Train – Lyons has two train stations, the Gare de Perrache on the central peninsula at Cours de Verdun and Pl. Carnot, and the newer Gare de la Part-Dieu, in the Part-Dieu urban complex on the left bank of the Rhône. Trains to and through Lyons, including *TGV* trains, usually stop at both stations; trains originating in Lyons leave from Perrache. For train information, call 78-92-50-50; to reserve a seat on the *TGV,* call 78-92-50-70).

SPECIAL EVENTS: Of increasing popularity is the *Salon des Métiers de Bouche,* a food trade fair that displays the culinary talent and gastronomic riches of the region, held in January or February of odd-numbered years. (In alternate years, it takes place in Paris.) For information about this year's fair, call 72-22-32-55. The *Foire Internationale de Lyon,* held for 2 weeks at the end of March and the beginning of April, is one of Europe's major trade fairs, an event that traces its origins back to 1420. Lyons's marathon is run in April. Held for the first time in 1987, the colorful *Les Pennons* enlivens the Lyons scene in June. In the style of Siena's famous *Palio,* horsemen garbed in the colors and arms of the quarters of old Lyons compete in a race around Place Bellecour. The *Brocante du Vieux Lyon,* a flea market (phone: 78-37-00-68), is also held annually in June, usually on the third weekend of the month. The *Festival Berlioz,* strictly a music festival, is held every 2 years (this is a festival year) and devotes 10 days in September to (almost exclusively) the music of Hector Berlioz. It takes place both in Lyons — mostly at the *Auditorium Maurice Ravel* and sometimes, when larger works are mounted, in the *Palais des Sports* — and in churches and an old château in the composer's birthplace of La Côte St.-André, 40 miles (64 km) away. Contact the festival office (127 Rue Servient, Lyons 69003; phone: 78-60-85-40) for details. In even-numbered years, the *Festival International Biennal de la Danse* now replaces the *Festival Berlioz.* Held during the same 10-day period in mid-September, this festival welcomes classical as well as contemporary artists and dance groups from around the world. The *Grand Prix de Tennis de Lyon* takes place in September. Two dates on the church calendar celebrated in a decidedly lay fashion are the long weekend of *Pentecost,* when a national *boules* tournament is held in the *Stade Edouard Herriot,* and December 8, the *Feast of the Immaculate Conception,* when candles are lighted in the windows of the city, the streets are illuminated, and the *Christmas* season is semi-officially ushered in to general merriment, Lyonnais style.

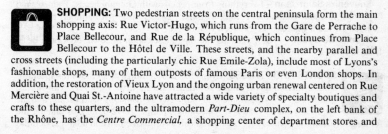

MUSEUMS: Give or take a few, there are two dozen museums in Lyons, of which the most important are listed in *Special Places*. Some others of interest include the following:

Maison des Canuts – An ensemble that includes a museum of silk weaving — looms set up with work in progress — and a shop with a limited selection of items, mostly silk ties, for sale. Open 8:30 AM to noon and 2 to 6 PM. Closed Sundays and holidays. Admission charge. 10-12 Rue d'Ivry (phone: 78-28-62-04).

Musée de l'Automobile Henri Malartre – More than 200 vehicles, including Hitler's Mercedes, housed in an imposing château high on the left bank of the Saône. Open daily 9 AM to 6 PM. Admission charge. Rochetaillée-sur-Saône, 7 miles north of Lyons (phone: 78-22-18-80).

Musée Guimet d'Histoire Naturelle – Collections of Far Eastern art and Egyptology as well as natural history. Open Wednesdays through Sundays from 2 to 6 PM. No admission charge. 28 Bd. des Belges (phone: 78-93-22-44).

Musée Historique de Lyon – In the Renaissance Hôtel de Gadagne, a survey of the city's history from Roman times. Open 10:45 AM to 6 PM. Closed Tuesdays. No admission charge. Pl. du Petit College (phone: 78-42-03-61).

Musée de l'Imprimerie et de la Banque (Museum of Printing and Banking) – In the 15th-century Hôtel de la Couronne, it commemorates the city's importance as the birthplace of French printing and banking. Open Wednesdays through Sundays from 9:30 AM to noon and 2 to 6 PM. No admission charge. 13 Rue de la Poulaillerie (phone: 78-37-65-98).

Musée International de la Marionnette – In the Hôtel de Gadagne along with the *Musée Historique*. The heart of this museum is a history of Lyons's own marionette, Guignol, along with a collection ranging from European puppets to Indochinese shadow theater. Open 10:45 AM to 6 PM. Closed Tuesdays. No admission charge. Pl. du Petit College (phone: 78-42-03-61).

Musée de la Résistance – Through documents and photographs, this museum commemorates Lyons's role as the center of the French Resistance during World War II. Open Wednesdays through Sundays from 10:30 AM to noon and 1 to 6 PM. No admission charge. 5 Rue Boileau (phone: 78-93-27-83).

Musée St.-Pierre d'Art Contemporain – Installed 7 years ago in the same former monastery that houses the *Musée des Beaux-Arts,* but with a separate entrance, this addition presents temporary exhibitions of the works of contemporary artists as well as its own collection of works dating from 1960. Open from noon to 6 PM. Closed Tuesdays. No admission charge. 16 Rue Edouard Herriot (phone: 78-30-50-66).

Musée de Train Miniature des Brotteaux – Lyons's newest mini-museum, with its collection of miniature trains, actually is an old favorite. Closed for the past 5 years, it is scheduled to reopen early this year. 4 Pl. Jules Ferry (phone: 78-34-31-17).

SHOPPING: Two pedestrian streets on the central peninsula form the main shopping axis: Rue Victor-Hugo, which runs from the Gare de Perrache to Place Bellecour, and Rue de la République, which continues from Place Bellecour to the Hôtel de Ville. These streets, and the nearby parallel and cross streets (including the particularly chic Rue Emile-Zola), include most of Lyons's fashionable shops, many of them outposts of famous Paris or even London shops. In addition, the restoration of Vieux Lyon and the ongoing urban renewal centered on Rue Mercière and Quai St.-Antoine have attracted a wide variety of specialty boutiques and crafts to these quarters, and the ultramodern *Part-Dieu* complex, on the left bank of the Rhône, has the *Centre Commercial,* a shopping center of department stores and some 200 boutiques, and *Les Halles,* the central food market at 102 Cours Lafayette. The city is rich in fine *charcuteries,* bakeries, pastry shops, cheese, wine, and other specialty food stores. Silk, historically a Lyons specialty, is another matter. A walk around the old silkworkers' quarter on the slope of Croix-Rousse is evocative of the past, but no longer a place to find small silk *ateliers.* The leading department store on the peninsula is *Au Printemps* (42 Pl. de la République); *Galeries Lafayette* and *Jelmoli,* a Swiss department store, are in the *Centre Commercial Part-Dieu.* For antiques, browse along the Rue Auguste Comte just south of the Place Bellecour or take a short taxi ride to the Boulevard Stalingrad behind the Parc de la Tête d'Or, where in 1988 an old market was transformed into an antiques forum containing nearly 100 stores. Stores generally are open from 9 AM to 7 PM, with a midday closing for smaller establishments. They all are closed on Sundays, except for food stores, many of which are open on Sunday morning and then closed until Tuesday morning.

Atelier d'Art – Typical Vieux Lyon handicrafts: painted silk, clothing, woven lamp-shades. 1 Pl. de la Baleine (phone: 78-37-72-76).

Ateyer de Guignol – Handcrafted marionettes: Guignol and others with heads made to order. 4 Pl. du Change (phone: 78-29-33-37).

Bernachon – A superb pastry shop and justly celebrated *chocolatier;* all the choco-lates are made from scratch on the premises and sold here only. 42 Cours Franklin-Roosevelt (phone: 78-24-37-98).

Boîte à Soie – Silk accessories, including scarves, sashes, ties, and handkerchiefs, for men and women. 3 Quai Gl. Sarrail (phone: 78-52-06-08).

Cavon de Lyon – A fine wine shop. 6 Rue de la Charité (phone: 78-42-86-87).

Chorliet – Perhaps the most Lyonnais of *charcuteries,* as well as a leading caterer. 12 Rue du Plat (phone: 78-37-31-95).

Clementine – Headquarters of Lyons's most successful contemporary designer, whose updated classics for women also are featured in shops in Paris and other Euro-pean cities. 18 Rue Emile-Zola (phone: 78-37-03-10).

Hermès – For elegant, susurrous scarves from the Paris purveyors of things silk and leather (the factory is in town; alas, not open to the public). 95 Rue du Président-Heriot (phone: 78-42-25-14).

Maréchal – Cheeses of enormous variety and superb quality. One of the two cheese merchants in *Les Halles* supplying the city's leading restaurants. 102 Cours Lafayette (phone: 78-62-36-77).

Au Petit Paris – For silk and other textiles by the meter. 9 Pl. des Jacobins (phone: 78-37-08-21).

Le Petit Train Bleu – Toys, in particular toy soldiers, model trains, and chess sets. 7 Rue de la Charité (phone: 78-37-61-81).

Pignol et Vital – For pastry, quiche, and the like, which can also be consumed at tables for a snack or lunch. 17 Rue Emile-Zola (phone: 78-37-39-61).

Renée Richard – More superb cheeses. The other *Les Halles* cheese merchant catering to the city's leading chefs. 102 Cours Lafayette (phone: 78-62-30-78).

Souvenirs Saint-Jean – Everything from pencils with Guignol heads, T-shirts, and key rings, to water colors and *cocons,* Lyonnais sweets made with almond paste and covered with chocolate. 8 Pl. St.-Jean (phone: 78-92-94-36).

A Vous de Jouer – Toys, perhaps the biggest selection in town. 30 Cours de la Liberté (phone: 78-60-88-49).

 SPORTS AND FITNESS: Lyons has a wide range of facilities for spectator sports, including the *Stade Municipal de Gerland* (239 Av. Jean-Jaurès; phone: 78-72-91-16), home field of the city's *Olympique* soccer team, and the *Palais des Sports* (350 Av. Jean-Jaurès; phone: 78-72-62-02), as much a site for large-scale music events (pop, rock, classical) as for basketball and boxing. Facilities for active sports are not lacking either, even though the real Lyonnais sport is *boules,* of which Lyons claims to be the birthplace. Its version differs somewhat from that practiced in Provence, but, as elsewhere in France, impromptu games take place almost anywhere there is flat dirt ground. A national tournament is held in the *Stade Municipal de Gerland* each year during the 4 days of *Pentecost* weekend.

Ice Skating – There are two *patinoires municipales* — municipal skating rinks (100 Cours Charlemagne; phone: 78-42-64-56; and 52 Rue Baraban; phone: 78-54-20-33). Both are open September to May; closed Mondays.

Swimming – The *Centre Nautique* (Quai Claude-Bernard; phone: 78-72-04-50) has outdoor pools on the Rhône, very centrally located (open June to September). *Piscine Garibaldi* (221 Rue Garibaldi; phone: 78-60-89-66) is open September to May; closed Tuesdays.

Tennis – Public courts can be found at the *Stade Municipal de Gerland* (89 Av. Tony Garnier; phone: 78-72-63-93).

 THEATER: Lyons is a lively theater town, and if you understand French, you'll have no trouble finding something worth seeing. As the country's second largest city, it has many resident theaters, ranging from the well known and well established to flocks of fly-by-nights, and it is on the circuit for touring French and foreign productions. Among the foremost theaters is the *Théâtre National Populaire (TNP)* (8 Pl. Dr.-Lazare-Goujon; phone: 78-03-30-30), run by the actor, author, and stage director Roger Planchon in the working class suburb of Villeurbanne. The *TNP* is one of France's leading state-subsidized theaters (one of its most talked-about theaters, too), a very official establishment yet at the same time avant-garde in its stagings and leftist in its political orientation — which used to mean a lot of Brecht, new leftist works, and daring productions of the classics, but the boundaries are getting fuzzy. At the opposite pole is the *Théâtre des Célestins* (Pl. des Célestins; phone: 78-42-17-67), a handsome 19th-century building where the repertory is quite eclectic (Molière, Wilde, Pinter, Feydeau, Balzac, Shakespeare) but quite traditional in style, appealing to a bourgeois audience — it's known familiarly as Lyons's *Comédie-Française.* Other leading theaters, appealing to a younger, rather serious public, are the *Carrefour Europeen/Théâtre du Huitième* (8 Av. Jean-Mermoz; phone: 78-74-32-08), which may do Dario Fo, Sartre, or Shakespeare — it tends toward modern plays, but not exclusively — or book a guest dance group; and the *Théâtre de Lyon* (7 Rue des Aqueducs; phone: 78-36-67-67), which stages both traditional and contemporary works, from Maupassant to Mrozek. On the lighter side, don't forget that Lyons is the birthplace of Guignol. One of several places to catch the puppet in action is the *Nouveau Théâtre du Guignol* (Palais du Conservatoire, Rue Louis-Carrand; phone: 78-28-92-57 or 78-37-31-79). It gives matinee performances of the classic Guignol repertory, mainly for kids, and evening performances of new pieces intended for adults ("adult" in the sense of political satire, not X-rated). *Maison de la Danse* (Pl. J. Ambre; phone: 78-29-43-44), a converted 1930s movie house, exists exclusively for dance, and books French and foreign companies from fall through spring. Ballet occasionally is presented at the *Auditorium Maurice Ravel* (82 Rue de Bonnel; phone: 78-60-37-13).

 MUSIC: The *Orchestre de Lyon,* under musical director Emmanuel Krivine, generally plays in the *Auditorium Maurice Ravel* (82 Rue de Bonnel, in the new Part-Dieu quarter; phone: 78-60-37-13). Some opera productions take place here, too, along with some of the *Festival Berlioz* concerts, other classical concerts (including those of the annual *Festival de la Musique du Vieux Lyon,* which takes place in November and December; phone: 78-30-00-86). As the main auditorium of the music conservatory, the *Salle Molière* (18 Quai de Bondy) used to be the primary concert hall, but as much of this activity has been transferred to the *Auditorium Maurice Ravel,* the *Salle* is being used more and more for other purposes (for information, phone the Lyons Tourist Office at 78-42-25-75). Visiting pop and rock groups that draw crowds usually check into the *Palais des Sports* (350 Av. Jean-Jaurès; phone: 78-72-62-02).

 NIGHTCLUBS AND NIGHTLIFE: Two parts of town to explore are the Rue Mercière–Quai St.-Antoine neighborhood on the peninsula and Vieux Lyon, across the Saône, both of them endowed with a rich choice of bars and clubs, some of which stay open all night. If you feel like a pub crawl in the first area, try the *Saint-Louis,* a piano bar (61 Rue Mercière; phone: 78-92-99-83); or the *Bar du Bistrot* (64 Rue Mercière; phone: 78-37-18-44), an annex to the *Bistrot de Lyon* restaurant, and certainly one of the most popular in a busy street. Nearby are *Le Saint Antoine* (37 Quai St.-Antoine; phone: 78-37-01-35), a nightclub/disco frequented by a sophisticated, well-dressed crowd. In the same area, a new bar, the *Fou du Roy* (50 Rue Mercière; phone: 78-42-81-02), offers the charm and elegance of a Renaissance court. Another stylish newcomer, the *Ambassadeur* (22 Quai R. Rolland; phone: 72-41-83-73), is open daily from 11 to 3 AM. In the old and slightly tawdry (but still popular) category, there is *Le Pub,* in Vieux Lyon (4 Rue de la Baleine; phone: 78-42-41-44). Elsewhere in Lyons, *Le Gourmandin,* Lyons's long-abandoned Brotteaux train station, was the inspiration for the dramatic relocation of the established Lyons restaurant of the same name. Owner Daniel Abattu successfully has combined existing turn-of-the-century murals with Italian high-tech and French modern art to create what is certainly Lyons's most avant-garde dining theater alternating, with vaudeville acts and experimental theater. Closed Sundays, reservations advised. (Gare des Brotteaux, 14 Pl. Jules-Ferry; phone: 78-52-02-52). *Eddie et Domino* (6 Quai Gailleton; phone: 78-37-20-29) has a stunning collection of old and straight malt whiskies, and Eddie, who is practically an adopted Scot, always is ready to discuss or instruct; it's open from 5 PM until everyone goes, except on Sundays and holidays. Among the more active jazz clubs are the *Hot Club* (26 Rue Lanterne; phone: 78-39-54-74) and, for modern jazz, *Le Bec de Jazz* (9 Quai Bondy; no phone). For dancing to an orchestra, go to the *Caveau* (50 Rue de la République; phone: 78-37-46-90), which is open every night. For gambling, *Lido*-like dinner shows, and cabaret, there's the sparkling, remodeled *Casino le Lyon Vert,* a short drive west of Lyons in Charbonnières (200 Av. du Casino, La Tour de Salvagny; phone: 78-87-02-70). Open daily 3 PM to 2 AM (3 AM on Fridays and Saturdays).

BEST IN TOWN

 CHECKING IN: It must be said that Lyons is not a great hotel town. Most of the city's hotels are aimed at the commercial traveler (apropos of which, expect the *complet* — sorry, full up — sign to go up early in the day during the week, even during the off-season when there are few tourists around). Most hotels in the central peninsula date from early in the century or were built between the wars and have subsequently been modernized (to a greater or lesser degree) or are still in the process of being brought up to date. While there are some very modern ones, there is a paucity of cozy, small, or quaint hostelries of the kind that one might find, say, on the Left Bank in Paris. In general, accommodations also are on the expensive side. For purposes of classification here, expensive means paying more, sometimes *much* more, than $75 for a double room with bath or shower, between $50 and $75 for moderate, while inexpensive means paying less than $50. Remember that here, as elsewhere in France, single occupancy of a double room will not mean much of a saving.

Concorde – Though traditional, modernized, and soundproof, this establishment (140 rooms) hardly is deluxe. 11 Rue Grolée (phone: 78-42-56-21). Expensive.

Cour des Loges – A luxurious property on a winding street in Vieux Lyon that combines the best of the old and the new. Creatively installed in three graceful, renovated Renaissance mansions, it features a spacious interior courtyard, 63 unusual rooms and suites (many of them duplexes), a restaurant, hanging gardens, a swimming pool, sauna, meeting rooms, and a garage. One of the city's most charming, unique, and priciest hotels. 2-4-6-8 Rue du Boeuf (phone: 78-42-75-75). Expensive.

Holiday Inn Lyon Atlas – Relatively new, with 159 comfortable rooms, it offers all the comforts and services typically found in the top of Holiday Inn's line. In the new part of town near the Part-Dieu station, it features a New Orleans–style restaurant. 29 Rue de Bonnel (phone: 72-61-90-90). Expensive.

La Maison de la Tour – When Philippe Chavent moved his highly rated restaurant, *La Tour Rose* (see *Eating Out*), into new quarters, he decided to crown it with this deluxe 13-room hotel. Scheduled to open as we went to press, the rooms have a warm, personal style, richly decorated with the textiles and silks for which this city is famous. 22 Rue du Boeuf (phone: 78-37-25-90). Expensive.

Metropole – With 119 rooms, this is slightly out of the center of town on the left bank of the Saône, but as compensation for any inconvenience, it has a swimming pool and tennis and squash courts as well as a restaurant, a grill, and a bar. 85 Quai Joseph-Gillet (phone: 78-29-20-20). Expensive.

Pullman Part-Dieu – Its 245 rooms are stacked on the top 10 floors of the city's only real skyscraper, the 41-story, cylindrical Crédit Lyonnais tower in the *Part-Dieu* center on the left bank of the Rhône. The view is unlimited, and the style is functional luxury. It also has one of the city's better restaurants, *L'Arc en Ciel* (see *Eating Out*). 129 Rue Servient (phone: 78-62-94-12). Expensive.

Pullman Perrache – A turn-of-the-century grand railroad hotel, renovated, but still with period charm. Its 120 rooms, many quite spacious, are only a few steps from the Perrache railroad station. 12 Cours de Verdun (phone: 78-37-58-11). Expensive.

Sofitel – Modern and well equipped; indeed, it has all the services one would find in a major hotel in an American city: shops, hairdresser, bank, florist, an outstanding restaurant, *Les Trois Dômes* (see *Eating Out*), a snack bar open until 2 AM. Not far from Place Bellecour, there are 196 rooms, some looking directly onto the Rhône. 20 Quai Gailleton (phone: 78-42-72-50). Expensive.

Royal – Another traditional grande dame that has been modernized, and now is part of the Best Western chain. Its 90 rooms are a few steps from the pedestrian shopping streets. 20 Pl. Bellecour (phone: 78-37-57-31). Expensive to moderate.

Altéa Park – Completely updated, this traditional place has 70 rooms, a garden, and a patio restaurant (in good weather). It is on the eastern side of the city. 4 Rue du Professeur-Calmette (phone: 78-74-11-20). Moderate.

Des Artistes – Plain and quiet, with 46 modern rooms, it is centrally situated on a peaceful square dominated by the *Théâtre des Célestins* (and a favorite of the actors playing there). No restaurant. 8 Rue Gaspard André (phone: 78-42-04-88). Moderate.

Créqui – This is a small, modern spot in the vicinity of the *Part-Dieu* center. It has 28 rooms, some opening onto an interior garden. No restaurant. 158 Rue de Créqui (phone: 78-60-20-47). Moderate.

Grand Hôtel de Bordeaux – A traditional establishment, next to the Perrache railroad station, it has a simple, pleasant style. Some of the 79 rooms are furnished with antiques. 1 Rue du Belier (phone: 78-37-58-73). Moderate.

Roosevelt – Quiet, modern, and attractive, with 87 rooms, in the Brotteaux quarter, the commercial neighborhood on the left bank of the Rhône. No restaurant, but there is a bar. 25 Rue Bossuet (phone: 78-52-35-67). Moderate.

Berlioz – Bright and cheerful, this newly remodeled hostelry, directly behind Lyons's Perrache station, has small but functional rooms. 12 Cours Charlemagne (phone: 78-42-30-31). Moderate to inexpensive.

La Résidence – Centrally located on the pedestrian shopping street between Place Bellecour and Perrache station. It has a somewhat sterile style, but it's clean, convenient, and reasonably priced. 18 Rue Victor-Hugo (phone: 78-42-63-48). Moderate to inexpensive.

Bayard – Not only is this the best situated of the city's less pricey hotels, but charm lurks behind the modern entrance. The 15 rooms are quite nicely outfitted. No restaurant. 23 Pl. Bellecour (phone: 78-37-39-64). Inexpensive.

Moderne – A functional establishment about halfway between Place Bellecour and Place des Terreaux. About half of the 31 rooms have private baths; and a few have lovely old fireplaces. No restaurant. 15 Rue Dubois (phone: 78-42-21-83). Inexpensive.

Morand – Timeworn stone stairwells, Renaissance courtyards, and funky floral carpeting on walls and doors make this hotel a quaint mix of ancient and modern. During summer, the proprietress plants flowers in the courtyards, and guests breakfast leisurely amid the blooms. 99 Rue de Crequi (phone: 78-52-29-96). Inexpensive.

 EATING OUT: Foremost among the solid reasons for Lyons's eminence in cuisine is geography. Wine flows in from the Beaujolais and Burgundy regions just to the north, from the Côtes du Rhône to the south, and from the Jura to the northeast. The chicken of Bresse, the beef of Charolais, the freshwater fish of countless nearby rivers, and the robust cheeses of surrounding dairy regions all funnel into the city's markets and restaurants. Nothing has to be imported any great distance. Thus Lyons (along with its surrounding region) has more than its share of great and near-great restaurants, but the distinctive and astonishing thing is that while the cooking in the great restaurants may be more complex, the standards are often as high in the least expensive places as in the most. At all economic levels the Lyonnais are very demanding, and although it may be possible to eat a bad meal in this city, there is no excuse for it.

Most of the world's (and Lyons's) great chefs may be men, but the cuisine of Lyons is basically a *cuisine des femmes,* home cooking raised to the *n*th degree. Many of the famous *mères de Lyon* have passed on now, but their names live on in the enduring influence of their hearty, straightforward style of preparing food, in the legacy of certain Lyonnais specialties — *volaille demi-deuil, fonds d'artichauts au foie gras, quenelles au gratin* — forever associated with them and, sometimes, in the names of restaurants (*Mère Brazier, Roger Roucou/Mère Guy*) descended from them and still operating. A corollary to this, perhaps, is that restaurants in the Lyons area seem to stay in the family for a long time, and even when (as in the case of the celebrated Bocuse) an establishment develops from a riverside inn into one of the world's most formidable restaurants, the contact with the past still seems to be there.

A small lexicon might be helpful. The simplest kind of Lyonnais restaurant is a *bouchon,* often an unpretentious mom-and-pop enterprise with marvelous beaujolais or Côtes du Rhône served in a *pot lyonnais* (a heavy bottle of 46 centiliters — about a pint) and simple cooking in which pork products weigh heavily. A *mâchon* used to be a hearty midmorning snack for the working stiff, but the word tends now to be used for the least expensive prix fixe menus, which might start with a *saladier lyonnais*, usually a rolling table with a dozen or so cold dishes such as potato salad, cold lentils, herring and onion in oil, pig's (or sheep's) feet *rémoulade*, and the like. Lyonnais gastronomic humor is reflected in the *tablier de sapeur* (literally, a fireman's or engineer's apron, referring to the thick leather apron of a Napoleonic army engineer), which is a slab of beef tripe breaded and grilled or sautéed, and *cervelle de canut* (literally, silkworker's brains), a soft white cheese into which a variety of herbs has been mixed. This does not mean that such places will not also have such familiar offerings as *boeuf bourguignon* or *coq au vin*.

In Lyons and its immediate region, the rough rule of thumb is that expensive means it is difficult (or impossible) to hold the bill to less than $150 for two people, and $200 is not uncommon; inexpensive means that it should not take too much effort to keep the bill to $60 for two; the price of a moderate meal lies somewhere in between. These prices usually include a service charge; wine, however, is not included. Reservations are always a good idea — and for the three-star establishments should be made in advance *in writing* — but if you are headed toward a popular *bouchon* on the spur of the moment for lunch, don't be much later than midday and don't be surprised to be turned away, for there may be only one sitting. Even in places noted as expensive, one can usually limit the financial damage by ordering from the more moderate prix fixe menu, while moderate places can rapidly become expensive if the temptation to sample fine wine takes over. In the case of month-long summer closings, exact dates can vary, so check carefully before visiting.

Georges Blanc – An institution, on the bank of the River Veyle in the picturesque village of Vonnas, where it has occupied the same premises since the great-grandmother of the present chef opened it in 1872. M. Blanc's award-winning menu — a combination of traditional regional and nouvelle cuisine — won him three stars in 1981. Outstanding features include braised sweetbreads in spinach, lamb tenderloin with fresh wild mushrooms, and a dessert cart brimming with 15 to 20 pastry selections. Reservations necessary. Closed Wednesdays, Thursday lunch, and January. 41 miles (66 km) north of Lyons in Vonnas (phone: 74-50-00-10). Expensive.

Paul Bocuse – One of France's best-known dining rooms, it earned its reputation after generations in the Bocuse family. This three-star institution is about 7 miles (11 km) north of Lyons on the right bank of the Saône. The quality of the food can suffer from M. Bocuse's frequent international journeys; still, there are those who'd cross continents to try the *soupe aux truffes noires* (truffle soup) and the *loup en croûte* (sea bass in a crust), two of the chef-host's most famous creations. Service can be indifferent to first-timers, but for some the hauteur is part of the appeal. Closed most of August. Reservations necessary. Pont de Collonges, Collonges-au-Mont-d'Or (phone: 78-22-01-40). Expensive.

Alain Chapel – Among France's greatest restaurants, this three-star Michelin luminary sparkled in a tiny village 12 miles (19 km) north of Lyons, where Chapel's parents ran a restaurant known as *Chez la Mère Charles* (his mother was Mère Charles). Regrettably, Monsieur Chapel passed away as we went to press and the future of his famous establishment is now uncertain. We hope his legacy will survive. A fabulous lobster salad, lobster with noodles, stuffed calf's ear, *gâteau de foies blonds* (a pie of chicken livers and foie gras), and other specialties that varied with the season (and his imagination) were his stock in trade. In warm weather, tables placed outdoors on a lovely patio make it hard to conceive of a nicer place to enjoy a midsummer lunch. There also are 13 rooms with bath. Closed Mondays, Tuesday lunch, holidays, and January. Reservations necessary. On N83 in Mionnay (phone: 78-91-82-02). Expensive.

Les Frères Troisgros – Pierre and Jean studied under the late Fernand Point at

La Pyramide, then returned in the 1950s to take over their father's 25-room hostelry, right across from the train station on Place de la Gare. The brothers became three-star chefs in 1968. The restaurant flies on one wing now, following the death of Jean Troisgros, although Pierre's son, Michel, second in command, now fills the gap. Pierre rejoices in the natural flavor of foods delicately enhanced and underscored. The menu changes with the season to use the area's fresh vegetables, poultry, shrimp, and snails to best advantage. Closed Tuesdays, Wednesday lunch, most of January, and most of August. Reservations necessary. *Hôtel des Frères Troisgros,* Pl. de la Gare, Roanne, 53 miles (85 km) northwest of Lyons (phone: 77-71-66-97). Expensive.

Léon de Lyon – Jean-Paul Lacombe continues to serve the traditional Lyonnais specialties his father served (*gras double* — finely chopped tripe sautéed with onion, parsley, garlic, and white wine — as done here would convert anyone to tripe), but he also has expanded his repertoire with nouvelle cuisine creations. The restaurant has two Michelin stars. It also has a newly opened nonsmoking dining room. Closed Sundays, Monday lunch, and for 10 days at *Christmas.* Reservations necessary. 1 Rue Pléney (phone: 78-28-11-33). Expensive.

Nandron – Gérard Nandron's one-star restaurant on a quay overlooking the Rhône is another place with a family tradition behind it and a menu midway between classic Lyonnais and innovative. Closed Friday evenings, Saturdays, and August. Reservations necessary. 26 Quai Jean-Moulin (phone: 78-42-10-26). Expensive.

Pierre Orsi – M. Orsi is an already well-established but still rising star (whose inspired and imaginative cooking has won him two Michelin stars). The already elegant dining room was undergoing extensive renovation as we went to press. Closed Sunday evenings and during August. Reservations necessary. 3 Pl. Kléber (phone: 78-89-57-68). Expensive.

La Pyramide – A French gastronomic shrine that was closed following the death of Mado Point, widow of renowned chef Fernand Point, it is beginning to shine again. Now owned by a Parisian real estate company, it reopened in July 1989 after extensive remodeling; its 60-seat dining room (one Michelin star) has a 1920s graciousness with a garden and terrace; 28 guestrooms were added, making this a fitting monument to what some consider this century's greatest French chef. Closed Wednesdays and Thursday lunch. Reservations necessary. 14 Bd. de la Pyramide, Vienne (phone: 74-53-01-96). Expensive.

Roger Roucou (La Mère Guy) – On the right bank of the Saône, south of the center, it was a river fishermen's eatery in the 18th century, but now is one of the city's most elegant establishments, although relatively little known. Closed Sunday evenings, Mondays, and August. Reservations necessary. 35 Quai Jean-Jacques Rousseau, La Mulatière (phone: 78-51-65-37). Expensive.

La Tour Rose – Philippe Chavent, one of Lyons's ambitious young chefs, has one Michelin star to his credit. He has established himself grandly on Vieux Lyon's winding, cobblestone Rue du Boeuf, where he recently moved from No. 18 to No. 22. Noted for very nouvelle cuisine and for a moderate prix fixe menu that makes it accessible to many, Chavent also runs a shuttle service with a London taxi between the restaurant and the parking lot on Quai Romain-Rolland. Closed Sundays and the last 2 weeks of August. Reservations necessary. 22 Rue du Boeuf (phone: 78-37-25-90). Expensive.

L'Arc en Ciel – A very fine hotel restaurant, not to mention the fact that from the 32nd floor of the Crédit Lyonnais tower on the left bank of the Rhône, it has the best view in town. Closed Sundays, Monday lunch, and from mid-July to mid-August. Reservations necessary. *Pullman Hotel,* 129 Rue Servient (phone: 78-62-94-12). Moderate.

Bistrot de Lyon – Jean-Paul Lacombe of *Léon de Lyon* (see above) is a partner in this booming enterprise. Open until 3 AM and full of all sorts of night people, including actors and their audiences after the theaters have rung down the curtain. The food is unpretentious, with a Lyonnais accent, and the wines are good. Closed 10 days at *Christmas*. Reservations advised. 64 Rue Mercière (phone: 78-37-00-62). Moderate.

Bourillot – Chef Christian Bourillot is known for his classic cooking and for maintaining a consistently high standard of excellence in this one-star restaurant on an attractive square. Closed Sundays and holidays, July, and for 10 days at *Christmas*. Reservations necessary. 8 Pl. des Célestins (phone: 78-37-38-64). Moderate.

Chez Raymond – Open only for lunch, when this prosaic-looking café is transformed into a trencherman's paradise of only about 20 seats. A *plat du jour* is preceded by a gigantic *saladier lyonnais* and followed by excellent cheeses and an immense choice of desserts set out buffet style. The *patron* is a former maître d'hôtel for *Bocuse,* and his wife presides in the large, well-equipped kitchen. Closed Sundays year-round and evenings during August. Reservations advised. 21 Rue des Rancy (phone: 78-60-58-67). Moderate.

Chez Rose – The ambience, food, and wines are those of a classic Lyonnais bistro. Closed Sundays and holidays year-round; Saturdays in July and August. Reservations advised. 4 Rue Rabelais (phone: 78-60-57-25). Moderate.

Les Fantasques – This is doubtless the outstanding seafood spot in Lyons. It has one Michelin star, and it serves a bouillabaisse that would hold its own in Marseilles. Closed Sundays and 2 weeks in mid-August. Reservations advised. 47-51 Rue de la Bourse (phone: 78-37-36-58). Moderate.

Henry – Among Lyonnais in the know, this is considered a sure bet for traditional food — particularly fish and game — prepared with finesse and served with style. One Michelin star. Closed Saturday lunch and Mondays. Just off Place des Terreaux. Reservations advised. 27 Rue de la Martinière (phone: 78-28-26-08). Moderate.

La Mère Brazier – The *mère* has gone (and so has her erstwhile Michelin three-star restaurant outside town), but her place in the city (one star) remains in family hands and adheres to the purest Lyonnais traditions. *Volaille demi-deuil* (chicken in half-mourning, in which the bird is poached with truffles under its skin, the black color of which gives the dish its name) is sacrosanct here, as are the artichoke bottoms with foie gras and *quenelles au gratin.* Closed Saturday lunch, Sundays, and August. Reservations advised. 12 Rue Royale (phone: 78-28-15-49). Moderate.

La Mère Vittet, Brasserie Lyonnaise – The best reason for keeping this spot in mind is that it closes only on May 1 (Europe's *Labor Day*) and always is ready to serve a meal, a rarity in France. It also is a well-run establishment with decent food and good wines. Reservations advised. Near the Perrache railroad station. 26 Cours de Verdun (phone: 78-37-20-17). Moderate.

Le Passage – Long a favorite with Lyonnais in the know, this lace-curtained Belle Epoque–style restaurant, hidden away in a passage near the Place des Terreaux, has earned a star from Michelin for its traditional fare. Closed Sundays. Reservations advised. 8 Rue Plâtre (phone: 78-28-11-16). Moderate.

La Tassée – The Borgeot family runs this marvelously classic Lyonnais bistro, an appealing place with amusing murals. The menu ranges from a *mâchon lyonnais* to solid bourgeois fare — served to about 10 PM — and there is a wide range of excellent regional wines. Closed Sundays and for 10 days at *Christmas*. Reservations advised. 20 Rue de la Charité (phone: 78-37-02-35). Moderate.

Christian Têtedoie – This talented young chef and his wife, Florence, moved to larger, more elegant quarters last year, after 2 successful years in their tiny wharf-side restaurant of the same name. Têtedoie's style — refined and rich in natural flavors — resembles that of Georges Blanc, the three-star Michelin chef whose kitchen Têtedoie helped run before moving to Lyons. Closed Sunday nights and Mondays. Reservations necessary. 54 Quai Pierre Scize (phone: 78-42-35-36). Moderate.

Les Trois Dômes – Another of the few hotel dining rooms to compete seriously in this city. This one, too, has a panoramic view, though only from the eighth floor, but it does take in three churches as well as the banks of the Rhône. Open daily. Reservations advised. *Hôtel Sofitel,* 20 Quai Gailleton (phone: 78-42-72-50). Moderate.

Tupinier – The Lérons, who formerly operated *Daniel et Denise,* changed their restaurant's name and format, putting more emphasis on local Lyonnais special-ties. Reservations advised. 2 Rue Tupin (phone: 78-37-49-98). Moderate.

La Voûte (Chez Léa) – Léa, probably the last of the great *mères lyonnaises,* has retired, but her successors are keeping the same down-to-earth Lyonnais tradition, and at last report Léa was still coming around from time to time to check on things. The reasonably priced prix fixe menu usually includes *tablier de sapeur* and the typically Lyonnais *salade de mesclun* (a mixture of wild greens). Closed Sundays and July. Reservations advised. 11 Pl. Antonin-Gourju (phone: 78-42-01-33). Moderate.

Chez Georges – The truculent Georges Drebet, who made this place, is long gone, but it is still in the genuine *bouchon* tradition. Closed Saturdays at midday and Sundays. Reservations advised. 8 Rue du Garet (phone: 78-28-30-46). Moderate to inexpensive.

Chez Hugon – Classic Lyonnais *bouchon,* complete with red-checkered tablecloths, tightly packed tables, rustic woods, and a motherly *cuisinière* at the stove serving up copious portions of simple, soul-satisfying local specialties. Reservations ad-vised. 12 Rue Pizay (phone: 78-28-10-94). Moderate to inexpensive.

Le Garet – A long-established *bouchon.* The menu is classic Lyonnais, the service, agreeable, and the Beaujolais, excellent. Closed weekends, holidays, August, and a week at *Christmas.* Reservations advised. 7 Rue du Garet (phone: 78-28-16-94). Moderate to inexpensive.

Les Adrets "Le Tire-Cul" – Delightful atmosphere, good quality, and reasonable prices make this place on a winding street in Vieux Lyon a local favorite. Reserva-tions advised. 38 Rue du Boeuf (phone: 78-38-24-30). Inexpensive.

Bar de l'Entracte (Chez Marcelle) – This popular *bouchon* on the left bank of the Rhône has relatively late service for the type of place it is — orders are taken until about 9:30 PM. Closed weekends and August. Reservations unnecessary. 71 Cours Vitton (phone: 78-89-51-07). Inexpensive.

Café des Fédérations – More typical Lyonnais *bouchon* fare, an excellent *pot de Morgon,* and a decor of sausages hanging from the ceiling and photos and old newspaper clippings on the wall. Closed weekends and August. Reservations unnecessary. 8 Rue du Major-Martin (phone: 78-28-26-00). Inexpensive.

Le Comptoir du Boeuf – Philippe Chavent has a successful low-budget alternative to *La Tour Rose* in this colorful little café-restaurant in Vieux Lyon. You can snack on oysters or terrines or order a *plat du jour* until midnight or later. Closed Sundays. Reservations unnecessary. 3 Pl. Neuve-St.-Jean (phone: 78-92-82-35). Inexpensive.

La Mère Jean – The reason this place always seems noisy and crowded, full of students, journalists, soccer players, and whatnot, with loud debates going on between tables, is that hearty Lyonnais home cooking has been served here for over a half century at minuscule prices. Closed Saturdays and Sundays. Reservations advised. 5 Rue des Marronniers (phone: 78-37-81-27). Inexpensive.

 BARS AND CAFÉS: Most Lyonnais are likely to feel that the best thing to do with the late afternoon–early evening happy hour is to split a *pot* of beaujolais with a friend, perhaps in the same place they had lunch. Other possibilities include most of the bars listed under *Nightclubs and Nightlife* or two hotel bars with a view: *Le Melhor* in the *Sofitel* hotel and the *Panache Bar* in the *Pullman Perrache* hotel. The *Grand Café des Négociants* (1 Pl. Francisque-Regaud) is just about the last example of an old-fashioned grand café of the turn of the century, while the *Cintra* (43 Rue de la Bourse) is a haven of anglophilic understatement. *Le Procope* (68 Rue Merciere) is a Lyons clone of the Paris establishment of the same name (which claims to be the oldest café in the world). The Lyonnais version is larger, more modern, and has an upstairs lounge where piano music and jazz are performed.

MARSEILLES

Some cities pass through a chrysalis stage as important ports before they emerge into greatness as commercial centers or industrial powers. Not so Marseilles. As it has been for 25 centuries, since before the Greeks controlled the wine-dark seas of the Mediterranean, modern Marseilles is above all else a port city. In 600 BC, Phocaean Greeks from Asia Minor founded the city, calling it Massalia, and then, as now, it acted as port of entry for goods, people, ideas, and most of all, history. (A commemorative block near Marseilles's thriving Vieux Port proclaims with perfect accuracy and stunning lack of modesty: "They founded Marseilles, from which civilization reached the West.")

With a population just brushing 1 million, Marseilles is among France's largest cities. But that may say more about the importance of the Mediterranean to France than of France's influence on Marseilles. Landlocked Paris, so gay in springtime and so gray in winter, is another country, 500 miles away, every mile of which must be traveled on land. It is a journey that traditional Marseillais, otherwise so effusive and warm, are reluctant to make. Marseilles and its people face steadfastly toward the sea, from which they have always drawn such strength.

When the city provisioned the Crusaders and welcomed back their booty, it was trading with Africa, the Near East, and the Far East. Today the names have changed, but France's major port does business with the same countries, and a lot more besides. Marseillais have as much in common with Italians and Greeks — fellow Mediterraneans — as they do with Parisians.

Unlike Paris, which has become predictable and bourgeois by comparison, Marseilles is France's connection to the sensuous, boisterous world of the Mediterranean. Sailors from all over the world roam the Canebière, the famous street leading up from the Vieux Port (Old Port), in search of women, excitement, or perhaps a little bit of smuggling on the side on their next tour of duty. And frequently violence still erupts, as it did in the gangland murder at the *Bar du Téléphone* not too many years ago. The milieu of the French underworld endures as a presence, for Marseilles remains, as both Interpol and Hollywood would have it, "the French connection." Even though many of the drug middlemen have moved on to Amsterdam or Berlin, Gene Hackman still would recognize the place. But an odd question lingers: Do we consider port cities wicked because of Marseilles, or do we feel such thrilling wickedness in Marseilles because it is so much the port city of our dreams?

As in all great port cities, numerous foreigners and immigrants have settled in Marseilles — particularly industrial workers from the island of Corsica and a large number of North Africans. Often poor, many Algerians, Tunisians, and Moroccans live in slums around the Porte d'Aix and the Rue Ste.-Barbe, where shops sell inexpensive North African items, but where few people feel comfortable wandering after dark. The area is perfectly safe in the daytime, however, and it's worth a visit for the colors and smells alone.

Life is lived boisterously in the Marseilles streets, particularly in the area around the Vieux Port, which now is a harbor for pleasure boats and for sidewalk restaurants offering bouillabaisse. Although the Germans dynamited much of the picturesque but seedy old quarter during World War II (because it was a center for the Resistance), some reminders of Marseilles's tradition still survive.

From the beginning, the city prospered at the hands of the Greek traders, declined under Roman rule, and was revived by the Crusaders, whom Marseilles supplied with food and weapons. Devastated by the great plague in 1720, in which 50,000 of its citizens perished, Marseilles rose again to support the French Revolution with enthusiasm. In 1792, 500 volunteers marched to Paris, singing a new war song composed at Strasbourg by a young officer named Rouget de Lisle. All the way to Paris, the Marseillais sang the new song with Mediterranean exuberance. Practice improved their performance, so that when the troops reached Paris, their expert chorus electrified all listeners. The song caught on and became France's stirring national anthem, named not for the city but for those staunch choristers, "La Marseillaise."

One hundred years later, the opening of the Suez Canal virtually assured the continued maritime success of Marseilles, and commercial traffic abandoned the small Vieux Port for a new one directly to the north. The new port was also destroyed during World War II, but it was rebuilt and expanded. Flat, nondescript, and soulless buildings have risen on the once vibrant site of the Old Quarter. Ironically, every new groundbreaking brings the possibility of unearthing still more traces of earlier civilizations, like the Roman docks discovered in the 1940s or the Greek ramparts found in 1967. Medieval churches now stand side by side with steel and glass apartment buildings. The ongoing excavations at the Centre Bourse are open to visitors.

Many visitors to Marseilles are heading off to the Côte d'Azur and are in the city only to change trains at the newly rebuilt Gare St.-Charles or planes at the modern Aéroport de Marignane. But there's sufficient reason to linger. Step into a café on the Vieux Port as the burning Mediterranean sun starts to sink in the sky and order a milky white *pastis,* an anise-flavored apéritif. (Or duck into the less seedy *La Samaritaine* at Bd. de la République.) Around you are spectacular white limestone hills and in front, a harbor filled with the cries and accents of far-off lands. Drink it all in, along with your *pastis.* Who knows? You may, like the American writer M.F.K. Fisher, fall in love with Marseilles and stay longer, soaking in its rich Mediterranean atmosphere and exploring its abundant historic remains.

MARSEILLES AT-A-GLANCE

SEEING THE CITY: Take the No. 60 bus up to this hilly city's most imposing height, a 531-foot limestone bluff crowned by the Basilica of Notre-Dame-de-la-Garde, known to the Provençal as La Bonne Mère. There's an extraordinary view — particularly at sunset — from the terrace: The boats on the Vieux Port, the white rocky islands, and the densely built city stretch out below. The half-Roman, half-Byzantine basilica itself, topped by a huge gilded statue of the Virgin, is far less of a draw than its view, but inside it does have interesting hand-painted offerings to the Virgin as thanks for curing various ailments. Pl. du Colonel Eden.

SPECIAL PLACES: If you walk down the Gare St.-Charles's monumental staircase and continue on the Boulevard d'Athènes, you'll come to a busy central shopping street, the Canebière. Visitors are sometimes disappointed at the modern, occasionally tacky appearance of this celebrated boulevard that runs into the Vieux Port. During the Middle Ages there were hemp fields here, or *chénevières* (hence the name Canebière); the broad plane-tree-lined concourse is still the key artery — and essential reference point — of Marseilles. During December, it becomes the backdrop for the colorful *santons* fair, where folk art takes center stage in the form of clay figures, some 2 to 3 feet tall, representing both the *Christmas* story and Provençal life in centuries past.

IN THE CITY

Vieux Port – Follow the Canebière down to the Quai des Belges and you'll arrive at the Vieux Port. Today a harbor for small fishing boats and yachts, it's far more picturesque than the burgeoning new port to the north. Its entrance is framed by the 17th-century forts of St. Jean and St. Nicholas (a Foreign Legion base). Terraced restaurants featuring bouillabaisse (at staggering prices) overlook the animated marina. A fresh-fish market does a lively business every morning. This is the heart of Marseilles. It still is possible to ferry from one side of the Vieux Port to the other, as in Marcel Pagnol's films. Ferries make the trip every 2 or 3 minutes from 7 AM to 7 PM daily. There also is a sightseeing train that leaves frequently from the Vieux Port to the Basilica of Notre-Dame-de-la-Garde from 2:15 to 6:15 PM.

Musée des Beaux-Arts – In the 19th-century Palais de Longchamp — noteworthy in its own right for impressive fountains and gardens (and even a zoo) — the museum offers a considerable display of art. Paintings from the Italian, Flemish, Dutch, and French (David, Courbet, Ingres) schools share the palace's left wing with works by Marseilles natives Honoré Daumier and Pierre Puget and by other Provençal artists. On the ground floor is a charming children's museum. The right wing of the palace contains a natural history museum. Open daily from 10 AM to 5 PM. Admission charge. Pl. Bernex (phone: 91-62-21-17).

Musée Grobet-Labadié – Near the Longchamp Palace, this l9th-century showplace is furnished opulently, exactly as it was when the musician Louis Grobet lived there. Stop by before or after visiting the *Fine Arts Museum.* Open daily from 10 AM to 5 PM. 140 Bd. Longchamp (phone: 91-62-21-82 or 91-08-96-04).

Outdoor Markets – Wander through the city's raucous market areas and take in their vivid sights and smells. They're particularly alive in the mornings on the Quai des Belges, where the fishermen and their wives sell their catch directly. Also, note the food market on Rue Longue des Capucins (at Rue Vacon, near the Canebière); the flea markets near the Porte d'Aix (that is, the triumphal arch in Pl. Jules-Guesde at the end of Rue d'Aix); the daily book market on Le Cours Julien; and Rue St.-Barbe in the Algerian quarter (but avoid this racially troubled area after dark).

Le Cours Julien – This unique public square has splashing fountains, interesting boutiques, bookstores, restaurants, and an innovative art gallery (see *Shopping*). It will take an hour to explore the whole plaza, but allow yourself the pleasure of real contact with the youth, vigor, and creativity of Marseilles. To get here, walk north from the Old Port, up the Canebière, then East onto Bd. Garibaldi, which crosses Le Cours Julien.

Musée des Docks Romains – An unexpected benefit came from the Germans' 1943 bombing of the old quarter. Fascinating remains of long-buried Roman docks and statuary were unearthed in the course of rebuilding the area, and the museum incorporates the original setting plus objects retrieved offshore. Open daily from 10 AM to 5 PM. Admission charge. 28 Pl. Vivaux (phone: 91-91-24-62).

Musée d'Histoire de Marseille – The excavations of the ancient Greek port and ramparts are now a museum. The open-air archaeological dig features the remains of a boat excavated on the site. Open daily from noon to 7 PM. Closed Sundays. Admission charge. Place Belsunce (phone: 91-90-42-22).

Le Panier – From the Quai du Port, the narrow streets climb toward what little remains of Old Marseilles. Reminiscent of Paris's Montmartre (and likewise beginning to suffer the same "renewal" fate), the Panier quarter is a maze of tiny streets reverberating with the exuberant sounds of daily life in a Provençal neighborhood. It is not lacking for art galleries or interesting bistros. Behind the Hôtel de Ville, climb the steps to the left of Notre-Dame-des-Accoules's bell tower, the remains of a 12th-century church.

Cathédrales de la Major – Reminiscent of Moslem mosques, the cathedrals' domes and cupolas dominate the Quai de la Tourette. The sadly battered Ancienne (Old) Major was built in the 12th century in pure Romanesque style on the ruins of the Roman Temple of Diana. The huge, ostentatious cathedral next to it was built in the 19th century in a Romanesque-Byzantine style. Pl. de la Major.

Basilique St.-Victor – The present fortified Gothic church dates from the 11th to the 14th century, but the real interest lies below, in its crypt, which actually is an ancient basilica founded in the 5th century in honor of the 3rd-century martyr St. Victor. This basilica contains a chapel and the tomb of two 3rd-century martyrs in addition to pagan and early Christian catacombs. The church also hosts concerts; call for the program. Crypt closed Sundays. Admission charge. At the end of Rue Sainte (phone: 91-33-25-86).

Cité Radieuse – Designed by the renowned Le Corbusier, the 17-story housing development — or *unité d'habitation* — was avant-garde for its time (1947–52) and is still a landmark in modern functional architecture. There is a moderately priced hotel with a number of shops on the premises. 280 Bd. Michelet.

Parc Borély – This is a lovely stretch of greenery where you can take some sun by the lake or rent a bicycle. There's also a quaint racetrack on the same site. The park itself closes after dark. Promenade de la Plage and Av. Clot-Bey.

OUT OF TOWN

Promenade de la Corniche – This scenic coast road that winds for some 3 miles (5 km) south of the Vieux Port passes in its course Marseilles's most spectacular homes and a breathtaking view of the sea and the islands, including the Château d'If and the Frioul Islands (see below). Also known as the Corniche Président-J.-F.-Kennedy, it passes a picture-postcard fishing port, Vallon des Auffes, and lovely rocky coves before it becomes the promenade de la Plage (with Parc Borély) and continues toward Cassis, a beautiful fishing town, now also a summer resort, that was celebrated by Derain, Vlaminck, Matisse, and Dufy. Cassis is 14 miles (22 km) from Marseilles. Beautiful, sandy Prado Beach is also along the Corniche road; watch for signs. Pick up Corniche Président-J.-F.-Kennedy at Rue des Catalans.

Château d'If – Set on a rocky island, this beautiful castle was built in the 16th century for defense, and then turned into a state prison whose most famous "guest" was Alexandre Dumas's Count of Monte Cristo. Inside some cells are carvings by Huguenot prisoners. Open daily; admission charge. The château can be reached by boats that leave about every 15 minutes for a 20-minute ride from the Quai des Belges (phone: 91-55-50-09).

Château Gombert – This village just outside the city limits claims the *Musée des Arts et Traditions Populaires du Terroir Marseillais* (Museum of Popular Art and Traditions), 5 Pl. des Héros (phone: 91-68-14-38). Among its exhibitions are pottery, pewter, and glass displays. Open only on Saturday, Sunday, and Monday afternoons. In summer the town holds a festival of Provençal folklore. Follow the autoroute north toward Lyons and exit at La Rose.

Allauch – On a cliff with a church on top and windmills all around, it offers a good view of Marseilles and the harbor and is known for *suce-miel,* a type of lollipop made of honey, and *croquants aux amandes,* almond biscuits. To get here, take Boulevard de la Libération out of Marseilles and follow signs north to St. Barnabé/Allauch.

Frioul Islands – These islands southwest of Marseilles have sparkling creeks that provide an idyllic retreat from the city's sometimes torrid atmosphere. Boats leave for the islands from the Quai des Belges every hour (in winter, every 1½ hours). Les Armateurs Côtiers (phone: 91-55-50-09).

■ **EXTRA SPECIAL:** For unsurpassed and unspoiled natural beauty, don't leave the region without seeing its spectacular *calanques* along the coast between Marseilles and Cassis. The *calanques* are crystal-clear narrow creeks running between stark white limestone cliffs that soar up to 650 feet, much like small fjords. They can be approached only by foot (about 1½ hours each way) or by boat, thereby ensuring a minimum number of tourists. The closest *calanques* — Sormiou and Morgiou — can be reached from Roy d'Espagne (take bus No. 44) and Les Baumettes (No. 22), respectively. For information on organized hiking ventures, visit *Les Excursionnistes Marseillais* (16 Rue de la Rotonde), Tuesdays through Saturdays from 6 to 8 PM. Otherwise, leave by boat from Quai des Belges (phone: 91-84-75-52).

SOURCES AND RESOURCES

TOURIST INFORMATION: The English-speaking staff of the Office du Tourisme (4 La Canebière; phone: 91-54-91-11) provides hotel reservations, maps, guides, and advice; also ask for *La Charte de la Bouillabaisse,* which gives the real recipe for this much maligned and poorly imitated fish soup and provides a list of those restaurants serving the authentic concoction. A second tourist office is at Gare St.-Charles (phone: 91-50-59-18).

For a closer look at Marseilles, read *A Considerable Town,* by the American M.F.K. Fisher; it's a charming and personal account of a city she loves.

A good street-indexed map is the *Carte et Plan Fréjet,* available at major bookstores along the Canebière. They also carry general English-language guidebooks, but no local English publications exist. Also, pick up a copy of *Trimestre,* a quarterly listing of what's happening.

From late May to October, 3-hour guided bus tours of Marseilles are available in English from Valadou (73 La Canebière; phone: 91-91-90-02), for about $13.

Local Coverage – If you read French, pick up *Le Mois à Marseille* or *Poche Soir* for current events. The local newspapers, *Le Méridional* and *Le Provençal,* are available at any newsstand.

TELEPHONE: The city code for Marseilles is 91, which is incorporated into all local 8-digit numbers. (*Note:* The area code for the airport is 42.) When calling a number in Marseilles from the Paris region (including the Ile-de-France), dial 16, wait for the dial tone, then dial the 8-digit number. When calling a number from outside Paris, dial only the 8-digit number. When calling from the US, dial 33 (which is the country code), followed by the 8-digit number.

 GETTING AROUND: Airport – Marseilles-Marignane Airport is about 18 miles (29 km) northwest of the city (phone: 42-78-21-00). International and domestic terminals are adjacent in the main airport concourse. For a taxi into town, 24 hours a day, call 42-78-24-44; the 20- to 30-minute ride will cost about 200F ($35). There are buses every 20 minutes in both directions from 6 AM to 8 PM and according to flight schedules; the approximate time to Gare St.-Charles, the main train station, is 30 minutes, and the fare is about 32F ($6). For information on regular bus service to the airport from Marseilles, call 91-50-59-34.

Boat – Boats leave for the Frioul Islands (see *Special Places*) from the Quai des Belges approximately every hour. Les Armateurs Côtiers (phone: 91-55-50-09).

Bus and Métro – Marseilles's attractive subway system is coordinated with the buses, allowing easy — and free — transfers between systems. The métro goes in only two directions, so it's difficult to get lost. Buy a *carnet* (packet) of six tickets instead of the single ticket. The métro shuts down each night at 12:30 AM and most buses stop running even earlier. For information, call 91-91-92-10. For information about regular bus service to Marseilles-Marignane Airport, call 91-50-59-34.

Car Rental – Major international firms are represented.

Ferry – For ferries to Corsica, inquire at *SNCM*, 61 Bd. des Dames (phone: 91-56-32-00).

Taxi – There are cabstands around the city, or call *Taxi Tupp* (phone: 91-05-80-80), *Marseille Taxi* (phone: 91-02-20-20), *Taxi 2000* (phone: 91-49-20-00), or *Taxi +* (phone: 91-03-60-03).

Train – Marseilles's train station is Gare St.-Charles (phone: 91-08-50-50 for information, 91-08-84-12 for reservations). The extension of the Paris-Lyons high-speed *TGV* line to Valence (expected to be completed by 1993) will cut travel time between Paris and Marseilles to just over 3 hours; until then, it takes about 4½ hours.

 SPECIAL EVENTS: There's an *International Folklore Festival* in early July at the Château Gombert, Pl. des Héros, as well as a live crèche at *Christmas*. The best events during the rest of the year are the *Santons Fair,* during which the traditional hand-painted clay statuettes fill *Christmas* crèches all over the city (December 1 to January 6); *La Fête de Mai,* when the Cours Julien and Place Carli are closed to cars and open to circus acts, theater troupes, and singers (late May); the *Garlic Fair,* when mounds of garlic cover the sidewalks of Cour Belsunce (June 15 to July 15); and the *Islands Festival* (July and August).

 MUSEUMS: Besides those described in *Special Places*, there are three other notable Marseilles museums:

Musée Cantini – Provençal ceramics and often outstanding contemporary art exhibitions. Open daily from 10 AM to 5 PM. Admission charge. 19 Rue Grignan (phone: 91-54-77-75).

Musée de la Moto – Just opened, the collection of motorcycles here includes a De Dion Bouton (1898), a Moto Guzzi (1947), a Motosacoche 215cc (1904), and many more. Open daily except Tuesdays from 10 AM to 6 PM. Traverse St.-Paul, Quartier le Merlan (phone: 91-63-25-36).

Musée du Vieux Marseille – A folklore museum set up in a 16th-century house, the Maison Diamantée (Diamond House), so called for the shape of its stone facing and best known for its *santon* collection (see *Shopping*). Open daily. Admission charge. Rue de la Prison (phone: 91-55-10-19).

SHOPPING: Major department stores, elegant couturier and gift shops, and enough shoe shops to make a centipede happy are clustered in the frenetic area around the Canebière (Rue de Rome, Rue Paradis, and Rue St.-Ferréol). The flashy and trendy *Centre Bourse* shopping center is north of the Canebière. Less expensive shops, usually selling North African items, are in the vicinity of the Porte d'Aix (Arc de Triomphe).

Typical Marseillais souvenirs include clay *santons,* which can be found in tourist shops or at numerous booths set up for the *Christmas Santons Fair* on the Canebière. The word *santon* is derived from the Italian *santibelli,* "the beautiful saints." These small, naively modeled and brightly colored figurines represent both biblical figures and traditional characters of Provence life such as the Gypsy, the shepherd, and the milkmaid.

Les Arcenaux – A bookstore and publishing house that sells new and old editions. It also has a tearoom, a restaurant, and an antiques shop. 25 Cours Estienne d'Orves (phone: 91-54-39-37).

Le Four des Navettes – Try some *navettes* (half bread, half cake loaves, which stay fresh for months) from this remarkable 200-year-old bakery. 136 Rue Sainte (phone: 91-33-32-12).

Galerie Roger Pailhas – An art gallery that promotes the work of international artists, including some of Marseilles's most original ones. 61 Cours Julien (phone: 91-42-18-01).

Parenthèses – Jazz bookstore and publisher, it's a storehouse of books on music, the arts, and architecture. 72 Cours Julien (phone: 91-48-74-44).

SPORTS AND FITNESS: Professional sports include auto racing, basketball, horse racing, ice hockey, rugby, and soccer. Inquire at the tourist office.

Fishing – Notably for gilt-head and mackerel: off the Corniche, in the *calanques,* the Frioul Islands, and in nearby fishing villages.

Golf – The nearest 18-hole course is 14 miles (22 km) away at the *Golf Club Aix-Marseille,* Domaine de Riquetti, Les Milles, Aix-en-Provence (phone: 42-24-20-41).

Horseback Riding – Inquire at the *Centre Equestre de la Ville de Marseille,* 33 Carthage (phone: 91-73-72-94).

Jogging – Take bus No.21 to Domaine de Luminy, about 4 miles (6 km) from the city center. Or try Parc Borély, 3 miles (5 km) south of the city by the Promenade de la Corniche.

Sailing – Contact *Centre Nautique Roucas-Blanc,* Plage du Roucas-Blanc (phone: 91-22-72-49).

Swimming – *Piscine Luminy,* Rte. Léon Lachamp (phone: 91-41-26-59).

Tennis and Squash – Try the courts at *Tennis Municipaux* (Allée Ray Grassi; phone: 91-77-83-89) or *Tennis Didier* (81 bis François Mauriac; phone: 91-26-16-05). Both *Set-Squash Marseille* (265 Av. de Mazargues; phone: 91-71-94-71) and *Prado Squash* (26 bis Bd. Michelet; phone: 91-22-03-45) provide facilities for tennis as well as squash.

Water Sports – For information, call or visit the *Fédération des Sociétés Nautiques des Bouches du Rhône,* 10 Av. de la Corse (phone: 91-54-34-88).

THEATER: Theater is booming in Marseilles, with more than 10 new stages opening in the past few years. There's a surprisingly good choice of theater activity year-round. The choices range from the intimate *Centre Culturel* for theater and music (33 Cours Julien; phone: 91-47-09-64) to the *Café-Théâtre du Vieux Panier* (52 Rue St. Françoise; phone: 91-91-00-74) and the *Théâtre de Poche* (2 Av. Maréchal-Foch; phone: 91-72-41-27) to the more ambitious national theater,

La Criée (30 Quai de Rive Neuve; phone: 91-54-74-54 or 91-54-70-54), where reservations are necessary. An especially interesting program is offered by the *Théâtre du Gyptis* (136 Rue Loubon; phone: 91-08-10-18). The *Théâtre Massalia* (60 Rue Grignan; phone: 91-55-66-06) has been converted into a unique marionette theater featuring performances by marionette companies from all over Europe. For experimental theater, visit *Théâtre de Poche* (2 Av. Maréchal-Foch; phone: 91-72-42-27) and *Théâtre de Lenche* (4 Pl. de Lenche; phone: 91-91-55-56 or 91-91-52-22). (*Note:* Those who don't speak French will endure no handicap while enjoying operettas or mime performances, which are presented frequently.) In addition, the *Opéra de Marseille* is the home of the *Compagnie Roland Petit,* France's well-known ballet company. For theater information and tickets, visit the office of the *FNAC* at *Centre Bourse,* north of the Canebière.

 MUSIC: The Marseillais know good opera and ballet as well as they know bouillabaisse. The sometimes outstanding *Opéra de Marseille* (Pl. Ernest-Reyer; phone: 91-55-14-99) and the recently launched *Théâtre de Recherche de Marseille* (*TRM*) (Espace Massalia, 60 Rue Grignan; phone: 91-55-66-06) both have devoted followings. Chamber music and organ recitals are frequent at major churches and occasionally outdoors on the Vieux Port. Popular music doesn't fare nearly as well. There are occasional acts at *Théâtre Axel Toursky* (22 Av. Edouard-Vaillant; phone: 91-02-58-35), although at press time, the theater was closed temporarily.

 NIGHTCLUBS AND NIGHTLIFE: Marseilles does not suffer from inactivity after dark, with action ranging from the sedate to the frenetic. In the former category, visitors will find soothing piano bars such as *Le Beauvau* in the *Pullman Beauvau* hotel (9 Rue Beauvau; phone: 91-54-91-00), whose barman really knows his trade, and *Le Garbo* (9 Quai de Rive Neuve; phone: 91-33-34-20), whose evocative decor recalls the period and style of its namesake. There's traditional Andalusian dancing at *Le Sangria* (145 Bd. Rabattau; phone: 91-79-64-35). The most "in" night spots include *Bunny's Club* (2 Rue Corneille; phone: 91-54-09-02), with a packed dance floor and an excellent sound system; *Abbaye de la Commanderie* (20 Rue Corneille; phone: 91-33-45-56), a cabaret that draws its neighbor's overflow with a *sympathique* evening of nonstop songs; and *London Club* (73 Corniche Président-J.-F.-Kennedy; phone: 91-52-64-04), a friendly nightclub/disco. At the moment, the young set favors *Le Rock A Billy* (5 Rue Molière; phone: 91-54-70-36) and the famous, as well as the would-bes, congregate at *Le Juke* (6 Rue Lully; phone: 91-33-14-88). Unique *Espace Julien* (33 Cours Julien; phone: 91-47-09-64) offers jazz occasionally and an open cabaret where anyone can perform; it's also a learning center for everything from musical instruments to dance to gymnastics.

BEST IN TOWN

CHECKING IN: Marseilles traditionally has had a meager selection of good hotels. With a recent spurt of hotel construction there's now an overabundance of higher priced, ultramodern rooms, but not much improvement in the lower price ranges. Expect to pay $75 or more for a double room (including breakfast) in expensive hotels; $50 to $75 for moderate; and under $50 for an inexpensive one.

Altéa – Just a 5-minute walk from the Old Port, this hotel belongs to a major French chain but distinguishes itself by its taste, pleasant piano bar, and an outstanding restaurant, *L'Oursinade* (see *Eating Out*). Its 200 rooms have all the expected luxury hotel amenities. Rue Neuve-St.-Martin (phone: 91-91-91-29). Expensive.

Concorde Palm Beach – A supermodern spot by the sea, with an outdoor pool and a good restaurant, *La Réserve.* 2 Promenade de la Plage (phone: 91-76-20-00). Expensive.

Le Petit Nice – Small (18 rooms and suites in 2 buildings) and gracious, it was built in the 19th century as a private villa. There's a shaded garden and a superb two-star Michelin restaurant (see *Eating Out*), all looking out over the Mediterranean from a magnificent position on the Corniche. The restaurant is closed Mondays, and Tuesdays during the winter; the hotel is closed during January and the first week in February. 160 Corniche Président-J.-F.-Kennedy (phone: 91-59-25-92). Expensive.

Pullman Beauvau – Next to the tourist office and just down the street from the *Opéra*, this is one of Marseilles's best properties. Most of its 72 rooms face the Vieux Port. 4 Rue Beauvau (phone: 91-54-91-00). Expensive.

Sofitel Vieux Port – Magnificent and modern, with a splendid view from its perch above the entrance to the Old Port, near the *Palais du Pharo*. It has some 200 rooms, air conditioning, a heated outdoor pool, a cozy bar, and a fine restaurant, *Les Trois Forts* (see *Eating Out*). 36 Bd. Charles-Livon (phone: 91-52-90-19). Expensive.

Astoria – One of a number of small, old, Marseilles hostelries that have been renovated, this turn-of-the-century relic now has a bright, skylit lobby filled with plants, and contemporary furnishings in the guestrooms. 10 Bd. Garibaldi (phone: 91-33-33-50). Moderate.

Bompard – In a quiet park on a hill not far from the sea, only a 5-minute drive (on the coastal road) from the bustle of the Vieux Port. Some of its 40-plus rooms — in the main building or surrounding bungalows — have kitchenettes. No restaurant. 2 Rue des Flots-Bleus (phone: 91-52-10-93). Moderate.

Le Corbusier – There are only 24 rooms, and each gives the experience of living in a city apartment. 280 Bd. Michelet (phone: 91-77-18-15). Moderate to inexpensive.

Capitaines de Vieux Port – Formerly the *Urbis,* this modern hotel has 148 rooms, a restaurant, a bar, and conference facilities. Close to the Vieux Port and 1 block above the Cours d'Estienne d'Orves. 46 Rue Sainte (phone: 91-54-73-73). Inexpensive.

Esterel – Small, comfortable, and convenient to the métro and shopping. Rooms are air conditioned and have color TV sets. No restaurant. 124 Rue Paradis (phone: 91-37-13-90). Inexpensive.

Grand Hôtel de Genève – Old, but now modernized, it is in a quiet pedestrian precinct just behind the Old Port. No restaurant. 3 bis Rue Reine-Elizabeth (phone: 91-90-51-42). Inexpensive.

EATING OUT: What it has traditionally lacked in hotels, Marseilles always has made up for in restaurants; they are among France's finest, and that is saying a lot. Besides classic French cuisine, be sure to try Provençal (from Provence — the southern region of France that straddles the Rhône River) specialties. The city virtually is synonymous with bouillabaisse, a dish not to be missed. In its classical form, this soup is based on Mediterranean rockfish (called *rouget*), but other fish and shellfish usually are added, particularly lobster and crab. The seasoning (cayenne, garlic, tomatoes, herbs) is very special, but the star ingredient is saffron, which gives bouillabaisse its golden color. It often is served with rouille, a relish made of red pepper, garlic, and fish broth, as well as with aioli, a delicious olive-oil-based garlic mayonnaise. Another dish common on menus in Marseilles is bourride, a fish stew that some prefer to bouillabaisse.

Other regional specialties include *anchoïade*, anchovies and olive oil mashed into a paste that accompanies raw vegetables; *poutargue*, fish eggs grated in oil, then pressed and dried to become a sort of white caviar; *navettes*, flat biscuits flavored with orange-flower water; and *fougasses*, flat, salty breads in leaf designs, flavored with walnuts, olives, bacon, or cheese.

You also may wish to sample *pastis*, the anise-flavored apéritif that tastes something like licorice. Usually colorless, *pastis* is served diluted with ice water, which turns it cloudy white. Also try wines from Provence, particularly the dry, pleasant rosé.

Expect to pay $80 and considerably higher in the expensive category (for two without wine); from $50 to $80 in the moderate range; and under $50 in the inexpensive category. Prices include a service charge.

Calypso – This outstanding dining room offers a classic sea view and Marseilles's best bouillabaisse. No meat or vegetables here, just impeccably served seafood. But the quality and quantity leave nothing to be desired. Its twin and peer — *Michel* — is across the street. Closed Sundays and Mondays. Reservations necessary. 3 Rue des Catalans (phone: 91-52-64-00). Expensive.

Chez Brun (Aux Mets de Provence) – At this venerable family-run place, you'll eat in the *ancienne* style. Up to 20 dishes of the true Provençal cuisine, which means fish and olive-spiced specialties. Closed Sundays, Mondays, and holidays. Reservations necessary. 18 Quai du Rive-Neuve, on the 2nd Floor; the entrance is hard to find, so watch closely (phone: 91-33-35-38). Expensive.

Michel (Les Catalans) – Across the street from the *Calypso*. The menu is short and the seafood is succulent, rating one Michelin star. Don't miss the bouillabaisse. Closed Tuesdays and Wednesdays. Reservations unnecessary. Rue des Catalans (phone: 91-52-30-63). Expensive.

Miramar – Touted by locals as one of the best sources on the *quai* of the Old Port for authentic bouillabaisse, this modern dining place also serves a wide variety of other fish dishes and regional specialties. Closed Sundays, Saturday lunch, and during August. Reservations unnecessary. 12 Quai du Port (phone: 91-91-10-40). Expensive.

Le Petit Nice – A two-star Michelin establishment that deserves a third rosette. Our favorite dining spot in Marseilles; the view alone is worth the price of admission. The tomato tart appetizer is the most beautiful single menu item we've ever had on our *plats*, and the lobster ragoût is equally impressive. Closed Mondays, and Tuesdays during the winter. Reservations necessary. 160 Corniche Président-J.-F.-Kennedy (phone: 91-59-25-92). Expensive.

New York – For seafood again, try this restaurant in the old harbor area. Especially good are the fish terrine and the bourride. The owner fell in love with New York when he was a sailor — thus the name. Open daily. Reservations unnecessary. 7 Quai des Belges (phone: 91-33-60-98 or 91-33-91-79). Expensive to moderate.

L'Oursinade – In the *Altéa* hotel, this place serves very fine Provençal dishes in an atmosphere of understated elegance. Closed Sundays and late July through August. Reservations unnecessary. Rue Neuve-St.-Martin (phone: 91-56-05-02). Expensive to moderate.

Les Trois Forts – You'll find a panoramic view of the Old Port here, and such inventive dishes as lamb's liver braised with melon and honey. Reservations unnecessary. *Sofitel Vieux Port*, 36 Bd. Charles-Livon (phone: 91-52-90-19). Expensive to moderate.

L'Avant-Scène – The food here runs to fairly light French, and the place actually is a café/art gallery/theater/magazine shop all rolled into one. The theater is downstairs, and there's a fashion designer's atelier upstairs. Open nightly from 8 PM to 2 AM. Reservations unnecessary. 59 Cours Julien (phone: 91-42-19-29). Moderate.

Chez Caruso – Where the locals go when they crave some delicious Italian food.

Closed Sunday nights, Mondays, and from mid-October through mid-November. Reservations unnecessary. 158 Quai du Port (phone: 91-90-94-04). Moderate.

Chez Fonfon – In an old fishing club, it's heavy on local color and boat scenes, real bouillabaisse, and other fish dishes. Reservations unnecessary. 140 Vallen des Auffes (phone: 91-52-14-38). Moderate.

Cousin, Cousine – Interesting nouvelle cuisine is served here, along with good local wines. Try the hot oysters with broccoli and pheasant in wine sauce. Closed Saturdays and Sundays. Reservations unnecessary. 102 Cours Julien (phone: 91-48-14-50). Moderate.

Au Pescadou – On entering, you'll be dazzled immediately by the spectacular array of fresh oysters, clams, mussels, and other seafood delicacies. With ingredients like these, only the simplest preparation is needed. Closed July and August. Reservations advised. Closed Sunday nights. 19 Pl. Castellane (phone: 91-78-36-01). Moderate.

Les Platanes (Restaurant des Abattoirs) – By the slaughterhouse, at the city's northern extreme, this immense old café is where the butchers themselves eat. Choose from beef, pork, veal, and a great selection of sausages. Lunch only; closed Saturdays and Sundays. Reservations advised. 7 Av. Journet (phone: 91-60-93-17). Moderate.

Texas Fiesta – Run by a Frenchman who used to live in Houston, this lively spot serves up Tex-Mex food, margaritas, American beer, and, on Tuesday nights, country music. Open daily. Reservations unnecessary. 70 Cours Julien (phone: 91-48-49-24). Moderate.

Aux Baguettes d'Or – Located just behind the *Opéra*, it offers authentic Vietnamese food and friendly service, and sometimes is frequented by singers after performances. Closed Wednesdays. Reservations unnecessary. 65 Rue Francis Davso (phone: 91-54-20-39). Moderate to inexpensive.

Dmitri – Hungarian and Russian specialties are the order of the day. Closed Sundays and Mondays. Reservations unnecessary. 6 Rue Meolan (phone: 91-54-09-68). Inexpensive.

La Kahenas – This Tunisian eatery offers daily specials, mint tea, pastries, and is crowded at lunch. Closed Sundays. No reservations. 2 Rue de la République (phone: 91-90-61-93). Inexpensive.

Tarte Julie – Every pie imaginable, sweet or salty, is here, along with pizza and salads. Closed Sundays. No reservations. 14 Av. du Prado (phone: 91-37-23-45). Inexpensive.

 BARS AND CAFÉS: At 5 PM the old Marseillais (barely a woman in sight) gather for *pastis* and tall tales at *Les Cafés du Panier*, a café just outside Marseilles (52 Rue St. Françoise). Facing the Vieux Port is *Le Petit Pernod* (30 Rue des Trois Mages) where the bourgeoise congregate. *Place Thiars* (38A Pl. Thiars) is an artists' haunt that becomes even more popular in the summer, when it attracts tourists and theater people to its alfresco dining. The barman really knows his stuff at *Le Beauvau* (9 Rue Beauvau). Expect a lovely evening at *Le Garbo* (9 Quai de Rive-Neuve), whose decor recalls the 1930s (call in advance to make sure the piano player is scheduled the night you plan to attend).

MONACO
(and Monte Carlo)

The independent principality of Monaco is one of the smallest states in Europe, but because of its wealth and glamor, it is also one of the most famous. Visually, it is a mixture of old and new, with sleek modern buildings next to the pastel stucco and tile of traditional French Mediterranean architecture and the extravagant silhouettes of the Belle Epoque. Everywhere the emphasis is on sumptuous elegance. Yachts of the rich and famous fill the port; the shops display vintage wine, rare jade and ivory, costly jewels, couturier clothes and furs. Tourists, dazzled by the spectacle, may sometimes forget that Monaco is more than just a stage for conspicuous consumption and that with its rare climate, its turbulent history, and the diversity of activities that take place within its borders, it has other resources besides manmade, tangible riches.

The location of this picturesque country, in something of a natural amphitheater between the Mediterranean and the foothills of the French Maritime Alps, gives it a climate much like that of Southern California. Winters are mild (in January and February, the average low temperature is 46F and the average high is 55); summers are warm (July and August have an average low of 72F and an average high of 79); and there is little rain. The vegetation, too, is like Southern California's, with orange and lemon trees, palms, and live oaks. The water temperature is ideal for swimming. In fact, the only shortfall in this natural endowment was an adequate supply of beach. Monaco's most exclusive stretch of beach is actually just over the border, in France, and its own beach is all manmade. The principality is divided into two parts: Monaco is its proper overall name and also designates the older neighborhood where the palace and the *Oceanographic Museum* are located; Monte Carlo is the center of tourism, with the classiest hotels, ritziest clubs, trendiest boutiques, restaurants, and casinos, which perpetuate the reputation of this unique enclave.

What Monaco had from the very beginning was a natural harbor next to a high, rocky promontory jutting into the sea — a natural fortress. The rock itself first was colonized in the 6th century BC by the Monoikos Ligurian tribe (the probable origin of the name Monaco). Later, it was inhabited by Romans, and Julius Caesar allegedly sailed from the port to do battle in Greece.

At the end of the 12th century, this strategic configuration belonged to the Genoese, who, in 1215, sent men and matériel to begin the process of fortifying the Rocher, or the Rock of Monaco, as it is called. In the 13th century, the Republic of Genoa (along with the rest of Italy) was torn by strife between the Guelphs and the Ghibellines, opposing political parties favoring the pope and the emperor respectively. When the Ghibellines came to power in Genoa in 1295, they threw out the Guelphs, including the noble Ligurian Grimaldi family and one Francesco Grimaldi, immortalized as Malizia (the Cunning One). Not intending to suffer insult for very long, Malizia, disguised as a monk and accompanied by a band of partisans, went to the Rock one night early in 1297 to ask for shelter. The guard agreed, opened the gates, and Malizia and his companions stormed the fortress and took it.

The two monks brandishing swords on the Grimaldi coat of arms commemorate this event. They can be seen above the main door of the palace that evolved from the fortress on the Rock and in which the Grimaldi rulers of Monaco still live, though the ensuing centuries were not without incident. For more than 100 years, the family fought Genoa to maintain — or regain — control of its conquest, and once the matter with Genoa was settled, the tiny state still had to contend with other foreign influences. From 1524 to 1641, it was a protectorate of Spain; from 1641 to 1793, a protectorate of France. Came the French Revolution, and in 1793 it was annexed to France as part of the Alpes-Maritimes *département,* under the name Port Hercules. The Treaty of Paris (1814) restored it to sovereignty, but from 1815 to 1861 it was again a protectorate, this time of the kingdom of Sardinia. The period was not a prosperous one for Monaco, given the economic deprivation of the revolutionary years and the constant threat of annexation by Sardinia. When the cities of Menton and Roquebrune, which separate the principality from the Italian border and which had been part of it for centuries, declared themselves free cities in 1848, Monaco was virtually beginning to come apart.

The turning point came with Prince Charles III, who ruled from 1856 to 1889. In 1861, he negotiated a treaty with France establishing Monégasque sovereignty without any doubt and without any protectors and then underscored that sovereignty by minting gold coins and issuing postage stamps. Because the loss of Menton and Roquebrune had reduced the revenues as well as the size of the principality, he took up his father's idea of opening a gambling casino to replenish the treasury. The Société des Bains de Mer (Sea Bathing Society), which was to run the enterprise and organize resort facilities, was formed, and a gaming house of sorts began to operate, but it wasn't until the prince put François Blanc — the "wizard" who had run the casino at Bad Homburg — in charge of the project that Monaco was on its way to solvency. In 1864 a luxury hotel, the *Hôtel de Paris,* opened on the Spélugues plateau across the harbor from the Rocher, and in 1865 the casino next door began to function. Through Blanc's efforts — he even hired boats and carriages to bring well-heeled tourists to Monaco from up and down the coast — the casino became so fashionable and successful that by 1869 the prince was able to abolish direct taxes for his citizens. Monte Carlo, or Mount Charles, as the development on the plateau was renamed in the prince's honor, had been born.

Charles's son, Prince Albert I (on the throne from 1889 to 1922), was another Grimaldi who proved critical in the development of the principality. Known as "the scholar prince" because of his passionate interest in oceanography, he was anything but a dilettante in his field. He undertook numerous scientific expeditions to study the seas and built the prestigious *Oceanographic*

Museum to house the results and promote further research (he also founded the Oceanographic Institute in Paris in 1906). In addition, Monaco is indebted to him for the Exotic Garden and the *Museum of Prehistoric Anthropology,* for the construction of the port, for the establishment of numerous schools and a hospital, for its first constitution, and for the automobile rally.

Prince Rainier III, the present ruler (and great-grandson of Albert I), came to the throne in 1949 and has changed the face of Monaco no less than his ancestors. His marriage to the late American actress Grace Kelly in 1956 turned the international spotlight on the principality as never before, making it a household word that was all but synonymous with fairy-tale romance. The great charm and beauty of Princess Grace (who died in an automobile accident in 1982), and the caliber of the international clientele she attracted to the social and cultural events of her new home, in no small way complemented the prince's efforts to bring about a major overhaul of the principality in the postwar period, especially of its tourist industry. Modern high-rise apartment buildings (which block the sunshine in some streets), roads and tunnels, underground parking lots, public elevators, a new port, new hotels, new parks, and new beaches have all been built and, indeed, some of the development has taken place on land that itself was built up, or reclaimed, from the sea (77 acres), enlarging Monaco's area to a total of 482 acres. Monaco also is becoming something of a banking center (there are no taxes), and after work, many an international deal is made at one of the city's luxury spots.

The modern *Monte Carlo Convention Center and Auditorium,* built in 1974, is part of an ongoing effort to attract the business traveler and the convention trade, while the gaming tables, nightclubs, fashionable galas, and arts and sporting events that traditionally have drawn visitors — gamblers, jet setters, the international *beau monde* — to this most chic of Riviera resorts continue to do so. The Société des Bains de Mer, the company with which François Blanc created the Monte Carlo scene and in which the principality today has a controlling interest, continues to be responsible for most of the luxurious resort installations and much of the resort activity. At latest count, SBM owned four of the most deluxe hotels, 18 restaurants, the *Monte Carlo Country Club,* the *Monte Carlo Golf Club,* the *Monte Carlo Sporting Club,* the *Monte Carlo Casino,* and more.

Although Monaco is a sovereign state, with its own postage stamps (favorites with collectors) and license plates, it exhibits a few peculiarities. It has a customs union with France and there are thus no formalities crossing the border — you may not even realize when you've done it. And French money is the medium of exchange, though Monégasque coins bearing Prince Rainier's likeness are circulated and are fully convertible in France. French, too, is the primary language spoken, though Italian also is common and English is spoken in hotels, restaurants, and at the casinos. Less frequently will you hear the singular Monégasque dialect, a mixture of Italian and Niçois, though it is officially encouraged and is taught in the schools. Finally, the majority of Monaco's population of 28,000 are foreign residents, largely of French, but also of Italian, Swiss, British, and American origin. Only approximately 5,000 are Monégasques — that is, citizens of Monaco. Citizenship is not easy to come by, is expensive, and is not necessarily granted even to those born here. Those who have it are excluded from the gaming tables, but in return do no military service and pay no income tax, privileges somehow fitting for the nationals of a country just about the right size for the pages of a storybook.

MONACO AT-A-GLANCE

SEEING THE CITY: Because the "old" city of Monaco is built on top of a promontory of rock and everywhere else the principality climbs from the coast toward the rocky mountain peaks behind it, panoramic places are not in short supply. The Place du Palais in Old Monaco is one. It offers a breathtaking view of the harbor and Monte Carlo, a view that should be seen again at night when the lights of this tiny enclave glitter against the mountainous backdrop. The Exotic Garden, set even higher on a steep slope behind the Rock, is another. From here (a sign points the way to the lookout point), the view takes in the whole of the principality and beyond to the Italian coast, including a grand expanse of blue Mediterranean. Some of the most spectacular views of Monaco are found about 1 mile (1.6 km) from the city, on the Cannes–Nice highway.

SPECIAL PLACES: Monaco's 468 acres are divided into four parts: Monaco-Ville, containing Old Monaco on top of the Rock; Monte Carlo, the "new" city with the casino, most of the hotels, shops, and beaches; La Condamine, the more commercial harbor area between Monaco-Ville and Monte Carlo (you'll often hear La Condamine referred to simply as Monaco); and Fontvieille, 20 acres of reclaimed land on the west side of the Rock, now developed into commercial, residential, and industrial areas. Most of what visitors want to see is in Monaco-Ville and Monte Carlo, two districts in marked contrast to each other. One is a traffic-free maze of narrow cobblestone streets and 3-story, tile-roofed houses tightly contained within a girdle of fortifications. The other is a seaside sprawl of modern luxury high-rises, broad avenues, and highways, with the respite of palm trees and gardens and several particularly opulent examples of the architecture of the last century.

OLD MONACO (LE ROCHER)

Palais Princier (Prince's Palace) – The first foundation stone of the manmade fortress on top of the natural fortress of the Rock was laid in 1215, and for a few hundred years thereafter the structure remained largely defensive. Its transformation into something more fit for habitation by a prince is largely the work of two of the 17th-century Grimaldis, Prince Honoré II and Prince Louis I. What they and their successors accomplished was then almost destroyed by the French Revolution, when the palace was looted and used for a time as a military hospital, its treasures dispersed. Nineteenth-century restoration, continued modification, and the return of much lost furniture and artwork brings us the palace of today. With its crenelated tower sporting a rather anachronistic clock and its cannons (a gift of Louis XIV) complete with neat piles of cannonballs, it looks like a castle from an operetta set, perfect for a miniature monarchy. The changing of the guard at the candy-striped sentry boxes takes place each day precisely at 11:55 AM (go early for a good view). From July through September, you also can go inside the palace. You'll see the Cour d'Honneur surrounded by mainly

17th-century frescoes, the sumptuously decorated State Apartments, and the Throne Room. Open daily from June to October; admission charge. Place du Palais (phone: 93-25-18-31).

Musée du Palais Princier – This museum in the south wing of the palace also is called the *Napoleonic Museum*. It houses souvenirs of Napoleon and his family — such as his field glasses, watch, and decorations — gathered by Prince Louis II, the grandfather of Prince Rainier. Documents relating to the history of the principality also are on display, along with a collection of rare 19th-century Monégasque postage stamps, a series of coins minted by the princes since 1640, and uniforms of the prince's guards. Closed lunchtime and Mondays, and from October 23 to December 5; admission charge. Palais Princier (phone: 93-25-18-31).

Jardins St.-Martin – The old fortifications surrounding the Rock have been turned into garden walks, a peaceful place to stroll amid Mediterranean flowers and shady trees. The gardens run roughly from the palace around to the point of the Rock at Fort Antoine.

Cathédrale – Near the St. Martin Gardens, Monaco's cathedral is an 1875 edifice built on the site of an earlier church (St. Nicholas), which was demolished to make way for the new one. The white stone exterior is Romanesque in style; the interior, which contains two 16th-century altarpieces by Louis Bréa preserved from the original church, shows a Byzantine influence. The burial chapel is in the west part of the transept and the tombs of the Princes of Monaco — among whom Princess Grace was laid to rest — are in the crypt. Av. St.-Martin at Rue de l'Eglise (phone: 93-30-88-13).

Musée Océanographique et Aquarium – Not only a museum, but a working scientific research institute, this was the brainchild of "the scholar prince," Albert I. Prince Albert wanted a museum to promote the science of oceanography and to house the results of his expeditions around the world, and this building on the Rock, at the edge of a sheer drop, was a bold construction for its day. Pillars had to be built from sea level to support it, and the rocks below had to be hollowed out to let in sea water for the aquarium. Though the work began in 1899, the inauguration did not take place until 1910.

Start your visit on the lowest level, with the aquarium. It's one of the finest in the world — not surprising when you learn that the director of the museum is Jacques-Yves Cousteau. His films are shown in the conference hall. On the ground floor are zoological exhibits, skeletons of large marine mammals, and specimens that Prince Albert brought back from his travels. The top floor is perhaps the most interesting, with the prince's whaleboat, 19th-century brass navigational instruments, and, in complete contrast, ultramodern diving equipment. Open daily 9:30 AM to 7 PM; admission charge. Av. St.-Martin (phone: 93-30-15-14).

MONTE CARLO

Casino de Monte Carlo – Even if you're not a gambler, this landmark is a must, but don't dress too casually or you won't get in. The original casino of 1865 quickly became too small, and in 1878 Charles Garnier, the architect of the Paris *Opéra,* was commissioned to design the casino seen today. Stop for a moment in front to appreciate the drama of the setting, the immaculate gardens with sculpture exhibitions, the coming and going of glamorous patrons in elegant limousines and sports cars, and the building itself, with its copper roof enhanced by a green patina. Then enter the Atrium, a grand foyer lined with brown marble columns supporting an elaborate second-story gallery and a stained glass ceiling. To the left are the gaming rooms, beginning with the American Room, a rococo splendor in gold with gambling by American rules and some 140 incongruous slot machines; the adjoining Pink Salon, now a bar but previously used as a smoking room (witness the cigar-puffing nudes painted overhead); and the red-carpeted and -curtained White Salon, also with American games. Next come the

European gaming rooms: the Touzet Rooms, swathed in paintings; the large and regal Salon Privé (Private Room), reserved for high rollers; and, finally, a Salon Super-Privé, which caters to visiting royalty, celebrities, and the super-rich, and is open by appointment only.

To the right of the Atrium, past glass cases holding memorabilia and costumes from famous performances, is the obscure entrance to the *Salle Garnier*, Monte Carlo's opera house. In 6 months, Garnier transformed what was once a small concert room into a jewel of a theater lavish with gold-leaf medallions, garlands, and scrolls, allegorical statues, a Romantic painted ceiling, and an 18-ton gilt bronze chandelier. Sarah Bernhardt starred on opening night in 1879 and the acts that followed were no less illustrious: Diaghilev created the *Ballets Russes de Monte Carlo* on this stage, Nijinsky danced here, and Caruso, Lily Pons, and other legends have sung here.

The casino is open daily (except May 1); the American Room and Touzet Rooms at 10 AM, other rooms later. You can go as far as the American Room and White Salon without restriction, though you may be asked to show a passport to prove you're over 21. A passport and an admission charge are required for the European gaming rooms. The *Salle Garnier* can be seen only by attending a performance. Pl. du Casino (phone: 93-50-69-31; for the opera house, 93-50-76-43).

Musée National – This is billed as perhaps the most complete collection of dolls and "automata" (mechanical dolls) in the world, objects that may seem unusual for a national museum unless the size of the nation and its penchant for play are taken into account. The 2,000-plus objects here, mostly from the 18th and 19th centuries and donated to the principality by the descendants of Mme. de Galéa, their collector, include not only the 400 exquisitely dressed dolls but also the delicately crafted miniature furniture and accessories that surround them in their elegantly composed settings; e.g., a quaint attic full of old treasures, a tearoom, and a wedding hall. The centerpiece of the collection is a remarkable 18th-century Neapolitan crêche. All of this is housed in another Garnier design, the beautiful Villa Sauber, the grounds of which are rampant with roses and scattered with sculptures by Rodin, Maillol, and others. Open daily, mornings and afternoons (except holidays and during the *Grand Prix*), but be sure to go between 3:30 and 5:30 PM, when the automata come to life. Admission charge. 17 Av. Princesse-Grace (phone: 93-30-91-26).

ELSEWHERE

Jardin Exotique – Another of the projects of Prince Albert I, this is a cactus garden, but no ordinary cactus garden. It clings to the side of a rocky cliff at the western approach to Monaco, more than 300 feet above the sea, and at one time was called "the suspended garden." The inclination of the cliff provides protection from northern winds and maximum exposure to the winter sun, and thus the 7,000 species of cacti and succulents, weird and wonderful examples from semi-arid climes around the world (particularly from Africa and Latin America), thrive as well here as they would in their native habitats. Equally impressive is the view from the garden, a sweeping one that embraces the whole of the principality.

Within the garden, actually at the base of the cliff, are the Grottes de l'Observatoire (Observatory Caves). Although today you're most likely to notice the stalagmites and stalactites, at one time the caves housed prehistoric man, whose bones have been found as a record of his stay. You can take a guided tour of the caves, but note that the climb up and down totals 558 steps. Open daily; a single admission charge covers the garden, caves, and the nearby *Museum of Prehistoric Anthropology*. Bd. du Jardin-Exotique (phone: 93-30-33-65).

Musée d'Anthropologie Préhistorique – This museum safeguards what archaeologists have found on the site and elsewhere in the principality and its environs. Fossils of animals now extinct, primitive tools, the remains of Cro-Magnon man, skeletons and fauna from 5000 to 500 BC, with some Roman jewelry, and other relics discovered during excavations at the harbor in 1879 are on display. Open May to September. The admission charge includes the Jardin Exotique and Observatory Caves (see above). Bd. du Jardin-Exotique (phone: 93-30-19-21 or 93-30-33-39).

Centre d'Acclimatation Zoologique – A tiny zoo at the foot of the Rock that has various monkeys and apes, lions and other large cats, wild birds, an elephant, and many specimens of tropical (mainly African) fauna. It opened in 1955, a creation of Prince Rainier. Open daily; admission charge. Place du Canton.

■ **EXTRA SPECIAL:** The south of France is noted for its colorful produce markets, and Monaco is no exception. To take the measure of one and meet some real Monégasques, go to Place d'Armes, a small square not far from the port, at the base of the Rock, in the Condamine district. Under the arches of the square stands a beautiful open-air market selling fruits and vegetables, flowers, pasta, bread, fresh fish, and more. You might have a bite to eat while savoring all this Mediterranean abundance. A typical snack consists of a glass of red wine with hot *socca* (a thin pancake made with chickpea flour) or a slice of *pissaladière* (a type of thick pizza with onions, a specialty of Nice). In addition to Monaco's market, there's the one at the totally renovated *Beausoleil,* open mornings only; it's just above Monte Carlo's Eglise St.-Charles, on Rue du Marche. There are both indoor and outdoor markets and many specialty food shops in the surrounding streets.

SOURCES AND RESOURCES

TOURIST INFORMATION: Monaco's Direction du Tourisme et des Congrès, or tourist and convention bureau, is in Monte Carlo at 2a Bd. des Moulins, just above the gardens of the casino (phone: 93-50-60-88; for weekly programs in English, 93-30-87-01). It is open daily (half days on Sunday) to provide maps, detailed brochures on the principality's sights, restaurants, and hotels, and, if necessary, to make hotel reservations. The free monthly brochure *Bienvenue à Monte Carlo* lists events and much other pertinent information, and a brochure featuring restaurant menus, *Le Guide de la Bonne Table* (in French), is available for a small fee. Postage stamps and posters also are sold here.

Local Coverage – The daily French newspaper *Nice Matin* covers the southeast of France, including Monaco. *La Gazette,* an attractive bimonthly newsmagazine that covers Monaco, the Riviera, and Europe, is more society-oriented (the magazine is printed in Monaco, in French and English), as is the slick *Riviera,* which is available in English. French and other international newspapers and magazines can be found at the *Café de Paris* on Pl. du Casino or at *Loews Monte Carlo* hotel on Av. Spélugues. The bookstore *Scruples* (9 Rue Princesse-Caroline; phone: 93-50-43-52) sells English-language books, maps, travel guides, and posters.

TELEPHONE: The city code for Monaco is 93, which is incorporated into all local 8-digit numbers. When calling a number in Monaco from the Paris region (including the Ile-de-France), dial 16, wait for a dial tone, then dial the 8-digit number. When calling a number from outside Paris, dial only the 8-digit number. When calling from the US, dial 33 (which is the country code), followed by the 8-digit number.

GETTING AROUND: Monaco is one of the few countries visitors can see from border to border by foot (though strictly speaking there is no border and you can suddenly find yourself in France by just crossing the street). Transportation is simple and well organized.

Bus – Of the four main bus lines, two depart from Place de la Visitation in Monaco-Ville (which is now closed to all traffic except local buses, taxis, and cars with Monégasque plates) and go as far as the casino, and two depart from the station at Av. Prince Pierre. Route 1 goes to the east border (Monte Carlo, the *National Museum,* the beaches, the *Monte Carlo Country Club*); Route 2 goes to the west border (the Exotic Garden); Route 4 goes east to the Larvotto beaches; and Route 5 does a sort of figure eight, one loop encompassing Fontvieille, the other the Princess Grace Hospital Center. (A fifth route, No. 3, is in operation at *Easter* and during the summer season only.) There are frequent stops; buses run every 11 minutes during the week; every 20 minutes on Sundays and holidays. A bus service also runs to and from Nice airport. For more information, contact the tourist office.

Car Rental – Given Monaco's modest size, a car is hardly a necessity, but if you intend to roam the surrounding region, rentals are available, with or without chauffeur, from a number of agencies. *Avis* (9 Av. d'Ostende; phone: 93-30-17-53), *Europcar* (47 Av. de Grande-Bretagne; phone: 93-50-74-95), and *Hertz* (57 Rue Grimaldi; phone: 93-50-79-60) are all represented, and the tourist office has a list of local firms.

Elevator – Public underground elevators have been installed to facilitate pedestrian traffic between the various sections of the principality and to eliminate some hill-climbing. They connect the Exotic Garden to the port (near the Pl. Ste.-Dévote end of Bd. Albert-I) and the center of Monte Carlo (Pl. des Moulins) to Av. Princesse-Grace and the Larvotto beach area.

Helicopter – *Héli-Air Monaco* (Héliport de Fontvieille; phone: 93-30-80-88) offers an aerial tour of the principality as well as 6-minute transfers to and from Nice–Côte d'Azur International Airport, 14 miles/22 km away (about $50 one-way). It also links Monaco to Italy. Reservations are necessary.

Taxi – Phone for a cab or walk to the nearest cab stand. The three major stands are at the train station (phone: 93-50-92-27), at the casino end of Av. des Beaux-Arts (phone: 93-50-56-28), and on Av. Princesse-Grace (phone: 93-50-47-26). Also try *Radio Taxi* (phone: 93-50-56-28 or 93-50-92-27). Taxis are expensive but worth it, since the fleets are composed mainly of comfortable Mercedes-Benzes, BMWs, and Peugeots.

Train – The Gare de Monaco–Monte Carlo, on Av. Prince-Pierre in the Condamine district, is a regular stop for French trains running along the Riviera, and several international trains stop here, too. In summer, the *Métrazur,* a special *SNCF* service shuttling along the Côte d'Azur between Menton and Cannes, stops here every half hour. For train information, call 93-25-54-54; from Nice airport call 93-21-34-62. For reservations, call 93-30-74-00. Currency exchange at the station is from from 8 AM to noon and 2 to 5 PM (phone: 93-30-74-00).

SPECIAL EVENTS: In January, specially made cars are in abundance for the *Monte Carlo Rallye,* a particularly prestigious motor rally because it's been on the calendar since 1911, almost as long as cars have been in existence. The *Festival of Ste.-Dévote,* on January 26 and 27, is a public holiday honoring the patron saint of the principality and its ruling family. February heralds the *International Circus Festival* and *International Festival of Television,* and March, the *Rose Ball.* The *International Tennis Championships* at the *Monte Carlo Country Club* are the highlight of April, and May brings an event that's been run almost uninterruptedly since 1929: Monaco's *Grand Prix,* when the best drivers in the world take state-of-the-art Formula 1 cars onto the Belle Epoque streets to compete on one of the most hazardous circuits in motor racing. In July, the *Open Golf Tournaments*

take place. In July and August, the *Festival International de Feux d'Artifice de Monte Carlo* (International Fireworks Festival) gives specialists of various nations a chance to fill the skies over the port of Monaco with color and excitement; a different country presents each of the several nights of pyrotechnics. November 19 is the *Fête Nationale* (National Day), an excuse for a small parade in Old Monaco, fireworks, and other merriment. In February, the Big Top is set up on the Fontvieille Esplanade and the *International Circus Festival* — 5 nights of competition to choose the best acts from the world's circuses — gets under way. Finally, though high-caliber musical performances, including an occasional opera, can be seen throughout the year, they are concentrated during the 2 weeks at *Easter* known as the *Printemps des Arts de Monte Carlo.*

 MUSEUMS: Monaco's major museums are described in *Special Places.* Other museums or exhibitions open to the public include the following:

Musée des Cires (Wax Museum) – This small museum, on one of Monaco's most picturesque streets, re-creates the history of the principality and of the Grimaldi dynasty in 24 life-size scenes. Open daily. 27 Rue Basse (phone: 93-30-39-05).

Porcelaines d'Art de Monaco et Monte Carlo – Locally handcrafted porcelain and small souvenirs bearing Monaco's national colors (red and white) are on display and for sale. Closed Sundays. 16 Rue des Géraniums (phone: 93-50-59-24).

 SHOPPING: The Place du Casino and the Avenue des Beaux-Arts in Monte Carlo are lined with the fabulous boutiques of *Cartier, Bulgari, Van Cleef & Arpels, Christian Dior, Yves Saint Laurent,* and other purveyors of luxury goods. To these has been added *Les Allées Lumières,* the elegant, new shopping arcade of the Park Palace building at the top of the casino gardens, which sells the wares of still better-known (and equally expensive) French designers. Shops offering moderately priced clothing, antiques, perfume, and gifts can be found among the immoderate ones on the Boulevard des Moulins and the Boulevard Princesse-Charlotte, Monte Carlo's major shopping streets. In the Condamine district, the two main commercial streets are Rue Princesse-Caroline and Rue Grimaldi. Another shopping arcade, the *Galerie du Sporting d'Hiver,* is across the street from the *Hôtel de Paris.* The new *Metropole* hotel houses *Les Galeries du Metropole,* with more than 100 elegant boutiques.

Atmosphere – Particularly outstanding leatherwear. *Les Allées Lumières,* 27 Av. de la Costa (phone: 93-25-00-03).

Benetton – The popular international chain has inexpensive cardigans, turtlenecks, and shirts for each season, in many colors. 37 Bd. des Moulins (phone: 93-50-50-42 or 93-50-63-84).

Christofle Pavillon – A glistening array of crystal, silverware, and china. 42 Bd. des Moulins (phone: 93-25-20-20).

Façonnable – Preppy pullovers, socks, shirts, and pants, supposedly for men only, but women like them, too. 23 Bd. des Moulins (phone: 93-50-50-66).

Jaguy – Good menswear — a wide range of attractive suits, pants, and sweaters — at affordable prices. 17 Bd. Princesse-Charlotte (phone: 93-30-84-56).

Katy – Christian Dior lingerie, but mainly an especially wide selection of women's bathing suits. 10 Bd. des Moulins (phone: 93-50-66-22).

Old River – Exclusive men's fashions at competitive prices. 17 Bd. des Moulins (phone: 93-50-33-85).

■ **Note:** The lovely *Boutique du Rocher,* created by Princess Grace to support local artisans, offers ceramics, embroidery, stuffed dolls, items made of Provençal fabrics, and other things suitable as souvenirs or gifts — all handmade. There are two locations: 1 Av. de la Madone (phone: 93-30-91-17) in Monte Carlo, and 11 Rue Emile de Loth (phone: 93-30-33-99) on the Rock.

SPORTS AND FITNESS: Archery – There's a stand at *Rainier* III (terre-plein de Fontvieille; phone: 93-30-32-80).

Golf – The 18 holes of the *Monte Carlo Golf Club* are actually in France, some 2,600 feet above sea level on top of Mont-Agel, a spot from which the view of the principality and the surrounding Riviera is particularly enchanting. The club, about 20 minutes from the center of Monte Carlo by car, is open all year (closed Mondays October through June), with numerous tournaments held throughout the year. For details, write to the *Monte Carlo Golf Club* (La Turbie 06320, France; phone: 93-41-09-11).

Sailing – The *Yacht Club de Monaco* (16 Quai Antoine-I; phone: 93-50-58-39) sometimes gives sailing lessons during July and August.

Swimming – A favorite year-round activity in Monaco, which has not only built numerous pools but has also given Mother Nature a hand by importing sand for its beaches. The *Plage du Larvotto,* the large, popular public beach off Avenue Princesse-Grace (phone: 93-30-28-63), is an example, an entirely artificial stretch of sand deposited along the shoreline between two strips of land that once upon a time did not exist. It's open from May to October (the rest of the year it's barricaded to hold the sand in place) and there's no charge. Next door, the *Monte Carlo Sea Club* (20 Av. Princesse-Grace; phone: 93-30-98-80), a private bathing complex with a double pool of heated seawater and a private beach, is open to season members only, but it also is open (free) to guests of the *Beach Plaza* hotel. Another, even more exclusive club, the *Monte Carlo Beach* (Rte. du Beach St.-Roman; phone: 93-78-21-40), is *the* place to be seen and to see the "who's who" of Monte Carlo. In addition to its cachet, it offers an Olympic-size, heated seawater pool, a snack bar, two restaurants, and a pebble beach lined with pretty striped cabanas, all of which are just beyond the eastern border of Monaco on French territory (perhaps the reason this is the only Monégasque establishment allowing topless sunbathing). The club is open from April to about mid-October and is free to guests of all SBM hotels (see *Checking In*). Others pay a daily admission charge.

Among the pools of Monaco are the Olympic-size heated seawater pool at the *Stade Nautique Rainier III* (Quai Albert-I; phone: 93-30-44-67), open to the public from April through October for a small admission charge, and the indoor heated freshwater pool at the *Stade Louis II* (2 Av. Prince Hereditaire Albert, in Fontvieille; phone: 93-15-40-00), closed in August. The stadium is part of a complex with facilities for just about every sport imaginable. Tours are conducted daily between 3 and 4 PM. The luxurious health spa *California Terrace* (2 Av. de Monte Carlo; phone: 93-25-57-58) has an indoor heated seawater pool and a restaurant besides its spa facilities, and it stays open year-round from 9 AM to 8 PM.

Tennis and Squash – The *Monte Carlo Country Club* has 23 tennis courts (4 lighted), 2 squash courts, and beautiful clubhouse facilities. The courts are laid out on terraces overlooking the Mediterranean above the private *Monte Carlo Beach,* just beyond the eastern edge of Monaco, and are open year-round. For details, contact the Monte Carlo Country Club (St.-Roman; phone: 93-78-20-45). The *Tennis Club de Monaco* (27-29 Bd. de Belgique; phone: 93-30-01-02) has 13 courts (5 lighted), a sauna, and a clubhouse that's open all year. The *Monte Carlo Squash Racquets Club* (Stade Louis II; phone: 93-25-40-00) has 4 courts and is open year-round.

Windsurfing – Skim the water's surface at the *Monte Carlo Beach* (Rte. du Beach St.-Roman; phone: 93-78-21-40), in July and August; or the *Monte Carlo Sea Club* (22 Av. Princesse-Grace; phone: 93-30-98-30), May to September.

THEATER AND MUSIC: The *Théâtre du Fort-Antoine,* an open-air theater in the old fortifications of the Rock, has a short season of plays, folkloric dance, and concerts from June through August. Tickets are sold at the theater 45 minutes before each performance; if you need details, call the Direction des Affaires Culturelles (phone: 93-15-80-00). The lovely *Théâtre Princesse Grace* (12 Av. d'Ostende; phone: 93-25-32-27), designed by the princess, presents a season of comedy and drama (anything from the French classics to the latest foreign plays in translation), variety acts, and concerts from October through May.

The *Orchestre Philharmonique de Monte Carlo,* with internationally known guest artists, can be heard from October through April in the *Convention Center*'s 1,100-seat *Auditorium Rainier III,* the largest theater in Monaco. Then, in July and August, it presents a series of gala summer concerts in the *Cour d'Honneur* of the Prince's Palace. The box office for information and advance tickets for both series is in the Atrium of the casino (phone: 93-50-76-54 or 93-50-93-00); closed Mondays. The orchestra also participates in the *Printemps des Arts de Monte Carlo,* 2 weeks of concerts by visiting chamber groups, singers, instrumentalists, and dance companies that take place around Easter in the convention center auditorium, the *Théâtre Princesse Grace,* or in the casino's *Salle Garnier,* also known as the *Monte Carlo Opera House,* a jewel of a theater where such legends as Diaghilev's *Ballet Russes de Monte Carlo,* Nijinsky, Caruso, Gigli, and Lily Pons have all performed. Today, Monte Carlo has an opera company whose season runs from December or January through March; a resident ballet company, created in 1985, and visiting troupes dance during the *National Day* (November 19), *Christmas,* and *New Year's* holidays as well as at *Easter* as part of the *Printemps* program.

NIGHTCLUBS AND NIGHTLIFE: Quite a bit of the excitement after dark takes place in the *Casino de Monte Carlo* (phone: 93-50-69-31), even though gamblers have been at it in some rooms since 10 AM (the slot machines in the American Room open at 10 AM, the tables at 4 PM; the White Salon opens at 4 PM; the Salon Privé opens at 3 PM; the Salon Super Privé by appointment). Dress is casual for gambling American style (women in slacks and men without ties are welcome), but if you penetrate as far as the European gaming rooms, coats and ties for men are required (and you won't feel ill at ease in black tie or chiffon). Monte Carlo also has two other casinos. There's an all-American casino in the *Loews Monte Carlo* hotel (12 Av. des Spélugues; phone: 93-50-65-00), and a "summer" casino is part of the lure of the *Monte Carlo Sporting Club.* This lavish, modern pleasure complex, built on a spit of land reclaimed from the sea at the far end of Avenue Princesse-Grace, opens at 10 PM in July and August. Its focal point is the large Salle des Etoiles, so called because of a roof that rolls back to reveal the stars. The room is the site of Monte Carlo's famous Friday night galas — grand dinner dances topped off with fireworks held to herald a new show or an international star's opening night and, not incidentally, to allow those in attendance to dress up (*tenue de soirée* is *de rigueur* for galas). On other nights, the dinner and show continue without the fireworks and without the formal dress requirement. The price of an evening at the Salle des Etoiles varies with the occasion. For information and reservations, call 93-50-80-80; after 6 PM, dial 93-30-71-71.

Also at the sporting club are *Jimmy'z de la Mer* (phone: 93-30-71-71), the most attractive (it overlooks a Japanese garden), most chic (sartorial slouches are not likely to be admitted), and most expensive (including a tip to the bouncer to get in) disco in Monte Carlo, open from 11 PM to dawn every night in July and August; *Parady'z* (also open July and August; phone: 93-30-71-71), a second, less formidable disco formerly run by Régine; and the *Maona* restaurant (phone as for the Salle des Etoiles above), a dinner-dance spot with a tropical theme.

From September through June, *Jimmy'z* moves to winter quarters (Pl. du Casino; phone: 93-50-80-80). *The Living Room,* a popular bar and disco (7 Av. des Spélugues; phone: 93-50-80-31) is open year-round. *Loews Monte Carlo* has the *Folie Russe* supper club (phone: 93-50-65-00), where an elaborate Las Vegas–type show goes on every night but Mondays. A sophisticated evening in a more formal, old-fashioned setting is possible at the *Casino Cabaret* (phone: 93-50-69-31 or 93-50-80-80), in what was formerly a concert room of the casino, open from September through June, but closed Tuesdays. An elevator in the Salon Privé takes you down or you can enter from Place du Casino.

BEST IN TOWN

 CHECKING IN: Choosing a hotel in Monaco is not easy, because the selection is wide and each hotel has its own charm or a special view. Note that the four Société des Bains de Mer (SBM) hotels (the *Hôtel de Paris, Hermitage, Mirabeau,* and *Monte Carlo Beach*) issue guests a Carte d'Or (Gold Card) at registration. The card provides free entrance to the European gaming rooms at the casino, to the indoor pool at the *California Terrace,* and to the *Monte Carlo Beach Club;* discounts of 50% on greens fees and court fees at the *Monte Carlo Golf Club* and the *Monte Carlo Country Club;* and the privilege of charging meals at any SBM establishment directly to your room. Note also that should you arrive in Monaco during the summer without a reservation, it will be practically impossible to find a room, though the tourist and convention bureau is ready to provide assistance.

For a luxurious double room in hotels listed in the very expensive category, expect to pay $250 and up; $130 to $250 in a hotel listed as expensive; a nice room in a moderate hotel will cost between $75 and $100; and a very adequate double room in a small, inexpensive hotel will cost $75 or less.

Hermitage – Like its sister, the *Hôtel de Paris,* though somewhat lower key, this is Belle Epoque splendor, the sort of Riviera "palace" where even the least creative imagination can easily picture a cat burglar dropping from balustrade to balcony to loggia en route to some dowager's emeralds. Opened in 1899, it has, besides its exquisite façade, two public rooms that are among the showplaces of the principality: the *Belle Epoque* dining room, where pink marble columns hold up an extravagant gilt and frescoed ceiling, and the Art Nouveau winter garden, a simpler, airier space encircled by a wrought-iron balcony and topped with a stained glass dome. The hotel is built on a rock that faces the harbor and Le Rocher de Monaco, and thus many of its 275 luxurious rooms have enchanting views. All of them have period touches, such as brass beds, though the fixtures and fittings are mostly modern. Sq. Beaumarchais (phone: 93-50-67-31 or 93-50-67-38). Very expensive.

Hôtel de Paris – This opulent Beaux Arts confection has been on the scene longer than the *Hermitage.* It opened in 1864, just before the casino, and still looks every bit the setting for the reigning royalty, deposed royalty, prima donnas, and plutocrats it has welcomed in its lifetime. The architectural tours de force here are the appropriately named *Salle Empire* dining room, a thoroughly imperial composition in cream and gold, with marble columns, classical statuary, and crystal chandeliers; and the glass-domed rotunda lobby (where a statue of Louis XIV on horseback has been rubbed to a luster by guests in need of luck at the casino, a roll of the dice away). *Le Grill* offers dining under the stars, and the three-star *Louis XV* offers spectacular Provençal cuisine by Alain Ducasse in an elegant setting (for both, see *Eating Out*). The 255 spacious rooms and 39 suites have modern comforts and beautiful views, and guests have access to the indoor pool of the *California Terrace,* via an underground passageway. There is also a spa and the well-known *Le Bar Américain.* Place du Casino (phone: 93-50-80-80). Very expensive.

Beach Plaza – Besides the *Monte Carlo Beach,* this is the only other hotel in Monaco with a beachfront location, and it's a great favorite with families. It has its own heated freshwater pool and private beach in addition to the facilities (2 more pools, more beach, and a mini-club for children) of the adjoining *Monte Carlo Sea Club.* The hotel is modern; its 320 rooms are nicely decorated, and many have a water view. In the summer, an open-air grill restaurant is set up by the pool. 22 Av. Princesse-Grace (phone: 93-30-98-80). Expensive.

Loews Monte Carlo – Huge and thoroughly modern, this American-managed hotel expresses a spirit entirely different from that of Monte Carlo's two landmark palaces — some would call it the spirit of Las Vegas. Set on pilings driven into the sea, it sprawls along the water at the foot of the casino. All the rooms (and suites) — there are 650 — have terraces, many with direct water views. The hotel has 5 restaurants (see *Eating Out* for *Le Pistou*), its own gambling casino, a nightclub, a lavish marble promenade level with attractive boutiques, an open-air heated pool on the roof garden, and a health and fitness club. Av. des Spélugues (phone: 93-50-65-00). Expensive.

Metropole Palace – Opened in the spring of 1990, the city's newest addition is a member of Conrad International (a division of Hilton Hotels of the US). In keeping with Monte Carlo's Belle Epoque architecture, $120 million was spent to restore this neo-classical–style hotel, located just a few blocks away from the casino. It features 170 rooms, plus an indoor-outdoor pool, 3 restaurants, and over 130 boutiques. 4 Av. de la Madone (phone: 93-15-15-15). Expensive.

Mirabeau – Small and elegant, it occupies several floors of a modern high-rise, centrally located not far from the casino. It has 113 comfortable rooms (all with terraces, some with a view of the water), 2 restaurants (see *Eating Out*), and its own heated seawater pool. Comfortable, if not particularly rich in character. 1 Av. Princesse-Grace (phone: 93-25-45-45). Expensive.

Monte Carlo Beach – A compromise between the sumptuously baroque and the brashly up-to-date look of the other deluxe properties. Built in 1928, this terra cotta–roofed structure in the shape of a crescent is on the edge of the sea just beyond the eastern border of the principality, about 1½ miles (2 km) from the casino. There are 46 small, elegant rooms, each with a balcony over the ocean; the ambience is quiet and private, a bit less formal than the "palaces," remote from the nightlife of Monte Carlo, but full of charm. The hotel shares the beach, 2 pools, cabanas, and restaurants of the exclusive *Monte Carlo Beach Club,* literally at its front door. Open from mid-April through October. Rte. du Beach (phone: 93-78-21-40). Expensive.

Abela – Recently opened, it overlooks the sea and has more than 200 rooms and suites with French windows and private terraces, plus 3 restaurants and a lobby bar. Conveniently situated in Fontvieille, 2 minutes from the heliport and 5 minutes from the train station. 23 Av. des Papalins (phone: 92-05-90-00). Expensive to moderate.

Alexandra – A modest hostelry at the intersection of two major shopping streets in the center of Monte Carlo, it has 55 comfortable rooms, many with bath or shower. 35 Bd. Princesse-Charlotte (phone: 93-50-63-13). Moderate.

Balmoral – Conveniently located, this traditional hostelry has 70 rooms, some overlooking the harbor, all with either bath or shower. A restaurant is on the premises. 12 Av. de la Costa (phone: 93-50-62-37). Moderate.

Louvre – A small hotel that is on the main shopping street of Monte Carlo. The 32 cozy and comfortable rooms all have a private bath and some have a view of the water. 16 Bd. des Moulins (phone: 93-50-65-25). Moderate.

Helvetia et Romain – Another small, clean hotel, this one has 28 rooms (18 with bath or shower), and its attractive restaurant, favored by locals, is a bargain for Monaco. It's in the Condamine district near the Place d'Armes market. 1 bis Rue Grimaldi (phone: 93-30-21-71). Inexpensive.

Terminus – Also in the Condamine district, adjacent to the train station; there's no view, but each of the 54 comfortable, air conditioned rooms comes with bath or shower, a television set, and radio. There is a restaurant. Closed in October and November. 9 Av. Prince-Pierre (phone: 93-30-20-70). Inexpensive.

■**Note:** Beaulieu, the French commune bordering Monaco several blocks to the north of the casino, has several hotels that are more down-to-earth and more modestly priced than those in the principality, and as conveniently located as any in Monte Carlo. Among them is the *Olympia* (Bd. General Leclerc — just east of the Credit Lyonnais building; phone: 93-78-12-70). Only 5 minutes from the casino, its 24 rooms are still affordable. Two traditional two-star hotels are nearby: the *Cosmopolite* (phone: 93-78-36-00), next door, run by the same management; and the *Boeri* (29 Av. General Leclerc; phone: 93-78-38-10). All are moderate.

 EATING OUT: The choice of restaurants in Monaco ranges from haute cuisine to typical corner bistros, and includes several Italian restaurants and pizzerias serving very good, inexpensive food. Traditional Monégasque cooking — reminiscent of the cooking of Nice — can be sampled at bistros near the marketplace or on the Rock. Among the specialties are *barbagiuan,* a fried pocket of dough with a rich filling of zucchini, eggs, cheese, and rice; *pan bagnat,* a round bun of country bread that is "bathed" in olive oil, vinegar, garlic, and basil, then stuffed with a *salade niçoise;* and stockfish, a type of dried codfish stewed in a succulent wine and tomato sauce, with garlic, onions, and olive oil. Generally speaking, however, the quality of the cuisine in Monaco is a cut below the level of the food found in surrounding France.

Dinner for two (excluding wine) will cost $100 and up in a restaurant listed below as expensive; $50 to $100 in one listed as moderate; and less than $50 in the inexpensive places. Despite its ritzy reputation, Monte Carlo offers a wide variety of inexpensive restaurants. Service usually is included.

La Coupole – The atmosphere is contemporary, soft, and elegant; the food refined nouvelle cuisine. One Michelin star. Closed for lunch during July and August. Reservations necessary. *Mirabeau Hotel,* 1-3 Av. Princesse-Grace (phone: 93-25-45-45). Expensive.

Le Grill – The rooftop restaurant of the *Hôtel de Paris* is swank and the view is delightfully romantic (it overlooks the turrets of the casino on one side and the harbor and Old Monaco on the other). In summer, the ceiling opens up to the sky and stars. Among the *grillades* are succulent lamb noisettes, *côte de boeuf,* and veal pailliard; there is a lobster tank; and, for dessert, there are delicate tangerine and raspberry soufflés. The hotel's wine cellar, carved out of the rock about a decade after the hotel was built, holds some 200,000 bottles. One Michelin star. Closed Mondays and mid-December. Reservations necessary. *Hôtel de Paris,* Pl. du Casino (phone: 93-50-80-80). Expensive.

Le Louis XV – The only hotel restaurant in the history of the *Michelin Guides* to be awarded three stars. The chef, Alain Ducasse, learned his trade in France's best restaurants before coming to work in Monaco. Sea scallops with black truffles, risotto with white truffles, and wild strawberries are his masterpieces. Closed

November 20 to December 19 and February 26 to March 13. Reservations necessary. *Hôtel de Paris,* Pl. du Casino (phone: 93-50-80-80 or 93-30-23-11). Expensive.

Il Novecento – In the *Galerie du Metropole,* this place is lavishly decorated, or perhaps overdecorated, in Belle Epoque style. It features a prix fixe menu and live music. Closed Sundays and Mondays for lunch. Reservations unnecessary. Av. des Spélugues (phone: 93-50-20-70). Expensive.

Rampoldi – Pleasant and very fashionable, this chic brasserie serves good French and Italian food in a 1930s setting of polished wood paneling and mirrors. Closed November. Reservations necessary. 3 Av. des Spélugues (phone: 93-30-70-65). Expensive.

Saint Charles – This small and very fine, though unpretentious, eatery specializes in seafood. Menu favorites include the flavorful Mediterranean snapper, sea bass (*loup*), fresh clams and mussels, and wonderful Bélon oysters. Closed Tuesdays, mid-May to June, and November 20 to December 11. Reservations necessary. 33 Av. St.-Charles (phone: 93-50-63-19). Expensive.

Café de Paris – A true French brasserie, with two terraces for outdoor dining, it's in a shopping-and-casino complex restored to turn-of-the-century grandeur. Note the stained glass windows representing the four seasons and the zodiac signs, designed by Charles Garnier of opera house fame. Reservations unnecessary. Pl. du Casino (phone: 93-50-57-75). Moderate.

Le Pinocchio – Not one of the pasta dishes is likely to disappoint in this very small, cozy spot with a vaulted ceiling in Old Monaco. Closed Wednesdays from September to April and from December 1 through January. Reservations advised. Rue Comte-Félix-Gastaldi (phone: 93-30-96-20). Moderate.

Le Pistou – Good Monégasque and Provençal cooking at reasonable prices is the draw of this rooftop hotel restaurant. Try the *pissaladière* (Nice's version of onion pizza) or the *tian d'aubergines* (eggplant gratin). Reservations unnecessary. *Loews Monte Carlo,* 12 Av. des Spélugues (phone: 93-50-65-00). Moderate.

Polpetta – Delicious food and a warm Italian atmosphere make this lovely dining room very popular. Closed 3 weeks in February. Reservations necessary. 2 Rue Paradis (phone: 93-50-67-84). Moderate.

Port – A charming place near the port, as its name suggests, with outdoor tables in summer. The menu leans to local fish, meats, and pasta. Closed Mondays and 3 weeks in November. Reservations unnecessary. Quai Albert-I (phone: 93-50-77-21). Moderate.

Santa Lucia – This upstairs place is recommended for its pizza, risotto, and grilled meat. A pianist performing Italian songs and, on request, old American tunes animates the quaint Italian setting. Open every evening. Reservations unnecessary. 11 Av. des Spélugues (phone: 93-50-96-77). Moderate.

Castleroc – From the outside tables of this informal eating place there's a view of the Prince's Palace and the water. It's one place to try stockfish or other Monégasque specialties. Lunch only; closed Saturdays and December and January. No reservations. Pl. du Palais (phone: 93-30-36-68). Inexpensive.

Le Périgordin – A small eatery near the railroad station serving good fare of southwest France. Closed Saturdays for lunch, Sundays, and 3 weeks in August. No reservations. 4 Rue Turbie (phone: 93-30-06-02). Inexpensive.

Saint Nicolas – The food is very good in this small place just behind the cathedral, and the price tag on a three-course meal makes it one of Monaco's better values. Closed Thursdays in January and 3 weeks in December. No reservations. 6 Rue de l'Eglise (phone: 93-30-30-41). Inexpensive.

Vin sur Zinc – Along with a fine selection of classic French wines, this wine bar offers a menu of salads and light fare as well as full meals. Closed Saturday lunch and

Sundays. Reservations advised at lunchtime. 24 Bd. Princesse-Charlotte (phone: 93-25-61-11). Inexpensive.

 BARS AND CAFÉS: Part outdoor café (with indoor tables, too), part drug-store (with a newsstand, cigarettes, stamps, and even slot machines), and part restaurant, the *Café de Paris* is open daily until 4 AM, but it's the perfect place to sip a Campari after 5 o'clock while watching the comings and goings on Place du Casino. *Le Bar Américain* in the *très* glittering *Hôtel de Paris* is a very posh place, definitely a spot where the elite gather to see and be seen as well as to find out the latest — the experience is fun but expensive, and reservations are necessary (phone: 93-50-80-80) if you want a good table, especially in summer. *Tip-top*, a comparatively plain, small snack bar with sidewalk tables (11 Av. de Spélugues; phone: 93-50-69-13), nevertheless becomes very popular with Monaco's jet set after midnight in the summer, and it stays open all night. Another unassuming place, the *Bar de la Crémaillère* (31 Bd. Princesse-Charlotte; phone: 93-50-66-24), is a simple bistro with small outside tables (closed Sundays). *Flashman's,* in the Sun Tower building (7 Av. Princesse-Alice; phone: 93-30-09-03), and *The Living Room* (7 Av. des Spélugues; phone: 93-50-80-31), are both piano bars, among other things: *Flashman's,* which is also a restaurant, is fancy, good for late snacking to easy-listening music until 5 AM; *The Living Room* has a dance floor, an Irish manager, and a pleasantly old-fashioned atmosphere.

NICE

Those who remember the halcyon days of ornate villas, swaying palms, and languid luxury under an azure sky may shake their heads sadly at the Côte d'Azur of today: a symphony in cement, a real estate speculator's orgy of high-rise apartment blocks, pillbox hotels, and honky-tonk pizza parlors. Its once-quaint little marinas are linked by a permanent shoreline traffic jam, and some of its renowned beaches now look more like a horde of people dangling their feet from the edge of a freeway.

But Nice, somehow, has managed to keep its head above the concrete and retain its special flavor — a mixture of Marseilles, the *Mardi Gras,* and the Mediterranean. Even in the dead of winter, there always is something faintly festive about Nice: Perhaps it's all that city strung along all that sea. And at the first shine of sun, the café tables come out, the awnings unfurl, and strollers in sandals are back clacking along the Promenade des Anglais. In the summer, the population of 340,000 burgeons with holiday makers from Paris, Piccadilly, and Peoria — though no longer from St. Petersburg — and an empty or moderately priced hotel room is harder to find than a winning lottery ticket. And a lot more scarce than a movie star.

The Greeks founded the city in 350 BC as a little market town and auxiliary port, and named it Nikaia. The stolid Romans, too, discovered the pleasures of the Riviera, and the remains of their lavish colonization are evident today in the Arena and the Baths on the hill at Cimiez — the city's elegant residential section. During the fall of the Roman Empire, barbarians from the north and pirates from North Africa invaded Nice and brought about its decline. In the 14th century, the House of Savoy wrested the growing city from the Counts of Provence (who brought the city back to its former state) and retained almost unbroken possession of it for close to 500 years. Napoleon lived for a time at No. 6 on what is today the Rue Bonaparte, later on Rue St.-François-de-Paule by the opera house. In 1860, the head of the House of Savoy and King of newly unified Italy, Victor Emmanuel II, ceded the region to France in return for military support against an Austrian invasion. Giuseppe Garibaldi, the Italian patriot, was born here, as was Masséna, the general Wellington admired most after Napoleon. In modern times, the beauty and climate of Nice have made it the amusement park of the European aristocracy, an off-season refuge from harsh northern climes and irritating revolutions. Today, the major portion of the city's income comes from various high-tech industries (e.g., electronics) rather than tourism.

The city, between Cannes and Monte Carlo, is one big easy-to-scan color postcard: the lapis lazuli of the Bay of Angels (Baie des Anges), the activity of the Vieux Port, and the timelessness of the towering Castle (Château) — the name given to the hill with the ruins of an old fortress that looms over the harbor. Along the bay runs the fabled Promenade des Anglais, a broad seafront avenue that resembles a mile-long outdoor café. At one end of the promenade is the city's pulse, Place Masséna: semitropical gardens set against crimson buildings and cool graceful arcades. Avenue Jean-Médecin (named after the former Mayor of Nice; his son is the current officeholder) is Main Street, bisecting the city in a straight line from the Place Masséna to the railroad station. The Old City, La Vieille Ville, is a little piano-shaped quarter — all narrow and cobbled and noisy, and pungently southern — that huddles in the shadow of the Château. La Vieille Ville's boundaries are the Quai des Etats-Unis and the Boulevard Jean-Jaurès beside the Paillon River, which is covered in parts by esplanades and divides the Old City from modern Nice to the west. In the past few years, Nice has spread farther to the west, past the airport that was expanded onto land reclaimed from the Baie des Anges.

Nice's heritage is culturally rich. Rodin, Modigliani, and Toulouse-Lautrec were among the numerous artists to have converged on the city starting in the 19th century. Matisse spent the last years of his life close to Nice, and for many years Chagall lived nearby; their works can be seen in the city's *Musée Matisse* and *Musée National Marc Chagall.* Music lovers flock to the renowned *Opéra de Nice,* and a variety of concerts are performed all year long throughout the city. And if you prefer fun and frolicking to art and music, Nice offers that too — not just with its usual festivities, but with a big bang during *Carnival.*

NICE AT-A-GLANCE

SEEING THE CITY: The long azure sweep of the bay, the compact jumble of red tile roofs in La Vieille Ville, the foothills of Provence, and the Maritime Alps rising sharply just outside the city are best seen from a viewing platform at the summit of the 300-foot Château. It can be reached by an elevator — or a 300-step climb — at the end of the Quai des Etats-Unis, where the quay joins the Rue des Ponchettes. Now there is a train from the Promenade des Anglais that goes through La Vieille Ville en route to the hills of the Château; from there, an exceptional panorama of Nice's port and the Bay of Angels unfolds before you. For information and reservations, call *Les Trains Touristiques* (phone: 93-71-44-77).

SPECIAL PLACES: Nice is a city to be seen casually, to be ambled through under a morning or late-afternoon sun, especially in and around the Old City and the renowned flower market, *Le Marché aux Fleurs.* Let your discoveries be guided by casual occurrences: the purchase of a peach in an open market, a cold glass of Corsican white wine at a portside café, the scent of thyme wafting from the flower market.

IN THE CITY

Promenade des Anglais – If you only have an hour in Nice, spend it strolling along this promenade from the Place Masséna to the *Négresco* hotel (see *Checking In*). Ornate hotels grace one side, and a narrow, crowded strip of pebbled beach separates you from the brilliant blue of the bay. The promenade takes its name from the city's English colony, which constructed the path (in the middle of the last century) that was the predecessor of this one. You can lunch in your bathing suit on several excellent private beaches along the Promenade des Anglais. Prices are moderate and carafe wines are good.

La Vieille Ville (Old City) – Old Nice is a tight labyrinth of winding streets and alleys, steep ascents between medieval buildings, and balconies festooned with rainbows of drying laundry. The character of the city as it grew down the slopes of the Château from the 14th to the 18th century is in striking contrast to the city of expansive patrician promenades that developed in more modern times. Of late, La Vieille Ville has shown indications of evolving into Nice's artists' quarter. Explore the Rue Rossetti, the Rue de la Boucherie, or the Rue du Collet. Crowd your way through the teeming street markets. Stop in at the Cathedral of Sainte Réparate and the 17th-century Church of St. James.

Le Marché aux Fleurs (Flower Market) – On the edge of the old city, just behind the Quai des Etats-Unis, you'll find the wholesale flower market that offers one of Nice's most colorful spectacles. The varieties of blossoms are dazzling, the aromas heady, and there are a few well-placed cafés, where you can see, sniff, and sip, all at the same time. Closed Mondays and Sunday afternoons. Cours Saleya.

Le Marché de la Brocante (Antiques Market) – On Mondays, the huge square where the flower market is held becomes an antiques and bric-a-brac market of unusual allure. In the late afternoon on Wednesdays, local artisans and painters display their often-expensive works. Cours Saleya.

Palais Lascaris (Lascaris Palace) – A splendid private palace of the 17th century in Genoese style, this is the former residence of the Count Lascaris-Ventimiglia. It is noted for its ceilings with frescoes, its decorative woodwork, and its regal staircase. Closed Mondays in summer; Mondays, Tuesdays, and some public holidays in winter; and November. 15 Rue Droite (phone: 93-62-05-54).

Vieux Port (Old Port) – To the east of the Château, the harbor of Nice is an artful array of multicolored boats, from one-man dinghies and kayaks to the white steamers that make the crossing to Corsica. Excursion boats leave from the port and putter along to nearby Riviera towns. To reach the port, go out around the base of the Château at the far end of Quai des Etats-Unis or take Rue Cassini south from Place Garibaldi.

Cathédrale Orthodoxe Russe – A reminder of the days when the royal Romanovs roamed the Riviera and the promenade bustled with grand dukes, ballerinas, and an occasional Bolshevik, the cathedral was built in the Belle Epoque of the 19th century, under the auspices of Czar Nicholas himself. Built from 1903 to 1914, it is considered one of the most beautiful churches of its style outside of Russia. The church supports a bouquet of ornate onion domes in the ancient Russian style. Inside are a rich collection of icons and an impressive, carved iconostasis — the traditional screen that separates the altar from the nave in an Orthodox church. No visitors are permitted during the Sunday morning service. Admission charge. Bd. du Tzarewitch (phone: 93-96-88-02).

Musée National Marc Chagall – Built on a wooded hill in Cimiez in 1972, this modern museum houses works donated by Chagall, including the 17 canvases, painted over a 13-year-period, that make up his *Biblical Message.* In addition to the many fine paintings, the museum has sculptures, mosaics, sketches, and lithographs, all by Chagall. In summer, a tearoom is set up in the garden. Closed Tuesdays. Admission charge. Av. du Dr. Menard and Bd. de Cimiez (phone: 93-81-75-75).

Musée Matisse et d'Archéologie – Henri Matisse had his studio in the Cimiez section of Nice, and a representative collection of his work — canvases, drawings, and sculpture done at various stages of his career — along with some of the artist's personal effects and his private art collection, are in the village here. A separate building houses the collection of archaeological objects found at the Roman site of Cimiez. Matisse's tomb is at the north end of a nearby cemetery, where Raoul Dufy also is buried. 164 Av. des Arènes de Cimiez (phone: 93-81-59-57).

ENVIRONS

Eze Village – Perched on a rock spike 1,550 feet above the sea, this unusual village — once a medieval fortress — offers a splendid panorama of the Riviera. It also has a tropical garden (Jardin Exotique) and a church with a beautiful 15th-century font. Nietzsche is supposed to have first worked out his masterpiece, *Thus Spake Zarathustra,* here. The walk from the Lower (Inferieure) Corniche up the Nietzsche Pass (Sentier Nietzsche) is picturesque and well worth the effort, and ends at Eze-Bord-de-Mer, by the water. Eze is less than 7 miles (11 km) from Nice, along the Middle (Moyenne) Corniche, on the way to Monte Carlo.

■ **EXTRA SPECIAL:** The Chapelle du Rosaire (Rosary Chapel), designed and decorated by Matisse between 1947 and 1951 (who thought it his masterpiece), is the main reason so many people have rediscovered Vence, a picturesque old market town some 13½ miles (22 km) northwest of Nice. The stunning stained glass windows, the murals, and the church vestments created by Matisse may bring you here, but you'll also enjoy the setting — on a rock promontory, sheltered by the last foothills of the Alps — and the charm of the old town, enclosed in elliptical walls and entered through five arched gateways. Restricted access and the small dimensions of the chapel can result in its being crowded, however, especially when a tour bus unloads its contents. The chapel, on Av. Henri Matisse, is open Tuesdays and Thursdays from 10 to 11:30 AM and 2:30 to 5:30 PM; other days by appointment made at least a day in advance (phone: 93-58-03-26). For those who are interested in exploring the town of Vence itself, a stop at the tourist office in the central plaza (Place du Grand Jardin; phone: 93-58-06-38) will provide ample ideas about what to see and how to get there.

SOURCES AND RESOURCES

 TOURIST INFORMATION: The Nice Office de Tourisme–Syndicat d'Initiative, whose hostesses speak English, has three branches: next to the railway station on Av. Thiers (phone: 93-87-07-07), 5 Av. Gustave (phone: 93-87-60-60), and at the Acropolis, 1 Esplanade Kennedy (phone: 93-92-82-82). There's also a welcome desk near the airport.

Local Coverage – The daily newspaper of the area is *Nice-Matin.* A free weekly directory of activities on the Riviera, *Sept Jours–Sept Nuits,* is distributed in the lobbies of most hotels. Also pick up the weekly *Semaine des Spectacles.* All are in French, but they're easy to decipher. *Riviera,* a glossy, expensive weekly, is an English-language Niçois publication that covers social life on the Côte d'Azur.

 TELEPHONE: The city code for Nice is 93, which is incorporated into all local 8-digit numbers. When calling a number in Nice from the Paris region (including the Ile-de-France), dial 16, wait for a dial tone, then dial the 8-digit number. When calling a number from outside Paris, dial only the 8-digit number. When calling from the US, dial 33 (which is the country code), followed by the 8-digit number.

GETTING AROUND: It's a good thing that central Nice is compact and easily accessible by foot, because traffic becomes ludicrous during the tourist seasons. Many areas have become pedestrian zones, such as Rue Masséna and some of its cross streets, as well as numerous streets in La Vieille Ville. If you want to move faster, rent a motorbike, moped, scooter, or bicycle from *Nicea Location Rent,* 29 Rue Paganini (phone: 93-16-10-30).

Airport – Nice–Côte d'Azur Airport (phone: 93-21-30-12 or 93-21-30-30), about 4 miles (6 km) west of the city, handles both domestic and international traffic. The approximately 10-minute taxi ride into town costs about 80F (about $14). The airport shuttle is part of the municipal bus network, *Transports Urbains de Nice* (24 Rue Hôtel des Postes; phone: 93-62-08-08). Leaving about every 20 minutes, it makes runs to the airport from 6 AM to 8 PM and continues to bring passengers into town from the airport until 11 PM. The shuttle leaves Nice from Av. Félix-Faure next to the information office at the Gare Routière; some of the buses into Nice go directly to the train station.

There also is a shuttle service from the Nice airport to Menton, which stops at the coastal resorts along the way — Villefranche, Beaulieu, Eze, Cap d'Ail, Monaco, Monte Carlo, and Roquebrune. Leaving approximately every hour from 7 AM to 8 PM, depending on the season, the trip takes about 1½ hours each way and costs 57F ($10) one way, 100F ($18) round-trip (phone: 93-21-30-83). In addition, helicopter service to Monaco is available. For details, call *Héli-Air Monaco* (phone: 93-21-34-62 at the airport, 93-30-80-88 at the Héliport de Fontvieille in Monaco).

Boats – *Gallus* boats cruise along the Riviera. Apply to *SATAM* (22 Rue Bottéro; phone: 93-55-33-33). For ferries to Corsica, inquire at *SNCM* (3 Av. Gustav V; phone: 93-13-66-99).

Bus – You can hop on a bus for outlying districts, such as Cimiez, at the Place Masséna. The central station for the urban bus network is at 10 Av. Félix-Faure (Traverse Flandres Dunkerque; phone: 93-62-08-08). Nearby, the main station for regional buses is the Gare Routière (Bd. Jean-Jaurès and Promenade Paillon; phone: 93-85-61-81).

Car Rental – Major international firms represented, both downtown and at the airport, are *Avis* (phone: 93-80-63-52 and 93-87-90-11); *Budget* (phone: 93-87-63-87 and 93-21-36-50); *Europcar* (phone: 93-88-64-04 and 93-21-36-44); and *Hertz* (phone: 93-81-51-21 and 93-21-36-72).

Taxi – Cabs are expensive, so watch the meter and remember streets often are clogged with traffic at certain hours. There usually are plenty of cabs at designated stands, and they also can be hailed in the streets; or call 93-52-32-32 or 93-83-62-82.

Train – The Gare *SNCF* is on Av. Thiers (phone: 93-88-50-50). Another station, Gare de Provence (33 Av. Malausséna; phone: 93-84-89-71), belongs to the *Chemins de Fer de Provence* (Provence Railways), a narrow-gauge railway that operates on a scenic route between Nice and Digne, approximately 100 miles (160 km) to the northwest.

SPECIAL EVENTS: The Nice event par excellence is *Carnival,* which begins 3 weekends before *Lent* and ends when His Majesty, King Carnival, is burned in effigy on *Shrove Tuesday*. The festivities include myriad parades and floats, marching bands and majorettes, fireworks and flowers, giant papier-mâché heads and masked balls. The *Fête des Mais* is a month of Sundays in May, with special merriment in the gardens of the Roman Arena at Cimiez. In July, the 10-day *Grande Parade du Jazz,* also in the Cimiez gardens, is the biggest jazz festival in Europe. To find out more about special events in Nice, contact *Comité des Fêtes* (5 Promenade des Anglais; phone: 93-87-16-28).

MUSEUMS: The Chagall and Matisse museums described in *Special Places* are the most impressive in Nice, but there are several others of interest.

Musée d'Histoire Naturelle or Musée Barla (Natural History Museum) – Exhibitions on marine life, paleontology, and mineralogy. 3 Cours Saleya (phone: 93-85-18-44).

Musée International d'Art Naïf Anatole Jakovsky (Anatole Jakovsky International Museum of Naive Art) – Jakovsky's collection of almost 600 paintings documenting naive art from the 18th century to the present, representing some 27 countries. Closed in November. Château Ste.-Hélène, Av. Val-Marie (phone: 93-71-78-33).

Musée Jules Chéret – Nice's municipal art museum, with works by Fragonard, Renoir, Degas, Picasso. This is one of the few authentic buildings remaining from La Belle Epoque. 33 Av. des Baumettes (phone: 93-44-50-72).

Musée Masséna – Memorabilia of Napoleon's trusted marshal and exhibitions on the history of Nice. 65 Rue de France (phone: 93-88-11-34).

Musée Naval – From its perch atop the Tour Bellanda (a former residence of Berlioz), this museum overlooks spectacular grounds. It houses the expected — ship models, arms, navigation instruments — and the not so expected, such as models of the port at various times in its history. Tour Bellanda, Parc du Château (phone: 93-80-47-61).

Musée de Terra Amata – Artifacts from this excavated prehistoric site that is about 400,000 years old. 25 Bd. Carnot (phone: 93-55-59-93).

SHOPPING: Street market shopping in La Vieille Ville is the least expensive and the most fun. Rue Masséna, Place Magenta, and Rue Paradis are the pedestrian zone of shops and cafés, with Rue Paradis noted for its elegant shops. There's also a flea market on Boulevard Risso every day except Sunday.

Alziari – Oils, spices, rustic wooden kitchenware, and olive oil soap. 14 Rue St.-François-de-Paule (phone: 93-85-76-92).

Comtesse du Barry – Toulouse food delicacies of every description; 57 varieties of foie gras. 5 Rue Halévy (phone: 93-88-49-16).

Confiserie du Vieux Nice – A sweets factory with Provence specialties such as candied fruits and flowers. Watch the stuff being made downstairs, then buy it upstairs. 14 Quai Papacino and Rue Robilante (phone: 93-55-43-50).

Galeries Lafayettes – Part of a nationwide chain of department stores that has a VAT rebate for tourists and an English-speaking staff. 6 Av. Jean-Médecin (phone: 93-85-40-21).

Nice-Etoile – A shopping mall with an art gallery on the second floor. 24 Av. Jean-Médecin.

Riviera Bookshop – A wide choice of books in English. 10 Rue Chauvain (phone: 93-85-84-61).

La Tour des Antiquaires – Houses a complex of 22 antiques galleries. 7 Promenade des Anglais.

Vogade – For chocolate lovers. 1 Pl. Masséna (phone: 93-87-89-41).

Louis Vuitton – Handbags, luggage, and other items with the status LVs. English spoken, prices high. Check erratic seasonal opening hours. 2 Av. de Suède (phone: 93-87-87-47).

SPORTS AND FITNESS: Boating – Various kinds of small boats are available for hire in the Vieux Port. Windsurfing craft, *planches à voile,* can be rented at bathing establishments along the promenade.

Bowling – At 5 Esplanade Kennedy (phone: 93-55-33-11); open from 11 AM to 2 AM.

Fitness Center – The *Centre Profil* at the *Méridien* hotel (1 Promenade des Anglais; phone: 93-82-25-25) has an American instructor and is open to the public.

Golf – The most spectacular course is at Mont-Agel in the hills above Monte Carlo (phone: 93-41-09-11). There also are two good 18-hole courses near Nice — *Golf de Biot* (Aix Avenue Jules Grec, Biot 06410; phone: 93-65-08-48) and *Golf du Valbonne* (Golf Opio Valbonne, Château de la Begude, Valbonne 06160; phone 93-42-00-08).

Horse Racing – Thoroughbred racing takes place at the *Hippodrome de Côte d'Azur* in nearby Cagnes-sur-Mer (phone: 93-20-30-30).

Horseback Riding – Horses can be rented at *Club Hippique de Nice* (368 Rte. de Grenoble; phone: 93-29-81-10); *Centre Regional de Randonnées et de Tourisme Equestre* (Rte. de Sain Cézaire St.-Vallier-de-Thiey 06460; phone: 93-60-73-48); and *Relais Equestre de la Ferme* (Rte. Nationale 98, Hyères 83400; phone: 94-66-41-78).

Jogging – The wide sidewalk on the sea side of the Promenade des Anglais is good for early morning jogging. The Parc de Vaugrenier, 5 miles (8 km) west of Nice on N7, has a jogging track equipped with exercise stations.

Skiing – From November to April, you can ski on the slopes at Valberg, Isola, Esteng d'Entraunes, Auron, and Gréolières-les-Neiges in the Alps, only an hour or two away.

Swimming – The Ruhl Plage is the most central of Nice bathing beaches. Castel Plage is set right into the rock of Pointe de Rauba Capeù below the Château. In winter, you can swim at *Piscine Municipale J. Médecin* (178 Rue de France; phone: 93-86-24-01) or try *Piscine Jean Bouin* in the *Palais des Sports* (next to the Acropolis, near the Palais de l'Exposition; phone: 93-13-13-13).

Tennis and Squash – Contact the *Nice Lawn Tennis Club* (Parc Imperial, 5 Av. Suzanne Lenglen: phone: 93-96-17-70). Squash is played at *Club Vauban* (18 Rue Mal Vauban; phone: 93-29-09-78).

 THEATER: In summer, all of Nice's best theatrical experiences take place outdoors: cabarets, concerts, theater, and folkloric shows at *Théâtre de Verdure,* in the Albert I Garden (just off Place Masséna; phone: 93-87-77-39 or 93-82-38-68) and at the *Roman Arena* in Cimiez. Check with the tourist office for more information. *Théâtre du Vieux Nice* (4 Rue St.-Joseph; phone: 93-62-00-03) is a music hall with operettas and dancing. The *Nouveau Théâtre de Nice* (Esplanade des Victoires; phone: 93-56-86-86) presents a season of plays in French from October through April. For modern theater, try the *Théâtre de l'Alphabet* (69 Rue Roquebillière; phone: 93-89-52-01).

 MUSIC: In addition to musical performances outdoors in summer, there is an opera season at the *Théâtre de l'Opéra* (Quai des Etats-Unis) from November through April. The box office is at 4 Rue St.-François-de-Paule (phone: 93-80-59-83 for information; 93-85-67-31 for reservations). The *Nice Philharmonic Orchestra* plays a musical spring and a musical autumn at the opera house. Jazz can be heard from October to June at Cimiez's *Centre Culturel et Sportif Municipal* (49 Av. de la Marne; phone: 93-81-09-09).

 NIGHTCLUBS AND NIGHTLIFE: Probably the best-known nightspot in Nice is the *Casino Ruhl,* on the ground floor of the *Méridien* hotel (1 Promenade des Anglais; phone: 93-87-95-87). Smaller than its counterparts in Monte Carlo, it has a full complement of *jeux,* not to mention a Las Vegas–style cabaret and a disco called the *Jok' Club.* *Le Sphinx* (29 Rue de Préfecture; phone: 93-62-28-62) hosts a cool crowd, features video clips, and serves breakfast from 5 AM on weekends. Gambling enthusiasts can also go to Cannes, 20 miles (32 km) southwest, or Monte Carlo, 13 miles (21 km) northeast.

BEST IN TOWN

CHECKING IN: Nice hotels can be divided into those along the Promenade des Anglais, with a view of the bay — and the traffic — and those set back on quieter streets. At an expensive hotel expect to pay above $150 per night for a double (although rates can be much higher for suites at hotels such as the *Négresco*); $100 to $150 at a moderately priced hotel; less than $80 is inexpensive. However, expect prices to leap upward by one-half in summer, and perhaps even double on the most expensive end. Do not show up in the summer high season without a reservation unless you want to become an expert in Riviera hotel lobbies. Be aware, though, that Nice has a good supply of furnished rooms for visitors who plan to stay a week or more; a brochure is available upon request from the Tourisme-Syndicat d'Initiative.

Beach Regency – A deluxe, modern, and fully air conditioned 332-room hotel. The management has established a very fine restaurant, *Le Regency* (closed in August), and such lively activities as *thés dansants* (tea dances) and festive buffet lunches on Sundays. And there's still a swimming pool on the roof as well as a good terrace restaurant, featuring Lebanese specialties, overlooking the bay. The location is a bit away from the center, toward the airport, but the street address still is right. 223 Promenade des Anglais (phone: 93-83-91-51). Expensive.

Elysée Palace – This elegant hostelry boasts all the amenities desired by travelers on holiday or business. It's set 100 feet from the sea, yet is near the center of town, with 150 rooms and suites. Facilities include a rooftop swimming pool with a bar, a fitness room and sauna, a garage, 2 conference rooms, and an excellent restaurant. Outside, the hotel's signature is a 250-ton, 80-foot-high bronze statue of a woman by Sacha Sosno. 33 Rue François-I (phone: 93-86-06-06). Expensive.

Grand Hôtel Aston – Recommended not only because it is in the center of town, but also because it faces the fountains in the Place Masséna and has a good restaurant. 12 Av. Félix-Faure (phone: 93-80-62-52). Expensive.

Holiday Inn – Opposite the airport, this place provides a regular free shuttle. Air conditioned throughout, it has modern luxury appointments, a pool, sauna, and solarium. Nice Airport, 179 Bd. René-Cassin (phone: 93-83-91-92). Expensive.

Méridien – Above the *Ruhl Casino* near the Albert I Garden, this shiny, modern, somewhat impersonal hotel has lots of glass and escalators, and is luxurious in a more streamlined way than the Victorian dowager hotels that gave the Riviera its reputation. There's a good restaurant, piano bar, and health club, as well as an underground parking lot that offers access to the pedestrian zone. 1 Promenade des Anglais (phone: 93-82-25-25). Expensive.

Négresco – One of those Côte d'Azur landmarks where everyone should stay at least once before doomsday. A great wedding cake hotel overlooking the promenade, with elaborately appointed rooms, a fine restaurant called *Chantecler* (see *Eating Out*), and staff in 18th-century rainment. In the central atrium, a ton of Baccarat crystal is suspended over what is allegedly the largest Aubusson carpet in the world (a similar chandelier is in the Kremlin). The building itself has been designated a national monument. 37 Promenade des Anglais (phone: 93-88-39-51). Expensive.

Plaza Concorde – A traditional palace, it is beautifully restored and in the center of town facing Albert I Garden and the sea. The view from the rooftop terrace is magnificent. 12 Av. de Verdun (phone: 93-87-80-41). Expensive.

Pullman – In the center of town, this deluxe hotel is a 5-minute walk from Place Masséna. The rooms are air conditioned and soundproof. Among the hotel's attractions are a Polynesian bar, pool and sauna, exotic interior gardens, and a great view from the rooftop terrace. 28 Av. Notre-Dame (phone: 93-80-30-24). Expensive.

Splendid-Sofitel – This 100-year-old dowager has been run by the same family for three generations, though it's been modernized, with television sets and air conditioning. One floor is reserved for nonsmoking guests. Only 500 yards from the sea, but it, too, has a pool as well as a sauna on the premises. 50 Bd. Victor-Hugo (phone: 93-88-69-54). Expensive.

Westminster Concorde – An old hotel in the grand tradition, facing the sea. All the air conditioned rooms have mini-bars and color TV sets, and there's a good restaurant, bar, and disco. 27 Promenade des Anglais (phone: 93-88-29-44). Expensive.

Albert I – One of the best situated properties in Nice, it is 50 yards from the beach and Place Masséna and a 2-minute walk from the pedestrian zone. Good views of the sea and the gardens. 4 Av. des Phocéens (phone: 93-85-74-01). Expensive to moderate.

Georges – Only 18 rooms, but each is comfortable, clean, well cared for, and looks as if it's been decorated with surplus *Négresco* furnishings. Rooms are understandably hard to come by in the summer, but it's well worth the necessary advance planning. 3 Rue Henri-Cordier (phone: 93-86-23-41). Moderate.

Grand Hôtel de Florence – Small, centrally located yet quiet, and air conditioned. There is no restaurant. 3 Rue Paul-Déroulède (phone: 93-88-46-87). Moderate.

Napoléon – This typical, gracious, Niçois building is on a quiet corner a few streets back from the beachfront, near the pedestrian zone. The owner also is the manager, and the atmosphere is warm and welcoming. Bar, but no restaurant. 6 Rue Grimaldi (phone: 93-87-70-07). Moderate.

La Pérouse – A charming small hostelry at the far end of the Quai des Etats-Unis, with a view of the entire bay, particularly spectacular at sunset. It offers gardens, pool, sauna. One drawback: traffic noise on an uphill curve outside. No restaurant. 11 Quai Rauba-Capeù (phone: 93-62-34-63). Moderate.

West End – Here is traditional elegance of a somewhat British flavor. A faithful clientele seems to have been coming back each year since the Crimean War. There are 101 rooms in this seafront location, but no restaurant. 31 Promenade des Anglais (phone: 93-88-79-91). Moderate.

Brice – This old hotel is 4 blocks from the Promenade des Anglais, in a delightful flower garden with orange and palm trees. 44 Rue Maréchal-Joffre (phone: 93-88-14-44). Moderate to inexpensive.

New York – An old white building with tropical flora in its entrance court, on a side street off the busy Avenue Jean-Médecin. Centrally located and remodeled despite its elderly-looking exterior. 44 Av. Maréchal-Foch (phone: 93-92-04-19). Moderate to inexpensive.

Résidencehôtel Ulys – Among the finest and most economical choices of Nice's many apartment hotels. The 88 studio and 1-bedroom apartments are clean, modern, and fully equipped with kitchens, and many have balconies overlooking the sea. Maid service by the day or week. 179 Promenade des Anglais (phone: 93-96-26-30). Moderate to inexpensive.

Berne – Small, comfortable, and completely renovated, it is directly opposite the train station. No restaurant, but there's a pleasant cafeteria decorated in a rustic style. 1 Av. Thiers (phone: 93-88-25-08). Inexpensive.

Impérial – In a garden with palm trees and exotic plants, this quiet hostelry is a bit out of town but close to the Exhibition Center and Congress Hall. Restaurant on the premises. Closed November through January. 8 Bd. Carabacel (phone: 93-62-21-40). Inexpensive.

Primotel Suisse – A small hotel in the traditional style, close to the Old City. Its restaurant offers a panoramic view of the Bay of Angels. 15 Quai Rauba-Capeò (phone: 93-62-33-00). Inexpensive.

 EATING OUT: The food found in Nice is a curious mixture of Parisian, native Provençal, and neighboring Italian. However, the city can claim specialties of its own, and some are described in the popular *Cuisine of Nice* (Penguin) by the city's flamboyant mayor, Jean Médecin, who is married to an American. Specialties include *pissaladière,* a kind of pizza topped with black olives, onions, and anchovies; *stocaficada,* a ragoût of stockfish, served with potatoes, tomatoes, peppers, and zucchini; *gnocchi à la niçoise,* a kind of potato dumpling,; and *pain bagnat,* a loaf of French bread split down the middle, soaked in olive oil, and garnished with tomatoes, radishes, peppers, onion, hard-boiled egg, black olives, and parsley. *Soupe au pistou* is a vegetable bean soup with garlic, basil, and herbs. *Socca,* a popular dish in bars of the old town and port, is an enormous pancake made from chickpea flour and olive oil, baked like pizza or fried in oil. It is usually washed down with a solid red wine or a little glass of *pointu* (chilled rosé). Fast food also has come to Nice; there are signs posted throughout the city giving directions to various quick eats.

Nice has the distinction of being the only major city in France, apart from Bordeaux, which grows its own Appellation Contrôlée wines within the city limits. These are the Bellet reds, whites, and rosés, which must be tried during your stay here. At a very expensive restaurant, expect to pay $200 or more for two for dinner; $100 to $150 at expensive restaurants; $50 to $100 at moderately priced restaurants; and less than $50 at inexpensive restaurants. Prices don't include drinks or wine; usually a service charge is included.

Jacques Maximin – The newest and currently the best restaurant in Nice. M. Maximin has brought the expertise to his own establishment that earned him two Michelin stars at *Chantecler* (see below). In addition to à la carte dishes, there are four fixed dinner menus, including Italian selections, egg dishes with fresh herbs, a "grand menu Provençal," and traditional French cuisine. Closed Sundays and Mondays. Reservations necessary. 2-4 Rue S. Guitry (phone: 93-80-70-10). Very expensive.

Le Moulin de Mougins – One of the most extraordinary dining experiences on the Côte d'Azur thrives in Roger Vergé's converted 16th-century mill in the charming market town of Mougins. The cuisine justifiably has earned three Michelin stars, and among the specialties to be enjoyed are braised slivers of Provençal duck in honey and lemon sauce, escalope of fresh salmon, lobster fricassee pâté of sole, and for dessert, cold wild strawberry soufflé. Closed Mondays, Thursday afternoons, and from January 29 to April 5. Reservations necessary. About 20 miles (32 km) west of Nice in Mougins (phone: 93-75-78-24). Very expensive.

L'Ane Rouge – Fine seafood specialties at this fancy restaurant include oysters in champagne, lobster, and bourride (fish stew) — or try the sweetbreads. Closed mid-July to September, Saturdays, and Sundays. Reservations necessary. 7 Quai des Deux-Emmanuel (phone: 93-89-49-63). Expensive.

Chantecler – Since chef Jacques Maximin left, the expensive, elegant fare certainly is less thrilling, though such specialties as *gourmandise de foie gras* (a luxurious pâté), a fish fantasy called *charlotte de St.-Pierre,* and inventive dishes like lobster ravioli still are consistent and rate one Michelin star. The *menu dégustation* features tiny, elegant portions of a dozen different dishes. Closed mid-November to mid-December. Reservations necessary. 37 Promenade des Anglais (phone: 93-88-39-51). Expensive.

Château de la Chèvre d'Or – For a special treat — one Michelin star — drive east out of Nice on the Moyenne Corniche to the perched village of Eze (see *Special Places*), where you will find this excellent restaurant in a restored medieval manor house with a garden. (It's also a hotel.) Dine on lobster mousse or rack of lamb, while enjoying a spectacular panorama of the sea. Closed from December 2 to March 2 and Wednesdays during off-season. Reservations necessary. Moyenne Corniche, Eze (phone: 93-41-12-12). Expensive.

Coco Beach – A large fish restaurant a few yards from the sea that is popular with residents who appreciate good food. Renowned for its bouillabaisse, lobster, and grilled fish of all kinds. *Very* crowded during summer months. Closed Mondays and Sunday evenings and mid-November to mid-December. No reservations. 2 Av. Jean-Lorrain (phone: 93-89-39-26). Expensive.

Colombe d'Or – This gallery–dining room in a small hotel (with a pool) just outside the gates of the old town in St.-Paul-de-Vence is most noted for its collection of post-Impressionist art. (It was here that the late Simone Signoret met Yves Montand, and later married him in the presence of the hotel owner.) Matisse and other artists sometimes paid their bills during the 1920s and 1930s with the paintings that now decorate the walls. The restaurant specializes in grills and roasts, and there is a lovely view from its terrace in summer. Closed early November to mid-December. Reservations advised. About 14 miles (22 km) northwest of Nice in St.-Paul-de-Vence (phone: 93-32-80-02). Expensive.

Chez Don Camillo – A tranquil, intimate place that offers an appetizing taste of Italy (in case you're not going to make it across the border), but with a Niçois accent. Closed Sundays, Mondays, the second half of August, and school holidays in November and February. Reservations necessary. 5 Rue des Ponchettes (phone: 93-85-67-95). Expensive to moderate.

Le Jardin Gourmand – Another good fish eatery; better known for the chef's preparation of vegetables. Closed Sundays. Reservations unnecessary. 15 Rue Biscarra (phone: 93-62-48-00). Expensive to moderate.

Rôtisserie de St.-Pancrace – Dine on prawn stew, *quenelles* of salmon, roast squab, or ravioli stuffed with foie gras, among other dishes that have earned the restaurant its Michelin star. A lovely view from the garden terrace. Closed Mondays except in July and August and from early January to early February. Reservations unnecessary. In the village of St.-Pancrace, about 5 miles (8 km) north of Nice on D914 (phone: 93-84-43-69). Expensive to moderate.

La Toque Blanche – This 10-table spot offers magnificent fish dishes and has a fixed-price lunch weekdays. Closed Sunday evenings, Mondays, and mid-July through August 1. Reservations necessary. 10 Rue de la Buffa (phone: 93-88-38-18). Expensive to moderate.

Albert's Bar – An American-style bar and grill with a decor reminiscent of the 1930s, it offers such traditional French dishes as *blanquette de veau* (veal stew) along with Slavic specialties such as blinis with salmon. Closed Sundays and August. Reservations unnecessary. 1 Rue Maurice-Jaubert (phone: 93-53-37-72). Moderate.

Auberge de Bellet – Beautifully decorated, it is the ideal place to sample the range of local Bellet wines. Accompany them with braised chicken with mint or the fricassee of fish with herb butter. In summer dine outdoors in the shaded garden. Closed Tuesdays and January 20 to March 1. Reservations unnecessary. A mile (1.6 km) to the west of St.-Pancrace in the village of St.-Romans-de-Bellet (phone: 93-37-83-84). Moderate.

Bông Laï – For a change of pace, this Vietnamese-Chinese restaurant is quite good, especially the lacquered duck and the fish in ginger — even the chop suey. Closed

Mondays, Tuesdays, and the last 3 weeks of June and 2 weeks in mid-December. Reservations unnecessary. 14 Rue Alsace-Lorraine (phone: 93-88-75-36). Moderate.

Le Champagne – The emphasis is on fish, delicately prepared with fine sauces and served in a comfortable setting. Closed Saturday afternoons and Sundays. Reservations unnecessary. 12 Av. Félix-Faure (phone: 93-80-62-52). Moderate.

Au Chapon Fin – This charming place in the old quarter has a limited menu of delicious regional food. Closed Sundays, holidays, mid-June to July 8, and 2 weeks at *Christmas.* Reservations unnecessary. 1 Rue du Moulin (phone: 93-80-56-92). Moderate.

Chez les Pêcheurs – The specialties of this seafood spot in the Old Port include fish pâté and grilled deep sea bass (*loup de mer*). Closed Wednesdays, Thursday afternoons, and from mid-November through December. Reservations unnecessary. 18 Quai Docks (phone: 93-89-59-61). Moderate.

Au Ciel d'Azur – Elegant dining where you'd least expect it — on the second floor of the airport. Very good fish, especially the sole, and luscious desserts. And if you find yourself at the airport with time to kill but little appetite, the restaurant's adjoining bar is a comfortable refuge from the crowded self-service restaurant-bar on the third floor. Open daily. Reservations unnecessary. Aéroport de Nice (phone: 93-21-36-36). Moderate.

Michel – Also called *Le Grand Pavois,* this place has very good seafood dishes, especially the fish soup, stuffed mussels, and the sole meunière. Closed Mondays and from the first Sunday in July to August 10. Reservations unnecessary. 11 Rue Meyerbeer (phone: 93-88-77-42). Moderate.

Au Passage – A Vietnamese eatery with French cooking, too. Excellent sauces; simple atmosphere. Closed Sundays and August. No reservations. 11 bis Bd. Raimbaldi (phone: 93-80-23-15). Moderate.

A la Ribote – The crazy-quilt menu lists oysters, fish, paella, and couscous, along with a daily special. Closed Saturdays. No reservations. 5 Av. de Bellet, Pl. de Caserne des Pompiers Magnan (phone: 93-86-56-26). Moderate.

L'Univers "César" – A great place for pasta, which is served in all shapes and styles (even flambéed) and with proper ceremony by César himself. *Loup de mer* (sea bass) with *cèpes* (mushrooms) and artichokes is another specialty of the house. The Niçois seem to come for the festive atmosphere as much as for the food, and at times it can be a bit of a circus. You might even bump into Jean-Claude Killy or some other French celebrity. Open daily until 2 AM. Reservations unnecessary. 54 Bd. Jean-Jaurès (phone: 93-62-32-22). Moderate.

La Coquille – A popular, unpretentious seafood restaurant that displays its wares on the street and also prepares food to take out. Good for oysters. No reservations. 36 Cours Saleya (phone: 93-85-58-82). Moderate to inexpensive.

Rendez-Vous des Sportifs – A cheery family-run place specializing in Niçois cooking. Here you can sample the whole range of regional specialties, including *pissaladière,* stockfish, and *aubergine* (eggplant) fried in olive oil. Closed Sundays. No reservations. 120 Bd. de la Madeleine (phone: 93-86-21-39). Moderate to inexpensive.

Ruhl Plage – The best of the beach restaurants along the Promenade des Anglais serves good grilled fish, salads, and carafe wines. A pool for children and all kinds of water sports facilities make it a popular summer lunch spot with the Niçois. Open from March through November, or as long as the weather stays warm. No reservations. Opposite the *Casino Ruhl,* which is at 1 Promenade des Anglais (phone: 93-87-09-70). Moderate to inexpensive.

Biererie Chez Nino – You may find yourself the only out-of-towner in this old bistro tucked away in a tiny street near the train station. The place features a hundred different beers (both bottled and draft) from 22 countries, and its friendly owner will help you choose the right one to accompany your meal. Good grills and stockfish. The pictures on display are painted by local artists and there's a guitarist singing songs by Jacques Brel and other *chansonniers*. The clientele is a democratic mix of business suits and leather jackets. Closed Sundays and August. No reservations. 50 Rue Trachel (phone: 93-88-07-71). Inexpensive.

La Méranda – Simple and plain but highly recommended by the Niçois, this tiny, crowded place near the flower market is run by a husband and wife team. Service is a bit slow, as each dish is prepared to order. Tripes *niçoises* and pâtés *au pistou* are splendid choices. Closed February, August, Saturday evenings, Sundays, and Mondays. No reservations. 4 Rue de la Terrasse (no phone). Inexpensive.

La Nissarda – In an attractive setting just a 10-minute walk from Place Masséna, serving many local specialties. Closed Wednesdays and for 2 weeks in July. No reservations. 17 Rue Gubernatis (phone: 93-85-26-29). Inexpensive.

La Pizza – The best pizza this side of Ventimiglia (and possibly Milan), and good pasta, too. Young folks congregate en masse here until midnight. No reservations. In the heart of the pedestrian zone, at 34 Rue Masséna (phone: 93-87-70-29). Inexpensive.

Rive Gauche – A small, friendly bistro with an Art Deco interior. Good food, like calves' liver and duck, and an excellent value. Closed Sundays, and August. No reservations. 27 Rue Ribotti (phone: 93-62-16-72). Inexpensive.

Taverne du Château – Good Niçois cooking in a lively family place in Old Nice. No reservations. 42 Rue Droite (phone: 93-62-37-73). Inexpensive.

 BARS AND CAFÉS: The *Scotch Tea House* (4 Av. de Suède; phone: 93-16-03-55) is very British and proper. *Café de France* (12 Bd. Gambetta; phone: 93-88-50-81) is a landmark where old and young Niçois alike, as well as out-of-towners, drink coffee or beer or dine from a light menu. An older crowd frequents *Le Mississippi* (5 Promenade des Anglais; phone: 93-82-06-61). At water's edge is *Le Queenie* (19 Promenade des Anglais; phone: 93-88-52-50), a café with a bamboo and glass decor. *Bar L'Hermitage* — also called *Bar des Oiseaux* (5 Rue St. Vincent; phone: 93-80-27-33) — is a colorful place where, legend has it, the owner carries a bird on her shoulder; ask for a *piconbière*, the house specialty. *Le Valentino* (3 Promenade des Anglais; phone: 93-87-09-27) features live music in decor centered on black lacquered wood. There's an exotic African ambience at *Le Pam-Pam Masséna* (1 Rue Desboutin; phone: 93-80-21-60). *L'Isle Au Zebre* is a *cave* restaurant with French Caribbean music, a dance floor, and a billiard table (19 Rue Droite; phone: 93-80-56-27). Late-night places include *Bar-Tabac des Fleurs* (13 Cours Saleya), a bar near the *Marché aux Fleurs* that *opens* at 4 AM; and *Le Frog,* where you can drink, eat Tex-Mex food, and listen to live music after the restaurant closes (closed Sundays; Rue Milton Robbins; phone: 93-85-85-65). *Le Cheap* features spare ribs, some French food, and good cocktails, and a great lineup of sounds from rock to jazz and soul (closed Sundays; 4 Rue de la Barillerie; phone: 93-80-46-76).

PARIS

It was Victor Hugo, the great French poet and novelist, who captured the true spirit of his native city when he called it "the heir of Rome, the mundane pilgrim's home away from home." If Rome, for all its earthly exuberance, never lets the visitor forget that it is the spiritual home of the West, Paris — with its supreme joie de vivre and its passion for eating, drinking, and dressing well — belongs unabashedly to the material world.

Like a magnet, Paris always has attracted visitors and exiles from all corners of the earth. At the same time, it remains not so much an international city as a very French one, and a provincial one at that. Paris has its own argot, and each neighborhood retains its peculiar character, so that the great capital is still very much a city of 20 villages.

But parochialism aside — and forgetting about the consummate haughtiness of Parisians (someone once remarked that Parisians don't even like themselves) — the main attraction of the City of Light is its beauty. When you speak of the ultimate European city, it must be Paris, if only for the view from the Place de la Concorde or the Tuileries toward the Arc de Triomphe, or similarly striking sights beside the Seine. Here is the fashion capital of the world and the center of gastronomic invention and execution. Here the men all seem to swagger with the insouciance of privilege, and even the humblest shopgirl dresses with the care of a haute couture mannequin. Paris is the reason "foreign" means "French" to so many travelers.

Paris is in the north-central part of France, in the rich agricultural area of the Seine River valley. With a population of over 2 million people, it is France's largest city, an industrial and commercial center, and an important river port. Roughly elliptical in shape, the city has more than doubled in size in the last century. Its limits now are the ring of mid-19th-century fortifications that once were well beyond its boundaries. At its western edge is the vast Bois de Boulogne and to the east the Bois de Vincennes — two enormous parks. Curving through Paris, the Seine divides the city into its northern Right Bank (Rive Droite) and southern Left Bank (Rive Gauche). The Right Bank extends from the Bois de Boulogne on the far west, through Place Charles-de-Gaulle (l'Etoile), which surrounds the Arc de Triomphe, and farther east to the Tuileries Gardens and the fabulous *Louvre.* North of the *Louvre* is the area of the Grands Boulevards, centers of business and fashion; farther north is the district of Montmartre, built on a hill and crowned by the domed Eglise du Sacré-Coeur, an area that has attracted great artists (and many of markedly less greatness) since the days of Monet and Renoir.

The Left Bank sweeps from the Eiffel Tower on the west through the Latin Quarter, with its university and bohemian and intellectual community. South of the Latin Quarter is Montparnasse, once inhabited jointly by artists and intellectuals and laborers, now a large urban renewal project that includes a suburban-style shopping center around the Tour Montparnasse.

In the middle of the Seine are two islands, the Ile de la Cité and the Ile St.-Louis, the oldest parts of Paris. It was on the Ile de la Cité (in the 3rd century BC) that Celtic fishermen known as Parisii first built a settlement they named Lutetia, "place surrounded by water." Caesar conquered the city for Rome in 52 BC, and, in about AD 300, Paris was invaded by Germanic tribes, the strongest of which were the Franks. In 451, when Attila the Hun threatened to overrun Paris, a holy woman named Geneviève promised to defend the city by praying. She succeeded — the enemy decided to spare the capital — and Geneviève became the patron saint of Paris. Clovis I, the first Christian King of the Franks, made Paris his capital in the 6th century. Relentless Norman sieges, famine, and plague curtailed the city's development, but at the end of the 10th century peace and prosperity came with the triumph of Hugh Capet over the Carolingians. Capet ascended the throne, the first of a long line of Capétian kings, and Paris became the "central jewel of the French crown," a great cultural center and seat of learning.

The Capétian monarchs contributed much to the growth of the city over the next few centuries. A defensive wall was begun in 1180 by Philip Augustus to protect the expanding Right Bank business and trading center as well as the intellectual quarter around the newly formed university on the Left Bank. He then built a new royal palace, the *Louvre,* just outside these ramparts, but he never lived there. Medieval Paris was a splendid city, a leader in the arts and in the intellectual life of Europe. The Sorbonne attracted such outstanding scholars as Alexander of Hales, Giovanni di Fidanza (St. Bonaventure), Albertus Magnus, and Thomas Aquinas.

The Ile de la Cité remained a warren of narrow streets and wood and plaster houses, but the banks of the Seine continued to be built up in both directions. Renaissance kings, patrons of the arts, added their own architectural and aesthetic embellishments to the flourishing city. Major streets were laid out; some of Paris's most charming squares were constructed; the Pont Neuf, the first stone bridge spanning the Seine, was completed; and Le Nôtre, the royal gardener, introduced proportion, harmony, and beauty with his extraordinary Tuileries.

Louis XIV, who was responsible for many of the most notable Parisian landmarks, including Les Invalides, moved the court to Versailles in the late 17th century. Paris nevertheless continued to blossom, and it was under the Sun King's rule that France and Paris first won international prestige. Visitors were drawn to the city, luxury trades were begun, and the Panthéon, Champ-de-Mars parade ground, and Ecole Militaire were built. In 1785, at age 16, Napoleon Bonaparte graduated from this military school with the notation in his report: "Will go far if circumstances permit!"

French history reflects the conflict between the two extremes of the French character, both equally strong: a tradition of aristocracy and a penchant for revolution. To the French aristocracy we owe magnificent palaces like the *Louvre,* the Luxembourg Palace, and Versailles, with their formal gardens. At the same time, the people of Paris have always been noisily rebellious and independent: from 1358, when the mob rebelled against the Dauphin, to the Fronde in 1648–49, the great French Revolution of 1789, the 1830 and 1848 revolutions that reverberated throughout Europe, the Paris Commune of 1870–71, and finally to the student rebellion of 1968, which nearly overthrew the Fifth Republic. The most profound one of all was the French Revolution at the close of the 18th century, the bicentennial of which was celebrated in grand style in 1989.

The excesses of the French court, the consummate luxury of the Versailles of Louis XIV, cost the French people dearly in taxes and oppression. The Parisians, fiercely independent, forced the French king to his knees with their dramatic storming of the Bastille in 1789. Inspired by the ideas of the French and English philosophers of the Enlightenment, just like the American founding fathers in 1776, the French subsequently overthrew their monarchy.

During the Revolution, unruly mobs damaged many of the city's buildings, including Ste.-Chapelle and Notre-Dame, which were not restored until the mid-19th century. Napoleon, who came to power in 1799, was too busy being a conqueror to complete all he planned, though he did manage to restore the *Louvre,* construct the Carrousel Arch and Place Vendôme victory column, and begin work on the Arc de Triomphe and the Madeleine. Though something of a tyrant, Napoleon's conquests spread the new ideas of the Revolution — including the Code Napoléon, a system of laws embodying the ideals of "Liberty, Equality, Fraternity" — to places as far away as Canada and Moscow.

Later in the 19th century, Paris was reorganized and modernized by a great urban planner, Baron Haussmann. He instituted the brilliant system of squares as focal points for marvelous, wide boulevards and roads; he planned the Place de l'Opéra, the Bois de Boulogne and Bois de Vincennes, the railway stations, the boulevards, and the system of 20 *arrondissements* (districts) that make up Paris today. He also destroyed most of the center of the old Cité, displacing 25,000 people.

During the peaceful lull between the Franco-Prussian War and World War I, the city of Paris thrived as never before. These were the days of the Belle Epoque, the heyday of *Maxim's,* the *Folies-Bergère,* and the cancan, whose spirit is captured so well in Offenbach's heady music for *Gaité Parisienne.* Montmartre, immortalized by Toulouse-Lautrec, was so uninhibited that the foreign press dubbed Paris the "City of Sin."

In the 2 decades before World War II, this free-spirited city attracted politically and socially exiled artists by the dozens: Picasso, Hemingway, Fitzgerald, and Gertrude Stein were just a few. Only in Paris could such avant-garde writers as James Joyce, D. H. Lawrence, and, later, Henry Miller find publishers. And Paris, which witnessed the first Impressionist exhibition in 1874 — introducing Monet, Renoir, Pissarro, and Seurat — heard the first performance of Stravinsky's revolutionary "Sacre du Printemps" (Rite of Spring) in 1913, even though the baffled audience jeered loudly.

As the quintessentially beautiful center of intellectual life and home of the arts, Paris can claim to have earned its City of Light title. Even though it, like other modern cities, is troubled by a rise in crime — at *Maxim's,* for instance, a precautionary bulletproof window has been installed — its beauty and libertarian atmosphere remain. Its supreme talent for civilized living has made the city beloved by the French and foreigners alike. After all, these are the people who made food preparation a fine art, and, despite the unfortunate presence of fast-food vendors on the Champs-Elysées, the French passion for haute cuisine remains unrivaled. And as the undisputed capital of fashion, male and female, Paris continues to be the best-dressed city in the world, and Rue du Faubourg-St.-Honoré remains the standard by which all other shopping streets are measured.

However avant-garde in dress, Parisians are a conservative lot when it comes to any changes in the appearance of their beloved city. When the Eiffel Tower was built in 1889, Guy de Maupassant commented, "I spend all my afternoons on the Eiffel Tower; it's the only place in Paris from which you can't see it." So today's Parisians grumble about the ultramodern *Centre Georges Pompidou,* a focus for every type of modern art: theater, music, dance, circus, painting, sculpture, photography, and film, and about *Le Forum,* a sunken glass structure filled with boutiques in what was once *Les Halles,* the bawdy produce market. They also don't seem especially thrilled by the I. M. Pei glass pyramids that form the new entrance to the *Louvre.*

Parisians accept innovations reluctantly because they want their city to remain as it has always been. They love their remarkable heritage inordinately, and perhaps it is this love, together with the irrepressible sense of good living, that has made Paris so eternally attractive to others.

PARIS AT-A-GLANCE

 SEEING THE CITY: It's impossible to single out just one perfect Paris panorama; they exist in profusion. The most popular is the bird's-eye view from the top of the Eiffel Tower on the Left Bank; there are several places to have snacks and drinks and enjoy a view (on a clear day) of more than 50 miles. (There also are three restaurants where you can enjoy fine dining.) The tower is open daily, 10 AM to 11 PM; admission charge (Champ-de-Mars; phone: 45-55-91-11). From the top of the towers of Notre-Dame, eager spectators enjoy closeups of the cathedral's Gothic spires and flying buttresses, along with a magnificent view of the Cité and the rest of Paris. Start climbing the steps at the foot of the north tower; admission charge (Rue du Cloître Notre-Dame, 4e; phone: 43-25-42-92). On the Right Bank there's a stunning view from the terrace of Sacré-Coeur. The observatory on Tour Montparnasse also offers a striking panorama, as does the landing at the top of the escalator at the *Centre Georges Pompidou.*

The most satisfying view, if not the highest, is from the top of the Arc de Triomphe. The arch is the center of Place Charles-de-Gaulle, once Place de l'Etoile (Square of the Star), so called because it is the center of a "star" whose radiating points are the 12 broad avenues, including the Champs-Elysées, planned and built by Baron Haussmann in the mid-19th century. Open daily, 10 AM to 5:30 PM; admission charge (phone: 43-80-31-31).

For the truly extravagant, there are helicopter tours that start at $80 per person from the Héliport de Paris at the foot of the *Sofitel* hotel. *Héli-France* (4 Av. de la Porte de Sèvres, 15e; phone: 45-57-53-67) offers tours daily for a minimum of 4 people, and *Héli-Cap* (phone: 45-57-75-51) offers weekday tours for a minimum of 4 people.

SPECIAL PLACES: Getting around this sprawling metropolis isn't difficult once you understand the layout of the 20 *arrondissements.* We suggest that visitors orient themselves by taking one of the many excellent sightseeing tours offered by *Cityrama* (4 Pl. des Pyramides, 1er; phone: 42-60-30-14) or *Paris Vision* (214 Rue de Rivoli, 1er; phone: 42-60-31-25). Their bubble-top double-decker buses are equipped with earphones for simultaneous commentary in English and several other languages. Reserve through any travel agent or your hotel's concierge.

Once you have a better idea of the basic layout of the city, buy a copy of *Paris Indispensable* or *Plan de Paris par Arrondissement* at any bookshop or newsstand. These little lifesavers list streets alphabetically and indicate the nearest métro station on individual maps and an overall plan. Now you're ready to set out by foot (the most rewarding) or by métro (the fastest and surest) to discover Paris for yourself.

Street addresses of the places mentioned throughout the chapter are followed by their *arrondissement* number.

LA RIVE DROITE (THE RIGHT BANK)

Arc de Triomphe and Place de l'Etoile – This monumental arch (165 feet high, 148 feet wide) was built between 1806 and 1836 to commemorate Napoleon's victories. It underwent a major cleanup and restoration for the bicentennial of the French Revolution. Note the frieze and its 6-foot-high figures, the ten impressive sculptures (especially Rude's *La Marseillaise* on the right as you face the Champs-Elysées), and the arches inscribed with the names of Bonaparte's victories as well as those of Empire heroes. Beneath the arch is the French Tomb of the Unknown Soldier and its Eternal Flame, which is rekindled each day at 6:30 PM. An elevator (or 284 steps) carries visitors to the top for a magnificent view of the city and the 12 avenues radiating from l'Etoile. Admission charge. Pl. Charles-de-Gaulle (phone: 43-80-31-31).

Champs-Elysées – Paris's legendary promenade, the "Elysian Fields," was swamp-land until 1616. It has come to be synonymous with everything glamorous in the city, though the "Golden Arches" and shlocky shops recently have replaced much of the glitter (a commission was formed in 1990 to try to restore some of the old elegance). The Champs-Elysées stretches for more than 2 miles between the Place de la Concorde and the Place Charles-de-Gaulle (l'Etoile). The very broad avenue, lined with rows of plane and horse chestnut trees, shops, cafés, and cinemas, is perfect for strolling, window shopping, and people watching.

The area from the Place de la Concorde to the Rond-Point Champs-Elysées is a charming park, where Parisians often bring their children. On the north side of the gardens is the Palais de l'Elysée, the official home of the President of the French Republic. Ceremonial events, such as the *Bastille Day Parade* (July 14), frequently take place along the Champs-Elysées.

Grand Palais – Off the Champs-Elysées, on opposite sides of Avenue Winston-Churchill, are the elaborate turn-of-the-century *Grand Palais* and *Petit Palais* (Large Palace and Small Palace), built of glass and stone for the *1900 World Exposition.* With its stone columns, mosaic frieze, and flat glass dome, the *Grand Palais* contains a large exhibition area and the *Palais de la Découverte,* the Paris science museum, and the planetarium. Closed Tuesdays; open Wednesdays until 9:45 PM. Av. Franklin-Roosevelt, 8e (phone: 42-89-54-10).

Petit Palais – Built contemporaneously with the *Grand Palais,* this is now the *Paris Musée des Beaux-Arts,* containing exhibits of the city's history as well as a variety of fine and applied arts. Closed Mondays. Admission charge. Av. Winston-Churchill, 8e (phone: 42-65-12-73).

Place de la Concorde – This square, surely one of the most magnificent in the world, is grandly situated in the midst of equally grand landmarks: the *Louvre* and the Tuileries on one side, the Champs-Elysées and the Arc de Triomphe on another, the

Seine and the Napoleonic Palais Bourbon on a third, and the pillared façade of the Madeleine on the fourth. Designed by Gabriel for Louis XV, the elegant square was where his unfortunate successor, Louis XVI, lost his head to the guillotine, as did Marie Antoinette, Charlotte Corday, Robespierre, and others. It was first named for Louis XV, then called Place de la Révolution by the triumphant revolutionaries. Ornamenting the square, the eight colossal statues representing important French provincial capitals were polished and blasted clean for the bicentennial celebration in 1989. The 3,300-year-old, 75-foot-high obelisk was a gift from Egypt in 1829.

Jardin des Tuileries – Carefully laid out in patterned geometric shapes, with clipped shrubbery and formal flower beds, statues, and fountains, this is one of the finest examples of French garden design (in contrast to an informal English garden, exemplified by the Bois de Boulogne). Along the Seine, between the Place de la Concorde and the *Louvre*.

Rue de Rivoli – This charming old street has perfume shops, souvenir stores, boutiques, bookstores, cafés, and such hotels as the *Meurice* and the *Inter-Continental* under its 19th-century arcades. The section facing the Tuileries, from the Place de la Concorde to the *Louvre*, is an especially good place to explore on rainy days.

In the *Orangerie*, a museum across the gardens, is a series of large paintings of water lilies by Monet called the *Nymphéas* and the collection of Jean Walter and Paul Guillaume, with works by Cézanne, Renoir, Matisse, Picasso, and others. Open 10 AM to 5:15 PM; closed Tuesdays. Admission charge. Pl. de la Concorde and Quai des Tuileries, 1er (phone: 42-97-48-16).

Louvre – Built on the site of a medieval fortress on the banks of the Seine, this palace was the home of the French kings during the 16th and 17th centuries, until Louis XIV moved the court to Versailles in 1682. In 1793, it became a museum and now is one of the world's greatest art repositories. It's easy to spend a couple of days here, savoring treasures like the *Venus de Milo, Winged Victory,* the *Mona Lisa,* and the French crown jewels — just a few of the 297,000 pieces in six different collections.

Nor is the outside of this huge edifice to be overlooked. Note especially the Cour Carrée (the courtyard of the old *Louvre*), the southwest corner of which, dating from the mid-1550s, is the oldest part of the palace and a beautiful example of the Renaissance style that François I had so recently introduced from Italy. Note, too, the Colonnade, which forms the eastern front of the Cour Carrée, facing the Place du Louvre; fully classical in style, it dates from the late 1660s, not too long before the Sun King left for Versailles. Newer wings of the *Louvre* embrace the palace gardens, in the midst of which stands the Arc de Triomphe du Carrousel, erected by Napoleon. From here, the vista across the Tuileries and the Place de la Concorde and on up the Champs-Elysées to the Arc de Triomphe is one of the most beautiful in Paris — which says a lot. The glass pyramids — designed by I. M. Pei and opened in 1989 — sit center stage in the *Louvre*'s grand interior courtyard, and the largest of the intrusive trio now is the museum's main entrance. The controversial structure is the first step of a major expansion; when completed (the target date is 1993), the *Louvre*'s underground galleries, shops, and exhibit space will connect the North and South Wings, increasing museum exhibition space by almost 80%.

Good guided tours in English, covering the highlights of the *Louvre,* are frequently available, although not every day, so be sure to check in advance. Open from 9:45 AM to 6:30 PM; closed Tuesdays. Admission charge. Pl. du Louvre, 1er (phone: 40-20-51-51, for recorded information in French and English or 40-20-50-50, for more detailed information).

Place Vendôme – Just north of the Tuileries is an aristocrat of a square, one of the loveliest in Paris, the octagonal Place Vendôme, designed by Mansart in the 17th century. Its arcades contain world-famous jewelers, perfumers, and banks, the *Ritz* hotel, and the Ministry of Justice. The 144-foot column in the center is covered with bronze from the 1,200 cannons captured at Austerlitz by Napoleon in 1805. Just off Place Vendôme is the famous Rue du Faubourg-St.-Honoré, one of the oldest streets in Paris, which now holds elegant shops selling the world's most expensive made-to-order items. To the north is the Rue de la Paix, noted for its jewelers.

Opéra – Charles Garnier's imposing rococo edifice stands in its own busy square, its façade decorated with sculpture, including Carpeaux's *The Dance.* The ornate interior has an impressive grand staircase, a beautiful foyer, lavish marble from every quarry in France, and Chagall's controversially decorated dome. Until a few years ago, the opera house only could be seen by attending a ballet performance (held September–June); now, however, visitors may explore its magnificent interior and enjoy its special exhibitions daily from 11 AM to 4:30 PM, except on the days when there are special performances. Pl. de l'Opéra, 9e (phone: 47-42-57-50).

L'Opéra Bastille – In sharp contrast to Garnier's *Opéra* is the curved glass façade of 20th-century architect Carlos Ott's brand-new Paris opera house. Set against the historic landscape of the Bastille quarter, this austere, futuristic structure houses over 30 acres of multi-purpose theaters, shops, and urban promenade. Inaugurated for the bicentennial of the revolution on July 14, 1989, the opera house opened in March 1990 with a production of Berlioz's *Les Troyens.* It looks a lot like the prison-fortress that started the French Revolution. Pl. de la Bastille, 11e (phone: 40-01-17-89).

La Madeleine – Starting in 1764, the Church of St. Mary Magdalene was built and razed twice before the present structure was commissioned by Napoleon in 1806 to honor his armies. The church is based on a Greek temple design, with 65-foot-high Corinthian columns supporting the sculptured frieze. From its portals, the view extends down Rue Royale to Place de la Concorde and over to the dome of Les Invalides. Nearby are some of Paris's most tantalizing food shops. Open from 7:30 AM to 7 PM as well as during concerts (held 4 PM Sundays) and other frequent musical events. Pl. de la Madeleine, 8e (phone: 42-65-52-17).

Sacré-Coeur and Montmartre – Built on the highest of Paris's seven hills, the white-domed Basilica of Sacré-Coeur provides an extraordinary view from its steps, especially at dawn or sunset. The area around the church was the artists' quarter of late-19th- and early-20th-century Paris. The more garish aspects of Montmartre's notoriously frivolous 1890s nightlife, particularly the dancers and personalities of the *Moulin Rouge,* were immortalized by the paintings of Henri de Toulouse-Lautrec. And if the streets look familiar, chances are you've seen them in the paintings of Utrillo; they still look the same. The Place du Tertre is still charming, though often filled with tourists and overly eager, mostly undertalented artists. Go early to see it as it was when Braque, Dufy, Modigliani, Picasso, Rousseau, and Utrillo lived here. Montmartre has the last of Paris's vineyards — and still contains old houses, narrow alleys, steep stairways, and carefree cafés enough to provide a full day's entertainment; at night, this is one of the centers of Paris life. Spare yourself most of the climb to Sacré-Coeur by taking the funicular from Place St.-Pierre. Butte Montmartre, 18e.

Les Halles – Just northeast of the *Louvre,* this 80-acre area, formerly the *Central Market,* "the Belly of Paris," was razed in 1969. Gone are most of the picturesque early morning fruit and vegetable vendors, butchers in blood-spattered aprons, truckers bringing the freshest produce from all over France. Their places have been usurped by trendy shops and galleries of youthful entrepreneurs and artisans, small restaurants with lots of charm, the world's largest subway station, acres of trellised gardens and playgrounds, and *Le Forum,* a vast complex of boutiques, ranging from the superchic designer ready-to-wear to more ordinary shops, as well as concert space and movie theaters. Touch-sensitive locator devices, which help visitors find products and services, are placed strategically. A few echoes of the earthy past remain, however, and you can still dine at *Au Pied de Cochon, Pharamond,* and *L'Escargot Montorgueil,* or have a drink with the few remaining workmen (before noon) at one of the old brasseries.

Le Centre National d'Art et de Culture Georges Pompidou (Le Centre Georges Pompidou) – Better known as "the Beaubourg," after the plateau on which it is built, this stark, 6-level creation of steel and glass, with its exterior escalators and blue, white, and red pipes, created a stir the moment its construction began. Outside, a computerized digital clock ticks off the seconds remaining until the 21st century. This wildly popular museum brings together all the contemporary art forms — painting, sculpture, the plastic arts, industrial design, music, literature, cinema, and theater — under one roof, and that roof offers one of the most exciting views of Paris. The old houses and cobbled, tree-shaded streets and squares vie for attention with galleries, boutiques, and the spectacle provided by jugglers, mimes, acrobats, and magicians in the plaza out front. The scene in the courtyard often rivals the exhibits inside. Open weekdays from noon to 10 PM; 10 AM to 10 PM weekends. Closed Tuesdays; no admission charge on Sundays except for special exhibitions. Rue Rambuteau, at the corner of Rue St.-Martin, 4e (phone: 42-77-12-33).

Le Marais – Northeast of the *Louvre,* a marshland until the 16th century, this district became the height of residential fashion during the 17th century. But as the aristocracy moved on, it fell into disrepair. Recently, after a long period of neglect, the Marais has been enjoying a complete face-lift. Spurred on by the opening of the *Picasso Museum* in the Hôtel du Salé, preservationists have lovingly restored more than a hundred of the magnificent old mansions to their former grandeur. They now are museums of exquisite beauty, with muraled walls and ceilings, and their courtyards are the sites of dramatic and musical presentations during the summer *Festival du Marais.* Among the houses to note are the Palais de Soubise, now the National Archives, and the Hôtels d'Aumont, de Clisson, de Rohan, de Sens, and de Sully (*hôtel* in this sense means private residence or townhouse). The Caisse Nationale des Monuments, housed in the last one, can provide maps of the area as well as fascinating and detailed tours. It also offers lectures on Saturdays and Sundays. 62 Rue St.-Antoine, 4e (phone: 42-74-22-22).

Place des Vosges – In the Marais district, the oldest square in Paris — and also one of the most beautiful — was completed in 1612 by order of Henri IV, with its houses elegantly "built to a like symmetry." Though many of the houses have been rebuilt inside, their original façades remain, and the newly restored square is one of Paris's enduring delights. Corneille, Racine, and Mme. de Sévigné lived here. At No. 6 is the *Maison de Victor Hugo,* once the poet's home and now a museum. Closed Mondays; admission charge (4e; phone: 42-72-10-16).

Musée Carnavalet (Carnavalet Museum) – Also in the Marais, this once was the home of Mme. de Sévigné, a noted 17th-century letter writer, and now its beautifully arranged exhibits cover the history of Paris from the days of Henri IV to the present. Its recent expansion through the *lycée* next door and into the neighboring *Le Peletier* hotel doubled the exhibition space, making it the largest museum in the world devoted to the history of a single capital city. The expansion, done primarily to house a permanent major exhibit on the French Revolution, was part of Paris's celebration of the Revolution's bicentennial. Watch for special exhibitions here. The museum also rents out its concert hall to various music groups. Closed Mondays; no admission charge on Sundays. 23 Rue de Sévigné, 3e (phone: 42-72-21-13).

Musée Picasso (Picasso Museum) – This long-awaited museum, which contains a large part of the artist's private collection, is at the Hôtel du Salé. To tell the truth, the building is at least as interesting as the artwork it houses — too many recent works, too few early ones — but a visit is worthwhile just to see Picasso's collection of works by other artists (the Cézannes are best). Closed Tuesdays; half price on Sundays. 5 Rue de Thorigny, 3e (phone: 42-71-25-21).

Cimetière Père Lachaise (Père Lachaise Cemetery) – For those who like ceme-teries, this one is a beauty. In a wooded park, it's the final resting place of many illustrious personalities. A map is available at the gate to help you find the tombs of Balzac, Sarah Bernhardt, Chopin, Colette, Corot, Delacroix, Héloise and Abelard, La Fontaine, Modigliani, Musset, Edith Piaf, Rossini, Oscar Wilde, and even Jim Morrison (of the *Doors* rock group), among others. Note, too, the legions of resident cats. Open daily from 8 AM to 5:30 PM. Bd. de Ménilmontant at Rue de la Roquette, 20e (phone: 43-70-70-33).

La Villette – The City of Sciences and Industry, a celebration of technology, stands in its own park on the edge of the capital and houses a planetarium, the spherical Géode cinema, lots of hands-on displays, and a half-dozen exhibitions at any given time. Restaurants and snack bars. Open 10 AM to 6 PM. Closed Mondays. 30 Av. Cotentin Cariou, 20e (phone: 40-05-70-00).

Bois de Boulogne – Originally part of the Forest of Rouvre, on the western edge of Paris, this 2,140-acre park was planned along English lines by Napoleon. Ride a horse or a bike, row a boat, shoot skeet, go bowling, smell roses, picnic on the grass, see horse races at *Auteuil* and *Longchamp*, visit a zoo, see a play, walk to a waterfall — and there's lots more.

Bois de Vincennes – As a counterpart to the Bois de Boulogne, a park, a palace, and a zoological garden were laid out on 2,300 acres during Napoleon III's time. Visit the 14th-century château and its lovely chapel; the large and lovely floral garden; and the zoo, with animals in their natural habitat. It's at the southeast edge of Paris (métro: Château de Vincennes).

Palais de Chaillot – Built for the *Paris Exposition of 1937* — on the site of the old Palais du Trocadéro left over from the *Exposition of 1878* — its terraces have excellent views across gardens and fountains to the Eiffel Tower on the Left Bank. Two wings house a theater, an aquarium, and four museums — *du Cinéma* (phone: 45-53-74-39), *de l'Homme* (anthropology; phone: 45-53-70-60), *de la Marine* (maritime; phone: 45-53-31-70), and *des Monuments Français* (monument reproductions; phone: 47-27-97-27). Closed Tuesdays and major holidays. Pl. du Trocadéro, 16e.

LA RIVE GAUCHE (THE LEFT BANK)

Tour Eiffel (Eiffel Tower) – It is impossible to imagine the Paris skyline without this mighty symbol, yet what has been called Gustave Eiffel's folly was never meant to be permanent. Originally built for the *Universal Exposition of 1889*, it was due to be torn down in 1909, but it was saved because of the development of the wireless — the first transatlantic wireless telephones were operated from the tower in 1916. Its centennial was celebrated with great fanfare in 1989. Extensive renovations have taken place, and a post office, three restaurants (*Jules Verne* is the best), and a few boutiques have opened up on the first-floor landing. On a really clear day, it's possible to see for 50 miles. Open daily. Admission charge. Champ-de-Mars, 7e (phone: 45-50-34-56).

Chaillot to UNESCO – From the Eiffel Tower, it is possible to look out over a group of Paris's 20th-century buildings and gardens on both sides of the Seine, including the Palais de Chaillot, the Trocadéro and Champ-de-Mars gardens, and the UNESCO buildings. Also part of the area (but not of the same century) is the huge Ecole Militaire, an impressive example of 18th-century French architecture on Avenue de la Motte-Picquet. The Y-shaped building just beyond it, facing Place de Fontenoy, is the main UNESCO building, dating from 1958. It has frescoes by Picasso, Henry Moore's *Reclining Silhouette*, a mobile by Calder, murals by Miró, and Japanese gardens by Noguchi.

Les Invalides – Built by Louis XIV as a refuge for disabled soldiers, this vast classical building has more than 10 miles of corridors and a golden dome by Mansart. For yet another splendid Parisian view, approach the building from the Alexandre III bridge. Besides being a masterpiece of the age of Louis XIV (17th century), the Church of St. Louis, part of the complex, contains the impressive red and green granite Tomb of Napoleon (admission charge). Also at Les Invalides is the *Musée de l'Armée*, one of the world's richest museums, displaying arms and armor together with mementos of French military history. Av. de Tourville, Pl. Vauban, 7e (phone: 45-51-92-84).

Musée d'Orsay (Orsay Museum) – This imposing former railway station has been transformed (by the Milanese architect Gae Aulenti, among others) into one of the shining examples of modern museum curating. Its eclectic collection includes not only the Impressionist paintings decanted from cramped quarters in the *Jeu de Paume*, but also less consecrated academic work and a panorama of the 19th century's achievements in sculpture, photography, and the applied arts. Closed Mondays. Admission charge; reduced on Sundays. 1 Rue de Bellechasse, 7e (phone: 45-49-11-11).

Musée Rodin (Rodin Museum) – The famous statue *The Thinker* is in the garden of this splendid 18th-century residence. The chapel and the mansion also contain Rodin sculpture. Closed Tuesdays. Admission charge. 77 Rue de Varenne, 7e (phone: 47-05-01-34).

Montparnasse – Just south of the Luxembourg Gardens, in the early 20th century there arose an artists' colony of avant-garde painters, writers, and Russian political exiles. Here Hemingway, Picasso, and Scott and Zelda sipped and supped in places like *La Closerie des Lilas, La Coupole, Le Dôme, Le Select,* and *La Rotonde.* The cafés, small restaurants, and winding streets still exist in the shadow of a new shopping center.

Tour Montparnasse – This giant complex dominates Montparnasse. The fastest elevator in Europe whisks Parisians and tourists alike up 59 stories for a view *down* at the Eiffel Tower, from 9:30 AM to 9:30 PM daily for a fee. The shopping center here boasts all the famous names, and the surrounding office buildings are the headquarters of some of France's largest companies. 33 Av. du Maine, 15e, and Bd. de Vaugirard, 14e (phone: 45-38-32-32).

Palais et Jardin du Luxembourg (Luxembourg Palace and Garden) – In what once were the southern suburbs, the Luxembourg Palace and Garden were built for Marie de Médici in 1612. A prison during the Revolution, the Renaissance palace now houses the French Senate. The classic, formal gardens, with lovely statues and the famous Médicis fountain, are popular with students meeting under the chestnut trees and with neighborhood children playing around the artificial lake. 15 Rue de Vaugirard, 6e.

Mosquée de Paris (Paris Mosque) – One of the most beautiful structures of its kind in the non-Muslim — or even in the Muslim — world, it is dominated by a 130-foot-high minaret in gleaming white marble. Shoes are taken off before entering the pebble-lined gardens full of flowers and dwarf trees. Inside, the Hall of Prayer, with its lush Oriental carpets, may be visited daily except Fridays, from 9:30 AM to noon and 2 to 6 PM. Admission charge. Next door is a restaurant and a patio for sipping Turkish coffee and tasting Oriental sweets. Pl. du Puits-de-l'Ermite, 5e (phone: 45-35-97-33).

Panthéon – This 18th-century "nonreligious Temple of Fame dedicated to all the gods" has an impressive interior, with murals depicting the life of Ste.-Geneviève, patron saint of Paris. It contains the tombs of Victor Hugo, the Resistance leader Jean Moulin, Rousseau, Voltaire, and Emile Zola. Open daily from 10 AM to noon and 2 to 5 PM. Admission charge. Pl. du Panthéon, 5e (phone: 43-54-34-51).

Quartier Latin (Latin Quarter) – Extending from the Luxembourg Gardens and the Panthéon to the Seine, this famous neighborhood still maintains its unique atmosphere. A focal point for Sorbonne students since the Middle Ages, it's a mad jumble of narrow streets, old churches, and academic buildings. Boulevard St.-Michel and Boulevard St.-Germain are its main arteries, both lined with cafés, bookstores, and boutiques of every imaginable kind. There are also some charming old side streets, such as the Rue de la Huchette, near Place St.-Michel. And don't miss the famous *bouqui-nistes* (bookstalls) along the Seine, around the Place St.-Michel on the Quai des Grands-Augustins and the Quai St.-Michel.

Eglise St.-Germain-des-Prés (Church of St.-Germain-des-Prés) – Probably the oldest church in Paris, it once belonged to an abbey of the same name. The original basilica (AD 558) was destroyed and rebuilt many times. The Romanesque steeple and its massive tower date from 1014. Inside, the choir and sanctuary are as they were in the 12th century, and the marble shafts used in the slender columns are 14 centuries old. Pl. St.-Germain-des-Prés, 6e (phone: 43-25-41-71).

Surrounding the church is the *quartier* of Paris's "fashionable" intellectuals and artists, with art galleries, boutiques, and renowned people watching cafés such as the *Flore* (Sartre's favorite) and *Aux Deux Magots* (once a Hemingway haunt).

Musée de Cluny (Cluny Museum) – One of the last remaining examples of medie-val domestic architecture in Paris. The 15th-century residence of the abbots of Cluny later became the home of Mary Tudor and now is a museum of medieval arts and crafts, including the celebrated *Lady and the Unicorn* tapestry. Closed Tuesdays. Admission charge. 6 Pl. Paul-Painlevé, 5e (phone: 43-25-62-00).

Eglise St.-Séverin (Church of St. Séverin) – This church still retains its beautiful Flamboyant Gothic ambulatory, considered a masterpiece of its kind, and lovely old stained glass windows dating from the 15th and 16th centuries. The small garden and the restored charnel house also are of interest. 3 Rue des Prêtres, 5e (phone: 43-25-96-63).

Eglise St.-Julien-le-Pauvre (Church of St. Julien le Pauvre) – One of the smallest and oldest churches (12th to 13th century) in Paris offers a superb view of Notre-Dame from its charming Place René-Viviani. 1 Rue St.-Julien-le-Pauvre, 5e (no phone).

THE ISLANDS

Ile de la Cité – The birthplace of Paris, settled by Gallic fishermen about 250 BC, this island in the Seine is so rich in historical monuments that an entire day could be spent here and on the neighboring Ile St.-Louis. A walk all around the islands, along the lovely, tree-shaded quais on both banks of the Seine, opens up one breathtaking view of Notre-Dame Cathedral after another.

Cathédrale de Notre-Dame de Paris (Cathedral of Our Lady) – It is said that the Druids once worshiped on this consecrated ground. The Romans built their temple, and many Christian churches followed. In 1163, the foundations were laid for the present cathedral, one of the world's finest examples of Gothic architecture, grand in size and proportion. Henri VI and Napoleon were crowned here. Take a guided tour (offered in English at noon Tuesdays and in French at noon other weekdays, 2:30 PM Saturdays, and 2 PM Sundays) or quietly explore on your own, but be sure to climb the 225-foot towers for a marvelous view of the city and try to see the splendid stained glass rose windows at sunset. Pl. du Parvis, 4e (phone: 43-26-07-39).

Palais de Justice and Sainte-Chapelle – This complex recalls centuries of history; it was the first seat of the Roman military government, then the headquarters of the early kings, and finally the law courts. In the 13th century, St.-Louis (Louis IX) built a new palace and added Sainte-Chapelle to house the Sacred Crown of Thorns and other holy relics. Built in less than 3 years, the chapel, with its 15 splendid stained glass windows and 247-foot spire, is one of the jewels of Paris. Open daily from 10 AM to 4:30 PM. Admission charge. 4 Bd. du Palais, 1er (phone: 43-54-30-09).

Conciergerie – This remnant of the Old Royal Palace was used as a prison during the Revolution. Here Marie Antoinette, the Duke of Orléans, Mme. du Barry, and many others of lesser fame awaited the guillotine. It was restored extensively for the celebration of the bicentennial of the French Revolution, and the great arch-filled hall is especially striking. Open daily. Admission charge. 4 Bd. du Palais, 1er (phone: 43-54-30-06).

Ile St.-Louis – Walk across the footbridge at the back of Notre-Dame and you're in a charming, tranquil village. This "enchanted isle" has managed to keep its provincial charm despite its central location. Follow the main street, Rue St.-Louis-en-l'Ile, down the middle of the island, past courtyards, balconies, old doors, curious stairways, the Eglise St.-Louis, and discreet plaques bearing the names of illustrious former residents (Mme. Curie, Voltaire, Baudelaire, Gautier, and Daumier, for example); then take the quai back along the edge.

■**EXTRA SPECIAL:** Versailles, by far the most magnificent of all the French châteaux, is 13 miles (21 km) southwest of Paris, accessible by train or bus (also see *Ile-de-France,* DIRECTIONS. Louis XIV, called the Sun King because of the splendor of his court, took a small château used by Louis III, enlarged it, and really outdid himself. The vast, intricate formal gardens, designed by the great Le Nôtre, cover 250 acres and include 600 fountains, for which a river had to be diverted. At one time, the palace itself housed 6,000 people, and the court numbered 20,000. Louis kept his nobles in constant competition over his favors, hoping to distract them from any opposition to his rule. It's impossible to see all of Versailles in one day, but don't miss the Hall of Mirrors, the Royal Apartments, and the Chapel. Also on the grounds are the Grand Trianon, a smaller palace often visited by Louis XIV, and the Petit Trianon, a favorite of Marie-Antoinette, who also liked Le Hameau (the hamlet), a model farm where she and her companions played at being peasants. More than 20 additional rooms — the apartments of the dauphin and dauphine — are open to visitors Thursdays through Sundays. The gardens are open daily from 9:45 AM to 5 PM; the château and Trianons are closed Mondays and holidays. Guided tours in English are available from 10 AM to 3:30 PM. Admission charge (phone: 30-84-74-00). A spectacular illumination and display of the great fountains takes place on Sunday evenings during the summer. For more information, contact the Versailles Tourist Office, 7 Rue des Reservoirs (phone: 39-50-36-22).

SOURCES AND RESOURCES

TOURIST INFORMATION: For information in the US, contact the French Government Tourist Office (610 Fifth Ave., New York, NY 10020; phone: 212-757-1125). In Paris, the Office de Tourisme de Paris (127 Champs-Elysées, 8e; phone: 47-23-61-72), open daily from 9 AM to 8 PM, is the place to go for information, brochures, maps, or hotel reservations. If you call the office, be prepared for a 4- to 5-minute wait before someone answers. Other offices are found at major train stations, such as the Gare du Nord (phone: 45-26-94-82) and the Gare de Lyon (phone: 43-43-33-24).

Local Coverage – *Paris Selection* is the official tourist office magazine in French and English. It lists events, sights, "Paris by Night" tours, places to hear jazz, some hotels, restaurants, shopping, and other information. Far more complete are three weekly guides, *L'Officiel des Spectacles, Paris 7,* and *Une Semaine à Paris–Pariscope.* All are in simple French and are available at newsstands. Most major newsstands carry *Paris Passion,* a tabloid in English that comes out ten times a year, listing cultural events and giving a youthful, lively, American perspective on Paris.

For insights on eating out and finding the best of French food and wine, consult *The Food Lover's Guide to Paris* (Workman, $12.95) by American-in-Paris Patricia Wells. (Though out of print, check the library.) She also contributes a weekly column on restaurants to the *International Herald Tribune*.

TELEPHONE: All phone numbers in Paris begin with the prefix 4 (incorporated into the numbers given here); in the area surrounding Paris, they are preceded by either 3 or 6. When calling a number in the Paris region (including the Ile-de-France) from Paris, dial only the 8-digit number. When calling a number from outside the Paris region, dial 1, then the 8-digit number. When calling from the US, dial 33 (which is the country code), followed by 1, and the 8-digit number.

The pay phones on Paris street corners accept only phone cards. They are available in 40- and 120-franc denominations at post offices and tobacco shops. Before dialing from a pay phone, put the card into the slot on the phone and close the hood. When the franc value remaining on the card is displayed, you can dial your call.

GETTING AROUND: Airports – Charles de Gaulle Airport (Roissy, 16 miles — 25 km — northeast of Paris; phone: 48-62-12-12) has two terminals: Aérogare 1, for foreign airlines, and Aérogare 2, for *Air France* flights. The two terminals are connected by a free shuttle bus. *Air France* airport buses (phone: 42-99-20-18), open to passengers of all airlines for 36F (about $6), leave for the Palais des Congrès (métro station: Porte Maillot) every 12 minutes from 5:40 AM to 11 PM and take between 30 and 50 minutes, depending on traffic. City bus No. 350 between the airport and the Gare du Nord train station also is available, but it generally is slow, taking up to an hour. *Roissy-Rail* runs between the airport and the Gare du Nord every 15 minutes and takes about 35 minutes. (A shuttle bus connects the airport to Roissy station, and from there to the Gare du Nord is by train.) Taxis into town cost 160F (about $26) or more for most destinations.

Orly Airport (10 miles — 16 km — south of Paris; phone: 48-84-52-52) has two terminals: Orly Ouest, mainly for domestic flights and flights to Geneva, and Orly Sud, for international flights. The two terminals are connected by a free shuttle bus. *Air France* buses (phone: 43-23-97-10) leave for a terminus on the Esplanade des Invalides (métro station: Invalides) every 12 minutes and take from 30 to 45 minutes, depending on traffic. You can purchase tickets ($9 one way, $18 round trip) in the US from *Marketing Challengers International* (10 E. 21st St., New York, NY 10010; phone: 212-529-8484). City bus No. 215, which links the airport to Denfert-Rochereau, in southern Paris, takes about a half hour. *Orly-Rail*, a combination shuttle bus to Orly station and train to various stops in the city such as Luxembourg, St.-Michel, and Invalides, runs every 15 or 30 minutes depending on the time of day and takes 35 to 50 minutes, according to the stop. A taxi into town costs 80F (about $13) and up.

Buses linking Charles de Gaulle and Orly airports run roughly every half hour and take from 50 to 75 minutes.

Boat – See Paris from the Seine by day and by night for about 25 francs (about $4). Modern, glass-enclosed river ramblers provide a constantly changing picture of the city. Contact *Bateaux-Mouches* (Pont d'Alma, 7e; phone: 42-25-96-10), *Les Bateaux Parisiens* (Pont d'Iéna, 7e; phone: 47-05-50-00), or *Vedettes Pont-Neuf* (Square Vert-Galant, 1er; phone: 46-33-98-38). In 1989, "bus-boat" service on the Seine was inaugurated: *Les Bateaux BUS* departs from the Hôtel de Ville (Town Hall) every 45 minutes from 10 AM to 8 PM daily, with stops at Nôtre-Dame, the *Louvre,* and the *Musée d'Orsay* (phone: 47-05-50-00). The fare is 35F (about $6). The seasonal operation runs through September 30.

Bus – Generally operates from 6:30 AM to 9:30 PM. Slow but good for sightseeing.

Métro tickets are valid on all city-run buses. Lines are numbered, and both stops and buses have signs indicating routes. One or two tickets may be required, depending on the distance traveled. The *RATP,* which operates both the métro and bus system, also has designated certain lines as being of particular interest to tourists. A panel on the front of the bus indicates in English and German "This bus is good for sightseeing." *RATP* has a tourist office at Pl. de la Madeleine, next to the flower market (phone: 43-46-14-14), which organizes bus trips in Paris and the region.

Car Rental – Book when making your plane reservation, or contact *Avis* (phone: 45-50-32-31), *Budget* (phone: 46-86-65-65), *Europcar* (phone: 45-00-08-06), or *Hertz* (phone: 47-88-51-51).

Métro – Operating from 5:30 AM to about 1 AM, it is safe, clean, quiet, easy to use, and, since the Paris rapid transit authority (*RATP*) began to sponsor cultural events and art exhibits in some subway stops in an effort to cut down on crime and make commuting more enjoyable, entertaining as well. The events have been so popular that so far they've been offered in about 200 of Paris's 368 métro stations.

The different lines are identified by the names of their terminals at either end. Every station has clear directional maps, some with push-button devices that light up the proper route after a destination button is pushed. Keep your ticket (you may need it to leave) and don't cheat; there are spot checks. Those caught in first class with a second class ticket are subject to an immediate fine, except from 6 PM until 9 AM, when anyone is allowed in a first class car.

A 10-ticket book (*carnet*) is available at a reduced rate. The Paris-Visit card, a tourist ticket that entitles the bearer to 1, 3, or 5 consecutive days of unlimited first class travel on the métro and on city-run buses, may be purchased in France upon presentation of your passport at 44 subway stations and 4 regional express stations, or at any of the 6 *French National Railroad* stations. In the US, the card is available by money order from *Marketing Challengers International* (10 E. 21st St., New York, NY 10010; phone: 212-529-8484) — $5 for a 1-day ticket, $15 for a 3-day ticket, and $20 for a 5-day ticket, plus $3 for postage and handling.

SITU – Handy streetside bus and subway directions are now available in some métro stations from *SITU* (*Système d'Information des Trajets Urbains*), a computer that prints out the fastest routing onto a wallet-size piece of paper complete with the estimated length of trip. The *RATP* (the rapid transit authority) service is free and augments the lighted wall maps that guide métro riders. High-traffic spots such as the Châtelet métro station, outside the Gare Montparnasse and on the Boulevard St.-Germain, now sport *SITU* machines, with more on the way.

Taxi – Taxis can be found at stands at main intersections, outside railway stations and official buildings, and in the streets. A taxi is available if the entire "TAXI" sign is illuminated (with a white light); the small light *beside* the roof light signifies availability after dark. But be aware that Parisian cab drivers are notoriously selective about whom they will pick up, and how many passengers they will allow in their cab — a foursome inevitably has trouble. You also can call *Taxi Bleu* (phone: 49-36-10-10) and *Radio Taxi* (phone: 47-39-33-33). The meter starts running from the time the cab is dispatched, and a tip of about 15% is customary. Fares increase at night.

Train – Paris has six main train stations, each one serving a different area of the country. The general information number is 45-82-50-50; for telephone reservations, 45-65-60-60. North: Gare du Nord (18 Rue de Dunkerque; phone: 42-80-63-63); East: Gare de l'Est (Pl. du 11-Novembre; phone: 42-03-96-31); Southeast: Gare de Lyon (20 Bd. Diderot; phone: 40-19-60-00); Southwest: Gare d'Austerlitz (51 Quai d'Austerlitz; phone: 45-84-14-19); West: Gare Montparnasse (17 Bd. de Vaugirard; phone: 40-48-10-00); West and Northwest: Gare St.-Lazare (20 Rue de Rome; phone: 42-85-88-00). The *TGV* (*train à grande vitesse*), the world's fastest train, has cut 2 hours off the usual 4-hour ride between Paris and Lyons; it similarly shortens traveling time to Marseilles, the Côte d'Azur, Switzerland, and the Atlantic Coast. It leaves from the Gare de Lyon, except for the Atlantic Coast run which departs from Gare d'Austerlitz; reservations are necessary.

SPECIAL EVENTS: After the *Christmas* season, Paris prepares for the January fashion shows, when press and buyers come to town to pass judgment on the spring and summer haute couture collections. (The general public can see what the designers have wrought after the professionals leave.) More buyers come to town in February and March for the ready-to-wear shows (fall and winter clothes), open to the trade only. March is the month of the first *Foire à la Ferraille et aux Jambons* of the year. This fair of regional food products held concurrently with an antiques flea market (not items of the best quality, but not junk, either) is repeated in September. The running of the *Prix du Président de la République,* the first big horse race of the year, takes place at *Auteuil* on the last Sunday of the month. From late April to early May is the *Foire de Paris,* the capital's big international trade fair. In mid-May there's the *Paris Marathon;* in late May (through early June), the *French Open Tennis Championships.* Odd years only, the *Paris International Air Show* is an early June attraction at Le Bourget Airport. Horse races crowd the calendar in June — there's not only the *Prix de Diane* at *Chantilly,* but also the *Grande Semaine* at *Longchamp, Auteuil,* and *St.-Cloud.* And in the middle of June, the *Festival du Marais* begins a month's worth of music and dance performances in the courtyards of the Marais district's old townhouses. *Bastille Day,* July 14, is celebrated with music and fireworks, parades, and dancing till dawn in every neighborhood. Meanwhile, the *Tour de France* is under way; the cyclists arrive in Paris for the finish of the 3-week race later in July. Also in July, press and buyers arrive to view the fall and winter haute couture collections, but the ready-to-wear shows (spring and summer clothes) wait until September and October, because August for Parisians is vacation time. Practically the whole country takes a holiday then, and in the capital, the classical concerts of the *Festival Estival* (from mid-July to mid-September) are among the few distractions. When they finish, the *Festival d'Automne,* a celebration of the contemporary in music, dance, and theater, takes over (it goes until December). The *Foire à la Ferraille et aux Jambons* returns in September, but in the even years it's eclipsed by the *Biennale des Antiquaires,* a major antiques event from late September to early October. Also in even years in early October is the *Paris Motor Show.* Every year on the first Sunday of October, the last big horse race of the season, the *Prix de l'Arc de Triomphe,* is run at *Longchamp;* and every year in early October, Paris holds the *Fête des Vendanges à Montmartre* to celebrate the harvest of the city's last remaining vineyard. On November 11, ceremonies at the Arc de Triomphe and a parade mark *Armistice Day.* An *International Cat Show* and a *Horse and Pony Show* come in early December; then comes *Christmas,* which is celebrated most movingly with a *Christmas Eve* midnight mass at Notre-Dame. At midnight a week later, the *New Year* bows in to spontaneous street revelry in the Latin Quarter and along the Champs-Elysées.

MUSEUMS: Many Paris museums (*musées*) are free or offer reduced admission fees on Sundays. "La Carte," a pass that can be used at over 60 museums and monuments in the city, is available at métro stations and at major museums (or in the US from *Marketing Challengers International,* 10 E. 21st St., New York, NY 10010; phone: 212-529-8484). Prices are the equivalent of $10 for a 1-day pass, $20 for a 3-day pass, and $30 for a 5-day pass. Note that "La Carte" is not valid for certain special exhibits. Museums of interest not described in *Special Places* include the following:

Archaeological Crypt of Notre-Dame – Under the square in front of walls and floor plans from later periods. Open daily from 10 AM to 4:30 PM. Parvis de Notre-Dame, 4e (phone: 43-29-83-51).

Catacombs – Dating from the Gallo-Roman era and also containing the remains of Danton, Robespierre, and many others. Bring a flashlight. Closed Mondays. 2 Pl. Denfert-Rochereau, 14e (phone: 43-22-47-63).

Egouts (Sewers of Paris) – Underground city of tunnels, a very popular afternoon tour, daily except Thursdays and Fridays, and on holidays and the days preceding and following them. In front of 93 Quai d'Orsay, 16e (phone: 47-05-10-29).

Maison de Balzac – The house where the writer lived, with a garden leading to one of the prettiest little alleys in Paris. Closed Mondays. 47 Rue Raynouard, 16e (phone: 42-24-56-38).

Manufacture des Gobelins – The famous tapestry factory, in operation since the 15th century. Guided tours of the workshops take place Tuesdays, Wednesdays, and Thursdays from 2:15 to 3:15 PM. 42 Av. des Gobelins, 13e (phone: 43-37-12-60).

Mémorial de la Déportation – Set in a tranquil garden in the shadow of Nôtre Dame at the tip of Ile de la Cité, this monument is dedicated to 200,000 French women and men of all religions and races who died in Nazi concentration camps during World War II. Square de l'Ile de France, 4e.

Mémorial du Martyr Juif Inconnu – A moving tribute to Jews killed during the Holocaust, this 35-year-old memorial includes World War II documents and photographs. Open daily except Saturdays from 10 AM to noon and 2 to 5:30 PM. 17 Rue Geoffroy L'Asniers, 4e (phone: 42-77-44-72). The French Government Tourist Office has published a booklet, *France for the Jewish Traveler,* that describes these two memorials as well as other places of interest to Jews visiting France. See "Tourist Information" in *Sources and Resources,* GETTING READY TO GO, for a list of the offices in the US.

Musée des Antiquités Nationales – Archaeological specimens from prehistoric through Merovingian times, including an impressive Gallo-Roman collection. Open daily, except Tuesdays, from 9 AM to noon and 1:30 to 5:15 PM. Pl. du Château, St.-Germain-en-Laye, 14e (phone: 34-51-53-65).

Musée des Arts Africains et Océaniens – One of the world's finest collections of African and Oceanic art. Closed Tuesdays. 293 Av. Daumesnil, 12e (phone: 43-43-14-54).

Musée des Arts Décoratifs – Furniture and applied arts from the Middle Ages to the present, Oriental carpets, and Dubuffet paintings and drawings. Galerie Art Nouveau–Art Deco features Jeanne Lanvin's bedroom and bath. It now also houses 3 centuries of French posters formerly displayed in the now-closed *Musée de l'Affiche et de la Publicité.* Closed Mondays and Tuesdays. 107 Rue de Rivoli, 1er (phone: 42-60-32-14).

Musée Cernuschi – Art of China. Closed Mondays and holidays. 7 Av. Velásquez, 8e (phone: 42-72-21-13).

Musée Cognacq-Jay – Art, snuffboxes, and watches from the 17th and 18th centuries. Closed Mondays. 25 Bd. des Capucines, 2e (phone: 42-61-94-54).

Musée des Collections Historiques de la Préfecture de Police – On the second floor of the modern police precinct, in the 5th *arrondissement,* are arrest orders (for Charlotte Corday, among others), collections of contemporary engravings, and guillotine blades. Open Mondays through Thursdays from 9 AM to 5 PM and Fridays to 4:30 PM. 1 Bis Rue des Carmes, 5e (phone: 43-29-21-57).

Musée Eugène-Delacroix – Studio and garden of the great painter; exhibits change yearly. Closed Tuesdays. 6 Rue de Furstenberg, 6e (phone: 43-54-04-87).

Musée Grévin – Waxworks of French history from Charlemagne to the present day. 10 Bd. Montmartre, 9e (phone: 47-70-85-05). A branch devoted to La Belle Epoque is in the *Forum des Halles* shopping complex. Open daily. Pl. Carrée, 1er (phone: 40-26-28-50).

Musée Guimet – The *Louvre*'s Far East collection. Closed Tuesdays. 6 Pl. d'Iéna, 16e (phone: 47-23-61-65).

Musée Jacquemart-André – Eighteenth-century French decorative art and European Renaissance treasures, as well as frequent special exhibitions. Closed Mondays and Tuesdays. 158 Bd. Haussmann, 8e (phone: 45-62-39-94).

Musée Marmottan – Superb Monets, though several were stolen in a daring 1985 robbery and have yet to be recovered. Closed Mondays. 2 Rue Louis-Boilly, 16e (phone: 42-24-07-02).

Musée de la Mode et du Costume – A panorama of French contributions to fashion in the elegant Palais Calliéra. Closed Mondays. 10 Av. Pierre-I de Serbie, 16e (phone: 47-20-85-23).

Musée de la Monnaie – More than 2,000 coins and 450 medallions, plus historic coinage machines. Open daily, except Mondays, from 1 to 6 PM. Admission charge. 11 Quai de Conti, 6e (phone: 40-46-56-66).

Musée Gustave-Moreau – A collection of the works of the early symbolist. Closed Tuesdays. 14 Rue de la Rochefoucauld, 9e (phone: 48-74-38-50).

Musée Nissim de Camondo – A former manor house filled with beautiful furnishings and art objects from the 18th century. Closed Mondays, Tuesdays, and holidays. 63 Rue de Monceau, 8e (phone: 45-63-26-32).

Musée de Sèvres – Just outside Paris, next door to the Sèvres factory, is one of the world's finest collections of porcelain. Closed Tuesdays. 4 Grand-Rue, Sèvres (phone: 45-34-99-05).

Musée du Vin – Housed in a 13th-century abbey that was destroyed during the revolution, the museum was restored in 1981. The history and making of wine is traced through displays, artifacts, and a series of wax figure tableaux. Open daily, except Mondays, from noon to 6 PM; Saturdays and Sundays to 5:30 PM. Admission charge includes a glass of wine. 5-7 Sq. Charles-Dickens, 16e (phone: 45-25-63-26).

Parc Océanique Cousteau – Based on the work of the French oceanographer, this museum houses ocean exhibits and interactive displays. Open Mondays, Tuesdays, and Thursdays from noon to 7 PM; Wednesdays, Saturdays, Sundays, and holidays from 10 AM to 7:30 PM. Admission charge. Forum des Halles, Pl. Carrée, 1er (phone: 40-26-13-78).

Pavillon des Arts – An exhibition space in the mushroom-shaped buildings overlooking the *Forum des Halles* complex. Presentations range from ancient to modern, paintings to sculpture. Closed Mondays and holidays. 101 Rue Rambuteau, 1er (phone: 42-33-82-50).

 GALLERIES: Few artists live in Montparnasse nowadays, as the center of the Paris art scene has shifted from the narrow streets of the Quartier Latin, which set the pace in the 1950s, to the Right Bank around the *Centre Georges Pompidou*. Here are some galleries of note:

Artcurial – Early moderns, such as Braque and Sonia Delaunay, as well as sculpture and prints, with a fine art bookshop. 9 Av. Matignon, 8e (phone: 42-99-16-16).

Beaubourg – Well-known names in the Paris art scene, including Niki de Saint-Phalle, César, Tinguely, Klossowski. 23 Rue du Renard, 4e (phone: 48-04-34-40).

Claude Bernard – Francis Bacon, David Hockney, and Raymond Mason are among the artists exhibited here. 5 Rue des Beaux-Arts, 6e (phone: 43-26-97-07).

Isy Brachot – Master surrealists, American hyper-realists, and new realists. 35 Rue Guénégaud, 6e (phone: 43-54-22-40).

Caroline Corre – Exhibitions by contemporary artists, specializing in unique artists' books. 14 Rue Guénégaud, 6e (phone: 43-54-57-67).

Agathe Gaillard – Contemporary photography, including Cartier-Bresson and the like. 3 Rue du Pont-Louis-Philippe, 4e (phone: 42-77-38-24).

Maeght-Lelong – The great moderns on display include Chagall, Tapies, Bacon, Moore, Miró. 13-14 Rue de Téhéran, 8e (phone: 45-63-13-19).

Daniel Malingue – Works by the Impressionists as well as notable Parisian artists from the 1930s to the 1950s — Foujita, Fautrier, and so forth. 26 Av. Matignon, 8e (phone: 42-66-60-33).

Nikki Diana Marquardt – Spacious gallery of contemporary work opened by an enterprising dealer from the Bronx. 9 Pl. des Vosges, 4e (phone: 42-78-21-00).

Hervé Odermatt Cazeau – Early moderns — among them Picasso, Léger, Pissarro — and antiques. 85 bis Rue du Faubourg-St.-Honoré, 8e (phone: 42-66-92-58).

Darthea Speyer – Run by a former American embassy attaché, now an art dealer. Contemporary painting. 6 Rue Jacques-Callot, 6e (phone: 43-54-78-41).

Virginia Zabriskie – Early and contemporary photography by Atget, Brassaï, Diane Arbus. Also painting and, occasionally, sculpture. 37 Rue Quincampoix, 4e (phone: 42-72-35-47).

SHOPPING: From new wave fashions to classic haute couture, Paris starts the trends and sets the styles the world copies. Prices are generally high, but more than a few people are willing to pay for the quality of the products, not to mention the cachet of a Paris label, which enhances the appeal of many things besides clothing. Perfume, cosmetics, jewelry, leather goods and accessories, wine and liqueurs, porcelain, and art are among the many other things for which Paris is famous.

The big department stores are excellent places to get an idea of what's available. They include *Galeries Lafayette* (40 Bd. Haussmann, 9e; phone: 42-82-34-56; and other locations); *Au Printemps* (64 Bd. Haussmann, 9e; phone: 45-22-66-59); *Aux Trois-Quartiers* (17 Bd. de la Madeleine, 1er; phone: 42-60-39-30); *La Samaritaine* (19 Rue de la Monnaie, 1er; phone: 40-41-20-20); *Le Bazar de l'Hôtel de Ville* (52 Rue de Rivoli, 4e; phone: 42-74-90-00); and *Au Bon Marché* (22 Rue de Sèvres, 7e; phone: 45-49-21-22). Two major shopping centers — *Porte Maillot,* Pl. de la Porte Maillot, and *Maine Montparnasse,* at the intersection of Bd. Montparnasse and Rue de Rennes — also are worth a visit.

There are several shopping neighborhoods, and they tend to be specialized. Haute couture can be found in the streets around the Champs-Elysées: Av. George-V, Av. Montaigne, Rue François-I, and Rue du Faubourg-St.-Honoré; famous designers are also represented in department stores. Boutiques are especially numerous on Av. Victor-Hugo, Rue de Passy, Bd. des Capucines, in the St.-Germain-des-Prés area, in the neighborhood of the *Opéra,* in the *Forum des Halles* shopping center, and around the Place des Victoires. The Rue d'Alésia has several blocks devoted solely to discount shops.

The Rue de Paradis is lined with crystal and china shops, and St.-Germain-des-Prés has more than its share of art galleries. The best and most expensive antiques dealers are along the Faubourg-St.-Honoré on the Right Bank. On the Left Bank there's Le Carré Rive Gauche, an association of more than 100 antiques shops in the area bordered by Quai Voltaire, Rue de l'Université, Rue des Sts.-Pères, and Rue du Bac. Antiques and curio collectors should explore Paris's several flea markets, which include the *Marché d'Aligre,* at the Place d'Aligre; *Montreuil,* near the Porte de Montreuil; *Vanves,* near the Porte de Vanves; and the largest and best known, *Puces de St.-Ouen,* near the Porte de Clignancourt.

A few more tips: Sales take place during the first weeks in January and in late June and July. Any shop labeled *dégriffé* (the word means, literally, without the label) offers discounts on brand name clothing, often last season's styles. Discount shops also are known as "stock" shops. The French value-added tax (VAT; typically 18.6% and as high as 33.33% on luxury articles) can be refunded on most purchases made by foreigners provided a minimum of 1,200F (about $211) is spent in one store. Forms must be filled out and the refund usually is mailed to your home. Large department stores and the so-called duty-free shops have facilitated the procedure, but refunds can be obtained from any store willing to cooperate. If the refund is not exactly equal to the tax — 15% to 25% refunds are common — it's because stores may retain some of it as reimbursement for their extra expense in handling the paperwork.

Here is a sampling of the wealth of shops in Paris, many of which have more than one location in the city:

Agnès B – Supremely wearable, trendy, casual clothes. 3 and 6 Rue du Jour, 1er (phone: 40-26-36-87 or 45-08-56-56); 13 Rue Michelet, 6e (phone: 46-33-70-20); 25 Av. Pierre-I-de-Serbie, 16e (phone: 47-20-22-44); and 81 Rue d' Assas, 6e (phone: 43-54-69-21). The latter store is for children only.

Azzedine Alaïa – The Tunisian designer who brought the body back. 17 Rue du Parc-Royal, 3e (phone: 42-72-19-19).

Arnys – Conservative and elegant men's clothing. 14 Rue de Sèvres, 6e (phone: 45-48-76-99).

Laura Ashley – The English designer's familiar Victorian styles. 94 Rue des Rennes, 6e (phone: 42-22-77-80); and 261 Rue St.-Honoré, 1er (phone: 42-86-84-13).

Baccarat – High-quality porcelain and crystal. 30 bis Rue du Paradis, 10e (phone: 40-22-11-00 or 47-70-64-30).

La Bagagerie – Perhaps the best bag and belt boutique in the world. 41 Rue du Four, 6e (phone: 45-48-85-88), and other locations.

Au Bain Marie – The most beautiful kitchenware and tabletop accessories. 10 Rue Boissy-d'Anglas, 8e (phone: 42-66-59-74).

Pierre Balmain – Couturier boutique for women's fashions. 44 Rue François-I, 8e (phone: 47-20-35-34), and other locations.

Beauté Divine – Antique perfume bottles, Art Deco bathroom accessories, glove stretchers, nail buffers, and mustache cups. 40 Rue St.-Sulpice, 6e (phone: 43-26-25-31).

Dorothée Bis – Definitely a trendsetter in women's wear. 33 Rue de Sèvres, 6e (phone: 42-22-00-45).

Brentano's – British and American novels, critiques on the American arts, and a variety of books on technical and business subjects — in English. 37 Av. de l'Opéra, 2e (phone: 42-61-52-50).

Cacharel – Fashionable ready-to-wear in great prints. 34 Rue Tronchet, 8e (phone: 47-42-12-61), and other locations.

Cadolle – Founded in 1889 by the woman credited with inventing the brassiere, it still sells corsets as well as other items of frilly, pretty lingerie. 14 Rue Cambon, 1er (phone: 42-60-94-94).

Pierre Cardin – A famous designer's own boutique. 83 Rue du Faubourg-St.-Honoré, 8e (phone: 42-66-62-94); 27 Av. Victor-Hugo, 16e (phone: 45-01-88-13); and other locations.

Carel – Beautiful shoes. 12 Rond-Point des Champs-Elysées, 8e (phone: 45-62-30-62), and other locations.

Carita – Paris's most extensive — and friendliest — beauty/hair salon. 11 Rue Faubourg-St.-Honoré, 8e (phone: 42-68-13-40).

Cartier – Fabulous jewelry. 11-13 Rue de la Paix, 2e (phone: 42-61-58-56), and other locations.

Castorama – One of 86 stores throughout France, this department store sells 45,000 European-designed housewares — from flower pots to home security systems. 1-3 Rue Caulaincourt, 18e (phone: 45-22-07-11).

Céline – A popular women's boutique for clothing and accessories. 24 Rue François-I, 8e (phone: 47-20-22-83).

Cerruti – For women's clothing, 15 Pl. de la Madeleine, 8e (phone: 47-42-10-72); for men's, 27 Rue Royale, 8e (phone: 42-65-68-72).

Chanel – Classic women's fashions, inspired by the late, legendary Coco Chanel, now executed by Karl Lagerfeld. 42 Av. Montaigne, 8e (phone: 47-20-84-45), and 29-31 Rue Cambon, 1er (phone: 42-86-28-00).

Charley – Excellent selection of lingerie at fairly low prices. 14 Rue du Faubourg-St.-Honoré, 8e (phone: 47-42-17-70).

Charvet – Paris's answer to Savile Row. An all-in-one men's shop, where shirts are the house specialty — they stock more than 4,000. Ties, too. 28 Pl. Vendôme, 1er (phone: 42-60-30-70).

Chaumet – Crownmakers for most of Europe's royalty. Expensive jewels, including antique watches covered with semi-precious stones. 12 Pl. Vendôme, 1er (phone: 42-60-32-82).

Chloé – Designs for women. 3 Rue de Gribeauval and 60 Rue du Faubourg-St.-Honoré, 8e (phone: 45-44-02-04).

Christofle – The internationally famous silversmith. 12 Rue Royale, 8e (phone: 42-60-34-07).

Commes des Garçons – Asymmetrical-style clothing for *des filles* and *des garçons.* 40-42 Pl. des Victoires, 1er (phone: 42-33-05-21).

Courrèges – Another bastion of haute couture, with its own boutique. 40 Rue François-I, 8e, and 46 Rue du Faubourg-St.-Honoré, 8e (phone: 47-23-00-73).

E. Dehillerin – An enormous selection of professional cookware. 18-20 Rue Coquillière, 1er (phone: 42-36-53-13).

Destination Paris – Glittering selection of knickknacks, hand-painted T-shirts, scarves, picture frames, and souvenirs. 9 Rue du 29 Juillet, 1er (phone: 49-27-98-90).

Christian Dior – One of the most famous couture names in the world. 28-30 Av. Montaigne, 8e; Miss Dior and Baby Dior for children also are at this location (phone: 40-73-54-44).

Hôtel Drouot – Paris's huge auction house operates daily except Sundays. Good buys. 9 Rue Drouot, 9e (phone: 48-00-20-20).

Les Drugstores Publicis – A uniquely French version of the American drugstore, with an amazing variety of goods — perfume, books, records, foreign newspapers, magazines, film, cigarettes, food, and more, all wildly overpriced. 149 Bd. St.-Germain, 6e (phone: 42-22-92-50); 133 Av. des Champs-Elysées, 8e (phone: 47-23-54-34); and 1 Av. Matignon, 8e (phone: 43-59-38-70).

Erès – Avant-garde sportswear for men and women. 2 Rue Tronchet, 8e (phone: 47-42-24-55).

Fabrice – Trendy, fine costume jewelry. 33 and 54 Rue Bonaparte, 6e (phone: 43-26-57-95).

Fauchon – *The* place to buy fine food and wine of every variety, from *oeufs en gêlée* to condiments and candy. 26 Pl. de la Madeleine, 8e (phone: 47-42-60-11).

Louis Féraud – Couturier fashions for women at 88 Rue du Faubourg-St.-Honoré, and men at No. 62, 8e (phone: 47-42-18-12); and other locations.

Fouquet – Beautiful displays of chocolates, fresh fruit candies, herbs, condiments, and jams. 22 Rue François-I, 8e (phone: 47-23-30-46), and other locations.

France Faver – Top-quality beautiful and comfortable shoes for women. 79 Rue des Sts.-Pères, 6e (phone: 42-22-04-29).

Fratelli Rossetti – All kinds of shoes, made from buttery-soft leather, for men and women. 54 Rue du Faubourg-St.-Honoré, 8e (phone: 42-65-26-60).

Freddy – A popular shop for gifts, perfume, gloves, ties, scarves, and other items at good prices. 10 Rue Auber, 9e (phone: 47-42-63-41).

Maud Frizon – Sophisticated, imaginative shoes and handbags. 79-83 Rue des Sts.-Pères, 6e (phone: 42-22-06-93 or 42-22-19-86).

Galignani – Books in English and French, run by the same family since the beginning of the 19th century. 224 Rue de Rivoli, 1er (phone: 42-60-76-07).

La Gaminerie – Reasonably priced, good sportswear; outstanding window displays. 137 Bd. St.-Germain, 6e (phone: 42-36-19-99).

Monique Germain – Unique hand-painted silk clothing at affordable prices: cocktail dresses, bridal wear, padded patchwork jackets. 59 Bd. Raspail, 6e (phone: 45-48-22-63).

Givenchy – Beautifully tailored clothing by the master couturier. 3 Av. George-V, 8e (phone: 47-23-81-36); *Nouvelle Boutique*, 66 Av. Victor-Hugo, 16e; and *Givenchy Gentleman*, 29 Av. George-V, 8e.

Guerlain – For fine perfume and cosmetics. 2 Pl. Vendôme, 1er; 68 Champs-Elysées, 8e (phone: 45-59-96-30); 29 Rue de Sèvres, 6e; and 93 Rue de Passy, 16e.

Daniel Hechter – Sportswear and casual clothing for men and women. 146 Bd. St.-Germain, 6e (phone: 43-26-96-36); 12 Rue du Faubourg-St.-Honoré, 8e; and other locations.

Hédiard – Pricey but choice food shop, notable for its assortment of coffees and teas. Chic tearoom upstairs. 21 Pl. de la Madeleine, 8e (phone: 42-66-44-36).

Hermès – For the very best ties, scarves, handbags, shoes, saddles, and accessories, though the prices may send you into cardiac arrest. 24 Rue du Faubourg-St.-Honoré, 8e (phone: 40-17-47-17).

IGN (French National Geographic Institute) – All manner of maps — ancient and modern, foreign and domestic, esoteric and mundane — are sold here. 136 bis Rue Grennelle, 7e (phone: 45-50-34-95); 107 Rue La Boétie, 8e.

Charles Jourdan – Sleek, high-fashion shoes. 5 Bd. de la Madeleine, 1er (phone: 42-61-50-07), is one of many outlets.

Kenzo – Avant-garde fashions by the Japanese designer. 3 Pl. des Victoires, 1er (phone: 40-39-72-02).

Lachaume – Stem for stem, the most beautiful flower shop in Paris. Buy a bouquet for an *ami(e)* or for *vous-même*. 10 Rue Royale, 8e (phone: 42-60-57-26).

Christian LaCroix – The first major new fashion house to open in Paris in 2 decades. Offers the "hautest" of haute couture. 73 Rue Faubourg-St.-Honoré, 8e (phone: 42-65-79-08).

Lalique – The famous crystal. 11 Rue Royale, 8e (phone: 42-65-33-70).

Lancôme – Cosmetics. 29 Rue du Faubourg-St.-Honoré, 8e (phone: 42-65-30-74).

Lanvin – Another fabulous designer, with several spacious, colorful boutiques under one roof. 15, 17, and 22 Rue du Faubourg-St.-Honoré, 8e; 2 Rue Cambon, 1er (phone: 42-60-38-83).

Ted Lapidus – A compromise between haute couture and excellent ready-to-wear. 23 Rue du Faubourg-St.-Honoré, 8e (phone: 44-60-89-91); 35 Rue François-I, 8e (phone: 47-20-56-14); and other locations.

Guy Laroche – Classic and conservative couture. 30 Rue du Faubourg-St.-Honoré, 8e (phone: 42-65-62-74), and 29 Av. Montaigne, 8e.

Marché aux Puces – Paris's famous *Flea Market,* with 3,000 dealers in antiques and secondhand items. Open Saturdays, Sundays, and Mondays. Bargaining is a must. Porte de Clignancourt, 18e.

Missoni – Innovative, original Italian knitwear. 43 Rue du Bac, 7e (phone: 45-48-38-02).

Issey Miyake – "In" shop, selling women's clothing made by the Japanese artist-designer. 201 Bd. St.-Germain, 7e (phone: 45-44-60-88).

Morabito – Magnificent handbags and luggage at steep prices. 1 Pl. Vendôme, 1er (phone: 42-60-30-76).

Hanae Mori – The grande dame of Japanese designers in Paris. 17 Av. Montaigne, 8e (phone: 47-23-52-03); 9 Rue Faubourg-St.-Honoré, 8e.

Le Must de Cartier – Actually two boutiques, on either side of the *Ritz* hotel, offering such Cartier items as lighters and watches at prices that, though not low, are almost bearable when you deduct the 25% VAT tax. 7 23 Pl. Vendôme, 1er (phone: 42-61-55-55).

Au Nain Bleu – The city's greatest toy store. 408 Rue St.-Honoré, 8e (phone: 42-60-30-01).

Marie Papier – Handsome marbled stationery and writing accessories. 26 Rue Vavin, 6e (phone: 43-26-46-44).

Au Petit Matelot – Classic sportswear and accessories for men, women, and children. Especially terrific are their Tyrolean-style olive or navy loden coats. 27 Av. de la Grande-Armée, 16e.

Le Petit Faune – A marvelous place to buy children's things. 33 Rue Jacob, 6e (phone: 42-60-80-72), and other locations.

Pixi & Cie – Terrific collection of dolls, toy soldiers, and antique windup cars. 95 Rue de Seine, 6e.

Porthault – Terribly expensive, but elegantly exquisite bed and table linen. 18 Av. Montaigne, 8e (phone: 47-20-75-25).

Puiforcat – Art Deco tableware in a beautiful setting. 22 Rue François-I, 8e (phone: 47-20-74-27).

Raymond – Charming and fairly inexpensive Porcelaine de Paris items. 100 Rue du Faubourg-St.-Honoré, 1er (phone: 42-66-69-49).

Nina Ricci – Women's fashions, as well as the famous perfume. 17 Rue François-I, 8e (phone: 47-23-78-88), and 39 Av. Montaigne, 8e (phone: 47-23-78-88).

Sonia Rykiel – Stunning sportswear and knits. 6 Rue de Grenelle, 6e (phone: 42-22-43-22).

Yves Saint Laurent – The world-renowned designer, considered one of the most famous names in high fashion. 38 Rue du Faubourg-St.-Honoré, 8e; 5 Av. Marceau, 8e (phone: 47-23-72-71); and other locations.

Jean-Louis Scherrer – A top designer, whose clothes are favored by the Parisian chic. 51-53 Av. Montaigne, 8e (phone: 45-59-55-39).

Shakespeare and Company – This legendary English-language bookstore, opposite Notre-Dame, is something of a tourist attraction in itself. 37 Rue de la Bûcherie, 5e (no phone).

W. H. Smith and Sons – The largest (and best) Parisian bookstore for reading material in English. It sells the Sunday *New York Times,* in addition to many British and American magazines and books. 248 Rue de Rivoli, 1er (phone: 42-60-37-97).

Souleiado – Vibrant, traditional Provençal fabrics made into scarves, shawls, totes, and tableware. 78 Rue de Seine, 6e (phone: 43-54-62-25), and *Forum des Halles,* Pl. Carrée, 1er.

Per Spook – One of Paris's best young designers. 18 Av. George-V, 8e (phone: 47-23-00-19), and elsewhere.

Chantal Thomass – Ultra-feminine fashions, 5 Rue du Vieux-Colombier, 6e (phone: 45-44-60-11); sexy lingerie, 11 Rue Madame, 6e (phone: 45-49-41-29), and other locations.

Vicky Tiel – Strapless evening gowns decorated with beads and bows, as well as contemporary sweaters and baseball-style jackets. 21 Rue Bonaparte, 6e.

Torrente – Women's fashions. 9 Rue du Faubourg-St.-Honoré, 8e; 60 Av. Montaigne, 8e (phone: 42-56-14-14).

Emmanuel Ungaro – Couturier boutique for women. 2 Av. Montaigne, 8e (phone: 47-23-61-94).

Upla – Sporty handbags, scarves, and casual clothing. 17 Rue des Halles, 1er (phone: 40-26-49-96).

Van Cleef & Arpels – One of the world's great jewelers. 22 Pl. Vendôme, 1er (phone: 42-61-58-58).

Victoire – Ready-to-wear, with attractive accessories. 12 Pl. des Victoires, 2e (phone: 45-08-53-29), and other locations.

Louis Vuitton – High-quality luggage and handbags. 78 bis Av. Marceau, 8e (phone: 47-20-47-00), and 54 Av. Montaigne, 8e (phone: 45-62-47-00).

BEST DISCOUNT SHOPS

If you're one of those — like us — who believes that the eighth deadly sin is buying retail, you'll treasure these inexpensive outlets.

Bab's – High fashion at low — or at least reasonable — prices. 29 Av. Marceau, 16e (phone: 47-20-84-74), and 89 bis Av. des Ternes, 17e.

Dorothée Bis Stock – Ms. Bis's well-known designs at about 40% off. 74 Rue d'Alésia, 14e (phone: 45-42-17-11).

Boétie 104 – Good buys on men's and women's shoes. 104 Rue La Boétie, 8e (phone: 43-59-72-38).

Boutique Stock – A vast selection of big-name knits at less than wholesale. 26, 30, 51, and 5 bis Rue St.-Placide, 6e (phone: 45-48-83-66), and other locations.

Cacharel Stock – Surprisingly current Cacharel fashions at about a 40% discount. 114 Rue d'Alésia, 14e (phone: 45-42-53-04).

Pierre Cardin Stock – Terrific buys on the famed designer's men's clothing. 77 Rue Faubourg-St.-Honoré, 1er (phone: 40-26-74-73).

Catherine – One of the most hospitable of the perfume and cosmetics shops. A 40% discount (including VAT) is given on purchases totaling 1,200F (about $211) or more. 6 Rue Castiglione, 1er (phone: 42-60-81-49).

Club des 10 – Christian Dior, Courrèges, and Louis Féraud clothing at discount prices. 58 Rue du Faubourg-St.-Honoré, 1er.

Drôles des Choses pour Drôles de Gens – Half-price clothes by Marithé and François Girbaud. 14 Rue des Colonnes-du-Trône, 12e (phone: 43-45-66-77).

Halle Bys – Haute couture as well as casual togs. 60 Rue Richelieu, 2e (phone: 42-96-65-92).

Emmanuelle Khanh – The designer's clothes at a substantial discount. 6 Rue Pierre-Lescot, 1er (no phone).

Lady Soldes – Prime fashion labels at less than normal prices. 221 Rue du Faubourg-St.-Honoré, 8e (phone: 45-61-09-14).

Lanvin Soldes Trois – Lanvin fashions at about half their normal retail cost. 3 Rue de Vienne, 8e (no phone).

Anna Lowe – Saint Laurent's styling, among others, at a discount. 35 Av. Matignon, 8e (phone: 45-63-45-57).

Mendès – Less than wholesale prices on haute couture, especially Saint Laurent and Lanvin. 65 Rue Montmartre, 2e (phone: 45-08-52-62 or 42-36-83-32).

Miss Griffes – The very best of haute couture in small sizes (up to size 10) at small prices. Alterations. 19 Rue de Penthièvre, 8e (phone: 42-65-10-00).

Mod Soldes – Names like Laroche and Lapidus at sale prices. 20 Rue Petit Champs, 1er (phone: 42-97-47-45).

Le Mouton à Cinq Pattes – Ready-to-wear clothing for men, women, and children at 50% off original prices. 6, 8, and 10 Rue St.-Placide, 6e (phone: 45-48-86-26).

Reciproque – Billed as the largest *"depot-vent"* in Paris, this outlet features names like Chanel, Alaia, Lanvin, and Scherrer. Several hundred square yards of display area are arranged by designer and by size. 95 Rue de la Pompe, 16e (phone: 47-04-82-24); men's clothing and accessories next door at No. 101.

Jean-Louis Scherrer – Haute couture labels by Scherrer and others at about half their original prices. 29 Av. Ledru-Rollin, 12e (phone: 46-28-39-72).

Stéphane – Men's designer suits by Pierre Balmain, Ted Lapidus, and André Courrèges at 25% to 45% discount. 130 Bd. St.-Germain, 6e (phone: 46-33-94-55).

Stock Coupons – Features discounted Daniel Hechter for men, women, and children. 92 Rue d'Alésia, 14e (phone: 45-42-82-66).

Stock Griffes – Women's ready-to-wear apparel at 40% off their original prices. 17 Rue Vielle du Temple, 4e (phone: 48-04-82-34).

Stock System – Prêt-à-porter clothing for men and women at a 30% discount. 112 Rue d'Alésia, 14e (phone: 45-43-80-86).

Michel Swiss – Huge selection of perfume, cheerful service, and discounts of almost 44% to American visitors who pay with cash or traveler's checks, and who buy more than 800 frances ($140) of scents. 16 Rue de la Paix, 2e (phone: 42-61-71-71).

Also, Rue du Paradis (10e) is the best area to shop for crystal and porcelain — Baccarat, Saint-Louis, Haviland, Bernardaud, and Villery & Boch — at amazing prices. Try *Cristalerie de Paris* at No. 10, *Boutique Paradis*, 1 bis, *L'Art et La Table*, 3, *Limoges-Unio*, Nos. 8 and 12, *Porcelain Savary*, 9, *Arts Céramiques*, 15, and *Cristallerie Paradis*, at No. 17.

■ ***Note***: For a modest price ($5 to $40), you can also take home a bit of the *Louvre*. The museum's 200-year-old Department of Calcography houses a collection of 16,000 engraved copper plates — renderings of monuments, battles, coronations, Egyptian pyramids, and portraits — dating from the 17th century. Prints made from these engravings come reproduced on thick vellum, embossed with the *Louvre*'s imprint. The Calcography Department (open daily, except Tuesdays, from 2 to 5 PM), is 1 flight up from the Porte Barbet de Jouy entrance on the Seine side of the *Louvre*.

 SPORTS AND FITNESS: Biking – Rentals are available in the Bois de Boulogne and the Bois de Vincennes, or contact the *Fédération Française de Cyclo-tourisme* (8 Rue Jean-Marie-Jégo, 13e; phone: 45-80-30-21); *Bicyclub* (8 Pl. de la Porte Champerret, 17e; phone: 47-66-55-92); or *Paris-Vélo* (2 Rue du Fer à Moulin, 5e; phone: 43-37-59-22). In addition to renting bicycles, *Paris by Cycle* (99 Rue la Jonquière; phone: 42-63-36-63) arranges guided group tours of the city, Versailles, and bike trips alternating with horseback rides. The world-famous *Tour de France* bicycle race takes place in July and ends in Paris.

Fitness Centers – The *Garden Gym* (65 Av. des Champs-Elysées, 8e; phone: 42-25-87-20; and 123 Av. Charles-de-Gaulle, Neuilly; phone: 47-47-62-62) is open daily to non-members for a fee.

Golf – For general information, contact the *Fédération Française du Golf* (69 Av. Victor-Hugo, 16e; phone: 45-02-13-55). It usually is possible to play on any course during the week by simply paying a greens fee. Weekends may be more difficult. *Ozoir-la-Ferrière* (Château des Agneaux, 15 miles — 24 km — away; phone: 60-28-20-79) welcomes Americans (closed Tuesdays); and *St.-Germain-en-Laye* (12½ miles — 19 km — away; phone: 34-51-75-90) accepts non-members on weekdays only. The *Racing Club de France* (La Boulie, Versailles; phone: 39-50-59-41) and *St.-Nom-la-Bretèche* (in the suburb of the same name; phone: 34-62-54-00) accept only guests of members. It's best to call at least 2 days in advance to schedule a time.

Horse Racing – Of the eight tracks in and around Paris, two major ones are in the Bois de Boulogne: *Longchamp* (phone: 42-24-13-29) for flat races and *Auteuil* (phone: 45-27-12-25) for steeplechase. *St.-Cloud* (phone: 43-59-20-70), a few miles west of Paris, and *Chantilly* (phone: 42-66-92-02), about 25 miles (40 km) north of the city, are both for flat racing. *Vincennes* (Bois de Vincennes; phone: 47-42-07-70) is the trotting track. Important races take place from spring through fall, but the *Grande Semaine* (Big Week) comes in late June, when nine major races — beginning with the *Grand Steeplechase de Paris* at *Auteuil* and including the *Grand Prix de Paris* at *Longchamp* — are scheduled.

Jogging – The streets and sidewalks of Paris may be ideal for lovers, but they're not meant for runners. There are, however, a number of places where you can jog happily; one of the most pleasant is the 2,500-acre Bois de Boulogne. Four more central parks are the Jardin du Luxembourg (reachable by métro: Luxembourg), the Champ-de-Mars gardens (just behind the Eiffel Tower; métro: Iéna), Parc Monceau (métro: Monceau), and the Jardin des Tuileries (métro: Tuileries, Louvre, or Concorde).

Soccer – There are matches from early August to mid-June at Parc des Princes (Av. du Parc-des-Princes, 16e; phone: 42-88-02-76).

Swimming – At the heart of Paris, rather unsuitably near the National Assembly, lies the *Piscine Deligny,* notorious in the summer for its acres of topless women bathers and, on the third-floor deck, nude sunbathers of both sexes. The pool is set in a floating barge on the Seine beside the Concorde bridge; it is, says the sign, filled with fresh water. Open May to September. 25 Quai Anatole-France, 7e (phone: 45-51-72-15). Other pools include *Piscine des Halles* (10 Pl. de la Rotonde, 4e; phone: 42-36-98-44), *Pontoise* (19 Rue de Pontoise, 5e; phone: 43-54-06-23), *Butte-aux-Cailles* (5 Pl. Paul-Verlaine, 13e; phone: 45-89-60-05), *Keller* (14 Rue de l'Ingénieur-Robert-Keller, 15e; phone: 45-77-12-12), *Jean-Taris* (16 Rue Thouin, 5e; phone: 43-25-54-03), *Tour Montparnasse* (beneath the tower at 66 Bd. de Montparnasse, 15e; phone: 45-38-65-19), and *Neuilly* (50 Rue Pauline-Borghèse, Neuilly; phone: 47-22-69-59).

Tennis – For general information, call *Ligue Régionale de Paris* (74 Rue de Rome, 17e; phone: 45-22-22-08), or the *Fédération Française de Tennis* (*Roland Garros Stadium,* 16e; phone: 47-43-48-00). Americans who wish to attend the annual *French Open Tennis Tournament* may write in advance to the *Fédération Française de Tennis Billetterie* (2 Av. Gordon-Bennet, Paris 75016; phone: 47-43-48-00).

 THEATER: The most complete listings of theaters, operas, concerts, and movies are found in the *Officiel des Spectacles* and *Une Semaine à Paris–Pariscope* (see *Tourist Information,* above). The season generally is from September to June. Tickets are less expensive than in New York and are obtained at each box office, through brokers (*American Express* and *Thomas Cook* act in that capacity and are good), via your hotel's trusty concierge, or with the high-tech Billetels at the *Galeries Lafayette,* the *Centre Georges Pompidou,* and other locations. Insert a credit card into a slot in the Billetel and choose an event from among over 100 upcoming theater events and concert performances. The device will spew out a display of dates, seats, and prices, from which you can order your tickets — they will be printed on the spot and charged to your account. Half-price, day-of-performance theater tickets are available at the kiosks at the Châtelet-les Halles, 1er (Tuesdays through Saturdays from 12:45 to 7 PM), and at 15 Place de la Madeleine, 8e (Tuesdays through Saturdays from 12:30 to 8 PM, Sundays from 12:30 to 4 PM). The curtain usually goes up at 8:30 PM.

For those who speak French: Performances of classical plays by Molière, Racine, and Corneille take place at the *Comédie-Française* (Pl. du Théâtre, 1er; phone: 40-15-00-15). Two other national theaters are *Théâtre de L'Odéon* (1 Pl. Paul-Claudel, 6e; phone: 43-25-70-32) and *Théâtre National de Chaillot* (Pl. du Trocadéro, 16e; phone: 47-27-81-15). Last, but not least, the *Théâtre du Soleil,* in an old cartridge factory, La Cartoucherie de Vincennes (on the outskirts of Paris in the Bois de Vincennes, 12e; phone: 43-74-24-08), offers colorful productions ranging from contemporary political works to Shakespeare.

It's not really necessary to speak the language to enjoy the opera, dance, or musical comedy at *L'Opéra* (Pl. de l'Opéra, 9e; phone: 40-17-33-33 or 40-17-34-10), the new *L'Opéra Bastille* (120 Rue de Lyon in the Place de la Bastille, 11e; phone: 40-01-17-89), *Salle Favart–Opéra Comique* (5 Rue Favart, 2e; phone: 42-96-12-20), or *Théâtre Musi-*

cal de Paris (1 Pl. du Châtelet, 1er; phone: 40-28-28-40). Theater tickets can be reserved through *SOS-Théâtre* (73 Champs-Elysées, 8e; phone: 42-25-67-07).

For those who consider French their second language, Paris's many café-theaters offer amusing songs, sketches, satires, and takeoffs on topical trends and events. Among them are *Café de la Gare* (41 Rue du Temple, 4e; phone: 42-78-52-51) and *Café d'Edgar* (58 Bd. Edgar-Quinet, 14e; phone: 43-22-11-02).

 CINEMA: With no less than 200 movie houses, Paris is a real treat for film buffs. No other metropolis offers such a cinematographic feast — current French chic, recent imports from across the Atlantic, grainy 1930s classics, and the latest and most select of Third World and Eastern European offerings. In any given week, there are up to 200 different movies shown, generally in their original versions with French subtitles.

Film distribution is erratic, to say the least, so the French often get their *Batman* and *Ghostbusters* flicks up to 6 months late. But the system works both ways: Many of the front-runners at Cannes first hit the screens here, which gives you a jump on friends back home.

Both *Pariscope* and the *Officiel de Spectacles,* which come out on Wednesday, the day the programs change, contain the full selection each week. *Pariscope* has thought of almost every possible way to classify films, sorting them into new releases and revivals, broad categories (for instance, the *drame psychologique* label means it will be heavier than a *comédie dramatique*), location by *arrondissement,* late-night showings, and so on.

Films shown with their original-language sound tracks are called VO (*version originale*); it's worth watching out for that crucial "VO" tag, or you may find yourself wincing at a French-dubbed version, called VF (*version française*). Broadly speaking, the undubbed variety of film flourishes on the Champs-Elysées and on the Left Bank, and it's also a safe bet to avoid the mostly French-patronized houses of les Grands Boulevards.

The timetables aren't always reliable, so it's worth checking by telephone — if you can decipher the recorded messages that spell out exactly when the five or so showings a day begin. A *séance* (sitting) generally begins with advertisements (often imaginatively made by out-of-work French film directors), and the movie proper begins up to 20 minutes later.

There's more room in the big movie houses on the Champs-Elysées, but the cozier Latin Quarter establishments tend to specialize in the unusual and avant-garde — often the only showing such films will ever get. For the ultimate in high tech, the *Géode* offers a B-Max hemispherical screen, cupped inside a reflecting geodesic dome, at La Villette Sciences and Industry complex. The program is, however, limited to a single scientifically oriented film at any given time, whereas the *Forum Horizon,* in the underground section of the *Forum des Halles,* offers a choice of four first-run movies and claims to have one of the city's best sound systems. Some more out-of-the-way venues like the *Olympique Entrepôt* and the *Lucernaire* in Montparnasse are social centers in themselves, incorporating restaurants and/or other theaters.

Paris's cinemathèque — at the Palais de Chaillot — runs a packed schedule of reruns at rates lower than those of the commercial cinemas. The *Videothèque de Paris,* in the *Forum des Halles,* was the world's first public video library. Visitors can select individual showings or attend regularly scheduled theater screenings of films and television programs chronicling Paris's history (phone: 40-26-34-30).

Then there are two period pieces almost worth a visit in themselves. *Le Ranelagh* (5 Rue des Vignes, 16e; phone: 42-88-64-44) has an exquisite 19th-century interior where films are screened and live theater performed. *La Pagode* (57 bis Rue de Babylone, 7e; phone: 47-05-12-15), with flying cranes, cherry blossoms, and a tearoom, is built around a Japanese temple that was shipped over to Paris by the proprietor of a department store in the 1920s.

MUSIC: The *Orchestre de Paris,* under the direction of Daniel Barenboim, is based at the *Salle Pleyel* — the *Carnegie Hall* of Paris (252 Rue du Faubourg-St.-Honoré, 8e; phone: 45-63-88-73). Other classical recitals are held at the *Salle Gaveau* (45 Rue La Boétie; phone: 49-53-05-07), at the *Théâtre des Champs-Elysées* (15 Av. Montaigne, 8e; phone: 47-23-47-77), and at the *Palais des Congrès* (Porte Maillot; phone: 46-40-22-22). The *Orchestre Philharmonic* performs at a variety of places, including the *Grand Auditorium* at *Maison de Radio France* (116 Av. du Président J.-F.-Kennedy; phone: 42-30-15-16 or 42-30-18-18). Special concerts frequently are held in Paris's many places of worship, with moving music at High Mass on Sundays. The *Palais des Congrès* and the *Olympia* (28 Bd. des Capucines; phone: 47-42-82-45) are the places to see well-known international pop and rock artists. Innovative contemporary music — much of it created by computer — is the province of the *Institut de Recherche et de Coopération Acoustique Musique (IRCAM),* whose musicians can be heard in various auditoriums of the *Centre Georges Pompidou* (31 Rue St.-Merri; phone: 42-77-12-33).

NIGHTCLUBS AND NIGHTLIFE: Organized "Paris by Night" group tours (*Cityrama, Paris Vision,* and other operators offer them; see *Special Places*) include at least one "Spectacle" — beautiful girls in minimal, yet elaborate, costumes, with lavish sets and effects and sophisticated striptease. Most music halls offer a package (starting as high as $90 per person), with dinner, dancing, and a half-bottle of champagne. It is possible to go to these places on your own, save money by skipping dinner and the champagne (both usually way below par), and take a seat at the bar to see the show. The most famous extravaganzas occur nightly at *Alcazar* (62 Rue Mazarine, 6e; phone: 43-29-02-20), *Crazy Horse Saloon* (12 Av. George-V, 8e; phone: 47-23-32-32), *Folies-Bergère* (32 Rue Richer, 9e; phone: 42-46-77-11), *Lido (Cabaret Normandie)* (116 bis Champs-Elysées, 8e; phone: 45-63-11-61), *Moulin Rouge* (Pl. Blanche, 18e; phone: 46-06-00-19), and *Paradis Latin* (28 Rue du Cardinal-Lemoine, 5e; phone: 43-25-28-28). An amusing evening can also be spent at smaller cabaret shows like *René Cousinier* (*La Branlette*) (4 Impasse Marie-Blanche, 18e; phone: 46-06-49-46), *Au Lapin Agile* (22 Rue des Saules, 18e; phone: 46-06-85-87), and *Michou* (80 Rue des Martyrs, 18e; phone: 46-06-16-04). Reserve all a few days in advance.

Discotheque or private club, there's one big difference. Fashionable "in" spots like *Le Palace* (8 Rue Faubourg-Montmartre, 9e; phone: 42-46-10-87), *Régine's* (49 Rue de Ponthieu, 8e; phone: 43-59-21-60), *Chez Castel* (15 Rue Princesse, 6e, members only; phone: 43-26-90-22), *Olivia Valère* (40 Rue de Colisée, 8e, members only; phone: 42-25-11-68), and *Elysées Matignon* (48 Av. Gabriel, 8e; phone: 42-25-73-13) super-screen potential guests. No reason is given for accepting some and turning others away; go here with a regular or look as if you'd fit in with the crowd. Go early and on a weeknight — when your chances of getting past the gatekeeper are at least 50-50. Don't despair if you're refused; the following places are just as much fun and usually more hospitable: *La Scala* (188 bis Rue de Rivoli; phone: 42-61-64-00), *Les Bains* (7 Rue du Bourg-l'Abbé, 3e; phone: 48-87-01-80), *L'Aventure* (4 Av. Victor-Hugo, 16e; phone: 45-01-66-79), and *L'Ecume des Nuits* (*Hôtel Méridien,* 81 Bd. Gouvion-St.-Cyr, 17e; phone: 47-58-12-30).

Some pleasant, popular bars for a nightcap include *Bar de la Closerie des Lilas* (171 Bd. Montparnasse, 6e; phone: 43-26-70-50), *Harry's New York Bar* (5 Rue Daunou, 2e; phone: 42-61-71-14), *Fouquet's* (99 Champs-Elysées, 8e; phone: 47-23-70-60), *Ascot*

Bar (66 Rue Pierre-Charron, 8e; phone: 43-59-28-15), *Bar Anglais* (*Plaza-Athénée Hôtel,* 25 Av. Montaigne, 8e; phone: 47-23-78-33), and *Pub Winston Churchill* (5 Rue de Presbourg, 16e; phone: 45-00-75-35).

Jazz buffs have a large choice with *Caveau de la Huchette* (5 Rue de la Huchette, 5e; phone: 43-26-65-05), *Le Bilboquet* (13 Rue St.-Benoit, 6e; phone: 45-48-81-84), *New Morning* (7-9 Rue des Petites Ecuries, 10e; phone: 45-23-51-41), and *Le Petit Journal* (71 Bd. St.-Michel, 6e; phone: 43-26-28-59).

Enghien-les-Bains, 8 miles (13 km) away, is the only casino in the Paris vicinity (3 Av. de Ceinture, Enghien-les-Bains; phone: 34-12-90-00). Open 3 PM to about 4 AM, it easily can be reached by train from the Gare du Nord.

BEST IN TOWN

CHECKING IN: Paris offers a broad choice of accommodations, from luxurious palaces with every service to more humble budget hotels. However, they all are strictly controlled by the government and must post their rates, so you can be sure that the price you are being charged is correct. Below is our selection from all categories; in general, expect to spend at least $300 and up per night for a double room in the "palace" hotels, which we've listed as very expensive; from $170 to $300 in the expensive range; $70 to $170 is considered moderate; $50 to $70 is inexpensive; and $50 or less is very inexpensive.

Except for July, August, and December, the least crowded months, hotel rooms usually are at a premium in Paris. To reserve your first choice, we advise making reservations at least a month in advance, even farther ahead for the smaller, less expensive places listed. Watch for the dates of special events, when hotels are even more crowded than usual. The apartment rentals offered by *Paris Accueil/Paris Séjour* are an alternative to the hotel options listed here (see *Accommodations,* GETTING READY TO GO).

Street addresses of the hotels below are followed by the number of their *arrondissement* (neighborhood).

Bristol – A palace with a special, almost intimate cachet. Service is impeccable, as are the 188 spacious, quiet rooms and huge, marble baths. The beautiful little restaurant and comfortable lobby cocktail lounge are additional pleasures. There also is another wing with a heated swimming pool on the sixth-floor terrace. 112 Rue du Faubourg-St.-Honoré, 8e (phone: 42-66-91-45; from the US, 800-999-1802). Very expensive.

Crillon – No sign out front, just discreet gold "C's" on the doors, it is currently the only "palace" hotel in Paris still owned by a Frenchman. The rooms on the Place de la Concorde side, though rather noisy, have the view of views; rooms facing the courtyards are just as nice and much more tranquil. The popular bar and 2 elegant restaurants, *L'Obélisque* and *Les Ambassadeurs* (which rates two Michelin stars), often are frequented by journalists and US and British embassy personnel. 10 Pl. de la Concorde, 8e (phone: 42-65-24-24). Very expensive.

George V – This nonpareil pick of movie moguls and international tycoons has 288 elegantly traditional or handsome contemporary rooms and 63 suites: some, facing the lovely courtyard, have their own balconies; those on the upper floors, a nice view. And there are 2 restaurants, *Les Princes* and a grill, as well as a tearoom. One of the liveliest and chic-est bars in the city is here, with a bartender who mixes a mean martini. The patio is a summer delight. 31 Av. George-V, 8e (phone: 47-23-54-00). Very expensive.

Meurice – Refined Louis XV and XVI elegance and a wide range of services are offered at prices slightly below those of the other "palaces." The hotel, a member of the CIGA chain, has 187 rooms and especially nice suites, a popular bar, a restaurant, *Le Meurice,* and the chandeliered *Pompadour* tearoom. The location and hospitality couldn't be better, and the first-floor public room has been restored. 228 Rue de Rivoli, 1er (phone: 42-60-38-60). Very expensive.

Plaza-Athénée – One of the legendary hotels, this favorite of the sophisticated seeking serene surroundings and superior service has 218 rooms, some now being refurbished. This is a haute bastion that takes its dignity very seriously (a discreet note in each bathroom offers an unobtrusive route in and out of the hotel for those in jogging togs). The *Relais* tables are much in demand at lunch and late supper, and the two-star *Régence,* summer patio, tea tables, and downstairs English bar are places to see and be seen. 25 Av. Montaigne, 8e (phone: 47-23-78-33). Very expensive.

Relais Carré d'Or – For those visitors who are in Paris for a long stay, this recently opened hostelry (with all the amenities of a luxury hotel) provides a variety of accommodations — from studios to multi-room apartments — all with modern kitchens, marble bathrooms, and lovely, understated furnishings. Most have a balcony overlooking the hotel's garden or Avenue George-V. 46 Av. George-V, 8e (phone: 40-70-05-05). Very expensive.

Résidence Maxim's – Pierre Cardin's luxurious venture is located near the Elysée Palace. No expense has been spared here to create sybaritic splendor. The 39 suites range in style from sleek modern to Belle Epoque, with original Art Nouveau pieces from Cardin's own collections, and every bathroom has been individually designed. *Le Caviarteria,* its restaurant, has made a name in the city, and has a pleasant terrace in summer; *La Tonnelle* serves tea and breakfast, and doubles as a tea salon; and the bar, *Le Maximin,* is open late. 42 Av. Gabriel, 8e (phone: 45-61-96-33). Very expensive.

Ritz – Optimum comfort, privacy, and personal service are offered here, in one of the world's most gracious and distinguished hotels. There is an extraordinary health club (with pool, sauna, squash courts, ozone baths, and massages), an extensive business center, and the Ritz Escoffier Ecole de Cuisine. The latest addition is the *Ritz Club,* a nightclub and discotheque on the hotel's lower level that is open to hotel guests and club members only. The 162 redecorated rooms still preserve their antique treasures. This turn-of-the-century monument is *the* place to splurge, and even its sale to Egyptian interests (some say the Sultan of Brunei is the real financial force) has not diminished the glow one iota. The bars are fashionable meeting places, and the two-star *Ritz-Espadon* restaurant carries on the tradition of the legendary Escoffier. 15 Pl. Vendôme, 1er (phone: 42-60-38-30). Very expensive.

Royal Monceau – This elegant, impeccably decorated property, not far from the Arc de Triomphe, has 3 restaurants — including one with an attractive garden setting — as well as 2 bars, a fitness center, pool, Jacuzzi, and beauty salon. 37 Av. Hoche, 8e (phone: 45-61-98-00). Very expensive.

St. James's Club – Located in a château in a residential section of the city, this hotel is really a private club (there are others: one in London, one in Antigua, another in Los Angeles). For an additional 50F ($9), non-members can stay here for a few nights and feel as if they are living in an elegant home. The penthouse suites have a winter roof garden. There's a health center, a 5,000-volume library, and 2 restaurants. 5 Place Chancelier Adenauer, Av. Bugeaud, 16e (phone: 47-04-29-29; in the US, 800-641-0300). Very expensive.

San Régis – This is an elegant place to feel at home in comfortable surroundings. 12 Rue Jean-Goujon, 8e (phone: 43-59-41-90). Very expensive to expensive.

Westminster – Between the *Opéra* and the *Ritz,* it was at one time quite prestigious, but declined somewhat before its recent renovation. The paneling, marble fireplaces, and parquet floors of its traditional decor remain; air conditioning has been installed; and a new restaurant, *Le Céladon,* and cocktail lounge replace the old grill and bar. Some of the 101 rooms and apartments overlook the street, some an inner courtyard. 13 Rue de la Paix, 2e (phone: 42-61-57-46). Very expensive to expensive.

Grand – This recently renovated property, part of the Inter-Continental chain, has long been a favorite of Americans abroad, with its "meeting place of the world," the *Café de la Paix*. It has 530 rooms and 10 luxurious suites, plus cheerful bars and restaurants — and a prime location (next to the *Opéra*). 2 Rue Scribe, 9e (phone: 40-07-32-32). Expensive.

Holiday Inn Place de la République – In the heart of town, in a 120-year-old edifice that evokes the grandeur of the Second Empire — its façade is unlike any *Holiday Inn* you've seen before. Of the 333 pleasantly decorated rooms, those facing the courtyard are preferable to those facing the square. Restaurant, piano bar, and air conditioning. 10 Pl. de la République, 11e (phone: 43-55-44-34). Expensive.

L'Hôtel – Small, but chic, this Left Bank hostelry is favored by experienced international travelers. The 27 rooms are tiny, but beautifully appointed (antiques, fresh flowers, marble baths). The attractive restaurant, complete with waterfall, is flanked by a piano bar, and the location can't be beat. 13 Rue des Beaux-Arts, 6e (phone: 43-25-27-22). Expensive.

Hôtel des Saints-Pères – In a great location in the heart of the Left Bank, its attractively decorated guestrooms, courtyard garden, and a charming bar make this one of Paris's best little hotels. Book far in advance — it's often difficult to get a room. 65 Rue des Saints-Pères, 6e (phone: 45-44-50-00). Expensive.

Inter-Continental – The 500 rooms and suites have been meticulously restored to re-create turn-of-the-century elegance with modern conveniences. The top-floor Louis XVI "garret" rooms are cozy and look out over the Tuileries. There's an American-style coffee shop, a grill, and a popular bar. 3 Rue de Castiglione, 1er (phone: 42-60-37-80). Expensive.

Lancaster – Small and still smart, this 57-room townhouse has quiet, comfortable accommodations. There are flowers everywhere, a cozy bar, and a topnotch restaurant with courtyard service in summer. Run by London's Savoy group. 7 Rue de Berri, 8e (phone: 43-59-90-43). Expensive.

Méridien – *Air France*'s well-run, 1,027-room, modern American-style property has all the expected French flair. Rooms are on the small side, but tastefully decorated, quiet, and with good views. There are 4 attractive restaurants, a shopping arcade, lively bars, and a chic nightclub, *L'Ecume des Nuits*. 81 Bd. Gouvion-St.-Cyr, 17e (phone: 40-68-35-35). Expensive.

Méridien Montparnasse – With 952 rooms, this ultramodern giant is in the heart of Montparnasse. It has a futuristic lobby, efficient service, a coffee shop, bars, and the *Montparnasse 25* restaurant, with a view, and in summer, a garden restaurant. 19 Rue du Commandant-René-Mouchotte, 14e (phone: 43-20-15-51). Expensive.

Paris Hilton International – Its 474 modern rooms are only a few steps from the Eiffel Tower. Those facing the river have the best view. The glass-walled rendezvous *Le Toit de Paris* has dancing and a glittering nighttime view; *Le Western* serves T-bone steaks, apple pie à la mode, and brownies (mostly to French diners). The coffee shop is a magnet for homesick Americans. 18 Av. de Suffren, 15e (phone: 42-73-92-00). Expensive.

Pavillon de la Reine – Supreme location for the Marais's only luxury hotel, owned by the management of the *Relais-Christine* (see below) and similarly appointed. Its 49 spacious rooms look out on a garden or courtyard. The setting on the Place des Vosges is regal, and the *Picasso Museum* is only a couple of minutes away on foot. 28 Pl. des Vosges, 3e (phone: 42-77-96-40). Expensive.

Prince de Galles – An excellent location (a next-door neighbor of the pricier *George V*) and impeccable style make this hostelry a good choice. All 160 rooms and suites are individually decorated. This Marriott member offers concierge services, a restaurant, and an oak-panelled bar; parking is available. 33 Av. George-V, 8e (phone: 47-23-55-11). Expensive.

Pullman St.-Jacques – This four-star hotel has 797 up-to-date rooms, a nice shopping arcade, a cinema, 4 restaurants (one Japanese, one Chinese, one French, and an informal coffee shop), and the lively *Bar Tahonga*. A bit out of the way, but the métro is close by. 17 Bd. St.-Jacques, 14e (phone: 40-78-79-80). Expensive.

Raphael – A very spacious, stately place, with a Turner in the lobby downstairs and paneling painted with sphinxes in the generous rooms. Less well known among the top Paris hotels, but favored by film folk and the like. 17 Av. Kléber, 16e (phone: 45-02-16-00). Expensive.

Relais Christine – This lovely small hotel, with modern fixtures and lots of old-fashioned charm, formerly was a 16th-century cloister. Ask for a room with a courtyard or garden view. 3 Rue Christine, 6e (phone: 43-26-71-80). Expensive.

Relais Saint-Germain – One of the Left Bank's best small hotels, it has 10 rooms just steps from Boulevard St.-Germain and the area's best shops, eateries, and galleries. 9 Carrefour de l'Odéon, 6e (phone: 43-29-12-05). Expensive.

Résidence du Roy – Within easy reach of the Champs-Elysées, this establishment offers self-contained studios, suites, and duplexes, complete with kitchen facilities. No restaurant. 8 Rue François-I, 8e (phone: 42-89-59-59). Expensive.

Le Vernet – With 36 modern rooms and suites, this new sister hotel to the elegant *Royal Monceau* is located just a few steps from the Arc de Triomphe. 25 Rue Vernet, 8e (phone: 47-23-43-10). Expensive.

Abbaye St.-Germain – On a quiet street, this small, delightful place once was a convent. The lobby has exposed stone arches, and the elegant public and private rooms are furnished with antiques, tastefully selected fabrics, and marble baths. There's a lovely garden and a bar, but there continue to be some complaints about the service. 10 Rue Cassette, 6e (phone: 45-44-38-11). Expensive to moderate.

Angleterre – Its 29 classic, clean, unpretentious rooms are in what once was the British Embassy, now a national monument. 44 Rue Jacob, 6e (phone: 42-60-34-72). Moderate.

Danube St.-Germain – The rooms, with their four-poster bamboo beds, are comfortable, and some of them overlook an attractive courtyard typical of the Left Bank. 58 Rue Jacob, 6e (phone: 42-60-34-70). Moderate.

Deux Iles – This beautifully redecorated 17th-century house is on the historic Ile St.-Louis. It has a tropical garden and the decor is in bamboo, rattan, and braided rope. The rooms have French provincial fabrics and Louis XIV ceramic tiles in the bathrooms. But there's one drawback: the rooms aren't very large. 59 Rue St.-Louis-en-l'Ile, 4e (phone: 43-26-13-35). Moderate.

Duc de St.-Simon – If you're in search of things past, this may be one of the best places in town, despite the rather small rooms. In 2 big townhouses in a beautiful, quiet backwater off the Boulevard St.-Germain, this elegant little spot veritably reeks of Proust. Just a 5-minute walk from the spectacular *Musée d'Orsay*. 14 Rue de St.-Simon, 7e (phone: 45-48-35-66). Moderate.

Grand Hôtel Taranne – Anybody anxious to get into the Left Bank scene should love it here, for the 35 rooms are literally on top of the *Brasserie Lipp*. Each room is unique: No. 4 has exposed beams, a TV set, and a mini-bar; No. 3 has a Louis XIII–style bed; No. 17, the oddest, has lights and a disco ball. 153 Bd. St.-Germain, 6e (phone: 42-22-21-65). Moderate.

Grand Hôtel de l'Univers – Modern and tucked away on a quiet street, it's also only

2 steps away from St.-Germain-des-Prés and the Latin Quarter. No restaurant. 6 Rue Grégoire-de-Tours, 6e (phone: 43-29-37-00). Moderate.

Jeu de Paume – The architect-owner of this former *jeu de paume* (tennis court) has artfully married old and new in this newest addition to the exclusive Ile St.-Louis hotels. High-tech lighting, modern artwork, and a sleek glass elevator are set against ancient ceiling beams and limestone brick hearths. There's a country feeling here. Rooms are comfortable and reasonably priced. 54 Rue St.-Louis-en-l'Ile, 4e (phone: 43-26-14-18). Moderate.

Lord Byron – On a quiet street off the Champs-Elysées, it has a pleasant courtyard and 30 comfortable, homey rooms. The staff is friendly and speaks good English, and a family atmosphere prevails. 5 Rue de Chateaubriand, 8e (phone: 43-59-89-98). Moderate.   *OII - 33-I*

Lutèce – Here are 23 luxurious rooms (one split-level) on the charming Ile St.-Louis. Positively ravishing, with exquisite toile fabric and wallpaper and raw wood beams. 65 Rue St.-Louis-en-l'Ile, 4e (phone: 43-26-23-52). Moderate.

Madison – Offers 55 large, bright rooms, some with balconies. 143 Bd. St.-Germain, 6e (phone: 43-29-72-50). Moderate.

Odéon – Small, modernized, and charming, it's in the heart of the St.-Germain area on the Left Bank. No restaurant. 3 Rue de l'Odéon, 6e (phone: 43-25-90-67). Moderate.

Regent's Garden – On a quiet street near the Etoile, it has 40 spacious rooms, some with large marble fireplaces. The property is run by young hoteliers who make you feel as if you are in your own home. A country atmosphere pervades. There's also a garden and parking. 6 Rue Pierre-Demours, 17e (phone: 45-74-07-30). Moderate.

Résidence Charles-Dullin – In a sleepy corner of Montmartre, near the leafy square of the *Théâtre de l'Atelier,* this residential hotel charges nightly, weekly, and monthly rates. The apartments have kitchens, and some overlook a peaceful garden. 10 Pl. Charles-Dullin, 18e (phone: 42-57-14-55). Moderate.

Ste.-Beuve – A stylish place in Montparnasse with rooms and lobby designed by David Hicks. 9 Rue Ste.-Beuve, 6e (phone: 45-48-20-07). Moderate.

Le St.-Grégoire – A small 18th-century mansion on the Left Bank, this recently renovated hostelry has an intimate cozy atmosphere, a warm fire in the hearth, and 20 tastefully furnished rooms, some with terraces overlooking a garden. 43 Rue de l'Abbé Gregoire, 6e (phone: 45-48-23-23). Moderate.

St.-Louis – On magical Ile St.-Louis, practically in the shadow of Notre Dame, this small hotel will make the first-time visitor fall in love with the city forever. The 21 rooms aren't large, but they're pretty, and the 3 fifth-floor rooms under the eaves are enchanting, with tiny balconies overlooking Parisian rooftops. No TV sets, but baths are clean and modern, and there's a charming breakfast room and a warm welcome. 75 Rue St.-Louis-en-l'Ile, 4e (phone: 46-34-04-80). Moderate.

St.-Merry – A stone's throw from the *Centre Georges Pompidou* arts complex, this mock-medieval establishment may be the most bizarre hotel in Paris. It not only backs onto the Eglise St.-Merry, but it has a communion rail as a banister and ancient oaken confessionals as broom closets. The rooms, hung with dark, demonic oil portraits, have church pews for benches, and some rooms are even spliced by a flying buttress. In dubious taste, perhaps, but there's nothing else like it. 78 Rue de la Verrerie, 4e (phone: 42-78-14-15). Moderate.

Tuileries – With a good location in a "real" neighborhood in the heart of the city, it has a well-tended look and attractive carved wood bedsteads. 10 Rue St.-Hyacinthe, 1er (phone: 42-61-04-17 or 42-61-06-94). Moderate.

L'Université – Its 28 charming rooms of all shapes and sizes are in a former 18th-century mansion. 22 Rue de l'Université, 7e (phone: 42-61-09-39). Moderate.

Vendôme – This older "house" has 36 immaculate high-ceilinged rooms with brass beds, and the location couldn't be better. There is a small restaurant with a limited menu, and a bar. 1 Pl. Vendôme, 1er (phone: 42-60-32-84). Moderate.

West End – Friendly, with 60 rooms, it's on the Right Bank. The front desk keeps a close, concerned watch on comings and goings, which some may find reassuring. 7 Rue Clément-Marot, 8e (phone: 47-20-30-78). Moderate.

Celestins – On a quiet residential street on the edge of the newly chic Marais (Paris's oldest neighborhood), this tiny hotel is a short walk from the Place des Vosges, the *Louvre,* the quais along the Seine, and the Bastille nightclubs. Dating from the 18th century, when it belonged to the Celestin Convent, it has 14 small rooms, which still have their original dark wood walls and ceiling beams. No. 18, the nicest, has an extra couch; No. 20 has a skylight in the bathroom. Historical status has barred installation of an elevator, however. 1 Rue Charles-V, 4e (phone: 48-87-87-04). Moderate to inexpensive.

Chomel – Sprucely decorated, this establishment is near the *Au Bon Marché* department store. 15 Rue Chomel, 7e (phone: 45-48-55-52). Moderate to inexpensive.

Ferrandi – Popular with international businessmen, this no-frills hostelry is done up in browns and blues, with a winding wood staircase and a quiet lounge. 92 Rue du Cherche-Midi, 6e (phone: 42-22-97-40). Moderate to inexpensive.

Parc St.-Severin – An interesting property in the heart of the 5th *arrondissement* on the Left Bank, it has a total of 27 rooms, including a top-floor penthouse with a wraparound balcony. The decor is modern but understated, and the overall ambience is appealing even though the neighborhood is less than the quietest in Paris. 22 Rue de la Parcheminerie, 5e (phone: 43-54-32-17). Moderate to inexpensive.

St.-Thomas-d'Aquin – Built in the 1880s, this unpretentious hotel is a simple, functional base from which to explore a shopper's paradise of new wave designer boutiques and tiny restaurants. The 21 rooms are clean and neat, and baths are modern (though tubs are half-size). Breakfast is included. 3 Rue d'Pré-aux-Clercs, 7e (phone: 42-61-01-22). Moderate to inexpensive.

Amélie – Centrally located, this comfortable spot has 15 rooms, each with color TV set, direct-dial telephone, and mini-bar. Breakfast is included in the rate, which makes this one of Paris's better bargains. 5 Rue Amélie, 7e (phone: 45-51-74-75). Inexpensive.

D'Argenson – The upper middle class residential district in which this hotel is located is off the typical tourist track but convenient to major department stores on the Bd. Haussmann and a 15-minute walk from the *Opéra.* The showplace rooms — Nos. 23, 33, 43, and 53 — feature fireplaces and up-to-date bathrooms. Room rate includes breakfast. 15 Rue d'Argenson, 8e (phone: 42-65-16-87). Inexpensive.

Bretonnerie – This restored 17th-century townhouse takes itself seriously, with petit point, dark wood furnishings, and several attic rooms with beams that overlook the narrow streets of the newly fashionable Marais area. 22 Rue Ste.-Croix-de-la-Bretonnerie, 4e (phone: 48-87-77-63). Inexpensive.

Ceramic – Close to the Champs-Elysées, the Faubourg St.-Honoré, and the métro, this 53-room establishment with an Art Nouveau façade has been designated a national historic treasure. Request a room facing the street, particularly No. 412 — enormous, with a crystal chandelier and wide bay windows. Room rates include breakfast. 34 Av. de Wagram, 17e (phone: 42-27-20-30). Inexpensive.

Delavigne – Good value and location (just down the street from the *Odéon* theater), it has an enlightened manager who says he isn't interested in simply handing out keys, but enjoys introducing foreigners to Paris. 1 Rue Casimir-Delavigne, 6e (phone: 43-29-31-50). Inexpensive.

Deux Continents – A cozy red sitting room looks invitingly onto the street here, in this 40-room establishment on the Left Bank. 25 Rue Jacob, 6e (phone: 43-26-72-46). Inexpensive.

Esmeralda – Some of the rooms look directly at Notre-Dame over the gardens of St.-Julien-le-Pauvre, one of Paris's most ancient churches. The oak beams and furniture round out the medieval atmosphere. Small and friendly, especially popular with the theatrical crowd. 4 Rue St.-Julien-le-Pauvre, 5e (phone: 43-54-19-20). Inexpensive.

Family – A longtime favorite with Americans — you're treated just like part of the family. There are 25 small but comfortable rooms. 35 Rue Cambon, 1er (phone: 42-61-54-84). Inexpensive.

Grandes Ecoles – Just the sort of place that shouldn't appear in a guidebook (even the proprietress says so) and that people recommend only to the right friends. Insulated from the street by a delightful courtyard and its garden, it is a simple 19th-century private house with plain comforts, but it's long on atmosphere. There aren't many like it in Paris. 75 Rue Cardinal-Lemoine, 5e (phone: 43-26-79-23). Inexpensive.

Hôtel de Bellevue et du Chariot d'Or – Slightly eccentric, but friendly, this is the best of more than a score of tiny hotels in the wholesale garment district. Although the hallway carpets and wallpaper are in dire need of replacement, the rooms are clean and comfortable, and most of the baths have been redone. Room no. 110 is on the courtyard (which means it's quiet) and has twin beds, a pink bathroom, and a marble fireplace. Some rooms are large enough to sleep four. Breakfast included. 39 Rue de Turbigo, 3e (phone: 48-87-45-60). Inexpensive.

Le Jardin des Plantes – In addition to a magnificent setting across from the Parisian Botanical Gardens, near the Sorbonne, there are 33 airy, spotless rooms and baths, each with its own floral motif. The owner, a psychologist, has anticipated the traveler's every need: All rooms have mini-bars, TV sets, and hair dryers; some have alcoves large enough for extra beds for children; a sauna is available in the basement. Breakfast can be enjoyed in the sunny ground-floor coffee bar or on the fifth-floor terrace and rose garden. Art exhibits and classical music concerts are held on Sundays in the vaulted cellar. 5 Rue Linné, 5e (phone: 47-07-06-20). Inexpensive.

Jeanne d'Arc – This little place on a quiet street in the Marais doesn't get top marks for decor and its facilities are simple, but somehow its appeal has spread from Minnesota to Melbourne. It's well placed at the colorful end of the Rue de Rivoli, and the management is friendly and speaks English. 3 Rue Jarente, 4e (phone: 48-87-62-11). Inexpensive.

Lenox – Between the busy St.-Germain area and the boutiques nearby, it's small and very tastefully done, with a small bar. Popular with the fashion crowd. 9 Rue de l'Université, 7e (phone: 42-96-10-95). Inexpensive.

London – In the heart of the business district, this comfortable hotel has 50 rooms, each with color TV set and direct-dial telephone. 32 Bd. des Italiens, 9e (phone: 48-24-54-64). Inexpensive.

Prima Lepic – A 38-room hotel in Montmartre, a busy neighborhood of winding little streets that evoke the romance of *la vie bohème,* Utrillo, Picasso, Toulouse-Lautrec and the *Moulin Rouge.* Decorated by cheerful young owners, rooms sport pretty floral wallpapers and one-of-a-kind furnishings — a wicker chair, a mirrored armoire, a 1930s lamp. No. 56, on the top floor, looks out over Paris, and travelers with a child should make special note of room No. 2, which connects to another room. There's an elevator, and the public spaces are charming. 29 Rue Lepic, 18e (phone: 46-06-44-64). Inexpensive.

Prince Albert – Despite its unprepossessing aura of faded glory, this has its site to recommend it: just off the quiet and unspoiled Marché St.-Honoré and a hop, skip, and jump from the Tuileries. 5 Rue St.-Hyacinthe, 1er (phone: 42-61-58-36). Inexpensive.

St.-André-des-Arts – A rambling old favorite among the chic and hip whose purses are slim but whose tastes are discerning. 66 Rue St.-André-des-Arts, 6e (phone: 43-26-96-16). Inexpensive.

Sévigné – If it's a little noisy (right on the Rue de Rivoli), the warm welcome and handy location make up for it. 2 Rue Malher, 4e (phone: 42-72-76-17). Inexpensive.

Solférino – A cozy place with Oriental rugs scattered about. The 34 tiny rooms have floral wallpaper, and there's a plant-filled breakfast and sitting room. 91 Rue de Lille, 7e (phone: 47-05-85-54). Inexpensive.

Le Vieux Marais – Near the *Centre Georges Pompidou,* this is one of the few agreeable hostelries in the Marais area, with brightly sprigged walls in the cheerful, if not very large, rooms. The breakfast room has an impressive wall-size engraving of the Place des Vosges, not far away. 8 Rue du Plâtre, 4e (phone: 42-78-47-22). Inexpensive.

Welcome – Overlooking the Bd. St.-Germain, it's simple but comfortable. 66 Rue de Seine, 6e (phone: 46-34-24-80). Inexpensive.

Boucherat – A plain, friendly establishment with no airs and with a clientele that returns. Near the Place de la République. 110 Rue de Turenne, 3e (phone: 42-72-86-83). Very inexpensive.

Du Globe – Tiny and charming, it's on a quiet street in the heart of the St.-Germain area. 15 Rue des Quatre Vents, 6e (phone: 43-26-35-50). Very inexpensive.

Henri IV – No one could call this modern — the fittings obviously haven't been changed for decades, and there's only a bidet and basin in the room, since the bathrooms are down the hall. But it has a reputation and a history, not least because it is the only hotel on the Place Dauphine on the Ile de la Cité — the real core of Paris. Prices are breathtakingly low. 25 Pl. Dauphine, 1er (phone: 43-54-44-53). Very inexpensive.

EATING OUT: Paris considers itself the culinary capital of the world, and you will never forget food for long here. Whether you grab just a freshly baked croissant and café au lait for breakfast or splurge on an epicurean fantasy for dinner, this is the city in which to indulge all your gastronomic dreams. Remember, too, that there is no such thing as "French" food; rather, Paris provides the perfect mosaic in which to try regional delights from Provence, Alsace, Normandy, Brittany, and many other delicious places.

Restaurants classed as very expensive charge $250 and way up for two; expensive is $150 to $200; moderate, $100 to $150; inexpensive, less than $100; and very inexpensive, $50 or less. A service charge of 15% is added to the bill, but most people leave a small additional tip for good service; wine is not included in the price. Street addresses of the restaurants below are followed by their *arrondissement* number.

Note: To save frustration and embarrassment, always *reconfirm* dinner reservations before noon on the appointed day. Also remember that some of the better restaurants do not accept credit cards; it's a good idea to check when making your reservations. It may come as a surprise to discover that many of the elite Paris restaurants close over the weekend; also note that many Paris restaurants are closed for part or all of July or August. It's best to check ahead in order to avoid disappointment at the restaurant of your choice, and it's also worth remembering that many offer special lunch menus at considerably lower prices. Here is a sampling of the best restaurants that Paris has to offer:

L'Ambroisie – Quietly elegant, beneath the arcade of historic Place des Vosges, this is the showcase for chef Bernard Paucaud's equally elegant cuisine. The menu is limited to only a few entrées, such as duck with foie gras, skate and sliced green cabbage in sherry vinegar sauce, veal sweetbreads with shallots and parsley on ultra-fresh pasta, delicately battered chicken thighs in a piquant sauce, and oxtail in a savory sauce, but the quality has earned the place three Michelin stars. Closed Sundays, Monday lunch, August, and holidays. Reservations necessary. 9 Pl. des Vosges, 4e (phone: 42-78-51-45). Very expensive.

Le Grand Véfour – Founded in 1760, this sedately elegant Empire-style establishment — with paintings on the mirrors — is known for refined menus and perfect service. It's famous for toast Rothschild (shrimp in crayfish sauce set in a brioche) and pigeon Aristide Briand (boned roast pigeon stuffed with foie gras and truffles). Closed Saturdays at lunch, Sundays, and August. Reservations necessary. 17 Rue Beaujolais, 1er (phone: 42-96-56-27). Very expensive.

Jamin – Due to the culinary talents of owner-chef Joel Robuchon, this is one of the city's finest restaurants — with a three-star ranking by Michelin — and one of the most difficult to get into. Robuchon calls his cuisine "moderne," similar to but not always as light as nouvelle. The dining room is *very* small, so reserve far in advance. Waiting time is almost 8 weeks. Closed weekends and July. Reservations necessary. 32 Rue de Longchamp, 16e (phone: 47-27-12-27). Very expensive.

Lasserre – The ultimate in luxury, with a magical ceiling that opens periodically during dinner to reveal the nighttime sky. Equally sublime is the food, served in the *style Lasserre* — that is, vermeil dessert settings, plates rimmed with gold, and extravagant garnishes with each dish. The classic menu is heavy on foie gras, caviar, truffles, and rich sauces. Michelin downgraded the food to two stars a few years ago, but we think it's still topnotch. Closed Sundays, Monday lunch, and August. Reservations necessary. 17 Av. Franklin-D.-Roosevelt, 8e (phone: 43-59-53-43). Very expensive.

Lucas-Carton – Once proprietor of the Michelin three-star restaurant called *L'Archestrate,* chef Alain Senderens dropped that name in 1985 when he moved to larger, more elegant quarters in a historic building that boasts a gorgeous Belle Epoque interior. Senderens enjoys the reputation as one of France's most innovative culinary talents, combining many tenets of nouvelle cuisine with Oriental and African influences. Closed Saturdays, Sundays, and most of August. Reservations necessary. 9 Pl. de la Madeleine, 8e (phone: 42-65-22-90). Very expensive.

Maxim's – A legend for its Belle Epoque decor and atmosphere. It's good for celebrations, but it's hard to feel comfortable if you aren't known here. Owned by fashion designer Pierre Cardin, this is one of the few places in Paris where you are expected to dress formally — on Friday evenings. There's an orchestra for dancing from 9:30 PM until 2 AM. Closed Sundays. Reservations necessary. 3 Rue Royale, 8e (phone: 42-65-27-94). Very expensive.

Olympe – Owner and chef Dominique Nahmias is the first female chef to be awarded three toques — very high honors — by Gault Millau. Her nouvelle cuisine is painstakingly prepared and simply glorious; an excellent wine list adds to the meal's enjoyment. Closed Saturday lunch, Sundays, Mondays, and August. Reservations necessary. 8 Rue Nicolas-Charlet, 15e (phone: 47-34-86-08). Very expensive.

Le Taillevent – Full of tradition, Louis XVI furnishings, 18th-century porcelain dinner service — all in a 19th-century mansion — this epicurean haven offers no-nonsense *cuisine classique,* which currently is the best in Paris. Try terrine of truffled sweetbreads, seafood sausage, duck in cider, and especially chef Claude Deligne's soufflés in original flavors like Alsatian pear and cinnamon chocolate. Three stars in the *Guide Michelin.* Closed weekends and August. Reservations necessary. Americans often have difficulty reserving here (although it's a bit easier if there are four in your party), and it's best to try at least 60 days ahead. No credit cards accepted. 15 Rue Lamennais, 8e (phone: 45-63-39-94). Very expensive.

La Tour d'Argent – Another of the five Parisian restaurants to be awarded three stars by the *Guide Michelin* and probably the best-known — though recent visits have not been up to the standards of years past. The spectacular view of Notre-Dame and the Ile St.-Louis competes with the food for the attention of a very touristy clientele. Pressed duck — prepared before you — is the specialty, but the 15 other varieties of duck are equally interesting. A single main dish here can cost $100, and to be quite frank, it just ain't worth it. Closed Mondays. Reservations necessary. 15 Quai de la Tournelle, 5e (phone: 43-54-23-31). Very expensive.

L'Ami Louis – This is the archetypal Parisian bistro, unattractive physically but with huge portions of food that we rate as marvelous. Though the original Louis is gone, his heirs have maintained the rough welcome and informal ambience. Specialties include foie gras, roast chicken, spring lamb, ham, and burgundy wines. A favorite among Americans, this is the place to sample authentic French fries. Closed Mondays, Tuesdays, and July and August. Reservations necessary. 32 Rue de Vertbois, 3e (phone: 48-87-77-48). Expensive.

Amphyclés – Since it opened in May 1989, Philippe Croult's tiny restaurant near the Arc de Triomphe has won praise and a prized Michelin star. A former student of star-chef Joel Robuchon of *Jamin,* Croult prepares wonderful dishes, including *crême de morilles au chou nouveau* (cream of mushroom soup flavored with new cabbage). Reservations necessary. 78 Av. des Ternes, 17e (phone: 40-68-01-01). Expensive.

Apicius – Jean-Pierre Vigato's highly original recipes have won him a reputation as one of Paris's finest chefs. Favorites include such delicacies as sweet-and-sour foie gras, *rougets* (a Mediterranean fish) with olive oil and potato purée, and a *panaché* of five mouth-watering chocolate desserts. Closed weekends and August. Reservations necessary. 122 Av. de Villiers, 17e (phone: 43-80-19-66). Expensive.

Le Carré des Feuillants – Alain Dutournier of *Le Trou Gascon* has set up shop right in midtown. The cuisine is still Gascon-inspired, but Dutournier is allowing his imagination more license, with, for example, such creations as frogs' legs with watercress sauce and salmon served with braised cabbage and bacon. Michelin has awarded him two stars. Closed Saturdays for lunch and Sundays. Reservations necessary. 14 Rue de Castiglione, 1er (phone: 42-86-82-82). Expensive.

Castel – You might be able to get a reservation at this, one of the few private clubs in Paris, if you ask for help from the concierge at one of the town's grand hotels. The Belle Epoque interior is breathtaking, and the cooking fine, and there's a disco in the basement. Specialties include lobster and chicken with cucumbers. Closed Sundays. Reservations necessary. 15 Rue Princesse, 6e (phone: 43-26-90-22). Expensive.

Chiberta – Elegant and modern, and boasting the acclaimed nouvelle cuisine of Jean Michel Bédier. Try *bavarois de saumon au coulis de tomates frais* (salmon mousse with fresh tomato sauce) and *marbré de rouget au fenouil* (red mullet with fennel). Closed weekends and August. Reservations necessary. 3 Rue Arsène-Houssaye, 8e (phone: 45-63-77-90). Expensive.

Le Divellec – This bright and airy place serves some exquisitely fresh seafood. Try the sea bass, the *rouget,* and the sautéed turbot. The latter is served with "black pasta" — thick strips of pasta flavored with squid ink — an unusual and delicious concoction. Closed Sundays, Mondays, and August. Reservations necessary. 107 Rue de l'Université, 7e (phone: 45-51-91-96). Expensive.

Dodin-Bouffant – Popular because it was set up by the gifted, imaginative, and long-gone Jacques Manière, it still offers excellent seafood and inventive dishes. Open late. Closed Sundays, 2 weeks at *Christmastime,* and August. Reservations necessary. 25 Rue Frédéric-Sauton, 5e (phone: 43-25-25-14). Expensive.

Drouant – Founded in 1880, this classic favorite reopened after an extensive face-lift, with an ambitious chef and menu. Open daily. Reservations necessary. 18 Rue Gaillon, 2e (phone: 42-65-15-16). Expensive.

Duquesnoy – Jean-Paul Duquesnoy, one of Paris's most promising young chefs, is in his element in nifty quarters. Warm carved woods and tasteful decor set the stage for specialties that include a new potato and caviar salad, terrine of leeks and *langoustine,* and a chocolate mousse and pistachio–filled *mille-feuille.* Two Michelin stars. Closed Saturday lunch and Sundays. Reservations necessary. 6 Av. Bosquet, 7e (phone: 47-05-96-78). Expensive.

Faugeron – Among the finest nouvelle restaurants, awarded two stars by Michelin, it rates even higher with us. Superb food, lovely service, and one of Paris's prettiest table settings in what once was an old school. Closed weekends and August. Reservations necessary. 52 Rue de Longchamp, 16e (phone: 47-04-24-53). Expensive.

Gérard Besson – Michelin has given this small and formal eatery two stars. The service is impeccable and the classic menu includes specialties such as fricassee of lobster. Closed Saturdays and Sundays July 13 to 30, and from December 22 to January 7. Reservations necessary. 5 Rue Coq-Héron, 1er (phone: 42-33-14-74). Expensive.

Jacques Cagna – The talented eponymous chef always provides an interesting menu at these charming premises on the Left Bank, very near the Seine. Closed August, *Christmas* week, two Saturdays a month, and Sundays. Reservations necessary. 14 Rue des Grands-Augustins, 6e (phone: 43-26-49-39). Expensive.

Lamazère – Truffle heaven. The menu is a triumph of rich products from the southwest of France. The owner is a magician in the real sense of the word, as well as with food. The elegant bar and salons are open late. Closed Sundays and August. Reservations necessary. 23 Rue de Ponthieu, 8e (phone: 43-59-66-66). Expensive.

Ledoyen – This grand dowager of Paris dining places received a major face-lift in 1988 when Régine, the capital's nightlife queen, took it over. Its look, and menus ordained by staff chef Jacques Maximin, have received generally favorable reviews, particularly from high-powered businesspeople. Closed Sundays and August. Reservations necessary. Carré des Champs Elysées, 8e (phone: 47-42-23-23). Expensive.

La Maison Blanche – Decidedly "in," it is fashionably elegant, and its talented young chef, José Lampréia, prepares an inventive, contemporary version of soul-satisfying *cuisine bourgeoise.* Closed Saturday lunch, Sundays, Mondays, the first 2 weeks of September, and from *Christmas* to *New Year's Day.* Reservations necessary. 82 Bd. Lefebvre, 15e (phone: 48-28-38-83). Expensive.

Le Petit Montmorency – In his location near the Champs-Elysées, chef Daniel Bouché presents one of the most exciting and unusual menus in Paris. Very, very popular. Closed weekends and August. Reservations necessary. 5 Rue Rabelais, 8e (phone: 42-25-11-19). Expensive.

Le Pré Catelan – It's the large restaurant right in the middle of the Bois de Boulogne, and believe it or not, the food here is very good. Ingredients are fresh and sauces are light. Specialties include four or five new dishes daily. Closed Sunday evenings, Mondays, and the first 2 weeks of February. Reservations necessary. Rte. de Suresnes, Bois de Boulogne, 16e (phone: 45-24-55-58). Expensive.

Quai des Ormes – Elegant dining on the Seine, with an English-speaking staff. In summer, try to sit on the first-floor terrace overlooking Notre-Dame. Closed weekends and August. Reservations advised. 72 Quai de l'Hôtel-de-Ville, 4e (phone: 42-74-72-22). Expensive.

Régine's – The food actually is good in this beautifully decorated nightclub, which is frequented by Parisians as well as the chic international set. Ask your hotel manager to get you in because it's nominally a private club. Try the foie gras (made on the premises) and the goose. Closed Sundays. Reservations advised. 49 Rue de Ponthieu, 8e (phone: 43-59-21-60). Expensive.

Relais Louis XIII – Old-style decor and new cuisine in one of Paris's prettiest houses. Closed Sundays, Monday lunch, and August. Reservations advised. 8 Rue des Grands-Augustins, 6e (phone: 43-26-75-96) Expensive.

Vivarois – Claude Peyrot is one of France's finest chefs. Specialties in his small, elegant eating place include curried oysters au gratin, turbot, and assortments of desserts. Closed weekends and August. Reservations necessary. 192 Av. Victor-Hugo, 16e (phone: 45-04-04-31). Expensive.

Auberge des Deux Signes – This place was once the cellars of the priory of St.-Julien-le-Pauvre; try to get an upstairs table overlooking the gardens. Auvergnat cooking à la nouvelle cuisine. Closed Sundays. Reservations necessary. 46 Rue Galande, 5e (phone: 43-25-46-56). Expensive to moderate.

Brasserie Lorraine – Bustling and convivial until late at night, this place pulls in the neighborhood's bourgeoisie for animated evenings over the foie gras salads. Open daily from noon to 2 AM. Reservations unnecessary. Pl. des Ternes, 8e (phone: 42-27-80-04). Expensive to moderate.

La Cantine des Gourmets – This restaurant specializes in light, inventive creations of high quality. Closed Sundays. Reservations advised. 113 Av. Bourdonnais, 7e (phone: 47-05-47-96). Expensive to moderate.

La Coquille – A classic bistro, where the service is unpretentious and warm, and the food consistently good. From October to May, the house specialty is coquilles St.-Jacques, a version that consists of scallops roasted with butter, shallots, and parsley. Closed Sundays, Mondays, holidays, and August. Reservations advised. 6 Rue du Débarcadère, 17e (phone: 45-74-25-95). Expensive to moderate.

Le Duc – The atmosphere is warm and comfortable, and Paul Minchelli is incomparably inventive with fish and shellfish (cooked and raw). Quality and variety are the rule here, with such specialties as curried oysters, tuna tartar, coquilles St.-Jacques *cru,* and an extraordinary seafood platter. Closed Saturdays, Sundays, and Mondays. Reservations necessary. 243 Bd. Raspail, 14e (phone: 43-22-59-59 or 43-20-96-30). Expensive to moderate.

Morot-Gaudry – On the top floor of a 1920s building with a great view of the Eiffel Tower, especially from the flowered terrace. Among the inventive dishes are calf's liver with raspberry vinegar, compote of chicken with leeks, and rice cake with ginger. Closed weekends. Reservations necessary. 8 Rue de la Cavalerie, 15e (phone: 45-67-06-85). Expensive to moderate.

Pavillon des Princes – Under the direction of Pascal Bonichon, it serves produces delicious duck sausage salad with avocado, coquilles St.-Jacques with fresh pasta, and lamb nuggets with cabbage and tomatoes. Open daily. On the edge of the Bois de Boulogne. Reservations advised. 69 Av. de la Porte d'Auteuil, 16e (phone: 47-43-15-15). Expensive to moderate.

Au Quai d'Orsay – Fashionable, sophisticated, very French, and very intimate. Traditional copious bourgeois cooking and good beaujolais. Closed Sundays. Reservations advised. 49 Quai d'Orsay, 7e (phone: 47-05-69-09). Expensive to moderate.

Le Trou Gascon – Alain Dutournier created the inspired and unusual cooking that features southwestern French specialties and a vast choice of regional wines and Armagnacs. He has moved on to a more elegant neighborhood, but his wife holds down the fort here. Closed weekends. Reservations advised. 40 Rue Taine, 12e (phone: 43-44-34-26). Expensive to moderate.

Allard – A very popular bistro with hearty country cooking and excellent burgundy wines. Snails, turbot, and beef bourguignon are the prime lures. Spring, when white asparagus and the new turnips arrive, is a special time here. Don't miss the chocolate charlotte for dessert. Closed weekends and August and for 10 days at *Christmas*. Reservations advised. 41 Rue St.-André-des-Arts, 6e (phone: 43-26-48-23). Moderate.

L'Amanguier – This series of garden restaurants serves an appetizing brand of nouvelle cuisine. Stick to a main course, which comes with a choice of appetizers, and the price is surprisingly low. The desserts are tempting. Open daily for lunch and dinner. Reservations advised. 51 Rue du Théâtre, 15e (phone: 45-77-04-01); 110 Rue de Richelieu, 2e (phone: 42-96-37-79); 43 Av. des Ternes, 17e (phone: 43-80-19-28); and 12 Av. de Madrid, Neuilly (phone: 47-45-79-73). Moderate.

Ambassade d'Auvergne – Its young chef creates delicious, unusual, classic Auvergnat dishes with a modern touch (try the lentil salad and the sliced ham). Also known for seasonal specialties and wonderful cakes. Open daily for lunch and dinner. Reservations advised. 22 Rue du Grenier-St.-Lazare, 3e (phone: 42-72-31-22). Moderate.

Astier – An honest-to-goodness neighborhood hangout that always is packed, because the clientele knows they can rely on it for the staples of bourgeois cooking, lovingly prepared. Closed Saturdays, Sundays, and August. Reservations advised. 44 Rue Jean-Pierre-Timbaud, 11e (phone: 43-57-16-35). Moderate.

La Barrière Poquelin – The excellent cooking *à la nouvelle cuisine* includes a splendid foie gras salad. Closed Saturdays for lunch, Sundays, and 3 weeks in August. Reservations advised. 17 Rue Molière, 1er (phone: 42-96-22-19). Moderate.

Bistro 121 – A hearty menu and excellent wines are offered in a modern setting that's always chic and crowded. Try *poisson cru mariné au citron vert* (seafood marinated in lime juice) and chocolate charlotte for dessert. Closed Sunday evenings, Mondays, and mid-July to mid-August. Reservations advised. 121 Rue de la Convention, 15e (phone: 45-57-52-90). Moderate.

Le Bistrot de Paris – Michel Oliver offers informality, original and classic bistro fare, and a good wine list, which attract a crowd. Closed Saturdays for lunch and Sundays. Reservations advised. 33 Rue de Lille, 7e (phone: 42-61-16-83). Moderate.

Le Boeuf sur le Toit – In the building that once housed a restaurant of the same name, a haunt of Jean Cocteau and other Paris artists in the 1940s, this eatery off the Champs-Elysées is managed by the Flo group, well known for good value in atmospheric surroundings. Piano bar until 2 AM. Reservations advised. 34 Rue du Colisée, 8e (phone: 43-59-83-80). Moderate.

Bofinger – For magnificent Belle Epoque decor, this is the place; it's one of Paris's oldest brasseries and it is beautiful, even if the food is occasionally disappointing. Order onion soup and *choucroute* and you won't be unhappy. Open daily. Reservations advised. 3 Rue de la Bastille, 4e (phone: 42-72-87-82). Moderate.

Cactus Bleu – High tech, trendy, and lighted by aqua-neon, this draws a chic young crowd to Paris's up and coming Bastille quarter for "Cal-Mex" food and margaritas at the bar. Reservations advised. 8 Rue de Lappe, 11e (phone: 43-38-30-20). Moderate.

Café de la Jatte – Only those in the know venture this far down the Seine for dinner. This leafy island, l'Ile de la Jatte, was ripe for a smart renovation, and this huge, high-ceilinged dining room, with half-moon-shaped windows and a pink floor, is now full of the chic-est local clientele. The fare is healthy and simple: generous salads and roast chicken along with more nouvelle items. Open daily for lunch and dinner. Reservations advised. 60 Av. Vital Bouhot, Neuilly, 15 minutes by car from central Paris (phone: 47-45-04-20). Moderate.

Chez André – A classic, bustling bistro near the chic shopping of Avenue Montaigne. Although a bit too noisy and crowded, it is quite popular with the well-heeled crowd, perhaps because it offers impeccably prepared *sole meuniere, blan-quette de veau, gigôt d'agneau,* and other traditional dishes. Reservations advised. 12 Rue Marbeuf, 8e (phone: 47-20-59-57). Moderate.

Chez Benoît – A pretty but unpretentious bistro with wonderful old-fashioned Lyonnaise cooking and exquisite wines. Just about at the top of the bistro list, it's rated one Michelin star. Closed weekends and August. Reservations necessary. 20 Rue St.-Martin, 4e (phone: 42-72-25-76). Moderate.

Chez Georges – This narrow, old-fashioned bistro — with a whole platoon of matronly waitresses in starched aprons — is a bastion of traditional French cooking. Closed Sundays and holidays. Reservations advised. 1 Rue du Mail, 2e (phone: 42-60-07-11). Moderate.

Chez Josephine and **La Rôtisserie Chez Dumonet** – Two restaurants share the same building and the same management. *Josephine* is an old-time bistro with traditional cuisine and an excellent wine cellar; the *Rôtisserie* is lively and more modern, with steaks and grills over an open fire. *Josephine* is closed weekends and July; the *Rôtisserie,* Mondays, Tuesdays, and August. Reservations advised. 117 Rue du Cherche-Midi, 6e (phone: 45-48-52-40). Moderate.

Chez Pauline – The perfect bistro. The tiny, wood-paneled downstairs room (ask to be seated there) is brightened by large mirrors and fresh flowers; the place settings look like Florentine marbeling. Try the oysters in a watercress sauce or the assortment of seafood with a saffron sauce, and save room for dessert — *mille-feuille* of orange with raspberry sauce is sublime. Closed Saturdays, Sundays, July, and from December 24 to January 2. Reservations advised. 5 Rue Villedo, 1er (phone: 42-96-20-70). Moderate.

Chez Pierre Vedel – Truly original cuisine. Closed weekends, from mid-July to mid-August, and at *Christmastime.* Reservations advised. 19 Rue Duranton, 15e (phone: 45-58-43-17). Moderate.

Chez Toutoune – This modest place specializing in Provençal dishes has become very popular for two good reasons: The food is tasty and the prices are fairly reasonable. The five-course, prix fixe menu features a rather short, but very interesting selection of appetizers, entrées, and desserts. Closed Sundays and mid-August to mid-September. Reservations advised. 5 Rue de Pontoise, 5e (phone: 43-26-56-81). Moderate.

La Coupole – A big, brassy brasserie, once the haunt of Hemingway, Josephine Baker, and Picasso, it is owned by the Flo group. The atmosphere is still great, the food still mediocre. Open daily until 2 AM. Closed August. Reservations advised. 102 Bd. du Montparnasse, 14e (phone: 43-20-14-20). Moderate.

Le Dômarais – This used to be the Crédit Municipal, or state pawnshop, and its elegant cupola now houses a sophisticated restaurant serving such inventions as Camembert fondue, grilled Bayonne ham, and a *petit salé* of duck. Closed Saturdays for lunch and Mondays. Reservations advised. 53 bis Rue des Francs Bourgeois, 4e (phone: 42-74-54-17). Moderate.

L'Escargot Montorgueil – The polished wood paneling, the brass fittings, and the spiral staircase at this beautiful place, which dates from 1830, only add to the pleasure of a meal that might include snails in any of half a dozen styles or duck with orange sauce. Closed Monday lunch. Reservations advised. 38 Rue Montorgueil, 1er (phone: 42-36-83-51). Moderate.

La Ferme St.-Simon – Among our favorites for wholesome *cuisine d'autrefois* (old-fashioned cooking). Nothing very chi-chi here, just well-prepared, authentic dishes — the kinds you'd expect from a traditional Left Bank restaurant. Leave room for dessert; the owner once was a top assistant to Gaston Lenôtre. A perfect place for lunch. Closed Saturday lunch, Sundays, and August. Reservations advised. 6 Rue de St.-Simon, 7e (phone: 45-48-35-74). Moderate.

Au Gamin de Paris – Combines the coziness of a classic bistro with the chic of a historic Marais building and serves well-prepared, imaginative food. Open daily. No reservations after 8 PM. 49 Rue Vieille du Temple, 4e (phone: 42-78-97-24). Moderate.

Jo Goldenberg – The best-known eating house in the Marais's quaint Jewish quarter, with good chopped liver and cheesecake and a range of Eastern European Jewish specialties. It's also a fine place to sip mint tea at the counter in the middle of a busy day. Open daily. Reservations unnecessary. 7 Rue des Rosiers, 4e (phone: 48-87-20-16 or 48-87-70-39). Moderate.

Le Grand Colbert – Bright and brassy, with delightful polychrome, Belle Epoque motifs, and traditional offerings such as *boeuf gros sel* (boiled beef with coarse salt) and *merlan Colbert* (lightly breaded, pan-fried whiting), this newly renovated 19th-century brasserie is next to the Bibliothéque Nationale. Open daily. Reservations advised. In the *Galerie Colbert,* 2 Rue Vivienne, 2e (phone: 42-86-87-88). Moderate.

Julien – Belle Epoque decor with all the flourishes. Reliable, if uninspired, meals are served in a bustling atmosphere until 1:30 AM. Open daily. Reservations advised. 16 Rue du Faubourg-St.-Denis, 10e (phone: 47-70-12-06). Moderate.

Le Manufacture – The second eatery of two-star chef Jean Pierre Vigato (of *Apicius*), this starkly modern place in an old cigar factory at the southern edge of Paris offers an excellent quality/price ratio. Closed Saturday afternoons and Sundays. Reservations advised. 30 Rue Ernest-Renan, Issy Les Moulineaux, 15e (phone: 40-93-08-98). Moderate.

La Marée – Unobtrusive on the outside, there is great comfort within — also the freshest of fish, the best restaurant wine values in Paris, and fabulous desserts. Closed weekends, holidays, and August. Reservations advised. 1 Rue Daru, 8e (phone: 47-63-52-42). Moderate.

Le Moulin du Village – Light and airy, especially in summer, when tables are put out on the cobbles of Cité Berryer, a tiny pedestrian alley very near the Madeleine, just off the Rue Royale. Cuisine is nouvelle and wines good. Closed Sundays. Reservations advised. 25 Rue Royale, 8e (phone: 42-65-08-47). Moderate.

Le Muniche – St.-Germain's best brasserie is a bustling place with a rather extensive menu, and it's popular until 3 AM. Open daily. Reservations advised. 27 Rue de Buci, 6e (phone: 46-33-62-09). Moderate.

La Petite Chaise – Founded in 1680, it occupies 2 stories of a 17th-century stone house on the Left Bank. The intimate (and slightly run-down) atmosphere of the home of an ancient aunt characterizes this place, with brocaded walls, brass chandeliers, and antique oils contributing to the period decor. The trout you see swimming in a tank also are on the menu, as are specialties like shellfish crêpes and veal Pojarsky, in which the meat is combined with minced chicken. Always open. Reservations advised. 36 Rue de Grenelle, 7e (phone: 42-22-13-35). Moderate.

Au Pied de Cochon – No more *choucroute* on the menu (sob!). Crowded and colorful 24 hours a day, its customers enjoy shellfish, pigs' feet, and great crocks of onion soup, all in the old *Les Halles* area. Unfortunately, the food and service aren't what they used to be, and a garish redecoration has mangled most of the old atmosphere. Reservations advised. 6 Rue Coquillière, 1er (phone: 42-36-11-75). Moderate.

Pierre Traiteur – A delightful place with admirable bourgeois cooking and lovely Chinon and Saumur wines. Closed weekends and August. Reservations necessary. 10 Rue de Richelieu, 1er (phone: 42-96-27-17). Moderate.

Le Récamier – The so-called garden is actually a courtyard between a couple of high-rise buildings, but as the sun goes down, it's a very congenial place to dine in good weather. Martin Cantegrit is a perfect host, and the menu features first-rate fish dishes (try the turbot, if possible). The apple tart for dessert is special (order it warm), and the wine list is one of the most fairly priced on the Left Bank. Closed Sundays. Reservations necessary. 4 Rue Récamier, 7e (phone: 45-48-86-58). Moderate.

Restaurant du Marché – Cuisine Landaise, which means solid, country-style cooking — foie gras, *confits d'oie,* and fine wines from the Landes region in the southwest of France, near Bordeaux. An amazing choice of herb teas and a pretty terrace for summer dining. Open daily for lunch and dinner. Reservations advised. 59 Rue de Dantzig, 15e (phone: 45-32-26-88 or 45-33-23-72). Moderate.

La Rôtisserie du Beaujolais – A de rigueur spot for Paris's "in set" is Claude Terrail's recently opened casual canteen on the quai in the shadow of his three-star gastronomic temple, *Tour d'Argent.* Most of the meat, produce, and cheese served come from Lyons. Closed Monday and Tuesday afternoons. No reservations. 19 Quai de la Tournelle, 5e (phone: 43-54-17-47). Moderate.

Le Soufflé – On the street just behind the Rue Rivoli, not far from Place Vendôme, this is the place to enjoy an orgy of soufflés. We suggest crayfish soufflé for an appetizer, cheese soufflé as a main course, and chocolate soufflé for dessert. Closed Sundays. Reservations advised. 36 Rue du Mont-Thabor, 1er (phone: 42-60-27-19). Moderate.

Tan-Dinh – The perfect pause from a constant diet of French specialties, it is the only non-French restaurant in Paris to earn a Michelin star, and its Vietnamese specialties are simply superb. Shrimp rolls, Vietnamese ravioli, and minced filet of beef are only three examples of the marvelous menu (ask for the version in English). Remarkable wine list. Closed Sundays and August. Reservations advised. No credit cards accepted. 60 Rue de Verneuil, 7e (phone: 45-44-04-84). Moderate.

Le Train Bleu – Fine food, good wine, and Baroque decor so gorgeous it's been made a national monument. And it's in a train station. Open daily for lunch and dinner. Reservations usually unnecessary. Gare de Lyon, 20 Bd. Diderot, 12e (phone: 43-43-09-06). Moderate.

Ty-Coz – Breton cuisine features fish, cider, and crêpes; no meat, no cheese. Closed Sundays and Mondays. Reservations advised. 35 Rue St.-Georges, 9e (phone: 48-78-34-61). Moderate.

Le Zeyer – After a hard morning discount shopping on the nearby Rue d'Alesia, here's a good neighborhood place for mussels *marinière,* grilled *lotte* with sorrel, or platters of shellfish. Open daily. Reservations unnecessary. 234 Av. du Maine, 14e (phone: 45-40-43-88). Moderate.

Androuët – There's a great cheese emporium on the main floor and, upstairs, a unique restaurant where cheese is the base of every dish. In recent years the quality has slipped somewhat, but it still is a unique experience. Closed Sundays. Reservations advised. 41 Rue Amsterdam, 8e (phone: 48-74-26-90). Moderate to inexpensive.

Brasserie Lipp – This famous café is fashionable for a late supper of *choucroute* and Alsatian beer and for people watching inside and out, but be aware that you are likely to be dispatched to second-floor "Siberia." The food's just as good there, however. Closed 15 days at *Christmas.* Reservations advised. 151 Bd. St.-Germain, 6e (phone: 45-48-53-91). Moderate to inexpensive.

Chez La Vieille – Adrienne's cooking is simple, savory, and very popular. For lunch only. Closed weekends. Reservations necessary. 28 Rue de l'Arbre-Sec, 1er (phone: 42-60-15-78). Moderate to inexpensive.

Clos de la Tour – This popular restaurant has "bistro moderne" decor. Closed Saturdays at lunch, Sundays, and August. Reservations advised. 22 Rue Falguière, 15e (phone: 43-22-34-73). Moderate to inexpensive.

Coup de Coeur – With a 2-level design reminiscent of Manhattan's stark Upper West Side eating establishments, this place features inventive cooking, eager waiters, and an interesting wine list. Closed Sundays. Reservations advised. 19 Rue St.-Augustin, 2e (phone: 47-03-45-70). Moderate to inexpensive.

L'Epicurien – Just 55 seats here, in three little rooms around a garden. Closed Saturday lunch and Sundays. Reservations advised. 11 Rue de Nesle, 6e (phone: 43-29-55-78). Moderate to inexpensive.

Joe Allen's – Just like the original on West 46th Street in New York City, it has good T-bone steaks, hamburgers, chili, and apple pie. Open till 1 AM. Open daily. Reservations after 8 PM advised. 30 Rue Pierre-Lescot, 1er (phone: 42-36-70-13). Moderate to inexpensive.

Les Noces de Jeannette – Under new management, this place now offers inventive cuisine at reasonable prices. Closed Sunday evenings. Reservations advised. 14 Rue Favart, 2e (phone: 42-96-36-89). Moderate to inexpensive.

Le Petit Niçois – This tiny bistro, serving delicious bouillabaisse, is a favorite of French TV news crews who broadcast from a nearby building. A few good specials vary from night to night. Closed Sundays and Monday lunch. Reservations advised. 10 Rue Amélie, 7e (phone: 45-51-83-65). Moderate to inexpensive.

Au Petit Riche – Genuine 1900s decor, subtle Touraine cooking, and inexpensive vouvray, chinon, and bourgueil wines. Closed Sundays and August. Reservations advised. 25 Rue Le Peletier, 9e (phone: 47-70-68-68). Moderate to inexpensive.

Le Pharamond – Serves only the best Norman food in a beautiful Belle Epoque, timbered townhouse that has been declared a historic monument by the French government. Famous for *tripes à la mode de Caen* and *pommes soufflés* since 1862. Closed Sundays, Monday lunch, and July. Reservations advised. 24 Rue de la Grande-Truanderie, 1er (phone: 42-33-06-72). Moderate to inexpensive.

Taverne de Nicolas Flamel – Tracing its beginning to 1407, this architectural relic serves anything but old-fashioned food. The young chef turns out what he calls *cuisine moderne,* including a bay scallop and mussel salad, and guinea hen with apricots. Closed Saturday afternoons and Sundays. Reservations advised. 51 Av. de Montmorency, 16e (phone: 42-72-07-11). Moderate to inexpensive.

Tour d'Argent Bastille – The "other" *Tour d'Argent,* this one completely unrelated to Claude Terrail's 3-star temple overlooking the Seine, is a bustling, turn-of-the-century-style brasserie serving oysters and shellfish platters, fish, and grilled meats. Located next to the new *L'Opéra Bastille.* Reservations advised. 6 Pl. de la Bastille, 11e (phone: 43-42-90-32). Moderate to inexpensive.

Atelier Maître Albert – Unlike most other eateries on the Left Bank, this one is pleasantly roomy, with a log fire in winter and an honest prix fixe menu year-round. Notre-Dame looms up in front of you as you walk out the door and onto the quai. Closed Sundays. Reservations advised. 1 Rue Maître-Albert, 5e (phone: 46-33-13-78). Inexpensive.

Aux Bigorneaux – A souvenir of the old *Les Halles,* this place is frequented by arty types and journalists. Especially recommended are the *foie gras frais maison,* the chicory salad, the steak au poivre, the Réserve Maison wine, and the sumptuous desserts. Closed Mondays. Reservations advised. 12 Rue Mondétour, 1er (phone: 45-08-49-33). Inexpensive.

Brasserie Flo – One of the last of the brasseries of the 1900s, owned by the enterprising Flo group. Hidden in a hard-to-find courtyard, it's excellent for oysters, foie gras, wild boar, and Alsatian specialties. Open daily and late. Reservations advised. 7 Cour des Petites-Ecuries, 10e (phone: 47-70-13-59). Inexpensive.

Brissemoret – Popular with Parisians, this eatery serves basic quality food at bargain prices. The tasteful ambience is a perfect setting for excellent foie gras, raw salmon marinated in fresh herbs, and great sauces (try the breast of duck in wine sauce). Closed Saturdays and Sundays. Reservations necessary. 5 Rue St.-Marc, 2e (phone: 42-36-91-72). Inexpensive.

Chez Fernand – A nondescript hole in the wall that produces surprisingly tasty dishes. *Pot au feu,* steak with shallots, and fish pâté all are first-rate, but the real lure is the huge tub of chocolate mousse served for dessert — a chocoholic's fantasy come true. Open evenings only. Reservations advised. 13 Rue Guirsade, 6e (phone: 43-54-61-47). Inexpensive.

Chez Jenny – A roisterous Alsatian brasserie, where the waitresses still wear white lace collars and dirndls. There are oysters year-round, though perhaps more in keeping with the place's character are the huge platters of *choucroute* (sauerkraut and assorted pork meats) accompanied by good Riesling wine. Open daily. No reservations. 39 Bd. du Temple, 3e (phone: 42-74-75-75). Inexpensive.

Chez Marianne – A friendly Jewish delicatessen and restaurant; the falafels make nourishing fuel for any exploration of the Marais. Closed Fridays. Reservations unnecessary. 2 Rue des Hospitalières-St.-Gervais, 4e (phone: 42-72-18-86). Inexpensive.

Chez Yvette – This excellent, small, bourgeois restaurant has good home cooking, lots of choices, and great desserts. Closed weekends and August. Reservations advised. 46 bis Bd. Montparnasse, 6e (phone: 42-22-45-54). Inexpensive.

Chicago Meatpackers – If homesickness strikes, head here for hamburgers or chili; finish your American food fix with apple pie or chocolate chip cheesecake. Open daily. Reservations unnecessary. 8 Rue Coquillière (phone: 40-28-02-33). Inexpensive.

Gérard – A hearty *pot-au-feu* and other country favorites are served at this bistro. Closed Saturday lunch and Sundays. Reservations unnecessary. 4 Rue du Mail, 2e (phone: 42-96-24-36). Inexpensive.

Le Jardin de la Mouffe – A choice of hors d'oeuvres, entrées, and desserts, plus a cheese course, half a carafe of wine, and a pretty garden view. Closed Sundays and Mondays. Reservations unnecessary. 75 Rue Mouffetard, 5e (phone: 47-07-19-29). Inexpensive.

Lunchtime – One of the few eateries in Paris that satisfies the desire for a light lunch, serving crispy mixed salads made with the freshest greens and a wide range of sandwiches, including blue cheese with cream, curried chicken with currants, and American standbys such as roast beef. The desserts are homemade and delicious. Lunch only. Closed Saturdays, Sundays, holidays, and August. Reservations unnecessary. Two locations: 156 bis Av. Charles-de-Gaulle, Neuilly (phone: 46-24-08-99), and 255 Rue St.-Honoré (phone: 42-60-80-40). Inexpensive.

Moulin à Vent (Chez Henri) – Located across the street from what was once Paris's wine market, this bistro's decor has remained intact for over 40 years. The bar is adorned with half-barrels and small lights that are inscribed with the names of different wines and growers. The menu of meats (especially sausages from the Ardèche) and salads also has stayed the same. Try the frogs' legs and the steak with shallots. Closed Sundays, Mondays, and August. Reservations necessary. 20 Rue des Fossés St.-Bernard, 5e (phone: 43-54-99-37). Inexpensive.

Paul – Once a secret bistro, it is now known by the whole world. There's good solid fare here, and the premises always are packed. Closed Mondays, Tuesdays, and August. Reservations advised. 15 Pl. Dauphine, 1er (phone: 43-54-21-48). Inexpensive.

Petit Zinc – A popular late (3 AM) spot for fish, oysters, foie gras, and an ample, reasonably priced wine list. Open daily. Reservations advised. 25 Rue de Buci, 6e (phone: 46-33-51-66). Inexpensive.

Polidor – Regulars here keep their napkins in numbered pigeonholes, and the place's history includes frequent patronage by such starving artists as Paul Verlaine,

James Joyce, Ernest Hemingway, and, more recently, Jean-Paul Belmondo. The College of Pataphysics, founded by Raymond Queneau and Ionesco, still meets here regularly for the good family-style food. Ask to see the house scrapbook. Closed Sundays, Mondays, and August. Reservations unnecessary. 41 Rue Monsieur-le-Prince, 6e (phone: 43-26-95-34). Inexpensive.

Le Procope – One of Paris's oldest restaurants, where the food is reasonably good and the atmosphere couldn't be more Parisian. Open daily. Reservations advised. 13 Rue de l'Ancienne-Comédie, 6e (phone: 43-26-99-20). Inexpensive.

Relais de Venise – There's always a crowd waiting outside this place near the Porte Maillot, better known as "L'Entrecôte." The prix fixe menu includes free second helpings of steaks with pepper sauce and French fries. Fancy strawberry desserts cost extra. Open daily. No reservations. 271 Bd. Pereire, 17e (phone: 45-74-27-97). Inexpensive.

Robert et Louise – Family bistro, with warm paneled decor and a very high standard for ingredients and cooking. Try the *boeuf bourguignon* or the open-fire–grilled *côte de boeuf*. Also good are the *fromage blanc* and the *wine en pichet*. Closed Sundays, holidays, and August. Reservations unnecessary. 64 Rue Vieille-du-Temple, 3e (phone: 42-78-55-89). Inexpensive.

Le Roi du Pot-au-Feu – A very good place to sample this delicious peasant dish. Closed Sundays. Reservations advised. 34 Rue Vignon, 9e (phone: 47-42-37-10). Inexpensive.

La Route du Beaujolais – It's a barnlike workers' bistro on the Left Bank, serving Lyonnaise specialties and Beaujolais wines. Don't miss the *charcuterie* and the fresh bread here, and try the *tarte tatin* (caramelized apple tart) for dessert. Closed Sundays. Reservations unnecessary. 17 Rue de Lourmel, 15e (phone: 45-79-31-63). Inexpensive.

Le Trumilou – The formidable proprietress sets the tone of this robust establishment, which serves huge, steaming portions of boar, pheasant, and venison in season under a frieze of some excruciatingly bad rustic oils. Closed Mondays. Reservations unnecessary. 84 Quai de l'Hôtel-de-Ville, 5e (phone: 42-77-63-98). Inexpensive.

Vagenende – An Art Nouveau spot with fantasy decor that has changed little since it opened in 1898. It features adequate, filling meals at low prices. Open daily until 1 AM. Reservations unnecessary. 142 Bd. St.-Germain, 6e (phone: 43-26-68-18). Inexpensive.

Assiette au Boeuf – Steaks, salad, and *pommes frites,* with music in the evening. Open daily until 1 AM. No reservations. 123 Champs-Elysées, 8e (phone: 47-20-01-13). Very inexpensive.

Bistro de la Gare – Michel Oliver offers a choice of three appetizers and three main courses with *pommes frites.* Excellent for a quick lunch. Open daily. No reservations. Ten locations, including 73 Champs-Elysées, 8e (phone: 43-59-67-83); 59 Bd. Montparnasse, 6e (phone: 45-48-38-01); 38 Bd. des Italiens, 9e (phone: 48-24-49-61). Very inexpensive.

Chartier – Huge, turn-of-the-century place with lots of down-to-earth food for the money. No reservations. 7 Rue du Faubourg-Montmartre, 9e (phone: 47-70-86-29). Very inexpensive.

Drouot – The younger member of the Chartier family, but less known, and with more berets and fewer tourists. The waiters and waitresses, clad in black and white, look as if they emerged from a Renoir painting, although the decor is 1920s, with brass hat stands. The simple food is a bargain. To avoid a long wait for a table, arrive before 9 PM. No reservations. 103 Rue de Richelieu, 2e (phone: 42-96-68-23). Very inexpensive.

L'Etoile Verte – Not much to look at, but always full, it serves fresh and generous helpings of standard French classics — quenelles, seafood timbales, and so forth — at rock-bottom prices. Open daily. Reservations unnecessary. 13 Rue Brey, 17e (phone: 43-80-69-34). Very inexpensive.

L'Olympic Bar – Crowded at all hours, this popular hangout is open for meals at lunch only. Blue-collar workers, students, executives, fashionable women, and others eat and drink with pinball noise as a background. The decor is nothing to speak of, but the food is good, the portions huge, and the price is right. Closed Sundays and sometimes for Saturday lunch. Reservations unnecessary. 77 Rue St.-Dominique, 7e (phone: 45-51-75-87). Very inexpensive.

Le Petit Gavroche – A hole-in-the-wall bistro-cum-restaurant with a lively clientele, an inexpensive and classic menu, and the feeling that nothing has changed in years. Reservations unnecessary. 15 Rue Ste.-Croix-de-la-Bretonnerie, 4e (phone: 48-87-74-26). Very inexpensive.

Le Petit St.-Benoît – French cooking at its simplest, in a plain little place with tiled floors and curlicued hat stands. Open weekdays. Reservations unnecessary. 4 Rue St.-Benoît, 6e (phone: 42-60-27-92). Very inexpensive.

Au Pied de Fouet – This former coach house has had its habitués, including celebrities as diverse as Graham Greene, Le Corbusier, and Georges Pompidou. Service is fast and friendly, and it's a place to order the daily special. Desserts, such as *charlotte au chocolat,* are marvelous. Arrive early; it closes at 9 PM. Closed Saturday evenings, Sundays, 2 weeks at *Christmas* and *Easter,* and August. 45 Rue de Babylone, 7e (phone: 47-05-12-27). Very inexpensive.

■**EXTRA SPECIAL:** Although we've noted the existence of *Fauchon* in *Shopping,* we would be remiss in omitting it from the restaurant listings. Actually three spectacular stores stocking elegant edibles (at 28 Place de la Madeleine), *Fauchon* is considered so much a bastion of the privileged that one of its stores was bombed by radicals back in 1978. But the shops thankfully have long been back in full working order, which is a blessing for every abdomen in town.

One *Fauchon* shop specializes in the most beautiful fruits and vegetables available anywhere, plus pâtés, terrines, and as many other incomparable carryout items as even the most jaded gourmet's palate could conceive. If you're planning any sort of picnic, and are looking for something out of the ordinary, this is the place to pack your hamper. There also is a new grocery and sweet shop on the street level.

But it's across the narrow street in the far corner of the Place de la Madeleine that all of Paris congregates for nonpareil pastries, coffee, and an occasional snack or drink. Chocolate *opéra* cakes and macaroons in many hues, as well as *mille feuilles* and other custardy concoctions, are sold by the slice and can be eaten standing at one of the narrow ledges right in the store. And last year, the two original shops were joined by a *Fauchon* coffee shop in the basement of the building located at 30 Place de la Madeleine and by a first class restaurant on the second floor. Breakfasts, lunches, snacks, and coffee are served downstairs throughout the day, while the restaurant upstairs is open for lunch and dinner. If you need a sugar surge during the course of your Paris meanderings, these are the places to take your high-caloric breaks.

For chocoholics: The very best hot chocolate in Paris (if not the universe) is served at *Angelina's* on the Rue Rivoli, 1er. The best chocolate ice cream in the City of Light is at *Berthillon's* on the Ile St.-Louis (31 Rue St.-Louis-en-l'Ile, 4e) and the new location near the Porte Maillot métro in the Palais de Congrès. The best (and most generous) servings of chocolate mousse are offered at *Chez Fernand,* 13 Rue Guirsade, 6e, on the Left Bank.

WINE BARS AND CAFÉS: Choosing a place to drink is not a pressing problem in Paris. Following is a selection of watering holes to suit a variety of tastes and thirsts. Prices tend to be higher than in the United States, with a *café crème* or a glass of red wine costing $3 or more in the more expensive establishments. The moderate ones charge $2 to $3 for the same, and you pay less than $2 in the inexpensive spots.

Café Costes – Paris's latest word in post-modernism, something of a revolution on the scene. It has an impressive marble stairway, a clock inspired by Fritz Lang's film *Metropolis,* some wild high-tech restrooms, and a fashionable complement of lounge lizards. Open daily. Reservations unnecessary. Sq. des Innocents, 1er (phone: 45-08-54-39). Expensive.

Fouquet's – All the cafés on the Champs-Elysées are overpriced and most are nasty, so it may be worth paying the inflated tab for a coffee at this one, which at least has more style than all the rest — as well as a large corner for outdoor tables in summer. Always open. Reservations advised for dinner; unnecessary for the café. 99 Champs-Elysées, 8e (phone: 47-23-70-60). Expensive.

Harry's Bar – The son of the original Harry, who opened this celebrated establishment in 1911, is still at the helm here. And the memories of past patrons like Ernest Hemingway, Gertrude Stein, and George Gershwin are almost as tangible as the university flags and banners that hang from the paneled walls. Open 10:30 AM to 4 AM every day but *Christmas.* Reservations unnecessary. 5 Rue Daunou, 2e (phone: 42-61-71-14). Expensive.

Willi's – An enterprising Englishman set up this smart little wine bar, a pleasant walk through the Palais Royal gardens and only minutes from the *Louvre.* The wine selection — a list of 150 — is one of the best in Paris, with an emphasis on Côtes du Rhône. The chef creates some appetizing salads as well as a *plat du jour.* Closed Sundays. Reservations unnecessary. 13 Rue des Petits-Champs, 1er (phone: 42-61-05-09). Expensive to moderate.

Blue Fox – On a cobbled market street behind the Madeleine, this wine bar has a list of about 20 reasonably priced wines by the glass that changes every 2 weeks. And there's good *charcuterie* to go with them. Closed Saturday evenings and Sundays. Reservations unnecessary. Cité Berryer, 25 Rue Royale, 8e (phone: 42-65-08-47 or 42-65-10-72). Moderate.

L'Ecluse – This unassuming bistro looking onto the Seine has fathered five others, more sophisticated, in the Rue François-I, at the Madeleine, at the *Opera,* in *Les Halles,* and in Neuilly. Its red velvet benches and wooden tables — not to mention its bordeaux and its fresh, homemade foie gras — remain unchanged. Open daily. Reservations unnecessary. 15 Quai des Grands-Augustins, 6e (phone: 46-33-58-74), and several other locations in Paris. Moderate.

Le Pain et Le Vin – An imaginative wine bar with daily hot luncheon specials. It's operated by four Parisian chefs, including Alain Dutournier of the *Carré des Feuilliants* and *Au Trou Gascon.* Closed Wednesday evenings. Reservations unnecessary. Several locations, including 1 Rue d'Armaille, 17e (phone: 47-63-88-29). Moderate.

Le Petit Bacchus – A wine bar specializing in unusual regional wines, displayed in crowded rows. You can buy wine by the bottle to take home or on a picnic, or sample them at the counter with cheese and *charcuterie.* Closed Sundays and Mondays. Reservations unnecessary. 13 Rue du Cherche-Midi, 6e (phone: 45-44-01-07). Moderate.

Taverne Henri IV – A selection of nearly 20 wines are offered by the glass, along with generous servings of simple food such as open sandwiches of ham, cheese, sausage, or a terrine of wild boar. You also can order cold food combinations by the platter. Closed weekends. Reservations unnecessary. 13 Pl. du Pont-Neuf, 1er (phone: 43-54-27-90). Moderate.

Zimmer – Centrally located and with new moldings and chandeliers, this is the place to stop off for a drink before or after a show at one of the nearby theaters. Reservations unnecessary. 1 Pl. du Châtelet, 4e (phone: 42-36-74-04). Moderate.

Au Duc de Richelieu – Specializes in the wines of Beaujolais, Chiroubles, Juliénas, St.-Amour, and so on. A cozy atmosphere and lots of wine tasting certificates on the walls. Closed Sundays and August. Reservations unnecessary. 110 Rue de Richelieu, 2e (phone: 42-96-38-38). Inexpensive.

Jacques Melac – An old-fashioned wine bar run by a young, extravagantly musta-chioed man from the Auvergne, who bottles and sells his own rustic wines. Closed Sundays and Mondays. Open until 6:30 PM except Tuesdays and Thursdays when a set dinner is served. No reservations. 42 Rue Léon-Frot, 11e (phone: 43-70-59-27). Inexpensive.

La Palette – This Left Bank hideaway on a quiet square, with outdoor tables during the summer, stays lively with a young crowd until 2 AM every morning except in August. Perhaps the monocled gentlemen on the 1930s tiles and the oils hung on the walls paid the bills of never-to-be-successful painters. Closed Sundays, holidays, and August. Reservations unnecessary. 43 Rue de Seine, 6e (phone: 43-26-68-15). Inexpensive.

Le Rubis – A tiny corner bar with an old-fashioned atmosphere and a big selection of wines — about 30 in all. With your glass of wine try the pork *rillettes*, a savory meat paste made on the premises. Closed on weekends and 2 weeks in August. No reservations. 10 Rue du Marché-St.-Honoré, 1er (phone: 42-61-03-34). Inexpensive.

Au Sauvignon – The no-nonsense couple in blue overalls who run this tiny corner bar look as if they just stepped in from the country. They seem to be in perpetual motion, pouring the white sauvignon and carving up chunky sandwiches from the famous Poilane bakery not far away. Closed Sundays, 2 weeks in January, *Easter*, and August. Reservations unnecessary. 80 Rue des Sts.-Pères, 7e (phone: 45-48-49-02). Inexpensive.

La Tartine – One of the old, authentic bistros, with a colorful local clientele and a good selection of wine by the glass. Closed Tuesdays and Wednesday mornings. Reservations unnecessary. 24 Rue de Rivoli, 4e (phone: 42-72-76-85). Inexpensive.

La Tour de Monthlery – Hidden away on a small street near *Les Halles,* this animated bistro with sawdust on the floor and hams hanging from the rafters serves hearty, simple fare at bargain prices. Reservations unnecessary. 5 Rue de Prouvaires, 1er (phone: 42-36-21-82). Inexpensive.

REIMS

This busy provincial center is in many ways more French than Paris. For one thing, it is far more representative of the majority of French cities. For another, it offers a little of everything that the mind's eye tends to include in a mental image of France. It has a glorious cathedral, impressive medieval churches, and elegant châteaux, sidewalk cafés and eminent restaurants, stylish shops, the headquarters of famous wine firms — even barges floating downriver and a canal through the center of town. And just outside the city are the celebrated vineyards of Champagne, as well as the not-so-celebrated battlefields of World Wars I and II, and many a place to linger for a lovely pastoral view.

The first settlement on the Vesle River had been for centuries the capital of a Gallic tribe, the Remi, before Caesar conquered Gaul from 58 to 51 BC. During the Roman occupation it became one of the main and most beautiful cities of Gaul, a crossroads rich in commerce and monuments, far outstripping the village of Paris in importance. The Romans called their city of more than 80,000 inhabitants Durocortorum. Later the name became Rheims, and in the 18th century the "h" was dropped, leaving today's Reims (pronounced *Rance*). It is still common in English to use the antiquated spelling, but in French and in France all signs and references are to Reims.

Four dates stand out in the exceptional history of this city: 496, 1429, 1914, and 1945. The history of France may be said to have begun in Reims in 496 when St. Remi, the Bishop of Reims, baptized and crowned Clovis I King of all the Franks in a church that preceded Reims Cathedral. Though Clovis (a name that in time evolved into "Louis") chose Paris as his capital, it was in memory of this ceremony that Reims later became the city of coronations. From Louis VII, who ascended the throne in 1137, to Charles X, who was crowned in 1825, it was customary for the Kings of France to be crowned in Reims Cathedral, and the extent to which this setting became a prerequisite to royal legitimacy is illustrated by the most famous of the coronations, that of Charles VII in 1429.

In an attempt to end the Hundred Years War with England, Charles's father had agreed to a treaty appointing the King of England heir to France. Though the disinherited Charles repudiated the treaty and undertook to rule, his authority was limited to a small realm and contested by both the English and their French allies. It was at this point that Joan of Arc, driven by visions and voices, appeared in aid of her beleaguered king. After rallying his forces and leading them to an important victory at Orléans, she insisted that he go to Reims, advising him that "there lies the salvation of France." "But I was crowned at Poitiers!" he is reported to have replied. "Poitiers can only crown the Kings of Bourges" was her response. "Kings of France are made at Reims."

In all, 37 Kings and 11 Queens and Regents of France went to Reims to be "made," and the city, which already enjoyed a reputation for the making of saints (13 came from Reims between the 3rd and 8th centuries), came to be regarded somewhat as hallowed ground.

Unfortunately, as far as geography is concerned, the ground on which Reims stands is in a rather fateful position. Its region — Champagne — is largely an expanse of open, level land that has been a route of invasion and a battlefield throughout European history. As a consequence, numerous wars, well before and well after the Hundred Years War, have raged in and around the city. In fact, between the 5th and 10th centuries, Reims was flattened to the ground seven times. In the modern age, however, no war left its mark on the body and spirit of the city more than World War I. The Germans occupied Reims for 10 days in 1914, but for almost 3 years they controlled the surrounding heights, from which they unceasingly bombarded it for 1,051 days. Reims was virtually leveled. Some 80% of its homes were destroyed, and most public buildings were severely damaged, including the cathedral.

In World War II, the German occupation lasted much longer, for 4 years, and war damage once again was not minimal. After Allied soldiers liberated Reims in 1944, General Eisenhower established his headquarters in a large technical high school here, and it was in one of its schoolrooms that the unconditional surrender of the Third Reich was signed on May 8, 1945.

Today, although quite a few things in Reims are of historical or artistic note, most visitors include the city in their itinerary for one of two reasons if not for both: the soaring Gothic Cathedral of Notre-Dame and the ancient, labyrinthine cellars of the great champagne houses, full of millions of bottles of truly sparkling wine. These two tourist "musts" rank with the best France has to offer. Notre-Dame de Reims is commonly ranked with Notre-Dame de Paris and Notre-Dame de Chartres as the most sublime of France's cathedrals and among the most magnificent in the world. Champagne is, considering its nearly universal connotation of joy and celebration, doubtless the most famous wine in the world, and it comes only from this area.

Reims also is a center of the textile industry, known especially for woolens as far back as the 12th century. It also has long been recognized for its university, which Pope Paul III founded in 1547. The destruction and rebuilding of this century have left it with extensive suburbs and its share of high-rise buildings, and it must be said that Reims today is not the most stunning of cities. However, its center is particularly lively, especially on the Rue de Vesle and on the long Place Drouet-d'Erlon, and enough of it has survived the wars and invasions to tell a fascinating tale of French history.

REIMS AT-A-GLANCE

SEEING THE CITY: The vine- and tree-covered hills that surround Reims provide more than one place for a panoramic view, and if you have a car, you no doubt will find your own spot, probably en route to the grape-growing region of the Montagne de Reims to the south. Be aware that the modern buildings on the outskirts of Reims sometimes block out the city's most impressive structure, the Cathedral of Notre-Dame, and that the ancient church you see may be the Basilique St.-Remi rather than the cathedral itself. In the center of the city, you can survey the area from the cathedral towers.

For leisurely, ground-level viewing, try a 45-minute jaunt on the sightseeing train called "Petit Train de Reims" or a horse-drawn carriage ride. Both are offered during July and August and depart from the cathedral.

 SPECIAL PLACES: Long, wide Place Drouet-d'Erlon, lined with hotels, cafés, and arcaded houses, is a good place to begin a tour of the city. Near one end of it is the Rue de Vesle, from which you can easily walk to the cathedral and surrounding sights. At the other end it runs into Boulevard Foch–Boulevard Général-Leclerc across from the railroad station and at the midpoint of a huge mall. The Place de la République, with the Porte Mars, is at the northern extreme of the mall, and from here it is the Rue de Mars that will set you toward the cathedral, while the Rue du Champ-de-Mars heads toward the Chapelle Foujita and the cellars of several of the major champagne firms. Other champagne firms are on the other side of town, clustered in the vicinity of the Basilique St.-Remi and Parc Pommery.

THE CITY

Cathédrale Notre-Dame de Reims – This magnificent cathedral is one of the most historic structures to be seen in France today. The first church on the spot was the Cathédrale St.-Nicaise, in which Remi baptized Clovis I and crowned him King of the Franks in 496. The event became the basis of a later precedent, and from the coronation of Louis VII in the second church on the spot in 1137 to the coronation of Charles X in the third and present church in 1825, the Kings of France, with few exceptions, were crowned here. The cathedral is also one of the most important monuments of the French artistic heritage. After the second church was destroyed by fire in 1210, construction of the edifice seen today began in 1211 and was all but complete a mere century later (the towers were added in the 15th century). Consequently, the style of Notre-Dame de Reims, conceived by master builder Jean d'Orbais and largely respected by his successors, is pure 13th century, representative — along with the cathedrals of Chartres, Paris, and Amiens — of the classic period, or the golden age, of French Gothic architecture. This unity endures, even though the cathedral suffered heavy shelling during World War I, which burned the roof, damaged the apse, and caused a section of the arches to fall down, requiring a long restoration. Also in this century, some of the statuary — either damaged or weatherworn — has been removed from the exterior and replaced by copies.

The cathedral's western façade is one of the most splendid conceptions of the 13th century. Its three deep doorways constitute a Bible in sculptured stone, with the central doorway dedicated to the Virgin, the left door to the saints and martyrs, and the right door to Christ and the prophets. Among the glorious statues, note the groups representing the Visitation and the Presentation to the Temple in the central door and the two angels flanking the scalped St. Nicaise in the left door. One of these, the *ange au sourire* (the smiling angel), is the most famous of the cathedral's many angels and also is known as the *sourire de Reims* (the smile of Reims). The upper part of the façade is ornamented with a gallery of colossal statues of kings.

Inside, the tall windows, the clerestory, and the spectacular stained glass windows provide superb lighting for the nave. Much of the 13th-century glass, including the awe-inspiring rose window of the western façade and the rose window in the northern transept, was restored after World War I. Other windows are completely modern, including the six windows in the axial chapel drawn by Marc Chagall and executed in

1974. Not to be overlooked is the interior sculpture, as in the remarkable ensemble of masterly statues in niches surrounding the smaller rose window of the façade and in the very beautiful capitals of the columns. In summer, the remaining bare walls come alive with 17 magnificent tapestries of the 16th century depicting the life of the Virgin. (At other times of the year, they are shown in the *Palais du Tau*, where the cathedral's treasures can also be viewed.)

No matter when you visit the cathedral, try to come back to see the façade and the stained glass–lit nave in the early morning or at twilight. Then, too, is when the face of the *ange au sourire* is most beguiling. For a lovely view of the spectacular flying buttresses, stand in the garden of the adjacent *Palais du Tau*. There's also an interesting view of the cathedral, and of surrounding Reims, from atop its towers (entry possible at 11 AM and 3, 4, and 5 PM). Two different light and laser shows are presented at the cathedral Thursdays, Fridays, and Saturdays from June through September. New *son et lumières* presentations of the coronations were begun last year. They are shown on Saturdays evenings at 9:30 PM from late June to mid-August. For information, call the tourist office at 26-47-25-69. Enter the cathedral from Pl. du Cardinal-Luçon.

Palais du Tau – Next door to the cathedral, this rebuilt archbishop's palace takes its name from the shape of the original plan of the building (the Greek letter "T," or "tau"). It was the residence of the king at the time of the coronations, and the site of post-coronation banquets. Now a museum, it contains monumental sculptures from the exterior of the cathedral, tapestries, and the cathedral treasury, including a 9th-century pendant said to have been the talisman of Charlemagne, a 12th-century chalice used in numerous coronations, and mementos of the coronation of Charles X. Open daily, except *Christmas* and *New Year's*. Admission charge. Pl. du Cardinal-Luçon (phone: 26-47-74-39).

Basilique St.-Remi – In almost any other city, the glories of this ancient abbey church of the Benedictines would be legend. It is the oldest of Reims's churches and, like the cathedral whose fame overshadows it, it has been beautifully restored following the damage of World War I. Most impressive are its Romanesque nave and transept, which date from the middle of the 11th century, and its immense choir, an example of the primitive Gothic style of the end of the 12th century. The Flamboyant Gothic façade of the southern transept dates from the 16th century. The church also contains the tomb of St. Remi (actually a 19th-century reconstruction of a previous tomb). Next door, the old abbey, which was begun at the end of the 12th century, now serves as the city's archaeological museum (see *Museums*). A sound and light show is presented free of charge Saturdays at 9:30 PM in July, August, and September. For information, call 26-85-35-22). Rue Simon.

Musée St.-Denis – Also called the *Musée des Beaux-Arts*, this houses a rich collection of tapestries and ceramics, 13 sketches of German princes by both the elder and younger Cranach, and French paintings from the 17th century to the present. With 27 canvases on display, Corot is the most heavily represented of the French painters, but there are also paintings by pre-Impressionists, Impressionists, and post-Impressionists, including Boudin, Pissarro, Monet, Sisley, Renoir, Dufy, Matisse, and Picasso. The gardens also may be visited. Closed Tuesdays, and Saturday and Sunday afternoons. Admission charge. 8 Rue Chanzy (phone: 26-47-28-44).

Place Royale – The main square of the city is a beautiful example of 18th-century architecture, a legacy of the reign of Louis XV, whose statue stands in the middle. The original statue by Pigalle was destroyed during the French Revolution, though this one, by Cartellier, is still set off by Pigalle's pedestal statues.

Porte Mars – A remnant of Gallo-Roman times when Reims was known as Durocortorum, this imposing 3rd-century triumphal arch is a memorial to Augustus Caesar. During the Middle Ages, it became a gate in the city's ramparts. Pl. de la République.

Chapelle Foujita – This striking chapel in the Romanesque style was designed and decorated by the famous Japanese painter of the School of Paris, Léonard Foujita, who converted to Catholicism late in his life. The color, freshness, and individuality of the stained glass windows and frescoes are stunning. A gift of Mumm Champagne to the city, the chapel, also known as Notre-Dame de la Paix, was opened in 1966. Closed Wednesdays and in very cold weather. Admission charge. 33 Rue du Champs-de-Mars.

Salle de Reddition – General Eisenhower's headquarters during the final days of World War II were in a high school behind the railroad station. The Germans signed an unconditional surrender in a simple schoolroom here on May 8, 1945 — VE Day — and the room has been preserved as it was that day, with operational maps on the wall. Closed Tuesdays and holidays. 12 Rue Franklin-Roosevelt (phone: 26-47-84-19).

CHAMPAGNE CELLARS

After a visit to the cathedral, a tour of one or more champagne cellars is a second "must" for visitors to Reims — especially for those who are not going on to the much smaller city of Epernay, which rivals Reims as the capital of the champagne industry. Reims is the home of a greater number of champagne houses, and some of its cellars are the oldest in the region, dating back to ancient times when the Romans excavated huge chalk pits (*crayères*) in the limestone base of the city, creating inverted funnels that they undoubtedly used as cool pantries. These gigantic cones often were connected underground, and in recent centuries, it was discovered that conditions in this nether-world were perfect for the aging of champagne. (For an introduction to the history of champagne and how it is made, see the beginning of the *Champagne* tour route in DIRECTIONS.) Today, the underground tunnels have been expanded so that there are miles and miles of them, some with the bare chalk walls still exposed, some covered by brick, tile, and other materials. Of the more than a dozen champagne houses in Reims that open their cellars to visitors, a number are beyond the Place de la République in the Champ-de-Mars section of the city; others are beyond the Basilique St.-Remi around Place des Droits-de-l'Homme and nearby streets including Avenue du Général-Giraud, Boulevard Henri-Vasnier, and Rue des Crayères.

Before descending into any of the caves, be sure to have a sweater or jacket handy; a constant temperature of 45F to 50F is one reason the cellars are ideal for making champagne. Also be reasonably well shod, because in most cases you'll be doing a fair amount of walking in a damp and dimly lit environment. All the champagne houses listed below offer guided tours; unless otherwise indicated, visits are weekdays, except holidays and the month of August, and by appointment only (9 AM to noon and 2 to 5 PM are accepted hours). All offer tours in English, though off-season travelers should verify that an English-speaking guide will be available when setting up an appointment. There is no charge for the tours, which sometimes end with a free champagne tasting.

Besserat de Bellefon – These are the most modern cellars, built when the company moved from nearby Ay to Reims in 1970. Allée du Vignoble (phone: 26-36-09-18).

Charles Heidsieck – Fifty rooms of pure chalk linked by galleries. The Gallo-Roman *crayères,* shaped like a bottle end, were rediscovered in the 18th century. Tours are not always available; call ahead. 3 Pl. des Droits-de-l'Homme (phone: 26-85-03-27).

Heidsieck Monopole – Eight miles of chalk cellars. 83 Rue Coquebert (phone: 26-07-39-34).

Krug – Here the cellars are standard, but the famous oak barrels used for the first fermentation are special. Write or call 2 months in advance for appointments. Krug family members conduct 2-hour tours. Closed in July. 5 Rue Coquebert (phone: 26-88-24-24).

Lanson – Beautiful wine presses are one of the things that make this an interesting visit. Open weekdays and by appointment. 12 Bd. Lundy (phone: 26-40-36-26).

Mumm – No appointment required to tour the 11 miles of gigantic cellars, open weekdays from 9 to 11 AM and 2 to 5 PM, year-round. The tour is very informative — one of the best. 34 Rue du Champ-de-Mars (phone: 26-40-22-73).

Piper-Heidsieck – No appointment is required here, either, where part of the visit is aboard an electric train. Open daily from late March to mid-November and weekdays only the rest of the year. 51 Bd. Henry-Vasnier (phone: 26-85-01-94).

Pommery – Fascinating cellars: Down 116 steps are 11 miles of avenues with their crossroads, statues (including a 14th-century Virgin), bas-reliefs, and extraordinary *crayères* that form pyramidal wells reaching through smooth white walls to daylight. Open all year; appointments required on weekends and public holidays. 5 Pl. Général-Gouraud (phone: 26-05-05-01).

Louis Roederer – The enormous oak tuns (casks) here are extraordinary. Make reservations to see them well in advance of a visit. Closed during July. 21 Bd. Lundy (phone: 26-40-42-11).

Ruinart Pere & Fils – The pyramidal *crayères* date from the 2nd century BC and are the only ones in the region classified as a historic landmark. 4 Rue des Crayères (phone: 26-85-40-29).

Taittinger – An interesting historical slide show precedes the tour of cellars set up in the crypt of the former abbey of St. Nicaise and remarkable for their pointed arches. Other cellars are in beautiful triangular *crayères* of the 3rd and 4th centuries. Open daily from March through November; closed weekends in winter. No appointment necessary. 9 Pl. St.-Nicaise (phone: 26-85-45-35).

Veuve Clicquot – No appointment is necessary to visit these extraordinary funnel-shaped *crayères,* which date from Gallo-Roman times. There are 15 miles of underground galleries with splendid bas-reliefs carved into the walls. Hours are seasonal: open daily, except Sundays, from 9 to 11 AM and 2 to 5 PM, April–July and September–October; shorter hours the rest of the year; and by appointment in February. 1 Pl. des Droits-de-l'Homme (phone: 26-85-24-08 or 26-85-00-68).

ENVIRONS

Fort de la Pompelle – This 1880-vintage fort, which stood in defense of Reims during World War I, contains a museum of war mementos — decorations, uniforms, arms, and an exceptional collection of German helmets — of interest to military history buffs. Open daily, 8:30 AM to 7 PM from mid-March to mid-November; 10 AM to 6 PM the rest of the year. Admission charge. About 5½ miles (9 km) east of Reims via N3 and then N44 (phone: 26-49-11-85).

■**EXTRA SPECIAL:** If you have a car, don't miss a drive through the undulating hills and valleys of the Montagne de Reims, the Valley of the Marne, and the Côte des Blancs — nearby areas where the grapes that go into champagne are grown. Not only will you glimpse some of the finest, most famous, and most expensive vineyards in the world, but you will glimpse the quintessential French provincial life, passing through tiny villages with fascinating churches, frequently of the 12th or 13th century, and through lovely pastoral settings. For a suggested itinerary, see *Champagne,* in DIRECTIONS. Better still is a breathtaking balloon flight, with licensed pilots, over Champagne vineyards and villages. Contact *Air Show* (15 bis Pl. St.-Nicaise; phone: 26-82-59-60).

SOURCES AND RESOURCES

TOURIST INFORMATION: The Reims Office de Tourisme is at the Square du Trésor, just to the left of the cathedral (2 Rue Guillaume; phone: 26-47-25-69). Besides some useful free brochures, it provides a walking tour of the cathedral and central city on an audio cassette, which can be rented for about $5. It also houses the Champagne branch of *Accueil de France,* which will book accommodations in or out of the city for a fee.

Local Coverage – Consult Reims's daily newspaper, *L'Union,* published in French.

TELEPHONE: The city code for Reims is 26, which is incorporated into all local 8-digit numbers. When calling a number from the Paris region (including the Ile-de-France), dial 16, wait for the dial tone, then dial the 8-digit number. When calling a number from outside Paris, dial only the 8-digit number. When calling from the US, dial 33 (which is the country code), followed by the 8-digit number.

GETTING AROUND: For much of your visit, probably the best means of transportation will be your own two feet. Many of the shops, restaurants, hotels, churches, and other monuments you will want to see are in the center of the city, within walking distance of the cathedral. It's a hike, though, from there to the Basilique St.-Remi and to many of the champagne cellars, so you'll probably want an alternative mode, especially if you plan to cover the surrounding area.

Airport – Aéroport Reims accommodates a limited number of regional flights (Reims-Lyons is one) and special charters. Betheny (phone: 26-07-18-85) and the Aérodrome Reims-Prunay (phone: 26-49-10-92) both have landing facilities for private planes.

Bus – There's a local bus company (phone: 26-88-25-38) and a long-distance bus company (phone: 26-65-17-07).

Car Rental – Among the firms with offices in Reims are *Avis* (18 Bd. Joffre; phone: 26-47-10-08), *Budget* (Cour de la Gare; phone: 26-40-01-02); *Europcar* (25 Rue du Temple; phone: 26-88-38-38), and *Hertz* (26 Bd. Joffre; phone: 26-47-98-78).

Taxi – Short of renting a car, a taxi is probably the most expedient way to see the city and its environs. Find one at a designated stand — at the station, for instance, and in plenty of other spots — or telephone for one (phone: 26-47-05-05).

Train – The station is on Bd. Joffre, across the mall from the north end of Pl. Drouet-d'Erlon (phone: 26-88-50-50). There are several trains daily to Paris (1½ hours) and to Epernay (25 minutes).

SPECIAL EVENTS: If you plan to be in Reims during January and February and have children with you, don't miss a series of annual special performances given by *Centre des Formations des Art du Cirque* (1 Rue du Cirque, Chalons sur Marne 51000; phone: 26-21-12-43), France's national circus school. An international horse show takes place in May. The second weekend in June, processions, historical parades, and secular and religious plays and songs are all part of the *Fêtes de Jeanne d'Arc,* celebrating her return to Reims with the dauphin for his coronation as Charles VII. Coinciding with these events is *Les Sacres du Folklore,* a weekend-long festival during which folkloric groups from around the world, dressed in native costume, parade through the streets. In early fall (usually the third weekend in September), the city's *Automnales* (Autumn Festival) annually draws 100,000 visitors for fairs and fireworks at the Place de la République. During the same weekend, there's a harvest car rally for vintage autos. St. Remi, the holy bishop who inspired the tradition of royal coronations in Reims, is honored on the first Sunday in October with a religious festival that includes fine concerts. The *Reims Marathon,* one of France's most important, takes place the third weekend of October and attracts 7,000 to 8,000 runners.

MUSEUMS: *The Palais du Tau* and the *Musée St.-Denis* are described in *Special Places.* There are three other noteworthy museums:

   Musée-Abbaye St.-Remi – An ancient abbey next door to the Basilique St.-Remi, this is now an archaeological museum, also known as the *Musée* *d'Histoire et d'Archéologie,* with items from prehistoric times to the Middle Ages, including some interesting Gallo-Roman mosaics and tombs. Ranked among France's 50 most beautiful museums, *St.-Remi* also has an exhibit on regional military history that was recently enlarged. There are free sound and light shows on Saturday evenings at 9:30 PM from July through September. Open weekdays from 2 to 6:30 PM, Saturdays and Sundays from 2 to 7 PM; closed some holidays. Admission charge to the museum. 53 Rue Simon (phone: 26-85-23-36).

Musée-Hôtel le Vergeur – Also known as the *Musée du Vieux Reims* (Museum of Old Reims), it contains sculptures, paintings, drawings, and plans relating to the history of Reims and to the splendors of the coronations; two rooms of Flemish and Dutch artists, including a collection of Dürer engravings; and attractive apartments with 19th-century furnishings. Open daily, except Mondays and holidays, from 2 to 6 PM. 36 Pl. du Forum (phone: 26-47-20-75).

Centre de l'Automobile Française – Reims's newest museum, it houses the private collection of engineer/inventor Philippe Charbonneaux, and includes 130 automobiles dating from 1897 to today. In addition, there is a remarkable collection of toy and model cars, and old posters. Open daily from 10 AM to noon and 2 to 7 PM (weekends and holidays to 5 PM) April to November; by appointment in winter. 84 Av. Georges Clémenceau (phone: 26-82-83-84).

SHOPPING: Much of the best shopping in Reims can be found on the streets and malls near the cathedral. Local specialties are champagne and biscuits, and if you wish to stock up on the former, the prices in the wine shops in the vicinity of the cathedral are slightly lower than those found in Paris. The best place to buy Reims *croquignolles* (dry biscuits) is *Fossier* (25 Cours Langlet; phone: 26-47-59-84). A good chocolate shop — it specializes in chocolate champagne corks — is *La Petite Friande* (15 Cours Langlet; phone: 26-47-50-44). Better shops for men and women line the Cours Langlet and the Rue de Vesle or can be found at *Galerie des Sacres,* on Rue Libergier, near the cathedral. For arts and crafts, try *La Garinie* (6 Rue de l'Université; phone: 26-88-43-91).

SPORTS: The huge *Parc Pommery* offers plenty of opportunity for outdoor recreation.

Golf – A private course, the 18-hole *Golf Club of Reims* (Château des Dames de France, in nearby Gueux; phone: 26-03-60-14), often admits non-members for a fee. From Reims take exit Reims-Tinqueux, turn onto N31 toward Soissons, but quickly turn off it onto D27 toward Gueux. Farther away on Route Monmirail (18 miles/29 km from Epernay; 31 miles/50 km south of Reims) is a public golf course with 18 holes, *La Vitarderie* (phone: 26-58-25-09).

Swimming – Among the public pools is the *Piscine Olympique* (41 Chaussée Bocquaine; phone: 26-82-60-00).

Tennis and Squash – Tennis courts at *Parc Pommery* (Av. du Géneral-Giraud; phone: 26-85-23-29); squash courts (10 Rue Gabriel Voisin; phone: 26-85-40-80).

THEATER: The *Théâtre de la Comédie* (1 Rue Eugène-Wiet; phone: 26-85-60-00 or 93-85-61-69) performs plays in repertory, in French, before a small audience (capacity is 100 seats). For ballet, the *Grand Théâtre* (9 Rue Chanzy; phone: 26-47-44-43).

MUSIC: The *Grand-Théâtre* (9 Rue Chanzy; phone: 26-47-44-43) is the place for opera and concerts. The ticket office is open from 10 AM to noon and from 2:30 to 5:30 PM except Mondays. Popular music can be heard in some of the bars and cabarets (see below).

NIGHTCLUBS AND NIGHTLIFE: Though the people of Reims are reputed to be serious, family-oriented stay-at-homes who do their champagne drinking over dinner with friends and relatives, somebody is keeping the bars, cafés, and cabarets open at night. The champagne bar at *Boyer "Les Crayères"* (64 Bd. Henri-Vasnier; phone: 26-82-80-80) is open Tuesdays through Sundays from 11 AM to 1 PM. Discos to try are *Le Club Saint-Pierre* (41 Bd. du Général-Leclerc; phone: 26-88-26-13) with music every night after 10 PM, and the newer *L'Aquarium* (93 Bd. du Général-Leclerc; phone: 26-47-34-29). Outside town, in the middle of a woods in Cernay-les-Reims, there's *La Bergerie* or the *Discothèque de l'Ermitage* (Rte. de Luxembourg; phone: 26-89-01-16) also open after 10 PM, except Mondays. Other bars and cafés with music are *La Boite à Cocktails* (6 Pl. du Forum; phone: 26-47-56-58), with a pianist nightly except Sundays and mid-July to mid-August, when it's closed; *Le Duke,* in the *Altéa* (phone: 26-88-53-64), an "American bar" where the live music includes some mild jazz that can be accompanied by three or four dozen brands of champagne; and *Le Palais* (114 Rue du Barbâtre; phone: 26-85-29-26), a bar-café with jazz until 8 PM nightly except Sundays.

BEST IN TOWN

 CHECKING IN: With a few exceptions, hotels are not among Reims's major assets. There are plenty of beds, but if you have a car you might consider staying in one of the lovely country inns nearby (see the "Checking In" sections in *Champagne,* in DIRECTIONS) before settling for an undistinguished hostelry. However, there are plenty of two-star chain hotels on the periphery, and future plans include the construction of new three- and four-star hotels. Due to the generally lower prices found outside Paris, rates are reasonable. Expect to pay $130 or more for a double room in hotels classified as expensive; $60 to $130 for those in the moderate range; and $40 to $60 for those listed as inexpensive.

Boyer "Les Crayères" – If you want the best — and are willing to pay for it — this is the place to stay. Though the château was built early in this century, it imitates the grand style of the past, and its setting, in a lovely private park, gives it an approach through elegant gates and a long driveway. All 16 rooms and 3 suites are large, individually (and beautifully) decorated in Provençal prints, and are complete with an entry hall, a dressing room, and a sizable bathroom. All have views of the majestic trees and green lawns of the park and some have views of the Basilique St.-Remi, which is nearby, and of the cathedral. The hotel's three-Michelin-star restaurant is one of the greats in France (see *Eating Out*). 64 Bd. Henri-Vasnier (phone: 26-82-80-80). Expensive.

Grand Hôtel des Templiers – This renovated 19th-century bourgeois mansion near the center of town is the latest addition to Reims's slim complement of luxury hotels. It has large, individually decorated rooms, sleek marble baths, a winter garden, and an indoor pool as well as a sauna, steambath, and tanning room. 22 Rue des Templiers (phone: 26-88-55-08). Expensive.

Altéa – If need be, you should be able to find a vacancy here; it's one of the largest hotels in the region (125 rooms). It's expensive for what's delivered, however, though the rooms are modern and reasonably comfortable (40 have color TV sets and air conditioning). Service is problematic; there's a bar and a restaurant, *Les Ombrages,* without much to recommend it. 31 Bd. Paul-Doumer (phone: 26-88-53-54). Expensive to moderate.

L'Assiette Champenoise – The newest hotel in the area, it has 30 rooms and is located in Tinqueux, just west of Reims. Modern and comfortable, it occupies a niche between the deluxe *Boyer* and the other, pricier Reims hotels. 40 Av. Paul-Vaillant-Couturier, Tinqueux (phone: 26-04-15-56). Moderate.

Novotel – Just outside Reims, this modern hotel-motel (part of the popular chain), with 125 rooms, is well run and convenient. Its bar and grill are open until midnight, and the amenities include a swimming pool. Rte. de Soissons (phone: 26-08-11-61). Moderate.

La Paix – The best bet in the city — a friendly, efficiently run property with 105 comfortable and well-equipped rooms. *La Taverne Kanter* restaurant is not very exciting, perhaps, but getting better. 9 Rue Buirette (phone: 26-40-04-08). Moderate.

Continental – A vintage hotel from the 1860s whose lobby has a tawdry charm, with wood-trimmed, print armchairs, frayed Oriental rugs, and a monumental ceiling lamp of brass and glass. Rooms are simple and comfortable. There is a recently enlarged breakfast room and a new meeting room. 93 Pl. Drouet d'Erlon (phone: 26-40-39-35). Inexpensive.

Du Nord – An old-fashioned hostelry in the heart of Reims, it recently was renovated to include comforts and charm that come as a surprise after passing through its drab lobby. Offers excellent value (and clean rooms) for a very reasonable price. 75 Pl. Drouet d'Erlon (phone: 26-47-39-03). Inexpensive.

 EATING OUT: There's no reason for not eating well in Reims or in the Champagne region in general. A similar statement surely could be made about any major French city or region, but in the case of Reims and its surrounding area it is particularly applicable. The curious part is that as far as food goes, there's not much of a regional cuisine, certainly not a distinguished one; indeed, this is the only wine region in France without an appropriate indigenous cuisine to accompany its wine. What Reims and its environs do have, however, is an increasing number of excellent restaurants — in and of themselves worth a visit. According to the tourist office, Reims now boasts more Michelin stars than any other French city of its size. At the better restaurants, expect dishes that marry particularly well with champagne — fish, seafood, poultry, and veal dishes — and expect dishes even to be made with the bubbly.

For a full lunch or dinner for two, excluding beverages (service often is included in the price, but check because this is becoming less common), expect to pay $150 or more at places we list as expensive; $80 to $150 for those in the moderate range; and $50 to $80 for those listed as inexpensive.

L'Assiette Champenoise – Still one of the best in town. The fish preparations are exquisite, the daily specials are a sure bet, but the desserts are forgettable — except for the bittersweet chocolate cake. Open year-round. Reservations necessary. 40 Av. Paul-Vaillant-Couturier, Tinqueux (phone: 26-04-15-56). Expensive.

Boyer "Les Crayères" – Nary a pilgrim leaves this temple of haute cuisine in less than a state of bliss. It isn't just the best restaurant in the region, it is one of the best in France (which to some gastronomes means the world). And even after Gérard Boyer and his wife, Elyane, have earned innumerable accolades, including a three-star rating from Michelin, they keep getting better. The greeting here is sunshine — some say the best welcome this side of heaven — and there is a warmth and glow in the restaurant that quickly converts to the comfort and contentment of its diners. The menu is seasonal, brilliantly inspired, and loaded with foods that have an affinity to Champagne. Try the *escalope de foie gras,* the delicate and elegant fish dishes, the cabbage stuffed with langoustines, Boyer's famous truffle in puff pastry, the no less famous *salade du Père Maurice,* the local cheeses, and save room somehow for the riches of the dessert cart. Closed Mondays, Tuesdays at lunch, and mid-December to mid-January. Reservations necessary. 64 Bd. Henri-Vasnier (phone: 26-82-80-80). Expensive.

Le Chardonnay – This was the site of Boyer's original restaurant. When they moved to new quarters across town, they left behind Dominique Giraudeau, a young chef with impeccable training, who continues to offer fine fare here. This restaurant earned its first Michelin star in its first year and now unfailingly serves meals that are the equal of (or superior to) many two-star operations. Try the steamed shrimp in a champagne-vinegar sauce, duck breasts with wild cherries, and exquisite desserts, especially the sherbet and the orange flan. Closed Saturdays at lunch, Sundays, most of August, and from December 22 to mid-January. Reservations advised. 184 Av. d'Epernay (phone: 26-06-08-60). Expensive to moderate.

Le Florence – This luxurious restaurant offers refined cooking characterized by delicate sauces, and some locals feel it offers the best food for the money in town. It's especially strong on fish dishes (crayfish, lobster, turbot, oysters) and on offal (which tastes better than the word suggests). Tantalizing desserts and a remarkable selection of champagne also are offered. One Michelin star. Closed Sunday evenings from November to *Easter* and from July 20 to August 11; terrace dining in summer. Reservations advised. 43 Bd. Foch (phone: 26-47-12-70). Expensive to moderate.

La Côte 108 – A bit out of town, and the first impression here can be disappointing — the dining room is large and seems to lack ambience — but the food will make you forget the decor. In the fall, there are wonderful *feuilletés* with wild mushrooms. Fish always is cooked to perfection, and dishes of wild duck *magrets* (slices of boneless breast) or lamb medallions with garlic cloves are superb. The balanced *menu dégustation* is a feast. Closed Sunday evenings, Mondays, and from December 20 through January. Reservations advised. In Berry-au-Bac, 12 miles (19 km) from Reims via N44 (phone: 23-79-95-04). Moderate.

Au Petit Bacchus – Old and new mix harmoniously in this recently opened wine bar/lunch spot located on a small street behind the cathedral. Ceiling beams, wood-paneled walls, and rose marble tables add warmth to an otherwise modern motif. Daily specials chalked on blackboards announce light lunchtime platters, including cheese trays, smoked salmon, and such extravagances as caviar. As the name hints, wines take priority; the cave is excellent. Open from 11 AM to 8 PM daily. Reservations unnecessary. 11 Rue de l'Université (phone: 26-47-10-05). Moderate.

Au Petit Comptoir – The bistro trend continues, and like many of France's starred chefs, Gerard Boyer (see "*Les Crayères*"above) has opened his version. A cozy, casual spot in the heart of Reims's old market area, it has all the requisite elements — a frosted glass façade, marble tables, zinc bar, and well-prepared, refined fare that can be had for an extremely fair price. Reservations advised. 17 Rue de Mars (phone: 26-40-58-58). Moderate.

Le Vigneron – Local cuisine par excellence is the stock in trade of the two small dining rooms in this 17th-century house. The rooms are decorated with old posters and a collection of rare wine labels; the atmosphere is friendly and very French. Among the menu choices are Reims ham with grapes, pike in a champagne sauce, and *potée champenoise* (a stew of smoked ham, bacon, sausages, and cabbage). The wine list is reasonably priced and features an extensive selection of champagne and local still wines. Closed Saturday lunch, Sundays, and 3 weeks in August. Reservations unnecessary. Pl. Jamot (phone: 26-47-00-71). Inexpensive.

Waida – A popular pastry shop with a classic 1930s tearoom, complete with ceiling fans, inlaid woods, and an Art Deco–stained glass backdrop. Open daily from 7 AM to 8 PM; closed Sundays from 1 to 3:30 PM. Reservations unnecessary. 3-5 Pl. d'Erlon (phone: 26-47-44-49). Inexpensive.

ROUEN

"Oh, Rouen, art thou then my final resting place . . . ?" With this plaintive cry, Joan of Arc was led off to her execution and to a destiny that bound her to this city forever. Indeed, so strong is this association, fueled by writers from Schiller to Shaw, that for the visitor it tends to obscure other aspects of Rouen's history, not to mention its current stature as a port and manufacturing center. Given its location, in Normandy on the Seine — near the mouth of the river at the English Channel — it is the country's fourth largest port, the port of Paris, in fact. The rich agricultural lands and forests surrounding Rouen and the chemical, petroleum, paper, metallurgical, and textile industries operating in Greater Rouen all profit by the port's proximity, fueling an economy that supports more than half a million people.

The Gauls had a settlement here called Ratuma, but it was the ever-efficient Romans who established this as the first point upstream from the Channel where a bridge could be built. The Romans settled on the right bank of the great loop in the river, in the natural amphitheater created by the steep surrounding hills that remains the heart of the city, and were still there when the earliest bishops arrived to convert the citizens and countryfolk to Christianity in the 4th century. Then both the Romans and their city disappeared into the shadows of the Dark Ages, when invading barbarians swept away nearly all of the physical and spiritual manifestations of the Pax Romana and plunged Europe into disorder.

That something of Rouen must have endured, or been rebuilt, seems likely, for when the city's recorded history resumed almost 5 centuries later, with the creation of the duchy of Normandy in 911, the new duke chose it as his capital. From the time of this Duke of Normandy — Rollo — until another Duke of Normandy — William — crossed the Channel, conquered England, and made himself its king in 1066, Rouen thrived as an independent capital. Even after the Conquest it was second only to London in importance among the possessions of the Norman-English kings, and it maintained that standing until 1204, when the luckless King John of England lost his Norman possessions to Philippe-Auguste of France, who annexed them to the French crown. From then on it became one of the most sought-after prizes in the on-again, off-again tug-of-war between France and England that reached its climax in the Hundred Years War (1337–1453). In 1418 and 1419, Rouen endured a 6-month siege that ended with its capitulation to the English, whom the Normans dubbed "Goddons" because of their noticeable addiction to the oath "Goddamn!" Under John of Lancaster, Duke of Bedford and brother of Henry V (the duke is buried in the cathedral), the Goddons controlled Rouen for the next 30 years.

It was during this time that Joan of Arc walked into the pages of history and the popular imagination. Born in Domrémy (Lorraine) in approximately 1412, she began at an early age to hear voices and see visions urging her to go to the aid of the feeble heir to the French throne, the future King Charles VII. In an attempt to end the Hundred Years War, Charles's father had agreed in 1420 to a treaty naming Henry V, King of England, his successor as King of France. Though the young Charles repudiated the treaty when his father died in 1422, he ruled over a small realm confined south of the Loire while the English, with the help of their French allies, the Dukes of Burgundy, extended their rule over an increasingly larger part of France north of the Loire. The important town of Orléans — on the Loire and thus considered the gateway to southern France — probably would have fallen to the English, too, had not the young peasant girl convinced the fainthearted Charles of her divine inspiration and led his troops to raise the months-long siege in 1429. Forever after known as the Maid of Orléans, she then led her king to be crowned in Reims Cathedral, adding legitimacy to his royal title, and went on to other battles. The next spring, however, she was captured by the Burgundians during the defense of Compiègne.

Joan had been captured after an astonishing series of victories in which her role seems to have been talismanic rather than tactical. Nevertheless, her influence was powerful even as a mascot, and the English commanders were anxious to see her destroyed. Having paid her Burgundian captors the requisite 30 pieces of silver at the inflationary rate of 10,000 ducats, Richard de Beauchamp, Earl of Warwick, handed her over to the ecclesiastical court of Rouen to be tried for heresy and witchcraft. Joan's prison was in a tower of the castle that Philippe-Auguste had built 200 years before. The keep, now called Tour Jeanne-d'Arc, is all that remains of the castle, and it was here that she was shown some convincing instruments of torture for the first time. Her trial, before Pierre Cauchon, the Bishop of Beauvois, lasted 3 months. Then, on May 24, 1431, she was taken to the cemetery of the Abbey of St. Ouen (now the garden of the Hôtel de Ville) where she publicly renounced the "voices" she had heard. In return for recanting, her inquisitors condemned her not to death but to life imprisonment, though one condition of their leniency was that she wear only women's clothes.

Not satisfied, the English pressed for more definitive measures until, by a trick, the Maid was forced to dress once more in the male garb she had worn while fighting, and she was accused of breaking her oath. On May 29, in a room of the Archbishop's Palace (only an outer wall of the room now remains on Rue St.-Romain), Warwick and Winchester and the other villains who have since enlivened stages around the world condemned her to death. The next day, on Place du Vieux-Marché, she was burned at the stake. Still the English feared her. Already she was being talked of as a martyr, and lest any of her mortal remains become a rallying point for the French, they were thrown into the Seine in what must rank as one of history's more spiteful moments. Twenty-five years later, at the instigation of the spineless Charles VII, she was rehabilitated by Cardinal d'Estouteville in the same room where she had been condemned.

The English finally left Rouen in 1449, and during the 100 years that followed, building flourished in the city on an unprecedented scale. One of the most perfect examples of the Flamboyant Gothic style in all Europe, the Eglise St.-Maclou, belongs to this period, as do the Cathédrale de Notre-Dame's Butter Tower and those superb Renaissance mansions, the Hôtel de Bourgtheroulde and the Palais de Justice. All of these, along with the famous Gros-Horloge, still form part of the city's backdrop. They seem even more spectacular set against the simple *maisons de pans de bois,* those exquisite examples of domestic architecture with exposed beams, gables, *colombages,* and leaded windows that survive in profusion in Rouen. During World War II, Rouen suffered the brunt of aerial and tank bombardments from the advancing German forces, then from Allied (mainly British) air attacks aimed at the entrenched invaders.

As an integral final stop en route to the capture of Paris, the city was taken by Rommel's 5th Panzer Division on June 10, 1940, and occupied for the next 4 years, experiencing near-total destruction. The area between the cathedral and the river was obliterated. It is estimated that during 1 night in 1944, 345 bombs were dropped on Rouen. But all the town's treasures — many of the oldest stained glass windows, paintings, ceramics, antiques, and book collections — had been stowed away for protection. The city was liberated by Canadian forces on August 30, 1944. The war had ravaged hundreds of acres of land, destroyed 9,500 houses and 14 monuments, and buried 1,600 people in debris. Ninety political prisoners and Resistance members, and 250 of the city's Jews, had been arrested, never to return.

Rouen is a survivor, though. Except for the destroyed Church of St. Vincent, the major architectural wonders remain — those damaged were repaired; those demolished have been rebuilt. Despite the losses of war, Rouen has maintained the profound spirit of its past with the continuing rush of its present, such that the ancient building at 31 Place du Vieux-Marché exists still as a restaurant, *La Couronne,* as it has for hundreds of years, serving the dishes — duck, ham, sheep's feet, cheeses — and the cider that are part of the Norman gastronomic heritage. So, too, the school that Pierre Corneille attended and that is now named for him still drums Latin, Greek, and logic into the heads of tomorrow's leaders, just as the city's hundreds of bells still call the faithful to mass and remind them twice a day of the Angelus, and as scenes depicted in the masterpiece *Madame Bovary* attract fans of native son Gustave Flaubert.

ROUEN AT-A-GLANCE

SEEING THE CITY: The best view of the city is from the viewing table on the Côte Ste.-Catherine (St. Catherine's Hill), southeast of the center. It takes in the towers and belfries of the city and the serpentine Seine and is especially attractive in the glow of early evening. From the summit of N182 in Canteleu, on the other side of town, there is a view eastward down the valley, over the docks to the city. Another fine view — across the roofs and over the gables of the Old Town — is from the Beffroi (Belfry) of the Gros-Horloge.

SPECIAL PLACES: In addition to one of France's major cathedrals, Rouen has other important churches as well as a number of secular monuments, museums, and picturesque streets. All of the sights below are within walking distance of each other in the Old Town, on the right bank of the Seine. On the left bank is the modern St.-Sever quarter.

Cathédrale de Notre-Dame – The best way to approach this famous cathedral the first time is from Rue du Gros-Horloge. As you walk along that narrow street into Place de la Cathédrale, the extraordinary contours of the great west façade beloved of Monet gradually appear, a mesmerizing spectacle of statues, pinnacles, and mismatched towers that amounts to an object lesson in 400 years of ecclesiastical architecture. Included, apart from the Romanesque base of the Tour St.-Romain (St. Romanus Tower), to the left as you face the church, are styles from four different Gothic periods: primitive Gothic, in the middle tiers of the Tour St.-Romain; pure Gothic in the portals of St.-Jean-Baptiste and St.-Etienne flanking the main door; Rayonnant in the windows above St. Stephen's door and the four major pinnacles of the façade; and Flamboyant in the famous Tour de Beurre (Butter Tower), so named because it was paid for by local gourmands who preferred to buy indulgences to eat butter during *Lent* rather than do without it for 40 days. The detail of the west portals, as well as that of the north door, the Portail des Libraires, and the south door, the Portail de la Calende, is absorbing, always full of narrative, often of humor. The sculptures surrounding the Portail des Libraires (Booksellers' Door), for instance, show beasts of fact, fable, and fantasy, among them a philosopher with the head of a pig and a pig playing a violin. In the Cour des Libraires leading to the door, there is a workshop where 20th-century sculptors chisel away at reproductions of the medieval saints that will replace those disfigured beyond repair. It is an intriguing sight, suggesting that the cathedral is a living work of art.

Though the exterior embraces several epochs and styles, beginning with vestiges of the ancient Romanesque church, which burned down in 1200, through to the finishing touches of the 16th century (the cast-iron spire of the central lantern tower was a final 19th-century flourish, replacing a wooden one), the interior speaks basically of only the pure Gothic style of the 13th century, when the nave with its 4 great stories of arches, false tribunes, triforia, and high windows was completed. The choir, also from the 13th century, was lovingly restored after extensive damage in World War II; the 15th-century misericords survived the bombing, and their carvings still provide a colorful illustration of the costumes, customs, trades, and work implements of the period. Some 13th-century stained glass survives in the ambulatory, most notably in the windows of St. Julian l'Hospitalier; here, too, are several 13th-century tombs, including that of Richard Coeur de Lion, whose lion heart alone is buried below his effigy, his other earthly remains resting elsewhere. (The heart of Charles V is entombed in the crypt, another of the few parts of the ancient Romanesque church still extant.)

In the north arm of the transept, the Escalier des Libraires (Booksellers' Staircase) dates from the 15th century and is famous for its lacelike banister. The Chapelle de la Vierge (Chapel of the Virgin) in the apse contains 14th-century stained glass windows depicting 24 of Rouen's bishops and archbishops, but it is dominated by two 16th-century tombs. On the right facing the altar, the two cardinals d'Amboise, Georges I and his nephew Georges II, kneel in prayer above their sumptuously decorated burial place. Constructed between 1515 and 1525 in the overlush style of the early Renaissance, the tomb is an ornate monument of arabesque and Italianate details at once gorgeous and grotesque. That of Louis de Brézé (he was the husband of Diane de Poitiers, mistress of Henri II of France), on the left facing the altar, reflects the more sober taste of the Renaissance not too many years later (1535); its simple Corinthian columns and graceful caryatids provide a marked contrast to the tomb of the cardinals. A wonderful 17th-century Spanish-style reredos adds confusion to the styles in the chapel. Painted in gold and crowned by a statue of the Virgin with Child standing in a high niche, it has a charming painting, *The Adoration of the Shepherds* by Philippe de Champaigne, at its center.

Guided tours of the cathedral (in French) take place several times daily during the summer (with a shortened schedule on Sundays and religious holidays), and on Saturday and Sunday afternoons the rest of the year; participants gather in the nave. Except for guided tours (check with the tourist office for times), the Chapelle de la Vierge is closed Mondays through Fridays. It is best seen early on Sunday mornings when, in preparation for the first mass at 7 AM, it is the only illuminated spot in the vast, gray gloom of the church. The Portail de la Calende on the Rue des Bonnetiers side of the cathedral is open at that hour to admit worshipers. The cathedral takes on a magical quality at night, when the spire is illuminated. Pl. de la Cathédrale.

Place de la Cathédrale – The cobbled square where Monet sat to paint is overwhelmed by the cathedral that inspired him. There is, in addition, the beautiful early-16th-century building that houses the tourist office, the former Bureau des Finances. Before checking out the brochures, look inside the marvelous courtyard. There are some largish brasseries on the south side of the *place* for beer swilling and people watching.

Gros-Horloge (Great Clock) – Rouen's best-known secular monument used to be in the Beffroi (Belfry) next to it, but in 1527 the town's proud burghers decided to show it off to greater advantage and built the present gatehouse-like clock tower that spans the street. The extraordinary conglomeration abutting, adjacent to, overshadowed by, and looming down upon the clock is best seen from the west side of the gatehouse, where the eye takes in all at once a collage of buildings and styles spreading across 4 centuries. The two lower stories of the Belfry are Rayonnant Gothic of the 13th century; the top story is Flamboyant; the clock tower itself is in the Renaissance style of the late 1520s and 1530s; the half-timbered houses nearby are in the simpler domestic style of the same epoch; the gatekeeper's house nestling against the clock tower and the Belfry is 17th-century classical; and the vaguely baroque fountain next to it dates from the reign of Louis XV in the 18th century. The gilded and painted clock face marks the hour with only one hand, and the clock also tells the days of the week and the phases of the moon. The clockwork mechanism inside the cupola is among the oldest still functioning in Europe. One of the clock's two bells, named the Cache-Rimbaud, has been in service since 1260; the other, Rouvel, cracked in 1904. The Belfry offers an interesting view of the roofs and gables of the old quarter and of the cathedral; it is open daily except Tuesdays and Wednesday mornings from *Easter* to October. Entrance to the *Musée des Beaux-Arts* and the *Musée Le-Secq-des-Tournelles* is included in the admission charge. Rue du Gros-Horloge.

Rue du Gros-Horloge – For close to 2 centuries, this, Rouen's most famous street, has been the city's main commercial strip. But in spite of the boutiques, burger joints, and bars, several old houses give just the faintest hint of what it was once like. The house at No. 161 dates from the early 1500s, No. 146 from a little later. The corner house next to the Belfry on the Rue Thouret side was the city's original town hall (1608).

Archevêché – The Archbishop's Palace behind the cathedral is a great Gothic mansion that can be visited only by special arrangement (ask at the tourist office). The outstanding reward is the Great Hall, called the Hall of the States of Normandy, with four 18th-century pictures by Hubert Robert of Dieppe, Le Havre, Gaillon, and Rouen itself. Entrance on Rue des Bonnetiers.

Rue St.-Romain – This picturesque street is famous for its half-timbered houses of the Middle Ages and late Renaissance. Some of these have overhanging upper stories, which meant that slops thrown from the top floors did not soil people passing close to the house or leaning from windows below. Two such are those at Nos. 11 and 13, which date from the early 1400s and were the only houses in the city never covered by plaster. The Cour des Libraires leading into the cathedral from the street is named for the booksellers that used to congregate here. Adjacent is the wall of the Archbishop's Palace with a plaque marking the spot below the room, no longer extant, where Joan of Arc was sentenced to death and where 25 years later Cardinal d'Estouteville proclaimed her innocence. Standing underneath the overhanging housefront, opposite the plaque, you peer through the moss-covered stonework of the walls of the archbishopric to view the cathedral's massive central spire. The old house at No. 56 almost certainly was standing in Joan's day. Leading off Rue St.-Romain into Rue St.-Nicolas is the narrow alley known as the Rue des Chanoines (Street of the Canons). Thoroughfares in Old Rouen had to be wide enough to permit the passage of a horse's hindquarters. This one qualifies — just.

Eglise St.-Maclou – Behind the cathedral across Rue de la République is this striking church built in the 15th and 16th centuries and dedicated to St. Maclou, the Welsh saint who turns up in Brittany as St. Malo. Connoisseurs agree that the west façade, with its fan-shaped porch of five pinnacled arches, is one of the most perfect examples of Flamboyant Gothic in France. Inside, the visitor is immediately struck by the soaring vertical lines of the nave, which give an impression of dynamic upward surge — in fact, when the organ swells during the recessional after 10 o'clock mass, it seems that the church might take off like a rocket. The decorative carvings on the door panels are splendid examples of wooden sculpture of the late 16th century. The famous one showing the baptism of Christ (left door of the two-door main entrance) is in a framed medallion supported by St. John, St. Luke, St. Mark, and St. Matthew. Recently, centuries of grime were scoured off the church's exterior, returning it to a gleaming white. Pl. Barthélémy.

Place Barthélémy – This square in front of the Eglise St.-Maclou was once several narrow streets and tiny blocks. Some years ago, the central buildings were torn down, producing a view of the church's façade that was so stunning, no one dared to replace the buildings. It was not only the church that profited; the half-timbered houses on either side also were seen in a new perspective that showed off their gables and fine exterior (but walled-in) staircases to excellent advantage. The lower floors of these handsome houses are almost all antiques shops.

Rue Martainville – A street of 17th-to-18th-century houses once occupied by prosperous merchants and professional men. Today some of them are bookshops and galleries. In the corner by the Eglise St.-Maclou is a "manneken-pis" fountain. Hidden behind No. 186 is the Aître St.-Maclou (see *Extra Special,* below).

Rue Damiette – Another street of ancient houses, many turned into antiques shops. Especially worth a glance is the 17th-century Hôtel de Senneville at the end of an alley at No. 30. Damiette leads into the colorful, small Place Lieutenant-Aubert, where there is an outstanding 15th-century house with a sculpted porch at No. 6. The view of the tower of St.-Ouen from Rue Domiette is splendid. The tower often is called the Ducal Crown of Normandy, and from this perspective it is clear why.

Rue Eau-de-Robec – Now lined with antiques shops, this is the street Flaubert described in *Madame Bovary.* The houses at the western end have overhanging eaves built so that their medieval residents, mostly dyers, could hang wool out to dry.

Eglise St.-Ouen – The abbey church of St. Ouen is longer and higher than the cathedrals of Rouen and Notre-Dame in Paris. It also is cool to look at, almost to the point of austerity. Although it took 300 years to build, beginning in 1318, the pure Gothic lines of the original plan were rigidly followed. Thus, the arches, triforium, and clerestory add up to a textbook example of how a Gothic church of the Middle Ages should look. Because of the lack of decoration, the visitor tends to focus on the windows. Most of the glass in these, from the 14th to the 16th century, was removed at the beginning of World War II and has now been returned. Especially remarkable are the rose windows in the north and south transepts, the latter a treatment of the tree of Jesse in blue and gold designed by Colin de Berneval, the son of the cathedral's architect. Note, too, the organ, built in 1630 and famous enough for its tone to draw organists from all over Europe. Outside on the north flank of the church are the one remaining gallery of the old abbey cloister and 18th-century abbey buildings now serving as the Hôtel de Ville (Town Hall). The gardens behind the Hôtel de Ville and the church were once the abbey cemetery, where Joan of Arc was brought to renounce her voices publicly. The view of the church from here includes its central tower, the *tour couronnée* referred to as the Ducal Crown of Normandy. Pl. du Général-de-Gaulle.

Musée des Beaux-Arts – One of France's greatest provincial collections. The emphasis is on European paintings, from the Flemish primitives (Gerard David's somber *Virgin and the Saints*) to the Impressionists and post-Impressionists (among them, Dufy's *Beach at Ste.-Adresse*). One room is devoted to Delacroix's *Justice of Trajan,* another to works by Géricault, a native of Rouen, including his *Slaves Stopping a Horse* and *Portrait of Delacroix.* There are views of Rouen by Van Ruisdael and Van Goyen in rooms devoted to Dutch and Flemish masters, and among the Monets there is one of the series of paintings he executed of the cathedral. A first-floor room contains portraits by Jacques-Emile Blanche of his contemporaries (Claudel, Cocteau, Stravinsky, Montherlant, Giraudoux, Maeterlinck) in the heady years before and after World War I. There also is a celebrated ceramics collection showing the development and decline of Rouen faïence (a type of ceramic) from 1550 to 1800. Closed Tuesdays, Wednesday mornings, and holidays. Admission charge. Square Verdrel (phone: 35-71-28-40).

Musée Le-Secq-des-Tournelles – Here are thousands of pieces of ironwork, from the Dark Ages to the 19th century. It is a feast of intricately wrought lamps, gates, balconies, grilles, keys, weapons, kitchen utensils, candelabra, and religious and secular ornaments beautifully hung or mounted in what was formerly the Eglise St.-Laurent, a Flamboyant Gothic edifice built in the 15th and 16th centuries. Closed Tuesdays, Wednesday mornings, and holidays. Admission charge. Rue Jacques-Villon (phone: 35-71-28-40).

Musée des Antiquités – A Gallo-Roman mosaic from nearby Lillebonne is one of the outstanding sights of this museum, which is in a former convent (Cloître Ste.-Marie) dating from the 17th century. Although there are items from the Middle East and farther afield, the emphasis is on holdings with a Norman connection. A 13th-century Virgin and Child in ivory and a famous 15th-century tapestry, *Les Cerfs Ailés* (Winged Stags), are especially appealing. Furniture, corbels, cornices, statues, ornaments, and household items from medieval Rouen throw a fascinating light on what some of the wonderful houses a few blocks from the museum originally contained. Closed Tuesdays and holidays. Admission charge. 198 Rue Beauvoisine (phone: 35-98-55-10).

Tour Jeanne-d'Arc – A round tower — the keep — is all that remains of the castle built by Philippe-Auguste in the 1st decade of the 13th century. The part of the castle in which the Maid was imprisoned is no longer standing, but the starkly simple round room in which she was interrogated and threatened with torture is open to the public. Closed Thursdays, holidays, and during November. Rue du Donjon (phone: 35-98-16-21).

Eglise St.-Patrice – This was the parish church of what was once upon a time Rouen's "Irishtown," the quarter where Irish merchants and traders lived. Flamboyant Gothic in style, though comparatively subdued inside, the church is famous chiefly for its 16th- and 17th-century stained glass windows, especially those illustrating the Passion and Resurrection of Christ and one based on a Dürer engraving of the legend of St. Eustachius. The church also contains a collection of religious paintings. Entrance on Rue de l'Abbé Cochet.

Palais de Justice – Students of architecture consider this an exquisite example of a municipal building in the Flamboyant Gothic style. Note, as you look at the famous façade, that the decoration becomes increasingly richer the higher it goes, so that the pinnacles atop the buttresses on the roof look like upended, intricately carved icicles. The main part of the building was built in 1508 and 1509; the left wing was begun slightly before that, from 1493 to 1508; and the right wing is a 19th-century reconstruction. Ironically, the newest part was spared the ravages of World War II, which particularly damaged the oldest part, including the Salle des Procureurs, where Pierre Corneille appeared as king's counsel and which is today a magnificent restoration. The Procurer's Room (take the staircase on the left) is open to visitors on weekdays only. Rue aux Juifs.

Monument Juif (Jewish Monument) – During excavations in 1976, the remains of a 12th-century Romanesque building were unearthed in the courtyard of the Palais de Justice. Certain graffiti and Hebrew inscriptions indicated that it had been a center of some importance to the Jews of Rouen, who lived in the adjacent ghetto until they were expelled by Philip the Fair in the early 14th century. Since there already was one synagogue serving the community, it has been suggested that the building housed a yeshiva, or school, making it one of the oldest universities in Europe. It can be visited at 11 AM Sundays from April to September, and at 2 PM Saturdays in winter months, by applying at least 2 days in advance at the tourist office. Admission charge. Rue aux Juifs.

Eglise Ste.-Jeanne-d'Arc – One of the most modern churches in France, it was built on the site where Joan of Arc was burned and is part of the revamping of Place du Vieux-Marché. It is worth visiting only for the stained glass windows it incorporates, which date from the 16th and 17th centuries; they were originally in the chancel of the old Eglise St.-Vincent, which stood here until it was destroyed in World War II. The windows are devoted to traditional religious themes such as the Passion, Crucifixion, and Resurrection of Christ, and Adam and Eve. In addition, many of them show typically garbed figures from the various trades and guilds that paid for them. In the background, bottom right, of the window devoted to St. Peter, the churches of St. Maclou and St. Ouen are clearly depicted in stained glass. The irregularly crested roof of Eglise Ste.-Jeanne-d'Arc has been intrepreted by some as a representation of tongues of flame; others see it as a stylized version of a ship. Both views seem reasonable. Pl. du Vieux-Marché.

Place du Vieux-Marché – Besides the Eglise Ste.-Jeanne d'Arc, the other modern building in the not quite square square is the covered marketplace, where flowers, produce, and fish are sold Tuesdays through Saturdays. On the west side of the square are the remains of the Eglise St.-Sauveur, from which a cross was brought to comfort the Maid at the stake. The south and east sides of the square are taken up largely by restaurants, among them the famous *La Couronne* (see *Eating Out*), which is near a waxworks museum, the *Musée Jeanne-d'Arc*.

Oceade (Aqua Park) – An aquatic center of particular interest to those traveling with children. There are rides, a solarium, and various exhibits. Open daily during the summer from 11 AM to 9 PM. The rest of the year, open Tuesdays, Thursdays, and Fridays from 4:30 to 9 PM; Wednesdays from 11 AM to 9 PM; Saturdays from 11 AM to midnight and Sundays from 11 AM to 8 PM. Admission charge. Ile Lacroix (phone: 35-07-03-30).

■**EXTRA SPECIAL:** Walk under the arch at 186 Rue Martainville, through an ancient courtyard and under a gatehouse, and suddenly you are in a tree-lined quadrangle enclosed by low, 2-story timbered buildings. This is the Aître St.-Maclou (St. Maclou Cloister), one of the few remaining charnel houses in France, used for the burial of plague victims. It was founded in 1348 when 100,000 people in Rouen succumbed to the Black Death. During the various plagues that raged from the 14th to the 17th century, the cemetery became overcrowded, and it was necessary to dig up the bones and place them in specially built gallery-like cloisters that served as ossuaries. Two were built in 1526, one in 1533, and a final one in 1640. On the supporting timbers carpenters carved macabre skulls, crossbones, spades, hoes, and crosses — all the iconography of death that still can be seen quite clearly today. It has not been used as a cemetery since the French Revolution. The grounds and building were restored in 1851, and the entire complex became a girls' school. Since October 1940 it has housed the Ecole des Beaux-Arts. In a corner by the entrance to the courtyard, a glass case embedded in the wall contains the mummified remains of a cat, supposedly a witches' familiar. This is the only grisly feature in what is otherwise, oddly enough, a very serene retreat in this ancient city. Open daily for visits.

SOURCES AND RESOURCES

TOURIST INFORMATION: For brochures, maps, and lists of hotels and restaurants, go to the Office de Tourisme, where English is spoken (25 Pl. de la Cathédrale; phone: 35-71-41-77). The beautiful Renaissance mansion, erected between 1505 and 1510, used to be the Treasury of Normandy. Go to the same address to take advantage of the *Accueil de France* accommodations service (for a small fee) if you need help finding a hotel room. The tourist office provides daily guided walking tours in French (although you can request an English-speaking guide) of Rouen's historical neighborhoods from mid-June to late September, and on weekends and holidays from *Easter* to mid-June. Visitors also can take a 40-minute guided tour of the city by miniature train, the *Rêves de France.* The train goes along the city's principal streets and crosses the river to the left bank. From April through November, the train leaves regularly starting at 10 AM from the Place de la Cathédrale. The tourist office's *Guide Officiel de Rouen,* in both French and English, is very good. The exhaustive *Le P'tit Normand,* in French, is available in bookshops all over Normandy and in Paris. A sort of yellow-pages-cum-encyclopedia of the city, it is an indispensable guide to Rouen and the region. *The City of Rouen,* published in English by Editions Ouest France, is a useful, illustrated guide to the city's most famous historical points. It is available for a few dollars in all bookshops and in most places where postcards are sold. There are no monthly or weekly guides to Rouen in English. Travelers on their way to Rouen via Paris can pick up brochures at the main Office de Tourisme in Paris (127 Champs-Elysées; phone: 47-23-61-72).

Local Coverage – The regional newspaper *Paris-Normandie* is published daily in Rouen. You'll find English-language books — mainly literature, cookbooks, and guidebooks — at the *ABC Book Shop* (11 Rue de Faulx; phone: 35-71-08-67).

TELEPHONE: The city code for Rouen is 35, which is incorporated into all local 8-digit numbers. When calling a number in Rouen from the Paris region (including the Ile-de-France), dial 16, wait for a dial tone, then dial the 8-digit number. When calling a number from outside Paris, dial only the 8-digit number. When calling from the US, dial 33 (which is the country code), followed by the 8-digit number.

GETTING AROUND: Bus – The best way to penetrate the suburbs and the hills above the Seine. The Station du Théâtre des Arts, at the foot of Rue Jeanne-d'Arc (phone: 35-71-63-86), is the main terminal for city and suburban buses, which are operated by two companies: *SATAR* (Rue des Charrettes; phone: 35-71-81-71) and *TCAR* (79 Rue Thiers; phone: 35-98-02-43). Monthly and weekly tickets and tickets for 20 journeys can be purchased at the main terminal at reduced rates, and 1- to 3-day Sympabus Tourism passes, allowing unlimited rides on local buses, also can be purchased at the tourist office or the bus station. The station also has timetables and maps of the 26 lines served. Long-distance buses (*autocars*) to cities such as Dieppe, Le Havre, and Fécamp are operated by *CNA* and leave from the Gare Routière (on Rue des Charrettes, close to the Station du Théâtre des Arts; phone: 35-71-81-71). Another line, *Bus Verts* (phone: 31-44-74-44), goes to Le Havre, Deauville, Honfleur, and Caen.

Car Rental – *Avis* (24 Rue Malouet; phone: 35-72-77-50) rents campers as well as cars. Also try *Europcar* (17 Quai Pierre-Corneille; phone: 35-70-18-30). *Hertz* (38 Quai Gaston Boulet; phone: 35-98-16-57) rents Fords and has special rates for trips from Rouen to Orly or Charles de Gaulle airports in Paris. *SNCF*'s Train + Auto rental plan also is available.

Taxi – Cabs are relatively inexpensive. They don't cruise, but they congregate outside the Gare *SNCF* and in Place Foch, and they can be flagged down when passing. The best way to get one is to telephone *Radio Taxis*, 67 Rue Thiers (phone: 35-88-50-50), or the group of independent drivers operating out of 18 Rue Wagner (phone: 35-80-34-34).

Train – The Gare *SNCF* (Gare Rive-Droite), at the top of Rue Jeanne-d'Arc, recently underwent a vast renovation. For information, call 35-98-50-50. The trip to Paris takes about an hour and 10 minutes, and there are frequent round trips daily.

SPECIAL EVENTS: Secondhand furniture is the order of the day at the *Puces Rouennaises*, a large flea market held at *Parc des Expositions* in mid-February. Late May to early June is the *Salon des Antiquaires*, an annual antiques fair at the *Halle aux Toiles*. Choral, jazz, and classical music concerts, modern dance, theatrical productions, marionette shows, and various other happenings are all part of the annual *Festival d'Eté* (Summer Festival), which is a high spot on the calendar from mid-May to mid-July. Concerts take place in the city's halls and churches and often in the sylvan charm of outlying abbeys and villages. The *Fêtes Jeanne d'Arc* (Joan of Arc Commemoration), on the weekend nearest May 30, her feast day, is a time for pageants and plays about the saint in the Place du Vieux-Marché and the Aître St.-Maclou. And the second half of October brings Rouen's major antiques event, the *Salon National des Antiquaires*. From mid-October to mid-November is the *Tapis de Fleurs*, a beautiful display of chrysanthemums, with patterns of vibrant colors that virtually carpet the square in front of the cathedral.

MUSEUMS: Apart from those discussed in *Special Places*, Rouen's museums tend to concentrate on some famous people.

Manoir Pierre-Corneille – A delightfully timbered, many-gabled house containing yet more books, manuscripts, prints, and pictures relating to the playwright, whose country place this once was. Rue Pierre-Corneille, in the suburb of Petit-Couronne, 5 miles (8 km) southwest of the city's center. For information ask at the *Musée Corneille*, below.

Musée Céramique – Collections of the highly decorative faïence de Rouen are exhibited here. The museum also houses rare pottery and porcelain from the 16th to the 18th century and from other regions in France, as well as China, Japan, England, and Italy. Closed Tuesdays and Wednesday mornings. Hôtel d'Hocqueville, 1 Rue Fauçon (phone: 35-07-31-74.

Musée Corneille – A fine old Rouennais town house that gives a wonderful idea of how a well-to-do professional man — in this case, a lawyer — lived in the 17th century. Since the lawyer was also one of France's greatest dramatists, there is the added charm of seeing his birth certificate and a library full of finely bound first editions and translations of his works and related tomes. Closed Tuesdays and Wednesday mornings. 4 Rue de la Pie (phone: 35-71-63-92).

Musée Flaubert et d'Histoire de la Médecine – The writer's birthplace is full of 17th- and 18th-century medical equipment in wood, metal, and faïence de Rouen as well as of statues of saints famed for curing incurable ailments. (Flaubert's father and brother were surgeons.) There is also a room where manuscripts, books, photographs, and other Flaubert memorabilia are displayed. Closed Sundays and Mondays. 51 Rue de Lecat (phone: 35-08-81-81, ext. 52467).

Musée Jeanne-d'Arc – Essentially a super-kitsch wax museum with life-size tableaux showing the saint's progress from her home in Domrémy to the spot in Rouen, a few steps away, where she was burned. The few contemporary seals and charters and intricately built cardboard models of the events in her life are more interesting than the grisly dioramas. Closed Mondays in winter. 33 Pl. du Vieux-Marché (phone: 35-88-02-70).

Musée d'Histoire Naturelle – Dioramas of animals *chez eux* — at home, that is. Local prehistoric finds and pre-Norman ethnography are well illustrated. Closed Sunday mornings, Mondays, and Tuesdays. Next to the *Musée des Antiquités* at 198 Rue Beauvoisine (phone: 35-71-41-50).

Pavillon Flaubert – All that remains of the riverside house where Flaubert wrote *Madame Bovary.* It contains furniture, bibelots, and other mementos of the author not found downtown. Closed Tuesdays and Wednesday mornings. Croisset, 3 miles (5 km) west of Rouen by D51 (phone: 35-36-43-91). For information, ask at the *Musée Flaubert.*

 SHOPPING: Not surprisingly, antiques are the shopping specialty in Rouen. Streets noted for this trade are Rue Eau-de-Robec, Place Barthélémy, Rue Damiette, and Rue St.-Romain, all in the heart of the Old Town. Prices can be up to 50% less than those asked in the United States, and though many stores sell country armoires, chests, tables, and other pieces too large for the average traveler to transport, most also have more portable items. In addition to the shops, antiques auctions are scheduled throughout the year at the *Salles des Ventes* (25 Rue du Général-Giraud; phone: 35-71-13-50; and 20 Rue de la Croix-de-Fer; phone: 35-70-32-89). Faïence de Rouen — ceramicware once made locally in traditional patterns — is easily obtained. Beautifully bound books, some with delicate tooling, and old prints also are abundant and comparatively inexpensive, though to find the latter one occasionally has to sift through considerable quantities of dross to get to the real thing. There is a flea market in Place St.-Marc each Saturday and Sunday and in Place des Emmurées on Thursdays, although both spots are heavier on blue jeans than antique christening mugs. The first Saturday of each month, bric-a-brac and antiques are sold at the market set up along the stream on Rue Eau-de-Robec. Ask at the tourist office for the leaflet *Rouen Ville d'Art,* which lists antiques shops, galleries, painters, stained glass, and so on.

Large French and European chains are represented among the many types of stores in Rouen, though on a modest scale compared to Paris, whose proximity diverts a lot of shoppers from Rouen. Most privately owned stores are closed Sundays and Mondays.

Antic St.-Maclou – Antique silver jewelry, ivory bibelots, and books with fine bindings are among the bargains. 178 Rue Martainville (phone: 35-89-52-61 or 35-98-36-31).

L'Armitière – A large, modern bookstore near the *Musée des Beaux-Arts,* with a wide selection of books on Normandy (in French) and a small group of English and American works in paperback. 5 Rue des Basnages (phone: 35-70-57-42).

Laura Ashley – Multi-level boutique featuring the usual selection of flowered frocks. 19 Rue du Gros Horloge (phone: 35-70-20-02).

Atelier St.-Romain – Old French and English prints plus a wide variety of antique objets d'art. 28 Rue St.-Romain (phone: 35-88-76-17).

Burton's – Basically British, though not exclusively, for men. English-cut jackets made from fine, sturdy tweeds are good bargains. 54 Rue du Général-Leclerc (phone: 35-71-58-80).

C & A – Another British company, now widespread in France thanks to the Common Market. Women's blouses and men's wool sweaters are among the many real bargains. 143 Rue du Gros-Horloge (phone: 35-88-04-73).

Michel Carpentier – Discriminatingly crowded with reproductions of engravings of Rouen's street scenes and churches. Carpentier also owns the faïence shop next door. Both are very reasonable. 26 Rue St.-Romain (phone: 35-88-77-47).

P. Chasset – Old glasses and bottles, fascinating antique playing cards, Tarot cards, and children's games in beautifully decorated boxes. 12 Rue de la Croix-de-Fer (phone: 35-70-59-97).

Aux Ducs de Gascogne – Specialties from the southwest of France, one of the country's most famous gastronomic regions: pâtés, foie gras, *confits,* and esoteric soups in aristocratic-looking cans. 7 Rue de l'Epicerie (phone: 35-88-06-04).

Echec et Mat – Jigsaw puzzles, building blocks, chess sets, and other games, with the emphasis on good design. 115 Rue St.-Sever (phone: 35-73-38-88) and 9 Rue Rollon.

M. et Mme. Ester – A colorful variety of eggcups, decanters, fluted champagne glasses, and other bibelots jam this beautiful, attic-like antiques store. 190 Rue Eau-de-Robec (phone: 35-98-04-26).

Michel Garnier – Antique lamps in faïence, ceramics, glass, and brass; Tiffany lamps and lamps from the Far East; lamps from the Belle Epoque, the Edwardian era, and Victoria's England. 11 Rue Damiette (phone: 35-88-66-85).

Herboristerie Saint-Romain – Time-worn domain of a local herbalist, worth a visit — if only to admire the half-timbered structure built in 1480 as the private residence of the director of Rouen's fine arts school. 74 Rue St.-Romain (phone: 35-71-28-23).

Minitrain – Model trains, reproductions, miniatures in wood and metal. 28 Rue Jeanne-d'Arc (phone: 35-70-70-58).

Monique – Ladies' hats that are soigné, outré, *raffiné,* and just plain passé, all at prices that Paris cannot cap. 6 Rue Pie (phone: 35-71-36-52).

Paillard – Chocolates, nougats, pastries . . . ecstasy. 32 Rue du Gros-Horloge (phone: 35-71-10-15).

Picadilly Antics – Antique lace and splendid silverware, much of it from England, languish casually among the pinewood cupboards and tables. 1 Pl. Lieutenant-Aubert (phone: 35-88-17-47).

Marie-Hélène Pottier – Dolls, dolls, dolls — mostly Victorian and many with fancy hats — and antique doll and baby clothes, and perambulators and cradles. The proprietress also restores old dolls. 1060 Chemin de Clères (phone: 35-98-10-46).

Au Printemps – One of France's major department stores, it is inclined toward the trendy rather than the traditional. 4-14 Rue du Gros-Horloge (phone: 35-71-74-75).

Vieux Rouen – A good source (with a large choice) for faïence de Rouen, the decorative tableware and accessories once made here. The items in this small shop near the cathedral are hand-painted, modern reproductions now made in the east of France. 44 Rue de la Tour-de-Beurre (phone: 35-70-54-36).

 SPORTS: Facilities are better in the suburbs than they are in the city.

Ballooning – *Paul Fleury* (1453 Rue de l'Eglise, Bois-Guillaume; phone: 35-60-59-59) will pilot your maiden — or umpteenth — flight over the Norman countryside for an hour or a day from nearby Bois-Guillaume.

Golf – There are 18 holes overlooking the city at *Golf de Rouen* (on Rue François Poulenc in Mont-St.-Aignan; phone: 35-88-99-87). It's more bracing at *Golf d'Etretat* (outside Etretat, a 40-minute drive from Rouen; phone: 35-27-04-89), and more posh at the *New-Golf Club de Deauville* (outside Deauville, an hour's drive away; phone: 31-88-20-53).

Hiking – Contact the *Association Rouennaise de Randonnée Pédestre* (58 Rue du Général-Giraud; phone: 35-62-02-49).

Horseback Riding – You can mount a steed at the *Centre Hippique des Cateliers* (Houppeville; phone: 35-59-14-06), for riding through the Forêt Verte, or at the *Centre Hippique de Génétey* (St.-Martin de Boscherville; phone: 35-32-00-44), for riding through the Forêt de Roumare.

Ice Skating – Glide away at *Patinoire Municipale de Rouen* (Rue Ste.-Amélie; phone: 35-71-05-69), on the Ile Lacroix in the Seine.

Rugby – This is the number one sport in the southwest of France, but since Rouen is in the north, the *Racing Rugby Club de Rouen* (phone: 35-34-45-69) might be considered bush. See them play at *Stade Jean-Mermoz* (Rue de la Motte; phone: 35-62-09-15).

Soccer – Rouen's soccer team, *FCR*, plays at the *Stade Robert-Diochon* (48 Av. des Canadiens, Petit-Quevilly; phone: 35-72-16-25).

Squash – Squeeze into *Rouen Squash* (1 Quai Gaston-Boulet; phone: 35-89-47-80), if you've brought your racket.

Tennis – There are three outdoor courts across the river at the *Centre St.-Sever La Maison* (10 Rue St.-Julien; phone: 35-72-10-32). For indoor courts, try the *Tennis Club de l'Ile Lacroix* (24 Rue Stendhal; phone: 35-88-85-36).

THEATER: The *Théâtre des Arts* (Rue du Docteur Rambert; phone: 35-98-50-98) is the place to see touring hits from Paris, variety shows, and plays put on by famous provincial troupes, besides opera, operetta, and ballet. Experimental theater and dance companies use the *Théâtre Maxime Gorki* (Rue Paul Doumer, in nearby Petit-Quevilly; phone: 35-72-67-55), though you are just as likely to catch a mime, an art exhibit, or a foreign film here. Similarly broad in scope is *L'Espace Duchamp-Villon* (Centre St.-Sever; phone: 35-62-31-31), the home of theater, dance, music, and film. The *Théâtre des Deux Rives* (48 Rue Louis-Ricard; phone: 35-70-22-82) is a local company that mounts experimental and avant-garde productions, and occasionally produces some unconventional versions of French classics.

MUSIC: Rouen is a regional opera center; a season of, usually, eight operas plus six operettas is presented at the *Théâtre des Arts* (Rue du Docteur Rambert; phone: 35-98-50-98). *L'Espace Duchamp-Villon* (Centre St.-Sever; phone: 35-62-31-31) has an annual program of concerts in which such international artists as Jean-Pierre Rampal perform with the *Orchestre de Chambre de Haute Normandie* and other local groups. A summer program of organ recitals, along with chamber music, takes place on the organ of the Eglise St.-Maclou each July and August (for information, call 35-70-84-90). The *Salle Ste.-Croix des Pelletiers* (Rue Ste.-Croix des Pelletiers; phone: 35-71-59-90) is used for classical concerts, including performances by young prizewinners of international competitions appearing under the auspices of the *Rencontres Internationales de Musique en Normandie* (phone: 35-71-43-61). The best jazz in Rouen is organized by *Rouen Jazz Action* (for information, call 35-98-15-91), which arranges appearances by well-known artists.

NIGHTCLUBS and NIGHTLIFE: Paris it ain't, nor, for that matter, Nice, Lyons, or Marseilles. Still, the disco habit has hit Rouen. At *La Bohème* (12 Pl. St.-Amand; phone: 35-71-53-99), expect an older crowd and the music to be mellower than that of *Le Rolls* (16 Av. de Bretagne; phone: 35-03-29-36), a new disco. *Sunset Boulevard* (66 Rte. de Bonsecours; phone: 35-71-12-18) boasts distorted mirrors as part of its idiosyncratic decor, making one question the rather strict dress code. *Père Bos* (59 Rue aux Ours; phone: 35-71-07-60) is at its most bearable when there are visiting chanteuses with gravelly voices. The couples at the *Green Onions Club* (29 Bd. des Belges; phone: 35-07-76-20) are generally over 30. There is a restaurant here, too.

BEST IN TOWN

CHECKING IN: Because Rouen is only an hour from the hundreds of hotels in Paris and less than an hour from the scores of fine hostelries along the Normandy coast, it has become a city that people visit rather than stay in overnight. The result is a dearth of first-rate hotels, especially in the expensive and moderate categories. Only a very few of the 40-some hotels have toilets and a bath or shower in every room. Others may have both in some rooms, a toilet and bidet in some, a shower and bidet in others, and some have rooms with just a wash basin. Many rooms have no facilities at all, though usually they are just "down the hall." Expensive means more than $75 for a double room with toilet and bath or shower. Moderate means $50 to $75; inexpensive, less than $50. In the moderate and inexpensive categories, accommodations are available at lower prices for anyone prepared to share some or all facilities.

Pullman Albane – In the heart of all that is interesting in Rouen, it is astounding how well this hotel fits into the old quarter. With 121 rooms, it has almost every amenity — mini-bars, TV sets, telex service — expected in an up-to-the-minute hostelry, yet you can sit on your burgundy bedspread and look out into streets redolent of the Middle Ages. Service at the front desk is sometimes distracted, though never quite rude, and all staff members who meet the public speak English. Rue de la Croix-de-Fer (phone: 35-98-06-98). Expensive.

Carmes – This centrally located property retains the cozy, intimate feel of an old family hotel while offering the comforts of modern rooms with baths. 33 Pl. des Carmes (phone: 35-71-92-31). Moderate.

Colin's – A new, contemporary hostelry, tucked into a medieval courtyard, that offers the most modern comforts in Rouen's charming Old Town. There's a bar, a garden court, a garage, and one of the city's best restaurants — *Bertrand Warin* (see *Eating Out*) — next door. Ask for a room with a view of the city's rooftops. 15 Rue de la Pie (phone: 35-71-00-88). Moderate.

Dieppe – Close to the station and 10 minutes by foot from old Rouen, this establishment has two wings. The older has the atmosphere of a far from sumptuous pre-war place. The newer wing is spare, clean-cut, and functional, with prints and the odd antique to alleviate what might otherwise be a rather spartan atmosphere. All 37 rooms have toilets and baths or showers. The hotel's *Le Quatre Saisons* (see *Eating Out*) is one of the city's better eating places. Pl. Bernard-Tissot (phone: 35-71-96-00). Moderate.

Le Manoir de Saint Adrien – A few miles outside of Rouen, this turn-of-the-century, Anglo-Normande–style manor house is located in a wooded setting overlooking the Seine. It is half-timbered and quaint outside, with a cozy charm inside. The restaurant serves traditional regional dishes. 6 Chemin de la Source, St.-Adrien (phone: 35-23-32-00). Moderate.

Bordeaux – In one of the modern (late 1940s, that is) blocks along the quays. New owners recently renovated many of the 45 rooms. Those overlooking the quay have views across the Seine; those at the back look out onto the celebrated ecclesiastical towers. 9 Pl. de la République (phone: 35-71-93-58). Moderate to inexpensive.

La Cathédrale – The most famous and colorful hotel in old Rouen is near the cathedral in a quiet, narrow street known for its old houses. There's nothing uniform about any of the 24 rooms: some are Norman rustic, some vaguely Mediterranean, some Directoire. Repeat visitors ask for the ones looking into the flower-filled courtyard. 12 Rue St.-Romain (phone: 35-71-57-95). Moderate to inexpensive.

Gros-Horloge – The elegance has faded somewhat from the Louis XVI furnishings, but the 62 rooms still exude an atmosphere of good, bourgeois comfort. Rooms on the Rue du Gros-Horloge offer a unique closeup of the famous clock. 91 Rue du Gros-Horloge (phone: 35-70-41-41). Moderate to inexpensive.

Normandie – This small, attractive property with 23 rooms in the heart of the Old Town is much favored by nostalgic alumni of the University of Rouen. Some of the plumbing is picturesque, but it usually is efficient. 19 Rue du Bec (phone: 35-71-55-77). Moderate to inexpensive.

Paris – On a nondescript street running down from the Seine, this place is comfortable; breakfast — served either in bed or in the large, salon-style front room — doesn't skimp on coffee. The beds are big, and most of the 24 rooms have a private bath and shower. Parking available. 12-14 Rue de la Champmeslé (phone: 35-70-09-26). Moderate to inexpensive.

La Cache-Ribaud – If it's character you're after, this is it. The 9 bedrooms are wallpapered in the autumnal colors — lots of russets, oranges, and dun browns — found all over Normandy, and they are generally rather cramped, dominated by huge armoires and double beds. Some have washbasins, but for most the facilities are down the hall, which is not too much of an imposition considering that this is like a large family house. The restaurant of the same name downstairs (see *Eating Out*) is beautiful to look at. 10 Rue du Tambour (phone: 35-71-04-82). Inexpensive.

Lisieux – Five minutes from the cathedral in the postwar complex close to the Seine, here is another hotel of little interior character compensated by a very pleasant management. The 27 rooms are clean and comfortable. 4 Rue de la Savonnerie (phone: 35-71-87-73). Inexpensive.

Solferino – A 1930s-style hotel owned by a local architect and his wife, with 14 simple rooms. Located midway between the train station and central Rouen, at 51 Rue Thiers (phone: 35-71-10-17). Inexpensive.

■**Note:** The *Union,* 16 rooms (13 Pl. du Général-de-Gaulle; phone: 35-71-46-55); *Viking,* 37 rooms (21 Quai du Havre; phone: 35-70-34-95), and *Préfecture,* 18 rooms (35 Av. Champlain; phone: 35-72-93-89), are all inexpensive hotels of little decorative distinction, where there are some rooms that have baths and showers with toilet. All are clean, comfortable, and what the French call *tranquille.* If you prefer modern, most of the major moderate-priced French hotel chains such as Ibis are found on the outskirts of town.

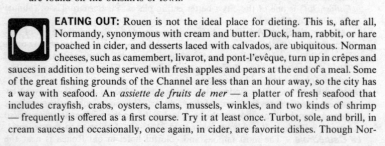

EATING OUT: Rouen is not the ideal place for dieting. This is, after all, Normandy, synonymous with cream and butter. Duck, ham, rabbit, or hare poached in cider, and desserts laced with calvados, are ubiquitous. Norman cheeses, such as camembert, livarot, and pont-l'evêque, turn up in crêpes and sauces in addition to being served with fresh apples and pears at the end of a meal. Some of the great fishing grounds of the Channel are less than an hour away, so the city has a way with seafood. An *assiette de fruits de mer* — a platter of fresh seafood that includes crayfish, crabs, oysters, clams, mussels, winkles, and two kinds of shrimp — frequently is offered as a first course. Try it at least once. Turbot, sole, and brill, in cream sauces and occasionally, once again, in cider, are favorite dishes. Though Normandy is not a prime wine region, it is nonetheless France, and Rouen's wine cellars can be spectacular. But cider, the local brew, often displaces the *grands crus* of Bordeaux and Burgundy in the hearts of the Rouennais. This is not apple juice but hard cider, harder than most Americans have ever experienced, and it can be bought in bottles in most restaurants. The bottled cider is almost always *doux* (sweet), however, and slightly carbonated, and real aficionados will tolerate only cider served in *pichets* (stone jugs), which is still and very dry and sometimes quite potent.

At restaurants below rated expensive, dinner for two excluding wine and drinks will come to more than $80. Moderate means $40 to $80; inexpensive, less than $40. Service usually is included.

Le Beffroy – Very Norman in atmosphere and one of the top dining spots in town. The fish dishes are superb, as are the classic *canette à la rouennaise* and the apple desserts. Closed Sundays, Mondays, and August. Reservations necessary. 15 Rue Beffroy (phone: 35-71-55-27). Expensive.

Les Capucines – This suburban place is in a modern building of little character, and the dining room is decorated in the autumnal tones that are common in Normandy. It's the duck pâté, apple sherbet, and braised sweetbreads with celery (and much besides) that make the 15-minute ride worthwhile. Closed Sunday evenings. Reservations necessary. 16 Rue Jean-Macé, Petit-Quevilly, southwest of central Rouen (phone: 35-72-62-34). Expensive.

La Couronne – The most famous restaurant in Rouen and reputedly the oldest in France. Don't be deceived by the timber and corbels of the exterior; the façade is barely 50 years old. But the interior is ancient and lovely, with exposed beams, carved woodwork, medieval porcelain in glass cases, and — in fall and winter — a fire that casts a warm glow over the pink napery and sienna ceilings. Duck *à la rouennaise* is the famous dish here, but many regulars prefer other local classics such as *pieds de mouton* (sheep's feet) and *cassolette d'homard* (lobster casserole with fresh vegetables). Open daily. Reservations advised. 31 Pl. du Vieux-Marché (phone: 35-71-40-90). Expensive.

Dufour – A huge stone fireplace, exposed beams, antique statues of saints in wall niches, and a vast display of fresh seafood in one corner; this is the sort of place where you expect to see the three musketeers drop by any minute to sample huge *assiette de fruits de mer,* oysters, *coquilles, barbue* (brill) in cider, the duck pâté, or duck *rouennais*. It's all worth fighting over. Closed Sunday nights, Mondays, and August. Reservations advised. 67 bis Rue St.-Nicolas (phone: 35-71-90-62). Expensive.

Gill – Gilles Tournadre, the young chef, has cultivated the culinary art of subtlety, making even simple dishes like *raviolis de langoustines* or duck liver with leeks seem special. The *feuillantine de fraises* and *panaché de poissons* both come highly praised. The pastel decor is modern and refreshing, an anomaly in Rouen. Closed Sundays, Mondays at noon, the first 2 weeks of January, and the last week of August through mid-September. Reservations necessary. 60 Rue St.-Nicolas (phone: 35-71-16-14). Expensive.

Le Quatre Saisons – A classic example of the truism that in France, unprepossessing-looking buildings close to railways can house exceptional restaurants. A favorite with discerning business types, its kitchen turns out a wonderful salad of smoked fish in sour cream, a splendid duck pâté, and a much-admired pressed duck. Open daily. Reservations advised. *Hôtel de Dieppe,* Pl. Bernard-Tissot (phone: 35-71-96-00). Expensive.

Bertrand Warin – M. Warin was trained by Michel Guérard but has relaxed the master's nouvelle cuisine strictures somewhat; his cuisine has won him one Michelin star. Menus vary with the season, but the *assiette de fruits de mer* is served year-round and tastes as it looks — delicious. Mirrors of the Belle Epoque, stately

Louis XIII chairs, and gleaming silverware add to the feeling of good living experienced here. Closed Sunday dinner, Mondays, and during August. Reservations necessary. 9 Rue de la Pie (phone: 35-89-26-69). Expensive to moderate.

La Cache-Ribaud – Atmosphere has run riot in this beguiling old dining place. Beams are exposed, like skeletons, on all sides, the intervening plaster and brick having generally been removed to add light and space to the dining rooms. Try the parsleyed ham, the duck in cider vinegar, or the brill in mushroom sauce. Closed Sunday dinner. Reservations unnecessary. *Cache-Ribaud Hôtel,* 10 Rue du Tambour (phone: 35-71-04-82). Expensive to moderate.

La Poule au Pot – The place to go is the rotisserie — the grillroom of this bar-hotel-restaurant. The fare consists of fine examples of regional specialties such as rabbit, duck, lamb, or veal served in cream or calvados. Seafood dishes also are plentiful. Closed Mondays. Reservations unnecessary. 13-15 Rue du Père-Adam (phone: 35-71-09-53). Expensive to moderate.

Les P'tits Parapluies – The Belle Epoque interior of this small, charming restaurant once housed an umbrella shop (*boutique de parapluies*). Hot oysters with salmon roe and sweetbreads with truffles will make you forget the rain. Closed Sundays, Monday lunch, and the first 3 weeks of August. Reservations unnecessary. 46 Rue Bourg-l'Abbé (phone: 35-88-55-26). Expensive to moderate.

La Toque d'Or – A warren of rooms with whitewashed walls, beams going every which way, and flagstone corridors make this the most rustic restaurant in Old Rouen. It's possible to eat here for as little as $15 a head, but dining well on a brioche of salmon with herbs, sweetbreads in port, salad, cream cheese, and *crème caramel* costs more. Open daily. Reservations necessary. 11 Pl. du Vieux-Marché (phone: 35-71-46-29). Expensive to moderate.

Le Bistrot d'Adrian – A pleasant spot to eat outdoors looking across to the modern Eglise Ste.-Jeanne-d'Arc. Although the service can be a little nervous when it's busy, the fish soup, calf's head, and many other items are fine. The menu changes weekly. Open daily. Reservations advised. 37 Pl. du Vieux-Marché (phone: 35-71-57-73). Moderate.

Le Boeuf Couronné – Terrine of snails and salmon (combined, that is) and oysters cooked in cream make dining here an unusual pleasure. As befits the name, there are also better than average beef dishes. Closed Saturday dinner and Sundays. Reservations advised. 151 Rue Beauvoisine (phone: 35-88-68-28). Moderate.

La Bourse – Actually several different dining rooms that are very popular locally and you are unlikely to see many tourists. Most soignée of the various *salles à manger* is the Corneille, which features prawn fritters in whiskey sauce and a fricassee of sweetbreads with brill among other unusual combinations. Open daily. Reservations advised. 9 Quai de la Bourse (phone: 35-70-31-30). Moderate.

Charles – An old café recently transformed into a trendy bistro by one of Rouen's most successful restaurateurs. There is a simple menu of cold items, including smoked salmon, carpaccio, and foie gras, as well as a daily hot special. Whiskey, exotic drink concoctions, and wines by the glass are served at the wooden bar and at classic café tables in the front. Reservations unnecessary. 6 Rue du Général-Giraud (phone: 35-70-73-39). Moderate.

Au Chat Bleu – It's hard to miss this busy, popular, and sometimes claustrophobic eatery: The blue lights outside gleam across Place Beauvoisine. Seafood is basically the thing, especially the English Channel version of bouillabaisse served on Fridays. Closed Sundays. Reservations advised. 113 Pl. Beauvoisine (phone: 35-71-22-76). Moderate.

Gentil – It is *très gentil.* This is, again, basically a seafood house, with the lively ambience of a brasserie. It's the perfect spot for sampling an *assiette de fruits de mer* and other marvels from the Channel in the open air. The terrace is wildly popular and the menu is enormous. Open daily. Reservations unnecessary. 2 Pl. du Vieux-Marché (phone: 35-71-59-09). Moderate.

La Marmite – Dining by candlelight until 2 AM at this small, comfortable spot is very relaxing. Specialties include duck in cider, lamb with white beans, and a casserole of sweetbreads with *cèpes,* a particularly tasty variety of mushroom. Closed Saturday lunch and Sundays. Reservations advised. 3 Rue Florence (phone: 35-71-75-55). Moderate.

Mirabelle – Another favorite for dining under the stars on a summer night. The accent is Alsatian, the *choucroute* of various kinds served in generous portions. Open daily. Reservations advised. 3 Pl. du Vieux-Marché (phone: 35-71-58-21). Moderate.

La Rose des Sables – The queen of the couscous houses, the name means the rose of the sands (whatever *that* means) and the restaurant is appropriately decorated in a sandy pink. In addition to couscous, it will produce a complete sheep on request. Open daily. Reservations unnecessary. 93 Rue Bouvreuil (phone: 35-07-00-39). Moderate.

Pain, Amour et Fantaisie – A funky little tea salon–cum–boutique, offering a variety of English cakes, scones, tarts — savory and sweet — and salads. Shelves are cluttered with teas, Crabtree & Evelyn jams, dried flowers, and other items for purchase. Open daily, except Sundays, from 11 AM to 6:30 PM. Reservations unnecessary. 25 Rue Cauchoise (phone: 35-07-52-74). Moderate to inexpensive.

La Petite Auberge – An undiscovered pearl worthy of attention. The tipoff is how shy the waiters are with foreigners, meaning they don't often cater to the tourist trade. Seafood is the specialty, and the fish soup and mussels in cream are recommended, though the chicken with lemon and curry also is excellent. The size of the portions is breathtaking, and if you didn't see similar quantities of food all around you, you'd think the chef wished you abdominal harm. Closed Monday dinner. Reservations unnecessary. 164 Rue Martainville (phone: 35-70-80-18). Moderate to inexpensive.

L'Absinthe – The *style normand* back room and the small patio are the most attractive spots here. Steaks and chops are among the main items on the menu, ham and fish terrines the most interesting. Closed Sundays at lunch. Reservations unnecessary. 60 Rue Bouvreuil (phone: 35-07-53-23). Inexpensive.

Les Flandres – Another ideal spot for those in a hurry, although the generous helping of *moules* does take time to consume. Entrecôte steaks and super French fries are typical of the menu. Closed Saturday nights, Sundays, and August. Reservations unnecessary. 5 Rue des Bons Enfants (phone: 35-98-45-16). Inexpensive.

Grande Poste – A local institution, with waiters *à l'ancienne* and a café-brasserie style that caters to patrons of all ages, at all hours, every day of the year. Reservations unnecessary. 43 Rue Jeanne D'Arc (phone: 35-70-08-70). Inexpensive.

Le Grutli – This popular brasserie serves chops, *coquilles,* salads, and a much-praised steak tartare. Open daily. Reservations unnecessary. 38 Rue de la République (phone: 35-71-09-34). Inexpensive.

Le Long-Van – One of the more elegant Vietnamese eateries in town, with a sleek, wooden latticework ceiling and wall-to-wall bamboo screens. Traditional Vietnamese and Thai dishes are served, though the menu leans toward the ocean. Portions are generous — more than you'd ever be served in a Vietnamese restaurant in Paris. Dinner only; closed Sundays. Reservations unnecessary. 51 Rue de la République (phone: 35-98-09-65). Inexpensive.

La Tarte Tatin – A *crêperie,* though a rather smart one. Camembert, ham, creamed mushrooms, and crab are among the many fillings available in the beautifully prepared crêpes. It is also a *salon de thé*. Closed Sundays. Reservations unnecessary. 99 Rue de la Vicomté (phone: 35-89-35-73). Inexpensive.

La Tour de Beurre – This small restaurant is, basically, another *crêperie*. There is a pleasant terrace for sunny days. Closed Sundays. Reservations unnecessary. 20 Quai Pierre-Corneille (phone: 35-71-95-17). Inexpensive.

Ty Briez – An ancient, crooked house in the winding old quarter harbors this cozy crêperie, where bowls of cider and variety of simple crêpes are served for a simple price. Closed Sundays and Mondays. Reservations unnecessary. 5 Rue du Père Adam (phone: 35-71-07-67). Inexpensive.

 BARS AND CAFÉS: Two favorites with young Rouennais and visitors are *Le Big Ben Pub,* in the shadow of the Gros-Horloge (30 Rue des Vergetiers; phone: 35-88-44-50), and *La Taverne* (11 Rue St.-Amand; phone: 35-88-51-38), a Rouen landmark that counted Sartre among its patrons in the 1930s. At *Le Bateau Ivre* (17 Rue des Sapins; phone: 35-70-09-05), there occasionally are visiting singers and jazz groups. For softer music in a Louis XV atmosphere, try *Le Club XV* (81 Rue Ecuyère; phone: 35-98-60-41). For a nightcap in an intimate ambience (with fellow countrymen usually on hand), there is the *Bar Pullman,* the cocktail bar of the *Pullman Alban* (Rue de la Croix-de-Fer). Many of Rouen's bars stay open until 2 AM most nights of the week. Some close at least 1 day a week.

ST.-TROPEZ

Rivaling Cannes as a favorite of the international set, St.-Tropez first became famous when Brigitte Bardot made it her home during the 1950s. Her arrival turned a fishing port that had for centuries been a target for pirates and then for painters into the headquarters for a whole coterie of starlets, swingers, and spectators, including those ready to give anything to be part of the action. When topless sunbathing appeared — it is said to have originated here at Tahiti Plage — it certainly did nothing to downplay the town's already considerable notoriety; rather, this curious folkway, as reported in newpapers, magazines, and TV programs around the globe, pinpointed St.-Tropez on the map for would-be hedonists everywhere. The miracle of St.-Tropez is how well it has survived its success. The charm of its setting remains, its marvelous climate — give or take a *mistral* bluster or two around August 15 — endures, and its mystique always seems to triumph over the formidable menace of the annual high summer invasion.

In May and early June, and again in September and October, St.-Tropez is at half pace and a joy. Not so in July and August, when people who do not like crowds of any kind should give the St.-Tropez mob scene a very wide berth. But those who do brave the traffic jam into town will find the multitudes at the portside cafés and boutiques magically endowed, if only for the short season of their stay, with a style and high spirit many of them never knew they possessed. The St.-Tropez look, whatever its ingredients, mixes them with a certain aesthetic flair and delightfully meretricious chic that are seductive to even the most blasé visitors. For years, for instance, the town set trends in summer fashions, with no apparent end to their colorful craziness, and while this heavy responsibility is now more evenly shared with other resorts, the clothes still manage to look their sexiest when worn in St.-Tropez at six in the evening at *Sénéquier,* the perennially "in" café on the waterfront.

Like many another Mediterranean port, St.-Tropez has seen the destruction of pillage and war, but it has resisted the equally devastating assaults of modern real estate development much better than some other coastal towns. The reconstruction after World War II was carried out by a municipality always sensitive to the enchanting allure of old buildings, especially such old buildings as the pink and ocher facades that used to line the main harbor and, in copy, do so once again. Elsewhere, the narrow streets of cream stone houses and the broad main square shaded by plane trees for the market and for the *boules* players are unmistakably Provençal. Considering the kind of commercial exploitation that St.-Tropez's fame had every reason to attract, the new architects have kept splendid faith with the old; and fast-food protrusions and condominial blockhouses have been kept to an inconspicuous minimum.

One very good reason that the original appearance of the town escaped wholesale distortion is St.-Tropez's sheer inaccessibility at the end of a rocky, hilly peninsula. No train, no expressway, no airport serves it, and people who come have to really want to; there's no simply passing by. It's a tribute to its charm that all those thousands are still prepared to struggle along the winding mountain route across the Massif des Maures or along the equally tortuous coastal route to the one road in — and out. The only other way in, and certainly the most romantic way in for first-timers or for sentimental regulars, is by sea; even if you don't have a yacht, there are boats from Port Grimaud or Ste.-Maxime. You'll be eternally grateful if you can make your first glimpse of town that view of the port from the Gulf of St.-Tropez rather than from the traffic jam on N98.

In the old days, everyone came by sea. First, the Greeks. The town that Bardot made famous in the 20th century originally was settled, so the story goes, by another sex goddess, Phrynea, a model and mistress of the great Athenian sculptor Praxiteles. That first Greek settlement, Athenopolis, under the Romans became Heraclea, a natural port of call for ships riding the current from Italy to Spain. On May 17 in the year AD 68 (like all really good legends, there's a precise date for it), the current brought in a boat with a weird trio of passengers — a headless Roman centurion accompanied by a dog and a cockerel. The Roman was Torpes, a converted Christian beheaded by the emperor Nero. The dog and cockerel were sent along, as was the custom, to devour his body. But they left the martyr — St. Torpes — intact, prompting pious fishermen to make a shrine that became St.-Tropez. Torpes is still venerated in Pisa, which claims to have the martyr's head, and the anniversary of his arrival is celebrated annually on May 16 and 17 in St.-Tropez by taking the statue of him (with the dog and the cockerel) out of the parish church and parading with it around the town. The city elects a captain to lead the parade. A similar festival takes place on June 15; this time to celebrate the city's victory over a Spanish fleet that tried to capture St.-Tropez back in 1637.

In the Middle Ages, St.-Tropez was prey to Saracen pirates from North Africa and underwent continuous destruction and reconstruction until Raffaele Garezzio arrived with 21 families from Genoa in 1470, authorized by the rulers of Provence to guarantee its defense in exchange for tax exemption. St.-Tropez thus became an independent republic, governed by a council made up of the heads of all families and two elected consuls, until Louis XIV incorporated it into France in 1672. For a few centuries thereafter it remained a quiet little fishing village, then Guy de Maupassant wrote about "this charming and simple daughter of the sea," which he visited on a Mediterranean cruise in 1888. His description attracted the attention of the painter Paul Signac, who made it his home, followed by Pierre Bonnard, Charles Camoin, Henri Matisse for a short while, and later André Dunoyer de Segonzac, all drawn by the bewitching light of this isolated port. The painters in turn attracted Colette to make her summer home here in the 1920s. Decades before it was to delight the paparazzi with its topless, even bottomless customs, St.-Tropez shocked the outside world because this emancipated novelist went around with *bare legs.* The influx of celebrity-hungry tourists drove her away in 1938, and, not for the last time, people lamented that St.-Tropez wasn't what it used to be.

In August 1944, the Germans nearly destroyed it completely. Faced with American landings along the Mediterranean coast, they blew up the whole port, leaving only a few of the old houses standing behind the Hôtel de Ville (Town Hall). The possibility that St.-Tropez would never be the same again was indeed real. Instead, it was lovingly restored, and the returning artists, this time joined by film stars and pop singers, discovered the added pleasures of the nearby, hitherto deserted beaches. Jean Cocteau and the St.-Germain-des-Prés crowd flocked here in the early 1950s. In 1953, the director Roger Vadim filmed *And God Created Woman,* starring a (for that time) shockingly nubile Brigitte Bardot, on location on the white sands of Pampelonne beach. Bardot made her home in a secluded beachfront villa, La Madrague, and she and her succession of playboy lovers created another St.-Tropez legend. The town soon was swarming with blond, pouty-lipped, long-legged lookalikes trailed — with poodle-like devotion — by bronzed Nordic gods.

And ever since, hordes of superbly narcissistic Scandinavians, Germans, Britons, Italians, Americans, and not a few French have come to look for each other at sunset on the quay, to dance and make love till dawn, sleep in the sun, and return to the quay the next evening to do it all over again. Tropezians, who've known other invasions, watch it all with a bemused eye — some fishermen, a lot of hotel, restaurant, and shop owners and artists, who are by no means all Signacs and Matisses but who do like painting in the sun. They know the place is infuriatingly irresistible.

ST.-TROPEZ AT-A-GLANCE

SEEING THE CITY: If you can't come into St.-Tropez by sea, be sure to make your way as quickly as possible to the Môle Jean-Réveille, the pier that runs along the north side of the harbor. Glance back frequently at the unfolding panorama of portside houses embracing yachts and fishing boats. At the lighthouse on the end of the pier, you can take in the Old Town at the foot of the Citadelle on the eastern heights and, to the west across the Golfe de St.-Tropez, the castle ruins of Grimaud set against a mountain plateau, the Massif des Maures. The play of light at daybreak is dramatically different from that at sunset, so catch both. For a rear view of the town and gulf, walk up to the ramparts of the Citadelle above the very pretty cemetery. The ultimate pleasure here is to combine the view with one of the concerts held in the summer.

SPECIAL PLACES: St.-Tropez is a fishing village turned resort, so it's short on monuments. If you're not staying here — that is, if you're popping in only for a quick visit — you'll find it won't take long to see it all. Except for the beaches, everything is within easy walking distance of everything else, and even the Citadelle requires only the slightest extra effort to make it up the hill. Those staying longer can see what there is to see in a series of walks — or rambles — before and after beach time. Never forget, however, that in St.-Tropez people are a very important part of the scene nor that wherever you go (and on the beach in particular), *you* are part of the scenery.

The Port – Fishing is secondary now, but the port is still the soul of the town. Most of the social and much of the commercial life takes place along the quays, and the spectacle around the cafés, boutiques, and the boats themselves is the essential sight of St.-Tropez. Smaller boats — fishing vessels and such — anchor around Quai Fréd-éric-Mistral, protected by the Môle Jean-Réveille. Luxury yachts, with the captains and their ladies drinking champagne at sundown, have choice moorings around the junction of Quai Jean-Jaurès and Quai Suffren. Farther along, a bronze statue pays tribute to Vice-Admiral Pierre André de Suffren, who grew up in St.-Tropez to become one of the great sailors of 18th-century France. Along the west side of the harbor, artists display their works on the Quai de l'Épi.

Musée de l'Annonciade – It comes as a surprise to some people consumed with the material hedonism of the place to discover that St.-Tropez has one of France's most exquisite little museums of modern art. Set back on the west side of the harbor, the *Annonciade* is a deconsecrated 16th-century chapel of the White Penitent friars, beauti-fully converted to a bright 2-story museum to display the collection of the connoisseur Georges Grammont: French paintings and sculpture spanning the half-century from 1890 to 1940. Around Maillol's sensual bronzes hang some fines canvases of Signac, Matisse, Bonnard, Seurat, Derain, Braque, Van Dongen, and Vlaminck. Some of the best pieces are studies of St.-Tropez itself. Closed Tuesdays and November; admission charge. Pl. Georges-Grammont, Quai l'Epi (phone: 94-97-04-01).

Old Town – One of the most ancient parts of town, La Glaye was spared the dynamite of the German army in 1944 and offers a delightful alternative to the quayside bustle. Start at the Tour du Portalet, where old men sit on their *banc des mensonges* ("bench of lies") spinning yarns of fish and other wild creatures that got away. The tower is part of the old fortifications in which the houses themselves, built right out of the rock on the little bay of La Glaye, still present a formidable barrier on the seaward side. A couple of blocks inland, the Place de la Mairie is graced by a remark-ably unbombastic Hôtel de Ville (Town Hall) and, opposite, by a house with a huge, splendidly ornate carved wooden door brought back by a local sailor from the Arab colony in Zanzibar. Northeast of the harbor.

Eglise Paroissiale (Parish Church) – This dignified, neo-classical 19th-century building with its simple bell tower dating from 1634 is most notable for housing in the chapel left of the entrance the bizarre bust of the city's patron saint. The gaily colored wooden sculpture of the mustachioed St. Torpes (or Tropez, if you prefer) wears a helmet and bejeweled crown, a bemedaled sash, and a slightly dazed look — perhaps because beneath this bust is another version of him *without* his head, watched over by the dog and cockerel in the boat that brought him to town. He's also surrounded by ex-voto gifts, including some smashed blunderbusses and a bosun's whistle. At *Christ-mas,* a beautiful 19th-century nativity scene with Provençal figures called *santons* is set up in the church. Rue du Clocher, in the Old Town.

Place des Lices – The town's main square is the traditional gathering place of true Tropezians — both year-round residents and seasonal regulars — who appreciate that moment at the end of the afternoon when the shade of the plane trees and the click of the *petanques* provide the perfect setting for a good cool *pastis.* There's a morning market Tuesdays and Saturdays for fruit, vegetables, old clothes, and older furniture. It's also the occasional site of the itinerant amusement park and the place that reminds you that St.-Tropez is as much a village as an international playground. Inland from Quai Suffren and identified on some maps by its little-used newer name, Pl. Carnot.

Musée de la Citadelle – On the eastern edge of town, the fortress that France's Henri IV ordered built at the end of the 16th century was the unpopular symbol of St.-Tropez's transformation from an independent republic into just another French town, an assertion of military authority over the region that was a constant bone of contention between Provençal nobles and the French monarchy. Its most recent mili-tary function was as the Germans' last bastion of resistance to the American invasion of 1944; Tropezians participated in its recapture on August 15. In the hexagonal dungeon today is a museum of St.-Tropez's history and of Mediterranean shipping, illustrated by an attractive collection of sailor's paraphernalia, ship models, engravings, paintings, and documents. They include a graphic account of the Tropezians' heroic routing of a Spanish fleet in 1637. Closed Thursdays and mid-November through mid-December; admission charge. On the eastern edge of town, in the Citadelle St.-Tropez (phone: 94-97-59-43).

Beaches – The dazzling stretches of white sand and umbrella pines are just outside town but absolutely inseparable from the total idea of St.-Tropez. *This* is where Vadim created Bardot. The elite arrive at the beach by boat. For ordinary people who walk, the easiest to get to is the Bouillabaisse, a popular family beach a quick 10 minutes southwest of the harbor. Almost as close, going east, is Les Graniers, favored by Tropezians during their lunch break. More fashionable are the Tahiti, around the southern side of the peninsula, and its glorious extension, the 3-mile-long Pampelonne, long enough to dilute the mob scene. These are a short car or taxi ride, or a more leisurely bike ride, 2½ miles (4 km) along the road toward Ramatuelle and are served by some good and a few terrible beach restaurants. The beach mattress rentals may seem a little high at Tahiti and Pampelonne, but the people are more beautiful. For the too mature or exhausted, gin rummy under the umbrella pines is strongly recommended.

■**EXTRA SPECIAL:** In St.-Tropez, all is vanity and it is most properly indulged at the café *Sénéquier.* What counts here is not just the place, but the time. If this town is the ultimate in street theater, the play must be seen from the beginning. So between 8 and 9:30 in the morning (at any rate, no later than 10), have breakfast in one of *Sénéquier*'s scarlet canvas chairs at the scarlet tables at the hub of the port. With a newspaper from the nearby *Maison de la Presse* and coffee and a fresh croissant or brioche from the café's own bakery, watch the performers, eccentric and otherwise, as this craziest of resorts comes to life (and a few of last night's owls head for bed). By 10:30 to 11 the mob is up and you'll no longer see the wonderful wood for the trees. Beach time. Act Two begins around 6 PM. Return to *Sénéquier* for the ritual *café glacé* (iced coffee) and watch the same crowd, a little more tanned than at breakfast, parade their stuff and prepare for their nights.

SOURCES AND RESOURCES

TOURIST INFORMATION: St.-Tropez's portside Office de Tourisme (Quai Jean-Jaurès; phone: 94-97-45-21) also covers the nearby towns of Ramatuelle and Gassin. It provides maps and brochures, details of hotel and camping accommodations, and programs of local events, and it is open year round. Inquire here for information about hotels and restaurants, museums, concerts, shopping, and sports for St.-Tropez and surrounding villages. The city opened a new tourist office at the Gare Routière (Av. du 8 Mai 1945). There also is an American Express office (23 Av. Général Leclerc; phone: 94-97-20-66).

Local Coverage – *Nice Matin* and *Var Matin,* competing regional daily newspapers, both have a special St.-Tropez and Ste.-Maxime edition, good for gossip. The English-language *Flash* is a glossy magazine of just one summer issue previewing the major events of the main holiday season.

TELEPHONE: The city code for St.-Tropez is 94, which is incorporated into all local 8-digit numbers. When calling a number in St.-Tropez from the Paris region (including the Ile-de-France), dial 16, wait for a dial tone, then dial the 8-digit number. When calling a number from outside Paris, dial only the 8-digit number. When calling from the US, dial 33 (which is the country code), followed by the 8-digit number.

GETTING AROUND: Bicycle – A bicycle or a motorcycle is the best way to beat the traffic jams. Rent from *Mas* (Rue Josef Quaranta; phone: 94-97-00-60).

Boat – Transport by boat is available from the *Messageries Maritimes du Golfe,* known as *MMG* (Quai Jean-Jaurès; phone: 94-96-51-00). Or rent your own, with or without captain, from *Suncap Company* (Passage du Port; phone: 94-97-11-23). For those who really like living in style, *Sport-Mer* (8 Pl. Blanqui; phone: 94-97-32-33) rents houseboats.

Bus – Buses serve the surrounding villages of Grimaud, Gassin, Cogolin, Rama-tuelle, La Garde-Freinet, and Croix-Valmer, as well as the railroad station in St.-Raphaël. For information, contact the new tourist office at Gare Routière (Av. du 8 Mai 1945; phone: 94-97-45-21) or the Gare de Saint-Tropez (Av. du Général Leclerc; phone: 94-97-62-77).

Car Rental – During the summer months, it's advisable to make a reservation well ahead of arrival, as demand is heavy. Among the major companies are *Avis* (Av. de 8 Mai 1945; phone: 94-97-03-10); *Europcar* (Résidence du Port; phone: 94-97-15-41); and *Hertz* (Rue Nouvelle Poste; phone: 94-97-22-01).

Taxi – Pick one up by the Quai de l'Epi or call 94-97-05-27.

Train – There is no train service to St.-Tropez. St.-Raphaël (see *Bus* above) is the closest station on the rail line. For information, call *SNCF (Société Nationale des Chemins de Fer Français* (phone: 93-99-50-50 in Cannes; 94-95-13-89 in St.-Raphaël).

SHOPPING: Resortwear, from sailor suits to monokinis, is the thing to buy here and, like fashion itself, an amazing number of shops in St.-Tropez change from season to season — name, management, location. This often is not because of failure or success but, just like the fads, because of a whim. Many big Paris names are currently taking over in town, and though St.-Tropez no longer dictates to other resorts what will or won't be worn on the beach or in the nightclubs each year, the flair remains, and the port provides the right ambience for the more outrageous clothes you might not risk back home.

Don't forget the Tuesday and Saturday morning markets at Place des Lices, good for clothing and antiques as well as for food and flowers. If you're around in late August or early September (it varies from year to year), don't miss the *Foire aux Antiquaires* (Antiques Fair) that also takes place at Place des Lices. Paintings can be bought from artists along the harbor.

There are three main shopping areas — the port, the galleries or *passages* between Quai Suffren and Place des Lices, and the Old Town around the Hôtel de Ville. As the "overnight successes" come and go, here are some of the mainstays.

Josiane Abrial – Specializes in silk, not only in slinky clothes, but also in grandly ornate bed linens. 3 Rue de la Ponche.

Choses – Caters to the passing port trade — dresses, bathing suits, shirts, jeans, and T-shirts with this year's "look"; many of the fashions are unisex. Quai Jean Jaurès.

Daniel Crémieux – Great for men's shirts and classic casual wear. Passage du Port and Rue Gambetta.

Façonnable – For beachwear and sandals. Passage Gambetta.

Galerie de la Colombe – Specializing in surrealist painters. Passage du Port (up-stairs).

Galeries des Peintres de la Mer – Marine paintings for sale. 3 Rue Allard.

Royal Navy – Offers somewhat classic clothes. 9 Rue de la Ponche.

SPECIAL EVENTS: Amid all the cosmopolitan frolic and the undeniably lucrative business of catering to tourists, the Tropezians celebrate a few annual events strictly for themselves. Visitors may watch, but there's no attempt to jazz up the folklore for the foreigners — which is what makes *Les Bravades* all the more attractive. The first and most important of these uniquely Tropezian commemorations, the *Grande Bravade,* begins on May 16, the eve of the legendary arrival of St. Torpes. Following a tradition dating back to 1558, the polychrome wooden bust of the martyr is taken out of the parish church and paraded through the streets for 2½ days by gaily uniformed men firing off blunderbusses behind a band of fifes, bugles, and drums. Starting at the Place de la Mairie, it's a raucous celebration of civic pride punctuated by an occasional solemn blessing of the *bravadeurs'* antique arms and by the less solemn tippling of *pastis* or vermouth. A slightly less boisterous *Bravade des Espagnols,* on June 15, celebrates the Tropezians' victory over the hostile Spanish fleet in 1637.

On June 29, *St. Peter's Day,* fishermen celebrate at the old Port des Pêcheurs at the end of Rue de la Ponche. On August 14 and 15, Americans are particularly welcome for the anniversary of the 1944 landings and *Libération,* with a midnight mass in the Chapelle Ste.-Anne. There also are music-filled evenings scheduled throughout July and August, as well as Provençal dancing, *boules* tournaments, and medieval jousting matches.

 SPORTS AND FITNESS: Other than people watching, the only serious spectator sport in town is *boules,* the court for which is Place des Lices.
Horseback Riding – The *Centre Hippique des Maures* is just outside town at Beauvallon (phone: 94-56-16-55).

Sailing and Windsurfing – The sailing school (*Ecole de Voile*) operates in July and August at the Baie des Canoubiers (phone: 94-97-12-58), and there is good windsurfing along the Pampelonne and Tahiti beaches. Learn to sail or windsurf at *La Moune* (phone: 94-97-11-05), and rent windsurfers at *Windsports* (Rue Paul-Roussel; phone: 94-97-43-25). Make sure not to go out when the mistral is blowing, you might have trouble getting back.

Scuba Diving – This is organized by *Les Plongeurs du Golfe,* whose boat is anchored off the Môle Jean-Réveille from June through September. Inquire at the *nouveau port* (new port) or call (phone: 94-97-08-39; at night, 94-79-27-77).

Tennis – Red clay courts, just like those at the *French Open.* Play and swim at *Tennis Club des Marres* (Rte. des Plages; phone: 94-97-26-68); *Tennis-Club de St.-Tropez* (Rte. des Salins; phone: 94-97-36-39); or *Tennis Municipal* (*UST*) (Route des Plages; phone: 94-54-82-40).

 MUSIC: Recitals and chamber music concerts are held in the *Renaissance* theater on Place des Lices, up at the Citadelle, and occasionally at the Château de la Moutte, at the east end of the peninsula. The Office de Tourisme has details.

 NIGHTCLUBS AND NIGHTLIFE: Most of the "boîtes" are super discos, distinguished from each other mainly by the people they let in or keep out, all with a sweet smile that leaves the banished with the surprisingly comfortable feeling that they wouldn't have been happy there anyway. The two smartest are both in the *Byblos* hotel: *Les Caves du Roy* (entrance off Place des Lices) offers a good live band in season for your gladdest rags; *Le Krak des Chevaliers* is a little more subdued (phone for both: 94-97-00-04). *L'Esquinade* (3 Rue du Four; phone: 94-97-38-09) prides itself on its exclusive taste and makes an interesting challenge for the not easily daunted — if they're pretty or amusing to look at. The *Papagayo* (Quai de l'Epi; phone: 94-97-07-56) has the most pleasingly insane atmosphere, Chinese exotica, and local eccentrics.

BEST IN TOWN

 CHECKING IN: Considering the enduring appeal and celebrity of the resort, hotels in St.-Tropez compare in price more than favorably with the rest of France. There is a good selection of expensive hotels, in the $125 and up range for a double room, but a majority are moderate, around $60 to $125, and a fair number are inexpensive at $25 to $60. For anything less expensive, inquire well in advance through the Office de Tourisme (phone: 94-97-45-21) about renting a furnished flat, available during the summer, or about camping and holiday villages (*villages de vacances*), available only around nearby Grimaud, Gassin, Ramatuelle, and La Garde-Freinet. The advice about booking far in advance for *all* accommodations applies here from June through mid-September.

Byblos – This manages to be a truly luxurious hotel without looking or feeling anything like the traditional "palaces" elsewhere along the Côte d'Azur. Built at the beginning of the 1970s and constantly modernizing its amenities to include Jacuzzis, a sauna, and air conditioning, it nevertheless retains the atmosphere of a self-contained Provençal village. The 107 rooms are beautifully, cheerfully furnished, and the youthful spirit of St.-Tropez is superbly captured with a personal, unpretentious touch to the service so often sacrificed at these prices. Lunch at the (heated) swimming pool is *the* great midday rendezvous away from the beaches (see *La Braiserie* in *Eating Out*). Closed mid-October to late March. Av. Paul-Signac (phone: 94-97-00-04). Expensive.

La Mandarine – Designed like a small village with pink-washed walls, it has 42 brightly furnished rooms and apartments separated by hedges, vines, and graveled walks around a quiet courtyard. There is a terrace restaurant. About half a mile from town, the hotel maintains a private beach out at Pampelonne in addition to its own swimming pool. Closed from mid-October to mid-April. Rte. de Tahiti (phone: 94-97-21-00). Expensive.

Le Mas de Chastelas – On the edge of town though only a few minutes from the harbor, this is an exquisitely renovated 17th-century country manor with 31 rooms, a haven of peace among the umbrella pines and grapevines that has become a favorite of the Paris movie and fashion world. Ten duplex apartments are in a tree-shaded annex. There are 4 clay tennis courts as well as a heated swimming pool. Closed from October through *Easter*. Quartier Bertaud, Rte. de Ramatuelle (phone: 94-56-09-11). Expensive.

La Ponche – One of the oldest and most charming of the in-town hotels, in the heart of the Vieille Ville (Old City) by the Port des Pêcheurs. The 23 rooms are small but nicely done, several with private terraces providing a splendid view of the Golfe de St.-Tropez, a delight at breakfast time. The service is exceptionally friendly. Closed from mid-October to *Easter*. 1 Pl. du Révelin (phone: 94-97-02-53 or 94-97-13-27). Expensive.

Résidence de la Pinède – This comfortable hotel, with 34 rooms and 5 suites right on Bouillabaisse Beach, caters very much to the sporting crowd. For those not content with the kidney-shaped pool in the shade of the pine trees, the saunas, or solarium, the private beach offers windsurfing and water skiing. The rooms are spacious and prettily furnished in traditional Provençal style. Closed from mid-October to February. Plage de la Bouillabaisse (phone: 94-97-04-21). Expensive.

Yaca – An intimate, shady, 22-room hostelry at the edge of the Old Town. It's quiet here — no mean claim in this noisy town. There is a restaurant that is open during the summer months. The cocktail bar has a nice jazz piano. Closed from the end of September to mid-April; open 2 weeks for *Christmas* and *New Year's*. 1–3 Bd. d'Aumale (phone: 94-97-11-79). Expensive.

Ermitage – Up on the road leading past the Citadelle, this is one of the few hotels with a panoramic view of the town. There are 29 rooms, and the service is excellent and very friendly. Open all year. Av. Paul-Signac (phone: 94-97-52-33). Expensive to moderate.

Le Levant – On the road where Colette used to live, it is tranquilly set in a lovely garden by the sea. It has a huge heated pool, beside which the restaurant serves a lunchtime barbecue. 28 modern rooms. Closed from mid-October to mid-April. Rte. des Salins (phone: 94-97-33-33). Expensive to moderate.

Sube – Set right on the harbor behind the statue of Vice-Admiral Suffren, this famous place has 28 very unpretentious rooms, with ringside views of the most amusing resort show on the Côte d'Azur, and a popular restaurant. Make room reservations well in advance. Open year-round; 35% discount on room rates in winter. 15 Quai Suffren (phone: 94-97-30-04). Expensive to moderate.

Le Pré de la Mer – This 12-room, modern motel offers comfort and good value. Closed from October to *Easter*. Route des Salins (phone: 94-97-12-23). Moderate.

Résidence des Lices – Modern and by the Place des Lices, its 41 rooms are nonetheless peaceful, and it's more attractive from its bougainvillea-festooned inner patio and swimming pool than the rather nondescript street façade suggests. Closed from mid-November to April 1; open for *Christmas*. Av. Augustin-Grangeon (phone: 94-97-28-28). Moderate.

Lou Cagnard – Not far from Place des Lices, it has 19 rooms, a garden, friendly service, and it's quiet. Consider it a great bargain, particularly for the off-season. Closed November 15 to December 26. Av. Paul-Roussel (phone: 94-97-04-24). Inexpensive.

Les Chimères – Right on the water, this charming guesthouse is nicely situated outside the hustle and bustle of town. Breakfast is served in the garden under cool palms and bougainvillea. Port du Pilon (phone: 94-97-02-90). Inexpensive.

Lou Troupelen – These two pink-washed Provençal houses in a delightful garden surrounded by vineyards contain 44 rooms only a short walk from the center of town and an easy ride to the beaches. Closed early November to *Easter*. Chemin des Vendanges (phone: 94-97-44-88). Inexpensive.

 EATING OUT: With a few noble exceptions, St.-Tropez is not a temple of gastronomy. Ambience, table hopping, and general people watching take precedence over sophisticated cuisine, but it's still possible to eat well if you choose the excellent local fish, cooked simply — grilled or baked in Provençal herbs. And the local wines (Côtes de Provence), which are less impressive transported back home, will taste perfectly good, especially the rosé. While you're sampling, try the local nougat and the *tarte tropézienne,* a pineapple-filled cream sandwich. A meal for two, without wine, in a restaurant listed as expensive will cost around $80 and up; in a moderate one, $40 to $70; and in an inexpensive one, $20 to $40. Service charge is usually included. Closing periods vary from year to year, but most places are open from *Easter* on through the winter onslaught.

Bistro des Lices – New owners are trying to make this restaurant a hit by featuring traditional cooking and a piano bar. Open daily for dinner in the summer; for lunch (except Tuesdays and Wednesdays) and dinner in the winter. Reservations advised. Place des Lices (phone: 94-97-29-00). Expensive.

La Braiserie – Fish and inventive dishes are the order of the day at this restaurant, poolside at the posh *Byblos* hotel. Open daily. Closed February to late March. Reservations unnecessary. Av. P. Signac (phone: 94-97-00-04). Expensive.

Le Chabichou – Considered by many the best in town for decor, service, and exciting food preparation; it's also a good place to spot celebrities. Dinner is worth the price, and weekday lunch is a bargain. It's the only place in St.-Tropez that has a Michelin star. Closed Mondays and mid-October to late May. Reservations necessary. Av. Foch (phone: 94-54-80-00). Expensive.

Leï Mouscardins – Old-fashioned Provençal cooking in the antique setting of the Old City fortifications leading to the Tour du Portalet, with a superb view of the Golfe de St.-Tropez. (Ask for one of the prized tables on the terrace.) The restaurant's habitués swear that the bouillabaisse cannot be beaten in Marseilles. The grilled sea bass is pretty good, too. Count on the best of the local wines. Open daily for lunch and dinner. Closed from November through January. Reservations advised. Rue Portalet (phone: 94-97-01-53). Expensive.

Le Mas de Chastelas – The most discreetly elegant clientele of St.-Tropez partakes of the very sophisticated fare here. Dinners only, except for hotel guests. Open daily for lunch and dinner. Closed from October to *Easter*. Reservations advised. Rte. de Ramatuelle (phone: 94-56-09-11). Expensive.

L'Olivier – A charming place just outside town. The chef hails from the southwest of France and experiments with Mediterranean flavors. Try his classic duck with honey. Open daily for lunch and dinner. Closed January to February, and mid-October to mid-December. Reservations advised. Rte. des Carles (phone: 94-97-58-19). Expensive.

Club 55 – Like all the beach eateries, this is in a category by itself, one where ambience is everything and cuisine most definitely secondary (however, the fish is very fresh). But the sheer lazy delight of a simple meal at tables set among the umbrella pines a few yards away from the white sands of Pampelonne epitomizes hedonistic St.-Tropez more than any other eating place. It grew out of a canteen set up for the film crew of the Vadim-Bardot movie that launched postwar St.-Tropez in 1953. Lunch only. Closed Mondays. Reservations unnecessary. Plage de Pampelonne (phone: 94-79-80-14). Expensive to moderate.

La Ponche – This pleasantly calm terrace spot by the Port des Pêcheurs serves a marvelous saffron mussel soup and giant *gambas* (shrimp) in tarragon sauce, but there's also a bargain menu with such things as a fine lamb stew (*navarin*) and a definitive lemon pie. Closed Mondays, and from mid-October to *Easter*. Reservations unnecesary. Pl. du Révelin (phone: (94-97-09-53). Expensive to moderate.

La Romana – The most fashionable of the town's several Italian *trattorie*. Fresh pasta and very good pizza in a lovely garden; dinners only. Open daily. Closed from end of September through March. Reservations unnecessary. Chemin des Conquettes (phone: 94-97-18-50). Expensive to moderate.

Café des Arts – A back room behind the bar and through the kitchen serves as one of the perennially fashionable hangouts that does not cold-shoulder newcomers, but welcomes a nice mixture of Tropezians and transients. The food is less brilliant than the clientele. (But try the cold lentil salad. It's only a bistro, so keep it simple and you'll have a good time.) Open daily for lunch and dinner. Closed from October through March. Reservations unnecessary. Pl. des Lices (phone: 94-97-02-25). Moderate.

Le Gorille – For the unserious eater. Open all night, all year — steaks and French fries in one of the town's great institutions, on the port, beside the newspaper shop. No reservations. 1 Quai Suffren (phone: 94-97-03-93). Inexpensive.

Lou Revelen – For the serious eater. Try the *tapenade* (an appetizer of anchovy paste, minced olives, and garlic), the great grilled sardines, and the bourride (a whitefish version of bouillabaisse with cream or milk). The restaurant has its own very honorable wines. Open daily for lunch and dinner; except from January 1 to *Easter,* when it is open only on weekends. Reservations unnecessary. 4 Rue des Remparts (phone: 94-97-06-34). Inexpensive.

 BARS AND CAFÉS: Hardened Tropezians spend nights at the *Café des Arts* on Place des Lices; they share elbow room with the *boules* players at the great zinc bar. *Le Gorille,* the classic French provincial bar on the port, is rich in sailors and those who went out for a pack of cigarettes and never came back (open all night, all year, on Quai Suffren). The most beautiful people on the port can be found at sundown in the bar at the back of *L'Escale* (Quai Jean-Jaurès). For quieter conviviality, try the bar of *La Ponche* (Pl. du Révelin). The "in" place for young locals is the *Bar Avins* (13 Rue des Fénier) where you can play billiards squeezed between the tile-covered walls and the small bistro tables where you can get a quick bite to eat.

STRASBOURG

Since 1949, the headquarters of the Council of Europe and, since 1979, the meeting place of the European Community's directly elected European Parliament, Strasbourg is the newest capital on the Continent. Given its international scope, it potentially could be the most imposing of capitals, too, except that the Strasbourgeois don't think of things that way. They seldom mention their newfound prominence and concentrate instead on being perhaps the most amiable and agreeable of capitals. The city fathers welcomed all the multinational activity and concomitant publicity and economic advantages that began with the arrival of the Council of Europe. But they quietly planted the first building to house it — now supplanted by the massively modern Palais de l'Europe — in the suburbs, where it wouldn't interfere with the daily comings and goings and almost casual meanderings of the citizenry.

Strasbourg is a warm, cozy kind of city, tiny, in fact, and very homey. Not every building dates from the 15th, 16th, or 17th century, although in certain sections it may seem that way. Some belong to the 18th and 19th centuries, and some are as recent as the postwar period, since the city suffered considerable damage during World War II. But the overall effect is that of a live-in museum, where the high, narrow half-timbered houses, the steep, massive tile roofs punctured by strange, birdhouse-like dormer windows, and the maze of winding walking streets are immensely photogenic. "Restorations" in Strasbourg — throughout Alsace, in fact — have established the practice of removing the plaster covering the wooden structures of traditional houses. The result may appeal to tourists, but the fact is that the houses originally were covered with plaster, except for carved wood decoration around the doors and windows.

The city is rich in art, music, and the intellectual excitement that comes from having a renowned, 4-century-old university, now with some 27,000 students, and major schools of medicine and both Catholic and Protestant seminaries. It is France's main Rhine River port and a major commercial center, but it is also a city on a human scale. Despite the bustle and frequent congestion (which remind you of its modern importance) on Rue des Francs-Bourgeois, the Grand'Rue, the Rue des Grandes-Arcades, and along the quays that circle the central city, around nearly every corner is a street set aside for pedestrians, an escape for the wanderer. Even some of the main streets are less than two cars wide, so traffic tends to roll at about the same speed as the pedestrians.

The Germans have a word — *gemütlich,* meaning comfortable and pleasant — for such a place, and as it happens, German is understood easily here. Strasbourg, the ancient capital of the province of Alsace, is at the very eastern edge of France. The center of the city is on the River Ill, but its port is on the Rhine and the city's neighbors across the water have occasionally considered it to be on the western edge of Germany, most recently in the Franco-Prussian War of 1870–71 and both world wars. As a consequence, and possibly out of a sense of resignation, most Strasbourgeois speak both French and German and sometimes their own Alsatian dialect, a sort of smoothed-out German. They have a strong sense of regionalism, a certain isolation from the rest of France, and especially from Paris. They listen, for example, to German radio for the weather forecast, because, they say, the French national radio spends too much time talking about Normandy and Brittany. It also is said that the Strasbourgeois have the discipline of the Germans and the grace of the French. Add their Alsatian individuality, and a visit to this part of the country is something like seeing three countries at once.

Only in the late 17th century did Strasbourg become French. Settled in 12 BC by Roman legions, who called it Argentoratum and later Strateburgum, or the City of the Roads, Strasbourg became in the 10th century a part of the Germanic kings' revival of the Roman state, the Holy Roman Empire. In the 13th century, it achieved a measure of independence as a free imperial city and as such carried on a flourishing trade, bringing about, in the 14th century, the first of its annual fairs, the first bridge across the Rhine, and its first customs house, which stands today. Prosperity, in turn, attracted artisans, artists, and intellectuals, including a German from Mainz, Johann Gutenberg, who may well have invented printing from movable type during the 14 years he lived here in the mid-15th century.

When the Reformation swept in from the east in the 16th century, Strasbourg became an important center of Protestantism. One result was the founding of the university (which in a later century would have alumni as distinguished as Goethe and Metternich). Another was that mass ceased being said in the cathedral in 1529 and was not said here again until Louis XIV, taking advantage of the effective undoing of the Holy Roman Empire by the Thirty Years War, surrounded the city with his army in 1681 and annexed it to France. Even so, he did not insist on immediate integration. While taking over the city's defense and diplomacy, he allowed it the free exercise of the Protestant faith and a measure of autonomy in political, economic, and social institutions, which endured until the French Revolution.

By then, the Strasbourgeois felt French enough to embrace the principles of "Liberty, Equality, Fraternity" and to defend them from enemies within and without. In fact, in 1792, with invasion by Austrian and Prussian forces imminent and in response to a request by the mayor of Strasbourg, Rouget de Lisle, a poet, musician, and soldier, wrote a rousing marching song for an elite Strasbourg volunteer battalion. The song, called the "Chant de Guerre pour l'Armée du Rhin," became instead the theme of a volunteer battalion from Marseilles and thus acquired its more familiar name, "La Marseillaise," and went on to become the French national anthem. A plaque on the Bank of France building at 4 Place Broglie commemorates the day — April 26, 1792 — when de Lisle first sang it as the mayor's guest.

In 1870, during the course of the Franco-Prussian War, the Germans laid siege to Strasbourg and captured it after 50 days and the loss of 600 French soldiers and about 1,500 civilians. Along with the rest of Alsace and part of

Lorraine, it remained German for 44 years, returning to French rule only as a result of Germany's defeat in World War I. From 1940 to 1944, it again was occupied by the Germans and suffered two aerial bombardments before French forces recaptured it as Allied armies moved into Germany. Thus today, with about 250,000 inhabitants and another 150,000 in the neighboring communities and villages making up the metropolitan area, it ranks as France's seventh largest city, although many of its older citizens were born German.

Perhaps because of its location, Strasbourg remains virtually undiscovered by Americans, who tend to visit Paris and points north, south, or west. (Most of the tourists here are Germans or Belgians, who seem to resemble the natives, and so the city is unselfconsciously itself.)

Yet there is plenty to see, beginning with one of France's most important cathedrals. Before the New World was even discovered, this was complete, the tallest building in the Old World, and it still towers over everything for miles around, a reassuring beacon that can be glimpsed from virtually everywhere in the city. A few yards away is what might inelegantly be called Museum Row — an 18th-century palace housing three museums, three more in neighboring, still older buildings, and a seventh just over the bridge across the Ill. A 10-minute walk from the cathedral, where the Ill breaks into several small canals, is an old half-timbered neighborhood, La Petite France, once a tradesmen's quarter, now a tangle of shops and artisans' *ateliers* (studios), restaurants, cafés, a tearoom or two, and even a few discos, wrapped in crooked streets and tiny bridges, odd angles, and picturesque corners. Nor elsewhere in Strasbourg are you ever very far from a café, a brasserie, or a pastry shop. Find a suitable one, sit down between sights, order a cold Alsatian beer or some rich *pâtisserie,* and relax as you savor France from a different perspective.

STRASBOURG AT-A-GLANCE

SEEING THE CITY: For a spectacular overview, climb the 330 steps up to the platform of the cathedral tower (there's an admission charge). During his student days in the city, Goethe did this frequently, not only to survey the scene, but also to conquer his fear of heights. The restaurant and tearoom atop the *Printemps* department store and the luxury 14th-floor *Valentin-Sorg* restaurant, both on Place de l'Homme de Fer, are other spots from which to contemplate the rooftops of Strasbourg, while the Barrage Vauban offers a view of the Ponts Couverts (Covered Bridges) and Petite France area such as a bird might have coming in for a landing — broad and explanatory, yet reasonably close to the ground.

SPECIAL PLACES: Central Strasbourg is a flat little island shaped more or less like a ham with the shank chopped short, an image that, as it happens, also symbolizes one of the staples of the Strasbourg diet. The River Ill bounds the south side of the island, and a narrow canal that once served as a moat — the Fossé du Faux-Rempart — lies like a strip of bacon over the north side. Most of Strasbourg's sightseeing attractions are on this central island, as are its main squares: Place Gutenberg, Place Kléber, and Place Broglie — in addition to Place de la Cathédrale. One of the main charms is that at an easy pace you can cross the island east to west in 25 minutes or so, north to south in about 15 minutes. But you wouldn't want to, because Strasbourg is for strollers, with history to be rediscovered at almost every corner. The natural starting point is the cathedral; after that, hardly anything else listed below is more than a 10-minute walk, except for the Palais de l'Europe, the park, and the Brasserie de Kronenbourg.

Cathédrale Notre-Dame – This is the physical and emotional heart of Strasbourg and one of Europe's most striking examples of Gothic architecture. Built of pink sandstone from the nearby Vosges mountains, the so-called *grés des Vosges,* the cathedral is bathed in a rosy hue, as though it were blushing at its own fanciful beauty. Work began in 1015 in the Romanesque style, the church burned several times in the 12th century, and work began again, this time in pure Gothic. When finally complete in 1439, the lacy openwork spire made it the tallest building in Christendom (466 feet), and so it remained for some 400 years. The building has witnessed much of the turbulent history of Alsace and even served the Protestant faith during the Reformation. Louis XIV and Louis XV both worshiped here, and in 1770, Marie-Antoinette was greeted formally here on the way to her wedding to Louis XVI. During the Revolution, many of the cathedral's statues were torn down (a good number of them have since been restored or replaced by copies, with the originals remaining in the *Musée de l'Oeuvre Notre-Dame*). The spire also was threatened (its height offended the principle of *égalité*), but was saved by being crowned with a huge red Phrygian cap. The wars of the 19th and 20th centuries also damaged the structure, which nevertheless survives to present the splendid sight we see today.

Before going inside, note the rich sculptural decoration of the west façade, especially that of the middle of the three doorways, which almost in itself sums up medieval religious belief. Then go around to the double doorway of the south transept, known as the Portail de l'Horloge (Clock Portal). The two female figures to the right and left of the doors, allegories for the Synagogue (the blindfolded figure) and the Church (the one with the Cross), are counted among the masterpieces of the cathedral's sculpture (though these are copies of originals kept in the *Musée de l'Oeuvre Notre-Dame*), as is the moving Death of the Virgin in the left tympanum, a 13th-century original.

Stained glass is the marvel of the cathedral's interior. The large rose window (ca. 1316) in the west front gleams like a jeweled eye, a star-flecked pupil of black surrounded by an iris of white, then rings of deep blue, amber, and muted greens. The windows of the Chapelle Ste.-Catherine (ca. 1340), showing the Apostles and two female saints surmounted by tall, thin, shimmering spires in gray-green grisaille are stunning. The oldest windows (late 12th and early 13th century) are in the north transept. The pale green of the robe of the Virgin in the topmost of four medallions in one window and the similar green of the robes of the two saints John in the window next to it is a rare, prized color. Also to be seen inside are an exquisitely intricate late Gothic pulpit in the nave and two other attractions in the south transept. If it is dark, put a franc in the box to light up the Pilier des Anges (Angels' or Doomsday Pillar) or you may miss this masterpiece of 13th-century sculpture. The other attraction, hard to miss, is the wonderful 16th-century astronomical clock, an ingenious device that tells so much to those who know it — the day of the week, sunrise and sunset, saints' days, eclipses of the sun and moon — that it's hard to remember it also, simply, tells the time. Set according to the meridian of Strasbourg, it strikes noon at precisely 12:31 PM each day, and this is the time to see it in action. Toward noon, visitors are asked to leave the south transept and to reenter by the Clock Portal (after paying a small admission charge). A taped recitation in French, German, and English begins at 12:15. When the small cherub on the left (look carefully) strikes the time, the cherub on the right turns over an hourglass, an old man (the last of the four ages of man) passes before Death, the Twelve Apostles parade before Christ, and the cock above flaps its wings, crowing three times. Guided tours of the cathedral are offered at 10:15 AM, 2:30, and 3:30 PM in French and German during July and August. There is a sound and light show from April through October nightly at 8:15 PM (commentary in German) and at 9:15 PM. Pl. de la Cathédrale.

Place de la Cathédrale – The half-timbered house to one side of the square, wonderfully carved with signs of the zodiac, biblical figures, and ancient and medieval heroes, is the Maison Kammerzell. It was built by a rich fabric merchant in the late 16th century (over a ground floor dated 1465) and must have been even then the finest house in the city as well as a prime business location. It takes its name from a grocer who owned it in the 19th century and is today a restaurant (see *Eating Out*). The less ornate timbered building facing the cathedral at the corner of Rue Mercière is the *Pharmacie du Cerf,* the oldest pharmacy in France. It dates from 1268, though it has undergone various transformations since then.

Château des Rohan – This episcopal palace off the south side of the cathedral was commissioned by Cardinal Armand-Gaston de Rohan-Soubise, one of several members of the famous French family to be Archbishop of Strasbourg in the 18th century. It was built from 1730 to 1742 according to the plans of Robert de Cotte and during the course of its history welcomed such illustrious guests as Louis XV, Marie-Antoinette, and Napoleon. Various rooms of the bishops' apartments can be seen — including a dazzling black and white marble salon with two giant faïence (ceramic) stoves, an inviting library, and a chapel — in addition to three museums. The *Musée des Arts Décoratifs* is especially notable for its collection of ceramics, in particular for that produced by the Hannong family of Strasbourg in the 18th century. The *Musée des Beaux-Arts* contains paintings by Italian (Botticelli, Tintoretto, Veronese, Tiepolo), Spanish (El Greco, Zurbaran, Murillo), Flemish and Dutch (Memling, Rubens, Van Dyck, De Hooch), and French (Lorrain, Watteau, Boucher, Fragonard) masters from the 14th to the 19th century. The *Musée Archéologique,* in the basement of the château (scheduled to reopen early this year after extensive renovation), traces civilization in Alsace from Paleolithic to Celtic, Gallo-Roman, and Merovingian times and is regarded as one of the most significant of its kind in France. All are open daily except Tuesdays from April through September and closed mornings the rest of the year. Half of the *Musée des Beaux-Arts* always is closed, with alternate halves of the collection visible on alternate days. Admission charge. 2 Pl. du Château (phone: 88-32-48-95).

Musée de l'Oeuvre Notre-Dame (Our Lady's Work Museum) – The Maison de l'Oeuvre Notre-Dame was built in various stages from the 14th through the 16th century to house the Oeuvre Notre-Dame, the medieval institution founded to collect money for and oversee the construction of the cathedral and then its maintenance. Now the *maison* houses part of this museum, the rest of which rambles through the adjoining 14th-century Hôtellerie du Cerf building and a 17th-century house that once stood on Rue d'Ors but was reconstructed here. Similarly, only part of the museum is devoted to the Cathédrale Notre-Dame. Its broader scope is the art of Alsace of the Middle Ages and Renaissance. Original working drawings of the raising of the cathedral from the 13th to the 15th century are on display, as well as originals of many of the cathedral statues replaced by copies, but so, too, are paintings, sculpture, stained glass, examples of the goldsmith's art, and rooms full of furniture and disparate objects not associated with the cathedral — everything from a head of Christ, made about 1070 for a church in Wissembourg (and considered to be the oldest piece of figurative stained glass in France), to a 17th-century dollhouse. Before leaving, you'll also have seen a courtyard sided with the carved wood balconies of a building demolished on the Grand'Rue. Closed Tuesdays and mornings from October through March. Admission charge. 3 Pl. du Château (phone: 88-32-06-39 or 88-32-48-95).

Musée Historique – The emphasis of this collection, which occupies a former

16th-century slaughterhouse (the Grande Boucherie), is on the military. There are arms, uniforms worn by the Strasbourgeois and Bas-Rhinois from the 18th through the 20th century, and regiment after regiment of antique *petits soldats de Strasbourg,* or toy soldiers — actually much like paper dolls. A highlight is a unique 1:600 scale model of the city made in 1727 by the military engineers of the king. Closed Tuesdays and mornings from October through March. The museum has been closed for renovation, and as we went to press, it had not yet reopened. Admission charge. 3 Pl. de la Grande Boucherie (phone: 88-32-25-63 or 88-32-48-95).

L'Ancienne Douane – This 14th-century customs building, renovated after World War II and formerly the home of the *Musée d'Art Moderne,* now houses special revolving exhibitions only. The city's impressive permanent collection of modern paintings, sculpture, and stained glass grew too large for these quarters and currently is awaiting a new building (it is not expected to be completed for several years). The collection includes works by Monet, Degas, Gauguin, Braque, Chagall, and Jean Arp (a native of Strasbourg), as well as *The Kiss* by Gustav Klimt. 1 Rue du Vieux Marché aux Poissons (phone: 88-32-46-07).

Musée Alsacien – The exhibits of this charming museum document the folk arts, traditions, and everyday activities of the past in rural Alsace. One room, for instance, is given over to a reconstructed early-19th-century *chambre paysanne* fitted out with a large iron stove, table and chairs, rocking horse, swinging cradle, and a plump alcove bed complete with bedside slippers and a chamberpot. The rest of the exhibitions — taking up three floors in a characteristic 17th-century house and spilling over into a courtyard and adjacent buildings — include other reconstructed rooms, furniture, ceramics, kitchenware, clothing, work tools and agricultural implements, and Protestant, Catholic, and Jewish religious items from baptismal certificates to Passover plates. Closed Tuesdays and mornings from October through March. Admission charge. 23-25 Quai St.-Nicolas (phone: 88-35-55-36).

Eglise St.-Thomas – Built in the 13th and 14th centuries, this has been an important Protestant church — called the cathedral of Lutheran Protestantism — since the 16th century. Architecturally, it is a hall church, a style common in Germany and the Netherlands but fairly rare in France. Inside, note the mausoleum of the Maréchal de Saxe, by the 18th-century sculptor Jean-Baptiste Pigalle, and the 18th-century Silbermann organ, on which Albert Schweitzer played concerts commemorating the death of Johann Sebastian Bach. Rue St.-Thomas.

Petite France – This most picturesque quarter of Strasbourg, extending roughly from the Eglise St.-Thomas to and including the Ponts Couverts (see below), used to be the home of the city's fishermen, millers, and tanners. It is full of postcard-perfect scenes of 16th- and 17th-century houses mirrored in the waters of the River Ill and small canals, of gliding swans, and of small boats and barges nudging through the locks — though explanations of the origin of its name conjure up less sublime images. (The French soldiers of François I used to frequent the area in search of amorous adventures, according to one version; there was once a hospital here to treat the "French" (venereal) disease brought to Alsace by the soldiers of Charles VIII, according to another.) Walk along Rue de la Monnaie and Rue des Dentelles to Place Benjamin-Zix, and the huge, balconied and flower-bedecked *Maison des Tanneurs,* dating from 1572 and now a restaurant, will be at the edge of the water to the left. Other buildings that formerly housed tanners are beyond the *place* in Rue du Bain-aux-Plantes (Plant Bath Street, so called because a bathhouse existed here as early as the 14th century). Be sure also to walk along Rue des Moulins, Quai Woerthel, and Quai de la Petite France. Both of the quays lead to the Ponts Couverts, but the latter, lined on one side with old houses, trees, and a willow or two dipping into the water, is especially appealing.

Ponts Couverts (Covered Bridges) – The three bridges and four towers at the dividing point of the Ill are vestiges of the city's 14th-century fortifications. Originally, the bridges were of wood and uncovered; from the 16th to the 18th century they had roofs; in the 19th century, they were rebuilt in stone. Today they are a promenade, uniquely scenic, and via the Quai de l'Ill, they give access to the Barrage Vauban.

Barrage Vauban (Vauban Dam) – When Strasbourg was annexed to France in the late 17th century, its fortifications were modernized and extended by the French military engineer Sébastien Vauban, who built this dam across the Ill near the Ponts Couverts. You'll find it identified on maps also as L'Ecluse (floodgate), because it allowed the flooding of the southern part of the city if necessary, and as the Terrasse Panoramique, because that is its function today. From here the view includes all the bridges and towers of the Ponts Couverts, the Petite France quarter, and the cathedral in the background. Opening hours vary with the time of year. Admission charge. Quai de l'Ill (phone: 88-36-16-98).

Eglise St.-Pierre-le-Vieux – Unusual because Catholic and Protestant churches are joined together in one structure, with rather different architectural design. Among its treasures are the 16th-century carved wall panels. Pl. St.-Pierre-le-Vieux.

Eglise St.-Pierre-le-Jeune – The most recent of three churches built on the same site since the 7th century, transformed from Catholic to Protestant along the way. The present church dates from the 13th century, though parts of its predecessors remain and the church has been much restored. Pl. St.-Pierre-le-Jeune.

Palais de l'Europe – This 1977 building is noteworthy for its striking modern architecture — in the design of its semicircular interior chamber (the hemicycle), in particular — and for its symbolism as the cornerstone of European cooperation. It is the seat of the 21-nation Council of Europe and the meeting place, for a week each month, of some 500 directly elected members of the 10-nation European Parliament (whose secretariat is in Luxembourg). The building is open to the public, guided tours in English are possible (contact the secretariat in Luxembourg at 352-43001), and if you wish to attend a session, it can be arranged by calling the Council (phone: 88-61-49-61) or the Parliament (phone: 88-37-40-01). Av. de l'Europe.

Parc de l'Orangerie – Across the road from the Palais, this park was created by Le Nôtre in 1692, although it was transformed in the 19th century. Besides a lake and a zoo, it contains a pavilion built for Empress Josephine in 1805, rebuilt after damage by fire, and now used for exhibitions.

Brasserie de Kronenbourg – This brewery in a northwestern suburb is the home of Strasbourg's most famous beer. Guided tours take place on weekdays (except holidays) at 9 and 10 AM and 2 and 3 PM from April to October, and at 10 AM and 2:30 PM from October to April. 68 Rte. d'Oberhausbergen (phone: 88-27-41-59).

■**EXTRA SPECIAL:** Simply wandering among the old streets and passages under restoration (or still untouched) provides special pleasures in this romantic city. For instance, just off Place du Corbeau is a large, pink-sand-colored building with an old-fashioned roof that is otherwise nondescript. Walk inside the cobblestone courtyard, however, and you will see the kind of high, angled wooden balconies, weathered by age, that musketeers used to leap from. This is the *Hôtellerie du Corbeau,* a coaching inn whose existence at least back to 1538 is documented and whose last guest was received in 1854. Notable travelers included Frederick the Great, King of Prussia, who stayed here incognito in 1740. The Quai St.-Nicolas is an architectural history book, offering side by side buildings from the 15th through the 19th century and best seen the first time from across the river. The Pont du Corbeau used to be the site of executions by drowning. Stroll up the narrow Rue de l'Ecurie, which begins at the Ancienne Douane, becomes Rue de l'Epine, and crosses Rue des Serruriers and Rue Gutenberg. En route, you will see 16th-to 18th-century homes and courtyards encrusted with sculptured lions and ugly faces to scare away the devil, pierced with oval *oeil-de-boeuf* (ox-eye) windows — also known as concierges' windows — and affixed with oriel windows, a form of bay window attached to the corners of the buildings. The rooflines have their own characters, and the steeply sloped tiled roofs of the buildings are pierced with myriad dormer windows. Such windows on each side of the roof provided air circulation and a kind of refrigeration for the Strasbourgeois, who used their attics for food storage. Look, too, for the occasional stork's nest on the roofs. The stork, now rare in Alsace, has long been considered a lucky bird and a symbol of the city.

SOURCES AND RESOURCES

TOURIST INFORMATION: The Office de Tourisme of Strasbourg and its region has a central branch (10 Pl. Gutenberg; phone: 88-32-57-07) open daily from June through September, closed Saturday afternoons and Sundays the rest of the year. Other locations are the Pavillon du Tourisme across from the train station (Pl. de la Gare; phone: 88-32-51-49) and one near the German border (Pont de l'Europe; phone: 88-61-39-23). Among the literature available is a booklet discussing facilities for the handicapped and access to museums, theaters, and other public buildings. The tourist office has an *Accueil de France* accommodations service, which will make hotel reservations for a fee, and it runs its own tours (in French) for a small charge, including 2-hour guided walking tours departing from 10 Place Gutenberg daily in July and August at 10 AM (check locally for other hours). The tourist office also offers a series of theme tours (in French), including "Strasbourg in the Middle Ages, Renaissance Strasbourg, and The Alsacienne House," for groups of 15 or more.

Other tours include the mini-trains that leave from the south side of the cathedral (Pl. du Château) from *Easter* through October and roll on a 45-minute route among the scenic sections of the Old City or on a slightly longer route that takes in the Parc de l'Orangerie and the Palais de l'Europe. Three-wheeled Vespacars, each carrying four passengers, make a similar circuit and can be reserved for day or evening tours for a small charge (phone: 88-23-23-10). Boat tours of the Ill are offered from March through December. Contact the *Port Autonome de Strasbourg* (25 Rue de la Nuée-Bleue; phone: 88-84-13-13). Cruises on the Rhine also are available from *Alsace Croisières* (12 Rue de la Division-Leclerc; phone: 88-22-38-81) and *Strasbourg Croisières* (5 Rue Deserte; phone: 88-32-67-95). *Alligator* (11 Bd. d'Anvers; phone: 88-61-10-00), a boat restaurant, offers *promenades gastronautiques* (cruises on the city's waterways) that include meals.

Local Coverage – The Strasbourgeois keep up with local news by reading *Les Dernières Nouvelles d'Alsace,* in French, daily, and refer to the monthly booklet *Strasbourg Actualités,* available at all newsstands, for listings of current activities such as theater and sporting events. A billboard in front of the *Marks & Spencer* department store (Pl. Kléber) also gives all the movie and theater timetables, and kiosks along the city streets have posters on the latest cultural happenings. The *Librairie Kléber* (1 Rue des Francs-Bourgeois; phone: 88-32-03-88) is a good source of books in English on various local topics including French and Alsatian history, the cuisine of both cultures, and other lore.

TELEPHONE: The city code for Strasbourg is 88, which is incorporated into all local 8-digit numbers. When calling a number in Strasbourg from the Paris region (including the Ile-de-France), dial 16, wait for the dial tone, then dial the 8-digit number. When calling a number from outside Paris, dial only the 8-digit number. When calling from the US, dial 33 (which is the country code), followed by the 8-digit number.

GETTING AROUND: Walking is the best and easiest way, because the city is small and many streets in the vicinity of the main points of interest are pedestrian zones.

Air – The recent inauguration of direct flights from New York to Strasbourg makes this city particularly accessible to US visitors. The Aeroport International de Strasbourg-Entzheim is about a 15- or 20-minute taxi ride from the heart of town (phone: 88-78-40-90). A taxi from the airport to the city should cost between 100 and 150 francs ($20 to $30). Shuttle buses leave for the airport from Place Kleber and Place de la Gare about an hour before the departure of major flights and cost about 30 francs ($5.50). The *Air France* office is at 15 Rue Francs Bourgeois (phone: 88-32-99-74).

Bicycles – Besides being small, Strasbourg is flat, ideal for cycling. Rentals are available at the train station (3 Bd. du Président-Wilson; phone: 88-32-48-12).

Bus – Service is good, although on Sundays it can be infrequent. *Carnets* of five tickets (representing a discount of about 30% off the price of singles) can be bought in *tabacs* near the bus stops — the nearest location is marked at the stop — or in the tourist office. Single tickets can be bought on the bus. Once punched, tickets are good for an hour.

Car Rental – Various firms at the airport and in town rent cars, and *SNCF*'s Train + Auto service is available at the train station. But a car is not required or even recommended for city touring because of the narrow streets and pedestrian zones. If you do have one, park it in an underground garage and leave it.

Taxi – Taxis are not inexpensive, but given the city's size, the longest ride to any likely tourist spot should be less than $5. They generally are plentiful, except on weekends. Call *Radio Taxis Strasbourg* at 88-36-13-11 or 88-36-13-13, day or night.

Train – The Gare Centrale *SNCF* is to the west of the Old City, across Pont Kuss at the end of Rue du Maire-Kuss. For train information, call 88-22-50-50; for reservations, call 88-32-07-51. Strasbourg is a rail hub of northeastern France, with good connections to such European cities as Basel, Zürich, Stuttgart, Frankfurt, and Brussels. Paris is less than 4 hours away; when completed, the *TGV* East line will cut travel time down to 2 hours.

SPECIAL EVENTS: Two events of international scope held annually in Strasbourg are the *Foire Européene,* held for 1 week at the end of April or beginning of May and 12 days in September, and the *Festival International de Musique,* for 2 weeks in June. The latter, a long-standing event, features classical concerts by first-rate guests and ensembles performing in the *Palais de la Musique et des Congrès,* largely but not exclusively; the cathedral and various other churches are other venues. Information and reservations are available from the festival office (24 Rue de la Mésange, 67081 Strasbourg; phone: 88-32-43-10) and bookings by mail can be made about 3 months in advance. A more recent tradition, *Musica,* a festival of contemporary music, takes place here from mid-September to the beginning of October, drawing more than 30,000 people each year. For information call 88-35-32-34. Other events include the *Schilig Sing Immer Noch,* an Alsatian song festival in several parts of Strasbourg and Alsace, but principally in the suburb of Schiltigheim (phone: 88-83-90-00 for information) in April; the *Marathon de Strasbourg,* held in mid-May; and *Christkindelmarik, Christmas* trees and decorations displayed from the first Saturday in December until December 24 at Pl. Broglie.

MUSEUMS: Most of the museums of greatest interest to visitors are in notable old buildings not far from the cathedral and are discussed in *Special Places.* Elsewhere, Strasbourg also has the following:

Musée Zoologique de l'Université – A small but interesting natural history museum, with special attention paid to endangered species and to Alsace's bird of good fortune, the stork. Open from 2 to 6 PM every day except Tuesday; Sunday 10 AM to noon and 2 to 6 PM. 29 Bd. de la Victoire (phone: 88-35-85-35).

Planetarium – One of the best in France; lectures on Wednesdays, Thursdays, Fridays, and Saturdays, and guided tours of the dome on the first Tuesday of the month. Rue de l'Observatoire (phone: 88-36-12-50).

 SHOPPING: Strasbourg is not particularly a shoppers' paradise. In range and variety of goods, it does not compare to Paris or Lyons, although there's an ample selection of the designer clothes, shoes, furniture, jewelry, tableware, and kitchen equipment for which France is well known. Most of the handicrafts and special products of the region are sold in the smaller towns outside Strasbourg where they originate: pottery and ceramics in Soufflenheim and Betschdorf, embroidery and needlework in Eckbolsheim, and weaving and table linens at Muttersholtz, all within 25 miles (40 km) of the city. In Strasbourg itself, the best shopping buys tend to be food and drink, including such things as the Alsatian white alcohols, or *eaux-de-vie* — the "waters of life" — distilled from local fruits, and *kugelhopf,* the sweet yeast cake baked in a characteristic fluted pan. The block-long Rue des Orfèvres, besides having some excellent clothing and jewelry boutiques, including *Laura Ashley* and *Celine,* also is the perfect place to shop for the ingredients of an Alsatian picnic. Among the establishments conveniently next to each other are *Au Vieux Gourmet* (No. 3), specializing in cheese; *Nicolas* (No. 18), in wine; *Fritz Lutz* (No. 16), in *charcuterie* and delicatessen; and *Naegel* (No. 9), in *pâtisserie.* Nearby, on Rue Chaudron, at No. 9, is *Winckelsass,* Strasbourg's oldest baker, and at No. 5, *Albert Henry,* producing foie gras. Dart through the small alley on Rue des Orfevres to *Ziegler* for fresh fruits and vegetables.

Strasbourg has more than one shopping center and more than one department store. The Centre Commercial, Pl. Kléber, has a score or so of stores featuring clothing, records, appliances, and plenty of noise and bustle. The *Centre Halles* complex at Quai Kléber has dozens of shops, fast-food restaurants, crowds, and chaos, but it does dispense a large stock of medium-priced merchandise. The *Galleries Arcadia* is on Rue des Grandes Arcades. *Magmod* (34 Rue du 22-Novembre) is an economical, functional department store that also repairs heels in a minute, develops photos in an hour, fixes watches, and has a food market on the third floor. *Au Printemps,* a branch of one of France's major department stores, is on Pl. de l'Homme de Fer, and *Marks & Spencer,* a branch of the British chain specializing in wearable clothing at moderate prices, is on Pl. Kléber. On Wednesday and Saturday mornings, a flea market takes place in Pl. du Marché-aux-Cochons-de-Lait and Rue du Vieil-Hôpital. It's not very big but worth picking through for books, prints, glassware, and the odd piece collected and discarded more than a few times during the course of the century.

Belles Choses – An interesting assortment of local and regional faïence. 30 Av. de la Marseillaise (phone: 88-35-35-94).

Boulangerie au Vieux Strasbourg (Charles Woerlé) – Cookies, sweets, bread in all shapes and sizes, a 2-pound *kugelhopf* of pure butter, and a smaller one with almonds and walnuts. 10 Rue de la Division-Leclerc (phone: 88-32-00-88).

Boutique des Tanneurs – Rather *touristique,* except for a good selection of small bottles of *eau-de-vie* packaged for easy shipment and a variety of small cake molds, copies of antique figures from Alsace, that make simple, unusual gifts. 29 Rue du Bain-aux-Plantes (phone: 88-32-93-05).

La Brocanterie – An eclectic collection of dolls, old glassware, lamps, vases, miniatures. Open afternoons only; all day Wednesdays and Saturdays. 18 Rue du Vieil-Hôpital (phone: 88-32-52-79).

A la Civette – A tobacco shop selling pricey but unusual faïence canisters hand-painted in old-fashioned designs and flower patterns, plus copies of antiques. 21 Rue des Grandes-Arcades (phone: 88-32-12-85).

Le Corbeau Gourmand – A gem of a wine and specialty-food shop, with a wide selection of good wines, foie gras, candies, and other treats as well as a vaulted basement cave dating from the Middle Ages. The owners are delightful and helpful. 6 Rue des Bouchers (phone: 88-36-75-25).

Faïancerie à la Petite France – This quaint shop, in a half-timbered building in the Petite France quarter of the city, is chock-full of pottery and porcelain — new and old — from all over France. Prices are fair, and the gentleman who owns the shop is friendly and very informative. 33 Rue du Bain-aux-Plantes (phone: 88-32-33-69).

Fruhauf – For admirers of original jewelry made by a passionate artist. Rue du Chaudron (phone: 88-32-52-27).

Maison Ritter – Table linens and dolls, some of them antique. 16 Rue des Serruriers.

La Sommelière – Local wines, Alsatian *eaux-de-vie* made from raspberries, plums, pears, and nearly every other available fruit of the region, and foie gras packed in handsome porcelain jars. 1 Rue du Fossé-des-Tailleurs (phone: 88-32-78-59).

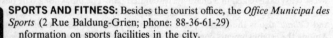 **SPORTS AND FITNESS:** Besides the tourist office, the *Office Municipal des Sports* (2 Rue Baldung-Grien; phone: 88-36-61-29)
nformation on sports facilities in the city.

Bowling – There are lanes at the *Bowling de l'Orangerie*, Parc de l'Orangerie (phone: 88-61-36-24).

Fishing – Licenses are obtainable from the *Fédération de la Pêche,* 1 Rue de Nomeny (phone: 88-34-51-86).

Golf – There is an 18-hole course on the Route du Rhin, Illkirch-Graffenstaden (phone: 88-66-17-22). There are two new golf courses in the Strasbourg area — *Golfy,* with 6 holes and training center (Route du Fort-Uhrich, Illkirch-Graffenstaden; phone: 88-67-30-31); and the 18-hole *Le Kempferhof Golf-Club* (Rue du Moulin, Plobsheim; phone: 88-98-72-72).

Horse Racing – Racing, with pari-mutuel betting, takes place at Hoerdt, 10 miles (16 km) north of Strasbourg, from March through October except in July and August (phone: 88-51-32-44).

Ice Skating – *Patinoire du Wacken* (Allée du Printemps; phone: 88-36-60-45) is open from December to March and rents skates.

Swimming – There's an indoor municipal pool (10 Bd. de la Victoire; phone: 88-35-51-56). Open-air pools are on Rue Pierre-de-Coubertin (phone: 88-31-49-10), in the suburb of Wacken, not far from the exhibition ground, and at the Parc du Rhin is the *Oceade Nautique* amusement park and club (phone: 88-61-92-30).

Tennis and Squash – You can rent both tennis and squash courts by the hour at *Tennis Loisirs,* 31 Rte. du Rhin (phone: 88-34-58-79).

 **THEATER:** The *Théâtre National de Strasbourg* (Rue Marseillaise; phone: 88-35-63-60; administrative offices: l Rue du André Malraux) is probably the institution of major interest among the city's resident theater companies. The *Théâtre Alsacien* performs at the *Théâtre Municipal* (19 Pl. Brogliel; phone: 88-75-48-00). The *Maillon* is a relatively new theater that presents contemporary works, as well as music and dance performances, and film (13 Pl. André-Maurois; phone: 88-26-12-66). *Le Choucrouterie* (20 Rue St.-Louis; phone: 88-36-07-28), is a lively, popular dinner theater featuring song and dance, comedies, and satirical pieces. General information on theater in Strasbourg is available from the *Maison des Arts et Loisirs — (MAL) —* (1 Rue du Pont-St.-Martin; phone: 88-32-74-04), and from the *Théâtre Jeune Public* (7 Rue des Balayeurs; phone: 88-35-70-10).

MUSIC: The *Palais de la Musique et des Congrès* (Av. Schutzenberger; phone: 88-37-67-97) is Strasbourg's main classical music hall. The *Orchestre Philharmonique de Strasbourg,* a leading European orchestra, plays here from October to June (phone: 88-22-15-60), most of the concerts of the *Festival International de Musique* take place here, and so do many concerts by visiting groups and soloists. The *Opéra du Rhin* performs, from November through June, at the 19th-century opera house, *Théâtre Municipal* (19 Pl. Broglie; phone: 88-36-43-41); besides subscription seats, a certain number of seats are set aside for drop-ins and can be reserved up to 6 days before each performance; remaining tickets go on sale 30 minutes before curtain time. Another local group, the widely known *Percussions de Strasbourg,* made up of approximately 150 percussion instruments from around the world, plays at the *Conservatoire de Musique* (7 Pl. de la République; phone: 88-36-55-02). Folk music and dancing are plentiful in summer. Check with the tourist office for information about Alsatian folk dances that are performed frequently during summer months in the courtyard of the Château des Rohan. Troops from other nations also occasionally give international folk music and dance shows. For popular music, check the weekly publications to find out who is in Strasbourg and where.

NIGHTCLUBS AND NIGHTLIFE: Although Strasbourg is an international capital with plenty of international tourism, it is still in many ways a provincial town offering provincial entertainment. On the whole, it becomes extraordinarily quiet right after dinner. Discos do come and go: *Club YG* (17 Rue des Moulins; phone: 88-32-05-11), which operates until about 4 AM (except Sundays), seems to flourish. *Le Stereo* (23 Rue Geiler; phone: 88-61-19-23) also attracts a middling crowd until about 4 AM, although it's a little away from the main tourist routes. Popular dance spots are *Le Charlie's* (24 Pl. de Halles; phone: 88-22-32-22), with a Star Wars motif, and *Le New Paradise* (27 Rue des Frères; phone: 88-36-42-02). *Le Retro* (43a Rte. de Bischwiller; phone: 88-81-05-43) is a relatively new addition to Strasbourg's dancing spots. Just outside of town, this club is true to its name, offering old-time ballroom dancing in elegant surroundings.

BEST IN TOWN

CHECKING IN: The *Accueil de France* service at the Office de Tourisme can help find you a place to stay if you arrive in Strasbourg unannounced. But this is not wise, because, while there are a good number of hotels for the size of the city, there are relatively few in the top class, and these are often taken by European bureaucrats and business travelers who visit frequently. On the other hand, since in many ways Strasbourg is still undiscovered by American tourists, prices are quite reasonable. The top hotels in town, listed as expensive, charge about $75 and up for a double room. Moderate means about $50 to $75 double, and inexpensive can be about $50 or less.

Hilton International – The chain's first French hotel outside Paris is large (246 rooms), modern, comfortable, and equipped with all the amenities, such as a health club with a sauna, good bars (including one named and decorated in honor of the classic Bugatti automobile, which was built nearby), a fine restaurant, the *Maison du Boeuf,* and another, less formal, eatery. Rooms are equally well equipped (with mini-bars, color TV sets, direct-dial telephones, and, in some cases, with king- or queen-size beds) and there are rooms for the handicapped and nonsmokers. The hotel is in a quiet area across from the park surrounding the Palais de la Musique et des Congrès — a bus ride or a 10-minute walk from downtown. Av. Herrensch-midt (phone: 88-37-10-01). Expensive.

Novotel Centre Halles – This member of a major French chain sits atop a bustling commercial center (with shops, restaurants, banks, and a post office) overlooking central Strasbourg. With 97 rooms, it's modern and straightforward, catering to businesspeople with all the necessary amenities. Quai Kléber (phone: 88-22-10-99). Expensive.

Le Régent Contades – Thirty-two well-appointed rooms and suites, a gym, sauna, bar, and 24-hour room service. 8 Av. de la Liberté (phone: 88-36-26-26). Expensive.

Sofitel – Also modern, this member of the reliable chain has an excellent location on a relatively quiet corner in the center of town — the bells of St.-Pierre-le-Jeune across the street provide a Sunday wake-up call. Among the amenities are a quiet bar (*Le Thomann*), a good dining room (*Le Chateaubriand*), boutiques, and a pleasant patio and garden, and the 158 rooms have all the comforts expected of a first class hotel. Pl. St.-Pierre-le-Jeune (phone: 88-32-99-30). Expensive.

Cathédrale Dauphin – An old building, in front of the cathedral, houses this new hostelry, with its crisply modern lobby and tastefully decorated rooms, many with fantastic views of the cathedral and square. Guests have access to a nearby health and fitness club. 12 Place de la Cathédrale (phone: 88-22-12-12). Expensive to moderate.

Des Rohan – Though it looks like a historic landmark, this small place on a pedestrian street near the cathedral has been completely modernized. The 36 rooms are all decorated differently in 17th- and 18th-century styles, but each has a private bathroom (tub or shower). The front rooms are the quietest because from the back you overlook, and overhear, the flea market in Rue du Vieil-Hôpital on Wednesdays and Saturdays. No restaurant. 17–19 Rue du Maroquin (phone: 88-32-85-11). Expensive to moderate.

Terminus Grüber – The best among the eight hotels facing the train station on Place de la Gare. It features lots of marble and crystal — an agglomeration of decor throughout — and includes a large country-inn kind of dining room, the *Cour de Rosemont,* with a fireplace, as well as a brasserie and a cozy bar. Many of the 78 rooms are decorated in grand style. Rooms and suites are soundproofed, but not air conditioned (a design quirk in many medium-priced Strasbourg hotels). 10 Pl. de la Gare (phone: 88-32-87-00). Expensive to moderate.

Dragon – An appealing hostelry located in a calm corner of town just slightly off the beaten track, it is 17th-century outside and Bauhaus modern inside. Rooms are in shades of gray with reproduction Mallet Stevens chairs; some rooms have views of the cathedral. It's already a favorite of members of the European Parliament. 2 Rue de l'Escarlate (phone: 88-35-79-80). Moderate.

L'Europe – Old and slightly worn but entirely functional and clean, it is furnished in heavy antiques and reproductions. It's well located for touring the Petite France quarter, with buildings under restoration on all sides. Not all of the 60 rooms have a private bath and there is no restaurant. 38 Rue du Fossé-des-Tanneurs (phone: 88-32-17-88). Moderate.

Le Relais de Strasbourg – Elegant façade and a high-ceiling lobby hint at the former grandeur of this relic, recently renovated in modern, minimalist style. Located between the train station and Strasbourg's center, it is clean and affordable. 4 Rue du Vieux Marché aux Vins (phone: 88-23-08-85). Moderate.

Royal – A pleasant little hotel on the street leading from the train station to the business center. It offers modern amenities such as meeting rooms and Jacuzzi, but is brimming with Alsatian touches — hand-painted furniture, prints by local artists, and handcrafted door plates — which add warmth and charm. 3 Rue du Maire Kuss (phone: 88-32-28-71). Moderate.

Gutenberg – Small and simple and in an old château just a few steps off Place Gutenberg; is clean if rather spare. About a third of the 50 rooms come with private bathrooms, and many of the rooms already have an extra bed for a third person or a child. 31 Rue des Serruriers (phone: 88-32-17-15). Inexpensive.

Ibis – A modern, austere hotel that is less expensive than its neighbor, the *Novotel,* atop the *Centre Halles* commercial center. There are 97 functional rooms with private bathrooms. Children under 12 can stay in their parents' room for free. Rue Sébastopol and Quai Kléber (phone: 88-22-14-99). Inexpensive.

 EATING OUT: If French nouvelle cuisine attracts the eye, Alsatian cooking attracts the nose. It is fragrant, and the aromas travel through the streets from early morning. Everything is heavy, rich, and has at least some acquaintance with either pork or cabbage or both. There is virtually no limit to the things Alsatians can do with pork, and cabbage may be Strasbourg's "national" flower — the fields around the city are filled with it. (Those that aren't are filled with hops — *houblon* — because when the Strasbourgeois aren't eating, they are drinking — beer or wine or *eau-de-vie.*) The city is jammed with restaurants, enough to fill several pages of the phone book in very small type. This includes the ones that remember they are, after all, in France and bring to the table some fine French fare. In the rest, emphasized here, where the food is neither French nor German but Alsatian, the terms may be uncommon even to practiced menu readers, requiring some translations. Almost every Alsatian restaurant has one or two versions of *choucroute garnie,* a mound of warm sauerkraut, often flavored with juniper berries, heaped with boiled potatoes and varying combinations of ham, slab bacon, smoked and fresh pork loin or shoulder or similar meats, and smoked and fresh sausage, at least three kinds. The lone diner may greet the arrival of such a monumental platter at once both daunted and drooling to dig in, which brings to mind another characteristic of Alsatian restaurants. Portions are usually large — often huge — and can easily be shared by two and sometimes three people, which restaurant staffs seem willing to accept. Other translations: *Baeckeoffe,* or "baker's oven," is a stew of pork, beef, lamb (sometimes without the latter), potatoes, onions, and spices served in its earthenware cooking pot (again, of generous proportion). *Jambon en croûte* is ham baked in a pastry crust. *Tarte à l'oignon* is a light onion pie; *tarte flambée* is a sort of Alsatian pizza, a thin crust covered with onions, cheese, cream, bacon chunks, and nutmeg, baked crisp enough to be slightly charred ("licked by flames") and served on a flat board. The white Alsatian wines flow easily — riesling (try the *coq au riesling,* the local version of *coq au vin,* served with tiny dumplings called *spaetzle*), gewürztraminer, sylvaner, and tokay d'alsace (pinot gris) — and so does the beer, notably Kronenbourg 1664 and Meteor. The Alsatians eat heartily, with great gusto, and, as a rule, early. Restaurants that are essentially wine bars with food are called *winstubs;* they are generally less formal than the classic restaurant and many are closed at lunchtime. In the list below, expensive means about $70 or more for a meal for two without wine and is reserved for the elegant French dining rooms. Moderate means about $35 to $50 for two, and inexpensive means anywhere up to $20 or $25 for two. A service charge is usually included.

Buerehiesel – The Alsatian equivalent of a big old château in a lovely park houses this beautifully appointed dining room where the ambience is softly personal, the service extraordinarily attentive, and the food rated worthy of two Michelin stars. It's favored by many of the visiting European parliamentarians, but that seems to make no difference to the gracious management: Everyone is greeted and treated with equal and unfailing courtesy. Excellent fish and, in season, game birds are on the basically French menu and there is a large selection of fine wines. Closed Tuesday evenings, Wednesdays, in mid-August, and for periods during the winter. Reservations necessary. 4 Parc de l'Orangerie (phone: 88-61-62-24). Expensive.

Le Crocodile – This restaurant won its third Michelin star in 1989 (the only restaurant in France to be elevated to three-star status that year), so it's unquestionably among the city's — and the region's — leading eating places. The cuisine is French, often with an Alsatian touch; the fish and game specialties, including eel and frogs, are outstanding; and the atmosphere is elegant — definitely a good choice for that special, well-dressed French evening. Closed Sundays, Mondays, from mid-July to early August, and for 1 week at *Christmas*. Reservations necessary. 10 Rue de l'Outre (phone: 88-32-13-02). Expensive.

Valentin-Sorg – On the 14th floor of an undistinguished-looking office building in the middle of town, it offers a fine French menu served in a pretty, surprisingly small dining room with a beautiful view of the quaint rooftops of Strasbourg and the towering cathedral above them. The overall tone may be slightly stiff, as though accustomed to looking down at the neighbors, but this is still another good choice for a romantic and elegant dinner. Closed Sunday evenings, Tuesdays, 2 weeks in February, and 2 weeks in August. Reservations necessary. 6 Pl. de l'Homme-de-Fer (phone: 88-32-12-16). Expensive.

Maison Kammerzell – A 16th-century architectural monument in its own right, it holds down the best corner in town. The elaborate wood carving continues in the restaurant inside, which has a comfortable dining room downstairs and a more formal room upstairs overlooking Place de la Cathédrale. The sale of this local institution — to Guy Baumann, an Alsatian chef who made it big in Paris with a chain of quality *choucroute* restaurants — doesn't seem to have diminished its popularity or quality. Some claim his classic *choucroute alsacienne* is the city's best. For the adventurous there's the less conventional *choucroute au poisson*. The menu offers a variety of "formulas," including some very reasonably priced offerings, service included. English-speaking waiters. Open daily. Reservations advised. 16 Pl. de la Cathédrale (phone: 88-32-42-14). Expensive to moderate.

Maison des Tanneurs – This beautiful, giant half-timbered building bedecked with balconies and flowers at the edge of a canal is a restaurant justly reputed to produce one of the best *choucroutes* in Strasbourg. In fact, it bills itself as "La Maison de la Choucroute," but it offers fine dining on other traditional dishes as well in lovely paneled surroundings in the heart of Petite France. Share the *choucroute*. English-speaking waiters. Closed Sundays, Mondays, the first 2 weeks in July, and from the end of December to mid-January. Reservations advised. 42 Rue du Bain-aux-Plantes (phone: 88-32-79-70). Expensive to moderate.

La Vieille Enseigne – Once a mere *winstub*, this cozy restaurant has a club-like atmosphere that makes it popular with politicians. The food and service have improved over the years, ultimately reaching a very high level in both. Closed Saturday lunch and Sundays. Reservations necessary. 9 Rue des Tonneliers (phone: 88-32-58-50). Expensive to moderate.

L'Ami Fritz – This is a small, neat, friendly place for Alsatian food in the midst of Petite France. It doesn't have the view that its bigger neighbors have, but it's less pretentious. Open nightly except Mondays; open for lunch from July through October. Reservations unnecessary. 8 Rue des Dentelles (phone: 88-32-80-53). Moderate.

L'Ami Schutz – A favorite of young businessmen getting away from downtown. It has a good location along the Ponts Couverts with a terrace overlooking the water and the Petite France quarter, and it's a pretty place, albeit slightly stuffy. The setting counts more than the cuisine, even though an effort is made to re-create traditional dishes. The hand-painted dishware can be purchased. Closed Sunday nights and Mondays. Reservations unnecessary. 1 Ponts Couverts (phone: 88-32-76-98). Moderate.

Le Clou – A straightforward *winstub*, and one of the best in town for rubbing elbows with the gusty Strasbourgeois. Businesspeople, professionals, plain folks, and students (with their allowances from home still fresh) jam together at shared tables with a sense of jovial well-being. The service is gracious and bustling, with portions easily, and willingly, divided for two. This is a good spot to be introduced to *baeckeoffe*, the savory stew of beef, pork, onions, and potatoes layered so the flavors mingle. Good local wines come by the pitcher. Dinner only; closed Sundays and holidays and the last 2 weeks in July. Reservations accepted only for four persons or more. 3 Rue Chaudron (phone: 88-32-11-67). Moderate.

La Maison du Boeuf – Those with an irresistible desire for T-bone steaks (imported from the US) or for some local beef specialties will feel at home here. Closed Saturdays and Sundays. Reservations unnecessary. In the *Hilton,* Av. Herrenschmidt (phone: 88-37-10-10). Moderate.

Au Pont du Corbeau – A modern little restaurant catering to businesspeople, only a few steps from the *Musée Alsacien.* It serves French rather than strictly Alsatian food, a half-dozen specialties each day, and you can finish your meal with a *tarte au fromage blanc,* a moist cheesecake about 3 inches high that should not be missed. Closed Saturdays, Sunday lunch, 2 weeks in February, and the last 2 weeks in July. Reservations unnecessary. 21 Quai St.-Nicolas (phone: 88-35-60-68). Moderate.

Au Pont St.-Martin – Another beautiful, giant half-timbered building in Petite France. The *winstub*-style restaurant has many tables overlooking the water and the locks, it stays open late at night, and it has a piano. When somebody plays, anybody sings, anything from anywhere. The mood is better than the food, but the view is fine. Downstairs there's a disco. Closed Sundays at lunch. 13–15 Rue des Moulins (phone: 88-32-45-13). Moderate.

Ziewelstub (L'Oignon) – A cozy place for insomniacs, also right in the heart of Petite France. It serves a full menu from midnight until 8 AM. Closed Sundays and Monday dinner. Reservations unnecessary. 4 Rue des Moulins (phone: 88-32-06-48). Moderate.

Le Pied dans le Plat – A small spot in pastel pink with lace tablecloths and paintings on the walls. Meats are tender here, desserts delicious. Closed Sundays and Mondays. Reservations unnecessary. 8 Rue du Renard-Prêchant (phone: 88-36-00-84). Moderate to inexpensive.

St.-Sépulcre – Small, noisy, crowded, close, and fun. Strangers share long tables for eight, the menu is postcard-size, the food good, the service fast. You'll see children of all ages, because the management happily splits dishes. Closed Sundays and Mondays. Reservations unnecessary. 15 Rue des Orfèvres (phone: 88-32-39-97). Moderate to inexpensive.

S'Burjerstuewel (Chez Yvonne) – This tiny place is a true *winstub,* chockablock with Strasbourgeois working from a light menu of heavy fare on crowded checkered tablecloths. The specialties include the onion pie and the baked ham that comes with cornichons and horseradish. Or you can perch at the small bar, drink the local wine, and watch the modish, noisy crowd. Serves to 12:30 AM. Closed Sundays, Mondays at lunch, holidays, and mid-July to mid-August. Reservations unnecessary. 10 Rue du Sanglier (phone: 88-32-84-15). Moderate to inexpensive.

Aux Armes de Strasbourg – The large, crowded room here has a dark wooden ceiling and walls yellowed by numberless winters of warmth. There's a good menu of solid food and the waitress tots up the bill on the paper tablecloth. Closed Tuesday evenings and Wednesdays. Reservations unnecessary. 9 Pl. Gutenberg (phone: 88-32-85-62). Inexpensive.

Chez Tante Liesel – If Norman Rockwell had had an Aunt Liesel, this would have been her kitchen. Friendly and cheerful, the tiny room has only nine wooden tables that are quickly crammed with traditional dishes from family recipes and unexpected treats such as a slab of Muenster cheese with a little pot of caraway seeds to dip it in or an apple pie topped with a crust filled with walnuts and cinnamon. Closed Tuesdays, *Christmas,* and *New Year's Day.* Reservations unnecessary. 4 Rue des Dentelles (phone: 88-23-02-16). Inexpensive.

Au Gutenberg – Small and friendly, with a stack of pretzels on each table and service from 10 AM to 1 AM every day of the year. On Thursday, Friday, and Saturday nights, the specialty is *tarte flambée.* Reservations unnecessary. 8 Pl. Gutenberg (phone: 88-32-82-48). Inexpensive.

Au Petit Bois Vert – A simple spot serving regional dishes, it has a pretty terrace under a giant canalside plane tree. Closed Sundays in winter. Reservations unnecessary. 3 Quai de la Bruche (phone: 88-32-66-32). Inexpensive.

Pfifferbrieder – This is in a little corner house that looks like something Disney would have drawn for Gepetto. The food is Alsatian — solid, plentiful, and reminiscent of home cooking — and it's served without frills or fanfare. Indeed, if the service is a little harried, you can fill the lapses by contemplating the hearty citizenry. Closed Sundays and August. Reservations unnecessary. 9 Pl. de la Grande Boucherie (phone: 88-32-15-43). Inexpensive.

S'Marikstuewele – A standard, no-nonsense eatery, with plenty of children in evidence. The *tarte flambée* served downstairs on Friday and Saturday nights — on a board about a foot long — makes an outstanding meal for two. Closed Sundays. Reservations unnecessary. 6 Rue du Marché (phone: 88-23-24-10). Inexpensive.

Strissel – Reliable Alsatian food, a good selection of Alsatian wines, traditional rustic decor, and quintessential Alsatian atmosphere have made this one of the more popular places among the Strasbourgeois. Its location in the midst of the pedestrian traffic pattern between the museums and the cathedral helps, too. Closed Sunday evenings, Mondays, a week in February, and 3 weeks in July. Reservations unnecessary. 5 Pl. de la Grande Boucherie (phone: 88-32-14-73). Inexpensive.

TAKING TEA: If something sweet suffices as a meal, Strasbourg has any number of tearooms. *Christian Meyer* (10 Rue Mercière; phone: 88-22-12-70) has a chocolate and pastry shop downstairs and a tearoom serving coffee, tea, and fine, rich pastries upstairs. The *Salon de Thé Suzel* (at the corner of Rue du Bain-aux-Plantes and Rue des Moulins; phone: 88-23-10-46) is a tiny, welcoming place to drop in for tea and homemade pastries after trooping through Petite France. It's open from 2 to 7 PM. And if you're an early jogger looking for coffee and a croissant or a slice of *kugelhopf* after a sprint along the quays, try the *Espresso* (17 Rue du Maire-Kuss; phone: 88-32-02-19), between the canal and the train station. It opens at 5 AM every day except *Christmas* and the day after.

BARS AND CAFÉS: Local watering holes include the *Bugatti Bar* at the *Hilton International* and *Le Thomann* at the *Sofitel.* Two popular bars located across the street from each other on Rue des Soeurs, behind the cathedral, are *Les Aviateurs* (12 Rue des Soeurs; phone: 88-36-52-69) and *Le Nid d'Espion* (3 Rue des Soeurs; phone: 88-37-02-83). A little off the beaten path is *L'Abreuvoir* (3 Pl. de l'Abreuvoir; phone: 88-36-09-36), a good, middle class drinkingman's bar. *Bar Jean et Jacques* (4 Rue des Païens; phone: 88-32-33-44) is a gritty sports hangout for the regulars, the old-timers, and the visitor in search of local color, the sort of place where they'll be knocking them back to open their eyes in the morning. You might try a Picon *bière* — orange bitters and beer — listen to the jukebox, and wait for Montand or Belmondo to come in. They probably won't, but if they were around, this is where they'd be.

DIVERSIONS

DIVERSIONS

For the Experience

Quintessential France

Modern France is much more than *baguettes*, bicycles, and berets, and there is a terrible temptation to describe the once-treasured glory of this now polyglot nation as gone forever. It's not hard to dismiss any real national identity in a country that sprawls from the shores of the Rhine to the far-flung *départements* of Guadeloupe and Martinique in the Caribbean, for France encompasses the Teutonic types of Alsace, the fractious faction of Basque separatists, the dour Celts of Brittany, and the topless Lolitas of St.-Tropez. All this while the smoky bistros fill with North African Jews in Belleville and the *Burger King* of the Champs-Elysées have become just as Parisian as the *Café de la Paix*. Still, it would be wrong to despair that the flavor of France had been boiled out of the new French melting pot. Rejoice that authentic bouillabaisse still requires *rouget* scooped fresh from the Mediterranean, that vin ordinaire sipped in a crowded café is somehow elevated far above pure plonk, and that the stubborn Gauls still smooch by the Seine, argue using every available limb for emphasis, and happily dance in the streets on *Bastille Day*. Here are some quintessential French experiences to prove the point.

BOULEVARD ST.-MICHEL, Paris: In the glitter of street lamps, and the evening glow from floodlit Notre-Dame, there is a simmering mix of arguing students, drumming youths and strumming guitars, roasting chestnuts, and sizzling streetcorner crêpes — a feast that hasn't moved since Hemingway's day. Latin no longer is the *lingua franca* of this quarter, but you'll hear plenty of Greek, Arabic, Farsi, and Wolof, and sharing billboard space in front of the multilingual movie theaters are posters for the latest films from India and Indiana Jones. The bookstalls along the Seine hold anything from a first edition of Proust to a paperback mystery from 1962 — or a single, illuminated page from a medieval manuscript.

MEGALITHS OF BRITTANY, Pérros-Guirec and Carnac: The Celts settled along the western rim of the liveable world, where the earth juts out into water and fog. And on this gray-green tongue of Europe they still speak a language closer to Gaelic and Galician than to French. On the northern coast of Brittany, the sea has chiseled and the wind has polished huge sculptures of rose-colored granite, challenging humans to match them. Across the Breton peninsula is the competition — thousands of great stone *menhirs* of Carnac, aligned since prehistoric times like petrified cheerleaders in some cosmic half-time show. Long after the Eiffel Tower has collapsed into a twisted heap of scrap metal, this druidic trail marker for the gods will remain a symbol of France. Luckily, there is no quick way to cross Brittany from north to south. So after lying on the sun-warmed, smooth pink boulders perched delicately on a cliffside with nothing below, wander from Carnac to St.-Malo, with plenty of stops for fish soups, cider, and seafood crêpes.

BUBBLES AND TRUFFLES AND STAINED GLASS, Reims, Champagne: The 11 miles of catacombs under the Pommery vineyards hold that celebratory essence of

France first brought to life by a 17th-century monk, Dom Perignon. Since then, conditions in Champagne have been honed to fastidious perfection, from the grapes grown close to the ground to absorb heat from the chalky soil, to the cellars' naturally constant temperature, to the patient *remueurs* who give each of millions of bottles the requisite fraction of a turn. At the restaurant *Boyer Les Crayères,* you will be treated as lovingly as a magnum of Roederer Cristal 1979. If one of the great stars of chefdom, Gérard Boyer, comes to your table in the mansion's lavish dining room to ask if everything is to your liking, the truffled foie gras with carrots and leeks should give you reason enough to be sincerely ecstatic. The only possible disturbance to dessert on the terrace overlooking the bucolic estate might be the whirr of a helicopter as it deposits a guest from Paris on the restaurant's private landing pad. After dinner, floodlights give a pale yellow tinge to the spikes, spires, and statues that bubble up the fluted façade of Reims's Gothic cathedral, made of the same chalky stone that gives champagne its fizz. But do try to get here during the day, when the principal ornament of the stark interior is a jeweled glimmer thrown by the stained glass windows on the gray stone floor.

ON HORSEBACK THROUGH CORSICA: Take a deep breath when you get to Corsica — in the late spring, the mingled scents from the undergrowth of honeysuckle, lavender, thyme, and mint mix with the salty froth of the Mediterranean and the last snow still clinging to the mountains. Avoid the resorts and the worn roads, and canter through the chestnut forests, the glacial streams, the olive groves, and terraced gardens carved out of steep granite and dense brush. Spend an evening listening to throaty *lamenti,* a kind of Corsican blues sung in the wine bars and cafés of miniscule port towns. This is an island created with a postcard palette — the *maquis* flowering white in May, the electric-colored houses on Cap Corse, the red rock of the Calanques dropping into a sapphire sea at Piana. This banished bit of France, with its Genoese watchtowers and its dialect akin to Sardinian, is so close to Italy that Napoleon could see his native Corsica from the Tuscan island of Elba where he was in exile.

LOIRE VALLEY BY BOAT, BALLOON, OR BICYCLE: Ever since the Middle Ages, aristocrats, with a love of rural living but no taste for roughing it, have made the Loire Valley into the ultimate exurb. Go in the fall, when the traffic thins on the rivers, gravel paths, and marble stairways, and when, from the basket of a balloon, you can see the châteaux ensconced in the auburn parkland of their thousand-acre backyards. Don't visit too many, and concentrate on the outside. Better to remember the fairy-tale turrets of Chambord or the graceful arches of Chenonceaux spanning the Cher River than to have it all meld into a sumptuous haze of polished wood and tarnished mirrors and the very chair where Louis the Something sat. Whether you float, fly, or pedal from the catapult-proof towers of Loches to the flower beds of Villandry, the point is to take it slow. Stop during the hottest part of the day for some goat cheese and a glass of dry Vouvray, and bask for a while in the delightful sounds of silence.

D-DAY BEACHES, Normandy: Save a gray day for this blowy, empty coast. Roll up your pants' legs and wade along these silent, sandy flats, and listen in a sea shell for the sputter of field radios and the crackle of machine guns and the long-ago crunch of boots on the beach. Or scan the coastline and see the scars from one of the greatest operations in military history — the vast American cemetery, the German pillboxes on the murderous cliff at Pointe du Hoc, the landing craft and giant bulkheads sunk in the sand at Arromanches. You cannot help but be moved, whether you're 20 and read about Omaha Beach in a book, or 70 and have a buddy buried under one of the white marble crosses or Stars of David at St.-Laurent-sur-Mer. June 6, 1944, the date of the Normandy landings (like the date the Normans landed in England in 1066) divides European history into before and after.

TURQUOISE, EMERALD, AND GOLD — THE CÔTE D'AZUR: Squeezed between mountains and the Mediterranean, the Côte d'Azur is a glittering strip of low-slung bathing suits and Alps-high prices, the meeting spot of Europe's wealthy worshipers of sun and self. With a croissant and *café crème* on the Promenade des Anglais in Nice comes a ringside seat for people watching — in July and August it's hard to see the beaches for the Swedes. After a long day of windsurfing and body-burnishing, take a sunset convertible ride on the Grande Corniche to the castle town of Roquebrune-Cap Martin, to look down on the sea trails left by waterskiers eking out the last drops of twilight. Look west over the pines and the cactus-covered cliffside of the Riviera toward Monte Carlo, where most of what glistens really is gold, and where suitable attire should include an extra shirt, in case you lose the one you're wearing. From a table in the *Grill Room* atop Monte Carlo's *Hôtel de Paris,* survey the yacht harbor, watering hole of the world's jet set. After dinner, take a deep breath of mimosa-scented air and walk across the Place du Casino for an evening of serious play among the mirthful rococo motifs and poker-face croupiers in the casino's Salon-Privé.

HARVEST TIME IN BURGUNDY, Beaune: The well-being of Beaune is safeguarded by the phalanx of vines laid out in disciplined rows on the hills outside the city's high medieval walls. The town's veneration of *vin* is such that there is no marked separation between church and grape — the brothers of the Order of the Chevaliers du Tastevin dress in priestly raiments for their tastings in the nearby Château du Clos de Vougeot, whose fabled vineyards were planted by Cistercian monks. Once the local seat of power, the Palace of the Dukes of Burgundy now houses the *Musée du Vin,* virtually a museum of Burgundian civilization. At harvest time, the ripening grapes and turning leaves give the vineyard-patterned hills the same hues as the wine-colored tile designs that adorn Burgundian roofs. Thousands of pickers, armed with shears and giant baskets, fan out among the vines and round up the fruit to be pressed, stomped, aged, and bottled in a Nuits-St.-Georges or a Pouilly-Fumé. Visit the cellars for a tour and a taste, even if you decide not to bring home a case — you're sure to learn something, whether you've never touched the stuff or already know the difference between an impudent little rosé and a flirtatious, full-bodied red.

RUE DU FAUBOURG-ST.-HONORÉ AND RUE ST.-HONORÉ, Paris: Like the *Grand Bazaar* of Istanbul, the souk of Marrakesh, and the agora of ancient Athens, the designer sidewalks of the mile-long stretch between the president's palace and the Palais Royal is one of the world's great shopping experiences. It has the finest names in everything, and an unsurpassed array of specialized retailers of chocolate, leather, and lingerie. Try *Au Nain Bleu* for a miniature tea set in Limoges porcelain, *Hermès* for an equestrian-print umbrella, or *Raymond* for gold-plated faucets. Nearby on Place Madeleine, go to *Fauchon* for plum mustard or a salmon mousse sprinkled with caviar, and if you can't live without something nobody else could have, tour the galleries and antiques dealers, and stop in at that ultimate purveyor of the unique — *Louvre des Antiquaires* on the Place du Palais-Royal.

THE BORDER BLEND, Alsace: Alsace often has been the rope in a Franco-German tug-of-war, and now is the French capital of both foie gras and *choucroute.* Although the air is tinged with riesling and the curvy Route des Vins defines the greatest distance between two nearby points, the people here do not live by wine alone — Alsace also produces France's best, most German beer. It is the birthplace of the anthem that got named for Marseilles and of the German invention of movable type. Over the years, the same Strasbourg artery has been named for Napoleon, Kaiser Wilhelm II, the French Republic, Adolf Hitler, and Charles de Gaulle. The city even has a French quarter — La Petite France. The town of Riquewihr, with its gables, cobbles, old wells, storks' nests, and ancient walls, has the Hansel-and-Gretel look of 16th-century Germany. In the fairly large medieval city of Colmar, the *Musée Unterlinden* houses the glowing *Issenheim Altarpiece* by Matthias Grunewald. A bedraggled, tortured Christ hangs from twisted limbs covered in crimson rivulets of blood and then is resurrected in a radiant aura, able-bodied and blond.

PAINTERS' PROVENCE, Arles and Aix-en-Provence: A brooding Dutchman came to Arles and saw the light that soaks the earth, and it gave him the luminous brushstroke that the world associates with Vincent Van Gogh. That same Provençal sun shines through the big picture windows of a studio in Aix, lighting up a canvas that still waits patiently on an easel for Cézanne to finish it. The painter came from this sleepy city cooled by fountains and shaded by the trees on the Cours Mirabeau. A walk out of town along the Route de Cézanne leads to the Montagne Ste.-Victoire, still dressed in ocher and pine-tree green, still posing for a post-Impressionist landscape. Arles, too, looks like a canvas come to life, with its brightly painted shutters, its rich surrounding fields of sunflowers and wheat, its sunbaked Arlésiens tossing *boules* on a dusty pitch. Paul Gaugin lived here for a while with Van Gogh, and Picasso loved the town so much that he gave it 57 drawings that are now housed in the *Musée Réattu.*

Romantic French Hostelries

 In an increasingly homogeneous and anonymous world, the fine French hotel remains one of the last bastions of charm and luxury. From the first warm, flaky croissant to the last turned-down eiderdown, a stay in one of them is a study in perpetual pampering which makes for an experience that is not to be missed on any account.

But France also boasts another unique species of hostelry, the wonderful establishment with a certain quality of romance that goes beyond mere splendor. Such a hotel may have a sleek, urbane lobby throbbing with the pulse of Paris. Or a languid arbor overlooking the Mediterranean in a garden full of flowers. It may be a château in the country with a dozen or so crackling fireplaces. These hostelries exist in a certain harmony with their settings; they seem to be a part of the local life rather than something aside from it. They also have a special warmth. And the staff has an ability to make you feel that you count and that they care. Excellent cuisine often is a feature, though not always.

The descriptive list of hotels that follows, a selection of some of the best rather than a comprehensive report, suggests the quantity of such accommodations that the adventurous traveler in France can discover.

HÔTEL DU CAP–EDEN ROC, Antibes, Alpes-Maritimes: A bastion of luxury in a miniature wilderness, this 100-room Riviera landmark and its piney 20-acre park — believed to be the setting for F. Scott Fitzgerald's *Tender Is the Night* — is set above the rocks at the tip of the promontory at the Cap d'Antibes, one of the most exclusive spots on the entire Côte d'Azur. It's *the* place to stay during the *Cannes Film Festival* — if you can get a room. From the edge of the turquoise swimming pool, it's possible to dive right into the aquamarine sea; whole afternoons can be spent simply inhaling the fragrance of wisteria between serves on the 5 private tennis courts. Sea-view dining on the patios of the *Pavillon Eden Roc,* one of the Côte d'Azur's most lordly restaurants, is another none too inconsequential feature here. And all for only pennies more than the price of a few Renoirs. Information: *Hôtel du Cap–Eden Roc,* Bd. du Cap, Antibes 06602 (phone: 93-61-39-01).

CHÂTEAU D'AUDRIEU, Audrieu, Calvados: One of the stately homes of France, this historic monument has been lovingly preserved by the family that built it some 2 centuries ago. Now, their castle is your home — complete with exquisite formal gardens, a heated swimming pool, a full complement of antique furniture, 2 splendid and serene dining rooms (see *Haute Gastronomie*), more than 60 acres of verdant parkland, and a location just a few miles away from the beaches of Normandy — so close, in fact, that the castle narrowly escaped destruction during the D-Day invasion. Many of the ancient trees still bear shell scars. A member of the Relais & Châteaux group. Information: *Château d'Audrieu,* Audrieu 14250 (phone: 31-80-21-52).

HÔTELLERIE DU BAS-BRÉAU, Barbizon, Seine-et-Marne: This charming inn is in the midst of a setting that inspired artists like Corot and Rousseau and writers like Robert Louis Stevenson. Indeed, Stevenson wrote *Forest Notes* here, and the inn served as an exhibition hall for Barbizon school painters in the early 20th century. Jean-Pierre Fava is now the proprietor, and he continues a family tradition of charm and comfort outdoors and in. The 12 rooms, 7 apartments, and villa are furnished with antique furniture and fine linen. Outside, the lawns are exquisitely manicured, the flowers meticulously tended. An airy restaurant offers a superb, sophisticated menu. A member of the Relais & Châteaux group. Information: *Hôtellerie du Bas-Bréau,* 22 Rue Grande, Barbizon 77630 (phone: 60-66-40-05).

HOSTELLERIE LE PRIEURÉ, Villeneuve-lèz-Avignon, Gard: A country inn par excellence (and another member of the Relais & Châteaux group), this ancient priory in the middle of a deep and shady wood now offers such modern pleasures as a swimming pool, tennis courts, and a friendly, highly reputed restaurant, where, when the weather is fine, meals are served in a delightful garden. The *gigot* (leg of lamb) in aromatic herbs or the betruffled tournedos will turn the steadiest head; the homemade *tapenade* is so popular that the kitchen packs it in jars to sell to departing guests. Note that as lovely as the hotel's modern section is, the ancient section is even more appealing. Information: *Hostellerie le Prieuré,* 7 Pl. du Chapitre, Villeneuve-lèz-Avignon 30400 (phone: 90-25-18-20).

OUSTAU DE BAUMANIÈRE, Les Baux-de-Provence, Bouches-du-Rhône: Eleven miles (18 km) east of Arles and tucked deftly into the rocky crags of the gleaming limestone Alpilles foothills, this gracious and lushly green oasis has as its centerpiece a venerable old manor house fitted out with accommodations that are no less than princely. Fireplaces crackle under vaulted ceilings. Tapestries surround diners in the two-star restaurant (see *Haute Gastronomie*). Wines are selected from the 35,000 bottles in the famous Baumanière cellars. Four-poster beds cradle bodies wearied from swimming or horseback riding. And no one goes away without sampling the dining room of the nearby one-star *Cabro d'Or,* the management's alternative pleasure dome. Both are members of the Relais & Châteaux group. Information: *Oustau de Baumanière,* Les Baux-de-Provence, Maussane 13520 (phone: 90-54-33-07).

HÔTEL DU PALAIS, Biarritz, Basses-Pyrénées: When this establishment's brochures describe the premises as "a hotel of dramatic extravagance," they demonstrate a commendable degree of self-knowledge. This most patrician of lodging places, in perhaps the most patrician of all French resorts, once was the imperial residence of Napoleon III's Empress Eugénie. There are stunning views of the whole coastline, an elegantly groomed private beach, a gently warmed seawater pool for those who prefer to admire the Atlantic at a distance, and, just down the street, a casino. None of this comes cheap, of course; the empress herself probably couldn't afford to stay here today. Open from *Easter* to October. Information: *Hôtel du Palais,* 1 Av. de l'Impératrice, Biarritz 64200 (phone: 59-24-09-40).

LA RÉSERVE, Beaulieu-sur-Mer, Alpes-Maritimes: Dining in the sleek salon of *La Réserve* feels a little like sitting at the captain's table on one of the old luxury liners, with the blue sea and bluer-than-blue sky stretching away just beyond the chandeliers. Here, one level down, there's a handsome pool, and a notch below that a stony beach and an amply stocked yacht basin. The grounds are enthralling; those who manage to drag themselves away will find charming Beaulieu to be well worth their effort. And the whole of the Riviera is just a corniche away. Information: *Hôtel La Réserve,* 5 Bd. Général-Leclerc, Beaulieu-sur-Mer 06310 (phone: 93-01-00-01).

CARLTON, Cannes, Alpes-Maritimes: This great white-turreted doyenne presides over La Croisette — the Riviera's principal main drag — like some permanent sand castle for seaside royalty, complete with swaying green palm trees and blue and white umbrellas to shade some of the most beautiful bodies in Europe. In this city, May is an especially merry month because of the film festival, but if you plan to see just how merry, count on reserving a decade or two in advance lest you find yourself in a sleeping bag on the beach. Information: *Hôtel Carlton,* 58 Bd. de La Croisette, Cannes 06400 (phone: 93-68-91-68).

NORMANDY, Deauville, Calvados: At its proudest during the city's August racing season, when the casino is wall-to-wall tuxedos and all of Paris has come down for a stroll on the boardwalk, this imposing Norman mansion of a hotel by the sea has a special, more solitary romance during the winter, when wind and rain froth the ocean and lash the Norman coast. Neither discourages the roulette players or the lobster-eaters at *Ciro's,* the hotel's boardwalk restaurant. Information: *Hôtel Normandy,* 38 Rue Jean-Mermoz, Deauville l4800 (phone: 31-98-66-22).

LE GRAND HÔTEL, Divonne-les-Bains, Ain: In a peaceful arboretum in a placid border village in the quiet foothills of the Jura mountain range. Golfers can test their skills on one of France's finest courses (see also *Great French Golf*); sailors can sample the winds on an extensive artificial lake; hedonists can experience a soak in each of 57 varieties of thermal baths. Anyone else may want to thumb his nose at such sedate pastimes and enjoy lavish predawn dining in the wheelside restaurant of France's busiest and most profitable casino. Geneva is only a quarter of an hour away, so at any given moment the town's demographics will strike a pleasant balance between farmers' daughters and international traveling salesmen. Information: *Le Grand Hôtel,* Divonne-les-Bains 01220 (phone: 50-20-06-63).

ROYAL CLUB EVIAN, Evian-les-Bains, Haute-Savoie: At this Belle Epoque beauty set in 28 acres of woodland high above Lake Geneva, nearly every room has a sunny balcony that faces across the lake to Switzerland or looks south toward the Mont-Blanc range. The modern management — gone pleasantly health and sports mad — has added to this formerly staid center for sylvan pastimes a bristling lot of athletic facilities and programs: a half-dozen Greenset tennis courts (3 lighted for night play) and a Tennis Academy; a regular shuttle service to the *Royal Golf Club;* an archery range and daily instruction; saunas, hydrotherapy facilities and hydrotherapists; calisthenic sessions; and a jogging circuit with obstacles. The 5 restaurants provide something to look forward to while sweating. Information: *Royal Club Evian,* Av. des Mateirons, Evian-les-Bains 74500 (phone: 50-75-14-00).

CHÂTEAU DE LA CHÈVRE D'OR, Eze-Village, Alpes-Maritimes: This small hotel in a medieval village is perched so splendidly high (1,300 feet) above the Côte D'Azur that it is quiet and calm even on the most intense summer days on the Riviera. Its 13 rooms all look out over the sea, and have the rustic appeal that stone walls and down comforters offer. The one-Michelin-star restaurant is excellent countrified-chic; try the wild strawberry soufflé. Monte Carlo and Nice are only a few miles away, but you just may decide to save them for another trip. Though it's a bit of a climb from the parking lot *up* to the hotel's front door, it's worth every step. A member of the Relais & Châteaux group. Information: *Château de la Chèvre d'Or,* Eze-Village 06360 (phone: 93-41-12-12).

CHÂTEAU DE LOCGUÉNOLÉ, Hennebont, Morbihan: A woodland park (250 acres) surrounds this family mansion, now a fine hotel, cushioning guests from the busy beaches of the Breton coast and any other brush with real life. Owned by the same family for more than 500 years, the antiques, paintings, and museum-quality tapestries in this courtly castle grace the stately, yet welcoming lounges. If your mood is correspondingly regal, choose a large velvety room with French doors on the second floor. If your tastes run to the rustic, the exposed beams and flowery prints of the attic floor will charm you. The views over Le Blavet Sound are dazzling from all the rooms. Leave time for sampling local seafood in the renowned restaurant. Swimming, tennis, and fishing are possible without ever stepping out into the rude world. A member of the Relais & Châteaux group. Information: *Château de Locguénolé,* Rte. de Port-Louis (Km. 5), Hennebont 56700 (phone: 97-76-29-04).

FERME SAINT-SIMÉON, Honfleur, Calvados: The Impressionist light of Monet, Renoir, and Corot brightened here at Honfleur. After a day of painting outdoors, the artists played dominoes and drank cider with the local farmers at this 17th-century inn. Today, a modern 19-room annex is cozy and bright, but the original 19 rooms are the most romantic. Ask for one with a view of the Atlantic, and then watch the clouds move against a brilliant blue sky. Dine on lobster stew on the terrace under the trees. Set the morning aside to explore the port of Honfleur and the evening to click chips at the *Deauville* casino. Information: *Ferme Saint-Siméon,* Rue Adolphe Marais, Honfleur 14600 (phone: 31-89-23-61).

LA CÔTE SAINT-JACQUES, Joigny, Yonne: Before self-indulgence goes out of style, explore its true meaning at this luxurious hotel-restaurant complex on the shore of the Yonne River, bordering Burgundy wine country. The superbly managed family-owned and run restaurant (see *Haute Gastronomie*) is housed in a traditional 18th-century country home, but the newer and more elegant accommodations are in the nearby *Résidence.* Many rooms have soothing river views. You can stagger from your three-star foie gras and truffles to a flower-bedecked bed by going through the glamorously lit vaulted tunnel. There are Parisians who make the 2-hour drive simply to dine here. Information: *Résidence de la Côte Saint-Jacques,* 14 Faubourg de Paris, Joigny 89300 (phone: 86-62-09-70).

HÔTEL MONT-BLANC and CHALET-MONT-D'ARBOIS, Megève, Haute-Savoie: Film buffs will never forget the suave actor Gérard Philippe on the slopes of sophisticated Megève in Roger Vadim's wicked 1959 picture *Les Liaisons Dangereuses.* In the French Alps, these establishments represent the ultimate in jet set chic now as they did then. Still *the* spots where the beautiful people brush the snow from their pastel stretch pants and sip mulled wine by the fire. The hotel is large and bustling, right in the center of the village; the 20-room chalet, at 4,000 feet, lies on a country road above the town. Information: *Hôtel Mont-Blanc,* Pl. de l'Eglise, Megève 74120 (phone: 50-21-20-02); *Chalet-du-Mont-d'Arbois,* Rte. du Mont-D'Arbois, Megève 74120 (phone: 50-21-25-03).

CHÂTEAU D'ARTIGNY, Montbazon, Indre-et-Loire: Many travelers who have spent the day visiting the châteaux of the Loire Valley experience an unquenchable desire to spend the night sleeping in one — and this is the spot. Built by François Coty (of perfume fame and fortune) on the site of an 18th-century château, this structure has a decorous mansarded exterior that cloaks an interior as ornate and resplendent as anyone could desire. A heated swimming pool and a pair of private tennis courts represent just a couple of the improvements that have been made since the establishment's construction; musical weekends enliven the fall and winter seasons. A member of the Relais & Châteaux group. Information: *Château d'Artigny,* Rte. d'Azay-le-Rideau, Veigné, Montbazon 37250 (phone: 47-26-24-24).

HÔTEL DE PARIS, Monte Carlo, Monaco: That this establishment, opened on *New Year's Day* in 1864, is the dowager queen of the Côte d'Azur is evident in nearly every bit of ornamentation in its nooks and crannies — from the fulsome frescoes in the Empire dining room to the bare-breasted caryatids that gaze across the rows of parked Rolls-Royces to the grand *Casino* across the square (see *Monaco,* THE CITIES). The guestbook reads like a *Who's Who* of the century; Winston Churchill stayed here so often that the management named one of its 30 palatial suites after him. The celebrated wine cellars, carved out of the rock on which the principality sits, are accessible to visitors. And it's possible to pick up a quick Dior in the lobby. The elegantly decorated Louis XV restaurant, awarded three Michelin stars, is one of the best on the Côte D'Azur. Whatever you do, don't forget that caviar and smoked salmon are available 24 hours a day, in case of emergency. Information: *Hôtel de Paris,* Pl. du Casino, Monte Carlo 98000 (phone: 93-50-80-80).

NÉGRESCO, Nice, Alpes-Maritimes: Though traffic whizzes along the Promenade des Anglais and cement-slab apartment buildings litter the coastline, this grande dame presides over Nice as serenely as ever, as if to remind us that there was once an era when every new building worth mentioning looked like a wedding cake. The whole edifice — from the gilded, inlaid ceilings and the canopied beds to the fluted columns — has been designated a National Historical Monument. Information: *Hôtel Négresco,* 37 Promenade des Anglais, Nice 06000 (phone: 93-88-39-51).

DOMAINE DES HAUTS-DE-LOIRE, Onzain, Loir-et-Cher: Less overwhelming than some of its fellow castles in the Loire Valley, this erstwhile hunting lodge of some forgotten count comes across as a family-size château; and with its rough oaken beams and gleaming copper cauldrons, it has a pleasant, residential feel that is mirrored in the friendly, thoughtful service. Spring, when flowers bloom in profusion around the velvety lawns and swans glide on the placid pond, is a particularly entrancing time to visit. Information: *Domaine des Hauts-de-Loire,* Rte. de Herbault, Onzain 41150 (phone: 54-20-72-57).

CRILLON, Paris: An apparent proving ground for the entire French automotive industry, the Place de la Concorde has a frenetic atmosphere today far at odds with its spirit in the 18th century. But within its Sienese marble foyers, guests here are insulated from all the brouhaha. Diplomats from nearby Embassy Row buy and sell countries in the bar, and journalists seem always on hand trying to overhear the parameters of the deals. The view from the suites facing the *place* are *sans pareil.* This is perhaps Paris's most expertly managed hotel; it is a member of the Relais & Châteaux group. Information: *Hôtel Crillon,* 10 Pl. de la Concorde, Paris 75008 (phone: 42-65-24-24).

GEORGE V, Paris: The lobby is a League of Nations of private enterprise, where wheelers and dealers of every nationality seem to be settling matters of planetary importance. It also seems to be where the *Cannes Film Festival* crowd spends the other 11 months of the year, so numerous are the stars and starlets, directors, producers, and other movie folk who pilgrim here. The Eiffel Tower is just across the river, the Champs-Elysées just down the block, and the Arc de Triomphe around the corner; most of the rest of Paris can be seen from the panoramic windows of rooms higher up in the hotel. Even those who can't afford one of them — or the tranquil chambers facing the gracious courtyard — should be sure to stop for one of the establishment's utterly lyrical croissants. Information: *Hôtel George V,* 31 Av. George-V, Paris 75008 (phone: 47-23-54-00).

PLAZA-ATHÉNÉE, Paris: A $6 million renovation is underway, carefully preserving the charm of this most charming of European hotels, much to the relief of those who love it — from the guest quarters done in Louis XV and XVI to the *Relais* grill, where *tout Paris* seems to be eternally lunching, and the idyllic *Garden Court* restaurant, which is like a set for some Parisian *Mikado,* with its cheeping birds, pools, and a bridge. On the elegant Avenue Montaigne, this hotel is a little more sedate and a little more French than the *George V* (above). Information: *Hôtel Plaza-Athénée,* 25 Av. Montaigne, Paris 75008 (phone: 47-23-78-33).

RITZ, Paris: The Right Bank establishment that César Ritz created and made synonymous with all the finer things in life is so much a part of French tradition and literature that every year an occasional perambulator, coming upon it suddenly, is startled to find that it still exists, much less reigns as majestically as ever over the Place Vendôme. Marcel Proust wrote most of *Remembrance of Things Past* in a cork-lined room here; Georges-Auguste Escoffier put France at the top of the culinary Olympus from its kitchen. The latest addition is the *Ritz Club,* a nightclub and discotheque built about the same time as its super spa, and open to guests and club members only. Like bagging a tiger under Kilimanjaro or owning a palazzo on the Grand Canal, this is one of those experiences that the truly discriminating owe themselves. Information: *Hôtel Ritz,* 15 Pl. Vendôme, Paris 75041 (phone: 42-60-38-30).

LE BRISTOL, Paris: A palace with a special, almost intimate cachet. Service is impeccable, as are the 188 spacious, quiet rooms and huge marble baths. The beautiful little restaurant and comfortable lobby cocktail lounge are additional pleasures. A wing built in 1985 includes a heated swimming pool on the sixth-floor terrace. Information: *Hôtel Le Bristol,* 112 Rue du Faubourg-St.-Honoré, Paris 75008 (phone: 42-66-91-45).

BOYER "LES CRAYÈRES," Reims, Marne: With its move to a stunning 19th-century château, this three-star restaurant added lodgings that match its menu. Set on 19 beautifully landscaped acres, just a stone's throw from the twin Gothic towers of Reims cathedral, it has 16 sumptuous rooms and 3 suites, some of which open onto terraces overlooking the gardens, and all of which are decorated differently, mainly in the styles of the Louis Philippe era. A member of the distinguished Relais et Châteaux group, its main attraction is, however, food. The menu's offerings reflect a finely tuned balance between nouvelle and traditional cuisine, and service is helpful rather than overbearing (see *Haute Gastronomie*). In support of the main local industry, the wine list includes more than 60 champagnes. Closed mid-December to mid-January. Information: *Boyer "Les Crayères,"* 64 Bd. Henry-Vasnier, Reims 51100 (phone: 26-82-80-80).

MAS D'ARTIGNY, St.-Paul-de-Vence, Alpes-Maritimes: How can a hotel with 25 swimming pools be ignored? This ultramodern, ultra-luxurious bastion of the 20th century (and another member of the Relais & Châteaux group) is a complex of suites, each graced by its own private garden and pool, arranged in an emerald and sapphire horseshoe around a main building, which itself boasts a more than adequate pool. And Nice, the sea, and the winding 16th-century ramparts of St.-Paul-de-Vence are only a short drive away. Information: *Mas d'Artigny,* St.-Paul-de-Vence 06570 (phone: 93-32-84-54).

L'ESPÉRANCE, Saint-Père-sous-Vezelay, Yonne: The best rooms in this serene country manor house overlook the beautiful garden and the Cure River. The principal indoor activity is dinner in the glass-enclosed dining room, where three-star food is served with just the right degree of unfussy concern for your comfort. The medieval town of Vezelay and the glowing Romanesque church of St. Madeleine are nearby. The hotel is closed in January, the restaurant on Tuesdays and Wednesday lunch. A member of the Relais & Châteaux group. Information: *L'Espérance,* Saint-Père-sous-Vezelay, Vezelay 889450 (phone: 86-33-20-45).

AUBERGE DU PÈRE BISE, Talloires, Haute-Savoie: Lakes, a principal drawing card for European vacationers in prewar days, are, like spas, coming back into fashion. Lake Annecy and its picturebook environs make a persuasive case for choosing a tranquil lake over a teeming seaside. The village of Talloires, elegant and serene, is the backdrop for the family-owned, three-star restaurant of the same name on the lakefront. Mountains to the left, water to the right, there's no choice but to concede to the temptation of lunching outdoors on duck, lobster tails, and wicked chestnut pastry. Spend the night in a deliciously plush room with a balcony, and start again the next morning. Closed from early December to early March. The restaurant is closed

Wednesdays for lunch and Tuesdays off-season. A member of the Relais & Châteaux group. Information: *Auberge du Père Bise,* Rte. du Port, Talloire 74290 (phone: 50-60-72-01).

LE VIEUX LOGIS, Trémolat, Dordogne: In one of the prettiest and least traveled regions of France, this old dwelling is one of the most picturesque and little known of French stopping places. Installed in a typical old Périgord house with rustic furnishings, ivied walls, and flowered bowers, it offers fine regional fare, all the truffles the fastidious could fancy, and lots of hunting and fishing nearby for those who want to procure some victuals on their own. An enchanting member of the Relais & Châteaux group. Information: *Le Vieux Logis*, Trémolat 24510 (phone: 53-22-80-06).

Haute Gastronomie

 Inspiring the same fierce passions and loyalties that soccer does in Brazil, eating is the French national sport. The French talk about food instead of the weather, reminisce about one meal while downing another, and select restaurants as if they were putting together an investment portfolio. The light, sauce-free fashion of the nouvelle cuisine brought a few mouthfuls of moderation to the nationwide gourmandizing — until the country's superchefs began to recant, labeling it "big plates with small ingredients and nothing in between."

So we're happy to report that France is once again awash in béchamel and ablaze with cognac, and the turbot once again reigns *suprême.*

Before you take to the field, a few morsels of advice. Once you're seated, don't be intimidated by the ritual or its priesthood. Remember that you are quite literally the consumer. While it is customary to conceive of the meal as a whole, insist on ordering one course at a time if you can't think about *moules* and *mousse* at once. In addition, consider that many restaurants are happy and even proud to present their guests with small portions of dishes they'd simply like to sample. And some restaurants also offer *dégustation* menus, which include a sampling of the chef's noblest creations. Ask the wine waiter for advice, but unless you're a true oenophile, don't spend unnecessarily for sought-after châteaux or venerable vintages. Local wines, many of which don't ever find their way out of the immediate neighborhood but are well known to a resident restaurateur, are likely to be the best tasting and least expensive choices. And if a dish is unsatisfactory, by all means send it back to the kitchen. Restaurateurs hold their reputation in deadly earnest (to such an extent that one eminent chef did away with himself on learning he'd been stripped of one of his three Michelin stars). And, above all, be sure to make reservations — if only a few days in advance. Far better, write for reservations months in advance of your anticipated arrival at one of France's authentic temples of gastronomy. There is very little impulse dining in France, and tables at restaurants that are among the most favored are sometimes booked months ahead. This also assures that you won't show up hungry — only to find that the chef has gone off on his annual holiday. In the list of some of the best restaurants in France that follows, we note the *fermetures annuelles* (yearly closings), but do bear in mind that last-minute changes can occur. What's more, don't forget to *reconfirm* reservations once you arrive on French soil — even if no request for reconfirmation has been made formally. Reservations at the top restaurants in France are routinely (and automatically) canceled without timely reconfirmation. When making your reservations, check to determine if credit cards are accepted.

Finally, *bon appétit!*

CHÂTEAU D'AUDRIEU, Audrieu, Calvados: According to local legend, the first lord of the 60-acre park that surrounds this beautiful 18th-century castle was the personal chef to no less than William the Conqueror. Today's cuisine, presented in a pair of tasteful and intimate dining rooms, is consummately majestic. The crown jewels are the *soupe de homard et d'escargots* (lobster and snail bisque) and the *aiguillettes de canard aux pêches* (duck in peach sauce). A very fine *dégustation* menu also may be ordered. Closed Wednesdays, Thursday lunch, and from early December to March. Information: *Château d'Audrieu,* Audrieu, Tilly-sur-Seulles 14250 (phone: 31-80-21-52).

OUSTAU DE BAUMANIÈRE and LA CABRO D'OR, Les Baux-de-Provence, Bouches-du-Rhône: These two restaurants, a snail's throw from each other and under the same management, are in charming old Provençal manor houses in richly verdant settings. Seated under vaulted ceilings and wooden beams or on a terrace overlooking a fairy tale duck pond, guests are graciously presented with some of the most highly reputed food in France. At the former, a recipient of two Michelin stars (true, it long had three), *filets de rougets au vinaigre* (fish fillets with a vinegar sauce) and *gigot d'agneau en croûte* (leg of lamb in a pastry crust) are among the specialties; the latter offers a fine *terrine de légumes au confit de tomates* (vegetable terrine with a tomato sauce). *Oustau* is closed Wednesdays and Thursdays from October 15 to mid-January for lunch and from mid-January to early March; *La Cabro* shuts down the kitchen on Mondays and Tuesdays from December 20 through March at lunchtime and November 15 to December 20. Information: *Oustau de Baumanière,* Les Baux-de-Provence, Maussane-les-Alpilles 13520 (phone: 90-54-33-07); La Cabro d'Or at the same address (phone: 90-54-33-21).

LE ST.-JAMES, Bordeaux, Gironde: Lavishly elegant, this establishment in a large, garden-rimmed stone villa pioneered the nouvelle cuisine revolution in Bordeaux. But still, amid all the watercress mousse, a bounty of sinful savories — most notably the duck liver terrine, the garlic-studded roast lamb, the thyme-perfumed rabbit, and the caramel-lined roast wild duck — can also be found. Meals are served inside the manor and, when the weather is fine, on a pleasantly shady terrace. Information: *Le St.-James,* Pl. Camille-Hosteins, Bordeaux-Floirac 33270 (phone: 56-20-52-19).

CIRO'S, Deauville, Calvados: If you eat one lobster in all of France, eat it here. Crowded but cozy, especially on a weathery Sunday when the Norman rains empty the beach, this bastion of the very rich on Deauville's celebrated boardwalk is under the management of the *Casino* and the *Hôtel Normandy,* which handles its guests with velvet gloves. The fine view of the ocean from which the maritime specialties on the menu have just been hauled is a bonus. Information: *Ciro's,* Promenade des Planches, Deauville 14800 (phone: 31-88-18-10).

LES PRÉS D'EUGÉNIE, Eugénie-les-Bains, Landes: Chef Michel Guérard is to French gastronomy what Joe DiMaggio was to baseball, and this little thermal resort in the southwestern corner of France is where he cooks his home runs. Guérard's *cuisine minceur* (slimming cuisine), the subject of his best-selling cookbook, is notable for allowing diners to make a *cochon* of themselves and stay trim and slender at the same time. The natural products of the region, the bases of this miracle, are selected by Guérard and his staff with the meticulous care of an art dealer shopping for a kilo of Renoirs. And the roster of refined delights seems to get longer, and more bewitching, by the year. Closed from early November to February. Information: *Les Prés d'Eugénie,* Eugénie-les-Bains 40320 (phone: 58-51-19-01)

LES BORIES, Gordes, Vaucluse: This tiny and utterly delightful stone-walled inn in the heart of Provence has an outdoor terrace with a view that allows for languid lunching in the shade of olive trees while stray shafts of sunlight glow pinkly through a bottle of rosé. Try the feather-light *salade folle* (crazy salad) with duck and crayfish as well as the lamb grilled on an open wood fire. Restaurant open daily except Wednesdays and during December; lunches only on Sundays, Mondays, and Tuesdays. Information: *Les Bories,* Rte. de Sénanque, Gordes 84220 (phone: 90-72-00-51).

AUBERGE DE L'ILL, Illhaeusern, Haut-Rhin: Serene and exceptionally elegant, this three-star establishment on the willow-feathered shores of the River Ill, surrounded by lovely gardens, serves Alsatian food at its pungent and aromatic best — a creative and elegant mix of the delicacy of the best French haute cuisine and the vigor of the German. This is the place to sample a wild hare salad (if you're in the mood for something light and gamey) or *choucroute garnie* (if you're feeling porky and Teutonic) or simply to dip into one of the almost uncountable number of pâtés. Flan of frogs' legs with watercress, venison in a light pepper sauce, and salmon soufflé are among the other delights. Whatever the selection, let the fruity local riesling flow like the nearby Rhine. Closed Mondays, Tuesdays, most of February, and the first week in July. Information: *Auberge de l'Ill,* Rue de Collonges, Illhaeusern, Ribeauvillé 68150 (phone: 89-71-83-23).

PAUL BOCUSE, Collonges-au-Mont-d'Or, Lyons, Rhône: The chef whose name this much-publicized culinary magnet bears is a member of the French Légion d'Honneur, and there are those who consider his truffle soup Valéry-Giscard-d'Estaing one of the most important achievements of the nation's previous government. Regrettably, M. Bocuse is often away from his restaurant, tending to gastronomic affairs from Tokyo to *Walt Disney World.* Still, even the supporting kitchen staff can create awesome comestibles well worth a visit. Information: *Paul Bocuse,* Pont de Collonges, Collonges-au-Mont-d'Or, Lyons, Rhône 69660 (phone: 78-22-01-40).

MICHEL (LES CATALANS) and CALYPSO, Marseilles, Bouches-du-Rhône: The seaport of Marseilles brought the world bouillabaisse, the fish stew which thou shalt not leave France without tasting; and these neighboring restaurants serve the best cauldron of it in town. Peek in, sniff, and take your choice. The Mediterranean fish stew called bourride and grilled fish also are available. The old and very traditional *Michel* is closed Tuesdays, Wednesdays, and July; elegant, sea-view *Calypso* is closed Sundays, Mondays, and August. Information: *Michel (Les Catalans),* 6 Rue des Catalans, Marseilles 13007 (phone: 91-52-64-22); *Calypso,* 3 Rue du Catalans, Marseilles 13007 (phone: 91-52-64-00).

ALAIN CHAPEL, Mionnay, Ain: About 12 miles (19 km) north of Lyons, this lovely little inn, with a whitewashed cloister and a manicured garden, was the base of operations of the late philosopher-chef Alain Chapel, another member of the "All Stars" of French cuisine. Sadly, M. Chapel passed away as we went to press and the future of his restaurant is uncertain. We hope that every morsel is first class, whether a simple omelette or a complex lobster assemblage; a certain well-known pair of French food writers once admitted to having shed real tears over one of Chapel's confections. Lodge in one of the 13 tasteful rooms and you can start all over again the following day. Closed Mondays, Tuesdays for lunch, and the month of January. Information: *Alain Chapel,* RN 83, Mionnay 01390 (phone: 78-91-82-02).

LE MOULIN DE MOUGINS, Mougins, Alpes-Maritimes: In the hills above Cannes, this 16th-century olive oil mill houses one of the Riviera's most gorgeous and glamorous restaurants — with a clientele to match. Dark wood beams stand out against the rustic white walls, and the exotic garden is the "beaker full of the warm south" for which an old French poet once pined. Chef Roger Vergé's braised slivers of Provençal duck in honey and lemon sauce stand out as one of the plainer selections on an entrancing menu, which to the food lover reads like the *Thousand and One Nights* and then some. Don't miss the cold wild strawberry soufflé, the escalope of fresh salmon, the lobster fricassee, and the pâté of sole. Closed Mondays, Thursday lunch, and from mid-November to mid-December and late January to mid-March. In the same town, Vergé also operates the simpler *L'Amandier de Mougins.* Information: *Le Moulin de Mougins,* 424 Chemin du Moulin, Mougins, Alpes-Maritimes 06250 (phone: 93-75-78-24).

L'ANE ROUGE, Nice, Alpes-Maritimes: *Moules farcies* (stuffed mussels), *oursins* (sea urchins), *loup de mer au fenouille* (sea bass grilled in fennel), *huîtres plates aux champagne* (oysters with champagne), bourride, and just about anything else from the sea can be ordered either in the pretty, flowered dining room of this establishment in Nice's old port or outdoors on the terrace. Closed Saturdays, Sundays, holidays, and from July 14 to September 1. Information: *L'Ane Rouge,* 7 Quai des Deux-Emmanuel, Nice 06300 (phone: 93-89-49-63).

CHEZ ALLARD, Paris: *Allard* still has the zinc bar, the smoky windows, and the terra cotta floor sprinkled with sawdust of the traditional Paris bistro of old. It also has some of the finest Burgundy country cooking this side of the Côte d'Or — including garlicky escargots, buttery scallops, turbot in *beurre blanc, coq au vin,* guinea hen, cassoulet, leg of lamb, and a chocolate charlotte that is one of the legends of the Left Bank. Closed Saturdays, Sundays, holidays, August, and 10 days at *Christmas.* Information: *Chez Allard,* 41 Rue St.-André-des-Arts, Paris 75006 (phone: 43-26-48-23).

L'AMI LOUIS, Paris: This is the archetypal Parisian bistro, unattractive physically but with huge portions of marvelous food. Specialties include foie gras, spectacular roast chicken, spring lamb, ham, and burgundy wines. It's a particular favorite among Americans, and *the* place to sample authentic French fries. Though its fabled owner has died, the new regime carries on gallantly. Closed Mondays, Tuesdays, and all of July and August. Information: *L'Ami Louis,* 32 Rue du Vertbois, Paris (phone: 48-87-77-48).

L'AMBROISIE, Paris: Promoted to three-star status by Michelin in 1988, this tiny, quietly elegant establishment on the Place des Vosges is the showcase for chef Bernard Pacaud's equally elegant cuisine. Matched in scale, the menu is limited to only a few entrées, such as duck with foie gras, skate and sliced green cabbage in sherry vinegar sauce, veal sweetbreads with shallots and parsley on ultra-fresh pasta, lightly battered chicken thighs in a piquant sauce, and oxtail in a savory sauce, but the quality more than compensates for the limited number of choices. Closed Sundays, Monday lunch, August, and holidays. Information: *L'Ambroisie,* 9 Pl. des Vosges, Paris (phone: 42-78-51-45).

ANDROUËT, Paris: Downstairs, it's a cheese shop with some 200 varieties, the constant tasting of which spawned one of the city's unique restaurants, upstairs. The *menu dégustation* is a seven-course parade of cheese platters accompanied by a basket of the crusty long loaves of bread known as *baguettes,* fresh from the bakery. The only decision left to make is whether to wash it all down with burgundy or bordeaux. Closed Sundays and holidays. Information: *Androuët,* 41 Rue Amsterdam, Paris 75008 (phone: 48-74-26-90).

L'ESCARGOT MONTORGUEIL, Paris: The polished wood paneling, the brass fittings, and the stunning spiral staircase at this beautiful restaurant dating from 1830 — the Second Empire period — only add to the pleasure of a meal, which might include snails in any of half a dozen styles or duck with orange sauce. Closed Mondays. Information: *L'Escargot Montorgueil,* 38 Rue Montorgueil, Paris 75002 (phone: 42-36-83-51).

JAMIN, Paris: Due to the culinary talents of owner-chef Joel Robuchon, this is one of Paris's finest restaurants, meriting a three-star ranking by Michelin. Robuchon calls his cuisine "moderne," similar to but not always as light as nouvelle. The dining room is very small, so reserve well in advance. Closed Saturdays, Sundays, and the month of July. Information: *Jamin,* 32 Rue de Longchamp, Paris 75016 (phone: 47-27-12-27).

LE GRAND VÉFOUR, Paris: In the stately courtyard of the Palais Royal, this 231-year-old corner of Paris at its most patrician is a place of thick carpets and frescoed mirrors, where the choice dishes have been named for dignitaries who have discussed affairs of state here since the time of Robespierre. The house specialties are every bit as enthralling as the history. In honor of both, gentlemen still are required to wear jacket and tie. Closed Saturday lunch, Sundays, and all of August. Information: *Le Grand Véfour,* 17 Rue Beaujolais, Paris 75001 (phone: 42-96-56-27).

LASSERRE, Paris: The waiters are in tails, the ceiling glides open to reveal the stars, the decanted burgundy is warmed by a candle, and the impeccable service makes diners feel that somehow they deserve all this. The cuisine is traditional French at its most heavenly, and the wine cellar is a virtual museum of French oenology. Not surprisingly, making dinner reservations is akin to booking seats for a sold-out Broadway musical, so think ahead. Way ahead. Closed Sundays, Monday lunch, and August. Information: *Lasserre,* 17 Av. Franklin-Roosevelt, Paris 75008 (phone: 43-59-53-43).

LUCAS CARTON, Paris: The splendid Belle Epoque premises were taken over several years back by the near-legend Alain Senderens, who made his reputation as owner-chef of *L'Archestrate,* once the capital's three-star temple of nouvelle cuisine. The change of surroundings took the chill off the old hauteur somewhat, and the lush, plush premises are the perfect place to sample a few bites of truffle salad, lobster with vanilla, or the *carpaccio de canard Eventhia.* This is innovative cuisine at its quirkiest best, and Michelin lost no time in awarding it three stars. The utensils and serving pieces are almost as alluring as the food. Be sure to reconfirm all reservations. Closed Saturdays and Sundays, most of August, and the last 10 days of December. Information: *Lucas Carton,* 9 Pl. de la Madeleine, Paris 75008 (phone: 42-65-22-90).

LE TAILLEVENT, Paris: The culinary classic that continues to rise to ever greater heights is currently the very best in the City of Light. This three-star dining room occupies a distinguished 19th-century mansion complete with fine paintings, porcelain dinnerware, and aristocratic decor that make it look as if the French Revolution was really just a bad dream. The salad of warm sweetbreads, the salmon with fresh mint, the tarragon-perfumed lobster casserole, and the rainbow assortment of soufflés are among the pillars of the Parisian gastronomic community. The most difficult restaurant reservation in France. A tip: Booking a table for three or more sometimes is easier than trying to book a table for two. Closed Saturdays, Sundays, holidays, February, and part of August. Information: *Taillevent,* 15 Rue Lamennais, Paris 75008 (phone: 45-63-39-94).

L'AUBERGE DU VIEUX PUITS, Pont-Audemer, Eure: The immensely charming proprietors of this establishment, in a rustic old Norman house not far from Deauville, receive guests as if they were highly valued and long-lost members of the family — and so the best course is to leave the task of selecting the buttery, creamy components of any given meal entirely in their deft culinary hands (though it is a good idea to let on that a taste of the bewitching local trout would be most welcome). Closed Monday evenings and Tuesdays, early July, and from mid-December to mid-January. Information: *L'Auberge du Vieux Puits,* 6 Rue Notre-Dame-du-Pré, Pont Audemer 27500 (phone: 32-41-01-48).

AUBERGE DES TEMPLIERS, Les Bezards-Boismorand, Loiret: Named for the austere order of religious warriors once headquartered here, this elegant eatery nestles langorously in a quiet oak grove. Guests can enjoy their drinks and relax in front of the immense brick fireplace before moving on to one of the dining rooms where 18th-century tapestries drape from the timbered ceilings to the Oriental carpeted floor. In summer, lunch is served under the rose-studded trellises on the terrace, where the sweet scents of flowers and soufflés stir even the drowsiest palate. The kitchen specializes in fish, which include a variety fresh from the nearby Loire, and the extensive wine list boasts a 1947 Château Lafite-Rothschild. Closed mid-January to mid-February. Information: *Auberge des Templiers,* Les Bezards-Boismorand, Nogent-sur-Vernisson 45290 (phone: 38-31-80-81).

HÔTEL DES FRÈRES TROISGROS, Roanne, Loire: Just a ramble across the street from the railroad station, this magnet for pilgrims of the plate would warrant the effort to cross the Loire in a colander. From the vegetable terrines and the sorrel-sauced escalopes of salmon to the chicken breasts served in vinegar-spiked and walnut oil–flavored bouillon and the warm honey soufflé, the three-star menu is a tribute to the kaleidoscopic richness of the French countryside, and dinners are composed with all the delicacy of an Impressionist painting. Closed Tuesdays, Wednesdays for lunch, January, and most of August. Information: *Hôtel des Frères Troisgros,* 22 Cours de la République, Roanne 42300 (phone: 77-71-66-97).

LA CÔTE ST.-JACQUES, Joigny, Yonne: Housed in an 18th-century villa overlooking the sleepy river Yonne, this three-star establishment is a Lorain family affair: Michel is chef, Jean-Michel his lieutenant in the kitchen, and Jacqueline is mistress of the wine cellar. Inside, fabric-covered walls, fresh flowers, porcelain, and silver tableware, all aglow in candlelight, set an elegant stage for the main event. The menu offers *cuisine traditionelle,* which includes three courses of lobster, and *cuisine créative,* which features such novel preparations as a ragôut of young pigeon, cooked with cocks' crests and crawfish tails. Closed January. Information: *La Côte St.-Jacques,* Joigny 89300 (phone: 86-62-09-70).

L'ABBAYE ST.-MICHEL, Tonnerre, Yonne: In the middle of the idyllic Burgundy countryside, this 13th-century Benedictine abbey has a cool, stone-vaulted dining room, a gently blossoming garden, a selection of almost lyrical wines from the surrounding vineyards, and a superbly refined cuisine that steals the thunder of even the celestial setting. Closed from January to mid-February, Sunday evenings, and Mondays except from June to September. Information: *L'Abbaye St.-Michel,* Montée St.-Michel, Tonnerre 89700 (phone: 86-55-05-99).

BOYER "LES CRAYÈRES", Reims, Marne: This three-star establishment is housed in a stunning 19th-century château, set on 19 beautifully landscaped acres, just a stone's throw from the twin Gothic towers of Reims cathedral. The offerings, which include dishes such as mussel soup with saffron and orange and salmon with lemon and ginger, as well as standards such as fois gras, bass with artichokes, and roast pigeon with garlic and parsley, reflect a finely tuned balance between nouvelle and traditional cuisine. Service is helpful without being overbearing. In support of the main local industry, the wine list includes over 60 Champagnes. Closed Mondays, lunch Tuesdays, and mid-December through mid-January. Information: *Boyer "Les Crayères",* 64 Bd. Henry-Vasnier, Reims 51100 (phone: 26-82-80-80).

Shopping Spree

For centuries, France has been producing some of the world's most fashionable clothing, its most delicious food and wine, and its most bewitching perfumes. And all of these items benefit from that same pinch of Gallic flair and good taste that characterize just about everything else to which the French put their hearts and hands. So it's no wonder that shopping in this country is such a delight.

In the provinces, regional specialties are among the best buys — calvados in Normandy, sausage in Toulouse, perfume in Grasse, and wine almost everywhere but especially in the Bordeaux, Burgundy, and Loire Valley growing areas. And all over France — particularly near the Côte d'Azur — there are little *ateliers,* studios, whose potters, weavers, wood carvers, and even glassblowers sell their wares either from tiny shops, in the sunny open-air markets of Nice and Cannes, or in the picturesque roving crafts fairs that periodically visit neighboring towns.

Elsewhere, buy a local newspaper or an information booklet, which may advertise crafts exhibits. Gift shop owners also may know how to contact artisans in their areas.

And the official tourist information office (the Office de Tourisme or the Syndicat d'Initiative) almost always can answer specific questions. Shopping in the French provinces offers its own pleasures, mostly related to the leisurely pace that affords time for personal contact between buyer and seller.

However, there seldom is any savings in buying a name-brand cast-iron skillet in the south of France and lugging it back to Paris. French storekeepers nationwide seem to adhere much more closely than their American counterparts to manufacturers' list prices, and if there is any price difference, it may well be that the skillet actually will cost *more* in that isolated shop than it would in a department store in Paris. By the same token, the French capital also boasts the widest selection available of practically every type of merchandise. And since most visitors to France pass through Paris at some point, the city rates as the most convenient place to shop as well.

Long considered the international capital of fashion, Paris excels in the area of stylish, high-quality clothing and accessories. Prices range from the wildly extravagant to the fairly reasonable; but in any case they are far lower than for the same merchandise sold outside France. Perfume, first-rate leather goods, food, wine, and cooking equipment and related items are good buys here.

PARIS SHOPPING STREETS: Stores selling similar merchandise tend to cluster along a certain one of the capital's celebrated boulevards and avenues, and for visitors who want to browse rather than go out of their way to find a specific shop, these are prime destinations:

Boulevard Haussmann – The *Galeries Lafayette* and *Au Printemps,* the city's two leading department stores, and the Paris branch of London's *Marks & Spencer* are here.

Place de la Madeleine – Several emporia purveying fine foods and wine — including *Hédiard,* specializing in exotic fruit and spices at No. 21, and the famous, fabulous *Fauchon* at No. 28 — can be found here.

Rue d'Alésia – Several blocks of discount shops.

Rue de Rivoli – This is not only the best place to find souvenir scarves decorated with Eiffel Towers and handkerchiefs imprinted with maps of the Paris métro system, but it also abounds in shops selling perfume and other gifts. Two of the city's more famous bookstores with an English-language stock are *W. H. Smith* at No. 248 and *Galignani* at No. 224.

Les Halles and St.-Germain-des-Prés – Trendy and often inexpensive clothing boutiques are concentrated in these two areas.

Rue du Faubourg-St.-Honoré – *The* shopping street for elegant fashions, chic shoes, and leather goods, including *Courrèges, Hermès, Lanvin, Guy Laroche, Yves Saint Laurent,* and others.

Rue des Sts.-Pères – Terrific shoes.

Place Vendôme – The *haute joaillerie* of France — the jewelry with the most splendid designs and the highest prices — is sold on this square adjoining the Rue de la Paix at shops such as *Cartier, Boucheron,* and *Van Cleef & Arpels.*

Place des Victoires – Stylish boutiques for women are the specialty, but there are some for men as well.

DEPARTMENT STORES NATIONWIDE: The *grands magasins,* as these emporiums are called, stock at least a little bit of everything, so it's hardly necessary to go from shop to shop for many types of items. In addition, these stores offer the opportunity to purchase several small gifts under one roof and thereby qualify to receive a refund of France's value-added tax (VAT).

Galeries Lafayette and *Au Printemps* – Of the nation's large stores, these two are deservedly the most popular with visitors. In addition to carrying an extensive and fashionable stock of men's, women's, and children's clothing, housewares, perfume, shoes, gifts, and all the miscellaneous merchandise ordinarily sold by such emporiums, they also provide tourists with special shopping information, translations, and instructions on how to obtain tax refunds on goods purchased here. In Paris, their main stores are next to each other near the *Opéra*.

Galeries Lafayette's main store in Paris is at 40 Bd. Haussmann (phone: 42-82-34-56); it has a branch in the *Maine Montparnasse Shopping Center* (22 Rue du Départ; phone: 45-38-52-87). There also are stores in Lyons (*La Part Dieu Shopping Center*; phone: 78-71-70-29), in Montpellier (the *Polygone Shopping Center*; phone: 67-64-83-00), in Nice (6 Av. Jean-Médecin; phone: 93-85-40-21), and in Nantes (18 Rue du Calvaire; phone: 40-48-62-55).

Au Printemps stores include the main one in Paris (64 Bd. Haussmann; phone: 45-22-66-59) as well as four others around Paris and almost 2 dozen in the French provinces, including branches in Auxerre (2 Rue de la Draperie; phone: 86-51-67-77), in Bayonne (32/38 Rue Victor-Hugo; phone: 59-59-00-64), in Bordeaux (15 Pl. Gambetta; phone: 56-52-67-01), in Caen (83 Rue St.-Pierre; phone: 31-86-15-98), in Deauville (104 Rue Eugène-Colas; phone: 31-88-21-83), in Dieppe (7 Grand Rue; phone: 35-84-11-35), in Le Havre (32 Av. du Président-Coty; phone: 35-42-45-05), in Lille (37/45 Rue Nationale; phone: 20-30-85-33), in Lyons (42 Pl. de la République; phone: 78-42-51-77), in Marseilles (*La Valentine Shopping Center* in the Chemin de la Sablière; phone: 91-44-00-66), in Metz (8/16 Rue Serpenoise; phone: 87-76-03-33), in Poitiers (Pl. du Maréchal-Leclerc; phone: 49-01-82-34), in Rennes (at the *Alma Shopping Center*; phone: 99-53-74-03), in Strasbourg (1/5 Rue de la Haute-Montée; phone: 88-32-33-34), and in La Valette near Toulon (in the *Grand Var Shopping Center* on the Av. de l'Université; phone: 94-75-90-65).

Monoprix and **Prisunic** – These low-priced stores are good to remember for attractive, inexpensive children's clothing and toys. The fashion accessories, housewares, and stationery departments also can yield treasures.

OPEN-AIR FOOD MARKETS NATIONWIDE: A visit to one of these colorful markets anywhere in France will provide an intimate, surprising, and usually delightful look at not only what the French eat but also how they live their daily lives. They're far too much fun to miss. So wherever you are, find out when the market is held and where, then plunge into the action with camera and shopping bag. Even if you buy no more than a bag of cherries — probably the sweetest you've ever tasted — you'll be glad you saw it all.

Dieppe – The market here reaches inland behind the port. Pots of jam made on nearby farms by the women who sell them are among the more alluring wares.

Lyons – It's at this city's outdoor market, which stretches along the Saône River, that great chefs like Paul Bocuse do their shopping; it's not necessary to be a three-star culinary wizard to do the same.

Mont-de-Marsan – Farm women pedal to the charming and memorable market held each Saturday morning under a high roof in the center of this small town in the Landes region of southwestern France, famed for good eating. Their bicycles are laden with cartons of just-gathered eggs and freshly pulled carrots and the like. Children will love the live chickens, ducks, and rabbits.

Nice – Markets in this area are especially colorful because of their settings — often within a pebble's throw of the brilliant Mediterranean.

Paris – The best and most enjoyable market here is probably the one set up on Wednesday and Saturday mornings on the Av. du Président-Wilson between Pl. d'Iéna and Pl. de l'Alma, both of which have métro stops. Butchers, bakers, and cheese and flower sellers abound here, along with all types of fresh fish, lettuce and herbs just pulled from the ground and trucked in from farms outside the city, and wonderful fruits and other vegetables. Other good roving markets appear in the Pl. Monge on Wednesdays,

Fridays, and Sundays; on the Bd. Raspail on Tuesdays and Fridays; and on the Bd. Edgar-Quinet on Wednesdays and Saturdays. Every neighborhood has one, and everyone has his or her favorite.

Sarlat-La-Canéda – This small Dordogne town full of ocher buildings, an irresistible destination for tourists, has a lively market every Saturday morning in the Pl. des Oies. It's also fun to buy foie gras, walnut oils, *cèpes,* and other Limousin food specialties in any of a handful of shops in the old town.

CRYSTAL AND CHINA NATIONWIDE: France has crystal and china to make the humblest table gleam like that in a royal banquet hall, and there are two good ways to get an overview of the nation's best: a visit to a porcelain producing center like the town of Limoges, in the Limousin region of southwestern France, and a stroll the length of the somewhat run-down Rue de Paradis in Paris.

Limoges – Do not expect to save money when buying porcelain in this porcelain manufacturing city 250 miles (400 km) southwest of Paris; shopping in France simply does not work that way. In fact, most major firms in Limoges sell no china at their factories, but simply refer purchasers to nearby retail stores, which follow the same price lists as the shops in Paris and other cities.

However, each July through September, Limoges holds a large free exhibition of Limoges porcelain, where 4 or 5 dozen small round tables each are set attractively with a sampling of place settings of the patterns currently produced by the principal firms; lists of stores selling the porcelain are available at the door. In addition, the *Musée National Adrien-Dubouché,* described in *Memorable Museums and Monuments,* shows off the city's creations of the past and puts its porcelain history in perspective.

Finally, Limoges does offer the visitor a chance to view the manufacture of porcelain in all of its stages, from the blending of the porcelain paste from feldspar, quartz, and kaolin through its molding into a multitude of forms and its elaborate decoration, much of it still done by hand.

Le Pavillon de la Porcelaine offers the city's most complete exhibition and reserves a special welcome for Americans, both because the firm was founded by the American David Haviland in 1842 and because it always has had a large proportion of Americans among its clients. Demonstrations are free and continuous, and are conducted daily year-round, from 8:30 AM to 7:30 PM. Information: *Le Pavillon de la Porcelaine, Z.I. Magré,* Rte. de Toulouse, Limoges 87000 (phone: 55-30-21-86).

La Maison de la Porcelaine, though less prestigious than *Le Pavillon de la Porcelaine,* also provides visitors with a complete view of the manufacturing process — from the raw and biscuit-fired stages to the hand decoration of the pieces with decals and fine brushes through the final firing in large gas kilns. At 14 Av. du Président-Wilson in Aixe-sur-Vienne, 6 miles (10 km) southwest of Limoges on N21 toward Périgueux, the factory offers its free guided tours at 9:45 AM and 3 PM daily, except Sundays from March through mid-September; additional tours are organized whenever the demand warrants. And there is an outlet on the premises for both first- and second-quality merchandise (phone: 55-70-14-68).

Pastaud, a small company at 36 Rue Jules-Noriac in Limoges proper, offers a very close look at its workers embellishing the porcelain that is produced away from a visitor's view — carefully applying intricate decals and painting the finished pieces with amazingly precise brushstrokes. The 19th-century kilns, which have been replaced by modern electric kilns, and some of Pastaud's past work, including a gold-decorated dinner plate made in 1938 for Franklin D. Roosevelt, are also displayed. Appointments are required (phone: 55-77-44-18).

Rue de Paradis, Paris – The entire street is lined with stores specializing in objects related to what merchants here call "the arts of the table."

Baccarat, a dazzling museum as much as a store at No. 30, is worth a visit even for those with no intention of purchasing an elegantly proportioned champagne flute or a multifaceted crystal champagne bucket (phone: 47-70-64-30 or 40-22-11-00). *Limoges-Unic* has a branch at No. 58, which carries many different types of Limoges china as well as a good supply of typically French Porcelaine de Paris patterns (phone: 47-70-61-49), and another at No. 12, which offers more expensive items, including china decorated with 18-karat gold (phone: 47-70-54-49).

Other Paris Locations – A couple of other places in Paris are worth a detour for those seeking French expertise in matters breakable:

Raymond (100 Rue du Faubourg-St.-Honoré; phone: 42-66-69-49) is noteworthy for its charming and relatively inexpensive Porcelaine de Paris items, including coffee and tea sets, plates, soufflé dishes, mustard pots, and jam jars, all bedecked with wild strawberries, herbs, and garlands of French flowers.

Lalique, famed for its large pieces of sculptured, decorative crystal, has a shop at 11 Rue Royale (phone: 42-65-33-70).

WOMEN'S CLOTHING: The haute couture designers who put Paris on the map as the center of the fashion world still are flourishing in the French capital, and still welcoming those able to afford their distinctive and luxurious made-to-order clothing. However, they often sell much less expensive clothing of very high quality in couturier boutiques, usually at the same address:

Pierre Balmain, 44 Rue François-I, 8e (phone: 47-20-35-34)

Pierre Cardin, 14 Pl. François-I, 8e (phone: 45-63-29-13)

Chanel, 29-31 Rue Cambon, 1e (phone: 42-86-28-00) and 42 Av. Montaigne, 8e (phone: 47-20-84-45)

Christian Dior, 30 Av. Montaigne, 8e (phone: 40-73-54-44)

Louis Féraud, 88 Rue du Faubourg-St.-Honoré, 8e (phone: 47-42-18-12)

Givenchy, 3 Av. George-V, 8e (phone: 47-23-81-36)

Lanvin, 15, 17, and 22 Rue du Faubourg-St.-Honoré, 8e; 2 Rue Cambon, 1er (phone: 42-60-38-83)

Ted Lapidus, 35 Rue François-I, 8e (phone: 47-20-56-14)

Guy Laroche, 29 Av. Montaigne, 8e (phone: 47-23-78-72)

Hanae Mori, 17 Av. Montaigne, 8e (phone: 47-23-52-03)

Nina Ricci, 39 Av. Montaigne, 8e (phone: 47-23-78-88)

Yves Saint Laurent, 5 Av. Marceau, 16e (phone: 47-23-72-71)

Jean-Louis Scherrer, 51 Av. Montaigne, 8e (phone: 43-59-55-39). This is the bigger outlet (see below).

Per Spook, 18 Av. George-V, 8e (phone: 47-23-00-19)

Torrente, 3 Rond Point des Champs-Elysée, 8e (phone: 42-56-14-14)

Emmanuel Ungaro, 2 Av. Montaigne, 8e (phone: 47-23-61-94)

High-Fashion Bargains – The concept of selling at a discount is gradually catching on in France, and new designs from the top couturiers are available a season (sometimes only a few months) later at many outlets.

Bab's is one of a trio with an especially devoted following. Most couturiers are represented, and the selection of evening gowns at reasonable prices is exceptional. Several locations include one at 29 Av. Marceau (phone: 47-20-84-74).

Mendès, another shop particularly well loved by knowledgeable French women, specializes in the creations of Yves Saint Laurent; the winter season's designs are available beginning in mid-January and his summer collection from July 1 — all at substantial markdowns. There are mirrors everywhere, but no dressing rooms; it's the kind of place that inspires a lady to wear her best underwear. 65 Rue Montmartre (phone: 42-36-83-32 or 45-08-52-62).

Jean-Louis Scherrer is a bit out of the way, but it's possible to make its very inconvenience part of the pleasure of shopping and exploring. Prices for very fancy couturier labels run about 50% less than original retail. 29 Av. Ledru-Rollin (phone: 43-43-58-34).

Other shops selling high-fashion clothing at discounted prices include the following: *Boutique Stock* (26, 30, 5l, and 5 bis Rue St.-Placide); *Cacharel Stock* (114 Rue d'Alésia); *Club des 10* (58 Rue du Faubourg-St.-Honoré); *Dorothée Bis Stock* (74 Rue d'Alésia); *Drôles de Choses Pour Drôles de Gens* (14 Rue des Colonnes-du-Trône); *Halle Bys* (60 Rue Richelieu); *Le Mouton à Cinq Pattes* (6, 8, and 10 Rue St.-Placide); *Miss Griffes* (19 Rue de Penthièvre); *Pierre Cardin Stock* (72 Rue du Faubourg-St.-Honoré); *Stéphane* (130 Bd. St.-Germain); *Stock Griffes* (17 Rue Vielle du Temple); and *Stock System* (112 Rue d'Alésia).

Boutiques – The attractive and innovative clothing that the French so nicely call *votre bonheur,* "your happiness," is stocked at thousands of small boutiques all over the country. But nowhere are these so abundant as they are in Paris, most notably at the following shops:

Agnes B offers colorful and chic yet wearable fashions from its namesake designer, who has committed herself publicly to holding her prices down. 3 and 6 Rue du Jour (phone: 45-08-56-56 or 40-26-36-87), and other locations.

Dorothée Bis, long established though still avant garde, specializes in sportswear with a young look. 17 Rue de Sèvres (phone: 42-22-02-90).

Kenzo, with its flashy colors and whimsical shapes, is especially fun for young shoppers. 3 Pl. des Victoires (phone: 40-39-72-02).

Victoire is slightly crowded but congenial and packed with all types of attractive clothing from top ready-to-wear designers — and coordinated accessories to add extra dash. 12 Pl. des Victoires (phone: 45-08-53-29).

Lingerie – It's true that many Americans living in France buy their own lingerie in the US, swearing that American products are not only better made and better fitting but even less expensive and prettier than their French counterparts. But the lacy, frilly, silk undergarments sold in France, often covered with polka dots or dripping with ribbons, are the stuff of which fantasies are made, and lingerie makes a delightful souvenir.

Department stores carry a wide selection of brands, styles, and sizes and display their wares clearly, making choices simpler than in small shops, where much of the stock may be tucked in boxes behind the counter.

Cadolle was founded in 1889 by the woman widely credited with inventing the brassiere and is still run by her great-great and great-great-great-granddaughters. They sell charming, ribbon-bedecked garters and lacy bras as well as sturdy, made-to-measure corsets. 14 Rue Cambon (phone: 42-60-94-94).

Charley, just a few doors away from *Hermès,* offers an excellent selection, personal attention, and relatively low prices. 14 Rue du Faubourg-St.-Honoré (phone: 47-42-17-70).

Christian Dior, while sold all over the world and in many stores in France, makes a few exceptionally lovely articles, including ensembles of gowns and robes, which are sold only in the exclusive collection one flight up from the main Dior saleroom. 28-30 Av. Montaigne (phone: 40-73-54-44).

MEN'S CLOTHING: Men's clothing is not generally considered to be a good buy, and many a male has gone into shock after looking at a price tag. But for some, the blend of classic styling and French flair is irresistible.

Arnys offers Anglo-French conservatism and elegance in suits, jackets, and the other components of a gentleman's wardrobe. 14 Rue de Sèvres (phone: 45-48-76-99).

Charvet specializes in shirts, ties, and everything else for the complete *gentilhomme.* 28 Pl. Vendôme (phone: 42-60-30-70).

Daniel Hechter has clothing for a sporty lifestyle; it all has a touch of class. 146 Bd. St.-Michel (phone: 43-26-96-36).

Saint Laurent Rive Gauche is well known for its classic designs in suits, shoes, socks, and accessories. 38 Rue du Faubourg St.-Honoré (phone: 42-65-43-76).

CHILDREN'S CLOTHING: Gorgeous hand-smocked and hand-decorated clothing for babies and older children can still be found in France but at prices that are painfully high. For all but the most indulgent grandparents, the best idea is to head for department stores, which generally display a wide selection of charming clothing for youngsters, often decorated with motifs that make them look very French.

FOOD AND WINE: At any given point in France, it's possible to put together a sumptuous picnic by making exactly four stops: the closest *charcuterie,* or butcher shop, often much like a deli; the *fromagerie,* or cheese store; the *marchand de vin,* or wine merchant; and the *boulangerie,* or bakery. Usually, these shops will be within a block or two of one another, sometimes right next door.

Bordeaux – In this city, a shop known as *Cadiot Badie* sells excellent bonbons in pretty tin boxes. 26 Allées de Tourny (phone: 56-44-24-22).

Lyons – Some people take the TGV all the way from Paris just to indulge in the chocolates sold at *Bernachon.* 42 Cours Franklin-Roosevelt (phone: 78-24-37-98).

Paris – There are dozens of specialty shops in the capital.

Androuët is devoted to cheese, and many varieties are available either to eat in the restaurant upstairs or to take out. 41 Rue d'Amsterdam (phone: 48-74-26-90).

Berthillon sells such delicious ice cream that Parisians often line up outside for a small carton for a special party. Flavors, which change with the season, include wild strawberry, calvados crunch, and candied chestnut. 31 Rue St.-Louis-en-l'Ile (phone: 43-54-31-61). Several cafés on the Ile St.-Louis also serve scoops of Berthillon.

Fauchon is one of the world's great purveyors of food, and every day there's a new exhibition of fresh and packaged food from all corners of France and around the world, lavishly laid out with taste and style found nowhere else. Fine wine also is available, along with delicacies prepared in the shop's own *charcuterie.* Lotus tea (*tchando*) makes a special souvenir. The store is very experienced in shipping gift packages. The two original shops are at 26 Pl. de la Madeleine (phone: 47-42-60-11); a grocery and sweet shop has been added to *Fauchon's* new premises a few doors away at 30 Pl. de la Madeleine.

Hédiard, in business since 1854, sells an array of products similar to Fauchon's, but specializes in exotic fruit and spices. 21 Pl. de la Madeleine (phone: 42-66-44-36).

Legrand Fille et Fils offers an excellent selection of wine, including bottles that are both good and inexpensive, in a charming old wine shop near the city's stock market. 1 Rue de la Banque (phone: 42-60-07-12).

Lenôtre specializes in pastries and other desserts, and everything is exquisite, from the simplest éclair to the fruit mousses, charlottes, and chocolates. 44 Rue d'Auteuil (phone: 45-24-52-52).

La Maison de l'Escargot prepares and sells more than 10 tons of snails annually following a secret recipe that is 75 years old. 68 Rue Fondary (phone: 45-75-31-09).

Poilâne is considered by many French to sell the best bread in the country, and the large and crusty round country-style loaves dubbed *pain Poilâne,* baked in wood-burning ovens, taste delicious with soup, pâté, cheese, or cassoulet. 8 Rue du Cherche-Midi (phone: 45-48-42-59).

Caves de la Madeleine, a wine shop tucked away in a charming little street near the Madeleine, is run by an Englishman who stocks a wide selection of top-quality French wine — and even some vintages from California. 24 Rue Boissy d'Anglas (phone: 42-65-92-40).

HOUSEWARES: *Castorama,* a chain with 86 branches throughout the country, carries 45,000 different European designed basics for the home — from a simple flowerpot to a sophisticated security system. Although you may not want to cart home a bidet or a set of wrought-iron andirons (*Castorama* does not arrange shipping), you will find dozens of moderately priced and stylish smaller items — doorknobs, soap dishes, coat hooks, decorative door plaques — that will travel well and add European panache to your home. Forget about electrical wall switches and anything else you have to connect to existing wiring; the two systems are not compatible.

Paris: Near the St.-Lazare railway station, in the basement of a shopping complex, 1-3 Rue Caulaincourt, 18e (phone: 45-22-07-11).

Antibes: Péage d'Antibes, Rte. de Grasse (phone: 93-33-53-30).

JEWELRY: Several of the world's greatest jewelers are clustered around the elegant Pl. Vendôme in Paris — a dazzling place to window shop if not to pick up an heirloom or two.

Boucheron, 26 Pl. Vendôme (phone: 42-61-58-16)

Cartier, 13 Rue de la Paix (phone: 42-61-58-56)

Van Cleef & Arpels, 22 Pl. Vendôme (phone: 42-61-58-58)

KITCHENWARE: In a country that reveres cooking among the highest of the arts, it is not surprising to find an abundance of kitchen items at nearly every turn.

Paris – Pots and pans that are almost sculptural in their classic beauty are everywhere, as are odd-looking gadgets that perform tasks that most cooks never even imagined. Department stores provide an overview of both the most traditonal and the latest utensils in the world of French cookery. But for real fun, a cook simply cannot beat a store devoted solely to kitchen supplies:

E. Dehillerin is where some of the finest chefs in France have gone to supply their kitchens for the last 150 years. The 2 stories are stacked from nearly floor to ceiling with pots and pans in copper, cast iron, and tin plate in an array that ranges from tiny saucepans to enormous stockpots; with fine carbon steel knives; and with all kinds of casseroles. A number of fascinating little bins contain just about every kind of kitchen accessory conceivable. 18 Rue Coquillière (phone: 42-36-53-13).

Villedieu-les-Poëles – This small, rural Norman town takes its name from the *poëles,* frying pans, that have been made here in copper for 300 years, and from one end of the main street to the other, copper gleams through the glass shop windows. Pots come in all different gauges and sizes, and the prices vary accordingly. It is possible to save money over stateside prices for comparable merchandise, but the variety is such that it's necessary to come armed with the exact specifications of the pots you want. About 200 miles west of Paris, 14 miles (22 km) northeast of Avranches, and 21 miles (33.5 km) south of St.-Lô.

LEATHER GOODS: It is a pleasure to shop for leather goods in France, especially in the best establishments, where every piece of merchandise from the key cases to the steamer trunks is impeccably designed and perfectly crafted. Bear in mind, however, that lower-quality leather goods are probably more expensive and not as well made as comparable items in the US.

Americans should be aware that some exotic skins that are sold legally in France — including certain species of alligator, crocodile, ostrich, and lizard — could be seized on arrival back home, since these animals are on the Endangered Species List in the United States. The best French stores will steer American shoppers to merchandise that meets US import laws, but it's still wise to check the latest regulations with the US Fish and Wildlife Service before leaving home.

Nice – In all of France, the seemingly ubiquitous Louis Vuitton handbags, capacious satchels, suitcases, and dozens of other items (most marked with LVs) — many for traveling — are sold at only three stores, one here (2 Av. de Suède; phone: 93-87-87-47) and the other two in Paris (78 bis Av. Marceau; phone: 47-20-47-00; and 54 Av. Montaigne; phone: 45-62-47-00).

Paris – The capital abounds in shops purveying the finest of leather goods.

Céline, whose subdued setting is as classy as its merchandise, offers especially nice small shoulder bags in a great variety of colors and skins. 24 Rue François-I (phone: 47-20-22-83).

Hermès, generally considered *the* place to find leather objects of quality and beauty (at extremely high prices), stocks classics such as the popular Constance and Kelly models in a wealth of sizes, skins, and colors. And there are attaché cases, suitcases, saddles, and small address books and coin purses that make useful and eminently packable gifts of great cachet. 24 Rue du Faubourg-St.-Honoré (phone: 40-17-47-17).

PERFUME: For centuries, the French have been making enticing scents that are synonymous with luxury and romance, and around the world, in all languages, the adjective that springs most quickly to mind to modify the word "perfume" is "French." Consequently, it's not surprising that perfume heads the shopping lists of more visitors to France than any other item. And department stores around the country, which generally carry the best selections of all the well-known brands (except Guerlain, which sells only from its own shops), do a booming business among tourists.

But today, with virtually all names and sizes of French perfume available in US stores, is there any reason beyond this mystique to buy French perfume in France?

The answer is yes. By shopping in the right places and following the rules for getting tax refunds as described below, it's possible to save considerable money — and to pay as little as a third of the price of some of France's most expensive and sought-after perfumes. Even without the additional reduction afforded by the tax refund, in fact, the cost of French perfume in a department store is roughly two-thirds of what you would pay stateside.

Do not be taken in by the flashy Tax Free signs sported by perfume stores all over the country. Most shops, the major department stores included, sell basically the same brands and sizes at rates set by the manufacturers. Regardless of where you shop, the perfume becomes tax free only after you have purchased enough of it at a single store to qualify for the tax refund set up by the government. The exception, airport duty-free shops, sell without tax even on small bottles of inexpensive perfumes; the selection is more limited in city stores, however.

Grasse – Visitors to this town, which is perched in the hills 11 miles (18 km) from Cannes and 26 miles (42 km) from Nice and has been an international perfume making center since the 16th century, probably will want to visit a perfume works to see for themselves how the floral essences that go into almost all of their favorite French perfume are extracted from tons of locally grown and imported flowers. They also can view the small plots where neighborhood farmers cultivate jasmine and roses (half a dozen tons of whose petals are required to produce just a quart of essence) or, about 20 minutes into the rocky heights above the town, gather their own fragrant bouquets of wild lavender that grow in beautiful violet patches by the roadside.

The large factories that produce vast quantities of perfume, soap, and cosmetics are closed to the public because of the volatile chemicals they use. However, the laboratories of three manufacturing concerns are open for free tours, during which guides explain in English, French, and other languages how the essences are extracted and distilled and show off magnificent old copper machinery full of curves and spirals:

Fragonard also has an attractive museum of objects associated with perfume since antiquity. 20 Bd. Fragonard (phone: 93-36-44-65).

Galimard is at Esplanade du Cours (phone: 93-36-08-21).

Molinard can be found about a mile from the heart of town. 60 Bd. Victor-Hugo (phone: 93-36-01-62).

The sales rooms in which the tours end are full of pretty souvenirs and small gifts to take home, such as scented candles, soaps, and sachets of lavender and potpourri as well as dozens of bottles of fragrance in all sizes and forms. Each *parfumerie* sells just its own creations — which include not only the brands that are associated with their houses but also many with unfamiliar names that are imitations of the popular scents of other houses (such as YSL's Opium). Discounts of about 5% are available here, and many of the virtually unknown scents are so inexpensive that no one has to think twice about taking a chance on a new perfume.

Paris – In the capital, there are two good addresses for buying perfume. *Michel Swiss* (16 Rue de la Paix; phone: 42-61-71-71) offers a voluminous selection, cheerful service, discounts of 25% for payment with cash or traveler's checks (20% for credit cards), and, in addition, a 25% tax refund on the balance to American visitors who spend more than 800 francs (about $133). That brings the total discount to almost 44%. *Catherine* gives a 40% discount — including VAT — on purchases totaling 1,200F (about $210) or more (6 Rue Castiglione; phone: 42-60-81-49).

SHOES: France is a country for shoe fiends, and it is full of places to buy footwear that is not only stylish but also — probably because the French walk a good deal themselves and refuse to clump around in ugly shoes — comfortable.

Nationwide, look for the *André* and *Raoul* chains, which stock surprisingly inexpensive shoes in the latest styles and colors — and are consquently the source for the shoe wardrobe of many a fashion-crazy French high school girl.

Paris – This city offers an additional supply of exceptional shoe stores that have few equals in the rest of the country:

Carel sells classy shoes in the latest shapes and colors — sometimes, but not always, suited to the American foot. At several locations, including 12 Rond-Point des Champs-Elysées (phone: 45-62-30-62).

France Faver offers stylish beauty and welcome comfort in its shoes. They are moderately expensive, but the quality makes them worth the price. 79 Rue des Sts.-Pères (phone: 42-22-04-29).

Maud Frizon offers some of the most sophisticated shoes in Paris. The designs are often lovely and usually costly, especially the boots. 79 Rue des Sts.-Pères (phone: 42-22-06-93).

Charles Jourdan sells high-fashion shoes of good quality. 86 Av. des Champs-Elysées and other locations (phone: 45-62-29-28).

FABRIC: The colorful and distinctive cotton fabrics of the south of France make a delightful souvenir. In Aix-en-Provence, bags, bedspreads, eyeglass cases, and other articles made of this cloth — as well as the cloth by the yard — are available at *Les Olivades,* 5 Rue des Chaudronniers (phone: 42-23-57-47).

HOW TO GET A TAX REFUND

The values available to visitors in France on certain merchandise become even more compelling when the refund offered by the French government of its special value-added tax (VAT) is added to existing bargains. (See *Shopping* in GETTING READY TO GO for a detailed discussion of the VAT system and tax-free stores.)

To qualify, visitors must be at least 15 years of age, must reside outside France, and must have visited in the country for less than 6 months. No refunds are offered for purchases of food, wine, or tobacco.

To receive a refund, a visitor must spend at least 1,200F (about $210) in a single shop and must show a passport to prove eligibility. The clerk will then give the buyer an export sales document in triplicate, which must be signed and saved, and an envelope addressed to the store. When leaving France, both the forms and the purchased goods must be taken to the French Customs *détaxe* (tax refund) booth. Note that tax formalities must be taken care of *before* checking baggage and *before* going through passport control at an airport or *before* boarding a train at a station.

The same person who signed the refund forms in the store must present the envelope and the three sheets to the customs officials (who will return one, countersigned, to the buyer in case of later difficulties). The tax refund may be paid immediately at an airport bank window, but more often the traveler will receive a check mailed from the store. Sometimes, if the buyer pays by credit card, the store makes out a credit slip for the amount of the tax and processes the credit after receiving the validated refund forms from French customs. Or the store may simply make up a separate charge slip for the tax and tear it up when the forms arrive.

Casinos Royal

 To anyone who has been brought up on the high-rolling, honky-tonk gambling supermarkets of Las Vegas and Atlantic City, the hushed elegance of France's 153 casinos, Europe's most elaborate gaming network, will require some adjustment — and perhaps some classier clothes. But even for those who only toss an occasional chip onto those lush meadows of felt, the spectacle at the great pleasure domes of Monte Carlo and Deauville is well worth the modest price of admission. Set in some of France's major resort towns (but forbidden within 60 miles — 96 km — of Paris by Napoleonic decree), they draw a crowd that is a heady mixture of Parisian chic and Arab sheik. The scenario is pure Hollywood. In fact, behind all the glitter is a system of tight surveillance by the Brigade des Jeux, France's special branch of gaming police, and a gambling code that regulates everything from the odds on the slot machines to the dinner jacket on the croupier — which has (by law) no pockets. The result is an almost totally aboveboard industry, though internecine squabbles among operators have occasionally evoked memories of Chicago in the 1920s. Players are nonetheless fairly certain to lose their money according to the inexorable laws of mathematics.

Passports are required for admission. Though marathon games of chemin-de-fer are allowed to continue until the players drop, most French casinos open in mid-afternoon and close at 3 or 4 AM day in and day out. Dress has become far more casual in recent years, but there still are many casinos where jacket and tie are de rigueur for gentlemen; in any case, it's always better to err on the side of decorum. A number of the larger casinos have glamorous, first-rate restaurants right on the gaming room floor; their waiters discreetly reheat the food of those kept away from their meal by a winning streak.

The staples of the French casino diet are roulette, baccarat, and boule; craps and blackjack increasingly are in evidence, the result of creeping Americanization. If you're not familiar with the rules or the vocabulary, many casinos will provide an explanatory booklet. And still others have roving *chefs de partie* (game chiefs), who will be more than happy to help a player who doesn't mind looking the greenhorn in the midst of all that savoir-faire.

AIX-LES-BAINS, Savoie: At this ancient thermal resort where the Romans once frolicked, titled matrons fresh from the sulfurous mudbaths hoard their chips in silver mesh purses. Hotels bear names like *Iles-Britanniques* and *Angleterre*. And streets are called Victoria and Pierpont Morgan. There is a faintly *fin-de-siècle* feeling to it all — from the gaming tables in the *Palais de Savoie,* one of France's most distinguished and stately casinos, to the more contemporary *Nouveau Casino* only a chip's throw away. The town lolls at the foot of the Alps on the east bank of lovely Lac du Bourget. When the chips are up, try the half-day boat tour of the lake, which includes the Royal Abbey of Hautecombe. Information: *Palais de Savoie,* Rue du Casino (phone: 79-35-16-16); and *Nouveau Casino,* 36 Av. Victoria, Aix-les-Bains 73100 (phone: 79-35-10-10).

LA BAULE, Loire-Atlantique: Gambling is so deeply ingrained in the spirit of this busy, pleasure-mad resort in southern Brittany that the main waterfront promenade, the Esplanade François-André, is reverently named after the founder of a great chain of French casinos. In a manicured park opposite the regal *Royal* hotel, the town's casino has a kitschy 1930s charm inside that comes as a surprise in view of its creamy façade and soaring arched windows. Its restaurant, *Le Bistengo,* serves the best fish in town until 1 AM, and its gold lamé night spot, the *Tropicana,* has dining and dancing until dawn in season. Anyone who should happen to rise before the next evening's gaming can shine for a few hours on the resort's splendid 3-mile sweep of beach or on the couple of dozen perfectly maintained clay tennis courts; yacht basins, equestrian centers, and all manner of other facilities effectively banish boredom at La Baule. Information: *Le Casino,* Esplanade François-André, La Baule 44500 (phone: 40-60-20-23).

BIARRITZ, Pyrénées-Atlantiques: The two casinos in this most aristocratic resort attracted kings and princesses to the Atlantic coast long before the reign of the Riviera. Queen Victoria vacationed here, and it was here that King Farouk, a regular, once flipped his solid gold lighter across the roulette table to a lady in need of a light — and then watched while she promptly handed it to the croupier as a tip. Both the *Bellevue,* set on the cliffs and guarding the beach below like a sentry, and the *Municipal Casino,* on the sand of the Grande Plage, still operate as casinos. Just beyond the Grande Plage, great gilt-edged hotels like the *Palais, Miramar,* and *Regina et Golf,* which line the Avenue Impératrice, gaze out to sea on a cluster of tiny islands scattered like dice on the blue table of the ocean. Information: *Casino Bellevue,* Pl. Bellevue, Biarritz 64200 (phone: 59-24-11-22).

CANNES, Alpes-Maritimes: The classy *Palm Beach,* whose receipts always are among the highest in France despite its short summer season, now has been joined by the *Casino Croisette* opposite the old harbor. As a result, it's now possible to go broke gracefully all year in this chic resort town. At the other tip of the fashionable Boulevard de la Croisette, the *Palm Beach* sports a swimming pool at the edge of the sea and outdoor dining and dancing by the water with the orchestra in full lilt. "Le Winter," as the *Casino Croisette* is known, has a theater that brings top talent from Paris — everything from *West Side Story* to Nureyev. Information: *Palm Beach Casino,* Bd. de la Croisette, Cannes 06406 (phone: 93-43-91-12); and the *Casino Croisette,* Palais des Festivals, Jetée Albert-Edouard, Cannes 06406 (phone: 93-38-12-11).

DEAUVILLE, Calvados: A gleaming vanilla villa by the sea, the *Deauville* casino and environs have often been called "the 21st Arrondissement of Paris." A playground of the 19th-century jet set, Deauville is in its patrician prime during the July-August horse racing season, when formal dress may still be de rigueur in certain of the casino's sanctums. Trouville, Deauville's neighbor across the River Touques, offers comparable sport, not to mention horseback riding from one end of the beach to the other. The *Deauville* casino also owns two of the town's other delights — the Norman, wooden-gabled *Hôtel Normandy* and a deluxe lobster joint named *Ciro's,* both on the eminently strollable boardwalk and both described at greater length in *Romantic French Hostelries* and *Haute Gastronomie* in this section. Information: *Casino de Deauville,* Rue Edmond-Blanc, Deauville 14800 (phone: 31-98-66-66).

DIVONNE-LES-BAINS, Ain: Open year-round, Divonne is France's top moneymaking casino. In a sleepy border village at the foot of the Juras, it is only about 10 miles (16 km) from vice-free Switzerland and a quarter of an hour from the Geneva Airport. Consequently, the clientele is both prosperous and varied and includes a number of people staying in Geneva for reasons of foreign commerce or private finance. The local thermal baths specialize in dunking "the fatigued, the anguished, and the insomniac"; the lush golf course ranks among France's finest; and there is tranquil sailing on the artificial lake. The centerpiece of a luxurious park and hotel complex, the casino sponsors most of the town's cultural events — most notably the highly reputed summer chamber music festival. Everything from Jura farmyard specialties to Persian caviar is available in the casino's excellent restaurant, which is right on the gaming room floor. Information: *Le Casino,* Av. de la Divonne, Divonne-les-Bains 01220 (phone: 50-20-06-63).

EVIAN-LES-BAINS, Haute-Savoie: Divonne's competitor for the Swiss connection, the town of Evian is about 25 miles (40 km) by road from Geneva or 40 minutes by boat across Lake Geneva; its casino — a late-19th-century gaming palace that complements that other Evian pleasure dome, the Thermal Baths — is just a few yards from the boat dock. Stroll past the Baths along the animated, flower-decked Quai de Blonay, where the high born and the high rollers alike contemplate the lake at cocktail hour, and savor the vestiges of the world of wealth and idleness enjoyed by Marcel Proust, who stayed here at the turn of the century. Take a a room at the *Royal,* the most sumptuous hotel in the region — it's a good place to spend any winnings. Information: *Casino Municipal,* Evian-les-Bains 74500 (phone: 50-75-03-78).

FORGES-LES-EAUX, Seine-Maritime: Just outside the 60-mile (96-km) roulette-free zone that Napoleon decreed must surround Paris, Forges attracts all the capital's players who don't want to risk the wheels at the city's various *clandés,* as its clandestine gaming dives are called. Those who can't face the predawn drive back to Paris can stay at the delightful *Grand Hôtel du Parc,* right in the casino complex — and those who lose enough in the course of the evening are guests of the management. Information: *Casino de Forges,* Av. des Sources, Forges-les-Eaux 76440 (phone: 39-09-80-12).

JUAN-LES-PINS, Alpes-Maritimes: The *Eden Beach,* the casino in Juan-les-Pins, actually was founded in 1928 by a Riviera regular, the American industrialist Frank Jay Gould. Nestled between those two specialties of Juan-les-Pins, the emerald pines and the royal blue sea, it became shortly thereafter — and remains today — a principal center for all that is sleekest on the Côte d'Azur nightlife scene. The restaurant is right on the beach, and those who go out for a breath of air between rounds of chemin-de-fer can hear the rhythmic throb of the all-night jazz clubs that animate the town. Nearby, in Antibes, there's the huge *Siesta* casino entertainment complex, which resembles nothing so much as a Mexican village for plutocrats, with 3 restaurants and 5 dance floors — a trio of which are under the stars. Gamble here if you will — but dine at *Le Bacon,* one of the Riviera's temples of the table. Information: *Eden Beach Casino,* Chemin des Sables, Juan-les-Pins 06160 (phone: 93-61-00-29).

MONTE CARLO, Principauté de Monaco: When the brash and brassy Las Vegas-style *Loews Casino* (see *Monaco,* THE CITIES) began to cut into the receipts of Monte Carlo's own staid dowager of a casino, the most legendary in Europe, the latter — designed by Charles Garnier, the architect of *L'Opéra* in Paris — pulled on a pair of jeans over its ball gown and turned its rococo and splendidly gilt Salon de l'Europe into the American Room, all a-clatter with slot machines, fitted out with craps and black-jack tables, staffed by Las Vegas-trained managers and bartenders adept at making screwdrivers and Bloody Marys — and imposing no entrance fee or dress regulations. Still, there are paintings, murals full of nudes, and other Belle Epoque touches throughout, and the old and elegant Salon Privé (Private Room) is as decorous as ever; a passport and admission fee must be presented at the door. The cloistered sanctum known as the Salon Super-Privé, equipped with one table for *banque-à-tout-va,* is available by appointment only; the very knowledge that you have played there should forever banish the need to wear Gucci loafers or drive a Ferrari to prove your worth. Try to get a glimpse of the casino's ornate and fabled theater, a lavish study in gold leaf, scrolls, and garlands, where Lily Pons, Nijinsky, Caruso, and Sarah Bernhardt all performed, the last on opening night in 1879. And to vary the summer gaming diet, stop in at the water's-edge *Monte Carlo Sporting Club,* built on a sea-rimmed, manmade promontory a few miles out of town; there is discreet lighting, a Starlight Room with a 3,300-square-foot roof that opens to the sky, and a Polynesian restaurant nestled amid tropical gardens. Information: *Société des Bains de Mer,* Pl. du Casino, Monte Carlo, Principauté de Monaco 98000 (phone: 93-50-69-31).

Most Visitable Vineyards

 It's hard to know just what to expect at a vineyard in France. Arrive when the winemaker is in a chatty, outgoing mood and you may end up staying for hours, sharing recent vintages and discussing French politics and the state of French wine. Another day, you may find yourself in the hands of an ambitious young peasant farmer just getting started in the business, and the next you'll be visiting a château where a wealthy wine maker follows family rules and techniques that go back centuries. In almost every case, a vineyard visit includes a wander through the château's tasting room, normally attached to the cellars, where guests settle down and the most recent vintages are uncorked. Usually, these tastings are free; the wine also is available for purchase. Though almost every vineyard in France welcomes visitors, it always is a good idea to call ahead. Spring and summer visitors are more welcome than those who come in fall, when the harvest keeps the vineyard's entire staff occupied nearly around the clock. Note that although many do not keep official hours — wine makers are farmers, after all — it's most polite to arrive between 10 AM and noon or between 2 and 5 PM.

Consider taking a summer course in wine wisdom with the *CIDD (Centre d'Information, de Documentation, et de Dégustation),* which includes in its program visits to vineyards and wine cellars. The center has a wide range of activities in English, and occasionally holds an open house to introduce little-known wines to the public. Open Monday through Friday from 1 to 7 PM. Information: *CIDD,* 45 Rue Liancourt, Paris 75014 (phone: 43-27-67-21).

The following is a sampling of France's vineyards; they offer a variety of styles of wine made by a wide assortment of wine makers, who espouse not only different methods of wine making but also varying merchandising programs.

ALSACE: The wines of this area are fragrant, fruity, and white, ordinarily drunk while still young. And they are named for the variety of grape that went into them. Gewürztraminer is dry and spicy, with a certain zing. Pinot Gris, also known as Tokay d'Alsace, is broad and full-bodied. Riesling is at once dry and fruity, crisp and elegant. And sylvaner, the most plentiful of all, has a distinctive freshness that makes it a fine apéritif.

Léon Beyer, Eguisheim, Haut-Rhin – The Beyer family, tending its vineyards since 1850, makes one of the best and best-known wines of the Alsace wine making region, which is in the foothills of the Vosges mountains facing the Rhine River — a region that, incidentally, offers some of the most charming and lovable villages in all of France. Beyer's riesling shows up on the wine lists of such famous three-star restaurants as *Taillevent* in Paris and *Auberge de l'Ill* in Illhaeusern. The firm's tasting room is in Eguisheim, a most historic and attractive Alsace town full of tidy stone and timber houses with geranium-filled windowboxes. The town, which is centered around a main square with a handsome Renaissance fountain, is on the Wine Road, which takes in several other wineries in the area. See also the tour route *Alsace,* DIRECTIONS. Information: *Léon Beyer,* Eguisheim 68420 (phone: 89-41-41-05).

Hugel et Fils, Riquewihr, Haut-Rhin – Visitors to these caves — in a pair of 16th-century houses that have been gutted to make room for the winery — see what's believed to be the oldest cask in the world still in constant use. It was made in 1715 and holds more than 8,800 quarts. Hugel is respected for its elegant, round, supple, well-balanced wines, particularly the dry riesling, with its round bouquet, and its rich, spicy, full-bodied gewürztraminer. The entire town is a historical monument, and the main street is so packed with remarkably well preserved houses that it would warrant a visit in its own right. Information: *Hugel et Fils,* Riquewihr 68340 (phone: 89-47-92-15).

BORDEAUX: From the flat terrain with its precise rows of vines punctuated by red roses near the roadsides to the attractive villages where the wine business occupies everyone — from the joiners who knock together the cases for the bottles to the printers who make up the labels — this region is the home of some of the richest wine country in the world. The vines of the Médoc, the region that stretches along the bank of the Gironde River between Bordeaux and the Bay of Biscay, set the standard. Margaux, Pauillac, St.-Estèphe, and St.-Julien are among the principal towns, and the area around them has road signs for nearly every château. The *Maison du Vin* in Bordeaux (1 Cours du 30-Juillet, Bordeaux 33075; phone: 56-00-22-66) can provide a list of those open to the public. See also *Bordeaux and the Médoc,* DIRECTIONS.

Château Palmer, Margaux, Gironde – Although the famous turreted château that's featured on the elegant and distinctive label of this vineyard's wine can be visited much of the year, it is most popular as a tourist attraction at vintage time, usually in September, since it is one of the few vineyards where visitors can see the old-fashioned destalking of grapes by hand on a wooden tray. The Dutch, French, and British flags fluttering outside honor its successful (if rather unusual) tri-national ownership. Visits are generally available weekdays from 9 to 11:30 AM and from 2 to 5:30 PM, but call ahead. See also *Bordeaux and the Médoc,* DIRECTIONS. Information: *Château Palmer,* Margaux 33460 (phone: 56-88-72-72).

Château Prieuré-Lichine, Margaux, Gironde – The late Alexis Lichine, the best known and most respected American wine maker in France, worked to make the wines of the Château Prieuré-Lichine — in a former Benedictine priory — among the finest and most fragrant produced on the 2,500 vineyard acres cultivated around Margaux. Visitors might find M. Lichine offering neighborly advice at the nearby Château Margaux or just back from a trip to the United States, where he does much to promote French wines in general through his writing and personal appearances. The old cloister remains are decked out with fanciful antique cast-iron firebacks that Lichine has collected from all over Europe, and the vat room with its craggy beams was built by the monks who tended the vines long before Lichine was a gleam in his father's eye. Visits are possible from 9:30 AM to 6 PM daily in winter, to 7 PM in summer. Call for an appointment. See also *Bordeaux and the Médoc,* DIRECTIONS. Information: *Château Prieuré-Lichine,* Margaux 33460 (phone: 56-88-36-28).

Château Beauséjour-Becot, St.-Emilion, Gironde – A visitor who comes to this friendly wine maker's château with a few hours on his hands almost certainly will hear, if not Baudelaire, at least the story of how the small but now prosperous 16-acre property was rescued from decline some years ago. M. Becot loves to quote Baudelaire, to sing the well-deserved praise of St.-Emilion (both the wine and the charming hilltop village), and to receive visitors — and when the spirit moves him, he sometimes passes out "before" and "after" samples to document the big changes that have occurred since his arrival. See also *Bordeaux,* THE CITIES. Information: *Château Beauséjour-Becot,* St.-Emilion 33330 (phone: 57-74-46-87).

BURGUNDY: Burgundian wines include the dry and flinty white made in Chablis; the aromatic, full-bodied reds and whites made south of Dijon in the Côte d'Or; and the light and fruity reds made in Beaujolais. Great wine producing villages are as common as corn in Kansas: Chambertin, Chassagne-Montrachet, Gevrey-Chambertin, Meursault, Mâcon, Morey-St.-Denis, Nuits St.-Georges, Pommard, Puligny-Montrachet, Pommard, and others. A *Musée du Vin de Bourgogne* in Beaune documents the cultivation of the grape and wine making down through history; there are tours on the hour. Rue d'Enfer (phone: 80-22-08-19).

Domaine de la Romanée-Conti, Auxey-Duresses, Côte d'Or – The main gate of one of the world's most famous vineyards is hidden in the back streets of Vosne Romanée and visitors are received by appointment only — but then the wines of the Domaine, including the fabulously expensive Romanée-Conti (of which only 6,000 bottles are produced each year) and the equally well known La Tache — are among the most expensive and revered in the world. Even the likes of Nikita Khrushchev have signed their names in the crimson and gold guestbook. For appointments, contact the *Négociant Leroy,* Auxey-Duresses, Meursault 21120 (phone: 80-21-21-10).

Domaine Henri Gouges, Nuits St.-Georges, Côte d'Or – The village of Nuits St.-Georges produces some admirable reds known for their characteristic earthy flavor (*gout de terroir*), and some of Burgundy's best known of these wines come from Domaine Henri Gouges, which supplies Paris's *Taillevent* with the remarkable and rare white wine of the region as well as full-bodied reds. M. Gouges, an amiable man, receives visitors by appointment only. Information: *Domaine Henri Gouges,* 28 Rue du Moulin, Nuits St.-Georges 21700 (phone: 80-61-04-40).

Georges Duboeuf, Romanèche-Thorins, Saône-et-Loire – Beaujolais, once a cheap bar wine, is now enjoyed the world over for its fresh, fruity flavor. The area in which it is produced is unquestionably one of France's most picturesque wine regions, and M. Duboeuf is highly respected by his neighbors and colleagues. When visiting him, take the time to drive at least a portion of Beaujolais's Route du Vin, beginning at Juliénas, passing through Chenas, Pontanevaux, then on to Romanèche-Thorins. Open to wine professionals only with an appointment. Information: *Georges Duboeuf,* Romanèche-Thorins 71570 (phone: 85-35-51-13).

CAHORS: This tranquil village, one of the principal gateways to the south of France, is most famous for the hearty red wine made from the grapes grown on the hills along the Lot to the west of town.

Clos de Gamot, Prayssac, Lot – This establishment is a good place to sample some of the "black wine of Cahors." Jean Jouffreau, an excellent and remarkably gregarious grower, tends his vines without chemical sprays and ages his wine in oak casks. The result is a liquid that is dark and weighty, with overtones of cassis, some say; others love it for its vigor and its ability to stand up to the robust food of the region — cassoulet, truffles, *confit,* and hearty breads. Information: *Clos de Gamot,* Prayssac 46220 (phone: 65-22-40-26).

CHAMPAGNE: It was the Romans who planted the first vines in this region an hour and a half from Paris, the northernmost vine growing area in the country; and despite a succession of wars, from the Hundred Years War to World War II, the Champenois have been tending their vines, harvesting their grapes, and bottling their vintages nearly ever since. The sparkling beverage known as champagne, made according to a process developed at the end of the 17th century, is still the lifeblood of the region. Tourist information offices throughout the area publish standard Champagne itineraries and maintain signs along the routes. And a colorful museum full of regional maps, agricultural tools, wine presses, and labels has been set up in the 19th-century Château Perrier. See also *Champagne,* DIRECTIONS.

Ricciuti-Révolte, Avenay-Val-d'Or, Marne – That this bubbly is often described as the champagne with the Baltimore flavor is because the wine maker, Albert Ricciuti, is a Baltimorean who married a Frenchwoman whose family also happened to produce champagne. It all started in 1944, when Mr. Ricciuti, then an American soldier, helped liberate the village of Avenay-Val-d'Or. He met a young Frenchwoman, corresponded with her for 18 years, then returned for a visit. Marriage followed, and since 1963 he's been part of the family champagne business. Mr. Ricciuti is an outgoing, jovial man who loves showing visitors around his vineyards and cellars. Information: *Ricciuti-Révolte,* Avenay-Val-d'Or, Ay 51160 (phone: 26-52-30-27).

Moët & Chandon, Epernay, Marne – The best way to learn about champagne is to watch the painstaking care with which it is made. And one of the best-organized spots to do this is at Moët & Chandon, whose vast and impressive cellars — if not the most beautiful in the area, then certainly the biggest, with their 17 miles of galleries — can be seen on entertaining guided tours daily from April through October, weekdays only the rest of the year. Most impressive is the sight of the *rémueurs,* the men who carefully, and rapidly, turn each bottle precisely one quarter turn (a process called "riddling"). Afterward, guides offer each visitor a drink of the famous white-and-bubbly. Open from 9:30 AM to noon or 12:30 PM and from 2 to 4:30 or 5:30 PM, depending on the day and the season. A museum devoted to the wine as well as several other cellars are along the Avenue de Champagne, and the Syndicat d'Initiative on the same street distributes a pamphlet listing their hours. Information: *Moët & Chandon,* 20 Av. de Champagne, Epernay 51205 (phone: 26-54-71-11).

CÔTES DU RHÔNE: The wines of this area usually are red and ordinarily robust; Châteauneuf-du-Pape, the most famous wine of the southern vineyards of this area, and the flavorful Gigondas, a close second, are just two examples. Those specifically labeled Côtes du Rhône and Côtes du Rhône Villages are particularly soft and flavorful.

Caves des Vignerons, Beaumes-de-Venise, Vaucluse – The sweet white wine from Beaumes-de-Venise and a fresh melon from nearby Cavaillon, in the south of France, make one of the finest food combinations in the world. The cooperative at Beaumes-de-Venise sells one of the better-known versions of the naturally sweet local dessert wines as well as a variety of other wines, including Côtes du Rhône Villages and Côtes du Ventoux. Information: *Caves des Vignerons,* Beaumes-de-Venise 84190 (phone: 90-62-94-45).

Domaine de Mont-Redon, Châteauneuf-du-Pape, Vaucluse – In the spotless tasting rooms at this largest, best known, and most respected of the Châteauneuf-du-Pape estates, visitors may sample various recent vintages of Châteauneuf-du-Pape red, a hearty blend of 13 different grape varieties, as well as a lesser-known white that rarely finds its way out of the region. The estate also is proud of its small production of *eau-de-vie,* a clear liquor made from grape pressings; only about 2,000 bottles are produced each year and most are sold at the château. Information: *Domaine de Mont-Redon,* Châteauneuf-du-Pape 84230 (phone: 90-83-72-75).

Gigondas, Vaucluse – Right in the center of this sleepy little village, visitors will find a tasting room where more than 20 different versions of the heady local red, Gigondas, may be sampled. One of the finest comes from Georges Faraud, whose farmhouse is at the edge of the village; his classic, long-lived red received praise from French as well as American critics, and visitors receive a most cordial welcome. Information: *Syndicat d'Initiative,* Gigondas 84190 (phone: 90-65-85-46).

Domaine de la Gautière, La Penne sur Ouvèze, Drôme – Deep in the heart of French lavender country, the Tardieus run a small organic farm where they raise bees for honey, tend ancient olive trees that yield exquisite black olives and fruity, golden olive oil, and produce a delicious red country wine that seems to taste even better when sipped on the family patio. The honey, the olives, the oil, and the wine are all for sale here, and there's a campground attached to the property. Information: *Domaine de la Gautière,* La Penne sur Ouvèze, Buis-les-Barronies 26170 (phone: 75-28-09-58).

Cooperative Vinicole Vinsobraise, Vinsobres, Drôme – The French of this region usually buy their wine in bulk, and usually from a cooperative such as that at Vinsobraise, a large, active group just outside the village of Vinsobres, which makes a strong, substantial wine that ages well and also some lesser-known whites and rosés. All can be sampled at the *Cooperative*'s bar, where visitors also will see local wine makers bringing in their wines and buyers coming in with huge plastic containers for refilling. Information: *Cooperative Vinicole Vinsobraise,* Vinsobres 26110 (phone: 75-27-64-22).

Learning the Culinary Arts:
Cooking Schools

The cooking schools of France are as varied as the nation's landscape and regional cuisine. Visitors can study with famous chefs such as Gaston Lenôtre and Roger Vergé. They can gain hands-on experience at the most classic of all cooking schools — Paris's Le Cordon Bleu. And they can take courses with farm wives in the rustic kitchens of the Quercy and the Dordogne in the southwest. Travelers who want to look behind the scenes at restaurant kitchens or to visit the wholesale markets where the chefs themselves shop can go on tour with Robert Noah in Paris. Many schools will tailor special courses for groups of ten or more. The choice is limited only by one's vision and by one's command of French, a knowledge of which goes a long way toward making the experience meaningful, even though translators are usually available. Programs tend to be casual and are geared to novices and experts alike. The point is to go with an open mind and a willing spirit, ready to acquire a few additional culinary skills and authentic French experiences — and have a good time besides.

A few words of advice on planning a trip. Don't be afraid to go alone. Many lifelong international friendships have been struck over magnificent soufflés. Most schools operate year-round, and courses in Paris are good anytime; those offered in the southwest and in Provence are probably better in late spring and early fall, when the countryside is at its most beautiful and the pace is a bit less hectic. In any case, be sure to send away for brochures and read them carefully before booking so that you know exactly what to expect.

PROVENÇAL COOKING SCHOOL, Gordes, Provence: Sylvie Lallemand — who speaks English — learned to cook at her Provençal mother's knee, and she passes on the best of the region's dishes and the skills necessary to prepare them as well as an appreciation of Provençal wines to guests who stay in her pine-rimmed country house with a swimming pool. Each morning they investigate the local food markets, afternoons are spent practicing and polishing the skills learned, and evenings are given over to gastronomic indulgence and critique. Week-long courses begin on Saturday afternoons. In Gordes, 30 miles (48 km) east of Avignon. Information: *Provençal Cooking School,* Sylvie Lallemand, Les Mégalithes, Gordes 84220 (phone: 90-72-23-41).

FARM COOKING WEEKENDS, Ladornac, Dordogne: Dany and Guy Dubois work a farm in the lush and hilly Dordogne in France's southwest. But they also conduct informal weekend cooking classes that may include a visit to the town bakery or to an antique but still working walnut oil mill. Students may choose either a weekend *du cochon,* which covers the preparation of pork products such as blood sausage and the curing of a ham, or a weekend devoted to that specialty made of fattened goose livers, foie gras, during which Dany Dubois helps students prepare their own, as well as *confit* and *rillettes,* using the force-fed geese raised on the family farm. Courses, which are taught in French, are limited to six students, and reservations must be made several months in advance. Meals and lodging are included, and the Dubois family will pick up students at the train station in nearby Brive. Information: *Dany and Guy Dubois,* Ladornac 24120 (phone: 53-51-04-24).

ROGER VERGÉ'S L'ECOLE DU MOULIN, Mougins, Provence: As the only

Michelin three-star chef to offer regular cooking classes, Roger Vergé runs a school designed for home cooks, and touring American couples come by the dozen for the week-long course taught by various chefs from Vergé's celebrated restaurants, the three-star *Le Moulin de Mougins,* just outside the charming village of Mougins, and the two-star *L'Amandier,* in the heart of it. The participation-demonstration classes take place above the latter; each weekday students prepare a different menu featuring the varied cuisine of Provence. Classes are available in English, French, German, and Japanese, and include lunch but not lodging. A similar program by Vergé also is offered in Nice at the *Beau Rivage* hotel. Information: *Le Moulin de Mougins,* 424 Chemin du Moulin, Mougins, Alpes-Maritimes 06250 (phone: 93-75-78-24).

LE CORDON BLEU, Paris: This famous school has been instructing an international group of students in French cooking and pastry making since 1895. During the summer, special 5-week courses are offered in cooking and pastry, while 11-week sessions that give credits toward certificates and diplomas are available during the year. Visitors may reserve a few days ahead for single afternoon demonstrations, with menus available about 30 days in advance for each month's program. There also are intensive 4- or 5-day sessions during holiday periods — *Christmas, Easter,* and throughout the summer. Both the demonstration and intensive courses often are translated into English. Students are responsible for their own lodging. Information: *Le Cordon Bleu,* 8 Rue Léon Delhomme, Paris 75015 (phone: 48-56-06-06).

ECOLE DE CUISINE LA VARENNE, Paris: This well-known cooking school run by the English cookbook author, journalist, and food historian Anne Willan — with Simone Beck and Julia Child as advisers — occupies small but well-equipped quarters near the Invalides. Devoted to French cuisine, with classes taught by a staff of French chefs and visiting Parisian chefs, the school remains particularly popular with Americans. Students may sign up for a year-long cycle of courses or visit for a single afternoon demonstration; week-long demonstration and participation courses in regional cooking, pastry, contemporary, and classic French cuisine also are available. Week-long sessions are held during the summer and fall at a château in Burgundy. Classes are in French, and though English translations are provided, an understanding of the language is most helpful. Courses are offered year-round except during part of August and over the French holidays, when the school generally closes. Reserve a few days in advance for daily demonstrations (limited to about 50 students), several months in advance for longer courses. Students are responsible for their own lodging. Information: *Ecole de Cuisine La Varenne,* 34 Rue St.-Dominique, Paris 75007 (phone: 47-05-10-16) or in the US, *La Varenne,* PO Box 25574, Washington, DC 20007 (phone: 800-537-6486).

ECOLE DE GASTRONOMIE FRANÇAISE RITZ-ESCOFFIER, Paris: Escoffier was to food what Daimler was to automobiles. Today, the *Ritz* hotel, where the legendary chef Escoffier made his debut in the last century, houses the ultimate cooking school. Courses last 1 to 6 weeks and involve 25 hours of instruction weekly. There also is a course in *pâtisserie* — the art of cake, ice cream, chocolate, and candy making — and a 12-week program for professionals. Instruction is in French and English. Information: *Ecole de Gastronomie Française Ritz-Escoffier,* 38 Rue Cambon, Paris 75001 (phone: 42-60-38-30).

ECOLE LENÔTRE, Paris: Working in groups of up to a dozen under France's best known and most respected pastry chef, Gaston Lenôtre, professionals and serious amateurs study French pastry, chocolate, bread, ice cream, *charcuterie,* and catering in the huge, modern, spotless Lenôtre laboratory in the suburb of Plaisir, about 17 miles (28 km) outside Paris. Courses, which are conducted in French, generally last 5 days and include breakfast and lunch (though students are responsible for their own lodging and transportation). Reserve several months in advance. Information: *Ecole Lenôtre,* Rue Pierre Curie, Plaisir 78370 (phone: 30-55-81-12).

PRINCESS ERE 2001, Paris: A well-appointed apartment in Paris and a château in Normandy are the sites for the programs offered by the outgoing, enthusiastic Princess Marie-Blanche de Broglie. In the capital, these include demonstration courses that deal with cooking professionally, the harmony of wines and foods, pastry, the art of entertaining, and French regional cooking. In Normandy, a month-long session in August — primarily for professionals — includes preparation of meals for visiting tourists. Courses may be arranged in English, French, and Spanish, with translations supplied as necessary. In Paris, the programs run year-round, and students are responsible for their own lodging. In Normandy, lodging is available in an 18th-century house on the estate. Reserve several months in advance. Information: *Marie-Blanche de Broglie, Princess Ere 2001,* 18 Av. de la Motte-Picquet, Paris 75007 (phone: 45-51-36-34).

PARIS EN CUISINE, Paris: Travelers who want to visit the wholesale market in the outskirts at Rungis, tour the kitchens of such well-known Paris restaurants as *Taillevent* or *Chiberta,* attend cooking classes with top chefs like Michel and Pierre Troisgros or Michel Guérard, or get an inside view of a chocolate shop, a *boulangerie,* a *pâtisserie,* or a *charcuterie* can arrange individual or group visits led by Robert Noah, an American based in Paris with excellent contacts in the French food world. The tours are excellent for those who do not speak French, for Noah is a careful translator and groups are small (usually about ten students, depending on the program). Reserve several months in advance. Students are responsible for their own lodging. Information: *Paris en Cuisine,* 49 Rue de Richelieu, Paris 75001 (phone: 42-61-35-23). Noah also publishes a lively, informative newsletter about food and wine in France. Information: *Paris en Cuisine,* PO Box 50099, St. Louis, MO 63105.

For the Body

Sensational French Skiing

 Unsophisticated skiers initially may think of Switzerland when they day-dream about the Alps, but savvier downhill devotees know that the Alps claimed by France boast ski slopes equal to any in the world. French ski resorts, isolated centers of pleasure concentrated in the Haute-Savoie, are scenic and relaxing — not to mention socially enjoyable — and nightlife amid the French mountains is such that France has given the rest of the world the term *après-ski,* the all-inclusive phrase that describes all that's fun at the end of a hard day on the slopes.

Most major French ski resorts offer economical packages that include room, board, equipment, and lift passes, and these can be irresistible for those looking for the highest quality of European ski experience at the lowest possible cost. It is best to insist on half-board — only breakfast and dinner — since returning to a lodging place for lunch almost always is inconvenient. Prices fluctuate according to the season. Late November and early December are considered low season, and *Christmastime* and February are high season. January, when conditions often are as good as they are a month later, usually falls somewhere in between.

For each ski center, we have included a few favorite hotels in each price range: Expensive (E), Moderate (M), Inexpensive (I) — or, at least, more moderate. Each town, no matter how small, has a tourist office that can provide up-to-date information about hotel availability, unusual tours, ski schools, etc.

ALPE D'HUEZ, Isère: Built after World War II, this is one of France's most up-to-date and well-cared-for ski resorts. With a dozen trails for experts (including a 10-miler that ranks as the longest in Europe), it has particular appeal for accomplished skiers. But among its 100 trails there is plenty for everyone, and the network of lifts connecting the three main sections of the skiing terrain is effective enough to keep waiting time down. Tennis, swimming, horseback riding, skating, and glacier skiing allow the resort to remain open year-round. Information: *Office de Tourisme,* L'Alpe d'Huez 38750 (phone: 76-80-35-41). Hotels: *Royal Ours Blanc* (E), *Les Bruyères* (M), *L'Eclose* (I).

LES DEUX-ALPES, Isère: This resort, incongruously modern in a mountain-crowded valley that cries out for quaint chalets, makes up for its lack of nightlife with an abundance of slopes and trails and vast mountainsides that are spectacular for skiers of all abilities. For summer glacier skiing, it's difficult to do better in France. Informa-tion: *Office de Tourisme,* Maison des Deux Alpes, Les Deux-Alpes 38860 (phone: 76-79-22-00). Hotels: *Farandole* (E), *Edelweiss* (M), *Brunerie* (I).

CHAMONIX, Haute-Savoie: Ever since the first *Winter Olympics* were held here in 1924, this valley town (sandwiched between the Mont-Blanc range and the Aiguilles-Rouges) has had a reputation as an important center for mountain pursuits, and it unquestionably is one of the best ski resorts in the French Alps. Since most of the more than 50 trails on the mountains above the busy, picturesque village are within sight of Mont-Blanc, whose 15,771-foot summit makes it the highest peak in the Alps, the scenery is as good as the skiing. Experts can join a guided tour down the challenging Vallée Blanche, an 11-mile-long glacier run. The swimming pool, gym, tennis court, saunas, and ice skating rinks in the sports center round out the offerings. Information: *Office de Tourisme,* Pl. du Triangle de l'Amitié, Chamonix 74400 (phone: 50-53-00-24). Hotels: *Mont-Blanc* (E), *Richemond* (M), *Roma* (I). See also *The Alps* tour route, DIRECTIONS.

COURCHEVEL, Savoie: With 92 trails and some 380 miles of skiing, this resort, which actually is a collection of skiing centers named according to their altitude in meters (1650, 1550, and 1300), offers some of the finest and certainly the most extensive skiing in France — lending credence to its sobriquet, "The Star." And there's a huge assortment of other activities to fill the time spent off the slopes: skating, swimming, hang gliding, concerts, language courses, and more. Courchevel will host the alpine ski events at the *Winter Olympics* in 1992. Information: *Office de Tourisme,* La Croisette, Courchevel 73120 (phone: 79-08-00-29). Hotels: *Byblos des Neiges* (E), *La Sivolière* (M), Tournier (I).

FLAINE, Haute-Savoie: With an altitude of 5,250 feet at the base and 8,860 at the summit, this small but appealingly modern ski station is the highest resort in the Grand Massif of the Haute-Savoie, and with more than 150 miles of slopes and trails served by 80 lifts, it offers skiing of a quality that vindicates the vision of its developers. Information: *Office de Tourisme,* Flaine 74300 (phone: 50-90-80-01). Hotels: *Totem* (E), *Gradins Gris* (M), *Aujon* (I).

MEGÈVE, Haute-Savoie: Built around a lovely little 13th-century Savoyard village, with Mont-Blanc as its backdrop and a burbling little stream as its backbone, Megève is one of the country's most fashionable ski resorts. And while the magnitude and quality of the 60 slopes and trails do not quite measure up to those at Val-d'Isère or Chamonix, Megève does attract a contingent of *World Cup* ski racers each winter. The sight of movie stars and other international personalities mingling in its expensive boutiques, pretty cafés, casino, and nightspots also makes this resort very special. Cross-country skiing is good, too. Since snow conditions are reliable only from January to March, the vacation season starts late and ends early here. Information: *Office de Tourisme de Megève,* Megève 74120 (phone: 50-21-27-28). See also *The Alps,* DIRECTIONS. Hotels: *Mont-Blanc* (E), *La Prairie* (M), *Sapins* (I).

MORZINE-AVORIAZ, Haute-Savoie: This resort actually is two towns — traditional Morzine, a sunny, spread-out valley village at an altitude of only 3,000 feet, and modern Avoriaz, perched on a high-altitude (5,400 feet) plain. Their ski trails interlock and there's plenty to challenge an adventurous skier. Off-slope hours can be spent at Morzine's beautiful indoor skating rink. Information: *Office de Tourisme,* Morzine-Avoriaz 74110 (phone: 50-79-03-45). Hotels: *Les Dromonts* (E), *Fleur des Neiges* (M), *Les Rhodos* (I).

LA PLAGNE, Savoie: In describing this large and bustling ski destination in the heart of the vast Tarentaise region, the numbers speak for themselves: 27,400 beds, mainly in chalets and private residences since there are only 12 hotels; close to a half dozen independent ski villages, each with its own eating and drinking spots; and 100 lifts serving 100 trails that take in wide valleys, massive glaciers (skiable even in summer), and picturesque forests alike. Because of the variety of activities, this is an ideal ski station for the skier who wants to mix some serious instruction — in English — with some relaxed enjoyment off the slopes. Information: *Office de Tourisme,* Aime 73210 (phone: 79-09-79-79). Hotels: *Christina* (M), *France* (M), *Graciosa* (M).

TIGNES, Savoie: One of the largest French ski resorts, this town — largely built during the 1960s after a new hydroelectric dam and its resultant lake forced the removal of the old village to a site 1,000 feet up the mountain — takes the spillover from neighboring Val-d'Isère during busy seasons. And since it is so easy to travel from one to the other on skis, there is even more skiing than suggested by the number of slopes and trails, 61, with 90 miles of runs in all and 2,100 acres of skiing off the main trails. The possibility of traveling between Tignes and La Plagne with a mountain guide or ski instructor increases the downhill possibilities still further. The town itself — full of boutiques, apartment blocks, and restaurants verging on the futuristic — is intimidatingly modern. Yet oddly enough, it all works with the setting, a treeless and almost lunar sort of landscape. Information: *Office de Tourisme,* BP 51, Tignes 73320 (phone: 79-06-15-55). See also *The Alps,* DIRECTIONS. Hotels: *Ski d'Or* (E), *Campanules* (M), *Gentiana* (I).

VAL-D'ISÈRE, Savoie: The highest resort in the Savoie, Val-d'Isère is neither as impressive as Chamonix nor as attractive as Megève, but it has been attracting serious Alpine enthusiasts since the turn of the century. It has produced no less an international champion than Jean-Claude Killy, and its world-famous downhill course traditionally is a regular stop on the *World Cup* ski racing tour. As a result, Val-d'Isère draws big spenders who ensure an atmosphere of high fashion. From morning, when the streets are clogged with skiers clumping to the lift base and village buses shuttling less energetic souls to the same destination, until late at night, when the little avenue rings with the cries of merrymakers making their way from one bar or disco to the next, Val-d'Isère is a glamorous, busy place. Summer skiing is available on the 10,000-foot Grand Pissaillas glacier. Information: *Office de Tourisme,* Val-d'Isère 73150 (phone: 79-06-10-83). See also *The Alps,* DIRECTIONS. Hotels: *Christiana* (E), *Altitude* (M), *Vieux Village* (I).

VAL-THORENS, Savoie: High and barren, this recently constructed Alpine resort is a place for the true sports enthusiast. From Val-Thorens, it's possible to ski virtually without interruption for half a day before arriving at Mottaret. Or to ski to Courchevel or Méribel, as many visitors do. And so, though the resort has only 34 slopes and trails of its own, it actually has access to a huge quantity of terrain. The altitude — 7,545 feet at the base and 11,155 feet at its highest point — assures good conditions throughout the season. Information: *Office de Tourisme,* St. Martin de Belleville 73440 (phone: 79-00-08-08). Hotels: *Fitzroy* (E), *Bel Horizon* (M), *La Marmotte* (I).

Great French Golf

 Food, wine, castles, and cathedrals are what first come to mind when thinking about France — not golf. But golf has been a tradition in Gaul since 1856, when the first course was laid out in Pau (in the Pyrénées). Since that time, it has grown enormously in popularity. By the end of 1989, there were 307 courses around the country, and 100 more are expected to be completed by the end of this year. In fact, except for England and Scotland, France has more courses than any other country in Europe (and by 1995, there will be *more* here than in Scotland!).

Until recently, Gallic golf was considered a sport for the rich and the old. But with the construction of 50 municipal courses since 1980, golf has become accessible to a far broader group of people — including foreign visitors. The *Fédération Française de Golf* and the French Ministry of Tourism set up a system whereby travelers and others who are not members of a local golf club can play. Greens fees vary according to the day and season, but average about $30, except during weekends, when prices rise. Call ahead to reserve. Information: *France Golf International*, c/o Maison de la France, 8 Avenue de l'Opéra, 75001 Paris (phone: 42-96-10-23) or *Fédération Française de Golf*, 69 Av. Victor Hugo, 75783 Paris (phone: 45-02-13-55).

France is filled with spots where you can tee off while taking in some of the country's most beautiful sights — layouts by the sea, in valleys, and near cities. Below is a list of courses that are among the best in the country. But be forewarned: golf is considered more sport than leisure in France. Carts are forbidden on most courses, and generally only the courses designed specifically for tourists allow them.

BIARRITZ: Wonderful weather year-round (similar to Monterey, California) makes this region perfect for tee-time anytime. The oldest golf area in the country is the site of Europe's most extensive golf training center, *Centre International d'Entrainement au Golf,* located in a valley right outside Biarritz. Information: *Centre d'Entrainement au Golf,* 10 Rte. National, Biarritz 64200 (phone: 59-23-74-65).

Chiberta – Built in 1927, it is one of the most famous layouts in France. The course (18 holes, 6,400 yards, par 72) varies widely, from 7 holes in a pine forest to wonderful holes at water's edge. Greens fees range from $30 to $40. Information: *Golf de Chiberta,* 104 Bl. des Plages, Anglet 64000 (phone: 59-47-18-99).

Golf Club d'Hossegor – Fifteen miles (24 km) north of Biarritz, this course (18 holes, 6,400 yards, par 72) is set in a pine forest typical of the Basque region. It is challenging, and high scores are solved somewhat by the excellent lunch at the club- house. Greens fees range from $25 to $45. For information: *Golf Club d'Hossegor,* Av. du Golf, Hossegor 40150 (phone: 58-43-56-99).

Golf Municipal de Biarritz-Le Phare – In its 100-year history, this lovely, short (5,900 yards) course has attracted some of the world's best players. It is a short walk from the *Hôtel du Palais* (see "Checking In" in *Biarritz,* THE CITIES). Greens fees range from $30 to $40, depending on the season and day of the week. Information: *Golf de Biarritz,* Le Phare, Av. Edith-Cavell, Biarritz 64200 (phone: 59-03-71-80).

Golf de Seignosse – Completed in 1989 by designer Robert Van Hagge, this 18-hole track (6,800 yards, par 72) is considered one of the most spectacular courses in France. Beautifully set in the midst of the Landes pine forest, it is demanding and hilly (luckily carts are available here). Greens fees range from $25 to $35. Information: *Golf de Seignosse,* Seignosse 40510 (phone: 58-43-17-32).

CÔTE D'AZUR: Famous for its beaches and casinos, the French Riviera is tops with tourists. Until recently, however, it was lacking in very many good golf courses. In addition to those listed, several more currently are under construction.

Cannes Mandelieu – One of France's oldest clubs, it is run by Lucien Barriére Hotels and Casinos (golf packages are available through the *Majestic* hotel in Cannes). This 6,300-yard course, set among beautiful pine trees, hosts 60,000 players each year. Closed on Tuesdays, the greens fees range between $40 and $50. Information: *Golf Club de Cannes,* Mandelieu 06120 (phone: 93-49-55-39).

Cannes Mougins – Home to 500 members from 28 countries, every year this club hosts the *Cannes Mougins Open* tournament (a stop on the PGA European Tour). The 18-hole course is 6,700 yards, par 72; the clubhouse is in a restored old olive mill. It is closed on Mondays; greens fees range from $40 to $50. Information: *Golf de Cannes Mougins,* 175 Rte. d'Antibes, Mougins 06250 (phone: 93-75-79-13).

Monte-Carlo – On a clear day, this hilly 6,200-yard course has splendid views of Monaco and the coast from St.-Tropez to Italy. It hosts the annual *Monte-Carlo Open* (on the PGA European Tour) in June. A private club, visitors should call in advance to make arrangements. Greens fees range from $40 to $50. Information: *Monte-Carlo Golf Club,* La Turbie 06320 (phone: 93-41-09-11).

LANGUEDOC-ROUSSILON: Running along the Mediterranean Sea to the Spanish border, this part of southern France is one of the fastest growing golf areas in the country. The weather here is ideal almost year-round. Most of the courses here are new and in excellent condition.

Golf du Cap d'Agde – Brand new and already something of a French hot spot, this course is a full 7,000 yards long, and very difficult. Better to play off-season than in the summer when it is jammed toe to tee. Greens fees range from $25 to $35. Information: *Golf du Cap d'Agde,* Cap D'Agde 34300 (phone: 67-26-34-40).

Golf de Nîmes Campagne – Built in 1968, these 6,800 yards are particularly challenging when the wind is blowing (which is quite often). In fact, the club suggests that only those with handicaps under 30 play at all. The 18th hole is next to a beautiful pond surrounded by weeping willows. The clubhouse is called the "White House," and is lined by a splendid alley of sycamore trees. Greens fees range from $30 to $60, depending on the time of year. Information: *Golf de Nîmes Campagne,* Rte. de St.-Gilles, Nimes 30000 (phone: 66-70-17-37).

La Grande Motte – Designed by Robert Trent Jones, Sr. and built in 1987, this resort has both a 9-hole and an 18-hole course. The warm climate, flat land, ponds, flamingos, and the US southern-style architecture of the club will make folks from Florida feel right at home. As with the *Nîmes* course (above), the wind can be a real challenge. Greens fees range from $30 to $40. For information: *Golf Club de la Grande-Motte,* La Grande Motte 34280 (phone: 67-56-05-00).

NORMANDY: Because of its relative proximity to the capital, Normandy has become a popular weekend haven for Parisians. Not only are its beaches steeped in history, they are gorgeous as well. That also goes for its golf clubs.

New Golf de Deauville – Designed in 1920, it is one of the oldest golf clubs in France. Its 6,600 yard, 18-hole course, plus another 9-hole layout, make this a golfer's "don't miss." The views of the Norman houses and the surrounding coast are spectacular from the back 9 of the championship course. Greens fees range from $25 to $35. Information: *New Golf de Deauville,* St. Arnoult 14800 (phone: 31-88-20-53).

Omaha Beach – There are three 9-hole courses near the historic D-Day beaches, ranging from 3,200 to 3,460 yards. Each has an entirely different design — the *Hedges,* quite flat and running along the Norman countryside; the *Pond,* which offers water hazards on three of its holes; and the *Sea,* with a superb view of the cliffs nearby. Greens fees run from $25 to $35. Information: *Omaha Beach Golf Club,* Port en Bessin 14520 (phone: 31-21-72-94).

BRITTANY: This region, similar to parts of Ireland and northern California and home to small fishing villages and wild moors, is becoming a growing golf center as well. Among some of the more interesting courses are the following three.

Golf de Dinard – One of the country's oldest courses, and one of the shortest. But be forewarned: if the wind is blowing, the 5,700 yards will seem far longer very quickly. Greens fees range from $25 to $30. Information: *Golf de Dinard,* St. Briac Sur Mer 35800 (phone: 99-88-32-07).

Golf Public de Baden – This public 18-hole, 6,700-yard forest layout was completed in 1989. A stone's throw from St. Laurent, it could make a great golf weekend in Brittany. Greens fees range from $20 to $30. Information: *Golf Public de Baden,* Kernic, Baden 56870 (phone: 97-57-18-96).

Golf de St.-Laurent Ploermel – Another 18 holes set in a forest, this 6,800-yarder has been the site of the *French PGA Championship* for the past 2 years, and is very popular during the summer. It is located near Carnac, known for its 500 giant prehistoric stones. Greens fees range from $20 to $30. Information: *Golf de St.-Laurent Ploermel,* Auray 56400 (phone: 97-56-85-18).

LOIRE VALLEY: Set among the famous châteaux of this region (many of which have been converted into luxury hotels) are many golf courses, with several more under construction. The mildness of the area's climate (except in winter) makes it ideal to play a few rounds after visiting the castles.

Golf d'Ardrée – Opened in 1988, this is the first of several courses scheduled to be built over the next few years by a group of French businesses. Located 8 miles (13 km) north of Tours, it is laid out on land that once was a private hunting preserve. The club still has a small château on the property and a modern clubhouse. Electric carts are available to get around the 6,500-yard course. Greens fees are $25 to $35. Information: *Golf d'Ardrée,* St.-Antoine du Rocher 37360 (phone: 47-56-77-38).

Golf des Bordes – Texas architect Robert Von Hagge was asked to design a championship course that would respect the landscape. The result is this 7,100-yard layout, set 10 miles (16 km) southwest of Orléans. There is water on 12 of its 18 holes. Greens fees range from $50 to $100; electric cars are available. Information: *Golf des Bordes,* St.-Laurent Nouan 41220 (phone: 54-87-72-13).

NEAR PARIS: Not only is the countryside around Paris enticing for an afternoon excursion (see *The Ile-de-France,* DIRECTIONS), but also for a round of golf. The two courses listed below are open to visitors.

Golf Club de Chantilly – Known for food and lace, Chantilly is also famous for Chateau de Chantilly, the home of French kings, and this elegant club, only 5 minutes from the historic castle. With its Old World charm and aristocratic ambience, this British-designed course winds through an impressive forest just 25 miles (40 km) north of Paris. Non-members may play for a fee on weekends. Closed Thursdays. Information: *Golf Club de Chantilly,* 60500 Vineuil-Saint Firmin, Chantilly, France (phone: 44-57-04-43).

Golf National – Owned and operated by the *Fédération Française de Golf,* this huge public golf complex is in St.-Quentin-en-Yvelines. The first of its three courses, the 18-hole, 7,400-yard *Albatros* (designed by Hubert Chesneau and Bob Von Hagge), was scheduled to open as we went to press. Water hazards abound. Information: *Fédération Française de Golf,* 69 Av. Victor-Hugo, 76783 Paris (phone: 45-02-13-55).

Golf des Yvelines – Set in a protected park, this 18-holer is a par 72 forest course 28 miles (45 km) from Paris. Its clubhouse is in a château. Greens fees are $35 during the week, $50 on weekends. Information: *Golf des Yvelines,* La Queue les Yvelines 78940 (phone: 34-86-48-89).

GOLF AND GOBLETS

Though great golf can be found through much of Europe, leave it to the French to make it even more attractive. With beautiful courses found in Bordeaux, Burgundy, and the Loire Valley, now it is possible to spend the mornings on the fairway and the afternoons at some of the world's finest vineyards. *Travelinks* (1015 18th St. NW, Suite 805, Washington DC 20036; phone: 202-659-5657) and *Marsans International* (19 W. 34th St., New York, NY 10001; phone: 212-239-3880 or 800-223-6114) are a couple of the US tour operators that offer wine and golf packages. Accommodations (often in châteaux), greens fees, tours of the area, and wine-tastings at one of the local vineyards are included in the cost. The following two courses, though included in the packages, also are open to non-teetotalers on their own.

Golf du Cognac – The Martell cognac vineyards are the setting for this 6,950-yard, par 72 course. During harvest time, players are treated to the aroma of fermenting grapes. It is an easy 18-holer, but well worth playing for the ambience. Information: *Golf Club du Cognac,* Rue St.-Brice, Cognac 16100 (phone: 45-32-18-17).

Le Golf du Médoc – Just 20 minutes from Bordeaux, each of the 18 holes here is named for one of the area's vineyards — the 18th, for example, is Mouton Rothschild. If you make a hole-in-one at the par 3, 155-yard Pontet Canet (the 5th), you get an imperial bottle of the wine. Regional wines also are served at the clubhouse's restaurant. Information: *Le Golf du Médoc,* Chemin de Courmateau, Louens, Blanquefort 33290 (phone: 56-72-01-10).

Game, Set, and Match: Tennis in France

 Like the United States, France has seen an enormous increase in the interest in tennis over the past 20 years — as a sport for spectators and participants alike. The number of tennis courts and camps in France continues to increase, and there are hundreds of tennis clubs — both private and public. The prime surface of choice is red clay, although there are a fair number of all-weather and hard courts scattered around the countryside. Though it can be hard to get court time in Paris, conditions are far less crowded outside the capital. Attendance at the country's leading international tournament, the *French Open,* has soared to the point where a major expansion of *Roland Garros Stadium* (in Paris) was necessary.

TENNIS CLUBS: The many tennis clubs in France — of which by far the most famous is Paris's *Racing Club,* unquestionably one of the greats among the world's athletic clubs — are organized by *département* or league. Most require annual membership, and virtually all are closed to outsiders who aren't personally acquainted with a member. However, some are less exclusive than others, and occasionally it's possible for business associates to provide an entrée. Also, in resort areas, the best clubs are open to any player willing to pay the sometimes substantial, but by no means prohibitive, admission fee. And many offer *stages,* or instruction sessions, to the general public on a weekend or weekly basis. Instruction usually is in French.

Aix-en-Provence, Bouches-du-Rhône – In this leafy southern town, the *Aixois Country Club* offers 5-day *stages* during the spring and summer, with instruction from 2½ to 5 hours a day. Information: *Country Club Aixois,* Bastide des Solliers, Puyricard 13540 (phone: 42-92-10-41).

Arcachon, Gironde – This breezy beach town has just the right climate for summer tennis. There are 22 courts at the *Tennis-Club* (Stade André Dupin) and 5 more at the *Abatilles Tennis Courts* (165 Bd. de la Côte-d'Argent). Information: *Office de Tourisme,* BP 42, Pl. Roosevelt, Arachon 33311 (phone: 56-83-01-69).

La Baule, Loire-Atlantique – The *Tennis Country Club* has decidedly the best tennis opportunities in a town that is full of them — 83 courts in all. An establishment worth crossing the Atlantic to experience, it boasts a half-timbered clubhouse with martially squared hedges, an active tournament schedule, 5 all-weather courts, and 25 superbly tended red clay courts. Suzanne Lenglen reigned here for many years, and Ellsworth Vines bowed to Bill Tilden in the men's final in 1933. Now owned by a hotel chain, it offers a wide variety of tennis packages that include lodgings. Information: *Tennis Country Club,* 113 Av. du Maréchal-de-Lattre-de-Tassigny, La Baule 44500 (phone: 40-60-23-44).

Biarritz, Pyrénées-Atlantiques – The tennis club at the *Parc des Sports d'Aguiléra* in this prosperous resort on the southern Atlantic coast is open year-round, and lessons are available by the day or by the week. Of the 12 courts, 10 are clay, and 2 are lighted. Information: *Parc des Sports d'Aguiléra,* Biarritz 64200 (phone: 59-23-93-24).

Deauville, Calvados – The town itself owns 23 courts by the sea and sponsors numerous tennis tournaments, but should you strike it rich at the casino, consider one of the two classic Deauville hotels — the *Normandy* and the *Royal.* The *Normandy,* an oversize Norman cottage in the heart of town, faces its own 21 tennis courts, as well as the Atlantic Ocean. Should the weather disappoint you, jog the underground passage to the casino or swim in the covered heated Olympic-size salt water pool. Down the street is the *Royal,* with 23 courts. Information: *Hôtel Normandy,* 38 Rue Jean-Memoz, Deauville 14800 (phone: 31-98-66-22). *Hôtel Royal,* Bd. Cornuché, Deauville 14800 (phone: 31-98-66-33).

Evian-les-Bains, Haute-Savoie – World famous for its casino (see "Casinos Royale" in *For the Experience*), Evian first developed as a spa. Today its water is a household word. A tennis club with 13 courts is another one of its many charms. If money is no object, the *Royal* hotel (phone: 50-75-14-00) — see "Romantic French Hostelries" in *For the Experience* — offers an intensive 6-day tennis program combining exercise and 2 hours of daily court play on its own 6 courts. Information: *Office de Tourisme,* BP 988, Evian 74502 (phone: 50-75-04-26).

Hendaye, Pyrénées-Atlantiques – The club in this beach town on the Spanish border has 12 clay courts, 10 of them outdoors. It is most active in July and August but is open year-round. Information: *Tennis Club Parc des Sports,* Rue Elissacilio, Hendaye 64700 (phone: 59-20-02-73).

Nice, Alpes-Maritimes – The *Nice Lawn Tennis Club,* delightfully away from the noisy beach and business districts in a residential section of the city, seems to attract a substantial number of better than average players. Suzanne Lenglen, who grew up just across the street (now renamed to honor her), developed her distinctive balletic playing style on its courts. There now are 19 in all, 13 of them clay. Information: *Nice Lawn Tennis Club,* Parc Impérial, Nice 06000 (phone: 93-96-17-70).

La Plagne, Savoie – The *stages* on the 16 hard courts at this popular ski and summer resort, which include full room and board, are available in July and August. Information: *Eric Loliée Résidence de Plagne Belle-Côte,* Aime 73210 (phone: 79-09-29-00).

Roquebrune-Cap-Martin, Alpes-Maritime – The *Monte Carlo Country Club* (see *Monaco,* THE CITIES) actually is across the border (in France) from Monaco proper, but don't let that stop you from experiencing one of the most sublime tennis layouts in the country — 23 courts arranged on terraces on a hillside with spectacular Mediterranean views framed by cypress trees, like columns. The clubhouse, with its sunny restaurant embellished with murals and its well-kept, old-fashioned locker rooms (complete with their original wooden lockers), is simply an extra delight. The fact that no less than Prince Rainier III still plays doubles here is some indication of the quality of the crowd. The best times for playing, as on the rest of the Riviera, are fall and spring. Information: *Monte Carlo Country Club,* Av. de Monte-Carlo, Quartier St.-Roman, Roquebrune-Cap-Martin 06190 (phone: 93-78-20-45).

Tignes, Savoie – The instruction program at this ski and summer resort is rather intensive, with more than 4 hours of instruction a day for 6 days. But after a day of tennis on the 15 hard courts, it's possible to go sailing in the mountain lake, golf, or even ski. Hotels, apartments, and studio lodgings are abundant. Information: *Stage Caujolle, Club Omni-Sports,* Tignes-le-Lac 73320 (phone: 79-06-53-87).

Trouville-sur-Mer, Calvados – Besides the 7 clay courts, the 2 hard courts, and the single indoor court, the tennis club in this Atlantic-pounded Normandy resort town offers golf, horseback riding, swimming, and windsurfing. Tennis instruction is offered on a weekly basis. Open from April to October. Information: *Trouville Tennis Club,* Trouville-sur-Mer 14360 (phone: 31-88-91-62).

TENNIS CLUBS NEAR PARIS: The following clubs are located close to the capital:

Aubervilliers, Seine-St.-Denis – Open year-round (except August), the *Tennis Forest Hill* offers lessons for an hour and a half each day in blocks of 4 days on 18 indoor courts. Information: *Tennis Forest Hill,* 111 Av. Victor-Hugo, Aubervilliers 93300 (phone: 48-34-75-10).

Bois-le-Roi, Seine-et-Marne – With 9 hard courts outdoors and 2 indoors, the

UCPA offers a 7-hour weekend instruction program year-round. Information: *UCPA,* Rue de Tournezy, Bois-le-Roi 77590 (phone: 60-69-60-06).

Boulogne, Hauts-de-Seine – At the *Tennis Club de Longchamp,* just down the road from *Roland Garros Stadium* in the Bois de Boulogne on the outskirts of Paris, it is possible to enroll for weekly instruction sessions on the 3 hard courts. There is a golf course nearby. Information: *Tennis Club de Longchamp,* 19 Bd. Anatole-France, Boulogne 92100 (phone: 46-03-84-49).

Nanterre, Hauts-de-Seine – Weekend lessons are possible here year-round at the *Tennis Club Défense.* Various periods of instruction and weekend lessons both are available on the 8 hard courts. Information: *Tennis Club Défense,* 45 Bd. des Bouvets, Nanterre 92000 (phone: 47-73-04-40).

Villepinte, Seine St. Denis – The *Villepinte Tennis Club* has 7 clay and 6 hard courts, with possibilities for indoor and outdoor play year-round. Weekend and extended courses are offered. Information: *Tennis de Villepinte,* Rue du Manège, Villepinte 93420 (phone: 43-83-23-31).

TENNIS CAMPS: French tennis camps, with highly qualified instructors, offer more intense tutoring than the clubs, usually by the week rather than for a shorter period of time.

Alpe d'Huez, Isère – A popular skiing center in the winter, this most up-to-date and well-cared-for of French resorts offers organized tennis instruction from mid-July to mid-August. Lessons are given on a weekly basis, with lodging in local hotels. Information: *Office de Tourisme,* Alpe d'Huez 38750 (phone: 76-80-35-41).

Les Arcs, Savoie – *Arc 1600* and *Arc 1800,* a pair of ski resorts whose numbers refer to their altitude in meters, offer 6-day tennis camps in July and August at both locations with 3 to 4 hours of instruction per day. There are a total of 40 hard courts and, at *Arc 1800,* a swimming pool and a golf course as well. Lodging is abundant. Information: *Maison des Arcs,* 94 Bd. du Montparnasse, Paris 75014 (phone: 43-22-43-32).

Arles, Bouches-du-Rhône – The camp at *Les Villages du Soleil* offers 4½-hour sessions for 5 days on either the 7 indoor courts or the 23 outdoor hard courts, depending on the season. Lodging with half-board is available at the camp, which also has a swimming pool, a sauna, and squash and volleyball facilities. Closed in January. Information: *Les Villages du Soleil,* Mas de Véran, Arles 13200 (phone: 90-96-50-68).

Bandol, Var – Open from March to October, the relatively inexpensive *Tennis Club Buding* offers 6-day sessions with 2-hour lessons daily from March to October on the 30 hard courts. The club is about a mile (1.6 km) from the Mediterranean coast. Accommodations are available on the premises. There are English-speaking instructors on staff. Information: *Tennis Club Buding,* Quartier du Pont-d'Aran, Bandol 83150 (phone: 94-29-43-36).

Cap d'Agde, Hérault – This famous camp in the Languedoc consumes the life of the village where the former tennis star Pierre Barthès founded it in 1973. From training films to specialty boutiques, tennis rules the day. The instruction programs last for 6 days, 4 hours a day. There are 62 courts with about as many surfaces as a tennis player can name. Students can lodge at the camp hotel or at any of numerous hotels and bungalows in the area. Similar programs are offered at *Pierre Barthès* centers in Val Thorens and Les Menuires, resort towns in the mountains of the Haute-Savoie. Information: *Club Pierre Barthès,* Cap d'Agde 34305 (phone: 67-26-00-06).

Flaine, Haute-Savoie – The tennis camp in this modern mountain ski and summer resort may have as many as 10 students per instructor, but there is ample room for practice on the 26 hard courts. *Stages* are offered in July and August. Students lodge in ski chalets or hotels in the area. Information: *Stages Georges-Deniau,* Sepad Loisirs, 23 Rue Cambon, Paris 75001 (phone: 42-61-55-17).

Les Hauts-de-Nîmes, Gard – Run by the same people who stage the camp at Flaine, the one here in the south of France offers sessions of either 2 or 4 hours for each of

6 days on 33 courts (4 indoors). Lodging is available at the camp or in town. Information: *Stages Georges-Deniau,* Sepad Loisirs, Les Hauts-de-Nîmes, Rte. d'Anduze, Nîmes 30900 (phone: 66-23-14-67).

Opio, Alpes Maritimes – Some of the very best spots for playing tennis in Europe are at the "vacation villages" of *Club Mediterranée,* which consistently offer extensive facilities, first-rate instruction, and settings maintained with ecological fervor. The *Club Med* not far from the Côte d'Azur at Opio spreads out over 125 acres and has 15 tennis courts, 7 of which are lighted. Other *Club Med* sites that are tops for tennis include Cargèse, Pompadour, and Vittel. All offer a variety of other sports as well and are fine for family holidays. Information: *Club Med,* 40 W. 57th St., New York, NY 10019 (phone: 212-750-1670; 800-CLUB MED).

TOURNAMENT TENNIS

There are two major international tournaments in France each year. The *French Open,* which takes place during the last week in May and the first week in June in Paris, is the world's premiere red clay court tournament and one of the four *Grand Slam* events (the other three being *Wimbledon,* the *US Open*, and the *Australian Open*), and most of the top international men and women players participate. Tickets for matches early in the tournament generally are easy to obtain at the box office in early May or by mail through the *Fédération Française de Tennis (FFT;* address below). However, seats for the semifinal and final matches go fast and must be requested well in advance.

The *Monte Carlo Open,* France's other big clay court event, also draws most of the world's best. The men's tournament takes place in early April. Information: *Monte Carlo Country Club,* Quartier St.-Roman, Roquebrune-Cap-Martin 06190 (phone: 93-78-20-45).

In addition, there are the handful of other French tournaments on the intermediate circuit of the *Grand Prix* professional schedule — that is, the *Challenge Series* tournaments — which, despite the absence of the most famous players, always attract competitors recognizable to anyone who follows tennis regularly. The event that takes place annually in Nice is one of the most popular; there are others in Nancy (March), Aix-en-Provence (April), Bordeaux (September), Toulouse (October), and Paris (November). The *FFT* can supply specifics.

FOR MORE INFORMATION: A complete list of addresses for tennis clubs in France, as well as a roster of club tournaments open to visiting players and competitive events of interest to spectators, may be obtained from the *Fédération Française de Tennis (FFT)* (Roland Garros Stadium, 2 Av. Gordon-Bennett, Paris 75016; phone: 47-43-48-00).

Sun, Sea, and Sand: France's Best Beaches

The Riviera is almost everything it is touted to be. The water is clear and tame, the sun reliable, the celebrities abundant. It is a paradise of cool drinks by day and casinos by night; topless tanning very definitely is the rule rather than the exception. And to those who are seeking this kind of getaway, the Riviera will not disappoint.

But most of the beaches are pebbled rather than sandy, and in August, when all of France shuts down so that workers can take the month of vacation that is guaranteed by law, it seldom is possible to find an open patch on which to spread a towel, let alone an empty hotel room.

France does boast some 1,200 miles of beachfront in all, and most of them have a lot more natural scenery to offer than the Côte d'Azur, however glamorous it may be. From the rugged cliffs of Normandy and Brittany down the expansive Atlantic coast to the Mediterranean hideaways of the Languedoc, there are scores of old fishing villages steeped in history, places where a beach vacation can be mixed with the pleasure of exploring a country and its culture.

Note that some beaches are specially designated *naturiste,* connoting nude bathing. However, sunning and swimming in the buff is common enough in other places as well — usually on the fringes of the greatest concentration of swimmers. And topless bathing is the norm for women.

Below is a sampling of the most interesting seaside resorts, following the French coastline counterclockwise from Normandy.

NORMANDY: Best known to the world nowadays as the site of the Allied invasion in 1944, the Normandy coastline is a rugged stretch of sandy beaches and craggy cliffs. Omaha Beach, Utah Beach, and other spots are legend (though they're not swimming beaches); others, among them the western side of the Cotentin Peninsula, are less well known and, therefore, more interesting for the visitor who wants to beat his own pathway. For information about any of these, contact the *Comité Régional de Tourisme de Normandie* (46 Av. Foch, Evreux 27000; phone: 32-33-79-00).

Deauville, Calvados – This town and neighboring Trouville-sur-Mer, both affluent former fishing villages with sandy beaches and seaside restaurants, have drawn the rich and famous over the decades for their casinos, racetracks, chic hotels, and other attractions.

Plages du Débarquement, Calvados – The landing beaches, as this stretch of coastline is known, bore the brunt of the Allied invasion. Luc-sur-Mer, with its museum of seashells, and Bernières-sur-Mer, whose 219-foot belfry is the highest on the Normandy coast, are especially pleasant.

Les Côtes des Grandes Marées, Manche – Before reaching Mont-St.-Michel, a motorist arrives at a stretch of magnificent beaches — Carolles, medieval Granville, Jullouville, and St.-Pair-sur-Mer. The cliffs just beyond Carolles give a fine view of the northern Brittany coast, while Vauville, farther up the Cotentin Peninsula, is noted for its sand dunes.

BRITTANY: The coastline of this especially scenic province, a picturesque mélange of rocky cliffs, small fishing ports, and sandy coves, has many faces. The northern area offers well-developed beach towns, some as glitteringly sophisticated as the Riviera and some very low-key and family-oriented. The south tends to be a little wilder, particularly around Quiberon.

St.-Cast-le-Guildo, Côtes-du-Nord – To avoid the confusion of the Riviera, many families prefer to spend the month of August at this resort known as the pride of the Côte d'Emeraude (Emerald Coast), one of Brittany's largest resorts. There are a dozen public tennis courts and a 9-hole golf course, among other diversions. Information: *Office de Tourisme,* Pl. Général de Gaulle, St.-Cast-le-Guildo 22380 (phone: 96-41-81-52).

Bénodet, Finistère – It is not always as warm on the pebbled beaches of Bénodet as it is on the sandy beaches farther south, and the water is often chilly. But this district at the mouth of the River Odet in folklore-rich Finistère is renowned for its beautiful camping areas and its fine sailing school. A few miles down the coast is the beautiful, piney Beg Meil. The boat ride along the Odet to Quimper is a popular diversion. Information: *Syndicat d'Initiative,* 51 Av. de la Plage, Bénodet 29118 (phone: 98-57-00-14).

Baie de Quiberon, Morbihan – The most widely heralded beaches in the area around the Morbihan Bay, in the south of Brittany, are at Carnac, which is as famous for its prehistoric megaliths as it is for its resort facilities, at nearby La Trinité, and at Quiberon, which is at the end of a long, rockbound peninsula. While the nights can be cool, the scenery is rugged — just what most visitors travel to Brittany to find. Quiberon is the departure point for trips to Belle-Ile, the largest island in the province and a beach lover's destination in its own right; the terrain rises sharply from the sands that border it and allows for some spectacular coastal views. Information: *Office de Tourisme,* 74 Av. des Druides, Carnac 56340 (phone: 97-52-13-52).

La Baule, Loire-Atlantique – Many believe that the 5 miles of sandy beach at this busy and fashionable resort, farther east along the stretch of Brittany coastline known as the Côte d'Amour, are the loveliest in the country; and the area — so built up as to be almost urban — draws what some French call the "bourgeoisie of the west" to its casino and discotheques, its 70 tennis courts, its pair of equestrian centers (with more than 200 horses), its 18-hole golf course, and its flying club. Information: *Office de Tourisme,* 8 Pl. de la Victoire, La Baule 44500 (phone: 40-24-34-44).

UPPER ATLANTIC COAST: L'Ile d'Yeu, Vendée – About 1¼ hours by ferry from Fromentine, this island is so notched by rocky promontories on the south that the coastline is known as the Côte Sauvage. But elsewhere there are lovely beaches and simple port towns. Marshal Pétain, head of the Vichy government during World War II, was imprisoned here from 1945 to 1951. It is possible to tour the island in a day on foot or by bicycle. Information: *Office de Tourisme,* 1 Pl. du Marché, L'Ile d'Yeu 85350 (phone: 51-58-32-58).

St.-Jean-de-Monts, Vendée – The vast beach of St.-Jean-de-Monts, back along the coast, has been described as the perfect beach for families because of its exceptionally calm waters. The fact that there are only a handful of hotels suggests just how quiet the place can be. Information: *Office de Tourisme,* Palais des Congrès, St.-Jean-de-Monts 85160 (phone: 51-58-00-48).

Les Sables-d'Olonne, Vendée – The 7 miles of beach here make these strands of sand among the most popular of all the Atlantic resorts. Many visitors like to go horseback riding through the dunes or visit the aquarium or zoo. La Tranche-sur-Mer, a few miles farther down the coast, is famous for its tulip fields in April and May and popular for its vast sandy beaches all summer long. Information: *Office de Tourisme,* Rue de Maréchal-Leclerc, Les Sables-d'Olonne 85100 (phone: 51-32-03-28).

L'Ile d'Oléron, Charente-Maritime – France's second largest island, linked to land by a bridge, has lost some of its charm to popularity. But it does have an abundance of marvelous sandy beaches that draw French youth by the thousands. At night, the island bustles; by day, you can visit oyster farms, take sailing lessons, and explore medieval ruins. Information: *Syndicat d'Initiative,* Le Château, L'Ile d'Oléron 17480 (phone: 46-47-60-51).

L'Ile de Ré, Charente-Maritime – Aptly named "the Bright Island" because of the plenitude of sunlight that graces it, this island is a 48-mile-long treasure of tiny villages, whitewashed cottages, and undeveloped land. There's a bird sanctuary, a bicycle livery, a satisfying number of well-marked beaches, and a handful of comfortable hotels. Access is provided by ferry from La Pallice. Information: *Office de Tourisme,* Quai Sénac, La Flotte, Ile de Ré 17630 (phone: 46-09-60-38).

La Rochelle, Charente-Maritime – A thriving port in medieval times, this city boasts the largest pleasure boat basin in all of Europe and a charming fortified old city that was English from the middle of the 12th until the 17th century, when it was besieged by Louis XIII. Now it is closed to traffic on summer weekend evenings. With a population of 85,000, it is no quaint small town; but the city is a dazzler, night or day, and there are bicycles to ride and an antique carousel, and the white sand beaches in its environs — including those at Ile de Ré (above) — are lovely. Information: *Office de Tourisme,* 10 Rue Fleuriau, La Rochelle 17025 (phone: 46-41-14-68).

Royan, Charente-Maritime – Largely rebuilt after World War II, this resort town just north of Bordeaux lacks the charm of many others in a region that has been called the Côte de Beauté (the Beautiful Coast) for its stretch of more than a dozen miles of beaches and rocky coves. The water is relatively chilly, but there are plenty of facilities for golf, tennis, horseback riding, sailing, and water skiing. And near Marennes are huge oyster beds where some of the finest oysters in France are cultivated. Information: *Office Municipal de Tourisme*, Palais des Congrès, Royan 17200 (phone: 46-38-65-11).

LOWER ATLANTIC COAST: With almost 150 miles of sand, this stretch of beach backed by the Landes forest and running from the mouth of the Gironde to the Basque country is one of the longest in the world. Environmental regulations have left some sections of the coast delightfully undeveloped; other sections have been allowed to grow so that there are comfortable hotels and restaurants aplenty. Note that the waters often are rough and dangerous, so it is advisable to swim only in designated areas and when there's a green flag flying — meaning that a lifeguard is on duty and swimming is safe.

Arcachon, Gironde – Along the 50-mile perimeter of the Arcachon Basin, where Celts were living around 500 BC, there are about 30 beaches and oyster farms, pine trees by the thousands, and, near Pilat Plage, an immense sand dune (380 feet and still growing) — taller than any other in France. Thousands of sailboats moor here, and in the town of Arcachon proper, the old beachfront hotels, the handsome 19th-century villas, and the promenade edged with feathery tamarisk trees still recall the town's Belle Epoque heyday, when English gentry came here to socialize and French artists like Manet and Toulouse-Lautrec visited to paint. Nearby, at La Hume, the restored medieval village is full of craftspeople costumed as basket makers, bell makers, candle makers, cane makers, clog makers, leaded glass workers, and other artisans of the period. Information: *Office de Tourisme*, BP 42, Pl. Franklin-Roosevelt, Arcachon 33120 (phone: 56-83-01-69).

Hossegor and Capbreton, Landes – Hossegor, a modern oyster center, and Capbreton, an ancient fishing village, combine to make one of the loveliest resorts on the south Atlantic coast. The beach is sandy, safe, and vast, and the lake between the two towns tends to be a few degrees warmer than the ocean. A little farther down the coast are other popular beaches as well, most notably Ondres and Labenne-Plage. Information: *Syndicat d'Initiative*, Pl. Louis-Pasteur, Hossegor 40150 (phone: 58-43-72-35) and *Office de Tourisme*, Av. Georges-Pompidou, Capbreton 40130 (phone: 58-72-12-11).

Lacanau-Océan, Gironde – Visitors to this clean, modern, and quickly developing resort can enjoy not only the sprawling beaches along the coast but also the forest immediately inland and a freshwater lake of almost 5,000 acres. There is an 18-hole golf course, a group of 23 tennis courts, and a sailing school on nearby Lacanau Lake, not to mention excellent cycling and windsurfing. Information: *Office de Tourisme*, Pl. de l'Europe, Lacanau 33680 (phone: 56-03-21-01).

Soulac-sur-Mer, Gironde – A thriving port even before the Middle Ages, Soulac was also one of the stops along the pilgrimage to Santiago de Compostela in Spain. Just south of the Pointe de Grave, this tidy little town full of colorfully trimmed brick houses welcomes about 70,000 holidaymakers each summer. There are tennis courts, a gym, a cinema, a casino, and horses for rent. But most visitors prefer to spend at least some of their time away from the strand to explore the old town with its 12th-century Romanesque church and other relics. Information: *Syndicat d'Initiative*, 95 Rue de la Plage, Soulac-sur-Mer 33780 (phone: 56-09-86-61).

BASQUE COUNTRY: Biarritz, Pyrénées-Atlantiques – Once a favorite residence of Napoleon III, this fashionable resort now is popular with the casino crowd. British sun worshipers congregate here in great numbers. Offshore reefs protect the long sandy beaches under the spectacular rocky cliffs from the force of the surf, so the strands are as fine for bathing as they are for strolls. Information: *Comité de Tourisme et des Fêtes*, Square d'Ixelles, Biarritz 64200 (phone: 59-24-20-24).

St.-Jean-de-Luz, Pyrénées-Atlantiques – Louis XIV was married to Maria Theresa of Spain in 1660 in the Eglise St.-Jean-Baptiste, and the old town has not changed much since. The harbor still bustles with fishermen bringing in their tuna and sardines. The vast and well-patrolled beach has a reputation for being one of the country's safest. Information: *Syndicat d'Initiative,* Pl. du Maréchal-Foch, St.-Jean-de-Luz 64500 (phone: 59-26-03-16).

LANGUEDOC-ROUSSILLON: There are more than 100 miles of good sandy beaches backed by the Pyrénées along the Mediterranean coast from the Spanish border — and resorts of all types, both ancient fishing villages and modern pleasure grounds. And in this part of the country, the sunshine is practically guaranteed.

Collioure, Pyrénées-Orientales – This ancient port, a favorite of the 19th-century painters Matisse and Braque, boasts a 15th-century dungeon which Philip II of Spain transformed into a citadel and a medieval château royal with a view of the beaches that constitute one of the area's other charms. Information: *Syndicat d'Initiative,* 2 Rue Camille Pelletan, Collioure 66190 (phone: 68-82-15-47).

Argèles-Plage, Pyrénées-Orientales – The population of this massive modern seaside resort swells from its normal level of 5,000 to 300,000 in summer, and together with its neighboring communities, there are literally dozens of places to lodge or camp. A casino is open in Argèles-sur-Mer, a mile or so inland, in the summer. Information: *Office de Tourisme,* Pl. de l'Europe, Argèles-sur-Mer 66700 (phone: 68-81-15-85).

Le Cap d'Agde, Hérault – More than 7 miles of white sand at the foot of an extinct volcano and some 5 dozen clay tennis courts only begin to suggest why this is one of the Languedoc's most outstanding modern summer resorts. The handful of hotels are expensive; it's better to rent a studio apartment by the week. Information: *Office de Tourisme,* Palais des Congrès, BP 544, Le Cap d'Agde 4305 (phone: 67-26-38-58).

Leucate and Le Barcarès, Pyrénées-Orientales – Between these two ports is a 6-mile stretch of beach that has developed rapidly in the course of the last decade and offers everything from sailing and tennis to water skiing. And the beach is large enough not to seem overcrowded, even when it's teeming with tourists. Information: *Syndicat d'Initiative,* Pl. du Village, BP 16, Port-Barcares 66420 (phone: 68-86-16-56).

St.-Cyprien Plage, Pyrénées-Orientales – This futuristic resort is one of a handful in France designed to give the impression of paradise. There's a lake inhabited by flamingos and surrounded by sweet-smelling trees, a pair of golf courses, a thousand acres of lovely landscaping, and miles and miles of sandy beach. Information: *Syndicat d'Initiative St.-Cyprien,* Quai Rimbaud, St.-Cyprien Plage 66750 (phone: 68-21-01-33).

CÔTE D'AZUR: Many of the beaches are more stony than sandy, but the Côte d'Azur has a multitude of them, and they attract thousands of tourists. While hardly the place to get away from it all, the Côte offers spectacular scenery: gracefully curved bays and wildly beautiful coves, often backed by blindingly white cliffs and mountains fuzzed by silvery olive and cypress trees and dark green pines. The water is a dazzling shade of turquoise that almost matches the brilliant, flawless blue of the sky, and the light still possesses the exquisite brightness that lured many of the nation's most distinguished painters to work here at one time or another. There are hotels in all price ranges all along the coast; for people watching, the famous resorts such as Bandol, Cannes, Nice, and St.-Tropez hardly can be beat, and for peace and quiet, there are scores of smaller resorts.

Juan-les-Pins, Alpes-Maritimes – About halfway between Cannes and Nice, Juan-les-Pins is as chic and as night-crazed as St.-Tropez, with activity focused on the casino, which occupies a cool garden set just away from the sea. During the annual *World Jazz Festival,* things are even more active. The diving and sailing schools have a good reputation, and some two dozen hotels rise along the white sandy beach. Information: *Office de Tourisme,* 51 Bd. Charles-Guillaumont, Juan-les-Pins 06160 (phone: 93-61-04-98).

Mandelieu and La Napoule, Alpes-Maritimes – Just west of Cannes, the ancient village of Mandelieu and nearby La Napoule, with its superb sandy beach, make up a spectacular resort with tennis courts, golf courses, and camping facilities. Anyone who scrambles down the stony cliffs from the Corniche de l'Esterel between Cannes and St.-Raphaël might claim some picturesque little crescent of sand for the afternoon — to enjoy completely alone. Information: *Syndicat d'Initiative,* Av. de Cannes, Mandelieu-La Napoule 06210 (phone: 93-49-14-39).

Ste.-Maxime, Var – While this resort lies just across the bay from St.-Tropez, its lifestyle is light-years apart. Most female sunbathers wear tops as well as bottoms, and disco takes second place to quiet dinners and daytime strolls through the many boutiques. Young families are the primary clientele. There also are more than a dozen tennis courts, a 9-hole golf course, a sailing school, a marina full of pleasure craft — and, most delightful of all, a sensational view of mountains and coast just a mile north at the Sémaphore. Information: *Syndicat d'Initiative,* Promenade Simon-Lorière, Ste.-Maxime 83120 (phone: 94-96-19-24).

Sanary-sur-Mer, Var – Not far from the famous beaches at Bandol and La Ciotat, Sanary is a quiet place with a beach, an old town, and an open-air theater. And together with the islands of Bendor and Embiez, it is also a fabulous center for water sports. Hotel facilities are limited, so inquire well in advance. Information: *Syndicat d'Initiative,* Jardins de la Ville, Sanary-sur-Mer 83110 (phone: 94-74-01-04).

Gone Fishing

 One of the most relaxing ways to enjoy the French countryside is to spend a few lazy hours angling in one of its many streams, lakes, and coastal waters. It also offers a fine opportunity to get to know a particular locale in depth by day and to sample regional food and wine by night. It's not surprising that the sport is so popular among the French and visitors alike, from the calm inland waterways of the Auvergne to the turbulent mountain streams of the Pyrénées.

SEA ANGLING: France's 2,550 miles of shoreline are open to ocean and sea anglers year-round, and even amateurs can fish freely for albacore, bass, bonito, conger eel, dogfish, gar, goby, mackerel, mullet, black and yellow pollack, ray, sea bream, sole, and tuna — the fish found off the French coast — as long as they observe the rules relating to military ports, sewage facilities, and bag limits. Amateur sea anglers do not need permits, as a rule, to fish with hand-held rods or lines or to gather shellfish. However, to fish with most nets, a permit must be obtained from the local maritime authority.

It is also possible to fish underwater off the Atlantic and Mediterranean coasts using a harpoon gun, a mask, a breathing tube, and rubber fins. But the most common quarry — moray, mullet, sea perch, ray, rock bass, and turbot — are beginning to get wise and are drawing fishermen increasingly deeper, so that 50 to 65 feet currently is about normal. (The *Conseil Supérieur de la Pêche* in Paris describes this underwater fishing as "a test of endurance and coolness requiring a strong heart, strong lungs, a normal blood pressure, and perfect self-control.")

Instruction centers can be found in resorts such as Aix-en-Provence, Biarritz, Marseilles, Nice, Paris, and Toulon.

For further information, contact local fishing clubs or the *Fédération Française d'Etudes et de Sports Sous-Marins* (24 Quai de la Rive Neuve, Marseilles 13007; phone: 91-33-99-31).

FRESHWATER FISHING: All freshwater fishing enthusiasts must belong to a French angling and fisheries association and must pay an annual fisheries tax. This can sometimes be done at tackle shops, but any town Syndicat d'Initiative can provide details about obtaining the necessary documents. General information is available from the *Conseil Supérieur de la Pêche* (34 Av. de Malakoff, Paris 75016; phone: 45-01-20-20). Inland waters are divided into two categories, each with different seasons and regulations. The first category includes waters stocked mainly with trout and salmon, which water pollution has made increasingly rare in France. The trout season normally runs from mid-March to mid-September; the best fishing is usually in June. The second category includes all other waters and a wide variety of fish, including the following:

Barbel (*barbeau*). Sometimes stretching a yard long and weighing 20 pounds, barbel is among the largest of France's river fish and will fight fiercely. Cheese is normally an excellent bait.

Bleak (*ablette*). A smallish fish that measures about 8 inches long and weighs about 2 ounces, bleak is abundant in a number of rivers with slow currents and in a few lakes. It is relatively easy to catch with a floating line.

Bream (*brème*). This fish fills most of the waters in the second category. They can weigh as much as 20 pounds and are known to be attracted by the smell of garlic.

Carp (*carpe*). An extremely prolific fish, the carp is found most frequently in rivers and pools. It is intelligent and therefore among the most difficult freshwater fish to catch, but it has been seen to bite at worms, potatoes, corn and beans.

Chub (*chevesne*). Almost every fast-running river in France is loaded with these, which can weigh up to 7 or 8 pounds. A chub eats just about everything it finds and can be caught with a flyrod, a floating line, or by trolling.

Grayling (*ombre commun*). Now becoming rare in France, it is found primarily in the fast-running cold rivers of the east and central regions. It normally takes skilled fly-fishing to have success with grayling, which spoils easily and therefore must be eaten promptly.

Gudgeon (*goujon*). Small, like the bleak, the gudgeon often is used as a bait for larger fish such as pike. Generally found near sandbanks, the gudgeon is most frequently caught with earthworms.

Perch (*perche*). Found in many rivers and lakes, the carnivorous perch is considered by many gourmands to be the tastiest of the freshwater fish. It is also among the most fun for the sports person because it can be caught by dapping, casting, or with ground bait.

Pike (*brochet*). The pike, which rarely weighs more than 20 pounds and normally grows to about a yard long in France, usually clusters at a particular place and waits for prey. Found in most of the second-category waters in France, pike is most easily caught by trolling with live bait.

Pike perch (*sandre*). As the name implies, this is a kind of cross between a pike and a perch. It is found in pools, lakes, and temperate rivers throughout France. Like the pike, it eats mainly smaller fish, which are recommended as bait. It is much more prolific than other carnivorous fish and can grow to be 3 feet long and weigh up to 25 pounds.

Roach (*gardon*). The national fish of France, sometimes carnivorous and sometimes vegetarian, usually weighs in at about a pound or so and is found in most waters of the second category. Worms and corn are the recommended baits.

Salmon (*saumon*). Born in rivers, salmon swim out to live in the sea for about 3 years and then head back upstream to spawn. They can grow to a length of 4 feet or more and can weigh up to 70 pounds. While becoming rarer in France as a result of pollution, heavy sea fishing, and other factors, salmon are still abundant in the rivers of Brittany, the rushing streams of the Pyrénées, and the Loire and Allier rivers. They are most commonly caught by fly-fishing from a large birch rod, minnow spinning, or by casting with worms; it is illegal to keep fish less than 20 inches in length.

Trout (*truite*). They can be found in the mountain torrents of the Pyrénées, the Alps, and the Massif Central, as well as in the smaller streams of the plains. Two types are common in France: the indigenous *fario* and the rainbow trout, which was introduced to Europe in the 19th century. There is also a subspecies called the sea trout, which, like the salmon, go to live in the sea before returning to the river to spawn. The *fario*, with its distinctive red spots, usually grows to 5 or 6 pounds. Most trout are caught by artificial-fly-fishing or by casting with worms or natural insects. Experts say that the chances are best at sunrise and immediately before or after a storm.

Some of the outstanding freshwater fishing regions in France include the following:

Auvergne – From the summits of the Massif Central to the plains of the *département* of Allier, the fishing in Auvergne is renowned. Both *fario* and rainbow trout are abundant in the *départements* of Cantal, Haute-Loire, and Puy-de-Dôme. In Allier, most of the water is of the second category, but there is good trout fishing in the streams running from Bourbonnaise Mountain and in those west of Vichy. Salmon of 10 to 20 pounds are abundant in more than 600 miles of stream from their spawning grounds in the Haut-Allier. The streams in Puy-de-Dôme and Haute-Loire are particularly scenic. Barbel, carp, eel, grayling, perch, pike, and roach also are abundant in Auvergne. For more information, contact the *Fédération de Pêche* in each *département:*

Allier: Fédération de Pêche de l'Allier, 25 Bd. du Général-de-Gaulle Cusset 03300 (phone: 70-97-90-42)

Cantal: Fédération de Pêche du Cantal, 14 Allée du Vialenc, Aurillac 15000 (phone: 71-48-19-25)

Haute-Loire: Fédération de Pêche de la Haute-Loire, 32 Rue Henri-Chas, Le Puy en Velay 43000 (phone: 71-09-09-44)

Puy-de-Dôme: Fédération de Pêche du Puy-de-Dôme, 65 Rue de l'Oradou, Clermont-Ferrand 63000 (phone: 73-91-42-33)

For a list of hotels in the area that are ideally situated for fishing, contact the *Comité Régional de Tourisme d'Auvergne,* 43 Av. Julien, BP 395, Clermont-Ferrand 63011 (phone: 73-93-04-03).

Aveyron – The French call the region stretching from the foothills of the Massif Central to the Causses dominating the Languedoc the "Green Country of the Midi," and with good reason. Serene, beautiful, and known for its many castles, cathedrals, and Roman chapels, it offers the angler 4,000 miles of rivers and 8,800 acres of lakes. From the large lakes of Le Lévézou to the valleys of Aveyron, Lot, and Tarn, the region is one of unspoiled natural scenery. The four best rivers for fishing are the Lot, the Aveyron, the Viaur, and the Tarn, which, together with their numerous tributaries, are loaded with barbel, chub, gudgeon, perch, and trout. Of the many lakes, the Castelnau-Lassouts and Golinhac are especially attractive and offer unusually extensive varieties of fishing. Hotels, camping spots, holiday farms, and country lodgings abound. Information: *Fédération de la Pêche,* 52 Rue de l'Embergue, Rodez 12003 (phone: 65-42-56-03).

Brittany – The small country city of Châteaulin on the Nantes–Brest Canal is a pleasant and practical starting point for the fisherman in Brittany. About a tenth of all the salmon caught in France each year, the best of them weighing 24 pounds, come from this waterway. But since some parts of the canal are much better than others, it's a good idea to get some advice first. Sea trout also are abundant here, especially in the section between Guilly-Glas and Châteaulin. The best time is from the end of February to the first of April, while summer salmon can be caught from mid-May to mid-June. The Aulne and Hyères rivers are excellent for other varieties of trout. June and October are the months for pike and whitefish, which normally weigh 5 or 6 pounds. The estuaries abound in bass, eel, mullet, smelt, and sole. Information: *Fédération de la Pêche,* 1 Rue Poher, Quimper 29000 (phone: 98-53-16-61).

Dauphiné – The mountainous Dauphiné region southeast of Lyons may be renowned for its winter sports, but it is popular in summer for its fine rivers, streams, and mountain lakes. The Isère, a first-category water upstream of Grenoble, for instance, has plenty of grayling and trout; the resorts of Brignoud, La Terrace, and Le Versoud make good headquarters for fishing there. Downstream of Grenoble, the stream is second-category water, primarily stocked with pike and roach; the nearest resorts are St.-Marcellin and Tullins. South of Grenoble is yet another stream, which splits to become the Drac and Romanche; grayling and trout prevail before the fork, second-category fish afterward. The region also has its lakes — most notably the Monteynard-Avignonet at Avignonet, filled with bream, gudgeon, perch, roach, and trout; the Paladru at Charavines-les-Bains and Paladru, stocked with bream, perch, pike, and trout; and the several lakes around Laffrey, where the fishing is quite varied. Information: *Fédération de la Pêche de l'Isère,* Rue du Palais, Grenoble 38000 (phone: 76-44-28-39).

Hautes-Alpes – Trout fishing is excellent in the torrential mountain streams southeast of Isère, both in the first- and second-category waters and in the mountain lakes. The second-category waters in the area are also rich with chub and barbel, and perch can be found in the Serre-Ponçon lake. A particularly invigorating area for the outdoorsman, this region near the Italian border also has many camping areas and navigable waterways. Information: *Maison des Hautes-Alpes,* 4 Av. de l'Opéra, Paris 75001 (phone: 42-06-05-08).

Normandy – After tracing the path of the Allied invasion and tossing back a few drams of the special apple brandy of Calvados, many anglers from abroad seek out the spectacular trout fishing of the heart of Normandy. The *département* of Orne, in particular, boasts of its rivers Huisne, Mayenne, Orne, and Sarthe and of smaller streams like the Egrenne, Noireau, Risle, Rouvre, and Varenne. For pike, try the Sarthe around Mêle-sur-Sarthe and Alençon. Information: *Fédération des Pêcheurs de l'Orne,* 1 Pl. à l'Avoine, Alençon 61003 (phone: 33-26-10-66).

Pyrénées – For trout and salmon fishing, it is hard to improve on the Pyrénées, both inside and outside the boundaries of the Pyrénées National Park, a scenic reserve created in 1967 along the Spanish border. About half of the 250 Pyrénées mountain lakes are stocked with various kinds of trout, and there is at least one good fishing stream in each valley; the Gave d'Ossau is particularly fine. Outside the park, the lakes of Barèges and Campan are excellent for a wide variety of fishing. In fact, one of the only problems with the angling in this area is that some of the waters are hard to find or are accessible only by foot. Anglers interested in this area should be sure to investigate the Gave d'Oloron, which is probably the most famous salmon torrent in the western section. One expert recommends following the salmon upstream in February and March from Peyrehorade to Sauveterre, from there in April and May to Navarrenx, and continuing upstream during the summer months to Orlon-Ste.-Marie. Information: *Le Parc National des Pyrénées,* Tarbes 65000 (phone: 62-93-30-60); and *La Maison des Pyrénées,* 15 Rue St.-Augustin, Paris 75002 (phone: 42-61-58-18).

Var – In the extreme southeastern section of France, where the climate almost always is pleasant and the air has the smell of the sea, this area has plenty of freshwater streams to keep the inland angler happy. The River Argens, with its scenic falls, begins near Seillons and is first-category water until Carces — fast, cold, and full of good trout; though the banks sometimes are steep, the stream always is accessible. In addition, there are a number of tributary brooks with their own population of trout — the Cauron, the Meironne, and the Rigoirds, for instance. Other good fishing waters include the Caramy, teeming with bream, perch, pike, roach, and, at least downstream of Vins, some large trout. Then there's the Issole, a pretty river with a rocky sand bed that draws fishermen from Besse, Cabasse, Flassans, Garéoult, and St.-Anasthasie, not to mention the Verdon, the clear green river that flows down from the Hautes-Alpes. The 232-acre Lake Carces, which stretches for 2½ miles from the dam at Caramy, is another favorite fishing hole; famous for pike perch, it also is rich in black bass, bream, carp, chub, pike, and roach. The artificial 1,384-acre St.-Cassien Lake, which reaches 28 miles behind Montauroux, is also popular. Information: *Fédération Départemental des Associations de Pêche et de Pisciculture du Var,* BP 104, Brignoles 83170 (phone: 94-69-05-56).

Horsing Around

Holidays on horseback in France unquestionably are among the country's best-kept secrets. That's too bad, because seeing the countryside astride a spirited steed can be pure delight. But whether the animal hauls your belongings while you walk alongside, pulls your wagon, or carries you from farm to village through deep woods, you will travel through stretches of France that few visitors ever see, a countryside whose rugged beauty is only enhanced by the creaking of saddle leather and the steady thud of hooves.

Equestrian holidays come in a variety of breeds. There are centers with riding instruction, multi-day horseback excursions, and week-long expeditions in horse-drawn gypsy carts. Highly organized centers provide expert instruction for every level of rider, including the beginner, while guest farms specialize in horseback *randonées* (rambles) along their area's wooded paths and country roads, with accommodations that can vary from tent to straw-littered barn to cozy hotel. Some programs are designed for teenagers as well. In any case, pastoral-pure air, authentic country food, a relaxed pace, and an almost total absence of tourist hordes (and sometimes even passing vehicles) are the chief allures. Each center can provide specific details on the *randonées* it offers. Reserve in advance since horse farms and riding hotels always are small, family-run affairs with a loyal clientele. And allow plenty of time for exchanges of correspondence.

For those who would rather limit their relationship with horses to admiration from afar, France offers a number of famous racecourses — nine around Paris alone. Deauville, Vichy, and Cagnes-sur-Mer also attract everybody who is anybody during the summer racing season. Chantilly has a most unusual horse museum that is well worth a visit. The *haras nationaux* (national stud farms) are equally fascinating.

For more information about riding in France, contact the *Association Nationale pour le Tourisme Equestre et l'Equitation de Loisirs,* Ile Saint-Germain, 170 Quai de Stalingrad, Issy les Moulineaux 92130 (phone: 45-54-29-54).

CENTRE EQUESTRE DE ZANIÈRES, Ardes-sur-Couze, Puy-de-Dôme: A friendly atmosphere prevails at this family-oriented center specializing in week-long *randonées* around the volcanoes, valleys, and lakes of this varied region. Accommodations are simple, both at the center and on trips into the surrounding area. The horses are knowledgeable. And the riders, who travel up to ten in a group, generally are highly accomplished. *Randonées* are scheduled from May through September. It's also possible to leave a teenager behind in a specially designed riding program for young people. Information: *Centre Equestre de Zanières,* Ardes-sur-Couze 63420 (phone: 73-71-84-30).

LA CHEVAUCHÉE DES DEUX MERS, Aubiet, Gers: Twice each summer, a dozen or so experienced riders cross southeastern France from the Atlantic to the Mediterranean, caravan style. The 300-mile trip is a wonderful fortnight's exploration of a seldom visited slice of the country and includes a stop in glowing Carcassonne. Information: *Le Cheval Vert,* Lussan, Aubiet 32270 (phone: 62-65-93-47).

FERME EQUESTRE DU VAL D'ADOUR, Bazillac, Hautes-Pyrénées: In the high valley of the Adour River, this farm offers week-long riding experiences in the lush farmland of a little-known corner of France not far from the national stud farm, the Haras de Tarbes, the home of some magnificent examples of Anglo-Arabian stallions from July through January. Run by a family of horse breeders, this is a serious professional center that can guide a visitor from his first time in the saddle to the highest level of horsemanship. Mornings are usually spent on the trail; afternoons are customarily devoted to group instruction. Every sort of accommodation is available, from camping on the farm itself to luxurious quarters at nearby hotels. The atmosphere is intimate, with no more than ten riders accepted at any given time. Information: *Ferme Equestre du Val d'Adour,* Bazillac, Rabastens de Bigorre 65140 (phone: 62-96-59-44).

CHANTILLY, Oise, Picardie: Known as "La Ville du Cheval," the city of the horse, Chantilly has an equestrian museum, a racetrack and training center, and a population of more than 3,000 thoroughbreds. The lordly 18th-century stables, which furnished mounts to the royal court in nearby Paris, are open to the public as the *Musée Vivant du Cheval* (the Living Museum of the Horse); they house stallions from all the country's national stud farms, as well as a unique collection of equestrian art. Less than an hour from the Champs-Elysées. Information: *Musée Vivant du Cheval,* Chantilly 60500 (phone: 44-57-13-13).

L'ETRIER DU MONT-HEDIN, Signy Le Petit, Ardennes: Is there any more romantic name in France than Champagne? As it turns out, this beautiful region is exceptionally well supplied with riding facilities. This one offers accommodations in rustic but comfortable quarters, and in addition to a complete program of riding instruction and excursions, there's glorious champagne to make every adventure just that much more effervescent. Information: *L'Etrier du Mont-Hedin,* Tarzy, Signy le Petit 08380 (phone: 24-54-32-52).

LES RANDONNÉES SAUVAGE DE L'HABITARELLE, Châteauneuf-de-Randon, Lozère: For the hardy and adventurous, there are 5-to-8-day riding odysseys here in the Cévennes National Park, of Robert Louis Stevenson and *Travels with a Donkey* fame. Other routes go around the volcanoes of the Haut Vivarais area, through the Gorges of the Tarn, or even across Corsica. This is for experienced riders only, those unfazed by tentless, sleeping bag, starlit nights. Information: *Les Randonnées Sauvage de l'Habitarelle,* Châteauneuf-de-Randon, Lozère 48170 (phone: 66-47-90-10).

CORSICA: More than 500 miles of riding trails crisscross this mountainous Mediterranean island, and many of them still are used by shepherds and forest rangers. Picturesque villages along the way offer accommodations ranging from the primitive to the comfortable, and dozens of equestrian centers will organize expeditions that run from a few days to a couple of weeks. Information: *Agence Régionale du Tourisme,* 22 Cours Grandval, BP 19, Ajaccio, Corsica 20176 (phone: 95-51-15-23).

DEAUVILLE, Calvados: A sunset gallop along the beach here still ranks among France's prime existential delights, and this is one of the equestrian capitals of Europe. Summer witnesses an orgy of polo and racing, but excellent riding programs and facilities are available year-round. The wonderful seafront mansion known as the *Hôtel Normandy,* for instance, offers vacation weeks that include free access to the *Club Hippique d'Oxer* (the Oxer Horse Club) and lessons in manège, dressage, and jumping. The food is sensational, the rooms princely, and the location just a canter from France's classiest gambling casino. Information: *Hôtel Normandy,* 38 Rue Jean-Mermoz, Deauville 14800 (phone: 31-98-66-22).

L'HOMME A CHEVAL, Eygalières, Bouches-du-Rhône: An enticing menu of long excursions — to Arles, Avignon, and the lonely landscape of the Camargue — or an equally appealing assortment of day trips from a home base should satisfy every rider's inclinations. The stay-putters can choose from dormitory to *grande luxe* lodgings in neighboring hotels. The excursioners sleep over in farms, inns, and camping sites. Information: *L'Homme à Cheval,* Eygalières, Bouches-du-Rhône 13810 (phone: 90-95-90-57).

LES BEIGES, La Roche-l'Abeille, Haute-Vienne: Set in a lush forest-bordered valley in a verdant and undisturbed region, this farm offers something for everyone — from 3 hours of daily instruction at the farm itself for the inexperienced to overnight excursions in the surrounding area with stops in neighboring farmhouses for the more expert. Non-riders can join the latter group each evening — arriving in style in horse-drawn carriages. Teenagers who ride well can join week-long excursions especially designed for them or stay on their own at the farm for daily instruction. Information: *Les Beiges,* La Roche-l'Abeille 87800 (phone: 55-00-70-92).

CERCLE HIPPIQUE DU CHATEAU LA DOUVE, Le Bourge d'Ire, Maine-et-Loire: This handsome hotel is a Loire château recently renovated and transformed with riders in mind. Riding facilities in the park around the hotel are open all year. Accommodations are more luxurious here than the often rustic lodgings found where riding is the star attraction. Information: *Cercle Hippique du Château La Douve,* Le Gourge d'Ire 49780 (phone: 41-61-54-54).

CHÂTEAU HÔTEL DE COATGUELEN, Pléhédel par Lanvollen, Côtes-du-Nord: This glamorous 19th-century manor is set in about 250 acres of meadows and parkland near Brittany's quaint ports, impressive cliffs, and sandy beaches. The invigorating Breton air will only enhance the daily riding routine. Moreover, the hotel offers golf facilities and cooking classes for the less athletically inclined as well as outstanding seafood, the crêpes for which the region is famous, and wonderful local cider. Open from April to December. Information: *Château Hôtel de Coatguelen,* Pléhédel par Lanvollen 22290 (phone: 96-22-31-24).

CLUB EQUESTRE LOISIRS "LA GRANDE VIGNOBLE," St.-Julien-de-Crempse, Dordogne: Surrounded by acres of woods and meadows deep in the countryside, this manor house built in the days of Louis XIV offers luxurious accommodations, gleaming stirrups, and saddles that look as if they were purveyed by Gucci. Aside from the outstanding riding facilities and instruction that completes the picture, there are tennis courts, a heated swimming pool, bikes to rent, and a sauna to soothe away sore muscles after an active day. Information: *Club Equestre Loisirs "La Grande Vignoble,"* St. Julien-de-Crempse, Villamblard 24140 (phone: 53-24-23-18).

CLUB MÉDITERRANÉE, Pompadour, Limousin: The efficient *Club Med* operation virtually guarantees a successful vacation, and the green paradise at Pompadour is no exception. While riders wander around chestnut-shaded paths or take lessons in the covered riding school, others can use the 22 tennis courts, a 9-hole pitch and putt golf course, and a heated swimming pool. The regal facilities include a pony club for children. A glorious place for riders and non-riders alike. Information: *Club Med,* Domaine de Noailles, Arnac Pompadour 19230 (phone: 55-73-31-33).

HORSE RACING

With Pigalle turf touts rubbing jodhpurs with the *beau monde* of the elegant Faubourg-St.-Honoré, the *Hippodrome d'Auteuil* in the Bois de Boulogne supplies a supremely Parisian day at the races; open year-round. Also worth attending are the evening races at the *Champs de Courses de Vincennes*. The restaurant here, *Le Paddock,* affords diners a splendid view of the track (phone: 43-68-64-94).

From June to mid-September, stately old Vichy offers the ultimate in stylish horse racing in an atmosphere of thermal baths, palm-lined promenades, and twirling white parasols. The *Grand Prix de Vichy* in late July is one of the high points.

And the August racing season at Deauville on the Normandy coast, France's answer to England's Ascot, is one of the country's major social and sporting highlights. The *Grand Prix de Deauville,* at the end of the month, is a highlight.

Some of the year's other major racing events include the *Grand Prix d'Amérique,* a late January annual in Paris (*Vincennes*); the *Prix du Président de la République,* in Paris (*Auteuil*) in the middle of April; the *Prix de Diane,* in Chantilly in mid-June; late June's *Grand Prix de Paris* in Paris (*Longchamp*); and the *Prix de l'Arc de Triomphe,* in early October in Paris (*Longchamp*).

Visitors to Paris also can pick up the flavor of the track by reading *Paris-Turf* (in

French), available at kiosks, or by dropping in at the *Champs-Elysées Horse Club* (34 Av. des Champs-Elysées), where all the action is on television and all the jockeying at the bar.

Freewheeling by Two-Wheeler

To understand just how seriously the French have always taken the sport of bicycling, a visitor has only to consider the annual *Tour de France* (won by an American twice in the last 5 years). The world's premier bicycle competition, it has the French people cheering from the valleys of the Loire to the mountain passes of the Alps. But though this competition is reserved for professional cyclists, the passion that spawned it is felt by many, and there are all kinds of other activities and competitions for less serious cyclists at every level. Among them, there also is a distance program, with merit certificates to recognize accomplishment in a variety of categories; those who cover a stipulated territory, and pass through certain checkpoints in the various *départements,* complete certain short but difficult itineraries, or make certain long-distance trips, and the like, may earn special certificates.

However, most visitors, who just want to pedal through the French countryside in a leisurely fashion, merely take advantage of the itineraries provided through the various regional societies of the *Fédération Française de Cyclotourisme* (*FFCT;* 8 Rue Jean-Marie-Jégo, Paris 75013; phone: 45-80-30-21). These (easy to hard) *Randonnées Permanentes,* which can be taken by individuals or by groups at any time of year and normally cover several hundred miles over country roads, are designed to be completed over a period of days or weeks, with stops specified at intervals of a dozen or so miles. While written in French, the place names, route numbers, and distances are comprehensible even to those who do not speak the language. The *FFCT* will supply specific information for all of the routes listed below.

BURGUNDY: Setting out from Dijon, the ancient capital of the duchy of Burgundy with its Louis XIV palace, this trip meanders along winding country roads, through villages full of flower-bedecked stone buildings that date from the 16th century, past immense cathedrals and imposing abbeys and châteaux. There is an undeniable tranquillity to it all. In Dijon proper, it takes in the Hôtel Chambellan and the typically Burgundian old Rue des Forges, the pure Gothic Cathédrale St.-Bénigne, the curious 15th-century Eglise St.-Michel, the Renaissance Palais de Justice, and the Palace of the Dukes of Burgundy. It skirts a crannied quarter of picturesque old streets and passes the Clairvaux wine cellars, which were built by 13th-century monks. Heading northwest and continuing roughly counterclockwise around Burgundy, it subsequently encompasses St.-Germain-Source-Seine, where the famous river begins, the ruins of a 12th-century château at Maisey-le-Duc, and Ancy-le-Franc, where one of the most magnificent Renaissance châteaux in Burgundy is open to the public. Tonnerre, a comfortable small town on a hill full of vines and greenery, is another stop, as is Noyers, a handsome fortified city that has changed little since the Middle Ages, right down to the twisty outdoor stairways, the ancient stone walls, and the half-timbered architecture. Beaune, famous for its wine, is one of some 3 dozen other towns on the tour. 750 miles (1200km).

CATHARIST SITES: This region in south-central France is known for its many fortresses and other remains from the 12th century, when it was inhabited by a group of Catharists, one of the medieval Christian sects who believed that Christ was of angelic and not human origin. The tour begins in Toulouse, known for its many churches and its famous Hôtel de Ville (Town Hall), and continues through Carcassonne, the 13th-century walled city that remains Europe's largest fortress. Subsequent stops include the ancient blockhouse of Mirepoix, the ruins of the Puilaurenx Château, the fortified 14th-century village of Lagrasse, and the wine city of Béziers. 482 miles (771 km).

BOURBONNAIS: The ancient province of Bourbonnais, famous for its landscape, lies almost in the dead center of the country west of Burgundy. In the *département* of Allier, the area covered on this tour begins and ends in Vichy, famous for its mineral water and for having been the collaborationist government headquarters during World War II. Traveling west and then clockwise around the *département,* the ride shows off soft mountains, an 11th-century church at Veauce, the Forêt Château-Charles, the Tartasse Valley near Ronnet, the ancient market town of Hérisson and its splendid ruined 14th-century château, the spa at Bourbon-l'Archambault that has been serving rheumatics since Roman times, the magnificent Romanesque church at Château-Montagne, and the museum of prehistory at Glozel. One of the most interesting areas is the Forêt-de-Tronçais, whose 26,000-acre oak grove is reputed to be the most beautiful in the country. In old French, *tronce* referred to huge oak trunks, hence Tronçais. 325 miles (520 km).

GIRONDE: Anyone familiar with fine wine will recognize many of the stops on this tour of the green Bordeaux region, immediately southwest of the Dordogne: attractive little Pauillac, St.-Emilion, Monségur, and the walled city of Blaye. Beginning in Bordeaux proper and moving through the Dordogne Valley before circling westward again, the tour spends a good deal of time southwest of the city in the quiet Landes forest, an amazing trail-crossed tract of regal conifers. Especially in the Médoc, the terrain often is flat, and the parallel rows of vines, with every plant trimmed to the same height, is a study in elegant precision. 478 miles (765 km).

DORDOGNE: That there are more than 1,000 châteaux and country manors in this lush area of rolling hills, fern-carpeted forests, and cliff-edged rivers — more than in any other *département* in France — is just one of the charms of this tour. It begins in Périgueux, the capital of truffles and foie gras, and proceeds through one of the sections of the country that is richest in ruins and religious art. Splendid vistas are the norm and there are innumerable small villages full of mellow stone churches and old houses dating to the Middle Ages. Serenely set Brantôme is one of the highlights, for its abbey founded by Charlemagne, its brace of excellent restaurants, and the hyacinth-choked Dronne River that meanders through it. 370 miles (592 km). See also the *Périgord* tour route, DIRECTIONS.

CHÂTEAUX OF THE LOIRE: Probably no region of France is better suited to quiet pedaling than this area surrounding the quiet Loire River. The lazy stream, the colorful villages, the spectacular valleys, and the beautiful châteaux combine to draw thousands of tourists each summer. The *FFCT* recommends four itineraries, all beginning in La Folie. The first takes in Balzac's birthplace at Tours and the châteaux near Vallière, Langeais, La Gaudinière, and Le Lude. A second travels southeast to Montbazon, famous for its ancient dungeon, and includes the châteaux near Azay-sur-Indre, Montrésor, Valençay, Orbigny, and Montpoupon. The third heads west to the châteaux near Candé, Pont-de-Ruan, Chinon, Saumur, and Montsoreau. And the fourth follows an easterly route through Montrichard, Fougères-sur-Bièvre, Chambord, and St.-Gervais-la-Forêt. 443 miles (709 km).

CALVADOS: Best known for its apple cider, this area of Normandy appeals to cyclists because of its diverse geography. The *FFCT* itinerary runs along the coast through the picturesque old port of Honfleur, takes in the splendid beaches of Deauville and Arromanches, visits the Louis XIII château and the beautiful, peaceful Cérisy-la-Forêt (Cerisy Forest), the Orne Valley, and the caves and high rocky cliffs of "Swiss" Normandy, which center on Clécy. 287 miles (459 km).

BRITTANY: Beginning in cosmopolitan Nantes, where Jules Verne was born in 1828, this itinerary quickly takes you to more rural scenery, taking in the fishermen's hamlet of Pont-St.-Martin, the fortified city of Guérande, the eerie megaliths at Carnac, the rocky and surf-pounded coast at Quiberon, and the folkloric center of Brittany at Quimper. Modern Brest and the famous islet of Mont-St.-Michel — perhaps France's best-known monument after Notre-Dame and the Eiffel Tower — also is on the tour. 852 miles (1,363 km).

JOAN OF ARC ROUTE: This pilgrimage, which runs from Lorraine through the Loire country to Normandy, begins in Domrémy-la-Pucelle, where the national heroine was born in 1412, and continues on a line through Tonnerre and Auxerre in Burgundy, passes through Chinon, and takes in Troyes, Reims, sections of Normandy, and Rouen, where she was executed in 1431. 934 miles (1,494km).

HAUTE-PROVENCE: Covered with lavender fields and olive groves, this dry, mountainous region in the extreme southeast of France offers exceptionally scenic terrain for the cyclist. The route begins at Dignes, the capital of "the Lavender Alps," and extends spoke-like in four directions. The southern spoke travels through Moustier-Ste.-Marie, an ancient village whose maze of alleys is set in the shadows of some fantastic boulders. East, there is picturesque Castellane, a village noted for Romanesque churches and magnificent views. To the north, there's Seyne-les-Alpes, where Louis XIV built an interesting citadel; the view from its ramparts now is a favorite with visitors. And the western route leads to the ancient fortress town of Sisteron, to Forcalquier, noted for its 15th-century Gothic fountain, and to the old market town of Manosque. 325 miles (520km).

EDELWEISS ARIEGEOIS: Ariège, in the Pyrénées, is perfect for the conditioned cyclist. Surrounded by these vast, beautiful mountains, the tour begins in the heart of the Pyrénées in tiny Pamiers and includes prehistoric sites, pine forests, and a moving 12th-century monastery at Montjoie. 538 miles (861 km).

MONT-BLANC TOUR: A demanding route that circles Mont-Blanc, the highest peak in the Alps, this itinerary begins in medieval Albertville at 1,132 feet, continues through the popular ski resorts of Megève and Chamonix, and penetrates into Switzerland, where, in the village of Col de la Forclaz at 5,009 feet, it descends rapidly — with the Rhône Valley always in view — to the pretty Swiss village of Martigny at 1,561 feet. This marks the beginning of a steep climb into Italy via an 8,100-foot mountain pass that has been well traveled since the Bronze Age. Aoste, founded by Caesar Augustus in 25 BC, and Bourg-St.-Maurice are among the final stops. 200 miles (320 km).

BASQUE PROVINCES: Using the seaside resort of Biarritz as the starting point, this excursion passes through the green hills of the French and Spanish Basque country to Bayonne, where there is a Basque museum, and to Bonloc, a popular rest stop along the pilgrimage to Santiago de Compostela. After crossing into Spain at Arnéguy, it takes in Santesteban, known for its picturesque houses, and San Sebastián, which has a magnificent beach. In Fuenterrabía there is a fine *parador,* once a medieval fortress and now an inn (phone: 943-642140), which makes a pleasant overnight stop before the route turns once again to France and the house of the composer Maurice Ravel in Ciboure. 337 miles (539 km).

FOR MORE INFORMATION

The main *FFCT* office (8 Rue Jean-Marie-Jégo, Paris 75013; phone: 45-80-30-21) can provide bicycling route maps as well as information about where to rent multi-speed bicycles; also available is a list of the train stations in France where simple one-speed bicycles may be rented and returned to another station. For information about organized biking tours all over France, contact *Bicyclub* (8 Pl. de la Porte Champerret, Paris

75017; phone: 47-66-55-92). Also see "Camping and RVs, Hiking and Biking" in *When and How to Go,* GETTING READY TO GO.

Great Walks and Mountain Rambles

 While no European terrain can rival the vast reaches of open land so abundant in the United States, Europe does offer an enormous range of scenic country close to wherever you happen to be visiting. This is particularly true of France.

Here the hiker will discover varied terrain suitable for all kinds, and angles, of walking. There are the high mountain ranges of the Alps and the Pyrénées, the green volcanic outcrops of the Massif Central, the forests of Burgundy and the Ile-de-France, and the gently rolling countryside of Brittany and Normandy. Add to this a climate that generally is benign and (south of the Loire) warm in summer, plus excellent food and wine whose consumption can be even more easily justified after a day on the trail, and, once you get into the *arrière pays* (the backcountry), very low prices. And although it was a Frenchman who coined the phrase "*une journée de sentier, huit jours de santé*" ("one day on the trail makes for eight healthy days"), the nation's footpaths are more or less empty — except, that is, during the month of August, France's peak holiday time.

France's star treks are the Sentiers de la Grande Randonnée, the more than 18,000 miles of footpaths that wend their way into even the most remote corners of the country. Each Grande Randonnée (GR) trail is numbered, and each is marked with distinctive red and white blazes on trees, telegraph posts, rock faces, walls, gateposts, and the like, wherever there is a shift in direction or point of ambiguity. Some are straight routes and some are circular, and the network covers an immense variety of landscapes. The GR5 alone spans the Alps from Lake Geneva down to the Mediterranean. The GR10, a 400-mile (640 km) hill walk that will take even the fittest hiker many weeks to complete, covers the Pyrénées. The GR3 meanders along the Loire through the château country. The GR65 follows the famous 620-mile (992 km) pilgrims' road from Le Puy to Santiago de Compostela and the Spanish frontier. In addition, there are six Trans-European footpaths like the 1,240-mile (1,984 km) E2 from Ostend to Nice, a little over half of which lies within France.

These are the long walks, several lasting for many weeks, but the French trail network offers a little something for everyone. Even the long trails contain a number of cutouts or feeder trail variations by which the route can be shortened to the needs of a brief vacation or weekend break. In addition, every province has at least one perfect center for hikes and its nearby *sentiers de pays* (country trails). In Brittany, for example, Huelgoat in wooded Finistère has an abundance of them, as do the Seine Valley and the hilly Suisse Normande area near Alençon in neighboring Normandy. In the Pyrénées, Ascain in the green Borique country is good, as are Luchon, which has walks across the border into Spain; Luz-St.-Sauveur, south of Lourdes and close to the spectacular Cirque de Gavarnie; or, in the east, Font-Romeau on the high plateau of the Cerdagne. In each case, you'll find spectacular scenery, plenty of inexpensive accommodations, and good, good walking.

Before choosing a specific area of the country for hiking, look at a general map of France that shows physical characteristics, so as not to opt for terrain too demanding for your level of fitness. For those who are sedentary, the choice of a mountainous region would be foolhardy; far more sensible are areas such as the Brittany heathlands, the open plateau of the Causse country south of the Massif Central, and the green Basque foothills of the southwest.

Since hot weather is not necessarily a welcome companion on a walk, it's best to avoid the southern half of the country in midsummer. And since it can get extremely warm anywhere south of the Loire between May and September, the wise walker will get most of his day's journey done before midday. Although it is possible to get caught in a snowstorm as late as April in the northern areas, the essential pieces of equipment are a hat, shorts, plenty of sunblock, rainwear, and something warm, just in case.

In more remote areas, a backpack, sleeping bag and pad, cookstove, food, and other gear are requisites. It's possible to camp out in the wild except in high summer, when certain sites are restricted because of the considerable risk of fire. In general, although *camping sauvage* never is actively encouraged (and actually is forbidden in the national and regional parks), the French tend to turn a blind eye to small tents in remote areas that are placed discreetly above 5,000 feet and in areas that are an hour or more away from alternative accommodation.

Throughout France, a hiker will have little difficulty finding simple, inexpensive accommodations in villages along the way. In fact, since French walkers prefer a real roof rather than mere canvas at night, GR trails are equipped, at intervals of 5 hours or so, with *gîtes d'étape* — small, usually unmanned hostels in a converted barn or other farm building that are fitted out with dormitory accommodations for around 20 people, but no bedding, and kitchen facilities (inexpensive and in demand; reserve by telephone a day in advance in summer). In mountainous regions, the *gîtes'* counterparts are the basic huts called *abris,* some staffed and some not — warm and dry, but not much more (free). Locations are noted invariably on the *Topo Guides* and on the IGN 1:50,000 or 1:25,000 series of maps (described at greater length below). Here's a sampling of some of the better areas for hiking in France.

ALPS: The Alps is the area where walking turns into scrambling, climbing, and mountaineering; where the times given in trail guides are as important as the distances; and where the best of the trails demand fitness, outdoor skills, and proper equipment. It should not be forgotten that every year the mountains claim the lives of hundreds of hikers, many of whom should never have ventured from the security of easy footpaths. Yet some of France's classic walks are in the Alps, and they are as irresistible to the committed hiker and climber as the *Louvre* is to lovers of fine art. Consider the best-known route, the Tour de Mont-Blanc; a 14-day adventure around Europe's tallest mountain, it offers plenty of scrambling and, for the upwardly mobile, a complement of climbing as well. The 240-mile (384 km) Grande Traversée des Alpes Françaises, GR5, dotted by 100 mountain refuges, is another major walk. And in the Vanoise, France's first national park, hikers can tackle the Tour Pédestre, which runs from the Tarentaise across to Maurienne, with winter ski resorts as stopovers. Huge numbers of day hikes complete the picture. Mondane, Val d'Isère, and Plan d'Amont give access to the 300 miles of trails in this park, and the summer and winter resort of Chamonix boasts an additional 180 miles of marked trails into the mountains around it. Local *Syndicats d'Initiative* and branches of the *Club Alpin Français* are the best sources of information for the surrounding areas. For other details: *Comité Régional du Tourisme* (*CIMES*), Maison du Tourisme, 14 Rue de la République, Grenoble 38019 (phone: 76-54-34-36); and the *Syndicat d'Initiative,* Bonlieu, 1 Rue Jean-Jaurès, Annecy 74000 (phone: 50-45-00-33). See also *The Alps,* DIRECTIONS.

AUVERGNE: The very center of France, this northern corner of the Massif Central provides an excellent introduction to France's spikier landscapes. The area's finest scenic assets lie in the domain of the fairly energetic backpacker. But because the land is predominantly rural and dotted with small market towns that serve the needs of the wheat farming, sheep raising, and vineyard tending population, the hiker will find a good variety of walks of all grades in each of its four *départements:* Allier, which the Bourbons called home, the least rugged quarter, with modest hills covered by forests and farmlands; the Haute-Loire, the source of its grand namesake river (no more than a trickle in summer); remote Cantal, with gorgeous valley scenery; and the volcanic core known as Puy de Dôme, whose 500-million-year-old green hills are hard to beat for anyone planning to day-hike out of a home base. GR routes, as well as sections of long-distance trails, ribbon the whole of the Auvergne. Particularly rewarding is GR40, the 96-mile (154 km) Tour du Velay, which circles some moderately hilly terrain in the Haute-Loire and Le Puy de Dôme. The GR400, known as the Tour des Volcans du Chantal, offers 87.6 (140 km) additional scenic miles. The GR65, covering 84 miles (134 km), was named the Sentier de St.-Jacques-de-Compostelle after the old pilgrims' trail that some of its sections follow. And GR441, called the Tour de la Chaîne des Puys, takes in more than 3 dozen extinct volcanoes as it makes the circuit of the Volcanoes National Park, one of a pair in the area. Morvan, the second, is full of woods, rivers, and primarily artificial lakes. Summers are hot and dry, though with an occasional thunderstorm and generally chilly nights. Information: *Maison de l'Auvergne,* 194 bis Rue de Rivoli, Paris 75001 (phone: 42-61-82-38); *Comité Régional du Tourisme,* 43 Av. Julien, Clermont-Ferrand 63011 (phone: 73-93-04-03).

BRITTANY AND NORMANDY: Good, fairly gentle trails, coupled with plenty of historical sights and good food, make this northwest corner of France a sensible choice for the less ambitious walker in need of wayside distractions. Both Normandy and Brittany primarily are fishing and agricultural regions, and the landscapes and the high quality of the cuisine reflect the fact. Normandy's most popular corner for walkers is the Cotentin Peninsula, the broad finger of land that pokes the English Channel; its delightful coastline is peppered with tiny fishing harbors such as Barfleur, St.-Vaast, and St.-Pierre-l'Eglise, which are linked by the 141-mile (226 km) GR223 coastal footpath. In Brittany, the prime terrain is in Finistère, the *département* where you'll find Breton culture at its most intense; delightful Huelgoat (an ideal center for tours), the Parc Naturel d'Amorique, and several Grands Sites (officially designated as such due to their natural beauty) are the chief lures for the walker. Although both provinces offer plenty of easy short walks, no fewer than 21 GR trails are found here, including GR34, which is known as the Tour de Bretagne since its 521 miles (834 km) cover the entire province, and a section of GR36, which runs from the Channel coast to the Pyrénées. Information: For details about walks in Normandy, write to the *Comité Régional de Tourisme de Normandie,* 46 Av. Foch, Evreaux 27000 (phone: 32-33-79-00); for walking information about Brittany, contact the *Comité Régional de Tourisme,* 3 Rue d'Espagne, Rennes 35041 (phone: 99-50-11-15). Also, for details about towpath trails that follow the more than 930 miles of canal, write to the *Comité de Promotion Touristique des Canaux-Bretons,* 12 Rue de Jemmapes, Nantes 44000 (phone: 40-47-42-94).

CÉVENNES: Those who enjoy backpacking in remote territory will particularly enjoy the five *départements* of the Languedoc-Roussillon region to the west of the Rhône Valley — Aude, Gard, Hérault, Lozère, and the Pyrénées-Orientales. Each has its merits, but for those with limited time, the best choices are Lozère and the Cévennes range. Full of steep, wooded hills and lovely, lonely rivers, it is mostly enclosed by the Cévennes National Park, the country's largest. Of the several miles of trails here, the most famous is the one that its namesake, Robert Louis Stevenson, followed with his donkey in 1878; it runs between Le Monastir, near Le Puy, and St.-Jean-du-Gard, and links this region with the Auvergne. Other GR routes include the 94.8-mile (152 km) GR67-67A, the Sentier du Tour des Cévennes; and the 48-mile (77 km) GR71, the Chemin des Templiers et Hospitaliers, which follows the routes once patrolled by the Knights Templar. Since the region is so large, a hiker should be prepared for a variety of climates, including snow as early as October. Information: *Comité Régional du Tourisme,* 20 Rue de la République, Montpellier 34000 (phone: 67-92-67-92); and *Office de Tourisme,* Pl. Gabriel Peri, Alès 30100 (phone: 66-52-32-15).

CORSICA: Easily overlooked when poring over a map of France with walking in mind, this island — the largest in the Mediterranean — lies about 100 miles from the southern coast of France (and is in fact far closer to Italy). So covered by myrtle, gorse, and heather that Napoleon reckoned he could recognize the place by its smell alone, it is rugged and mountainous, and its best-known trail, GR20, represents 103.8 (166 km) miles of hard, isolated going that should be tackled only by the extremely fit. Information: *Agence Régionale du Tourisme,* 22 Cours Grandval, BP 19, Ajaccio 20176 (phone: 95-51-15-23).

ILE-DE-FRANCE: Despite its proximity to Paris, the many miles of marked trails here, all with gentle gradients, thread their way through some of France's finest forest scenery, the old hunting terrain of the Bourbon kings. The area's classic route is the GR1, a 372-mile (595 km) circle around Paris that begins and ends at the Parc de Saint-Cloud. But the single most attractive terrain undoubtedly lies to the east in the Ardennes, a region of lush woodlands, steep valleys and magnificent castles, all strung together like beads on the network of footpaths. Most of these are suitable for day trips, but a few cover real distances; witness the l86-mile (298 km) GR12-12a, which crosses the Oise and Aisne rivers. The best centers for day hiking include Charleville-Mézières and Sedan, a town on the Meuse that boasts the largest castle in Europe. The *FFRP-CNSGR* describes 30 marked trails in its two-volume *Petite Randonnée en Ile-de-France.* And the Comité Départemental des Ardennes in Charleville-Mézières covers several attractive routes in its *Sentiers de Grande Randonnée et Sentiers Pédestre.* Information: *Centre d'Information de la Randonnée Pedestre,* 64 Rue de Gergovie, Paris 75014 (phone: 45-45-31-02).

MIDI-PYRÉNÉES: Stretching from the Auvergne in the northeast to the Basque country in the southwest and to Languedoc-Roussillon in the southeast, this vast region in the south comprises no less than eight *départements.* The population is sparse and the scenery is spectacular — defined as it is by the mountains of the Pyrénées and its foothills and by the courses of several rivers, including the Aveyron, Blais, Garonne, Gers, and Tarn (which also has stupendous gorges). Consequently, for walkers of all abilities — particularly backpackers and long-distance day hikers who don't need villages at frequent intervals to supplement the pleasures of the trail — the area is a natural. Most of the region's *Syndicats d'Initiative* are sympathetic to a walker's needs, and towns like Aveyron, St.-Bléat, and Luchon boast an impressive density of footpaths on their very doorsteps; the last, for instance, is the departure point for 25 marked trails. In addition, there are a number of GR routes in the area. The GR60 (58 miles/93 km) follows an old trail along which herds of animals used to be driven to market. The GR65 and GR65-651 continue the Sentier de St.-Jacques-de-Compostelle, the historic western European footpath that Christian pilgrims have been following for 1,500 years. Generally speaking, the walking gets easier as you move north through the area, though even in the south, the river valley trails don't demand anything like a bionic constitution. The summer months are extremely hot, so the optimal seasons are spring and fall. Information: *Comité Régional du Tourisme,* 12 Rue Salambo, Toulouse 31222 (phone: 61-47-11-12).

PYRÉNÉES: Several of the routes in the Pyrénées demand a fair measure of scrambling and even climbing ability, and crampons (spiked steel frames that attach to boots) and an ice ax are essential. But there are many miles of more amenable trails in addition to those involving rock faces. The Pyrénées National Park, which runs along the Spanish frontier, has 240 miles of marked trails; they range from comfortable valley walks that follow the courses of the Aspe or Ossau River to the more rugged treks in the Pays Toy area around Luz-St.-Saveur and take in such attractions as the *cirques* of Gavarnie and Troumouse, spectacular glacial amphitheaters. There also are the two famous long-distance walks — the 420-mile (672 km) GR10, between Hendaye on the Atlantic and Banyuls on the Mediterranean, and the Haute-Route, a demanding hike requiring as much as a couple of months on the trail. Luchon in the Haute-Garonne, Aix-Les-Thermes in Ariège, and Font-Romeau in the Pyrénées-Orientales make good centers for day hiking. *Département* information offices are at Carcassone, Foix, Paul, and Tarbes; and the *Club Alpin Français* has branches in many towns and villages. Information: *Comité Régional du Tourisme,* 12 Rue Salambo, Toulouse 31200 (phone: 61-47-11-12).

PLANNING A HIKE

As the popularity of walking has increased in France, the French have improved upon their natural advantages by providing well-organized facilities at both the national and local level. An abundance of literature also exists, and before ever setting foot on the trail, savvy hikers will investigate their routes through both avenues.

ORGANIZATIONS: The principal organization for walkers in France is the magnificently titled *Fédération Français de la Randonnée Pedestre–Comité National des Sentiers de Grande Randonnée.* The *FFRP-CNSGR* has branches throughout France and, from its main office in Paris (8 Av. Marceau, Paris 75008; phone: 47-23-62-32), organizes the marking of long-distance trails, negotiates rights of way, urges local authorities to maintain and blaze their own paths with the assistance of *FFRP* members, and produces an excellent series of *Topo Guides* — one for every trail in the Grande Randonnée network and some for regional and local footpaths as well. The *FFRP* also has produced a series of *Topo Guides* for the regional long-distance footpaths known as the GR de Pays and for the shorter day walks of a particular region, such as the forests of the Ile-de-France near Paris. The *FFRP-CNSGR* magazine, *Randonnée GR,* not only details new trails but also has tear-out pages with which to update the *Topo Guides.* The *FFRP*'s efforts are supplemented by those of the many walking groups such as *CHAMINA,* in the Auvergne; *ADDRAM,* for the Alpes-Maritimes; the *Randonnées Pyrénéan,* which looks after the interests of hill walkers in the hot, high mountains of the south; and the *Club Vosgian,* France's oldest walking organization, which maintains an excellent network of paths and hostels in the green Vosges hills and the Moselle River valleys.

The *Club Alpin Français* (7 Rue La Boétie, Paris 75008; phone: 47-42-36-77) oversees matters relating to strenuous walking and climbing.

It's also useful to know about the *Fédération Française du Camping-Caravanning* (78 Rue de Rivoli, Paris 75004; phone: 42-72-84-08) and the *Fédération Unie des Auberges de la Jeunesse* (French Youth Hostel Association; 10 Rue Notre-Dame de Lorette, Paris 75009; phone: 42-85-55-40). Unfortunately for walkers, most of this group's 200-odd hostels are in large towns, not in country districts.

MAPS AND GUIDES: Each of the GR routes is described fully in one of the excellent *Topo Guides.* The only snag with these, and with the bulk of the information provided by the various organizations noted above, is that nearly everything is in French. But the maps are clear, regardless of language, and, with the aid of a smattering of high school French, plus a small dictionary, the text, too, can be followed.

That said, the maps in the *Topo Guides* clearly indicate the route of the trail on a 1:50,000 scale as well as provide information on shelters, campsites, transportation, food replenishment, points, timings, and distances. The various timings and stages assume 7 hours' walking a day as a fair average, at a speed of roughly 2 or 3 miles per hour.

The most popular series of topographical maps for walkers is the series published by the *Institut Géographique National (IGN,* 107 Rue La Boétie, Paris 75008; phone: 42-25-87-90). Its shop, just off the Champs-Elysées, is well worth visiting.

As for inspiration, the best single source is the IGN 1:1,000,000 Map 903, *Sentiers de Grande Randonnée,* which shows all the GR trails. The *FFRP-CNSGR* also produces a guide called *Randonner,* which includes a general map and a list of the *Topo Guides* that describe the GR trails. The IGN series of 1:50,000 maps (roughly 1¼ inches to the mile) and 1:25,000 maps (2½ to the mile) are detailed enough for trail use. Showing both the marked trails and local paths, these maps are available all over France.

The series published by the Editions Didier et Richard of Grenoble, especially those covering eastern France, the Alps, and the Jura, are also good.

Since there are roughly three times the number of *sentiers de pays* as there are GR routes, you'd be well advised to call at the local tourist office of the *Syndicat d'Initiative,* for maps of the shorter trails in the immediate vicinity as well as general background information on the region.

If the area receives a large proportion of British or American visitors, these materials usually will be in English.

WALKING HOLIDAYS: Since the British are among the most enthusiastic walkers in France, it is hardly surprising that the largest number of accompanied walking holidays are led by English-speaking guides and are based on the opposite shore of the Channel. Two of the best are the following:

> *Ramblers Holidays,* 13 Longcroft House, Fretherne Rd., Welwyn Garden City, Hertfordshire AL8 6PQ, England (phone: 70-733-1133)
> *Waymark Holidays,* 295 Lillie Rd., London SW6 766, England (phone: 71-385-5015)
> Also see "Camping and RVs, Hiking and Biking" in *When and How to Go,* GETTING READY TO GO.

THE LAW AND THE WALKER: Apart from the official trails, walkers are free to walk on all footpaths and unmade tracks. You may find a path barred to prevent animals straying, but although the obstruction is inconvenient, you still are allowed to pass along the route. Similarly, the frequently spotted "Chasse Privé" signs or "Réserve de Chasse" refer to shooting rights and do not exclude access by walkers. Private land is encircled by a wall, fence, or boundary ditch and usually has a "Proprieté Privée" or "Défense d'Entrer" sign at frequent intervals around the perimeter. You are not allowed to walk across such property, nor over cultivated land, which includes orchards, mushroom fields, chestnut groves, and snail "fields" — all less obvious than fields of wheat or barley. (Snails, please note, are cultivated under piles of stones.)

Although not entirely backed by the force of law, the Country Code, as the country's environmental rules are called, should be respected by all walkers in France. This code prescribes that all hikers should love and respect nature; avoid unnecessary noise; destroy nothing; reclose all gates; protect and preserve the habitat; refrain from smoking or building fires in the forests (the one rule that is actively enforced); stay on the footpath; respect and understand the country way of life and the country people; think of others as they would think of themselves. In addition, hikers should not leave litter; should not pick flowers or plants; and should not disturb wildlife.

CLIMBING

ALPS: Among the more than 2,000 trails in this massive chain of mountains, there is climbing for everyone from the expert to the rank beginner (although the latter will not be able to notch up all that many peaks). Though there are some 40-odd huts and bivouac spots so the climber does not have to pack a tent, even relatively easy climbs demand a high degree of fitness, plus navigational and rope handling skills. Sometimes a climb can be tackled in a single day; in other cases, a party goes as far as a climbers' hut on the first afternoon, then makes the final ascent beginning early the next morning, in time to assault the peak and return to the base by dusk.

The 15,771-foot Mont-Blanc and its surrounding peaks offer climbers innumerable Himalayan challenges and require the highest level of competence. Sometimes the climb requires primarily technical skills; sometimes, as in the case of Mont-Blanc itself, the challenge lies primarily in the mountain's well-known sudden weather changes, which can render the visibility close to zero, and the danger of avalanches. The main center for climbs on the popular north ridge is Chamonix; the favorite ascent from there begins with a trip via cable car and train to Nid d'Aigle and then on to the Aiguille du Gouter hut for an overnight before the peak assault on the following day.

The Swiss cartographers Kummerly and Frey produce a pair of maps of the Alpine region as a whole. Individual sections of the Alps are best covered in the Didier et Richard 1:50,000 and 1:25,000 series. The *Vallot Guides,* published in French, assess the difficulty of all climbs on a scale that runs from *facile* (F), easy, through *extrêmement difficile* (ED), extremely difficult.

Further information is available from the *Fédération Française de la Montagne — FFM —* (20 bis Rue La Boétie, Paris 75008; phone: 47-42-39-80), the umbrella organization for the Alpine associations for the various individual regions; and the *Club Alpin Français* (7 Rue La Boétie, Paris 75008; phone: 47-42-36-77), which coordinates 80 local divisions in the main French towns and mountain resorts and administers nearly all the high-altitude shelters.

PYRÉNÉES: Though this wall of mountains dividing France from Spain is one of Europe's most challenging ranges for the able climber, it is also ideal for the less experienced climber. That is in large part a result of the weather, which tends to be more reliable than in the Alps. But it is also because most of the summits are both relatively modest in stature and comfortably reached from the more than 50 huts operated by the *Club Alpin Français* and by the government authority that manages the 75-mile stretch of the mountains between the Col du Somport and the Cirque de Gavarnie.

The most popular of the rock climbs for which the Pyrénées are particularly noted are the walls around the Cirque de Gavarnie, a hollow measuring about half a mile in diameter with a floor at about 5,400 feet and peaks at 9,900 feet — the ascents here can challenge even the most competent mountaineers. The granite faces of the Balaitous, particularly in the west, the north face of the Vinnemale, the Pic du Midi d'Ossau, and the Pic Long are also good.

The best books on the area are *Pyrénées East* and *Pyrénées West,* published in Great Britain by West Col Productions and in France by the Ollivier/FEM series.

Boating:
France's Wonderful Waterways

 Given France's vast coastline and its 5,000 miles of inland rivers, canals, and lakes, it's little wonder that when the weekend rolls around, scores of French pleasure-seekers roll back the tarps of their boats and head out for some serious cruising. Avid sailors can challenge the waters of the Atlantic or Mediterranean and dock overnight in a charming old port town for a fine seafood meal in a waterside café. Or they may relax on the tame inland lakes. The canoe or kayak enthusiast can find adventure on the Loire, Rhône, and Vézère rivers or in the white-water of the Alps and Pyrénées. And then there are the leisurely cruises on hired craft through the canals of Burgundy, Bordeaux, and the south of France. Boating novices can sign up for any number of sailing, cruising, or canoeing courses of varying duration.

Foreigners sailing their own boats in France must have a *permis de circulation,* a license that is available free of charge at French government tourist offices in foreign countries; depending on the size and type of vessel, other permits may be necessary as well, so it's wise to check with the French tourist authorities before sailing to France. Communities along the French rivers usually have canoeing and kayak clubs to advise on conditions and arrange lessons and group outings.

Here are some choice destinations for boat-lovers of every sort.

SAILING

BRITTANY COAST: Many sailors rave about the Raz de Sein, that stretch of rugged water off the westernmost point in France between the Pointe de Raz and the stony, isolated Ile de Sein. The rocky scenery is unequaled anywhere, but the wind can be fierce, and widows on the island call these waters "the Sailors' Graveyard" — be prepared. Farther down the coast in the Baie de la Forêt are the lovely fishing ports of Pont-Aven, a favorite retreat of the painter Gauguin, and Concarneau, where 1- and 2-week sailing courses are available throughout the year. Information: *Ecole de Voile les Glénans,* 1 Quai Louis-Blériot, Paris 75781 (phone: 45-20-01-40).

EASTERN MEDITERRANEAN COAST: The Port de Fos, just west of Marseilles, handles large commercial ships and is usually closed to pleasure craft. But on the other side of the peninsula west of the gulf is the mouth of the Grand Rhône, and from Port St.-Louis-du-Rhône it's possible to drive on up to Arles, Cézanne's favorite hideaway. En route, just shy of the fork of the Petite Rhône, there's the exceptional bird sanctuary of the Camargue National Park. Near Sète at St.-Gilles along the Petite Rhône is the fortification of Aigues-Mortes, whence St.-Louis departed on an Egyptian crusade in 1248. Farther toward Sète and the Etang de Thau, a small bay, are the picturesque ports of Balaruc, Bouzigues, Marseillan, and Mèze, where there are sailing courses year-round. Information: *Comité Régional de Tourisme de Provence,* 22A Rue Louis-Maurel 22A, Marseilles 13006 (phone: 91-37-91-22).

NORTHERN COAST: The small port of St.-Valéry-en-Caux, about 20 miles (32 km) west of Dieppe, just a bit removed from the heavy Channel traffic, makes a good starting point for northeasterly sails under the spectacular white cliffs that edge the English Channel. Before setting out, visit Notre Dame du Port, a 13th-century church and the former residence of Henri IV next door. In busy Dieppe, visit the bustling farmers' market on Saturday. The Somme estuary, farther along, is enlivened by the many varieties of birds that emigrate there; on one side, there's the beach-blessed Le Croitoy, and on the other, St.-Valéry-sur-Somme, a recommended port of call and one of the many points from which you can navigate by canal to Paris. Sailing lessons are available in July and August. Information: *Comité Régional de Tourisme,* 46 Av. Foch, Evreux 27000 (phone: 32-33-79-00).

RIVIERA: The coastline of the Mediterranean teems with sailboats in summer, and it is easy to navigate the entire French coastline — perhaps stopping in Monte Carlo for an evening at the casino and then setting out for a couple of days in Corsica. However, the loveliest section is the stretch between Cap Croisette and Cassis, where there are scores of secluded *calanques,* the Mediterranean creeks with ports that are accessible only by water. The opportunity that these destinations offer to escape the madness of Marseilles and the other large Riviera harbors may well justify wrestling with a stiff eastern wind or even the *mistral* to reach them. Cassis is a charming port, with pebble beaches, and in July and August, sailing courses lasting from 1 to 3 weeks are available. Information: *Maison de Cassis,* Pl. Pierre-Baragnon, Cassis 12260 (phone: 42-01-71-17).

SOUTHERN ATLANTIC COAST: The 125 miles of coastline along the Landes forest south of Bordeaux offer very few ports for yachts, and the Atlantic is generally rough and dangerous. However, there is nice, leisurely boating in the Bay of Arcachon and near St.-Jean-de-Luz not far from the Spanish border. The former is relatively calm, and the port itself has fine beaches and oyster beds. The rocky coastline outside the latter is more challenging, but the port at Ciboure is small enough that it may be necessary to sail on into Spanish waters to find docking facilities. Information: *Comité Régional de Tourisme,* 24 Allée de Tourny, Bordeaux 33000 (phone: 56-44-48-02).

CANOEING AND KAYAKING

Possibly because canoes and kayaks are so easily transported and because it's possible to take them out on so many waterways, canoeing and kayaking are extremely popular in France. As in North America, streams are graded in order of difficulty from classes I through VI, with category VI being the most difficult and therefore suited to only the most accomplished sportspersons.

AVEYRON: The Aveyron is only one of several fast-flowing rivers in the forested northwestern section of the *département* of Tarn; the Tarn and the Agoût also are recommended. Information: *Comité Régional de Tourisme,* 12 Rue Salambo, Toulouse 31200 (phone: 61-47-11-12).

DORDOGNE: The trip on this stream toward the Garonne is magnificent, especially the 75 miles or so before Sarlat-le-Canéda, with its forested gorges and limestone rocks. From Argentat to Trémolat, the water is category I and II. The only non-navigable point is at Beaulieu, about 15 miles downstream from Argentat, where it is necessary to portage past an obstruction. Information: *Office Départemental de Tourisme de la Dordogne,* 16 Rue Wilson, Périgueux 24000 (phone: 53-53-44-35).

LOIRE: France's longest river, which runs from its source high in the Massif Central to Nantes in Brittany and its mouth in the Atlantic, offers a wealth of possibilities. There are some lovely ruins of a château not far from the source, between Arlempdes and Goudet, and there are torrential waters farther downstream at the Gorges de Peyredeyre. The river is navigable all the way to the Atlantic and is rated category I from Roanne to Nantes. Information: *Comité Régional du Tourisme,* 3 Pl. Saint-Pierre, Nantes 44000 (phone: 40-48-15-45).

RHÔNE: One of the most popular rivers among French canoeing and kayaking enthusiasts because it is navigable for almost 500 miles, from the Swiss city of Brig all the way to the Mediterranean. Anyone who manages to go the distance ends up on the Riviera — a suitable reward. The water is category II from Geneva to Lyons, category I the rest of the way.

VÉZÈRE: This tranquil river in the Dordogne is perfect both for newcomers to the canoe-kayak scene and for experienced boaters who are looking for not too strenuous good times. Except just after a storm, when the waters swell and the current speeds up, the waters are swift but not dangerous. Points of interest en route include the unusual caves in the hills around Les Eyzies and the charming medieval village of Sarlat farther downstream. Information: *Office Départemental de Tourisme de la Dordogne,* 16 Rue Wilson, Périgueux 24000 (phone: 53-53-44-35).

RIVER CRUISING

There hardly exists a finer way to see the French countryside than to travel on a slow boat along some section of the nation's thousands of miles of river. Dozens of companies in France rent riverboats for leisurely cruises, with or without captains and accommodations. A handful of American firms also offer cruising through specified areas.

Below are three organizations that can provide information and ideas:

Floating Through Europe (271 Madison Ave., New York, NY 10016; phone: 212-685-5600). Operates leisurely cruises complete with guide, comfortable sleeping quarters, and sumptuous meals.

Syndicat National des Loueurs de Bateaux de Plaisance (Port de la Bourdonnais, Paris 75007; phone: 45-55-10-49). Can advise about riverboat rentals with or without sleeping quarters.

Blue Lines (Le Grand Bassin, BP21, Castelnaudary 11400; phone: 68-23-17-51). Rents hundreds of boats, all with sleeping quarters, on waterways all over France.

BRITTANY: The Nantes–Brest Canal, which ribbons through the heart of Brittany, provides access to many fine country hotels. But since the cruising speed on all canals in Brittany is limited to 3.5 mph (5.5 km), be prepared to take your time. The River Vilaine, which flows north to St.-Malo, is another good destination. Information: *Comité de Promotion Touristique des Canaux Bretons,* 12 Rue de Jemmapes, Nantes 44000 (phone: 40-47-42-94).

BURGUNDY: The Canal du Nivernais provides a window on the beauties of Burgundy. Stopping every half hour or so to pass through the locks and exchange pleasantries with the lockkeepers, tasting the marvelous wines and cheeses of the region, and docking in the afternoon to visit an interesting old Roman church or a charming medieval town like Corbigny make for an unforgettable cruise. A good starting point is Auxerre, which has a splendid Gothic cathedral. Most boats have full living accommodations. Information: *Office de Tourisme,* Pl. Darcy, Dijon 21022 (phone: 80-43-42-12).

THE SOUTH: The Canal du Midi, which runs southeast from the center of Toulouse through the corn and wheat fields of the Lauragais to Carcassonne, Béziers, and the Languedoc coast, gives you a real feeling for the south of France, with its red tile rooftops, its powder blue sky, and its dark green cypress trees at every turn. Most boats in the area offer accommodations and meal facilities to allow for extensive cruises. Information: *Syndicat d'Initiative,* Donjon du Capitôle, Rue Lafayette, Toulouse 31000 (phone: 61-23-32-00).

PARIS: Everyone knows about the *bateaux-mouches* that parade from morning to evening along the Seine. Less well known, but perhaps even more charming, are the morning and afternoon cruises along the Canal St.-Martin, between the métro stops at Jean-Jaurès and Bastille, and the full-day excursions on the Canal de l'Ourcq, which take in some lovely green areas starting at the Paris-Bassin de la Villette near the métro stop at Jean-Jaurès. Information: *Office de Tourisme,* 127 Champs-Elysées, Paris 75008 (phone: 47-23-61-72).

FOR MORE INFORMATION

The following organizations can provide countrywide information on a variety of on-the-water subjects. (For further information, see *Traveling by Ship* in GETTING READY TO GO.)

Fédération Française de Canoe/Kayak, BP 58, Joinville-le-Pont 94340 (phone: 48-89-39-89). Specifics on local canoeing and kayaking clubs.

Fédération Française de la Voile, 55 Av. Kléber, Paris 75016 (phone: 45-53-68-00). Details about sailing in France.

For the Mind

Memorable Museums and Monuments

 The stunning achievements of French art are an exhilarating hymn to human possibility, from the halls of Mont-St.-Michel to the shores of Cap d'Antibes, from the prehistoric cave paintings of Les Eyzies to the science fiction Tinkertoy that is Paris's *Centre Georges Pompidou.* There is a breathtaking elegance to French artistic endeavors, whatever the century. It can be seen in the intricate weave of an Aubusson tapestry, in the airy geometry of the Eiffel Tower, in the angular grace of a Lautrec chanteuse; everywhere, the cool complexity of the Gallic mind is in evidence, together with that exquisite sense of taste, as orderly and yet as exuberantly fruitful as a Burgundy vineyard.

Sip these pleasures — don't gulp them. Mix monuments with merriments. Try a few casual nibbles at a museum rather than a single marathon banquet. As soon as you feel a sense of duty creeping over you, it's time to look for the nearest glass of beaujolais. And always remember that a rainy Monday in February is far better for quiet contemplation than tourist-mad midsummer. But if you must travel in August, at least present yourself at the gates for their early morning opening — or visit at lunch hour, when the hordes usually forsake Leonardo da Vinci for pâté.

MUSÉE D'ALBI, Albi, Tarn: Born of noble family in this charming town on the banks of the Tarn, Henri de Toulouse-Lautrec, that crippled and tormented genius, became a creature of the Parisian night and immortalized its prostitutes, cabaret dancers, and café dwellers. The museum installed within the austere, brooding walls of the 13th-century Palais de la Berbie bursts with the multicolored animation of Lautrec's special world. The more than 500 works here, including the famous posters that marked the beginning of a whole new art form, make this the richest Lautrec collection anywhere. Nearby, you can visit the artist's family's house, the Hôtel du Bosc. And don't miss the red brick monolith of the Basilique Ste.-Cécile, on the same square as the museum (see *Celebrated Châteaux and Cathedrals,* below). Open from *Easter* through September. Information: *Musée D'Albi,* Palais de la Berbie, Albi 81000 (phone: 63-54-14-09).

MUSÉE PICASSO, Antibes, Alpes-Maritimes: Picasso lived and worked at the 16th-century Château Grimaldi in 1946 — one of the most prolific years of his career — and later donated the entire production of that happy period to the town of Antibes on the condition that the works remain forever at their birthplace. The 23 major paintings of the collection, displayed in a stunning site overlooking the sea, fairly sing with the Mediterranean's marine joys; there are also lithographs, drawings, etchings, and a fine assortment of ceramics. Wander out on the exotic, flower-filled terrace to gawk at the gull's-eye view that kept Picasso inspired. Information: *Musée Picasso,* Château Grimaldi, Pl. du Château, Antibes 06600 (phone: 93-34-91-91).

TAPESTRIES OF AUBUSSON, Aubusson, Creuse: During the Renaissance, the methods and products of this ancient Limousin town, which had been an important center of tapestry weaving as early as the 9th century, were world-renowned; during the 20th century, they have had their own renaissance at the hands of master weaver Jean Lurçat. On the Avenue des Lissiers, the *Centre Culturel et Artistique Jean Lurçat,* a tapestry museum, documents the art from ancient days to the present; there also are films and animated demonstrations. And in the Rue Vieille, it's possible to visit an ancient weaver's studio, the *Maison du Vieux Tapissier,* and a score of private galleries full of tapestries to buy — or just ogle. Information: *Syndicat d'Initiative,* Rue Vieille, Aubusson 23200 (phone: 55-66-32-12).

CITÉ DE CARCASSONNE, Carcassonne, Aude: This fortress-village perched on a hilltop above the Garonne Valley, a movie-set forest of turrets, battlements, and drawbridges, is Europe's most perfect example of medieval military architecture. Romans, Gauls, Visigoths, Arabs, Franks, and the royalty of France assembled it over a period of some 13 centuries, and the celebrated architect Eugène Viollet-le-Duc restored it lovingly in the 19th century. For the best views of its 52 towers, make the promenade around the Lices between the inner and outer ramparts, starting from the Porte Narbonnaise. Don't fail to see the Basilique St.-Nazaire, a wonderful marriage of Romanesque and Gothic blessed by Renaissance stained glass. Whatever you do, stay until nightfall; the illumination of the Cité is high drama. Information: *Syndicat d'Initiative,* 15 Bd. Camille-Pelletan, Carcassonne 11012 (phone: 68-25-07-04).

CAVES OF LES EYZIES, Les Eyzies-de-Tayac, Dordogne: Ever since the caves at Lascaux were closed to the public, sleepy little Les Eyzies, at the confluence of the Vézère and the Beune rivers, has been France's center for the prehistoric. Of the huge numbers of cave dwellings unearthed by extensive excavations in the cliffs that rise above the town, most fascinating are the Grottes de Font-de-Gaume, with their 200 remarkably fluid wall paintings of 15,000-year-old bison, deer, mammoths, and horses colored with red and black oxides; the Grotte des Combarelles, for the 300 engravings; the Abri du Cap-Blanc, for its superb frieze of horses; and the Grotte du Grand Roc, which is rich in stalactite formations and offers, from its entrance, a panorama of the entire valley. The way so-called primitive man could convey the contours of the cave walls to convey the shape and bulk of the animal he was painting is particularly fascinating. The *Musée National de la Préhistoire,* installed in an 11th-century castle, houses one of the world's most important collections of prehistoric tools and weapons, tombs, ornaments, and Cro-Magnon skeletons — and models and explanations enough to help you understand what you saw in the caves. Note that the best caves are closed on Tuesdays and from November 25 to December 25 annually. The caves of Lascaux, one of the greatest prehistoric finds in Europe, have been re-created by artists from the *Beaux-Arts* in Paris, using the same vegetable dyes and oxides used by primitive man, in the hills above Montignac, about 12 miles (19 km) from Les Eyzies. Information: *Syndicat d'Initiative des Eyzies,* Les Eyzies-de-Tayac 24620 (phone: 53-06-97-05).

MUSÉE NATIONAL ADRIEN-DUBOUCHÉ, Limoges, Haute-Vienne: For centuries, this town has been Europe's most celebrated center of the porcelain and enamel crafts, and its museums are consecrated to their glories. The *Musée National Adrien-Dubouché* has the world's most extensive porcelain collection, more than 10,000 pieces in all. Delft and Wedgwood and the work of China and France — modern and ancient alike — are all represented. The *Musée Municipal de l'Evêché* shows off 300 of the finest Limoges enamels from the 12th century to just yesterday; and the Syndicat d'Initiative will arrange a visit to the studio of an artisan currently working in the discipline. The *Biennale Internationale de l'Email,* a summer-long porcelain fair held in even-numbered years, attracts artists from all over the globe. Information: *Musée National Adrien-Dubouché,* Pl. Winston-Churchill, Limoges 87000 (phone: 55-77-45-58); or *Syndicat d'Initiative,* Bd. Fleurus, Limoges 87000 (phone: 55-34-46-87).

LOURDES, Hautes-Pyrénées: Every year, more than 4 million people, the faithful and the curious alike, flock to this mountain village where, in 1858, a 14-year-old farm girl named Bernadette Soubirous had her famed visions of the Virgin Mary. The official recognition of this miracle by the Catholic church has made Lourdes one of the world's major pilgrimage sites. Thousands of pilgrims — particularly the ill and the handicapped — join in passionate group prayer. Cast-off crutches dangle at the entrance to the Cave of Apparitions. Although the town is full of religious supermarkets stocked with windup Virgins and Holy Water hip flasks, Lourdes is unique and unsettling, whatever your faith — or lack of it. Information: *Syndicat d'Initiative,* Pl. du Champ, Lourdes 65100 (phone: 62-94-15-64).

LE MONT ST.-MICHEL, Manche: Normandy's answer to the Pyramids, this 11th-century Benedictine monastery carved out of natural granite is one of France's — and the world's — most spectacular sights. On what was once an island separated from the mainland by quicksand shoals, the Bishop of Avranches built a shrine in the 8th century. Later, the original Romanesque church flared up into a Gothic riot of spires and flying buttresses that all seem to swirl and spiral heavenward. Since 1879, a 2,000-yard causeway has connected the mainland and the island's single main street, thereby permitting visitors to flock to the island in droves. Be sure to sample the special *omelettes Mère Poulard* at the restaurant of the same name, on the way up to the abbey gates. Better still, plan in advance to stay overnight in one of the unpretentious small inns on the island itself. Once the day tourists are gone, the place has a resonant silence that speaks more eloquently of its long history than all the tourist literature ever written. Information: *Syndicat d'Initiative,* Porte du Roi, Le Mont St.-Michel 50116 (phone: 33-60-14-30).

MUSÉE NATIONAL DE L'AUTOMOBILE, Mulhouse, Haut-Rhin: The *National Automobile Museum* documents the history of the automobile with some 500 cars representing nearly 100 different makes, from an 1878 Jacquot to a freshly minted Formula I Ferrari — a collection that two Swiss industrialists forfeited in lieu of paying taxes owed to the French government. Ranged between mile-and-a-half-long rows of antique lanterns, the jam-packed exhibition contains Hispano-Suizas, vintage Rolls-Royces (including a 1910 Silver Ghost with silver-plated fittings), and gems like the Dion Bouton (like an open stagecoach on wheels) and the Bugatti T16 Garros, which the French aviator had built with a transparent plastic body that reveals the motor, not to mention the vehicles that once belonged to Charlie Chaplin, Juan Fangio, and the Emperor Bao-Dai — all in perfect, gleaming condition. See also *Alsace,* DIRECTIONS. Information: *Musée National de l'Automobile,* 192 Av. de Colmar, Mulhouse 68100 (phone: 89-42-29-17); or the *Office de Tourisme,* 9 Rue Maréchal-Foch, Mulhouse 68100 (phone: 89-45-68-31).

MUSÉE NATIONAL MARC CHAGALL, Nice, Alpes-Maritimes: A collection of 17 major canvases, enriched by all of their preparatory sketches, as well as hundreds of gouaches, engravings, lithographs, sculptures, mosaics, and tapestries make this wonderful institution a concentrated communion with the spirit of one of our century's most original creators. The unity of Chagall's poetic vision of man, nature, and the Bible is clear and present in every room. And the lovely grounds and gardens, the reflecting pool, and the chapel glowing with stained glass all enhance the experience. While in the area, consider making a side trip to visit the *Fondation Maeght,* a splendid modern art museum that contains yet other works of Chagall and his contemporaries, and to the nearby hill town of St.-Paul-de-Vence (see also "Special Places" in *Nice,* THE CITIES). Information: *Musée National Marc Chagall,* Av. du Docteur-Ménard, Nice 06000 (phone: 93-81-75-75).

ROMAN AMPHITHEATER, Nîmes, Gard: A virtual twin of the arena in nearby Arles, the Nîmes amphitheater, which dates from the 1st century AD, is one of the most stunningly preserved Roman remains in Europe. Used as a fortress by the Visigoths, it had long since degenerated into ghetto dwellings pieced together with chunks of Roman rubble when it was rehabilitated in the 19th century. But now, every spring and summer, more than 20,000 spectators jam its elliptical grandstands for bullfights. Equally well preserved is that other jewel of Nîmes, the Maison Carrée, a Greek temple from the 1st century BC that looks like a piece of the Acropolis on permanent loan. Information: *Comité Départemental du Tourisme du Gard,* 3 Pl. des Arènes, Nîmes 30000 (phone: 66-21-02-51).

LE PONT DU GARD, Remoulins, Gard: Another wondrous and perfectly preserved relic of ancient Rome's far-flung empire: a 3-tiered, 180-foot-high, 2,000-year-old stretch of the aqueduct that once brought water to Nîmes from the mountain springs near Uzes. The pastoral setting in the middle of the Gardon Valley has a way of putting you in closer contact with the grandeur that was Rome than the more obvious and far more frequented sites in Italian cities. It's even possible to walk across the bridge where the Roman waters once ran. About 14 miles (22 km) northeast of Nîmes on the way to Avignon. Information: *Comité Départemental de Tourisme du Gard,* 3 Pl. des Arènes, Nîmes 30000 (phone: 66-21-02-51).

CENTRE GEORGES POMPIDOU, Paris: Known to Parisians as "the Beaubourg," this potpourri of multicolored geometry was a source of great controversy when it first splashed onto the sober Gothic cityscape in 1977. Since then, its annual admissions have been more than double that of the staid *Louvre,* as French and foreigners alike come to savor its quixotic feast of exhibitions with the basic theme of "the art and culture of the 20th century" — anything from Einstein memorials and the development of the pinball machine to solar heating and disco dancing. The *Beaubourg* also has a vast library and a regular program of concerts, poetry readings, and dance recitals. But it would be worth a visit if only for the sci-fi architecture, the fishbowl escalators, and the plaza outside, where swords are swallowed, fire is eaten, and *commedia dell' arte* is enacted by roving mimes. Information: *Centre National d'Art et de Culture Georges Pompidou,* 120 Rue St.-Martin, Paris 75191 (phone: 42-77-12-33).

LA TOUR EIFFEL, Paris: Measuring 1,056 feet in height, 412 feet in breadth, and 8,500 tons in weight, this famous pre-fab — the world's first, whose 18,000 pieces are joined by 2,500,000 rivets — was built to commemorate the centenary of the French Revolution. At the time of its March 1889 inauguration, it was the world's tallest structure; early critics predicted it would keel over in the first high wind, reviling it as a grotesque edifice that marred the city's skyline. From the very start, it was destined to be dismantled, and when its lease expired in 1909, it escaped destruction only by a narrow margin. Since then, it has been scaled by alpine climbers, a plane has flown through it, and an elephant was hoisted up into it. To celebrate its centennial, the lights that illuminate it at night were reworked — a dazzling success. Hundreds upon thousands of visitors have braved the 1,789-step climb to its summit (although most take the elevator), and it is safe to say that visiting Paris and missing the E.T. is like visiting France and skipping Paris. There are three snack shops as well as three restaurants in the tower. Information: *La Tour Eiffel,* Champ-de-Mars, Paris 75007 (phone: 45-55-91-11).

MUSÉE D'ORSAY, Paris: The Impressionist paintings that once crowded intimately into the joyfully informal *Jeu de Paume* museum have found a more spacious and sober home. The brilliant transformation of a vast turn-of-the-century glass and cast-iron train station into a museum has brought the best artistic production of France from 1848 to 1914 under one vaulted, translucent roof. Now Degas, Monet, and Renoir are displayed in specially designed spaces within this former railroad-cathedral, along with the works of 600 other painters and 500 sculptors. No detail of light, humidity, or acoustics has been left to chance, making this voyage around the art world a very comfortable one. Don't miss the museum's *pièce de résistance* — the Van Goghs on the top floor, glowing under the northern Parisian skylight. Open 10 AM to 6 PM daily, except Mondays; Sunday mornings and in summer the museum opens at 9 AM, and Thursday evenings it stays open until 9:45 PM. Information: *Musée d'Orsay,* 1 Rue de Bellechasse, Paris 75007 (phone: 45-49-11-11).

MUSÉE DU LOUVRE, Paris: This colossus on the Seine, born in 1200 as a fortress and transformed over the centuries from Gothic mass to Renaissance palace, served as the royal residence in the 16th and 17th centuries until it was supplanted by suburban Versailles, becoming a museum when François I donated a dozen masterpieces from his private collection. Napoleon later turned it into a glittering warehouse of artistic booty from the nations he conquered. Today its 200 galleries cover some 40 acres; to view all 297,000 items in the collections in no more than the most cursory fashion, it would be necessary to walk some 8 miles. In addition to the *Mona Lisa, Venus de Milo,* and the *Winged Victory of Samothrace,* it has many delights that easily are overlooked — Vermeer's *Lace Maker* and Holbein's portrait of Erasmus, for instance; not to mention Van der Weyden's *Braque Triptych,* Ingres's *Turkish Bath,* Dürer's *Self-Portrait,* Cranach's naked and red-hatted *Venus,* and the exquisite 4,000-year-old Egyptian woodcarving known as the *Handmaiden of the Dead.* More of our favorites include Michelangelo's *The Slaves,* Goya's *Marquesa de la Solana,* Watteau's clown, *Gilles,* and his *Embarkation to Cythera,* Raphael's great portrait, *Baldassare,* Veronese's *Marriage at Cana,* Titian's masterpiece, *Man with a Glove,* both *Mary Magdalen* and *The Card Sharps* by Georges de la Tour, Rembrandt's *Bathsheba,* and Frans Hals's *Bohemian Girl.* Try to save time for any one of David's glories: *Madame Recamier, The Oath of the Horatti, The Lictors Bringing Back to Brutus the Body of His Son,* or *The Coronation of Napoleon and Josephine.* And don't miss *Liberty Leading the People* and *The Barque of Dante,* both by Delacroix, and Courbet's *The Artist's Studio, Burial at Ornans,* and *Stags Fighting* — just for openers! I. M. Pei's controversial glass pyramid, which was unveiled in time for the celebrations of the bicentennial of the French Revolution in 1989, constitutes a step toward expanding gallery space by about 80%. Information: *Musée du Louvre, Palais du Louvre,* Paris 75058 (phone: 40-20-51-51 for a recording in both French and English or 40-20-50-50 for more detailed information).

MUSÉE RODIN, Paris: This is one of France's most complete and satisfying museum experiences. Ambling in a leisurely way through one of the great 18th-century aristocratic homes and its grounds, it's possible to follow the evolution of the career of that genius of modern sculpture Auguste Rodin. Among the broad terraces and in the serene and elegant gardens are scattered fabled statues like the *Thinker,* the *Bourgeois de Calais,* the superb statues of Honoré de Balzac and Victor Hugo, and the stunning *Gate of Hell,* on which the master labored a lifetime, and much, much more. The celebrated *Ugolin* group is placed dramatically in the middle of a pond. Information: *Musée National Auguste Rodin,* 77 Rue de Varenne, Paris 75007 (phone: 47-05-01-34).

LA STE.-CHAPELLE, Paris: Tucked away in the monumental complex of the Palais de Justice, the 13th-century Ste.-Chapelle was built by the monarch Louis IX (St.-Louis) on the site of the former palace of the early kings of the Capétian dynasty as a reliquary for the recently obtained Sacred Crown of Thorns. The 15 soaring stained glass windows, with more than 1,100 brilliantly colored and exquisitely detailed miniature scenes of biblical life, are one of the unquestioned masterpieces of medieval French art, and the graceful, gleaming spire is one of the city's most beautiful and understated landmarks. Information: *La Ste.-Chapelle,* 4 Bd. du Palais, Paris 75004 (phone: 43-54-30-09).

MUSÉE PICASSO, Paris: Showing works still amazingly modern, this museum is in a 17th-century mansion in Paris's oldest neighborhood. It houses a part of the collection with which Picasso could never bring himself to part, and gives a panoramic view of the versatile doyen of this century's art. His varied career went from the contemplative self-portrait painted in shades of blue in 1921, through the cubist newspapers and guitars, to the 1961 iron-sheet sculpture of a soccer player looking like an ice cream on a stick. Especially interesting is the master's collection of works by other artists. Information: *Musée Picasso,* 5 Rue de Thorigny, Paris 75003 (phone: 42-71-25-21).

ROCAMADOUR, Lot: This ancient shrine-city in the south of France, a reputed source of miraculous cures whose origins are wrapped in a tangled cloth of legend, has been a goal of pilgrims for 900 years. Breathtakingly built onto the face of a sheer rock canyon wall some 500 feet above the gorge, the town has seven churches teetering on its blade of limestone cliff, a cluster of houses clinging precariously to its rock, massive fortified gates, a citadel, and a château, all stacked on top of one another as if to ascend to the azure Périgord sky. When seen at dawn in spring or at sunset in summer, Rocamadour is almost as intoxicating as the tantalizing quail steeped in gin that the local restaurants brew. Since the village likes to call itself the "Deuxième Site de la France" — the second best tourist attraction in the country after Le Mont St.-Michel — there are a few too many souvenir vendors along the sloping main street. But if you use your imagination you will not be disappointed. Information: *Syndicat d'Initiative,* Hôtel de Ville, Rocamadour 46350 (phone: 65-33-62-59).

The Liveliest Arts:
Theater, Opera, and Music

When a Frenchman utters the word *province,* usually with a certain wrinkling of the nose, he is referring to any part of the country that isn't Paris. Nothing of any significant artistic interest was deemed to occur there, for the capital held an unquestioned monopoly on culture. But the byword of the past decade has been *décentralisation,* and the theatrical-musical map of France has undergone some startling changes. *Province* now fairly bristles with first-rate repertory companies and orchestras financed by generous subsidies from the central and regional governments. Top French directors like Patrice Chéreau and Roger Planchon chose working class areas in Nanterre and Lyons as their base of operations. The renowned center for electronic music is situated in the otherwise quiet town of Bourges. The operas of Nancy and Toulouse have been outdoing their staid Parisian cousins in critical acclaim.

Many of these companies spend a good part of their season on tour, bringing the word and the note to other parts of the country and to smaller towns in their region. So keep an eye on kiosks and wall posters; if you miss the *Théâtre de la Salamandre* in Lille, you might still catch it in some Breton upland village.

And don't bypass an evening in the theater just because your French is a high school relic, because it's a fine way to become a part of local life. In your favor is the current style for splashy, highly visual productions where spectacle trumps text. Where classics are concerned, English copies generally can be found in a city of any size — and at any rate, France's most-performed playwright is the *formidable* Guillaume Shakespeare.

CATHÉDRALE NOTRE-DAME, Chartres, Eure-et-Loir: Twenty years ago, a massive restoration of the cathedral's 14th-century organ once again placed it among Europe's noblest instruments. Frequent recitals, masses, an organ festival held in the spring, and an international competition should give most visitors plenty of opportunity to hear the instrument's rich and majestic tones swelling and rising into the cathedral's celestial heights. And only about 58 miles (93 km) away, at that other Notre-Dame in Paris, there are concerts by France's foremost organists every Sunday afternoon. Information: *Syndicat d'Initiative,* Place de la Catédral, BP 289, Chartres 28007 (phone: 37-21-54-03).

CENTRE DRAMATIQUE NATIONAL DES ALPES, Grenoble, Isère: Grenoble was one of the first of the provincial cities to be alloted one of the cultural centers known as Maisons de la Culture during the reign of de Gaulle's renowned minister André Malraux. The *Centre des Alpes,* like many another of the more successful centers, eventually became a flourishing theater group. The elegant and original productions often dismantle and reassemble traditional works like *Lorenzaccio* and *King Lear* with a flashy theatricality; the productions are always lively, often controversial, and never predictable. Information: *Centre Dramatique National des Alpes,* 4 Rue Paul-Claudel, Grenoble 38000 (phone: 76-25-05-45).

ORCHESTRE NATIONAL DE LILLE, Lille, Nord: The thriving commercial-industrial complex of Lille-Roubaix-Tourcoing, just at the Belgian border, enjoys one of the richest cultural lives outside Paris. This excellent young orchestra is under the direction of Jean-Claude Casadesus of the famous French musical dynasty, and he has stocked it with the finest new talent. If you have trouble hearing them on their home ground, you may just as well find them performing at major music festivals like the one at Aix-en-Provence. Information: *Orchestre National de Lille,* 3 Pl. Mendès Frances, Lille 59000 (phone: 20-54-67-00).

THÉÂTRE DE LA SALAMANDRE, Lille, Nord: One of the first-ranking provincial theaters subsidized by the national government,this company of 15 performs under the direction of the exciting Gildas Bourdet. The repertoire may include anything from works by Racine and Corneille, those twin pillars of French classical theater, to Gorky's *Lower Depths* or stage versions of Jack London stories. An offer to perform with this troupe is prestigious enough to pull first class talent away from Paris. Information: *Théâtre de la Salamandre,* Pl. Général-de-Gaulle, Lille 59200 (phone: 20-40-10-20).

AUDITORIUM MAURICE RAVEL, Lyons, Rhône: Part of an architectural complex that also includes a huge tower-shaped hotel and a shopping center, this auditorium is an enormous, ultramodern music palace whose stage is surrounded by a horseshoe-shaped seating area. Concertgoers might hear anything from a flute sonata to Beethoven's "Ninth" — the spaces and the acoustics are equally suited to both — and all the top names in French music appear in the course of any year. In September of odd-numbered years, the auditorium hosts a Berlioz festival. Information: *Auditorium Maurice Ravel,* 149 Rue Garibaldi, Lyons 69003 (phone: 78-60-37-13).

THÉÂTRE NATIONAL POPULAIRE, Villeurbanne-Lyons, Rhône: In the working class suburb of Villeurbanne, the *TNP* has been France's most successful experiment in bringing dynamic theater to a wider, less educated audience, and with the support of local management and labor agencies, it has built a huge permanent roll of subscription holders that includes patricians and proletarians alike. Director Roger Planchon, one of the boy wonders of French theater, alternates easily between startling new visions of classics like Molière's *Tartuffe* and freshly minted works by young unknowns. Whatever happens in Lyons is usually the talk of Paris. Information: *Théâtre National Populaire,* 8 Pl. Docteur-Lazare-Goujon, Villeurbanne-Lyons 69627 (phone: 78-03-30-30).

COMPAGNIE ROLAND PETIT, Marseilles, Bouches-du-Rhône: France's best-known dance company, which makes its home in Marseilles but travels incessantly both at home and abroad, presents dance pieces that cross the austerity of the classical tradition with American musical comedy brashness to produce a personable style all its own that is never dark, stark, or aggressively experimental. Since all of this is further enlivened by Zizi Jeanmaire (Madame Petit), the ageless and inimitable prima ballerina, the *compagnie* provides a fine introduction for people who secretly are worried that they may be bored by ballet. Don't miss the marvelously original *Coppelia,* in which the character that most companies portray as a lonely old man is a decadent roué in white tie and tails who attempts to bring to life the doll he has created, not to be the daughter he never had — but as a lover. Information: *Ballet National de Marseille Roland Petit,* 1 Pl. Auguste-François-Carli, Marseilles (phone: 91-92-06-06).

ORCHESTRE PHILHARMONIE DE LORRAINE, Metz, Moselle: The entire population of this stately town on the banks of the Moselle is music-mad and music-proud, and at any given performance at the ornate, 19th-century *Théâtre Municipal* those who manage to procure a ticket will find themselves surrounded by an audience of both long-haired, tight-jeaned high schoolers and elders of the Légion d'Honneur — and a great many others in between. The orchestra excels especially at works by composers in the royal family of the French repertoire — Berlioz, Bizet, Debussy, Fauré, Franck, Gounod, and Saint-Saëns. Information: *Orchestre Philharmonie de Lorraine,* 57 Rue Chambière, Metz 57000 (phone: 87-32-66-30) and the *Théâtre Municipal de Metz,* Pl. Comédie, Metz 57000 (phone: 87-75-40-50).

THÉÂTRE DES AMANDIERS, Nanterre (near Paris), Hauts de Seine: Known for its continually evolving and inventive style, the theater is now under the hands of impressario Jean-Pierre Vincent, whose career has taken him all the way from actor with the theatrical school at the Lycée Louis-le-Grand, in 1959, to administrator of the *Comédie Française* in 1983. Recent presentations have included such time-honored classics as the Greek trilogy *Oedipe et les Oiseaux, Oedipe Tyran,* and *Oedipe à Colone* by Sophocles, but a trip to the box office can turn up any number of theatrical surprises. About 20 minutes by the *RER* city-rail from downtown Paris. Information: *Théâtre des Amandiers,* 7 Av. Pablo-Picasso, Nanterre 92022 (phone: 47-21-22-25).

LA COMÉDIE-FRANÇAISE, Paris: The undisputed dowager queen of French theater, as much a national monument as the Eiffel Tower, this dramatic doyenne presents a steady diet of lavish productions of great classics by Corneille, Racine, Molière, Rostand, and the happy few 20th-century playwrights like Anouilh, Giraudoux, and Sartre who have been received into the inner circle of French culture. The *CF* is streamlining its fin-de-siècle image, but even at its stodgiest, it's well worth seeing. Information: *La Comédie-Française,* 2 Rue de Richelieu, Paris 75001 (phone: 40-15-00-15).

IRCAM, Paris: The versatile musicians of this *Institut de Recherche et de Coopération Acoustique Musique,* France's current center of contemporary music activity, perform in the various auditoriums of the *Centre Georges Pompidou* — including the *Salle Polivalente,* whose rotating walls, rising floor, and lowering ceiling make it the last word in acoustical acrobatics. Computers are as common as clarinets, and the whole enterprise is under the aegis of Pierre Boulez, who conducts some of the major *IRCAM* concerts. Information: *IRCAM, Centre Georges Pompidou,* 31 Rue St.-Merri, Paris 75004 (phone: 42-77-12-33).

MAISON DE RADIO FRANCE, Paris: This round white fortress on the banks of the Seine is mission control for French radio and television. It also is the principal residence of two of the country's finest orchestras, the *Orchestre National de France* and the *Nouvel Orchestre Philharmonique,* which subdivides into a number of smaller ensembles specializing in various instrumental combinations or musical periods. Consequently, there is some vintage music making at this *maison* virtually every day of the week. Watch kiosk posters for appearances of the two orchestras in the capital's other major concert halls. Information: *Maison de Radio France,* 116 Av. du Président-Kennedy, Paris 75016 (phone: 42-30-15-16).

OPÉRA DE PARIS, Paris: In a futuristic opera house on the Place de la Bastille, the new *L'Opéra Bastille* began regular performances in 1990 under the baton of Myung-Whun Chung, and the grand *Palais Garnier* (former home of grand opera) at the melodramatic end of Av. de l'Opéra now is the site of the best in ballet. The other mainstays of Paris opera are the *Théâtre Musical de Paris,* in the old *Châtelet Theater,* and the *Opéra Comique*, at the *Salle Favart*. The latter isn't especially comic. The theater is smaller, the performers, as a rule, less well known; but the administration is the same, and the repertory is comparably vast. The *Théâtre Musical de Paris*, once the stronghold of the frothy operetta, now does everything from early Offenbach to late Verdi, importing productions from other European operas as well. The touch is light and stylish, the accent utterly French. Information: *L'Opéra Bastille,* 120 Rue de Lyon, Paris 75011 (phone: 40-01-17-89 or 40-01-16-16); *Théâtre National de l'Opéra,* Pl. de l'Opéra, Paris 75009 (phone: 47-42-57-50); *Théâtre National de l'Opéra Comique,* 5 Rue Favart, Paris 75002 (phone: 47-42-53-71); *Théâtre Musical de Paris,* 1 Pl. du Châtelet, Paris 75001 (phone: 40-28-28-40).

SALLE PLEYEL, Paris: Often called the *Carnegie Hall* of Paris, the renovated *Pleyel* is so admirably suited to all types of music that it even houses the Paris jazz festival, held most recently in February 1990. The greatest names in European music visit here, and the superb *Orchestre de Paris* lives at this elegant address on the Faubourg-St.-Honoré. Other temples of Parisian music include the smaller, charming *Salle Gaveau* on nearby Rue La Boétie; the *Théâtre des Champs-Elysées* on Av. Montaigne; and the massive *Palais des Congrès* at Porte Maillot. Any of the city's major orchestras may perform at the latter two, but if you turn up at the *Palais* on the wrong night, you may trade sacred Bach for punk rock. Information: *Salle Pleyel,* 252 Rue du Faubourg-St.-Honoré, Paris 75008 (phone: 45-63-88-73; and, for the *Orchestre de Paris,* 45-63-07-40).

L'ODÉON–THÉÂTRE DE L'EUROPE, Paris: The chameleon-like *Odéon* has, for years, been the joker in the French theatrical pack. After the turbulent period when it housed the fabled company under Jean-Louis Barrault and Madeleine Renaud and ranked among the most popular houses in the city, it became an annex of the *Comédie-Française.* Now it can be seen in yet another incarnation, as the *Théâtre de l'Europe.* Under the direction of one of Europe's foremost men of the theater, Giorgio Strehler of Milan's *Piccolo Teatro,* it became a kind of theatrical Common Market, with original-language productions from all over Europe. It presently is under the direction of a Spaniard, Luis Pasqual. But there's no telling whether, by the time we go to press, the *Odéon* will be transformed once again — perhaps into a circus arena or a House of Parliament. Information: *L'Odéon–Théâtre de l'Europe,* Pl. Paul-Claudel, Paris 75006 (phone: 43-25-70-32).

THÉÂTRE NATIONAL DE CHAILLOT, Paris: The rightful heir to the great *Théâtre National Populaire* created by the legendary Jean Vilar in the same building, this three-ring theatrical circus consists of a large room, a small room, and Grand Central Station–size corridors that themselves can be transformed into performance spaces. Everything happens here, from *Hamlet* and *The Three Sisters* to *Faust* for children — performed by marionettes — to new texts by Algerian workers, and contemporary musical happenings. New formats, odd curtain times, and a constant redefining of theater and its audience are the watchwords. Information: *Théâtre National de Chaillot,* Pl. Trocadéro et du 11-Novembre, Paris 75116 (phone: 47-27-81-15).

THÉÂTRE DU SOLEIL, Paris: In the Cartoucherie de Vincennes, an old cartridge factory on the outskirts of Paris, this theater always has had a colorful, sweeping style with a popular mood and political overtones. That was true in the dazzling *1789,* which made the troupe's international reputation during that other year of French upheaval, 1968, and in the more recent Shakespeare series as well. Information: *Théâtre du Soleil,* La Cartoucherie de Vincennes, Bois de Vincennes, Paris 75012 (phone: 43-74-24-08 or 43-74-87-63).

THÉÂTRE NATIONAL DE STRASBOURG, Strasbourg, Bas-Rhin: Today, this Strasbourg theater, an outgrowth of the general government effort to make Alsace completely French after the war, has a decidedly international flavor and outlook. One week you'll see *Tartuffe* with François Périer and Gérard Dépardieu; the next, a play by Pirandello directed by an Italian and performed in French. At the same time, the group also has tried to move out of conventional theatrical spaces; recent productions have been presented at a horse stud farm, in an 18th-century military barracks, and on the roof of the city's cathedral. Information: *Théâtre National de Strasbourg,* Rue Marseillaise, Strasbourg 67000 (phone: 88-35-63-60 or 88-35-44-52). The address of the administrative office is 1 Rue du André Malraux (even though it's located in the same building).

THÉÂTRE DU CAPITOLE, Toulouse, Haute-Garonne: A longtime rival for national preeminence with the *Opéra de Paris,* it has often been a proving ground for the finest new singers in French opera. The orchestra, which usually plays for both opera and concert seasons in the stately 19th-century *Capitole,* even did a triumphal tour of the United States, and has brought both operas and a memorable Beethoven's "Ninth" to sellout audiences in the city's sprawling *Palais des Sports* as well. All of France is in the throes of a frantic opera renaissance, so to avoid all-night lines of sleeping-bagged *mélomanes* (music lovers), it's wise to book seats well in advance. Information: *Théâtre du Capitole,* 687 Pl. Capitole, Toulouse 31000 (phone: 61-22-80-22).

Festivals à la Française

 Festivals, direct descendants of the Greek drama marathons and the first Olympic games, are annual celebrations of the pleasures of creating, competing, or just plain existing. They let a visitor cram the best and most of any given experience into the shortest possible time — whether it's auto racing or chamber music, wine tasting or bullfighting.

A word of sober caution to those planning to hurl themselves into the merriment at one of France's frothiest celebrations. Crowds are very much a part of most festivals, so be prepared for crowded hotels, crowded restaurants, crowded auditoriums, and crowded toilets. Though advance planning will ward off much of the discomfort (reserve rooms ahead of time and write ahead for seats), it's still necessary to prepare yourself mentally for being jostled, for waiting in line, and for paying $2 for a can of warm cola — all part and parcel of festival going. Just remember that you and your fellow merrymakers share a common passion and that everybody is in the same boat. Also keep in mind that festivals tend to offer some of France's most savory street eating, so avoid the meals offered in jammed, festival-priced restaurants in favor of crêpes stands, oyster bars, and wine booths. You'd be surprised how well Beethoven's Ninth goes with French fries.

FESTIVAL D'AIX-EN-PROVENCE, Aix-en-Provence, Bouches-du-Rhône: Of France's 250-odd music festivals, this one ranks among the best since it combines a high musical level with meticulous organization and a delightful setting in a leafy town in the south of France. From mid-July to early August, the festival offers works of all vintages, from early Rameau to late Berio, and of all instruments, with a special emphasis on voice. Operas are performed in any one of three theaters, and concerts make lyrical use of the beautiful Cathédrale St.-Sauveur and its cloister. A recent festival featured performing groups from the English *Baroque Soloists* to the *Ensemble Intercontemporain,* with Pierre Boulez wielding the baton. Information: *Festival International d'Art Lyrique et de Musique,* Palais de l'Ancien Archevêché, Aix-en-Provence 13100 (phone: 42-23-37-81 or 42-23-11-20).

FESTIVAL D'AVIGNON, Avignon, Vaucluse: This rendezvous for the most active stage people from all over France turns a modest provincial town of 90,000 into a polyglot United Nations of theater from early July to early August. Groups from all over the world — from Stuttgart's *Staatstheater* and England's *Footsbarn Travelling Theatre* to Milan's *La Scala* and a Japanese ritual dance troupe — perform in more than a dozen different sites such as the Cour d'Honneur of the Palace of the Popes, the Chapel of the White Penitents, and the courtyard of the Faculty of Science. Dance, music, debates, and creative electronics are the daily side orders. Information: *L'Office de Tourisme,* 41 Cours Jean-Jaurès, Avignon 84000 (phone: 90-82-65-11).

FESTIVAL DE MUSIQUE DE BESANÇON ET DE FRANCHE-COMTE, Besançon, Doubs: Based in an ancient town tucked into a lyre-shaped bend of the Doubs River, this September festival begun after World War II has spread to a whole cluster of other towns in the region. Chamber music has a special preeminence. A number of the charming settings here cannot accommodate a full symphony orchestra but seem to have been created for the string quartet. New York's distinguished *Beaux-Arts Trio* has been a highlight along with pianist Claudio Arrau and soprano Teresa Berganza. The international competition for young conductors that is a festival tradition has all the drama of a musical Wimbledon. For an unforgettable philharmonic orgy, try the Abonnement Complet, a subscription ticket that provides admission to every one of the festival's concerts. Information: *Festival de Musique de Besançon et de Franche-Comté,* 2-d Rue Isenbart, Besançon 25000 (phone: 81-80-73-26).

MAI MUSICAL DE BORDEAUX, Bordeaux, Gironde: Quite apart from its fine artistic value, the *May Musical Festival* also provides a lovely opportunity to get to know the Aquitaine in the spring. The concerts alternate between town and country: Venues include Bordeaux's 18th-century *Grand-Théâtre,* one of Europe's most beautiful halls; the Cathédrale St.-André; the 13th-century Château de la Brède, on Bordeaux's outskirts; a cruise boat on the Garonne; and castles and churches in the wine-rich villages of the Bordeaux countryside. It's particularly tempting here to uncork a bottle of St.-Emilion before a madrigal concert in the town's ancient Collégiale and, between performances in the city, to visit the Maison du Vin and taste enough wine to make Wagner sound like Gilbert and Sullivan. Information: *Mai Musical de Bordeaux,* Grand-Théâtre, Pl. de la Comédie, Bordeaux 33000 (phone: 56-90-91-60) or the tourist office (phone: 56-44-28-41).

LES TROIS GLORIEUSES, Beaune, Clos-de-Vougeot, and Meursault, Côte d'Or: The event whose name translates as "the three glorious days" — France's most important wine festival — takes place in three different Burgundian towns on the third Saturday, Sunday, and Monday in November. The weekend begins with the great banquet of the oenophiles of the Chevaliers du Tastevin at Clos-de-Vougeot; it continues on Sunday with the famed *Les Hospices de Beaune* wine auction, which attracts merchants and bon vivants from all over the drinking world; and its grand finale is *La Paulée,* a celebration in Meursault, the village that produces some of the world's most exquisite white wines. Some of the activity is for professionals, and tickets for the banquets often disappear a year in advance. But there is plenty of wine tasting, folk dancing, and general merrymaking for casual visitors — and in any case, this is a fine opportunity to visit some of the region's legendary vineyards. Information: *Conseil Régional Bourgogne,* 1 Rue Nicolas-Berthot, Dijon 21035 (phone: 80-55-24-55); or Office de Tourisme, Beaune 21200 (phone: 80-22-24-51).

FESTIVAL INTERNATIONAL DU FILM, Cannes, Alpes-Maritimes: The suntanned starlets in leopard skin sunglasses, the stogied producers, and the phalanxes of tuxedoed moguls who are always portrayed in the tabloids are indeed all part of the *Cannes Festival.* But that's only the glamorous tip of the moviedom iceberg. The festival also is a 24-hour-a-day bazaar where moguls hailing from as far away as Hong Kong and Ankara and New Delhi peddle and purchase hundreds of items like *Rocky X vs. the Teenage Mutant Ninja Turtles.* Some 40,000 cinema pros throng the *Palais du Festival* and the dozens of theaters and screening rooms between Rue d'Antibes and the sea. Some 400 pictures are shown that are not even competing for the coveted Golden Palm. For just plain film fans, the mid-May fantasia is a chance to see everything that is old, new, borrowed, and especially blue in an atmosphere that blends Hollywood, the Riviera, and the souks of Damascus. Information: *Office de Tourisme*, Palais des Festivals-La Croisette, Cannes 06400 (phone: 93-39-24-53).

LE QUATORZE JUILLET, Carcassonne, Aude: July 14, *Bastille Day* — France's biggest and most colorful holiday — is celebrated in especially high style at the medieval citadel of Carcassonne. The nighttime fireworks spectacular known as *"L'Embrasement de la Cité"*, literally, "the setting on fire of the ancient fortress-town," conjures up visions of boiling oil, flaming arrows, and besieging Crusaders as it illuminates the city's 50 fantastic towers like a stupendous blaze. The holiday also is the centerpiece of the *Festival de la Cité*, a 2-week feast of ballet, music, and theater; Ray Charles, Yehudi Menuhin, Rudolf Nureyev, and the major orchestras of France have all made appearances. Here, as in the rest of France, there really is dancing in the streets. Information: *Syndicat d'Initiative*, Bd. Camille-Pelletan, Carcassonne 11012 (phone: 68-25-07-04); or *Festival de la Cité*, Théâtre Municipal, BP 236, Carcassonne 11000 (phone: 68-25-33-13).

FESTIVAL INTERNATIONAL DE FOLKLORE ET FÊTES DE LA VIGNE, Dijon, Côte d'Or: Really a double-feature festival, this international bacchanal combines folklore with wine lore the first week in September. Some 20 foreign traditional singing and dancing groups from countries such as Israel, Japan, Romania, Sri Lanka, Turkey, the USSR, and points east and west join 2 dozen of their French counterparts to make merry through all the wine-dark vineyard villages of the Côte de Nuits and the Côte de Beaune. A concomitant wine exposition allows for endless *dégustations* (tastings) — on the spot and in all the villages and châteaux nearby. Information: *Office de Tourisme*, Pl. Darcy, Dijon 21000 (phone: 80-43-42-12).

LES 24 HEURES DU MANS, Le Mans, Sarthe: June's *24 Hours of Le Mans*, a grueling 2-day endurance contest at which speeds can reach 210 mph — one of the great events of European auto racing since its debut in 1923 — is actually only the centerpiece of a week-long celebration of man and motor that begins with *le pesage* (the weighing in) and gathers steam with the trial heats. A ticket for the Enceintes Générales gets you inside the 7.8-mile circuit, where there is space for cars and camping; the classiest observation post is a loge seat in the Tribune Citroën beside the dignitaries of the *Automobile Club de l'Ouest*. During the festivities, don't fail to visit the *Musée de l'Automobile*, inside the circuit, which has 150 stunning vintage vehicles starting with an 1884 De Dion Bouton. Information: *Automobile Club de l'Ouest, Circuit des 24 Heures*, Hôtel des Ursulines, Rue des Ursulines, Le Mans 72040 (phone: 43-28-17-13).

SON ET LUMIÈRE, Loire Valley, Indre-et-Loire and Loir-et-Cher: Invented in the Loire Valley in the early 1950s, these 30-to-90-minute sound and light pageants are offered today by virtually every major château. Undeniably corny yet undeniably gripping, they are an ingenious weave of mellifluous voices, music, and roving floodlights — part slick spectacle, part crash course in French history. Some start as early as *Easter* week, and most run until mid-September, with several châteaux offering performances in English on alternate nights. The best are held at the castles of Chambord and Chenonceau, described at length in *Celebrated Châteaux and Cathedrals*, in this section. Information: *Syndicat d'Initiative*, 3 Av. Jean-Laigret, Blois 41000 (phone: 54-74-06-49); or *Office de Tourisme*, Pl. de la Gare, Tours 37042 (phone: 47-05-58-08).

CARNIVAL, Nice, Alpes-Maritimes: The history of the Nice *Carnival* goes back to the 13th century, but it was the city's emergence as a fashionable winter resort during the last century that brought it to the full flower that visitors encounter today, beginning 3 weekends before *Shrove Tuesday* with the first of the Saturday night torchlight processions. The following Sunday afternoon's parade, the *Grand Corso Carnivalesque*, features fabulous floats and huge, leering dummies. On Wednesdays, there are the famous *Batailles des Fleurs* — the battles of flowers. And every week is crammed to the gills with all manner of regattas, masked balls, confetti wars, and fireworks until the very moment on that riotous *Mardi Gras* when King Carnival is burnt in effigy. With its throbbing music, its steaming street food, the prancing drum majorettes, and all those emphatically thronging throngs, Nice's *Carnival* is not a party for the faint of heart or, for that matter, for the faint of eardrum. Information: *Comité des Fêtes*, 5 Promenade des Anglais, Nice 06000 (phone: 93-87-16-28).

GRANDE PARADE DU JAZZ, Nice, Alpes-Maritimes: The biggest and brassiest riff in Europe, this Nice event held annually for 10 days in July attracts just about every major jazz musician from America and the Continent. Chick Corea, Fats Domino, Ella Fitzgerald, Dizzy Gillespie, Lionel Hampton, Woody Herman, Sonny Rollins, Muddy Waters, and a whole hall of fame's worth of others have performed, in styles ranging from the best vintage New Orleans Dixieland to the last 12-tone word, from hot and bop to blue and mod and cool. And the music never stops: From late afternoon until midnight, a music lover can hear concerts in the gardens of the Roman amphitheater at Cimiez and after that can track down all-night jam sessions in the city's jazz joints. Food stalls dish out shrimp creole and *salade niçoise* in appropriately marathon fashion. Information: *Office de Tourisme*, 5 Av. Gustave-V, Nice 06000 (phone: 93-87-60-60).

FOLK-EPIC SPECTACLE, Puy du Fou, Vendée: A remarkable marriage of oral tradition and high-tech computer sound and light effects, this outdoor spectacular is a retelling of the history of France from the Middle Ages to the present, through the eyes of a Vendean peasant family named Maupillier. A modern descendant of the *son-et-lumière* shows developed in the Loire, it is set against the stark background of a ruined château, but the hundreds of local actors and superb effects — as well as the renewal of area folk traditions — make this a unique experience. Performances take place Fridays and Saturdays from mid-June through July and from mid- to the end of August. Thousands attend each show, so it is advisable to reserve ahead. Information: *Secretariat Puy du Fou*, 30 Rue Georges-Clemenceau, Les Epesses 85590 (phone: 51-57-65-65).

FESTIVAL ESTIVAL AND FESTIVAL D'AUTOMNE, Paris: The former, which begins in mid-July and lasts until mid-September, brings a musical kaleidoscope of Gregorian chants, Bartók string quartets, Rameau opera, and more to the city's most picturesque and acoustically delightful churches. The *Festival d'Automne* takes up where the *Estival* leaves off and concentrates on the musically contemporary, generally focusing on one or two main themes or composers and including a certain number of brand-new works. Its moving spirit is Pierre Boulez, France's top musical talent. Information: *Festival Estival de Paris*, 20 Rue Geoffroy l'Asnier, Paris 75004 (phone: 48-04-98-01); and *Festival d'Automne*, 156 Rue de Rivoli, Paris 75001 (phone: 42-96-12-27).

GRAND PÈLERINAGE DE MAI, Les Stes.-Maries-de-la-Mer, Bouches-du-Rhône: On every May 23, 24, and 25, some 15,000 Gypsies from all over Europe flock to the Mediterranean village of Stes.-Maries-de-la-Mer in the Camargue to honor their patron saint, Sarah of Egypt, who was the servant of two legendary followers of Jesus, Mary Salome and Mary Jacobe. According to the story, the two Saint Maries were expelled from the old kingdom of Judea and cast adrift with their serving girl, but they miraculously were washed ashore at this site that now bears their name. The colorful ceremonies include a candlelight vigil in the church crypt and an exuberant procession to the sea with the sacred statues of the saints borne aloft in a sculpted boat. For 3 days, the whole town — itself already richly atmospheric with its bullfights, flocks of flamingoes, marshes, and legends of wild white horses — fairly vibrates with the gaudy rhythms and colors of Gypsy life. Information: *Syndicat d'Initiative*, Av. Van-Gogh, Stes.-Maries-de-la-Mer 13460 (phone: 90-47-82-55).

An Odyssey of the Old: Antiques Hunting in France

 The history of France may best be seen in fortresses and châteaux and the Bastille, but it is best felt by holding a fragment of a sculpted choir stall or an Art Deco soup ladle, by touching the satiny surface of a marquetry wedding chest or by slipping on the signet ring that once belonged to a scheming marquise. Such morsels of the nation's past can be savored at some 13,000 French antiques shops and auction houses or at a countrywide and year-long array of fairs and markets from Abbeville to Zonza.

SOURCES FOR ANTIQUES NATIONWIDE

SHOPS: No little village in France would be complete without its *Petite Galerie* (Little Gallery) or its *Au Bon Vieux Temps* (In the Good Old Days). Some are true *antiquaires,* antiques dealers, who handle pieces of established value and pedigree. Others are *brocanteurs,* secondhand shops, whose stock may run the gamut from Second Empire snuffboxes to broken 78 rpm Edith Piaf records. Many dealers belong to either the *Syndicat National des Antiquaires* (National Antique Dealers' Association) or the *Syndicat National du Commerce de l'Antiquité* (National Association of Antique Businesses), two highly reputable guilds whose members have pledged to tell the truth about all items they are selling.

For an important purchase, the wise buyer will request a certificate of authenticity. With furniture, in particular, the dealer should be precise about just which parts have been restored and how; a number of "antiques" are really superbly carpentered composites of partly salvaged pieces, and there is a thriving industry in the recycling of genuinely ancient wood into pieces of "antique" furniture that were actually born yesterday.

A trend of the past decade has been the clustering of individual shops into *villages d'antiquaires,* which are something like shopping centers for antiques, with dozens of dealers housed under a single roof. The prototype is the giant *Louvre des Antiquaires* (2 Pl. de Palais-Royal), whose 250 different shops are in an old Paris department store. But there are others: *La Treille des Antiquaires,* 23-25 Rue des Chats-Bossus, Lille; the *Cour des Antiquaires,* 7 Rue de l'Industrie, Nantes; the *Village Ségurane,* 2 Rue Antoine-Gauthier, Nice; the *Marché des Antiquaires,* between Cannes and Antibes at Vallauris. Most are open on weekends and make a pleasant excursion — even if you are only in the market for a very contemporary sandwich and a beer.

The richness and tradition of the French antiques trade has spawned a high degree of specialization, both by genre and by period. Some shops deal exclusively in dolls, maritime instruments, chimneys and mantelpieces, locks and keys, and postcards. Several antiquarians in Paris stock only items from the 1950s. Passionate collectors with a one-track mind should consult the *Guide Emer* (50 Rue-Quai de l'Hôtel-de-Ville, Paris 75004; phone: 42-77-83-44) for information about where in the whole of France to indulge their most exotic whims.

EXPOSITIONS, FAIRS, AND SALONS: These are three words for roughly the same ritual — an annual antiques fair that lasts a week, give or take a few days, and attracts dealers from all over the region, the nation, or Europe, depending on its importance in the trade. There are so many salons in France now that many dealers have no home base at all; they simply travel the circuit from one fair to the next, selling, buying, trading, and sizing up the competition.

One of the biggest and best is the *Salon des Antiquaires Languedoc-Midi-Pyrénées* at Toulouse. For 10 days, usually beginning the second week in November, more than 400 dealers spread their wares throughout the giant *Parc des Expositions.* The merchandise is some of Europe's finest, and the crowd includes all of the country's top professionals. It's a bit like ambling through an out-of-town *Louvre* where everything is for sale.

A few other three-star salons include: *Salon des Antiquaires du Sud-Ouest,* an early February annual at the *Parc des Expositions,* Bordeaux-Lac; *Salon Européen des Antiquaires,* staged in late January or early February at *Alpexpo,* Grenoble; *Salon Indépendent des Antiquaires de Marseille,* held the last week in October at the *Parc Chanot* in Marseilles; and the *Salon des Antiquaires et Brocanteurs,* which takes place in late April in Nancy.

FLEA MARKETS: The range of France's countless *marchés aux puces* — literally, "markets with fleas" — extends from the vast, sprawling bric-a-brac city that is Paris's *Porte de Clignancourt* flea market to two folding tables in the town square in Poubelle-les-Bains. The merchandise varies from lower-echelon antiques to very rare rubbish, and it may be necessary to comb your way through ten boxes of bent spoons and a decade of back copies of *Paris-Match* before finding the Picasso of your dreams.

But dealers stock up in precisely this fashion, and flea markets are where everybody in Paris or Poubelle seems to be on nearly every sunny Saturday. The Syndicat d'Initiative in whatever town you may be visiting can tell you the time and the place of the nearest *marché.* A baker's dozen of the most delightfully dilapidated are in the following towns at the following times:

Aix-en-Provence, Tuesday, Thursday, and Saturday mornings, Pl. de Verdun
Antibes, Thursdays and Saturdays, Pl. Aubertini
Avignon, Saturday mornings, Place Crillon; Sundays, Pl. des Carmes
Cannes, Saturdays, Allée des Fleurs
Lille, Sunday mornings, Marché Wazemmes
Lyons, Thursdays and Saturdays, and Sunday mornings, Brocante Stalingrad
Nantes, Saturday mornings, Pl. Viarme
Nice, Daily except Sundays and holidays, Village Ségurane
Nimes, Monday, Rue Jean-Jaures
St.-Tropez, Tuesday and Saturday mornings, Pl. de Lices
Toulon, Sunday mornings, Quartier Ste.-Musse
Toulouse, Saturdays, Sundays, and Mondays, Marché Saint-Germain

AUCTIONS: Once something of a professional club for dealers only, auctions — known in French as *ventes aux enchères* — have become the favorite indoor sport of the *haute bourgeoisie* in the last few years, and in the *salles des ventes* (salesrooms) of France, there are fewer bargains around than there used to be. However, those who know their market may still save as much as a third of the retail price; and even for those who don't, auctions are hard to beat for pure theater.

But the auction situation in France is a bit different than those in the US, Great Britain, and Ireland, for all sales take place under the aegis of a government-authorized auctioneer known as the *commissaire-priseur.* And the auction houses in the various cities, including Paris's venerable *Hôtel Drouot,* are basically cooperatives managed by the local guild of *commissaires-priseurs,* and it is they who are known for their probity and expertise rather than salesrooms or specific companies. By law, French auctioneers are responsible for the authenticity of any item they sell for 30 years after the sale.

Besides the houses in Paris, the most important *salles des ventes* are in Angers, Brest,

Cannes, Chartres, Dijon, Enghien, Fontainebleau, Lille, Lyons, Morlaix, Toulouse, Versailles, and L'Isle-Adam.

The weekly *Gazette de l'Hôtel Drouot* prints a calendar of auction sales all over France as well a running tally of the results (99 Rue de Richelieu, Paris 75002; phone: 42-61-81-78). Remember that provincial sales, often held on Sundays, can help liven up a rainy day in a place like Rouen.

HOT SPOTS FOR ANTIQUERS

With the possible exception of those in the mountain regions like the Haute-Savoie and the Pyrénées, all roads in France lead to antiques. The city of Paris plus the four regions described below are perhaps the richest, both historically and commercially. A word to the wily: The Riviera has the thinnest stylistic traditions and the thickest prices in the country. Save your money for areas where the local antiques were once household objects rather than bathing season baubles.

PARIS: Just as Vienna specializes in *Carnival* balls, the French capital is a feast of antiquing activity.

The greatest concentrations of antiques shops are at the *Louvre des Antiquaires* (2 Pl. du Palais-Royal; phone: 42-97-27-00), open daily except Mondays, and Sundays in the summer; at *Le Village Suisse* (78 Av. de Suffren and 54 Av. de la Motte-Picquet; phone: 43-06-69-90), open daily except Tuesdays and Wednesdays; at *La Cour aux Antiquaires* (54 Rue du Faubourg-St.-Honoré; phone: 47-42-43-99), open daily except Sundays and Monday mornings. Then there's *Le Carré Rive Gauche*, an association of more than 100 antiques shops in the square of streets formed by Quai Voltaire, Rue de l'Université, Rue des Sts.-Pères, and Rue du Bac.

Other good hunting grounds include Bd. St.-Germain, Rue Bonaparte, and Rue Jacob on the Left Bank; and Rue du Faubourg-St.-Antoine, Rue St.-Honoré, Rue du Faubourg-St.-Honoré, Av. Victor-Hugo, Rue La Boétie, and Rue de Miromesnil on the Right Bank.

As for the Paris auction world, the center is the *Hôtel Drouot* on the Right Bank, not far from Bd. Montmartre. Some 600,000 lots go through its 16 salesrooms every year, and the activity is frantic. If you find yourself in a room full of plumbers' fittings or vintage cognacs when what you really wanted was antiques, just go up to the next floor. Information: *Drouot-Richelieu*, 9 Rue Drouot, Paris 75009 (phone: 48-00-20-20). Sales also are held at the *Drouot-Montaigne*, 15 Av. Montaigne, Paris 75008 (phone: 48-00-20-80).

A new bidding-free variation on the auction theme is the *dépot-vente*, a salesroom where private sellers leave lots on consignment with a dealer who sets the price and takes a 15% commission. These generally are well patronized by bargain-hunting professionals. The largest is the immense *Dépot-Vente de Paris*, 81 Rue de Lagny, Paris (phone: 43-72-13-91).

Among flea markets, the best known is the *Marché aux Puces de St.-Ouen* at the Porte de Clignancourt, open Saturdays, Sundays, and Mondays from 8 AM to 8 PM. St.-Ouen actually comprises a number of submarkets — the *Biron*, the *Paul Bert*, the *Vernaison*, and the *Serpette* among them — and there are some 3,000 stalls, ranging from the equivalent of chic boutiques to rickety tables to blankets on the curbstone. You may have to hack your way through a million pairs of Taiwan Levi's to get to the Marie-Antoinette miniatures.

Lesser known and lower brow are *Les Puces de Montreuil* (literally, "the fleas of Montreuil"), held on Saturdays, Sundays, and Mondays at the Porte de Montreuil; and *Les Puces de Vanves*, held on Saturdays and Sundays at the Porte de Vanves. Both run from 7 AM to 7 PM.

And then there are the salons and expositions. The classic is the *Biennale International des Antiquaires,* held astride September and October in even-numbered years in the *Grand Palais.* With its stock of the finest pieces available in Europe and a range of exhibitors that includes all the top dealers from France and abroad, the *Biennale* may set the tone of the market for the following 2 years.

Ranking next in importance is the *Salon des Antiquaires,* held every year in late November or early December and sponsored by *Arts-Expo,* 10 Rue Thénard, Paris 75005 (phone: 46-34-05-80).

The *Grande Foire à la Ferraille et au Jambon* is a curious event that takes place in March and September every year and mixes antiques, handicrafts, and regional foods from all over France; fairgoers do lots of wine tasting, cheese nibbling, and bric-a-brac browsing.

The *Foire Nationale à la Brocante* at Ile de Chatou, 10 minutes from Paris, also is held twice a year — in early March and late September. This party is organized by *SNCAO,* 18 Rue de Provence, Paris 75009 (phone: 47-70-88-78).

In Ivry-sur-Seine, the new *FIBA (Foire Internationale Brocante Antiquité)* attracts over 1000 exhibitors every March, June, and September. Organized by *SODAF,* 2 Placette Fauconnières, Ivry-sur-Seine 94200 (phone: 46-71-66-14).

BURGUNDY: In addition to antique vintage burgundy wines, you'll find the flower of French furniture and sculpture in Burgundy. The town of Beaune is a good bet, and, especially for those in search of an antique mantelpiece, the villages of Mâcon and Nevers also can yield treasures.

Dijon – One big deal is the *Salon des Antiquaires et de la Brocante,* which takes place every May at the *Parc des Expositions.* But for those who travel at other times of the year, there's the flea market on Rue Delaborde the last Sunday of each month. And there are a handful of shops on Rue Verrerie and Rue des Forges.

LOIRE VALLEY: The forest of princely châteaux here was synonymous with France itself in the 16th and 17th centuries, and many of its treasures have remained in the region. Drive from Blois to Orléans along one bank of the Loire and back along the other, and you'll find dozens of shops in all the villages en route.

Chartres – There's a flea market held in the Place St.-Pierre on the fourth Sunday and Monday of each month from May to October.

Tours – The most rewarding browsing is at the *Salle des Ventes* at 20 Rue Michel-Colombe; at the *Salon des Antiquaires,* held annually on the fourth weekend in March; and in the shops along Rue de la Scellerie. Wednesdays and Saturdays are flea market days at Place des Victoires.

PROVENCE: An antiques hunter will turn up all manner of oldies but goodies in the south of France at a handful of exceptional locations.

Aix-en-Provence – After the 80 antiques shops in town, the *Village des Antiquaires,* 5 miles (8 km) from Aix on RN7 toward Avignon, and the *Marché aux Puces,* held on Tuesday, Thursday, and Saturday mornings on the Pl. de Verdun, are the best bets.

Avignon – Dedicated browsers here haunt the flea markets on Saturday mornings on Pl. Crillon and on Sunday mornings on Pl. des Carmes; and auction mavens patronize the regularly scheduled auctions at the *Hôtel des Ventes,* 2 Rue Rempart St.-Lazare. And, about 13 miles (21 km) southeast of Avignon, there are a handful of good shops in the *Village d'Antiquaires* at l'Isle-sur-Sorgue, open Saturdays through Mondays. Twice yearly, in May or June and August or September, there's the big *Foire à la Brocante.*

Montpellier – On Saturday mornings, the town's antiques lovers all can be found prowling through the *Marché aux Puces* on the Pl. des Arceaux. And every year in late April or early May, all eyes turn to the good-size *Salon des Antiquaires et de la Brocante* at the *Parc des Expositions.*

Nîmes – On Mondays, dealers congregate at the *Marché à la Brocante* in the Allée

Jean-Jaurès. On Sundays, there's the little flea market in the Pl. des Carmes. And the year's activity climaxes in December with the *Salon des Antiquaires* at the *Parc des Expositions.*

NORMANDY: Wonderful Norman carvings in oak are among the more splendid finds in this corner of France.

Caen – There's often a treasure or two at the *Marché aux Puces,* held on the first Saturday of every month on Rue du Vaugueux and the shops on Rue Ecuyère. The *Salon des Antiquaires,* held in mid-June at the *Palais des Expositions,* brings new dealers and new wares.

Honfleur – Antiques shops are a special attraction of this picturesque port town. The greatest concentration is around Place Ste.-Cathérine and in the half-timbered houses along its side streets.

Rouen – Supplementing the city's roster of shops, which are concentrated on Rue Damiette, are the auctions scheduled regularly at the *Salles des Ventes* at 25 Rue du Général-Giraud and at 10 Rue Croix-de-Fer. And during the second half of October, the *Parc-Expo* hosts the big *Salon National des Antiquaires.* Look for the flea market on Thursdays at Place des Emmures, and on Saturdays and Sundays at Place St.-Marc.

RULES OF THE ROAD FOR AN ODYSSEY OF THE OLD

Buy for sheer pleasure and not for investment. Forget about the carrot of supposed resale values that French dealers habitually dangle in front of amateur clients. If you love something, it probably will ornament your home until the next Revolution.

Don't be afraid to haggle. This is true even in the most awesomely elegant boutique on the Rue du Faubourg-St.-Honoré. Everything is negotiable, and the higher the price, the harder (and farther) it falls.

Buy the finest example you can afford of any item, in as close to mint condition as possible. Chipped or broken "bargains" will haunt you later with their shabbiness.

Train your eye in museums. These probably are the best schools for the acquisitive senses, particularly as you begin to develop special passions. Collections like those of tapestries at Aubusson, of porcelain at Limoges, and of furniture in the *Louvre* will set the standards against which to measure purchases.

Peruse French art and antiques magazines. French newsstands abound in them. The best include *Connaissance des Arts, L'Estampille, Beaux-Arts,* and *L'Oeuil. Trouvailles* deals with bric-a-brac and flea markets. The weekly *Gazette de l'Hôtel Drouot* details auction action.

Get advice from a specialist when contemplating a major acquisition. Members of the various national guilds of antiques experts are well distributed throughout the country. For more information, contact the *Chambre Nationale des Experts Specialistes en Antiquités* (4 Rue Longchamp, Nice 06000; phone: 93-82-21-40) or the *Syndicat Français des Experts Professionnels en Oeuvres d'Art* (81 Rue St. Dominique, Paris 75007; phone: 47-05-50-26).

Celebrated Châteaux
and Cathedrals

For half a millennium, the Gothic cathedral and the Renaissance château reigned as the most sublime reflections of the French spirit. As their massive stone shadows colored the life of the whole town and the surrounding countryside, these structures were the peaceful statements of the power, both religious and secular, that was France.

The Gothic mode took shape in the northern part of the country during the middle of the 12th century and then spread throughout Western Europe. With its vaults and spires straining heavenward and its pointed arch, which the sculptor Rodin called "a pair of hands in prayer," the cathedral was a celebration of both God and engineering. Searching for ever greater elevation and ever more light, its architects replaced the massive walls of earlier styles with airy windows and raised the vaulting higher and higher like stakes in some Olympian poker game. The result was a whole new system of stress and support, characterized most obviously by the famous *arc boutant,* flying buttress.

The onset of the Hundred Years War in 1337 put an end to the golden age of Gothic cathedral building. But the end of the conflict in the middle of the 15th century marked the beginning of the château building years, when new generations of royalty subjected the placid Loire Valley to an orgy of regal real estate development. And as decoration replaced defense as a prime architectural motivation, the once stolid and brooding medieval fortress gave way to the fanciful wonder that became the Renaissance château.

One brief caution: Since cathedrals and châteaux share a number of stylistic features, there's a risk of aesthetic indigestion if you try to see a great group of them on successive days. So to get the most out of your visits, vary your sightseeing menu as much as possible. Take in an evening organ concert at one cathedral and attend early morning mass at another, for instance, or try bicycling between a pair of Loire castles and tour the interior of one and visit only the gardens of another; stop at Azay-le-Rideau after an icy bottle of Vouvray, then see Chambord dramatically lit at night. It is also less than original sin to leave a few stones unturned.

CATHÉDRALE STE.-CÉCILE, Albi, Tarn: This great crimson citadel — together with the Palais de la Berbie across the square — was built for defense as well as worship beginning with the laying of its cornerstone in 1282 by the Archbishop of Albi. Set in a corner of France where the Church had led holy wars against the heretical Cathars, it is the country's finest example of the simple, bare Midi Gothic. Characterized by a column-free nave whose 100 feet of elevation equals the span of its base, the interior was richly decorated at the beginning of the 16th century by a team of sculptors from Burgundy and painters from Bologna. The breathtaking view from the tower over the town and the River Tarn is worth the heavenward trudge. Information: *Office de Tourisme,* 19 Pl. St.-Cécile, Albi 81000 (phone: 63-54-22-30).

CATHÉDRALE NOTRE-DAME, Amiens, Somme: While its 261,400 cubic yards make this cathedral at Amiens the largest in France, its harmony of style and the airy grace of its immense spaces make it one of the most beautiful as well, and the statuary of the west portal is one of the high points of Gothic art. Inside, don't miss the oaken choir stalls, where some 3,600 carved figures depict scenes from the Old and New Testaments, and be sure to see the unique bronze reclining statues of the two bishops who spent their part of the 13th century supervising the construction of these precious stones. Information: *Office de Tourisme d'Amiens,* Rue Jean-Catelas, Amiens 80000 (phone: 22-91-79-28).

CATHÉDRALE ST.-PIERRE, Beauvais, Oise: At Beauvais, an easy hour's journey from Paris, the Gothic architects' ceaseless quest for ever more height and light ended in disaster. With too much space between the support piers and too little mass in the ribbing, the choir collapsed in 1284. Reconstruction, begun shortly thereafter, was ultimately broken off until the 16th century, when the tower above the transept crashed. It was never repaired. As a result, the 20th century's inheritance at Beauvais is an unfinished symphony of Gothic art with splendid stained glass windows and a priceless collection of Beauvais, Gobelin, and Flemish tapestries. Information: *Office de Tourisme,* 6 Rue Malherbe, Beauvais 60000 (phone: 44-45-08-18).

PALAIS DES PAPES, Avignon, Vaucluse: The residence of the popes during the 14th-century schism in the Catholic church, this massive, imposing sprawl is a kind of French Vatican City. By turns military, religious, and residential, it sometimes seems like some fanciful sand castle that any one of half a dozen capricious popes might have built during a long stay at the beach. The cavernous frescoed interior may be visited on guided group tours, and the cloisters and the courtyard hold dramatic musical and theatrical productions during Avignon's summer festival. Information: *Syndicat d'Initiative,* 41 Cours Jean-Jaurès, Avignon 84000 (phone: 90-82-65-11).

AZAY-LE-RIDEAU, Azay-le-Rideau, Indre-et-Loire: Often described as the most "feminine" of French châteaux, Azay-le-Rideau was built between 1518 and 1529 under the supervision of a woman, the wife of the great financier Gilles Berthelot. A cheerful white manor, military in style but not in spirit, it stands gracefully astride a branch of the Indre and is reflected in its waters; with its surrounding English gardens and its beautiful avenue of trees, it has a certain domesticity that seldom fails to inspire thoughts of how lovely it would be to live there. In fact, François I liked it so much he confiscated it. Those who tire of lounging about the luxuriant grounds should note the fine collection of Renaissance furniture and tapestries inside. Information: *Office du Tourisme,* Pl. du Maréchal-Leclerc, Tours 37000 (phone: 47-05-58-08).

PALAIS JACQUES COEUR, Bourges, Cher: A banker to King Charles VII and one of the 15th century's most powerful merchants, Jacques Coeur built his palace at Bourges with profits, not an inheritance, and for many years the *palais* functioned as much as a warehouse as a sumptuous bourgeois dwelling. The practical burgher spirit is evident in everything from the efficient modern plumbing to ornamental details like the embellishments of cattle and turnips instead of the more usual unicorns and fleurs-de-lis. The ample courtyard is the site of June's annual *Festival of Experimental Music,* a major international event on the busy French contemporary music calendar. Information: *Syndicat d'Initiative,* 21 Rue Victor-Hugo, Bourges 18000 (phone: 48-24-75-33).

CHÂTEAU DE CHAMBORD, Chambord, Loir-et-Cher: This quintessentially elegant, marvelously balanced 440-room creation in the Italian Renaissance style was the brainchild of the château-mad François I, who, at the outset of the 16th century, diverted a river to make way for it and emptied church coffers and melted down silverware to finance it. On the site of an old hunting lodge in the middle of the great forest domain of the Counts of Blois, it is the largest castle in the Loire Valley and is renowned for its roof terrace that is crowded with black slate turrets, chimneys, dormers, and buttresses ornamented with an almost frenzied array of pediments and capitals and statues, and for the double spiral staircase that twists from the central lantern turret at the top to the ground floor. There are 84 additional staircases within its maze-like interiors as well as 365 chimneys. Molière was a house guest of Louis XIV here, and *Le Bourgeois Gentilhomme* had its world première at Chambord. The castle was sacked during the Revolution, and since many of the rooms have not yet been refurbished, much of it is empty. Be sure to stroll on the splendid roof terrace, the lookout from which the royal court stargazed, watched falcons, and applauded the jousting of the tournaments below. The lawns that edge the château are broad and green, and the surrounding 14,000-acre deer park, rimmed by a 20-mile-long wall, may be seen on rental horses — a special delight in the golden light of late afternoon and when a bluish mist fogs the château's base. The château also was the site of the world's first *son et lumière* performance, first presented in 1952 and still breathtaking, thanks in part to the accompanying music of Jean-Baptiste Lully, who composed and performed here in the 17th century. Information: *Syndicat d'Initiative,* 3 Av. Docteur Jean-Laigret, Blois 41000 (phone: 57-42-02-45).

CATHÉDRALE NOTRE-DAME, Chartres, Eure-et-Loir: When an 1194 fire destroyed an earlier Romanesque church on the same site, a vast community effort produced this masterpiece of the human spirit in only 30 years — record time for a Gothic cathedral. As a result, this medieval marvel at Chartres has an architectural unity unrivaled by any of its sisters. The intricate webbing of flying buttresses so lightens the stone colossus that it seems almost poised for flight; the Royal Portal is one of the pinnacles of medieval French sculpture; and the stained glass windows in famed "Chartres blue" bathe the interior in subtle shades that modulate with the time and tonality of the day. Try to hear one of the frequent recitals on the restored 14th-century organ, which is among the best in Europe. Information: *Office de Tourisme de Chartres,* Pl. de la Cathédrale, Chartres 28000 (phone: 37-21-54-03).

CHÂTEAU DE CHENONCEAUX, Chenonceaux, Indre-et-Loir: A haunting way to see this most majestic and graceful of French castles is the *son et lumière* spectacle performed on the grounds on summer evenings. As the languid River Cher whispers under the enchanting gallery built on a bridge by Catherine de Médicis, Renaissance music and courtly voices emerge from the woods, and lights dart on and off in the bedchamber where Diane de Poitiers amused Henri II. Wife and mistress respectively to the king, these two women ruled and embellished the castle during its heyday in the mid-16th century, and their rival gardens still face each other across an ancient drawbridge. Built in the first part of that century by a royal tax collector named Thomas Bohier, who died with his debts to the throne unpaid, Chenonceau came under the ownership of the French Crown, and Henri II gave it to his mistress upon his coronation in 1547; Catherine de Médicis confiscated it after Henri's death 12 years later. The interior, unlike that of Chambord, is largely intact, if somewhat worn, and there is a warm feeling about the place that makes it especially pleasant to visit. This is also one of the few Loire châteaux where visitors are permitted to amble about without a guide; there's a small café for coffee or lunch. Information: *Syndicat d'Initiative,* 2 Pl. Libération, Bléré 37150 (phone: 47-57-93-00).

CHÂTEAU DE FONTAINEBLEAU, Fontainebleau, Seine-et-Marne: Set in the midst of a verdant forest 39 miles (63 km) south of Paris, Fontainebleau was built, expanded, redecorated, or otherwise touched by all the greats of French royalty. François I transformed it from hunting lodge to palace, Henri IV created its lakes and carp-filled pond, Louis XIII was born here, Louis XV was married here. And Napoleon turned Louis XIV's bedroom into his own throne room, signed his abdication here, and bade farewell to his Old Guard from the great Horseshoe Staircase. The most beautiful sections of the interior are the Gallery of François I and the Ballroom — but Josephine's bedroom and Marie-Antoinette's boudoir are worth a look as well. Information: *Syndicat d'Initiative,* 31 Pl. Napoleon-Bonaparte, Fontainebleau 77300 (phone: 64-22-25-68).

CATHÉDRALE NOTRE-DAME, Paris: Along with the Eiffel Tower, Paris's other great perpendicular, this noble structure rising above the Ile de la Cité in the middle of the Seine rules the skyline with all the accumulated authority of Church and State — who, in fact, split its original cost. Built on the site of a Gallo-Roman temple that dated back to the earliest pre-Christian days of Paris, it took more than 200 years to erect, from the middle of the 12th century until the middle of the 14th, and was built from the plans of a single anonymous architect. Napoleon was crowned emperor here in 1804 by Pope Pius VII, and the distances from the rest of France to Paris are measured from the Place du Parvis in front. Among its myriad wonders are the main portals, the portal to the cloister, the portal of St. Stephen, the 13th-century rose windows, and the heart-stopping view from the tower. Information: *Cathédrale Notre-Dame,* Pl. du Parvis de Notre-Dame, Paris 75004 (phone: 43-26-07-39).

CATHÉDRALE NOTRE-DAME, Reims, Marne: The history of Notre-Dame de Reims is intimately bound up with that of the French monarchy. On *Christmas* night in the year AD 496, Clovis, the first Christian King of France, was baptized on the site by that pious politician the Bishop St.-Remi, and from its construction in the early 13th century until the Revolution, virtually every sovereign was crowned in this cathedral. It was here that Joan of Arc, having driven out the hated English, presided over the coronation of Charles VII to the strains of the *Te Deum.* Badly damaged in World War

I, Notre-Dame has been painstakingly restored, and the simple and elegant interior contrasts strikingly with the Flamboyant Gothic exterior. Be sure to admire the walls full of 15th-century tapestries, the lapis lazuli rose window, and the stained glass windows by Marc Chagall. Information: *Office de Tourisme de Reims,* 2 Rue Guillaume de Machault, Reims 51100 (phone: 26-47-25-69).

DOMAINE DE VAUX-LE-VICOMTE, Melun, Seine-et-Marne: On the evening of August 17, 1661, Louis XIV's superintendent of finance, Nicolas Fouquet, proudly welcomed his 23-year-old king to see the new castle on whose construction he had just spent his entire personal fortune. Serenades especially composed by the renowned Lully, a new stage production by Molière, a fabulous five-course banquet, and a fireworks display all heralded the occasion. Three weeks later, the jealous and fearful Louis XIV had Fouquet clapped into jail for life on trumped-up charges and hired his former superintendent's architect, painter, and landscapist to whip him up a pied-à-terre called Versailles. Vaux-le-Vicomte, Fouquet's castle, is today the largest private property in France; its magical, stylized gardens alone cover more than 125 acres. And it is full of lovely fountains, placid pools, sculpted lawns, and fields of flowers that look like giant illuminated medieval manuscripts. The Vaux-aux-Chandelles (Vaux-by-Candlelight) tours show off all of the château's splendors at their most dramatic. Information: *Service Touristique,* Domaine de Vaux-le-Vicomte, Maincy 77950 (phone: 60-66-97-09).

CHÂTEAU DE VERSAILLES, Versailles, Yveslines: In 1682, 2 decades after its founding, the town and castle of Versailles became the French court's new suburban home. Besides a nucleus of a thousand nobles, Louis XIV's retinue consisted of some 9,000 men-at-arms and an equal number of servants. At any given moment between 5,000 and 6,000 people were living here, which only begins to suggest the scale of this royal commune, and seeing it all in one visit is about as relaxing as running the *Boston Marathon.* But before you drop, be sure to squeeze in the cream and gold chapel where the kings said mass, the State Apartments, the fabled Hall of Mirrors, the Royal Suites, and, on the grand green grounds, the Petit Trianon, Marie-Antoinette's rustic small castle. Between May and September, on specified afternoons, the 600 jets of water in the 50-odd fountains and pools in the park outside the palace are all turned on; it's a spectacular sight. Versailles is accessible by public transportation from downtown Paris. Information: *Office de Tourisme,* 7 Rue des Réservoirs, Versailles 78000 (phone: 39-50-36-22).

DIRECTIONS

The Ile-de-France

The first thing to know about the so-called Island of France (l'Ile-de-France) is that it is not an island at all. It is the region surrounding Paris to a radius of roughly 50 miles, and its name alludes to the fact that its boundaries are delineated by rivers and waterways — The Epte, the Aisne, the Eure, the Ourcq, the Autonne, the Essonne, and others form an irregular circle around the area, while the mighty Marne and the regal, ubiquitous Seine coil and curve through its heart.

In fact, it's the rivers that define the land here, lending their names to the valleys that lie between them. Officially, the Ile-de-France can be divided into eight subregions: Paris and seven other *départements* (Seine et Marne, Yvelines, Essone, Hauts de Seine, Seine St.-Denis, Val de Marne, and Val d'Oise) that wrap snail-like around the French capital, cradling it in a temperate basin.

Richly blessed with both natural and manmade treasures, the Ile-de-France constitutes what art critic and author John Russell described as "one vast national park of fine living." Russell added, "I doubt, indeed, if there is anywhere in France a greater abundance of unexplored marvels." This is the region of the French kings, of their regal châteaux, and the châteaux of their ministers and mistresses. The special quality of the light has inspired nearly as many painters (and often the same ones) as those who worked in Provence, while writers and poets have found their inspiration in the region's character.

Through this area passed Charlemagne, St.-Louis, Joan of Arc, and Napoleon, each leaving an imprint. Almost every illustrious Frenchman or woman has ties to the Ile-de-France. The homes of historical, literary, and artistic notables are here, many of these now memorials or museums honoring their famous former occupants.

No other region of France has a higher concentration of cathedrals and abbey churches, exquisite Gothic stone witnesses to a fervent religious past played out over centuries. The same locally quarried stone chiseled for these masterpieces also defines the châteaux — not just Versailles and Fountainebleau — and the other countless small gems that dot the countryside.

The modern landscape of the Ile-de-France is full of sometimes jarring contrasts: quaint market squares, medieval fortresses, deep woods, and the ever-present serpentine rivers juxtaposing the bleak industrial pockets and urban sprawl that can dishearten the casual traveler. But, despite the encroachment of modern times and suburbanization, nature still firmly holds its own. And there are places within minutes of the Paris periphery that are secret havens — so near and yet seemingly so far removed from the capital's crowds and traffic.

Apart from the rivers and their soft green valleys, the most characteristic natural feature of the region are its tens of thousands of acres of majestic forests, including Fontainebleau, Compiègne, Chantilly, and Rambouillet, as well as small, lesser known woods, such as Fausses Reposes. Head out of Paris in almost any direction and you're likely to run into one of these woodlands, some tended and tamed, others wild and untouched by time. Once princely hunting grounds, these forests, and the peaceful country-style inns that frequently can be found in their shadows, are rare pleasurable retreats for modern travelers.

We suggest that you make Paris your base for forays into the region, particularly if your time is limited. The route suggested here begins at St.-Denis in the north, then winds clockwise around the capital, occasionally spilling over into areas that are outside the official boundaries of the Ile-de-France. Every site on the route makes a comfortable day trip or can be combined with other stops to fill out a weekend jaunt. To strangers, Paris — the City of Light — can seem rather dark on Sundays and Mondays, when its shops and many restaurants are closed. These are ideal days to take advantage of the nearby countryside. For tourist information on sights of interest and accommodations in the Ile-de-France, write the *Comité Regional d'Ile-de-France* (73 Rue Cambronne, Paris 75015; phone: 45-67-89-41), or visit the Ile-de-France booth at the Paris Tourist Office (127 Champs-Elysées; phone: 47-23-61-72).

Because of their proximity to Paris, country inns in the Ile-de-France tend to have city prices. Reservations almost always are required. Expect to pay $95 and up per night for a double room in hotels listed as expensive; $50 to $95 in those listed as moderate; and under $50 for inexpensive rooms. The restaurants range in price from $95 and up for a dinner for two in the expensive category; $50 to $95 in the moderate range; and under $50 for an inexpensive meal. Prices do not include wine or drinks, although service usually is included.

ST.-DENIS: Worth a visit to this otherwise dreary suburb is the Cathedral of St.-Denis. Located at the northern gate of Paris (off the A1 autoroute, less than 2 miles (3 km) north of the Porte de la Chapelle), it is perhaps one of the greatest, albeit one of the least visited, of the Ile-de-France's greatest ecclesiastical monuments. Considered the cradle of French Gothic style, its basilica is noteworthy not only as an architectural milepost, but also for its magnificent tombs. French kings and queens have been buried here for 12 centuries, since St.-Louis commissioned the chiseling of a series of effigies to commemorate his ancestors — rulers of France going back to the 7th century.

A church has stood on this holy ground since before the 5th century. St.-Denis, who is depicted repeatedly in the church in stained glass and stone with his severed head in hand, was an evangelist. Along with two fellow missionaries, he brought Christianity to pagan Lutetia (later named Paris) in about 250 AD. So successful were the trio's preachings that they were decapitated at Montmartre (named the Martyr's Mount in their honor) by leaders jealous of their influence. Legend has it that the decapitated St.-Denis rose, picked up his head, and walked north into the countryside until he collapsed. The spot where he fell and was buried became a pilgrimage sight, where a modest abbey eventually was erected.

At the behest of St.-Geneviève, work on a larger church began in the 5th century, and in 638, King Dagobert sponsored the construction of the abbey church. Nearly 600 years later, the Abbot Suger, Louis VII, and architect Pierre de Montreuil conspired to promote a new style that included the first rose windows, ogival arches, and buttresses (concealed at this early stage), marking the earliest manifestations of Gothic architecture. Much of what the visitor sees today is a result of excellent 19th century restorations undertaken by Viollet-le-Duc in an effort to correct the ravages of time.

Note the restored central portal representing the last judgment. The one on the right depicts the last communion of St.-Denis, and the portal on the left shows the torture of the saint and his fellow missionaries, Rustique and Eleuthere.

St.-Denis's early Gothic architectural grandeur notwithstanding, an equally impressive wealth is represented by the tombs grouped around the transept, a sketchbook in stone of France's monarchs and their loved ones. Among those buried here are Clovis, the first King of France, Dagobert, Charles Martel, and Pepin the Short. Elaborate Renaissance structures, many of them created by the sculptor Germain Pilon, represent Catherine de Médicis and Henri II, Louis XII and Anne de Bretagne, and, most moving of all, Louis XVI and Marie Antoinette. Most of the tombs now are empty — the royal remains were exhumed during the revolution and heaped into a nearby communal grave. There are other tombs in the crypt, as well as excavations of the churches that preceded the present one on this site. Regular guided tours (for a fee) of the transept are available. Visitors also may rent headphones with commentary in several languages.

EATING OUT: *Mets du Roy* – An inviting, creamy stone façade fronts this rather formal restaurant serving traditional fare. Located directly across the square from the cathedral. 4 Rue Boulangerie (phone: 48-20-89-74). Expensive.

Cour de l'Abbaye – Also within walking distance of the cathedral, this lunch-only, casual restaurant leans heavily on the hearty fare of France's southwest. The prices are reasonable and the service is friendly. Closed evenings and weekends. Rue de Boucherie (phone: 48-09-84-13). Inexpensive.

ECOUEN: Travel north from St.-Denis about a dozen miles (19 km) on N16 to reach Ecouen, a rather drab town of about 5,000 inhabitants that easily could be bypassed if it weren't for the superb Château d'Ecouen and the *Musée National de la Renaissance* (National Museum of the Renaissance) that it houses. Dating from the early 16th century, perched on a hill and surrounded by a park, Ecouen rivals Chenonceaux — one of the great Loire valley châteaux — in elegance, though far fewer travelers visit it. Its columned interior porticoes, delicately chiseled stone, and ribbed vaulting exhibit elements of the Renaissance. Anne de Montmorency, a powerful adviser to François I, commissioned two of the epoch's masters — Jean Goujon and Jean Bullant — to construct this palace for the king.

It would be hard to imagine a more appropriate home for the museum devoted entirely to the Renaissance. Its collection, much of it formerly stored at Paris's *Musée de Cluny,* represents an outstanding assemblage of 16th and early 17th century pieces, particularly works from the decorative arts — furniture, carved wood panels, tapestries, ceramics, and enamels. Not to be missed is the 250-foot long series of tapestries depicting the story of David and Bethsheba. Woven in silk, wool, and silver threads, it dominates the west wing of the museum's first floor and ranks among the most beautiful 16th-century tapestries in France. Note also the painted mantelpieces depicting biblical scenes in the style of the Fontainebleau School. The museum is open daily, except Tuesdays and holidays, from 9:45 AM to 12:30 PM and from 2:00 to 5:15 PM. Admission charge.

Before leaving Ecouen, visit the Church of Saint Acceul near the center of town. Its remarkable stained glass windows, attributed to Jean Cousin, date from 1545. Italian influences can be detected in the windows devoted to the life of the Virgin, while those depicting members of the Montmorency family and the church's benefactors clearly follow the French style. Jean Bullant, who was responsible for much of the design of the Château d'Ecouen, is thought to be the architect of this church.

En Route from Ecouen – On the way to Chantilly, wander north on N16 about 4 miles (6 km), and then turn west on to D922 and D909 to visit Royaumont, one of the best preserved medieval abbeys in France. Founded in 1228 by Blanche de Castille, then Regent of France, and her 12-year-old son, the future Louis IX (St.-Louis), this immense Cistercian abbey has a regal character that is reflected in its name. The wealth and beauty that still are apparent here attest to the protection and interest lavished on Royaumont by kings after Louis IX. Visit the vaulted refectory with its five monolithic columns and the tomb of Henri of Lorraine sculpted by the artist Coysevox.

CHANTILLY: Only a few miles northeast of Royaumont via N16, Chantilly is famous for its château, its park, and of course, the track where horse races have taken place since 1836. The surrounding 5,187-acre Chantilly Forest is crisscrossed by roads and horse trails, many of them closed to automobiles. Over the last 2,000 years, five different châteaux have stood on this site. The Montmorency family owned Chantilly's château until it passed into the possession of the noble French family, Grand Condé, in 1632. The present one was built between 1875 and 1881 by Nicolas-François Mansart at the behest of the Duke of Aumale, a son of King Louis-Philippe. Resembling an island rising out of the surrounding moat, the château is small by French standards, but exceptionally elegant. It now houses the *Musée Condé,* an excellent museum with over 2,000 artworks, including more than 600 oils by French, Flemish, and Italian masters of the 16th–18th centuries, and some superb illuminations from the 15th and 16th centuries. Open from 10 AM to 6 PM, March 1 to October 31; and 10:30 AM to 5 PM, November 1 to February 28; closed Tuesdays; (phone: 44-57-03-62). Tour the interior of the château to see the library, with its prodigious collection of rare books.

Also visit the 18th-century stables and the chapel where — to this day — the descendants of the last owner gather for Sunday services. Take time, as well, to wander through the 17th-century gardens and park, created by the renowned royal landscaper, Le Nôtre. There are several additional buildings of interest in the park, including the Maison de Sylvie, named for the Duchesse de Montmorency, who hid Theophile de Viau after he was condemned to death for his licentious poems. The house, rebuilt in 1684, later was the site of a mysterious romantic liaison that ended in the death in a "hunting accident" of the Duc de Joyeuse, Louis de Melun. Connected to the main château is the Petit Château, a lovely castle built in 1560 by Jean Bullant.

CHECKING IN: *Hostellerie du Lys* – A modest 35-room hotel in a calm, beautiful park. Av. Septième, Lys-Chantilly (phone: 44-21-26-19). Moderate. *Angleterre* – A pleasant, simply furnished inn. 9 Pl. Omer-Vallon, Chantilly (phone: 44-57-00-59). Inexpensive.

EATING OUT: *Le Relais Condé* – Small and bright, with a beamed ceiling and huge stone fireplace, this restaurant serves classic fare, including grilled kidneys and a good selection of fish. Closed Sunday evenings and Mondays. 42 Av. du Maréchal-Joffre, Chantilly (phone: 44-57-05-75). Moderate.

En Route from Chantilly – St. Leu-d'Esserent lies 3 miles (5 km) northwest of Chantilly via N16 on D44. Renowned for its architectural excellence, its mellow and beautiful 12th-century stone church sits on a commanding site overlooking the Oise River.

Route N924 east leads to the charming town of Senlis, dominated by the Ancienne Cathédrale de Notre-Dame (Pl. Notre-Dame) that was begun in 1153. Of particular interest is the portico, dedicated to the Virgin and used as the prototype for the porticoes of Chartres, Notre-Dame-de-Paris, and Reims. Also worth a visit are the ancient Eglise St.-Pierre (Pl. St.-Pierre), the Château Royal (for its Gallo-Roman walkway), and the *Musée de la Venerie* (Hunting Museum) in front of the château. The Gallo-Roman walkway, a defense wall on the château's perimeter, provides a good vantage point from which to view all the principal monuments.

COMPIEGNE: On the banks of the Oise, 49 miles (79 km) north of Paris via N17, is this village justly famous for its palace (Pl. du Palais). The exterior is somewhat austere, but the rich and exquisite interior is preserved beautifully.

Compiègne has played a significant and paradoxical role in French history: Most of the Kings of France visited it at one time or another, and Joan of Arc was taken prisoner here in 1430. More recently, the armistice of November 11, 1918 was signed here (the exact site — Clairière de l'Armistice — is marked in a clearing in the woods surrounding the palace). Sadly, from 1941 to 1944, Compiègne served as a deportation center for some members of France's Jewish community en route to concentration camps.

The forest of Compiègne, with nearly 35,000 acres, has majestic avenues, ponds, and picturesque villages, such as Vieux-Moulin and St.-Jean-Aux-Bois. Just beyond the forest, via D85, is the splendid 12th century château-fortress of Pierrefonds, once the property of Napoleon.

CHECKING IN/EATING OUT: *Auberge à la Bonne Idée* – In a peaceful setting is a 15-room hostelry with a fine restaurant (closed Tuesdays and Wednesday lunch). St. Jean-aux-Bois, Compiègne (phone: 44-42-84-09). Moderate.

En Route from Compiègne – Retrace your route back to Senlis, turn east onto N330 toward Meaux. Seven miles (11 km) south of Senlis in the town of Chaalis are the picturesque ruins of a 13th-century abbey, a château, a park north of the entrance to the château, and a museum — with three rooms devoted to the works of Jean-Jacques Rousseau, who died in 1778 in Ermenonville (2 miles/3 km) south. The countryside is dotted with numerous ponds. The Mer de Sable (Sea of Sand) — a mini-desert and a small zoo — is at Ermenonville.

MEAUX: Continue on N330 about 15 miles (24 km) south to Meaux (pronounced *Mow*), a market town of about 50,000 in the center of the wheat fields of the Brie plain — Paris's breadbasket. Meaux is renowned for its rich, creamy brie cheese and a bishop named Bossuet (known for his controversial oratories). Though just 25 miles (40 km) from Paris, it is quite removed from the frenzied hubbub of the French capital.

A diocesan see since the 4th century, Meaux has a significant religious importance. Its 14th-century Cité Episcopale is one of the rare bishopric ensembles in France that remain almost entirely intact. The complex consists of St.-Etienne Cathedral, the Episcopal Palace, the chapter house, and a garden laid out in the form of a bishop's miter by the famous landscape artist, Le Nôtre.

Not to be missed on even the shortest visit to Meaux, the Cité Episcopale is located in the heart of the Old City. Start at the St.-Etienne Cathedral. Constructed between the 12th and the 13th centuries, it illustrates the evolution of the Gothic style: The elegant south façade is radiant Gothic, while the main façade is Flamboyant Gothic. Connected to the cathedral is the 13th-century chapter house with its covered 16th-century staircase.

The Ancien Evêché (Episcopal Palace) forms a rectangular courtyard with the chapter house and the cathedral. Today the palace (built during the 12th century and modified in the 17th century) houses a museum that displays Bossuet's personal effects and writings. The chapel has a collection of sacred art, including medieval sculpture, fabrics, and religious relics. Part of the palace is devoted to local history and displays works of art by regional painters and other artists including Millet, Courbet, and Van Loo. From here, visit Le Nôtre's beautiful miter-shape garden and the old ramparts, parts of which date from the 4th century. The terrace affords a beautiful view of the garden, the palace, and the cathedral.

One of the city's most illustrious citizens was Jacques-Bénigne Bossuet, an intellectual who served as the dauphin's tutor for 12 years, and subsequently was named Bishop of Meaux in 1682 by a grateful Louis XIV. Bossuet held the post for 22 years and his religious and moral convictions, as well as his gift for rousing oratory, earned him a place in posterity under the title of L'Aigle de Meaux (the Eagle of Meaux). In his vast library, Bossuet composed five famous eulogies — most notably the funeral oration for Marie-Thérèse, Louis XIV's wife. To commemorate the tricentennial of Bossuet's appointment as bishop, Meaux inaugurated a spectacular *son et lumière* show with over 2,000 performers that takes place on summer evenings in the court of the old chapter house. Check with the local tourist office (2 Rue Notre-Dame; phone: 64-33-02-26) for times and days of performances.

Meaux's bishopric weathered the Revolution better than most, though in 1792 it was the sight of the bloody "Massacres de Septembre," where 14 prisoners and several priests were killed in the palace courtyard. On his flight to La Varennes, Louis XVI spent the night in this palace, and Napoleon also stayed here.

The city was spared destruction during the German invasion of 1914, though the area directly north of it was the sight of devastating and decisive battles.

Before leaving town, visit the nearby market area and the core of medieval streets that wrap around it. The first *halle* (market) was built here in 1722. The current structure — a metal-frame, covered market reminiscent of Paris's central *halles* (torn down in the 1960s) — is stocked with the best food products from the generous Brie plain. Be sure to pick up a wedge of the area's famous brie — a fragrant, runny cow's milk cheese.

 EATING OUT: *Champs de Mars* – Locals recommend this traditional establishment for its consistent good quality and pleasant ambience. Closed Monday evenings, Tuesdays, and during the month of August. 16 Av. Victoire (phone: 64-33-13-96). Expensive.

Le Rustique – True to its name, this small eatery near the cathedral has a rough charm. Couscous and paella are the specialties; grilled meat also is offered, and unlike many provincial restaurants, it serves meals continuously from noon on. 42 Rue St. Remy (phone: 64-34-09-60). Inexpensive.

En Route from Meaux – Take A4 to N36 south and follow it to the junction of N19, then turn east to reach Provins. On the way you'll pass the future home of *EuroDisneyland,* slated to open in 1992. The cost of the project is estimated at over $2.5 billion — 1½ times the cost of the tunnel (still not finished) under the English Channel.

PROVINS: Roses thrive throughout the Ile-de-France, but nowhere are they more prevalent than in Provins, dubbed the "town of roses." According to legend, it was Thibaud IV, King of the Navarre, Comte de Champagne, and religious crusader, who imported the first rose to France on his return to Provins from the Holy Land in the 13th century. He brought it as a gift to Blanche de Castille, his cousin, and the mother of St.-Louis. The red "rose Gallica," later "*La Rose de Provins,*" flourished in the fertile Brie plain and became the object of cults. It symbolized the prosperity and flowering of this town, which remains one of France's most important (and least discovered) relics of the Middle Ages.

Today, Provins has barely 13,000 inhabitants, but during the Middle Ages, it boasted some 80,000 residents and was the third largest city in France after Paris and Rouen. Behind the city's wealth was the *Foire de Champagne,* a twice-yearly trade fair sponsored by the powerful Counts of Champagne that attracted merchants from all over Europe.

The Ville Haute (Upper Town), a fortification on a promontory jutting out over the valleys of the Voulzie and the Durteint rivers, already was a key post in 800 when Charlemagne sent his governors to oversee the settlement. The Lower Town was founded later in 1049, when one of the Counts of Champagne built a chapel in the chestnut forest below. Provins gained power and prestige, and by the 10th century, it was minting its own currency and was one of France's most powerful cities.

Today, numerous vestiges of Provins's former prominence remain. The wide stone ramparts of the Upper Town — which date from the 12th and 13th centuries — are reminiscent of the famous walled city of Carcassonne. Visit the St.-Jean and the Jouy gates, and walk along the ramparts or stroll down the quaint, interior cobbled streets. Near the edge of the Ville Haute is the pride of Provins, the Tour César, a curious 150-foot high stone tower built over the foundations of a 12th-century dungeon. The wall at its base, added by the British in 1432 when they occupied the tower, was dubbed "English Pie." When the French recaptured the tower, they hurled the executed English into the moat, which henceforth became known as the "English Pit."

Nearby is the Church of St.-Quiriace. Work on the present structure began in the 12th century, and although church canons had hopes of creating a cathedral to rival the one in Reims and other great edifices, its completion was plagued by lack of funds; the façade wasn't added until nearly 4 centuries later. Shortly afterward, a fire destroyed many of St.-Quiriace's early treasures, though the 12th-century choir stalls remain, as well as the north and south doorways (built during the 12th and 13th centuries).

Provins has an exceptional number of underground passages, some of which are open to visitors. Dug over 1,000 years ago, these passages formed a bizarre labyrinth, winding from the Lower to the Upper Town. Whether these were used as simple refuges, places of worship, or for meetings of the secret societies (whose symbols are carved in the earthen walls) is unknown. Guided tours in English of one portion (the only one open to tourists) of the passages begins at the 12th-century palace of the Comtesses de Blois and Champagne, which was later transformed into a hospital, and now is empty. Note the 13th-century portal and the Renaissance stone altarpiece, donated by the Seigneurs de Chenoise in 1506. Below is the vast vaulted gallery from which tours exit. Check with the tourist association (Pl. Honoré Balzac; phone: 64-00-16-65) for details on days and times.

Also worth visiting is the Church of St. Ayoul, which stands on the site of the first chapel built in the Lower Town. Portions date from the 12th century, though much of it was rebuilt during the 16th century. The damaged Romanesque doorway recently has received a new bronze tympanum, the subject of considerable local controversy. If you visit in June, be sure to attend the colorful medieval festival that takes place every year in the Upper Town. (Check with the tourist office for dates.)

En Route from Provins – Before leaving the area, drive 5 miles (8 km) southwest of Provins to see the St.-Loup-de-Naud church. A beautiful little building, it has a magnificent 12th-century main door and is surrounded by sculpture that rivals Chartres's cathedral portals. In 1432, the English destroyed the monastery that stood here.

CHECKING IN/EATING OUT: *Aux Vieux Remparts* – Reputed to offer the "best table in town," this hotel in the Upper Town has a garden and modern rooms in a newly constructed wing. The rustic, beamed restaurant is in the older part. Its menu features refined interpretations of local specialities, with a strong emphasis on fish. 3 Rue Couverte, Ville Haute (phone: 64-08-94-00); hotel, moderate to inexpensive; restaurant, expensive to moderate.

Croix D'Or – Claiming to be the "oldest inn in France," this 13th-century stone hostelry has a handful of spacious old rooms, some recently redecorated. It also has 2 dining rooms, each warmed by a great hearth. 1 Rue des Capucines, Provins (phone: 64-00-01-96). Moderate to inexpensive.

En Route from Provins – Return via N19 to the junction of N36 and follow it south to Vaux-le-Vicomte, a 17th-century château and park that ranks among the most beautiful in Europe. The château was commissioned by Fouquet, minister of finance under Louis XIV. Unfortunately, Fouquet's exquisite taste required greater resources than his personal fortune could accommodate, and his access to state funds was convenient. To build Vaux-le-Vicomte, Fouquet hired the greatest talents of the day: Le Vau as architect, Le Brun as Decorator, Le Nôtre as landscape architect. A total of 5 years, 18,000 laborers, and the equivalent of $10 million later, his château was finished. But Fouquet had committed the fatal error of being grander in scope than his sovereign. In August 1661, he gave a fabulous dinner for Louis XIV. The decoration, the food, and the entertainment were so dazzlingly elegant that they provoked the king's jealous curiosity, and in no time Fouquet's embezzlement was exposed. A few days later, Fouquet was in prison and his property confiscated. But the magnificent château had whet the self-indulgent king's appetite, and in the mid-17th-century, Louis XIV employed the same people to build his own dream palace at Versailles, the site of his father's hunting lodge. Many of the splendidly decorated rooms of Vaux-le-

Vicomte are open to the public daily from 11 AM to 6 PM in summer, 5 PM in winter. Admission charge. Closed *Christmas* (phone: 60-66-97-09).

FONTAINEBLEAU: Continue south via N36 past Melun to the forest and town of Fontainebleau — the fabulous Renaissance palace that is set within 50,000 acres of forest and was the ancient hunting preserve of the Kings of France. Today the grounds are open to the public, and picnicking, hiking, or horseback riding among the trees, ravines, and ponds makes a perfect counterpoint to a day of city sightseeing. There are references as early as 1137 to Fontainebleau as a royal hunting site. Philippe IV was born and died here, but it wasn't until the early 16th century that the palace itself was transformed by François I — with the help of some of Italy's most talented artists — from a 12th-century medieval château to a Renaissance palace. Later kings made further alterations and added wings. Louis XIII was born here and Louis XIV signed the Revocation of the Edict of Nantes here in 1685.

Napoleon lived in Fontainebleau during most of his reign. He abdicated on April 6, 1814, but that wasn't his final good-bye. He returned from Elba in March 1815 to rally his troops again.

In August 1944, following 3 years of German occupation, US General Patton liberated Fontainebleau; the château then was used as headquarters for the Allied army.

Some people find Fontainebleau more beautiful than Versailles. It certainly is more intimate, full of surprising little corners. It's open daily except Tuesdays (admission charge), and there's a guided tour (in English) through the Throne Room, the Queen's Bedroom, which was redone for Marie-Antoinette, the splendid Royal Apartments with their Gobelin tapestries, the Council Room, and the Red Room, where Napoleon abdicated in 1814.

The Cour des Adieux or Cour du Cheval Blanc – The Court of Farewells, or Court of the White Horse, named respectively for the site of Napoleon's farewell to his guard on April 20, 1814, and for the equestrian statue of Marcus Aurelius that formerly stood here. An elegant horseshoe shaped staircase leads to the first floor.

Salle de Bal – The work of Philibert Delorme, this splendid 100-foot long ballroom, the site of feasts and celebrations, includes mythological paintings conceived by Primaticcio and painted by Dell'Abate.

Chapelle de la Sainte-Trinité – The medieval château's original chapel was consecrated by Thomas Becket in 1169. Its replacement, located to the left of the vestibule, was built by Philibert Delorme and was the site of the marriage between Louis X and Marie Leczinska in 1725.

Galerie de François I – Named for the king responsible for the transformation of Fontainebleau, this long gallery dates from the 1530s and includes the original works of Italian masters such as Rosso and Scibec de Capri.

Appartments Royaux – These regal apartments are composed of several rooms, notably the Salon Louis XIII, the Appartements de la Reine, decorated by Marie-Antoinette, and the Salle de Trône, the king's bedroom from the reign of Henri IV to Louis XVI — transformed into a throne room by Napoleon.

In addition, don't miss the Salle du Conseil, the Appartment de l'Empereur (including Napoleon's bedchamber and abdication room), and the Appartements des Reines Mères et du Pape. Before leaving, visit the *Musée Napoleon* and the extensive and beautiful gardens — particularly the Jardin de Diane created for Catherine de Médicis.

CHECKING IN/EATING OUT: *L'Aigle Noir* – An elegant, family-run establishment facing the château gardens and near the heart of the city. The style is Napoleonic — fittingly grand lodgings for visitors to the château of which the emperor was so fond. There are 27 rooms, 4 suites, and 2 restaurants, an indoor pool, a workout room, meeting rooms, and an interior garden. 27 Pl. Napoleon-Bonaparte, Fontainebleau (phone: 64-22-32-65). Expensive.

En Route from Fontainebleau – Just on the edge of the forest lies Barbizon, made famous as an artists' colony in the 19th century by the likes of the painters Honorée Daumier and Constant Musset, the poet Alfred de Troyon, and the writer George Sand. You can visit Rousseau's house on Grand-Rue, just behind the Monument aux Morts, and you can stop for lunch or a drink at the celebrated, half-timbered inn *Bas-Breau* (see below), an elegant second home to many Parisians.

CHECKING IN/EATING OUT: *Hotellerie du Bas-Breau* – An elegant hotel (a member of the Relais & Châteaux group) that welcomes fashionable — and well-heeled — Parisians. In existence since 1867, it has housed such celebrities as Robert Louis Stevenson and Napoleon III. With modern bathrooms, an intimate bar, and a superlative haute cuisine restaurant, this place is expensive but worth it. An absolutely perfect place for a Sunday drive from Paris. Closed January through mid-February. 22 Rue Grande, Barbizon, via N7, N37, and D64 from Fontainebleau (phone: 60-66-40-05). Expensive.

From here travelers can opt for several different routes depending on their interests and the time available. Nearly due west by some 70 miles (113 km) is Chartres. (For a detailed report on the city, its sights, and restaurants, see *Chartres*, THE CITIES.) Returning toward Paris via A6, then turning west on N446 will lead you through an area that many of the French consider the prettiest countryside in the Ile-de-France — the Vallée de Chevreuse. Picturesque villages abound: Châteaufort, with its 12th-century fortress; St. Rémy-lès-Chevreuse; St.-Lambert; Dampierre, the site of a 16th-century château; and Les Vaux de Cernay, one of the loveliest valleys in France. Just south of Les Vaux de Cernay on N306 is Rambouillet, the château that served as a rural retreat for Louis XVI and Napoleon and is used today by President François Mitterand. Originally a medieval fortress, it retains its impressive 14th-century tower. President Mitterand uses the château for some political meetings and visits on Mondays, Wednesdays, Fridays, and Saturdays. Tourists can tour the château (admission charge) when he is not there. In nearby Chatenay-Malabry (via N186) is the home of the writer Châteaubriand (Maison de Châteaubriand; 87 Rue de Châteaubriand, Vallée aux Loups; phone: 47-02-08-62). It recently was transformed into a museum in tribute to the author and his fellow Romantics. Continue west on N186 to reach Versailles.

CHECKING IN: *Château d'Esclimont* – Built in 1543, this turreted feudal castle was restored and now is a luxury hotel. Its 60 rooms are furnished beautifully with period pieces; their shape varies depending on whether they're in the castle, dungeon, stables, or a separate pavilion. The restaurant overlooks a 150-acre walled park that surrounds the hotel. Tennis, swimming, and hunting are available. St. Symphorien-le-Château, off N10 between Rambouillet and Chartres (phone: 37-31-15-15). Expensive.

VERSAILLES: The construction of Versailles nearly bankrupted France. About 6,000 people once lived in this incredibly lavish palace, and its vast gardens, designed by the famous royal gardener Le Nôtre in the formal French style, are spread over 250 acres. A river was diverted to keep the 600 fountains flowing. A gleaming monument to the French monarchy at its most ostentatious, Versailles epitomizes the excesses that sparked a revolution that changed the course of history.

Its beginnings were modest enough. In 1624, Louis XIII ordered a hunting lodge to be built on a hill above the small village of Versailles, 14 miles (22 km) west of Paris. Versailles's evolution from this simple lodge to the grandiose palace of the Sun King and the seat of the French government from 1682 to 1789, was the result of a complex, and ultimately condemning, set of circumstances.

There is so much to see at Versailles that a full day is almost the minimum required for a visit. If time allows, plan to spend 2 days. The château is under continuous restoration, so be prepared for temporary closings of certain rooms from time to time. The château is closed on Mondays. Admission charge.

Before crossing the wide avenue that passes in front of the château, notice the king's stables (*écuries royales*) and carriage house constructed by Jules Hardouin-Mansart. Once past the Louis XVIII gates, three successive courtyards lead up to the visitors' entrance: the Minister's Courtyard and the Royal Courtyard, separated by a bronze statue of Louis XIV on horseback, which give way to the internal Marble Courtyard.

The main entrance to the right of the Royal Courtyard leads to a vestibule and ticket booth through which some 4 million visitors pass annually. To get the most from your visit, join an English-language lecture tour (leaves every 20 minutes from Gate C) or read up in advance.

The Chapel – Built between 1699 and 1710 by Mansart, this masterpiece of white stone and multicolored marble — punctuated by great gilded doors and the bas-reliefs of masters such as Puget and Vasse — was dedicated to St.-Louis. Its construction was vehemently opposed by Mme. de Maintenon (mistress and subsequently second wife of Louis XIV) who, according to Voltaire, was preoccupied with the poverty of the people. This did not deter the Sun King, whose aim was to offer God the most magnificent of all chapels. Note the elaborate ceiling paintings dedicated to the Holy Trinity and the magnificent gilded organ loft.

Grand Apartments – Some of the château's most extraordinary rooms are found in this first floor wing. Start at the Salon d'Hercule, named for François Lemoine's ceiling painting, the *Apotheosis of Hercules*. Next is the Salon de l'Abondance, which marks the beginning of the king's State Apartments. Each of the following five rooms was dedicated to a Greek god: the Salons of Venus and Diana, with their Italianate marble decors; the Salon of Mars, with an early Gobelins tapestry depicting the life of the king; the Salon of Mercury, a card room where Louis XIV lay in state for 8 days after his death; and the Salon of Apollo, the former throne room and the last of the king's state apartments.

The Hall of Mirrors – Flanked on either side by the Salon de la Guerre and the Salon de la Paix, the Galerie des Glaces is, for many visitors, the most memorable of all of Versailles's rooms. Extending along the west façade of the château, it measures 240 feet long, 33 feet wide and 40 feet high. Seventeen tall, arched windows facing east are reflected in 17 sparkling mirrors on the opposite wall, each separated by red marble and gilt bronze pilasters. Gilded scrolls and cherubs, ornate candlesticks, crystal chandeliers, and a celebrated ceiling painting by Le Brun add to the pomp and splendor of this hall, once the scene of magnificent balls and the place the Sun King chose to grant audiences to ambassadors from Persia, Siam, and other distant lands. The Treaty of Versailles was signed in this gallery on June 28, 1919, putting an end to World War I. In 1923, John D. Rockefeller donated funds for repairing the roof of the Hall of Mirrors, thus initiating the restoration of this great monument.

Queen's Apartments – The queen's bedchamber, her private suite, antechamber, and guard room were created for Marie Thérèse, first wife of Louis XIV. Most outstanding is the sumptuous bedchamber, unveiled in 1975 after an intensive 30-year restoration. The elaborate floral motifs amid rococo ornamentation reflect the queen's love of flowers. It is said that royal gardeners replanted the garden outside these windows daily so that the queen would see a new assortment of blossoms each morning. Nineteen royal children were born in this room, including Louis XV and Philippe V of Spain, and it was here that Marie Antoinette spent her last night at Versailles.

King's Apartments – The king's state and private chambers comprise a series of some 15 rooms arranged in a "U" around the Marble Court on the east façade of the palace. Completed in 1701, these rooms clearly illustrate the evolution of the decorative style known as Louis XIV. Included are the "public" bed chamber where the king's waking and retiring were attended by members of the court and the public, as well as his private bedchamber and rooms — the king's most secret quarters.

Museum of French History – Louis-Philippe converted the palace's south wing — the apartments of Louis XIV's brother and some of the royal children — into a museum. The centerpiece of the museum is the Hall of Battles where huge paintings, busts, and bronze plaques constitute a survey of French history from the 17th to the 19th century. Other parts of the palace museum include the 16th through the 19th-century rooms, including many royal apartments recently opened.

Royal Opera – Louis XV commissioned this dazzling display of carved and gilded wood, colorfully painted imitation marble, and glittering crystal in honor of the marriage of his grandchildren, in particular that of the dauphin to Marie-Antoinette on May 16, 1770. It was the first theater in France to have an elliptical shape and levels graded in tiers. Built in just 21 months, it was designed by Gabriel with decorative motifs by Pajou. It was stripped during the Revolution and later used for Assembly and Senate meetings from 1870 to 1875; it was restored to its original splendor in the 1950s.

Gardens – Le Nôtre created the gardens between 1661 and 1668, with mechanical assistance for the fountains by Mansart and magnificent sculpture by Le Brun. The gardens spread over 2,470 acres and represent the pinnacle of French formal landscaping. An in-depth visit requires nearly as much time as a tour of the château and can uncover a multitude of delightful surprises. On summer Sundays, the fountains dance to a son et lumière presentation. (For information, check with the Versailles Tourist Office, 7 Rue des Reservoirs; phone: 39-50-36-22 or 39-50-53-90.)

Grand and Petit Trianons – Apparently not content with the size of the domain encompassed by Versailles's palace and its immense gardens in 1668, Louis XIV bought the small village of Trianon located at the edge of his gardens and ordered his architects to construct a pavilion for casual gatherings and rustic fetes. The resulting House of Porcelain, completed in 1670, was covered with blue and white Delft tiles. However, it proved too small and quaint for the king and in 1687, he commissioned a more glamorous, marble palace — the Grand Trianon — that remains today. Nearby is the Petit Trianon, a small masterpiece by Gabriel set in the midst of a botanical garden and a sort of experimental farm, commissioned by Louis XV in 1761. After the king's death, his son gave the Petit Trianon to Marie Antoinette, who went there frequently in an effort to escape the pressures and confusion of Versailles. She decorated its rooms in the style of the period. Several other structures also are grouped in this area, including Le Hameau, a collection of cottages emulating the small hamlet of Chantilly. Though legend has it that Marie Antionette amused herself here by playing the peasant, most sources refute this, saying that the queen's sense of propriety would have prevented such behavior. What seems certain is that she enjoyed the simplicity and privacy afforded by this hidden hamlet.

 CHECKING IN: *Le Trianon Palace* – Versailles's most prestigious hotel, in operation since 1911, has a covered swimming pool and 2 terraces facing the chateau's park. The 130 rooms are furnished with antiques, and its elegant restaurant, *Clemenceau,* serves modern and classic cuisine. 1 Bd. de la Reine (phone: 39-50-34-12). Expensive.

Les Ibis – Set in a large park in an attractive residential area, the rooms are simple but comfortable. The restaurant (closed July and August) offers good food and a warm atmosphere. Ile du Grand-Lac, Le Vesinet, via N321 (phone: 39-52-17-41). Moderate.

 EATING OUT: *Trois Marches* – Warm, intimate decor, charming service, and highly original cooking mark this celebrated restaurant (two Michelin stars), which would be worth the trip even if you weren't visiting the palace. Chef Gérard Vié invents new recipes daily, but his foie gras is famous, as are his oysters and wild goose. The wines here, especially the burgundys, are excellent, too. Closed Sundays and Mondays. 3 Rue Colbert, Versailles (phone: 39-50-13-21). Expensive.

SCEAUX: Even in this region of lush woods and kings' gardens, Sceaux (pronounced *Sew*) — located 10 miles (16 km) east of Versailles via N12 — with its cascading fountains, reflecting pools, grand canal, and precisely manicured emerald lawns, stands out. A park worthy of any monarch, Sceaux's gardens and château were commissioned not by the king, but by his audacious minister of buildings, Colbert.

In 1670, Colbert called on the greatest architectural and landscaping talents of the epoch, including Claude Perrault, le Bru, Girardon, Coysevox, and Le Nôtre, to collaborate in the realization of his grandiose project. The inauguration in 1677, before honored guest Louis XIV, was a spectacular affair during which Racine's *Phèdre* first was presented.

Transformed from a small, anonymous hamlet in the center of vineyards to a de rigueur stop for royalty and nobility, Sceaux entered its golden age. About 2 decades after the Sun King and his mistress (later wife) Mme. de Maintenon were received at Sceaux, their son, the Duc of Maine, bought the château and its gardens. His ambitious wife, the Duchesse of Maine, added to Sceaux's renown with her lively salons and spectacular *nuits de Sceaux* (festive evenings) that drew *tout* Paris and Versailles. Habitués included Voltaire, Racine, and Molière, some of whose works were performed in the Orangerie (northeast of the château) constructed by Jules Hardouin-Mansart in 1684. To the right of the Orangerie is the Pavillon de l'Aurore, built by Perrault, and behind it a series of neatly kept French gardens.

Colbert's sumptuous 17th-century château was replaced in the 19th century by the more modest one that still stands today and nearly is overwhelmed by the park's grandeur. Since 1937 the château has housed the *Musée de L'Ile-de-France* (Museum of the Ile-de-France) documenting the history and topography of the region through drawings, photographs, and objects such as the ceramics of Sceaux, St.-Cloud, and Sèvres. Open Mondays and Fridays from 2 to 6 PM (5 PM in winter); Wednesdays and Thursdays from 10 AM to noon and 2 to 6 PM (5 PM in winter); Saturdays and Sundays from 10 AM to noon and 2 to 7 PM (5 PM in winter). Admission charge.

After a visit to the museum, wander through the grounds to the west and south. Laid out by Le Nôtre, it is one of the most beautiful public parks in the Paris region. Most spectacular is the Allée de la Duchesse leading to the Grandes Cascades, where ten broad platforms of tumbling water and fountains empty into the sculpture-flanked, octagonal pool. To the west is the Grand Canal and beyond a putting-green-perfect lawn is the curious Pavillon de Hanovre. Constructed in 1760 on Paris's Boulevarde de Capucines, with funds extorted from Hanoverians during the Seven Years War, the structure was picked up and moved to Sceaux in 1832. (It is not open to the public.)

Exit the park at the northwestern gate to visit the town. The French fabulist Florian is buried in the Jardin des Félibres behind the church where there are busts of Mistral and other provincial poets. In the local cemetery are the tombs of Pierre and Marie Curie. Also visit the 16th-century Eglise St.-Jean-Baptiste, which houses some mementos of the Duc and Duchesse du Maine, as well as a medallion of the Virgin attributed to Coysevox. Nearby is yet another garden, the Jardin de la Ménagerie.

The winding little main street of Sceaux is a quaint pedestrian walkway lined with shops — many selling cheese, meat, and bread perfect for a picnic. Beautifully displayed cheeses, *pain Poilane* (a French country bread), *tourtes* (savory tarts), and prepared dishes that use cheese, are among the offerings in *Le Fromagerie*, a jewel-like boutique (37 Rue Houdan; phone: 46-61-01-50). They also sell excellent wines. Also try *Au Porcelet Rose* (41 Rue Houdan; phone: 46-61-01-71), a rosy-hue, high-tech *charcuterie,* featuring everything from roast chicken and prepared salads to foie gras and steamed lobsters.

En route from Sceaux – Northeast of Sceaux via N13 is the château of Malmaison, bought by Josephine Bonaparte in 1799, 3 years after her marriage to Napoleon. It became the empress's favorite residence; she settled here after her divorce in 1809 and stayed until her death in 1814. It now is a museum containing many impressive artworks of the Napoleonic period as well as some of the house's original furnishings and a survey of the era's history as seen through war documents and mementos.

ST. GERMAIN EN LAYE: Return to N13 and travel 5 miles (8 km) farther west to reach St.-Germain-en-Laye. This former home of kings is today a favorite weekend retreat for Parisians. The château was begun during the 12th century but completely rebuilt in the 16th century to bring it up to Renaissance standards. Two floors now are occupied by the *Musée de Antiquités Nationales,* which displays tools, jewelry, ceramics, and other objects through the time of Charlemagne as well as prehistoric and Celtic artifacts. The gardens and terraces are splendid, and the extensive forest surrounding the town offers all manner of recreational activity.

The town itself is one of the chicest and best-heeled in the environs of Paris. The pedestrian shopping street that curves away from the château (Pl. Charles de Gaulle) leads to more boutiques-lined streets that are worth exploring. Also visit the *Musée du Prieure* (2 bis Rue Maurice-Dénis; phone: 39-73-77-87), a few minutes' walk southwest of the main shopping streets. Dedicated to the works of artists from the Symbolist and the Nabis schools, and particularly to the museum's benefactor, artist Maurice Dénis, who made this former hospital his home and studio from 1914 to 1943, the museum has a noteworthy collection of works from the mid-19th to the mid-20th century. Be sure to see La Chapelle St.-Louis, the chapel of the old hospital, decorated in blue frescoes and stained glass by Dénis. Open Wednesday through Friday, 10 AM to 5:30 PM; weekends and holidays from 10 AM to 6:30 PM. Admission charge.

CHECKING IN: *La Forestière* – A charming, traditional country inn with modern conveniences; set among beautiful gardens, it also has a fine restaurant, *Cazaudehore,* which serves classic cuisine as well as several Basque specialties such as *pipérade* (eggs cooked with peppers, ham, and hot sausages). Closed Mondays except holidays. 1 Av. Président-Kennedy, St. Germain-en-Laye (phone: 39-73-36-60). Expensive.

Pavillon Henri IV – An old-fashioned hostelry with 42 plush rooms and apartments, a delightful atmosphere, and a pleasant restaurant overlooking the Seine Valley. This is where béarnaise sauce was created. 21 Rue Thiers, St. Germain-en-Laye (phone: 34-51-62-62). Expensive.

Alpes Franco-Suisse – In a wonderful country setting, this is a modest place with modern facilities. Closed the last 2 weeks in August and from *Christmas* to *New Year's.* Rte. Nationale 1, Warluis (phone: 44-89-26-51). Moderate to inexpensive.

Auberge Morainvilliers – This very attractive country inn and restaurant are set in private gardens with a swimming pool. Morainvilliers-Orgeval, via N13 and D198 from St. Germain-en-Laye (phone: 39-75-87-57). Moderate to inexpensive.

EATING OUT: *L'Esturgeon* – Sturgeon no longer are served here (they no longer frequent the Seine), but there is a good *coulibiac* of salmon, the house specialty. Closed Thursdays and August. 17 miles (27 km) northwest of Paris via N190, at 6 Cours du 14-Juillet, Poissy (phone: 39-79-19-94 or 39-65-00-04). Expensive.

Brasserie du Théâtre – The front room of this bustling archetypal eatery provides a great view of the château, located just across the square. The decor is Art Deco and the service friendly. The food is classic brasserie fare, including a fresh raw bar, grilled meat, steak tartare, and *choucroute* (sauerkraut). Pl. Charles-de-

Gaulle, St.-Germain-en-Laye (phone: 30-61-28-00). Open daily until 1 AM. Moderate.

En Route from St. Germain En Laye – North of St.-Germain-en-Laye via D927 is *Mirapolis* (outside Pontoise), France's first theme park. If you have children along, it's worth a visit. Open year-round.

But if art and gardens are more to your liking, take a detour to the west (via A13) for a visit to Giverny and the *Museum of Claude Monet.* (For a complete description, see "Vernon" in *Normandy,* DIRECTIONS.) If time still allows, continue north to Beauvais — 45 miles (72 km) from Paris via A15 and D927. Although technically it too lies outside the boundaries of the Ile-de-France in a less-than-attractive area, a visit to the imposing Cathédrale St.-Pierre makes the trip worthwhile.

The cathedral, whose Gothic style is in rather jarring contrast to that of the rest of the city, has had an erratic history, plagued by overambition and underfinancing. The soaring choir section, begun in 1247, was a challenge to architects throughout Europe. They did not prove equal to the challenge, and in 1284 the choir collapsed. In 1500, another generation of bishops decided to continue the work and undertook to finance it by the expedient sale of indulgences. But again the architects literally let Beauvais down: An experimental cross tower was constructed, but the supporting pillars gave way in 1573. Since then, the cathedral of Beauvais has remained a magnificent, if unfinished, monument.

The vaulted interior of the cathedral appears to rise to startling, almost dizzying, heights. Through the well-preserved stained glass windows streams a luminous light in which to view the church's magnificent tapestries, attesting to the city's renown as a center of weaving.

Before leaving the city, also look at the Eglise St.-Etienne (Rue de L'Etamine and Rue de l'Infanterie). The stained glass of the Choir section has some of the most beautiful examples of Renaissance windows.

 CHECKING IN: *Mercure Beauvais* – Modern facilities and an outdoor pool are offered at this comfortable hotel. Av. Montaigne, SAC Quartier St.-Lazare, Beauvais (phone: 44-02-03-36). Moderate.

N1 will take you to Paris.

The Loire Valley

The Loire Valley is one of the most strikingly beautiful portions of a country renowned for its beauty. Here the turrets of a medieval castle soar above the deep green branches of a forest in which the Kings of France once hunted wild boar; there the bright waters of a broad river part to curve around a lushly wooded island with children splashing on its shore; and everywhere neatly tended vineyards, orchards, and vegetable fields stretch between water and rolling slopes under a wide, pale blue sky that is almost always speckled with a few puffs of cloud. "Peaceful" is the word most often used over the centuries to describe the Loire Valley, and that it still is — gentle, tranquil, and calm. An important element in this mildness is the climate, tempered by winds blowing inland from the Atlantic, into which the Loire — at 625 miles the longest river in France — flows 100 miles (160 km) west of the city of Angers, by general agreement the western limit of the Loire Valley. Spring comes early here — Loire Valley gardeners send asparagus and strawberries to Paris street markets before Parisians are out of their winter coats — and summer often lingers late.

But for all this sweetness and softness that the French term *douceur,* the Loire Valley has seen considerable drama, intrigue, and outright bloodshed. Kings and counts have fought over each piece of high ground here — and over the affections and dowries of a long list of wealthy, titled, sometimes beautiful, and often scheming women — obtaining naturally well defended positions and, in the process, spectacular views.

Today the people you meet in the Loire Valley are warm and charming 20th-century innkeepers, restaurateurs, and vintners, but you are likely to come away with equally vivid impressions of dramatic, sometimes blood-thirsty characters who lived, and in some cases died, long ago in the châteaux and abbeys of the valley, among them Richard the Lion-Hearted, François I, Marie de Médici, Honoré de Balzac, and Leonardo da Vinci. It was here that Joan of Arc won the allegiance of the dauphin and rode into history and immortality under his banners. To walk the Loire Valley's heavy stone corridors and ancient flower gardens is to be touched by hints of what life must have been like for these fascinating people centuries ago.

Going back some 5,000 years, you also can visit remarkable prehistoric stone monuments called dolmens and menhirs, especially in the Saumur-Gens area. Everywhere you will see troglodyte dwellings and cave homes, often large and comfortable, dug right into the region's soft cliffs; people live in them (though they must seem very unusual "basement" apartments) or use them for garages or wine cellars.

Gentle as well as more vigorous sports are available here for visitors. Much of the area is flat, with well-surfaced country roads meandering through pretty fields and along enchanting waterways, so bicycling has become popular. Bicycles can be rented in several towns and at four locations in Tours, in the heart of the region: the train station (Pl. de la Gare; phone: 47-20-50-50), *Barat* (156 Rue Giraudeau; phone: 47-61-03-58), *Au Col de Cygne* (46 bis Rue Docteur-Fournier; phone: 47-46-00-37), and *Grammont Motocycles* (93 Av. de Grammont; phone: 47-66-62-89).

You can canoe, kayak, and even windsurf on the Loire and its tributaries; fishing is so popular that places like Chinon and Langeais are full of shops selling *articles de pêche* (fishing tackle). The truly adventurous can fly over the Touraine region in hot air balloons; tours are organized by a number of companies, including *B. Bombard* (phone: 47-41-69-37) or *De Sade* (phone: 47-58-56-70).

For most visitors, though, the Loire Valley is a place simply to slow down and enjoy the exercise inherent in climbing château steps (some have many) and in strolling across flowery fields under a gentle noonday sun to find an ideal picnic place. Evening entertainment here is correspondingly quiet: perhaps a *son et lumière* at the closest castle or a chamber concert in a nearby cloister.

Many of the churches and châteaux have superb acoustics, and many musical events are scheduled, especially from July through September. The best-known musical festival in the Loire Valley is probably the 20-year-old *Fêtes Musicales en Touraine* (see the city of Tours, below).

Mealtime is a particular pleasure in the Loire Valley. Not surprising in a region laced by sparkling rivers and bursting with agricultural abundance, you will find delicious fish, tasty sausage, and fine meat of all kinds, often exquisitely sauced and accompanied by excellent vegetables and fruits, the freshest of local cheeses, and delightful wines. Regional dishes include *saumon à l'oseille* (salmon with sorrel sauce), *andouillette* (sausage made from chitterlings) from Tours or Angers, *coq au vin* (chicken cooked in wine sauce) made with regional bourgueil or chinon red wines or even white vouvray, *matelote d'anguille* (stewed eel), and *rillons* (spicy, cubed pork) and *rillettes* (minced pork usually spread on crisp bread) from Tours. The house specialty in the Loire Valley may be a terrine made from deer, pheasant, or boar from a nearby forest, freshly caught fish (such as the tasty Loire River *sandre*), or vegetables from a nearby garden. Pâtés usually are worth sampling, as are *chèvres* (goat cheeses) and fruit tarts. For all of these, prices usually are very reasonable.

Travelers brought up on the idea that a hotel restaurant equals a bad restaurant should prepare to change their thinking in the Loire Valley. First of all, if you decide to stay in some of the charming small towns (strongly recommended) rather than in Orléans, Blois, Tours, or Angers, there may be few restaurants other than hotel dining rooms. Luckily, some of the finest restaurants *are* connected with hotels. And what a pleasure after a rich meal and good wine simply to climb the stairs to a comfortable bed instead of driving on dark and unfamiliar roads.

In 1882, Henry James said: ". . . it is half the charm of the Loire that you can travel beside it. A wide river, as you follow a wide road, is excellent company." The Loire Valley route covers about 300 miles (480 km), beginning at Blois, 113 miles (181 km) and 2 hours by autoroute south of Paris. It progresses generally west past châteaux, through forests, and along rivers on the southern side of the Loire to Angers, then turns east, following the northern bank of the river back to Tours, where you can take the autoroute north to Paris or south toward Bordeaux. It's also possible to zigzag back and forth across the river west of Tours and end the route at Angers in order to continue into Britanny. Michelin map No. 64 contains all but a short southern dip of the route.

A caveat: To cover all the stops mentioned in a single trip might be wearying and could lead to the malady known as being "châteauxed out." Distances between one point of interest and the next are short — Blois and Angers are only 100 miles (160 km) apart, and the direct distance from Angers to Tours is a scant 66 miles (106 km) — so it is highly possible to cover the entire route, with stops, in 3 or 4 days. You may, however, choose to concentrate on the sections of the route that most intrigue you and save the rest for return trips.

Other tips: Reserve as early as possible for hotels and special restaurants; this area is as popular with Parisians as it is with tourists, and some towns have only one or two specially pleasant hotels. Hotels usually charge extra for breakfast; check the card on the back of your hotel room door for both room and breakfast rates. Some châteaux and museums close 1 day a week, most commonly Monday, and many are closed daily from noon to 2 PM. You may welcome a lunch break yourself, but if you are trying to squeeze in as much sightseeing as possible, study brochures from the regional tourist offices ahead of time. Be forewarned, though, that closing dates, not only of châteaux and museums but also of restaurants and hotels, may change.

Admission prices to the châteaux vary dramatically. Some are run by the government; others are privately owned and are usually more expensive; still others include visits to adjacent museums in the cost.

For up-to-date information on all aspects of life in this area, consult regional and local Syndicats d'Initiative, or tourist offices. The main tourist office in Tours, opposite the train station, is an especially dynamic operation, publishing each year a detailed series of brochures in English covering food and wine, hotels, monuments and museums, concerts and *son et lumière* performances, routes for tourists, and even unusual things to do and see in Touraine. Write to the Office de Tourisme de Tours, Place du Maréchal-Leclerc, Tours 37042 (phone: 47-05-58-08).

Expect to pay $90 or more for a double room in an expensive hotel; $50 to $90 in a moderate one; and less than $50 in one listed as inexpensive. A meal for two with a bottle of regional wine will cost $95 and up in an expensive restaurant; $50 to $90 in a moderate one; and under $50 in an inexpensive restaurant. Service usually is included.

ORLÉANS: No one has received quite the rousing welcome Joan of Arc did when she liberated this city from the English in 1429, but it is still often chosen as the beginning of a tour of the Loire Valley. World War II was not kind to Orléans, now as in centuries past an industrial center and with a current population of 106,000; yet a few treasures remain, and the city is a good point from which to explore the surrounding Loire region. Though not as stunning as its castle-flecked counterpart to the west, it still is special in its own right.

A visit to Orléans should include the following three sights, all conveniently on or just off Rue Jeanne-d'Arc: First, the Gothic Cathédrale Ste.-Croix, as large as Notre-Dame in Paris, which was begun in the 13th century. Partially destroyed by the Huguenots (who made Orléans their headquarters briefly in 1568), it was not completed until the 19th century. Its chancel contains outstanding woodwork from the early 18th century executed by Jules Degoullons, who also designed the stalls in Notre-Dame and contributed to the decoration of Versailles. The *Musée des Beaux-Arts* is in the splendid old Town Hall, which dates from the 15th century; it contains some outstanding works of primitive art from the 15th century, pastel and oil portraits from the 18th century, and 19th- and 20th-century art, including works by Gauguin and Max Jacob. The *Musée Historique et Archéologique,* in the restored 16th-century Hôtel Cabu, is small and lovely, with examples of local arts and crafts from the 17th through the 19th century.

A statue of Joan of Arc on horseback, erected in 1855, dominates Place du Martroi, into which Rue Royale dead-ends. Every May 7 and 8, the city celebrates its Maid with great pageantry.

From Orléans, excursions can be made easily into the Forêt d'Orléans, 124,000 acres of pine and oak, and beyond it to the Basilique St.-Benoit-sur-Loire, 19 miles (30 km) upstream from Orléans on the north bank of the river. This exquisite Romanesque structure, perhaps the finest in France, stands on foundations that date to 806 and is crowned with a beautifully carved belfry on the 11th-century chancel; a Roman mosaic brought from Italy in 1531 graces the floor, and the restored crypt looks the same as it did 8 centuries ago.

A few miles south of Orléans via RN20 is the Château La Ferte Saint-Aubin, a private castle recently opened to the public. Though there has been a château on this site since the 11th century, most of this exceptional building was built in the 17th century by Henri de Saint-Nectaire. Open daily from 10 AM to 7 PM from late March to mid-November (phone: 38-76-52-72).

Follow N152, or the speedier A10, west for 37 miles (59 km) to Blois.

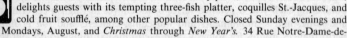

CHECKING IN: *D'Arc* – One of Orléans's most comfortable hotels, it has 35 rooms that are decorated with rattan furniture. Located in the center of town. 37 Rue de la République (phone: 38-53-10-94). Expensive to moderate.

EATING OUT: *La Crémaillère* – This lovely place, with two Michelin stars, delights guests with its tempting three-fish platter, coquilles St.-Jacques, and cold fruit soufflé, among other popular dishes. Closed Sunday evenings and Mondays, August, and *Christmas* through *New Year's.* 34 Rue Notre-Dame-de-Recouvrance, Orléans (phone: 38-53-49-17). Expensive to moderate.

BLOIS: Rising above the right bank of the wide Loire River, its skyline dominated by a historic château, this pleasant city of 50,000 is mainly a business center for the surrounding farming region. Blois prides itself on its complex history as a residence of French kings and on its rich architecture from the 13th to the 17th century, expressed most dramatically in the château itself. The multi-winged whole reads like a summary of the evolution of French architecture over 400 years: its separate sections date from the 13th-century feudal period, the 15th-century Gothic-Renaissance transition period, the Renaissance of the 16th century, and the 17th century's Classicism. Dastardly deeds and intrigues aplenty are evoked on a visit here: The Duc de Guise was assassinated in King Henri III's bedroom on the second floor in 1588; Marie de Médici, as a stout, middle-aged woman, inched down a rope ladder into the moat by night in 1619 to escape after 2 years of banishment here ordered by her son, Louis XIII; and 237 carved wooden panels in Catherine de Médici's study still conceal her secret cupboards.

Other places to visit in Blois include the fine Eglise St.-Nicolas, the Cathédrale St.-Louis, and the picturesque streets stretching down from it toward the Loire, and the former Bishop's Palace, now the Hôtel de Ville (Town Hall), with a terrace overlooking the river and an 18th-century humpbacked bridge across it. The statue of Joan of Arc on the terrace is the work of an American sculptor, Anna Hyatt Huntington. There also is a statue of Denis Papin, Blois's most famous son, who discovered the principle of the steam engine in 1707 and also invented what he called a "digester," the forerunner of the pressure cooker. Follow D951 and D84 upriver to Chambord.

On a clear day, a flight by helicopter or plane, lasting from 10 minutes to more than an hour, can be organized at the tourist office in Blois (3 Av. Jean Laignet; phone: 54-74-06-49).

CHECKING IN: *Le Médicis* – Located just behind the train station, this small hostelry recently was renovated. Some of its 12 individually decorated rooms have Jacuzzis. Despite the new look, a homey atmosphere still prevails in both the hotel and its restaurant. 2 Allée François I (phone: 54-43-94-04). Moderate.

EATING OUT: *La Bocca d'Or* – Set in a 14th-century vaulted cellar, this dining spot is run by well-known chef Patrice Gallard and his Californian wife. Closed from the end of January to March 7, and Sundays. 15 Rue Haute, Blois (phone: 54-78-04-74). Moderate.

En Route from Blois – Cross Blois's main highway bridge over the Loire, with lovely views of sandbars and sometimes small boats, toward Chambord, turning right just at the south end of the bridge and then right again under it to follow D951 along the picturesque south bank of the river. Like many in the Loire region, the road has only two lanes but a good surface. It passes well-tended fields, pretty camping areas, and the remains of an old aqueduct on the right, and then on the left there's an excellent view across the river of the Château of Menars and its terraces. Turn south on D84, which curves gently through cornfields and tiny villages, until you reach a sign warning you to limit your speed since deer and wild boar roam freely through the forest of Chambord.

CHAMBORD: The largest of all the Loire Valley châteaux, this is also one of the most spectacular. To reach it, you pass through a gateway in the longest wall in France — 20 miles around! — into the immense national game reserve of 13,600 acres that surrounds the château, then proceed straight down a long alley carved through the forest to frame the central spire of the château until the road at last opens onto the whole magnificent structure. François I built this extravagant 440-room hunting lodge in the 16th century; the Renaissance inspired the fantastic terrace atop the château, a forest of spires, gables, turrets, and chimneys decorated with black slate, which offers visitors an extraordinary view. A remarkable interior feature is François I's ingenious double staircase, which soars from ground floor to roof terrace in two spirals superimposed on one another so that one person can ascend and another descend simultaneously without meeting. The apartments of the château, long nearly bare, have been refurnished. The world's first *son et lumière* performance was presented here in 1952, and the Chambord shows, set to the music of Jean-Baptiste Lully, who composed and performed in this very château, remain breathtaking.

CHECKING IN/EATING OUT: *Grand St.-Michel* – An old rambling establishment with bright flowers in the windowboxes and a pleasant staff, this would be a comfortable place to stay anywhere, but it happens to be idyllically located directly across a narrow road from Chambord castle, far from any town and surrounded by Chambord's vast, game-filled forest. Stay here and at dusk, after the busloads of tourists have gone, drive to an observation platform to spy on deer and perhaps even boar. Return to the hotel's spacious dining room, which specializes in game during the hunting season and also offers such Loire specialties as *rillons* (spiced, cubed pork) and poached salmon and trout. Then, in season, watch a *son et lumière* performance from your bedroom window, or simply gaze at the château as it glows silver by moonlight or rosy with dawn. Both hotel and restaurant are closed from mid-November to mid-December. Chambord (phone: 54-20-31-31). Inexpensive.

CHEVERNY: Only 10 miles (16 km) south of Chambord via D112, which cuts through the cool forests of Chambord and Boulogne, then west on D102 from the pleasant little town of Bracieux, the Château de Cheverny is a lordly mansion, unusual in the Loire for having been built all in one piece in the 17th-century classical style. Many of its handsomely furnished rooms can be toured. Even more memorable is the hunting museum, in an outbuilding with one room containing 2,000 sets of stag antlers, and the kennel, where you can see a pack of 70 hounds that are a crossbreed between the English foxhound and the French poitevin. Your ears will guide you right to it.

From Cheverny, head south on D102 for just under 30 miles (48 km), cutting across an edge of the Cheverny forest; at Contres, pick up D956, which crosses the Cher River at Selles-sur-Cher, whose château towers are reflected in the water. Then on to Valençay.

CHECKING IN: *St.-Hubert* – Close to the Château de Cheverny, this 20-room quiet inn has been in the same family for 45 years. The restaurant specializes in game. Closed from early December to mid-January and Tuesday evenings and Wednesdays until *Easter,* after which it's closed only on Wednesdays. Cour-Cheverny (phone: 54-79-96-60). Restaurant, moderate; hotel, inexpensive.

EATING OUT: *Trois Marchands* – A former coaching inn, this pleasant restaurant bustles, especially at noon, and the food (lots of fish specialties) is fresh and good. Closed from January 15 to March 1 and Mondays from October to mid-January. Cour-Cheverny (phone: 54-79-96-44). Moderate to inexpensive.

VALENÇAY: Just far enough off the main route of Loire Valley tour buses to preserve its tranquillity even at the peak of summer, Valençay is small and pleasant, with tree-shaded avenues that lead to a château whose builder, Jacques d'Estampes, was inspired by Chambord. Dating from 1540, the château was owned in the early 19th century by Talleyrand. King Ferdinand VII of Spain was comfortably confined here by Napoleon from 1808 to 1814. And you can see the table used for the Congress of Vienna in 1814–15, when a new map of Europe was drawn up. Its elegantly furnished 17th-century west wing can be visited, now the scene of musical and theatrical productions in the summer (Information: Château de Valençay, PO Box 23, Valençay 36600).

Probably its most unusual feature is its large park filled with deer, llamas, buffalo, peacocks, swans, and flamingos, a joy especially for youngsters. There is a museum filled with souvenirs of Talleyrand as well as a well-kept automobile museum on the grounds.

CHECKING IN/EATING OUT: *Espagne* – A beautiful old coaching inn, its main connection with Spain seems to be that the staff of King Ferdinand VII was housed here while he was confined to Valençay's château, a few steps away. Since 1875, four generations of the Fourré family have welcomed guests to the elegant lodgings (10 rooms and 6 suites, many with private balconies) built around a flower-filled courtyard. The dining room serves specialties including *ris de veau aux morilles* (sweetbreads with morels), lamb filet with tarragon, *sandre* (pike perch), and flambéed peaches. This is one of the many little towns in this area that produces its own wine, so you may want to try a bottle of the rather nondescript dry white valençay just for the fun of it. Closed January and February. Reservations advised. 9 Rue du Château, Valençay (phone: 54-00-00-02). Expensive.

En Route from Valençay – Head west along pretty, sunflower-bordered D960 for 14 miles (22 km) to the tiny village of Nouans-les-Fontaines; watch for its strangely shaped church spire, which looks something like a rocket soaring over the fields, or you may drive through without realizing it. Oddly enough, this unassuming village church contains one of the finest French works of art of the late 15th century, a moving *Descent from the Cross*, also called the *Nouans Pietà*, painted on wood in somber colors by artists from the school of Jean Fouquet. A 5F piece placed in a slot illuminates the painting and sends a detailed commentary in French, English, or German echoing through the usually empty church.

MONTRÉSOR: In this pretty town on the right bank of the Indrois River, 5 miles (8 km) west of Nouans-les-Fontaines across rolling fields of sunflowers, are an interesting church and château, and somebody has gone to the trouble of lining the main road with trees of alternating red and green foliage. The church is known for its fine doorway and the 16th-century tomb of the Basternays, overlords of Montrésor. The castle is one of 20 in the Loire Valley built by Foulques Nerra (971–1040), a Count of Anjou and one of the most dramatic and violent personalities in the region's history. He spent his life battling the Counts of Blois, building fortresses to use in this fight; then, during periodic fits of repentance for his unscrupulous and sometimes criminally violent acts, he raised churches and went on pilgrimages to Jerusalem. You can walk around the fortified promontory on which the château is perched, high above the Indrois.

Follow D760 5 miles (8 km) west to the long wall that denotes the Chartreuse du Liget.

CHARTREUSE DU LIGET: Though these are only the ruins of a Carthusian monastery founded in the 12th century, supposedly by Henry II of England in expiation for the murder of Thomas à Becket, Archbishop of Canterbury, impressive ruins they are. Park near the monumental 18th-century gateway, walk through it, and obtain permission from the caretakers to visit the open, grass-floored ruin of the 12th-century chapel and, near the brook called the Liget, the vast cloisters, where now a child's swing is set up. Chapelle St.-Jean-de-Liget, standing alone in a field west of the monastery, contains interesting 12th-century frescoes. You can stage a memorable picnic amid tiny wildflowers just outside the walls of the monastery.

Continue west on D760 west for 16 miles (26 km) to Loches.

LOCHES: Relatively unknown, yet one of the special treasures of the Loire Valley, this attractive little town on the Indre River, with modern stores and friendly inhabitants, has preserved a large and fascinating medieval quarter, the Cité Médiévale, on the heights in its center, with a château full of history and dungeons with grim memories. Loches has been fortified from its earliest history; captured in a 3-hour surprise attack by Richard the Lion-Hearted in 1195, it was regained for France 10 years later by Philippe-Auguste after a year-long siege. Loches then became the state prison of the Kings of France. In the keep, a group of fortified towers at the southern end of the medieval city, are some of the most gripping dungeons you are ever likely to see, complete with torture instruments and inscriptions carved or painted on the walls by the prisoners. During World War II, Nazi collaborators were jailed here. Also interesting in the medieval city are the *Musée Lansyer* (1 Rue Lansyer; phone: 47-59-05-45) and the *Musée du Terroir* (Folklore Museum; same address and phone number). The former is devoted to the works of a local landscape artist; the latter affords a lovely view of Loches, both on Rue Lansyer. Eglise St.-Ours has two unusual pyramids rising between its towers; and the château, at the northern end of the promontory, holds the lovely, sculpted tomb of Agnès Sorel, mistress of Charles VII. The remains of "*la dame de beauté,*" as she was known, are no longer here; originally buried in St.-Ours, they were scattered to the winds during the French Revolution by soldiers who mistook Agnès for a saint. Loche's château and dungeon are closed Wednesdays off-season and all of December and January.

In mid-July, the town stages an old-fashioned "peasants' market," with costumes, artisans selling their wares, and singing and dancing in the streets.

Head north from Loches on D31 for 17 miles (27 km) through fields and vineyards, then twist through the busy little town of Bléré and turn east on N76 toward Chenonceaux, 4 miles (6 km) away.

CHENONCEAUX: Leapfrogging splendidly across the Cher River like a fantasy bridge, with views of decorative gardens and water from almost all of its beautiful furnished rooms, Chenonceaux, perhaps the most photographed of all the region's châteaux, is not to be missed even on the briefest tour of the Loire Valley. You approach it down a long avenue shaded by plane trees, with ducks and swans swimming in canals alongside, then cross a drawbridge onto a terrace surrounded by moats. To the left is the Italian garden of Diane de Poitiers, who was given the château in 1547 by her lover, King Henri II, 20 years her junior; to the right, that of Catherine de Médici, the king's wife, who evicted Diane and took over Chenonceaux herself after Henri II was killed by a lance thrust in a tournament in 1559. Several other women played major roles in the history of the beautiful château, including Catherine Briçonnet, who supervised its building from 1513 to 1521, and Louise of Lorraine, daughter-in-law of Catherine de Médicis, who retired to Chenonceaux to mourn after the assassination of her husband, Henri III. Louise became known as "the White Queen" because she wore white, widow's clothes until her own death 11 years later. One of the special pleasures of Chenonceaux is that you can stroll through it on your own, without the guided tour that is obligatory in most châteaux, reading full descriptions of each room from a free brochure available at the ticket booth. An English version is available.

The entire château is fascinating, but make a special effort to see the tiny library, with windows overlooking the Cher, that was used by Catherine de Médici; the downstairs kitchens, a labyrinth of rooms set almost at water level into the château's piers; and, above the kitchens, the beautiful gallery spanning the river, built by Catherine on top of a bridge previously constructed by Diane de Poitiers. A plaque informs you that in the bright, 65-yard-long gallery, where today taped Renaissance music plays softly, 2,254 wounded people were given medical care during World War I; the entire château was turned into a temporary hospital by its owners, members of the Menier chocolate manufacturing family. Follow signs to the *Musée de Cires* (Waxworks Museum), where 15 scenes depict château life.

The most scenic route for the approximately 8 miles (13 km) from Chenonceaux north to Amboise is D81, which passes through vineyards and countryside dotted with hay in big round bales at harvesttime and under the overhanging greenery of the Forest of Amboise.

CHECKING IN/EATING OUT: *Château de Chissay* – Between Chenonceaux and Montrichard, this 12th-century castle was converted into a luxury hotel in 1986, complete with mosaic bathrooms and a heated swimming pool. Closed January and February. 4 miles (6 km) east of Chenonceaux on D176, Chissay en Touraine (phone: 54-32-32-01). Expensive.

Domaine des Hauts de Loire – Less than 10 miles (16 km) north of Amboise on N152, this gracious 18th-century manor set in a 75-acre park was once the hunting lodge of the Count de Rostaing. Most of the 22 rooms and 4 suites, in a newer but equally charming annex, are exquisitely decorated with antiques and have modern bathrooms. The elegant dining room more than deserves its one Michelin star; fresh salmon, parsley mousse in hazelnut oil, and hot apple tart star among the house specialties. There also is a tennis court and an 8-acre lake stocked with pike and carp. Closed December to March. Outside Onzain on N152 (phone: 54-20-72-57). Expensive.

Château de Gué Péan – Stop by just to visit or stay on a while in this 17th-century castle, which is set in a private forest and furnished in the style of the 18th century. You will be welcomed by the charming Marquis de Keguelinet, who speaks excellent English and dines with his guests in the elegant dining room. Open year-round. Less than 10 miles (16 km) east of Chenonceaux, Monthou sur Cher (phone: 54-71-43-01). Expensive to moderate.

Bon Laboureur et Château – *The* place to stay in tiny Chenonceaux. A short walk from the château and the *son et lumière* performances, it is as charming as its name, *Hotel of the Good Plowman.* Low and vine-covered, it proffers windowboxes bright with flowers and a dining room that serves an abundance of well-prepared Loire Valley fish, other specialties, and good regional wines. A breakfast of fresh croissants and jam served in the 26 rooms (some in an annex) is especially pleasant. Closed from late November to mid-March. Chenonceaux (phone: 47-23-90-02). Hotel inexpensive; restaurant moderate to inexpensive.

Hostellerie de l'Isle – Relax in the warm family atmosphere of this cozy 18th-century manor house. The well-prepared meals are served by the fire on chilly days or under the trees in the surrounding garden-park on warmer ones. Closed December 10 to January 10. On scenic D176 at Civray de Touraine, 1 mile (1.6 km) before Chenonceaux (phone: 47-23-80-09). Moderate to inexpensive.

AMBOISE: The village of Amboise offers a fine château perched high on a promontory, magnificent views over the Loire and surrounding countryside, and a lovely 15th-century clock tower. It also has a rich history, featuring 15th- and 16th-century kings (this was the birthplace of the dauphin) and even a massacre — of the Huguenots (French Protestants), who were hanged from its castle walls or thrown from its battlements into the river in 1560. Its most illustrious resident was Leonardo da Vinci, who spent his last years working here and was buried here (his remains are in the château's Chapelle St.-Hubert, in the north transept). After touring the château, stroll about a third of a mile east along Rue Victor-Hugo to the Clos Lucé, the charming 15th-century manor house that François I, a patron of the arts, turned over to Leonardo after bringing him here from Italy in 1514. Pass through a gateway under a pretty little gallery with wooden arches, the oldest part of the red brick house, and by a lovely park with paths and benches to find this quotation from Leonardo just inside the front door: "A well-filled day gives a good sleep. A well-filled life gives a peaceful death." Past 60 when he arrived here and with a paralyzed right hand, the artist nevertheless painted and sketched actively until his death on May 2, 1519, in an upstairs bedroom with a view of rose gardens and, in the distance, the château. Some say François I was with him when he died. The lowest floor of the Clos Lucé holds a fascinating collection of 40 models of intricate machines constructed by IBM from plans by Leonardo, demonstrating his engineering genius in precursors of the first airplane, helicopter, military tank, and bridge designed to swing open.

Tours lies only 15 miles (24 km) downriver from Amboise and good roads lead to it on both sides of the Loire; D751 on the south bank and N152 on the north provide good views of the river, its islands, and sandbars.

CHECKING IN: ***Château de Pray*** – Less than 2 miles (3 km) northeast of Amboise via D751 on a bluff overlooking the Loire, this picturesque old château with 16 rooms has a dining room with a fireplace and a beamed ceiling and, for pleasant summer lunches, a terrace overlooking part of its own walled-in garden and the Loire — the perfect spot to linger over salmon in sorrel sauce. Adjoining the more formal garden with its graveled paths and geraniums in big pots is a wild, woodsy park with leafy trails and even a swing set in a clearing.

Closed from December 31 to mid-February. D751, just northeast of Amboise (phone: 47-57-23-67). Hotel moderate to inexpensive, restaurant moderate.

Au Lion d'Or – Choose one of the back rooms in this comfortable 7-room dwelling, for an undisturbed quiet spot with shuttered windows that open onto the wall of the château. The dining room, long and spacious, exudes the atmosphere of a hunting lodge: A large fireplace fills one end and game trophies line the walls. Try the *foie gras frais de canard* (fresh duck foie gras), *pain d'épinards à la crème* (spinach soufflé covered with a delicate cream sauce), or *navarin de cidre* (pork stew with potatoes, turnips, and a pungent cider sauce). Closed Sunday evenings, Mondays, and January. 17 Quai Charles-Guinot, Amboise (phone: 47-57-00-23). Moderate.

Le Manoir St.-Thomas – A Renaissance manor house that has the best reputation in town, and deservedly so. Its excellent menu and fine selection of wines have earned it a Michelin star. Closed Mondays and mid-January to mid-February. Pl. Richelieu, Amboise (phone: 47-57-22-52). Moderate.

L'Auberge du Mail – This calm, comfortable 14-room inn is on the Loire River, near the Amboise château. The restaurant has an old-fashioned atmosphere, with wooden beams, an iron candle chandelier, high-backed chairs, and a sideboard laden with wines and cognacs. The house specialties include salmon mousse, asparagus with a mousseline sauce, and fish stew with baby eel. Closed Fridays. 32 Quai du Général-de-Gaulle, Amboise (phone: 47-57-60-39). Moderate to inexpensive.

EATING OUT: *La Bonne Etape* – Near the Château de Pray, this quaint little restaurant has lovely gardens with a graceful willow, winding paths, and neat hedges. The dining room (recently renovated by its new owners) is warm and informal, and potted geraniums decorate its terrace. The specialties here are seafood, such as *friture* (small fried fish served with lemon) and *sandre* (pike perch). Closed February 17 to March 4. Rte. 2, about a mile east of Amboise (phone 47-57-08-09). Inexpensive.

En Route from Amboise – One advantage of taking the northern route, N152, to Tours is that you can make a short detour to follow a marked Route du Vouvray past vineyards and through the hamlets of Noizay and Vernou to the little town of Vouvray, which produces the best-known white wine of Touraine. Watch for the signs of wine producers offering visits and tastings.

TOURS: The major city of a region rich in magnificent châteaux, fine food and wine, and some of the most beautiful countryside in France, Tours has been an important metropolis since Gallo-Roman times. It was bombed heavily in World War II, so it greets you with ugly 20th-century apartment towers instead of the elegant château towers of its Loire neighbors. Yet Tours, the home of 136,000 people (and another 114,000 in the outlying areas), is an ideal base for visitors who prefer to sleep in the same bed every night while exploring the Loire Valley, and it is easy to reach from Paris, 3 hours by autoroute or a little less by train. The charms of this city must simply be sought out. Stop at the large and well-run tourist office in front of the train station (Pl. du Maréchal-Leclerc; phone: 47-05-58-08), then visit Cathédrale St.-Gatien, which could illustrate an art history text on the evolution of the Gothic style; it was begun in the early 13th century and not finished until the 16th. Be sure to see the fine stained glass windows that date from the 13th to the 15th century. The cathedral's cloister was the setting for native son Honoré de Balzac's novel *Le Curé de Tours* (The Vicar of Tours). Nearby, in the *Musée des Beaux-Arts,* formerly the archbishop's palace, hang paintings by Mantegna, Rubens, Rembrandt, Degas, and Delacroix. A few blocks to the west, on Rue Nationale, are the Eglise St.-Julien, part of a former Benedictine abbey, whose cellars now house a Touraine wine museum that includes a 12th-century cellar, and the *Musée du Compagnonnage* (Museum of the Craft Guilds), where the work and tools of a variety of craftspersons are displayed. Keep walking west to reach Vieux Tours (Old Tours), with half-timbered houses that lean into charming narrow streets. The *Musée du Gemmail* (open late March to mid-October), which focuses on the "gemmail" artistic technique of superimposing pieces of glass to produce painting-like works, is in this area, as is a honeycomb of little streets called Les Artisans du Petit St.-Martin, featuring painted jewelry, marionettes, lampshades made to measure, and many other items of silk, wood, and leather.

Especially in the summer, there are frequent concerts. A classical music festival, the annual *Fêtes Musicales en Touraine,* is held the last weekend in June and the first weekend in July at the Grange de Meslay, a vast, 13th-century barn that was part of a fortified farm; it is about 5 miles (8 km) north of Tours on N10, toward Château-Renault. Another festival, the *Semaines Musicales de Tours,* takes place in churches and halls in Tours itself, usually during July. The city also stages a folksy *Garlic and Basil Fair* each summer on *St. Anne's Day,* July 26.

Follow D7 12 miles (19 km) west to Villandry.

 CHECKING IN: Near Montbazon, 8 miles (13 km) south of Tours on N10, are two elegant hotels that allow you to fulfill the fantasy of "living" in a luxurious Loire Valley château after a day of touring others.

Jean Bardet – Installed in a grand old mansion set in a park near the center of Tours, Monsieur Bardet established his hotel-restaurant as one of the most outstanding in a region rich with luxurious hostelries. Dining specialties include fresh steamed salmon in soy sauce, farm rabbit with artichokes, and oven-roasted lobster. 57 Rue Groison, Tours (phone: 47-41-41-11). Expensive.

Château d'Artigny – This world-famous château, once the property of the perfumer François Coty, perches in a fairy tale setting of gardens and woods above the Indre River. You can swim in a heated pool, play tennis, fish, or even listen to a string quartet if you arrive for one of the "Soirées Musicales" during the winter; golf and horseback riding are nearby. The dining room rates one Michelin star; try the sweetbreads casserole and fish specialties. Closed from November 27 to January 6. (See also *Romantic French Hostelries,* DIVERSIONS.) A little more than a mile (1.6 km) southwest of Montbazon via D17 (phone: 47-26-24-24). Expensive.

Domaine de la Tortinière – Smaller and slightly less illustrious than its neighbor across the valley of the Indre, this storybook château can provide an equally memorable stay. Romantic but small rooms surrounded by towers and turrets overlook grounds that slope gently toward the river. A garden-style restaurant with one Michelin star adds to the pleasure, with fine fish and good sauces. The chef sometimes holds week-long cooking classes for groups of 10 or more at the hotel; English translation is provided as needed by Americans living in this area. The château is closed from October 15 to April 1; the restaurant also is closed Tuesday and Wednesday noons from October 15 to November 15 as well as in March. A mile (1.6 km) north of Montbazon on N10 — watch for signs on the right if you're driving south from Tours (phone: 47-26-00-19). Expensive.

EATING OUT: *Charles Barrier* – This venerable chef has garnered top culinary ratings in Tours for decades and continues to merit two stars from Michelin for his refined versions of regional specialties. A reasonable fixed-price menu puts the pleasures of *Barrier's* elegant dining room within reach of those of moderate means. Closed Sunday evenings, Mondays, and during July. 101-103 Av. de la Tranchée, Tours (phone: 47-54-20-39). Expensive.

Les Charmilles – In a village house facing the Loire, this charming restaurant features fresh fish of all kinds, from lobster salad to brill and turbot in béarnaise sauce. The dining room is rustic, the garden beyond it, lush. Open year-round.

Closed Thursday evenings. 49 Quai des Maisons Blanches, St.-Cyr-sur-Loire, about a mile (1.6 km) west of Tours on N152 (phone: 47-54-02-01). Moderate.

La Poivrière – Romantically situated in a beautiful 15th-century house in Vieux (Old) Tours, this spot offers a commendable prix fixe menu. Closed Sunday evenings and Mondays. 13 Rue du Change, Tours (phone: 47-20-85-41). Moderate.

Rôtisserie Tourangelle – A longtime favorite of residents, this brasserie is noted for good service and a fine menu. House specialties include smoked breast of duck simmered in local borgueil wine. Closed Sunday evenings, Mondays, and 2 weeks in March. 23 Rue du Commerce, Tours (phone: 47-05-71-21). Moderate.

Les Tuffeaux – Highly regarded, it boasts a special location in the old quarter, near the cathedral. Loire fish are especially good here, as well as puff pastry desserts. Closed Sundays and Monday lunch. 19 Rue Lavoisier, Tours (phone: 47-47-19-89). Moderate.

Les Trois Rois – A pleasant bistro that serves lunches of toasted sandwiches and salads, but no evening meals, in a 15th-century house on the most charming square in Vieux Tours. It's a wonderful place to sip a cold drink on a hot summer afternoon. Closed Sundays. 1 Rue du Change, Tours (phone: 47-20-61-20). Inexpensive.

En Route from Tours – For those interested in such curiosities, the three-quarter mile "petrifying grottoes" are 10 miles (16 km) west, on D7 at Savonnières, less than 2 miles (3 km) from Villandry. The caves, which are connected to the Villandry château by an underground passage, are the scene of continuous dripping that allegedly petrifies objects left there in a matter of months. Hour-long guided tours are available daily except from December 16 to February and Wednesdays from February 9 to March 30; bring along a sweater to ward off the 57F chill.

VILLANDRY: This is the one place in the Loire Valley where the gardens are much more spectacular than the château they adjoin, and these are amazing: 3 tiers of large, superimposed terraces that include a lake, hedges, and bushes trimmed into precise patterns representing, among other things, different kinds of love (tender, passionate, adulterous), an extensive garden of herbs and medicinal and aromatic plants, and, most unusual, a large 16th-century kitchen garden whose beautiful patterns in a wealth of colors are formed by carefully planted ordinary fruits and vegetables. Villandry, the hamlet of the same name, faces the Cher River near the point at which it joins the Loire; it was the last great Renaissance château to be built in this area, and Jean le Breton, a financier and minister to François I, finished it in 1536. Unlike many neighboring châteaux, Villandry has always been privately owned, and the interests of its owners have given it a special flavor. Le Breton had served as the French ambassador to Italy and was knowledgeable in both architecture and garden design. His château, attractive and of moderate size with a moat and elegant courtyard, is purely French in style, but the gardens, which manifest both French and Italian influences, were always the more famous. The Cardinal of Aragon is said to have visited Villandry's kitchen garden around 1570 and wrote to the pope that there he had seen "finer salad vegetables than in Rome." The 16th-century gardens were lost temporarily when the 19th-century owners tore them out to follow the fashion by planting a garden landscaped in the English style. Happily, they were replanted according to old plans and drawings early in this century by Dr. Joachim Carvallo, whose grandson now owns and lives in the château with his family. The part of the château open to the public includes a fine collection of Spanish paintings and even an intricate Moorish ceiling brought from Spain by Dr. Carvallo. Visitors ultimately should climb to a vantage point over the gardens and then wander through them at leisure. The château is open daily from *Palm Sunday* to November 12, the gardens from 9 AM to nightfall year-round.

Follow D39 due south to Azay-le-Rideau.

EATING OUT: *Cheval Rouge* – An extremely pleasant provincial restaurant a short stroll from the château gardens, it has homemade foie gras and smoked salmon, Loire fish, including *sandre* (pike perch), and good regional wines on the menu. Meals are served until 9 PM. Closed Mondays and November to mid-March. Villandry (phone: 47-50-02-07). Moderate.

AZAY-LE-RIDEAU: Pocket-sized and charming, Azay boasts a handful of pictur-esque old streets, some interesting shops, and in its heart, a Gothic château so visually satisfying in its setting of woods and water that it is considered one of the jewels of the Loire Valley. Because it stands where the road between Tours and Chinon crosses the Indre River, Azay was fortified early in its history. Named for one of its overlords, Ridel, or Rideau, of Azay, the village today contains immense trees and expanses of greenery. It is hard to believe that it was known as Azay-le-Brulé (Azay-the-Burnt) from 1418 — when Charles VII, then dauphin, retaliated after a verbal insult from a guard by executing 350 soldiers and torching the town — until the early 16th century, when the present château was built. Although it was owned by a financier, Gilles Berthelot, the château, built partly over the Indre and surrounded by water, actually was constructed under the supervision of his wife, Philippa Lesbahy, and she usually is given credit for its grace. The *son et lumière* performance here is especially striking, with woods and water dramatically illuminated and the château perfectly mirrored in its moat as spectators follow elaborately costumed youths carrying tall torches on a 1-hour stroll around the grounds.

Saché is about 4 very pleasant miles (6 km) from Azay-le-Rideau; take D84 east past tall stands of trees, then turn south on D9 across four very narrow bridges.

 CHECKING IN/EATING OUT: *Grand Monarque* – If a stay here doesn't relax you, probably nothing can. Located in the center of town, the hotel and its outbuildings ramble around a large, graveled, tree-shaded courtyard, where tables are set up for summer lunch. The 30 rooms are old-fashioned, quiet, and comfortable. The dining room, prettily decorated and filled with flowers, serves tasty meals, with the *andouillette* (chitterling sausage) and several good fish dishes especially recommended. The château is a 3-minute walk away, and for a treat after the *son et lumière,* return to the hotel lobby for a cognac or raspberry liqueur. The hotel is open, and serves breakfast, all year; the restaurant is closed from early November to mid-March. Pl. de la République, Azay-le-Rideau (phone: 47-45-40-08). Moderate.

SACHÉ: This tiny village has served as the home of two very creative men. A striking stabile with blue and red arms outside the Town Hall testifies to the presence of Alexander Calder, whose home and workshop were near the village, and a block away, at the Château de Saché, in a park by the Indre River, the bedroom of Honoré de Balzac remains as it was when he lived and wrote here from 1829 to 1848. That and other rooms have been turned into a Balzac museum.

From Saché, zigzag west and south (D17 to D217) for 3 miles (5 km) to Villaines-les-Rochers.

VILLAINES-LES-ROCHERS: An entire village of basket makers, little Villaines has long been known for its wickerwork. Some 80 families, many working in troglodyte homes dug into walls of rock, belong to the wickerwork cooperative that was founded here in 1849 by a village priest. The cooperative's big showroom is an excellent place to buy baskets of all shapes and sizes, wicker furniture from baby chairs to large sofas, and even cleverly designed wicker babies' rattles with pebbles woven inside the wicker. In an adjoining workroom, you can watch craftspeople at work on similar objects. Individual artisans invite visitors to their own workrooms as well; the shop of Joël Metezeau, with a big sign on the right as you enter the village from Saché, is a pleasant place with a clutter of picnic baskets, cradles, armchairs, and bracelets, all produced by amiable men weaving skillfully on the floor in the back room. They seem happy to break the monotony of their routine by chatting with visitors.

Return to Azay-le-Rideau, then head southwest on D751 to Chinon. The 13 miles (21 km) to Chinon literally are straight as an arrow on the map; they are indeed straight but the road includes long, roller coaster dips through the green Chinon Forest.

CHINON: The mention of Chinon makes one think first of the delightful red wine that is produced here and only later of this pleasant town astride the Vienne River. In its castle, Joan of Arc recognized the dauphin, Charles VII, in 1429 as he tried to hide himself in a crowd of followers, and here she persuaded him to trust her. Chinon was the site of the deaths of the English King Henry II, in 1189, and his son Richard the Lion-Hearted, in 1199, and in 1321 of all the Jews in the town (by fire) on Ile de Tours, the island in the Vienne River opposite the town, after a local uprising and accusation of well poisoning, only a year before all the Jews were expelled from France. François Rabelais was born just outside Chinon, in La Devinière, in 1494, and spent his early years in this area; his birthplace, a mile (1.6 km) from Chinon, is open to the public.

The château is mostly in ruins on a hilltop spur that dominates the town; you enter them through a clock tower that contains a small Joan of Arc museum. Peacocks stroll near historic walls, and there is a deep moat and good views of the countryside. From the château, a short walk brings you to the wine-tasting shop of the Couly-Dutheil vintners; their Clos de l'Echo is among the best of all chinons. A few dozen yards more, down a road marked cryptically "To the Echo," you can try one of the most amusing simple pleasures of the Loire Valley. A small sign adjacent to a vineyard denotes "l'Echo." Climb up on a concrete platform, face the walls of the castle (which stands across a ravine), give a few shouts of different pitches, and enjoy the fun. When the weather is clear and there aren't too many people around to muddy the acoustics, the echo is amazingly clear and strong. If possible, try the rhyme that generations of residents have relied on to tease their wives and girlfriends:

"*Les femmes de Chinon, sont-elles fidèles?*"

Echo: "*Elles?*"

"*Oui, les femmes de Chinon.*"

Echo: "*Non.*"

(The women of Chinon, are they faithful? Echo: Them? Yes, the women of Chinon. Echo: No.)

Below the castle, "taste" medieval Chinon with a walk down Rue Voltaire, where red and yellow banners stretch between old stone buildings and rosebushes bloom in lovely courtyards. Pedestrians have priority on the narrow street and can admire at leisure the pretty 17th-century Hôtel du Gouvernement and the *Maison des Etats-Généraux,* now an interesting museum, in which, according to local tradition, Richard the Lion-Hearted died of a wound he received at Châlus. A few steps farther is the reconstruction of a well on whose rim Joan of Arc supposedly placed her foot while dismounting from her horse. Chinon holds a medieval fair the first weekend in August, when residents dress in period costumes and everybody makes merry.

Take D751 west 14 miles (22 km) to Fontevraud-l'Abbaye.

CHECKING IN: *Château de Marçay* – This 15th-century fortress has metamorphosed into a luxury hotel with 35 elegantly appointed rooms and 3 suites. Surrounded by its own park, the château also has a swimming pool and tennis courts. In the dining room, try the soft-boiled eggs with puréed morels. Wealthy Parisians relax here on weekends, so be sure to make reservations. Closed from January to mid-March. 4 miles (6 km) south of Chinon by D749 and D116 in Marçay (phone: 47-93-03-47). Expensive.

La Poitevinière – A touch of the US in the Loire Valley, this château recently was purchased and renovated by a group of Americans in love with France. Stay in one of the 6 rooms or the 3-bedroom suite, or if you prefer, rent the entire château for about $4,000 a week. Huismes 37420 Avione (phone: 47-95-58-40). Expensive.

Hostellerie Gargantua – A charming 15th-century hotel, in the heart of Old Chinon just beneath the château. All 13 rooms have been entirely redone, as has the kitchen. On Friday evenings, guests are received by staff dressed in medieval costume. The house specialty is the *omelette Gargamelle,* with herbs and mushrooms. Closed Wednesdays, Thursday for lunch, and mid-November to mid-March. 73 Rue Voltaire, Chinon (phone: 47-93-04-71). Moderate.

La Giraudière – In the attractive countryside just to the west of town, by the road to Bourgueil and the turnoff to Savigny, this picturesque manor house offers simple charm and the convenience of kitchenettes in some of its 25 rooms. Breakfast is served, but there is no restaurant. Swimming, tennis, and horseback riding are available nearby. Closed January to mid-March. 3 miles (5 km) west of Chinon (phone: 47-58-40-36). Moderate to inexpensive.

En Route from Chinon – Shortly before the turnoff for Fontevraud-l'Abbaye, D751 becomes especially pretty; tree-shaded, it passes fields, small châteaux, and the scenic Vienne River close on the right. The stretch through La Chausée and St.-Germain-sur-Vienne is most charming and you may want to pull off the road for a picnic. At the very least, slow down a bit, both to admire the flowers in the windowboxes of the storybook houses and to be prepared for the occasional herd of cattle or flock of sheep crossing the road.

FONTEVRAUD-L'ABBAYE: Another relatively unknown treasure of the Loire Valley, the vast Royal Abbey of Fontevraud gives visitors a chance to explore one of the most intact complexes of monastic architecture standing today in France. Founded in 1099 by Robert d'Arbrissel, a Breton hermit, the Fontevraud order was remarkable for its aristocratic nature, for having been ruled over by a succession of 36 abbesses, all members of noble families, and for opening the doors of five separate monasteries to monks, nuns, lepers, the sick, and aristocratic women who wished to withdraw to a life of prayer and contemplation. The abbey church, consecrated in 1119 by Pope Calixtus II, is a huge Romanesque structure with a single nave. It contains the tombs of Henry II Plantagenet, Count of Anjou, who became King of England in 1154 and who asked on his deathbed to be buried at Fontevraud; Eleanor of Aquitaine, his widow, who withdrew to the abbey for the 15 years preceding her own death; Richard the Lion-Hearted, their son, who also requested that his remains be buried here; and Isabelle of Angoulême, the second wife of Richard's brother, King John Lackland. Their four beautiful, recumbent statues lie just to the right of the nave. There also are tranquil cloisters with noteworthy Renaissance and Gothic carving and an extremely unusual octagonal tower that served as the abbey kitchen, said to be the only one from the Romanesque period remaining in France. French revolutionaries destroyed some monastery buildings in 1793 and put an end to the monastic life. In 1804, Napoleon converted most of the remaining buildings into a cloister of another kind, a national prison, which functioned until 1963. Today the French government and regional cultural agencies administer Fontevraud and use it for concerts, art exhibitions, and theatrical productions. Also of note in the small town are St. Michael's parish church, across Place des Plantagenets and Rue du Logis Bourbon from the abbey, and the 13th-century chapel of St. Catherine, off a pretty avenue of lime trees leading from the church.

Route D947 follows the river west to Saumur.

EATING OUT: *La Licorne* – Attractive and elegant, with a young and hospitable owner, this small restaurant adds extra sparkle to a visit to Fontevraud-l'Abbaye. If the weather is good, try to reserve one of the two or three little tables on the patio adjacent to a walled flower garden. The inside is pleasant, too, with artwork focusing on the unicorn (*la licorne*). Loire fish with sorrel sauce, beef with tarragon sauce and homemade, carrot-tinted noodles, and the house's special chocolate cake all are excellent. The restaurant is closed Sunday evenings, Mondays, and late January to mid-February. Allée St.-Catherine, Fontevraud-l'Abbaye (phone 41-51-72-49). Moderate.

En Route from Fontevraud-l'Abbaye – The 7-mile (11-km) stretch of D947 west along the Loire to Saumur starts at Montsoreau, with a pretty château and the *Musée des Goums* (French cavalry units recruited in Morocco; the museum contains souvenirs of the Moroccan conquest), and includes a string of charming villages. Watch for picturesque troglodyte houses, an old windmill on a ridge, and cellars in which to taste wine, mainly Saumur.

SAUMUR: With a many-arched old bridge over the Loire, attractive shops, and busy streets, Saumur is famous for its wines, especially the sparkling mousseux variety, and its riding school, the Cadre Noir (Black Squadron), which draws eager crowds to a military tattoo and riding spectacle at the end of July each summer. Tasting the wine is no problem; a Maison du Vin run by the wine producers' association is next door to the tourist office (phone: 41-51-03-06) on Rue Beaurepaire. You also can visit the Ecole d'Application de l'Armée Blindée de la Cavalerie (Cavalry and Armored Corps School), founded when the best horsemen in the French army were sent in an elite regiment to Saumur in 1763 to become the original Cadre Noir. Saumur has a dramatic castle that soars high above the town on a sheer promontory. Several fortresses have stood here; the present one dates from the late 14th century and contains both a museum of decorative arts and one tracing the history of — what else? — the horse.

En Route from Saumur – Route D751 snakes along for 32 miles (51 km) to Angers. For an interesting detour, follow N147 through Saumur, over the Thouet River and into the suburb of Bagneux, which has one of the largest dolmens (prehistoric stone structures with side and roof slabs) in France. Standing in a yard by a café at the end of Rue du Dolmen, the monument, built some 5,000 years ago, is 70 feet long and divided into two chambers. The granite slabs that make up its sides and roof weigh as much as 35 tons.

Another Loire Valley curiosity is just west of Saumur's northwest suburb of St.-Hilaire-St.-Florent: a mushroom museum called *Caves Louis Bouchard*. Here you can take a half-hour tour of a labyrinth of caves carved out of the porous limestone called *tufa* during which you see all the stages of growth of the white mushrooms known as *champignons de Paris*. According to the guide, 40% of the world's canned mushrooms come from the Saumur region, where a full 500 miles of caves are used to grow mushrooms. One of the secrets of their successful cultivation here is that much of the manure in which they thrive comes from the nearby riding school. You can buy your own mushrooms, fresh or canned, at the museum entrance (Routes de Gennes, Saumur; phone: 41-50-25-01); closed mid-November to mid-March.

A beautiful church dating from the 11th to the 13th century graces the very pleasant village of Cunault, 3 miles (5 km) west of Chênehutte-les-Tuffeaux on D751. The belfry is Romanesque; the west front is fortified, with a fine 13th-century sculpted portrayal of the Adoration of the Virgin. Inside are traces of the painted decoration used to emphasize the main architectural lines of medieval churches: the richly carved capitals and a rare painted wooden shrine from the 13th century, riddled with wormholes but still lovely. The nave of this large church is tapered slightly to make it appear even longer than it is. In Gennes, just beyond Cunault, four dolmens rise dramatically in the hills behind the village; several upright stones called menhirs stand in nearby fields.

The 20 miles (33 km) from Gennes to Angers along D751 is a pastoral jaunt through sleepy villages where little seems to stir except the church bells that mark the hours. Fields of corn and sunflowers, vineyards, and old windmills, some of them overgrown with vegetation, beckon the wanderer to follow.

CHECKING IN/EATING OUT: *Le Prieuré* – One of the most splendid hostelries of the Loire Valley, famous for its quiet, wooded setting with a sweeping view of the Loire, elegant rooms in a 12th- and 15th-century priory, and an excellent dining room, it sits on a bluff above Chênehutte-les-Tuffeaux. There is a tennis court, a heated swimming pool, and 35 rooms, with 15 in the château itself ("Americans prefer these," says a staff member) and the rest in bungalows scattered over the grounds. Reserve several months in advance for the summer and as early as possible the rest of the year. The dining room features *foie gras de canard* (duck foie gras), a *panaché,* or mix, of *sandre* and turbot served with wild rice and curry, *magret de canard* (duck breast) with raspberry vinegar, and a *menu dégustation* (tasting menu), with small portions of many specialties. The view from your table will be spectacular, especially at sunset. Closed January 5 to March 5. Chênehutte-les-Tuffeaux, 5 miles (8 km) west of Saumur by D161 and D751 (phone: 41-67-90-14). Expensive.

Hostellerie de la Loire – Some 11 rooms are available here, and for a copious, tasty meal in cheerful surroundings, the restaurant is an excellent choice. Especially on weekends, you're likely to be among happy local families, which means children will feel at home here, too. Try the menu (the prix fixe meal), starting with the mushrooms in a pastry shell — irresistible if you've just toured the mushroom caves — and progressing to fish, steaks, or chicken, then salad, cheese, and dessert. The hotel and restaurant are closed Monday evenings, Tuesdays, and January. Gennes (phone: 41-51-81-03). Inexpensive.

ANGERS: Although the Loire River flows on for another 80 miles before reaching Nantes and the Atlantic Ocean, the city of Angers, population 143,000, is generally considered to mark the western end of the Loire Valley. Conquered by the Romans and later by the Normans in its early history, Angers lived through an especially brilliant period under the Counts of Anjou, from the 10th to the 12th century. A major city today, though not noted for its charm, Angers boasts an imposing castle in a feudal architectural style patterned on the crusaders' castles of Palestine; its 17 large towers are connected by a high curtain wall, and deer grazing in the dry moat add a whimsical note. Displayed in the castle is the huge Apocalypse Tapestry, woven in Paris between 1373 and 1380 for Louis I of Anjou. The Cathédrale St.-Maurice, the other sightseeing highlight in Angers, claims a single nave with the first Gothic vaulting constructed in Anjou, an impressive late Romanesque façade with fine sculptures surmounted by three towers, and a good collection of original stained glass windows. The oldest window, in the north aisle, dates from the 12th century. Angers also has a fine arts museum, the *Logis Barrault,* and, on the streets around Hôtel Pincé on Rue Lenepveu, some interesting 16th- and 18th-century buildings. The popular *Festival of Anjou,* held here from mid-June to mid-July, includes ballets, concerts, plays, and other cultural activities.

Backtrack east from Angers along the Loire's northern bank on D952, N152, and D749 to Bourgueil.

CHECKING IN: *Concorde* – This modern hotel in the center of town has 73 rooms, a pleasant restaurant, and a brasserie open until 11:30 PM. 18 Bd. Maréchal-Foch, Angers (phone: 41-87-37-20). Moderate.

France – Opposite the train station and the tourist office, this hostelry has 57 attractive rooms and a restaurant, *Plantagenets,* that offers fine food and service.

The restaurant is open daily. 8 Pl. de la Gare, Angers (phone: 41-88-49-42). Moderate to inexpensive.

EATING OUT: *Le Logis* – Endowed with one Michelin star, it specializes in seafood. Closed Saturday nights and Sundays, and the last 2 weeks of July. 17 Rue St.-Laud, Angers (phone: 41-87-44-15). Moderate.

L'Entr'acte – Popular, rustic, and near the post office, it is notable for its *coquilles St.-Jacques au champagne* (scallops in champagne) and *saumon du Bourgueil* (salmon). Closed Saturdays, Sunday evenings, and during August. 9 Rue Louis-de-Romain, Angers (phone: 41-87-71-82). Moderate.

Le Toussaint – A comfortable place that features simple and creative cooking such as vegetable cake, *foie gras au Layon,* and fresh fruit sherbets. Closed Sunday evenings and Mondays, late February, and 1 week in August. 7 Rue Toussaint, Angers (phone: 41-87-46-20). Moderate to inexpensive.

Le Vert d'Eau – Well known in the area, it serves original dishes that include *poissons de Loire beurre blanc* (fish with a white butter sauce), *fricassée de poulet à l'angevine* (chicken fricassee with anjou wine), and strawberries in season. It's closed Sunday evenings, Mondays, and 1 week in February. 9 Bd. G.-Dumesnil, Angers (phone: 41-48-52-86). Moderate to inexpensive.

En Route from Angers – Route D952 provides enchanting views of the river and its tree-covered islands as well as glimpses of towns and villages with big stone quays that were once prosperous river ports. The highway hugs the edge of the river through Saumur, where it becomes N152 to continue its scenic route eastward. Follow it to Port-Boulet, across the Loire from the enormous stacks and globes of the Avoine nuclear power plant, begun in 1957 and one of the first in France. Then turn north for 3 miles (5 km) on D749 to Bourgueil.

BOURGUEIL: A charming little town containing the remains of a powerful Benedictine abbey founded in 990, Bourgueil produces one of the two acclaimed red wines of the Loire Valley (the other being that of Chinon, 10 miles/16 km south). You can drive for miles past vine-covered slopes and find innumerable wine merchants happy to let you taste their full-bodied ruby red bourgueil and to sell you as many bottles as you wish. It was in Bourgueil that the deaf French poet Pierre de Ronsard met the object of the inspiration for his famous love poems.

Route D35 east connects with N152, which leads to Langeais.

LANGEAIS: This crowded town 12 miles (19 km) east of Bourgueil boasts store windows filled with enough fishing gear to tempt any visitor into testing the waters of the Loire, a few steps away. In its center reposes another of the region's idiosyncratic and memorable castles. Although much smaller than those of Chambord and Blois, the Château of Langeais is unusual in having all been built by Louis XI within a 5-year period in the 15th century and for having remained unaltered since then. The building, which you enter by a drawbridge between two solid towers, looks like a powerful medieval fortress. It was intended to serve as a strong defensive position in case of an attack from Bretons heading from Nantes up the Loire Valley toward Touraine. Such worries were put to rest on December 16, 1491, when the son of Louis XI, Charles VIII, married Anne of Brittany in this very castle, thereby uniting Brittany and France. Viewed from the inner courtyard, the château clearly is the residence of a 15th-century lord. Its apartments are furnished with an excellent collection of 15th- and 16th-century antiques, the marriage chest of Anne of Brittany among them.

Continue 3 miles (5 km) east on N152 to Cinq-Mars-la-Pile.

CHECKING IN/EATING OUT: *Hosten* – This charming, comfortable country inn is only a short stroll down the street from the château in Langeais. Most of the 12 rooms are on winding corridors over an inner courtyard, well isolated from traffic noise. The rustic decor of chintz and country furniture is confined to the cozy bedrooms; bathrooms are completely modern and include such amenities as shower caps and scales. Its restaurant, elegant and comfortable with dark wood and fresh flowers, has one Michelin star and it serves specialties like lobster salad with foie gras, sole with *cèpes* (mushrooms), and duck cooked in bourgueil wine. Reservations are advised. The hotel and restaurant both are closed Monday evenings and Tuesdays, from mid-June to early July, and mid-January to early February. 2 Rue Gambetta, Langeais (phone: 47-96-82-12). Hotel moderate, restaurant expensive to moderate.

CINQ-MARS-LA-PILE: This tiny village has two noteworthy monuments: its château and "La Pile," a unique Gallo-Roman tower. The château, now only two movingly overgrown 11th- and 12th-century towers, provides a fine, clifftop view over the Loire and its south bank. It was once the property of a favorite courtier of Louis XIII, Henri d'Effiat, the Marquis de Cinq-Mars, who was convicted of conspiracy against Richelieu and beheaded at the ripe age of 22. La Pile, visible from the highway, is a square masonry structure 98 feet high surmounted by four small pyramids. A path leads up a ridge to its base, but its solid interior doesn't invite climbing. Its purpose remains a mystery, as does the name of the town, which in earlier times was called St.-Mars.

To get to Luynes, the last stop on this route and only 8 miles (13 km) west of Tours, turn off N152 onto D76, a little more than 2 miles (3 km) beyond Cinq-Mars.

LUYNES: This town lies under the shadow of a strictly feudal 13th-century castle. Privately owned and occupied (by the same family since 1619), the castle can be viewed only from below. There are many troglodyte houses in this area, and signs lead through the pretty countryside behind and above the town, past horses pulling wooden farm carts, to the ruins of a Roman aqueduct.

CHECKING IN/EATING OUT: *Domaine de Beauvois* – Another luxurious Loire Valley château, this one 2 miles (3 km) northwest of Luynes via D49 is both a hotel with 40 rooms and suites, surrounded by woods and offering amenities such as a swimming pool, tennis court, and a one-star Michelin restaurant. Specialties include a terrine made of eel, bass cooked with truffles and leeks, and *beuchelle à la Tourangelle,* a Touraine dish combining sweetbreads and kidneys served in a delicious sauce. The hotel and restaurant are closed from mid-January to mid-March. Luynes (phone: 47-55-50-11). Expensive.

Normandy

Normandy owes its name to the Northmen, or Norsemen, those Scandinavian invaders who swept down the Seine Valley in AD 820. It was neither the first nor the last time invasions would play a momentous part in the province's history.

Whether the early Celts, whose descendants remain in neighboring Brittany, were settlers or conquerors is unsure. The Romans who sent many of them fleeing to the west were certainly the latter, though the legions stayed long enough to build towns where Evreux, Rouen, and Coutances now stand and to leave evidence of their presence in the ruins at Lillebonne. Saxon and German raiders disturbed the Roman peace, and toward the end of the 4th century the legions withdrew, leaving Normandy as a battleground between warring factions, a condition that was to be repeated on several occasions.

Under Frankish domination from 500 to the early 9th century, the foundation was laid for Normandy's major religious houses such as those at Mont-St.-Michel, Fécamp, and Jumièges, which, rebuilt and refashioned in later years, became part of the architectural glory of France.

Although the Norsemen plundered and sometimes destroyed many of these establishments, by the early 10th century the invaders had become settlers, and in 911 at the Treaty of St.-Clair-sur-Epte the Norman chieftain, Rolf the Ranger, became Rollo, Duke of Normandy. He subsequently was baptized at St.-Ouen in Rouen.

The most famous of all the dukes descended from Rollo was William the Bastard, the illegitimate son of Robert the Devil and a tanner's daughter. After William's successful invasion of England in 1066 history accorded him the sobriquet William the Conqueror. It is to him and his wife, Matilda of Flanders, that we owe the two great religious houses at Caen, the Abbaye aux Hommes and the Abbaye aux Dames.

Normandy's potential as a threat to the French throne and realm dominated its history for the next 138 years, especially after the English King Henry II added to his empire the vast territories of Aquitaine by his marriage to the colorful duchess Eleanor. Henry's son Richard, realizing that the duchy's position not only was threatening but also vulnerable, built the formidable Château Gaillard on the Seine, close to the border of the French territories. Its romantic ruins still can be seen. Richard's foresight notwithstanding, his brother, the unloved and unwise John Lackland, managed to lose Normandy in 1202 when Philippe Auguste invaded the duchy to avenge John's murder of his nephew Arthur of Brittany at Rouen.

From 1204, Normandy was united with the French crown, first as a duchy held by the sovereign and later as a province with its own governing body at Rouen. However, it still served as a battleground during the dynastic quarrels of the French and English kings, especially in the Hundred Years War

(1337–1453), when parts of Normandy were occupied by the English for 30 years.

The English finally were driven out in 1453, and Normandy enjoyed a period of peace and prosperity until the religious wars of the late 16th century. During this time of calm, great châteaux, such as those of O (*sic*) and Fontaine-Henry, were built, not just as fortifications but as country residences. Ornate and sumptuous mansions such as the Parlement de Rouen (now the Palais de Justice) and the Hôtel de Bourgtheroulde in the same town gave expression to the Renaissance passion for elaborate architectural design in the province's capital. Rouen and Caen became free cities during this period, and the increasingly important merchant classes began to construct the lovely half-timbered houses that still line the old streets of Rouen (but were destroyed in Caen in World War II).

The Wars of Religion did little to alter the face of Normandy, though they are recalled in the names Arques-la-Bataille, near Dieppe, and Ivry-la-Bataille, near Dreux. The great cathedrals at Evreux, Rouen, Bayeux, and Coutances and the abbeys at Fécamp, Mont-St.-Michel, Jumièges, Cérisy-la-Forêt, and Caen remained almost completely unscathed. The first mindless acts of destruction came during the French Revolution, when few cathedrals or churches escaped some form of desecration, particularly Mont-St.-Michel and Fécamp, which were stripped of their treasures, and Cérisy, which had some of its bays removed.

Worse destruction was to come in June, July, and August 1944, when in the battle to liberate France from the Nazis more than 200,000 buildings and 586 towns and villages, among them Le Havre, St.-Lô, Caen, Lisieux, and Evreux, were almost totally destroyed. Of all the great, ancient Norman cities, only Bayeux and its two great treasures, the cathedral and the *Tapisserie de la Reine Mathilde* (Queen Matilda's Tapestry), remained virtually intact.

The war changed the urban face of Normandy radically and in a way that only the patina of a century or so will make palatable. The landscape, more resilient, retains much of the lush green pasturage and forest that must have attracted the early Norsemen.

Normandy is bordered on the west by Brittany and the English Channel, on the north by the Channel as it narrows toward the Straits of Dover, on the northeast and east by the ancient region of Picardy, the Ile-de-France around Paris, and on the south by the Loire Valley.

Although a small area by American standards, the province is divided by geography and tradition into quite distinct regions. The Cotentin Peninsula in the northwest, stretching to the Channel around Cherbourg, is famous for horse breeding and dairy farming. Dairy farming also is important in the Bessin, the area between Bayeux and the coast, a region famous also for its handsome, fortified, gray stone farmhouses. The town of Isigny-sur-Mer, between the Cotentin and Bayeux, gives its name to a butter that is a household staple throughout France. In the Norman *bocage* ("open woodland," literally, but usually stone walls thickly overgrown with hedges) south of the Bessin there is more dairy farming and some celebrated cider from the apples that blossom with an astonishing beauty all over the region during April and May. On the prairie-type terrain around Caen, cereals have become a major postwar crop. East of Caen, in the Pays d'Auge are more apple orchards, often surrounded by half-timbered farms and rundown barns that make this part of France seem particularly idyllic. The dairy farms in the Pays d'Auge provide the milk that is turned into three celebrated cheeses, camembert, livarot, and pont-l'evêque. South of the plains around Caen, tributaries of the Orne have dug deep into the hilly pastures and woods around Flers, Clécy, and Falaise to form dramatic gorges. Ambitious promoters have dubbed the region Suisse Normande (Norman Switzerland), a name that even the spectacular view from La Roche d'Oëtre does not quite make plausible. Across the Seine, in the triangle formed by Dieppe, Le Havre, and Rouen, are the rolling hills and valleys of the Pays de Caux, bordered on the Channel by great white chalk cliffs that drop precipitously into the sea. The main cash crops of the hinterland are flax and sugar beet.

The Seine, which curves through Normandy in a half-dozen or so serpentine loops, is the region's economic lifeline. Its strategic position between the English Channel and Paris and its navigability have drawn major industries such as paper and textile manufacturing to Rouen and have caused huge petrochemical works to flourish along the river between Rouen and Le Havre, where there also are important shipbuilding and iron industries. The old cottage industries have all but disappeared. Ivory, for which Dieppe was famous, lace, wrought iron, and faïence de Rouen (ceramicware) now are mostly seen in museums, although there still are lace schools with small boutiques at Alençon and Bayeux, and ironwork still can be bought from small foundries at Gaillon and Monceau.

The one ancient activity other than farming that survives is commercial fishing, most of it local, but some in waters as far off as Newfoundland, where fishermen from Dieppe, Fécamp, and Honfleur harvest the cold North Atlantic for cod. The fruit of their labors graces the tables of most Norman restaurants and homes. The regional specialty, *assiette de fruits de mer* — a platter of fresh seafood and shellfish — is a visual and culinary delight and might include crayfish, crabs, several kinds of shrimp, oysters, clams, cockles, mussels, and winkles, often served on a bed of damp seaweed. Another favorite, *marmite dieppoise,* is served along the coast as far south as Isigny-sur-Mer; it can consist of a mixture of sole, turbot, brill, mackerel, whiting, shrimp, and crab, all simmered in their own juices to make a substantial half stew, half soup, to which is added another Norman staple, fresh cream. Rich, fattening, and irresistible — cream is used to enhance almost every type of dish found on the Norman table, from vegetables to poultry, game, and fish to fresh fruit and pastry.

Often what is not cooked in cream in Normandy is cooked in cider — not apple juice but a hard cider with an alcoholic content. Ham, chicken, duck, rabbit, and hare braised this way can be unforgettable. Although cider is bottled and can be purchased, most of it sold this way is *doux,* on the sweet side, and its consumption is considered effete. Cider bought from farmers who brew their own is dry, still, and has a powerful bite. Normandy's other famous beverage is calvados, a kind of applejack with class that takes 12 to 15 years to mature. It usually is served as a liqueur, although there are places, especially in and around Caen, where chefs cook tripe in it.

Tripe is a gastronomic specialty of the Caen region. Other regional delicacies are oysters from St.-Vaast-la-Hougue; *agneau pré salé,* lamb fed on saltwater grasses near Mont-St.-Michel; and another Mont-St.-Michel specialty, *omelettes Mère-Poulard,* named for a famous restaurateuse on the island who created these enormous, soufflé-like concoctions.

Normandy cheeses are savored all over the world, although pont-l'evêque never tastes quite as good as when eaten in or near the small village of lovely half-timbered houses for which it is named; and camembert is not camembert if it is made anywhere else.

This concentration on the culinary arts is not to suggest that the fine arts have been neglected in Normandy. Often the former has inspired the latter. The painters Gustave Courbet and Eugène Boudin were frequent visitors at the *Ferme St.-Siméon* (see *Romantic French Hostelries,* DIVERSIONS) near Honfleur, where they came to drink cider and sample the cooking of Mère Tatin, the proprietress. Boudin brought along his painter friends whose experiments with light led them to be called Impressionists. Jean Renoir was one, Alfred Sisley another, but the most notable visitor was Claude Monet, whose pictures of the cliffs at Etretat and studies of Rouen Cathedral are among his most famous works. Monet bought a villa at Giverny (just inside Normandy's border with the Ile-de-France), which is now a museum open to the public. Norman painters and subjects are well represented in the art museums at Rouen, Le Havre, and Caen as well as in some smaller galleries.

Some of Normandy's cathedrals, monasteries, and châteaux may be considered artistic masterpieces as well, including such buildings as the abbeys at Jumièges, Cérisy-la-Forêt, and Caen. In fact, medieval Norman architecture became so widespread and idiosyncratic that it was called the Norman style in England, which can be discerned in certain details at Canterbury, Westminster, and Durham.

Normandy also has its literary lights. Pierre Corneille, one of France's great tragedians, was born in Rouen in a house that still can be visited and practiced law in the Palais de Justice. Gustave Flaubert also was born in Rouen and describes his father's apartments in the hospice there in the novel *Madame Bovary.* Guy de Maupassant, another Norman, went to a school in Rouen, now called the Lycée Corneille, and used to relax at Etretat, one of his favorite resorts. Marcel Proust often stayed at the resorts on the Côte Fleurie, especially Cabourg.

This tour starts at Vernon, leaving autoroute A13 from Paris to cross the Seine for a visit to Monet's home at Giverny. The route continues via Rouen on D982 to Lillebonne and then goes across the Pays de Caux to Dieppe. It then travels down the coast to Le Havre, backtracks a short way along the Seine, and crosses the river by the great bridge at Tancarville heading for Honfleur, Trouville-sur-Mer, Deauville, and Cabourg, where it turns inland to Caen. There, a detour can be made to visit the Normandy beaches that were made famous on *D-Day* before returning to Caen and continuing the main itinerary via Bayeux, St.-Lô, and Coutances to Granville on the west coast of the Cotentin Peninsula. The route then takes the coast road along Mont-St.-Michel Bay to Avranches and the mount itself.

Expect to pay $100 and up for a double room in hotels listed as expensive;

between $50 and $80 in places listed as moderate, and less than $50 in those listed as inexpensive. Note that hotels in Deauville and Cabourg are very expensive in July and August, often charging closer to $150 for a double room, and in any season, all along the Norman coast, a sea view can add $30 to $40 to a room's price. Note, too, that there still are many inexpensive *auberges* (inns) and small hotels in Normandy where clean rooms with a minimum of amenities — usually just a sink; not always that — can be found for under $40. Dinner for two in the restaurants listed as very expensive is $150 and up; in the expensive category, $100 to $140; in the moderate range, $60 to $100; and in the inexpensive range, less than $60. Prices do not include wine or drinks, though service usually is included. A caveat: An *assiette de fruits de mer* — which everyone not allergic to fish should try at least once — will cost double if it is crowned with a lobster.

VERNON: Although much of the town was destroyed in World War II, its site on the left bank of the Seine backed by the forest of Bizy and opposite the great forest of Vernon has attracted visitors ever since the 12th century, when Louis IX (St. Louis) used to come here to escape the heat of Paris. So enamored of the place was that most likable of princes that he allowed Vernon to add the fleur-de-lis, the Capetian family emblem, to the three bunches of watercress on its escutcheon. The collegiate church of Notre-Dame, which largely escaped damage in the war, was originally built in the 12th century and was added to and modified in the 15th and 16th centuries. There is a splendid rose window on the west front, adorned on both sides by galleries with flying buttresses. The 15th-century nave, taller than the transept, is lofty and narrow, its cool lines enhanced by the grace of the triforium and the elegance of the high windows. In the precincts of Notre-Dame are a few 15th-century half-timbered houses that escaped the devastation caused by the bombing, including one next door to the church and others on Rue Carnot.

About a mile (1.6 km) outside the town, hidden behind stately trees, is the Château de Bizy (open April through October; closed Fridays), which still is the home of the Duke of Albufera. The exterior has no great distinction, but the interior is decorated handsomely in the Empire style and contains some splendid tapestries and paneling as well as a collection of souvenirs of the Napoleonic era. The gardens, laid out to provide a suitable context for the original château (1740), are adorned with waterfalls and baroque fountains that suggest Italy rather than northern France. From the bridge linking Vernon to the suburb of Vernonnet, across the Seine, there is a pleasant view of forested islands upstream and down. You also can see the remains of the original 12th-century bridge and the *donjon* (keep) of the small fortress that guarded it on the right bank.

Just over a mile (1.6 km) upstream from the bridge on D5 is Giverny, a charming little village nestling against the hillside, where Claude Monet lived from 1883 to 1926. Monet's house, now the *Musée Claude-Monet* (open daily, except Mondays, from April through October; phone: 32-51-28-21), is a delightful, homey contrast to the great residential châteaux and manor houses of Normandy; beautiful though they undoubtedly are, they tend toward a certain monumental quality even in their most domestic moments. Apart from the great studio where Monet painted some of his most famous works, everything about the artist's house is intimate and serene. It owes its present condition, which is a somewhat idealized version of the way it was when Monet lived here, to an international group of sponsors who rescued it from decay and dilapidation and subsidized the founding of the museum under the auspices of the Institut de France.

The painter's love affair with color can be appreciated from the exterior's pink walls, white highlights, and green jalousies to the blue motif of the old-fashioned country kitchen and the wonderful primrose yellow dining room. The interior — platters on the walls, dressers in the dining room, and pots on the yellow chimneypiece — has all been restored to look as it did when Renoir, Sisley, Cézanne, Manet, and Pissarro dropped by for a bite and a chat. Monet's much-loved Japanese prints have been restored as far as possible to the places he allotted them. His bedroom is an unexpectedly elegant enclave, with none of the Bohemian ambience one associates with 19th-century painters. Most appealing is his drawing room/studio, complete with couch, armchairs, and basketwork chairs, which conjures up the atmosphere of good talk, cigar smoke, wine, and absinthe that must have prevailed.

One of Monet's great passions, again associated with color, was his garden. This too has been re-created, and what one sees at any time of the year is, as far as possible, what he saw, down to the particular flowers growing in a particular place. The gardens were a frequent theme of his paintings after 1900, and in later years his only theme. Anyone who has seen pictures of the water lily pool with its Japanese bridge will recognize the original immediately, now regrettably separated from the main gardens by a road. The irises, peonies, heliotropes, and Judas trees — not to mention the willows and the water lilies — are all here just as they are on canvas. In spring, wisteria blooms over the bridge, and in the extensive gardens closer to the house, fruit trees burst into a blizzard of white and pink flowers not far from great masses of daffodils. In summer, morning glories appear, along with snapdragon, nasturtium, foxglove, sweet pea, stock, columbine, phlox, gentian, and sage — virtually the whole inventory of flowers found in the gardens of northwestern Europe at this season. In fall, the garden is ablaze with the gaudy, outrageous colors of the teeming autumn, brazen dahlias and sunflowers, subtler asters, and lofty hollyhocks. Seen in any of the three flowering seasons, Giverny leaves an indelible impression.

CHECKING IN/EATING OUT: *Hôtel d'Evreux* – This 18th-century townhouse became an inn more than 100 years ago. Today, it's a typically French family-run hotel/restaurant with homey touches, fine food, and friendly service. The hotel is open year-round, the restaurant is closed Sundays and from July 15 to August 15. 7 Pl. d'Evreux (phone: 32-21-16-12). Moderate.

En Route from Vernon – Take route D313 to Les Andelys to see Château Gaillard, the remains of a beautiful 12th-century fortress built by Richard the Lion-Hearted overlooking the Seine. The view over Les Andelys along the river, romantically dominated on the left bank by cliffs, is spectacular. From Les Andelys take D1 north to D2 and Ecouis, where there is one of the most famous churches in the Vexin (as the surrounding territory is known); it was built in 1310 and contains a 14th-century wooden sculpture of St. Veronica and an unusual statue supposedly of St. Agnes, whose robe is formed of her own flowing hair. Farther along D2, the church at Lisors is worth a stop to see the beautiful 14th-century statue of Our Lady, Queen of Heaven. A right turn onto D715 leads to the picturesque ruins of the Cistercian Abbaye de Mortemer, surrounded by trees and lawns.

Turning left on D6, you pass through Lyons-la-Forêt, the center of a beech forest, once the favorite hunting grounds of the Norman dukes and still the site of formal hunts with much scarlet livery and black velour headgear in evidence between April and September. The town's 15th-century church contains several huge wooden statues. Another left turn, this time onto D321, leads to the Abbaye de Fontaine-Guérard, on the banks of the River Andelle. This Cistercian foundation for nuns, initially sponsored by Robert, Earl of Leicester, in 1132, eventually came under the protection of John Lackland and Louis IX (St.-Louis) and now is owned by the Salvation Army. There are interesting early Gothic features in what remains of the abbey church, chapter house, nuns' parlor, and the study hall. (Open daily, except Mondays, from April through October; phone: 32-49-03-82.)

Backtracking about a mile (1.6 km) along D321, one comes again to D1, which passes the restored Château de Vascoeuil (open April through October, weekends only in winter; phone: 35-23-62-35), where one finds — surprisingly — sculptures by Braque, Léger, and Calder as well as works by David and Bernard Buffet. A few yards north of Vascoeuil off D1, N30 leads to Martainville and its château, a somewhat small, red brick affair built by a Rouen merchant. This sensible-looking house with stout turrets (which do not remotely suggest fortifications) has been turned into a showplace of Norman arts, crafts, and traditions. The kitchen, with its huge brick fireplace and dozens of implements, is a joy. (Closed Tuesdays and holidays; phone: 35-23-40-13.) Route N31 continues west to Rouen.

ROUEN: For a detailed report on the city, its sights, hotels, and restaurants, see *Rouen* in THE CITIES.

En Route from Rouen – Take D982 to Canteleu, where there is a good view along the Seine from the top of the hill. You can reach St.-Martin-de-Boscherville by crossing the corniche on D982, but a more interesting though circuitous route is via the turnoff on D51, running along the clifftop above the river to Sahurs, then turning right on D351 to drive through the Roumare Forest. St.-Martin boasts the first of the great abbeys along the Seine between Rouen and Le Havre. The abbey church of St. George was founded in 1050 by Raoul de Tancarville (who first was tutor and later chamberlain to William the Conqueror) and is one of the finest examples of Romanesque art in Normandy. The church is astonishingly pure in design, with a minimum of Gothic trappings to distract from the simple Romanesque arches. Two jousting knights, typical of the era in which the church was constructed, adorn the capitals in the south transept.

From St.-Martin it once again is possible to skirt the looping Seine by taking a road that becomes D65 at Duclair, to swing round to Jumièges, or to continue on D982 and make a short left backtrack to the Jumièges Abbey from Yainville. The ruins of the great Benedictine abbey of Jumièges are among the most romantic in France. The monks were here from the 7th century until the Revolution, during which time Jumièges was one of the great church establishments controlling life along the Seine, materially as well as spiritually. The remains include the entire nave and parts of the transept and chancel. In the center of the square cloister is an ancient yew tree, which romantics claim is almost as old as the abbey. (Open daily, 10 AM to noon and 2 to 4 PM, in winter; 9 AM to 6 PM in summer; phone: 35-37-24-02.)

Route D928 continues past Le Triat to St.-Wandrille, a splendid abbey whose Benedictine community still thrives. The monks have been here, with interruptions, since the 7th century. St. Wandrille was a count at the court of Dagobert who decided just after his marriage to become a monk. He was ordained at St.-Ouen in Rouen and eventually founded the abbey named for him. Because of his angelic qualities and his physical carriage, he was known as "the athlete of God." The cloister, seen only on a guided tour, has an interesting 16th-century lavabo. The monks still use a medieval barn brought stone by stone from the department of Eure and reconstructed here as the abbey church. Mass is said and vespers sung in Gregorian chant each day (phone: 35-96-23-11).

 CHECKING IN/EATING OUT: *L'Auberge du Bac* – A Normandy farmhouse transformed into a fine country inn at the ferry crossing. On sunny days you can dine on the terrace and watch the ships go up and down the Seine. The food and service are very good. Closed Tuesday evenings and Wednesdays. Jumièges (phone: 35-37-24-16). Moderate.

Auberge des Ruines – This hotel/restaurant is wonderfully rustic, with a charming fireplace for winter dining, a romantic arboreal bower for summer, and those exquisite ruins nearby. The fare is not particularly imaginative — duck à l'orange, turbot with hollandaise — but it is good and no one minds if you linger. There are 4 inexpensive rooms. 1 Pl. de la Mairie, Jumièges (phone: 35-37-24-05). Moderate.

CAUDEBEC-EN-CAUX: An extraordinary view over the Seine makes Caudebec an attractive spot, even though only a few of the half-timbered houses that lined its streets before the Germans set fire to the town in 1940 remain. The panorama over the river is best seen from the steps of the Hôtel de Ville (Town Hall). Occasionally a huge merchant ship plying between Le Havre and Rouen obliterates the vistas on the opposite bank; to see these large boats against such an idyllic setting can be awesome.

The fine Flamboyant Gothic church of Notre-Dame, with its celebrated organ, dates from the 15th and 16th centuries. Sculpted on the balustrade surrounding the church are some of the words from the Magnificat and the Salve Regina. The 15th-century window over the north door is of English glasswork, rare in France. The *Musée Biochet-Bréchot,* in the wonderful old building known as the Maison des Templiers (Templars' House), has pictures and artifacts of local history from prehistoric times to the present. (Open *Easter* through September; phone: 35-96-20-65.)

VILLEQUIER: Take D81 out of Caudebec to this charming riverside spot sheltered by wooded hills where the road reaches down off the cliff to the water's edge. Victor Hugo stayed here often at his son-in-law's family home overlooking the river. It is now the *Musée Victor-Hugo* and contains manuscripts, autographs, and letters by or concerning the author as well as portraits and furniture. (Closed Tuesdays in summer, Mondays and Tuesdays from mid-October to mid-April; phone: 35-56-78-31.)

LILLEBONNE: The Romans called this town Juliobona and, in the days when they controlled Gaul, it was a major city. Today only the grass-covered remains of the Roman theater recall its early importance. Apply to the *Café de l'Hôtel de Ville* (Place Felix Square, Lillebonne, 76170) for permission to wander through the site. William the Conqueror also found Lillebonne strategically useful, and he built a fortress here; the formidable walls of the keep and several towers remain. It was here that William gathered his barons before crossing to Hastings in the eventful year of 1066.

En Route from Lillebonne – Take D173 to Bolbec, where there are four handsome 18th-century houses on Rue de la République, then take meandering D149 into Dieppe. The road passes through typical Pays de Caux countryside, which is characterized inland by large half-timbered farmhouses, with barns and outhouses around a central courtyard. These in turn often stand in orchards, with the whole farm sometimes ringed by windbreaking rows of oak and beech trees. Here and there, barns have been remodeled with chic doors and windowboxes testifying to their new role as country retreats for city dwellers.

At Longueville there is a ruined castle that once belonged to Dunois, the Bastard of Orléans, who appears sympathetically in Shaw's *Saint Joan.* Farther on, at Arques-la-Bataille, poised high on a rock are the remains of a much larger castle, dating from the 12th century and surrounded by a moat. There are good views over the valley from the keep, the highest point of the castle, though the temptation to wander inside the walls should be avoided since crumbling masonry can be a danger.

CHECKING IN/EATING OUT: *Auberge du Clos Normand* – Regional specialties, the order of the day here, are served either in the wood-beamed and copper decor of the dining room or in the garden, which has a footbridge-laced stream running through it. Quiche lovers should request the *tarte aux moules,* with mussels. There are 9 rooms available except in winter. The restaurant is closed Monday nights and Tuesdays off-season and from mid-December to mid-January. Martin-Eglise, 22 Rue Henri-IV (phone: 35-82-71-01). Moderate.

Auberge de la Durdent – This small inn has a wooden balcony out front, lots of oak beams, plenty of chintz — and a river running through that divides the bar from the dining room. Trout, not surprisingly, is a specialty and good in any of the several ways in which it is prepared. In typical Norman fashion, cream is used with just about everything. There are 15 rooms with showers. Both the rooms and the cooking are traditional. Closed Wednesdays, 2 weeks in February and 3 weeks in November. At the crossroads of D149 and D131. Héricourt-en-Caux (phone: 35-96-42-44). Inexpensive.

DIEPPE: The main attraction of this major Channel seaport is the beachfront, which stretches for nearly a mile between cliffs dominated at the west end by a castle and at the east by the port itself. The basins of the port, lined here and there with 18th-century houses, extend deep into the town along the Quai de Quesle and the Quai de Norvège. Dieppe became a fashionable seaside resort in the 19th century when it was visited by Duchesse de Berry as well as by Empress Eugénie and her consort, Napoleon III.

Eglise St.-Jacques, dating from the 13th century but with later additions, is the most interesting of the town's churches. In its Flamboyant Gothic Sacred Heart Chapel, a frieze shows Brazilian Indians, recalling the time in the 16th century when Dieppe was an important point of embarkation for Atlantic explorers. There still are some pictur-esque old houses in the neighborhood of St.-Jacques, especially along Grande-Rue leading to Dieppe's other interesting church, the part Gothic, part Renaissance St. Rémy. Beyond St. Rémy via Rue de Chastes is a much-restored but still imposing 15th-century castle, offering excellent views of the town and its surroundings from the terraces. The château-museum is notable for its extensive collection of ivory carvings. (Open daily, June through September; closed Tuesdays the rest of the year; phone: 35-84-19-76.)

On August 19, 1942, Dieppe was the scene of the first Allied landing after the retreat from Dunkirk when 7,000 men, mostly Canadians, crossed the Channel in Operation Jubilee, hoping to secure a foothold on the northern shore of the continent. But the Allies did not know how strongly the port was defended, and the operation was a failure, costing the lives of 5,000 soldiers. However, the Dieppe Raids, as they became known, taught the Allies two major lessons: first, that the Germans expected any major attack to come via the ports and that, therefore, plans should be made to attack via the beaches and cliffs; second, that aerial and naval bombardment would be essential before land forces could gain a foothold. Almost 2 years later, these lessons were put into effect successfully on *D-Day* to the west of Dieppe, beyond the River Orne.

CHECKING IN: *La Présidence* – This inviting place has 88 comfortable rooms and a fourth-floor restaurant, *Le Queiros,* that offers good seafood dishes and wines, and a fine view of the water. 1 Bd. Verdun, Dieppe (phone: 35-84-31-31). Moderate.

Univers – A small and very popular hotel, its 28 rooms are decorated with beautiful antiques; a restaurant is on the premises. Be sure to make reservations. The hotel is closed from mid-December to February. 10 Bd. Verdun, Dieppe (phone: 35-84-12-55). Moderate.

EATING OUT: *Auberge de la Bucherie* – On the road to Rouen, this is the best dining spot in the Dieppe region. Small and flower-filled, it features traditional fare. Closed Sunday evenings and Mondays. Rte. de Rouen, Of-franville (phone: 35-84-83-10). Expensive.

Marmite Dieppoise – The obvious choice here is the *marmite dieppoise,* mussels, crayfish, crabs, sole, and turbot in a cream sauce of potatoes and leeks with fennel. There also are other delicious seafood dishes and Norman classics. Closed Sunday and Thursday nights, Mondays, June, and from *Christmas* to *New Year's Day.* 8 Rue St.-Jean, Dieppe (phone: 35-84-24-26). Moderate.

En Route from Dieppe – D75 climbs the cliff just beyond the castle and runs for a little over a mile along the coast before it turns inland to reach Varengeville-sur-Mer. There one can visit the Manoir d'Ango, the country home of a famous Dieppe merchant-adventurer whose privateers broke the Portuguese trade monopoly on the west coast of Africa in the 16th century. The manor house, dating from 1530, is a wonderful asymmetrical pile of brick and stone with sturdy Romanesque arches and a famous circular dovecote of ornate red and black brickwork. (Open Tuesdays, Thursdays, weekends, and holiday afternoons from *Easter* to October 31.) Varengeville itself contains some fine old houses on wooded hillsides and the Eglise St.-Valéry. Dating from the 12th century but much modified, the church stands in a rather lonely spot on the cliff's edge, bordered by a cemetery in which the painter Georges Braque is buried. The Tree of Jesse window inside the church was designed by the celebrated Cubist.

From the Phare d'Ailly (Ailly Lighthouse), at nearby Ste.-Marguerite, it is possible to see about 40 miles up and down the cliff-lined coast. The lighthouse is open from 8 AM until about an hour before dusk, and the lighthouse keeper who admits visitors to the first-floor platform is not averse to accepting a small tip. The 12th-century church at Ste.-Marguerite, much altered in the 16th century, is notable for its high altar, dating from 1160. Turn left off D75 at St.-Aubin-sur-Mer to make a delightful detour along the Dun Valley to Bourg-Dun to see the unusual spire on the church tower: It's shaped like the head of an ax. Return on the same road and turn left onto D68, the coast road, for Veules-les-Roses, picturesquely situated in a wooded valley through which runs what is supposed to be the shortest river in France.

EATING OUT: *Les Galets* – Its name means "the shingles," and this small, modern restaurant could hardly be closer to the shingled beach. Its seafood specialties, desserts, and superb selection of local cheeses have won it a Michelin star. Closed Sunday evenings off-season, Mondays, Tuesday lunch, and February. 3 Rue Victor-Hugo, Veules-les-Roses (phone: 35-97-61-33). Expensive.

ST.-VALÉRY-EN-CAUX: Like many other coastal towns, the fishing port of St.-Val, as it is locally known, is a breach in the great chalk cliffs, and most of its arterial streets run more or less parallel to the colorful yacht and fishing basin that penetrates deep into the town. St.-Val was badly damaged in 1940, during the retreat of the British 10th Army, but was rebuilt and became a popular seaside and sailing resort. A few old houses remain on the left bank, but most of the villas and small hotels date from the 1950s. Take the clifftop road D79 to Fécamp.

EATING OUT: *Port* – Unusual combinations of fish and sauces make this restaurant overlooking the port an occasionally esoteric culinary experience. For example, the chef-owner may cook fish in red wine. Closed Sunday evenings, Mondays, and mid-December to mid-January. 18 Quai d'Amont, St.-Valéry (phone: 35-97-08-93). Expensive to moderate.

FÉCAMP: Set between great white cliffs where the Pays de Caux meets the sea, this town is France's fourth largest fishing port. The colorful boats lying placidly at anchor along the quays may be waiting for a tide that will take them to the cold, rough fishing grounds off Newfoundland. Fécamp also is a seaside resort, with a gambling casino and a shopping center for people from surrounding villages.

The most interesting sight here is La Trinité, an early Gothic abbey church. The present structure, built between 1175 and 1225 and subsequently embellished, is the successor to earlier buildings. Apart from the application of a baroque façade in the 18th century, the church is impressive. Its massive lantern tower, 210 feet high, dominates the valley of Fécamp. The interior is no less commanding: At 416 feet in length, it's one of the longest churches in France. The ten awesome bays in the nave are marvelously free of ornament. Decoration, when present, is elaborate, especially in the sumptuous gilded baldachin, which hovers above the high altar poised on marble pillars. The cross on the altar is bronze and has an unusually poignant figure of Christ. The chapels in the ambulatory are hidden behind splendid stone screens playfully sculpted with classical vases, chimera, palms, hearts, and olives. In the Lady Chapel are four famous medallions carved in wood, including one with a veiled figure of Christ on the cross. Opposite the Lady Chapel at the back of the high altar is the Tabernacle of the Precious Blood, carved in white marble in 1505. People still come in large numbers to venerate the relic on the Tuesday and Thursday following *Trinity Sunday.* In the Chapelle du Calvaire you can see fragments from the old rood screen: John and Peter asleep during Christ's watch at Gethsemane; James with his face turned to the wall; Judas shaking his fist. In the south transept there is a remarkable Dormition of the Virgin with nine saints and friends in attendance, all sculpted in wonderful detail. In the humanistic tradition of the early Renaissance — it was worked in 1495 — the attending figures are all idiosyncratic personalities, suggesting that real models were used.

This abbey was the home of the Benedictine Brother Vincelli, who in 1510 experimented with the herbs he found on the nearby cliffs to produce a soothing distillation in the form of a liqueur. The secret recipe, closely guarded by the monks, was lost during the Revolution. However, searching through family papers one day in 1863, a local businessman named Alexandre Le Grand came upon an ancient manuscript with scarcely decipherable writing that turned out to be a recipe for a concoction based on herbs and spices. After lengthy experiments, Le Grand produced an elixir to his taste and called it Bénédictine. The factory where it is made, *Le Musée de la Bénédictine* (110 Rue Alexandre-Le-Grand; phone: 35-28-00-06), is open to the public daily from 9:30 to 11:30 AM and 2 to 5:30 PM (winter hours are shorter). It houses a sweet-smelling room piled with sacks of dried herbs and lined with bottles from all over the world. In the distillery, there are handsome old copper vats, and in the cellars, casks where the liqueur matures. And there is much more: Le Grand, who collected paintings and objets d'art, commissioned a part Renaissance, part Gothic palace adjoining his distillery in which he could display his burgeoning collection. The building is a rather ugly and pretentious piece of architecture, but Le Grand's collection, predominantly religious in theme, contains some extraordinary pieces — an ivory Spanish triptych of the life of Christ; an ivory, wood, and marble bas-relief of the Presentation at the Temple; and a 12th-century missal that alone would merit a visit to the museum. There also are scores of other bas-reliefs, statues, and a variety of items rescued from the abbey at the time of the Revolution as well as a fine ironwork collection and 600 oil lamps from the days of the Roman Empire.

CHECKING IN: *L'Universe* – A small, family-run hotel in the center of town, it offers a warm welcome to travelers who'd like to spend a night or two in Fécamp. Some of the 10 rooms include television sets. 5 Pl. St.-Etienne (phone: 35-28-05-88). Inexpensive.

EATING OUT: *La Marine* – There is nothing spectacular about this brasserie except the value. As the name suggests, seafood dishes are best: simply and expertly prepared and certainly ample. There is a fine view of the bay and the yacht basin from the first floor. Closed Tuesday evenings, Wednesdays, and during January. 23 Quai Vicomté, Fécamp (phone: 35-28-15-94). Moderate.

En Route from Fécamp – At St.-Léonard on D940, just at the top of the hill, there are some beautiful old half-timbered cottages and farms on the right. Take the coast road D211 down to Yport, which passes tidy middle class homes with neat yards and gardens lined with rows of vegetables. From Yport, the road to Etretat climbs over cliffs that look like moorland, covered with gorse, ferns, and brambles and often shrouded in mist. Along the way, look for signs offering fresh fruit and *chèvre* (goat cheese) for sale.

ETRETAT: Etretat is a small quiet resort that's barely more than a cleft between the precipitous Falaise d'Aval (Aval Cliff), to the left as you face the ocean, and the Falaise d'Amont (Amont Cliff), to the right. The famous opening in the cliff to the left, which looks like a flying buttress, is known as the Porte d'Aval (the Aval Gate), and jutting from the sea close by is the needle rock. Claude Monet painted these cliffs many times.

By taking the stairway and path from the Aval end of the beach you can see the cliffs from above, a much more thrilling perspective, especially when the fog swirls and eddies below, around, and above you. The path (which is steep and not recommended for anyone who has difficulty walking) leads past grim gun emplacements from World War II over firm, springy turf and past an enormous bramble bush, which in September is laden with luscious blackberries. Beyond the brambles, you reach the edge of the cliff and on a clear day can see to another "gate," the Manne, to the left, and the lighthouse atop the Cap d'Antifer. At the cliff's edge a very narrow pathway, which falls away treacherously on either side, permits you to reach what looks like ramparts on the cliff. The flat, milky, blue-white of the ocean here explains why this is known as the Côte d'Albâtre (Alabaster Coast). A warning about the path: It is narrower on the inland side than on the ocean side; jumping from the narrow side to the cliff's edge, where it is broader, is not too difficult; jumping back, especially in a high wind, can be very dangerous.

The Amont Cliff, on the other side of Etretat, is accessible by car. It is less dramatic than the Aval Cliff, although the nearby Chapelle Notre-Dame-de-la-Garde is worth seeing. On the beach at Etretat there's a small open-air bar where the fishermen may be found in the late morning, sometimes breaking into song, sea chantey-style, though they tend to be inhibited if they think they are attracting too much attention.

 CHECKING IN: *Dormy House* – A small, tranquil inn in which the rooms offer an exceptional view of the Etretat cliffs. Open weekends only from November 1 to March. Rte. du Havre (phone: 35-27-07-88). Moderate.

LE HAVRE: About 90% of this port, the second largest in France, was destroyed in World War II. Its proximity to the English coast made it the target of a series of RAF bombings meant to preclude a German invasion of Great Britain, and by 1945 it was the most damaged port in Europe. After the war, the architect Auguste Perret rebuilt the center of the city following the grid pattern of the old, 18th-century town, although the present concrete buildings do not convey the charm of the original. The *Musée des Beaux-Arts André-Malraux* contains paintings dating from the 16th century, but the outstanding collections are of works by Eugène Boudin (296 pieces, of which 50 are on permanent display) and Raoul Dufy, who was born in Le Havre. There also are important paintings by Corot, Sisley, Monet, and Pissarro (closed Tuesdays and holidays; Bd. John-F.-Kennedy; phone: 35-42-33-97). Also interesting is the Cathédrale Notre-Dame on Rue de Paris. Although it was devastated in the war, it has been almost completely and attractively restored. As a result, it has a certain pristine quality that one does not sense in some of the more ornately decorated churches in Normandy.

Another ecclesiastical site worth visiting is the Abbaye de Graville (Vierge Noir; phone: 35-47-14-01), in what is now a suburb of Le Havre. There has been a church here since the 6th century, but the present edifice is a restoration of the one built in the 12th and 13th centuries as an adjunct to the abbey. The buildings to the right, where Henry V stayed during the siege of Harfleur in 1415, are now a museum (closed Mondays and Tuesdays). On view are beautiful medieval pieces and fragments of the original abbey, along with religious statues, gravestones, bas-reliefs, documents, and processional crosses.

Ste.-Adresse, on the cliffs northeast of Le Havre, is a suburb with clifftop villas from the Edwardian period. There also is a tiny chapel, Notre-Dame-des-Flots (Our Lady of the Tides), which is lined with plaques thanking the Virgin for guiding a loved one to a safe harbor. Ste.-Adresse was the provisional capital of Belgium during World War I, and the Belgian coat of arms is incorporated into that of the village.

Another de facto suburb of Le Havre, even though it still boasts its own Town Hall, is Harfleur. Like the similar-sounding Honfleur on the Seine Estuary, Harfleur was a port of considerable importance until François I's edict created "Le Havre de Grace" in the 16th century. In grisly testimony to its stature, during the Hundred Years War the English laid siege to the town no less than nine times, though successfully only once. This was in 1415, when Henry V was a guest at Graville and the walls finally were penetrated. In Shakespeare's *Henry V,* the king says, "Once more into the breach, dear friends, once more, or close the wall up with our English dead." By the bard's time, the Breach (la Brèque) was the common name for the neighborhood of Harfleur where the wall was broken through.

The striking bell tower, 272 feet high, that dominates Harfleur belongs to the Eglise St.-Martin, built in the 15th and 16th centuries. Inside, the decorative capitals on the pillars on the north side and the Renaissance organ are worth noting. Parts of the old wall of Harfleur are visible near the Porte de Rouen (Rouen Gate). Among the not always attractive 19th- and 20th-century buildings, you still can glimpse parts of the old town; the Rue des 104, Rue de l'Eure, and Rue Thiers are likely to be the most rewarding.

 CHECKING IN: *Bordeaux* – This hotel is modern, quiet, and comfortable, with a minimum of service (in the American motel fashion). All 31 rooms have a bath or shower, refrigerator-bar, TV set, and telephone, and some rooms overlook the marina. 147 Rue Louis-Brindeau, Le Havre (phone: 35-22-69-44). Expensive.

 EATING OUT: *Cambridge* – The dark blue decor actually suggests Oxford, but since the coat of arms is Cambridge's, why quibble? Try the Norwegian smoked salmon, brill in sorrel, warm apple tart and Normandy cream. Not surprisingly, this restaurant is very popular with visiting Britons. Closed Sunday evenings, Mondays, and most of August. 90 Rue Voltaire, Le Havre (phone: 35-42-50-24). Moderate.

Nice-Havrais – The best eating in Le Havre is here, in a seaside suburb. This restaurant is noted for its menu selections and their presentation. Seafood and other regional specialties abound. Closed Sunday and Monday evenings year-round, and all day Monday in August. 6 Pl. F.-Sauvage, Ste.-Adresse (phone: 35-46-14-59). Moderate.

Mon Auberge – For 2 decades, this place has delighted customers with its ambience and its Périgord-Norman specialties. The duck dishes are especially good. Closed Sunday evenings and Mondays. 35 Rue du Général-Sarrail, Le Havre (phone: 35-42-44-36). Moderate to inexpensive.

En Route from Le Havre – Take N182 to Tancarville and cross the spectacular Pont du Tancarville, a suspension bridge completed in 1959 to replace the slow ferry service across the Seine. The bridge is almost a mile long and never less than 158 feet above the river at high tide. The south side of the Seine here is known as the Marais Vernier

(Vernier Marsh), which was drained by Dutch engineers and laborers during the reign of Henry IV. It is surrounded by an amphitheater of wooded hills that mark the old course of the river before it found a new channel eons ago. The marshy plain left behind is today a rich alluvial pastureland crisscrossed by canals and dotted with cattle and fruit farms. Both the plain and the surrounding hills can be seen to great advantage from the Pointe de la Roque, just off route D178 between Tancarville Bridge and Foulbec, from where a coast road takes you into Honfleur.

HONFLEUR: Imagine a bright blue sky in the west and nervous gray clouds in the east, and where they blend, luminous edges shedding a watery, silver light. See, illuminated by this, a small old port where picturesque fishing boats, their nets drying, lie at anchor, and tall narrow houses, their sides lined with gray slates, loom over the quays. This is Honfleur, a colorful antique, but a working one. The boats may be decorative but they also are functional, and their casual comings and goings may be to and from places as remote as St. Pierre and Miquelon, off Newfoundland. Honfleur on a Sunday is quiet and still, but on weekdays the fishermen, ships' engineers, and carpenters lend a sense of urgency.

The painter Eugène Boudin was born here and brought Monet, Renoir, Sisley, Pissarro, and others to Honfleur, where they experimented with the light in painting that eventually gave the world Impressionism. Honfleur also was the birthplace of some famous explorers, including Paulmier de Gonneville, who sailed the South Seas, and Samuel de Champlain, who set off from here in 1608 on an expedition that resulted in the discovery of Quebec. The Vieux Bassin (Old Dock), from which he sailed, still is the most celebrated sight in Honfleur.

The *Musée du Vieux-Honfleur* (Rue de la Prison, 14600 Honfluer; phone 31-89-14-12), in the former Eglise St.-Etienne, contains antique arms, costumes, ceramics, and furniture illustrating the town's past back to Gallo-Roman times. (Open July to mid-September, weekends off-season, and holidays).

The most celebrated curiosity in Honfleur is the double-naved Eglise Ste.-Catherine, shaped like an upturned keel, an ancient concept that has special poignancy here because the ceilings of its two naves were built by shipwrights, not masons. Even though the naves are unequal in length and there is a makeshift quality to the church (though it has been here for 500 years), the church is exceptionally appealing. Chief among the decorative items are a number of wooden statues, which harmonize beautifully with the rustic atmosphere of the church. Seventeen carved panels on the 16th-century banister of the organ loft show mythological figures playing what amounts to an inventory of the musical instruments of the period. The church belfry, also of wood, was built across the road from the church and now seems to exist almost independently as a small museum, *La Tour Ste.-Catherine* (St. Catherine's Tower), with liturgical objects and the records of the Confrérie de St.-Léonard, a local guild. The church and tower frequently appear in paintings by Boudin, Monet and others. (Open *Palm Sunday* through September, except Tuesdays.)

The *Musée Eugène-Boudin* (Pl. Erik-Satie) is a modern, 3-story building that shares a courtyard with a typical 19th-century apartment house. Oblivious to the high-minded tourists coming and going below, residents put eiderdowns and colorful bedspreads out to air on their windowsills — a delightful scene — just as they would have in Boudin's day. Besides the work of Boudin, Monet, and other Impressionists, the museum displays antique lace caps, children's bonnets, and collars as well as the instruments used in making them. From the third-floor gallery there is a good view over the town, showing just how it is placed in relation to the Seine Estuary and the Channel. (Closed during January and February, Tuesdays from mid-March through September, and weekday mornings in winter; phone: 31-89-16-47, ext. 27.) There are some fine old houses within easy walking distance of one another; apart from those surrounding the

Vieux Bassin and the church, the Rue Haute and the Rue de Puits are especially rewarding.

CHECKING IN: *Ferme St.-Siméon* – This half-timbered 17th-century inn (a member of the Relais & Châteaux group), overlooking the Seine estuary, was much frequented by the Impressionists. Now a modern, 19-room annex has been built, but the original 19 rooms are charming and cozy, and the kitchen turns out such well-prepared specialties as lobster stew, which won it a star from Michelin in 1990. Apéritifs are served on the terrace amid flowerboxes and under colorful umbrellas. Open daily. Rue A.-Marais, Honfleur (phone: 31-89-23-61). Very expensive.

Le Cheval Blanc – On the quai overlooking Honfleur's port, this half-timbered 15th-century inn has a traditional style about it and attractively refurbished rooms. Winter weekend packages include painting courses taught by Beaux Arts instructors. 2 Quai des Passagers, Honfleur (phone: 31-89-13-49). Moderate.

EATING OUT: *Le Bistrot du Port* – Although it looks out on the port rather than the Vieux Bassin, the view can be delightful when fishing boats are chugging to and fro along the quays. Indoors, the exposed beams and fireplace provide a congenial setting for this restaurant's spectacular *assiette de fruits de mer,* a platter of mixed seafood that includes oysters, mussels, shrimp, crab, and other crustaceans. Closed Monday evenings, Tuesdays, and November 11 to early February. 14 Quai de la Quarantaine, Honfleur (phone: 31-89-21-84). Moderate.

En Route from Honfleur – Take D513 for a scenic ride past old farms and views of the Channel through the apple orchards. The apple trees and flowers blooming on the cliffs that bracket the fine sandy beaches in this region, together with the sometimes exotic plantings by hillside villas and seaside homes, have given this corner of Calvados the name Côte Fleurie (Flowered Coast). At Cricqueboeuf, just before entering Villerville, look for a romantic, ivy-covered, 12th-century church next to a pond. Villerville itself is little more than a cleft in the cliffs, which shelter a small, attractive beach.

EATING OUT: *Le Moulin à Grains* – The dining room in this old Norman grain mill, with exposed beams and two fireplaces, is known for its generous portions of meat and seafood. The tripe in white wine and calvados and the *cochonnailles* (an assortment of sausage, pâté, and sliced ham) platter are very popular locally. Closed Sunday nights, Mondays, and July. Trouville-Aliquerville (phone: 35-38-04-46). Moderate to inexpensive.

TROUVILLE-SUR-MER: In the heady days of Napoleon III, the affluent *boulevardiers* (men about town) of Paris brought their wives, children, and children's nannies to this fishing village–turned–resort for the season while they disported themselves with their mistresses a stone's throw away, across the River Touques at Deauville. Boudin's masterly drawings and paintings of the beach at Trouville, showing women with bustles and parasols, illustrate what it must have been like when Empress Eugénie made it the most fashionable beach in France. The *Montebello Municipal Museum* (64 Rue Marechal, Leclerc; phone: 31-88-16-26) exhibits paintings by Boudin and others.

Today, Trouville stays busy long after Deauville has put up its shutters and started to doze for the winter. The fishing boats still go out in the morning; and at day's end, the nets still hang out to dry along the wall by the side of the river while the fishermen, in dungarees and navy sweaters, smoke their pipes and chat.

Bearing right at the Trouville seafront and walking toward the yacht club, you will find several blocks of villas, most of them still privately owned, which add up to an extravaganza of Gothic, Norman, and half-timbered follies that vie to outdo one another in turrets, towers, arches, and fantastical windows. The golden sand beach beyond the yacht club at the end of Rue Lieutenant-R.-Morane lies under a low cliff and is much quieter than the Deauville end of the beach. Toward the end of July there is a sandcastle contest at the Deauville end, in front of the casino, in which amateur architects attempt to reproduce some of the more dramatic buildings in the neighborhood. Also in July is Trouville's most important festival, the annual *Fête de la Mer,* and in May and November, the city hosts antiques shows.

There is still gambling at the *Deauville* casino (Pl. du Maréchal Foch; phone: 31-88-76-09) — its atmosphere is decidedly less snooty than that of Deauville — though part of the building has been turned into a cinema and a concert hall where entertainers from Paris sometimes perform during the season. The fish market on the riverbank is open daily; try *Chez Saiter* (phone: 31-88-13-55) for carry-out *soupe de poisson* (fish soup) and *bisque de homard* (lobster bisque).

EATING OUT: La Roches Noires – For fine fare, locals recommend this slightly out of the way restaurant, perched above a sandy beach on the road to Honfleur near an old mansion by the same name. Arrive in time to watch the sun set over the channel. 16 Bd. Louis-Bréguet (phone: 31-88-12-19). Moderate.

Les Vapeurs – The name means "the steamships," which are represented in red and white Art Deco tiles. This brasserie has a dedicated jet set following for several reasons: The service is exceptionally friendly, the *moules marinières* (marinated mussels) generous, and the *saucisse de Morteau* (sausages served warm with potatoes in oil and vinegar) satisfying. Closed Tuesday evenings, Wednesdays, the last half of November, and January. 160 Quai Fernand-Moureaux, Trouville (phone: 31-88-15-24). Moderate to inexpensive.

DEAUVILLE: It was Napoleon III's half-brother Charles, Duc de Morny, who established Deauville as the summer headquarters for the smart set, and its cachet lingers even today. This fashionable resort has a very short season — mid-July through September — during which visitors flock here to shop (in the town center are such famous designer boutiques as *Cartier, Chanel, Hermès, Yves St. Laurent*); sail in regattas; golf on two fine courses; gamble in an elegant casino; and gambol on the beaches. The highlight of the season is the *Grand Prix de Deauville,* a horse race in late August that draws some of the most famous breeders and punters from around the world. Anyone interested in ogling celebrities will certainly find them here then; the Aga Khan and the Rothschilds are just a few of the fancy folk who may have reservations for lunch at the "in" spot, *Le Ciro's* (see *Eating Out*). Besides the casino, the racetrack, and *Ciro's,* the place to be seen is on the *planches,* the wooden walkways along the beach, or on the beach itself, which is filled with the innumerable, brightly colored beach umbrellas of sunbathers. For a less rarefied experience, walk along the jetty in town on the west side of the Port-de-Deauville; it's especially nice at sunset, when pleasure craft make their way through the buoys into the harbor.

Deauville's casino is grander and more sparkling than ever, following a major face-lift, polish, and remodeling in 1988, and now remains open year-round. The winter casino is closed indefinitely.

CHECKING IN: Hostellerie de Tourgeville – A steeply pitched roof and half-timbered walls give this modern hotel a traditional Norman look. Inside, the bedrooms also are modern and comfortably furnished, decorated in earth tones, and have lovely picture windows and large baths. There is a pool, a sauna, and tennis facilities. Chemin de l'Orgueil, Tourgeville-Deauville (phone: 31-88-63-40). Expensive.

Normandy – Its half-timbered gables and balconies make this property one of Deauville's focal points. Inside it's as sumptuous as could be: huge plump pillows and soft velvet spreads adorn the beds in the 300 rooms and 20 suites. The tables and easy chairs are elegant reproductions of the Louis XVI era, and the bathrooms are spacious. Although the place has a reputation for snobbery, the staff seems pleasant enough. (See also *Romantic French Hostelries,* DIVERSIONS.) Open year-round. 38 Rue Jean-Mermoz, Deauville (phone: 31-98-66-22). Very expensive.

Royal – The other traditionally luxurious hotel in town, its 293 rooms and 17 suites are decorated comfortably yet somewhat formally in mock French Provincial-style. This slightly stiff note is carried into the restaurant and lobby, both dominated by floor-to-ceiling windows, crystal chandeliers, ornamental plasterwork, and a gold and white color scheme. A heated swimming pool, a sauna, and parking all are available. Closed mid-October to April. Bd. Eugène-Cornuché, Deauville (phone: 31-88-16-41). Expensive.

Le Trophée – It offers modern rooms (some with balconies), a rooftop sun deck, a pleasant restaurant, and a complete range of services for a moderate price. Conveniently located in the center of town, just a short walk from the beach. 81 Rue de Général Leclerc (phone: 31-88-45-86). Moderate.

 EATING OUT: ***Le Ciro's*** – Make no mistake about it, this is *the* place to eat during the high season when the jet setters are in town from Paris, London, and Hollywood. Crisp white napery and well-polished silver and glassware provide an appropriate setting for the classical dishes served. And it is right on the *planche,* so tables have fine views of the sea. Promenade des Planches, Deauville (phone: 31-88-18-10). Expensive.

Le Spinnaker – If *Le Ciro's* is the place to be seen, this increasingly popular spot near the main drag is the place to dine. The young chef shows considerable promise; his preparations have earned the establishment a Michelin star. 52 Rue Mirabeau (phone: 31-88-24-40). Moderate.

Chez Miocque – Noisy, friendly, and unpretentious, it's the kind of place where people talk across tables, bring their dogs and children, and taste one another's dishes. Order *moules marinières* (marinated mussels) to start (you'll receive at least 100 per person). Follow that with steaks and a large platter of perfectly cooked *pommes frites* (French fries). Other standard Norman fish and poultry dishes, as well as tripe and pigs' feet, also are served. Closed Tuesdays and Wednesdays in off-season, and January. 81 Rue Eugène-Colas, Deauville (phone: 31-88-09-52). Moderate to inexpensive.

En Route from Deauville – Blonville, Bénerville, Villers-sur-Mer, and Houlgate are four popular Norman resorts that D513 passes through on the way to Cabourg. Blonville and Bénerville nestle at the foot of pleasant, wooded hillsides studded with summer homes and are the quietest of this quartet of seaside spots. The beach at Villers is long but crowded in summer, with a promenade along much of it. Houlgate is the brassiest of the bunch and is much favored by the citizens of nearby Caen. Between Villers and Houlgate is one of the chief sights of the Côte Fleurie, the Falaise des Vaches Noires (Black Cow Cliffs), which, unlike the almost sheer chalk cliffs of the Pays de Caux, seem to tumble like a series of canyons down to the water. Geologically they consist of dark clay and marl and are famous for yielding fossils. It is possible to walk underneath the cliffs from Villers to Houlgate or vice versa (remembering to start when the tide is going out) or to walk on top of them from Auberville, a tiny hamlet between the two resorts.

EATING OUT: ***Auberge de l'Escale*** – Rustic Norman furniture and walls lined with fishnets suggest the menu here: seafood Norman-style, abundant and good. Closed Tuesdays and Wednesdays, 2 weeks in December and the month of January. Pl. de l'Hôtel-de-Ville, Blonville (phone: 31-87-93-56). Moderate.

CABOURG: A long stretch of beach and the most pleasant formal promenade of the Côte Fleurie are Cabourg's chief charms. The center of the promenade is dominated by the *Grand* hotel (see below) and the *Cabourg* casino. Proust loved Cabourg and often stayed at the *Grand* as a child; he used Cabourg as one of the prototypes for Balbec in "A l'Ombre des Jeunes Filles en Fleurs," the "Within a Budding Grove" section of *Remembrance of Things Past.* There is a pleasant walk at the east end of the beach along dunes above the estuary of the River Dives.

CHECKING IN: *Grand Hotel Pullman* – Dripping with lavish, turn-of-the-century details — marble columns, crystal chandeliers, elaborate plasterwork, plush draperies — this hotel has 70 bedrooms, all of which overlook either the sea or the adjacent casino gardens. Its fine restaurant, *Le Balbec,* also rich in decor, serves well-prepared basics such as lobster, tournedos, rack of lamb, shrimp and avocado salad, and lush desserts. Restaurant open till 10 PM. Parking available. Promenade Marcel-Proust, Cabourg (phone: 31-91-01-79). Expensive.

EATING OUT: *L'Amiral* – The white tables and chairs with blue umbrellas outside this beachfront bar-restaurant look quite inviting, as does the interior — light, modern, and airy, with exposed, bleached beams and some tiles of Norman and Breton women in traditional dress. *Fruits de mer* (seafood), tripe in cider, and shrimp in butter sauce are among the specialties. The food is well prepared and, except on crowded Sundays, the service is good. Closed mid-November to *Easter.* Promenade Marcel-Proust, Cabourg (phone: 31-91-50-66). Moderate.

CAEN: Of all the towns ravaged by the bombs of World War II, none was so severely wounded as Caen. Its old central quarter, which burned for 10 days, was completely destroyed; some buildings have been nicely restored. Fortunately for Caen, its two restored great churches, the Abbaye aux Hommes, also known as Eglise St.-Etienne, and the Abbaye aux Dames, also known as Eglise de la Trinité, survived. These, together with Caen's *Museum of Peace* (open daily from May through September; closed Mondays from October through April) and the ruins of William the Conqueror's castle, are most of what is worth seeing in the town.

Abbaye aux Hommes is best viewed from Place Louis-Guillouard, across a broad vista of lawns and formal gardens, beyond which are the 18th-century residential quarters of the abbey, now the Hôtel de Ville (town hall). Crossing the Place and turning into the Rue Guillaume-le-Conquérant and then left again brings you around the church to a point right under the domineering west front, its simple Romanesque lines almost, it seems, as massive and forbidding as the cliffs at Etretat. The lovely 14th-century apse and choir are early Gothic but blend subtly with the earlier parts of the church to form a monumental whole. In front of the pink marble high altar is the tombstone of William the Conqueror, who was buried ignominiously in the abbey in 1087. His wife, Matilda, was buried in the Abbaye aux Dames, the sister foundation. The couple built the abbeys as a penance following their marriage without papal dispensation for an impediment of consanguinity: They were cousins.

Abbaye aux Dames is smaller and appears more human in scale despite the great arches over the nine lordly bays. There is a delightful 13th-century Gothic chapel in the south transept, with delicately worked ribs and columns and female heads carved on the supporting arches. The 16 pillars in the 11th-century crypt make it look like a stone copse. A slab marking the spot where Matilda was buried can be seen in the choir, although the tomb itself was desecrated during the Revolution.

Caen's castle, built by William in 1060 and now a truly magnificent ruin, encloses lawns and sylvan walkways where its great towers once stood. A platform provides a pleasant view over the city, but the chief attraction is the splendid *Musée des Beaux-Arts.* (Closed Tuesdays and holidays; Esplanade du Château; phone: 31-85-28-63.) Few modern buildings sit so well in ancient surroundings; here the great gray stone slabs of the museum building merge handsomely with the medieval battlements. The collection is quite impressive and includes many pieces plundered by Napoleon in his forays across the Continent. Highlights include a magnificent *Marriage of the Virgin* by Pietro Vannucci (who called himself Perugino) and Bordon's *Annunciation.* Veronese, Titian, Tintoretto, and Van Ruysdael all are notably represented. The museum also houses the Mancel Collection, more than 40,000 prints including works by Rembrandt, Callot, Van Dyck, and Rubens.

The *Caen Mémorial Musée Pour la Paix* (Museum of Peace), which opened in 1988, was built on the site of a German underground command post to commemorate the 1944 *D-Day* landings and the ensuing battles. Its sobering exhibits emphasize not the military victories but the suffering of people in wartime. It's open from 9 AM to 7 PM daily, except *Christmas* and *New Year's.* Bd. Montgomery (phone: 31-06-06-44).

CHECKING IN: *Hôtel Saint Pierre* – A simple traditional-style place in the heart of Caen at Place Courtonne, recently purchased by a couple whose sincere welcome sets this apart from other hostelries in its class. Ten of the 19 rooms have private baths. 40 Bd. des Alliés, Caen (phone: 31-86-28-20). Inexpensive.

EATING OUT: *La Bourride* – In this 400-year-old dwelling, chef Michel Bruneau has earned two Michelin stars for his cooking, which features the best and freshest ingredients from Normandy's farms and fishing ports. Closed Sundays, Mondays, January 3-23, and 2 weeks in August. 15 Rue Vaugueux, Caen (phone: 31-93-50-76). Expensive.

Relais des Gourmets – Silver candelabra, gleaming glassware, and fresh white napery set the scene for some very fine Norman cooking and a superlative wine cellar. Try the *rognons grillés au bacon* (whole grilled kidney with English-style bacon) or the *turbot fourré de langouste* (turbot stuffed with sea crayfish), and a chocolate cake so rich it's almost pudding. There also are 32 clean, very comfortable rooms with bath upstairs. Restaurant closed Sundays. 15 Rue de Geôle, Caen (phone: 31-86-06-01). Expensive to moderate.

Alcide – The place most recommended for sampling Caen's famous *tripe à la mode:* tripe simmered in calvados, the region's apple brandy, and served with boiled potatoes and a calvados chaser. Closed Sundays, holidays, and August. Pl. Courtonne (phone: 31-93-58-29). Moderate to inexpensive.

D-DAY INVASION BEACHES: From Caen it is easy to make a detour to Sword, Juno, Gold, Omaha, and Utah beaches, the 50 miles of shore that played such an enormous role in the events of *D-Day,* June 6, 1944. Take D515 out of Caen to Bénouville and Pegasus Bridge. Here the road becomes D514 and continues to Ouistreham and Riva-Bella, where you turn left to follow the coastline via St.-Aubin-sur-mer, Arromanches-les-Bains, Port-en-Bessin, Pointe du Hoc, and Grandcamp-les-Bains. The route then turns inland to join the N13 highway just before Isigny-sur-Mer, passes through Carentan, leaves N13 after a few miles to follow D913 past Ste.-Marie-du-Mont, then heads north along the coastal D421 to Quinéville. Return inland to Montebourg on D42, making a left back onto N13 through Ste.-Mère-Eglise and continuing to Caen.

Virtually no one comes away from a visit to these famous beaches on Normandy's Calvados coastline without at least some twinge of patriotism. Looking out over sweeping stretches of seascape, now so picturesque and serene, it's difficult to imagine the devastation that took place on *D-Day.*

First it might be useful to contemplate some of the events of that period. It had been agreed at meetings between Winston Churchill and Franklin D. Roosevelt in 1942 and 1943 that an Allied invasion of Europe through France would be launched somewhere in the north of the country at some propitious time. Following the abortive attempt to seize Dieppe in 1942, it became clear that the beaches of Calvados were ideal. They were considered the least likely landing spot from the German viewpoint, for the Allied troops would have to overcome unreliable weather patterns, strong sea currents, and steep cliffs in order to succeed. The umbrella name for the invasion was Operation Overlord; General Dwight D. Eisenhower was appointed Supreme Commander of the Allied Expeditionary Forces in charge of strategic planning, and tactical coordination of all ground troops fell into the hands of General Bernard Law Montgomery of Great Britain. The unusual preparations for the invasion included training special British Commando and American Ranger units in cliff climbing; building vast floating docks for an artificial port; and creating an elaborate intelligence plan to convince the Germans — successfully, as it turned out — that the action would take place at Calais. The invasion was projected for the early part of June, when the weather could be expected to be good, the tides would be right, and the moon would be full enough to provide light for the airborne troops scheduled to be dropped behind the German coastal defenses ("the Atlantic Wall") a few hours before the landings.

In the early hours of June 6, the US 101st and 82nd and the British 6th Airborne divisions dropped into France, the first two on the western flank of the beaches just north of Carentan, the latter on the eastern flank around Bénouville, on the Orne River. Their mission was to divert the enemy as much as possible from the seaborne assault troops steaming across the English Channel: General Omar Bradley's 1st American Army, headed for Utah and Omaha beaches, where they landed at 6:30 AM; and the British 2nd Army under General Miles Dempsey (whose forces also included the 3rd Canadian Division), headed for Gold, Juno, and Sword beaches. Low-lying Utah Beach proved fairly easy to capture. By about noon on June 6 it was taken, and the 3rd Battalion of the 8th Infantry Regiment had managed to forge a unit inland about 8 miles to meet up with the 82nd Airborne. By the end of the day, 23,250 men and 17,000 vehicles had come ashore there.

Of all the Normandy beaches, Omaha was the hardest to conquer. The cliffs along its shoreline proved a predictably tough barrier, especially with rough seas at their foot. These harsh conditions became even worse for the troops that followed the initial landing force, since by then the Germans had opened fire. Losses were heavy. Nevertheless, 225 US Rangers managed to scale and capture Pointe du Hoc and hold it against heavy counterfire until they were relieved on June 8. The almost legendary Northumberlands, the 50th British Infantry Division, were part of the British 2nd Army that landed at Gold Beach around 7:25 AM, and the Royal Marine Commandos pushed west to Port-en-Bessin where they joined the American troops on June 8. The Canadian 3rd Infantry Division landed at Juno Beach around 7:10 AM, and by 5 PM the 7th Brigade had taken the beautiful hamlet of Creully, a few miles inland. The British 3rd Infantry Division, its objective Caen, came ashore on the part of Sword Beach between Lion-sur-Mer and Riva-Bella at about 7:30 AM. They captured a few small villages but met heavy resistance from the German 21st Panzer Division after 4 PM. A Franco-British Commando unit under Commander Philippe Kieffer managed to take Riva-Bella and continue on to Bénouville, where they met up with the British 6th Airborne.

June 6 was an extraordinary day's work, pivotal in mankind's history. The Battle of Normandy lasted about 11 weeks more, finally ending shortly after the capitulation of the German 7th Army on August 19 at Chambois.

Route D515 out of Caen leads to Bénouville, where a sign with a blue flying horse marks Pegasus Bridge on the Orne. This important crossing was liberated in the early hours of *D-Day* by members of the British 6th Airborne Division, who landed near the swing bridge in three gliders that had been towed across the Channel by Halifax bombers. The Town Hall of Bénouville was the first in France to be liberated. Details of what happened can be seen at the *Musée des Troupes Aéroportées* (Airborne Museum; 10 Av. Commandant-Kieffer; phone: 31-44-62-54), which is open daily from mid-March. Bénouville also has an interesting 18th-century château, famous for its monumental staircase.

Ouistreham and its neighbor Riva-Bella formed the ancient port of Caen. Now this is a popular pleasure boating center, and in summer the harbor is filled with the colorful sails of yachts from many northern European countries. British frogmen swam ashore here just before the invasion to clear the canals of obstacles. The *Musée du No. 4 Commando* (Pl. Alfred-Thomas; phone: 31-97-18-63) is open weekends from *Palm Sunday* through May; daily from June through mid-September. It concentrates on the French involvement in the invasion under Commander Kieffer with displays of arms, equipment, documents, uniforms, and photographs.

At Lion-sur-Mer, halfway along Sword Beach, there is little evidence of the chaos of *D-Day*. It is a typical Côte de Nacre resort, with a sandy beach, small hotels, tennis courts, and beachfront cafés. At Bernières-sur-Mer, a little farther on, two monuments commemorate the Canadian forces that created one of the essential bridgeheads in the operation. The 13th-century belfry of the church, with charming corner turrets over a small porch, is exceptionally fine, rising to a height of 220 feet. At Courseulles-sur-Mer, known for its oysters, ships were deliberately sunk during Operation Overlord to form a temporary harbor. Early in the operation, Winston Churchill, George VI, and Charles de Gaulle landed here to visit the battlefields. Just before entering Arromanches, there is an orientation table at the point called St.-Côme-de-Fresne, high on the cliff. It still is surrounded by German gun emplacements. The table, at the top of a flight of steps, provides the visitor with a perfect perspective of the beaches from Sword to Utah. In front are the remains of the breakwaters of the great artificial port that was built at Arromanches and still ranks as one of the most extraordinary examples of military marine engineering in the history of warfare.

Arromanches, set between cliffs around a sandy beach, has the finest of all the museums in Normandy commemorating Operation Overlord: the *Exposition Permanente du Débarquement* (Permanent Exhibition of the Landings; Pl. du 6-Juin; phone: 31-22-34-31), closed *Christmas, New Year's Day,* and the first 3 weeks of January. The museum is famous for its vivid models and dioramas. Chief among them is one of the great artificial ports called Mulberry Harbor B, which was built because the coast had no natural protection. Eighteen old merchant ships were scuttled to form the first shelter behind which smaller units could unload their cargoes. Soon after the ships were scuttled, more than 100 concrete pontoons each weighing between 3,000 and 6,000 tons were towed into position by tugs, and they too were sunk, forming a breakwater 7 miles long. (Forty of them remain more or less intact, although their life expectancy in the rough seas of the Channel was estimated at less than 2 years; they can be seen in a semicircle offshore.) Pierheads, floating steel platforms, also were established for unloading purposes. These were linked to the shore by floating roadways made of small pontoons connected by "Bailey" bridges, each about 4,000 feet long and capable of withstanding the weight of jeeps and other heavy cargo. Just 6 days after the invasion had begun 326,000 men and 54,000 jeeps had been put ashore. A model of this stupendous operation can be seen at the museum. Also on view are parachutes of the 101st and 82nd Airborne divisions, aerial bombs, high explosives, uniforms of various regiments and squadrons, and other items such as General Matthew Ridgway's jump boots. A Royal Navy film shot on June 6, 1944, shows what took place around Arromanches that day.

A few miles beyond Arromanches, a turnoff to the right leads down to the fishing harbor of Port-en-Bessin, a cleft in the cliffs at the mouth of the Drôme River, where American and British forces finally made contact on June 8. Even in summer, Port-en-Bessin is relatively quiet, although the granite jetties occasionally are jammed with fishermen, and the action at the early morning fish auctions on Mondays, Wednesdays, and Thursdays can be colorful.

A road to the right off D514 between Colleville-sur-mer and St.-Laurent-sur-Mer leads to the Normandy American Military Cemetery and Memorial, on a cliff right above Omaha Beach and the Channel. An overlook with an orientation table details the landing beaches. The 172½-acre cemetery contains the graves of 9,386 military personnel, including 307 unknown, each marked by a plain white marble cross or Star of David. The sight of these simple headstones in crisp, sharp rows on neatly clipped lawns is very moving. In one instance they mark where a father and son lie side by side; in about 30 others, where brothers lie next to one another.

There is another right turn off D514 at St.-Laurent onto a small road that follows the beach at sea level as far as Vierville-sur-Mer, about 1 mile (1.6 km). At the east end, a post marks the spot where the first American casualties were buried originally. The western end of this pleasant seafront road was called Dog Green on *D-Day*. This is where the heaviest casualties on Omaha took place, with the majority of the 116th Regiment killed or injured.

The church at Vierville-sur-Mer is worth noting. Its current belfry replaces one that was an important German lookout and stronghold; it was destroyed on *D-Day* by offshore shelling in order to assist the American Rangers who scaled the nearby cliffs to Pointe du Hoc.

Pointe du Hoc is reached by a short side road off D514. On *D-Day*, 225 American Rangers under Colonel James Earl Rudder climbed the 9-story-high cliffs using grappling hooks and firemen's ladders (among other equipment) amid smoke from offshore barrages and constant German fire from the clifftop. General Bradley called the operation "the most difficult assignment I ever had to give anyone." Today the clifftop that was taken and held by these men is still shell-scarred. There are potholes and gun emplacements, though they are now covered with grass, gorse, and brambles, and linnets and larks twitter and trill where guns blazed. At the cliff's edge is a modest stone column that reproduces the rock needle just offshore that gives the "pointe" its name. The dedication reads: "To the Ranger Commandos of the 116th Infantry."

About a mile (1.6 km) after D514 runs into N13 is Isigny-sur-Mer, which was liberated on June 9, 1944. Today, the town is famous throughout France for its butter. Carentan, the next town on the route, another prosperous dairy farming market town, is bordered by the marshes typical of the southeastern corner of the Cotentin Peninsula. There is a memorial to the 101st Airborne Division near the Hôtel de Ville (Town Hall).

Beyond Carentan, turn off N13 onto D913, passing Ste.-Marie-du-Mont to reach the monument at La Madeleine at the south end of Utah Beach on route D421. The memorial consists of a former German blockhouse honoring the 1st (American) Engineer Special Brigade. Route D421 follows the coast, though the sea is often obscured by dunes. Utah Beach stretches for nearly 2 miles, as far as Les Dunes-de-Varreville. This is where the 4th American Division met tough German resistance on *D-Day*, although before nightfall they were able to meet up with the paratroopers who had been dropped inland around Ste.-Mère-Eglise. Just off the road marked Route des Alliés at Les Dunes-de-Varreville, a pinkish granite marker, similar in shape to the forward part of a ship, is a reminder of French General le Clerc's arrival on August 1, 1944, with his 2nd Armored Division.

A little beyond Varreville, turn left and pick up D15 to Ste.-Mère-Eglise, where parachutists of the 82nd and 101st Airborne dropped just before dawn on *D-Day*. Unfortunately, this air drop wasn't the surprise it was meant to be, since a fire had awakened just about everyone in town, including the German soldiers. Many American soldiers were shot as they touched the ground. The best known of these soldiers was John Steele, who came down on top of the church spire and dangled there for hours, pretending to be dead. Outside the Town Hall there is the first milestone of Liberty Way, marked out by the American troops as they crossed France. The *Musée des Troupes Aéroportées* (Airborne Troops Museum) contains documents, photographs, arms, uniforms, and, outside, a Sherman tank — all part of the story of the early morning hours of the invasion. Some of the exhibits give a special, almost intimate flavor to the events of those historic days: dog tags, a chocolate vitamin ration, a French phrase book, and a photograph of a soldier reclining in front of a wooden sign reading Ste.-Mère-Eglise. (Open daily April through September, weekends in winter; closed mid-December to mid-January; Pl. du 6-Juin; phone: 33-41-41-35.) The town has commemorated *D-Day* with a stained glass window over the main portal of its 13th-century stone church that depicts the Virgin Mary and Child surrounded by American soliders parachuting from the sky to liberate Ste.-Mère-Eglise. From here you either can take an hour's drive back to Caen via N13 or stop at Bayeux along the way.

EATING OUT: *Manoir d'Hastings* – At this restored 17th-century country manor a few miles from Caen, the emphasis is on seafood and on a "lightened" version of Norman cuisine. Local ciders also are served and used in many dishes. One Michelin star. Closed the first week of February. 18 Av. de la Côte de Nacre, Bénouville (phone: 31-44-62-43). Expensive.

La Marine – Not promising from the outside, this restaurant is comfortable and relaxing, with views of the sea through huge picture windows. It is as good a place as any to try a *marmite*. Depending on what's available that day, the stew may contain sole, turbot, *lotte* (monkfish), crab, mussels, and scallops. The fish soup is scarcely less substantial, and one serving usually is enough for at least three helpings. Closed December through the first week of February. 5 Quai Letourneur, Port-en-Bessin (phone: 31-21-70-08). Expensive to moderate.

Auberge Normande – Brill with oysters is among the specialties that draw people again and again to this Norman restaurant with one Michelin star. Guests also appreciate the fire that is kept roaring whenever there is a nip in the air. Closed Sunday nights and Mondays off-season, 1 week in October, and 3 weeks in February. 17 Bd. de Verdun, Carentan (phone: 33-42-02-99). Moderate.

BAYEUX: Few towns in the world are famous for a piece of embroidery, but such a possession has indeed made this beautifully preserved town in the north of France celebrated for centuries. Bayeux could claim notice for other reasons. It has a fine cathedral, ancient streets, and it is the only town close to the Norman coast unscarred by the devastation of World War II. It also has a colorful history. Bayeux was an important city in Caesar's day, and successive waves of Celts, Saxons, and Vikings later came to occupy the city. Around 1050, William the Conqueror gave the episcopal land here to his half-brother Odo, who, as bishop, built the original cathedral. In ensuing years, the Conqueror's three sons engaged in various power struggles for the English throne and the duchy of Normandy. It was during one of these conflicts that Henry I came to Bayeux and burned the cathedral along with the rest of the city (most of the present structure dates from the 13th century). Much later, in the 19th century, the novelist Honoré de Balzac used to enjoy well-earned respites in Bayeux, and on June 7, 1944, Bayeux became the first town in France to be liberated by the Allies.

But it is the tapestry that draws most people here — justifiably, since it is one of the great treasures of France. Called in France *La Tapisserie de la Reine Mathilde* (Queen Matilda's Tapestry, or sometimes simply the Bayeux Tapestry), it is on display daily at *Centre Guillaume-le-Conquérant* (Rue de Nesmond; phone: 31-92-05-48). The tapestry, 19 inches wide and 231 feet long, tells the story of the events surrounding the Norman conquest of England, including the flight of the English after King Harold's death in the Battle of Hastings. Legend has it that the tapestry was commissioned by Bishop Odo and worked by William's wife, Matilda, and her ladies-in-waiting, although more prosaic minds have insisted that the stitching suggests it was sewn by Saxon women in England. Regardless, the tapestry is a remarkable and lively document consisting of 58 distinct scenes, each with a Latin legend summarizing the picture. The costumes, uniforms, food, boats, furniture, and pets of the period are all vividly illustrated, and the borders are decorated with an awesome bestiary of real and imaginary monsters. The tapestry is laid out in a glass case and can be followed section by section with an excellent commentary in English on a listening device. It originally was kept in the cathedral, one of the few major churches in lower Normandy to escape damage in World War II.

The two Romanesque towers with 13th-century Gothic spires that dominate Bayeux and the surrounding countryside belong to the Cathédrale Notre-Dame on Rue du Bienvenu. Entering the cathedral from the west door, one is immediately struck by the formidable Romanesque arches of the nave contrasting with the light, airy Gothic arches directly below. The walls of the nave are profusely decorated with saints, leaves, flowers, and abstract designs as well as with various creatures both exotic and mythical. The nine chapels all date from the first half of the 14th century. In the Chapelle de Bonne Nouvelle, an extraordinary stone tableau shows the Virgin with all the sacred symbols connected with her. The Chapelle de St.-Michel has a 15th-century fresco worked in a variety of blues and pinks showing Mary's Visitation to Elizabeth following the Annunciation.

Behind the cathedral is the *Musée Baron Gérard* in the charming Place des Tribunaux (open daily; phone: 31-92-14-21). Lacework, for which Bayeux was famous, and local porcelain are important among the museum's collections.

On Saturdays, Bayeux is enlivened by brightly dressed shoppers on Rue St.-Jean, the town's main shopping street, as well as on Place St.-Patrice, which is transformed into a bustling market with stalls selling clothes, bric-a-brac, finely bound old books, and especially food. From the beautiful, fortified farms of the surrounding Bessin countryside and from the nearby channel ports come farmers and fishermen with refrigerated trailers laden with cheeses, especially Normandy's own camembert, pont l'evêque, and *livarot,* seafood, *charcuterie,* and vegetables and fruit — predominantly apples in the fall.

The countryside east of Bayeux, between highway N13 and the coast, is considered one of the most beautiful and serene parts of Normandy. Along N13 near Caen the landscape tends to be flat — acres and acres of fields of grain; closer to the coast, tiny roads undulate through gentle valleys and around modest hills and twist through copses. An interesting architectural note is that the farmhouses are not half-timbered as in the neighboring Pays d'Auge around Lisieux and in the Pays de Caux, but are built of stone. Often these farmhouses are quite large, with arched stone gateways and barns that look like small fortified châteaux.

From Bayeux, it is possible to wander along dozens of very appealing country roads that ramble from Bayeux to points north and east, but we suggest taking N13 southeast for a short distance, then picking up D35 and following it to St.-Gabriel-Brécy. Here is an 11th-century priory, a delightfully haphazard conglomeration of buildings with towers, turrets, arched windows, and stone entrances, staircases, and balconies. It is now a horticultural college for the region, but permission to look around can be obtained at the reception office. About a mile (1.6 km) farther is Creully, one of the most perfectly preserved feudal villages in Normandy. At the adjacent community of Creullet is a charming manor house in a pasture, where General Montgomery established his headquarters in a trailer just after *D-Day.* In Creully itself is a château (with parts dating from the 12th through the 16th century), which was the BBC's headquarters just after the invasion. This building, standing in lordly fashion on a hill above the River Seulles, is now the town hall and can usually be visited every day.

From Creully, continue south on D22 and pick up D141 to Château Fontaine-Henry, home of the family d'Harcourt for centuries and one of the triumphs of Renaissance domestic architecture in Normandy. The château is most notable for its steeply pitched roof, which is actually taller than the buildings it caps. Inside is a fine Gothic staircase dating from the reign of François I, and a charming private chapel is on the grounds. In the main room there is a portrait by Mignard of the infant Louis XIV. (Open

Wednesdays, weekends, and holidays from *Easter* through May and mid-September through October; daily except Tuesdays and Fridays from June through mid-September; closed November through *Easter;* phone: 31-80-00-42.)

CHECKING IN: *D'Argouges* – This 18th-century mansion has become a comfortable hotel combining Old World charm with modern amenities. The 25 rooms and suites face either the inner courtyard or the back garden. Breakfast is served in the dining room, but there is no restaurant. Television set available on request. 21 Rue St.-Patrice, Bayeux (phone: 31-92-88-86). Moderate.

EATING OUT: *Lion d'Or* – The best restaurant in Bayeux, perhaps in Normandy, it has been open since 1640 and in the same family since 1929. The entrance is through a cobblestone courtyard overlooked by windows with red awnings and boxes of red geraniums. A menu of classic Norman cooking features brill, lobster, sole, salmon, and other favorites. Service is friendly and unhurried. There are 30 clean, airy rooms upstairs, all with bathrooms; in summer, half-board only. One Michelin star. Closed mid-December to mid-January. 71 Rue St.-Jean, Bayeux (phone: 31-92-06-90). Moderate.

En Route from Bayeux – Take D572, turning almost immediately onto D67 for about 3 miles (5 km) to the sign on the left saying Abbaye de Mondaye. Although this 18th-century abbey of the Prémontré's order (phone: 31-92-58-11) is open only for guided tours on Sunday afternoons, the classical church and conventual buildings can be seen at any time. In the manner of the period they form a graceful unity, often offset by cows grazing almost up to the abbey walls. Continue along D67 until it meets D13, then turn right to the Château de Balleroy, built in the early 1600s by François Mansart, for whom the mansard roof is named. The symmetrical main buildings are built of brick and stone, with gardens by Le Nôtre adding to the overall formality. The painted ceiling in one of the halls shows classical allegories of the four seasons and contains portraits by Mignard of Louis XIII, Anne of Austria, Louis XIV, and Madame de Maintenon. The château also houses the *Musée de Ballons* (Museum of Balloon Flight), with old prints, blueprints, maps, documents, and instruments pertaining to lighter-than-air flight from the experiments of the Montgolfier brothers in the late 1700s to the present. Among the interesting dioramas is one showing the part dirigibles played in the *D-Day* invasions. (Open daily except Wednesdays from mid-April through October; phone: 31-21-60-61.)

Continue on D13 through Cérisy de Forêt (phone: 33-56-10-01) to the ruins of the 11th-century abbey (open Sundays and holidays from April through October), which has *son et lumière* shows on Saturday evenings from mid-July through August. Since the Revolution the church has had only three bays (there were once seven), but it still is imposing, especially when seen through the trees across the nearby meadows. Inside, the Romanesque choir with its simple oak stalls is considered by experts to be the finest in Normandy. The 13th-century conventual buildings, the chapel, the porter's lodge, and the hall of justice have been converted into a museum containing 14th- and 15th-century religious manuscripts and books and 16th- and 17th-century furniture. Retracing route D13 from Cérisy toward Balleroy, turn right on D572 (which becomes D972) into St.-Lô.

ST.-LÔ: So devastated was this ancient town in the 1944 Battle of Normandy that it was dubbed "the capital of the ruins." One of the very few buildings to escape complete destruction was the church of Notre-Dame, which today has been almost completely rebuilt, although some portions were left damaged as a memorial to those terrible times. For centuries St.-Lô was an important fortified city, and the ramparts — ironically, beautifully exposed now as a result of the bombardments — are a favorite promenade from which to view the rebuilt town. The museum in the basement of the

Hôtel de Ville (Town Hall) is worth a visit for a series of eight Flemish tapestries worked in Bruges in the 16th century. They provide a humorous, down-to-earth glimpse of peasant life, showing the flora, fauna, work implements, and musical instruments that would have been part of the contemporary Flemish scene. The museum also has a collection of portraits of the Matignon-Grimaldi family, ancestors in a circuitous line of the Prince of Monaco. There also are paintings by Corot, Rousseau, and Boudin. (Closed Tuesdays; Pl. du Général-de-Gaulle; phone: 33-57-43-80.)

Continue along D972 to Coutances.

 CHECKING IN/EATING OUT: *Crémaillère* – Close to the ramparts, this restaurant sticks to a fairly simple menu. There also are 12 clean and modestly furnished rooms. Closed Saturdays and mid-December to mid January. 27 Rue du Belle, St.-Lô (phone: 33-57-14-68). Moderate.

COUTANCES: This city on a hill is dominated by a cathedral that can be seen from whichever direction you approach: a gray stone beacon that appears almost silver in sunlight. Go to the Place du Parvis for your first close look at the west façade, which has two towers with spires and pinnacles. The cathedral was begun in 1030 but ravaged by fire in 1218, and soon after a Gothic structure was superimposed on the original shell. The result is a fine example of Norman Gothic, notable for its harmonious proportions. Especially interesting is the large octagonal lantern tower, which crowns the transept and reaches a height of about 135 feet, and the chapels, which are separated from one another by delicately worked stone screens. The central chapel in the apse is much revered locally as the setting for the 14th-century statue of the Virgin known as Our Lady of Coutances. The St. Francis Chapel has a 17th-century wood carving showing Judas's betrayal of Christ with a kiss. The three 13th-century windows in the north transept depict St. George, St. Blaise, and St. Thomas à Becket.

The Jardin Public (Public Garden) is quite fine, with terraces and rose-filled flowerbeds, stone staircases leading down grassy slopes, and lots of trees. The gardens are open from 8 AM to 8 PM in summer, when there is a son et lumière involving the gardens and the cathedral, and from 9 AM to 5 PM in winter. The town's small museum (2 Rue Quesnel-Morinière, Coutances; phone: 33-45-11-92; generally closed Sunday mornings and Tuesdays) has an interesting bust of Emperor Hadrian, and among what remains of its collection of paintings (much damaged in World War II) is a Rubens.

Follow D971 south to Granville.

GRANVILLE: Granville is basically a town with a split personality. The old upper town, planted firmly on a promontory surrounded by ramparts, is seen to its best advantage on a sunny day (it looks rather grim and gray otherwise). The church of Notre-Dame, on the summit of the Roc de Granville in the upper town, looks out over the ocean with all the certainty of canonized granite. The seaward views from the upper town are stunning. The newer lower town, with its port and 19th-century resort hotels, is less appealing.

EATING OUT: *Le Phare* – This eatery has a terrace and a view of the hustle and bustle of Granville's harbor, and the food has hints of nouvelle cuisine about it. The seafood mousse and lamb chops in tarragon sauce are among the tastiest dishes. Closed Tuesday evenings and Wednesdays except in July and August, December 20 through January, and the last 2 weeks of September. 11 Rue du Port, Granville (phone: 33-50-12-94). Moderate.

En Route from Granville – The most picturesque route is the turning and twisting coast road, D911, which occasionally has splendid views over Mont-St.-Michel Bay and distant prospects of the abbey itself, especially from Cabane Vauban. It is a favorite spot for viewing the mount and the coast of Brittany.

AVRANCHES: Avranches is chiefly famous for having such a splendid view of Le Mont St.-Michel, especially at sunset in late spring or early fall. It is most romantic by moonlight, when the great rock and its crowning glory, La Merveille (the Marvel), swim against a shimmering silver backdrop of sea, sand, rivulets, and tides. The best spot for seeing what is certainly one of the world's most famous silhouettes is from the viewing table on the terrace of the Jardin des Plantes (Botanical Gardens), on Place Carnot. It was a bishop of Avranches, St. Aubert, who was initially responsible for establishing a place of worship on the nearby rocky islet in the bay, though only after some prodding — literally speaking, if legend is to be believed — by St. Michael the Archangel. Aubert's skull, with a dent in it where Michael somewhat zealously drove home his point, is one of the relics now housed in the St. Gervase Basilica (Pl. St.-Gervase). This, together with some superb relics of the Middle Ages, can be seen by contacting the sacristan. Manuscripts from or connected with the monastery of Le Mont St.-Michel and dating from the 8th to the 15th century are some of the principal holdings of Avranches's museum (closed Tuesdays and November through March; Pl. Jean de St.-Avit; phone: 33-68-31-89). Among these are Abelard's famous *Sic et Non* (a collection of religious writings by the church hierarchy), an account by Abbot Robert de Torigni on the founding of Le Mont St.-Michel, and wonderful illuminated manuscripts. The museum also has rooms and artifacts illustrating the life and work of the people of rural Normandy, including the interior of a farm kitchen, with benches, tables, dressers, and armoires.

Avranches also is where Henry II of England did his first public penance (in 1172) for the murder of Thomas à Becket, a deed performed on the orders of Abbot Torigni of Le Mont St.-Michel. The scene took place at the old cathedral. Though the cathedral was destroyed in 1794, the stone where he knelt in repentance can still be seen in La Plate-forme, near the police station, off Bd. des Abrincates.

LE MONT ST.-MICHEL: Victor Hugo called it "the pyramid of the seas" while to Guy de Maupassant it was "a fantastic manor"; indeed, it is hard to talk about the abbey on the island mount without resorting to simile or metaphor. Whether you see Le Mont St.-Michel first from Granville, from the public gardens at Avranches, or from any number of side roads that extend toward it from the coasts of Normandy and Brittany, it looks magical and mystical; profane and sacred; something from a fairy tale or an ancient saga.

It can be reached by car via the causeway that leads from La Digue, the small mainland village opposite the rock; but the ideal approach is to walk across the causeway, stopping first to look at the mount and its extraordinary assemblage of buildings from the bridge over the Couesnon River on the landward side of the causeway. There, when the tide is in, you can see Le Mont St.-Michel twice, as a jagged and formidable reality and as a shimmering, mysterious watery reflection. The walk across the causeway, slightly less than a mile, is an essential part of experiencing the island and its history. At first the path is a bit rocky, but it soon levels out so that one can concentrate on the shades and shadows as it comes more and more into focus, the vague gray shapes slowly turning to precise forms and lines.

Legend has it that Michael the Archangel himself wanted a chapel or oratory built on what was then known as Mont-Tombe, a rocky outcrop in the forest. With the casual facility ascribed to such luminaries, he appeared in 708 to St. Aubert, Bishop of Avranches, suggesting that a sanctuary be built on the mount in his honor. Aubert, it is said, was somewhat skeptical about the project, and it was only after the archangel had prodded him hard enough to leave a dent in his skull that he decided that, the forest notwithstanding, a small church might not be impossible. Accordingly, St. Aubert dutifully constructed a small oratory on the island. (Geologists say some phenomenon, probably tidal waves, occurred in the region during the first part of the 8th century, which would explain the sinking of the forest around the mount.)

But the abbey had its real beginnings in 966 when Richard I, Duke of Normandy, brought Benedictine monks to the site and began building a grander Le Mont St.-Michel. Most of what remains of the Norman Romanesque parts of the abbey were completed during the 11th and 12th centuries (much was destroyed in a 13th-century fire). This was also the period in which the monastery became a powerful force in Normandy; the abbot soon became the feudal lord over dozens of nearby villages and other fiefdoms and usually played an important role at the ducal court. While a reputation for sanctity was not always prevalent, a reputation for learning and miracles soon attached itself to the mount and its denizens.

The attention and fame that Le Mont St.-Michel enjoyed meant that ideally its buildings should be monumental, beautiful, and in harmony with the latest taste, so Flamboyant Gothic was built upon Gothic, which was built upon Romanesque, which has Carolingian foundations. Under the great Abbot Torigni, scion of a Norman noble family and chronicler of the island's history, the abbey reached the zenith of its fame and influence. Torigni's assets were worldly rather than spiritual, and he obtained royal confirmation of the abbey's fiefdoms and holdings in France and England. He received Henry II of England and was instrumental in persuading him to do penance for the murder of Thomas à Becket in front of the cathedral at Avranches. Less than 20 years after Torigni's tenure as abbot ended, Normandy had passed into the hands of the Kings of France. To ensure the good will of the abbey and those whose spiritual and temporal allegiance it commanded, Philippe Auguste showed that Capetian favor could be just as generous as Plantagenet. His munificence was instrumental in starting the construction of La Merveille (The Marvel) — as the French call the abbey church and buildings on the mount's north side, the Gothic crown on top of earlier Gothic and Romanesque buildings underneath — which was completed by 1230. The abbey continued to gain in political power, and although canonical hours were observed and mass was said daily, the monks' tasks often seemed more for the glory of the abbey than of God, and the abbey was managed not just as a community of brothers but as a small city with a comptroller, chancellor, and administrator for the vast tracts of forest in the abbatial domains.

During the 13th century, Le Mont St.-Michel's potential as a military stronghold became increasingly apparent; fortification began in earnest in the 1250s with the help of Louis IX (St. Louis). When it was completed, a garrison was maintained by the abbot with at least a token presence of soldiers of the crown always on hand to uphold the king's rights as the prelate's feudal overlord. During the long and dreary skirmishes of the Hundred Years War, its military role often seemed to supersede its spiritual one. Clearly, the close relationship between the monastery and the French crown could not escape the notice of the marauding English, and the island was the object of three major assaults in the early 1400s, all of which were repulsed even though most of Normandy was in the hands of the King of England.

Later, during the Revolution, most of Le Mont St.-Michel's treasures, pictures, and furniture were destroyed, leaving the abbey scarred and empty except for prisoners; "the Marvel" dedicated to God became a jail. Despite the mindless ravages that took place, enough remains today to satisfy even the greatest hunger for the past.

A day — at least — is needed to begin to appreciate the island and its wonders. Turning left through the Porte de l'Avancée, the outer gate, which is the only opening through the ramparts, one passes the Guardhouse and goes through a second gate called the Porte du Roi (King's Gate) onto the Grande-Rue. This narrow street of granite houses, some with mullioned windows and windowboxes full of geraniums, is the secular heart of Le Mont St.-Michel. A proliferation of souvenir shops and restaurants has not destroyed the street's charm, although the summertime throng can be unnerving. The street climbs past small garden plots nestling behind low stone walls to the medieval Eglise St.-Pierre, the island's parish church. The church is totally overshadowed by the abbey physically and historically, but it is well worth a stop. Inside, it is dim and damp, with the smell of the sea permeating the solid stone walls. In the morning you may see pilgrims singing hymns in front of a burnished and bejeweled statue of St. Michael battling a dragon. The street climbs up past more terraced lawns and rose gardens to the Ramparts, where there is a fine view over the great tidal flats to the Grand Degré (Great Stair), which leads in turn to the only entrance to the abbey. Past the fortified gateway under the Châtelet, stairs lead to the Salles des Gardes (Guards' Room), where a small entrance fee is paid. More steps leading up pass the abbey lodgings, the cistern, and then finally reach Gautier's Leap. Just beyond is the West Platform, an open terrace with wonderful views south to La Digue and west to Brittany.

It is here that guided tours begin (in English at 10:30 AM and 2:30 PM). For anyone unfamiliar with the abbey buildings, it is foolish to proceed without a guide since the interior is labyrinthine. From the terrace, the tour leads into the abbey church. The stained glass windows, ornaments, and furniture are gone, but the mellow pink stone of the Romanesque arches in the nave and the spartan bareness of the Flamboyant Gothic choir add up to a whole that is exceedingly graceful. In the traditional Norman Romanesque manner, the roof is supported not by vaults but by a timber ceiling. From one of the 16th-century chapels in the chancel — the second on the right — a doorway opens onto the *escalier de dentelle* (lace stairway), which leads up between elaborately carved stone balustrades to a gallery 394 feet above the sea, from which one can look across the sands and streamlets to the mainland over the heads of snarling gargoyles. Leading out of the church is a favorite spot for many people, the cloister. The garden-side perimeter here is lined with two rows of columns staggered evenly on a low wall. The garden-side capitals are plain and unadorned, but on the enclosed side there are sculpted flourishes of flowers, leaves, and vines occasionally enclosing figurines. The cloister's most interesting feature, however, not visible from inside, is that it is constructed above the Knights' Hall on the level below and not, as the center garden might suggest, on rock.

Similarly, the adjacent refectory is built over the 13th-century Guests Hall. About 50 slit windows in the refectory provide an effect of suffused light that is hard to forget. It is easy to imagine a monk reading the day's lesson from the lectern at the southern end of the hall as the brethren ate the midday or evening meal in this serene, otherworldly atmosphere. Descending to the old cloister on the next level down, one can see where the 7-foot-thick walls meet the cold, damp rock. Also on this level is the catacomb-like chapel of Notre-Dame-sous-Terre, the Chapelle de St.-Martin, with its spartan altar and simple crucifix, and the Crypte des Gros Piliers, directly underneath the chancel of the church. The two major rooms on the middle level are the Salle des Hôtes (Guests' Hall) and the Salle des Chevaliers (Knights' Hall). Although the abbey closes at 11:30 AM for 2 hours, anyone wishing to remain for the noon mass may do so. If the number of visitors is not large, they are invited into the sanctuary for the service with the Benedictine monks and sisters.

Leaving the church by the Grand Degré one passes a gate and a small souvenir shop, on the other side of which are the abbey gardens. The west end of the lower garden, above St. Aubert's Oratory (on a rock just above the beach), is the best spot from which to watch the incoming tide. It comes first as a trickle, then streamlets merge to become rivulets, pools join pools and become lagoons, until all the island except the causeway is surrounded by rippling water. Because of silting in the bay, only the highest tides of the year produce the spectacular effect for which the mount was long famous. The best times are in March, September, and sometimes October. Tide tables are available at most tourist offices along the Norman coast. As the tide comes in, improperly parked cars are sometimes inundated with salt water. To obtain a parking spot on high ground, arrive before 8 AM. (High tide warnings are always posted to advise visitors where and for how long they may park.) Le Mont St.-Michel is open all year from 9 to 11:30 AM and from 1:30 to 4 PM mid-May through September. Additional summertime hours (9 PM to midnight) now allow tourists to visit the abbey at night. The 50-minute guided tour features a sound and light show along the 1-mile walk. For more information, contact the tourist office (phone: 33-60-14-30).

The tide also cuts off the St. Aubert Oratory, which is outside the ramparts. To reach it (after making sure that the tide is well and truly out), walk around the rocks to the left of the Gabriel Tower. It is a simple stone edifice with a small, humble altar that can be seen through an aperture in the door. It may have been all that the archangel wanted.

There are a handful of small guesthouses right on the mount, which are delightful for an overnight stay — not particularly for their fine accommodations and amenities, but simply because Le Mont St.-Michel minus the daytime crowds is a completely different experience. Hearing your footsteps echo on medieval cobblestone streets while beholding the abbey washed in moonlight is unforgettable.

CHECKING IN: *Altea K* – The best motel of its kind near the mount, now that every room has its own bathroom. The beds are quite comfortable and the long white Formica desks fitted against the walls are ideal for spreading out all the accumulated bric-a-brac of travel. Closed from mid-November to mid-March. Rte. D976 at Le Pré Salé (phone: 33-60-14-18). Moderate.

Relais du Roy – Just on the mainland side of the causeway to the mount, this is the best of three or four motel-type hostelries in the immediate neighborhood. An old gray stone part of the building lends the place some character. The 27 bedrooms (some overlook Le Mont St.-Michel Bay), all with bath, shower, and toilet, though sparsely furnished, are attractively decorated in off-white tones. Fresh flowers usually are added for a touch of color. Two large stone fireplaces (there's a third in the bar) dominate the dining room, in the middle of which is a refectory table generously laden with fresh fruit, tarts, and other desserts. The *agneau pré-salé* (lamb grazed in saltwater marshes) is splendid, served with green beans and potatoes au gratin. Also good are the *omelettes à la Mère Poulard* and the *assiettes de fruits de mer* (platter of mixed seafood). Closed Tuesdays and mid-November through mid-March. Rte. D976 at La Digue (phone: 33-60-14-25). Moderate.

EATING OUT: *Mère Poulard* – This restaurant is famous for its huge ome-lettes, which are actually more like soufflés; the most dramatic version of *les omelettes à la Mère Poulard* is flambéed, for dessert. Another specialty is *agneau pré-salé* (lamb grazed in saltwater marshes) served with *flageolets* (beans). The dining room lives up to its location, with flagstone floors, a fireplace, and gleaming glassware. Open daily till 9:30 PM. Le Mont St.-Michel (phone: 33-60-14-01). Expensive to moderate.

Brittany

Surrounded on three sides by water, Brittany always has been something of an anomaly with respect to the rest of France. Something quiet and mysterious in the nature of the land itself, the dark mountains and the forests that once covered the inland sections, and the sea that crashes on the shoreline boulders and cliffs inspired a deep mysticism in the people from the very beginning, as early as 3500 BC, when a race of early men began constructing huge monuments of rough stone slabs weighing several tons each. The population claims as ancestors the Gauls, who arrived in the 6th century BC and called the country Armor (the country by the sea) and Argoat (the country of wood); the Romans, who came at about the time of Christ; and the Celts, who were fleeing the Angles and the Saxons in Britain in the 5th century. The Celts brought their keenly felt Catholicism, their saints (whose numbers they increased by granting sainthood to some of their own leaders), the seeds of a religious approach to life that found fertile ground in the Breton spirit, and a Celtic language not unlike Welsh, which immediately opposed itself to early French and reached its zenith in the wake of one Nominoé, who established a dynasty that controlled the area for a century.

Thus established, Breton independence from the then nascent French monarchy was guarded fiercely against further onslaughts for 400 tumultuous years. But in the end, it was no match for the tremendous power of the throne. Anne of Brittany married two French kings, Charles VIII and his successor, Louis XII, but maintained control of the duchy for herself. Her daughter Claude was another matter entirely. More interested in gardening than politics (she gave the world the species of plum known as the Reine Claude), she married Anne's husbands' successor, François de Angoulême, and quickly was persuaded to allow the duchy to become part of the legacy of their son Henri II, the future King of France. Brittany was lost.

Yet, even as a part of France, the province always stood apart. Habitually resistant to any central control, the Bretons banded together against the throne in the 18th century and fomented the Revolution in its early years; then, when the rest of France arose, they fought passionately on the other side; anti-Revolutionary Breton peasants known as the Chouans were engineering revolts as late as 1832. During World War II, the Bretons again resisted control by outsiders — this time the Germans. World War II was a great turning point in the history of the area. Young men for the first time in Breton history left the province by the thousands, and when they came back, it was with a broader worldview that seemed to dim the clarity of the folk legends of Brittany's past. At the same time, young people began leaving their homes to seek their fortune in the large cities, further eroding the culture. The cost of traditional Breton furniture and clothing rose; modern clothing and modern furniture were inexpensive and efficient by comparison.

Thus the traditional became a luxury rather than the outgrowth of a simple lifestyle. Nowadays, travelers seldom see the traditional lace headdresses known as *coiffes* except on great holidays, even in rural hamlets and villages.

Yet the legacy of the past remains. Most obvious to the first-time visitor are the strange Breton place names, comprised in part of Celtic words — *coat, goat, goët,* and *hoët,* which signify "wood" (as in Huelgoat, high wood, and Penhoët, end of the wood); *ker,* which means "village" or "house" (as in Kermaria, Mary's village); *loc,* which means "holy place" (as in Locmaria, Mary's place), or Locronan, St. Ronan's place); *pleu, plo, ploe,* and *plou,* which mean "parish"; *tre* or *tref,* which means "parish subdivision."

Then there are the legends, which the people nourish by the score. The story of Tristan and Iseult is said to have taken place here. And it was in the Forest of Brocéliande, now known as the Forest of Paimpont, that Christ's disciple Joseph of Arimathea is believed to have vanished with the Holy Grail. In the same forest, the renowned Merlin is said to have met and been inflamed by love for the fairy Viviane, who enclosed him in a magic circle in order to keep him forever. Then there is the story of the good King Gradlon, who reigned over a section of Brittany known as Cornouaille in an exquisitely beautiful capital city, Is, which was contained from the sea by a dike. Seduced by the devil in the form of a suitor, his beautiful but dissolute daughter stole the key to the seawall and flooded the city. Gradlon escaped on horseback and was saved only after he tossed his offspring into the sea — but Is was lost, and Gradlon went to Quimper to rebuild his kingdom. His daughter turned into a mermaid and charmed sailors to their deaths.

The people's considerable religious fervor, which went hand in hand with their belief in such legends, found an enduring expression in stone. Nine cathedrals, some 20 large churches, country churches and chapels by the thousand, and even greater numbers of calvaries and simple crosses were erected at crossroads throughout the province as expressions of thanks for prayers answered. The native building material, granite, was so hard as to be nearly impossible to cut. Yet, motivated by their faith, artisans wrought wonders with the substance.

When the desired effects could not be achieved in stone, they turned to wood and carved organ casings, pulpits, baptistries, choir screens, rood screens, rood beams, confessional enclosures, and other structures in the church; not a square inch was left unadorned. Thus, in many Breton houses of worship, there is a striking contrast between the simplicity of the stonework and the profusion of wooden ornament. The liveliness of the individual sculptures in both stone and wood further distinguishes Breton cathedrals and churches from their Norman counterparts, as do their ornate and imposing belfries and handsome porches on the south wall (used in the past for meetings of parish notables), which can be found even on small chapels.

In some communities, there are the uniquely Breton parish closes as well. Built primarily in the 15th and 16th centuries, these consist of the church; a calvary carved with episodes from the Passion, a type of monument that harks back to the menhirs of Brittany's earliest inhabitants; a cemetery; a triumphal arch guarding its entrance and heralding the arrival of the just into heaven; and, adjoining the cemetery, a charnel house, used to house bones that were exhumed when a cemetery ran out of room. (Its proximity to the church vividly recalls how close death was to life in those days of plagues and wars.) That Bretons saw it not without a sense of humor is revealed in an inscription near a bas-relief that portrays death menacing a group of figures from all walks of life on one of Brittany's largest ossuaries: "I'll kill you all," it reads.

Perhaps the belief in such legends is not what it once was, but neither does disbelief hold sway. Many Breton churches and chapels are the scenes of great religious processions known as *pardons,* and they still draw huge crowds for long walks, masses, and bonfires. If the celebrants do not believe as unreservedly as their grandparents, neither do they turn their back upon the blessings that their participation may bring, so they join the throngs and make a holiday of it. If the saint to which the *pardon* is devoted can heal colic or headaches, bring justice or wealth, or satisfy other earthly needs, so much the better.

A visitor sees this tapestry of fact, folkway, legend, and belief against the backdrop of one of the greatest landscapes in France. Fringing Brittany is a seacoast so notched and indented, so cliffbound, gorge-riven, and seapounded that the simple word "rocky" does not do it justice. Formed by movements of the earth that took place millions of years ago and by the tidal erosion, the action of the rivers, and the storms of the centuries, the coast consists of huge piles of rocks, tall escarpments, grand peninsulas, and bizarre rock formations. Inland, the woods that the Gauls called Argoat have been effectively decimated, but in a few spots it's possible to envision the dark mystery of the country that nourished the legends. The patchwork of fields and pastures separated by thickly overgrown hedgerows known as *bocages* lends a serenity to the place that makes for exceptionally restorative touring.

Neither is the food designed to exhaust the digestive tract. Breton fare is plain, by and large. But here the ingredients are so fine as to require little in the way of elaborate cooking. The lambs that graze on the salt meadows within sight of the sea, the cauliflowers and artichokes, onions, peas, strawberries, and string beans that grow on the edge of the escarpments along the north coast, draw an additional tang from the salt air. There are excellent lobsters — *homards,* which resemble the Maine crustaceans, as well as *langoustes,* which are more like the creatures of the Pacific coast. Oysters, *huîtres,* abound. They show up on menus (usually raw, on the half shell), at roadside stands, and in every fishing port. *Bélons,* one of the two main varieties, are mild, smooth-shelled, firm, and subtly flavored — the truffles of oysterdom. *Portugaises* have rough shells and a briny taste. Both are bred in the oyster beds in the Gulf of Morbihan, and then shipped for fattening to estuaries in other sections of Brittany and nearby areas, where they gain a distinctive flavor from the mix of food substances in the water — and at the same time acquire the name by which they are known in the market. (*Cancalaises,* for instance, are oysters fattened around Cancale.) Fish generally is broiled or poached or served with a straightforward sauce. The simple soup known as the *cotriade* — Brittany's answer to bouillabaisse — is about as elaborate as the local cuisine gets. The crêpes also are worth noting. These thin Breton pancakes are served in *crêperies* in almost every small town, and it's easy to make a meal of them — with those made of buckwheat flour and stuffed with cheese or tomatoes or bacon or other hearty ingredients as a main course, and with the more delicate ones made of wheat flour and stuffed with butter and sugar or jam, perhaps flamed with a liqueur, as dessert. The cost is low, and the meal filling and delightful — especially when consumed with a bottle of Breton cider, which is mildly apple flavored, not very sweet, and gently alcoholic.

The route outlined below shuttles between Armor and Argoat and takes in fishing villages and inland market towns, sophisticated resorts and back-woods farming centers. With the exception of Nantes, which provides an introduction to the folk art of the past and to some of the more interesting periods in Breton history, the tour avoids big cities — including Rennes and Brest, which are on the whole less rewarding for visitors than the countryside. Our suggestion is that you use the route as an outline. Then, with a detailed map, follow the unnumbered byways to the *artisanats* (craft shops), *moulins* (mills), *chapelles* (chapels), or châteaux signposted off the main roads. In general, the smaller and more obscure the road, the more appealing the scenery, and detours help avoid the congestion of primary routes at the height of the season. Note: The recent inauguration of the new *TGV-Atlantic* high-speed train has reduced travel time from Paris to Rennes or Brest to just over 2 hours — a good reason to think about taking a train to either of these cities and, on arrival, renting a car to begin a Breton circuit. (Major car rental companies have kiosks at or near the train stations.)

May and September are ideal times for visiting Brittany — the weather is fine and there are no crowds. From October through March, increasing numbers of hotels and restaurants post signs proclaiming *fermeture annuelle* (annual closing), so that it sometimes seems that whole communities have turned into ghost towns. However, there usually are a few tourist facilities open in every town. In summer, reserving hotel rooms and seatings at well-known restaurants far in advance is a must. No matter when you travel, expect to pay $75 and up for a double room in hostelries listed as expensive, from $55 to $75 for those described as moderate, and under $55 at places classed as inexpensive. A meal for two will run $80 and up in an expensive restaurant, $50 to $80 in a moderate one, and under $50 in one that is rated inexpensive. Prices do not include wine or drinks. Service usually is included.

NANTES: Its outskirts now predictably full of auto dealers and apartment towers, Brittany's largest city became a prosperous shipping center thanks to its location about 30 miles from the point at which the Loire River flows into the ocean. During the 18th century, before the abolition of the lucrative slave trade between West Africa and the Antilles after the Revolution and before the later tonnage increases made it impossible for ships to travel upstream as far as Nantes, the town laid out gracious boulevards edged by stately rows of trees, and wealthy merchants built themselves fine mansions. A walk that takes in the Place du Pilori, the Place Royale, the Rue Crébillon, the Place Graslin, the octagonal Place Mellinet with its eight identical townhouses, and the Cours Cambronne, a smaller version of Paris's Jardin du Luxembourg, will show off a number of mansions. It also passes scores of glossy shops; the 19th-century *Palais Dobrée*, now a museum filled with its wealthy builder's collections of prehistoric and medieval antiquities, religious relics, and paintings; and the Passage Pommeraye, a mid-19th-century shopping arcade with polished wood floors, a glass roof, pedestrian bridges, and much ornate cast ironwork.

In addition, Nantes offers the Cathédrale de St.-Pierre et St.-Paul, which also is in the center of the city on the Place St.-Pierre. This truly is a fabulous structure, from its elegantly carved façade to its soaring interior. Unlike most Breton cathedrals, which are built of granite, Nantes's is constructed of Vendée stone; its lightness allowed the vaults to soar to 120 feet, about twice that of other large cathedrals in Brittany and even higher than that of Notre-Dame in Paris. The softness of the stone permitted the sculptors to give sharp definition to every bit of Flamboyant Gothic ornamentation and to outline the slender ribs and groins with a crispness difficult to achieve in granite. And unlike most other cathedrals in France built over the centuries as this one was (between 1434 and 1893), it is architecturally harmonious, its pure Gothic lines undarkened by any shadow of other building styles. There is a fine tomb for François II and his second wife, Marguerite de Foix, a memorial ordered by Anne of Brittany for her father and carved by the Breton sculptor Michel Colombe between 1502 and 1507. Note its interesting statue of Prudence, one of four corner sculptures. She is depicted holding a mirror, which stands for the future and in which is reflected the visage of an old man, representing the past (the idea being that sagacity comes from consulting the past before determining a course for the future). Also note the fine modern windows: one, 80 feet high and 17 feet wide, portrays various Breton saints in unusually intense hues of scarlet and gold; others, ingenious and surprisingly beautiful, are done in oddly shaped glass pieces shading from pale to dark gray, which give the scenes the appearance of Cubist paintings from outside.

The cathedral — like the excellent *Musée des Beaux-Arts,* one of the best of its kind in the country (closed Tuesdays; 10 Rue Georges-Clemenceau) — is very far from the little harbor towns, simple chapels, pastures, and woodlands that most people expect of Brittany. But the city's tenacious attachment to its Breton identity is not as far-fetched as first appearances would indicate. The 15th-century Château des Ducs de Bretagne (closed Tuesdays), with round towers and a placid moat edged by graceful willows in front, makes this apparent. One of the most important Breton historical structures, it was first of all the birthplace of Anne of Brittany. Rebuilt in 1466 from a 9th- or 10th-century structure by her father, it was luxurious and full of intrigue as ministers, councils, chamberlains, majordomos, secretaries, equerries, and footmen danced attendance on him and each other. In 1598, Henri IV came here to discuss the epochal Edict of Nantes, which granted freedom of worship to French Protestants. Today, the château houses three museums accessible through a spacious courtyard. Most interesting as an introduction to a tour of Brittany is the one devoted to local popular arts; *coiffes,* embroidered costumes, pottery, ironwork, and carved oak box beds and chests can be seen here in numbers not encountered elsewhere in the province. Displays are organized by region to facilitate methodical study, but even a cursory perusal turns up dozens of interesting exhibits like the array of carved wooden marriage spoons and the bright yellow mourning costumes of the Bigouden area. Also on the premises are a decorative arts museum displaying modern textiles and a maritime museum.

The Syndicat d'Initiative on the Place du Change (closed Sundays; phone: 40-47-04-51) has maps and a wealth of other material, including an inexpensive, liberally illustrated book of walking tours. It also can provide information for events such as the *Festival des Arts et Traditions Populaires,* which takes place during the first 2 weeks of July every year.

CHECKING IN: *Le Domaine d'Orvault* – Ten minutes from the center of Nantes in an attractive residential area, this luxurious establishment (a member of the Relais & Châteaux group) with 29 rooms is the logical choice for peace and quiet. The restaurant, which merits a Michelin star, is closed Monday lunch and during February. Chemin des Marais-du-Cens, Nantes (phone: 40-76-84-02). Expensive.

 EATING OUT: Pike, a local specialty, is found on many Nantes menus, either poached or in the form of the small dumplings known as *quenelles* and often doused with white butter sauce called *beurre blanc*.

Les Maraíchers – This moderndining place serves nouvelle cuisine inspired fare. Duck may be presented with turnips, for instance, or spiny lobster offered in a stew flavored with mushrooms. Closed Saturday lunch and Sundays. 21 Rue Fouré, Nantes (phone: 40-47-06-51). Expensive.

La Cigale – Chic Nantais throng to this warm, busy museum piece of a café-brasserie not so much for the food, which is simple, but for the sumptuous turn-of-the-century surroundings — heavy iron-edged doors filled with beveled glass, walls partially faced with turquoise tiles, ceilings full of gilt plaster, rosy-cheeked cherubs, and buxom damsels with masses of hair and angelic robes. 4 Pl. Graslin, Nantes (phone: 40-69-76-41). Moderate to inexpensive.

La Rôtisserie de Palais – Small and unprepossessing but very popular, with a fairly substantial menu that changes with the market's offerings. Closed Sundays. 1 Pl. Aristide-Briand, Nantes (phone: 40-89-20-12). Moderate to inexpensive.

LA BAULE: This full-blown basically middle class French resort boasts discos, a casino, a yacht harbor, villas perfumed with honeysuckle and jasmine, the pine forest known as the Bois d'Amour, and dozens of boutiques just as sophisticated as those in the South of France. It is the most famous part of this short stretch of coast west of Nantes thanks to a wide crescent of white sandy beach that stretches for some 3 miles from end to end. Protected from the wind by the pines on the dunes to the north, by the Pointe de Penchâteau on the east, and by the Pointe du Croisic on the west, it is thronged with vacationers packed bikini to bikini in season and bounded with nearly identical white high-rise hotels jammed edge to edge like giant bricks in a fortress wall. These are a sight to be sure — especially in the off-season, when tightly closed shutters conceal any evidence of human life.

 CHECKING IN/EATING OUT: *Castel Marie-Louise* – In a handsome villa, complete with gables and towers, this stylish 31-room hostelry strikes a note of Edwardian grace in the nondescript symphony of contemporary beachfront high-rises that flank it on either side. The restaurant's cuisine is elegant and inventive enough to satisfy even that bon vivant François André, who founded La Baule in the 19th century. Tennis, a saltwater swimming pool, golf, and bicycling are available at this member of the Relais & Châteaux group. Esplanade du Casino, 1 Av. Andrieu, La Baule (phone: 40-60-20-60). Expensive.

En Route from La Baule – For huge Breton cliffs, tiny new moons of beach, and sweeping ocean vistas, you have to leave La Baule and make the superscenic drive along D45, which skirts the Grande Côte between the Pointe de Penchâteau and the Pointe du Croisic. Salty Le Croisic, whose port shelters fishing boats and pleasure craft alike, has a colorful fish market, with auction action from about 7 to 10 in the morning; you can get a fine view of the coast and the *marais salants* (salt marshes) to the north from the top of Mont-Esprit, a hill constructed from ships' ballast.

From there, follow D774 through Guérande to La Roche-Bernard, an erstwhile shipbuilding center that overlooks the Vilaine River. Turn west on N165 toward Vannes and you will cross the river on a 160-foot-long suspension bridge that fairly leaps out of the cliffsides.

 CHECKING IN/EATING OUT: *Domaine du Château de Rochevilaine* – This luxurious 27-room hostelry sprawls over a rockbound nipple of land, a former estate, which thrusts into the English Channel near the mouth of the

Vilaine River. Since the guest quarters are in the old manor house and its outbuildings, each is different; some are huge, with lofty ceilings, crystal chandeliers, velvet-covered furniture, tapestries, and Oriental rugs, spacious bathrooms, and fantastic views out over the sea-pounded boulders. The dining room is particularly gracious, with its beamed ceiling, dark floors, and linen tablecloths. Closed Sunday evenings and Monday lunch in low season, and most of January and February. Pointe de Pen-Lan, Billiers-Muzillac (phone 97-41-69-27). Expensive.

QUESTEMBERT: Zigging and zagging between *armor* and *argoat* — between sea and woodland — a traveler's next logical stop after Nantes is this minuscule town full of buildings constructed of a steely gray granite that seems hard and implacable even by Breton standards. The 16th-century covered market pavilion that dominates the town, crowded on all sides by more stores, is particularly attractive inside, where you can see the massive timbers that support the steeply pitched roof that sweeps practically to the ground.

CHECKING IN/EATING OUT: *Le Bretagne* – By the time a diner discovers that there are around 900 calories in the special "dietetic" menu that chef Georges Paineau offers at this Relais & Châteaux establishment, he probably is ready to throw caution to the wind and gobble every bite of the meal, from the langoustine-stuffed, lettuce-wrapped oysters flavored with tarragon to the last drop of espresso. The old stone structure wrapped in a tight net of vines is sheer visual delight inside, with its tapestry covered chairs, gleaming silver, and polished walnut paneling. The 6 guestrooms bring to mind the phrase *tout confort* (every comfort) with their modern bathrooms and firm double beds. Restaurant closed Sunday evenings and Mondays except in July and August; hotel closed from January to mid-March. 13 Rue St.-Michel, Questembert (phone: 97-26-11-12). Expensive.

MALESTROIT: The small bridge over the River Oust on the fringes of town is the best introduction to this charming, decidedly untouristy village. From here, the visitor sees a fine view of the stream, the *allées* of trees reflected in its still waters, and the town's mountain range of rooftops bristling with antennas, chimneys, and steeples. Curiously, in this land of steely gray granite, the town has done its building in a stone that is vaguely rust-colored streaked with shades of gray, green, and brown. Many structures along the narrow streets near the 12th- and 16th-century Eglise de St.-Gilles have carved beams adorned with folksy carvings, like the one of the *bourgeois* flailing an errant wife.

JOSSELIN: The Rohan family has been a force in this attractive village full of half-timbered houses for more than half a millennium. The Rohan coat of arms can be seen in an intensely colored stained glass window in the Basilique Notre-Dame-du-Roncier, a simple but elegantly detailed structure in the center of town; and towering over the Oust River nearby is the imposing fortress-mansion that has been the family seat for 600 years.

Constructed in the 11th century as a palace, the Josselin château was fortified with nine perfectly cylindrical towers and 12-foot-thick walls by Olivier de Clisson in 1370. The Rohans, the family of de Clisson's wife, Marguerite, acquired it upon his death in 1407. In 1488, the castle was partially destroyed on the orders of the Duke of Brittany, François II, after Jean II de Rohan had fought against him, on the side of the French crown, in the struggle for national unification. Subsequently, François II's daughter Anne of Brittany (who had married the King of France) made funds available to her husband's Rohan supporter to restore the castle. It was then that the façade of the mansion inside the walls was endowed with its granite carvings, as ornate and profuse as if they had been worked with wood, that are one of the château's distinctions. Of de Clisson's towers, only three survived the often bloody years since then. The satiny gloss to which the conical slate roofs have been burnished by the centuries, together with the wedding-cake carvings outside and the regal interiors (seen on guided tours), are the chief attractions of the château. A great *pardon* takes place here annually on the second Sunday in September. (Closed in winter; phone: 97-22-22-50.)

En Route from Josselin – Worth a small detour is the town of Elven to see the spectacular *son et lumière* show inspired by the legend of Tristan and Iseult. It is presented on Friday and Saturday evenings from mid-July to September at Tours de Largoet in Elven (7 ½ miles/12 km from Vannes). For information and exact times, get in touch with itd office (Rue Robert de la Noë, Elven 56250; phone: 97-53-52-79).

VANNES: Though the real joy of a tour of Brittany lies in picturesque villages like Josselin, the larger towns offer their pleasures, too. Vannes, an agricultural center with a population of about 45,000, is worth noting for its particularly handsome and extensive old quarter, which dates from the days that the Kings (later the Dukes) of Brittany headquartered here. Extending on all sides of the Cathédrale de St.-Pierre, a particularly infelicitous architectural hodgepodge noted primarily for its soaring 16th-century Italian Renaissance chapel, this area is edged on one side by the town ramparts and, at their base, by gardens full of sharply clipped hedges laid out with geometrical precision. One of the most stunning sights in Vannes, seen from the Rue Alexandre-Le-Pontois near the Porte Poterne, is the view of these gardens and a cluster of ramshackle old washhouses, their terra-cotta tile roofs punctuated whimsically with chimneys and reflected in a placid little river with the ramparts and the cathedral's steeple looming behind.

The old quarter proper, reached by crossing a narrow bridge just above the washhouses, is a labyrinth of narrow pedestrian streets crowded by half-timbered houses. Particularly attractive are the Rue St.-Guenhaël, which skirts the mossy-walled cathedral, the Rue de la Monnaie, and the Place Henri-IV, an enclave of gabled 300-year-old houses. The 15th-century Gaillard Château (2 Rue Noë; phone: 97-47-24-34) displays archaeological relics from the paleolithic period to the Iron Age. It is open daily, except Sundays (afternoons only in winter). The explanatory notes in the cases (in French) give a cursory overview of the finds at the excavations at Carnac, a later stop on the tour. The *Musée de la Cohue* (opposite the cathedral; phone: 97-47-35-86; closed Sundays and Tuesdays) has two exhibitions: seascape paintings and other sea-related subjects, and an explanation of oyster cultivation — a subject that will take on increased interest after several days of watching fishermen unload their harvest in little Breton harbor towns. Also worth a visit is the new *Aquarium Oceanographique et Tropical de Vannes* (Parc du Golfe, Vannes 56000; phone: 97-40-67-40). Open daily from 9 AM to noon, and 1:30 to 7:30 PM; July and August from 9 AM to 7 PM. Summer events in Vannes include a *Festival de Jazz,* held in early August (phone: 97-54-18-22).

CHECKING IN/EATING OUT: *La Marébaudière* – Set back from the road a bit and therefore quieter than other town hostelries, this establishment is only a couple of decades old (and the premises are accordingly up-to-date). But the pretty wallpaper, draperies, brass or antique bedsteads, and other handsome furniture in its 40 rooms give the place rather more character than most of its vintage. Seafood, straightforwardly prepared, is offered in the hotel's simple, modern restaurant *La Marée Bleue,* in its own building across the street (8 Pl. Bir-Hakeim; phone: 97-47-24-29). Closed Sunday evenings off-season and from mid-November to mid-March. 4 Rue Aristide-Briand, Vannes (phone: 97-47-34-29). Moderate.

Le Richemont – This simple hotel opposite the train station is done up with quasi-medieval beams and chandeliers that recall the château where its 14th-century namesake, Arthur de Richemont, the Constable of Brittany, was born. It has 29 very comfortable old-fashioned rooms with enough charm to overcome the occasional quirks of the older structure that houses the guest quarters. In the restaurant next door (under different management but also called *Le Richemont*), low beams, stained glass windows, a carved stone fireplace, and Genoese velvet chairs produce an air of luxury quite in keeping with the elaborate menu of seafood, grills, and Breton specialties. 26 Av. Favrel et Lincy, Vannes (phone: hotel, 97-47-12-95; restaurant, 97-42-61-41). Hotel, inexpensive; restaurant, moderate.

GULF OF MORBIHAN: This nearly circular body of water, very much "the little sea" to which its name refers, measures 12 miles across and 10 miles (16 km) from Vannes on the northern end to Port Navalo, on the south. It is a pretty area, flatter than an oyster shell and known for its rosy sunsets, its subtle light, the oyster beds in the rivers that open onto it, and its dozens of islands of all shapes and sizes, some woodsy and natural, some immaculately landscaped.

The best way to experience the area is by boat. Pack a picnic lunch and climb aboard one of the *Vedettes Vertes* boats at the Gare Maritime (Maritime Station) in Vannes (phone: 97-63-79-99). These craft call at most of the major islands, where passengers can stroll on landfalls like the 4-mile-long Ile-aux-Moines (Monks' Island), where dolmens guard heather moors and fishermen pedal home to thatch-roofed cottages along quiet roadways.

Skirting the shoreline by car, with glimpses of the sea here and there, is another alternative. South and east of Vannes, a tour might take in St.-Armel; St.-Colombier; the grand, windswept ruins of the 14th-century Suscinio château, where the Dukes of Brittany once summered; and St.-Gildas-de-Rhuys, the site of the church of the abbey to which the learned 12th-century philosopher Pierre Abélard repaired after his forced separation from his beloved Heloïse.

Moving west from Vannes, several highways connect small roads that reach to the very tip of the little points of land that notch the coast. In the Marais de Pen-en-Toul, a visitor might spot a lonely heron standing sentry over a sawtoothed patch of grass, and in harbors like the ones at Arradon and Larmor-Baden, a traveler might spy fishermen unloading their day's harvest in the dark blue twilight that follows a particularly scarlet sunset. Near Moustoir, where a handful of signs point to obscure villages along lanes more suited to bicycles than to cars, cows being herded from field to barn block the road. At Port-Blanc, there are boats to the Ile-aux-Moines, and Larmor-Baden has service to the Gavrinis Tumulus, one of the most interesting megalithic monuments in Brittany due to the extent and preservation of the chambers.

CHECKING IN: *Les Vénètes* – White, modern, and very small, this 12-room hostelry occupies a pleasant spot on the harbor at Arradon, just a short walk along the base of the cliffs from Arradon Point, where there are fine views of the sunset. Closed October through March. On the point in Arradon (phone: 97-44-03-11). Expensive to moderate.

AURAY: Much smaller than Vannes and far more manageable, Auray also has a charming old quarter. Occupying a point created by a bend in the Auray River and connected to the town proper on the opposite bank of the stream by a one-lane bridge, it has cobbled streets compressed to one lane by shuttered stucco and stone houses dating from the 15th century. The heart of the area is Place St.-Sauveur, which is full of brasseries and cafés whose site by the river makes them especially charming for afternoon coffee. Be sure to note the quay that leaves the square. Benjamin Franklin, sailing to France in 1776 to enlist aid for the Revolutionary cause, spent the night in a house 150 yards away when stiff headwinds stopped his ship from traveling up the Loire to Nantes.

CHECKING IN: *Fairway* – Golfers especially should take note of this addition to Brittany's lodging places, some 4 ½ miles (7 km) outside Auray. Though its modern facilities and rooms lack the charm of the region's old stone inns, it has a pristine 27-hole golf course. There also is a pool, a gym, and tennis courts. Closed mid-December to mid-January. Mailing address: *Golf St. Laurent,* Auray (phone: 97-56-88-88). Moderate.

En Route from Auray – Ste.-Anne-d'Auray, a few miles north, is the setting not only for some of Brittany's most important *pardons* in late July but also for the more minor pilgrimages that take place from Monday to Thursday nearly weekly between *Easter* and October. The elaborate costumes of the faithful are as impressive as the fervor with which they undertake their journeys; some will struggle up the double staircase known as the Scala Sancta, leading from the square to the basilica, on their knees.

CARNAC: Megalithic monuments may seem dull stuff, but not at Carnac, whose concentration of these rough-hewn stones has few equals in all of Europe. Here they stand, some 3,000 of them, aligned with the points of the compass or with stellar and solar trajectories — a silent testament to the ingenuity of man in service to his gods, eerie mementos that vibrate with a piety that, however antique, is fully the equal of that of the Ste.-Anne pilgrims. To get a sense of the magnitude of the force required to erect them, consider that when the 220-ton Luxor obelisk was set up in the Place de la Concorde in 1836, Parisians hailed it as an extraordinary feat. Yet megaliths typically weigh as much as 350 tons.

Sometimes the stones are impressive for sheer size. Witness the Tumulus St.-Michel, a huge mound of earth that conceals several burial chambers (accessible near Carnac's *Tumulus* hotel, off N781). Or the almost mystical allure derived from the stones' number, as in the case with the Ménec Lines, on the left of D196 as it heads north from Carnac, where more than a thousand stones of varying heights punctuate the fields of golden broom in several straight lines for about three-quarters of a mile. A visitor scarcely has time to absorb this sight before the Kermario Lines — still more of the same — appear along the road. The Kercado Tumulus, off the beaten path on the grounds of a private château, is only a bit farther. To see the tumulus, go down a long, straight, tree-lined lane that shoots off to the right past the Kermario Lines, stop at the gatehouse and speak to the gatekeeper, pay the small fee, and pick up the key to the barrow's locked door, a flashlight, and an information sheet. The turnoff is not marked by a sign, so the site is nearly always deserted and feels every bit the tomb that it probably once was. At the Kerlescan Lines farther along, the stones are taller than a man and even more mystically powerful.

The *Musée de Préhistoire,* a museum in town, displays the prehistoric findings of the excavations of the Carnac monuments — necklaces, axheads, vases, and the like. Closed Tuesdays. 1O Pl. de la Chapelle, Carnac 56340 (phone: 97-52-22-04.)

 CHECKING IN: *Lann Roz* – From the small, cheery garden to the salon full of pretty caged birds to the 13 daintily wallpapered rooms upstairs, this inn is a delightful spot to spend a night or two. Closed January. 13 Av. de la Poste, Carnac (phone: 97-52-10-48). Moderate.

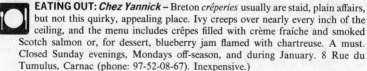 **EATING OUT:** *Chez Yannick* – Breton *crêperies* usually are staid, plain affairs, but not this quirky, appealing place. Ivy creeps over nearly every inch of the ceiling, and the menu includes crêpes filled with crème fraíche and smoked Scotch salmon or, for dessert, blueberry jam flamed with chartreuse. A must. Closed Sunday evenings, Mondays off-season, and during January. 8 Rue du Tumulus, Carnac (phone: 97-52-08-67). Inexpensive.)

QUIBERON: This busy resort center, extending landward from its beach and its harbor, is something of a carnival in season and has hotels, villas, a casino, bars, discos, tearooms, fishing supply stores, and boutiques by the dozen. Some are modern and some old-fashioned, so the place has an appealing mixed quality. What makes it particularly noteworthy, however, is the coastline all around it, which is some of the most spectacular in southern Brittany. Near town at the Pointe du Conguel, the waves hurl themselves onto low-lying rocks that afford a fine view of Belle-Ile (Beautiful Island) and the islands of Houat and Hoëdic. To the north of town, they crash upon tiny beaches at the base of tall cliffs. It is easy to understand why this stretch of shoreline was dubbed the Côte Sauvage (the Wild Coast).

Much of it is visible from the road that twists and climbs and rolls through the moors at the top of the cliffs. For a better view, park the car and walk the 2 miles (3 km) of coast between Port-Pigeon, midway along the peninsula's west coast, and Portivy, just north of the Pointe du Percho on the north. *Note:* Strong currents make swimming dangerous.

CHECKING IN: *Ker Noyal* – Well-kept and modern, this luxurious club-like establishment a short walk from the beach has two square buildings that face each other across a courtyard. Most of the 100 modern rooms have terraces with views of either the sea or a well-tended garden massed with bright flowers and pine trees. Closed from November to March. Rue de St.-Clément, Quiberon (phone: 97-50-08-41). Expensive.

Le Neptune – Small, modern, and right on the harbor, this establishment is not long on charm, but the 22 rooms have decent beds and small-patterned wallpaper, and the view from the terraces of the quarters facing the harbor and the gleaming bathrooms, sometimes done in handsome dark blue tiles, are a genuine pleasure. Closed from late December to mid-February, and Mondays off-season. 4 Quai de Houat, Quiberon (phone: 97-50-09-62). Moderate.

Gulf Stream – An older hostelry, this simple 20-room inn on the harbor gets its charm from the classic balustrades and windowboxes splashed with color. The whole place seems to gleam. 17 Bd. Chanard, Quiberon (phone: 97-50-16-96). Moderate.

BELLE-ILE: Of all the islands off the Breton coast, Belle-Ile is most often mentioned as a must. It is accessible by steamer from Port-Maria, which dominates 10-mile-distant Quiberon. The scenery is impressive — the shoreline cliffs, the deep valleys, the verdant pastures, the wheat and potato fields interspersed with patches of weeds and stately trees, and the small complexes of whitewashed farmhouses and barns. From several of the small villages there are fine walks to places on the coastline where the sea has carved caverns and odd shapes out of the cliffs. Don't miss the Grotte de l'Apothicairérie (Apothecary Grotto), named for the cormorant nests that used to be lined up along niches in the cave walls like bottles in a pharmacy. Especially in the late spring and early fall, there is a delightful serenity to this island that is hard to beat. (For steamer information, call 97-31-80-01.)

CHECKING IN: *Castel Clara* – Boasting bathrooms paved with marble and balconies opening onto the sea, this comfortable, gleaming white 43-room member of the Relais & Châteaux group occupies a secluded hillside on the peaceful west coast of the island. There also is a terrace, a heated saltwater pool, and tennis facilities. Closed from mid-October to mid-March. Port-Goulphar (phone: 97-31-84-21). Expensive.

Manoir de Goulphar – Thanks to its fine views and chic decor, this posh white structure with 53 rooms on the peaceful coast has far more character than its modern construction might suggest. Closed from November to mid-March. Port-Goulphar (phone: 97-31-80-10). Moderate.

KERNASCLÉDEN: The care with which pious Bretons decorated their simple churches immediately is apparent in the 15th-century, lichen-splotched house of worship that dominates this little town about 10 miles (16 km) north of Hennebont. The slender belfry is elegantly proportioned and finely embellished with small ornamental motifs, as are the tops of the buttresses. The archway above the front door is topped with one layer after another of decorative grooves. And the porch is lined with niches, each one edged with a wealth of lacelike details that frame realistic statues of the apostles.

Of particular interest inside this church (which has been restored) are its frescoes — some depicting musical angels and scenes from the life of Christ and the Virgin; others, underneath a beautiful rose window, showing macabre images like the Dance of Death between skeletons and courtiers and the weird pictures of horned devils in hell smashing anguished sinners into pots of boiling oil with pitchforks.

CHECKING IN/EATING OUT: *Château de Locguénolé* – Visiting this stately castle, now an inn, owned by the same family for more than 500 years, is like attending a courtly house party in some past century. The restoration of the 37 rooms and apartments has been masterfully done; those on the second story, originally consecrated to the gentry, have high ceilings, velvet curtains, soft rugs, and refined furniture, while those on the floor above, under the eaves, are handsomely rustic, with country prints and exposed beams. Views over the well-tended grounds, which slope down to the edge of the River Blavet in the rear, are stupendous. Antiques, paintings, and tapestries collected over the centuries ornament the salons, which manage to be comfortable and welcoming despite their formality. People come for miles around to sample the well-conceived and finely executed nouvelle specialties on the menu (rated two Michelin stars), which changes regularly from one season to the next but remains innovative — witness the red mullet cooked in a salt crust, the sweetbread salad flavored with sorrel, and the light crayfish bisque served with a vegetable mousse and fresh mint. Closed Mondays, off-season, and January. About 2½ miles (3 km) south of Hennebont, just off D781 (phone: 97-76-29-04). Expensive.

LE FAOUËT: An old town with a 16th-century covered market building not unlike the one at Questembert, with a veritable forest of pillars inside, Le Faouët is well worth visiting for the two fine chapels nearby and the beautiful countryside in between the district's Inam and the Ellé rivers.

By far the better known of the two is the one devoted to the Irish hermit St. Fiacre, the patron saint of gardeners. Somewhat asymmetrical but nonetheless balanced on the outside, this rather simple structure set alongside a simple farm is ornamented inside with a carved Gothic choir screen; its lifelike carvings, though executed in a rather primitive style, demonstrate the heights to which the Breton woodcarvers' skill eventually rose. On the nave side, note the thieves contorted on their crosses and, along the border, the crowd of curious faces, looking and leering and grinning. Facing the chancel, don't miss the pie-eyed peasant vomiting a fox (an image that represents drunkenness) and the man with the woman lifting her skirts flirtatiously (symbolizing lust).

The chapel of Ste. Barbe, a few miles on the other side of Le Faouët, is remarkable not so much for its interior, which is small, as for its site; it clings to the side of a cliff just beneath the crest of a hill whose summit overlooks the fields and forests of the Ellé Valley. To get to the chapel, it's necessary to walk through the woods for about 10 minutes up a switchbacked trail that begins immediately across the road from the *Café de l'Ellé*. There are two ways to go, one considerably steeper than the other, and the signs are no help. Inquire before starting out. The trail ends at a finely proportioned Renaissance stairway, which in turn leads to the chapel and the viewful hilltop where the only sounds may be the roaring of the wind across your ears or the occasional bark of the caretaker's fierce dogs. It is of such apparently inconsequential sites that the best Breton memories are made. *Pardons* are held here on December 4 and on the last Sunday in June.

QUIMPERLÉ: This unprepossessing hill town is well known to the fishermen who come for the salmon and trout in the placid little Isole and Ellé rivers, which here form the Laïta. But it is more interesting for the variation it offers on the Gothic church theme, the Romanesque Eglise de Ste.-Croix, which is laid out not in the shape of the rectangular, Latin cross but in that of the square Greek cross, like the Holy Sepulcher in Jerusalem. The round arches, the barrel vaulting, the small apse with its vividly colored windows, and the cool crypt supported by capitals carved with vaguely Celtic designs make this a spot to remember.

Not far from the church, along the Rue Brémond-d'Ars and the narrow, alley-like Rue Dom-Morice, there are some pretty half-timbered houses with walls that lurch and lean with the abandon of a drunkard.

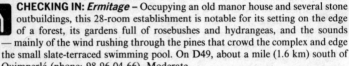

CHECKING IN: *Ermitage* – Occupying an old manor house and several stone outbuildings, this 28-room establishment is notable for its setting on the edge of a forest, its gardens full of rosebushes and hydrangeas, and the sounds — mainly of the wind rushing through the pines that crowd the complex and edge the small slate-terraced swimming pool. On D49, about a mile (1.6 km) south of Quimperlé (phone: 98-96-04-66). Moderate.

FOREST OF CARNOUET: Legend has it that this 1,852-acre preserve, which flanks D49 south of Quimperlé, once was inhabited by the Count of Comorre, a fearsome fellow who, under the spell of a prophecy that he would be murdered by his son, killed four wives, one after another, as soon as they became pregnant, then slaughtered the son of a clever fifth wife who had managed to bear her child. But the prophecy was fulfilled, nonetheless: St. Trémeur, as the son was later known, lived long enough to pick up his head and toss a handful of dirt at the count's castle with a force that made the building collapse. The fearsome Bluebeard of Cornouaille was buried alive in the rubble.

The reverberations of this legend add an extra dimension to the vision of the beautiful tall, straight trees, and many Bretons make a point of taking a walk along the many footpaths that shoot into the woods from the road — perhaps to the ruins of the Abbaye St.-Maurice (accessible via D224, off D49); to the Rocher Royal, a ridge that overlooks the serene Laïta River (a little over a mile/1.6 km from D49 via a footpath); or perhaps to the Château de Comorre itself.

CHECKING IN: *Les Moulins du Duc* – A tiny lake, swans, white doves, a waterwheel velvety with moss, comfortable quarters in a handful of rustic houses, a swimming pool, and a woodsy valley setting make this 22-room, 5-suite establishment one of the most inviting in the province. The intriguing hors d'oeuvres and entrées that reflect the chef's Oriental background are another major drawing card. Closed mid-January through February; restaurant closed Wednesdays for lunch off-season. Near Moëlan-sur-Mer, about 5 miles (8 km) from the southern edge of the Carnouet Forest (phone: 98-39-60-73). Expensive to moderate.

Chez Mélanie – This historic *auberge*, where a legendary gastronome named Curnonsky spent the war years, is worth noting for several reasons: its location on the shores of the Bélon River, which produces some of the finest oysters in France; the food, deceptively simple but delicious; and the distinction of the premises themselves, where every wall seems practically paved with Impressionist and post-Impressionist paintings. The 7 rooms, which have their own showers or bathtubs but share the toilet down the hall, are charming and old-fashioned, with chintz bedspreads and ornate French headboards, and neat as a pin; their acres of polished antique oak and mahogany and burnished brass reflect years of meticulous care. The specialties of the restaurant, which is full of old Breton armoires and chests and ceramic, include a lusty *timbale de fruits de mer* (seafood casserole) based on a flavorful fish stock, *palourdes farcies* (stuffed clams), a rich *pâté de volaille* (chicken liver pâté) — and, of course, Bélon oysters in various shapes, sizes, and preparations. Hotel closed October to *Easter;* restaurant closed mid-November to mid-December and Tuesdays off-season. Pl. de l'Eglise, Riec-sur-Bélon (phone: 98-06-91-05). Hotel, inexpensive; restaurant, moderate to inexpensive.

EATING OUT: *Chez Jacky* – Just down the road from *Chez Mélanie* is not just another rustic restaurant, but a seafood lover's paradise. Grilled lobster served with a creamy house sauce is the specialty, and Bélon oysters are available. Appetites can be appeased from 10 AM to 10 PM. Closed Mondays and October through *Easter*. Port de Belon, Riec-sur-Bélon (phone: 98-06-90-32). Moderate.

PONT-AVEN: It was in yet another simple Breton chapel, Chapelle Trémalo, that the Impressionist Paul Gauguin found the 16th-century wooden Christ on which he modeled his well-known *Yellow Christ*. The chapel can be seen today just less than a mile from this pleasant little town by following D24 and a climbing, twisting side road through the cow pastures edged by romantic lines of tall, straight trees. The celebrated carving is still there, but the real allure of the place is the granite structure itself — simple and asymmetrical and seemingly at the top of the world. The scene is especially beautiful at dusk, when the light makes the cows nearby look almost like statues and imbues the whole scene with a mystical quality.

In fact, it was this very quality of light that attracted Gauguin before his voyage to Tahiti, along with Maurice Denis, Paul Sérusier, Emile Bernard, and other painters, who together were known as the Pont-Aven School. The town is said to have been particularly picturesque then, with its valley setting, its little white houses, and its numerous mills driven by the Aven River.

But it is no less so today. There are several galleries and a town museum that mounts art exhibitions. Visit the *Musée de Pont-Aven* (Pl. de l'Hôtel de Ville; phone: 98-06-14-43) to see works by artists from the Pont-Aven School, as well as temporary exhibits of contemporary painters. Open 10 AM to 12:30 PM and 2 to 7 PM, from April through December. A few shops that sell the absolutely delicious butter cookies for which Pont-Aven is known, and some antiques shops and boutiques of more than usual interest; the clientele is as apt to be clad in suede trousers and one gold stud earring — male and female alike — as in blue jeans and T-shirts. Even the simplest bars and *crêperies,* with their whitewashed stucco walls, beamed ceilings, and polished antique furnishings, have atmosphere to spare. And, though the mills no longer are operating, the sound of the rushing waters that powered them still reverberates between the stone walls.

CHECKING IN: *Le Manoir du Ménec* – This hotel and leisure center installed in a gracious 15th-century stone manor northeast of Pont Aven has cozy individual cottages, each named for a famous painter, as well as 10 deluxe guestrooms. The restaurant, with ancient stone walls and elegant chandeliers, is in the oldest part of the manor, while the heated pool, Jacuzzi, sauna, and gym are in the newer addition. There also are facilities for small conferences. Bannalec (phone: 98-39-47-47). Expensive to moderate.

EATING OUT: *Moulin de Rosmadec* – The sounds of the mill stream that borders it on three sides are only part of the reason that this reconstructed 15th-century stone mill is such a delightful dining spot. Consider also the antiques scattered around the cozy dining rooms inside and the profusion of honeysuckle and roses and rhododendrons crowding the mill walls and edging the terrace outside. Then look at the menu itself, which offers a lemony *soupe de poisson* (fish soup), *palourdes farcies* (stuffed clams), *homard grillé à l'estragon* (grilled lobster flavored with tarragon), *aiguillettes de canard au poivre frais* (peppered duckling), and more — all rated one Michelin star. Closed Sunday evenings,

Wednesdays, the last 2 weeks in October, and all of February. Near the center of Pont-Aven (phone: 98-06-00-22). Expensive.

La Taupinière – Surrounded by a beautiful garden and coiffed with a straw roof, this restaurant serves giant crayfish grilled in the fireplace, raw tuna marinated in lime, angler fish in butter, and farmers' cider. Closed Monday evenings, Tuesdays, and from mid-September to mid-October. Rte de Concerneau, 1½ miles (2 km) from Pont-Aven (phone: 98-06-03-12). Expensive.

CONCARNEAU: This walled port, an erstwhile coastal fortress town, wears two faces — one as a popular summer resort, with a long stretch of beach and a *ville close* (walled city), where cars usually are prohibited; the other as a fishing center whose boats, which can be seen in all sizes in the *nouveau port* (new port) behind the Old City, haul in some of the biggest tuna catches in France between midnight and dawn.

The *ville close* has narrow streets attractively crowded by high, shuttered houses, but it also has souvenir shops that tend toward the trinkety and galleries where seascapes are the staple; some people find their tolerance for such fare limited. But when fishermen are unloading their catch by the basket and buyers are scrambling to bid for the best, even travelers who can't stand tourism are fascinated. And as a result of the continual influx of sailors, the city's middle class side is balanced appealingly by a certain raunchiness.

Don't miss the drive along the Boulevard Katerine-Wily, which wends its way between a wall of nondescript apartment towers and a glorious postcard sweep of bay. Buy a ticket at the clock tower just over the bridge at the entrance to the *ville close* and climb the ramparts for another view of the harbor. And explore the *Musée de la Pêche* and its exhibits on commercial fishing.

CHECKING IN: *Manoir du Stang* – This particular one of Brittany's handful of 16th-century château-hotels, on the outskirts of sleepy La Forêt-Fouesnant, proclaims the stateliness of the early life here, from the tall *allée* of trees to the neatly clipped lawns beyond them, from the imposing stone gate to the formal square of the graveled courtyard beyond it. The interiors are absolutely seductive — all paneling and crystal and velvet and silk and antiques. Closed September through May. Off D783, 6 miles (10 km) from Concarneau, near La Forêt-Fouesnant (phone: 98-56-97-37). Expensive.

Grand – Of the various Concarneau hostelries, this old-fashioned 33-room inn, on a busy corner overlooking the port bristling with ships, is most convenient to the *ville close.* Closed from October to *Easter.* 1 Av. Pierre-Guéguin, Concarneau (phone: 98-97-00-28). Inexpensive.

EATING OUT: *Le Galion* – The velvet curtains on the windows and the white linen and silver and crystal on the tables contrast strikingly with the low rough beams and rugged granite walls of this lovely, one-Michelin-star establishment. But attractive though the atmosphere may be, it's the food that constitutes the real draw — mainly seafood that seems to have come straight out of the surf. The chef excels when he uses his imagination, as in the *civet de lotte* (a stew made from monkfish), the *fricassée de langoustine* (lobster stew), the *filet de barbue avec coulis de poivrons* (a filet of brill with a purée of peppers), and the *turbot braisé avec champagne* (turbot with champagne). Closed Sunday evenings and Mondays except in summer, and also during January. In the *ville close,* 15 Rue St.-Guénolé, Concarneau (phone: 98-97-30-16). Expensive to moderate.

QUIMPER: Sprawling though it is, with a population of nearly 61,000, there still is something of the sleepy Breton village in this city, whose name in Breton (*kemp-er,* "junction") refers to the meeting point of the placid Steir and the Odet rivers in the town. Narrow streets miraculously spared damage during the war angle this way and that between tall half-timbered houses whose second stories are cantilevered out over the street. Walk through the old section of the city, following the Rue Elie Fréron, the Place au Beurre, the Rue du Sallé (with many restored structures), the Rue de Kerguelen, the Rue Valentin, the Place Mesgloaguen, the Rue St.-Nicolas, the Rue des Gentilshommes, the Rue des Boucheries (Butchers' Street, which once ran with the blood of slaughtered animals), and the Rue du Guéodet (distinguished by a house whose ground floor is guarded by caryatids in antique costumes). Fairly detailed maps and guided walking tours (in warm weather) are available at the town's tourist office (3 Rue du Roi-Gradlon; phone: 98-95-04-69). The whole area is full of boutiques purveying carved wood, embroideries, Breton musical instruments, regional clothing, handwoven cloth, its world-famous *faïence,* and more. If nothing else, Quimper is Brittany's best regional shopping center outside the major cities.

At the heart of the town and only a block from the graceful tree-lined quais of the Odet and the Rue Ste.-Catherine, where one of a half-dozen bridges lace together the riverbanks is the Cathédrale St.-Corentin, rather clunky and awkwardly proportioned compared to the one in Nantes but worth seeing nonetheless. The structure is named for the legendary spiritual adviser of the good King Gradlon, who is said to have subsisted on the meat of a single perpetually regenerating fish; he also is, incidentally, one of a handful of Breton saints not recognized by Rome. The church was erected between the 13th and the 15th century except for its pair of 250-foot towers, which were built in 1856 with funds provided by some 600,000 diocesans — each paying one *sou* annually for 5 years. Inside, note that the choir and the nave are out of alignment — possibly a result of some construction problem, though no one knows for sure. There are some richly colored stained glass windows. Sunday visitors are in for a treat: The organ is one of the best in Brittany, and after high mass, the air fairly vibrates with its chords.

Immediately adjacent, in the 16th-century bishop's palace, is the *Musée Départemental Breton* (1 Rue Roi Gradlor; phone: 98-95-21-60; closed Mondays and Tuesdays in low season, and from October to late March), with displays of Breton pottery, musical instruments, embroidered regional dresses and starched *coiffes,* and furnishings of lower Brittany. The carvings on the furniture demonstrate the considerable skill attained by rude Breton woodworkers; the resemblance of the ornamentation on a 19th-century *coffre à blé* (wheat storage chest) near the entrance to that often found in Great Britain and Ireland emphasizes Brittany's ties to Celtic culture — and is uniquely appropriate to an institution based, as this one is, in the capital of the region named La Cornouaille by its original settlers, who came from Cornwall, England. Also interesting is the Quimper ceramics display, which shows its development from the very crude to the extremely refined and illustrates the evolution of the *petits Bretons* (little Bretons) who have been found on almost every traditional Quimper plate from their debut in the 1880s to the present.

This white ceramicware, painted in blue and yellow with Breton figures and flowers and fruits, has been one of the city's primary claims to fame since the 17th century, when artisans came from Rouen and elsewhere to work in the Quimper potteries, and it is featured in nearly every prominent shop window in the older part of town. Guided tours of the factories that produce them also are available. Contact the *Faïenceries de Quimper Henriot* at 98-90-09-36 or the *Faïenceries Keraluc* at 98-53-04-50. (The latter does not offer guided tours; visitors are free to observe.)

It's also pleasant to board a boat for the 3-hour round trip down the forest- and cliff-edged Odet as far as the slick resort of Bénodet at its mouth. Also note that the restored *Musée des Beaux-Arts* boasts one of the best collections of paintings in provincial France; works from the Italian, Spanish, Flemish, and Dutch schools hang next to paintings by members of the Pont-Aven School and others who took their inspiration primarily from Breton scenes. (Closed Tuesdays; Pl. St.-Gorentin; phone: 98-95-45-20.)

Visitors expecting to arrive the week ending the fourth Sunday in July should plan to attend the important *Festival de Cornouaille,* which has been preserving and promoting Breton music and dance since 1923.

CHECKING IN: *Tour d'Auvergne* – A block from the Odet River, this older but renovated establishment boasts a subdued 1930s look that has been updated in many of the 45 guest quarters by warm, country-like red wallpaper. Bathrooms generally are commodious. There also is a restaurant. Closed over the *Christmas* and *New Year* holidays. 13 Rue des Réguaires, Quimper (phone: 98-95-08-70). Moderate to inexpensive.

PONT-L'ABBÉ: The area around this town of about 7,700 offers plenty of exceptions to the rule that traditional Breton costumes — the richly embroidered velvet skirts, lace aprons, and starched white *coiffes* — seldom are seen nowadays, even in the country. Here, not only do the old women wear their Bigouden costume to the town's *pardon* in mid-July, but they also can frequently be seen pedaling bicycles down lonely lanes at dusk, piling fruits and vegetables into net shopping bags on market day, or trudging to Mass on a Sunday, their black velvet skirts swishing and their wondrously tall headdresses bobbing with their every movement. The town's 14th-to-17th-century fortress-château has a museum that displays a collection of the historical versions of these colorful outfits. (Guided tours twice daily from late September to early June; closed Sundays; phone: 98-87-24-44.)

CHECKING IN: *Bretagne* – When 18 rooms were installed on the upper floors of this longtime favorite local restaurant a few years ago, the friendly proprietors let themselves be guided by their excellent taste and paid great attention to details such as flowered wallpapers and spacious bathrooms. Simple, but a real find. 24 Pl. de la République, Pont L'Abbé (phone: 98-87-17-22). Moderate to inexpensive.

Château de Kernuz – Reached by a winding, tree-lined lane with stone farm buildings huddling up next to the stone wall that bounds the property on one side, this comfortable 16th-century establishment with 16 rooms and a pool has wonderful salons full of antiques, chandeliers, beamed ceilings with refined paneling, and massive hearths big enough to make a playhouse for a fourth-grader. Things are a bit worn in spots, but the ensemble is charming. Closed October to April. 1½ miles (2 km) from Pont l'Abbé on N785 (phone: 98-87-01-59). Moderate to inexpensive.

EATING OUT: *Relais de Ty Boutic* – Light, fresh foods served by an innovative chef about 2 miles (3 km) from town. Closed Mondays and February. Rte. de Plomeur, Pont l'Abbé (phone: 98-87-03-90). Moderate.

En Route from Pont l'Abbé – The west coast of Brittany offers a study in the many meanings of the word "shoreline." Le Guilivinec, a fairly undistinguished commercial fishing port, is worth a detour around 5 PM, when the sardine and tuna boats come into port and the fishermen unload their catch. There is no question that fishing is important throughout the area; that it has been so historically is evident in Penmarch, where the doorways of the 16th-century Flamboyant Gothic St. Nonna's Church are embellished with carved reliefs of the ships of the wealthy merchants who built it. The Pointe de Penmarch, where low tides reveal a liberal scattering of smooth, sea-pounded rocks that might be cliffs squashed flat as pancakes, offers a vision of one of the types of coastline with which Breton sailors have always had to contend. Rising above it are the two lighthouses that have been warning sailors to steer clear of these waters ever since the 19th century; one of them, the Phare d'Eckmuhl, can often be toured. From its

213-foot-high gallery, it's possible to see nearly the length of the coastline in fine weather; half a dozen lighthouses can be seen in a single glance.

From here, D80 hugs the water's edge as far as the resort of St.-Guénolé, where there still are more boulders along the shore. At high tide, when the surf is beating against them, it's easier to envision that a great wave could come along and sweep away a whole family, an event of 1870 commemorated by an iron cross attached to one of the rocks. The road turns inward, and the sea becomes accessible only by spur roads from a larger highway like D57 until Pouldreuzic, where D40 turns westward to Penhors. Site of the annual *pardon* of Notre-Dame-de-Penhors on September 8, one of the largest in Cornouaille, the area is thronged with the faithful, who join a procession through the countryside to the shoreline for a blessing of the sea. The unnumbered northbound continuation of D40 passes through charming tiny villages like Keristenvet, Plozévet, and Ports-Poulan before turning inland again.

At Audierne, an attractive small fishing port at the base of a woodsy hillside on the Goyen River estuary, lovers of Breton folklore will want to stop on the Quai Pelletan, not far from the beach, to see La Chaumière (the Thatched Cottage), where wonderful 17th- and 18th-century carved oak furniture has been set up to suggest the interior of an old Breton cottage (open in July and August; 5 Rue Amiral Guépratte; phone: 98-70-12-20). Here, too, a traveler anxious to get far away from it all can catch the 90-minute boat trip to the wild, bare, and rocky Ile de Sein (Island of the Womb). The inhabitants, pagan until the 18th century, still furnish their houses as they have done over the ages — from ships that did not see the sentinel light and were wrecked off the coast. (For boat information, call 98-70-02-38.)

CHECKING IN/Eating Out: *Le Goyen* – This gracious, 34-room establishment right on the harbor in Audierne and decorated in fine French style is clean, well-kept, and very comfortable. Out in front there is a long front porch, brightened with pots of geraniums and plenty of white chairs, on which to while away a summer afternoon. It also boasts a first-rate restaurant that earned one Michelin star for specialties like mushrooms in walnut oil sauce and lobster sautéed with mushrooms. The chef follows his whim and the market offerings, so there's always something new. Closed from mid-November to February and on Mondays off-season. Pl. Jean-Simon, Audierne (phone: 98-70-08-88). Hotel, moderate; restaurant, expensive to moderate.

POINTE DU RAZ: A far more common destination for travelers leaving Audierne is the Pointe du Raz, a mass of craggy, tumbled cliffs and rocks assembled to look like the fin of a prehistoric animal. It is habitually battered by the sea with a ferocity that prompted Baudelaire to exclaim: "Nul n'a passé le Raz sans peur ou sans douleur" ("No one has passed through the Raz without fear or sadness"). The two good sized parking lots and the square full of rinky-tinky souvenir shops only begin to suggest the popularity of the spot. But even when there is not a single free space and the area guides have their hands full of tourists wanting to sign up for one of the walking tours along the footpaths that squiggle to the sea, the grandeur of the scene is undeniable. The Baie des Trépassés (Bay of the Dead), to the right of the headland, is believed to have been the point of embarkation for druids bound for the Ile de Sein to bury their dead. Legend has it that the town of Is, the beautiful capital of Cornouaille at the time of the good King Gradlon, was inundated offshore.

En Route from Pointe du Raz – There are equally scenic points at the end of the spur roads from D7 to Douarnenez — notably the Pointe du Van, less overwhelming than Raz and accessible only by a half-hour's walk, but a good deal more peaceful; and the Pointe de Brézellac, farther along, where the viewing area is close to the road.

DOUARNENEZ: Businesslike Douarnenez, a town of about 18,000 with packing plants and efficient docks, offers a certain respite from touristy Raz. The quays are lined with straightforward bars with names like *Le Voyageur* and *Le Navigateur,* meant for sailors. A stop at the New Port, which looks more industrial than nautical with its seawalls, ramps, and warehouses, offers another look at the seafaring life while its jetty provides a broad view of the town's namesake bay. Visitors who pass through Douarnenez in the morning should make a point of pausing at the open-air market near the Place Gabriel-Péri, where ladies in *coiffes* sometimes can be seen. Boat lovers should not miss the *Musée du Bateau* (Pl. de l'Enfer; phone: 98-92-65-20), with its fascinating marine memorabilia. Open daily from 10 AM to noon and 2 to 7 PM.

Offering another view of the craggy coast to the west are the harbor cruises (phone: 98-27-09-54 or 98-92-10-38), available from June through September, which visit the seabird refuge, the Réserve de Cap Sizun; pass by the Grottes de Lanvilo, hollowed out by the sea; and take in Ile Tristan, the legendary setting for the palace of King Mark of Cornwall. His nephew, Prince Tristan, was sent to Ireland to fetch his bride, Iseult. But the pair accidentally consumed a love potion intended to cement Mark's own union. Breton fancies embroider the end: Some people say that Tristan is murdered by Mark. Others marry off Tristan and Iseult and let them live happily ever after.

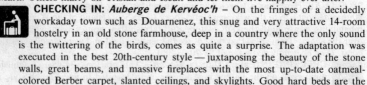 **CHECKING IN: *Auberge de Kervéoc'h* –** On the fringes of a decidedly workaday town such as Douarnenez, this snug and very attractive 14-room hostelry in an old stone farmhouse, deep in a country where the only sound is the twittering of the birds, comes as quite a surprise. The adaptation was executed in the best 20th-century style — juxtaposing the beauty of the stone walls, great beams, and massive fireplaces with the most up-to-date oatmeal-colored Berber carpet, slanted ceilings, and skylights. Good hard beds are the frosting on the cake. Closed from mid-October to *Easter.* Rte. de Kervéoc'h, 2½ miles (4 km) from Douarnenez on the Rte. de Quimper (phone: 98-92-07-58). Moderate to inexpensive.

LOCRONON: Some visitors find this little inland town too pretty to be real; others lament the number of tourists who clog its narrow lanes and tiny craft stores and boutiques throughout the season. Nonetheless, if you have time to visit only one of Brittany's inland towns during your stay, it probably should be this one.

It is an enchanting village, a real gem. Its perfectly preserved 16th-to-17th-century square is rimmed by old houses built of granite gone mossy with age, brightened with pots of geraniums, and punctuated by a small old well where a handful of children usually can be seen peering over the edge. And the 15th- to 16th-century Eglise et Chapelle du Pénity forms a relatively simple ensemble that strikes just the right note in the setting.

Inside are several statues, some carved out of relatively soft Kersanton granite by a busy local workshop of the 17th century, and others made from wood — Christopher the ferryman with the baby Jesus on his strong shoulders, Barbara and her tower, Fiacre with his spade, the Virgin Mary, and others; the most notable is the one sculpted in Kersanton granite on the tomb of St. Ronan, an Irish bishop who came to the area (and gave it his name) in search of a solitary environment in which to lead a life of self-denial and mortification during the Viking invasions of the 9th century. Tradition has it that passing underneath the statue, which is supported by a sextet of yard-high figures also carved from granite, will suppress symptoms of arthritis. On the pulpit, be sure to note the series of paintings that tell the story of St. Ronan's arrival in the area, his conversion of a peasant, his persecution by neighbors and by the peasant's wife, his rescue of a child from the dead, and his ultimate defeat of the devil. The very fortunate traveler will arrive at the church when the rich, sonorous organ is being played.

Just as much of the history of Locronan is bound up with St. Ronan, so too the physical town owes its current appearance to the weaving business that flourished here between the 16th and 18th centuries. The architectural harmony of the square and the richness of the ecclesiastical embellishments are the legacy of the prosperous times — when literally acres of sailcloth were shipped to England, Spain, and Holland, among other places — and their preservation is mainly a result of the poverty of the village in the intervening years. The town was so poor by the beginning of the 19th century that when the church steeple collapsed, struck by lightning, the villagers could not afford to rebuild it and had no recourse but to finish pulling it down. This abject poverty has been eroded by the influx of tourists, and the old houses and other granite structures have now been given over to shops where the merchandise, mainly hand wovens and hand knits and other one-of-a-kind wares, is decidedly above average. These, together with a handful of studios where craftsmen can be seen at their looms and workbenches, are scattered on the perimeter of the main square and along the streets and narrow alleyways leading from it.

Locronan is also the site of an elaborate *pardon* at which pilgrims follow the path to the top of the Mountain of Locronan that St. Ronan, barefoot and fasting, used during his life in the area. Cars can drive up the mountain throughout the year, and there's a small chapel with pretty stained glass windows and a fine view over the area at the top. But it is more colorful during the *pardons* — both the minor ones held on the second Sunday in July most years and the larger "Grande Troménie," as the procession is called, when the route is extended to 7 miles and broken up with 12 stops, held in mid-July every 6 years; the next will take place in 1995.

CHECKING IN: *Hôtel au Fer à Cheval* – "The Horseshoe" is handsome and contemporary if not particularly endowed with the charming atmosphere of the establishment's sister restaurant on the Locronan square — itself quite acceptable and decidedly friendly, considering its location in the heart of one of the most heavily visited villages in Brittany. All 35 rooms are modern and have a television set. Closed Mondays. Rte. du Bois-de-Nevet-Locronan, Locronan (phone: 98-91-70-67). Moderate.

En Route from Locronan – Follow D63 to Plonévez-Porzay, then take D61 to Ste.-Anne-la-Palud, where a 19th-century chapel peers out over the flattest of seaside meadows, gilded beautifully in summer by little yellow flowers. Every year, on the last Sunday of August, the area is the setting for a massive Breton *pardon* to which the faithful come in such numbers that the narrow roads become nearly impassable. From here, go inland again to Ploeven and turn toward the sea and travel through St.-Sebastian to Lestrevet, the southernmost crossroads settlement along the Lieu de Grève (Place of Beach), where there is a remarkable long, wide, straight, flat, Atlantic-pounded strand on one side of the road and an expanse of green pastures on the other.

Next, turn toward St.-Nic and travel through some wide open country patched with fields and strips of trees. Then take D108 for about 2 miles (3 km) and D887 for about a third of a mile in the direction of Châteaulin to the turnoff for the steep D83, which ascends the Menez-Hom; its utterly bald, windswept, 1,082-foot summit is one of the finest viewing points in the province. On cloudy days, you won't see a thing; don't even bother to leave the main road. The rest of the time, it is possible to see Locronan Mountain, Douarnenez, Van Point, and more. A viewing table identifies them all.

CHECKING IN/EATING OUT: *Hôtel de la Plage* – Embraced on one side by the gorgeous Lieu de Grève and nuzzled by a garden and a couple of handsome cypress trees, this charming white stucco hostelry (a Relais & Châteaux member) is tranquil as can be. There's a pool and tennis and sunsets to admire (right from your room if it faces west). The good food — lamb with a tarragon cream sauce, frozen raspberry soufflé, and other items according to the chef's inspiration — is the bonus. Closed from mid-October through March. On the beach in Ste.-Anne-la-Palud (phone: 98-92-50-12). Expensive.

Relais de Porz-Morvan – Staying at this hostelry, whose clean and comfortable if not particularly stylish 12 rooms were installed in a granite farmhouse and the neighboring stables, is a reason for winnowing your way into the most rural heart of the Breton countryside. Absolute quiet reigns. Tennis, too. The adjacent *crêperie,* which displays a collection of Breton antiques that only adds to the coziness, serves fine crêpes. The specialty of the house, crêpes stuffed with apples and flamed with calvados, is worth a try. Closed October to *Easter.* 1¼ miles (2 km) from Plomodiern (phone: 98-81-53-23). Moderate.

CROZON PENINSULA: Route D887 — a fine road that races through sweeping fields and pastures full of black and white cows — leads west onto this peninsula, another grand Breton meeting ground for sea and sky. Each of the handful of rock-bound points begs to be explored: the most southerly, the Cap de la Chèvre (the Goat's Cape), which pushes across Douarnenez Bay toward the Pointe du Van and the Pointe de Brézellac and their neighbors on the Raz peninsula; the somewhat more impressive Pointe de Dinan, which ends in a rather castle-like rock formation; and the most northerly, the Pointe des Espagnols, on the end of a peninsula that boasts shoreline roads with exceptional scenery.

Those who have time to see only one should head toward the Pointe de Penhir, where there are high cliffs from whose edge the sea is 229 feet away — straight down. It is perpetually windy on these heights, the view is nothing but grand, and it would be easy to spend a couple of hours here clambering over the rocks or, on a weekday in the off-season, celebrating life with a picnic.

Of the trio of small towns on the peninsula, Camaret is most notable. It seems a random little place, neither rich nor obviously poor but simply utilitarian. It is well known as one of the most important French lobster ports, a fact confirmed by the abundance of boats in the harbor. There also is a building by the 17th-century military architect Vauban, a castle-like, red stucco structure full of slits that now houses a naval museum, and, nearby, a very simple, yellowish chapel, the Chapelle de Notre-Dame de Roc'h-Amadour, where a *pardon* is held every year on the first Sunday in September. With the rotting wooden ships left foundering on their sides like beached whales by the low tide, the whole scene is picturesque enough to warrant a detour. On the outskirts of town are the Lagatiar menhirs, megalithic standing stones arranged in a semicircle. Even awkwardly situated opposite some nondescript vacation houses, these boulders exert a deep Celtic power.

En Route from the Crozon Peninsula – Head back to D887 and thence to D791. This fast road ribbons through the woods, crosses the Aulne River and follows the coast (plenty of good views), and traverses tiny Le Faou, where you should watch for D42 in the direction of Rumengol, where *pardons* are held throughout the year. Route D42 then winds through the hilly Forêt de Cranou, whose oak and beech woods eventually give way to the great windswept plateaus of the Parc Naturel Régional d'Armorique, which preserves the Arrée Mountains. These are not high — only 1,200 feet at the most, their once lofty peaks ground down and eroded to hills by the ages — but they seem elevated enough thanks to their barren windswept summits and the wide open vistas they provide when clouds are not swirling around their summits.

At Croas-ar-Go, turn left onto D342 and make your way to Sizun, which has the first of a handful of parish closes. This one has an organ (1683–84) whose carved and gilded case compares favorably with the most beautiful baroque instruments in central

Europe. Its builder, the Englishman Thomas Dallam, had come to work in Brittany with his father, Robert, who was fleeing persecution by Queen Elizabeth I. Go north on D764 as far as Lanviguer, then turn north toward La Roche-Maurice. At La Martyre there is another parish close, where *pardons* are held on the second Sunday in May and July. Note the angels carved on the archway that frames the Nativity scene above the porch. Next, turn right on D35 toward Ploudiry, whose parish close has a bizarre ossuary on whose façade a Dance of Death is carved in relief.

LAMPAUL-GUIMILIAU: The parish close in this otherwise insignificant inland town is most notable for the incredible richness of the decoration inside the 16th-to-17th-century church. The idea seems to have been to cover every square inch of wall with ornamentation — not merely idle decoration but also a sort of bible for the poor. Wood carving, for instance, covers both sides of a 16th-century rood beam overhead, where angels catch the blood dripping from the feet of the crucified Christ; blankets the 18th-century pulpit; and overlays two panels flanking the altar. Particularly notable is an altarpiece divided into eight compartments, each one containing a scene from the Passion packed with figures carved with such skill that they almost seem to move. In addition, at the front of the church are lively paintings that portray square faces distinctive enough, one from the other, to suggest that they were modeled from life, and with formidable skill.

GUIMILIAU: This former weaving center is named for a good and pious 8th-century prince who was decapitated after 7 years on the throne at the instigation of his evil brother. With a population of only about 800, it is even smaller than Lampaul-Guimiliau. But its parish close, which includes a 16th-century church whose style foreshadows the Renaissance as well as several other structures, is even more striking. There literally are dozens of statuettes in the church. On the Renaissance porch, the arch that forms its entrance is articulated with three rows of figures representing angels and saints, and the corners seem to be sprouting curious gargoyles that look like bearded dragons. Inside the porch, both walls are lined with niches occupied by statues representing the 12 apostles; other figures, depicting scenes from the Old Testament, alternate with rose medallions in an ornamental frieze below. In one, a monk-exorcist stands near a grimacing sinner above whose head is a horned devil; in another, God can be seen pulling Eve by the arm out of the side of a sleeping Adam.

The large calvary (1581–85) is adorned by some 200 figures. Many depict scenes from Christ's life, but there also are local motifs such as the story of Catell-Gollet or Catherine la Perdue (Catherine the Lost), a servant girl who steals a consecrated Host as a present for her lover, actually the devil in disguise, and is subsequently condemned to all manner of hellish tortures. Young women with flirtation on their minds were meant to take note. The images are arranged on two levels, each of which seems to have been sculpted by a different artisan; the bodies of the lower statues seem dry and rigid and a bit naive, particularly in comparison to those outlined against the sky on the upper level, which are so full of curves and so dynamic that they seem almost ready to march off.

Be sure to note the late-17th-century baptismal font inside the church, one of the most exuberant pieces of carved oak anywhere in Brittany. Garlands, leaves, vines, tiny birds pecking at berries, saints, evangelists, angels, and more, embellish the structure. The organ and the pulpit, supported by a column comprised of four cherubs, are also elaborately ornamented. A visitor might find the same sumptuous carving in a great cathedral. But here, as at Lampaul-Guimiliau, the profusion of work is concentrated in a relatively limited space, so a sense of the talent and energy of the artists who wrought the wonders is brought home all the more clearly.

ST.-THÉGONNEC: Another magnificent Breton parish close can be found in the center of this little town. Note the calvary, built in 1610; the Passion is depicted on the base. The figure in the niche underneath is of St. Thégonnec, who is portrayed with a cart to which he harnessed a wolf after his donkey had been consumed by its fellows. The town's namesake also is portrayed over the porch of the church and in a niche above the pulpit inside. The figure bearing a trumpet atop the canopy is the Angel of Judgment.

The organ has been classed as a historical monument since December 1973. Ordered in 1670, it was the subject of a pair of suits — one by a local noblewoman, who insisted that her coat of arms be put on the organ case rather than on the bay window at the rear of the church, the other by the men of the church, who complained that the factory had not delivered a satisfactory instrument. The suits only increased its cost, and the organ had to be rebuilt by another manufactory before finally being installed in 1684. It was restored and transformed on a regular basis for the next 2 centuries. Far from harming the sound, these restorations, together with the most recent one (1978), only enhanced the original, so that now the instrument has a sonority all its own, as rich as the gilded carvings that encase it. Lucky are the travelers who arrive when an organist or a student is playing. Note the images on the console — among them Ste. Cecilia, the patroness of musicians.

EATING OUT: *Crêperie Steredenn* – Large photographs of Breton scenes decorate the stone walls here. A fire crackles in the huge hearth and, at dusk, throws a warm, flickering light on the low beamed ceiling. Breton and Irish music play on a sleek stereo tucked away in a vast oak armoire. Without question, this neat, friendly establishment rates kudos as one of the most pleasant *crêperies* in the province. Particularly tasty is the *crêpe druidique* — slathered with bitter orange marmalade and almonds flavored with Grand Marnier. Just up a hill on a street leading from the parish close. Open Fridays, Saturdays, and Sundays off-season. 6 Rue de la Gare, St.-Thégonnec (phone: 98-79-43-34). Inexpensive.

En Route from St.-Thégonnec – Take N12 west and D230 and D30 north to the coast. In contrast to the wild shoreline terrain in southern Brittany, this area is fertile — with fields of cauliflowers and artichokes that stand up straight as if looking out to sea. Sometimes you even can smell the vegetables in the fields. The unnumbered coast road takes in farm settlements like Forban, Poulfoën, Kervaliou, Moguériec, and Santec. Even these insignificant hamlets seem to have their imposing granite churches, their perforated belfries shooting high into the horizon. Even a slight rise in the road opens up a huge panorama. In Roscoff, an attractive resort center with shops selling *vêtements marins* (seafaring clothes) and a pretty harbor fixed up with new landscaping and contemporary lampposts, there is regular ferry service to the Ile de Batz, itself little more than a quaint village undiscovered by tourists, with huge stretches of coastline that cry out for picnickers. Ferry service to Cork, in the Irish Republic, and to Plymouth, England, is also available from Roscoff.

CHECKING IN/EATING OUT: *Brittany* – The dining salon has stone floors, walls made of huge granite blocks, and a baronial fireplace; the bar is done up with red tartans; there are crystal chandeliers and an overall air of stateliness about the lobby; and the rooms, in a new tower in the back, have balconies, views, and the 20th-century comforts appropriate for a middle class clientele. This property adjoins a small pebbly beach. Closed off-season. Bd. Ste.-Barbe, Roscoff (phone: 98-69-70-78). Expensive to moderate.

Gulf Stream – Fresh seafood, often innovatively sauced with something like a cucumber purée or made into a terrine encased in aspic, is the specialty at this 32-room establishment overlooking a great sweep of Roscoff's bay. Closed from late October to April. Rue Marquise-de-Kergariou, Roscoff (phone: 98-69-73-19). Hotel, moderate; restaurant, expensive to moderate.

ST.-POL-DE-LÉON: Between January and September, the modern market here bustles with activity as tractor trailers, vans, carts, and vehicles of all descriptions haul in artichokes, cauliflowers, onions, potatoes, and other vegetables from the fertile fields that surround the town. This commerce adds another dimension to what is already a very worthwhile place to visit.

The chief attractions of the town, which was named for a Celtic religious leader who came here from Britain in the 5th century, are two ecclesiastical structures. The Cathédrale de St.-Pol-de-Léon, built between the 13th and the 16th century, is especially elegant, in part because of its fine proportions, in part because of the use of Norman limestone, whose pale hue lends a lightness to the interior. There is a beautiful 15th-century rose window, whose bright colors often are thrown on the polished wood floor of the sanctuary. Note the wooden statue of Ste. Apolline, now the patron saint of dentists, whose torturers pulled out all her teeth. Just to the rear of the sanctuary are a few rows of skulls, collected by families to keep relics of the dead formerly buried in the cemetery; some are enclosed in boxes ornamented by heart-shaped perforations that reveal a bit of bone inside. The carved oak bishops' stalls are also very fine. The organ dates from the 17th and 19th centuries.

The Kreisker Chapel, down the road a short distance and now part of a boys' school, is known for its tall belfry set at the transept crossing, made to seem even taller than its 246 feet by the vertical tracery articulating the windows. Inspired by the spire of St. Peter's in Caen, Normandy, which was destroyed during the war, it has itself been the inspiration for many others. The tall steeple at the top is stabilized by four bell towers; the whole structure is supported inside by a stone vault joining four massive uprights. The rest of the roof inside is of wood.

En Route from St.-Pol-de-Léon – The narrow roads that hug the coast, with their vistas of ocean and artichokes, are the most scenic way to travel south. Farm compounds and resort communities, which nudge each other like the black and white squares of a chessboard, add still more variety. Particularly on a sunny day, a traveler making a hurried tour of Brittany yearns for an extra couple of days in which to sprawl in the sun on a pretty stone terrace or to stroll along a promenade by the sea. Carantec, on a point well off the highways and all the more pleasant as a result, is particularly delightful. The roads that wind through the residential areas are almost too narrow for even a single tiny French vehicle. Houses crowded with hydrangeas are angled this way and that to maximize the minuscule amount of space. There are fine views, like the one from the Pointe de Pen-Lan.

Going south, D73 toward Locquénolé hugs the west shore of the Morlaix estuary, crossing gently rolling countryside occasionally patched with trees. Now and then you can see a sailboat chugging back to its moorings at Morlaix or out to sea for a day on the water. By the time D73 joins D769, the estuary has narrowed to the dimensions of a stream. High cliffs line it on one side and a wooded slope plunges on the other.

CHECKING IN: *La Falaise* – The yachtsmen who often patronize this small stucco and brick hotel set quietly on a high cliff above the Bay of Morlaix give the place a particularly relaxed air, and the rosy-cheeked proprietor adds the perfect touch of friendliness. The 24 guestrooms are simple and clean with high ceilings. The long dining room, where oysters may be served flavored with sorrel in puff pastry or the turbot in a creamy casserole, seems austere, but only because it lacks the antique bibelots to which Breton restaurants accustom their patrons. Closed from mid-September to mid-May. Plage de Kélenn, Carantec (phone: 98-67-00-53). Inexpensive.

Pors-Pol – This very simple family hotel, set in a residential neighborhood, provides rooms with sea views and a small beach nearby. Closed from late September to late March. 7 Rue Surcouf, Carantec (phone: 98-67-00-52). Inexpensive.

MORLAIX: Typical of many towns of the same size (pop. 20,000), this erstwhile port dominating the estuary of its namesake river boasts an extremely handsome old quarter with narrow, twisting streets and lanes, row upon row of houses dating from the days of half-timbers through the 19th century, and fashionable shops purveying shoes, faïences (ceramicware), and clothing. Especially noteworthy are the Grand'Rue, the Place Salvador Allende, the Place des Jacobins, and the Place des Viarmes. The corbelled 16th-century Maison de la Reine Anne, whose overhanging half-timbered second story seems to be supported by caryatids carved in the form of saints, is on the Rue de Mûr, which parallels the Grand'Rue.

What makes Morlaix different is its topography — immense hills that demand perpetual downshifting in the car. From the topmost of the city's tiers, there are fine views of the estuary and the old town not far away. There is also a mammoth 2-story viaduct across the Morlaix. Measuring 190 feet in height and 935 feet in length, it can be seen from most open areas in the city.

CHECKING IN: *Europe* – A traditional, 66-room hotel, with a restaurant whose chef is considered one of France's most promising young talents. His preparations are classical, yet original, served in elegant surroundings. 1 Rue Aiguillon, Morlaix (phone: 98-62-11-99). Hotel, moderate; restaurant, expensive.

EATING OUT: *La Marée Bleue* – In an old stone building that has been renovated to reflect contemporary design, the food is fully the equal of the extremely gracious reception accorded to guests. Seafood and fish are presented either plain or with the kinds of sauces that are simply not found in every Breton restaurant. The lengthy, detailed wine list is an education in its own right. Closed Mondays and February. 3 Rampe St.-Mélaine, Morlaix (phone: 98-63-24-21). Moderate.

HUELGOAT: Breton scenery lovers come here by the score to walk through the forests to which the woodsy scenery along D769 from Morlaix provides a good introduction, and to see the unusual arrangements of huge sandstone and granite boulders, some coated with intensely green moss, which are tumbled through the woods and along the little Argent River in ways that have suggested names like Chaos du Moulin (Mill Rock Chaos), Grotte du Diable (Devil's Grotto), Ménage de la Vierge (Virgin's Household), Roche Tremblante (Trembling Rock), and others. The latter, which weighs in at about 100 tons, can be made to sway on its base if you push hard enough. Great old oaks, beeches, and spruce and pine trees tower over these landmarks, which are reached by well-marked footpaths. Because the forest floor has no underbrush, the area has an unusually open feeling.

There also is a little lake, where anglers try for carp and perch, and a handsome square, the Place Aristide-Briand.

However, the whole area abounds in hiking trails that take in fine scenery, and it would be easy to spend more than the hour and a half that it takes most visitors to whiz in and out of Huelgoat. In nearby Locmaria-Berrien, a pretty chapel is fronted by two immense oak trees, one of them completely hollow inside and bound together by rusting bands. Nearby, a caravan center in the old railroad station, *Rouloete Bretagne,* rents cozy, bright carriages reminiscent of Gypsy wagons and the gentle horses to pull them for anywhere from a few days to weeks at a time. The proprietors will help plan the route to include as many of the local calvaries, chapels, manors, farms, and granite hamlets as you have time to see. A carriage costs about $600 per week. April through late September. (Gare de Locmaria-Berrien, Huelgoat 29218; phone: 98-99-73-28.)

CHECKING IN/EATING OUT: *Auberge de la Truite* – The very gracious *patronne,* who has presided over this neat establishment for some half a century and is now well into her eighties, nevertheless still keeps 6 comfortable rooms, a fine wine cellar, and a good restaurant, where the *truite maison* (housestyle trout) comes with a *beurre blanc* (white butter) sauce flavored with lemon and chives. Closed January and February, Sunday evenings and Mondays except in July and August. Locmaria-Berrien, 4¼ miles (7 km) from Huelgoat via D764 (phone: 98-99-73-05). Hotel, moderate; restaurant, expensive to moderate.

En Route from Huelgoat – The fields and forest scenery of the Argoat is at its best to the east, especially off the main roads. Follow the signs along the swooping curves of D769 through Poullaouen; then head along D154 to beautiful St.-Gildas, where there is a picturesquely situated chapel just at the base of a hill where the Romans once camped — ideal for picnics. Follow the signs south through Carnoët to D787, then turn north toward Callac. From there, follow D18 to St.-Servais, then go north on D31 to Burthulet, in whose lonely chapel the devil is said to have died of cold, and Bulat-Pestivien, whose 15th-to-16th-century church is one of the oldest in the Renaissance style in Brittany.

Retrace your steps along the beautiful D31 as far as Ty-Bourg and D28, then continue south on D31. At Croas-Tasset, there is a turnoff on D20 for the Gorges du Corong. Large trees planted atop the hedgerows arch over the road to the south. At N164, about 9 miles (14 km) farther south on D31, turn east toward Rostrenen.

From here it's possible to follow many beautiful country roads, turning this way and that, to skirt the massive impoundment of the Blavet River known as the Lac de Guerlédan. Routes D15A and D15 both cross the woods and heath plateau country of the 6,916-acre Forêt de Quénécan. For a more direct route, head directly toward Gouarec along N164. A short distance from town are the deep Gorges du Daoulas, some almost vertical, formed where the Daoulas River joins the Blavet. Just off the N164 bis about 3 miles (5 km) shy of Gouarec are the exciting ruins of the 12th-century Abbaye de Bon Repos, where the ivy grows thick as plush on the granite stones and ferns feather the broken tops of the walls.

At Gouarec, turn north along D8 for more exploring in the Argoat. At the Gorges de Toul Goulic, about 8 miles (13 km) north, a rather steep footpath leads to the point at which the sizable Blavet River totally disappears into a cleft. About 3 miles (5 km) farther, the Chapelle de Notre-Dame-de-Guiaudet suddenly appears almost out of nowhere, its immense belfry crammed with bells outlined against the sky. Accessible via a road lined on both sides with straight rows of trees, it occupies a piece of property that itself is laid out in a cruciform with the Stations of the Cross, a fountain, and a war monument.

CHECKING IN/EATING OUT: *Blavet* – For peace and quiet, this *auberge* on a sometimes busy highway is not ideal. But the simplest rooms have real charm with their old-fashioned wallpaper, Breton armoires, antique headboards, high ceilings, and modern bathrooms; and some of the rooms are quite elaborate, with four-poster beds and such. (One wishes that the rather soft mattresses were equally satisfactory.) There is a homey quality about the hairless doll, the high chair, and other debris of children that may occupy a corner of the breakfast room during the off-season. The dining room, with its rosy pink linen tablecloths, is elegant, as is the food — such as crayfish salad doused with raspberry vinegar or tournedos topped with wild mushrooms. Closed Sunday evenings and Mondays (except in July and August), a week in December, and during January. N164 bis, Gouarec (phone: 96-24-90-03). Moderate.

Hostellerie de l'Abbaye – Set at the end of a path of sycamores within a few hundred yards of the ruins of the Abbaye de Bon Repos, this longtime restaurant has acquired 5 rooms that can't be beat for tranquillity. Closed Wednesdays, 2 weeks in January, and 2 weeks in October. Just off N164 bis, St.-Gelven, west of Gouarec (phone: 96-24-98-38). Moderate to inexpensive.

GUINGAMP: This erstwhile feudal city is another one of those beautiful Breton towns with a tree-bordered square, a batch of half-timbered houses, and a fine Gothic church. Here, though, there also is a wonderful tiered fountain full of carved horses with goose wings, dragon tails, and goat faces. And the Basilique de Notre-Dame de Bon-Secours (Basilica of Our Lady of Perpetual Help) is Gothic only on one side. When the south side collapsed in the 16th century, the town held a competition and awarded the commission to a young architect whose plans were in the Renaissance style. Inside and out, the two faces are obvious — the round Renaissance arches with their keystones and pilasters on one side, and the Gothic ogives on the other. The best views are from the side yard (the opposite side of the church from the one edged by the Rue Notre-Dame). The Black Virgin, the basilica's patroness, has a chapel of her own opening into the Rue Notre-Dame; her altar is always massed with flowers. A *pardon* held annually on the Saturday night before the first Sunday in July attracts thousands.

CHECKING IN/EATING OUT: *Le Relais du Roy* – The presence of this hostelry in an old house on the main square is reason enough for travelers to seek out Guingamp. The 7 rooms, reached by climbing a 16th-century stone-walled stairwell, are decorated in the best of taste, with oh-so-French furnishings and appropriate wallpapers, generally striped or flowered. The same is true of the small and intimate dining room, where several carefully conceived *table d'hôte* dinners usually are available. The cozy bar, all polished mahogany and brass with Empire-style armchairs and walls of a golden brown raw silk that lends a certain formality, is a fine place for a quiet afternoon coffee. Be sure to note the Renaissance doorway in the courtyard, edged with carvings of many droll faces. 42 Pl. du Centre, Guingamp (phone: 96-43-76-62). Expensive to moderate.

En Route from Guingamp – Lannion and the coast can be reached in a flash by D767, but it's far more pleasant to make the trip along meandering country roads. Take N12 to the turnoff to the Menez-Bré, where a narrow, bumpy road climbs to lush meadows, where there is a simple stone chapel, like one a child might draw, and a fine view that stretches for miles. Return to N12, and turn right toward Gollot and Manaty. Then make your way to D11 following D31A, D31, and D30.

From D11, you can turn off for the Kergrist castle, whose gardens may be toured. Farther along, signs point to the moss-splotched Chapelle de Kerfons, which sits on a rutted road opposite a stone barn where the pigeons bill and coo as if to fill the quiet countryside with noise, and to the ruined 15th-century Château de Tonquédec, a hulk of granite topping the crest of a precipitous hill surrounded by beautiful woods. The keep has walls 13 feet thick.

CÔTE DU GRANIT ROSE: This stretch of shore, which runs between Morlaix and St.-Brieuc, is aptly named for the beautiful rosy hue of the rocks. This route explores it beginning at Trébeurden.

From this little beach town to the larger resort city of Perros-Guirec, the ocean has carved and chiseled the granite rocks offshore into fabulous shapes. Any drive in this area turns up a handful of signs pointing to boulders that only occasionally resemble the armchairs, corkscrews, elephants, gnomes, horses, rabbits, rams, thimbles, turtles, umbrellas, whales, witches, and such for which they are named; viewing points like the high, windy Pointe de Bihit at Trébeurden provide a panorama of such rocks both up and down the coast. In Trégastel, there is the Tire-Bouchon (Corkscrew), which looks much like a pile of cow dung, and an improbable Roi Gradlon (King Gradlon). The hour-long walk along the Grève Blanche (White Sandbank), roughly between the beach at the end of the Rue Grève-Blanche and the far end of the Plage de Coz-Pors (Coz-Pors Beach), skirts the coast, where imaginative travelers can make up a few names for the rock formations along the way. Still others — the Tête de Mort (Death's Head) and the Tas de Crêpes (Pile of Pancakes) — lie just beyond.

Ploumanach, a not particularly scenic fishing port and seaside resort farther along, has its own spate of rock formations, which surround a lighthouse a few yards from the sea. A platform close to the top provides a bird's-eye view of the coast. Nearby, the rocky landscape has been preserved as a municipal park. The Pointe du Squewel shows off the sawtoothed, rockpiled shoreline at its best. Those with a penchant for walking can follow the celebrated Sentier des Douaniers (Customs Agents' Footpath) along the tops of the 100-foot-high red and black stone cliffs within sight of more of these bizarre formations all the way to Perros-Guirec (about 2½ hours round-trip); sometimes there are berries to pick en route. Offshore are the Sept-Iles, a sanctuary for the auks, cormorants, gannets, gulls, guillemots, and puffins that nest on the island cliffs. Bird watchers interested in coming here should contact the Office de Tourisme in Perros-Guirec (phone: 96-23-21-15).

Every rocky point along this shoreline offers similar scenery. Sometimes there are grand vistas from the road or from a viewing point with a parking lot; sometimes a short walk is required. Adventure-minded travelers can follow their own whims, twisting through the crannied lanes of the residential neighborhoods that always seem to cluster near the shore, glimpsing bits of sea and sky between the houses, or swooping and soaring along as the road rises and falls with a full panorama of rocks and ocean off to the side. Often the road will end within a few feet of a beach. The long crescent of sand at Perros-Guirec, presided over by a casino that looks like a Moorish temple without the minarets, is wide and long and usually moderately to extremely crowded; but others that are quieter, less heavily endowed with facilities like trampolines and changing tents, are not hard to find. Sometimes, as in the area near Porz-Hir and the Pointe du Château, people are selling *homards* (lobsters) and *huítres* (oysters). The whole landscape is littered with boulders, and often the houses are built right up beside them. On these roads, it is impossible to hurry.

Tréguier, the site of an extravagant *pardon* honoring Brittany's beloved St. Yves, is another pretty Breton town. Its Cathédrale de St.-Tugdual is unusual for its handsome cloister and its relatively unspoiled vertical lines, and the inside walls are full of simple carved plaques thanking the saint for miraculous rescues. "Merci à St.-Yves," they read. Known for righting wrongs, this legendary figure once heard a suit in which a wealthy man complained about a beggar who loitered at his kitchen window to sniff the odors of the food cooking inside. Tossing a coin on the bench, Yves informed the plaintiff that the ring of the coin was his recompense for the smell of the food.

Particularly beautiful among the rocky viewing spots is the Pointe de l'Arcouest, where the shoreline slopes gently to the sea with a jumble of rocks whose hollows are filled with little pools of water that sparkle like sequins in the sun. The view is of the Ile de Bréhat, a mile long and twice that in width, where there are parks and gardens and villas, fields crossed by footpaths, and lots more rocky, cove-notched coast. It is beautiful, silent, and incredibly pastoral — well worth a trip. According to local legend, Christopher Columbus learned about the existence of the New World, nearly a decade before his milestone voyage, from a seafaring man from Bréhat whose fellow fishermen had been traveling there for years.

South of Paimpol are the farm-ringed ruins of the 13th-to-14th-century Abbaye de Beauport, built of warm, rose-colored granite furred with ivy, ferns, and other greenery. The beautifully articulated rose window is worth noting even without stained glass.

Binic, once a codfishing center, still is a seagoing place, with its serviceable jetty and a plethora of marine stores that really mean business. Some of the buildings that edge the harbor are modern and not particularly picturesque, but the town is not overbuilt and seems more relaxed than most. Notre-Dame-de-la-Cour, named for the small 15th-century chapel at its center, lies inland; it has harmonious proportions, elegant detailing, and a dollhouse quality that is particularly appealing.

On D786 from here to St.-Brieuc, tiny spur roads run down to the sea. There are no obvious stops, no musts except the sunrises over the Baie de St.-Brieuc, which are well worth the trouble it takes to see them. The point of this coast is to follow your hunches, to pick a road and follow it to the end just to see what's there.

CHECKING IN: ***Château de Coatguélen*** – This mid-19th-century château with 16 rooms rises like a fairy tale fantasy in the middle of an expansive park. Tennis, swimming pool, fishing, and golf. Closed from mid-November to mid-March. On D7, between Lanvollon and Paimpol (phone: 96-22-31-24). Expensive.

Manoir de Lan-Kerellec – This 13-room hotel (a member of the Relais & Châteaux group), whose restaurant has earned one Michelin star, occupies a handsome old stone building with smartly squared hedges twice the height of a man and comfortable rooms with ocean views. The dining salon, with its vaulted ceiling and baronial paneling, is especially striking. Closed from mid-January to mid-March. Trébeurden (phone: 96-23-50-09). Expensive.

Ti al-Lannec – Rarely in Brittany do you find a hostelry like this one, in which the conversion from bourgeois mansion to hotel has been executed with such taste and attention to detail. Lively wallpapers add cheer to bedrooms, which already have sloped ceilings or fine views or even terraces to their credit. There might be eyelet embroidery edging the sheets, or an antique white coverlet on the bed, a quaint hooked rug on the floor, or a handsome bouquet on the dressing table. Bathrooms are capacious as can be, with plenty of big, thick towels. As if that's not enough, the management sparkles with friendliness, and there are salons where guests can play Bach on an excellent stereo and enjoy after-dinner coffee and chocolate truffles over a game of cards or Scrabble. The food is excellent in the best nouvelle manner. Consider, for instance, the seafood terrine with two sauces, a symphony of pinks and whites that is almost fragile to the fork, or any other fish on the menu, whose English names the waiters are only too glad to share. Restaurant closed Monday lunch except in season; hotel closed from mid-November to mid-March. Allée de Mézo-guen, Trébeurden (phone: 96-23-57-26). Expensive.

Le Barbu – Many a beautiful point in Brittany has its hotel, but few are as pretty as this old-fashioned, 19-room establishment, with its panoramic restaurant above the sea, its small swimming pool, its hedge of hydrangeas, its chandeliered salon, and its lace curtains. On the Pointe de l'Arcouest, about 3½ miles (6 km) from Paimpol (phone: 96-55-88-60 or 96-55-86-98). Expensive to moderate.

La Colombière – Spectacularly set on a pine-fuzzed cliff overlooking a swooping curve of beach and acres of blue water, this is a friendly place. Though close to the highway, it is in a hollow so that the chief noise is not of traffic but of the crash of the surf. The garden is full of hydrangeas, paths run down to the sea, and bleating goats roam a section of the lawn. The comfortable rooms vary from antique to contemporary in style, and many have fine sea views. The menu is mainly seafood. Closed the first 2 weeks of October. Bd. du Littoral, Etables-sur-Mer (phone: 96-70-61-64). Expensive to moderate.

Printania – The atmosphere at this half-century-old establishment straddles the fine line between being very outmoded as a result of its age and very contemporary thanks to stylish refurbishings. Some rooms have balconies and narrow doors, and others have huge round windows. Closed from mid-December to mid-January. 12 Rue des Bons-Enfants, Perros-Guirec (phone: 96-23-21-00). Expensive to moderate.

Repaire de Kerroc'h – Firmly planted at the end of a little port overlooking a harbor full of pleasure boats and delicate masts, this handsome 7-room establishment comprises two imposing 18th-century townhouses. Open year-round. 29 Quai Morand, Paimpol (phone: 96-20-50-13). Moderate.

EATING OUT: *La Cotriade* – A former cook from New York City's *Lutèce* now holds forth in a tiny harbor establishment named for Brittany's fish stew; he offers some of the most inspired cooking in Brittany and has elevated regional dishes to works of art by his deft touch. His *homard grillé* (grilled lobster) and *turbot au beurre rouge* (turbot in red butter) are just two of the dishes for which he has earned one Michelin star. Closed Monday nights, Tuesdays, January, and February. Port de Piégu, about ½ mile (1 km) from Pléneuf-Val-André (phone: 96-72-20-26). Expensive.

Lorand-Barre – The decor is country, the menu lengthy and well balanced (with one Michelin star), and the *homard grillé* (grilled lobster), the *ris de veau au porto* (sweetbreads in port), and the *poulet sauté à l'estragon* (chicken sautéed with tarragon) as professionally presented as they are delicious. Closed Sunday nights, Mondays, and winter. Les Ponts-Neufs, about halfway between St.-Brieuc and Lamballe (phone: 96-32-78-71). Expensive.

La Vieille Tour – Seafood is the specialty at this highly regarded establishment with one Michelin star near St.-Brieuc, and it is as innovatively prepared as it is fresh. Unusual egg yolk sauces, lobster cooked with herbed oysters, and light dessert pastries with caramelized strawberries are among the culinary stars here. Closed Saturdays for lunch and Sundays. 75 Rue de la Tour, Port de St.-Brieuc-Le-Légué, about 2 miles (3 km) from St.-Brieuc on D24 (phone: 96-33-10-30). Expensive to moderate.

CÔTE D'EMERAUDE: Reaching from St.-Brieuc to Dinard, this scalloped coastline takes in a string of pretty resort and harbor towns along D786. At both points of every scallop, there are fine views and pleasant walks.

At Le Val-André, which is noted for its beautiful long beach, a visitor might stroll along the cliff path high above the Bay of St. Brieuc to the Pointe de Pléneuf, or on the Promenade de la Guette (Watchman's Walk), where there are still other sea views. At Erquy, a cluster of beautiful little houses wrap around a huge bay where a small scallop fishing fleet anchors at night, and an evening walk might lead along the harbor, where the sun can be seen setting through a grid of masts. There are beaches to explore at Sables-d'Or-les-Pins, which is full of hotels, and at Le Vieux Bourg.

But there are two particularly fine experiences — the ride from here to Cap Fréhel, on a road that skims the clifftops along the fringes of the gold-tinged fields, then drops off to perfect little beaches; and a walk on the cape itself, across moors flecked with tiny golden flowers where the constant wind has bent the heather to its will. The cliffs are rocky and high, reaching to some 229 feet, and the panorama stretches from the Ile de Bréhat on the left to the Pointe de Grouin on the right. When the weather is very clear, it's possible to see all the way to the Channel Islands. The whole area is crossed by paths; be sure to view the seagulls and cormorants crowded on the Fauconnière rocks just offshore, and at dusk, when the light transforms the landscape into a study in pastels, try to get off by yourself for a while to muse on the grandeur of the spectacle. Just to the east on this hefty notch of land, it's possible to see Fort La Latte, a massive 13th-to-14th-century stronghold — everyone's idea of a medieval fort. You can visit the fort (signs near Fréhel point the way), and it's well worth the long walk from the parking lot to the drawbridge, for here the thick stone walls that make so many French castles so impressive frame not ordinary scenery but some of Brittany's most stunning sea views. Incredible as it may seem, sections of the structure still are inhabited.

Dinard, which marks the eastern end of the Emerald Coast, is tame by comparison.

But its own charms, representing the civilized side of the province, are considerable: high Victorian villas that crane toward the view; narrow lanes and pine-shaded residential neighborhoods; a large casino; a beach pinned at one end by a ruined priory; and a glittering round of resort life to be lived in dozens of hotels. (See *France's Best Beaches* in the DIVERSIONS section.)

DINAN: Of the many medieval towns in Brittany, this rampart-bound town of 14,000 stands out among the prettiest. It is guarded by a handsome castle and laced by winding streets lined with half-timbered houses in a quantity unusual even in Brittany. Certainly, if you see no other inland towns during your stay, it should be this one. And you should allow at least a couple of hours if you intend to dally among the shops in the picturesque old quarter.

The best place to begin is the Jardin Anglais, which snuggles up against the ramparts and offers a fine view of the valley of the Rance River and the 250-foot Romanesque bridge that spans it. The Promenade de la Duchesse Anne, shaded by beautiful rows of chestnut trees and punctuated with benches that would be perfect for a picnic, skirts the ramparts, then descends to the street, which eventually leads to the 14th-century castle, a section of which contains a museum of local history. Yet another gracious walkway, the Promenade des Petits-Fossés (Walk of the Little Ditches), skirts the base of the castle.

From the statue of the great 14th-century Breton soldier Bertrand du Guesclin, which stands at the midpoint of this Promenade, it's only a short walk via the Rue Ste.-Claire and the Rue de l'Horloge into the Old Town, one of the chief charms of Dinan. The Place des Merciers, the Place des Cordelièrs, the Rue de la Lainerie and its extensions, the Rue du Jerzual and the Rue du Petit-Fort, which are bounded by shops where artisans usually can be seen at work (but seldom on Mondays), all evoke another age. The Eglise St.-Sauveur, where Romanesque and Gothic are in gentle counterpoint, shelters the heart of du Guesclin, whose body was buried at St.-Denis, near Paris.

CHECKING IN/EATING OUT: *D'Avaugour* – A pleasant 27-room hotel, with a parrot who squawks "Bonjour" in the lobby. It overlooks the square in the front and a garden in the rear. The restaurant, presided over by a chef who ventures beyond the usual *plat de fruits de mer* (assorted seafood platter) into the nouvelle, in which diners might find their salads flavored with walnut oil and fruit or studded with turnips and oranges, or their platter of hot oysters served with curried carrot mousse. 1 Pl. de Champs Clos, Dinan (phone: 96-39-07-49). Expensive.

Manoir du Vaumadeuc – Built of Breton granite and fitted out with objets d'art from around the world, this former manor house is surely one of Brittany's most sumptuous hostelries. Its site deep in the quietest country is only part of the attraction. There are 9 elegant rooms, each one with a fireplace and some with massive overhead beams. And the cuisine is classic and ambitious, with lobster *gratiné* keeping company on the menu with *quenelles de brochet Nantua* (pike dumplings with a lobster sauce). Closed early January to mid-March. Pléven, near Plancoët, about 14½ miles (23 km) from Dinan (phone: 96-84-46-17). Expensive.

La Caravelle – The young J. C. Marmion, the chef at this comfortable 11-room establishment, lets the market determine his menu to a great degree. Tomato and fresh green peas might figure in the summer, while hare and rabbit might appear in the fall in his fricassees, mousses, terrines, sauces, and salads. Closed Sunday evenings and Wednesdays off-season, and the last 2 weeks of October. 14 Pl. Duclos, Dinan (phone: 96-39-00-11). Hotel, inexpensive; restaurant, expensive.

ST.-MALO: Many a fine town would lose its charm altogether if forced to endure the onslaught of visitors to which this one-time privateering and shipbuilding center is subjected nowadays — throughout the season and on weekends the rest of the year. But the crowd is a mixed lot: Americans who visit St.-Malo if they stop nowhere else in Brittany; Englishmen who arrive on their yachts or on huge, sleek white ferries from Portsmouth, Guernsey, Jersey, or Sark; and the professional seamen from the French navy or merchant marine who tie up here periodically. The mix gives the old city an air of festive good cheer such as that more commonly found at a *Mardi Gras* or a house party. The bars, most notably the one at the *L'Univers* on the Place Chateaubriand, are gleaming studies in brass and wood, with photographs of famous racing yachts. The restaurants are the kinds of comfortable and appealingly decorated eateries, seldom all that formal, that people like to find on vacation. And there are plenty of attractive shops in which to while away an afternoon or two. Not to mention the natural beauties: the scenery of rooftops and water seen from the ramparts, which are remnants of when St.-Malo was a republic in its own right and stayed aloof from attacking Normans, French, and English alike. (In fact, though St.-Malo seems very old, the structures themselves are restorations, since the *ville close* was largely destroyed during the war.)

The center of town is the Place Châteaubriand, named for the Romantic novelist who was born here. There is a museum devoted to Malouin history on the right, built into the ramparts; the exhibits, which include pirate paraphernalia like treasure chests and cannon, memorabilia of Châteaubriand and of the French explorer Jacques Cartier, are handsomely lighted and displayed elegantly enough to warrant a visit. A stairway nearby leads to the breezy ramparts for which the city is famous. Also worth visiting is the handsome Cathédrale de St.-Vincent, which has a 12th-century nave and a set of stunning, almost fiery, modern windows.

If there's time, take the 25-minute breezy walk out to the islets of Grand and Petit Bé, where Chateaubriand wished to be buried. (Check the tide tables, go at low tide, and plan to return before the tide rolls in again.)

CHECKING IN: *Central* – The Best Western chain's associate in the Old Town has 46 large, attractively furnished (if somewhat spare) rooms that substantiate its status as the premier hotel here, not to mention a creditable if somewhat formal restaurant. It is not long on warmth, however. 6 Grande-Rue, St.-Malo (phone: 99-40-87-70). Expensive to moderate.

Elizabeth – Notable for its small but attractive rooms, this snug 17-room establishment off the beaten path is certainly the most atmospheric and comfortable in the old city — a gem in a town where the polished exteriors too often conceal rundown guest quarters. No restaurant. 2 Rue des Cordiers, St.-Malo (phone: 99-56-24-98). Moderate.

EATING OUT: *Duchesse Anne* – Charming, brightly lit, and done up with reddish walls, this polished place with one Michelin star in the center of town serves fine fish and shellfish, including plain oysters from Cancale and occasional surprises like *pétoncles farcies* (garlicky buttered scallops sizzling on the half shell). Closed December, January, and Wednesdays. 5 Pl. Guy La Chambre, St.-Malo (phone: 99-40-85-33). Expensive to moderate.

En Route from St.-Malo – Don't miss the Pointe du Grouin, accessible from the scenic D201, which squiggles along the coast eastward.

CANCALE: This port of 5,000 has been famous for its oysters for centuries. And though the native shellfish population was decimated by a disease whose origins have never been pinpointed, Cancale has maintained its claim by using the oysterian equivalent of seedlings (*spats*), imported from the community of Auray in the south. The *spats* are shoveled into bags made of tough netting, taken out to sea, and left to grow for a couple of years before harvesting. Late in the afternoon, visitors gather along the port to watch the oyster boats come in and unload their huge sacks full of the delicacies, and shopkeepers display baskets of oysters in all shapes and varieties. No need to bemoan the lack of a picnic table: They can be opened and consumed with a squeeze of lemon on the spot, and the juices left to drip on the pavement.

EATING OUT: *Bricourt* – Situated in a charming village, this is the perfect place to savor the sea's best bounty. Choose from among anything with fins or shells. Closed Tuesdays, Wednesdays, Thursdays during July and August, and from the end of December to March. 1 Rue Duguesclin, Ille-et-Vilaine, Cancale (phone: 99-89-64-76). Expensive.

The Atlantic Coast

"The Green Venice." "The Coast of Beauty." "Bright Island." "The Savage Coast." "The City Built on a Balcony." All are tag names for places lying along this route through the Charente and Charente-Maritime departments of France. About 400,000 people live in the Charente, more than 500,000 in the Charente-Maritime. Just across the Gironde estuary from Bordeaux, they are accessible to travelers via autoroute A10, which goes from Paris to Bordeaux. The region attracts oyster lovers, cognac lovers, lovers of history and pastoral beauty — lovers period (they should go directly to La Rochelle and Ile de Ré). Though residents are quick to defend the distinction between the two departments, there is one unifying thread: The 220-mile Charente River, which Henry IV once called "the most beautiful stream in my kingdom," meanders past Angoulême and Cognac, in the Charente department, through Saintes and on to the sea at Rochefort, both in the Charente-Maritime.

Beginning at Angoulême, the route through the region heads west to Royan, then north to La Rochelle and the Marais Poitevin. It passes open meadows, rolling hills covered by lush vineyards, fields of corn or cows, rocky coastlines, enticing beaches, and more than its fair share of charming towns that history left in its wake. The French president François Mitterrand was born in the Charente-Maritime, in Jonzac, as well as Samuel de Champlain, the founder of Quebec who was born in Brouage. It was from this area that French pioneers set sail for the new land in Canada and America. Huguenot emigrants departed from La Rochelle and settled just north of New York City in a town they named New Rochelle. Settlers of Prince Edward Island, New Brunswick, and the rest of what became known as Acadia (in Canada), also hailed from here.

Still centuries after these adventurers helped tame the New World, many modern voyagers have yet to discover the charms of the area the Charentais left behind — one of France's most varied and fascinating regions. Too many travelers tend to dash through its mellow landscape en route to southern Atlantic seaside resorts. But those who take the time to linger find no lack of pleasures in this gentle countryside.

Nestled snugly between Brittany and Bordeaux, Charente and Charente-Maritime share characteristics with both neighbors, particularly the fishing culture of the north and the vineyards of the south. The landscape is dotted with marshlands and pastures and touched by sea breezes. Wealth derives equally from land, sea, and the estuaries in between. Stately châteaux stand as monuments to the prosperity the region has enjoyed. The most outstanding among them are the 15th-century Château de la Roche Courbon near Saintes (a few minutes' walk from prehistoric caves) and the 12th-century and Renaissance Château de la Rochefoucauld, where weekend *son et lumière* shows during the summer months trace 1,000 years of history.

Art and architecture tell the region's history — read it in the whimsical façade of Cathédral St.-Pierre, the amphitheater in Saintes, or the fairy tale stone towers guarding the entrance to La Rochelle's little port.

The regional character also is expressed eloquently through the food, which is simple and relies on the fine-quality products of land and sea, rather than on culinary sleight of hand. The famous oysters of Marennes-Oleron are eaten *au nature* or accompanied by small eels and escargots, the latter prepared with wine, onions, and garlic. Another specialty is *chaudrée,* a fish soup made with white wine and the fresh catch of the day (such as pike, merlan, or sole). Rich pasturelands produce beef, pork, and the succulent *pre-sale* lamb, named for the salt-water-washed feeding grounds that give the meat its special flavor. The butter of the Charente is prized by purists for its delicate flavor. And then there is cognac.

A substantial 236,000 acres in the Charente and Charente-Maritime produce the white grapes from which cognac, France's number one export, is made. The highest-quality grapes and resulting *eau-de-vie* come from the area immediately surrounding the towns of Cognac and Segonzac, named Grande Champagne. Cognac is a brandy, but most brandy is not cognac and cannot bear the name unless it is from this region and has been distilled twice, then carefully aged in oak barrels. The cognac industry began in the 17th century, and today more than 300 firms produce cognac; fewer than half of them export it, however. The large firms offer free tours and tastings and go out of their way to cater to tourists. Before tasting cognac, it is traditional to hold the bulb-shaped glass in your palm for a few minutes to warm it and release the spirit's vapors; sniff and then sip. Drinking cognac is a smelling and tasting experience, one to savor slowly.

Pineau, a regional drink rarely found elsewhere in France, is a mixture of one-third cognac and two-thirds unfermented grape juice, with an alcohol content of 16% to 22%. It remained a home brew from the 16th century until 1935, when it was first sold commercially.

The Charente River is navigable from Angoulême to Rochefort, with 21 tidegates over the 100-mile stretch. From April to July, boats carrying 70 to 180 people depart from Angoulême or Châteauneuf; from April to October, they leave Rochefort, St.-Savinien, Saintes, Cognac, and Jarnac. For information, contact the regional tourist office at Place Bouillaud in Angoulême (phone: 45-92-24-43). Barges also can be hired for 4- to 7-day cruises. For information, contact *Maison Poitou-Charentes,* 68-70 Rue de Cherche Midi, Paris 75006 (phone: 42-22-83-74).

There also are quite a few land activities in the region. The Charente area now offers a total of 12 golf courses, the majority of which opened in the last 2 years (for information, contact the regional tourist office in Poitiers; phone: 49-88-38-94). Add zoos, parks, aquariums, bird preserves, peaceful islands, and Venice-like canals winding through marshlands, and there's more than enough to justify an extended visit here.

The Charente and Charente-Maritime regions have a vast selection of good hotels at reasonable prices. Though good restaurants aren't as plentiful except in La Rochelle, they do exist, and the regional dishes they prepare deserve ample tasting. In hotels listed as expensive, expect to pay between $45 and

$65 for a double room; $35 to $45, moderate; and less than $35, inexpensive. In an expensive restaurant, you will pay $60 or more for a meal for two, without wine; between $30 to $60, moderate; and less than $30, inexpensive. Service charge usually is included.

ANGOULÊME: Nicknamed "the town built on a balcony," Angoulême is perched on a rocky ridge overlooking the Charente Valley. The principal town and the administrative center of Charente, it has a population of 50,000, with another 100,000 people living in the outlying area. Finding the center of town is easy: Just keep climbing until you can't go any higher. All the sites are well marked, and the tourist office has two handy locations: 2 Pl. St.-Pierre (phone: 45-95-16-84), and in a kiosk across from the train station, Place de la Gare (closed Mondays; phone: 45-92-27-57). Each year the city holds an international comic book festival at the end of January and an international jazz festival at the end of May and the beginning of June. The main post office, open weekdays and Saturday mornings, is at Place du Champs de Mars; another, a more convenient one is at Place Francis-Louvel. A large covered market is held every morning at Place Guillon; Rue des Postes and Rue Beaulieu are pedestrian streets conducive to strolling and browsing.

The crowning glory of Angoulême is Cathédral St. Pierre, just off Rue de Friedland. The fourth building on this site (the first was built in AD 560) and the work of Bishop Gérard II, it was consecrated in 1128 and remains one of the oldest and most venerable cathedrals in France. Its façade, unique to the point of whimsy, contains 114 figures depicting not only the Last Supper and the Ascension of Christ but also Samson and the lion, St. George slaying the dragon, and scenes from the "Song of Roland." Monsters, birds, and winged horses all are part of the decoration. Across the street is a fine promenade along the ramparts of the city. The views both near and far are splendid. Two small churches in Angoulême deserve a look: Eglise St.-Martial, a Gothic structure that is lovely inside, and the 12th-century Roman Eglise St.-André (rebuilt in 1585 to 1660 in Plantagenet style), which has a 19th-century façade, three naves, and a tranquil garden.

The excellent *Musée de Beaux-Arts* is tucked away in what used to be the bishop's palace. It has striking ceramics by Alfred Renolleau, a master potter from the Charente during the late 19th and early 20th centuries whose work also can be viewed in *Faïencerie d'Art D'Angoulême,* a shop and museum. Open Sundays and Tuesdays through Fridays from 8 AM to noon and 2 to 7 PM; Saturdays and Mondays from 2 to 6 PM (5 Rue Renolleau; phone: 45-95-01-75). One gallery is devoted to the works of another Charente artist, Léonard Jarraud, and two other rooms display stunning art from west and central Africa and a number of Pacific islands. There is even a comic strip hall of mirrors. Not to be missed is a haunting painting by Pierre Vafflard, *Richard Young Burying His Daughter* (1804). (Closed Tuesdays and holidays off-season; 1 Rue de Friedland; phone: 45-95-07-69.)

The modest entry to the Maison St.-Simon (phone: 45-92-34-10) is misleading. What used to be the old *Renaissance* hotel, dating from 1550, now houses the *Association du Centre d'Arts Plastiques,* the place to see art and meet artists. One gallery, *Arthothèque,* rents pieces of modern art, which are on view for all to visit; another has changing exhibitions of work by emerging artists; and *FRAC (Fund Régional d'Art Contemporain)* of Poitou-Charentes displays its collection in another gallery (closed Sundays; 15 Rue de la Cloche Verte; phone: 45-92-87-10). The cultural center, or *CAC (Centre d'Action Culturelle),* has concerts, cinema, video, exhibitions, theater, dance, and much more (Bd. Berthelot; phone: 45-95-43-45). The *Musée Archéologique,* an archaeology museum, provides information about the history of the Charente region (closed Mondays; 44 Rue de Montmoreau; phone: 45-38-45-17). The city's newest museum, *Centre*

National de la Bande Desinée et l'Image (121 Rte. de Bordeaux; phone: 45-95-87-20), opened in January 1990. Devoted to the world of comic strips, it has, in addition to a permanent collection of over 8,000 original works, many excellent temporary exhibits. Open Wednesdays through Saturdays, 11 AM to 7 PM, and Sundays 2 to 6 PM. The city's theater is on Avenue des Maréchaux beside tree-lined Place New-York (phone: 45-95-38-40).

For a sweet-tooth fix, *Rimpault* is good. It's a *pâtisserie–salon de thé* on a pedestrian walk (32 Rue St.-Martial). Ask for a *gâteau ganage,* a small cake with chocolate icing and a layer of semisweet chocolate inside, or a regional cake filled with cognac called *Le 16.* Some say an even better *pâtisserie* is *Geslin* (on Place F.-Louvel).

Be sure not to overlook the Old Town; it's filled with very short, interesting streets: Rue du Soleil, Rue des Trois-Notre-Dame, Rue de la Cloche-Verte, as well as Rues Marengo, Genève, Massillon, Trarieux, and Taillefer. Place du Palet, a renovated square with a fountain, is one entrance to the old town. Also check out the beautiful view from the ramparts of the Charente River valley.

CHECKING IN: *Hostellerie du Moulin du Maine Brun* – Comfortable and chic, this member of the Relais & Châteaux group has 20 rooms, a fine restaurant, a swimming pool, and its own park. Closed November and December. 5 miles (8 km) west of Angoulême on N141, in La Vigerie, near Asnière-sur-Novère (phone: 45-90-83-00). Expensive.

Grand Hôtel de France – Right in the center of town with a good view of the valley and an exquisite garden, this great old hotel boasts 62 rooms, a large terrace built on 12th- and 13th-century ramparts, a restaurant, and a garage, and claims to be "the best place to stop between England and Spain." Pl. des Halles, Angoulême (phone: 45-95-47-95) Moderate.

Palais – In the center of the Old Town, it has 52 rooms on 3 floors and a comfortable sitting room. This is a clean, quiet place in a great location. 4 Pl. F.-Louvel, Angoulême (phone: 45-92-54-11 or 45-92-55-10) Moderate.

Trois Piliers – Convenient to both downtown and the train station, this pleasant hotel has 50 rooms, a bar, a terrace, and a garage. 3 Bd. de Bury, Angoulême (phone: 45-92-42-11). Moderate.

■ **Note:** Excellent municipal camping is available on the Ile de Bourgines, a quick bus ride (No. 7) from downtown or half an hour's walk (phone: 45-92-83-22); there also is an open-air municipal pool. In addition, the island has a very nice youth hostel; though it only has 16 rooms, it looks like a small motel (phone: 45-92-45-80). Ile de Bourgines also offers canoeing, kayaking, and other sports.

EATING OUT: *La Ruelle* – Exposed ceiling beams and ancient stone walls lighted by a blazing fire in the hearth set the stage for preparations by Jean François Dauphin and his daugher Veronique. Their style is traditional but original. There's a good, well-priced wine list, and wines are served by the glass. Closed Sundays, Monday and Saturday lunch, and February. 6 Rue des Trois-Notre-Dame (phone: 45-92-94-64). Expensive.

Ecole St.-Joseph – For a wonderful lunch and a special travel experience, dine at this private French cooking school, where the meal is prepared and served by students who are supervised very closely. Menus for the week are posted; on the day you want to visit, call before 10 AM and arrive between 12:15 and 12:30 PM. The formal dining room serves 100 people — teachers, students, and visitors — daily. The food is very good, and wine is available. 20 Rue Froide, Angoulême (phone: 45-95-11-45). Moderate.

Le Margaux – Traditional dishes prepared with contemporary finesse make this a favorite among locals. An extremely appealing decor adds to the pleasurable experience of dining here. Closed Sundays, 2 weeks in August, and 2 weeks at *Christmas*. 25 Rue Genève (phone: 42-92-58-98). Moderate.

En Route from Angoulême – Before heading to Cognac, the traveler who truly wants to savor the environs of Angoulême should consider two possibilities: one, a pleasant afternoon outing of a couple of hours, the other, a summertime day trip. If you have a free afternoon, take D674 south to D104 (go toward Libourne through the tunnel under the town) to the tiny town of Puymoyen, about 16 miles (26 km) away. Then follow the signs to the Verger paper mill, Moulin du Verger, about 3 miles (5 km) along a narrow, winding, forested road through the Eaux Claires Valley. The mill has been in operation since 1539 and continues to be self-supporting, selling its fine handmade paper to buyers in the United States, England, and Europe (there are only two other mills that aren't subsidized in France — in Couze in the Dordogne and in Auvergne). You actually can watch the paper being made — a mixture of fibers (cotton, manila, and linen, with flowers or straw sometimes added for decoration) and water; in one year this mill produces the same amount of paper it would take a machine to make in half an hour, but this paper will last for 500 or 600 years. Tours of the mill and explanations (in English) of the process are given daily at no charge (afternoons only on Sundays). There is a shop that sells paper. If you have no car, take bus No. 8 from Place du Champs de Mars and walk the mile (1.6 km) to the mill (phone: 45-61-10-38). Another mill in the area, Moulin de Fleurac, on D699 near Nersac, is government-subsidized; it has a museum with exhibitions of old documents as well as an explanation of the history of paper and writing. (Closed Tuesdays; phone: 45-91-50-69.) Also of interest is the *Atelier Musée du Papier* (134 Rue de Bordeaux, Angoulême; phone: 45-95-87-20).

An excellent day trip out of Angoulême follows N141 about 14 miles (22 km) northeast to the 1,000-year-old town of La Rochefoucauld (pop. 4,000). It has a 9th-century castle with an 11th-century keep, a 15th-century tower, and a 16th-century galleried staircase and chapel. It is open only in July, August, and the beginning of September. In July and August a historical *son et lumière* festival is held in the garden. Some 500 costumed citizens, including 60 horseback riders and coachmen, relate 11 centuries of local history in 11 tableaux. The show is held on Friday and Saturday nights; an admission fee is charged.

Another pleasant detour is the 15th-century Château de l'Oisellerie, where visitors can taste and buy *pineau* and cognac (3 miles/5 km south of Angoulême on N10). A bit farther is the 11th-to-13th-century abbey of La Couronne; an adjacent 18th-century building boasts a beautiful, ironwork Louis XV door.

The tourist office in La Rochefoucauld is in a 14th-century cloister on Rue des Halles and is open from June 15 to September 15 (phone: 45-63-07-45). At 39 Grande-Rue, Jacques and Mady Brun run a *salon de thé* that was started by his father in the late 1940s. M. Brun the elder created a delicious chocolate candy, unique to this town, called *pichottes;* of course, there is a story behind the name. In the 17th century, the monks used to grow mulberries, but migratory birds called *pichottes* would swoop down on them every year. The already weary birds would fall to the ground because of the small amount of alcohol in the fruit, and the monks would collect them and give them to hunters. The hunters then carried them to neighboring towns to sell, crying "Voilà la pichotte; la pichotte est arrivée!" People from La Rochefoucauld became known as *pichottiers,* and today they eat *pichottes* of the featherless variety. M. Brun the younger created a candy, as well: *calines,* dark chocolates made with cognac and wrapped in gold paper. The store is closed Mondays and Tuesdays, and at lunchtime.

A quick connection with D939 at Mareuil takes you back to Angoulême; from there N141 leads west for 26 miles (42 km) to the small town of Cognac.

CHECKING IN/EATING OUT: *La Chouette Gourmande* – For those who will go out of their way for a good meal, drive 22 miles (35 km) southeast of La Rochefoucauld via the road to Nontron (D6 to D65 to D4) to the small village of St.-Front-sur-Nizonne. This restaurant may be in the middle of nowhere, but you need a reservation to get in. There also are 3 guestrooms. St.-Front-sur-Nizonne (phone: 53-56-14-70). Moderate.

La Vieille Auberge – A visit to La Rochefoucauld should include lunch or dinner (and perhaps a night) at this 27-room inn, which serves regional dishes. You even can call and place your order. Closed Sunday evenings and Mondays off-season. 13 Faubourg de la Souche, La Rochefoucauld (phone: 45-62-02-72). Moderate to inexpensive.

COGNAC: To look at the unassuming town of Cognac (pop. 23,000), you'd never guess that the equivalent of more than a billion bottles of cognac was aging in its warehouses. The town is a virtual storehouse for the coveted brew, and it's possible many days to catch a whiff of it in the air. The equivalent of 20 million bottles evaporates from the porous oak aging casks each year; people call this "the angels' share" and perhaps it accounts for the advanced age some of the residents attain. The vapors may contribute as well to the softness of the light in the afternoons, so beautiful that even the busiest sightseers are bound to stop to admire it. The light and the cognac firms, all of which give free tours, are why most visitors stop here. The town itself has become commercial; billboards mar its walls and the roads leading into town. The town looks dingy because of a black fungus that lives on the fumes of the evaporating cognac and turns buildings gray. (It's impossible to store cognac illegally and get away with it!)

Cognac was the birthplace, in 1494, of François I, whose image and name appear around town as much as the word "cognac;" the town square features an equestrian statue of him, the municipal park (which has a swimming pool) is a woodsy 138 acres named after him, and the best hotel in town claims his name (see *Checking In*). François I was born in the Château Valois, which is beside the Charente River and now is the home of the Otard Cognac firm. Nearby is the 15th-century Porte St.-Jacques, all that's left of the old fortifications around the town, and beyond it, the Hennessy company, whose main building is a 17th-century abbey. The gate marks the entrance to the oldest part of town, which has dwellings from the 15th to the 18th century, many of them now restored. In the old town, near the tourist office, you can buy regional drinks, glasses, and cognac drenched chocolates from *La Cognathèque* (Pl. Jean-Monnet; phone: 45-82-43-31). Try its "cigar-drink," a test tube with a tobacco leaf wrapped around it like a cigar but with cognac inside.

The tourist office (phone: 45-82-10-71), between Place Jean-Monnet and Place François-I in the center of town, has a map of the cognac firms and their tour hours. These include Hennessy (whose tour features a visit to its barrel museum and its warehouse and bottling plant across the river), Martell, Camus, Remy Martin, and Prince H. de Polignac. Most are open only on weekdays. The Courvoisier company is in Jarnac, 9 miles (14 km) east of Cognac along N141; as you cross the bridge into town, the building looms majestically to your right. (In 16th-century Jarnac, the Catholics lived on one side of the river and the Huguenots on the other.)

The priory church of St. Léger, at 55 Rue Aristide-Briand in Cognac, was built between 1130 and 1140; its tower makes it the tallest edifice in town. The façade, walls of the nave, and base of the bell tower remain from the 12th century. The rose window dates from the 15th century, and if you look closely at the outermost section of the sculpted doorway, you'll recognize the signs of the zodiac. Cognac has a good museum, *Musée Municipal,* with exhibitions of wine making tools and regional ethnography. The museum is in the Jardin Public, 25 acres of shaded walkways and quiet ponds (no admission charge; closed Tuesdays and holidays, and mornings off-season; 48 Bd. Denfert-Rocherereau; phone: 45-32-07-25).

The municipal theater has film festivals, classical concerts, and theatrical productions of classical and modern works (Pl. Robert-Schuman; phone: 45-82-17-24). The *Convention Center,* near the tourist office, has changing exhibitions; there is no admission charge and it's open daily. A statue depicting a grape harvester at work is in front of the Palace of Justice (Pl. Charles-de-Gaulle) and is worth a look, especially if you miss seeing the real thing in October.

For nightlife, there's an inviting atmosphere at *Pub Victor-Hugo* (Av. Victor-Hugo) piano bar. Or have a drink at the popular but noisy *La Belle Epoque* bar (25 Rue Angoulême at Rue du Travail); it's open from 7 PM to 1 AM (closed Sundays).

For a down-home experience, try to arrive on the weekend of the *Fête de la Vendange* (Harvest Festival). The town's streets, closed to traffic, fill up with colorful floats, majorettes, and marching bands to kick off the harvest. There is an admission charge for the festival. Cognac's grapes are among the last to be picked in France, and the harvest usually begins around the middle of October.

CHECKING IN: *Moulin de Marcouze* – Definitely worth the 25-minute drive south of Cognac, is this charming old mill converted to a first class inn and restaurant by Dominique Bouchet, former head chef of Paris's famous *Tour d'Argent*. From Cognac, take D732 south to Pons, then N137 to Belluire and Mosnac. Closed Wednesdays, except in July, August, and holidays. Mosnac/ Saint-Genis de Saintonge (phone: 46-70-46-16). Expensive.

Moulin de Cierzac – About 8 miles (13 km) from Cognac via D731, this 10-room inn is located at the water's edge in a park. Its restaurant has earned one Michelin star for specialties such as *navarin de sole aux herbes de Marennes* (ragout of sole with vegetables and herbs). Closed Sunday evenings in November and December, Monday afternoons from June through August, and late January to late February. Cierzac (phone: 45-83-01-32). Expensive to moderate.

Le Valois – Near the post office, it offers 30 rooms with mini-bars as well as one large bar and parking. Closed December 22 to January 2. 35 Rue du XIV-Juillet, Cognac (phone: 45-82-76-00). Expensive to moderate.

Moderne – Here are 40 quiet, comfortable rooms, with gardens and parking right across the street. The Martell firm is nearby. Closed December 20 to January 4. Pl. de la Sous-Préfecture, at 24 Rue Elisée-Mousnier, Cognac (phone: 45-82-19-53). Moderate.

L'Auberge – A small, 2-story hotel that is on a quiet side street near Place François-I. The quality of the 24 rooms varies, but some are very nice; the large bathrooms are a treat. 13 Rue Plumejeau, Cognac (phone: 45-32-08-70). Moderate to inexpensive.

François I – This historic hostelry where General de Gaulle once stayed overlooks the town square and has 29 rooms on 3 floors. It used to be an inn, and what now is the garage was a stable. Ask for a room facing the plaza. Pl. François-I, Cognac (phone: 45-32-07-18). Moderate to inexpensive.

EATING OUT: *L'Echassier* – Under the supervision of one of the finest chefs of the region, this turn-of-the-century dwelling was transformed into an elegant dining spot where rich local food (one Michelin star) marries well with Bordeaux wines. 72 Rue de Bellevue, Cognac-Châteaubriand (phone: 45-32-29-04). Expensive to moderate.

Le Moulin de Cierzac – Very comfortable and pleasant, with its own park on the river, this restaurant also has 10 guest rooms. Closed Mondays and during February. St.-Fort Sur-le-Né, 9 miles (14 km) southeast of Cognac on D731 (phone: 45-83-01-32). Expensive to moderate.

Pigeons Blancs – In a lovely, wooded setting, this excellent dining room in a château-hotel (6 rooms) of the same name offers nouvelle cuisine, including a good *sole à la vapeur de cognac* (steamed sole). Don't miss cocktails on the terrace, overlooking the garden. Follow D731 north a short distance, toward Cherves. 110 Rue Jules-Brisson, Cognac (phone: 45-82-16-36). Expensive to moderate.

La Ribaudière – Only 5½ miles (8 km) from Cognac on the road to Angoulême, this restaurant offers a variety of grilled dishes and meats. It has a terrace facing the Charente River. Closed Mondays and January. Follow N141 east to Bourg-Charente; the restaurant is on the left-hand side of the road (phone: 45-81-30-54). Moderate.

SAINTES: Route N141 heading west from Cognac very quickly leads to the charming town of Saintes, reminiscent of St.-Emilion in Bordeaux, with its cathedral and houses with red tile roofs. Everything about Saintes has a gentle quality — the people, the curve of the river, the arch of the two bridges in the center of town, the shape of the plantain trees shading the sidewalks along Cours National. It might be called the city of markets and museums, of petunias and marigolds. It's the kind of place that is perfect for wandering aimlessly. Turn almost any corner and you're bound to happen upon a quaint street or an ancient landmark such as the 1st-century Roman arch (the votive arch of Germanicus) and amphitheater. The elliptical amphitheater, a large green basin between two hills, is amazingly well preserved, though it is said that unthinking citizens were in the habit of taking some of the evenly cut stones to build their own homes until the middle of the last century. Once, as many as 20,000 spectators could sit and watch gladiator battle gladiator or beast. Its outer dimensions are 336 by 415 feet; the arena itself is 129 by 211 feet.

Saintes is a grand place to shop; walk along the small pedestrian Rue St.-Michel or the larger Rue Victor-Hugo or Rue Alsace-Lorraine. The prices for food and clothing are more reasonable than anywhere else in the region. There are plenty of markets to stroll through. The one beside the library is open Wednesdays and Saturdays; there is an open-air market on Tuesdays and Fridays at Cours Reverseaux and Rue St.-Macoult and one on Thursdays and Sundays, near the train station. The first Monday of each month, a merry band of sellers comes into town and the streets fill up with vendors; look for them particularly near the arch at the abbey. To have a drink and listen to music, drop by *Le Vaudeville* (Quai de la République; phone: 46-93-11-91).

The tourist office (Villa Musso, 62 Cours National; phone: 46-74-23-82) provides a map with a walking tour of the city; it is open Tuesdays through Saturdays as well as the Monday the vendors come to town (closed the day after) and daily in summer.

The local food specialty is a *galette Charentaise,* a glazed sugar cookie. It's usually the size of a small pizza (some places make smaller ones, but they're hard to find) and impossible to eat without the help of half a dozen friends. For a brief respite, duck into the old-fashioned *Le Sainclair Salon de Thé,* tucked away under a couple of arches on Rue St.-Michel, near Rue Desiles; some say that *Arnaudin* (12 Rue St.-Michel) is better. To actually sample cognac where it is produced, visit M. Bossuet, who welcomes visitors at "Logis de la folle blanche," Senouches (Chaniers on N141; phone: 46-91-51-90). If you want to take home samples of pottery from Saintes and Angoulême, visit Mme. Bovet in the little town of St.-Porchaire (on the main road); for a less traditional sampling, go to *Alexiu* (La Chapelle des Pots, 5 miles/8 km from Saintes, near Brizambourg; phone: 46-91-51-04).

Cathédrale St.-Pierre has been built and destroyed a number of times. It originally was built in the late 12th century, then reconstructed in the Ogival Gothic style in the 15th century. Most of what remains today is from that period — the western portal at the base of the steeple, for instance, which is a beautiful piece of sculpture and deserves special attention. (The north and south walls of the base of the clock tower, on the other hand, appear to be part of the pre-Roman church.) The 240-foot clock tower dates from the 12th century, as does the southern part of the transept and its dome. Note the Renaissance chapel, the spiral staircase, and the ancient cloister of Chapitre St.-Pierre, next to the cathedral. The inside of the cathedral is surprisingly well lit by the sun during the day.

The Abbaye aux Dames, a Romanesque church dating from the 12th century, was administered for 7 centuries by abbesses from distinguished French families, from among whom will come the future Marquise de Montespan. Destroyed during the war, it was used as a supply house and a stable. Today the abbey houses a vibrant, living church; modern tapestries hang on the walls, and concerts of medieval music are held here in July. The central portal is intricately carved and the bell tower is worthy of note.

The remarkable Eglise St.-Eutrope was built on the road to Santiago de Compostela on the spot where St. Eutrope became a martyr. Consecrated in 1096, the vast crypt, which contains St. Eutrope's tomb, is the most interesting part of the church. The bell tower, the spire of which is almost 200 feet high, was built in the late 1400s. Across the street is a small, inviting park as well as a good *salon de thé.*

The *Musée des Beaux-Arts,* in a restored, 3-story, 17th-century hotel (Rue Victor-Hugo; phone: 46-93-03-94), is worth a visit if only for the building. The collection includes pottery from the 16th to the 18th century, including some of the work of the famous 16th-century artisan Bernard Palissy. There is an interesting framed fragment of a tapestry from the 17th century portraying St. Peter holding the keys to heaven. Nearby, the *Musée de l'Echevinage* (Rue Alsace-Lorraine; phone: 46-93-52-39) has a dozen noteworthy paintings from the 19th and 20th centuries as well as Sèvres china. Neither museum has an admission charge and both are closed Tuesdays; during the winter, closed Mondays.

If you have time for only one museum, let it be the *Musée d'Art Régional Dupuy-Mestreau,* in the former town house of the Marquis de Monconseil, which was built in 1738 and completely renovated in 1974 (Rue Monconseil and Rue St.-Maur). It has one of the best collections of French folklore anywhere, with excellent exhibitions of clothing, lace, and peasant and upper class headdresses (including the *quichenot* — "kiss me not" — that occasionally still is worn by women to gather oysters but was supposedly used originally to keep the English soldiers from trying to kiss the maidens). It also has 18th- and 19th-century dolls, jewelry from the reign of Marie-Antoinette, ceramics, furniture, and a re-creation of a 19th-century bedroom and kitchen in a Saintonge house as well as the bedroom of the Marquese de Monconseil. Don't overlook the Tarot cards from 1854 and the tiny mustache brush. A guided tour is included with the admission charge. Open afternoons only, except Tuesdays in summer and Sundays, Mondays, and Tuesdays in winter (phone: 46-93-43-27). There also is the *Musée du Folklore* (89 Rue St.-Palais; phone: 46-93-67-09), open daily, except Sunday afternoons, from June to October.

The *Musée Archéologique,* beside the tourist office on the east side of the river, has been around since 1815 but now is more a warehouse for Roman relics than a museum; it's free and should be (closed Tuesdays; phone: 46-74-20-97). Nearby is a pleasant public garden with a gazebo and large dovecote. The municipal library, in the old Hôtel Martineau at Place de l'Echevinage, houses the extensive collection of Maurice Martineau, more than 75,000 volumes. Notice the beautiful wood door; the entrance is through the courtyard. Open Tuesday to Saturday afternoons from 1:30 to 6 PM; Wednesday and Saturday mornings from 9:30 to 11:30 AM. Closed the first 2 weeks in August (phone: 46-93-25-39).

CHECKING IN: *Le Mancini* – Centrally located, this stately hotel (actually several adjoining houses) has 44 stylish rooms, a bar, a breakfast room, and a seafood restaurant. Diners can pick their lobster fresh from a tank, or try one of the duck or oyster specialties. Rue des Messageries, Saintes (phone: 46-93-06-61). Expensive to moderate.

Le Relais du Bois St.-Georges – This inn, which looks like a country estate at the end of a tree-lined drive, has 27 rooms and 3 suites, all delightful and tastefully decorated, from the antique furniture to the teal blue carpeting and wallpaper. Each of the 20 tables in the restaurant has a view of the lawn, since the walls are all glass; the room also has a raised ceiling, Oriental rugs, and a fireplace faced by comfortable leather chairs. Bass and turbot dishes are the house specialties; vegetables come straight from the garden. Indoor pool. About a mile (1.6 km) outside Saintes on Rue Royan and Cours Genêt (phone: 46-93-50-99). Expensive to moderate.

France – Across from the train station, this cozy hotel is a little removed from the downtown area but is a very pleasant place to stay. It has 28 rooms; request one facing the garden. There is a seafood restaurant, *Le Chalet,* and in summer you can dine outside under the trees. The hotel is closed in November; the restaurant is closed Fridays from December to *Easter.* Pl. de la Gare, Saintes (phone: 46-93-01-16). Moderate to inexpensive.

EATING OUT: *Le Logis Santon* – Self-taught chef Alain Sorillet has turned the family residence into one of the best restaurants in the region, combining tradition (local specialties) and creation (particularly in sauces) in a charming setting that accommodates only 20 guests. Closed Sundays and Monday lunch, the last week of February, and the last 2 weeks of September. 54 Cours Genêt, Saintes (phone: 46-74-20-14). Moderate.

Le Jardin du Rempart – This pleasant piano bar-dining spot, filled with hanging plants and skylit during the day, offers a fine salad bar as well as beef, duck, and grilled dishes. Open daily for brunch and dinner. Music nightly. 36 Rue du Rempart, Saintes (phone: 46-93-37-66). Moderate to inexpensive.

Le Procopio – At this large Italian eatery, the best seating is upstairs, in the garden, and on the enclosed terrace. Almost anything you order is large enough to be shared by two. Closed Sundays and Mondays. Near the cathedral, at 5 Rue de la Comédie, Saintes (phone: 46-74-31-91). Inexpensive.

En Route from Saintes – Before continuing west on N141, consider a 10-mile (16-km) detour north on N137 to St.-Porchaire to see the most elegant of the handful of large châteaux in this region that are open to the public. This one, La Roche Courbon, with two towers, manicured lawns, and a large reflecting pool, is a real beauty. Built during the 15th century and renovated 2 centuries later, the impressive structure is in a forest on a riverbank; within walking distance are prehistoric caves that can be explored. The interior of the château is ornate and filled with furnishings from a number of periods; one room is full of paintings on wood dating from 1662, and the Louis XIII room has noteworthy painted beams. The gardens are open daily year-round; the château is open daily from mid-June to mid-September and daily except Thursdays from mid-September to mid-June. Closed February 15 to March 15 (phone: 46-95-60-10).

The environs of Saintes are filled with tiny 15th- to 18th-century churches and chapels, usually off the main road, but the turnoffs are well marked. You can take pot luck or, one suggestion, follow D129 south to Rioux, a tiny Roman church 10 miles (16 km) from Saintes; the carvings make the detour worthwhile. Route N150 leads from Saintes to Royan, 23 miles (37 km) southwest.

ROYAN: A resort town that has known better days, Royan (pop. 18,000) was destroyed in World War II and has been completely rebuilt, leaving it with a mishmash of buildings, streets glutted with traffic, and none of its former charm. People still flock to its beaches every summer, but better spots lie to the south and north. The only real attraction here is Eglise Notre-Dame, designed by Guillaume Gillet and built in the late 1950s. It's impossible to miss it, rising like the hull of a great ship moored at the highest point in the city. Inside, it is even more boat-like, and you should stand in the center as well as at either end to get the full effect. The church is in the shape of an ellipse, and the ceiling soars high overhead, with nothing — neither column nor arch — obstructing the inner space. Vertical strips of pale stained glass set into slabs of reinforced gray mortar add to the unexpected beauty of the church. In summer an organ festival is held here. Signs point the way to the church from the center of town; it's uphill all the way.

Good maps of the Charente-Maritime region are available at the Royan Tourist Office (Palais des Congrès; phone: 46-38-65-11) and in a kiosk to your left just as you come into town (Rond-Point de la Poste; phone: 46-05-04-71). Regular ferries (phone: 56-09-60-84) travel from Royan to Pointe de Grave, where routes can be picked up either along the Atlantic coast or through the wine producing region of the Médoc.

CHECKING IN: *Residence de Royan* – A few miles north of Royan is this elegant 19th-century manor house that has been converted into a tranquil 40-room country inn. Closed mid-November to *Easter*. Pl. de Nauzan (phone: 46-39-00-75). Moderate.

En Route from Royan – Before heading north to the more interesting town of Rochefort, take time to follow the beach road, banked by pine-covered boulders plunging into the sea, a few miles south to the small, peaceful beaches of Meschers. Then continue 7 miles (11 km) farther south to Talmont. The sight of the tiny 12th-century church clinging to a wall by the side of the sea is what travel, and prized travel photographs, are all about. Built by Benedictine monks and damaged over the years by sea, wind, and war, this simple church, called Ste.-Radegonde, has retained its dignity and beauty and now is designated a national monument.

Route D733 leads directly from Royan to Rochefort, 25 miles (40 km) north, but it would be a shame to miss Marennes, the most important center for oyster cultivation in France, and the 17th-century fortified town of Brouage along the way. On a clear day, going to Marennes via the coastal road, D25, is especially worthwhile. There is a zoo along this route, in La Palmyre. Open year-round, it has 900 birds and animals in 24 acres of hills and valleys (phone: 46-22-46-06). Stop at Pointe de la Coubre to admire the lighthouse, and its spectacular view of Ile d'Oléron and the cliffs to the south; just south of the lighthouse is a nude beach, but be warned that the water can be treacherous here. North of the lighthouse stretches the Côte Sauvage (Savage Coast); let the name alone, with its inherent images of beauty, desolation, and danger, be enough to discourage a quick dip, no matter how refreshing it might seem.

Try to plan a stop in Marennes as close as possible to the outgoing tides in order to see the huge oyster beds and the people gathering the delicacies from the sea. Purportedly the finest oysters in all of France, they are green due to the algae in the water in which they thrive. Parisians are said to prefer these expensive, green oysters, though the people from the Charente-Maritime stick to the flat or long varieties that are a "normal" color. Stop to enjoy fresh oysters, mussels, and other seafood in La Cayenne, the oyster-fishing harbor at Marennes. There is an oyster museum here in the 17th-century Fort Louvois (also called Fort du Chapus), which is open only from June to mid-September. In Marennes it also is possible to visit the elegant Château de la Gataudière, part of which is now a maritime museum; the architecture and furnishings remain as they were when the château was built, in the mid-18th century, by François Fresneau, also known as "the father of the raincoat." The château is closed November to March (phone: 46-85-01-07). You can reach Marennes on D728 (turn left on D733 from Royan) if you don't take the coast road.

A country road full of hairpin turns, D3 leads from Marennes 4½ miles (7 km) to Brouage, whose walls rise up out of the road like a medieval mirage.

BROUAGE: Founded in 1555, Brouage was a port city until land encroached upon the sea and changed its history. It was here that Samuel de Champlain, the founder of Quebec, was born, in 1570, and from here French colonists set sail for the New World. The ancient ramparts, built in the 1630s by order of Richelieu, still encircle the town, which seems to have fallen asleep several hundred years ago. The walls, 3 miles of them punctuated with 22 watch towers, are still beautiful though crumbling in places. The best way to see the town and the surrounding area is to walk halfway around the ramparts; go up the stairs to the left of the tourist office (beside the northern entrance) and come back down again when you reach the main street, Rue du Québec, which passes by the town's early-17th-century church. Once you look out over the ramparts, it's easy to imagine the water that once lapped these walls, the workers loading salt for export onto waiting ships, and the tragic heroine Marie Mancini bidding farewell to Louis XIV, the lover she was never to see again, as he sailed south to marry Maria Theresa for political reasons in 1659. Driving through the portals of Brouage is like stumbling into a hidden garden, and an hour's visit here will leave you feeling peaceful and nostalgic for something not quite definable.

The 8 miles (13 km) of road, still D3, are pastoral and winding; on either side, sea grass grows profusely and cows are kept penned in by narrow moats rather than fences.

ROCHEFORT: The friendliness of this place and its people is apparent immediately. Today a bustling city of 30,000, Rochefort was founded in the 17th century as a military port, and it contains one of the greatest pieces of architecture from the reign of Louis XIV, the Corderie Royale, an incredible 1,236-foot arsenal. It burned in May 1944 and has been almost completely restored. The Corderie extends majestically along the Charente River, beginning at the Jardin du Roy (Garden of the King) and ending at the boat basin. Today it is a living museum to the seafaring life, complete with exhibitions and videotapes (Centre International de la Mer; open daily in season, afternoons off-season; phone: 46-87-0190).

The city has a transporter bridge dating from 1900, the last of its kind in France. It ceased service in 1967, when its duties were taken over by the neighboring Pont à Travée Levante. The new bridge allows the number of vehicles that cross the Charente to expand from 2,500 to 25,000 a day.

Place Colbert, in the center of town, is an open, graceful plaza. A few blocks away is the tourist office (Av. Sadi-Carnot; phone: 46-99-08-60), which is open daily except Sundays, and closed at lunchtime off-season. Also nearby is the only store in the region where cameras with serious problems can be repaired, *Vidéophot,* where M. Deserson offers reliable service and reasonable prices (111 Rue de la République; phone: 46-99-63-84).

On Tuesday, Thursday, and Saturday mornings, Avenue Général-de-Gaulle and Avenue Lafayette become a street fair, where vendors of prepared foods and produce, not to mention hamsters and chickens, file into town. This is one of the largest, liveliest, and most colorful markets in the Charente region. Use it as a chance to sample a regional specialty, *tourteau fromagé,* a round cake made with cottage cheese and oddly charred on top.

One of France's greatest novelties and best-kept secrets — at least to outsiders — is in Rochefort: the Maison de Pierre Loti, the birthplace and lifelong home of the famous French writer, soldier, and adventurer who collected an impressive number of souvenirs in his travels. The house can best be described as an extravagant curiosity inside; it contains, among other things, a medieval room, a Turkish room, a Renaissance room, an Islamic mosque with a sunken floor, an exquisite ceiling, and marvelous tiles and Oriental rugs. These rooms were backdrops for Loti's lavish parties, to which guests came decked out in magnificent costumes, many of them provided by their host. The weapons randomly placed throughout the house are works of art. (Closed Sunday mornings year-round, Monday mornings and Tuesdays off-season; 141 Rue Pierre-Loti; phone: 46-99-16-88. Tours are included in the admission charge.)

The *Musée de la Marine* is in the 17th-century Hôtel de Cheusses and pays homage to the sea, its vessels, and their crews. Downstairs are enormous models of ships from the 17th through the 19th century; upstairs, a modern section includes replicas of an ocean liner, a submarine, and much more. On the ground floor but with its own entrance is the Grand Salle, which has an exhibit of nautical knots (47 in all). The museum is next to the Porte du Soleil (Sun Gate), the principal entrance to the ancient marine arsenal. (Closed Tuesdays and holidays; Pl. de la Gallissonnière; phone: 46-87-11-22.)

There also is the *Musée d'Art et d'Histoire de la Ville de Rochefort* (closed Sundays and Mondays; 63 Av. Général-de-Gaulle; for information, phone 46-99-83-99) with paintings and ethnographic collections from the 16th through the 19th century. The city's theater, the 18th-century *Théâtre de la Coupe d'Or,* has concerts and plays year-round, including light opera and the works of such playwrights as Pinter and Anouilh; in the summer it sponsors open-air concerts and in the spring, lyric art festivals (101 Av. de la République; phone: 46-99-03-32).

Rochefort has gained a reputation in recent years for its thermal springs, sought out by those seeking relief from rheumatism, circulatory ailments, and skin problems. Visitors who come for treatment — some 5,000 a year — need to have a reservation; there is a hotel for their convenience. For more information, write to the *Etablissement Thermale de Rochefort* (Av. Camille-Pelletan, Rochefort 17300; phone: 46-99-08-64.

Route N137 leads to La Rochelle, 20 miles (32 km) north of Rochefort.

CHECKING IN: *Le Soubise* – This comfortable hotel has 22 rooms and an outstanding restaurant (closed Sunday nights and Mondays) that specializes in regional dishes. It's in the little town of Soubise, 5 miles (8 km) southwest of Rochefort on D238E. Closed during October. 62 Rue de la République, Soubise (phone: 46-84-92-16). Hotel, expensive to moderate; restaurant, expensive.

***Vitahôtel Corderie Royale* –** Regally housed in a 17th-century building, this recent addition to the city's accommodations offers 50 modern rooms with baths and a mini-health club for guests (no additional charge). Each room has a TV set, a direct-dial phone, and a mini-bar. Rue Audebert, Rochefort-sur-Mer (phone: 46-99-35-35). Expensive to moderate.

***La Belle Poule* –** An attractive hostelry on the Royan road into Rochefort, it has 22 rooms and a fairly expensive restaurant. Rochefort (phone: 46-99-71-87). Moderate.

***Roca-Fortis* –** Near the center of town and only a short walk from the boat basin, this spacious hotel has 16 rooms. 14 Rue de la République, Rochefort (phone: 46-99-26-32). Moderate to inexpensive.

***Le Bassin III* –** This little inn with lace curtains on the windows is certainly *charmante.* You'll find it just before the bridge on the road to Saintes out of Rochefort (near the boat basin). It has only 8 rooms, and there is a good, small restaurant with regional specialties such as *entrecôte à l'ardoise* (steaks cooked on slate). 6 Av. William-Ponty, Rochefort (phone: 46-99-01-88). Inexpensive.

EATING OUT: *Le Tourne-Broche* – Meats are grilled over a wood fire, but regional fish dishes are the real specialty here. Closed Sundays, Monday evenings, and July 1–15. 56 Av. Général-de-Gaulle, Rochefort (phone: 46-99-20-19). Moderate.

***Café "Le Flore"* –** Snuggled up against the boat basin, this is the local spot for a daily special of steaks with fries, seafood, a burger, or drinks. Weather permitting, you can sit on the porch in one of the ten rocking chairs. Closed Wednesdays. Pleasure Boat Basin, Rochefort (phone: 46-87-21-06). Inexpensive.

LA ROCHELLE: Called "the City of Lights," this is a dazzling town, night or day, and it also is the cultural and administrative center of the Charente-Maritime *département.* La Rochelle was a fishing village that was developed in the 12th century between two points of land jutting into the Atlantic, Minimes Point and Pallice Point. Two commanding towers — Tours St.-Nicolas and de la Chaíne — guard the entrance to the old port, as they have done for 6 centuries, and make entering this city of 85,000 all the more dramatic. And La Rochelle has the largest number of streets with covered archways in France as well as many houses dating from the 15th century, including Revival timbered houses. To add a modern note, it also has impressive high-rise condominiums and the biggest pleasure boat basin in all of Europe. The unflagging interest in ecology of Mayor Michel Crepeau, who used to be France's minister of the environment, is apparent throughout the city.

The old port has existed since the 13th century and probably was always fortified. The St. Nicolas and the Chain towers actually used to have a chain stretched between them to keep out unknown ships as well as to keep others from leaving without paying taxes. Tour de la Chaíne is connected by a rampart to yet another tower, Tour de la Lanterne (The Lantern, or Four Sergeants, Tower); it was used as a lighthouse as well as a prison and for defense. The names of former inmates still are visible where they were carved on the walls. This tower, with its Gothic spire, offers an impressive view of the city and the harbor. All three towers are open for visits.

Plentiful free parking is available at the old port. On Saturday and Sunday nights in the summer the main street of the port is closed to traffic, making it even more pleasant to stroll and admire the beautifully lit sweep of buildings along the seafront, with the medieval gate to the old town, the Porte de la Grosse Horloge, right in the center, beckoning wayfarers into the heart of town. The faint music of the 100-year-old carousel on Valin Square fills the air, advertising a free ride for anyone in the mood. Bicycles are provided (with proof of ID) at Valin Square and the Esplanade des Parcs at no charge every morning and afternoon except on Sundays, Mondays, and holidays, and are especially fun to take to Parc Charruyer, a mile-long, 660-foot-wide strip of green with a stream running through it.

The tourist office is at Place de la Petite-Sirène, Le Gabut, near the port (phone: 46-41-14-68; generally closed Sundays and holidays). The *Musée du Nouveau Monde* (10 Rue Fleuriau; open daily except Tuesday and Sunday mornings; closed lunchtime) is housed in the superbly restored 18th-century *Hôtel Fleuriau,* itself a marvelous exhibition piece. It has 17 rooms on 4 floors open to the public, 10 galleries, and 7 period rooms with beautiful wainscoting and fireplaces. This museum describes the opening of Louisiana by Louis XIV and depicts the lives of the early French settlers there. Objects on display date from the 16th through the mid-19th century and were chosen for their historic as well as artistic value. One room is devoted to the American Indian. For Americans especially, a visit to this museum is a chance to learn more about a very rich part of our heritage (phone: 46-41-46-50).

Rue Dupaty leads to a small square where you will find the central post office and the Hôtel de Ville (Town Hall), a striking building with a Gothic surrounding wall dating from the 14th century. The main part of the building dates from the 15th and 16th centuries and is very decorative; the façade and staircase are Henri IV. Throughout, visitors will see many mementos from the siege of 1628 as well as Jean Guiton's study with its marble table. Guided tours are given every 20 minutes during the summer; off-season, afternoons only.

La Maison de Culture (Rue St.-Jean at Cours des Dames, beside the old port; phone: 46-41-45-62) has a full and ever-changing agenda of films, music, dance, art exhibitions, and theater. The *Maison Municipale des Jeunes* (Municipal Youth Center) has similar offerings, but the acoustics aren't as good (closed Mondays; 10 bis Rue Amelot; phone: 46-44-43-11).

The *Musée d'Orbigny-Bernon* has quite a menagerie; of special note are the 18th-century apothecary and the carved, oval Oriental bed on the third floor. (Open daily except Sunday mornings and Tuesdays; 2 Rue St.-Côme; phone: 46-41-18-83.) The aquarium, France's largest, with fish from all over the world, is between the harbor and the beach at Les Iles du Ponant (open daily; phone: 46-44-00-00). Right across from the harbor, on Rue de la Désirée, in a small section of wooden houses, is an automaton museum filled with 300 robots (open daily; phone: 46-41-68-08). The *Lafaille Museum of Natural History* is a bit of a hike from the center of town, but it has a nice garden where you can rest once you get there (28 Rue Albert-I; phone: 46-41-18-25). Finally, there is a *Musée des Beaux-Arts* (Rue Gargoulleau; phone: 46-41-64-65) with paintings from the 16th through 20th century (open daily except Tuesdays). One ticket gains admission to the *Beaux-Arts, D'Orbigny,* and *Nouveau Monde* museums.

There's more to do in La Rochelle at night than simply admire the city lights. *Le Crystal,* the Art Deco café and piano bar with a striking chartreuse interior, is next to the Tour de la Chaîne. It serves cocktails, ice cream, and tea, and the concoctions dreamed up here are delightful (phone: 46-41-43-10). *Le Café de la Paix* sometimes has live jazz or classical music (54 Rue Chandrier, Pl. de Verdun; phone: 46-41-39-79). A local hangout that tourists might not ordinarily happen upon is the intimate *Piano Pub;* it's the epitome of "out-of-the-way" (12 Cours du Temple, just off Rue du Temple via Petite Rue du Temple; closed Sundays; phone: 46-41-03-42). Numerous nightclubs are scattered around the old harbor.

La Rochelle is a good city for shopping and eating out, though prices often are high. For local pottery, there is *Poterie de la Rochelle* (29 Quai Maubec; phone: 46-41-38-14). Gastronomic pleasures revolve around seafood, of course, and regional specialties on most menus include *mouclade* (mussels in a curry cream sauce), *chaudrée* (fish chowder), and *cagouilles* (small snails). For scrumptious chocolates and other sweets, visit *Boutet* (5-7 Rue du Temple).

For a real bird's-eye view of the city and surrounding area, you can take a sightseeing trip in a small airplane. The planes also go to Ile d'Oléron or Ile de Ré (the latter is the preferred stop — despite the new bridge that moors it to the mainland — because Oléron has become very populated in recent years and has lost much of its charm). For more information, call 46-41-78-95. You also can get a couple of breathtaking views without ever leaving the ground: Stroll along the walkway around the old port at sunset, or drive out for a look at the new pleasure boat basin.

There is a produce market on Wednesday and Saturday mornings at Place du Marché and a Saturday flea market in Quartier St.-Nicolas. In late May or early June there is a sailboat festival; in late June and early July, a contemporary art festival; also in July, *Francofolies,* a festival of French songs; and in September, the *Grand Prix de la Rochelle* boat race.

 CHECKING IN: *Le Yachtman* – Facing the old port, this hotel offers 40 rooms that look out on either the port or its swimming pool, which is enclosed by ivy-covered walls. Each room has a refrigerator, TV set, and direct-dial phone. Open year-round. 23 Quai Valin, La Rochelle (phone: 46-41-20-68). Expensive.

La Monnaie – In a stately stone building that once served as 17th-century Paris's mint and treasury, this hotel offers plush modern rooms and proximity to both the sea and the old port. 3 Rue de la Monnaie (phone: 46-50-65-65). Expensive to moderate.

St.-Jean d'Acre – This pleasant place, with 49 soundproof rooms (some overlooking the port) is tucked behind the Tour de la Lanterne. It has a good restaurant, *Au Vieux Port,* with a terrace on the wharf. Among the regional specialties are grilled lobster, salmon, and turbot. Pl. de la Chaîne, La Rochelle (phone: 46-41-73-33). Moderate.

St.-Nicolas – Quiet, and only a few blocks from the flow of traffic and activity, this

74-room establishment is still within walking distance of everything. Though totally redecorated in an ultramodern style, the friendly staff makes staying here still seem more like being in a home than in a hotel. 13 Rue Sardinerie, La Rochelle (phone: 46-41-71-55). Moderate.

EATING OUT: *Le Pavillon* – Recently opened by a chef from Lyons, this eatery is fast gaining high ratings for extremely refined cooking. Housed in an old building, it specializes in fish and seafood. Try the salmon filet and the fish *terrine* (pâté). Le Belvadere, La Repentie, La Rochelle (phone: 46-43-80-80). Expensive.

Richard Coutanceau – With two Michelin stars, it has a view of the sea to accompany such specialties as *salade de goujonnettes de sole et langoustine aux senteurs de Provence* (sole and lobster salad with Provençal herbs) and *bar en feuilles vertes au fumet de St.-Emilion* (bass in green leaves with St.-Emilion). There is a pleasing dessert selection and myriad white wines from which to choose. Closed Sundays and Monday evenings. Behind Tour de la Chaíne, Plage de la Concurrence, La Rochelle (phone: 46-41-48-19). Expensive.

La Marmite – Another Michelin star holder, its chef holds to traditional bourgeois cooking and does it well, with the accent on quality of preparation and richness of ingredients. Closed Wednesdays and January 15–31. 14 Rue St.-Jean-du-Pérot, La Rochelle (phone: 46-41-17-03). Expensive.

La Maison des Mouettes – In summer, grab a table on the terrace and order *langoustines au court bouillon d'algues* or *l'effilade de volaille au crabe.* The selection is as expansive as the seaside view. Closed Mondays and during February. Route de la Plage, in Aytre, 3 miles (5 km) south of La Rochelle via D937 (phone: 46-44-29-12). Expensive to moderate.

Serge – Well known, with one Michelin star, it is surprisingly small and cozy, with a wood ceiling and walls and lace curtains at the windows. Seafood delights include lobster, crab, prawn pâté, and oysters on the half shell, served on silver platters on a bed of ice. Everything is accompanied by mayonnaise and butter, *à la charentaise.* The restaurant is open for lunch and dinner; closed Tuesdays off-season. Facing the old port, at 46 Cours des Dames, La Rochelle (phone: 46-41-18-80). Expensive to moderate.

En Route from La Rochelle – From La Pallice Point, you can take the ferry to Ile de Ré, a 48-mile-long treasure of tiny villages, small whitewashed cottages, beaches, and mostly uninhabited land except in summer, with the tourist migration. A bird sanctuary is at the northern end of the island. In the summer you can rent a bike near the ferry terminus, as well as in other locations, for some personal exploration; bike paths are plentiful.

■ **Note:** It is dangerous to swim in the inlet, called Fiers d'Ars, at the northeast end of the island, but there are plenty of safe, well-marked beaches elsewhere. Ile de Ré is rightfully called "the bright island" because of the bounteous sunlight that graces it. Route N11, the road to Niort, leads north from La Rochelle to "the Land of the Great Green Silence," the Marais Poitevin.

MARAIS POITEVIN: Also called "the Green Venice," the unique Marais Poitevin comprises 212,000 acres, some 40,000 of which are filled with canals and islands, flooded areas interspersed with clumps of forest, houses with thatch roofs, and friendly country people. The Parc Naturel Régional du Marais Poitevin is a protected area, and within it lie many diversions, among them 34 miles of hiking trails, a "zoorama" containing 600 animals on 62 acres in Chizé Forest, 15 miles (24 km) south of Niort, ethnography museums, castles, and abbeys. Only a flat-bottom boat can maneuver you deep into this region, however, where lime green algae blankets the water and trees intertwine overhead to give all the nicknames credence. People who live here year-round depend on boat travel to get them to solid ground to buy groceries or mail a letter. Boat rentals and guided tours are available in several towns in the area: In Coulon, try *J. Fichet* (8 Rue de l'Eglise; phone: 49-33-90-88) or *D. Thibaudeau* (54 Quai L. Tardy; phone: 49-35-91-71); in La Garette, *Largeaud-Bouyer* (phone: 49-35-93-35); in Magné, *A. Cardinaud* (la Repentie; phone: 49-35-90-47). They're also available in Arçais and the old abbey of Maillezais, where there is a *son et lumière* show in summer. Now in ruins and lost in the moors, Maillezais was the home of the writer Rabelais from 1523 to 1527. The drive from Arçais to Coulon, 6 miles (10 km), follows a canal; La Garette is 1½ miles (2 km) from Coulon. To get to Coulon, go via Courçon, Frontenay-Rohan-Rohan. The canals are named and well marked on maps;take a picnic, tie up your boat along the way, and go ashore for a secluded feast in France's "green land." For information, call 46-27-82-44, or visit the information center in the town of La Ronde, near Courçon.

Bordeaux
and the Médoc

The Bordeaux region is a peninsula in southwest France that lies between the Gironde River and the Atlantic Ocean. Its base stretches from the city of Bordeaux to the resort town of Arcachon, where the splendid Arcachon Basin meets the sea. It contains the Médoc, some of the richest wine country in the world, glorious unsung beaches, two huge lakes and the Basin itself, 2 million acres of serene, trail-covered pine forest, and seaside towns and tiny fishing villages that entice even the most blasé travelers. The best part is that this bounty, in all its diversity, is only an hour or less from Bordeaux, no matter the direction chosen: north to the Médoc, south to the Basin, or west to the Côte d'Argent (Silver Coast).

The Médoc extends with hardly even the suggestion of a hillock along the bank of the Gironde from Bordeaux to Pointe de Grave, where the river enters the ocean. Its flat terrain may not be the most interesting, but many people find beauty in the elegant precision of the parallel rows of burgeoning vines, every plant trimmed to identical height. The all-encompassing greenness is punctuated by red roses planted at the roadside ends of the rows (now just a nice touch, but at one time a sort of early warning system against fungus attacks, since the weaker roses would be the first to succumb). From one end of the Médoc to the other, the villages along the vineyard road derive their sustenance from wine: In workshops around the town square, joiners put together the wine cases for the châteaux, and vineyard workers bicycle from their cottages to the fields; even the printing of wine labels is an important subsidiary trade. Although the wines of the Médoc make up only about 8% of those produced in the Bordeaux region, these thoroughbreds set the standard to which the remaining 92% aspire.

An old Médoc saying has it that if you can see the river and feel the pebbles under your feet, you can make good wine. The proximity of the river moderates the winter cold and softens the impact of the spring frosts. In this temperate climate, cool nights follow mild days, and abundant sunshine in the summer inspires the development of natural sugars that produce fermentation. The sand and gravel that the river has tossed onto its banks — no rich alluvial silt here — are perfect for drainage and the development of good wine producing grapes. Pebbles on the soil surface reflect the sunlight to help ripen the grapes. The vines of the Médoc are extremely strong and hardy and can live up to 80 years, with roots that delve as far as 10 to 15 feet down toward the water table. The finest wines come from old stock, and 8 to 10 years of age, corresponding to the maximum of root development, is considered the absolute minimum for top quality. In fact, local law forbids making wine from vines less than 4 years old.

In most wine making districts, the cellar master will invite you into a cool, low-ceilinged *cave* hewn out of bedrock. In Bordeaux, where the soil is sand rather than rock and where, because of the proximity of the river, the water table is high, traditional wine cellars are impractical. With few exceptions, the Médoc wine maker goes about his business in the *chai,* a long shed with a sloping roof of sunbaked terra-cotta tiles. The *chai* resembles a kind of warehouse, with whitewashed walls and good ventilation. There usually is a central row of columns supporting the roof over the earthen floor, and the barrels are stacked two or three high in orderly rows that run the length of the *chai.*

The terms first growth (or *cru*), second growth, bourgeois growth, and so on, refer to a system of ranking the top wines of the Médoc that was formulated more than a century ago. In 1855, Napoleon III ordered a classification of bordeaux wines by quality for the *Exposition Universelle de Paris,* a kind of *World's Fair.* This classification still is used, and although it remains accurate in its assessment of the very top of the great growths, there are many who argue that some wines deserve to be upgraded by rank and others lowered. The fun is to compare the wines from the various *crus* and other excellent selections that may not have a ranking (remember, the classification was of the best of the best), find those that particularly appeal to your taste and pocketbook, and perhaps return home with a case of your favorite. Some 25% of all Médoc wines are *crus classés.*

There is no great mystery to tasting wines at the Médoc vineyards (or anywhere else, for that matter). You'll find the people who work with wine completely free of the jargon and pretension that wine snobs like to invoke to intimidate lesser mortals. Just hold the glass by the stem or the base, not by the bowl, and raise it to the light. The wine should be a rich, vibrant red, perfectly clear and limpid. Swirl it gently in the glass, then smell it. Take a small sip and hold the liquid in your mouth. Let the wine tumble about the tip and sides of your tongue while you think about the taste. Then spit it out, especially if you're trying several different wines. This may be embarrassing at first, but it is a common practice. In the first place, young wine is not the most digestible drink, and for another, if you want to continue your tour by car and visit several châteaux in the course of the day, common sense will tell you that you can't afford to drink. Some châteaux provide sawdust-filled tubs for spitting; at others, use the floor as professionals do, but remember to turn your head to the side to avoid unnecessary dry cleaning bills for your fellow tasters. Even the best-brought-up tyro soon will be spitting with the rest.

Opposite the Médoc, along the western side of the peninsula jutting out from Bordeaux, a string of unsung beaches lazes in the French sunshine. The stretch of Atlantic from Soulac-sur-Mer, just below the mouth of the Gironde River, to Cap-Ferret, at the entrance to the Arcachon Basin — 60 miles of beautiful coastline backed by towering pine trees — has long been enjoyed by vacationing Bordelais and visiting Germans, Belgians, Dutch, and Swiss. The British are beginning to take advantage of its proximity, and soon other travelers are bound to follow — with good reason. These beaches, though certainly popular, are not as crowded as those along the southern expanse of the Côte d'Argent around Biarritz, and they rub elbows with two large freshwater lakes that offer boating, sailing, and swimming with no waves or undertow to battle. And the bountiful pine forest of the Landes (pronounced *Land*) — what one sees here is merely a hint of its vast acreage — has many convenient trails for hiking and biking.

Bordeaux's backyard beaches make up almost a third of the largest coastline in the world, the Côte d'Argent, and they are rapidly being developed, especially in Soulac-sur-Mer, in Lacanau-Océan, and — a brief hop inland — at lakeside Maubuisson, to provide hospitality, good food, and comfortable lodging for wayfarers. At the same time, parts of the coast are deliberately being left alone, a tribute to the foresight of environmentally minded regional planners.

Always keep in mind that these beaches suffer from a strong undertow; be especially attuned to flags posted to indicate the safety of the waters on any given day. A green flag means you can swim safely and that a lifeguard is on duty; a yellow flag warns you to proceed with caution; a red flag orders you to limit yourself to sunbathing and reading. Don't expect to collect shells when the waves are off-limits, however; you'll usually find only smooth stones and pebbles and occasionally ravenously hungry insects (carry repellent). Some beaches are especially designated *naturiste,* meaning that bathers *must* be nude. However, swimming and sunning in the buff occur openly at most places, though somewhat off to one side or the other of the central cluster of swimmers. Topless bathing is a common phenomenon wherever sand and water exist in tandem; those from countries where this is not the custom should gawk as unobtrusively as possible.

Almost directly west of Bordeaux lies the tidy triangle called the Arcachon Basin: a mooring spot for thousands of sailboats; an important breeding ground for several varieties of oysters; a source of livelihood for a handful of small fishing villages and beach communities; and an exquisite backdrop for the resort town of Arcachon, which still bears vestiges of the Belle Epoque days when it was Queen of the Ball, wooed by English gentry and French artists alike.

The largest sand dune in Europe, Pilat, sprawls a few miles south of Arcachon, at Pyla-sur-Mer. Scale its 380-foot height (and still growing!) for the best view of the region's odd juxtaposition of pine trees, sea, and dunes.

The regal conifers of the Landes, so evident along the coastal area to the north, become even more prevalent around the Basin. In fact, the Parc Regional des Landes de Gascogne (Gascony Moors Regional Park) begins at the southeast corner of the Arcachon Basin and extends about halfway to Biarritz. But it is only a 515,000-acre part of the Landes area. If one were simply to extend the sides of the peninsular triangle formed by Bordeaux, Arcachon, and Pointe de Grave (at the mouth of the Gironde River) down to Biarritz along the coast on the west and along the route of the Garonne River on the east, a new and larger triangle, its base falling just north of Gascony, would be created to encompass the 3 million acres of the Landes.

Until the end of the 18th century, the coastline here was barren and the Landes region was desolate, disease-harboring, swampy moorland. Even worse, strong Atlantic winds were blowing coastal sand farther and farther inland yearly, threatening to turn the inhospitable moor into a more inhospitable desert. The amazing metamorphosis of this tract into the biggest and most important forestland in France began in 1788, when engineer Nicolas Brémontier devised a plan to barricade the coastal dunes with wooden planks, ground cover, and pine trees. Once the dunes had been fixed in place, the swamp inland could be drained, a problem that was settled by 19th-century engineers. The job was completed with the large-scale planting of trees on the former swamp. Landes was once an area where people eked out a meager living herding sheep, which they did quite adroitly on stilts because of the soggy terrain. Now the inhabitants are more gainfully employed in the timber and paper industries and in the cultivation of corn, trout, and chickens. The tastiness of the poultry comes from the fact that it is allowed to roam free in the Landes forest, dining on the delicacies it finds there.

By no means a private preserve, the forest is very much open to and used by the public. In the bird sanctuary in Le Teich, at the southeast corner of the Basin, the land has been left in its natural, unforested state. Here it's possible to commune with the feathered residents and go back in time to see just how forlorn this part of France used to be.

Fire has proved a serious hazard here. From 1944 to 1949, it wiped out more than a third of the forest (fortunately, it has been replanted). Needless to say, campsites are regulated carefully. For more information about the Landes regional park, see tour routes in *Gascony* and *The Pyrénées,* DIRECTIONS.

Hotels in each of Bordeaux's three quick getaway regions — the Médoc, the Coast, and the Arcachon Basin — charge about the same rates as the city: $90 and up for an expensive double room; $50 to $90 for a moderately priced one; and under $50 for an inexpensive but adequate room. In restaurants, expect to pay $90 or more for a meal for two (not including wine or drinks) in the expensive category; between $50 and $90, moderate; and under $50 for an inexpensive meal. Service usually is included.

THE MÉDOC

Most of the châteaux in the Médoc make sure that an informed representative is available to greet visitors, take them on a tour of the *chais,* explain the processes involved in making the wine, and perhaps invite them to taste the most recent vintage from the barrel. An appointment often is necessary — most châteaux are open from 9 or 10 AM to noon and from 2 to 5:30 PM, but it's good insurance to call ahead. Tours generally include visits to the *chais* only, not to the châteaux themselves. Drop by the Maison du Vin in Bordeaux (1 Cours 30-Juillet; phone: 56-00-22-66) weekdays and get a list of châteaux that are open to the public; this includes the times they are open as well as which ones have English-speaking guides. The Maison du Vin also offers tastings of the region's wines on weekdays from 10:30 to 11:30 AM and 2:30 to 4:30 PM. Bottles or cases of recent vintages usually are available for purchase at the châteaux, but if you intend to make a substantial purchase, consult reliable vintage charts ahead of time and ask the advice of a reliable wine dealer. Be forewarned that the *maître de chai* probably won't speak English, although your tour guide may, and that most châteaux do not allow visits during the grape harvest.

Despite its importance to the city, the Médoc is poorly marked from Bordeaux. Follow the signs for Soulac, or find the directions to the Barrière du Médoc. The vineyard road, D2E, branches off to the right about 2 miles (3 km) beyond the turnoff for the Paris autoroute. At this point it's impossible to get lost — especially with ample signs that say Route Touristique du Médoc Nord (or Sud) pointing the way. All the châteaux, large and small, are individually marked right along with the towns. This is the way to all the greatest châteaux and some of the wonderful wines of the region — truly the road to happiness.

The first noteworthy property comes into view on D2E in about 11 miles (18 km).

Château La Lagune – The house and *chai* of this château are visible behind a lacy wrought-iron gate to the right of the vineyard road. The third-growth château, which was built in 1730 by Victor Louis, the architect of the *Grand Théâtre* in Bordeaux, is in the *chartreuse* style typical of the 18th and early 19th centuries in the Bordeaux region. The château produces about 25,000 cases of high-quality wine yearly. Closed in August. Visits are by appointment only and generally reserved for wine professionals (Ludon; phone: 56-30-44-07).

Château Cantemerle – About a mile (1.6 km) up the vineyard road from Château La Lagune, the handsome stone manor house of Château Cantemerle nestles deep amid grand old trees in a beautiful parkland setting. The fifth-growth wine of this château enjoys continuing popularity. By appointment only (call the château, 56-30-41-52, or Domaines Cordier, 56-31-44-44).

MARGAUX: No fewer than 21 classified growths as well as a good many unclassified labels are found among the 2,625 vineyard acres of Margaux that produce 5.5 million bottles of wine a year. This world-famous village allows its name to be hyphenated to those of four neighboring hamlets: Arsac, Labarde, Cantenac, and Soussans. Half a million cases of wine entitled to sport the name Margaux are produced here each year, 65% of which are classified growths. About 75% to 80% of the total is exported to eager foreign buyers. Margaux boasts the deepest beds of pebbled earth in what is known as the Haut-Médoc, which includes the townships of Margaux, St.-Julien, Pauillac, St.-Estèphe, Moulis, and Listrac. For more information, visit the Maison du Vin de Margaux (closed Sundays and Monday mornings; Pl. la Trémoille, Margaux; phone: 56-88-70-82).

Château Giscours – This is a third growth that, like many Bordeaux properties, lay in virtual desolation from the German occupation until the mid-1950s. Under the supervision of the father-son team that has owned the property in the succeeding decades, the vineyards have been restored to full production and the quality of the wine has been recaptured. Land unsuitable for vine cultivation has been planted with many varieties of rhododendrons, which make a magnificent display of bloom in the parkland behind the château. By appointment only; English is spoken (Labarde; phone: 56-88-34-02).

Château Prieuré-Lichine – At the bend in the vineyard road where D2E becomes D2, you'll catch your first sight of the fourth-growth Château Prieuré-Lichine, whose late owner, American Alexis Lichine, also was the author of the informative *Guide to the Wines and Vineyards of France.* Sacha Lichine, Alexis's son, currently manages the vineyard. The original part of the château was built as a Benedictine priory (*prieuré*), which served the village of Cantenac through the adjacent church until the dissolution of religious houses at the time of the Revolution. To visit, leave your car on the side of the road opposite the gateway and walk through the arch into the courtyard. The remains of the old cloister are decorated with the fanciful designs of antique cast-iron firebacks collected by the owner from all over Europe. At the office at the end of the gravel walk, you'll find an English-speaking guide who will take you through the *chai*. The vat room, which was built by the monks who tended the vines for centuries, features the original 16th-century beams, but the gleaming stainless-steel vats and wine making equipment are among the most modern in the Médoc. The *maître de chai* may invite you to sample wines in the attractive tasting room; purchases are easily arranged. Unlike most châteaux, Prieuré-Lichine is open every day until 7 PM in summer; until 6 PM in winter (Cantenac; phone: 56-88-36-28).

Château d'Issan – A stroll from Château Prieuré-Lichine along a grassy avenue of stately plane trees leads to this 16th-century château, which, with its pepper pot turrets and a moat, looks like some honey-colored castle bewitched in a fairy tale. In the spring, the grounds are carpeted with wildflowers. One of the *chais* is so magnificent that it has been designated a historic monument; it should not be missed. The property is owned by a prominent Bordeaux family of wine shippers, and visits to the château are not permitted. To arrange a visit to the *chai*, call 56-44-94-45.

Château Palmer – The compact and attractive Château Palmer, on the right side of the vineyard road, flies a flag to honor each of its three proprietors, who are English, French, and Dutch. A pretty feature of the 19th-century château is the rose border at the base of the courtyard walls. Open to the public on weekdays; appointments recommended (Cantenac; phone: 56-88-72-72).

Château Margaux – Take the vineyard road three-quarters of a mile to the marked turnoff to Château Margaux, which, along with its *chai* and grounds, has been classified a historic monument. The grand house with its Ionic columns was built in 1802 and remains an acknowledged perfect example of the Empire style. An intensive program of restoration of the house and modernization of the vineyards and wine making areas has been undertaken since 1977, when the first-growth property was bought by a couple who headed one of France's largest supermarket chains. Widowed and remarried since the purchase, the owner has sought the advice of the country's leading authorities on architecture and decoration to return the house to its Empire splendor; she has applied the same meticulous care to the production of Margaux's fabulous wines.

The enormous *chai* is a most impressive sight: Visitors enter by a kind of dais that is raised slightly above the earth floor to look out over row upon row of barrels, their glass bungs (stoppers) aligned in perfect precision. All splatters and droplets falling onto the wood in the course of sampling are wiped off by workers whose job it is to maintain the order and neatness of the *chai*.

Château Margaux is one of the few places whose production is large enough to justify making its barrels in the property's own cooperage. This is a vast room, with walls of the characteristic pale gold stone of the region, heated by flames leaping from crackling vine clippings in a fireplace large enough to roast an ox and illuminated by daylight streaming in through clerestory windows. In front of the fireplace, burly coopers wrestle the hoops down over the barrel staves in a scene that gives you the sensation of entering the world of medieval woodcuts instead of touring France by car in the 1990s.

The château itself is not open to visitors, but an English-speaking guide is available by appointment to take you through the *chai* (Margaux; phone: 56-88-70-28). In the tasting room are displayed interesting documents and photographs covering the history of the property.

CHECKING IN: *Le Relais du Margaux* – Luxury is the key in the 27 rooms and 3 suites of this well-equipped hotel. It has tennis courts, a swimming pool, and a beautiful, serene park. Its restaurant offers specialties such as asparagus with truffles and fish filet with herbs. Open March 1 to November 30. The restaurant is open daily when the hotel is open. About 1 mile (1.6 km) north of Margaux (phone: 56-88-38-30). Expensive.

EATING OUT: *Relais du Médoc* – It has good home cooking, Bordeaux style. Open for lunch and dinner. Closed Monday and Wednesday evenings and in October. A few miles north of Margaux in Lamarque; turn right off D2E onto D5 and you're as good as there (phone: 56-58-92-27). Moderate.

Le Savoie – This inn serves straightforward cooking and offers a wide variety of local wines. Eat in the garden in season. Closed Sundays and holidays. Pl.-la Trémoille, Margaux (phone: 56-88-31-76). Moderate to inexpensive.

ST.-JULIEN: As you continue on the vineyard road toward St.-Julien, note the contrast between low-lying fields of rich, loamy soil, where fat, contented dairy cows amble about the pasture, and the raised vineyard plantations, where the fast-draining, pebbly soil fosters a king's ransom in wines but could hardly feed a cow for a week! Here, 1,875 acres produce 4.2 million bottles of wine every year.

Château Beychevelle – The first vineyard in St.-Julien, this was once, like Château Prieuré-Lichine, a monastery. It was rebuilt in 1757, and the long, low, elegant château is considered a particularly lovely example of the *chartreuse* style. At the end of the 16th century, the property belonged to the Chief Admiral of France. Mariners plying the river saluted him by dipping their sails, and the name Beychevelle (*baisser voile,* to lower the sail) commemorates that salute. Open Mondays through Fridays until 5:30 PM. Guided tours, in English in July and August, of the *chais* and parklike gardens are given, though appointments are necessary (phone: 56-59-23-00).

Château Ducru-Beaucaillou – The vineyards of this château, a second *cru,* adjoin those of Beychevelle. The name *beau caillou* (beautiful pebble) honors the soil on which the life of the château depends. The *chais* have been sunk slightly into the ground and have a cool, damp atmosphere that is especially conducive to the preservation of old wines. In surroundings that are too dry, corks will dessicate and crumble, allowing air to enter the bottle and oxidize the wine as well as letting precious wine evaporate. English is spoken. Visits by appointment only; closed weekends, August, and at harvest time (phone: 56-59-05-20).

PAUILLAC: This attractive little town (pronounced more or less *Po*-yak) is one of the oldest in the Médoc and certainly the most central, lying halfway between Bordeaux and Pointe de Grave. The Médoc is not known for great lodgings, and the available hotels are modest at best. Still, it's nice not to have to turn around and go back to Bordeaux or rush to Soulac-sur-Mer if you're caught up in the spirit and the beauty of the area. Pauillac has several things going for it: a tourist office and Maison du Vin that are open daily (Quai Léon-Perrier at La Verrerie; phone: 56-59-03-08); the stationery store of M. Lafon, on Quai Léon-Perrier, which sells a number of English newspapers as well as good maps and postcards; and a handy camera store just up the street. The post office is at Place Gachet, and there are several quick-service dry cleaner–laundries. For a break from driving, go for a swim at the town pool or drive 11 miles (18 km) to Lamarque, leave the car, and take the ferry over to the walled city of Blaye (see *Bordeaux* in THE CITIES). Or for a unique opportunity to spend some time in a real Bordelais château, go to Moulis, where, in season, Château Clarke is open (for groups of 15 or more) for lunch or for viewing a slide show or art exhibition (by appointment only, Cercle Oeunologique de Château Clarke; phone: 56-88-88-00). Back in Pauillac, stroll along the promenade by the river or out onto the piers, admire the pleasure boats, and, of course, visit some of the most famous châteaux in the world, whose mailing address is this quiet little town, where 2,750 acres produce 5.2 million bottles of wine a year.

Château Latour – This great first-growth château, surprisingly modest in appearance, is the last vineyard in St.-Julien or, in some eyes, the first in the district of Pauillac, straddling the boundary as it does. The fortress that once stood on the site was built to repulse the river pirates and bands of pillaging mercenaries who roamed Europe in the wake of medieval wars. By the end of the Hundred Years War, which pitted England and France against each other until 1453, the fort was little more than a heap of rubble. The sole vestige is the tower (*la tour*), which stands today like a sentinel keeping watch over the vineyards. Château Latour will accept visitors by appointment only, on weekdays; it's closed in August (phone: 56-59-00-51).

Château Mouton-Rothschild – Classed as a second growth in 1855, only 2 years after the Rothschild family bought the property and before they had time to restore the vines, this has been ranked with the first *crus* of the Médoc since 1973 thanks to the unremitting efforts of the now deceased owner, Baron Philippe de Rothschild. The grounds here are kept meticulously, and the château is surprisingly small, because it was the last of the existing buildings to be added and there wasn't much room left except in the courtyard. An appointment is required (and difficult to get) to visit the *chais*, where the rows of barrels extend for about 3,000 feet, and the *Musée du Vin*. The museum, set up by the baron's late wife, Pauline, an artistic and creative American, is in former wine cellars. Here paintings, tapestries, finely wrought silver, and all manner of antique and contemporary works of art collected by the Rothschilds celebrate the history and pleasures of vines and wines. Closed in August. English is spoken (call Miss Courtiade at 56-59-22-22).

Château Pontet-Canet – Right across the road from Château Mouton-Rothschild is the largest vineyard, at 170 acres, and one of the loveliest properties in the Médoc: Château Pontet-Canet. A narrow driveway leads through the shade trees to the simple 18th-century stone château, with its white shutters and clean lines. The rose garden and gray, vine-covered outbuildings with claret-colored shutters only add to the beauty of the place. The château was owned by the same family, the Cruses, for a century before it changed hands in 1975. Unlike most châteaux in the region, this one is lived in year-round. Many believe that the wine produced here deserves far better than its fifth-*cru* status. Visits by appointment on weekdays (phone: 56-59-04-04 or 56-52-15-71).

Château Lafite-Rothschild – The word "Lafite" is a corruption of the local dialect term *la hite* (the height), referring to the elevation on which the château, with its medieval tower, is built. Since 1868, the owners of Château Lafite have been another branch of the Rothschild family, cousins of Baron Philippe de Mouton-Rothschild. The reputation of Château Lafite extends far back beyond the Rothschilds, however; wine making has been carried on here for as long as 800 years, by some accounts. The wine of Château Lafite is said to have been the favorite of two royal mistresses: Mme. de Pompadour served little else to Louis XV, and Mme. du Barry put away a few cases while she helped to while away the evenings for Louis XVI. The Nazi field marshal Hermann Göring declared his intention of taking the first-growth Lafite, with its exquisite vaulted *chais*, as his share of the spoils of France after Germany's inevitable victory in World War II. It is our good fortune, and France's, that matters didn't turn out quite the way he planned. Closed from September 15 to November 1; visits by appointment only on weekdays (phone: 56-59-01-74, or, in Paris, 42-56-33-50).

CHECKING IN: *Château Cordeillan-Bages* – Extensive renovation has turned this 17th-century château into a deluxe 18-room hotel. There also is a restaurant known for specialties such as *lamproie en rémoulade bourgeoise* (lamprey eel in an herb and anchovy-mayonnaise sauce) and *noisette d'agneau de Pauillac à la citronelle* (medallions of Pauillac lamb with lemon grass). Closed Mondays and the month of January. BP 90, Pauillac (phone: 56-59-24-24). Expensive.

La Coquille – This hotel has 9 rooms with private bathtub or shower but no private toilet. Its restaurant has three prix fixe menus as well as à la carte selections, all southwest French cuisine. The restaurant generally is closed in November but will open if you call. 18 Quai Léon-Perrier, Pauillac (phone: 56-59-07-52). Hotel, inexpensive; restaurant, moderate to inexpensive.

Hotel-Restaurant de la Renaissance – The views from this modern 8-room hotel make it worth a stop. Its restaurant serves traditional French food. Closed Sundays. St.-Laurent-Médoc (phone: 56-59-40-29). Inexpensive.

 EATING OUT: *Relais du Manoir* – Set in an old manor house, the kitchen prepares regional foods in original ways; be sure to try the assortment of salads with foie gras. It also has 8 reasonably priced rooms. Closed Sunday evenings. Just outside Pauillac, on Rte. de la Shell (phone: 56-59-05-47). Moderate.

La Salamandre – The price is right and the food's good at this little brasserie. Open daily for lunch and dinner, June to August; open daily except Sundays for lunch only and dinner on Saturday evenings, September to April. Pauillac (phone: 56-59-08-68). Inexpensive.

ST.-ESTÈPHE: Some 6.9 million bottles of wine are produced on 2,750 acres in this tiny village yearly, although less than 20% percent of the total is from classified growths. The soil of St.-Estèphe has the least gravel of the Médoc areas, and its heavier, moisture-retaining clay imparts a somewhat "heavier" quality to the wine. The Maison du Vin sells all the wines from the region and presents an audio-visual show; it also exhibits a collection of old wine cellar tools. Closed Sundays off-season, and February (phone: 56-59-30-59).

Château Cos d'Estournel – The second-growth wine produced here is first class, but you're likely to remember Cos d'Estournel for its bizarre architecture. The château, whose first owner traveled in the Far East, was put together in the 19th century with such incongruous details as pagoda towers and massive carved wooden doors from the palace of the sultan of Zanzibar. Of all the châteaux, it casts the most exotic outline against the already dramatic Médoc sky. Open to the public afternoons only (except Mondays) in July and August; tours are available in English, Dutch, and German, and an audiovisual show (also multilingual) is given. Make appointments at least 2 months in advance; this château is very popular in season (phone: 56-59-35-69).

Château Montrose – This château has the distinction of being run by a mother-and-son team in a business where father-and-son teams are the norm. They maintain the brilliant standard of the full, long-lived wine that was recognized as a second growth back in 1855. Open by appointment only. Closed July (phone: 56-59-30-12).

Château Calon-Ségur – A third *cru*, this is the northernmost classified growth of the Médoc. "Calon" refers to the small boats that were once used extensively by ferrymen to transport timber across the Gironde from the heavy forests of St.-Estèphe. The name Ségur recognizes a man who was not only a president of the Parlement de Bordeaux in the 18th century but also proprietor of both Château Lafite and Château Latour, along with his property here. The heart design on Calon-Ségur's label commemorates Ségur's great love for this property, and the motto carved in stone at the arched entrance to the château echoes this sentiment: "I make wine at Lafite and Latour, but my heart is at Calon." Open by appointment only; tours given in French (phone: 56-59-30-27).

CHECKING IN: *Vieux Acacias* – This pleasant 14-room hostelry amid a peaceful park and gardens provides a good stopping point between the vineyards of the Médoc and the Atlantic Coast. Queyrac, Lesparre (phone: 56-59-80-63). Moderate.

EATING OUT: *Château Layauga* – An 18th-century château that was converted into a small luxury hotel with 7 rooms, decorated in Louis XV style. Its restaurant serves updated French classics prepared by chef/owner Philipe Gorand. Gaillan en Médoc (phone: 56-41-26-83). Hotel, moderate; restaurant, expensive to moderate.

En Route from the Médoc – After looking at nothing but straight vine rows along most of the vineyard road, travelers may find its northern remnant a surprising, perhaps welcome, change. The flatness of the lower reaches gives way to wooded slopes and fields of more conventional farm crops — potatoes, corn, and other vegetables. A salty breeze is a reminder that this last stretch of the Gironde is the estuary where fresh water meets the Atlantic.

Note: Although D2E/D2 is known as the *route des châteaux* because it leads to a remarkable number of great châteaux, smaller roads, notably D5, also will take you to a number of châteaux that produce sound, reliable wines that often equal the products at least of the lesser Margaux, St.-Julien, Pauillac, and St.-Estèphe vineyards. In a few cases, the wines are really distinguished. Two of the most outstanding châteaux along D5 are Château Chasse-Spleen, "banish blues," as by drinking the wine (phone: 56-58-02-10), and Château Maucaillou, "bad pebbles" in contrast to the *beaucaillou* back in St.-Julien (phone: 56-58-01-23). Both châteaux are in the township of Moulis, northwest of Margaux.

THE COAST

The opposite side of the Bordeaux peninsula from the Médoc, and the northern third of the increasingly popular Côte d'Argent (also known here as the Côte Aquitaine), this string of beaches is easily accessible from Bordeaux and still refreshingly under-populated. A small coast road links most of the beach communities, which are about half an hour's drive apart. If you're in a hurry or don't want to explore each beach, it's quicker to take the more inland route, D101, from Soulac-sur-Mer as far as Hourtin and then D3. This route passes just east of two large lakes, Lac d'Hourtin-Carcans and Lacanau, and links the forested towns of Soulac, Vendays-Montalivet, Hourtin, Carcans, Lacanau, Le Porge, and Lege-Cap Ferret; connector roads lead from the towns to their respective beaches. Good accommodations are available near the beach in both Soulac-sur-Mer and Lacanau-Océan as well as in Maubuisson and at the recreation area called Bombannes, both on Lac d'Hourtin-Carcans.

SOULAC: The largest town along this part of France's Atlantic coast, Soulac is a tidy, bustling place with brick houses that have especially colorful shutters and trim. The town has a market every morning, and there is a museum, the *Fondation Soulac-Médoc* (phone: 56-09-83-99), open from 3 to 7 PM, June to October, which features the paintings, drawings, and sculpture of more than 100 Aquitaine artists. There also is the *Musée d'Archeologie* (28 Rue Victor Hugo) which includes prehistoric, protohistoric, and Gallo-Roman pieces. Open daily May 1 to September 15 from 3 to 7 PM. Soulac also has a municipal swimming pool, 21 tennis courts (2 of them covered), a gym, a cinema, a casino (open from June to September), and a nightclub, *Memphis;* the casino and nightclub are on Bd. Charcot (phone: 56-09-82-74). Visitors can rent horses for rides or trips (call the *Poney-Club* at 56-09-73-85 or, in winter, 56-50-41-17). Adventurous travelers can try parachuting with the *Centre Départemental de Parachutisme* (Aérodrome de Soulac; phone: 56-09-84-50). The nearby beach at L'Amélie-sur-Mer, just south of Soulac, is especially striking with its black rock formation and dunes. But the crowning attraction is the Eglise Notre-Dame de la Fin des Terres, a splendid 12th-century Roman church that was completely covered by sand in the 18th century and not unearthed until 1860. In July and August, a music festival takes place in the church. Soulac is close to the famous vineyards of the Médoc (N215 connects with the vineyard road, D2, at the village of St. Vivien du Médoc). It is also only 3½ miles (6 km) south of Le Verdon, where ferries depart every half hour or hour, depending on the time of day, for Royan from the end of June to the end of August; other months, every hour to hour and a half. For a city map, drop by the tourist office

(Place du Marche, near the Eglise Notre-Dame; phone: 56-09-86-61); it's open year-round.

The first 19 miles (30 km) of the drive south from Soulac are especially pastoral and pleasant, the backside of beaches masquerading as farmland.

CHECKING IN/EATING OUT: *Margaux* – Also known as "La Dame de Coeur," this is one of the handful of hotels that don't close in the off-season, and it's in the heart of downtown. All rooms come with a bath, and the restaurant serves hearty fare. Pl. de l'Eglise, Soulac-sur-Mer (phone: 56-09-80-80). Moderate.

Pins – In the small community of L'Amélie, 2½ miles (4 km) from Soulac, it's about 100 feet from the beach. The hotel has 35 rooms and is open year-round, except January and February. Its restaurant closes on Fridays and Sunday evenings off-season. L'Amélie-sur-Mer (phone: 56-09-80-01). Moderate.

L'Hacienda – With its lush garden and terraces, this hotel looks as though it was transported intact from Spain. It has 12 bedrooms, and its restaurant offers paella, seafood, and chicken dishes and meat grilled over a wood fire. Closed from the end of September through March. 4 Av. Du-Perier-de-Larsan, Soulac-sur-Mer (phone: 56-09-81-34). Moderate to inexpensive.

Lescorce – This comfortable hotel has a game room for Ping-Pong and billiards, a tennis court (make your reservation in the hotel bar; you don't have to be a guest to play), a TV room, and a homey ambience. Guests are required to take lunch and dinner in the hotel. The owner speaks English. Open from June to the end of September. 36 Rue Trouche, Soulac-sur-Mer (phone: 56-09-84-13). Moderate to inexpensive.

MONTALIVET-LES-BAINS: This long stretch of beach officially is designated *naturiste*. It is large enough to afford plenty of privacy and is used mostly by young couples with children. People simply park by the side of the road and walk across the dunes. Take along insect repellent and carry your valuables with you; it's not safe to leave them in the car.

EATING OUT: *La Clef des Champs* – Elegant and off the beaten track, this restaurant-farm is managed by a mother-and-daughter team, the *mesdames* Lussagnet. Whatever game and vegetables are in season will appear on the menu. Closed for lunch during July and August. Reservations are necessary, for the word's out. Between Vendays and Montalivet, 3 miles (5 km) from Montalivet; watch for signs (phone: 56-41-71-11). Moderate.

CARCANS: The streets in this town of 500 people dead-end into a large sand dune 20 feet high; you have to climb over it to get to the ocean. This beach is more crowded than Montalivet and more conservative. There is a small museum of arts and crafts that is open daily in the late afternoons in July and August (phone: 56-03-37-53). For information, contact the Carcans–Maubuisson Tourist Office (phone: 56-03-34-94).

En Route from Carcans – If at this point you've had enough sun and salt water and want a break, if only for a few hours, visit Lac d'Hourtin-Carcans, a pebble's throw away on D3E. Maubuisson, a tiny resort town on its southern shore, has a couple of decent hotels and restaurants right across the street from the lake. If you want to play or lie in the shade of a pine tree, the lakeside resort complex of Bombannes, about 5 miles (8 km) north of Maubuisson, is a must. Apartments are available only for minimum 1-week rentals. Facilities include open-air and enclosed tennis courts, a gym, and picnic areas, and the ocean is a short drive away. Don't be surprised to find bright pink heather everywhere, blanketing the base of the pines and sweetening the air. The complex is open from 8 AM to 10 PM; closed December and January (phone: 56-03-31-01).

LACANAU-OCÉAN: This is the cleanest of all the beaches and the one best equipped for demanding travelers. It has a couple of large, seafront hotels as well as a tourist office (Pl. de l'Europe; phone: 56-03-21-01). The dwellings look like gingerbread houses made of brick. Sculpted dunes speckle the beach, and a "sandwalk" runs parallel to the ocean. Activity-prone vacationers will never want to leave: They can rent surfboards, windsurfers, and Hobie Cats from *Lacanau Lou* (phone: 56-03-23-54), take surfing lessons by the week at the *Lacanau Surf Club* (phone: 56-26-38-84), learn windsurfing at the surf club or the *Voile Lacanau Guyenne* (phone: 56-03-05-11), go horseback riding (phone: 56-03-52-74), take golf lessons (phone: 56-03-25-60), undertake a 5-day tennis course, including one for children (phone: 56-03-24-91), or learn to water-ski (phone: 56-03-01-39 or 56-03-09-01). Lacanau Lake is nearby. During *Easter*, there is a festival of sports movies and sports medicine; there's also a 1-day *Mai Musical* (May Music Fest) at the Eglise St.-Vincent, in the inland town of Lacanau. July brings a windsurfing day, an international tennis tournament, and a dance festival. August heralds a surfing competition at the beach.

CHECKING IN: *Hôtel du Golf* – A modern hostelry at the edge of one of the region's best golf courses, it offers comfortable rooms and apartments with terraces overlooking the greens. It is surrounded by trees and is just a 4-minute walk from the ocean. Domaine de l'Ardilouse, Lacanau Océan (phone: 56-03-23-15). Moderate.

***L'Etoile d'Argent* –** Right by the water, this impressive hotel has 14 rooms facing the beach and another 9 in the equally nice annex right behind it. Closed from mid-November to mid-January. Place de L'Europe, Lacanau-Océan (phone: 56-03-21-07). Inexpensive.

EATING OUT: *La Taverne de Neptune* – Sit inside by the glow of candlelight or out on the porch by the glow of your fondue flame. (They do three kinds of fondue, plus other dishes such as duck, snails, lots of fish.) Service is slow but the food is delicious. English, Dutch, and German are spoken, and the menu is translated for you. Open daily for dinner; closed Tuesdays off-season, and from October to *Easter*. Av. de l'Europe, Lacanau-Océan (phone: 56-03-21-33). Moderate.

LE PORGE-OCÉAN: This lovely beach has a well-kept 114-acre municipal campground nearby, not to mention a nudist colony called La Jenny. It's worth it to arrive via the inland road, D3, from Lacanau and then drive west to the ocean along D107 from Le Porge. This way you can truly appreciate the stately, dense pine forest and get a good sense of the peacefulness, even solemnity, it imparts. The drive to the beach may be the most serene 8 miles (13 km) of your trip, especially if you go in the morning when the mist still hovers in the forest.

Diehards who want a sample of the Atlantic coast between the Gironde River and the Arcachon Basin can continue south from Le Porge on D3, which links up with D106 to lead to Cap-Ferret.

CAP-FERRET: This beach town has two beaches, one facing the ocean, the other facing the still, safe waters of the Basin. A train trundles visitors back and forth, and bicycles can be rented for further exploration. For more information, see the Cap-Ferret listing in the Arcachon Basin route, below.

THE ARCACHON BASIN

The most popular close destination for Bordelais who have set their hearts on sunning, swimming, and sailing is a day or two at the Arcachon Basin, via N250 to N650 to D650. The Basin is trianglular and has a road that loops 112 miles around it, connecting a baker's dozen communities. The most appealing spots, however, all fall along the base (or southern part) of the triangle, on D650, from Le Teich to Arcachon. Cap-Ferret, across the channel from Arcachon, is a boat ride away and a pleasant day trip. No cars are allowed on the boats, so those who insist on four wheels can get there only by making the tedious, traffic-riddled trip around the Basin.

LE TEICH: The first point of interest southwest from Bordeaux is Parc Ornithologique, a bird park and sanctuary in Le Teich. The town (not to be confused with nearby La Teste) is in the southeast corner of the Basin, 25 miles (40 km) from Bordeaux. The park comprises 296 acres, 173 of which contain still, brackish water used as a fish preserve. In winter, more than 25,000 birds inhabit the park. Ducks, geese, swans, herons, storks, and flamingos are among the 280 species to be found here at that time of the year. Two hiking trails offer a 1- or 2-hour diversion, but the longer one, which follows a flat course with no shade trees, is of interest only to committed bird watchers, who visit in winter. Buy a small bag of grain at the entrance or the ducks waddling in your wake will probably make you feel very guilty. The paths are gravelly, so don't wear sandals. Observation booths, which are plentiful, contain useful information about yearly migrations. Open daily from from 10 AM to 6 PM, March 1 to September 30 (after September, it's open only on weekends and holidays), but if you don't arrive before 4 PM, you may not be allowed to enter; admission charge.

En Route from Le Teich – Just 2 ½ miles (4 km) west on D650 is Ker *Helen* (phone: 56-66-03-79), a lovely campground dotted with roses and striped with grapevines. The proprietors are especially helpful to visitors, and it's open year-round.

GUJAN-MESTRAS: Nicknamed "the oyster capital," this tiny village 11 miles (18 km) west of Le Teich on D650 contains no less than seven ports. A small tourist office on D650 is open daily, mornings only; look for it on the Basin side of the road. If you want to taste some of the local oysters, drop by *Castaing-Druart* or *Beynel-Daney* on the main road.

EATING OUT: *La Coquille* – Try the oysters at this restaurant with a cheerful black and white tile floor and tables covered with crisp white cloths. Other specialties include stuffed mussels and fish soup. Closed January 15 to February 15, and Sunday evenings and Mondays off-season. On the main road through Gujan-Mestras (phone: 56-66-08-60). Moderate to inexpensive.

LA HUME: Although La Hume is only about 6 miles (10 km) west of Gujan-Mestras, it seems eons away in time. In the summer, the restored medieval village here comes alive with craftspeople dressed as they would have been long ago: a leaded-glass worker, coppersmith, candle maker, clog maker, basket maker, caneworker, herbalist, bell maker, silk painter, blacksmith, cabinet maker, enameler — 40 artisans in all. After a few hours of wandering through the village, you'll be ready to stop by the tavern for a refreshing drink. La Hume is open in July and August only, from 2 to 7:30 PM daily as well as from 9 to 11:30 PM on Saturdays. Just follow the signs marked "Artisans d'Art." Nearby, close to the crossroad between N250 and D625, the Parc Aquatique Aquacity is open daily from June to September; the admission charge covers swimming and amusements.

ARCACHON: This seaside resort, once sought out for its curative waters, enjoyed its heyday in the middle to late 1800s, when European high society filled its streets, cafés, casino, hotels, and beaches. Arcachon also lured artists such as Manet and Toulouse-Lautrec and the composer Debussy. Today it enjoys continued popularity, primarily among the Bordelais and Germans. Especially appealing are the old beachfront hotels, sidewalk cafés, the promenade lined with feathery tamarisk trees, and the beach itself. The tourist office is open daily in season and weekdays off-season (Pl. Roosevelt; phone: 56-83-01-69). The casino, a white, castle-like building complete with turrets, is open afternoons and evenings in season; off-season it is open Friday and Saturday evenings and Sunday afternoons and evenings (Bd. de la Plage and Av. Général-de-Gaulle; phone: 56-83-41-44). The aquarium, on Rue Jolyet just off Pier D'Eyrac, has an exhibit on oyster cultivation and a number of local fish, including eels, on view. It is open daily, mornings and afternoons; there is an admission charge. The Ville d'Hiver (Winter City), behind the tourist office in the opposite direction from the Basin, is Arcachon's old town. It is a jumble of purposely winding streets (for protection from the wind) filled with 19th-century villas and chalets; Allées Alexandre-Dumas, Pasteur, Faust, Pereire, Bremontier, Velpeau, Docteur-Lalesque, and Avenue Victor-Hugo are notable. Oddly, a walking tour guide of the Ville d'Hiver can be purchased at the tourist office in Bordeaux; in season, the tourist office in Arcachon offers walking tours of the town. Small boats, *pinasses,* make regular trips between Arcachon and Cap-Ferret daily. Boat trips also are available to nearby Ile aux Oiseaux (Bird Island), to an oyster park, and for deep-sea fishing excursions. For information, contact the tourist office or, for groups, Union des Bateliers d'Arcachon (phone: 56-83-06-62 in season; 56-54-60-32 year-round).

CHECKING IN: *Grand Hôtel Richelieu* – This impressive establishment overlooks the Arcachon Basin and the Grand Pier, and has direct access to the beach. Centrally located, it has 43 rooms, a tearoom, a bar, and free parking. Closed November through mid-March. 185 Bd. de la Plage, Arcachon (phone: 56-83-16-50 or 56-83-16-51). Expensive.

***Les Ormes* –** A pleasant modern hotel a short distance from the center of town. It has 24 rooms, 12 with terraces overlooking the sea, and a restaurant. Open year-round. 77 Bd. de la Plage at Rue Hovy, Arcachon (phone: 56-83-09-27). Expensive.

***Roc* –** Cheerful brown-and-white-striped awnings beckon you inside to try one of the 54 modern, comfortable rooms. Near the casino. Closed mid-October through March or April. 200-202 Bd. de la Plage, Arcachon (phone: 56-83-07-43). Moderate.

EATING OUT: *Chez Yvette* – Exceedingly popular through the the entire region, this old inn has ceiling fans that lazily circulate the soft sea air. The specialty of the house is *lamproie à la bordelaise* (lamprey eel in red wine sauce); for the less adventuresome, the owner recommends delicious sole, turbot, and bass (*bar*) dishes. The bread, ice cream, and sorbets are homemade. Across from the tourist office. 59 Bd. du Général-Leclerc, Arcachon (phone: 56-83-05-11) Moderate.

***La Guitoune* –** This commendable eatery is just a few kilometers away in Pyla-sur-Mer. It's also a small hotel (22 rooms). 95 Bd. de l'Océan, Pyla-sur-Mer (phone: 56-22-70-10). Moderate.

En Route from Arcachon – People who live here praise the stretch of beaches south to Biscarosse. Take D112 south, stopping along the way at Pilat-Plage to be awed by the Dune du Pilat. Like a gigantic glacier made of sand, this dune — 6½ miles long and about 35 feet high and still growing — encroaches on forest, town, and beach. Rugged beach buffs hike over it to get to the water; others take the stairs. Some 19 miles (30 km) farther south on D112, on the right-hand side of the road, is La Lagune, a quiet picnic area with a lovely, secluded beach where nude swimming is officially sanctioned.

CAP-FERRET: A quick boat ride across the Teychan Channel from Arcachon takes you to the seaside community of Cap-Ferret. A small train carries tourists from the town to the ocean, though the channel-side beach is by far recommended because it is both safer and cleaner. The tourist office is at 12 Avenue de l'Océan in Le Panier Fleuri building in season; off-season it's harder to find — in a booth opposite the market, in the Town Hall (phone: 56-60-63-26). In fact, none of the streets here is clearly marked, so expect to be lost most of the time whether you are on foot or wheels. There is a splendid view from the Croix-des-Marins lighthouse, which is open daily from June through September; otherwise, by request. Bikes can be rented at 47 and 51 Avenue de l'Océan; sailboats, at 65 Avenue de Bordeaux. Ocean conditions are given daily in French on radio channel 102 at 1 PM.

Périgord

Wedged neatly between the high plateau and volcanic formations of the Massif Central, the plains of the Guyenne, and the sun-soaked lands of the Midi is the lush green province of Périgord, corresponding approximately to the modern *département* of the Dordogne (the second largest in France). The Dordogne also encompasses parts of other ancient provinces, such as the Limousin and Quercy, but the geography and roads of Périgord make it natural to include certain sites in the Lot and Haute-Vienne *départements* in our itinerary here.

It is one of France's richest areas of both natural and manmade treasures and remains, if no longer undiscovered, at least still relatively unspoiled.

Coming into the Dordogne from the north, one notices a gradual change — not only in the terrain, but also in the rhythm and tempo of life. The autoroute gives way to tiny roads that wind their way through deep, cool, fern-carpeted forests, rolling hills, opulent valleys strewn with wild flowers, and tall white limestone cliffs that drop dramatically into deep river gorges.

You can drive for miles on these picturesque roads without passing another soul — the only signs of life, an occasional group of grazing cows or a stray goose. At times it seems that the 20th century has passed over the region or, at most, touched down just long enough to deposit its telephone lines and TV antennas before moving on, leaving it in the calm of another era.

The region owes much of its beauty to its rivers, among them the Dronne, Isle, Auvézère, and the Vézère, all flowing into the majestic Dordogne, considered by many to be the most beautiful river in France. The river valleys are dotted with charming towns of mellow stone churches and houses dating from the Middle Ages. And firmly entrenched on the heights are the châteaux. Their proud military bearing, a sharp contrast to the elegance of the Loire Valley palaces, reflects a troubled, war-torn past.

Prehistoric man walked in these valleys some 40,000 years ago. The awesome proof of his presence is in the region's many cliff shelters and caves whose walls are decorated with beautiful, enigmatic symbols and paintings. Carbon dating places the majority of these incredibly advanced works in the Magdalenian era of the upper (late) paleolithic period. The discovery, only about a century ago, of the wealth of prehistoric sites in and around Les Eyzies, in the heart of Périgord, has earned it the title of the capital of prehistory, drawing anthropologists from all over.

About 35,000 years after their paleolithic predecessors, the Romans settled here, even before Caesar forced the Gauls to capitulate. The vestiges of their arenas, baths, and temples are signs of the prosperity of the Roman forerunners of Périgueux and the other principal cities. The province was in turn conquered by the Visigoths and then taken by Clovis.

These serene valleys were turned into battlefields during the Middle Ages thanks, in large part, to Eleanor of Aquitaine, whose divorce from Prince Louis, son of the King of France, freed her to marry Henry Plantagenet, who ascended to the throne of England 2 years later, in 1154. Eleanor brought her precious dowry, the ancient duchy of Aquitaine, to the British crown, thereby upsetting the already tenuous balance of power between the two countries and launching a bitter war for possession of the region that lasted for 300 years. During much of that period, Périgord suffered incredible devastation as the dividing line between the French and the British camps. It wasn't until the end of the Hundred Years War, in 1453, that the area reverted to French hands.

But the suffering didn't stop then; in the 16th century the Wars of Religion brought more conflict. Périgueux was a Protestant stronghold between 1515 and 1581 after being taken by Geoffroi de Vivance, the Huguenot leader. Neighboring Bergerac, at one time the headquarters of the Reformed church, was taken by Catholics in 1562, then lost and, in turn, recaptured.

Finally, in the 17th century, the political situation began to stabilize, and from the reign of Louis XIV on, the history of Périgord pretty much parallels that of the rest of France.

Not surprisingly, considering its history, the area is almost as rich in architecture as it is in natural beauty. Most of its churches are in the Romanesque style. Purely Gothic edifices are fairly rare, since the turbulence of the Hundred Years War discouraged the building of anything less practical than fortified castles and *bastides,* the defensive towns constructed under orders of the opposing Kings of France and England. According to some estimates, there are close to 1,500 châteaux in the region. Many of them combine different types of architecture, having been added to, embellished, and in some cases almost entirely rebuilt at various periods without regard to the original design.

In addition to the varied scenic, architectural, and historical appeal of Périgord, it has rich gastronomic traditions — by themselves reason enough for a visit. The specialties are known and loved throughout France and the world. This is the land of foie gras, *confit d'oie* (preserved goose), and *magret de canard* (sliced duck breast), truffles and *cèpes* (wild mushrooms), walnut cakes and liqueurs, fresh river trout, beef *à la périgourdine* (in a red wine sauce similar to *à la bordelaise*), and the hearty wines of Cahors and Bergerac. The food is traditional and hearty — honest and refreshingly simple. Nouvelle cuisine has made few inroads here (though some chefs are lightening the classics somewhat), and the prices often match the down-home fare. A meal for two in an expensive restaurant can run to $80 and up. In the moderate range (most of the restaurants), the bill for two will average between $50 and $80, and in an inexpensive place (there are plenty) two can eat for well under $50. Prices do not include wine or drinks, though service usually is included. Hotel prices parallel those of the restaurants. A room for two in an expensive hotel will range from $80 and up; a moderate room, between $40 and $80; and an inexpensive room, less than $40. Although there are a few grand places, the majority of the hotels and restaurants in this region are cozy, comfortable, and traditional. In general, it's not an area for those who insist upon four-star luxury and modern conveniences such as air conditioning, television sets in their rooms, and overnight dry cleaning service.

Our tour route starts in Limoges, then curves southwest to Brantôme and Périgueux before turning into the heart of the region where the majority of the grottoes and prehistoric sites are found. Just a little to the east are the two most intriguing and most heavily visited towns, Sarlat and Rocamadour. The route then sweeps south to Cahors and the nearby grotto of Pech-Merle, then follows the wine route west of Cahors before turning north again, up to Bergerac and eventually back to Limoges.

LIMOGES: "The men are noted for their wit and the women for their whiteness." Whether the author Jean de La Fontaine's portrait of the people of Limoges still holds true or not, there clearly is a special appeal to this busy city of some 150,000 inhabitants. About 250 miles (400 km) southwest of Paris in what is technically the Limousin, Limoges straddles the Vienne River on the site of the Gallo-Roman town of Augustoritum. It owes much of its modern strength and the title of "City of Art" to its world-renowned porcelain factories and enamel works.

Porcelain has been produced here since the end of the 18th century, when kaolin, the pure white clay from which it is made, was discovered 38 miles (61 km) south of the city, in St.-Yrieix. (The Impressionist painter Auguste Renoir worked for a time in his native Limoges as a porcelain decorator.) The *Musée National Adrien-Dubouché* (open daily except Tuesdays; Pl. Winston-Churchill; phone: 55-77-45-58) has more than 10,000 pieces of pottery and porcelain, tracing the evolution of china making from antiquity to the present. More than 50% of all French porcelain is made in the factories here, some of which are open to visitors. (Ask at the tourist office on Boulevard Fleurus for information on tours; phone: 55-34-46-87.) Plenty of shops in the center of the city sell lovely porcelain. The best shops line the Boulevard Louis-Blanc, including *Prestige de Limoges* and *Charme du Logis.* Also worth a visit is the *Pavillon de la Porcelaine* (Rte. de Toulouse; phone: 55-30-21-86). Be sure to stroll the Boulevard Victor-Hugo or Rue Jean-Jaurès.

The art of enameling (called *émaux;* the various techniques are *émaux cloisonnés, émaux champlevés,* and *émaux peints*) has been practiced since antiquity, but it wasn't until the 12th century that Limoges's enamelers perfected their craft using the lead silicates and oxides of rare metals, including gold, silver, and cobalt, found in the primary faults of the area. Enamels still are made in tiny kilns at the rear of each enameler's workshop. Several of these shops are clustered around Place Wilson and in the old part of the city; visitors are welcome to wander in and observe the process. (For a frank and enlightening discussion on the current state of the art, stop in at 19 Rue des Tanneries, where Boris Veisbrot creates striking contemporary pieces. Both his work and his opinions are refreshing.) Two interesting shops for modern enamel are *René Restoueix* (2 Rue Haute Cité), and *Vincent Pécaud* (23 Rue Elie-Berthet). Appropriately, porcelain and enamel are the subjects of special exhibitions held in Limoges in July and August. The porcelain exhibition is held annually; an international exposition dedicated to the enamel arts is held in even-numbered years. For information on dates, contact the tourist office (phone: 55-34-46-87).

The *Musée Municipal,* in a beautiful 18th-century building that once was the bishop's palace (Palais de l'Evêché), has a wonderful collection of enamels dating from the 12th century to the present. It includes many pieces by Léonard Limousin, enameler to the Kings of France in the 16th century, and a fine group of post-Impressionist paintings. Closed Tuesdays (Mairie de Limoges; phone: 55-45-60-00).

A short walk from the museum is Limoges's striking Cathédrale St.-Etienne, begun in 1273 on the site of a Romanesque church, part of whose crypt and belfry remain. The cathedral is the only one in the Limousin to be completely in the Gothic style. Of particular interest are the Flamboyant Gothic St. John doorway, the delicately chiseled limestone screen inside at the end of the nave, and the three tombs flanking the chancel. The expansive gardens behind the cathedral are magnificent — neat rows of carefully tended flowers of all varieties and lanes of tall trees, all set against the backdrop of the cathedral and the river. Before leaving this area, wander the crooked streets of Vieux (Old) Limoges just to the north of the cathedral entrance. Especially charming is the Rue de la Boucherie, lined with half-timbered houses where the city's butchers have lived since the 10th century.

Also of interest are the Orsay Gardens, where the ruins of a Gallo-Roman arena were discovered during excavations in 1966. Near the tree-shaded Place de la République are two other churches, St.-Michel-des-Lions, begun in 1364, and St.-Pierre-du-Queyroix, its Flamboyant façade built in 1534. It was here, under the Place de la République, that the crypt of the former Abbey of St. Martial, dating from the 4th century, was found during excavations in 1960. Inside is the sarcophagus of St. Martial, the Limosin apostle who came to the area to convert people to Christianity in about AD 250. The abbey, destroyed in 1791, once was an important stop for pilgrims on the route to Santiago de Compostela.

CHECKING IN: *Royal Limousin* – A very comfortable, modern 75-room hotel that is one of the city's best. Recently renovated by its new management. Pl. de la République, Limoges (phone: 55-34-65-30). Expensive to moderate.

Luk – On one corner of the Place Jourdan opposite Limoges's 19th-century replica of the Hôtel de Ville in Paris, this 56-room hotel offers modern comforts and a convenient location. In addition to an existing dining room, there is a "gastronomic" restaurant, the *Luk Epoch.* Breakfast is included in the room rate and parking is available. 29 Pl. Jourdan, Limoges (phone: 55-33-44-00). Moderate.

L'Europe – This modest but congenial establishment is a typical, old-fashioned French hotel on a small square, with an outdoor café. The amiable patroness, Mme. Fouché, presides over the dual-purpose front desk and bar. The 23 guest rooms, some with private bath, are simple but clean, and the restaurant offers a good selection of local specialties, such as *omelette aux truffes* (truffle omelet), foie gras, and *cèpes de Limousin* (wild mushrooms). Closed Sundays. 2 Pl. Wilson, Limoges (phone: 55-34-23-72). Inexpensive.

EATING OUT: *La Chapelle St.-Martin* – About 6 miles (10 km) northwest of Limoges in the Limousin countryside is this elegant inn with one Michelin star, a former 19th-century home, surrounded by a park with tennis courts and peaceful *étangs* (ponds). Everything served in the restaurant is excellent and original, including the *bar à la vinaigrette aux herbes* (bass in vinaigrette sauce) and *carré d'agneau du limousin à l'ail confit* (rack of lamb in garlic). In addition, owner Jacques Dudognon has furnished the inn's 13 rooms with lovely antiques, paintings, and porcelain. Closed January and February. St.-Martin-le-Faux, near Nieul, on D35 (phone: 55-75-80-17). Expensive.

Le Chanplève – This recently opened eatery serves traditional cuisine presented on elegant porcelain with a touch of La Belle Epoque. Pl. Wilson (phone: 54-34-43-34). Expensive to moderate.

Les Petits Ventres – The setting is a 15th-century house; the menu offers good, hearty food. Closed Sundays and for lunch on Mondays. 20 Rue de la Boucherie, Limoges (phone: 55-33-34-02). Moderate to inexpensive.

En Route from Limoges – Head south, turning onto D78 at St.-Yrieix-la-Perche to reach Jumilhac-le-Grand, a romantic, turreted château on the rocks overlooking the Isle River. The core of this château was built during the 14th century, the two lateral wings added in the 17th century. Inside one of the wings is a great hall with wood carvings and a Louis XIV fireplace. Legend has it that the mistress of the castle, Louise de Hautefort, nicknamed La Fileuse (The Spinner), was locked up in the tower for life when her husband returned from the wars of Henri de Navarre to find his beautiful wife with a lover. Today you can visit the room where Louise is said to have sat spinning wool, making decorations, and painting her portrait on the door. In 1927, the château was purchased by Count Odet de Jumilhac, who gradually restored the badly neglected castle.

BRANTÔME: Continue on D78 to Brantôme, a peaceful little town on the Dronne River dominated by a Benedictine abbey founded by Charlemagne in 769. The abbey, which was sacked by the Normans and rebuilt in the 11th, the 14th, and again in the 18th and 19th centuries, once was presided over by Pierre de Bourdeille, better known as Brantôme, the chronicler whose literary fame derives mainly from his witty, spirited, and often cynical accounts of the lives of the *grands capitaines* and *dames galantes* of the late 16th century, an era rich in scandal.

Of particular interest here is the gabled Romanesque belfry, the oldest of its kind in the Limousin, erected in the 11th century apart from the abbey church on a 40-foot-high rock. Behind the abbey, in the caves that housed the monks' bakery and wine cellar, are huge 16th-century carvings in the rock of the Last Judgment and the Crucifixion. Every year, an exhibition of classical dance is held in these caves. Also noteworthy are the monastery buildings, with two 18th-century wings and a beautiful 17th-century staircase. The buildings house the Town Hall, the schools, and the *Musée Fernand-Desmoulin.* The museum has many prehistoric artifacts found in the area as well as the rather bizarre paintings of Desmoulin, produced while this 19th-century Périgord artist was under the influence of a medium.

But the real pleasure of Brantôme lies in its serene, storybook setting. It's a pleasure just to stroll among the willows on the banks of the Dronne, cloaked with white water hyacinths and spanned by asymmetrical stone bridges.

CHECKING IN/EATING OUT: *Moulin de l'Abbaye –* Régis and Catherine Bulot have transformed an old mill on a gentle bend in the Dronne River into one of the most delightful spots in the entire region. Its 9 rooms and 3 suites (elegantly furnished and decorated with French provincial fabrics) and the Louis XIII dining room, which opens onto a tree-shaded, riverside terrace, all contribute to the genteel, quiet luxury that charaterizes the inn, a member of the Relais & Châteaux group. Chef Rabinel's menu is an adroit blend of such up-to-date dishes as mullet with currants and more traditional Périgord fare; his kitchen has been given one Michelin star. Closed from mid-November to May. Rte. de Bourdeilles, Brantôme (phone: 53-05-80-22). Expensive.

Moulin du Roc – In a nearby village, on the verdant banks of the River Dronne, this 17th-century walnut mill has been converted by Solange and Lucien Gardillou into a romantic and peaceful inn. The 12 rooms are furnished with period pieces and have stocked mini-bars and television sets. The cozy but elegant dining room and sitting rooms are decorated with antiques as well as with objects from the old mill, and there are two terraces for outdoor dining and lounging. The imaginative regional cuisine, created by the talented Mme. Gardillou, has earned one Michelin star. Among the specialties are cod, guinea hen, and preserved duck. The wine list features an extensive selection of fine bordeaux. The inn is about 3½ miles (5 km) northeast of Brantôme. Champagnac-de-Bélair (phone: 53-54-80-36). Expensive.

Chabrol – This refined and comfortable hostelry overlooking the Dronne is a particularly good value. The 20 rooms, some with river views, are small but charming; each comes with private bath and a TV set. The hotel is owned by the two Charbonnel brothers, who do the cooking while their amiable wives act as hostesses. Its one-star restaurant, *Les Frères Charbonnel,* offers a very satisfying three-course meal — for a very fair price — in a wonderfully appointed dining room with a river view. Try the scallops in shells with truffles, the squab, and, for dessert, sweet Dordogne strawberries marinated in champagne. 57 Rue Gambetta, Brantôme (phone: 53-05-70-15). Hotel, moderate; restaurant, expensive to moderate.

En Route from Brantôme – Take D78 southwest for about 6 miles (10 km) to reach Bourdeilles, one of the four feudal seats of ancient Périgord (Biron, Beynac, and Mareuil were the other three). This small town and its towering château on a cliff over the Dronne are perhaps more interesting than Brantôme, certainly worth a visit of several hours. What makes the castle here particularly intriguing is that it actually is two châteaux: a massive medieval fortress started in the 13th century next to a Renaissance palace filled with wonderful pieces dating from the 15th to the 17th century.

There are Flemish and Aubusson tapestries, Italian paintings and porcelain, and Spanish furniture inlaid with gold and ivory. The palace was started in the 16th century by Jacquette de Montbron, a sister-in-law of Pierre de Bourdeille (the famous Brantôme), in anticipation of a visit by Catherine de Médicis, but she never arrived, and so the castle was never completed. The contrast between the imposing 13th-century towers and ramparts and the airy, festive palace with its sculpted gardens and sparkling treasures is wonderful. One of the most magnificent features is the Golden Room, decorated by Ambroise Le Noble, one of the painters of Fontainebleau. There also is a 12th-century church nearby.

 CHECKING IN: *Les Griffons* – This cozy inn, just a short walk from the château, has 8 rooms and a restaurant; it's a good place to keep in mind. Closed from October to April. Bourdeilles (phone: 53-03-75-61). Moderate.

PÉRIGUEUX: The capital of the Dordogne, this modern town in the center of the fertile Isle Valley is one of the oldest settlements in France and retains ample evidence of its long and eventful history. There is scarcely a period of architecture that is not represented here. During Gallo-Roman times, Vesunna, as it was then called, was one of the most prosperous towns in Aquitaine. Remnants of the Tour de Vésone, a round temple dedicated to the deity for whom the settlement was named, can be seen today as well as the ruins of the 20,000-capacity elliptical amphitheater. Vesunna was sacked by the Alemans in the 3rd century AD.

During the Middle Ages, two rival cities shared the site — Puy St.-Front, a commercial and monastic center on the hill, and the nearby Cité, where the aristocrats lived on the site of Vesunna. The two towns were reluctantly united under the name of Périgueux in 1251, but it was some time before these bitter rivals reconciled their differences and came together during the Hundred Years War under the motto "My strength is in the loyalty of my fellow countrymen." A good example of the early Périgord-Romanesque style is the Eglise St.-Etienne de la Cité, built in the 12th century and topped with four domes (two of which were destroyed during the Wars of Religion), but the most arresting and curious sight is the Cathédrale St.-Front, a sprawling, Byzantine structure built in the shape of a Greek cross and crowned with five cupolas similar to St. Mark's in Venice. The basilica was completed in 1173. Around 1755, the cathedral's five cupolas were covered to prevent water infiltration. They remained covered until 1852, when architects Abadie and Boeswillwald began restoring them to their original state, a project that wasn't completed until 1901. Visitors can see the cloisters — half Romanesque and half Gothic — as well as the crypt and confessionals. In summer you can walk around the domes of the cathedral roof, which has an excellent view of the old section. Back on the ground level, wander through the streets of this old quarter to discover remnants of Renaissance mansions. One of the most appealing streets is Rue Limogeanne, where 15th- and 16th-century houses have been renovated by their owners. Other picturesque streets, recently restored, are Rue de la Clarté and Rue de la Sagesse and streets of the Quartier Sauvegard.

Well worth a leisurely visit is the *Musée du Périgord* (22 Cours Tourny) which has an impressive collection of prehistoric objects found in the area. Included are tools from the paleolithic era, the skeleton of Chancelade man (late paleolithic), and engraved bones and mammoth tusks. A separate Gallo-Roman gallery on the main floor displays objects found during the excavation of the arena and the tower of Vésone, including mosaic floors that once flanked an altar on which bulls were sacrificed. Other sections of the museum are devoted to the paintings and arts of the region, such as enamels (open daily, except Tuesdays, from 9 AM to noon and 2 to 5 PM; phone: 53-53-16-42).

For a decadent detour, stop in at *La Chocolathèque* (2 Rue Taillefer; phone: 53-53-40-48) to sample *croquant du Périgord* (nougat and cognac covered with milk chocolate and almonds).

There's also a colorful local market every Wednesday morning in front of the cathedral. And the public market at Place Coderc can be of interest on a busy day, here in the heart of the area renowned for truffles and foie gras. On the street near the market there are plenty of unpretentious little restaurants in which to sample the regional specialties. During July and August, guided walking tours of the old section of Périgueux are offered in French and English, departing from the tourist office (1 Av. Aquitaine; phone: 53-53-10-63) at 2 and 4 PM, Tuesdays through Fridays.

CHECKING IN: *Le Saint Laurent* – Just outside of town and set in a private park, this modern hotel has 43 rooms, 13 of them duplexes that accommodate up to five people — perfect for families. A telephone and a color TV set are in every room, and the restaurant is noted for its regional dishes. St.-Laurie-sur-Manoire, St.-Pierre-de-Chignac (phone: 53-04-28-28). Hotel, moderate; restaurant, inexpensive.

Hôtel du Périgord – Part of the Logis de France chain, this property has 20 rooms and a flower garden with a pond (with real fish). Its restaurant specializes in regional and Spanish fare (the chef is Spanish). 74 Rue Victor-Hugo (phone: 53-53-33-63). Inexpensive.

EATING OUT: *L'Oison* – A one-star dining room fills this old hosiery workroom in the old part of the city near the cathedral. Specialties include grilled fish with olive oil. 31 Rue St.-Front, Périgueux (phone: 53-09-84-02). Expensive.

Le Tournepiche – A medieval structure in front of the cathedral is home to this rustic restaurant, which serves regional fare for reasonable prices under the vaulted stone arches. 2 Rue de la Nation (phone: 53-08-09-76). Moderate.

En Route from Périgueux – Follow D5 about 24 miles (38 km) northeast to Hautefort, possibly the most handsome of Périgord's châteaux. This fine 17th-century palace has stately towers crowned with Renaissance domes and turrets.

The château that stood on this spot in the 12th century belonged to the Born family and was fought over by the two sons, Bertran (of troubadour-knight fame) and Constantin. Though he had the support of Henry II of England, Bertran eventually lost the château to Constantin, whose ally was Richard the Lion-Hearted. Years later, the property passed into the hands of the Gontaut family, who took the Hautefort name and crest and rebuilt the château during the early 1600s with the help of architect Nicolas Rambourg. Today the château looks much as it did more than 350 years ago, though it was restored following a serious fire in 1968.

Luckily, several important pieces — including 16th- and 17th-century tapestries and urns by the sculptor Torod — survived the fire and are on view. In the guard tower is a small museum dedicated to Eugène Le Roy, one of France's most respected authors, born here, the son of servants, in 1836. The 17th-century chapel contains 16th-century paintings on leather, the altar at which Charles X was crowned, and other noteworthy objects.

The château is surrounded by neatly manicured and sculpted gardens and a 99-acre park. Down below, in the town, is a charity hospital and church built in the same style as the restored château. A gift to the village from the Marquis d'Hautefort, it was designed to house 33 sick people, one for every year of Christ's life.

LES EYZIES-DE-TAYAC: "Few regions in the world are more rewarding to the visitor than the valley of the Vézère," wrote André Maurois in *A History of France*. "The river's murky waters flow between two walls of stone, and its high banks are pierced by black openings, the mouths of caves or shelters." It was in these caves near Les Eyzies, a sleepy little village at the confluence of the Vézère and the Beune valleys, that evidence of one of our most distant ancestors was found.

In 1868, when a path was being cut through the valley for the railroad, workers unearthed bones that, on examination by experts, proved to be the remains of Cro-Magnon man. There are at least a dozen grottoes and prehistoric sites in the vicinity of Les Eyzies, once dubbed "the cradle of history." It is, without question, one of the areas in the world richest in vestiges of prehistory. One of the most spellbinding grottoes (and one of the few to offer a tour in English once a day) is the Font-de-Gaume, a deep, narrow cave whose rock walls are decorated with beautifully fluid paintings of bison, deer, mammoths, and horses colored with black and red oxides. More than 200 drawings here date from the early paleolithic period, many of them, unfortunately, defaced by those who frequented the caves in recent centuries, unaware of the existence of the prehistoric art. In an effort to preserve the paintings from deterioration, the number of visitors is limited to 100 a day, so arrive early. In season, tickets are sold only in the morning. Closed Tuesdays.

In the nearby Combarelles cave there are some 300 animal drawings, albeit very faint, dating from about the same period. Most intriguing is how "primitive" man used the rock contours in the caves to convey the shape and bulk of the animal. Again, entrance is limited, so arrive early to get your tickets.

The *Musée National de la Préhistoire*, in the restored medieval castle of Tayac halfway up a cliff near Les Eyzies's main street, houses one of the world's most important collections of prehistoric items (closed Tuesdays; phone: 53-06-97-03).

Also nearby, at Abri du Cap Blanc, there is a superb frieze of horses, and there are many remarkable stalagmite and stalactite formations at Grotte du Grand Roc. Signs for both are clearly posted.

CHECKING IN/EATING OUT: *Le Centenaire* – At one end of the short main street is this sparkling hotel — more modern than the *Cro-Magnon* (below) but equally deserving of praise. The main building has 29 rooms; the old mill in the garden has been made over and now has 20 rooms. Amenities include a swimming pool, a sauna, and a gym. Chef Roland Mazère, who apprenticed with such noted French chefs as the Troisgros brothers, Mark Haeberlin, and Jacques Manière, won his second Michelin star in 1981. His resolutely modern approach contrasts with the traditional kitchens in the area. Closed November to April. Les Eyzies (phone: 53-06-97-18). Hotel, moderate; restaurant, expensive.

Cro-Magnon – It is speculated that this wonderful, vine-covered inn stands where the Cro-Magnon skeletons were discovered in the 1860s. The hotel, which literally clings to the side of the massive, overhung rocks characteristic of the region, has been in the Leysalles family since 1910 and manages to provide modern luxury and efficiency without forfeiting a certain somnolent charm. There are 20 rooms, a swimming pool, and extensive grounds. The kitchen, rated one Michelin star, still can be counted on for the classic traditional fare for which it has been known, although these days the menu has begun to feature "some suggestions of the moment," such as *turbot aux herbes* or *saumon verdurette et ragoût de champignons* (salmon with mushroom sauce). Closed from mid-October to April. Les Eyzies (phone: 53-06-97-06). Hotel, moderate; restaurant, expensive to moderate.

MONTIGNAC: In the hills above Montignac about 12 miles (19 km) from Les Eyzies (D706) are the Lascaux Caves, the site of one of the greatest prehistoric finds in Europe. These caves, which have been dubbed the Sistine Chapel of prehistory, contain magnificent friezes of bulls, horses, deer, and unicorn-like creatures, some larger than life and delicately shaded with black and red. The drawings are remarkable not only for their quantity but for their grace and life-like quality. Carbon dating indicates that the caves were occupied about 15,000 to 13,000 years before Christ, and it is thought that they were used for primitive rites and magic. The caves were discovered in the 1940s by some children playing on the hill; they were opened to the public for about 20 years until it was realized that the atmospheric imbalance created in the small space by the carbon dioxide exhaled by large numbers of visitors was causing bacteria to grow and gradually destroy the paintings. As a result, Lascaux was closed to the general public in 1963 and now can be visited only with special permission from local authorities (about five people a day are admitted). But in July 1983, Lascaux II, an exact replica of the most interesting sections of the original, finally was completed after 6 years of work. Artists from the *Beaux-Arts* in Paris re-created the many hundreds of paintings in four chambers inch by inch, even using the same vegetable dyes and oxides that primitive man must have used. Lascaux II is open daily July and August, closed Mondays off-season. Tickets, which can be purchased only at the Montignac tourist office (Pl. Bertran-de-Born; phone: 53-51-82-60) during high season, include admission to Le Thot, in nearby Thonac, which offers a video presentation on prehistoric man and an exhibition on the construction and painting of Lascaux II.

CHECKING IN/EATING OUT: ***Château de Puy Robert*** – A turreted storybook château in a wooded park about 1½ miles (2 km) from Lascaux, it has been converted into a deluxe hotel with 15 comfortably furnished rooms, a swimming pool, and a restaurant (rated one Michelin star) serving regional cuisine. Montignac en Périgord (phone: 53-51-92-13). Expensive.

Soleil d'Or – This 38-room hotel, with a swimming pool, is set in a wonderful park. The restaurant features *cuisine bourgeoise.* Closed January. 16 Rue du 4 September, Montignac (phone: 53-51-80-22). Hotel, moderate; restaurant, expensive.

Hôtel-Restaurant des Iles – Overlooking a park on the Vézère River, this nicely located property offers 23 rooms and a restaurant. Closed January and Mondays off-season. Thonac (phone: 53-50-70-20). Moderate.

SARLAT-LA-CANÉDA: Take D704 to Sarlat, the capital of Périgord-Noir and one of the best-preserved medieval and Renaissance towns in France. The city was a religious center from the 14th to the 18th century, which accounts, in part, for its fine standard of architecture. Many of the old buildings are still standing thanks to the efforts of Prosper Mérimée, an inspector of historical monuments during the last century. And since 1964, Sarlat's appeal has been enhanced according to a plan sponsored in part by André Malraux and adapted by the city to restore and safeguard the old quarter. Not surprisingly, it is an irresistible destination for tourists; one hopes that the souvenir vendors won't break the spell cast by the ocher buildings and their crooked stone-covered roofs.

The first glimpse of Sarlat may not be impressive, particularly if you enter via Rue de la République, a "new" road built in the late 1800s and now lined with modern shops. It unfortunately cuts right through the center of old Sarlat, bisecting the medieval world. You'll enjoy the city more if you park the car, then wander aimlessly through the maze of curving streets and passageways.

You might want to start at Maison de La Boétie, the lovely Renaissance house in which Etienne de La Boétie, magistrate, poet, and close friend of the writer Montaigne, was born. Across the street is the 16th-century Cathédrale St.-Sacerdos, which weds Romanesque and Gothic elements. Behind the cathedral past the terraced garden is the curious Lanterne des Morts (Lantern of the Dead), a 12th-century tower with a cone-shaped roof commemorating the miracle of healing performed here by St. Bernard in 1147. To the north on Rue Landry is the Présidial and its gardens, and farther on are Rue de la Salamandre and Place de la Liberté, which during July and August are transformed into open-air theaters where plays by Molière and Shakespeare are performed. On Rue des Consuls is the magnificent House of the Consuls, built between the 14th and 17th centuries and now a restaurant called *Le Jardin des Consuls* (phone: 53-59-18-77). Colorful Saturday and Wednesday morning markets are held in the Place du Marche and Place de la Liberté; there also are a number of shops selling foie gras, walnut oils, *cèpes* (wild mushrooms), and other Périgord delicacies. Nearby are several foie gras factories that can be visited, one of which even provides a tasting. Inquire at the tourist office (Pl. Liberté; 53-59-27-67) for details. During the summer, guided walking tours of the old city start at the Place du Peyrou at 10:30 AM and 10 PM Mondays through Fridays. Check with the tourist office for hours of weekend tours. Also of interest is the *Musée d'Art Sacré* (a museum of religious art of the area) on Rue Jean-Jacques Rousseau.

CHECKING IN: *Hostellerie Meysset* – Just north of Sarlat, this ivy-covered manor house with 20 rooms and 6 suites also has a fine restaurant serving many duck dishes. Rte. des Eyzies, Sarlat (phone: 53-59-08-29). Expensive.

***La Hoirie* –** Outside Sarlat, this 15-room hotel, a Périgourdine house set in a garden and with a swimming pool, is pleasant and reasonable. About 1½ miles (2 km) south on Rte. 2, Sarlat (phone: 53-59-05-62). Moderate.

***La Madeleine* –** A distinguished and traditional hostelry in the old part of town, its 19 rooms and 3 suites are air conditioned. The restaurant serves classic cooking, well prepared and presented. Try the *magret à la bordelaise* (sliced duck breast, Bordeaux-style) or *confit de canard en pot au feu* (preserved duck) but leave plenty of room for walnut cake, a house specialty. In high season guests are required to take breakfast and dinner at the hotel. 1 Pl. Petite-Rigaudie, Sarlat (phone: 53-59-10-41). Moderate.

***La Couleuvrine* –** A charming hotel in a restored 12th-century structure. Its 25 rooms have antique reproductions but modern comforts; the halls and dining room feature genuine antiques. 1 Pl. de la Bouquerie, Sarlat (phone: 53-59-27-80). Inexpensive.

EATING OUT: *Auberge de la Lanterne* – The aroma, seasonal dishes, and atmosphere emanating from this corner restaurant draw diners like a magnet. A variety of menus are offered. Closed Thursday evenings and Fridays. 18 Bd. Nessmann, Sarlat (phone: 53-59-05-54). Moderate.

En Route from Sarlat – Take a short detour on D57 south to Beynac-et-Cazenac, another of the four feudal seats of the Périgord. The château here looms up magnificently some 500 feet above the Dordogne, like an extension of the rock on which it was built. In the 12th century, during the continuing struggle between the Plantagenets and Capetians, Richard the Lion-hearted gave the fortress on this site to his defender, the bloodthirsty Mercadier. In 1214, it was demolished by the Crusader Simon de Montfort, who overran much of the South of France. The castle was rebuilt by the Barons of Beynac in the early 13th century and added to from the 14th to the 17th century. The panorama from the terrace here is superb. The sinuous course of the Dordogne seen below marked the dividing line in the struggles between the British and the French during the Hundred Years War. On the river's opposite bank are the Fayrac Castle (privately owned) and, beyond, the ruins of English-occupied Castelnaud, the bitter enemy of the French-controlled Beynac. Among the most interesting things to see here at Beynac are the 14th-century frescoes found in a small oratory in the impressive state hall, where the nobility of the four baronies of Périgord met once a year. The château is undergoing a meticulous restoration program that will continue until 1995.

Just a few miles away and worth another detour is the town of Domme, a well-preserved *bastide* (fortified town) on a rocky cliff with a panoramic view of the Dordogne Valley.

CHECKING IN/EATING OUT: *Hostellerie de la Guérinière* – This 17th-century noble's residence perched on a hill just south of Domme offers panoramic views of the lush Dordogne countryside; comfortable rooms in Louis XIV-, XV-, and XVI-style; and a rustic restaurant serving regional fare as well as French classics. Cénac, Domme (phone: 53-28-22-44). Expensive to moderate.

SOUILLAC: Much less sensational than its neighbors Sarlat and Rocamadour and about midway between the two, where the D703 meets N20, Souillac grew up around a Benedictine abbey built in the 12th century. The monastery was sacked by the English during the Hundred Years War and by the Protestants during the Wars of Religion, then destroyed by fire in 1572. The abbey church survived and still is the town's main attraction. Its domed Romanesque-Byzantine style is similar, though on a much smaller scale, to that of the cathedral in Périgueux. Inside, the bas-reliefs of the prophet Isaiah and St. Joseph on either side of the doorway are beautiful for their detail and motion — particularly the one of Isaiah, who appears to be dancing. Equally well executed is the bas-relief over the doorway, delicately chiseled scenes from the life of the monk Theophilus, framed by carvings of St. Peter and St. Benedict.

CHECKING IN: *Château de la Treyne* – This lovely château was transformed into a luxurious bed and breakfast inn by a charming and enterprising Parisian, Mme. Michele Gombert-Devals. It has 12 beautifully furnished rooms and sits on the edge of a cliff, attached to a 120-acre private park with a pool, tennis courts, and a sauna. Breakfast and dinner are included in the room rate. Closed January to Easter. Lacave, 2 miles (3 km) southeast of Souillac, via D43 (phone 65-32-66-66). Expensive.

***La Vieille Auberge* –** One of the nicest of several traditional inns near the center of old Souillac, it has 45 simply decorated rooms, some of them down the street in an annex with a swimming pool. In the kitchen, owner-chef Robert Véril adds a delicate touch to local classics such as *émincé de pigeonneau aux figues* (squab with figs), *farandole de poissons* (an array of fish), or hot *foie gras quercinois.* Pl. de la Minoterie, Souillac (phone: 65-32-79-43). Moderate.

EATING OUT: *Le Pont de l'Ouysse* – In Lacave, close to *Château de la Treyne,* this terrace restaurant features a good but expensive à la carte menu. Specialties include foie gras, *foie du canard,* and hen served with mushrooms. Closed Mondays, and mid-November to March. Lacave (phone: 65-37-87-04). Expensive.

En Route from Souillac – The caves of Lacave are about midway between Souillac and Rocamadour on D23. Though less impressive in size and grandeur than the caves at Padirac to the northeast, the stalagmites and stalactites here have a more delicate beauty. It doesn't take much imagination to see the shapes of small people and animals in these fine crystalline deposits. Most intriguing is the Salle du Lac (Lake Chamber), which is suffused with the natural, dim, purple-white fluorescence of the formations still growing.

ROCAMADOUR: The first glimpse of Rocamadour from the L'Hospitalet road across the Alzou Canyon is unforgettable, particularly if you arrive in the morning when the sun shines on the rugged face of the cliff to which this village of medieval dwellings, towers, chapels, and ramparts clings. Its precarious position almost 500 feet above the river gorge seems to defy the laws of nature; however, Rocamadour has clung steadfastedly to this rock for centuries. In addition to its spectacular setting, Rocamadour has been an important point of religious pilgrimage for 900 years. In 1166, the remains of a man believed to be St. Amadour were unearthed near the threshold of the Chapel of the Virgin. Though the man's identity has long been debated, legend has it that he was Zaccheus, a disciple of Christ and husband of St. Veronica. As the story goes, after Christ's death, the couple was persecuted in Palestine and escaped to this part of France. When Veronica died, Zaccheus retreated to the rock high on the plateau and, when he died, was buried there.

Shortly after the discovery of the saint's remains, miracles began to occur, word spread, and the pious began to arrive in droves, among them the English King Henry Plantagenet. Until the 13th century, Rocamadour ranked in religious importance with Rome, Santiago de Compostela, and Jerusalem. Although it is still the site of an annual pilgrimage, the floods of worshipers have now been superseded by waves of tourists. The village, which has only about 800 permanent residents, bills itself as the Deuxième Site de la France (the second best tourist attraction in the country; picturesque Mont-St.-Michel is considered the first). Unfortunately, Rocamadour carries the scars and blemishes that accompany such renown. One can imagine how appealing the tiny, sloping main street guarded at either end by fortified gates might have been before any of its medieval structures were taken over by souvenir vendors. Nonetheless, if you make your way through it all and climb to the top of the 216 steps (called Escalier des Pèlerins and climbed by pilgrims on their knees), your effort will be rewarded by the sight of a lovely little square surrounded by no fewer than seven chapels. This is the Cité Religieuse, with several fine buildings: the fortified bishop's palace, Evêché; the 11th- to 13th-century Basilique St.-Sauveur; the Chapelle St.-Michel, known for its fresco of the Annunciation; St. Amadour's crypt; and, most entrancing of all, the Chapelle Miraculeuse. This last, the successor of the Chapel of the Virgin, was destroyed twice, then rebuilt during the 19th century; it houses the intriguing Black Virgin and Child, made of carved walnut covered with silver plate blackened by age and the elements. It is believed to have been carved in about the 9th century. Here also, suspended from the roof, is the miraculous bell that is said to ring of its own accord to foretell miracles.

On the wall outside the chapel are 13th- and 14th-century frescoes that depict St. Christopher and the Dance of Death between three living and three dead men. On the square near the Miraculous Chapel is the *Musée Tresor,* in which valuable religious items are displayed. Farther up the hill via a crooked dirt path is a fortress built in the 14th century to protect pilgrims. The adjacent 19th-century château now is inhabited by the chaplains of Rocamadour. The only part open to the public is the ramparts, from which there is a breathtaking view of the village and the surrounding countryside.

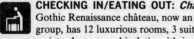 **CHECKING IN/EATING OUT:** *Château de Roumégouse* – This lovely Gothic Renaissance château, now an inn and a member of Relais & Châteaux group, has 12 luxurious rooms, 3 suites, and a restaurant. Ideal for those who appreciate elegance and isolation, it's in a wooded park and provides magnificent

views of the Causse foothills. Closed November to *Easter*. Off N140, almost 2 miles (3 km) from Gramat and 9 miles (14 km) from Rocamadour (phone: 65-33-63-81). Expensive.

Beau Site et Notre-Dame – Wedged between souvenir stands on the sloping main street, the distinguished façade of this solid and venerable 55-room establishment offers a warm welcome to the modern pilgrim. There also is a reasonably priced restaurant with a terrace that offers a beautiful view. Closed November to late March. Rue Roland-le-Preux, Rocamadour (phone: 65-33-63-08). Moderate.

Ste.-Marie – Perched on a landing about halfway up the Escalier de Pèlerins, this hotel with 22 comfortably decorated rooms is agreeably removed from the noise and traffic below. The cozy, well-appointed dining room and adjoining covered terrace (which has a fine vista of the Alzou Canyon) seem to be the best in town for trying the classics of the Quercy and Périgord. Some of the house specialties that should be sampled include *cassoulade d'escargots à la périgourdine* (snail casserole Périgord style), *magret au genièvre* (sliced duck breast with juniper berries), *omelette aux truffes* (truffle omelet), and walnut cakes, as well as one of the fine Cahors wines. Closed October to mid-March. Pl. des Senhals, Rocamadour (phone: 65-33-63-07). Moderate.

GOUFFRE DE PADIRAC: About 9 miles (14 km) northeast of Rocamadour (via D673 and D90) is the famous Gouffre de Padirac (Padirac Chasm), one of nature's more dramatic feats in the region. This series of underground caverns dug out over the centuries by an underground river is adorned with fascinating limestone concretions. Start your journey by descending into the gaping hole 325 feet across and 328 feet deep, the natural entrance to this surreal underground world. Part of the journey is by boat on the cool, clear river and part on foot, up, down, and around the intriguing formations of stalagmites and stalactites. (Note that the tour is 1¼ miles long — a third of that by boat — and that the climbing is at times strenuous.) The most impressive features of the chasm are the Grande Pendeloque (Great Pendant), a giant stalactite overhanging and nearly touching the river's surface, and the Salle du Grande Dome (Hall of the Great Dome), which, at 250 feet high, is the largest and most beautiful of Padirac's chambers.

Not surprisingly, superstition surrounds this awesome natural phenomenon; according to legend, the great gaping hole in the earth was the work of the devil. It's said to have been the site of a showdown between St. Martin, returning from an excursion in search of souls to save, and Satan, who was toting a sack of souls condemned to hell. Satan offered St. Martin a deal. He would surrender the doomed souls if the holy man could make his reluctant mule cross an obstacle created by the devil. An agreement was struck, the devil stamped the earth with his hoof, and the great chasm yawned open. When St. Martin's mule heroically jumped clear of the hole, Satan was forced to give up the souls and retreated to hell through the mouth of the chasm.

En Route from Padirac – If time allows, make a special side trip north from Padirac via N140, D23, and D38 to Collonges-La-Rouge, an ancient red village lost in the rugged hills of the Corrèze. Its quaint, vine-covered houses and churches, some dating from the 12th century, are all built in striking red brick, a dramatic contrast to the somber gray stone of the surrounding towns. In recent years Collonges has been carefully restored by artists and local merchants, making it one of France's most beautiful villages, well worth the detour. Rejoin route N140 and follow it southeast before continuing to Cahors to visit one of the region's newest museums, the *Musée Champollion* (on Enpasse Champollion). Named after the French Egyptologist, this museum of Egyptian artifacts is in the house where Champollion was born.

CHECKING IN/EATING OUT: *Le Relais de St.-Jacques de Compostelle*
– Arrive at dusk to sip an apéritif on the terrace as the sun sets over Collonges's
red brick. The quaint inn has 12 simple rooms, a terrace, and a pleasant dining
room which serves well-prepared regional dishes. Closed December, January, and
Tuesday evenings and Wednesdays off-season. Collonges-La-Rouge (phone: 55-25-
41-02). Moderate.

CAHORS: South of the Dordogne Valley in a deep loop of the Lot River is Cahors,
one of the main gateways to southern France (via D677, N20, or any number of
wandering country roads). It is most famous for the red wine made from the grapes
grown on the hills along the Lot west of the city.

Founded on the site of a spring (called Fontaine des Chartreux), the city was first
known as Divona Cadurcorum and later as Cadurca; it grew prosperous under the
Gauls and the Romans, acquiring the requisite forum, theater, baths, and temples. By
the early Middle Ages, Cahors was already an important commercial and university
center, but it reached its zenith in the 13th century when an influx of Lombard
merchants and bankers earned it the reputation of the first banking city in Europe. The
Lombard firms, known not only for their business acumen but also for their usurious
lending habits, soon made Cahors world famous. However, the city's fortunes fell
during the Hundred Years War, and eventually wine production replaced banking as
the chief industry.

The two most compelling sights in Cahors are the Pont Valentré and the Romanesque Cathédrale St.-Etienne. The first, one of the few surviving examples of a medieval
fortified bridge, is still used. Its three crenelated towers rise for 130 feet and its narrow
gateways allow only one modern vehicle to pass at a time. The best view of this proud,
unusual structure (another construction that the devil had a hand in, according to
legend) is from the right bank of the Lot, slightly upstream. It is particularly impressive
when lighted at night. St. Stephen's Cathedral, in the old part of town, dates from the
11th century, when Bishop Géraud of Cardaillac began building here on the site of a
6th-century church. Particularly noteworthy is the north door, an intricate, Romanesque carving of the Ascension executed about 1140.

The Cahors Tourist Board (Pl. A. Briand; phone: 65-35-09-56) provides a map that
outlines a pleasant walking tour of the old part of the city. It takes visitors past such
medieval and Renaissance structures as the late-15th-century Roaldès Mansion, with
crooked timberwork on one side and a rose window and mullioned doors and windows
on the other. Also of interest is the *Musée Municipal* (Rue Emile Zola; phone: 65-30-15-
13) in a former episcopal palace; its collection ranges from a Roman sarcophagus to
15th- and 16th-century sculpture to mementos of Cahors's most famous sons, including
Pope John XXII, the French magistrate Léon Gambetta, and the 16th-century writer
Clement Marot.

 CHECKING IN: *Château de Mercues* – In a turreted 12th-century castle
perched above the Lot River, this inn has 16 rooms, 7 luxury suites, tennis
courts, and a swimming pool. There also is an excellent restaurant (with
commanding views) serving fine cuisine. Located about 6 miles (10 km) from
Cahors in Mercues (phone: 65-20-00-01). Expensive.

Terminus – Across from the train station, this traditional hotel with lovely stained
glass windows from the early part of this century has 31 clean, bright rooms. The
husband and wife team who run it are particularly friendly and helpful. The
inexpensive restaurant features nouvelle fare. 5 Av. Charles-de-Freycinet, Cahors
(phone: 65-35-24-50). Moderate.

ST.-CIRQ-LAPOPIE: Wander along the course of the Lot east of Cahors via D662
to this picturesque village of less than 200 people. Dominated by its 15th-century

church, it sits precariously on the top of a rocky escarpment, high above the meandering river. Albeit tiny, the village is not short on historical interest. This cliffsite, a natural stronghold for the valleys below, was long a source of strife. In the 8th century, it was the site of the Duke of Aquitaine's last stand against Pepin the Short. And in 1198, Richard the Lion-Hearted unsuccessfully attempted to seize it. St.-Cirq was contested fiercely by the British and French during the Hundred Years War and by the Huguenots during the Wars of Religion. Both Louis XI (in 1471) and Henri de Navarre (1580) ordered the strategic castle destroyed. What remains of the castle sits at the highest point of the cliff (accessible by a dirt path), from which there is an inspiring view of the surrounding terrain. The half-timbered and stone houses of the village climb up the steep lanes (which are closed to traffic during the summer months). Many of them are inhabited by artisans, including potters, puppeteers, and a wood-turner, carrying on the former livelihood of the village.

 CHECKING IN/EATING OUT: *Auberge du Sombral* – This particularly comfortable little inn, on one corner of the town's sleepy central square, has 10 rooms furnished in a delightful country style with private baths or showers. The spacious dining room provides a most pleasing setting in which to sample owner-chef Gilles Hardeveld's renditions of regional specialties. Closed from mid-November to mid-March. St.-Cirq-Lapopie (phone: 65-31-26-08). Moderate.

La Pélissaria – Owned by François and Marie-Françoise Matuchet, this lovely 13th-century house has 6 rooms with whitewashed walls, exposed beams, and hand-turned wooden furniture, each with a private bath. All rooms, including the dining room, have views of the garden or village or, most spectacular, of the River Lot with its limestone cliffs. Mme. Matuchet now devotes most of her time to the hotel, so the restaurant offers a simple *menu gastronomique,* but the regional fare is quite good (terrines, desserts, and homemade bread). Closed mid-November to May. St.-Cirq-Lapopie (phone: 65-31-25-14). Moderate.

GROTTE DU PECH-MERLE: The route north from St.-Cirq to the caves at Pech-Merle is well marked, and it takes only a few minutes on the tiny back roads to reach this vast underground cave of tremendous geological and archaeological interest. These caverns, inhabited by prehistoric man some 20,000 years ago, were only discovered by modern man in 1922 when two boys happened to venture into the huge chambers. They found what you still can see today: marvelous and mysterious prehistoric paintings as well as weirdly beautiful stalagmites and stalactites. In the Galerie des Peintures are stunning, spotted horses and silhouetted handprints; and in the Salles des Hiéroglyphes, the outlines of feminine forms are just vaguely visible on the low clay roof of the cave. Nearby are the footprints of primitive man, petrified in the calcite-rich clay of the cave floor. The Salle des Disques contains more works of nature: strange, slanted disk-shaped formations as unexplained as the works of early man. Scientists don't know how or why these disks formed. In the hall of the broken column is a frieze of mammoths and bison believed to date from the Aurignacian age. The price of admission to this, one of the most intriguing of France's many grottoes, entitles the visitor to view a film before entering the cave and to visit the *Abbé Lemozi Museum,* where more prehistoric artifacts are on view.

En Route from Grotte du Pech-Merle – Follow the winding course of the Lot back to Cahors and drive west along the picturesque wine route; then head north on D710. Scattered through this area south of Bergerac are a number of *bastides,* the small feudal fortress towns constructed in the 13th century by both the French and the English when the two countries claimed sovereignty of the region. Monpazier, on D660, is perhaps the best-preserved *bastide* in France. Built by the English in 1284 in the name of Edward I, its layout is common to most *bastides.* The streets are arranged in a grid, with alleys between the houses to form fire breaks. (The alleys are called *andronne,* an old southwest term for man; it describes the width of these narrow passageways.) The central square and covered market are flanked by vaulted arcades and surrounded by houses, some with lovely Gothic bays. Nearby is the Eglise St.-Dominique and the 13th-century Maison du Chapitre (Chapter House). Three of the six gates to the village still remain, protected by towers set in the ramparts. Other *bastides* of interest are at Lalinde, Villeneuve-sur-Lot, Villeréal, Puylaroque, Sauveterre de Guyenne, and Domme.

BERGERAC: Take D660 back to Bergerac, a wine and tobacco center whose name will be familiar to lovers of wine and literature. The hills nearby produce the fine, dry bergerac reds and a sweet, white monbazillac, a perfect companion to foie gras. And, on the Place de la Myrpe, a statue of playwright Edmond Rostand's immortal hero, Cyrano de Bergerac, marks the town's literary connection.

Tobacco has helped make Bergerac prosperous, so it's fitting that it should have the only tobacco museum in France. In the old part of the town, the *Musée du Tabac* (10 Rue Ancien Pont) has a number of displays and exhibits on the history of the plant, how it's produced, and how it's consumed (closed Sunday mornings and Mondays; phone: 53-63-04-13). Next door is a small municipal museum with prehistoric items, the works of Bergerac painters, and a section on local history.

Near the tobacco museum is the Couvent des Récollets (Monastery of Recollects), a former cloister built between the 12th and 17th centuries, where the area's Consuls de la Vinée now meet.

The Eglise Notre-Dame, built in the 19th century in an imitation Gothic style, has two Italian paintings from the early Renaissance and an immense Aubusson tapestry depicting the Bergerac coat of arms.

Leave town via the scenic Tobacco Route to take a small detour south (D13) to the lovely Monbazillac château and vineyard.

 CHECKING IN: *Bordeaux* – Though neither plush nor charming, this 42-room hotel is adequate, and it has a restaurant. 38 Pl. Gambetta, Bergerac (phone: 53-57-12-83). Moderate to inexpensive.

 EATING OUT: *Le Cyrano* – A charming little dining spot where Jean-Paul Turon directs the kitchen, generally sticking to the classics of the area — try his *escalope de foie chaud de canard grillotin* (slices of hot duck liver) and, for dessert, his *gratin de fruits rouges au sabayon de Monbazillac* (baked fruit in a warm custard sauce). 2 Bd. Montaigne, Bergerac (phone: 53-57-02-76). Moderate.

MONBAZILLAC CHÂTEAU AND VINEYARD: Set among the vineyards that produce the famous sweet white wine of the same name is this pristine, small gray stone château. The reputation of the monbazillac wine goes back centuries. Legend has it that when a group from Bergerac made the pilgrimage to Rome in the Middle Ages, they were asked by the pope where their home was. "Near Monbazillac" was the reply, to which the pope is said to have responded with the benediction "*Bonum vinum.*"

Built in about 1550, the château is a pleasing amalgam of fortified castle and Renaissance palace. The surrounding grounds are well kept and the view of the Bergerac Valley below is superb. Today the château is owned and operated by the Monbazillac wine cooperative. Following a tour of the nobly decorated castle, guests are invited to visit the 17th-century wine cellar, now a tasting room, to sample (and, if they wish, purchase) both bergerac and monbazillac wines. The cooperative also runs a small restaurant (open for lunch only) in what were once the stables.

 CHECKING IN: *Château Rauly Saulieut* – South of Monbazillac, this lovely, vine-covered, 19th-century château was transformed into a hotel-restaurant in the summer of 1988. Its 8 spacious rooms are exquisitely furnished with antiques belonging to the owner, who also is an antiques dealer. More of his items are on sale in a shop here. There are gardens, a pool, a cozy restaurant, and conference rooms. Monbazillac (phone: 53-63-35-31). Expensive.

EATING OUT: *Closerie St.-Jacques* – With one Michelin star, this restaurant features *aiguillette de canard au jus de noix verte* (sliced duck in green walnut sauce), *escalope de foie poëlée sauce raisin et monbazillac* (sliced liver in a monbazillac wine sauce). Closed November and January and Mondays and Tuesdays, except in July and August. Monbazillac (phone: 53-58-37-77). Expensive to moderate.

En Route from Monbazillac – In an area such as Périgord, where splendid vistas of peaceful green valleys are as common as potholes in New York City streets, it's easy to become blasé about the scenery. There is, however, a particularly arresting view at the crest of a hill just outside Trémolat near D703 that's worth a detour. From here you can see the Cingle de Trémolat, a wide loop in the Dordogne River that encircles a resplendent valley of walnut orchards and soft, flat fields sprinkled with flowers.

Gascony

For travelers with a passing knowledge of French literature, history, and gastronomy, reference to the province of Gascony is likely to conjure up vivid and romantic images. This is the land of d'Artagnan and the musketeers, Henri IV, the troubadours, and Blaise de Monluc. It was part of the province of Aquitaine, that area keenly contested and controlled alternately by the French and the English during the Middle Ages. It also is the source of some of France's best-loved dishes, including cassoulet (a casserole of beans, pork, and sausage), foie gras, *garbure* (a thick vegetable soup), *tourin* (garlic soup), duck and goose prepared in a variety of ways, including *confit* (preserved) and *magret* (grilled), and succulent game birds in heady dark sauces, as well as Armagnac, the fiery brandy dubbed "the soul of Gascony." It's a proud and independent area that clings to old traditions and customs; the past is ever present here, the 20th century less insistent than in other areas.

In the heart of France's southwest, Gascony, as much a historical as an official appellation, does not have strict boundaries. It generally is considered to take up the modern *départements* of Gers and the Landes, bordered to the north by the mighty Garonne River, to the east by Toulouse, extending south into the foothills of the Pyrénées and all the way west to the Gulf of Gascony on the Atlantic coast.

The region is one of physical contrasts: The Gers is characterized by scenic rolling hills dotted with villages, vineyards, and neat fields of sunflowers and wheat. The Landes, to the northwest, is a flat, sandy expanse of sparsely settled land, a full two-thirds of which is a vast manmade forest. The two *départements* meet in an agricultural area that supplies this and many other regions of France with an abundance of fruit and vegetables.

When Roman armies penetrated these areas half a century before Christ, they found a large number of independent settlements whose people shared a physical stature and language that linked their origins more closely to those of the Basques in the Pyrénées than to those of the peoples in the rest of Gaul. The region prospered under Roman rule, as remnants of Gallo-Roman villas, particularly those in Séviac, unearthed near Montréal, bear witness.

The Vandals invaded in 410, followed by the Visigoths, and then by the Francs in 507. Around the beginning of the 7th century, the Basques moved north from their base in the Spanish Pyrénées, penetrating southwestern France and Gascony and imposing their will and ways on this kindred culture.

By the 10th century, Gascony had become a strong, almost totally independent duchy, but in 1062 the Count of Armagnac was forced to cede his realm to the Duke of Aquitaine. Ninety years later, Gascony was part of the dowry that Eleanor of Aquitaine presented to her new husband, Henry Plantagenet, heir to the British crown, and when he ascended to the throne 2 years later, in 1152, Gascony became part of England. For the next 300 years, Gascony and its neighbors to the north and west suffered continuous turmoil as the French and English battled for sovereignty. Several of the *bastides* (fortified villages) constructed by the opposing kings during this period still stand; particularly interesting are the remnants of these fortifications at Fourcès (near Montréal), Beaumarchés and Marciac (near Plaisance), and Bassoues (near Mirande).

Around the middle of the 14th century, the Counts of Armagnac regained control of their turf and for a time, under Bernard VII, champion of the French cause, Gascony's valiant soldiers controlled almost the whole of France.

During the Wars of Religion, the area once again was plunged into bitter conflict. Thanks to Jeanne d'Albert, mother of Henri de Navarre (the future King Henri IV), Nerac, in the north of Gascony, became an important Protestant stronghold and a frequent target of the Catholics. It was only after Henri ascended to the throne in 1589 that peace returned to the area, and in 1607 the lands of the counts of Armagnac were incorporated into the royal domain under his rule.

The Gascons did not, however, forfeit their independence to the French throne. The strong spirit and individuality of the region lives on today, embodied by the legendary d'Artagnan, certainly Gascony's most famous native son. Born Charles de Batz in 1615 near Auch (you still can see his birthplace at Castelmore), d'Artagnan presented himself at the court in Paris, taking his mother's family name to win royal acceptance more easily. After gaining the confidence of Louis XIII, he was appointed the first captain lieutenant of the king's company of musketeers, that gallant band of men whose swashbuckling exploits were immortalized (and certainly embellished) by Alexandre Dumas in *The Three Musketeers.*

Today, a visitor to this unspoiled area is likely to be charmed by the Gascon spirit, conveyed by the contagious warmth and bravado of its people. Though it frequently is overlooked by travel guides and foreign as well as French tourists, the region has a serendipitous appeal. Its attractions are subtle: narrow, tree-lined roads winding through sunflower-dotted landscapes; calm, inviting lakes; crumbling stone fortifications; and the arcaded squares of Gascony's countless pleasing villages that seem to exist in a time warp. It takes little imagination to suspend reality temporarily and let oneself drift back to another era.

Gascon cuisine also is reminiscent of another time — when portions were generous, food hearty and satisfying, and prices reasonable. The region is rich in family-run inns, where the quality of food is only outdone by the character-istic warmth of the Gascon welcome. They represent some of the best dining values in France today. The Gascons are serious about their food, a fact exemplified by an organization of chefs, "Ronde des Mousquetaires," whose members meet frequently at each other's establishments to share fine food, ideas, and comradeship. The gastronome will do well to seek out these restau-rants, each with its own style and character but offering an extremely high level of cooking. Food lovers also will find guidance in a small paperback entitled *Le Guide des Restaurants Inconnus de Gascogne* (Guide to the Unknown Restaurants of Gascony), available in most bookshops in the region; it lists undiscovered, out-of-the-way places of particularly good value.

A visit to this region can be particularly rewarding in summer, when the weather is warm and sunny and the sleepy little villages come alive with festivals and celebrations. It is even more enjoyable because it is less crowded than other rural areas in July and August, when practically the entire French population heads for the country. Plaisance is the site of an incomparable annual *Bastille Day* (July 14) goat cheese fair, *dégustation* (tasting), and judging (if you stop here, a meal at *La Ripa Alta,* a wonderful restaurant under the arcade of the main square, is a must; phone: 62-69-30-43). There's motor racing in Nogaro; in Marciac, an annual jazz festival in August; and in Vic-Fezensac, an annual 3-day *corrida,* when bulls run through the streets before testing their might against Gascons in the arena. (For information about dates for these and other festivals, contact Mme. Baron at the Maison de Gers et Armagnac, 16 Bd. Haussmann, Paris 75009; phone: 47-70-39-61, or visit any of the local *Syndicats d'Initiatives* — almost any town big enough to have a hotel and a post office has one) Mme. Baron also can supply you with information on the Gers's many pleasant lakes and other recreational possibilities.

This tour route starts in Auch, at the heart of the Gers; it then moves north to Lectoure and on to Condom, the center of Armagnac production. It continues west through the southern edge of the pine forests of the Landes, then over to the Gulf of Gascony and the seaside resorts of Hossegor and Capbreton.

Accommodations in Gascony range from the expensive, where rooms are $80 or more a night for two, to many moderate hotels, ranging from $40 to $80, to the bargain inns, where an inexpensive room for two is under $40. In the restaurant listings, the expensive category rates dinner for two at over $80; moderate, $40 to $80; and inexpensive, under $40. Prices do not include wine or drinks. Service usually is included.

AUCH: The administrative capital of Gascony, and the largest town (pop. 25,000) between inland Toulouse and Bayonne, Auch (pronounced *Osh*) is a lively market center on the banks of the Gers River. Its old town sits on a hill, grouped around the majestic, 16th-century, pale ocher cathedral that dominates the horizon for miles around.

People lived on this hill long before the arrival of Emperor Augustus in 25 BC. It became an important Roman town called Augusta Ascorum, a crossroads on the busy route from Toulouse to the Atlantic, and has continued to play a key role in the life and commerce of the region.

This is d'Artagnan's town, and it pays homage to its valiant musketeer, who was immortalized by Alexandre Dumas *père* in *The Three Musketeers,* with a swashbuckling statue perched midway up the monumental 232-step staircase that connects the lower, "new" town to the high ground on which the old town sits. At the top of the staircase is the serene, tree-shaded Place Salinis, overlooking the valley of the Gers and the rooftops of the ever-expanding modern part of town. Nearby rises the 15th-century Tour d'Armagnac, formerly a prison. In the same vicinity, picturesque narrow lanes (*pousterles*) wind steeply down the hill to the Gers past crooked structures dating from the Middle Ages.

More antiquities, such as the intriguing 15th-century structure that houses the tourist association, line Rue Dessoles, a lively pedestrian street near the cathedral. On Saturday mornings the cathedral square is transformed into a colorful open-air market. Nearby is the prefecture, housed in a superb yellow brick, 18th-century structure that once was the archbishop's residence. Also of interest is the *Musée des Jacobins,* on Rue Charras; a former Jacobin cloister, it now has a somewhat eclectic collection that includes Gascon furniture, old porcelain, a sizable grouping of pre-Columbian pieces, and the rather disquieting works of a local 19th-century painter, Jean-Louis Roumeguère. The Maison de Gascogne, on Rue Gambetta, exhibits regional foods and drinks, art, and crafts.

Auch's most precious treasures, however, are found inside the Cathédrale Ste.-Marie. Construction of this magnificent work, whose twin bell towers are reminiscent of those of St. Sulpice in Paris, was started in 1489 by Cardinal de Savoie, Archbishop of Auch, and it was not completed until the 17th century. The Renaissance windows of the Gascon painter Arnaut de Moles are remarkable not only for their vivid colors but for the strikingly expressive, caricaturish faces of the elaborately clothed figures. Equally awesome are the 113 intricately carved choir stalls bearing more than 1,500 different figures. This masterpiece, sculpted out of oak that had been soaked in the Gers for a year, took more than 50 years to complete and represents some of the finest Renaissance wood carving in France.

Other artworks worth the 40-mile (64-km) detour southwest of Auch to the town of Mirande are found in the *Musée des Beaux-Arts Décoratifs,* which groups together paintings of the Italian, Flemish, and French schools from the 15th to the 19th century, along with a collection of French faïence. It's open daily in summer from 10 AM to noon and from 3 to 6 PM. (13 Rue de L'Eveche; phone: 62-66-68-10.)

CHECKING IN: *Château de Larroque* – About 19 miles (30 km) from Auch, in Gimont, on the route to Toulouse, this stately pink brick château set in a park has 12 pleasant rooms, a serene terrace overlooking the gentle hills of Gascony, and a well-regarded restaurant. Restaurant closed Sunday evenings, Mondays, and during January. Rte. de Toulouse RN124, Gimont (phone: 62-67-77-44). Expensive to moderate.

France – This venerable establishment, the domain of the Daguin family since 1884, sits like a duchess benignly surveying the activity of Place de la Libération. It is a lively meeting place for French and foreigners alike, drawn here by the renown of chef-owner André Daguin's superb restaurant (see *Eating Out*), perhaps the best reason for an extended stay. Its 32 rooms, each individually decorated, have old-fashioned charm. Daguin and his wife, Jo, a witty and charming pair, create an atmosphere of elegance and familial warmth. Don't miss the impressive array of breads and jams that accompany *le petit déjeuner* (breakfast). Closed January. Pl. de la Libération, Auch (phone: 62-05-00-44). Expensive to moderate.

D'Artagnan – Once the residence of the Comtes de Monlaur, this terraced hotel between the old and new parts of the city offers 20 simple rooms, outdoor dining in summer, and a warm welcome. Pl. Villaret de Joyeuse (phone: 62-05-00-49). Inexpensive.

EATING OUT: *France* – Endowed with a d'Artagnan-like dash and bravado, André Daguin, founder of "La Ronde des Mousquetaires," is Gascony's biggest booster and one of its most loved and lauded chefs. His reputation — as well as two Michelin stars — is well earned. Dinner in this lush dining room, at once grand and homey, is a memorable experience whether you choose from among the traditional Gascon specialties — *magret de canard* (grilled duck breast) or *rôtie d'agneau aux anchois* (roast lamb with anchovy sauce) — or from Daguin's inventive variations on a theme — foie gras and rock lobster or a delicately sauced *feuilletté de saumon* (salmon in puff pastry) and *ris d'agneau* (lamb sweetbreads). Closed Sunday evenings, Mondays, and January. Pl. de la Libération, Auch (phone: 62-05-00-44). Expensive.

Claude Laffitte – Tucked away near the cathedral, this cozy restaurant operated by Claude Laffitte offers regional character and a fine selection of well-prepared Gascon specialties: *la cuisse d'oie en daube* (leg of goose braised in wine), *salmis de palombe forestière* (pigeon with mushrooms, bacon, and potatoes), and an exceptional *croustade landaise* (bridal-veil-thin pastry laced with prunes and armagnac). Dine downstairs in the bistro atmosphere or upstairs amid wooden beams and flowers. Closed Sunday evenings and Mondays, 2 weeks in April, and the first 2 weeks of October. 38 Rue Dessoles, Auch (phone: 62-05-04-18). Moderate to inexpensive.

En Route from Auch – To get the flavor of the Gascon countryside, drive northwest on D930, a pleasant tree-lined route that winds over verdant hills and dales before passing through Castéra-Verduzan, a somnolent thermal village of about 700 residents. The therapeutic properties of the town's two natural mineral springs were appreciated even in Roman times: The 3rd-century author Flagius Vegelius wrote about the Roman camp here called Castéra-Vivant. The Counts of Armagnac and French royalty came to take the cure; it was no doubt a livelier place during the reign of Louis XV, when going to take the cure reached its zenith. In modern times, this quaint village seems to have been all but forgotten, passed up for more dramatic attractions. Though it has no grand archaeological or architectural treasures, it's worth a stop, if only to take the waters (a visit to the pavilion housing *les sources* provides a glimpse of what thermalism is all about in France).

 CHECKING IN: Ténarèze – Bernard Ramouneda, the chef at *La Florida* (below), and his family operate this hotel, just up the street from the restaurant. It has 23 modern, simple rooms and is a real bargain. Castéra-Verduzan (phone: 62-68-10-22). Inexpensive.

 EATING OUT: La Florida – The dining rooms and chestnut-tree-shaded terrace are full of provincial charm, and chef Bernard Ramouneda serves a wonderful combination of the homey, traditional fare learned from his grandmother (the former chef) and dishes of his own contemporary cooking style. Try the foie-gras-and-*confit*-laced Gascon salad, the impeccable *terrine de légumes au coulis de tomate* (vegetable terrine with a light tomato purée), or his rich *cou d'oie farci* (stuffed goose neck in a prune-scented sauce). Closed Sunday evenings, Mondays, 2 weeks in November, and 2 weeks in February. Castéra-Verduzan (phone: 62-68-13-22). Inexpensive.

En Route from Castéra-Verduzan – Travel the vineyard-flanked D42 north to St.-Puy, a tiny hillside village at the foot of Château Monluc. This hill was lost and regained by the French four times during their battles with the English, and the châteaux that stood here were repeatedly destroyed and rebuilt. Mostly what remains today is a small, welcoming château dating from the 15th and 18th centuries, though part of the crumbling stone walls around it date from the 12th century. Between 1502 and 1577 it was the property of Blaise de Montluc, a marshal of France who fought fiercely against the Protestants during the Wars of Religion and who later recorded his regrets at having done so in his famous memoirs, *Commentaires* (1592), called "the soldier's bible" by Henri IV. Only part of the château is open to visitors, as it is the home of M. and Mme. Lassus, producers of Monluc, a dry sparkling wine that is the base for the most Gascon of apéritifs, the *pousse rapière* ("the sword's thrust"), a mixture of sparkling wine and Armagnac. The château tour includes a visit to the cellars, where the wine is aged under the old vaulting of an earlier château, and a tasting of the wine and the *pousse rapière*.

LECTOURE: Continue on D42 about 6 miles (10 km) to Lectoure, a town noted, even in this region filled with lofty villages, for the stunning vistas of the Gers Valley. On a clear day, the Pyrénées can be seen in the distance from the lovely tree-shaded Promenade du Bastion near the gardens of the Hôtel de Ville (Town Hall). This was the home of the Counts of Armagnac (a hospital now stands on the ramparts of their château), and it later became an important episcopal seat. Numerous *hôtels particulaires* and religious structures in the characteristic pale yellow stone of the region line the old streets; their scars bear witness to the town's stormy past. This was the site in 1473 of a terrible battle between the troops of Louis XI and the Counts of Armagnac. Jean V, the last count, was killed during this battle, which marked the fall of the house of Armagnac and the beginning of royal authority over the area. The old cathedral was badly hit during the siege of 1473 and suffered more abuse during the Wars of Religion. The remnants of the original spire were finally torn down in 1782. The oldest segments of the present cathedral, built in the Gothic style of the southwest, date from the 16th century.

Also of special interest here is the *Musée Municipal* in the Hôtel-de-Ville (Pl. Hôtel de Ville; phone: 62-68-76-98) which houses a famous collection of *tauroboles* (sacrificial altars) emblazoned with the head of a bull, and other mysterious objects and inscriptions. These marble altars, on which actual bulls were sacrificed in the purification rites of priests, are relics of the cult of Cybèle, believed to have existed 2,000 years ago. Twenty of the 40 *tauroboles* known to exist in France are assembled here.

CONDOM: A town of about 8,000 set on a hill above the Baïse River, Condom is the capital of the Ténaréze, the region between the Garonne and Adour rivers and one of the three armagnac producing areas in Gascony. It is an excellent base for excursions to the surrounding countryside, particularly rich in antiquities, including an old abbey, bishops' residences, *bastides* (fortified villages), and Gallo-Roman ruins.

The town itself has some interesting old structures, among them the 18th-century Hôtel de Cugnac and the Hôtel de Riberot, at 36 and 38 Rue Jean-Jaurès, respectively. The riverside quays here, in times past crowded with boats carrying armagnac to market in Bordeaux, are pleasant for a leisurely stroll. But the chief sight is the Cathédrale St.-Pierre. Rebuilt between 1507 and 1531, it is one of the last large cathedrals constructed in the Gers and is certainly one of the most stunning examples of Flamboyant Gothic in the southwest. Particularly beautiful are the elaborate south doorway with its 24 statuettes, and the neo-Gothic choir enclosure, adorned in 1844 with the magnificently delicate, almost lacy terra-cotta figures of saints and angels. The tourist office is across the street from the cathedral (Pl. Bossuet; phone: 62-28-00-80).

Condom also offers the *Musée de l'Armagnac* (Rue Jules Ferry) which displays antique tools and equipment, including alembics, used in the production of the brandy.

CHECKING IN: *Hôtel des Trois Lys* – Located in the heart of Condom, this new hostelry in an 18th-century mansion has 10 rooms, each individually decorated in keeping with the period. There's a swimming pool, a bar, a terrace, parking, and seminar rooms. 38 Rue Gambetta, Condom 32100 (phone: 62-28-33-33). Expensive.

Cordelièrs – This modern hotel with 20 simple rooms sits in a serene walled garden. Its unique restaurant, *Table des Cordelièrs*, makes a stop here worthwhile. The dining room, set under the warm brick archways and vaulted ceiling of a 14th-century Gothic chapel, would make it special even if the food were not so superb. Closed Sunday evenings, Mondays, and from mid-January to mid-February. Rue des Cordelièrs, Condom (phone: hotel, 62-28-03-68; restaurant, 62-68-28-36). Hotel, moderate; restaurant, expensive.

En Route from Condom – The first of several antiquities in the countryside here is the 12th-century Cistercian Abbaye de Flaran, a few miles south of town on D930. Set back from the road in an isolated, tranquil spot near the confluence of the Baïse and the Auloue rivers, this abbey, founded in 1151, is one of the most important remnants of the keen religious activity in the region in the 12th and 13th centuries. It consists of a predominantly Romanesque church of warm ocher stone, a small, elegant 14th-century cloister, and an adjoining, renovated 18th-century refectory. Particularly lovely is the small chapel on the east side of the cloisters; it has a low vaulted ceiling and columns of the black, red, and white marble of the Pyrénées. Damaged during the Wars of Religion, it later was neglected by private owners. Now owned by the *département* of the Gers, it is being restored and transformed into a regional cultural center. The cloister houses two exhibits: one on the abbey itself and the other on the pilgrimage routes to Santiago de Compostela, which passed through the Gascon region and included a stop here. Special changing exhibits are mounted in the refectory.

Life in this area revolves around armagnac, and you should be sure to visit one of the many cellars to taste this earthy brandy that in recent years has begun to chip away at the cognac market, even in the US. One of the most congenial places to taste and learn about it is Château Cassaigne, a handsome country château that once was the retreat of the Bishops of Condom. The original structure, built in 1247, was renovated at various periods. It retains architectural features of Gascony's three grand epochs: The thick-walled stone *cave* (cellar) where the Armagnac is aged dates from the 13th century; the intriguing kitchen, whose vaulted ceiling was constructed like a bread oven, is 16th century; and the classic Renaissance façade is 18th century. It was here that the Gascon warrior Blaise de Monluc (from nearby Château Monluc) came to recuperate and write his memoirs after being injured in the Siege of Rabastens. One room is devoted to old documents of the bishops and other residents of the château, another to the explanation of local viticulture. If you are lucky enough to see Henri Faget, an armagnac producer and the present owner of the château, your visit will be enriched by this lively Gascon's evocative account of the history of the region and of armagnac.

Return to Condom to pick up D15 westbound, which will take you past Larressingle, perhaps the smallest fortified town in France. This dreamy, moat-encircled fortress overhanging the Osse Valley was also the work of the Bishops of Condom, who built it as a lookout and haven for the Barons of Armagnac traveling through the region. Inside its stone walls, square tower, and arched gateway is a Roman church, an inn, a flower-filled courtyard, and pretty little houses that still are inhabited.

Continue on D15 to Montréal, one of the first *bastides* in Gascony, completed in 1289 by order of the King of England. Although it seems to have held up well during the disputes between the French and the British, Montréal was almost completely destroyed during the Revolution. Today, only the ruins of Eglise St.-Pierre-de-Genens, the ramparts, and one fortified gate remain.

 CHECKING IN: *La Ferme de Flaran* – This old Gascon farm transformed into a provincial inn has a pool, a terrace, and a comfortable, rustic dining room serving regional cuisine. Less than a mile (1.6 km) from the Cistercian Abbaye de Flaran. Closed Monday evenings and Tuesdays in winter. Valence-sur-Baïse (phone: 62-28-58-22). Moderate.

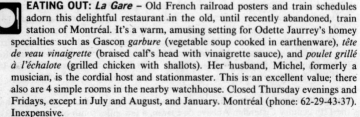 **EATING OUT: *La Gare*** – Old French railroad posters and train schedules adorn this delightful restaurant in the old, until recently abandoned, train station of Montréal. It's a warm, amusing setting for Odette Jaurrey's homey specialties such as Gascon *garbure* (vegetable soup cooked in earthenware), *tête de veau vinaigrette* (braised calf's head with vinaigrette sauce), and *poulet grillé à l'échalote* (grilled chicken with shallots). Her husband, Michel, formerly a musician, is the cordial host and stationmaster. This is an excellent value; there also are 4 simple rooms in the nearby watchhouse. Closed Thursday evenings and Fridays, except in July and August, and January. Montréal (phone: 62-29-43-37). Inexpensive.

En Route from Montréal – About a mile (1.6 km) southwest on an unnumbered road is Séviac, the site of an important Gallo-Roman settlement. The rich carpet of mosaics here is a reminder of the opulent villa that stood on this plateau some 12 to 18 centuries ago. The first of the colorful, detailed mosaics was discovered in 1861. In 1911, further digs unearthed marble columns and, later, the remnants of the luxurious public baths. Today you can walk through the ruins, tracing the layout of the villa from its vast inner courtyard to the residential apartments with vestiges of an underground heating system, and on to the public areas and pools. Throughout, you'll see the rich and varied mosaic designs (even more brilliant when doused with water) that are the real treasures of Séviac. Digs still are under way here under the direction of Mme. Aragon Launet, a woman passionate about her work. Ask for her especially; her explanation of life in the villa is enlightening and memorable.

Follow D29 north from Montréal along the Auzoue River to Fources, another English *bastide,* whose curious circular plan makes it one of the most unusual in France. It was founded in the mid-1200s by Robert d'Anjou, Duke of Aquitaine, as a small and sturdy defense against the attempts of the French to regain their lost territory. Off the tourist route, it was all but forgotten in past decades and was threatened with destruction by modern developers. Mme. Launet, a self-appointed defender of regional antiquities, lobbied against the demolition and was the catalyst for the renovation now going on. In addition to the lovely circular core, flanked by stone and typically Gascon split-timbered houses, there is also a 15th-century château and a Gothic bridge.

CHECKING IN/EATING OUT: *La Belle Gasconne* – Food lovers can continue north of Fources to Mézin and a little beyond to the tiny town of Poudenas, where they'll find one of France's favorite female chefs, Marie Claude Gracia, at the stove of this quaint former wine cellar next to a mill. Specialties such as *civet de canard au Buzet* (duck braised in the wine of nearby Buzet), *agneau rôti et farci aux rognons* (roast lamb stuffed with kidneys), and *cèpes du pays en persillade* (wild local mushrooms sautéed with parsley and garlic) have earned this ebullient Gasconne one Michelin star. Marie Claude and her husband, Richard, who acts as host, have transformed the small mill next door into a cozy inn with 6 individually decorated rooms and 1 suite. Closed Sunday evenings and Mondays in off-season, and from December 15 to January 15. Poudenas (phone: 53-65-71-58). Expensive to moderate.

BARBOTAN-LES-THERMES: This thermal station on D15 west of Montréal, on the wiggly border between the undulating hills of the Gers and the sparsely populated, majestic forests of the Landes, benefits from the distinct beauties of both regions. It's one of the region's most popular spas, attracting thousands of French each year, looking for cures. In fact, it seems there must be more inns and hotels here than permanent homes. Nonetheless, it retains an agreeable quaintness and flavor of times past, somewhat reminiscent of the holiday towns in the 1950s films of the late moviemaker Jacques Tati. Its natural springs, popular in Roman times, are particularly therapeutic for those with circulatory problems. There is a lovely park across from the thermal establishment as well as a handsome old stone and wood clock tower, the ancient gateway to the city, and an old church. The real charm of the place, however, is its provincial character and serene isolation.

CHECKING IN/EATING OUT: *La Bastide Gasconne* – This 18th-century monastery, set elegantly among tall shade trees and terraces, has 35 comfortable rooms, a number of them decorated in a hokily appealing Gascon style. The atmosphere is refined and soothing and the staff particularly congenial. There also are thermal baths, a pool, and tennis courts. Even if you're not planning to spend the night, enjoy a meal in the charming, wood-beamed dining room, supervised by the owner's son-in-law, none other than three-star chef Michel Guérard, founder of the slenderizing *cuisine minceur* which helped make his nearby Eugénie-les-Bains spa famous. The menu has a strong regional character but reflects Guérard's fresh, light style. Closed November to April. Barbotan-les-Thermes (phone: 62-69-52-09). Expensive to moderate.

En Route from Barbotan-les-Thermes – Travel west along D626 to D933 and D932, across the southern edge of the vast pine forests of the Landes; they start above Bordeaux, extend down the Atlantic coast to Biarritz, and east to where the Landes meets the Gers, near Nerac, and cover 5,500 square miles. *Lande* means "moor," and until the end of the 18th century the region was just that: desolate, inhospitable land, sandy at the coast and swampy inland. Swept progressively farther east by the Atlantic winds, the sand dunes of the coast threatened to turn the region into a desert until 1788, when a clever engineer named Nicolas Brémontier came up with a solution to stop the annual encroachment of the sands. After barricading the dunes with wooden planks, he planted them with hardy, strong-rooted ground cover. With the sands no longer a problem, the marshy areas inland could be drained and planted with pine groves, and this poor, barren region became the richest source of France's timber and resin for turpentine and varnish. As in earlier times, the region remains sparsely populated, dotted with tiny isolated villages, sawmills, and furniture factories. The most dramatic attraction here is the forest itself, part of which constitutes the 509,026-acre regional park, Landes de Gascogne.

If you are smitten with the forest, amble leisurely through the region above Mont-de-Marsan (D932), the capital of the Landes, on your way west to Hossegor and Capbreton, the Landes' coastal resorts and most popular tourist attractions. A few miles from Sabres, which is 22 miles (35 km) northwest of Mont-de-Marsan on N134, a 45-acre open-air museum, the *Ecomusée de Marquèze,* welcomes visitors. (It is named for the person first responsible for the reclamation of this region.) Created in 1969, this unique museum includes a sheep park, a mill, an outdoor oven for baking bread, Maison le Mineur (the Lesser House), which dates from 1772, Marquèze's house, which was built in 1824, and much more. A small train makes the trip between Sabres and the museum; the visit takes about half a day. The museum is open daily from mid-June to mid-September; otherwise, only on Sundays and holidays. Closed completely from October 30 to the Sunday before *Easter* (phone: 58-07-52-70). Those who want to extend their stay can try the inn in Sabres, *Auberge des Pins,* except when it closes from mid-January to mid-February (phone: 58-07-50-47).

Continue west from Mont-de-Marsan along N124 to Hossegor and Capbreton on the Atlantic coast. En route you'll pass Dax, on the Adour River. Along with Mont-de-Marsan and Arcachon (about 90 miles/144 km to the north), it is one of the three major towns in the Landes and it has thermal springs (which used to ease the aches and pains of the Romans), a casino, a good assortment of hotels and restaurants, and lovely Parc Théodore-Denis, where vestiges from Roman days still can be seen.

Or, if you prefer, turn south at Mont-de-Marsan and travel the tiny roads (N124 to D11) through agricultural land to Eugénie-les-Bains, a tiny thermal village named for Empress Eugénie, who came here frequently to take the waters. Its name has become world-famous ever since Michel Guérard opened his elegant spa, *Les Prés et les Sources d'Eugénie* (see *Checking In/Eating Out*). There is not much of interest in the town itself, centered as it is around a short main street with only a few cafés and shops. Guérard's *Les Prés,* however, is a destination in itself. More than any other spa in the area (and perhaps more than any other in France), this establishment conforms to the American idea of a spa, offering not only the therapeutic hot springs treatments but also a full range of modern spa amenities, including saunas, gymnastic equipment, a swimming pool, mudbaths, massages, weight-loss programs, and beauty treatments.

The cost of all this luxury is high, and the experience is definitely for those who like deluxe treatment and don't mind paying for it.

Pick up D924 at Grenade-sur-l'Adour about 6 miles (10 km) north of Eugénie-les-Bains and travel west to N124 and A63 to the coast. Hossegor and Capbreton lie just a couple of miles off A63 via D33 and D28, respectively.

CHECKING IN/EATING OUT: *Les Prés et les Sources d'Eugénie* – This white Second Empire mansion with its baroque lounge and tranquil, arcaded terrace sits back from the road; it is graced by a lush tropical garden and flanked by two newer white buildings. The 36 rooms are large, modern, and elegantly furnished with a pleasing mix of antique and contemporary pieces chosen by Christine Guérard. Those willing to pay three-star prices should not miss the pleasure of dining in the elegant but relaxed dining room. Those who have come to shed pounds can opt for Michel Guérard's *menu minceur,* refined and delicate dishes lightened somewhat of excess fat and calories, though by no means bare bones or lifeless. The more sybaritic will choose the *cuisine gourmande,* creative, beautifully presented dishes that have earned him the highest accolades from critics in France and abroad. Hotel reservations necessary; restaurant reservations advised. Eugénie-les-Bains (phone: 58-51-19-01). Expensive.

HOSSEGOR: The pine forests of the Landes meet the sea here at wide sandy beaches and a tranquil blue lake fed by the tide through a canal built in 1886. Although Hossegor, and Capbreton like it, lacks some of the chic of the larger Atlantic resorts of Biarritz and St.-Jean-de-Luz to the south, their beaches are cleaner and less crowded, their towns have a provincial charm, their hotels are more reasonably priced, and their surroundings are wild and unspoiled.

Until the turn of the century, the area around Hossegor's marine lake was little more than a sweep of desolate sand dunes, like much of the Landes coastline. It grew up somewhat haphazardly in the 1920s and 1930s, its pleasing climate and recreational potential attracting a quick following of nature lovers and sports enthusiasts.

Hossegor's town center, clean, white, and planted with flowers, has a lazy, relaxed holiday mood and lies between the lake and the ocean. Pretty little villas and quaint Basque hotels speckle the lakefront and nestle in the deep pine groves that stretch east from the beach and the lake. This place is ideal for those who would forgo sightseeing (there is little of historical interest here anyway) for sailing, windsurfing, golfing, tennis, hiking or horseback riding through the forests, or just basking in the sun.

Hossegor's sports casino (Av. de Gaujac) has a saltwater pool, five tennis courts, and a miniature golf facility. The town also has a jai alai arena, a yacht club, a surfing club, and a golf course. The tourist office, in the center of town (phone: 58-43-72-35), has information about these and other sports facilities.

EATING OUT: *Le Regalty* – A pleasant portside restaurant with a dining terrace where good Landes-style cuisine is prepared with a nouvelle touch. Quai Pecherie, Capbreton (phone: 58-72-22-80). Expensive to moderate.

CAPBRETON: Just a couple of miles south of Hossegor, Capbreton is so close that it seems almost an extension of its neighbor. Its past is a bit more colorful, though: Due to its location at the mouth of the Adour River, Capbreton grew into a lucrative fishing port and maritime city between the 10th and 16th centuries. Before the river changed its course and the harbor filled with silt, it was known as "the port of a hundred captains," and the 16th-century tower that guided navigators and fishermen to it still stands witness to its prosperous past. It was from Capbreton that seafarers set off for their new home on Cape Breton Island, in northeastern Nova Scotia (the island was a French possession from 1632 to 1763). A deep geological fault formed with the shifting of continents that produced the Pyrenean range tends to tame the force of the ocean here and, fortunately for visitors, makes the waves on this beach particularly gentle and pleasant for bathing.

The season in the resorts of Capbreton and Hossegor begins in June and runs through September 15, although a few hotels and restaurants stay open year-round.

 CHECKING IN: *Océan* – A neat white hotel rimmed with balconies, it looks like a small ocean liner moored on the quay facing the colorful marina. Its rooms, many of which overlook the marina, are simple and comfortable, and the management is congenial. Closed October to March. Av. de la Plage, Capbreton (phone: 58-72-10-22). Moderate to inexpensive.

 EATING OUT: *La Sardinière* – This rustic restaurant with seafaring motifs and an outdoor terrace facing the marina serves a good rendition of *ttoro,* a rich fish soup that is the Atlantic Coast's alternative to bouillabaisse. It also prepares plentiful seafood platters and a wide choice of other fish and meat dishes. Closed mid-November to December. 89 Quai Georges-Pompidou, Capbreton (phone: 58-72-10-49). Moderate.

The Pyrénées

The Pyrénées Mountains stretch from the rocky shores of the Atlantic in the west of France to the lush Vermilion Coast of the Mediterranean in the east, forming a natural frontier between France and Spain and offering the most varied and enchanting panoply of scenery, culture, and history imaginable. Legend has it that the goddess Pyrene, the lover of Hercules, is buried somewhere in this range — whence, presumably, it derives its name.

The range extends some 275 miles from west to east, its highest peaks reaching about 10,500 feet, only slightly lower than those of the French Alps. These peaks still play second fiddle to the Alpine range, perhaps due to their greater distance from Paris (800 miles/1,280 km). All the better for the visitor: Their isolation has left them pristine and unspoiled and has allowed their peoples to hold strongly to old ways, preserving to this day the languages, customs, cuisines, architectural styles, and independence of their ancestors. In these ways they resemble their Gascon neighbors to the north.

So varied are the areas that make up the Pyrénées range that it is almost impossible to generalize about them. Physically they can be divided into three groups: The western Pyrénées are characterized by harmonious terrain, verdant hills rising inland from the ocean in roller-coaster fashion and growing into high, forested slopes. The central Pyrénées are the most dramatic. Magnificent, rugged mountains — the highest peaks in the range — are crossed by dizzying, barren passes and overlook glacial valleys that intrude like splayed fingers between the heights. In the eastern region, the peaks, still quite high at first, ease into the heavily wooded slopes and the chalky cliffs and gorges of the Ariège Valley, eventually giving way again to gentler terrain and tumbling down to the lush, semitropical vegetation of the Roussillon's red, baked soil.

Equally varied are the culture and history of these areas. To the west is Basque country, dotted with postage-stamp villages of split-timbered houses. The origins of the highly individualistic people, who share a language (l'Euskara), traditions, and physical characteristics with their neighbors on the Spanish side of the border, are still a mystery. According to some theories, their civilization goes back 25 centuries, starting with Homo Pyrénéus, a contemporary of Cro-Magnon man. (But an abundance of caves in the Pyrénées gave shelter to even earlier inhabitants, whose traces were found — in the form of a human jaw 300,000 to 400,000 years old — near Montmaurin in 1949.) The Basque are a proud and keenly nationalistic people whose culture is worth thoughtful study. Their rustic, flower-bedecked inns are perfect Pyrenean retreats, and their hearty cuisine is the most distinctive in the entire region.

The central and eastern Pyrénées are a mix of modern ski resorts and lazy sun-warmed thermal spas, whose springs have been popular since Roman times. The impenetrable peaks behind these valleys protected them from attack from the south and allowed them to develop into strong, independent states during the Middle Ages, ruled over respectively by the Counts of Béarn, Bigorre, and Foix and later by the Kings of Navarre. Their strong stone châteaux still stand proudly on the heights, souvenirs of their lords' former power and glory.

Vestiges of prehistoric life are sprinkled throughout the numerous caves and grottoes that lie beneath the hills of the chain. Most notable, perhaps, are those at Niaux, whose well-preserved Magdalenian wall paintings rival those of the famous Lascaux in the Dordogne.

In 72 BC Romans founded Lugdunum Convenarum, which later became St.-Bertrand-de-Comminges. Sixteen years later, Crassus, Julius Caesar's lieutenant, conquered this area, establishing thriving settlements and the first spas. Remnants of their civilization can be seen at Montmaurin and St.-Bertrand-de-Comminges. In the 3rd century, the region was invaded by Germanic tribes, followed by the Normans in the middle of the 9th century.

During the Middle Ages, the area was marked by keen religious activity. Scores of religious pilgrims from all over Europe regularly converged at St.-Jean-Pied-de-Port and Sare in the Pays Basque (Basque Country) on their way to the important shrine of Santiago de Compostela in Spain. At about the same time, Romanesque churches and cathedrals were being erected in the central area (see St.-Bertrand-de-Comminges, below), while farther east battles were being waged by the papacy and the ruling Capetians against the Cathari (or Albigensians), the religious dissenters who shunned the evils of earthly life and attacked the worldly ways of the established Church. At least four of the hilltop châteaux where the Cathari sought refuge before being wiped out in the mid-13th century still can be seen around Foix. England gained control of the area in 1360, during the Hundred Years War. France won it back in 1463.

It wasn't until 1659 that the Peace of the Pyrénées was signed between Louis XIV and Philip IV of Spain at St.-Jean-de-Luz, finally establishing this grand range as the official boundary between France and Spain. Only then did much of this territory come under French dominion. But 3 centuries of French rule have not erased the strong regional identity of the Pyrenean people. Indeed, many of its citizens consider themselves to be first Basque, Béarnais, or, to the far east, Catalonian, placing secondary emphasis on their membership in the French republic.

To appreciate fully the distinct charms of each area and the depth of its incredible natural beauty, it's necessary to get around by car and on foot. A good pair of sturdy walking or hiking shoes is mandatory. Not surprisingly, the recreational possibilities are vast here: camping, hiking, climbing, horseback riding, skiing, and fishing in clear mountain streams. If you happen to be in Paris first, stop at the Maison des Pyrénées (15 Rue St.-Augustin; phone: 42-61-58-18), where several very helpful English-speaking employees will fill you in on upcoming events and sites of particular interest in the area. They also can arrange packages, such as 3- to 7-day hiking itineraries which include hotels and luggage transport from one destination to the next. (See "Great Walks and Mountain Rambles" in *For the Body,* DIVERSIONS.) Open Monday through Friday, closed in August.

As in many of the "undiscovered" regions of France, most of the hotels fall into the moderate and inexpensive price ranges. In a few, modern comforts such as air conditioning, TV sets, and room service are lacking, but they are compensated for by the rustic charm of flower-bedecked balconies, antique armoires, and down quilts.

The price categories for the hotels listed in this section are expensive, $80 and up per night for a double room; moderate, $40 to $80; and inexpensive, under $40. Dinner for two, including service, in an expensive restaurant is $80 and up; in the moderate category, between $40 and $80; and in the inexpensive category, under $40. Prices do not include wine or drinks.

The tour route starts at Bayonne, the gateway to the Basque country and beautiful mountain vistas. It follows the coastline south to St.-Jean-de-Luz before turning inland and starting to climb into the heart of the Pays Basque. After a short detour north to Pau, the cultural capital of the region, it climbs into the high Pyrénées, zigzagging from mountain ski resort to thermal spa, including stops at Lourdes and Cauterets. Finally it picks up the Route des Pyrénées, crossing three mountain passes before Luchon and then continuing into the lovely Ariège Valley and the romantic lands of the counts of Foix.

If there's time at the end of this itinerary, you may choose to head south to the tiny mountain state of Andorra, Europe's last feudal protectorate, the main draw being its duty-free status. Or you can continue east through the Pyrénées as they roll into the green hills, vineyards, and orchards of the Roussillon on their way to meet the Mediterranean at the beautiful beach resorts of the Vermilion Coast.

BAYONNE: This lively port just 4½ miles (7 km) inland from the white beaches and rocky precipices of Biarritz manages to combine a busy commercial life with a light-hearted holiday spirit. It is where Gascony meets the Pays Basque, the natural starting point for an itinerary through the Pyrénées, and it exhibits the distinct characteristics of both cultures. Its proximity to Spain adds yet another cultural dimension. A city full of personality and life, it is marked by a colorful past.

Like many of the cities in this part of France, Bayonne was inhabited in Roman times and called Lapurdum, from which the coastal Basque province of Labourd takes its name. As part of the province of Aquitaine, it passed into English hands in the 12th century along with the rest of the southwest when Eleanor wed the British monarch Henry Plantagenet.

The city fared badly after the resumption of French rule in 1451. But in 1578, under Charles IX, canals were dug that reopened the silted-up port to the sea. In 1784 Bayonne was declared a free port and its already healthy trade tripled.

Bayonne's golden hour came in the 18th century, when it benefited from a brisk trade between Europe and the West Indies. This was the port through which cocoa beans first entered France, and the city still is known for its fine chocolate. (It is equally famous for its smoked hams, which resemble Parma hams from Italy.) Bayonne also was known for its ironworkers and gunsmiths, who are credited with inventing the bayonet in the 17th century.

During the Revolution, Bayonne's fortunes once again turned downward with preemption of its free port status and the end of its trade with the British due to the blockade. When the Duke of Wellington trekked over the Pyrénées from Spain in 1813, leading an army of English, Portuguese, and Spanish soldiers, he dispatched a division to take Bayonne. But the city's garrison held out valiantly, capturing the English general. Again under siege in 1814, the garrison was equally heroic.

After the restoration, Bayonne did not return to its former position of glory. But the city experienced a renaissance in this century with the discovery of oil and natural gas at Lacq, 75 miles (120 km) to the east. By 1980, the port's traffic had passed the 3-million-ton mark, four times its volume in 1960.

Two of the best reasons to visit this city are its museums: the *Musée Basque* and the *Musée Bonnat,* both in Petit Bayonne, the area between the Nive and the Adour, the two rivers around which the city was founded. The *Musée Basque,* in a characteristically Basque structure on Rue Marengo by the bridge, is an excellent introduction to Basque culture, with traditional costumes, furniture, simulated interiors of Basque homes, and an exhibition of that very Basque sport *pelote,* which resembles jai alai. The *Musée Bonnat* (5 Rue Jacques-Lafitte) is built around the private collection of the painter Léon Bonnat, who willed it to his native city upon his death in 1922. A treasure trove of artworks from the 13th century to the Impressionist period, it includes the works of Van Dyck, El Greco, Goya, Degas, da Vinci, Raphael, Dürer, Rubens, Rembrandt, Fragonard, and Delacroix and is one of the finest and richest art museums in France.

On the opposite side of the Nive are the active pedestrian streets of the old city and, nearby, on Rue des Gouverneurs, the Gothic Cathédrale Ste.-Marie, whose delicate spires dominate the horizon. The cathedral was begun in the 13th century and wasn't completed until the 16th. It has a 14th-century cloister, lovely Renaissance windows, and in one chapel, a curious plaque commemorating "the miracle of Bayonne," when a strange white light is said to have appeared in the sky, signifying the imminent surrender of the English in 1451.

Also on Rue des Gouverneurs is Château Vieux, a massive, square fortress with round towers that was once the home of the viscounts of Labourd. It was in this fort, which no longer is open to the public, that the Spanish collected the ransom of 1,200,000 *écus* (crowns) demanded for the release of François I. Before leaving town, walk down the pedestrian Rue du Pont-Neuf and drink hot chocolate (really chocolate sauce in a cup) under the arcades where the city's famous confectioners have been making their sweet delicacies for more than 300 years. Continue on to the animated Place de la Liberté and nearby public gardens (half of the area has been turned into a parking lot), the Hôtel de Ville (Town Hall), and the municipal theater; both are in the same building as the tourist office (phone: 59-59-31-31).

Each year at the beginning of August, the city holds a colorful week-long festival that includes bullfights, dancing, singing, and *pelote* games. The rest of the year rugby games are held on Sundays.

Just a quick hop to the Atlantic via D260 leads to the bright lights, lovely beaches, and beckoning waves of Biarritz.

CHECKING IN: *Mercue* – An ultramodern, almost high-tech hotel on the outskirts of town, it seems out of place in this old city full of split-timbered houses and ethnic charm. Nonetheless, it provides modern conveniences — TV sets, air conditioning — in its 105 comfortable, contemporary rooms. Av. J.-Rostand, Bayonne (phone: 59-63-03-90). Moderate.

Aux Deux Rivières – This graceful, traditional establishment flanked by the sidewalk cafés and shops of the main commercial street has 63 unassuming but comfortable rooms and a cozy little lounge, but no restaurant. 21 Rue Thiers, Bayonne (phone: 59-59-14-61). Moderate to inexpensive.

EATING OUT: *Cheval Blanc* – Regional and fish dishes are offered at this eatery, housed in a half-timbered Basque house (ca. 1710) in the old part of town. The wine cellar is well-stocked with local varieties. Closed Sunday evenings and Mondays, except in July and August, and the last 3 weeks of January. Reservations necessary: 68 Rue Bourgneuf, Bayonne (phone: 59-59-01-33). Moderate.

Euzkalduna – The decor and ambience at this cozy bistro on a narrow street in Petit Bayonne are as typically Basque as its name and its former chef, Geneviève Muruamendiaraz. She has received laurels for almost 3 decades for her honest, inexpensive, and authentic Basque fare. Her daughter, Arroxa Aguirre, has taken over the kitchen and retained the food's high standards. Try the cuttlefish in its own sauce. A meal here is a perfect preface to an excursion into the Pays Basque. Closed Sunday evenings, Mondays, June 1–5, and October 15 to November 1. 61 Rue Pannecau, Bayonne (phone: 59-59-28-02). Moderate to inexpensive.

BIARRITZ: For a detailed report on the city, its sights, hotels, and restaurants, see *Biarritz,* in THE CITIES. Route N11 leads from Biarritz south to St.-Jean-de-Luz.

ST.-JEAN-DE-LUZ: If Biarritz is "the Queen of Beaches," then St.-Jean-de-Luz, 9 miles (14 km) down the coast, certainly is the crown princess, whose casual, fresh, and impulsive character is in many ways more appealing than the distinguished charm of Her Royal Highness.

Its biggest attraction is the expansive, gracefully curving white beach. Sandy and wide, and usually very crowded, the beach is in a naturally protected horseshoe-shaped bay between the sea and the mouth of the Nivelle River. In addition to being one of the most popular resorts on France's Atlantic coast, it also is the principle fishing port of the Basque coast, and its restaurants always are supplied with an abundance of fine, fresh seafood — perhaps its second biggest attraction.

Like Biarritz, St.-Jean-de-Luz was already an important whaling center in the 9th century. Its old name, St.-Jean-de-la-Boue ("St. Jean in the mud"), leads us to believe that its environs were not always so inviting. When the whales disappeared from this area, the fishermen turned to cod; today the big catch is tuna.

Its proximity to the Iberian border made the city a frequent target of the Spanish, who burned it to the ground in 1558 and again in 1635. Thus there are few ancient structures.

Without question, the finest hour of the city's history was in 1660, when Louis XIV married Maria Theresa, the daughter of King Philip IV of Spain, to fulfill one of the terms of the peace treaty signed by the two monarchs the previous year. The marriage took place on June 9, and the city still talks about and remembers the event. Today you can visit the Maison Lohobiague (Pl. Louis-XIV), where the Sun King stayed for 30 days before the wedding. It was the home of a wealthy shipbuilder and is filled with ornate furnishings and intriguing souvenirs of the king's stay. (The guided tour is in French, so ask for the English crib sheet to take along.)

The marriage was held in Eglise St.-Jean-Baptiste, not far from Place Louis-XIV, and the door through which the royal couple passed after the elaborate street processional was permanently walled over after the ceremony so that no other human would again cross this threshold. The church's interior is typically Basque, its walls stacked with three tiers of wooden galleries accessible only to the men of the congregation. Rebuilt after the fire of 1558 to replace the original 13th-century structure, this is perhaps the most sumptuous of Basque churches. Its magnificent retable, which dates from about 1670, contains large gilt statues of the popular saints of the Pays Basque.

Also of architectural interest is the gracious brick and stone Maison de l'Infante, where Maria Theresa stayed before the wedding, and, across the river in Cibo, at 12

Quai Ravel, the 17th-century house in which the composer Maurice Ravel was born in 1875.

Explore the streets behind the port (Rue de la République and Rue Gambetta) and stop for a drink at one of the cafés on the lively Place Louis-XIV. On summer Sundays, there is Basque music and dancing here.

Route D918 leads southeast from St.-Jean-de-Luz to St.-Jean-Pied-de-Port.

 CHECKING IN: *Chantaco* – A mile (1.6 km) or so south of town via D918, this genteel, peach-colored Basque mansion has gracious archways and quiet gardens as well as 24 tranquil, pleasingly furnished rooms and a restaurant that matches the quality of the hotel. It's also right across the street from a golf course. Book well in advance. Rte. 918, St.-Jean-de-Luz (phone: 59-26-14-76). Expensive.

Le Madison – This conveniently located, pleasant hotel features 25 attractive rooms and a very congenial management. 25 Bd. Thiers, St.-Jean-de-Luz (phone: 59-26-35-02). Expensive to moderate.

Prado – A small, family-run place, the only one in town that stays open year-round. Six of the 38 rooms overlook the beach. Pl. de la Pergola, St.-Jean-de-Luz (phone: 59-51-03-71). Moderate.

La Plage – Just a few steps from the beach, this homey, Basque-style family establishment has 30 simple rooms. During the summer, guests are required to take half- or full-board. Closed from mid-October to *Easter*. 33 Rue Garat, St.-Jean-de-Luz (phone: 59-51-03-44). Moderate to inexpensive.

 EATING OUT: *Chez Margot* – On the opposite side of the bay, in front of the harbor, and below the fortress of Socoa, this country-style restaurant-bar offers a variety of simple and ample Basque food, especially fish. Closed Wednesdays and the month of October. Port de Socoa (phone: 59-47-18-30). Moderate.

La Taverne Basque – Seafood and tasty sheep's-milk cheese are the fare here, as well as the delicious light local wines. Located in the center of the city. Closed Wednesday lunch and Thursdays during off-season, and from January 15 to February 15. 5 Rue de la République (phone: 59-26-01-26). Moderate.

■ **Note:** Two words sum up the restaurants in St.-Jean-de-Luz: Basque and seafood. You can't go too far wrong in any of the dozens of warm, inviting places with wooden beams and colorful Basque linen tablecloths that line these narrow streets. Two such restaurants are the *Petit Grill Basque* (closed Fridays and December 20 to January 20; 4 Rue St.-Jacques; phone: 59-26-80-76) and *Ramuntcho* (closed Mondays during off-season and November 15 to February 1; 24 Rue Garat; phone: 59-26-03-89); both are inexpensive.

En Route from St.-Jean-de-Luz – You can follow the road (D912) around the bay to Socoa, along the Corniche Basque with its magnificent vistas, and south to Hendaye, another popular resort, on the Spanish border. According to some, the beaches here are the French coast's most beautiful.

Or turn south on D918 and follow the Nivelle River into the heart of Basque country through tiny villages of split-timbered houses with rust-colored shutters and wooden balconies. Every town, no matter how small, has a *pelote* court where the Basque sport is played by young and old. If you are lucky enough to visit on a Sunday, you'll see the Basques dancing the fandango. Turn onto D4 and drive through Ascain, the village where Pierre Loti wrote *Ramuntcho* and continue on this curving route south to Sare, a storybook village huddled in the climbing hills that announce the ascent of the Pyrénées. (Just a couple of miles before this town is a curious little railroad car on a steep hillside; in summer it takes visitors up to the summit for an awesome view of the coast, including the beautiful Bay of San Sabastian in Spain.) Sare was a resting place for the 12th-century pilgrims who made the trek from all over Europe to Santiago de Compostela in Spain. As such it had, and still has, a tradition of welcoming hostelries.

CHECKING IN/EATING OUT: *Arraya* – This hotel is all wooden beams and stucco, with colorful fabrics and linen. Owner Paul Fagoaga upholds 400 years of Basque innkeeping tradition, and at the same time maintains a refinement and plushness rare in this province, where some comforts are forfeited for rusticity. The 21 rooms and 2 suites, most facing an interior garden, offer provincial luxury. The hotel's hearth-warmed dining room has earned one Michelin star and is particularly well known for its preparation of game birds in the fall. The Basque specialties also are very tasty. Closed November to May 1. Reservations necessary. Sare (phone: 59-54-20-46). Expensive to moderate.

ST.-JEAN-PIED-DE-PORT: One wouldn't be at all surprised to see a bent, gray-cloaked, 12th-century pilgrim, staff in hand, emerge from behind the ramparts here, so convincing is the ambience of this Basque village, the last stop along the ancient road to the Spanish border. Its location required heavy fortification, and the old, or high, town, *ville haute,* is encircled by 15th-century stone ramparts that climb up the hill to a citadel. Inside the old town are steep, narrow stone streets, a church built into the ramparts, and Basque houses, their rickety, flower-entwined balconies overhanging the Nive River. This place is like a medieval stage set for a movie. Wander through the old streets and climb up to the 13th-century citadel built by the King of Navarre and let your imagination take wing.

Just outside the gates of the old town is the modern town, the capital and market center of the Basse Navarre, one of the three French Basque provinces. On Mondays the sloping main street, with lively Basque cafés and *auberges,* turns into a bazaar where vendors sell food, clothing, books, and just about anything you might need. Many of the shops here specialize in colorful Basque linen.

For a glimpse of Basque camaraderie, stop at the *Etche Ona,* a provincial *auberge* on the main street where bereted, ruddy-cheeked Basques take an animated afternoon break.

St.-Jean-Pied-de-Port is an excellent point of departure for several excursions, north to the grottoes of Isturits and Oxocelhaya, with their prehistoric carvings, and south to the Iraty forest, one of the most lush in the Pyrénées.

CHECKING IN/EATING OUT: *Arcé* – About 7 miles (11 km) west on D15, this is a perfect Pyrenean retreat — with 19 rooms and 6 suites — secluded on the banks of a clear mountain stream. In the summer, guests dine on the garden terrace that overhangs the stream, the source of deliciously fresh trout that chef-owner Pascal Arcé, who rates one star in Michelin, puts on the table. Closed mid-November to mid-March. Reservations necessary. St.-Etienne-de-Baïgorry (phone: 59-37-40-14). Expensive to moderate.

Pyrénées – A white stucco house with neat flower-bedecked balconies and a very pleasing tree-shaded dining terrace that looks out on the main street and the city's ramparts. It has 2 suites and 18 simply decorated, comfortable rooms and a fine restaurant, whose chef, Firmin Arrambide, prepares excellent fare. His reputation and his two Michelin stars are well deserved; a meal on his terrace can be memorable whether you order from such traditional offerings as an incomparably flavorful Basque fish soup or from Arrambide's slightly more *recherché* creations like roast pigeon with ravioli of wild mushrooms or cod-stuffed peppers. Try the irouleguy wines from the vineyards nearby. Closed most of December and January, as well as Monday evenings, and Tuesdays during off-season. Reservations necessary. Pl. Général de Gaulle, St.-Jean-Pied-de-Port (phone: 59-37-01-01). Expensive to moderate.

En Route from St.-Jean-Pied-de-Port – Leave by D933, turning onto D918 and crossing the Osquich Mountain pass before reaching the charming little town of Mauléon Licharre, which has a small château worth seeing. Then continue on to Oloron-Ste.-Marie via D24, D25, and D936. Beret lovers might recognize the name of this town at the junction of two swift mountain streams as that stamped inside most of the world's authentic Basque hats. The best reason for stopping here, other than to buy a beret, is to visit Eglise Ste.-Marie, a small 13th-century cathedral with an incomparable Romanesque façade. Carved of Pyrenean marble that has mellowed to an ivory-like patina, it is peopled by scores of curious, intricately detailed creatures and deserves careful examination.

Up the hill in the old town are 15th- and 17th-century houses and the Eglise Ste.-Croix, the oldest Romanesque edifice in Le Béarn.

Route N134 leads from Oloron-Ste.-Marie to Pau.

PAU: The largest and most cosmopolitan city of the western Pyrénées, Pau combines all the advantages of a metropolitan area with the genteel atmosphere of a mountain resort. Its graceful Boulevard des Pyrénées, the work of Napoleon I, offers magnificent vistas of the surrounding hills and the peaks of the high Pyrénées; to the east lies the 9,504-foot Midi de Bigorée peak and to the south, the slightly higher Midi d'Ossau peak. The peaks are especially spectacular summer mornings and at sunset.

Now the capital of the Pyrénées-Atlantiques *département,* it once was the capital of the historical Béarn region, land of the Kings of Navarre and of Henri IV, one of France's most colorful and best-loved monarchs. The best introduction to the history of the Béarn and to all the fascinating lore surrounding Pau's dear Henri is found in the magnificent château where he was born in the middle of the 16th century. Set on high ground at the end of the Boulevard des Pyrénées and overlooking the River Gave de Pau (or Pau's mountain torrent), it is surrounded by the narrow structures and streets of the old town.

The château has a wonderfully ornate Renaissance character, having been renovated in the 16th century by Marguerite of Angoulême, the beautiful and celebrated wife of Henri d'Albret, King of Navarre; she wrote the *Heptameron,* a collection of tales modeled after Boccaccio's. (The château also was embellished in the 19th century by both Louis-Philippe and Napoleon III.) Marguerite and Henri's daughter, Jeanne d'Albret, gave birth to Henri IV here on December 13, 1553, and the curious tortoise-shell cradle the infant slept in is on display. Other treasures here include richly carved Renaissance furniture, priceless artwork, and, most awesome of all, the world's richest and most precious collection of Gobelin and Flemish tapestries. On the third floor is a fascinating exhibit of the history and culture of the Béarn as well as a curator who will gladly explain the furnishings, art, models, and any other parts of the exhibit that interest you.

The massive square stone tower at the entrance to the château was built by Gaston Fébus, actually Gaston III of Béarn, who modestly dubbed himself *"fébus,"* which means "brilliant." This legendary hunter, poet, and military strategist managed to build the Béarn into a strong and independent state in the 14th century. (Many of his castles still can be seen throughout the Béarn.) The tower is all that remains of the militaristic medieval structure that once stood here.

At the opposite end of the Boulevard des Pyrénées is Beaumont Park, a graceful, verdant city park with a small lake and tawdry casino. Nearby, on Rue Mathieu-Lalanne, the *Musée des Beaux-Arts* has important Italian, Dutch, Flemish, Spanish, and French works from the 17th to the 20th century. The *Musée Bernadotte* is housed in the birthplace of and devoted to Marshall Jean-Baptiste Jules Bernadotte (1764–1844), who in 1818 became King Charles XIV of Sweden after being adopted as heir to Charles XIII. The tourist office is in the Hôtel de Ville (Pl. Royale; phone: 59-27-27-08).

The city's benign climate, made famous by a much-translated book by the Scottish doctor Alexander Taylor, made it a favorite destination after it was published in 1842. At one point, almost 15% of the town's population was British. Though the English left with the World Wars, some of their customs, such as afternoon tea, remain. *L'Isle au Jasmin* (28 Blvd. de Pyrénées) is a charming place to enjoy one of more than a dozen varieties of teas and half a dozen coffees. In June and early July, Pau's streets come alive with music, dance, and theater festivals, many of the performances free.

CHECKING IN: *Continental* – A grand old establishment in the heart of Pau, most of its 110 rooms have been renovated in a modern functional decor. Ask for one of the four less modern, more charming rooms in the rotunda. 2 Rue Maréchal-Foch, Pau (phone: 59-27-69-31). Expensive to moderate.

Gramont – On gracious Place de Gramont, this quiet, traditional hotel has 33 simple, spacious rooms and a breakfast room. Friendly staff. 3 Pl. de Gramont, Pau (phone: 59-27-84-04). Moderate.

EATING OUT: *Pierre* – Still considered by many to be Pau's finest for classic cuisine, service, and appointments, it has one Michelin star. Closed Saturday lunch, Sundays, and the last 2 weeks in February. Reservations necessary. 16 Rue L. Barthou (phone: 59-27-76-86). Expensive.

Au Panache d'Henri IV – A particularly welcoming bistro between Place Royale and the château, with a warm, wood-beamed interior and big windows flung open to the street in fine weather. Its menu consists of pleasing, simple, and solid regional fare. Closed Mondays and Tuesday lunch off-season and 2 weeks in June and September. Rue Adove, Pau (phone: 59-27-56-19). Moderate.

La Goulue – A tiny, rather curious little café near the château, its walls are plastered with art and theater posters and its crude wooden tables are covered with red paper. The menu includes southwest specialties, such as *magret* (grilled duck breast) and *confit* (duck or goose simmered in its own flavorful fat and aromatic spices). Try the jurançon wines produced near Pau. Closed Saturday lunch. 13 Rue Henri-IV, Pau (phone: 59-27-44-44). Inexpensive.

En Route from Pau – Take D937 to Lourdes, stopping on the way at the Grottoes of Bétharram. A rickety aerial tram takes visitors up over a giant hill and down to the entrance of these stalactite- and stalagmite-filled caves where one travels by boat, foot, and train past nature's awesome work.

Not far away is the curious Eglise Notre-Dame-de-Bétharram, where several miracles are said to have occurred, particularly between 1620 and 1640. Once an important pilgrimage site, it was overshadowed in the 19th century by nearby Lourdes. Most intriguing is the painted ceiling under the organ loft, depicting the ancestors of Christ according to the Gospel of St. Matthew.

LOURDES: On February 11, 1858, Bernadette Soubirous, the 14-year-old daughter of an impoverished Lourdes miller, claimed to have seen a vision of the Virgin Mary in a rocky grotto surrounded by woods near the Gave de Pau. More apparitions occurred in the girl's presence (18 in all), and on one occasion the vision was accompanied by the spouting of a spring when Bernadette scratched the dry ground with her fingers. Miracles were reported that were attributed to the healing power of the spring's waters; word spread and pilgrims began to flock here. In 1862 the church officially recognized this as a holy place, constructing a sanctuary at the grotto, and in 1933 Bernadette was canonized. Today the small grotto chapel by the mountain stream is overshadowed by a monstrous, double-decker basilica, its monumental semicircular staircase leading to the upper church and embracing a large open plaza.

Lourdes is the destination of more than 4 million pilgrims a year, many of them the sick and disabled, who come here to bathe in the waters of the miraculous spring in hopes of a cure. The pilgrims support this not so appealing town of 18,000, which seems to consist only of hotels and saintly souvenir shops selling blue and white plastic bottles in the shape of the Virgin (people fill them with water from the central fountain). There are more than 400 hotels here, modern structures stacked one next to the other on the hilly streets like so many pastel matchboxes. In fact, Lourdes has the largest number of hotel rooms of any French city except Paris. Despite that, don't try to get a room around August 15, the most important of six annual pilgrimage dates. (In 1983, Pope John Paul II came for the August pilgrimage and rooms were booked as far away as 100 miles.)

This is a city built on faith and hope — and, some say, on their exploitation — and it is certainly worth seeing, although many touristic pilgrims choose to pass it by, disturbed by the commercialism and the sad spectacle of the disabled and sick waiting patiently for miracles.

If you do stop, see the fortified château (pre-miracle) high on a hill above the town. It is an impressive piece of medieval architecture and has an interesting museum on the culture and traditions of the Pyrénées. You also can visit the house where Bernadette was born and see a film on her life or, on Sunday afternoons, watch a rugby game; the local club is one of the best in France.

Though there are, needless to say, plenty of hotels to choose from, you might do well to leave the crowded city via N21 south and drive for 10 miles (16 km) into the nearby valley, where there are many pleasing rural hotels near Argelès-Gazost. Or you may continue driving to where the flat valley suddenly climbs into the mountains to the resort of Cauterets, about 19 miles (30 km) from Lourdes.

 CHECKING IN/EATING OUT: *Le Relais de Saux* – For those who choose to visit Lourdes, 1½ miles (2 km) north of the city this charming hostelry and restaurant offer a splendid view of the mountains. The owners, M. and Mme. Héres, make their guests feel very welcome. Hameau de Saux (phone: 62-94-29-61). Moderate.

CAUTERETS: This small, appealing resort compactly grouped at the feet of sharply rising peaks serves double duty, as both a ski resort and a health spa, and is as lively in the summer as in the winter. Its large thermal establishment attracts "curists" with respiratory ailments. (The waters also are said to benefit sterile women!)

The town is a pleasant base for excursions into the National Park of the Western Pyrénées, which begins a couple of miles beyond Cauterets. To reach the park, drive the scenically winding and climbing route to the Pont d'Espagne, where there is a magnificent waterfall. The road ends here, so you have to continue on foot into the forest, or you can take a chair lift to the lovely, clear lake of Gaube, about 6 miles (10 km) away. Hikers can continue through the mountains to another lovely work of nature, the Cirque de Gavarnie, a superb semicircular formation of mountains with tall, awesome waterfalls — the product of glacial erosion. The easier way, however, is to drive from Cauterets to Luz-St.-Sauveur and then take the narrow roads to the town of Gavarnie. From here you have to walk or take ponies to the Cirque.

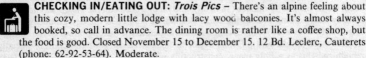 **CHECKING IN/EATING OUT:** *Trois Pics* – There's an alpine feeling about this cozy, modern little lodge with lacy wood balconies. It's almost always booked, so call in advance. The dining room is rather like a coffee shop, but the food is good. Closed November 15 to December 15. 12 Bd. Leclerc, Cauterets (phone: 62-92-53-64). Moderate.

La Fruitière – This little *auberge* with 8 rooms in the mountains on the road to the Pont d'Espagne is the choice of regulars for creative, well-prepared fare. Closed Sunday dinner, and for a month after *Easter* and from October to mid-December. On N21, Cauterets (phone: 62-92-52-04). Moderate to inexpensive.

Etche Ona – A friendly Basque hotel between the slopes and the thermal establishment, its rooms are modern and comfortable, the dining room and lounge very pleasant. The homey food with an occasional Basque flavor also is quite good. Closed November 1 to December 20 and mid-April to mid-May. Rue Richelieu, Cauterets (phone: 62-92-51-43). Inexpensive.

En Route from Cauterets – At Luz-St.-Sauveur pick up the Route des Pyrénées (D918, then D618) again and follow its breathtakingly scenic path to Luchon, crossing three great mountain passes. These are in the high Pyrénées, ruggedly beautiful and dotted with quaint old spas and modern ski resorts. Cross the dizzying Col de Tourmalet (*col* means "pass"), south of the Pic du Midi de Bigorre (9,455 feet). Farther down the sinuous route is the Col d'Aspin, and finally you'll cross the Col de Peyresourd before reaching Luchon. This stretch is one of the most important stages of the annual *Tour de France* bicycle race that takes place in July. Traditionally the victor of this section wins the entire event.

LUCHON: Though it's billed as the premier spa of the French Pyrénées, and in fact it still may be, this quiet resort in a lush, flat valley shadowed by the highest of Pyrenean peaks seems to have lost some of its former cachet in recent years.

It does retain the vestiges of a premier spa, however: the park-encircled thermal establishment, its dimensions and façade reminiscent of a theater or opera house, and the elegant tree-lined main street with smart shops and cafés. The sulfur springs, named Ilixo by Romans who were the first bathers here, are particularly therapeutic for respiratory and throat problems. In the winter, Luchon welcomes skiers drawn to the steep, snowy slopes of the nearby Superbagnères ski station. If the weather is clear, you'll have a magnificent view of the surrounding valleys and the Maladetta range at the Spanish border.

Like many of France's thermal towns, this seems to be something of an anachronism and as such retains a certain flavor, charm, and tranquillity of times past that makes a stop here especially enjoyable.

Travel D125 north from Luchon to St.-Bertrand-de-Comminges, 19 miles (30 km) away.

CHECKING IN/EATING OUT: *Corneille* – A gracious old white mansion in its own private garden, it provides 4 suites and 50 cozy rooms, each individually decorated. The staff here is extremely personable and the atmosphere familial and warm, and the food in the provincial dining room is good. Closed November to March 31. 5 Av. Alexandre-Dumas, Luchon (phone: 61-79-36-22). Expensive to moderate.

Les Bains – This traditional, turn-of-the-century hotel has 50 spacious rooms with high ceilings and wrought-iron balconies and 3 restaurants — Italian, Spanish, and French. Closed October 20 to March 31. 75 Allées-Etigny, Luchon (phone: 61-79-00-58). Moderate to inexpensive.

ST.-BERTRAND-DE-COMMINGES: Not far out of Luchon on D125 you can't help but notice an immense mellow stone cathedral surrounded by ramparts rising high on a hill in the distance and dominating the flat valley below. It compels one to draw nearer. The narrow, winding road leads to St.-Bertrand-de-Comminges, no mirage, but a dreamy walled village of no more than 20 or 30 inhabitants. This practically deserted, storybook place above the Garonne River, and the town on the plain below (inhabited by another 300), were livelier 2,000 years ago. In its earlier life it was called Lugdunum Convenarum, apparently founded in 72 BC by Pompey on his return from a Spanish campaign. Because it was on the busy route from Toulouse to the popular baths of

Luchon, the town grew rapidly and by the end of the 1st century had about 60,000 inhabitants. (According to the Jewish historian Flavius Josephus, it was here that Herod and his wife, murderers of St. John the Baptist, were exiled.)

In the 6th century the city was wiped out, by the barbarians according to some chroniclers, others say by the plague. The Roman city silted over, and archaeological digs have only recently unearthed remains of the old forum and some public monuments. The plain and the hillside apparently remained uninhabited until the 12th century, when Bertrand, Bishop of Comminges and later St. Bertrand, decided the magnificent acropolis was an ideal site for a cathedral, which he began building in 1120. At the end of the 13th century, Bertrand de Got, the future Clement V, first Pope of Avignon, began to enlarge the cathedral, completing the work in 1352. The Romanesque cloister, part of which was added in the 15th century, is lovely and provides a stunning view of the river and valley below. The cathedral's interior, embellished during various periods, is a fascinating lesson in religious architecture. It includes pure examples of Roman, Gothic, Renaissance, and baroque design. Perhaps its most beautiful treasures are the magnificent, intricately carved wood choir stalls. Sculpted by craftsmen from Toulouse in 1535, they tell the story of the redemption. Behind the altar is the frescoed stone tomb of St. Bertrand. There also is an exhibition of religious antiquities, such as richly embroidered bishops' capes dating from the 13th century.

Before leaving this lovely site, wander through the steep, curving, stone streets of the walled village surrounding the cathedral.

Travel east along N117 and D117 to Foix, the capital of the *département* of the Ariège.

En Route from St.-Bertrand-de-Comminges – In the valley just north, at Valcabrère, is the 10th-century basilica of St. Just. A graceful yellow stone example of early Romanesque design, it sits serenely in a cemetery surrounded by cypresses.

Nearby are the well-preserved remains of an opulent Gallo-Roman villa at Montmaurin (follow N125 and D633 north to D69C) and, close by, the Grotto de Gargas (northeast of D26), a cave inhabited by Aurignacien man, whose mysterious engravings of more than 200 mutilated hands, perhaps associated with some cult or ritual, have earned it the title of "Cave of the Cut Hands."

Traveling east on N117, then turning southeast on D117, the route soon passes into the department of the Ariège, the former domain of the Counts of Foix, an area whose romantic and colorful past is only outdone by the natural beauty of its glacial valley. This splendid wooded country is punctuated by chalky cliffs and commanding green mountains topped with the ruins of the medieval fortresses and stone strongholds of the 12th-century religious "heretics" known as the Cathari, or Albigensians.

The area also is rich in natural caves, where prehistoric man lived and left mystical clues to his activities drawn and engraved on the porous rock surfaces. One such cave is the Mas-d'Azil, north of St.-Girons via D119. This curious tunnellike grotto, 1,400 feet long and 165 feet wide, was carved out by the Arize River under the Plantaurel range. It was inhabited by prehistoric man from 40,000 to 8,000 BC and bears graceful, scratched images of bison and horses. Digs have turned up a wealth of implements used by Magdalenian man. Later the early Christians hid here, followed in the 12th and early 13th centuries by the Cathari and by the Huguenots 4 centuries later. You can see the hiding place, the Salle du Temple, where the Protestants sought refuge in 1625 from the fierce attacks of Cardinal Richelieu.

Return to D117 and travel east about 25 miles (40 km) to Foix.

FOIX: This sleepy little town, the unassuming capital of the *département* of the Ariège, is notable for the 11th-century château of the Counts of Foix, set commandingly on a rock high above the town. (From the Middle Ages up to the 19th century, crowds used to pan for gold in the Ariège River at its base.) In 1002 Roger le Vieux, Count of Carcassonne, to the north, bequeathed this part of his realm to his son, who took the title of Count of Foix, the first in a line of illustrious characters such as the previously mentioned Gaston Fébus (see Pau, above). A famous battle took place here in 1272 when one of the counts refused to recognize the sovereignty of the King of France, Philip the Bold, who mounted a dramatic and victorious attack against the château. When the Counts of Foix acquired the Béarn in 1290, they lost interest in the town and the château. They returned under French jurisdiction during the reign of Henry IV in 1607. What remains of the château today — the central tower and the core of the original structure, flanked by two separate stone towers added later — is only a small part of the fortress that once stood here. The three towers, nevertheless, form an extremely romantic silhouette. In the 1800s they were used as a prison and the graffiti of political prisoners can still be seen on the walls of the round tower. Today, the three floors of the tower show collections of prehistoric, Gallo-Roman, and medieval artifacts found in the region. The central structure has an exhibit of the arts and traditions of the Ariège. A week-long festival, the *Journées Médiévales Gaston Phoebus,* takes place the second week of July, with parades of citizens in medieval garb, street fairs, and other festivities. Sound and light displays happen in an open-air theater in July, August, and September. For details, visit the tourist office (45 Cours G.-Fauré; phone: 61-66-12-12).

The potential for side trips, detours, and unexpected adventures is great along the winding roads between Foix and Collioure, a resort town on the Mediterranean coast, where good food and lodging and beaches await the weary wanderer.

En Route from Foix – Take N20 south to the Grotto of Niaux (near the town of Tarascon), one of the most superb repositories of prehistoric paintings in France. The graceful bison, horses, and deer-like animals, colored with oxides and manganese, that line the walls here date from 20,000 BC and represent the height of Magdalenian art. In recent years, authorities have started regulating the number of visitors to preserve the cave's atmosphere and to prevent the deterioration of these treasures. The caves are open all day from June through September and for limited hours from October through May. Groups are restricted to 20 people, so it's wise to arrive early and to make reservations (phone: 61-05-88-37).

Pick up D117 again, turning south on D9 to Montségur (about 19 miles/30 km from Foix), the last stronghold of the Cathari, the religious rebels whose doctrines so angered the Church that Pope Innocent III mounted a vicious crusade against them. The infamous warrior Simon de Montfort, bent on eradicating the cultists in the name of his church and country, pursued them mercilessly, leaving a path of death and destruction from Toulouse to Montpellier and south to the Pyrénées. The final showdown was here, in 1244, when the last 207 "pure ones," as the spiritual leaders of the cult were called, had sought refuge in this high fortress on a seemingly impregnable mount against the Catholic army, almost 10,000 men strong. The siege began in July of 1243 and continued until the following March, when, according to some chroniclers, the château was set ablaze and the 207 Cathari burned alive. (Other accounts hold that they finally came out and surrendered.) Only the ruined stone walls and part of the square dungeon remain today. The ruins sit on a curious mount on top of a mountain pass above the small village of Montségur, where there is a Catharist museum. Though you can drive up to the pass, you have to climb the final mount on foot — no small task, as the trail is steep and rugged. It takes about 45 minutes to reach the château. Non-climbers can admire the crumbling stone walls from below. Those who do make the climb will be rewarded with a marvelous view of the surrounding valleys and mountains. There are two other Catharist châteaux in the area, one at nearby Roque-fixade (follow D9), also on top of a rocky mount; the other is at Puivert (D9 and, continuing east, D117).

Take D117 east from Lavelanet and pick up D613 southwest just before Quillan. At Ax-les-Thermes the road runs into N20, which follows the course of the Ariège River south into ruggedly beautiful mountain terrain, across the high pass of Col de Puymor-ens (open only in the summer). Continue southeast on N20 into the Roussillon region, picking up D618 past a string of winter resorts and mountain spas, including Font-Rameau, Mont-Louis, and Prades, where in May the annual *Prades Music Festival* is held at the nearby Abbaye St.-Michel-de-Cuxa. From nearby Vernet-les-Bains, a small winding road goes south to the magnificent 11th-century Abbaye St.-Martin-du-Cani-gou, renowned for the grace and harmony of its church and cloister as well as its magnificent location — and resultant commanding view — on the slopes of towering Mont-Canigou. The abbey can only be reached on foot from the small town of Casteil. It is, however, a memorable sight, worth the almost-2-hour trek for those with comfort-able shoes and time for an afternoon walk.

Return to N116 and travel east about 9 miles (14 km) to pick up D618, which winds slowly and picturesquely southeast to Amélie-les-Bains-Palalda, where the thermal springs have attracted people with respiratory and muscular ailments from Roman times to the present. This is the perfect starting point for some pleasant walks; a 30-minute stroll due south, for instance, leads to the impressive Mondony Gorges.

Only 5 miles (8 km) away, due east on D618, is Céret, a tiny Catalonian town set among orchards that once attracted the likes of Picasso, Braque, and others.

 CHECKING IN/EATING OUT: *Château de Riell* – Formerly a private man-sion, this hotel affords spectacular views from its 21 romantic guestrooms. Chef Marc Baudry presides over the one-star restaurant, specializing in Catalan-French fare. Closed November 5 to April 1. Molitg-les-Bains, Prades (phone: 68-05-04-40). Expensive.

CÉRET: With a population of only 6,200 people, Céret, called "the Mecca of Cub-ism," is best known for the artists who used to live and work here (as well as in nearby Collioure, on the coast) and for the *Musée d'Art Moderne,* filled with their paintings and sculpture. Its collection includes works by Matisse, Picasso, Chagall, Juan Gris, Miró, Dali, Maillol, and Manolo, the sculptor who is credited with luring the other artists here initially. One room is devoted to Picasso, and in the old part of town there is a plaza named after him, as well as a monument to this well-loved "adopted" son. Be sure to see the restored 14th-century Pont du Diable (Devil's Bridge), which rises 73 feet over the Tech River in a single arch.

Continue east on D618 through the vineyards of the Tech Valley and, via N114, to the resorts of the Vermilion Coast.

COLLIOURE: This tiny fishing port about 12 miles (19 km) north of the Spanish border has been called "the Pearl of the Côte Vermeille"; it is certainly one of the most picturesque and pleasant bathing resorts on the Languedoc coast. The tranquil beauty of the spot, with its two tiny bays separated by an impressive fortified château, drew artists such as Dufy, Matisse, Picasso, and Braque around the turn of the century and became a favorite subject for them. Collioure is considered the birthplace of the Fauvist movement, the precursor of Cubism.

The sprawling brick château here was the summer home of the Kings of Majorca during their short but remarkable reign (ca. 1276–1344) over Perpignan and Catalonia. It is open to the public and has changing exhibits. A 17th-century church set at the edge of the old port near the beach has a magnificent gilded retable (1698) by Joseph

Sunyer, a Catalonian craftsman; the church's tower once served as the port's light-house.

Collioure, a port for Phoenician and then Roman merchants, was an important center of commerce during the Middle Ages, when the Catalonian coast dominated Mediterranean trade, but like many Languedoc ports, it lost commercial importance after the Peace of the Pyrénées in the mid-17th century and the later annexation of Provence to France. The French military architect of Louis XVI, Marshall Vauban, destroyed almost half of the city and gave it its present look. Today its principal attractions are sandy beaches, albeit relatively small and crowded, and the charm of tiny streets lined with inviting little outdoor restaurants serving such simple pleasures as tender, fresh anchovies and great iced platters of fresh seafood, accompanied by the wine of neighboring vineyards.

The winding coast road that leads south from Collioure is a magnificently scenic stretch, flanked on one side by the vine-covered slopes that produce the famous, sweet banyuls wine, on the other by a breathtaking expanse of clear blue sea. Port-Vendres and Banyuls-sur-Mer (the birthplace of the sculptor Aristide Maillol), both only a few miles from Collioure, are extremely enjoyable places in which to soak up the Mediterranean sun and relax after a trek through the Pyrénées.

 CHECKING IN: *Hostellerie des Templiers* – This rustic inn on the quai facing the Château Royal was the gathering place for the Fauvists who lived and worked here around the turn of the century, and the walls of its charmingly cluttered dining room are lined with their sketches and paintings. Between the inn and its nearby annex, there are 52 simple rooms. Do stop for at least an apéritif to look over the intriguing art collection. Closed from November to *Easter,* except for 2 weeks at *Christmas.* Quai de l'Amirauté, Collioure (phone: 68-82-05-58). Moderate.

EATING OUT: *La Bodega* – Roussillon natives travel from miles around for the well-prepared Catalan specialties in this *bodega* (wine cellar), complete with wine barrels and rough wooden tables. And no wonder; it is one of only two or three genuinely Catalan restaurants in the region. Closed November 9 to *Christmas,* as well as Monday evenings, Tuesdays during the off-season, and 1 week in December. 6 Rue de la République, Collioure (phone: 68-82-05-60). Moderate.

San Vicens et Vieux Remparts – One of a number of simple, outdoor café-restaurants overlooking the beach, this place offers fresh anchovies, salads, and copious platters of fresh seafood for a very reasonable tab. Closed November 1 to *Easter.* Av. Boramar, Collioure (phone: 68-82-05-12). Inexpensive.

The Languedoc

Just the name of this large, infinitely diverse, and colorful region in France's sunny southwest promises a certain magic. Languedoc literally means "the language of *oc,*" *oc* meaning "yes" in the southern dialect — the tongue of the troubadours that long ago gave way to the official language of the north and its affirmative *oïl,* which became *oui.*

But even if the province today submits to the language and jurisdiction of the north, its heart and soul remain proudly independent, retaining the fiery spirit that underlies the language of *oc,* its art, culture, and traditions. This is France's deep south — a very Mediterranean province blessed with sun, a beautiful coastline of sandy beaches, lush valleys resplendent with vineyards and orchards, and, to the north, the rugged, mysterious terrain of the Causses and the Cévennes mountains, some of the wildest and most beautiful country in all of France.

The regional boundaries of the Languedoc, as much a historical as an official entity, are not distinct. However, the region generally is considered to take in the *départements* of Lozère, Gard, Hérault, Aude, Pyrénées-Orientales, and, historically, portions of Tarn and Haute-Garonne. The ancient region of the Languedoc was much larger. At one time the language of *oc* was spoken in nearly all the areas south of what might be considered the French Mason-Dixon Line, starting at the confluence of the Garonne and Dordogne rivers in the west and curving up to Angoulême, across to Vichy, St.-Etienne, and the Italian border in the east. Physically cut off from the north by the Massif Central, this region had reached a much more advanced level of art and culture by the 9th and 10th centuries than the barbarian north. The seeds of this early development were planted by the Phoenicians, who colonized the Mediterranean coast in 600 BC. They were followed in the 1st century BC by the Romans, who settled in the Bas Languedoc around Narbonne, making it the capital of the rich province of Gaule Narbonnaise. The remnants of their stay here are most visible in Nîmes, which boasts one of the world's best-preserved Roman temples.

The Visigoths held sway over this territory from the 5th century until their defeat in the 8th century by Charles Martel. The 9th century saw the establishment of the Counts of Toulouse, who controlled much of the Languedoc until the Albigensian Crusade, combined with the assaults of the jealous Capetian rulers in the north, brought their dynasty to an end in the 13th century and marked the beginning of the north's preeminence. The short but terrifying crusade against the religious dissenters (who took their name from the city of Albi, where they found refuge early in their movement) left deep scars in the area. At the same time, other religious groups, among them Catholics and Jews, were massacred in Béziers. A period followed during which the Church sought to underline its restored authority by constructing grand and powerful religious edifices such as those in Toulouse and Albi.

Farther south, the Roussillon, the southern coastal area that along with the adjacent northeast corner of Spain forms Catalonia, was alternately under the jurisdiction of France and Spain during this period. Perpignan's formidable Palais des Rois de Majorque (Palace of the Kings of Majorca) bears witness to the strength and glory of that dynasty. It wasn't until the Treaty of the Pyrénées in 1659 that this area came under French rule permanently. Religious upheaval violently rocked the lands of the Languedoc again during the Wars of Religion, which were particularly cruel and destructive here. Even today, an undercurrent of dissension against authority and northern rule seems to exist here, expressed from time to time in hazy separatist movements for a free Occitan state or, in Roussillon, a united Catalonian state. These are, to be sure, minority movements. Nonetheless, they reflect the strong and assertive sense of regional identity and independence you will soon discover. Along with this character and a warm southern style of hospitality, the Languedoc offers a range of cuisine: the much-heralded cassoulets of Toulouse, Carcassonne, and Castelnaudry; the traditional *cargolada* feast of Catalonia; bouillabaisse and a wealth of seafood along the coast; and rich, flavorful cheeses, including the famous roquefort, from the Causses area. The region's most important product is the grape — one *département* alone, Hérault, produces almost one-fifth of all the wines of France — and a visit would not be complete without tasting some of the many local wines.

In addition to precious souvenirs from its colorful past — the pink cathedrals of Toulouse and Albi, the Palace of the Kings of Majorca in Perpignan, the magnificent Roman arena and temple in Nímes, to name a scant few — the region offers wonderfully diverse and dramatic countryside, the highlight of which certainly is the 30-mile-long Gorges du Tarn, one of France's natural wonders. There also are darkly wooded mountains, the arid plateau of the limestone Causses, the wild Cévennes range rolling down into *garrigues,* rugged, brush-covered areas, and, of course, the long Mediterranean coastline backed by sun-baked vineyards for as far as the eye can see (and much farther still).

This tour route starts at Toulouse, the ancient capital of the Languedoc and home of the troubadours, and moves east to the great walled city of Carcassonne, then loops north to Albi and Cordes. From Albi it continues east to the rugged Causses area, through the Gorges du Tarn and down the southern slopes of the Cévennes range to Nímes, on the eastern border of the Languedoc. From Nímes it curves down to Montpellier and follows the Mediterranean coast to Perpignan. Though this area hardly can be considered undiscovered, it is less crowded than its Mediterranean neighbor, Provence, with its Côte d'Azur. Its hotels and restaurants, many of which are relatively new, are comfortable and still relatively reasonable — downright bargains compared to those on the Côte d'Azur. Our price categories for the hotels listed in this section are expensive, more than $90 for a double room; moderate, between $50 and $90 a night; and inexpensive, less than $50. For restaurants, the expensive category is more than $90 for dinner for two; moderate ranges from $50 to $90; the inexpensive category is $50 or less. Prices do not include wine or drinks, though service usually is included.

TOULOUSE: A poetic observer once described Toulouse as "a city pink at dawn, red at midday, and mauve at dusk." His characterization of what others have called the pink brick city aptly captures the face of this warm, animated metropolis. Toulouse is a colorist's dream, owing much of its charm to terra cotta brick, red roof tiles, and the southern sun that plays off them in so many hues. But the city has much more to offer than a magnificent façade: It is the old capital of the Languedoc, one of the largest French regions — larger, in fact, than Belgium but with only one-third the population. It now is the fourth largest city in France, a cultural capital and university center, and the heart of the nation's aerospace and electronics industries (the *Concorde* and the *Airbus* are built here). It is, as well, one of France's most appealing *villes d'art*.

This spot at a ford in the Garonne River was settled even before Rome; its early inhabitants were a tribe called the Volques-Tectosages. Later colonized by the Romans, it grew and had become the third city of Gaul by the 3rd century AD. About this time the evangelist St. Sernin (to whom Toulouse's most magnificent cathedral is dedicated) arrived, converting much of the populace to Christianity. The Visigoths invaded in 410, making this the capital of their vast territory. Next came the Francs and a period of chaos. Order returned under Charlemagne. When Louis le Pieux (the Pious) became King of Aquitaine, he designated advisers from his family to oversee the city, thereby starting the lineage of the great Counts of Toulouse. For centuries to come these counts, whose lands spread from the Pyrénées to Auvergne, ruled over one of the liveliest courts in Europe. This was the home of the troubadours (who later founded France's first literary society here, the Académie des Jeux Floraux, around 1323 for the preservation of the *languedoc*). This brilliant and gay court was brought to its knees in the early 13th century during the bitter conflicts between the north and the south over the Cathari, or Albigensians, religious "heretics" against whom Pope Innocent III and the ruling Capetians of the north mounted a fierce crusade led by the notorious Simon de Montfort. Count Raymond VI of Toulouse, accused of complicity with the heretics, fought to defend his city against the attacks of de Montfort, who finally was killed here in 1218. In 1229, Raymond VII, demoralized by continued attacks from the north, agreed to abide by the clauses of the Peace of Paris, which marked the beginning of the gradual incorporation of this area into the royal domain. Following the Albigensian Crusade and the devastation of the Hundred Years War, Toulouse experienced a renaissance thanks to a small plant called *coquanhas*. The blue dye yielded by this plant became so popular and was in such great demand that its production brought great fortunes to the city. Many of the superb palaces built by the newly rich *pastel* (dye) merchants in the early 16th century still remain.

You could spend several days wandering through the old quarters of Toulouse, most of them named after and grouped around the city's great churches; they abound in architectural gems from 11th-century stone dwellings to Renaissance *hôtels particuliers*. If time is short, you may want to concentrate on two districts, both near the heart of town and Rue d'Alsace-Lorraine, Toulouse's main commercial street. The first district centers around the Hôtel de Ville (Town Hall), a marble-pillared baroque marvel dominating the Place du Capitole, an immense open square lined with arcaded cafés and shops. (It is next door to the regional tourist office, at Donjon du Capitole; phone: 61-23-32-00.) Nearby are two of the city's loveliest Renaissance structures: Hôtel de Bernuy, at 1 Rue Gambetta, and farther south, off the broad shopping street Rue de Metz, Hôtel d'Assézat. The latter was built in the 1550s by Toulouse's greatest Renaissance architect, Nicolas Bachelier, for one of the city's wealthy *pastel* merchants. On Rue Lakanal are the church, cloister, and convent of Les Jacobins; the church is an example of the unusual Gothic style of the region with four single rows of tall supporting pillars across the middle of the nave, its spacious interior a wonderful polychrome play of light and color. The remains of St. Thomas Aquinas were brought here in 1974, the 700-year anniversary of his death, and are on exhibit. Continue on to Rue du Taur, where you'll pass the church of Notre-Dame-du-Taur, said to have been constructed on the spot where, in 250, the body of the martyred St. Sernin was left after he had been dragged through the streets by a bull until he died. At the end of Rue du Taur is Toulouse's gem, the magnificent Basilique St.-Sernin, the largest and most beautiful Romanesque church in the south of France, some say in the Western world. Consecrated in 1096, it is laid out in the form of a Latin cross. Notice the nine chapels surrounding the apse, the superb 12th-century 5-story bell tower, and the Renaissance Miègeville Gate with its magnificently carved marble figures that include Christ, St. Peter, King David, and Adam and Eve.

The second district centers around Cathédrale St.-Etienne (Pl. St.-Etienne, off Allée François-Verdier). In comparison to the exquisitely harmonious St. Sernin, it appears jarringly lopsided and disparate. Constructed from the 13th through the 17th century, it incorporates many styles. Not to be missed by even the most hurried visitor is the *Musée des Augustins,* where Rue de Metz and Rue d'Alsace-Lorraine intersect. It is filled with paintings and sculpture from all periods and, most noteworthy, the richest collection of chiseled stonework in France, all in the pleasing medieval setting of the old Augustinian convent. The *Notre-Dame-de-Grace* here is one of the most celebrated medieval sculptures of the Virgin and Child. *Musée Paul-Dupuy* (13 Rue de la Pleau) is devoted to applied arts from the Middle Ages to the present; the displays include clocks, coins, metalwork, and stamps. The *Musée du Vieux-Toulouse* (7 Rue du May, off Rue St.-Rome) contains regional art and information about the history and traditions of the city; the *Musée d'Histoire Naturelle,* in the Jardin Botanique, has a significant prehistoric collection. Also in this district are the law courts, the residence of the Counts of Toulouse, and, along Rue de la Dalbade, the Eglise Notre-Dame-la-de-Dalbade, which has a lovely Renaissance doorway, the Hôtel de Clary, with its 17th-century stone façade, and the 16th-century houses of members of Parliament. Don't leave Toulouse without strolling through one of its many delightful small parks or tasting its cassoulet, the hardy white bean, duck (or goose), and sausage dish that it (along with two other Languedocian cities, Carcassonne and Castelnaudry) claims as its own.

CHECKING IN: *Altéa Wilson* – What this modern hotel lacks in old-fashioned charm it makes up for in modern comforts and efficiency. It has 95 rooms with color TV sets, mini-bars, and luxurious baths. 7 Rue Labéda, Toulouse (phone: 61-21-21-75). Expensive.

Crowne Plaza Holiday Inn – Opened in 1989, it offers contemporary comfort in the center of the city. 7 Pl. du Capitole, Toulouse (phone: 61-61-19-19). Expensive.

Grand Hôtel de l'Opéra – This gracious old edifice, once quarters for opera students, has been completely renovated and transformed into what is now one of the most charming and comfortable hostelries in town. Its entrance is secluded in a tranquil courtyard, and its 15 suites and 48 contemporary rooms have air conditioning and television sets. Its restaurant, *Les Jardins de l'Opéra* (see *Eating Out*), has earned two Michelin stars. 1 Pl. du Capitole, Toulouse (phone: 61-21-82-66). Expensive.

Chaumond – Small and charming, overlooking a lovely garden, it offers 28 comfortable rooms. 19 Rue Lafayette, Toulouse (phone: 61-21-86-42). Moderate to inexpensive.

EATING OUT: *Darroze* – On a small back street, this bistro is full of rustic regional charm, as is the very well-prepared traditional fare that has earned it one Michelin star. Sample the foie gras with purée of truffles or *canette* (duckling) *du Gers.* Closed Saturday lunch, Sundays, the first 2 weeks of August, and 1 week in February. 19 Rue Castellane, Toulouse (phone: 61-62-34-70). Expensive.

Les Jardins de l'Opéra – Dominique Toulousy, one of France's most promising young chefs (he has earned two Michelin stars), concocts such heavenly specialties as *raviolis de foie gras frais* (ravioli filled with fresh foie gras) and *feuilleté au chocolat et écorces d'oranges confites* (chocolate-filled puff pastry with glazed orange peel), all served amid the flowers of the lovely winter and summer garden dining rooms of the *Grand* hotel. Closed Sundays, the first week of January, and the second and third weeks of August. 1 Pl. du Capitole, Toulouse (phone: 61-23-07-76). Expensive.

Vanel – Lucien Vanel is the venerable gastronomic star of Toulouse, rating two Michelin stars. His cuisine is at once traditional and highly creative. In summer, try his salad of melon, Bayonne ham, and artichokes or his fish dishes with delicate sauces; in winter, his hardy variations on Gascon specialties. The surroundings are modern and refined but pleasingly relaxed. Closed Sundays, Monday lunch, and 1 week in August. 22 Rue Maurice-Fonvielle, Toulouse (phone: 61-21-51-82). Expensive to moderate.

Colombier – A pleasingly unpretentious restaurant near the train station, it is reputed to serve the best cassoulet in town. Closed weekends, *Easter* week, and August. 14 Rue Bayard, Toulouse (phone: 61-62-40-05). Moderate.

La Grillothèque – You might mistake this modern eatery, with its limited, standard menu, for a transplanted American steakhouse; but you'll know it's completely French once you've tasted the ample entrecôte, the house specialty. And you'll understand why it's always busy. 16 Bd. de Strasbourg, Toulouse (phone: 61-62-87-31). Inexpensive.

En Route from Toulouse – Parallel to the road from Toulouse to Carcassonne is France's engineering masterpiece from the Louis XIV era — the Canal du Midi. Completed in 1680, the 150-mile waterway linking Toulouse to the Mediterranean port at Sète was the main connection between the Atlantic Ocean and the Mediterranean Sea. Boats transported wine, wheat, sand, wood, and passengers until the railroad, built during the second half of the 19th century, cut the trip from 9 days to 12 hours. Today vacation houseboats and wine barges ply the waters. Route A61 makes a wide sweep southeast to the great fortified city of Carcassonne, passing Castelnaudary on the way. Both of these cities lay claim to the quintessential cassoulet, challenging Toulouse. So, if you like to make gastronomic comparisons, a lunchtime stop at Castelnaudary is a must. The *Mapotel Palmes et Industrie* (10 Rue Maréchal-Foch, Castelnaudary; phone: 68-23-03-10 or 68-83-17-10) comes highly recommended, though you'll find cassoulet on nearly every menu in town.

CARCASSONNE: Thus satisfied with Castelnaudary's cassoulet, you'll be ready for a long ramble through the meandering streets of the walled city of Carcassonne, about 17 miles (27 km) southeast on A61. One of the largest fortified cities in Europe, it stands like a turreted Walt Disney creation high on a plateau overlooking the Aude River. Its imposing ramparts are even more impressive at night when illuminated. Leave your car in the lot on the city's east side and walk through the lovely Narbonne gate and across the drawbridge into the oldest part of the city, La Cité. The medieval mood inside is jarred somewhat by the inevitable scores of souvenir stalls, but the city's curving streets and half-timbered and stone dwellings retain enough charm to allow one to look past the kitsch and drift back into the time of Raymond-Roger Trencavel, Viscount of Carcassonne, under whose dynasty many of its grandest structures, including the walled Château Comtal and the Basilique St.-Nazaire, were constructed. Long before the reign of Roger and the Trencavels, the Romans had fortified this spot, and later the Visigoths added their share of stones to the ramparts of this strategic site, for centuries the border between the lands of what are now France and Spain.

Charlemagne besieged the city for 5 years in the 9th century and eventually was outwitted, according to legend, by Dame Carcas, a clever townswoman said to have tossed the city's last remaining pig, stuffed with everyone's last rations of wheat, over the ramparts of the town, thereby giving Charlemagne the impression that their larders still were well stocked and their spirit unbroken. Discouraged, Charlemagne retreated, his departure announced by Dame Carcas's trumpet call and the townspeople's jubilant cries of "Carcas sonne" ("Carcas sounds the horn"). It's an amusing tale of how the city got its name, although historians generally discredit it as no more than a romantic invention of the troubadours.

During the Albigensian Crusade of the 13th century the Trencavel dynasty and the city fell to Simon de Montfort, who subsequently established this fort as his base in the south. Later, Louis IX (St. Louis) and then his son Philip III (Philip the Bold) further strengthened the city with a second series of ramparts encircling the first, making it, they believed, impregnable. The strength of this double-walled system was never tested, however, because the city lost its strategic importance when the Treaty of the Pyrénées established that mountain range as the new boundary between France and Spain in 1659. Carcassonne was neglected and in danger of falling into ruin until 1835, when a resident brought it to the attention of the French government and Prosper Mérimée, the inspector of historical monuments (and author of the short story from which the opera *Carmen* was drawn). In 1844 the famous architect Eugène Viollet-le-Duc was commissioned to restore the city. His work was criticized by purists, since his efforts resulted in a very personal vision of how the city looked during the Middle Ages.

The tour of 12th-century Château Comtal, its museum, and the surrounding ramparts is a must, as is a visit to Basilique St.-Nazaire, with its lovely Gothic windows, considered among the most interesting in the Midi. The city's winding streets are alive with cafés and pleasant restaurants, many featuring the cassoulet in which this town also excels. In summer there are frequent concerts in the open-air amphitheater. The city is particularly spectacular during traditional fireworks on July 14 (*Bastille Day*). For 2 weeks in August, the city organizes various shows on medieval life. For information, contact the tourist office (15 Bl. Camille-Pelletan; phone: 68-25-07-04).

 CHECKING IN: *La Cité* – This elegant former pope's palace within the ramparts sustains the medieval mood with wonderful carved wood and appropriately heavy and grand decor. Its 50 large, renovated gracious rooms have high ceilings and balconies and are the most comfortable accommodations in La Cité. A garden overlooks the ramparts. Pl. de l'Eglise, Carcassonne (phone: 68-25-03-34). Expensive.

Domaine D'Auriac – Just 2½ miles (4 km) south of Carcassone and in a charming 23-room hotel, this is the best restaurant in the region. A Michelin star justly compensates Bernard Rigaudis's efforts in the kitchen. His foie gras, done in salt, is a must, as well as cow's cheek with pig's ear *à la carcassonaise*. Trust us! Closed Sunday evenings, Mondays, and January 10–31. Rte. de St.-Hilaire, Auriac (phone: 68-25-72-22). Expensive.

Donjon – A small, pleasing hotel in the heart of La Cité, it has a light, airy mood, a particularly pleasant manager, and 36 simply decorated rooms, some with small balconies. A nice garden restaurant is open only in the evenings, and closed on Sundays. 2 Rue du Comte-Roger, Carcassonne (phone: 68-71-08-80). Moderate to inexpensive.

EATING OUT: *La Crémade* – This light and cheery dining spot offers well-prepared regional specialties and relaxed, gracious service. Closed Sunday nights and Mondays off-season, as well as 1 week in January. 1 Rue du Plo, Carcassonne (phone: 68-25-16-64). Moderate to inexpensive.

Château St. Martin Trencavel – It's worth a trip outside the ramparts of La Cité, via N113, to this rustic *auberge* with its large, welcoming terrace. Although there are new owners, it still is reputed to serve the best cassoulet in Carcassonne — no small claim. It also offers a wide choice of other tempting and creative specialties. 290 Av. Général-Leclerc, Carcassonne (phone: 68-71-09-53). Moderate.

Le Plo – Stone walls enclose this curious, cozy little shell of a restaurant in La Cité, with nothing overhead but a vine-covered trellis and the stars. It has a simple, limited menu of salads, pâtés, and grilled items cooked over aromatic vines. Closed from November 15 to March 10. Rue du Plo, Carcassonne (phone: 68-25-51-85). Inexpensive.

En Route from Carcassonne – Traveling north on D118, you'll soon drive into the Montagne Noire. These gentle mountains are the extreme southeastern limit of the Massif Central. Their southern slopes are arid, almost Mediterranean, while on the other side, where rainfall is extremely heavy, they are cloaked with lush, deep forests so thick and dark that they have earned this range the name Black Mountains. Its highest peak is the 3,699-foot Pic de Noire. Its northern slopes roll down into the Parc Régional du Haut Languedoc, an area dotted with lakes and beautiful scenery too often overlooked by visitors. The traveler with time and a love of nature will want to make a small circuit of the small, often unnumbered roads of the Montagne Noire and the regional park. The town of Mazamet makes a convenient base for excursions.

From Mazamet head northwest on N112 to Castres, the birthplace of the socialist leader Jean Jaurès, which has a museum in his honor as well as the *Musée Goya,* with a collection of paintings that span 50 years of the artist's life. There's also the Hôtel de Ville (Town Hall), formerly a bishop's palace, with an elegant, sculpted garden, Jardin de L'Evêché; it is the 1676 work of André Le Nôtre, most celebrated for designing the gardens of Versailles.

Before continuing north to Albi, take a short detour east on D622 to the area known as the Sidobre, a granite plateau with strange and fascinating rock formations. The site is cut with grottoes and deep gorges of the Agout and Durenque rivers and there also are gigantic granite quarries. At first, the great round boulders piled precariously on top of one another seem to be the work of human hands, stacked, perhaps, for some mysterious ritual. In fact, the picturesque curiosities, with names like "the Priest's Hat," "the Rock of the Goose," "the Trembling Rock," and "the Three Cheeses," are the work of nature.

ALBI: Pick up N112 north again to Albi, a city on the northern edge of the Languedoc, therefore somewhat off the tourist route and too often omitted from itineraries. The first glimpse of this enchanting pink city and its powerful brick cathedral above the Tarn River should make you glad to be here. Like Toulouse, Albi la Rouge, as it is called, is built of terra cotta brick and red roof tiles, and the tones and moods of the city change with the movement of the sun.

Albi was an important religious center during the 12th and 13th centuries, not only for the Church but also for the Cathari, the religious "heretics" also known as Albigensians, named after this city where they found refuge and gathered strength early in their movement. They were later chased south by Simon de Montfort, the warrior who led Pope Innocent III's fierce crusade against them. Albi's great Cathédrale Ste.-Cécile was built in the mid-13th century after the martyrdom of the last of the Cathari, a symbol of the restored strength and irrefutability of the Catholic church. It stands like a fortress with high towers, sheer brick walls, and narrow windows; in fact, it was built to serve as a fortress as well as a place of worship and has an unusual exterior design. The main entrance, added in the 15th century, is on the south side, a wonderfully ornate and frilly contrast to the stark simplicity of the walls. The richly ornamented interior is considered one of the purest examples of the Gothic style of the Midi, with its superb carvings of biblical characters and saints around and inside the choir and an almost surrealistic fresco of the Last Judgment behind the altar. In addition, you can climb up into the tower for a view of the rooftops of Albi and the surrounding countryside. Next door is the 13th-century Palais de la Berbie, formerly the archbishop's palace and now the *Musée Toulouse-Lautrec* (see "Memorable Museums" in *For the Mind,* DIVERSIONS). It has the most important collection in France of the artist's work — more than 500 paintings, posters, sketches, and lithographs assembled by his mother. It is in itself reason enough for a visit to this city.

Toulouse-Lautrec was born here in 1864, and you can visit some of the rooms in his birthplace, now the Hôtel du Bosc, on Rue Toulouse-Lautrec in old Albi. This section of town is filled with charmingly lopsided, half-timbered houses, craftsmen's workshops, and cozy little restaurants. The plaques of the Circuit Pourpré (the Crimson Circuit) mark a self-guided tour of old Albi, which passes by the beautiful church and cloister of St. Salvy, created in several styles over several centuries (the 12th through the 15th). During the summer Albi holds several festivals, including the *Festival de Musique* in August. Stop in at the Palais de la Berbie (Pl. Ste.-Cécile; phone: 63-54-22-30) for information and schedules.

 CHECKING IN: *Hostellerie St.-Antoine* – Though this establishment, founded in 1739 and half hidden on a quiet street near the center of Albi, claims to be one of the oldest hostelries in France, it looks relatively modern because it was rebuilt in the 1960s. Its lobby is studded with antiques and flowers, its tranquil garden where guests take breakfast is lovely, its 56 rooms are pleasant and comfortable, and its restaurant is very good. The Rieux family, which has managed the hotel for 5 generations, also operates *La Réserve* (below). The restaurant is closed Saturday afternoons, and Sundays off-season. 17 Rue St.-Antoine, Albi (phone: 63-54-04-04). Expensive.

La Réserve – A plush 24-room country hotel just outside town at the edge of the Tarn Gorge. A swimming pool and tennis courts are on the property. Reservations are necessary at its fine restaurant. Both the hotel and restaurant are closed from November 1 to March 31. Rte. de Cordes; phone: 63-60-79-79). Expensive.

Auberge Landaise – At the edge of the old city and just off a large *place* with ample parking, this 17-room inn also is a good value; it houses the *Relais Gascon* (see *Eating Out*). 1 Rue Balzac, Albi (phone: 63-54-26-51). Inexpensive.

Parc – There are 20 simple but very comfortable rooms in this small hotel, just around the corner from the city's lush Rochegude Park. The rooms offer particularly good value for the money. 3 Av. du Parc, Albi (phone: 63-54-12-80). Inexpensive.

 EATING OUT: *Relais Gascon* – The flavor and spirit of Gascony live in this cozy, wood-beamed *auberge,* where you can dine on foie gras, *magret de canard* (breast of duck), and other hearty, satisfying specialties of the Landes and Gers regions. Closed Sunday evening and Monday afternoon. 1 Rue Balzac, Albi (phone: 63-54-26-51). Moderate.

La Viguière d'Alby – A tiny, homey place in the old part of town, it is filled with lace-draped tables, grandfather clocks, and vases of flowers. The food is simple and good — like dining at Grandma's or a favorite aunt's house. Closed Sundays. 7 Rue Toulouse-Lautrec, Albi (phone: 63-54-76-44). Inexpensive.

CORDES: Travel about 16 miles (26 km) northwest on D600 through pastoral countryside to the medieval town of Cordes, often called Cordes-sur-Ciel (Cordes on the Sky) because of its dramatic location on the crest of a steep hill. It's also called La Dame en Pierre ("The Woman in Stone") because of the lovely stone structures that line its steep, narrow streets. The Counts of Toulouse built their hunting lodges on this hill in the early 13th century. Later, Count Raymond VII fortified the town, making it a stronghold against the advances of Simon de Montfort and a place of refuge for the Cathari. After the turmoil of the Albigensian Crusade, the city prospered and grew into a center for leatherwork and weaving. During the 16th century it again offered refuge, this time to the Catholics, who in 1568 were attacked and overrun by the Protestants here. In later centuries, as a result of the bubonic plague and several wars, the town was virtually abandoned until Prosper Mérimée, the inspector of historical monuments under Louis-Philippe, ordered its restoration. Among its structures are some of the finest examples of Gothic civil architecture in France. Particularly beautiful are the old hunting lodges and the grand façades of homes built during the city's heyday. Today, a handful of artists and craftspeople have boutiques here, and there are pleasant cafés and hotels. Although you can drive into the city, the streets are very narrow and maneuvering is difficult. It's best to leave your car in one of the lots near the entrance to the city and explore on foot.

CHECKING IN: *Le Grand Ecuyer* – This magnificent medieval edifice, once the hunting lodge of Count Raymond VII of Toulouse, has 12 large, elegant rooms, some with fireplaces and all furnished with antiques. The warmly lighted lounge and restaurant with their carved wood pieces and stone walls are grand and welcoming, and Yves Thuries's creative cuisine has won him a Michelin star. Closed from November to mid-March; restaurant closed Mondays off-season. On the tiny, unnamed, cobblestone main street, Cordes (phone: 63-56-01-03). Expensive.

Cité – A very small hotel (only 8 rooms) but also very quiet and comfortable. On the main street, Cordes (phone: 63-56-03-53). Inexpensive.

En Route from Cordes – Return to Albi and take D999 east toward Millau. You'll see a gradual change in the scenery from the vineyards, green farmland, and hills around Albi as you move into the region known as Les Causses, roughly translated as "the chalky lands." Here the land has been pushed up by the same cataclysmic shifting of continents that produced the Pyrénées, forming in this area great plateaus and mesas not unlike those in Arizona and New Mexico. The Causses dominate the landscape, rising dramatically above the surrounding valleys and gorges. The limestone plateaus are arid and largely uninhabited except for herds of *brebis*, the sheep whose rich milk produces flavorful cheeses such as the famous roquefort. The road passes near Roquefort-sur-Soulzon, a dreary, minuscule town huddled against a gigantic mass of fallen rock known as Mount Combalou, whose caves' unique atmosphere produces the only blue-veined cheese in the world allowed to be called roquefort. Cheese is the town's only product, the huge, rather glum factory its main tourist attraction. The factory tour is somewhat anticlimactic, however, as the cheese is only aged here; it is fabricated in small lots throughout the region. Since there usually is a very long line to get into the caves, this stop might well be bypassed by all but the true *fromage*-ophile. If you do decide to visit, turn off D999 onto D23 just after St.-Affrique, about 50 miles (80 km) from Albi.

MILLAU: Millau sits placidly at the confluence of the Tarn and the Dourbie rivers in a rich green valley rimmed with the limestone walls and forested slopes of the Causses. The largest city in the Causses and the western gateway to the magnificent Gorges du Tarn, it is an excursion center filled with a holiday spirit in summer. The Romans settled here in 121 BC near a rich bed of very fine clay that ancient craftspeople fashioned into the pottery known as Graufesenque, famous throughout the Roman world. Digs in the area have turned up many examples of this red glazed pottery, which also has been found in Italy (near Pompeii), Germany, and Scotland. Since the 12th century Millau has been known for fine leatherwork, particularly gloves made from the skins of the mountain sheep that produce the cheeses of the area. The city still produces about a third of the gloves made in France as well as a vast array of other leather goods that can be purchased in the many shops that line Millau's commercial streets. Although there are some sights of interest — the Eglise Notre-Dame, the Gothic belfry, the museum with a collection of Graufesenque pottery, and the quaint old section of town — Millau's real appeal is its scenic location, its pleasant arcaded squares, and its unhurried pace of life.

CHECKING IN: *La Musardière* – This 120-year-old hotel, a former *maison particulière,* truly retains the atmosphere of an elegant private home, with a grand central stairway and 12 large, individually furnished bedrooms. The lively patroness, Mme. Canac, completes the "at home" feeling. Her plush dining room offers traditional fare. Hotel closed in January; restaurant closed from November to *Easter*. 34 Av. de la République, Millau (phone: 65-60-20-63). Expensive to moderate.

L'International – Although this establishment has more than 100 rooms, service is very personalized. Rooms on higher floors have breathtaking views. The restaurant (closed Sunday afternoons in off-season and Mondays) features typically French dishes. 1 Pl. de la Tine, Millau (phone: 65-60-20-66). Moderate.

Château de Creissels – On a hill overlooking Millau (a mile/1.6 km or so west via D992) is this old château with a crenelated tower, 30 rooms, comfortable lounges, and a garden where guests take breakfast. The dining room is under the warm stone vaulting of the oldest part of the castle, which dates from the 8th century. The rooms are simply furnished but quite comfortable and a particularly good value. Closed February. Creissels (phone: 65-60-16-59). Moderate to inexpensive.

EATING OUT: *Buffet de France* – Next to the train station in what at first appears to be a cafeteria (it was once the *buffet de la gare*), this restaurant is a diamond in the rough, serving carefully prepared specialties such as *coufidou de boeuf Millavoise* (Millau-style braised beef), *ris de veau à la Rouergate* (veal sweetbreads Rouergue-style), *foie frais de canard aux raisins* (duck liver with grapes), and *truite meunière* (sautéed trout). It's much more than what one might expect from the "buffet" appellation. There is a pleasant covered dining terrace in back. Closed January, and Tuesdays — except in July and August. Pl. de la Gare, Millau (phone: 65-60-09-04). Moderate to inexpensive.

En Route from Millau – Follow D110 northeast about 9 miles (14 km) to the Chaos de Montpellier-le-Vieux, an extraordinary group of bizarre rock formations built up over centuries by the slow dripping of water on the surface of the Causse Noir. This rock forest in the middle of nowhere looks, from a distance, somewhat like a city in ruins; it once was feared by the inhabitants of the area as a cursed place haunted by the devil. Signs for the Chaos lead from the main road to the Auberge du Maubert, in a clearing, where one can purchase tickets before driving a couple of miles (3 km) farther to a parking lot at the entrance. A walk through this rock labyrinth takes about 1½ hours. Signposts guide you past these masses of tall rocks shaped (at least to some eyes) like bears, sphinxes, and other creatures. One is even labeled Queen Victoria, although it takes some imagination to see the resemblance.

GORGES DU TARN: From Montpellier-le-Vieux travel northeast on D110 to D29, to Le Rozier. There pick up D907 north, which for the next 30 miles (48 km) or so winds its way through the Gorges du Tarn, one of the most extraordinarily scenic stretches of country in all of France. Like the Causses, these gorges probably were formed at the same time as the Pyrénées, the gigantic shifting of land causing this limestone plateau at the southern extreme of the Massif Central to split apart. The River Tarn, flowing down from Mont-Lozère in the Cévennes range, ran into the giant fissure and over millions of years carved its deep dramatic path through these canyons. The road snakes along the Tarn in the shadow of sheer limestone cliffs and magnificent rock formations towering high above the riverbed. A number of quaint villages are nestled amid these canyons, lost in another time, with rustic *auberges* and cozy restaurants. Some of the most beautiful rock formations are found around Les Vignes, one of the first villages you'll encounter. For a magnificent vista of the gorges, take the small side road at the village up a hill to Point Sublime, some 1,320 feet above the river. A little farther is the town of La Malène, the starting point for one of several boat trips through the gorges; this one leads through the beautiful *détroits* (straights) and the Cirque des Baumes, a circular rock formation inaccessible by car. A couple of miles past La Malène on D907 is one of the loveliest hotels in the gorges, the 15th-century *Château de la Caze* (see *Checking In/Eating Out*), worth a look even if you don't plan to spend the night.

At a northern loop in the river a bit farther along D907 is the medieval village of Ste.-Enimie, a particularly picturesque place with lively cafés and shops. There is an ancient convent with a Romanesque chapel, said to have been built by Ste.-Enimie, a young noblewoman who was cured of leprosy at this spot and thereafter devoted her life to God. See the Burle Fountain, whose waters cured the saint, and the grotto chapel in the rocks above the village. There also is a small medieval museum.

From Ste.-Enimie, a short southern detour via D986 (about 16 miles/26 km) leads to the grottoes of Aven Armand, whose exceptional stalagmites reaching as high as 99 feet are said to be the most magnificent in this grotto-rich area. Then return to Ste.-Enimie to complete the circuit of the Gorges du Tarn, following the windings of the river, along D907 and N106, to Florac, the eastern gateway to the gorges. From here follow the sinuous N106 down through the Cévennes range, the beautiful, wild, green mountains that Robert Louis Stevenson traveled through on a donkey more than 100 years ago. Continue southeast on N106 to Nîmes, about 60 miles (96 km) away.

CHECKING IN/EATING OUT: *Château de la Caze* – This wonderful, pale stone château, built in the 15th century, sits in a low meadow on the banks of the Tarn under the shadow of a tremendous looming rock. The mood is late medieval and tranquil, the large rooms are decorated with antiques, and the restaurant's food is very tasty, rating one Michelin star. Closed from October 30 to May 1. La Malène (phone: 66-48-51-01). Expensive.

NÎMES: Although this appealing southern city lies in the area still generally considered to be the Languedoc, its mood and pace are much like that of neighboring Provence. There is a certain sweetness of life here, heightened by the physical beauty of the city, with its wide tree-lined boulevards and its remarkable monuments. Nîmes often is called the French Rome, and for good reason: Two Roman emperors were born here, and the city is generously endowed with magnificent remnants — most notably an imposing stone temple called the Maison Carrée and a 21,000-seat amphitheater — of the prosperous Roman settlement that grew up around a sacred spring here a century before Christ. This spring was said to have been frequented by the god Nemausus — whence the city's name was derived.

The first glimpse of Nîmes's double-arched stone amphitheater in the center of town is arresting, recalling chariot races and gladiator games. Built early in the 1st century AD, it looks very much like a smaller version of the Colosseum in Rome. It is one of the best preserved of the some 70 amphitheaters known to have been built by the Romans and ranks 20th in size in that group. Visitors can ramble at will through the galleries of the arena, which still is used for bullfights in May and September, during the town's two most colorful annual festivals, and for other public events. In the winter months the arena is covered with a rather ugly inflated plastic roof. Sporting matches and various shows are offered in the heated atmosphere.

Not far away on the Place de la Comédie is the *Maison Carrée,* built in the 2nd century AD; the temple is in exceptionally good condition, perhaps the best preserved of its style in existence. It now is a museum containing Roman artifacts, including a statue of Apollo, found during excavations of the area. Less well preserved but no less evocative of Roman times is the Temple of Diana in the beautiful Jardin de la Fontaine (Fountain Garden). The name of this crumbling remnant of what was a much larger structure is unfounded, as there is no proof to whom it was dedicated or even for what it was used, though many chroniclers feel it was part of the city's public baths. To the north is the Tour Magne, a watchtower, on Mont-Cavalier; climbing the 140 steps to the top offers not only a good workout but also a splendid view of the city, its environs, and, on a very good day, the Pyrénées. This was the biggest of the towers built into the walls surrounding the Roman city and dates from about the 1st century BC. The Porte d'Auguste (Gate of Augustus), also called Porte d'Arles, and other remnants of the old ramparts — the longest in Gaul, they extend more than 4 miles — are visible around the city. The Castellum (Roman water tower), which received the town's water supply via an aqueduct from Uzès, is on Rue Lampeze, east of Mont-Cavalier. The graceful Pont du Gard, 13 miles (21 km) northeast of Nîmes, is all that remains of the aqueduct.

In addition to these awesome Roman souvenirs, the city has numerous monuments to more modern times: the Jardin de la Fontaine, the Eglise St.-Perpétue, the Palais de Justice built by Gaston Bourbon, and the Esplanade, with a fountain designed by Jacques Pradier. All date from around the mid-19th century. Place d'Assas has been rebuilt, giving Nîmes a small and curious sculpture garden. Nîmes also has some fine museums, including a fine arts museum, a natural history museum, an archaeological museum, and the *Musée du Vieux-Nîmes* (Pl. de la Cathédrale), formerly the episcopal palace, which displays a fine collection of 17th- and 18th-century furniture. Colorful parades, dancing in the streets, and *corridas* (bullfights) take place in May and September during the city's annual spring and harvest festivals, and in July there are opera and jazz festivals. A *Festival des Santons* (the quaint clay figurines of Provence used in creating *Christmas* crèches) takes place during the second and third weeks of November in the nearby town of Garons. For information, contact the tourist office (6 Rue Auguste; phone: 66-67-39-11).

CHECKING IN/EATING OUT: *Imperator* – An elegant dowager facing the lovely Jardin de la Fontaine, there are 3 suites and 59 large rooms, a gracious lobby, and a delightful garden where guests can dine in the summer. Its restaurant, *Enclos de la Fontaine,* one of the city's most highly rated, serves fine and inventive fare — for example, *rouget* (red mullet) with leeks and thyme, and lightly sauced *feuilleté de légumes* (vegetable-filled pastry) — all in plush surroundings. Restaurant closed Saturday lunch. Quai de la Fontaine, Nîmes (phone: 66-21-90-30). Expensive.

Cheval Blanc – This traditional 40-room hotel has a restaurant with a pleasant shrub-enclosed dining terrace facing the Roman amphitheater. The traditional menu includes specialties of the Landes and Gers regions: *magret de canard* (breast of duck), *confit* (preserved duck), and, in summer, light fish dishes. 1 Pl. des Arènes, Nîmes (phone: 66-67-20-03). Moderate.

En Route from Nîmes – Before continuing southeast to Montpellier via A9, take a short northeastern detour on N86 to the Pont du Gard aqueduct near Remoulins. This remarkable piece of Roman architecture was built in the 1st century BC to carry Nîmes's water supply from a spring in the town of Uzès, about 12 miles (19 km) north. Visitors can walk across all levels of the 3-tiered, arched stone structure that spans the Gardon River. The bottom tier has 6 arches, the middle tier 11, and the top tier, which carried the water, has 35 arches. Stop and have a drink of Perrier at Vergéze, 10 miles (16 km) from Nîmes (phone: 66-87-62-00).

MONTPELLIER: The capital of Bas Languedoc and an important university town, Montpellier is a busy and animated metropolis whose wide avenues, tree-lined promenades, and superb 17th-century public monuments give it a grace and charm unmatched by other cities in the region. In recent years, ultramodern structures such as the multilevel *Polygone* shopping center, on Place de la Comédie, have added a new dimension to this vital city. The area was settled in the 9th and 10th centuries by spice merchants engaged in trade with the East, and it remained a dominant Mediterranean trading center until Provence, with its major port of Marseilles, became part of France in 1481. The first French medical school was established here around the beginning of the 13th century, an outgrowth of the herb and spice trade, whose merchants were aware of the therapeutic qualities of their plants and who nurtured a curiosity about medicine. One of the school's most famous graduates was François Rabelais, who studied here in the 1530s. Some of the original buildings, dating to the 14th century, are still in use (Rue de l'Université).

The university area is the oldest section of town, and its crooked streets are lined with ancient stone dwellings and the elaborately decorated *hôtels particuliers* of wealthy 17th- and 18th-century merchants. Near the medical school is the former chapel, now the Cathédrale St.-Pierre, the only church in Montpellier not completely demolished during the devastating Wars of Religion. The cathedral was built in 1364 and, though restored in the 17th and 19th centuries, it retains a fortress-like façade, with romantic stone towers and a vaulted entrance. Next door, in a 14th-century structure, is the *Musée Atger,* which has a collection of baroque drawings.

Across Boulevard Henri-IV from the cathedral and the museum is the Jardin des Plantes, France's first botanical garden (1593). The boulevard leads to the Promenade du Peyrou, the exquisite 17th-century public garden and promenade that sit at the crest of the hill on which the city was built. At one end is the Arc de Triomphe, built in 1691 to honor Louis XIV; an equestrian statue of the Sun King stands in the center of the gardens; and at the opposite end is the Corinthian-columned Château d'Eau, a superb decorative structure perched on the highest point of the promenade like the crowning flourish on an ornate wedding cake. It cleverly conceals the tank in which the city's water supply was stored after being transported via an aqueduct from a spring 9 miles (14 km) away. From this point, the view of Montpellier and the surrounding area is superb. On a clear day, the sparkling Mediterranean coast is visible. On Tuesdays there is a colorful flower market under the arches of the aqueduct beside the Promenade du Peyrou.

The town's center of activity is the Place de la Comédie, a giant marble plaza surrounded by outdoor cafés. Nearby is the tree-lined Esplanade and the *Musée Fabre,* with a rich collection of paintings and sculpture, including the works of Ingres, David, Delacroix, Courbet, Houdon, and Barye. Among the many beautiful *hôtels particuliers* that stud the old sections of town, the 18th-century Hôtel de Rodez-Bénavent is perhaps the loveliest. A 5-minute walk from the Place de la Comédie brings you to Montpellier's link to the past — Antigone. A 60-acre recreated metropolis, Antigone is being built by Spanish architect Ricardo Bofill in classic architectural style, using modern materials. Upon completion (scheduled for 1992), it will house various cultural institutions and will accommodate 10,000 people. There also are several beaches within a couple of miles of Montpellier, and sparkling new resorts are just a short drive east. Other sites worth an excursion include Pic St.-Loup, 14 miles (22 km) north via D986 to D113, and the Grotte des Demoiselles (Grotto of the Fairies), 12 miles (19 km) farther along D986. St. Loup Peak rises 2,171 feet at the end of a long, stark ridge and provides a stunning panorama of the area. The grotto, discovered in 1770, is filled with white calcite stalactites and stalagmites; one formation, "La Vierge et l'Enfant," is said to resemble the Virgin, and the largest cavern, with just a short leap of the imagination, could be a huge cathedral with a ceiling that soars 165 feet overhead. The cave is open daily.

 CHECKING IN: *Noailles* – This romantic hostelry, a former 17th-century *hôtel particulier,* is a treasure, not only for its vaulted stone lobby and lounge and its delightfully furnished rooms (some overlooking the Esplanade) but also for its extremely reasonable rates. It's on a tiny street in the charming Aiguillerie quarter of Old Montpellier. Closed December 22 to January 15. 2 Rue des Ecoles-Centrales, Montpellier (phone: 67-60-49-80). Moderate.

EATING OUT: *Chandelier* – Wonderful seafood specialties are featured at this very pleasant, often-recommended restaurant that has earned one Michelin star. Closed Sundays, Monday lunch, and the last 2 weeks of August. 3 Rue Leenhardt, Montpellier (phone: 67-92-61-62). Moderate.

La Marée – Just a 2-minute walk from the Place de la Comédie, this eatery specializes in fine fish and seafood. 7 Rue Boussairolle (phone: 67-58-44-10). Moderate.

Le Vieil Ecu – A warm, homey little place tucked away on a small square in the old part of the city. The tables and chairs are all moved outdoors in summer. Its varied but simple menu includes many fish and seafood dishes. Closed Sundays, Monday lunch, and February. 1 Rue des Ecoles-Laiques, Montpellier (phone: 67-66-39-44). Inexpensive.

En Route from Montpellier – Before traveling south along the Languedoc coast, take a short detour east via D21 and D62 to the resorts of the lagoon area known as the Camargue (see *Provence*, DIRECTIONS). Most of this region was mosquito-infested swampland until the 1960s, when the government, hoping to reduce pressure on the overcrowded Riviera, decided to dredge these lagoons and create eight new resorts at the southwest corner. La Grande-Motte, 12 miles (19 km) from Montpellier, is the most famous of these developments; its beaches now are lined with the futuristic pyramidal hotels and apartment buildings that have come to symbolize the project. Although the architecture is somewhat jarring, the beaches here are wide and sandy.

Continue east on D62 another 9 miles (14 km) to Aigues-Mortes, a medieval remnant in sharp contrast to the modern development. This western edge of swampy Camargue Regional Natural Park stands out against a flat background. Visitors can walk around the massive ramparts and towers of this fortified city founded by Louis IX (St.-Louis), who set off on his first crusade in 1248 from this port. Up to the middle of the 14th century, the city rivaled nearby Marseilles, but the receding sea and development of Sète Port turned Aigues-Mortes into only a local agricultural center. As it was not near major roads, it escaped the destruction of war and is one of the most authentic remnants of the Middle Ages. The largest tower, Tour de Constance, was used as a prison.

Return to Montpellier and travel west on N109, then north on D32 and D27 (about 25 miles/40 km) to another fascinating antiquity, St.-Guilhem-le-Desert, a small village of warm yellow stone houses and narrow streets curiously wedged into the mouth of the Gorges de l'Hérault. The town, somewhat reminiscent of Les Baux-de-Provence, is grouped around a beautiful old abbey, part of the cloisters of which were dismantled by the American sculptor George Grey Barnard in 1906 and re-created as the *Cloisters* (a museum) in New York City. Nearby is the Grotte de Clamouse, with its dramatically lighted interior.

SÈTE: Take A9 south from Montpellier to Sète, a delightful fishing port and resort on a spit of land reached by a narrow causeway. Curiously set on and around Mont-St.-Clair and lined with canals, it once was Montpellier's access to the sea. Sète was granted free trade status by Louis XIV in the 17th century and prospered as the fifth most important port in France until the mid-19th century. Today Sète is both an important port for car-ferry crossings to North Africa and a fishing center. The seafood in its restaurants is renowned. It's definitely worth a stop for a meal or simply a plate of oysters in any of the simple, outdoor open fish restaurants that line the Quai de Bosc. For more refined ambience and more elaborate presentation, try *Palangrotte* (1 Rampe Paul-Valéry; phone: 67-74-80-35). Closed January, 1 week in November, Sunday evenings, and Mondays in off-season. Moderate.

Route A9 continues south to Narbonne.

NARBONNE: In Roman times, this peaceful, slow-paced city was a key Mediterranean port and the capital of Gallia Narbonensis, a large and flourishing Roman province that stretched all along the coast and inland toward Carcassonne. Later it served as a base for the Visigoth kings. When its port silted up, the city's fortunes waned, but it remained an important religious center, evidenced by its beautiful cathedral and archbishop's palace. The building of the Cathédrale St.-Just, Narbonne's most impressive monument, began in 1272, but the interior never was completed. Nonetheless, its high Gothic choir is, at 135 feet, one of the tallest in France, surpassed only by those in the cathedrals in Amiens and Beauvais. A 14th-century cloister connects the cathedral to the archbishop's palace, which today has two museums, one of art and history, another of archaeology, as well as the Hôtel de Ville (Town Hall). The beautifully ornamented palace was built between the 10th and the 17th century. The lapidary museum, on Place Lamourguier, is also worth a visit.

Narbonne vies with nearby Béziers as the center of the region's flourishing wine trade; the Maison Vigneronne (a former Dominican church), near the cathedral, has regular exhibits on wine production. The wide boulevards, pleasant parks, and Mediterranean mood make the city an appealing stop on the route south. Narbonne-Plage, a sandy beach lined with small hotels and holiday homes, is about 8 miles (13 km) east via D168 through the rugged hills of the coast. Autoroute A9 continues south from Narbonne to Perpignan.

En Route from Narbonne – About 9 miles (14 km) southwest via N113, D613, and a small unmarked road is the solitary late-11th-century Cistercian abbey of Fontfroide. This harmonious ensemble of Romanesque church, beautiful cloister, and stone abbey is hidden away in a grove of cypresses and poplars surrounded by a wild, deserted valley. The stained glass windows are a modern addition. Farther south on N9, near the town of Sigean, is the Réserve Africaine de Sigean, a drive-in wildlife park with Tibetan bears, white rhinoceroses, prides of lions, birds, and other animals living on the edge of a saltwater lagoon.

PERPIGNAN: The last important metropolis before the Spanish border, Perpignan is a city whose heart, soul, and history are divided. Culturally, linguistically, and to a certain extent commercially, it is tied to Catalonia, the distinctive region that encompasses both sides of the border from Perpignan to Barcelona. Its loyalties, in fact, seem stronger to Catalonia than to France, and though certainly not totally Spanish in character, the city cannot be said to be totally French either.

Perpignan and the surrounding Roussillon territory, of which it was the fortified capital, bounced back and forth between France and Spain for hundreds of years. It wasn't until the Peace of the Pyrénées, signed by Louis XIV in 1659, that they shifted permanently into the French domain.

The 20th century has brought a new prosperity to this once poor and war-torn area. Since 1914, the city of Perpignan has almost tripled in population (now 115,000). Its economic vitality comes chiefly from the orchards and vineyards of the surrounding plains and coastal area, which now supply a significant share of France's fruit and table wines. Though the area's fertile valleys have produced wine for centuries, during the past few decades local cooperatives have made great strides in dispelling their image as producers of "plonk" by making wines of considerable style and quality. Perpignan also has renewed its past academic glories. In 1954, its 600-year-old university was reopened after being closed for almost 200 years.

Throughout Perpignan the Spanish influence is apparent, from the orange and yellow Catalonian flag that flies proudly throughout the city to the clean white stucco dwellings with bougainvillea-laced wrought-iron balconies. But the most stunning souvenir of Spanish rule is the immense Palais des Rois de Majorque (Palace of the Kings of

Majorca), and a tour of the city might well start at this formidable Gothic fortress enclosed by ramparts. A long, curving ramp under brick vaulting leads to the upper level, where a lovely garden and an elegant arcaded inner courtyard are surrounded by great meeting halls and two Gothic chapels. The top of the palace keep offers a lovely view of the city.

From the palace, it's only a short walk north to the heart of the old city. The tourist association gives a walking tour of this area every afternoon from June to September, starting from its offices on Quai de Lattre-de-Tassigny (phone: 68-34-29-94). The first stop is the Castillet, an elegant red brick fort-like château built in 1368, originally the gateway to the town and later a prison. Today it houses the *Casa Païral,* a museum devoted to the arts and traditions of the Catalan culture. Nearby is the paved pink marble Place de la Loge, the animated center of the old city, still a favored meeting place and the spot where on summer nights residents dance the traditional Catalonian *sardana.* Here also is the lovely 14th-century Gothic Loge de Mer; once the trade exchange, it now has a lively café. Next door is the Hôtel de Ville, a beautiful 18th-century edifice whose courtyard shelters Aristide Maillol's graceful bronze statue *The Mediterranean.* Ask the concierge for permission to see the marriage hall, with its magnificent 15th-century Moorish wood ceiling and 19th-century wall paintings. See also the façade of the small 15th-century Palais de la Députation. On a small back street nearby, at 2 Rue des Fabriques d'en Nabot, is the Maison Julia, an exquisite private residence with an interior courtyard encircled by 14th-century Gothic arches and a gallery.

Take Rue St.-Jean to Place Gambetta and the Cathédrale St.-Jean, founded in 1324 by Sanche, the second King of Majorca. Particularly noteworthy here is a truly lovely treasure in a small chapel near the right entrance, the *Devout Christ,* a haunting wood carving of Christ on the cross, believed to have been made in Germany in the 14th century and brought here 2 centuries later. In this poignant work, Christ's head hangs very near his shoulders and is said to move infinitesimally closer each year. According to legend, when the head touches his shoulders, the world will come to an end.

Perpignan also has the *Musée d'Histoire Naturelle* (Rue Emile-Zola) and the *Musée Hyacinthe Rigaud,* a block southeast of Place Arago; the latter exhibits paintings of early Catalonian and Spanish masters from the 14th, 15th, and 16th centuries as well as several works by Rigaud, a native of Perpignan who was a 17th-century portrait painter and an official artist for Louis XIV and Louis XV. Ask the tourist association or go to the tourist office (Palais de Congrès; phone: 68-66-30-00) for information about weekly bus tours of the surrounding vineyards. The best way to see them, though, is by car, driving into the valleys of the Têt, the Tech, and the Agley rivers. These lush areas of gently rolling vine-covered hills are among the loveliest sights in the Languedoc. Springs and summers are lively in Perpignan; especially colorful is a procession of Pénitents de la Sanch on *Good Friday,* and during the annual modern dance festival in July.

CHECKING IN: *Park* – This modern hotel with 67 rooms offers comfort and hospitality. Its restaurant, *Le Chapon Fin,* is the best in the city and the only one with a Michelin star. It has a noisy Mediterranean atmosphere and inventive French and Catalan dishes. Restaurant closed Saturday evenings, Sundays, August 13 to September 4, and *Christmas* to *New Year's.* 18 Bd. J. Bourrat (phone: 68-35-14-14). Expensive to moderate.

France – A comfortable, established hotel, it overlooks the Basse River and is only a few feet from the Castillet. The style is traditional French, and the rooms are large and well furnished, some with luxurious, big, beautiful baths. The restaurant here, *L'Echanson,* is highly regarded for traditional brasserie fare. 16 Quai Sadi-Carnot, Perpignan (phone: 68-34-92-81). Moderate.

Aragon – A small, modern hotel near the Palais des Rois de Majorque, it may lack regional charm, but it does have 33 contemporary air conditioned rooms. 17 Av. Gilbert-Brutus, Perpignan (phone: 68-54-04-46). Inexpensive.

EATING OUT: *L'Apero* – An appealing Belle Epoque bistro that serves sophisticated contemporary cooking. Closed Saturday afternoons. 42 Rue de la Fusterie, Perpignan (phone: 68-51-21-14). Moderate.

L'Hostal – This bucolic restaurant definitely is worth the 9-mile (14 km) detour southwest of Perpignan for both the food and the setting. In the fortified hilltop outpost of Castelnou, surrounded by the wild and romantic Roussillon landscape, it is reached via D612 (toward Thuir) and tiny, winding D48. The food is as authentically Catalonian as you'll find in France, featuring the traditional *cargolade,* a feast consisting of snails, local sausages, lamb chops, and *boles de picolat* (spicy meatballs), all grilled outside over aromatic vine branches. After lunch, wander through the winding streets of this walled village, a pedestrians-only unspoiled treasure reminiscent of St.-Paul-de-Vence without the crowds. Closed Mondays, Wednesday evenings in off-season, and January 4 to March 15. Castelnou (phone: 68-53-45-42). Moderate.

Le Vauban – Simple, well-prepared fare — at very reasonable prices — is served at this brasserie. Closed Sundays and the last week of January. 29 Quai Vauban, Perpignan (phone: 68-51-05-10). Moderate.

Provence

Quintessentially Mediterranean in landscape, temperament, and culture, the essence of Provence is often more like that of Italy and Spain than that of the rest of France.

Some geographers like to define the northern limits of the Mediterranean region by the latitude where the olive stops growing. Certainly the silver-leaved and gnarled old olive trees are dominant features of the Provençal landscape. So, too, are the umbrella pines and cypresses, almond groves and shady *micocoulier de Provence,* the vineyards, and the arid but fragrant scrubland of wild lavender, thyme, rosemary, and the other familiar *herbes de Provence.* All are characteristic of the Mediterranean's celebrated back-country.

The sunny climate, brilliant blue skies, siesta-inducing afternoons, and mellow evenings make for an easygoing folk who, for many visitors, provide a welcome change from the more sober and abrupt temperaments of Paris and the rest of the north of France. Even the leisurely lilt of the Provençal accent seems imbued with the warmth of the climate. The cultural kinship is clear. Beneath the plane trees on a village square in, say, St.-Rémy, it's not hard to imagine a Neapolitan *boccie* buff trying to hustle in on the locals' lazy game of *pétanque* — and losing. And if the bullfights at Arles or Nîmes lack some of the elegance of a *corrida* in Madrid, they make up for it in the grandiose setting of their Roman arenas.

Provence owes much of its Mediterranean flavor to the Romans. While the Celts and Germanic tribes were settling the rest of France, Rome colonized Provence (Provincia Romana) in 125 BC after Marseilles, which was then a Greek trading port, had asked them for help against Ligurian pirates and Gallic tribes in its hinterland. With the first Roman foothold at Aix (Aquae Sextiae), Provence became a vital communications link between Rome's Spanish possessions and Italy.

Emperor Augustus intensified the Roman presence by giving the town of Nîmes to the war veterans who had defeated Anthony and Cleopatra, and the town's coat of arms still bears a symbol of that victory: an enchained Egyptian crocodile. Orange was a center of Roman commercial prosperity, and Emperor Constantine made Arles his home.

Something of a backwater in the Middle Ages, Provence reemerged in the 14th century as a congenial alternative home for the popes, who had fled the turmoils of Italy to set up headquarters at Avignon. While the French kingdom acquired most of the region in 1486, Avignon and the papal lands of the Comtat Venaissin (including Apt, Carpentras, and Cavaillon) remained independent until the French Revolution. During World War II, Provence was part of the *zone libre* (unoccupied zone) until the Germans invaded at the end of 1942.

Even the sunlight figures in the history of the region. The dazzling Provençal light, which drives sane locals into the shade, was the inspiration for Paul Cézanne's most mature realizations. Disgusted with the uncomprehending Parisian art world, he returned to his native Aix-en-Provence and found in the surrounding countryside the inspiration for the powerful and intense colors of his greatest landscapes. For the modern visitor, there's a special joy in seeking out the original locations depicted on those canvases, most notably around the Montagne Ste.-Victoire area east of Aix.

At the same time, over in Arles, the sun was having its effect on Van Gogh, for whom the contrast with the cooler light of his native Holland was creatively explosive. In his work, the light bursts all over the streets and squares of Arles, the fields outside of town, and the country road to Tarascon. Again, with his famous images in your head, it is a wonderful adventure to try to track down his subjects or their equivalents. All over Provence, even when you're indoors and the morning sun invades your hotel room, you'll be tempted to exclaim "That's a Van Gogh" or, outside in the ocher glow at the end of the afternoon, "Look, pure Cézanne!"

Away from the main roads, the most characteristic Provençal landscapes abound around the lovely Luberon hill villages east and southeast of Avignon and the spectacular springs of Fontaine-de-Vaucluse. Stop for the sweet and indolent life of Gordes, Roussillon, Bonnieux, Ménerbes, and Oppède-le-Vieux, and you may never want to move on.

South of St.-Rémy the terrain becomes wilder, more rugged — with stark outcroppings reminiscent of Arizona or New Mexico. These are the last splutterings of the Alpilles, the western end of the Alpine mountain range that begins its great arc on the Adriatric coast of Yugoslavia. The most dramatic spot in the region is the formidable Les-Baux-de-Provence, a medieval fortress high atop a ravine that was held for centuries by robber barons.

While driving around Provence, it's easy to imagine what the Roman Empire must have looked like in its heyday. Ruins are often better preserved here than in Italy: the magnificent theater and triumphal arch at Orange, the grand arenas of Nímes and Arles, the gigantic aqueduct at Pont du Gard, the ruined houses of Vaison-la-Romaine and St.-Rémy. And every now and again you will find yourself trundling along a stretch of original paving from the Via Aurelia, the ancient precursor of a freeway linking Rome and Arles via Genoa, Nice, and Aix.

But summer in Provence is a region-wide celebration of modern culture, attracting the top international stars to the tiniest villages. Apart from the great theater and music festivals in Avignon and Aix, there's opera, ballet, and choral works in Carpentras, in the amphitheaters of Orange and Vaison, and in the arenas at Nímes and Arles. In addition to the attraction of first class performances, the settings and atmosphere of a balmy Provençal evening lend a particular magic to the experience.

The festivals usually are held during July and early August, but for the best seats, book tickets (and hotel rooms) by early March. Fervent music lovers usually rent a house in one of those Luberon villages for the entire month in order to make the rounds of all the festivals.

While the region's cuisine may lack some of the sophistication and finesse of Lyons's or the richness of Périgord's, it is nonetheless admirably adapted to the sunny, outdoor life found here, with enough "high temples" of gastronomy and examples of innovative culinary arts to satisfy even the most demanding palate.

At almost every table, garlic and onions dominate — but they're sweet garlic and young onions — joined by tomatoes, green peppers, zucchini, eggplant, and the ubiquitous olives, all marvelously enhanced by the aromatic local herbs. *Ratatouille* is a hot or cold stew of the whole kit and caboodle. The salads are heaven, and the whole of France swears by the melons of Cavaillon. Fig jam makes a wonderful spread on a breakfast brioche.

Of the seafood coming up fresh from the coast, go for the *daurade* (gilt head), the delicate *rouget* (red mullet), or the royal *loup de mer* (sea bass) served with fennel, or — not to be snubbed — a plate of grilled sardines. Lamb, with the local rosemary, takes pride of place over beef.

The wines have none of the aristocratic pretensions of Burgundy or Bordeaux, but as you come down the Rhône Valley, you'll come across some great Croze Hermitage and Châteauneuf-du-Pape reds and some refreshing Tavel rosés. In Provence proper, beware of the punch of the splendid gigondas reds before nightfall.

If you're coming down from Paris, you'll find Provence a strong contrast. Hence we've chosen an itinerary that eases you into the region gently. First, stop just south of Lyons at Valence, then take a 20-mile (32-km) trip down the west bank of the Rhône to a fine hostelry at Baix before taking the aptly named Autoroute du Soleil to the Provençal gateway town of Orange. From there head southeast to the Fontaine-de-Vaucluse, then across to the Luberon and a circuit covering a couple of hundred miles or so, around Avignon, St.-Rémy, the Alpilles, and Les Baux, southwest to Arles, and then slightly southeast again via Salon-de-Provence to end up at Aix in grand style.

The price of a double room in places we list as expensive is around $90 and up; moderate (the large majority), $50 to $90; inexpensive, under $50. The price of dinner for two, with a good local wine, in a restaurant we list as expensive is about $90 and up; in a moderate restaurant, from $50 to $90; and inexpensive, under $50. Service usually is included.

VALENCE: An ideal break in the journey from Paris (the TGV will whisk you south of the perpetual traffic jams of Lyons where you can rent a car), this market town is the distribution point for the great fruit and vegetables of the Rhône Valley. Valence provides the first whiff of the good life of the south. François Rabelais spent his student days here in the 15th century, and Valence today pays fitting homage to the gargantuan appetite celebrated in his lusty writings. In a civilization where restaurants rival cathedrals and palaces as national monuments, the town boasts the much revered gastronomic sanctuary, *Pic* (see *Eating Out*).

From the esplanade of the Champ de Mars, there's a fine view across the Rhône River to a ruined château atop the white stone Crussol mountain, a challenge to any climber — not least of all to Napoleon Bonaparte, who is said to have scaled it when he was a cadet at the Valence Artillery School in 1785.

At the town museum (*Musée des Beaux-Arts*), south of the austere and over-restored cathedral, there's a fine collection of 18th-century *sanguines* (red chalk drawings) by Hubert Robert that will set the mood of your Provençal trip. His studies of Rome's ancient ruins evoke something of the wistfulness of Provence's imperial monuments.

CHECKING IN: *Hôtel 2000* – Of the town's hotels where efficiency wins out over charm, this one is modern and clean, with the asset of a quiet east side location and breakfast served in the garden. It has 3l rooms, good service, and a restaurant, the *Des Lys.* Av. de Romans, Valence (phone: 75-43-73-01). Moderate.

EATING OUT: *Pic* – For many it's the only, but also a totally justifiable, reason for stopping in or making a trip to Valence. If you can't get a table in the charming shady garden, the dining room is elegant without being overdone in exactly the same way that Jacques Pic's three-Michelin-star cuisine manages to be sumptuous without losing its delicacy and subtlety. There is no routine of "specialties," but langouste salad, sea bass, veal sweetbreads, and ingenious desserts are some of the triumphs of his repertoire. The local côtes du Rhône wines are excellent. If you're staying overnight or have time for a siesta, risk the cornucopia of the menu Rabelais. Reserve a month or two in advance if you wish to stay in one of the house's 2 beautiful bedrooms and 2 suites. Closed Sunday evenings, Wednesdays, February, and August. Reservations necessary. 285 Av. Victor-Hugo, Valence (phone 75-44-15-32). Expensive.

En Route from Valence – Before entering Provence proper, coast along the west bank of the Rhône, up in the wooded Vivarais hills of the Col de Ayes and Col de Rôtisson. Take the N532 west over the river to winding D279 and D479, connect with D232 and D266 till you rejoin the N86 highway past orchards of apricot, pear, and peach trees to the pretty little village of Baix. (From there, back up 4 miles/6 km to get on the Autoroute du Soleil, A7, near Le Pouzin, for the 45-minute drive to Orange.)

CHECKING IN/EATING OUT: *Hostellerie la Cardinale* – This pleasant hotel-restaurant (once again a member of the Relais & Châteaux group) offers a delightful Rhône view from the flowery waterside terrace while you try the house specialties of *cassolette d'escargots* (snails stewed out of their shells), *lotte* (angler fish) *à l'orange,* and chicken fricassee in tarragon. Besides 5 comfortable rooms in the 17th-century manor house above the restaurant, there are 10 more secluded rooms in an attractive property with a swimming pool in the hills just 2 miles (3 km) up the N86 highway. Open daily; restaurant and hotel closed from the beginning of November to March. Quai du Rhône, Baix (phone: 75-85-80-40). Expensive.

ORANGE: This is the true beginning of Provence. Cheerful as its name — with a few orange trees in the gardens to legitimize it — the town historically has nothing at all to do with that bright citrus fruit. The name is a corruption of the pre-Roman town of Arausio, which was once dedicated to the Celtic god of the local water source. Orange is charmingly sleepy today, but sleep often is broken by the noise of jet planes flying in and out of a nearby military base. Its magnificently preserved monuments recall its ancient role as a major center of Roman trade. Orange was (and still is) an important agricultural center. For a panoramic view, drive up the Colline St.-Eutrope south of town to the park where first Celtic, then Roman, armies had encampments.

On the northern side of town, the Arc de Triomphe dates from AD 21. Its sculpted reliefs on the northern façade commemorate Roman victories over local Gallic tribes and the Greek merchant ships of Marseilles. It stands astride the old Via Agrippa (at this point the N7 highway), once the link between Arles and Rome's Gallic capital at Lyons.

At the foot of the hill, the *Théâtre Antique* (amphitheater) is a few decades older than the arch and is revered by scholars as the most handsome and best preserved of its kind in the Empire. It is the only one with its monumental scenic wall still standing, complete with a heroic statue of Augustus Caesar at its center. Today, it offers opera lovers a magical backdrop for the summer festival that attracts the world's greatest singers. The acoustics are stunning. Reservations for the July festival — opera, symphony concerts, and lieder recitals — begin in mid-January, and tickets are often gone by May; get details and ticket order forms from Chorégies d'Orange (Pl. Fréres Mounet; phone: 90-34-24-24) or the tourist office (Cours A. Briand; phone: 90-34-70-88).

CHECKING IN: *Château de Rochegude* – Eight miles (13 km) from town, this small hotel, with 4 suites and 25 rooms, has a park, tennis court, and swimming pool. Its one-star Michelin restaurant offers regional fare cooked with local herbs as well as Rhône wines. Closed from January to the end of March. Rochegude (phone: 75-01-81-88). Expensive.

***Arène* –** Terrific value for the money, this hotel is in the center of town and miraculously quiet. The service is intelligent and considerate, and most of the 30 comfortable little rooms have balconies. Closed November to mid-December. Pl. de Langes, Orange (phone: 90-34-10-95). Inexpensive.

En Route from Orange – Archaeology buffs may like to head 20 miles (32 km) northeast along the D975 to Vaison-la-Romaine, where the ruins do not have the dramatic impact of the great monuments of Orange or Arles, but the excavated sites do resemble the layout of a Roman town. You'll see its houses and streets, together with a little museum where the more valuable finds are displayed and an explanation of the ruins given. Concerts and operas are held during the summer months in the amphitheater. For information, contact the tourist office (Pl. Abbé-Sautel; phone: 90-36-02-11). Vaison is worth a visit just for the cobblestone Haute Ville medieval quarter huddled around a 12th-century fortress atop the hill above the little Ouvèze River. A 2,000-year-old Roman bridge connects it to the rest of the town. The *Galerie du Vieux Marché* (Haute Ville, Vaison-la-Romaine; phone: 90-36-16-05) sells superb olivewood kitchenware and sculpture by a man with the most un-Provençal name of Niels Christiansen. Closed from mid-November to mid-December.

From Vaison travel on D938 20 miles (32 km) south to Carpentras, home of France's oldest synagogue (signposted near the Hôtel de Ville). The 14th-century structure still has the ritual bath (*mikvah*) in its basement, a baking oven for matzos on the ground floor, and a fine paneled hall of worship upstairs. Before the French Revolution, 20% of the town's population was Jewish; they lived in a walled ghetto and were forced to wear yellow hats.

FONTAINE-DE-VAUCLUSE: This is one of those beautiful natural wonders, like Niagara Falls or Yellowstone's geysers, that have become so popular that they can only really be enjoyed out of season. The mob scene surrounding the gushing springs of the Sorgue River can be hard to take in summer. If possible, visit during the spring or winter, when the waters are both higher and more spectacular. Among lush fig trees, at a rate of up to 7,000 cubic feet per second, they pour out of a great cavern at the base of a 750-foot-high cliff in marvelous emerald green cascades. The site is a 15-minute walk from the parking lot along a well-marked path. The Italian poet, Francesco Petrarca (Petrarch), lived in the valley on and off for 25 years. It was here that he wrote of his love for Laura (De Noves) from nearby Avignon.

Nearby, to the west and slightly south of Fontaine-de-Vaucluse, is Ile Sur La Sorgue, an island village in the middle of the Sorgue River, noteworthy for its unique location and Saturday flea market/antiques fair. The market takes place along the western riverbank every Saturday (in season) and offers some of the best Art Deco pieces to be found in France.

LUBERON: These rugged mountains at the southern end of the Vaucluse plateau, the villages with their pretty gardens and tasteful boutiques, and a surrounding countryside of fragrant heathland blend to form the classic Provençal landscape, protected here as a national park. It's an area where visitors should get out of the car and walk. Stock up on melons and other picnic goodies at Cavaillon's street market before heading east on the D2. First stop: Gordes. The village's spotless houses, solid *bastides,* and drystone *bories* (stone huts intricately constructed without mortar) hug the hill, which is topped by a medieval and Renaissance château. (The elongated farmhouses, called *mas,* are seen mainly in the valleys.) The *Musée du Vitrail,* a museum devoted to stained glass (particularly from the Middle East), is nearby on Rte. de St.-Pantaleon (open daily from 10 AM to noon and from 2 to 7 PM; phone: 90-72-22-11). From Gordes, drive a couple of miles north along the winding D177 to a valley of lavender fields and the exquisitely restored 12th-century Cistercian Abbey of Sénanques, now a striking setting for two permanent exhibitions: Symbolism and Architecture; and Desert and Man, Sahara of the Nomads (closed Sunday mornings; phone: 90-75-88-34).

Back on the D2, go 7 miles (11 km) east to Roussillon, a provocation for any painter as it rises rust-colored from its wreath of ocher quarries and red cliffs dotted with Mediterranean pines and green oaks. The little D149 heads south across a main road to Bonnieux, again perched on a hill with a terrace behind the town hall, from which there's a panorama back across to Roussillon and Gordes. For a good view back at Bonnieux, take the D3 west toward the hilltop citadel of Ménerbes (with a pretty 14th-century church on its outskirts), then continue on to the strange but beautiful ruined village of Oppède-le-Vieux, which gradually is being restored by painters. Writers come here from all over France for a little peace of mind; the dilapidated castle is a melancholy poem all to itself.

CHECKING IN: *Domaine de l'Enclos* – On the northern outskirts of Gordes, this luxurious hotel comprises a collection of houses clustered around a first class restaurant. Each of the 9 rooms and 5 apartments is airy and brightly furnished, with its own little garden in front of the window. The view over the Luberon alone is worth half of the considerable price. The restaurant serves a very sophisticated cuisine using classic Provençal ingredients: zucchini charlotte, salmon grilled with fennel, lamb roasted with sage, and stuffed young rabbit. There's a tennis court and swimming pool to help work off the considerable calories. Rte. de Sénanque, Gordes (phone: 90-72-08-22). Expensive.

***Mas de Garrigon* –** Two miles (3 km) north of Roussillon, this inn has only 7 small, very comfortable rooms, charmingly decorated in traditional Provençal style. The big fireplace in the lounge creates the ambience of a large country house. Other features: a swimming pool and a good restaurant, which is closed Sunday evenings, Mondays, and from mid-November to December 27. Rte. de St.-Saturnin-d'Apt, Roussillon (phone: 90-05-63-22). Expensive.

***Mas des Herbes Blanches* –** In the very heart of Provence, between Lubéron and Ventoux, this traditional stone house (a member of the Relais & Châteaux group) has 18 rooms, a swimming pool, tennis courts, and a delightful restaurant that offers both nouvelle and classic cuisines. 1½ miles (2.5 km) on D102A/Rte. de Murs (phone: 90-05-79-79). Expensive.

EATING OUT: *La Tarasque* – A pleasant bistro in Roussillon proper, with an accent on seafood, excellent fish soup, and grilled bass. Closed Wednesdays and from mid-February to mid-March. Reservations necessary during the week in winter. Rue Richard-Casteau, Roussillon (phone: 90-05-63-86). Moderate.

En Route from Luberon: Route N100 takes you west to Avignon (for a detailed report on the city, its sights, hotels, and restaurants, see *Avignon* in THE CITIES).

ST.-RÉMY-DE-PROVENCE: The village is one of those Provençal market towns with great charm and more than a little cultural interest in its nearby Roman ruins that is, above all, a simple pleasure in which to relax. It's worth planning at least a couple of days (more, if you get hooked) just to soak up the atmosphere of the carefree daily life: Watch the world go by over a coffee or *pastis* at the *Brasserie du Commerce* on Place de la République; check out the local goat cheeses, olives, almonds, freshest of fruits and vegetables at the market; toss a *boule* or two in a game of *pétanque* with the locals; become, for a brief moment, a St.-Rémois. The town's annual *Festival de Musique* begins in mid-July and lasts until the end of September.

On the southern outskirts of town, down the D5, is the ruined Greco-Roman city of Glanum (signposted as Les Antiques), which dates back to the town's colonization by the Greek merchants of Marseilles in the 3rd century BC. It was destroyed by Germanic tribes 900 years later. Its two most important monuments are the mausoleum erected to the memory of Augustus Caesar's grandson and an older, more dilapidated (but still impressive) triumphal arch from the end of the 1st century BC. The rest of the site shows the layout of the town — houses, forum, fountains, and bathhouse. Back in St.-Rémy, in the Hôtel de Sade on Rue du Parage, there's a museum housing the town's sculptural treasures and an archaeological account of Glanum's daily life.

Near the ruins, look for the medieval monastery of St.-Paul-de-Mausole, now converted into a sanatorium; Van Gogh was its most celebrated patient. Visit the graceful Romanesque cloister for a contemplative moment out of the sun.

CHECKING IN: *Château des Alpilles* – Five minutes west of town you'll find the peace and quiet of a tastefully modernized country manor on tree-shaded grounds — 15 large rooms, with tennis courts, swimming pool, and a poolside barbecue. Closed January 2 to April 1. Rte. D31, St.-Rémy-de-Provence (phone: 90-92-03-33). Expensive.

Le Castelet des Alpilles – No relation to the *Château des Alpilles,* this old, formerly private mansion is a stone's throw from the central square but seems in a world of its own, thanks to tranquil rooms that overlook a soothing garden surrounding the house. Closed November to March 20. Pl. Mireille, St.-Rémy-de-Provence (phone: 90-92-07-21). Moderate to inexpensive.

EATING OUT: *Le Bistrot des Alpilles* – Also not related to the *Château,* this unpretentious old-style eatery offers the best of simple, unadorned Provençal cuisine, with top honors going to that pungent celebration of garlic, the *brandade de morue* — cod cooked in olive oil with garlic, mashed and stirred until it's the texture of mashed potatoes. The *gigot* of local lamb also is excellent. Closed Sundays. 15 Bd. Mirabeau, St.-Rémy-de-Provence (phone: 90-92-09-17). Inexpensive.

Café des Arts – Not at all fancy, this is a lively local rendezvous for what once might have been described as the town's bohemians. Its walls are decorated with the works of local artists (for sale). The wise stick to the steaks, chops, salads, and omelettes. There also are 17 serviceable rooms upstairs. Closed Wednesdays, the first 2 weeks in November, and February. 30 Bd. Victor-Hugo, St.-Rémy-de-Provence (phone: 90-92-08-50). Inexpensive.

En Route from St.-Rémy-de-Provence – The vineyards, olive, and almond groves around St.-Rémy, against the backdrop of the craggy Alpilles mountains, make this great cycling — and hiking — country. (Rent a bike at *Agence Florelia,* 35 Av. de la Liberation, St.-Rémy; phone: 90-92-10-88.) The St.-Rémy Syndicat d'Initiative (tourist office; phone: 90-92-05-22) can propose several ambitious tours for experienced cyclists, but for an easy 10-mile (16-km) circuit, head northwest on D5 to Maillane (an exquisite little village and the birthplace of Provençal poet and Nobel Prize winner Frédéric

Mistral), returning on D27 across the main N99 highway toward Les Baux, then cutting back east on the Chemin de Roussan to St.-Rémy.

By car, drive 2½ miles (4 km) south along the winding D5 south toward Les Baux; make a little detour east to the observation point of La Caume (near a TV relay station) for a magnificent view of the mountains and the Camargue plain west of Marseilles.

LES-BAUX-DE-PROVENCE: This ruined medieval citadel, with an astonishing position high on a promontory of sheer rock ravines overlooking the Provençal plain and the Val d'Enfer (Valley of Hell), has long been a privileged tourist destination — so much so that, like the Fontaine-de-Vaucluse, it is now a tiresome crush in midsummer. But don't hesitate to visit in spring or autumn — and in winter when it is even more spectacularly desolate. Even in summer, hedonists make the pilgrimage just for the gastronomic indulgences of *L'Oustaù de Baumanière* and its companion *La Cabro d'Or* (see *Romantic French Hostelries* and *Haute Gastronomie,* DIVERSIONS).

This splendid feudal redoubt was defended for centuries by robber barons against French kings and the Avignon popes. As the star of Christ's Nativity on their coat of arms proudly indicates, the original Lords of Les Baux claimed descendance from Balthazar, one of the Three Kings who traveled to Bethlehem. From the 11th to the 15th century, they ruled more than 80 Provençal townships and their court was a center of medieval chivalry. When it became a focus of rebellion for the region's Protestants in the 17th century, Cardinal Richelieu, head of Louis XIII's government council, decided quite simply to do away with the citadel, rubbing salt into the wound by making the residents pay for the demolition of the fortress and ramparts.

This footnote may partly explain why the job was never completed and why, today, large sections of the baron's 13th-century castle and its chapels are still visible outside the main village, in what is known as the Ville Morte (dead town). Each structure affords superb vantage points overlooking the Val d'Enfer to the east or the Vallon de la Fontaine to the west. The hill on which the fortress stands contains the bauxite mineral to which the town gave its name. The bottom slopes on the southern side are covered with thousands of olive trees — some planted by the Greeks and Romans — and the oil they produce is considered the best in France.

The "modern" village is in fact a delightful maze of Renaissance houses, with hidden courtyards and gardens. Besides the unavoidable souvenir junk, the myriad boutiques and galleries have their fair share of genuine craftsmanship in olivewood items and patchwork quilts.

CHECKING IN: *Cabro d'Or* – Despite its fairy tale setting at the foot of the ancient Cité des Baux, this member of the Relais & Châteaux group offers modern amenities, including TV sets and telephones in each of its 22 rooms; there also is a fine restaurant which serves traditional Provençal food. Closed November 12 through December 21; restaurant closed Tuesday afternoons, and Mondays October 31 through March 31. Les-Baux-de-Provence (phone: 90-54-33-21). Expensive.

L'Oustaù de Baumanière – More elegant than the *Cabro d'Or* (and also a Relais & Châteaux member), this venerable old manor house tucked into the rocky crags of the gleaming limestone Alpilles foothills boasts accommodations befitting a prince: fireplaces, vaulted ceilings, tapestries, and four-poster beds. In regal settings guests are presented some of the most highly reputed food in France. *Filets de rougets au vinaigre* (fish fillet in a vinegar sauce) and *gigot d'agneau en croûte* (leg of lamb in pastry crust) are among the two-star restaurant's specialties. Closed from mid-January to March; restaurant also closed Wednesdays and for lunch Thursdays during the off-season. Reservations necessary. Les Baux-de-Provence (phone: 90-54-33-07). Expensive.

La Benvengudo – A perfectly respectable alternative to *L'Oustaù* in a superb secluded setting southwest of the town, this classic Provençal country house offers 18 traditionally furnished rooms with good, big bathrooms. The restaurant does an admirable job with regional products on a rich and varied menu — the bass with *cèpe* mushrooms is a special treat. Restaurant closed Sunday evenings and from November to mid-February. Rte. D78F, Les Baux-de-Provence (phone: 90-54-32-54). Moderate.

Bautezar – If the town is not overcrowded, try this attractive little place with 10 comfortable rooms and a stupendous dining room view past the terrace to the Val d'Enfer and the Vallon de la Fontaine. Closed January and February. Grande-Rue Frédéric-Mistral, Les Baux-de-Provence (phone: 90-54-32-09). Moderate.

EATING OUT: *Le Bistro du Paradou* – A short drive from Les Baux (east on D17) stands a white house with blue shutters that Jean-Louis and Mireille Pons have transformed into a genuine country bistro-café featuring one daily menu, one wine, and one price — about $20. Daily specials include *lapin à l'ail nouveau* (rabbit with fresh garlic) and *gigot d'agneau* served with *gratin de pommes de terre* (leg of lamb with potatoes gratin). Lunch only in off-season. Dinner served from *Easter* to August. Rte. D17, Le Paradou (phone: 90-54-32-70). Inexpensive.

ARLES: A major link in Rome's chain of communications with its Spanish colonies, Arles today uses its imposing ancient arena for colorful bullfights that recall the more brutal sports of the Romans. If you don't visit during the summer bullfight season, be sure to climb the tower beside the entrance for a walk along the roofs of the arena's arches. Imagine the roar of the spectators (capacity 26,000) cheering on the gladiators or taking sides when the lions met the Christians.

Southwest of the arena and a century older, the amphitheater is less well preserved than the one at Orange since it was in great part dismantled in the Middle Ages to build the city's churches. But it still serves as a striking setting for open-air theater, an international photo festival at the beginning of July — when there also are outdoor slide presentations in the Place de Forum — and folklore festivals in the summer.

There is a rare jewel of Provençal Romanesque architecture in the Church of St.-Trophime (Pl. de la République), with its beautifully sculpted portal depicting the Last Judgment. Unfortunately, the restoration of the portal still is not finished and the scaffolding obstructs the view. But don't miss the church's cloister and the richly carved pillars of the arcade, especially those on the northwest and northeast corners.

Arles was also the home of Vincent Van Gogh in the late 1880s. (The town commemorated his arrival with *Centenaire Van Gogh,* a year-long festival, in 1988.) The artist's house has disappeared, and only the noonday sun baking the surrounding countryside reminds you of his ghost, though one of his subjects remains: the melancholy alley of sarcophagi at the Roman cemetery of Les Alyscamps, in the southwest corner of town.

Picasso loved the town so much that he gave it 57 drawings that are now housed in the *Musée Réattu,* 10 Rue du Grand Trieure.

CHECKING IN: *Jules César* – A large (60-room) hotel converted from a 17th-century convent — complete with a baroque chapel — makes a comfortable old-fashioned stop near the center of town. Besides the room of the Mother Superior, the most coveted are those overlooking the cloister. Its restaurant, the *Lou Marquès,* does fine scrambled eggs with an anchovy and olive *tapenade* and *gigot* of baby lamb. Closed November to December 20. Bd. des Lices, Arles (phone: 90-93-43-20). Expensive.

d'Arlatan – Amazingly quiet in the center of town — 46 exquisitely furnished rooms in a medieval and Renaissance building overlook a lovely garden. 26 Rue du Sauvage, Arles (phone: 90-93-56-66). Expensive to moderate.

Le Cloître – This modest little place is centrally located, quiet, comfortable, and clean. Several of the 33 rooms face the cloister of St.-Trophime. Closed mid-November to mid-March. 18 Rue du Cloître, Arles (phone 90-96-29-50). Inexpensive.

En Route from Arles – South of Arles on D570 is Camargue National Park, one of Europe's most important wildlife preserves. There are almost 200,000 acres of swamps, shallow lakes, sand dunes, and natural and artificial canals, spread across the estuary of the Rhône. Although summer visitors disturb the various wildlife — pink flamingos, wild horses, Camargue bulls, birds, and fish — they still manage to thrive in these lowlands. Two cities dominate the Camargue swamps — Saintes-Marie-de-la-Mer in the south and Aigues-Mortes in the southwestern corner (see *The Languedoc*, DIRECTIONS).

Legend has it that the three Marys — Mary Magdalene, Mary Jacob, Mary Salome — and Sarah, their Egyptian servant — landed in this area in a boat with no sails or oars, steered by the divine hand. In the 15th century, a chapel was built and the local Gypsies began to worship the three Marys and Sarah. Twice a year — at the end of May and the end of October — Gypsies from all over Europe gather here to pay hommage to Sarah, their patron saint. Contact the tourist office for information (Av. Van Gogh; phone: 90-47-82-55).

Return to Arles. Heading east toward Aix on N113 to the autoroute, stop at Salon-de-Provence, which commands the expressway entrance. Though in many ways it's an unexceptional southern town, it is interesting to see how the region's handsome ocher sandstone has been ingeniously used to blend the modern architecture of its boutiques, cafés, and apartments with the old castle of Empéri towering above them. Drink a fresh fruit milkshake on the terrace of the *St.-Michel* brasserie (Pl. de la Salomenque). Military buffs will want to visit the castle museum for the collection of French army uniforms and weapons from the 17th century to World War I.

Take the autoroute toward Aix-en-Provence — the perfect climax to any tour in the south of France. (For a detailed report on the city, its sights, hotels, and restaurants, see *Aix-en-Provence* in THE CITIES section.)

CHECKING IN/EATING OUT: *Abbaye de Sainte-Croix* – A 12th-century Romanesque abbey converted, with considerable taste, into a luxury hostelry — a member of the Relais & Châteaux group — with a grand view over the Salon plain (3 miles/5 km northeast of town). Its 23 rooms each are named after a saint, but the comfort is far from monastic. It has a great swimming pool set among wild shrubs in the hillside, and the hotel can arrange temporary membership in the exclusive tennis club just down the road. The one-Michelin-star restaurant serves regional cuisine with great subtlety, notably bass with basil and purées of garlicked zucchini and pumpkin. The chef could lay claim to the best apple pie in Provence. Reservations necessary. Closed Monday lunch and from November to March. Rte. D16, Val de Cuech, Salon-de-Provence (phone: 90-56-24-55). Expensive.

The Côte d'Azur

The term "Côte d'Azur" can be confusing. It usually describes that privileged part of the Mediterranean coastline from Menton in the east to just beyond St.-Tropez in the west, embracing part of the Riviera (which extends from La Spezia in Italy to Cannes in France) and forming part of the ancient province of Provence. But ask the French themselves exactly how far west the Côte d'Azur stretches and you're likely to get half a dozen answers because it is not an official administrative *département*. Purists (especially natives of Nice) insist that the true Côte d'Azur is the coastal region of the Alpes-Maritimes *département*, which ends at Miramar, 15 miles (24 km) west of Cannes. But most people agree that it reaches into Var, the neighboring *département*, and some say as far as Les Lecques, 6 miles (10 km) west of Bandol.

It is an area of spectacular beauty, with dazzling white or red cliffs rising from the sea, gracefully curved bays, and some of the most luxurious and palatial hotels in the world. The past decade has seen the urbanization of most of the coastline. Except for parts of the bottom slopes of the Massif de l'Esterel, east of Cannes, it is difficult to find spots that are not filled with vacation retreats. Yet, this is the place for sunning, swimming, gambling, eating, nightclubbing, and for seeing some of the finest collections of modern paintings in France (many of the most prominent figures in 20th-century art lived here at one time or another, drawn by the beauty of the terrain and the extraordinary quality of the light).

The statues of Queen Victoria in Menton and of Lord Brougham (a Victorian aristocrat and politician) in Cannes are reminders that the Côte d'Azur was discovered and developed by upper-crust English during the last part of the 19th century. In those days it was the exclusive resort of the rich and leisured who were attracted by the mild climate, a result of the warming influence of the Mediterranean and the screen of mountains to the north. (In January, the average temperature in Nice is 48F and it can reach the high 70s on a sunny day. Winter nights, though, can be cold, and it's much colder inland.) For many years, no self-respecting monarch, cabinet minister, or business tycoon would miss spending a part of the winter in one of the elegant, wedding cake hotels of Menton, Monte Carlo, or Nice, or in an Edwardian villa tucked away behind the bougainvillea and frangipani along the splendid Cap d'Antibes.

More recently, especially since the 1950s, visitors have begun to forsake the sedateness of these towns for the frivolity and frenzy of St.-Tropez and the Ile de Porquerolles. And, although the coast is lively year-round, nowadays the high season is July and August, when the French themselves as well as people from all over the world flock here for vacation. (Indeed, the mass influx of people can be something of a nightmare; for example, the traffic in St.-Tropez becomes so congested that entering the town is virtually impossible.)

One happy result of this burgeoning of tourism is that despite the Côte d'Azur's reputation as a playground of the rich and famous (which indeed it is), you'll find a remarkably wide spread of prices and a fairly reliable level of quality. This is because the vacationing French (who are, after all, the most demanding of people) have contrived to keep standards high across all price ranges, from simple bistros and *auberges* to the most haute restaurants and luxury hotels. Thus, whatever your taste and however deep your pocket, the simple pleasures of the Mediterranean — food, wine, sun, and the sea — will prove enormously satisfying.

Many beaches are rocky or pebbly, but there are plenty of sandy beaches, especially between Antibes and St.-Tropez. Some beaches are public and free of charge, others are "private," which usually means they belong to a restaurant or hotel. But it's worth renting an air mattress and a beach umbrella at one of them for around $5 a day. Topless sunbathing (said to have originated at Tahiti Plage near St.-Tropez in the early 1970s) is ubiquitous but hardly the rule. One of the great delights of the Côte d'Azur is that everyone does his or her own thing — the French are consummate individualists. So relax.

Of course, there's more to do than just sit on the beach. If you feel the need to escape wall-to-wall people, take a day trip to Grasse, the famous perfume center, or to any of the other villages in the mountains. It will be cooler and less humid in the higher elevations than down on the coast. Or indulge in some lazy people watching: Seek out the heart of any Provençal village and its charming central square, which usually is graced by a fountain, shaded by plane trees, and often edged by small cafés. Sit on a café terrace with a kir (white wine with a dash of black currant brandy, deliciously cooling in summer) or a *pastis* (a very potent anise-flavored drink) and watch the residents play the traditional *boules* (lawn bowls). Or, if you're feeling energetic, visit one of the abundant flower markets or perhaps an art museum, a special treat on the Côte d'Azur. The work of the modern masters is exhibited in delightful settings — Renoir's paintings at his house in Cagnes-sur-Mer, where his simple studio is still set up just as he left it; Picasso's ceramics (a new medium he explored after World War II) in the Château Grimaldi in Antibes or at Vallauris; Matisse's drawings and paintings, a selection of which spans his whole life, in a museum in his native Nice.

There are gastronomic masterpieces to sample as well: bouillabaisse, the classic fish stew made with onions, tomatoes, garlic, olive oil, and saffron; rouille, a fiery mayonnaise made with red chili pepper; aioli, also a mayonnaise but based on olive oil and garlic; and *pissaladière,* a kind of pizza topped with onions, anchovies, and black olives. Provence is not one of France's great wine regions, but there are several local vintages. Try the dry whites from Cassis, the Bandol red, or the Bellet reds or whites. The Côtes de Provence rosés are light and fruity and can be enjoyed with most fish or meat dishes.

In an effort to provide the quintessential Provençal experience, we have suggested three complementary tour routes that either can be followed separately or combined, depending on the amount of time available. Motorists might find it useful to buy the Michelin green map No. 195, Côte d'Azur–Alpes Maritimes, or the Michelin yellow map No. 245 Provence–Côte d'Azur, which extends slightly farther west. The first route explores Les Corniches, between Nice and Menton, three roads that hug the coast and provide spectacular views of the sea and mountains for a distance of 17 miles (27 km). The second route is from Nice to Cannes and back, venturing slightly inland to Grasse and to St.-Paul and Vence as well as visiting Antibes on the coast. Our third route is from Cannes to St.-Tropez, a distance of 47 miles (75 km), and takes in St.-Raphaël, Ste.-Maxime, Port Grimaud, and other beach resorts.

Although our narrative assumes that the reader is driving a car, it is possible to cover the Côte d'Azur by train. The railway line, squeezed between the beach and the coast road, burrows through cliffs and sweeps past bays, offering some pretty remarkable views. The trains also are inexpensive, and they stop at dozens of little stations, which are clean and well-kept with wrought-iron canopies and tubs of flowers. An unexpected plus is that you never have far to walk; Cannes's station, for example, is only 5 minutes from the luxury resorts and beaches of the Croisette.

Despite the Côte d'Azur's extravagant reputation, there is a wide range of accommodations at various prices (except in Monaco, which caters mostly to the well-heeled tourist). In general, you can expect to pay $100 and up (occasionally way up) for a double room in hotels listed as expensive; $60 to $100 in moderate; and under $60 in an inexpensive one. (It is possible to to find perfectly decent rooms for as little as $80, especially in Nice.) The tab for dinner for two might come to about $100 and up in restaurants listed as expensive and from $50 to $100 in moderate; and under $50 in the inexpensive category. A few last caveats: Price ranges do not include wine or drinks (though service usually is included); set *menus* are always more economical than ordering à la carte; and in high season you may need to buy lunch or dinner in order to get a room, called "pension complète" for both meals and "demi-pension" for just one (plus breakfast in both cases).

LES CORNICHES

NICE: For a detailed report on the city, its sights, hotels, and restaurants, see *Nice* in THE CITIES. To start this tour, drive east along the Corniche Inférieure, which skirts the coast and offers many grand views of the sea.

VILLEFRANCHE: The first stop is a town full of steep, old streets with a magnificent backdrop of soaring mountains. Its deep harbor is a safe anchorage for oceangoing cruise ships and naval warships that frequently arrive on courtesy visits (you're quite likely to rub shoulders with sailors from the giant carriers *Nimitz* and *Kennedy* in the town's bars and restaurants). Not to be missed is the 16th-century Citadelle and the Chapelle St.-Pierre, which was decorated in 1957 by Jean Cocteau, the French painter and poet.

   CHECKING IN: *Welcome* – Across from the chapel, it has a fine restaurant, *Le St.-Pierre,* with food prepared in the Escoffier tradition and served on an open terrace overlooking the sea. 32 rooms and parking available. Closed from November 12 through December 20. 1 Quai Courbet, Villefranche (phone: 93-76-76-93). Expensive to moderate.
   Riviera – A comfortable, pleasant hotel where all the rooms have private baths, telephones, and terraces overlooking the sea. 2 Av. Albert-I (phone: 93-76-62-76). Inexpensive.

ST.-JEAN-CAP-FERRAT: Across the water from Villefranche is the wooded peninsula of St.-Jean-Cap-Ferrat, which is reached by turning right onto D25. Cap-Ferrat,
an old fishing port now taken over by pleasure craft, is worth visiting for a look at the
Villa Ephrussi de Rothschild, a museum (on the former property of the late King
Leopold II of Belgium) containing the family's collection of paintings, china, tapestries,
and furniture. Also notable are the botanic garden and zoo. Bd. Denis-Semeria.

CHECKING IN: *Grand Hôtel du Cap Ferrat* – A luxury 57-room hotel right
on the water, with lovely grounds, a beach, tennis, a pool, and indoor and
outdoor restaurants. Isolated, recently remodeled, this is arguably the finest
hotel on the Riviera. Closed from November through April 25. Bd. Général-de-
Gaulle, St.-Jean-Cap-Ferrat (phone: 93-76-00-21). Expensive.

Voile d'Or – This elegant hotel (though a bit on the stuffy side) on the harbor with
a fine restaurant (one Michelin star) features fish specialties, which seems to be
slipping, a heated pool, and superb views of the port. Closed from November
through February. Port de St.-Jean, St.-Jean-Cap-Ferrat (phone: 93-01-13-13).
Expensive.

EATING OUT: *Cappa* – A good yet reasonably priced (for this area) seafood
restaurant overlooking the port. Closed from November through January. Av.
Jean-Mermoz, St.-Jean-Cap-Ferrat (no phone). Expensive.

Le Provençal – The specialties of this beautiful dining spot are the light nouvelle
cuisine dishes. Closed Sunday evenings and Mondays in off-season. 2 Av. D.-Sem-
eria (phone: 93-76-03-97). Moderate.

BEAULIEU-SUR-MER: Leaving St.-Jean-Cap-Ferrat, turn right onto D125, which
takes you into Beaulieu. Protected by the surrounding hills from the cold north winds,
this village is one of the warmest spots on the Riviera. Among the many glamorous
homes built here by wealthy visitors is Villa Kerylos, a beautiful reconstruction of an
ancient Greek dwelling. The villa, which dates from 1900 and is open to the public
(except Mondays), sits on a promontory overlooking the Baie des Fournis and has
magnificent views of Cap-Ferrat, Eze, and Cap-d'Ail.

CHECKING IN/EATING OUT: *Le Métropole* – Reminiscent of an Italian
palazzo, this luxurious, 50-room member of the Relais & Châteaux group has
a private swimming pool, an excellent restaurant that boasts one Michelin star,
and a private helicopter landing pad. 15 Bd. du Maréchal-Leclerc (phone: 93-01-
00-08). Expensive.

La Réserve – Once one of France's top luxury hotels, it has experienced a decline
in recent years (and its restaurant no longer boasts a Michelin star), but it's right
on the sea and has a heated swimming pool. Parking is available. Closed from
November 20 to December 22. 5 Bd. du Général-Leclerc, Beaulieu-sur-Mer
(phone: 93-01-00-01). Expensive.

MONACO: For a complete report on the principality, its sights, hotels, and restaurants, see *Monaco (and Monte Carlo)* in THE CITIES. Leaving Monaco, follow the signs
to Cap-Martin. The road climbs gently, the mountainside becomes more densely
wooded, and it's worth stopping for a moment at one of the bends to look back for some
marvelous views of Monaco and the bay to Cap-d'Ail. Around the cape the road is
flanked by handsome villas with luxuriant gardens of pines, palms, and olive trees.
There are fine views of the bay of Menton on your right as you swing toward Roquebrune.

ROQUEBRUNE: This town merges in to Menton as you follow D52 along the
beachfront. Roquebrune and Menton are also linked historically: They date from about
the 10th century and have been held successively by the Counts of Provence, the

republic of Genoa, and the Grimaldis of Monaco before electing to become part of France in 1793, following the French Revolution. They reverted to the Princes of Monaco under the Treaty of Paris in 1814, and after a short period as free towns, they finally joined France in 1860. The medieval village of Roquebrune is particularly worth a visit, with its steep, narrow passageways and carefully restored castle, the oldest in France. At Rue de la Fontaine and Route de Menton, about 200 yards from the village, is a thousand-year-old olive tree said to be one of the oldest trees in the world. In 1467, survivors of the bubonic plague held performances of a Passion Play here. The town continues that tradition on its esplanade every August 5.

 CHECKING IN/EATING OUT: *Vista Palace* – This luxurious, recently renovated 42-room and 6-suite hotel beautifully set on a cliff has exceptional views of Roquebrune and the coast. A fine restaurant, a pool, gardens, and parking complete the amenities. About 2 miles (3 km) from the center of Roquebrune on the Grande Corniche (phone: 93-35-01-50). Expensive.

Reine d'Azur – A good, simple hotel with 10 rooms. Guests who take their meals here are in for a bargain. Closed from October 16 through January 10. 29 Promenade Cap-Martin (phone: 93-35-76-84). Inexpensive.

MENTON: Like Beaulieu, Menton is protected from the cold northern winds by mountains and as a result has the mildest climate on the Côte d'Azur. Menton's average winter temperature is about 54F (compare 46F for Cannes). Thanks to its warm and sunny climate, Menton and the surrounding region is famous for a profusion of flowers and citrus fruit, especially lemons. The delicate lemon tree (which dies if it freezes) produces fruit year-round; this fecundity is celebrated in the charming *Fêtes du Citron* during February.

Also due to its mild weather, Menton for many years was considered the traditional winter resort for older people; although the character of the town has changed somewhat, it's still a good deal more sedate than Cannes and Nice. In recent years, Menton has become something of a cultural center, with a *Chamber Music Festival* held in August. (For details, inquire at the tourist office at the Palais de l'Europe, Av. Boyer; phone: 93-57-57-00.)

A good way to start a visit is to stroll along the Promenade du Soleil, which runs along the beaches and is lined with luxury hotels (it's a slightly more decorous version of Nice's famous Promenade des Anglais). At the end of the promenade is the *Musée Cocteau* with drawings, paintings, and tapestries by Jean Cocteau. (Open from June 15 to September 15; closed Mondays and Tuesdays.) Continue past the museum along the Quai Napoléon-III for a magnificent view of the Old Town. In the heart of the Old Town, among its many narrow streets, is the Eglise St.-Michel, the finest baroque church in the region, with a beautiful Italianate square in front.

The Rue St.-Michel leads into the pedestrian precinct, just behind the Promenade du Soleil. Close by is the Hôtel de Ville (Town Hall), which has a "marriage room" decorated with murals by Cocteau. The ticket for this includes admission to the *Musée Cocteau.* Not to be missed is the indoor market, which is housed in an old wrought-iron building reminiscent of a Victorian train station.

The centerpiece of the modern town is the Jardin Biovès. With your back to the *Casino Municipal,* the garden is an impressive sight — bordered with plane and palm trees, interspersed with lemon trees. Among the fountains and statues is a memorial commemorating the annexation of Menton and Roquebrune to France in 1793. On the right is the vast Palais d'Europe, which houses the tourist office and is the center of the town's many cultural activities.

 CHECKING IN: *Hôtel Alexandra* – Quiet, and its wonderful view of the mountains and sea that stretches all the way to Italy make this 1950s hotel one of the best places to stay in town. Located at the entrance of the charming Cap

Martin Peninsula at the western end of Menton Bay. 93 Av. Sir Winston Churchill, Roquebrune Cap Martin (phone: 93-35-65-45). Moderate.

Chambord – Here is a pleasant 40-room hostelry overlooking the Jardin Biovès. No restaurant. 6 Av. Boyer, Menton (phone: 93-35-94-19). Moderate.

Pin Doré – A charming 18-room hotel, it has a pool, a bar, and a garden, but no restaurant. Open from December 20 through October 20. 16 Av. Félix-Faure (phone: 93-28-31-00). Moderate to inexpensive.

 EATING OUT: *Petit Port* – This family-run place offers a variety of fish cooked on a wood stove, and is one of the rare eateries to serve grilled sardines. Caen-style tripe is on the menu, reflecting the origins of the owner. Closed Mondays in off-season. Reservations necessary on Saturday evenings. Place de Port (phone: 93-35-82-62). Moderate.

STE.-AGNES: Take D22 out of Menton and head north, following the signs to Ste.-Agnes. The road climbs rapidly and tortuously, offering a magnificent view of the valley. From higher still, you'll see the whole of the Bay of Menton spread out below. After 9 miles (14 km) of this serpentine ascent, you'll enter the medieval village of Ste.-Agnes, which clings precariously to the mountainside. At an altitude of 2,262 feet, it claims to be the highest coastal village in Europe.

This is one of the most unaffected places on the Côte d'Azur. Its steep, cobbled streets contain many shops in which genuine bargains in woolens, ceramics, and leather goods may be found. Essences of lemon and lavender, which are distilled locally, are also sold. As in Menton, Ste.-Agnes has a "marriage room" decorated by Jean Cocteau, located at the *Mairie* (Town Hall).

En Route from Ste.-Agnes – Continue on D22. This is not a road for inexperienced drivers; you'll often have to stop to let other cars get past as the road winds up to an elevation of 2,600 feet at the Col de la Madone. Turn right at D53 into Peille. This town is not as interesting as Ste.-Agnes, but it's worth visiting the 11th-century ramparts and the chapels of St. Joseph and St. Antoine. From the lower part of the village, you have to backtrack the way you came. Don't follow the signs to Nice but continue on D53, which winds down to La Turbie.

LA TURBIE: At 1,575 feet, this is the highest point of the Grande Corniche. The town is best known for its Roman relic, the Trophée des Alpes (Tropea Augusti in Latin), which was built in the 6th century BC to commemorate Augustus Caesar's victory over the Gallic tribes of the region. There are only two structures of this kind still standing (the other is in Romania). The round pillar originally stood 160 feet high and on the base was engraved a list of the 44 conquered tribes. Above, between Doric columns, were statues of the generals who took part in the campaign. The top was surmounted by a statue of Augustus himself, flanked by two prisoners. A large part of the monument was destroyed by the Lombards in the 6th century, and villagers took much of the fallen stone for their houses. From the ruins you can catch some spectacular views (particularly at night) of Monaco and down the coast as far as Bordighera in Italy. The adjacent museum has interesting photographs of the restoration of the area, done some 40 years ago. Both the monument and musuem are open daily except Tuesdays and holidays (phone: 93-41-10-11).

CHECKING IN/EATING OUT: *Le Napoléon* – A comfortable, modernized hotel with 24 rooms, bar, restaurant, and flowered terrace. Closed February 18 to March 20. 7 Av. de la Victoire, La Turbie (phone: 93-41-00-54). Moderate.

Césarée – Modest but pleasant, it has 11 rooms and a terrace restaurant with a panoramic view. Closed December 1 to January 20. 16 Av. Albert-I, La Turbie (phone: 93-41-16-08). Inexpensive.

EZE: Follow the signs to the Moyenne Corniche and the village of Eze. Perched like an eagle's nest (1,300 feet) on the mountainside, this ancient settlement is famous for its vertiginous views of the sea — you can even see Corsica on a clear day. Aside from its breathtaking setting, Eze is mostly notable for its 14th-century Chapelle des Penitents-Blancs, which contains a fine Catalan crucifix dating to 1258 as well as several paintings and enamels of the crucifixion.

This completes the first route on the Côte d'Azur.

CHECKING IN/EATING OUT: *Château de la Chèvre d'Or* – This restored medieval manor house, in the heart of the village with splendid views of the sea, is a member of the Relais & Châteaux group. It has 13 rooms, a pool, and a dining room that offers classic French cuisine rating one Michelin star. Hotel closed from November to March; restaurant closed Wednesdays and from December to March. (See also "Romantic Hostelries" in *For the Experience,* DIVERSIONS). Rue du Barri, Eze (phone: 93-41-12-12). Expensive.

Château Eza – Once the residence of Prince William of Sweden, this 7-room hostelry offers splendid views of the Mediterranean (you actually can see St.-Tropez on a clear day) and a luxurious decor that more than make up for the overpriced food at its one-star restaurant. All of the rooms have private baths, mini-bar, and color TV; there also are 2 suites with fireplaces. Hotel and restaurant are closed from October 31 through April 1. Eze (phone: 93-41-12-24). Expensive.

NICE-CANNES ROUND TRIP

The next portion of this route is a loop between Nice and Cannes. Turn right out of Eze on D46, which winds up the mountain to rejoin the Grande Corniche. From here descend back into Nice. Leave Nice by the Promenade des Anglais and follow the coast road (N98) west to Cros-de-Cagnes (just past the airport and *Cap 3000,* a vast shopping center which is worth a visit). Follow the signs through Cagnes-Ville (the modern town) to Haut-de-Cagnes.

CAGNES-SUR-MER: This includes the medieval village of Haut-de-Cagnes, perched on a hillside covered with olive, citrus, cypress, and palm trees, a mile back from the sea; Cros-de-Cagnes, the somewhat tacky coastal strip; and Cagnes-Ville, the mundane modern neighborhood.

Head straight for the castle in the old village, which dates from the early 14th century and whose history has been dominated by the ubiquitous Grimaldi family. The castle museum — an old olive oil mill — has rooms devoted to several dissimilar subjects: the history and cultivation of the olive tree; a trompe l'oeil ceiling fresco of the *Fall of Phaeton* by the Genoese artist Carlone; and paintings by 20th-century artists who lived near the Mediterranean, including Marc Chagall and Raoul Dufy. The museum (closed Tuesdays and from October 15 through November 15) also is the home of the *Cagnes International Festival of Painting,* held during July, August, and September. In the castle precincts are a number of bars and restaurants, one of which, *Jimmy's,* is a good place to stop for a refreshing drink or snack. In Haut-de-Cagnes there are some interesting nightclubs (both gay and straight).

Les Collettes, the house where Pierre-Auguste Renoir lived for the last 12 years of his life, is on Avenue des Collettes in Cagnes-Ville (phone: 93-20-61-07). His studio on the first floor has been left just as it was and in the garden is his magnificent bronze statue of Venus. (Closed Tuesdays and from October 15 to November 15.) There also is a race track, *Hippodrome de la Côte d'Azur,* near the sea, that is open from December to March and in August and September. Blvd. Kennedy, Cagnes sur Mer (phone: 93-20-30-30).

ST.-PAUL-DE-VENCE: From Cagnes-sur-Mer follow D36 and D2 to St.-Paul. Half-way between Cagnes and Vence, it is set in olive groves with splendid views on all sides: to the north are the Alps, and to the south, the Mediterranean and Cap-d'Antibes. The town is enclosed by massive ramparts arranged in the form of an acropolis. A single cannon, which guards the entrance, is named Lacan and dates from the battle of Cerisilles in 1544.

The town is something of an artists colony (Modigliani, Bonnard, Soutine, and Chagall lived here) and is filled with studios, boutiques, and galleries. Don't miss the *Fondation Maeght,* a museum with one of the finest collections of contemporary art in France. Within the house, courtyard, and garden are beautifully displayed works by Braque, Chagall, Kandinsky, Miró, Giacometti, Bonnard, Dérain, Matisse, Bazaine, and many other artists. Special exhibitions featuring various other artists are also presented during the year as well as films, ballet, and poetry recitals. The building itself is worth a visit. For details, contact the tourist office on Rue Grande (phone: 93-32-86-95).

Also worth a stop is the Eglise St.-Paul-de-Vence, a 12th- and 13th-century church whose collection includes such treasures as a painting of St. Catherine of Alexandria by Tintoretto and a 15th-century alabaster Madonna.

CHECKING IN: *La Colombe d'Or* – Famous for its remarkable art collection — works by Miró, Calder, Picasso, Chagall, and others — this once sumptuous small hotel has begun to show its age. It has 24 rooms, a pool, and a terrace restaurant. Closed from mid-November to mid-December. 1 Pl. du Général-de-Gaulle, St.-Paul-de-Vence (phone: 93-32-80-02). Expensive.

Mas d'Artigny – This modern luxury hotel (a member of the Relais & Châteaux group) has 59 balconied bedrooms and 25 villas, each with a private patio and a pool, as well as tennis courts, air conditioning, and parking. The restaurant, with one Michelin star, serves fine seafood; try the *bourride de baudroie provençale.* Rte. de la Colle, D7, and des Hauts de St.-Paul, St.-Paul-de-Vence (phone: 93-32-84-54). Expensive.

Le Hameau – A pleasant hostelry in a garden setting, it has 16 reasonably priced rooms but no restaurant. Closed from mid-November through mid-December, and mid-January to mid-February. 528 Rte. de la Colle, D7, St.-Paul-de-Vence (phone: 93-32-80-24). Moderate.

EATING OUT: *Le Bougainvillier* – The specialties of this fine establishment include quail dishes, terrines, and fish casseroles. Closed November. 7 Rempart Ouest, St.-Paul-de-Vence (phone: 93-32-89-30). Moderate.

La Marmite – Good food in a pleasant environment; the service also is good. Closed Sundays, Mondays, and the month of January. Rue Grande, St.-Paul-de-Vence (phone: 93-32-92-49). Moderate.

VENCE: This picturesque Roman town on a plateau at 1,400 feet is separated from the sea by low, wooded hills and has fine views of the mountains. Unlike St.-Paul, Vence has spread out into a complex tangle of suburbs, but don't be put off: Head straight for the old walled town. Take note of the 10th-century cathedral, with handsomely carved choir stalls and a Chagall mosaic of Moses parting the waters; the urn-shaped fountain in the Place du Peyra, on the site of the old Roman Forum; and the Chapelle du Rosaire, which was cleverly designed by Matisse so that the sunlight streaming through its luminous stained glass windows creates striking patterns on the white ceramic walls. Open Tuesdays and Thursdays; closed November to mid-December (phone: 93-58-03-26). For tourist information, stop in at Place Grand-Jardin (phone: 93-58-06-38).

CHECKING IN: *Château du Domaine St.-Martin* – A posh place filled with antique furniture and tapestries, it is perched on a hillside amid 35 acres of parkland and has 17 bedrooms and 10 villas, a pool, and tennis courts. Its restaurant was awarded one Michelin star in 1990. Closed mid-November to mid-March. Rte. de Coursegoules, Vence (phone: 93-58-02-02). Expensive.

Auberge des Seigneurs – This comfortable and atmospheric old Provençal inn has 9 rooms and a good restaurant. Closed from mid-October through December 1. Pl. du Frene, Vence (phone: 93-58-04-24). Moderate.

Closerie des Genets – It's small (11 rooms and 2 suites) and quiet, with a terrace, garden, and restaurant. Closed from mid-November through December 18. 4 Av. M.-Maurel, Vence (phone: 93-58-33-25). Moderate.

La Roseraie – A restored 12-room manor house that is comfortably furnished in Provençal style, with gardens and a restaurant featuring the cuisine of southwest France. Closed Tuesdays, Wednesdays, and the month of January. Av. Henri-Girard, Vence (phone: 93-58-02-20). Moderate.

 EATING OUT: Les Portiques – This small bistro in the Old Town has a reputation for fine food and service. Closed Tuesdays and August. Reservations necessary. 6 Rue St.-Véran, Vence (phone: 93-58-36-31). Moderate.

En Route from Vence – Take D2210, which winds west through lushly wooded countryside with views of the Gorges du Loup unfolding on your right. Stop at the medieval village of Tourrette-sur-Loup to visit the 15th-century church for its triptych by Bréa and the Chapelle St.-Jean for its frescoes rendered in the naïf style by Ralph Soupault. As you approach Pont-du-Loup, there's a fabulous view of the waterfalls streaming from the heart of the mountain hundreds of feet above. The town has many artists and artisans' shops. The road climbs out of Pont-du-Loup past the ruins of the old railroad viaduct, which was destroyed in 1944. Two miles (3 km) farther is the village of Le Bar-sur-Loup, set among orange terraces and jasmine and violet fields, which supply ingredients for the perfume factory on your right. A fine view of the Gorges du Loup and the hills behind Vence can be seen from the porch of the Eglise St.-Jacques. At Le Pré du Lac, at the junction of D2210 and D2085, turn right for Grasse, 4 miles (6 km) down the road.

GRASSE: The very name of this city is synonymous with perfume. Three out of four bottles of perfume sold in the world contain essences distilled here. Ten thousand tons of flowers (jasmine, mimosa, and lavender) are used every year by the three major manufacturers, Fragonard, Galimard, and Molinard. Guided factory tours are given; visitors may observe how perfumes are still made in the traditional manner and watch the master perfumer (usually called *le nez* — the nose) blending essences. Each factory has its own museum and welcomes visitors. Details are available from the tourist office on Place de la Foux, on your right as you enter town (phone: 93-36-03-56) or call the factory direct: Fragonard, 93-36-44-65; Galimard, 93-36-08-21; Molinard, 93-36-01-62.

Also of interest is the Old Town, which has hardly changed since the 18th century. Here is the Cathédrale Notre-Dame-du-Puy, which dates from the 12th century and contains paintings by Rubens as well as a fine tryptych by Louis Bréa; the *Fragonard Villa*, a museum honoring the painter Jean-Honoré Fragonard (closed Mondays and November); and the *Musée d'Art et Histoire de Provence*, which is housed in an 18th-century mansion and contains exhibits on the art and history of Provence from prehistory to the end of the 19th century (closed Saturdays, the second and third Sundays of each month, and November). The *Musée de la Marine* (Hôtel Particulier Pontèves–Morel; phone: 93-09-10-71) has an interesting collection of 18th-century model boats. Closed Saturdays and Sundays, and the month of November.

 EATING OUT: Maître Boscq – Authentic regional cuisine and M. Boscq's warm welcome await diners at this small eatery in the Old Town. Closed Sundays and the month of November. 13 Rue de la Fontette, Grasse (phone: 93-36-45-76). Inexpensive.

MOUGINS: This quiet old village (12,000 people) perched on a hilltop retains little of its early fortifications except a 15th-century gate. At nearby Notre-Dame-de-Vie is the house where Picasso spent his last years. Mougins is known mostly for its fine restaurants (which have a total of six Michelin stars), so it's the place to stop if you've a taste for some rich and elaborate food. Three miles (5 km) from Mougins on the road to Cannes (N85) is an interesting vintage car museum, *Musée de l'Automobile* (722 Chemin de Font-de-Currault).

EATING OUT: *L'Amandier de Mougins* – Roger Vergé's "other" restaurant, which serves simpler and somewhat less expensive food worthy of one Michelin star, is in a former olive oil mill. The standouts here are the appetizers — foie gras with raisins, marinated salmon and sea bass with dill and coriander, and an array of courses incorporating the delicious local cheeses and fruits. Closed Wednesdays, and Thursday afternoons. Reservations necessary. Pl. du Commandant-Lamy, Mougins (phone: 93-90-00-91). Expensive.

Le Moulin de Mougins – Also set in a 16th-century olive oil mill, accented with exotic plants outside and paintings within, this is one of the most famous restaurants in France, with three Michelin stars. Chef Roger Vergé's specialties include zucchini stuffed with truffles, lobster and artichoke salad, fresh *palangre* (a Mediterranean fish) in a light tomato and basil sauce, noisettes of Alpine lamb, and filet of duck in margaux wine. Desserts make delicious use of fresh fruit: peaches and melon, cold wild strawberry soufflé, and lavender ice cream. The restaurant also has 5 delightful suites (book ahead) and a cooking school (see *Learning the Culinary Arts,* DIVERSIONS). Closed Mondays, Thursday afternoons from the end of January to the beginning of April, and mid-November through December 23. Reservations necessary. Notre-Dame-de-Vie, southeast 1 mile (1.6 km) via D3, Mougins (phone: 93-75-78-24). Expensive.

Le Bistrot de Mougins – Good food at reasonable prices is the keynote at this cheery little bistro. Closed Tuesdays, Wednesdays, and from December 4 through January 15. Pl. du Village, Mougins (phone: 93-75-78-34). Moderate.

CANNES: For a detailed report on the city, its sights, hotels, and restaurants, see *Cannes* in THE CITIES.

En Route from Cannes – A pleasant excursion would be to the nearby Iles de Lérins. Boats also leave from Golfe-Juan and Antibes; information on boat service may be obtained by calling 93-39-11-82. The trip takes half a day, including stops at Ile Ste.-Marguerite, fragrant with eucalyptus and pine forests, and at Ile St.-Honorat, the site of an ancient fortified monastery. It is said that the legendary "Man in the Iron Mask" was imprisoned on Ste.-Marguerite in the Fort de l'Ile; however, his identity remains the subject of much debate.

Another possible excursion is to Vallauris (take D803), known as a pottery center and the home of the *Biennial International Festival of Ceramic Art.* (For details, contact the tourist office at 93-63-82-58 or the Palais des *Festivals et des Congrès* at 93-39-24-53.) Picasso spent several years here working in clay and in 1952 was asked by the town council to decorate the chapel of the local priory. The resulting fresco, called *War and Peace,* can be seen at the *Musée National La Guerre et La Paix* (phone: 93-64-18-05). Along the Avenue Georges Clemençeau, there are a number of pottery shops, including the *L'Atelier Madoura,* that still sell some of Picasso's ceramics.

A mile (1.6 km) down the road (D135) from Vallauris is the old fishing port of Golfe-Juan, now mostly given over to pleasure craft and popular for water sports of all kinds. It has good, sandy beaches; there's a sailing school and club that holds regular regattas; and wind surfing and water skiing are easily arranged. The town has historical as well as sporting associations. A plaque on the quayside commemorates Napoleon's landing here on March 1, 1815. He chose this spot for his return from exile on Elba because Cap d'Antibes and the headland of the Croisette provided protection from the guns of the forts of Antibes and Cannes. The South of France was Royalist territory, so Napoleon quickly headed north, on what later became known as the famous Route Napoléon, with his small army of 1,200 men.

Along the seafront, Golfe Juan merges imperceptibly into Juan-les-Pins, which comes alive in the summer, its cafés and discos throbbing with activity and young people. The nightlife centers mostly around the casino, which is in a cool garden just set back from the sea. In July, a *World Jazz Festival* is held in the Palace of Congresses and outside among the pine trees. For details on this and other events, contact the tourist office (phone: 93-61-04-98).

 CHECKING IN: *Juana* – An excellent location just 100 yards from the beach affords most of the rooms of this elegant hotel lovely sea views. Its restaurant, *La Terrasse,* has two Michelin stars. Closed from November until 10 days before *Easter* each year. Av. G. Gallice, Juan-les-Pins (phone: 93-61-08-70). Expensive.

Astoria – This newly renovated, comfortable 55-room hotel is one of the few in the area that is open all year. 15 Av. Maréchal-Joffre, Juan-les-Pins (phone: 93-61-23-65). Moderate.

Mimosas – A small (36 rooms), pleasant hostelry in a garden setting. There is a swimming pool, and parking is available. Closed October through March. Rue Pauline, Juan-les-Pins (phone: 93-61-04-16). Moderate.

EATING OUT: *Tétou* – Grilled lobster and bouillabaisse are good choices here. Closed from October 20 through December 20 and March 1 through March 29. Bd. des Frères-Roustan, on the beach, Golfe-Juan (phone: 93-63-71-16). Expensive.

Le Bistro du Port – A great place for steaks or broiled fish. Closed Sunday evenings and Mondays, and December through January. 53 Bd. des Frères-Roustan, Golfe-Juan (phone: 93-63-70-64). Moderate.

On the seafront in Juan-les-Pins, there are restaurants and cafés every few yards, each with its own section of beach.

CAP D'ANTIBES: Cap d'Antibes is one of the most exclusive spots on the Côte d'Azur, where the sun is worshiped in utter luxury. For a beautiful drive, follow D2559 around the cape from Juan-les-Pins and ignore the "direct to Antibes" signs. Lovely villas line the approach to Cap d'Antibes, a peninsula covered with lush pine forests and rocky creeks (*calanques*). Take a few minutes to walk around the *Hôtel du Cap d'Antibes* (see *Checking In*) or enjoy a drink on the terrace or swim at the leafy pool of the *Hôtel Résidence du Cap;* the experience will convince you that Cap d'Antibes deserves its romantic reputation. After your feet touch the ground again, the *Musée Naval et Napoléonien* (Batterie du Grillon) is worth a look for its memorabilia of Napoleon's landing at Golfe-Juan, as is the Jardin Thuret, a 10-acre botanic garden established in 1856 to introduce tropical vegetation to the surrounding area.

CHECKING IN: *Cap d'Antibes* – Over the years this grand and exclusive luxury hotel (also known as *Hôtel du Cap*) has welcomed many celebrities and is said to be the hotel described by F. Scott Fitzgerald in *Tender Is the Night.* Set above the rocks, it has gorgeous grounds and views, 130 handsomely decorated bedrooms, a swimming pool, a tennis court, and a well-known restaurant, the *Pavillon Eden Roc.* (See also *Romantic French Hostelries,* DIVERSIONS.) Closed mid-October to end of April. Bd. Kennedy, Cap d'Antibes (phone: 93-61-39-01 or 93-61-39-01). Expensive.

Gardiole – This simple, quiet hotel among the pines has 20 rooms, some of which face the sea. Closed November 5 to February 28. Chemin de la Garoupe, Cap d'Antibes (phone: 93-61-35-03). Moderate.

EATING OUT: *Bacon* – Here on a terrace overlooking the sea, diners may choose bouillabaisse or excellent fresh fish from a menu that has been awarded one Michelin star. Closed Sunday evenings and from mid-November through January. Reservations necessary. Bd. de Bacon, Cap d'Antibes, right on the northeastern point of the cape as you approach the town of Antibes (phone: 93-61-50-02). Expensive.

ANTIBES: Antibes is one of the oldest settlements on the Côte d'Azur. Originally called Antipolis, the city was founded by the Greeks in the 4th century BC and quickly developed into an important port of trade between Marseilles and Italy. Several centuries later, Antibes proved valuable to the Kings of France for its strategic military position on the border of Savoy, and from approximately the 15th to the 17th century they built and rebuilt its fortifications. (Of these efforts, only Fort Carré, just to the north of the harbor, and some of the ramparts along the seafront remain.) Still later, during the French Revolution, the city was Napoleon's base when as general he was made responsible for the defense of the southern coast; after the downfall of Robespierre in 1794, Napoleon was imprisoned at Fort Carré.

Nowadays, Antibes has a more tranquil reputation as a center for commercial flower production; primarily roses and carnations are cultivated. The town also is notable for its *Musée Picasso,* a collection of some of the artist's best paintings and drawings as well as a fabulous selection of his ceramics. The museum is in the Château Grimaldi, a castle in the Old Town built in the 12th century and rebuilt in the 16th century. (No admission charge on Wednesdays; closed Tuesdays and November; details from the tourist office at Place du Château; phone: 93-34-95-91.) Just behind the Château Grimaldi is the marketplace (Cours Masséna), where the townspeople buy their fish, cheese, fruit, and vegetables — a walk through here and the Old Town, which buzzes with activity all year, and along the city ramparts are a must.

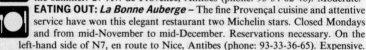

CHECKING IN: *Mas Djoliba* – This small, quiet hotel with 13 rooms has a beautiful park setting right in the center of town. Half-board is required during the summer. 27 Av. de Provence, Antibes (phone: 93-34-02-48). Moderate.

EATING OUT: *La Bonne Auberge* – The fine Provençal cuisine and attentive service have won this elegant restaurant two Michelin stars. Closed Mondays and from mid-November to mid-December. Reservations necessary. On the left-hand side of N7, en route to Nice, Antibes (phone: 93-33-36-65). Expensive.

L'Armoise – A tiny, utterly charming restaurant serving inventive fare. Closed Wednesday nights during off-season, and from mid-November to mid-December. 2 Rue de la Touraque, Antibes (phone: 93-34-71-10). Expensive to moderate.

La Famiglia – Authentic Italian dishes excellently prepared in a friendly atmosphere. Closed Wednesdays. 34 Av. Thiers, Antibes (phone: 93-34-60-82). Inexpensive.

L'Oursin – Although its setting is rather plain, this popular little eatery has the best seafood in the downtown area. Reservations necessary; closed Sunday evenings, Mondays, and July 23 to August 26. 16 Rue de la République, Antibes (phone: 93-34-13-46). Inexpensive.

En Route from Antibes – A few miles along the coast (N7 or N98), perched on a hilltop, is Biot, a village renowned for its ceramics. It was founded by Greeks and Romans, and in the 13th century was fortified by Templars. At the Biot Glassworks (reached via D4), visitors can watch glass blowing or buy the finished article. Also off D4 and worth visiting is the *Musée Fernand Léger,* devoted entirely to the work of this artist — paintings, mosaics, and sculptures. Route N98 will take you back to Nice via the coast.

CANNES–ST.-TROPEZ ROUND TRIP

As one drives along the coast between Cannes and St.-Tropez, the seascapes become incredibly vast and beautiful. It's a good idea to take the autoroute (A8) west through the mountains and then to return to Cannes along the coast road, stopping at the beach resorts of Ste.-Maxime, Fréjus, and St.-Raphaël along the way. With the sea on your right, the views are even more magnificent. From A8, exit at Le Muy and cross the Massif des Maures via D25 to Ste.-Maxime, or stay on A8 for another 12 miles (19 km), take the exit at Le Cannet des Maures, and strike south on D558. This road climbs up the steep mountains to La Garde-Freinet, then winds down through the delightful village of Grimaud and connects with the coast road to St.-Tropez.

LA GARDE-FREINET: Surrounded by cork forests and perched on the crest of the Massif des Maures, this little town is notable for its ruined, allegedly Saracen castle, abandoned in the 10th century. From here there's a fine view out to sea.

EATING OUT: *La Faücado* – This attractive terrace restaurant has a magnificent view of the wooded valley below and offers a fine set menu at lunchtime. Truffles and mushrooms are specialties. Closed Fridays in off-season, and from mid-January to mid-February. 31 Bd. de l'Esplanade, La Garde-Freinet (phone: 94-43-60-41). Moderate.

PORT GRIMAUD: Stop here for a look at this modern replica of an old-fashioned Provençal fishing village designed by François Spoerry. The architect's grand concept provided for the traditional main square; connecting canals; privately owned homes, each with its own mooring; the usual complement of shops, a church, and such.

CHECKING IN/EATING OUT: *Giraglia* – A comfortable lodging in a lakeside setting, it has a pool and a fine restaurant, *L'Amphitrite.* Closed October to April. Pl. du 14-Juin, Port Grimaud (phone: 94-56-31-33). Expensive.

ST.-TROPEZ: For a detailed report on the city, its sights, hotels, and restaurants, see *St.-Tropez* in THE CITIES.

En Route from St.-Tropez – Although the heart of the Côte d'Azur more or less ends at St.-Tropez, the scenery found in the region to the west is still quite dazzling. Before you start back to Cannes, we suggest a short detour in this direction along the coast road or a visit to Ramatuelle, 8 miles (12 km) from St.-Tropez, a picturesque medieval village with a magnificent view of the whole St.-Tropez peninsula. To head for the coast, drive west on N98 and D559 toward Cavalaire-sur-Mer for a view of its dramatic high cliffs and expansive seascapes. Farther west on D559 is Le Lavandou, a former fishing village that is now a resort with fine sandy beaches. From here, a boat may be taken to the Iles d'Hyères — Porquerolles, Port Cros, and Levant — where you may swim, sunbathe, picnic, bicycle, or walk among the fragrant pine and eucalyptus. (For details about boat schedules, call 94-71-01-02.) Still farther west (N559 to D41) is Bormes-les-Mimosas, a charming old village set on a steep hill among pine, eucalyptus, and mimosa and overlooking the sea; it's another departure point for the Iles d'Hyères as well as offering sandy beaches and a marina. From here, turn right on the mountain road, N98, and go back to St.-Tropez.

STE.-MAXIME: Ten miles (16 km) east along the coast road (N98) from St.-Tropez (which can be seen across the gulf) is Ste.-Maxime, a quiet seaside resort popular with young families. It has a fine sand beach, plenty of water sports, and the marina is always busy with pleasure craft. Follow the signs 1 mile (1.6 km) north (via Bd. Bellevue) to the Sémaphore, at an altitude of 400 feet, for a sensational view of the coast and the mountains. East of Ste.-Maxime, past the Cap des Sardinaux, is La Nartelle, where the Allies landed in August 1944. From here to St.-Aygulf are a number of small beach resorts, including Vald'Esquières, San Peïre, Les Calanques, and Les Issambres.

 CHECKING IN: *Calidianus* – A simple hotel with 33 comfortable rooms, beach, tennis courts, and pool, but no restaurant. Open year-round. Bd. Jean-Moulin, Ste.-Maxime (phone: 94-96-23-21). Moderate.

 EATING OUT: *La Gruppi* – Excellently prepared fish and seafood dishes, and friendly service. Closed Mondays. Av. du Charles-de-Gaulle, Ste.-Maxime (phone: 94-96-03-61). Expensive.

FRÉJUS: Founded by Julius Caesar in 49 BC, as Forum Julii, Fréjus was an important Roman naval base, with a population of 40,000 and a large inland harbor connected to the sea by canal. By the Middle Ages the port had declined in importance and gradually became occluded from the sea. Outbreaks of plague in the 14th century and endemic malaria caused the inhabitants to abandon the Roman site, and by 1780 the population had declined to 2,000. Today, Fréjus consists of two entities: Fréjus Plage, 3 miles of magnificent sandy beach that blend into that of St.-Raphaël; and the Old Town, which is now about a mile from the sea and a treasure trove of both Roman remains and medieval buildings, all of which can be visited. Among the former are some fortifications, houses, and baths as well as a huge amphitheater with space for 10,000 people (there are bullfights here in July and August; closed Tuesdays). Also noteworthy is the episcopal quarter, which was built in the Middle Ages on a small area of the Roman site; it consists of a cathedral with a 4th-century baptistry (one of the oldest ecclesiastical buildings in France) and magnificent cloisters. Try to visit the *Museé Archéologique* just behind the cloisters; it contains some splendid Roman mosaics, a marble statue of the god Hermès, and a 1st-century BC bust of Jupiter. For details on hours and tours, contact the tourist office in the Place Calvini (next to the cathedral; phone: 94-51-53-87) or from *Easter* to September at Fréjus-Plage (Bd. Liberation; phone: 94-51-48-42).

 CHECKING IN: *Les Résidences du Colombier* – It's a quiet hotel with individual bungalows designed in the Provençal style and set among pine trees in a private park. It has a restaurant, beach, and tennis facilities. Rte. de Bagnols, Fréjus (phone: 94-51-45-92). Moderate.

 EATING OUT: *Vieux Four* – Regional cuisine is stylishly served at this restaurant in an old wine cellar close to the cathedral. Closed Sunday afternoons, Mondays, the first 2 weeks in November, and in February. 57 Rue de Grisolle, Fréjus (phone: 94-51-56-38). Moderate.

ST.-RAPHAËL: The sister town to Fréjus, it also was founded by the Romans, although no ruins of their occupation remain. A pyramid on the harbor (Av. Commandant-Guilbaud) commemorates Napoleon's return to France from his Egyptian campaign; he landed here in 1790 and was dispatched from here in 1814 to exile on Elba. From the promenade along the water can be seen the reddish, offshore twin rocks called Lion de Terre and Lion de Mer (Land Lion and Sea Lion).

While less frenetic than St.-Tropez, St.-Raphaël is a very pretty and popular resort. In addition to its splendid beach and marina, the town has a full and varied program of cultural and sports events from February right through to November. Visit the tourist information office near the train station on Rue Rousseau for details (phone: 94-95-16-87). The *Museum of Underwater Archaeology* (Av. de Valescure) has an important collection of amphorae dug up in the area by diving club members. Closed Sundays off-season and Tuesdays in-season.

CHECKING IN: *La Potinière* – This quiet, modern hotel set in a garden has 25 rooms with balconies and is near the beach. Closed from mid-November to mid-December. Av. des Plaines, at Boulouris, 3 miles (5 km) along the N98 to Cannes (phone: 94-95-21-43). Moderate.

En Route from St.-Raphaël – During this last leg east along the Corniche de l'Estérel to Cannes (some 27 miles/43 km) the views are breathtaking, so drive slowly. You'll pass through the resorts of Boulouris, Le Dramont, Camp Long, Agay, Anthéor, Le Trayas, Miramar, Théoule, and La Napoule, all with marvelous sand beaches. You even might discover some tiny hidden strands if you scramble down the rocky cliffs from the road. As you pass the Pointe de l'Aiguiulle, just before Théoule, the coastline softens into the magnificent Gulf of Napoule, with Cannes to the northeast.

CHECKING IN: *Loews* – A luxury hotel right on the beach in the town of Mandelieu, it has a heated pool and a good restaurant, *Chez Loulou,* done up as a yacht. Open all year. Bd. Henri-Clews, Mandelieu (phone: 93-49-90-00). Expensive.

Sainte-Christophe – Just a few miles from Miramar and Théoule-sur-Mer, this 40-room hostelry is isolated among pine trees and red rocks on the L'Esterel Corniche. Rooms have TV sets, a balcony or a terrace, with garden or sea view. It has 2 restaurants specializing in fish, a private beach, a small pool, and a spectacular view. Corniche D'Or, 47 Av. De Miramar, Miramar Par Théoulle (phone: 93-75-41-36). Expensive.

EATING OUT: *L'Orangerie* – A kitschy dining room, with an excellent menu, a Provence wine list, and lots of flowers. Closed Sunday lunch, Mondays, and the last 2 weeks in October and January. Promenade R. Coty (phone: 94-83-10-50). Moderate to inexpensive.

Pastorel – Considered by most to be the best in St.-Raphaël, this charming place has consistently good food, nice wines, and great service. Closed Sunday dinner, Mondays, mid-November to mid-December, and for Monday lunch during August. 54 Rue de la Liberté (phone: 94-95-02-36). Moderate to inexpensive.

The Alps

Waterfalls crashing over rocks, glacial streams racing through valleys enclosed by snow-capped mountains, pine forests alluring as sirens, meadows of gentian and edelweiss, a dizzying array of breathtaking vistas and of pass after vertiginous pass — rev up those eyes and fasten those seatbelts, you're in the Alps.

Most travelers in the Alps find little need for volumes on culture and history. Goggling at the magnificent scenery, skiing, fishing, swimming, and pursuing other pastimes usually replace any preoccupation with Roman ruins, medieval ramparts, and the like. However, there is more to this region than just wildflowers and ski resorts, even if it is known to most people as the home of Mont-Blanc, one of the highest peaks (15,771 feet) in Europe.

Made up of two ancient provinces, Dauphiné and Savoie, the French Alps are bordered by Italy and Switzerland and, to the north and west for about 200 miles, by the Rhône River. The Dauphiné, occupying the southern half of the high Alps and taking in the offical *départements* of Hautes-Alpes, Isère, and Drôme, belonged first to the kingdoms of Provence and Arles and then to the Holy Roman Empire. It came under French control without violence fairly early, when it was sold to France by the pious and profligate King Humbert II of Dauphiné in 1349.

Savoie, on the other hand, because of its position astride many militarily and commercially important mountain passes, was the object of repeated assaults by countries who wanted to control the area not so much for its own sake but for the potential access to the land of the enemy. Ruled first by the kingdom of Burgundy, then Arles, then made part of the Holy Roman Empire, in the 11th century it was consolidated with other fiefdoms under Humbert the White-handed, who founded the House of Savoie. Over the years, through marriage and acquisition, Savoie became a powerful duchy that governed parts of France, Italy, and Switzerland. In the 16th century, the ducal seat was moved to Turin, making Savoie Italian rather than French, and in the 18th century, it became part of the kingdom of Sardinia. A plebiscite was held in 1860 to determine if the Savoyards wished to be returned to France or stay with Italy. The vote was overwhelming: 130,533 for France, 235 for Italy; and the subsequent Treaty of Turin ceded the region to France.

Today the French Alps have a very special character of their own. The people are feisty, industrious, and laconic — the Gallic equivalent of New Englanders. They speak a regional *patois* (dialect) that can confound the unsuspecting traveler: They pronounce words ending in *oz* or *az* as if those last two letters didn't exist; e.g., Sierroz is *Sierre;* Clusaz, *Cluse;* and so on.

The Alpine cuisine is straightforward, hearty, healthy. Regional menus feature many kinds of freshwater fish — trout, pike, carp — as well as ham, sausage, and wild game. Crayfish and wild mushrooms (*morilles*) are two favorite delicacies. Several excellent cheeses are produced, including *chèvre* (goat cheese); *reblochon,* a creamy, mild cheese; *tomme de Savoie,* also mild; and *beaufort,* a type of gruyère. The wines of the region marry well with the cuisine; the sparkling white wine seyssel is considered one of the best. The liqueurs, gentian (flavored with the flower) and the famous chartreuse, are interesting finales to dinner; also try the local marc de Savoie, made from the residue that remains after brandy is 'pressed. (But beware, this is a sneaky potion, much like tequila in its aftereffects.)

The Alps have two important seasons — both summer and winter — when thousands of tourists come to enjoy the beauty and majesty of the mountains. At the risk of stating the obvious, winter is not a time for touring but rather for skiing, hiking, and other Alpine sports. The major mountain passes generally are closed, the weather is unpredictable, and the roads get treacherous. The tour that's laid out here is designed for summertime, when most of the highest roads are open. (Even in July, some mountain passes such as the Col de l'Iseran can be closed, so be sure to inquire before you set out.)

Another precaution would be to check your car, especially its tire pressure and suspension. On the road, you'll notice that when people are asked for distance and directions, they answer in hours, not miles (or kilometers); mileage is irrelevant on these winding mountain roads that require special attention and careful driving. Also be aware of the peculiar French habit of occasionally ignoring center lines in taking hairpin curves.

The suggested tour of the French Alps forms an extended oval, starting in the extreme north at Lake Geneva (Lac Léman), going through the eastern side of the Alps, passing along the southern part of Dauphiné through Gap. It then moves back up the western ridge of the Alps, through the parks of Vercors and Chartreuse, through Grenoble, and ends up in the idyllic lakeside city of Annecy. Lovely villages and spectacular views are so abundant that it is impossible to begin to capture them all; if you take an alternate route, you can hardly go wrong.

The Tarentaise Valley in Savoie, home to some of the area's most famous ski resorts (Courcheval, Val d'Isère, and Tignes), will host the *1992 Winter Olympics*. Already a plus to visitors this year is the increase in the number of lodgings and sports facilities, and the improvement to the roads and highways to facilitate access to the Olympic sites.

A caveat: In a way, the Alps are too beautiful. They attract hordes of tourists, and during the high season, it is easy to be put off by the disappointing lack of tranquility and by the sheer volume of people just like yourself. The best way to deal with this is to visit off-season or to seek out the lesser-known areas. For example, Vercors, on the western side of the Alps, is not as famous as Chamonix or Val d'Isère, but it is also very beautiful.

The Alps traditionally have been heavily developed for the tourist trade, so there's a plethora of hotel rooms in every price range. In general, you can expect to pay $100 and up for a double room listed as expensive; between $60 and $90 in the moderate category; and less than $50 for an inexpensive room.

Dinner for two with wine in a restaurant listed as expensive will cost $85 or more; from $60 to $80, moderate; and below $50, inexpensive. Prices do not include aperitifs or after-dinner drinks, but service usually is included.

EVIAN-LES-BAINS: About two-thirds of the southern coast of Lake Geneva belongs to France, and its principal city is Evian-les-Bains, a familiar name because of the drinking water that takes its name from the town. Before the discovery of the health-restoring properties of its waters in the 19th century, Evian-les-Bains was a tiny fortified city. While traces of the pre-spa city remain (three towers, remnants of the city walls, a few old buildings), what Evian really has to offer is not the quaintness of the Middle Ages but the grandeur of the Belle Epoque. Though no longer only for the very rich, it looks as if it were, with an elegant casino, opulent hotels, exquisitely manicured gardens, and a long lakefront promenade. Every May the *Rencontres Musicales d'Evian,* a well-known music festival, takes place at the casino. The festival includes a competition for string quartets (phone: 50-75-03-78).

Stroll along the boulevards or the promenade, treat yourself to a drink or dinner in one of the hotels, perhaps the *Royal Evian* (see *Checking In*), and drift into Marcel Proust's world of idleness and wealth. Proust, who stayed at the now-defunct *Splendid* at the turn of the century, fashioned his "Balbec baths" after Evian's, and his train that runs from Paris to Brittany is in fact the train from Geneva to Evian. Some 60 years later, the negotiations that led to the independence of Algeria took place in one of Evian's grand hotels.

Numerous short outings can be taken from Evian. Thonon-les-Bains, some 5½ miles (9 km) to the west, also is a spa, but more bustling and modern. About a mile (1.6 km) north of Thonon is the Château de Ripaille, which the Savoyard King Amadeus VIII made his home two times, once after abdicating his throne in 1434 and again, 15 years later, after renouncing his papal (or rather anti-papal) title as Félix V. Lake Geneva, which is shaped like a giant boomerang sailing across Europe, lends itself to innumerable boat trips. A tour of the entire lake takes about 10 hours; an alternative is to take a boat into Switzerland, to the lakeside cities of Lausanne-Ouchy, directly across the lake, for instance, or to Montreux, 23 miles (37 km) to the east and the site of the Château de Chillon, where Byron was imprisoned.

If fitness, health, and beauty rank high among your preoccupations, you can take advantage of your stay in Evian for some à la carte treatment. For more information, get in touch with the tourist office (Pl. d'Allinges; phone: 50-75-04-26) or the *Centre Evian Equilibre* (phone: 50-75-02-30).

The most efficient way to get to Chamonix from Evian is through Switzerland. Head east along the lake on N5 to the French border town of St.-Gingolph, then south on route 21 through Vouvry and Monthey. At Martigny, take the Col de la Forclaz back into France; the border town is Vallorcine. Route N506 leads to Chamonix.

 CHECKING IN: *Royal Club Evian* – Built in 1907 for King Edward VII of England, this "palace" offers both refinement and modern comforts in its 158 rooms and spa facilities. Guests staying a minimum of 2 days have free access to the hotel's 18-hole golf course — located 2 miles (3 km) away. Closed mid-December to mid-February. Route du Mateirons, Evian-les-Bains (phone: 50-75-14-00). Expensive.

La Verniaz et Ses Chalets **–** This elegant and lovely hotel has 35 rooms and 5 chalets as well as a swimming pool, tennis courts, and a first class restaurant that has earned one Michelin star. Closed December to mid-February. Rte. Abondance, Evian-les-Bains (phone: 50-75-04-90). Expensive.

Terrasse **–** A much humbler hotel but also attractive, it has 32 rooms. 10 Rue B.-Moutardier, Evian-les-Bains (phone: 50-75-00-67). Moderate.

EATING OUT: *Bourgogne* – At a place that serves fine, traditional fare (one Michelin star), the seafood is especially good. There also are 29 comfortable rooms for those who want to stay the night. Reservations necessary. 73 Rue Nationale, Evian-les-Bains (phone: 50-75-01-05). Expensive.

La Toque Royale – Excellent cooking, rating one Michelin star, is featured on an extensive menu, and it's easy to spend any money left after the meal since the restaurant is in a casino. Reservations advised. Château de Blonay, Evian-les-Bains (phone: 50-75-03-78). Expensive.

CHAMONIX: At the base of 15,771-foot Mont-Blanc, the highest mountain in France and the second highest in Europe, Chamonix is probably Europe's most important center for serious alpinism. Compared to nearby neighbors such as Megève and Val d'Isère, it is a no-frills town: Chic is out in Chamonix; in its bustling, hyperactive downtown, along with the inevitable hordes of sedentary types, the streets are thronged with determined alpinists loaded down with pitons, carabiners, and the other accoutrements of mountaineering. The town is sandwiched into a narrow valley with the Mont-Blanc range on one side and the Aiguilles-Rouges on the other, an awe-inspiring setting. Cable cars pass on slender cables between peaks many thousands of feet above the ground. An ancient glacier descends to less than 1,000 feet above a major thoroughfare, and avalanches, with accompanying cracks and rumbles, occur periodically. In Chamonix, perhaps more than anywhere else in the Alps, the mountain gods make their intimidating presence felt.

A multitude of activities demand attention in Chamonix. Visits to nearby peaks, which can be accomplished via cog railway or cable car, are a must. A relatively tame trip is the one taken by train from the Gare du Montenvers to the Mer de Glace (Sea of Ice), a glacier 6,313 feet high. Farther up, at the summit of Montenvers, you'll find an ice grotto and a small museum. On the other side of the valley, there is the trip up Le Brévent to an altitude of 8,285 feet. The most spectacular excursion of all, however, is undoubtedly to the summit of the Aiguille du Midi, alongside the great Mont-Blanc itself. This trip is accomplished in two stages, first with a relatively normal cable car, picked up at the end of Avenue Aiguille-du-Midi, that takes you up to 7,500 feet, and then by a second one, which takes what seems like an almost vertical route to the summit of the Aiguille, an altitude of close to 12,600 feet. This is heart-stopping indeed, especially when distances of more than 1,600 feet separate you from good old terra firma.

Those who wish more land-based activities will find more than enough to do in the valley. *Les Praz,* an 18-hole golf course designed by Robert Trent Jones, is just outside town (phone: 50-53-06-28), and there's also swimming, tennis, riding, and ice skating. A fitness center offers a good selection of the usual facilities as well as Turkish baths and a wall to practice mountain climbing. The serious alpinist, of course, can spend a lifetime in Chamonix without getting bored. For more information, contact the tourist office (Pl. de l'Eglise; phone: 50-53-00-24).

Some 22 miles (35 km) down the road from Chamonix, via N205, D902, D909, and N212, lies Megève, another major resort.

CHECKING IN/EATING OUT: *Auberge du Bois-Prin* – An 11-room Savoyard chalet, it offers a view of Mont-Blanc and an opportunity to use the pool and tennis courts at the *Albert I et Milan,* almost a mile (1.6 km) away (see below). 69 Chemin de l'Hermine, Les Moussoux, Chamonix (phone: 50-53-33-51). Expensive.

Labrador – This 32-room hotel is right on the *Les Praz* golf course. Route du Golf, Chamonix (phone: 50-55-90-09). Expensive.

Mont Blanc – Centrally located, this recently redecorated hostelry has 44 rooms and 9 suites, a swimming pool, and an attractive garden. Pl. de l'Eglise, Chamonix (phone: 50-53-05-64). Expensive.

Albert I et Milan – This hostelry has 34 rooms and apartments, a pool and tennis courts, a flower garden with a children's play area, and a splendid view of the peaks. Its restaurant has been awarded one Michelin star, and offers such well-prepared specialties as fricassee of scallops and squab baked in salt. Reservations necessary. 119 Impasse du Montenvers, Chamonix (phone: 50-53-05-09). Expensive to moderate.

Alpina – The amount of luxury and the price of each of the 136 rooms is determined by whether it faces Mont-Blanc. The seventh-floor restaurant offers a panoramic view. Closed mid-October to mid-December. 79 Av. du Mont-Blanc, Chamonix (phone: 50-93-03-10). Expensive to moderate.

Beausoleil – Amid cow-filled pastures at the foot of Chamonix's peaks, this hotel has 17 rooms, a restaurant, and a tennis court. The owner, M. Bossonney, also is a high-mountain guide and willing to help you explore the rocky terrain. 60 Allée Peupliers, Le Lavancher (phone: 50-54-00-78). Moderate to inexpensive.

Les Gentianes – This chalet overlooking the Chamonix Valley is a good choice for a peaceful and comfortable stay. It has 14 rooms, a terrace, a restaurant, and an 18-hole golf course just a few miles away at Grands-Montets. Le Lavancher (phone: 50-54-01-31). Moderate to inexpensive.

MEGÈVE: Compared to Chamonix, Megève is effete, but this is not to say that it is unattractive. It has a lovely little downtown area bisected by a mountain stream and filled with appealing but expensive boutiques and outdoor cafés. Like Chamonix, it is a center for outdoor sports, with some of the finest skiing in the world. Among the many hikes and Alpine tours in the area, the prime attraction is probably the cable car ride to the top of Mont-d'Arbois, where you have a view of the surrounding ranges of Mont-Blanc, Fiz, and Aravis. The point of departure is Petit Bois, 2 miles (3 km) north of town on Route du Mont-d'Arbois. In late August, a tournament is held at *Golf du Mont-d'Arbois* (phone: 50-21-29-79), an 18-hole golf course.

 CHECKING IN: *Chalet–Mont-d'Arbois* – A 20-room hotel in a tranquil setting. It's 3 miles (5 km) up the road to Mont-d'Arbois, on Rte. de Mont-d'Arbois, Megève (phone: 50-21-25-03). Expensive.

Les Fermes de Marie – A group of old farmhouses was brought here in pieces and then put back together to make up this 42-room hostelry. There's a swimming pool, Turkish baths, and a fitness center. Chemin de Riante-Colline, Megève (phone: 50-93-03-10). Expensive.

Mont-Blanc – There are 51 pricey rooms (including 8 suites) from which to choose and the hotel's fine restaurant features frescoes by Jean Cocteau from *Les Enfants Terribles.* Pl. de l'Eglise, Megève (phone: 50-21-20-02). Expensive.

Parc des Loges – This luxury hotel, a pension before its renovation, has 51 rooms, suites, and apartments, many of them with a fireplace. The 2 restaurants, *La Rotonde* and *Le Grand Café,* are under the supervision of five well-known chefs. Full or half-board only. 100 Rte. d'Arly, Megève (phone: 50-93-05-03). Expensive.

Idéal-Mont-Blanc – Only 3 miles (5 km) from Megève, this hotel has 28 rooms. Combloux (phone: 50-58-60-54). Moderate.

St.-Jean – An attractive place, it has 15 comfortable rooms. Chemin du Maz, Megève (phone: 50-21-24-45). Moderate.

EATING OUT: *Auberge Les Griottes* – This fine restaurant features a good choice of fish dishes. Closed Mondays and during December. Reservations advised. Rte. Nationale 1117, Megève (phone: 50-93-05-94). Moderate.

En Route from Megève – Head southwest on N212 toward Flumet, Ugine, and Albertville, which will be the site of the *1992 Winter Olympics.* Albertville also is the headquarters for the Olympic Organizing Committee (COJO). As we went to press, a

30,000-seat stadium for the opening ceremonies and a new train station that will be equipped to handle the *TGV "Bullet"* train were under construction . The tourist office (Pl. de la Gare; phone: 79-32-04-22 or 79-37-49-50) or the Maison des Jeux Olympiques (265 Chemin de la Charrette; phone: 79-45-19-92) can provide detailed information on the Olympic events. *Olson-Travelworld,* Olympic Division (100 No. Sepulveda Blvd., El Segundo, CA 90245; (phone: 800-US4-1992 or 213-615-0711) has the exclusive US distribution rights for tickets to the games.

From Albertville, you might want to pay a quick visit to the pleasingly restored walled village of Conflans, with buildings dating back as far as the 14th century. Leaving Albertville, head south on N90; just before Moûtiers, take N915 to Pralognan-la-Vanoise, which will host the *1992 Olympic* curling matches. Pralognan is one of the gateways to the Vanoise, the first national park created in France (1963). With its outlying areas, this wonderland for hikers and campers encompasses some 80,000 acres of spectacular mountains and meadows. Automobile traffic is barred in the park itself, and exotic mountain animals such as the ibex and chamois roam unthreatened.

Other access points also lead to the Vanoise. The road back from Pralognan (the only way out except by foot) branches off toward Champagny-en-Vanoise; follow it through the village and on to its very end to cross a lovely high valley that passes through rugged mountainscapes and arrives at a much less populated jumping-off point for the Vanoise.

For an unexpectedly breathtaking bit of shunpiking (taking side roads) on the way back to Moûtiers from Champagny-en-Vanoise and neighboring Champagny-en-Haut, take the serpentine back road that leads up to Feissons-sur-Salins. This is the real Savoie: tiny untouristed hamlets clinging to the sides of steep hills, and successions of spectacular views. Back in Moûtiers, pick up N90 heading northeast for the summer and winter sports center of Bourg-St.-Maurice, and then follow lovely, winding D902 south (and up) to Val d'Isère. Just before that center of ski activity, you will happen upon the remarkable resort of Tignes. With the construction of a hydroelectric dam, the old village of Tignes was displaced and reestablished some 1,000 feet higher, by a small natural lake. There is something unbelievable about the new town, where even the oldest buildings date back only to the 1950s — surely a phenomenon in France. Apartments, boutiques, and restaurants are strung together in an oddly mechanical, modern style that, while undeniably unattractive, manages somehow to blend in perfectly with the imposing moonlike landscape. Grotesque yet oddly appropriate, Tignes is pure resort, offering superb skiing with 90 miles of runs. Only a small portion of these will be used for free-style skiing, which will become an *Olympic* sport during the 1992 games. In summer, the resort offers 32 miles of runs, an entry into the Vanoise, and a variety of activities about which the tourism office (right on the lake; phone: 79-06-15-55).

 CHECKING IN/EATING OUT: *Million* – This fine 29-room hotel houses one of the best kitchens in France, rating two Michelin stars, and includes on its menu *coquilles St.-Jacques* (scallops with cream sauce served in a shell) and numerous fish dishes. The restaurant is closed Sunday evenings and Mondays. Reservations advised. 8 Pl. Liberté, Albertville (phone: 79-32-25-15). Expensive.

Ski d'Or – A mile (1.6 km) outside Tignes, this particularly pleasant lodging has 22 inviting rooms and a good restaurant. Closed from May to November. Val Claret, Tignes (phone: 79-06-51-60). Expensive.

Berjann – Attractively furnished, this 11-room hostelry also offers good cooking. 33 Rte. Tours, Albertville (phone: 79-32-47-88). Moderate to inexpensive.

Petite Auberge – An appealing inn slightly off the main road, it offers 15 comfortable rooms, a pleasant terrace restaurant, and a family atmosphere. Rte. de Moûtiers, Le Reverset, on the outskirts of Bourg-St.-Maurice (phone: 79-07-05-86). Inexpensive.

VAL D'ISÈRE: Physically, this town is not as picturesque as Megève or as imposing as Chamonix, but its nightlife is renowned, and the surrounding landscapes provide their own magic. Val d'Isère is thought by many to feature the best skiing in the world. There are innumerable slopes for every level of skier, and one can whoosh along at altitudes of well over 11,000 feet. Jean-Claude Killy, who was born here, has designed a difficult track on the side of Rocher de Bellevarde for the *1992 Olympic* men's downhill events. Killy, the hero of the 1968 Grenoble games, has commented, "It will be very impressive. I'm glad I don't have to run anymore." It is being built so that spectators will be able to watch 80% of the run. Summer provides a wide variety of outdoor activities, too. Val d'Isère is in the heart of the Vanoise and offers any number of hikes and excursions. Particularly memorable outings include the cable car ride to the Rocher de Bellevarde and the ascent to the Tête du Solaise. Summer skiing is possible on the 10,000-foot-high Grand Pissaillas glacier. For more information, check at the tourist office, at Maison de Val d'Isère, close to the town center (phone: 79-06-10-83).

Most of the area around Val d'Isère has become very touristic; those hankering for a taste of the real Savoie can find it in out-of-the-way villages such as La Gurraz and Les Masures.

En Route from Val d'Isère – Head almost due south (as the crow flies, anyhow) to Briançon, the next major town on the itinerary and 98 miles (157 km) away; follow D902 to N6-E70, to D902, to N91.

For those who love the high, high Alps, this route offers everything a traveler could hope for, including two unbelievably beautiful mountain passes. (Incidentally, the French seem to have a good time crossing these passes on bicycles, a pastime that may strike the four-wheeled visitor as tinged with lunacy.)

The first pass is the Col de l'Iseran, whose summit is about 9,000 feet above sea level. Historically, it was so hard to get to that until the mid-19th century, cartographers simply guessed at its location on their maps. And it was only in 1937 that the first road over the pass was opened. As might be expected, the air here is bracing, the views spectacular, and the road, with its intermittent railings, cause for occasional palpitations of the heart.

Properly equipped and experienced (this trail is not for the inexperienced or easily frightened), climbers can hike from the summit of the Col de l'Iseran to the Pointe des Lessières, about 1,000 feet higher, for a magnificent Alpine panorama. Before setting out, make sure conditions are favorable.

The Col de l'Iseran descends into the Maurienne Valley, through which the Arc River courses. This relatively industrial yet nonetheless pleasant route goes through the towns of Bonneval-sur-Arc, Lanslevillard, Termignon, Modane, and St.-Michel-de-Maurienne. Bonneval is particularly attractive; its ambience arises mostly out of the delightfully unpretentious Alpine architecture of its buildings. Another especially pleasing village, about 25 miles (40 km) farther, is Aussois. In addition to the attractions of the town itself, there are a couple of interesting sites in the immediate neighborhood: the Monolith of Sardières, a spectacular, isolated rock face that was first scaled in 1960, and the massive fortress of the Esseillon, which was constructed at great labor and expense in 1815 by the Sardinian regime to protect against a French invasion and then was never used.

After St.-Michel-de-Maurienne, the road starts to climb steeply; the Col du Télégraphe is some 2,500 feet above St.-Michel, and the slowly expanding resort of Valloire, a little farther down the road, is close to a mile above sea level. For those for whom altitude is everything, this whole strip, valley and pass included, is a lovely preparation for the second great pass of the tour, the Col du Galibier, which takes you from the Maurienne to the Briançonnais, the area surrounding the town of Briançon. Rising to

8,500 feet above sea level, the Col du Galibier is fully as spectacular as the Col de l'Iseran. A magnificent view awaits those who leave their car at the road's high point and climb to the viewing station.

Taking on the Col de l'Iseran and the Col du Galibier in a single day is possible but taxing. Fortunately, a number of attractive places offer lodging along the way, and there is a splendid stopover just south of Col du Galibier.

CHECKING IN: *Auberge du Choucas* – This 1770 farmhouse, completely renovated in 1988, nestles in an Alpine village just beyond the Col du Galibier. The inn has 12 rooms and 6 independent studios, and easy access to Ecrins National Park and the skiing area of Serre-Chevalier, just 500 yards away. Full or half-board only. Le Monêtier-les-Bains (phone: 92-24-42-73). Expensive to moderate.

Club Les Carrettes – Here you'll find 30 modern, comfortable rooms, a swimming pool, and an owner with a sense of humor; he doubles as a nightclub performer in his hotel. Weekly arrangements with full board only. Valloire (phone: 79-59-00-99). Expensive to moderate.

Le Choucas – Some 28 comfortable, simple rooms are available here. Closed May, October, and November. Aussois (phone: 79-20-32-77). Inexpensive.

La Marmotte – Attractively situated and reasonably priced, it offers 28 rooms. Closed mid-May to mid-June and mid-September to mid-December. Bonneval-sur-Arc (phone: 79-05-94-82). Inexpensive.

BRIANÇON: Poised at an entry point into Italy and at the foot of several mountain passes, Briançon has long been an important military and commercial center. Today its excellent climate and beautiful location — at 4,333 feet, it is supposedly the highest town in Europe — make it a major tourist center, but unlike many of the more ski-based Alpine resort villages, Briançon has a palpable historical foundation. This city has been lived in. While the newer part of the town is attractive, the real highlight is the Old Town, called Ville Haute or Briançon-Vauban, for the engineer who controlled its reconstruction in the late 17th and 18th centuries after a fire had destroyed the village. Briançon-Vauban is positively redolent with a sense of the past. With no traffic and surrounded by ramparts, cute but not kitschy, it invites the visitor to stroll, to explore, to relax. Leave the car at the Champ de Mars and enter by the Pignerol gate, next to the tourist office (phone: 92-21-08-50). The Grande-Rue is relatively broad and bustling, and each of its numerous side streets has its own special charm. The graceful, twin-towered Eglise Notre-Dame, built by Vauban from 1703 to 1718, is just off Grande-Rue, and beyond it is a lovely view. From the citadel above the old city, there is an excellent panorama of the surrounding peaks and the Durance Valley. The Pont d'Asfeld, constructed in 1754, arcs audaciously over the river gorge at a height of 17 feet; those who can get there (by footpath) can walk across.

Those who wish to stay in the most "alpish" part of the Alps should head back up to the Col de Lautaret, via N91, and continue on to Grenoble, 73 miles (118 km) away. Consider stopping at a major ski resort such as Les Deux-Alpes or L'Alpe-d'Huez.

En Route from Briançon – The southern route to Grenoble is much more extensive, covering, with its various windings, well over 200 miles (320 km). It is worth the detour, however, and in no case should spectacular Vercors Regional Park be missed, be it along this route or as a day trip from Grenoble. The whole area can be covered in a day, but only by going at such a pace that much of the pleasure of the low mountains, steep buttes, and small villages is lost. It is best to follow this route in a leisurely fashion over a few days.

South of Briançon, the terrain begins to change. With some noteworthy exceptions, the mountains grow tamer, the views become longer and flatter. The area is less majestic somehow, and more subdued, but filled with beauties of its own. Route N94 and then D994 take the traveler through the Vallouise, an area named after the 15th-century King Louis XI. Nearby Queyras Regional Park, attainable by D902 out of Briançon, benefits from excellent weather and a wide variety of flora and fauna; Château-Queyras, a 13th-century fortress, is at its heart.

Route D902 meanders through the park and on to Guillestre, a lively market and resort town; a couple of miles (3 km) west, pick up N94 for a trip through the Durance Valley. About 12 miles (19 km) down N95, just before the enormous (7,410-acre) artificial lake of Serre-Ponçon, is the town of Embrun. As Eburodunum under the Romans, then as a major ecclesiastical center, Embrun was for many years a town of major importance. Now it is little more than a village, with a lovely church, Eglise Notre-Dame, well worth visiting, and a commanding view of the Durance Valley.

After the magnificent lakes of the Alps, the sprawling, mountain-splayed Serre-Ponçon is something of a letdown. Nonetheless, it is a popular sports center and on some summer days seems filled with windsurfers.

Just before the hamlet of La Bâtie-Neuve, about 7 miles (11 km) beyond the lake, D942 branches south off N94. Shortly thereafter, a small road heads north (right) toward Ancelle, St.-Léger-les-Mélèzes, Chabottes, and then to Chaillol. This little roundabout offers a wide assortment of scenery: pine forests, farm country, Alpine views — all lovely and definitely off the beaten track.

Pick up N94 again and continue west to Gap, a bustling commercial center with an attractive downtown area. It is also a center from which some serious trout (not to mention perch, chub, and barbel) fishing can be done. For more information about the area's mountain streams and lakes as well as more general information, write to the *Comité Départemental du Tourisme des Hautes-Alpes,* BP 46, Gap 05002, or contact the tourist office (phone: 92-51-57-03). From Gap, pick up the famous and much-traveled Route Napoléon (now N85) and head north. Corps, an especially comely little town perched above Lake Sautet, lies 25 miles (40 km) on N85 north of Gap. If you prefer to bypass Gap, head for St.-Bonnet from Chaillol.

A special treat awaits the traveler who leaves N85 at Corps and takes off on back roads through the villages of La Croix-de-la-Pigne, Mens (D66 west of Corps), Lavars (D34A off D34), and Clelles (D526 west of Mens). Far more bucolic than the high Alps, the scenery — pastures, rock faces, and pine forests — is nonetheless splendid in its own right. With each new turn, it appears utterly changed, as if the voyager was looking through a kaleidoscope.

Clelles is at the edge of Vercors Regional Park, a marvelous agglomeration of buttes, boulders, and ravines reminiscent of the scenery in movie westerns. By heading from Clelles to Châtillon-en-Diois on the D7 and D120 and thence to the distressingly mistitled town of Die (actually pronounced *Dee*), on D539 and D93, one gets not only a beautiful tour through Vercors but also a glimpse of the narrow, lavender-planted valley of the Drôme. Die is lovely and renowned for its bubbly white wine, Clairette de Die. The main road back into Vercors from Die, D518, scales the Col de Rousset and passes through the resort town of St.-Agnan-en-Vercors and on to another resort, St.-Eulalie-en-Royans, where D531 leads to yet another resort, Villard-de-Lans, then on to Grenoble.

 CHECKING IN: *Les Barnières I and II* – These two hotels, one beside the other, have 74 rooms furnished with all the modern amenities and offer tennis and swimming as well as a superb view of the Durance Valley. Full board required during July and August. Guillestre (phone: 92-45-04-87 and 92-45-05-07). Moderate.

Paris – A stately old hotel, it is in Vercors Regional Park in an attractive private park of its own. There is something vaguely and pleasingly anachronistic about this place, which has 54 rooms and a tennis court. Villard-de-Lans (phone: 76-95-10-06). Moderate.

Ferrat – On the doorstep of Vercors park and at the foot of the striking and legendary Mont-Aiguille (legendary because until it was first climbed in the 15th century, supernatural creatures reportedly populated it), this 16-room hotel is handsomely furnished and well managed. The only problem is its excessive proximity to the much-traveled N75. While extremely accessible, it also is quite noisy. Closed mid-November through February. Clelles (phone: 76-34-42-70). Inexpensive.

La Louzière – This mountain-modern, 29-room hostelry nestles in a small resort just above the village of Chaillol, not far from Gap. It affords a spectacular view. Chaillol (phone: 92-50-48-44). Inexpensive.

EATING OUT: *La Poste* – A popular and excellent eatery, it also has 15 rooms. Reservations necessary. Bordering Rte. Napoléon, Corps (phone: 76-30-00-03). Moderate to inexpensive.

La Petite Auberge – Across from the train station, this restaurant has good food for the prices; there are 13 rooms as well. Av. Sadi-Carnot, Die (phone: 75-22-05-91). Reservations advised. Hotel, inexpensive; restaurant, moderate to inexpensive.

GRENOBLE: Grenoble, which has been around since the year 1 BC and is the French Alps' major urban center, claims a population approaching 400,000. The host of the *1968 Winter Olympics,* it is a thriving commercial and intellectual center and handsome as well as historical (it was in Grenoble, for example, that the French Revolution really began). The University of Grenoble was founded in 1339; today it has some 35,000 students.

A walk through the bustling downtown area, with its elegant squares, well-designed parks, and old buildings, gives you a good sense of the city's attractions. Pick up a map at the tourist office (14 Rue de la République; phone: 76-54-34-36). For a bird's-eye view, however, take the little *téléphérique* at Quai Stéphane-Jay and rise across the Isère River to Fort de la Bastille. From the fort, it's possible to explore the neighboring Parc Guy-Pape and the Jardin des Dauphins, sip a cup of coffee or have a bite to eat, and, above all else, gaze ad infinitum at the city and mountain spires (Mont-Blanc included on clear days).

Grenoble has a number of interesting museums, foremost among them the *Musée des Beaux-Arts* (Pl. de Verdun), which has an excellent collection of paintings, including works by Corot, Renoir, Monet, Picasso, Modigliani, and Tanguy. The *Musée Stendhal* (in the old Hôtel de Ville — Town Hall — on Rue Beyle-Stendhal) contains memorabilia pertaining to the author of *Le Rouge et Le Noir* (The Red and the Black) and *La Chartreuse de Parme* (The Charterhouse of Parma), who was born in Grenoble in 1783. Devotees of the writer will find a visit here entertaining (though others may be less enthusiastic). The *Centre National d'Art Contemporain* ("Le Magasin"), a contemporary art museum, is in a former factory at 155 Cours Berriat. The small *Musée de la Résistance et de la Déportation* (Museum of the Resistance and Deportation; 14 Rue Jean-Jacques-Rousseau) is a moving tribute to the heroes and martyrs of World War II; it was built on the site of the birthplace of Stendhal.

Grenoble is undeniably a clean, modern city that has seen tremendous growth in the last few decades, but historic enclaves remain amid the proliferating new buildings. Make your way to Place Grenette in the old part of town and wander among the streets and gardens around it. Across the river, on Quai Xavier-Jouvin, is Eglise St.-Laurent, which contains one of the oldest crypts in France.

The Dauphiné region may be best known for its skiing, but it also is abundantly rich in fishing. In every direction from Grenoble, well-stocked rivers, streams, and lakes await visiting anglers. For specific information, write to the *Fédération de la Pêche de l'Isère* (1 Rue Cujas, Grenoble 38000; phone: 76-44-28-39). Follow A41-E712 north to Chambéry, 34 miles (54 km) away.

CHECKING IN: *Lesdiguières* – This 36-room hotel, albeit in the city, has a park nearby and is very comfortable. 122 Cours Libération, Grenoble (phone: 76-96-55-36). Moderate.

Les Oiseaux – Six miles (10 km) due south of Grenoble via D269, this hostelry offers an especially appealing setting, 20 pleasant rooms, and a swimming pool. Closed January. Claix (phone: 76-98-07-74). Moderate.

Chalet-Hôtel Rogier – Travel about 13 miles (21 km) north of Grenoble for the height of seclusion and your choice of 15 rooms. It is 3 miles (5 km) north of Le Sappey-en-Chartreuse at Col de Porte, La Tronche (phone: 76-88-82-04). Inexpensive.

Napoléon – A simple but adequate 50-room lodging right in town. Be aware that the street side can get noisy. 7 Rue Montorge, Grenoble (phone: 76-87-22-46). Inexpensive.

Skieurs – In a pleasant little village about 10 miles (16 km) north of Grenoble on N512, this hostelry has 18 clean, simple rooms and a swimming pool. Le Sappey-en-Chartreuse (phone: 76-88-80-15). Inexpensive.

EATING OUT:

Chavant – Among the more elegant restaurants in the area, a few miles south of Grenoble via D264, this one has one Michelin star. The service is good and the menu, which is vast, features traditional as well as more creative fare. There also are 8 rooms. Closed Saturday lunch and Wednesdays. Reservations advised. Bresson (phone: 76-25-15-14). Expensive to moderate.

L'Antarctique – Recently opened, this eatery specializes in exotic and traditional fish dishes. Open daily until midnight. Reservations advised. 9 Bd. Gambetta, Grenoble (phone: 76-46-63-64). Moderate to inexpensive.

L'Epicurien – Ham cooked in hay is the specialty of this fine dining spot. Closed Saturday afternoons and Sundays. Reservations advised. 1 Pl. Aux Herbes, Grenoble (phone: 76-51-96-06). Moderate to inexpensive.

Au Petit Vatel – A first-rate if simple bistro, it takes its name from a famous French chef who committed suicide when a fish dish turned out to be a failure. Closed Sunday evenings and Mondays. Reservations advised. 3 Pl. de Gordes, Grenoble (phone: 76-44-68-26). Inexpensive.

En Route from Grenoble – Due north lies the Chartreuse mountain range, the highest in France. One of its tranquil valleys harbors a unique history, reason enough to bypass the autoroute to Chambéry and head into the thick of the forest via D512 over the Col de Porte.

In 1084, St. Bruno and seven followers bushwhacked their way 16 miles (26 km) into these unruly hills to found the Carthusian order of monks, which has been there ever since (with the exception of the years 1903 to 1941, when they were expelled). For the past several hundred years the monks, who are isolated not only from the world but from each other most of the time, have been making a well-known green (also yellow) liqueur, chartreuse, whose formula has always remained a secret to all but three of them. The charterhouse of the monks, La Grande Chartreuse, is not open to the public, although in an outbuilding about a mile away is a small museum devoted to the daily life of these recluses. Called La Correrie, off D520-B, it is open from *Palm Sunday* to *All Saints' Day* (November 1). It is possible to hike to the charterhouse gate, but no farther. Those interested in seeing the liqueur distilled may do so in Voiron, 19 miles (30 km) northwest of Grenoble on N75. The proceeds from the million bottles of chartreuse sold annually, half of them to the French, support 460 Carthusian monks in 24 monasteries worldwide.

An easy exit out of the Chartreuse is D520-B west to St.-Laurent-du-Pont; then continue to Chambéry on D520 to N6.

CHAMBÉRY: An appealing little city of 57,000, the namesake of a pale vermouth, and the capital of Savoie from the 13th to the 17th century, it exists today as a compact assemblage of squares and boulevards, arcades and alleyways. Marking the bull's-eye of a map of Chambéry, the Fontaine des Eléphants is a charming tribute to the Count of Boigne, commemorating this local hero's (and benefactor's) trip to India; ensconced where Rue de Boigne and Boulevard de la Colonne merge, the four bronze behemoths date from 1838. The ancient château of the Dukes of Savoie still stands, and Rue de Boigne and Rue Juiverie lead pleasantly to it; the large, oblong Place St.-Léger, filled with fountains and lampposts, is nearby. Located at the other end of the Boulevard de la Colonne from Fontaine des Elephants, the tourist office can provide information on the guided tours of the city and its environs (phone: 79-33-42-47). A little over a mile (1.6 km) out of town via D4 is Les Charmettes, where Jean-Jacques Rousseau lived blissfully with Madame de Warens for 6 years; the place is filled with his memorabilia. Try to taste some of the luscious raspberries and strawberries that grow on the surrounding mountainsides.

Autoroute A41 continues from Chambéry 31 miles (50 km) north and east to Annecy.

CHECKING IN: *Hôtel du Château* – Just 3½ miles (6 km) out of Chambéry, this 10-acre property was the home of the Counts of Challes in the 15th century. Now a 70-room Best Western hotel, it features a restaurant serving regional fare, tennis courts, a swimming pool, a casino, and meeting facilities. Challes-Les-Eaux (phone: 79-72-86-71). Expensive.

***Château de Trivier* –** A quick 4 miles (6 km) east of Chambéry via N6, this lovely hotel, the ancestral home of the Seigneurs de Trivier, is a pocket of tranquility. It is surrounded by a small park complete with its own pond. Challes-les-Eaux (phone: 79-72-82-87). Moderate.

***La Cérisaie* –** Perched on a height above Lac du Bourget, just off the N504, about 9 miles (14 km) north of Chambéry, it offers a relaxing stay. The 7 rooms offer only the bare comforts, but a pleasant view of the lake and mountains adds to its appeal. Rte. Dent-du-Chat, just north of the village of Bourget-du-Lac (phone: 79-25-01-29). Hotel inexpensive, restaurant moderate.

EATING OUT: *Roubatcheff* – This popular and oft-heralded eating spot with one Michelin star makes every seafood dish a delicacy; try the *blinis de saumon fumé* (small pancakes packed with smoked salmon); *terrine de saumon frais*, salmon again, this time fresh and in a terrine; or *turbot à la crème de persil* (turbot with parsley cream); among many other delicious, Russian-inspired dishes. The prix fixe meals are decidedly less expensive. Reservations necessary. Esplanade Curial, Chambéry (phone: 79-33-24-91). Expensive.

En Route from Chambéry – A lovely road heads north toward St.-Jean d'Arvey, then through La Feclaz, a local winter sports center, and over Mont-Revard to Aix-les-Bains. This grand old spa is on Lac du Bourget, the lake that inspired the romantic poet Lamartine's tragic lament, "Le Lac." A stroll through Aix's elegant streets or on its long, handsome promenade is well worth the time. Across the lake is the Abbaye de Hautecombe, which deserves a visit, either by boat from Aix or by car. On Sundays at 9:15 AM and weekdays at 9:30 AM, mass includes Gregorian chants.

CHECKING IN: *L'Orée du Lac* – A jewel close to both Aix-les-Bains and Le Bourget du Lac, this small (10 rooms) but complete hotel boasts its own park, a pool, and tennis courts. La Croix Verte (phone: 79-25-24-19). Expensive.

EATING OUT: *Le Bateau Ivre* – Set in a former 17th-century barn that was used to store salt, and now surrounded by a garden full of flowers, this restaurant has earned two Michelin stars. Closed Tuesdays and November to April. Reservations necessary. La Croix Verte (phone: 79-25-02-66). Expensive.

ANNECY: Annecy has boomed into a major urban center in the last 20 years for several reasons, not the least of which is a sage town government that has encouraged industry while recognizing the importance of the city's physical setting. Its tourist office is housed in the very modern *Centre Banlieu,* a shopping mall that includes shops and a theater (1 Rue Jean-Jaurès; phone: 50-45-00-33).

Annecy is also a city of the past. It was the home of St.-François de Sales (1567–1622), the Savoyard nobleman, missionary, and writer who was canonized in 1665. Annecy also played an important part in the life of Jean-Jacques Rousseau (he lost his heart to Madame de Warens here). Today the old city of Annecy is charming and well preserved, with a number of attractive churches, including the Eglise St.-Maurice and the Eglise St.-François. The château, the former residence of the Counts of Geneva and the Dukes of Savoie-Nemours, also deserves a visit.

The lakefront at Annecy is popular, crowded, and active, but you can get quite a different sense of the lake by taking its east coast around to Talloires. This little village, nestled behind a point and across from the striking (and privately owned) château of Duingt, is a model of elegance, tranquillity, and taste. A picnic lunch at the lakeside here is a pleasure, as is the water, at an ideal temperature for swimming. A few miles beyond the south end of the lake is the village of Faverges, a good starting point for some pleasant meandering; take a right at the junction here and head toward Tertenoz and perhaps beyond it for a sense of the real Savoyard countryside, an enticing blend of gently rolling pastures and soul-stirring alpine vistas.

CHECKING IN/EATING OUT: *Abbaye* – On the east side of Lake Annecy, this former abbey has a handsome decor, 31 rooms, a garden, and a terrace. Talloires, 8 miles (13 km) south of Annecy (phone: 50-60-77-33) Expensive.

Auberge du Père Bise – This restaurant, on the eastern shore of Lake Annecy, is renowned throughout France for the quality and richness of its cuisine; Michelin gives it two stars. Duck is a specialty here, as witnessed by the *tourte de canard* (duck pie) and the *pot-au-feu de canard* (duck stew), among other dishes. Count on a meal you won't forget, but expect to pay for the pleasure. Reservations necessary. Some 20 rooms and 10 suites also are available at this member of the Relais & Châteaux group. Talloires, 8 miles (13 km) south of Annecy (phone: 50-60-72-01). Expensive.

Pavillon Ermitage – Seafood lovers should seek out this one-Michelin-star establishment, midway between Annecy and Talloires. Specialties include *omble chevalier* (salmon fresh from the lake) and *soufflé de brochet* (pike soufflé). After a filling dinner, it's possible to retire to one of 11 rooms. Reservations necessary. Chavoires (phone: 50-60-11-09). Expensive to moderate.

Florimont – A recently opened hotel with 27 rooms, it has a terrace garden. Its 2 restaurants offer quality food at reasonable prices. Faverges, 2 miles (3 km) toward Albertville on N508 (phone: 50-44-50-05). Moderate to inexpensive.

Marceau – Perched on a hilltop, this 20-room hostelry is quiet and restful. Closed mid-December to mid-January. Doussard, just south of Lake Annecy's southern shore (phone: 50-44-30-11). Moderate.

Gay Séjour – Aptly called "gay sojourn," this family-run enterprise off the beaten track offers 11 rooms with lovely mountain views. Closed during January. Tertenoz, just south of Faverges, which lies 16 miles (26 km) south of Annecy on N508; go 2 miles (3 km) toward the Col de Tamie on the D12 (phone: 50-44-52-52). Inexpensive.

Burgundy

When most people hear "Burgundy," they think of wine. But while it is true that the wines of this region are world-renowned, Burgundy offers much more than the pleasures of wine to the visitor. Its countryside is remarkably varied, ranging from the bucolic rolling pastures of Aix-en-Othe to the rough and striking hill country around Cluny to the lakes and forests of the Morvan. Burgundian villages seem to be caught in an enchanting time warp: Driving along a pleasant, winding country road, visitors suddenly find themselves among beflowered stone buildings that date from the 16th century. However, Burgundy's unchanging, timeless quality is due not only to the landscape, with its cathedrals, châteaux, and abbeys, but also to its people. Like so many agrarian folk, they are profoundly conservative, rooted to their land, and suspicious of the city and modern ways. Though Paris is only a few hours' drive away on the autoroute, it is a trip that not a few Burgundians have made only once, if at all. And it may well be that the quietude and tranquillity of today's Burgundy is due to a collective, subconscious memory of past glories. Some 5 centuries ago, the power and influence of the Dukes of Burgundy rivaled that of any crowned head in Europe. Whatever the reason, Burgundy is now a land in semiretirement, ripe with age and leaning back in its rocking chair, enjoying its repose after a most successful career.

Burgundy's history is as long as it is rich. At Solutré, a village at the foot of an imposing precipice in the Mâconnais region, archaeologists came upon the skeletons of 100,000 horses. Their theory is that the horses were herded together and then driven over the cliff, probably by fire, about 15,000 years ago, at the same time that Egypt's New Kingdom was reigning supreme in the so-called cradle of civilization many thousands of miles to the east. Some 10,000 years later, Burgundy was a center of Celtic civilization and subsequently of Celtic resistance to Rome's northern expansion. It was at Bibracte, the present Autun, that Vercingétorix held a war council of tribes committed to contest Rome's drive into Burgundy, and at Alésia (Alise Ste.-Reine), Vercingétorix with his 250,000 troops went down in defeat at the hands of Julius Caesar. With the fall of the Roman Empire, the area changed in character and in name. The Burgund tribe originally was from the Baltic Sea. They gradually emigrated south and west, and in the 5th century AD, Aetius, a general charged with defending the crumbling Roman Empire, invited them to settle in Sapaudia (Savoie). The Burgundians soon extended their hegemony to west of the Saône, and the kingdom of Burgundy was born.

It was not until the 14th century, however, that Burgundy's halcyon days began. Philip the Bold, John the Fearless, Philip the Good, Charles the Bold — this succession of dukes had enough power to challenge that of the Kings of France. Palace life in Dijon was opulent, and the Burgundian Renaissance preceded the French one by several decades. During the 1470s, this power was sharply reduced, with Burgundy itself being annexed by Louis XI and the remaining provinces of Flanders, Artois, and Franche-Compte going over to Austria by marriage. By then, though, the legacy already had been established; the century of glory had lent to Burgundy the luxurious sheen of royalty. It is an aura that remains today.

Burgundian cuisine is part and parcel of its history. It was one of the central luxuries in the life of the grand Dukes of Burgundy, and today Dijon still enjoys a reputation as a gastronomic capital. It is a cuisine for gourmands as well as gourmets, with the servings as generous as they are delicious. Burgundian dishes are hearty and based on the region's produce, including carefully bred chickens from Bresse, lean beef from Charolais, and freshwater fish from the Saône and Rhone rivers. Two universally recognized Burgundian specialties include *coq au vin* (chicken in wine sauce) and *boeuf bourguignon* (beef in red wine sauce). Cassis, the local liqueur made from black currant, is well worth sampling; try a kir (*aligoté,* a dry white wine, with cassis) or the sweeter *suze cassis* (a combination of cassis and suze, the gentian-derived liqueur). Naturally, every visitor should sample the famous Burgundian wines, which include the dry white made in Chablis, the full-bodied and aromatic reds and whites produced along the Côte d'Or south of Dijon, and the light, fruity reds made in the Beaujolais. Burgundian wine lists are a pleasure to the connoisseur and novice alike, although the latter may find the *vins de table* far less expensive and eminently satisfactory.

The best way to see Burgundy is by car — put it into gear, start traveling the byways, and you will have great trouble being bored. The route outlined below starts in the Pays d'Othe, in the northern tip of Burgundy, and works its way south, culminating with visits to Beaune, home of the Hôtel-Dieu, and to Cluny, the seat of the ancient abbey. For those who seek a change of pace, there is an alternative to the automobile — the boat. More than 600 miles of navigable canals run through Burgundy, and motorcraft with sleeping capacities of up to seven are available for rent. Write to *Canal-Plaisance,* La Marina, Montbard 21500 (phone: 80-89-44-04).

Accommodations, as throughout France, are pretty uniformly comfortable and clean. There are numerous château- and mill-hotels, which are surprisingly moderate in price and provide a special experience. In general, you can expect to pay $80 and up for a double room in hotels listed as expensive; $50 to $80 in moderate; and under $50 at inexpensive places. Burgundy also has a highly developed system of *gîtes ruraux,* private homes whose owners take in paying guests in a sort of bed and breakfast arrangement. The lodgings are often very pleasant, the meals fresh and tasty, and, perhaps most important, one gets off the beaten track and into contact with the "real" Burgundy. The *gîtes* can be quite inexpensive. Bed, breakfast, and dinner (including wine) for two can run as little as $60. Directories of *gîtes* are available at the local Syndicats d'Initiative. Meals tend to run higher; dinner for two with wine costs about $90 and up in a restaurant listed as expensive; from $60 to $90 in moderate; and below $60 in one considered inexpensive. Service usually is included.

SENS: Originally called Agendicum, this was one of the most important towns in Roman Gaul. Made a regional capital in AD 395, the boundaries of its domain were soon adopted by the church, and Sens became a major archbishopric. It was split up in 1622, after which Sens began its slow decline to its present status as a modest provincial town.

Sens's centerpiece, as in so many Burgundian towns, is the Cathédrale St.-Etienne, a prime example of early Gothic architecture. Particularly noteworthy are the stained glass windows, constructed between the 12th and 17th centuries. Be sure to visit the Trésor (Treasure); it's one of the richest in France, offering a unique collection of fabrics, liturgical vestments, shrouds, tapestries, and holy reliquaries. The Palais Synodal was the seat of the Officialité, a major ecclesiastical tribunal. It is architecturally elegant and historically grisly: Included in the tour is a visit to the dungeon where heretics and sinners awaited trial. The Synodal Palace was restored in the 19th century by the famous Eugène Viollet-le-Duc, an architect whose name crops up frequently in the cathedrals of Burgundy.

A stroll through Sens is imperative if you want a real sense of the town. In particular, look for the two interesting old buildings, called Abraham's House and the House of the Pillar, which sit beside each other at the intersection of Rue de la République and Rue Jean-Cousin.

 EATING OUT: *Palais du Sens* – A local favorite for two reasons: good cooking and reasonable prices. Closed Sunday evenings, Mondays, and 2 weeks in January. 18 Pl. de la République, in front of the cathedral, Sens (phone: 86-65-13-69). Moderate to inexpensive.

En Route from Sens – Head south on N6 to Joigny, the "gateway to Burgundy," worth a stop for its three-star restaurant, *La Côte St.-Jacques* (see *Checking In/Eating Out*) as well as for its streets lined with half-timbered houses and two picturesque churches, St. Thibault and St. Jean. Leave Joigny via D943 traveling east, then turn south onto D905, which will take you southeast toward château country to visit two indisputably fine châteaux near each other, Tanlay and Ancy-le-Franc. Tanlay, 5½ miles (9 km) to the east of Tonnerre on D965, was built in the 16th century, and its stately elegance reflects the spirit of Louis XIII. The Little Château, as it is called, is most notable for its frescoes, but a tour of the interior reveals a fine display of antique furniture as well. A few miles farther east via D965, in the town of Châtillon-sur-Seine, is a fine museum with exhibits from the Treasure of Vix, a sepulcher from the 6th century BC. Among the most striking of many impressive artifacts is an enormous bronze vase — almost 5½ feet tall and weighing well over 400 pounds.

Ancy-le-Franc, which can be reached from Tanlay via Pimelles, was built a few years before Tanlay by Antoine de Clermont, Earl of Tonnerre, according to plans drawn up by the famed Italian architect Sebastien Serlio. Among the many impressive rooms in the palace, the most striking is the Guards Hall, an immense space of almost 3,000 square feet.

From Ancy-le-Franc, take D905 and D965 toward Auxerre; along the way you'll pass through Chablis, home of the famous wine. Cellars in the area usually allow visitors, so ask around if you're interested in wine tasting.

 CHECKING IN/EATING OUT: *La Côte St.-Jacques* – An 18th-century former *maison bourgeoise* that won its third star from Michelin in 1986 and is now the weekend destination of connoisseurs from Paris and beyond, who come to savor such specialties as sea bass in caviar cream sauce and fresh asparagus in truffle-scented butter sauce. Many of the 33 rooms and suites have been redecorated in Flamboyant style — with prices to match. Closed January. 14 Faubourg de Paris, Joigny (phone: 86-62-09-70). Expensive.

Auberge des Vieux Moulins Banaux – This converted mill not far from the village center has 17 rooms, most with antique furnishings, and a handsomely appointed dining room. Closed Sunday evenings, Mondays, and mid-December to March. Villeneuve l'Archevêque, Joigny (phone: 86-86-72-55). Moderate.

La Vaudeurinoise – A 7-room hostelry, praiseworthy for the tranquility of its surroundings and a tradition of gracious service and excellent cuisine. Nearby are tennis courts and horseback riding. Hotel closed in February; restaurant closed Wednesday evenings and Thursdays off-season. Rte. de Grange-Sèche, Vaudeurs (phone: 86-96-28-00). Moderate.

AUXERRE: This attractive and bustling city on the left bank of the River Yonne has been the home of a number of French celebrities, including Germain, the famed bishop of the 5th century AD, and Marie-Noël, the 20th-century "poetess of love."

With its sculpted portals and elegant nave, the Cathédrale St.-Etienne is a first class example of 13th-century Flamboyant Gothic architecture. Be sure to visit the Romanesque crypt; hauntingly beautiful, it features a rare and remarkable 11th-century fresco titled *Christ on Horseback.* Also impressive are the frescoes in the crypts of the Abbaye St.-Germain, which was established in the 6th century by Queen Clothilde on the spot where that saint was buried in AD 448. Numerous old houses are notable, including the Coche d'Eau, at the foot of the Abbaye St.-Germain in the Marine quarter, and the buildings at 16-18 Pl. de l'Hôtel; 3-5 Pl. Charles-Surugue; 14-16 Rue Sous-Murs; and 21 Rue de Paris.

En Route from Auxerre – Head toward Noyers-sur-Serein via St.-Bris-le-Vineux and D956. (Incidentally, the wine of St.-Bris-le-Vineux is less well known than that of Chablis, but it's thought by many Burgundians to be superior.) Noyers is a special treat: It's a very well preserved little medieval town that sees surprisingly few tourists. Not far away, via D86 and D11, Montréal is another pretty medieval town; at the crest of the hill on which it sits is a small church, from the back of which appears a superb panorama of the surrounding countryside.

 CHECKING IN/EATING OUT: *Moulin de Ste.-Vertu* – The kind of place you hear about only in legend: a country inn where you can have a six-course meal for almost nothing. It's an old farmhouse with antique furnishings. Ste.-Vertu (phone: 86-75-90-09). Inexpensive.

AVALLON: High on a hill above the Vallée du Cousin, Avallon was a major stronghold during the Middle Ages. As weaponry became more sophisticated, however, its military significance declined until Louis XIV finally sold the ramparts to the citizens of the town.

Though an attractive city in its own right, as far as tourism is concerned, Avallon is resigned forever to play second fiddle to its near neighbor, Vézelay, whose cathedral is widely considered the gem of Burgundy. Nonetheless, Avallon has much to offer. The Eglise St.-Lazare is an ancient edifice dating from the 4th century AD. Around AD 1000, the church received a relic of St. Lazarus, the patron saint of lepers, and pilgrimages to the church by lepers began en masse. The church was too small — it proved always to be too small — and was expanded a number of times through the following centuries. Its most interesting features are the two Romanesque portals, with varied sculptures showing musicians of the Apocalypse, signs of the zodiac, wine, acanthus leaves, and more. No visit to Avallon is complete, however, without a leisurely stroll of the ramparts and a look at the 15th-century clock tower on the Butcher's Gate.

 CHECKING IN/EATING OUT: *Hostellerie de la Poste* – An atmospheric little inn with only 23 rooms, it dispenses consistently fine food and wines. The chef is an American, trained in France. Closed mid-November to March. 13 Pl. Vauban, Avallon (phone: 86-34-06-12). Expensive.

En Route from Avallon – Head southwest toward Vézelay via the Vallée du Cousin, a lovely, shaded road that wends its way beside the Cousin River. There are numerous places where you can pull off the road for an undisturbed, feet-in-the-water picnic. Turn left at Pontaubert and follow D957 into Vézelay. Or, if you're in the mood for something exotic, pick up N6 out of Avallon or after the Vallée du Cousin head for the Grottes d'Arcy-sur-Cure, some 12 miles (19 km) north of Vézelay. There are approximately 1½ miles of subterranean grottoes here, about half of which can be explored; it's a fantastic underground world of stalactites, stalagmites, and lakes.

CHECKING IN/EATING OUT: *Moulin des Ruats* – This converted mill on the banks of the River Cousin has 24 simple rooms and a restaurant. It's a soothing place to sojourn, with the stillness of the glade disturbed only by the rush of water through the millrace. The inn is closed for a month and a half in winter. Vallée du Cousin, Avallon (phone: 86-34-07-14). Hotel, moderate; restaurant, expensive.

Moulin des Templiers – Well managed and tiny (14 rooms), this place has an eccentric country charm — its owner keeps a small menagerie (goats, turkeys, and so on) across the road. Closed November through mid-March. Vallée du Cousin, Avallon (phone: 86-34-10-80). Moderate.

VÉZELAY: About 9 miles (14 km) up the road from Avallon is Vézelay, a town famous for that jewel of Romanesque architecture, the Basilique Ste.-Madeleine. The basilica has a long history. It is part of the Abbey of Vézelay, which was founded in the 9th century, according to popular memory, by the legendary Girart de Rousillon, an early Count of Burgundy, and was consecrated by Pope John VIII in AD 878. In the 11th century, the abbey was taken over by the powerful Abbey of Cluny. A multitude of miracles were reported to have taken place thanks to the relics of Mary Magdalene that were housed here, and so began an onslaught of pilgrimages to the church. In 1122, this precipitated a disaster. A massive fire broke out and the church collapsed, burying thousands of pilgrims alive. But the church soon was rebuilt, this time with a narthex (a vestibule leading to the nave) added to provide overnight lodging for the many pilgrims. Some years later, other relics of the saint were found in Provence, and this decreased Vézelay's appeal. Later still, the basilica suffered destruction during the religious wars and then the French Revolution; eventually, it went into decline. It was the poet Prosper Merimée, working in his capacity as inspector of historical monuments, who "discovered" the beauty of the basilica and undertook an immense restoration of the building that lasted from 1840 till 1859. Again, the architect Viollet-le-Duc played a leading role in the restoration.

Today, the church is a masterpiece of light and space. As the novelist André Malraux wrote, "Romanesque architecture, in its organization of interior space, is not striving after decorative effects, but . . . to release a feeling of sacredness, to express the inexpressible." The Basilique Ste.-Madeleine accomplishes these goals admirably. Note particularly the tympanum over the central entryway and the sculpted details of the interior columns. For energetic visitors, a hike to the top of the tower is well worth the effort. The view of the surrounding countryside is nothing short of magnificent.

CHECKING IN: *L'Espérance* – A quintessentially elegant 17-room hotel that's furnished with antiques and overlooks a flower garden. Its glass-enclosed restaurant is almost as great a magnet as Ste.-Madeleine, and has been awarded three Michelin stars. (See "Romantic Hostelries" in *For The Experience,* DIVERSIONS.) Closed during January. Restaurant closed Tuesdays and Wednesday lunch. St.-Père-sous-Vézelay (phone: 86-33-20-45). Expensive.

Le Pontot – Classified as a "historic private home," this 15th-century residence in the Town Hall Square offers 8 double rooms, each uniquely appointed. A large Louis XVI–style room has canopy beds, a fireplace, and a dressing room; another apartment has stone floors, a 16th-century beamed ceiling, and antique peasant furniture. All have modern baths. Breakfast is served in the paneled Louis XVI Salon or in a walled garden. No restaurant, since *L'Espérance* (see above) is nearby, but boat trips and even balloon rides can be arranged. Town Hall Square, Vézelay (phone: 86-33-24-40). Expensive.

En Route from Vézelay – Head south toward Autun through the Morvan, the northern reaches of France's Massif Central and of Burgundy's hill country. *Morvan* is derived from the Celtic for "black mountain," and it captures the spirit of the region well. Less prosperous and less bucolic than the rest of Burgundy, like so many backwoods areas it is looked down upon as something of a poor sister by many Burgundians. Nonetheless, with its many lakes and forests, it is a regional center for sports lovers and a popular weekend spot for Parisians.

There are innumerable ways to cut through the Morvan, almost any of which will yield a host of striking vistas. A good midway point is Château-Chinon, the capital of the area. A hike to the top of Calvary hill in Château-Chinon provides an excellent view of the surrounding landscape. South of Château-Chinon is the High Morvan, the more mountainous part of the region. Take D27 through the Forêt de la Gravelle, then head toward St.-Léger, 5 miles (8 km) to the east of which is Mont-Beuvray; from there, on clear days, one can see as far as Mont-Blanc, hundreds of miles to the east.

AUTUN: This city owes its name to Augustus Caesar; originally called Augustodonum, it was a major Roman garrison and served as a base of operations for the destruction of the Bibracte. In Gallo-Roman times, it became an important commercial center on the route between Lyons and Boulogne. Autun's prominence made it a popular military target, and after many invasions, the city went into decline.

However, Autun enjoyed a renaissance in the 15th century, thanks largely to the efforts of Nicolas Rolin, Philip the Good's chancellor and a native of Autun, and his son, the Cardinal Rolin, who made Autun a major church center.

Today, Autun is a thriving provincial town of some 20,000 inhabitants, with several sights of interest. The Cathédrale St.-Lazare, built between 1120 and 1146, is most celebrated for the tympanum over the central portal. Rendered by the sculptor Gislebertus, it portrays the Last Judgment and is less gloomy than many such depictions; heaven occupies the greatest portion of the tympanum, with hell confined to a small corner on the right. Just a few steps away is the *Musée Rolin* (3 Rue de Bancs; phone: 85-52-09-76), in a house built for Nicolas Rolin; it has a fine collection of Gallo-Roman artifacts as well as of 14th- and 15th-century sculpture and paintings (closed Tuesdays). Among the latter are two depictions of Old Autun that seem to combine the qualities of map and painting, which gives the viewer a good sense of what the city was like. La Porte St.-André (St. Andrew's Gate), on the north side of town, is a remnant of the ancient Roman walls that used to surround Autun; this great edifice has two large arches through which vehicles may pass and two smaller ones for pedestrians.

CHECKING IN/EATING OUT: *Hostellerie de Vieux Moulin* – A lovely waterside garden distinguishes this 16-room hotel and its dining room. Closed mid-December through February; restaurant also closed Sunday evenings and Mondays off-season. Porte d'Arroux, Autun (phone: 85-52-10-90). Hotel, moderate to inexpensive; restaurant, expensive to moderate.

En Route from Autun – The surrounding area offers many short excursions. La Cascade de Brisecou (Breakneck Waterfall) is about 1½ miles (2 km) south of Autun via D256. Leave the car at the church at Couhard and take the 20-minute walk to the waterfall. On the return trip, note the odd, pyramidal Pierre de Couhard, believed to date from Roman times. Also of interest is the Château de Sully. Built in the 15th century, it was the birthplace of Marshal MacMahon, President of the French Republic from 1873 to 1879. To visit the château, take D973 out of Autun, then take a left onto D326 at Creusefond. (Unfortunately, visitors may enjoy only the exterior of the château; the interior is closed to the public.) Head back northwest along the eastern edge of the Parc Régional du Morvan to the town of Saulieu.

CHECKING IN/EATING OUT: *La Côte d'Or* – This 22-room hostelry has two sections — an old part dates from the 19th century and a modern one has rooms with a garden view. The two Michelin stars awarded its restaurant attest to the fine food prepared here by chef Bernard Loiseau. Try the *aiguillettes de canard* (sliced duck). 2 Rue d'Argentine, Saulieu (phone: 80-64-07-66). Expensive.

La Tour d'Auxois – It has 30 modest but clean and comfortable rooms, somewhat reminiscent of those found in a college dormitory. The restaurant is more appealing, with a small terrace for apéritifs and very tasty prix fixe meals. Closed December to January 15; restaurant also closed Sunday evenings and Mondays. 10 Rue Sallier, Saulieu (phone: 80-64-13-30). Inexpensive.

SEMUR-EN-AUXOIS: Just a few miles southeast of Montréal via D11 and D954 is the lovely town of Semur-en-Auxois. During the Middle Ages, it enjoyed a reputation as a virtually impregnable fortress, and it still has all the lineaments of its past might. The approach to Semur via the flower-lined Pont Joly gives the visitor a striking first glimpse of this medieval town, although a walking tour is probably the best way to enjoy it. You might stroll along the ramparts for a look at the many attractive old buildings and a view of the surrounding countryside, or stop in at Eglise Notre-Dame, which originally was built in the 11th century but contains elements added from the 13th to the 16th century. The church also underwent restoration under the direction of the 19th-century architect Viollet-le-Duc.

Not far from Semur, and within a few miles of each other, are a number of unusually interesting places. The first of these, some 12 miles (19 km) due east of Semur and more than a little reminiscent of Montréal, is Flavigny-sur-Ozerain. This medieval walled city at the top of a hill and surrounded on three sides by water is very appealing for its sleepy, scarcely trafficked streets, pretty old houses, and ancient ramparts. Flavigny was a fortification of some significance during the Middle Ages, but it's mostly notable these days for the popular lozenges produced by a nearby abbey.

About 4½ miles (7 km) from Flavigny via D29 is the town of Alise-Ste.-Reine, the site of ancient Alésia, where the 250,000-strong army of Vercingétorix succumbed to the siege of the amassed Roman legions in 52 BC. The saga of Vercingétorix's defeat is tragic. He was taken as a prisoner to Rome, kept there for 6 years, forced to participate in Caesar's triumphal march, and, after that humiliation, summarily executed. In the 19th century, Napoleon III had an enormous statue of Vercingétorix built at the site of ancient Alésia, where it still stands in all its kitschy glory.

A few miles down the road from Alise-Ste.-Reine is the Château de Bussy-Rabutin, small (by château standards), handsome, and positively bubbling over with effrontery. The château reflects the spirit of its irrepressible owner, the soldier and writer Roger de Rabutin, Comte de Bussy, whose barbed verses incurred the wrath of Louis XIV. He was sent into exile at Bussy-Rabutin, where he continued his literary endeavors and wrote *An Amorous History of the Gauls*. For this effort, which mocked members of Louis's court, Roger de Rabutin landed in the Bastille; upon his release, he found much to his dismay that his mistress, for whom he had written his splendid lines, had lost patience and left him.

The château at Bussy-Rabutin was known to contemporaries of the count as the Temple of Impertinence, and it deserved the title. A typically irreverent touch is the series of moons at the entrance, a not-so-subtle counterpoint to that glorious symbol so often used to represent the Sun King, Louis XIV, in Paris.

A quite different experience is found at the Abbaye de Fontenay, north of Bussy-Rabutin toward Montbard. This 12th-century Cistercian monastery has gone through a number of changes since its heyday. It first was abused by avaricious abbots, then converted into a paper factory after the French Revolution. Nonetheless, most of the buildings are intact, and a visit to the tranquil, elegant site gives a fine sense of the monastic life some 800 years ago. The guides at Fontenay can be prim to the point of schoolmarmishness — a point against the abbey, especially after a tour given by the lighthearted guides at Bussy-Rabutin. If one is prepared to wear a fittingly pious expression, however, the visit is worth it.

 CHECKING IN/EATING OUT: *Hostellerie du Val-Suzon* – It has a tranquil atmosphere, a pleasant little garden, a fine kitchen, and 17 rooms, 10 of them in a neighboring chalet. Hotel closed January to mid-February; restaurant also closed Wednesdays and Thursdays for lunch off-season. Rte. N71, Val-Suzon (phone: 80-35-60-15). Hotel, moderate; restaurant, expensive to moderate.

Auberge Chez Guite – Part of a functioning farm, this *gîte* offers 11 rooms, all clean and simple; meals are similarly unpretentious but hearty and good. The owners are M. and Mme. Frelet. Open year-round. St.-Seine-l'Abbaye (phone: 80-35-01-46). Inexpensive.

En Route from Semur-en-Auxois – From Saulieu, travel east along D977, then pick up the autoroute east, which leads to the capital and true heart of Burgundy, Dijon.

DIJON: For a detailed report on the city, its sights, hotels, and restaurants, see *Dijon* in the CITIES section.

En Route from Dijon – Just south is the part of Burgundy with which most people are familiar — the famed Côte d'Or (Golden Slope). Here the grapes are grown for several wines — le montrachet, for example — whose very names set oenophiles' palates a-tingling. Leave Dijon via D122, known as the Route des Grands Crus, and follow it south until it rejoins N74 at Vougeot; follow this road to Beaune and beyond. Along the way you'll pass through some of the great wine producing villages, among them Gevrey-Chambertin, Morey-St.-Denis, Chambolle-Musigny, Vougeot, Vosne-Romanée, Nuits-St.-Georges, Pernand-Vergelesses, Aloxe-Corton, Savigny-les-Beaune, Pommard, Volnay, Meursault, Puligny-Montrachet, Chassagne-Montrachet, and Santenay; you might stop to visit their vineyards. The people at Morin et Fils, in Nuits-St.-Georges, are particularly friendly and offer a broad selection of wines for tasting.

One highly recommended stop on the Côte d'Or is the Château du Clos de Vougeot. This ancient building houses the Confrérie des Chevaliers du Tastevin, the Burgundian wine tasting society. Tours of the château, along with descriptions of the activities of the Confrérie (which include the promotion of burgundy wines), are given on a regular basis. Although the tour devotes too much time to hailing the glories of the rather Elk-ish Confrérie, it also takes the visitor through rooms full of ancient wine making apparatus, and this aspect of the visit is fascinating.

 CHECKING IN: *Château de Gilly* – Located midway between Dijon and Beaune at the edge of the Citeaux forest, this palatial old abbey has been transformed into a luxurious 37-room hostelry. The romantic complex has vaulted hallways, Gothic dining rooms, fireplaces, and Louis XV bedrooms, as well as more contemporary amenities, such as conference facilities for up to 100. Closed January and February. Gilly Les Citeaux, Vougeot (phone: 80-62-89-98). Expensive.

 EATING OUT: *La Rôtisserie du Chambertin* – About a 20-minute drive from Dijon in the quaint town of Gevrey-Chambertin, this wonderful restaurant rates a Michelin star thanks to the talents of chef Jean-Pierre Nicolas, who turns out such dishes as *fricassee des grenouilles et escargots.* The town is famous for its powerful red wine and its semisoft cow's milk cheese — be sure to try them both here. The wine list is extraordinary. Closed Sunday evenings, Mondays, February, and the first week of August. Gevrey-Chambertin, 7 miles (11 km) south of Dijon on N74 (phone: 80-34-33-20). Expensive.

BEAUNE: This thriving city of 20,000 is renowned not only as the heart of Burgundy's wine country but also for its many fine treasures of art and architecture. By far and away Beaune's most famous structure is the Hôtel-Dieu, built in the 15th century by the Chancellor (and tax collector) of Burgundy, Nicolas Rolin. This striking example of Flemish-Burgundian architecture, though somewhat somber overall, is topped by an eye-catching roof of colorful ceramic tiles laid out in an intricate geometric pattern. The Hôtel-Dieu, which was founded by Rolin to provide care and comfort for the poor, sick, and aged, functioned as a hospital right up through 1971; today it is an old age home. (One story, perhaps apocryphal, has it that King Louis XI thought it only fitting that Rolin, who had made so many people poor, should then found a charity hospital.)

The tour of the Hôtel-Dieu includes a visit to its museum, which contains some very beautiful tapestries as well as the remarkable polyptych, *The Last Judgment,* painted by the 15th-century Flemish artist Rogier van der Weyden. The painting is a masterpiece of color and detail, which viewers can best appreciate by using a special magnifying mirror.

Nicolas Rolin also bequeathed to the hospital his vineyards, the wine from which is sold at the annual wine auction held at Beaune's marketplace. Although these wines frequently command a fairly high price because the proceeds go to the hospital and other charities, they also usually set the trend for the sale of other Burgundian wines. Thus, if this year's prices for Hospice wines are generally bid up, so too will the prices be for other wines. The auction, held on the third Sunday in November, draws buyers and wine lovers from all over the world.

Near the Hôtel-Dieu is the *Musée du Vin de Bourgogne* (Rue d'Enfer; phone: 80-22-08-19), in the old mansion of the Dukes of Burgundy, which documents the history of wine making and the cultivation of the grape. Guided tours in English are given every hour; closed on Tuesdays, *Christmas,* and *New Year's Day.* Of interest to summer visitors is Beaune's annual music festival, held during the first 2 weeks of July.

 CHECKING IN/EATING OUT: *Hostellerie du Vieux Moulin* – There are 12 rooms with TV sets in this inn. Chef Jean-Pierre Silva made big news on the Côte d'Or last year when the Michelin guide awarded him a second star for such creations as *estouffade de poireaux et jambonette de grenouilles en meurette* (a delicate stew of leeks and frogs' legs) and *pigeonneau rôti dans son jus* (young squab roasted in its juices). Closed Thursday afternoons, Wednesdays (except holidays), mid-December to mid-January, the last week of February, and the first week of March. About 10 miles (16 km) outside of Beaune in Bouilland (phone: 80-21-51-16).

Hôtellerie de Levernois – Set in a 10-acre park just 2 miles (3 km) outside of Beaune, this gracious 12-room hotel-restaurant was opened by Jean Crotet, former chef-owner of the highly rated *Côte d'Or* in nearby Nuits-St. Georges. The rooms, furnished by Mme. Crotet, are spacious and very comfortable, and the inviting, terraced dining room offers the same excellent food for which Crotet previously gained two Michelin stars. Beaune (phone: 80-24-73-58). Expensive.

Bernard Morillon – Trained in Lyons and the recipient of accolades from critics and consumers alike, chef Bernard Morillon offers light traditional *bourguignon* fare, with a heavy accent on fish. Guests dine in a covered outdoor garden. Closed Monday and Tuesday afternoons; also in February. 31 Rue Maufoux, Beaune (phone: 80-24-12-06). Expensive.

La Poste – At this old favorite with 25 comfortable rooms, travelers will find tasty regional cuisine prepared by chef Marc Chevillot and a good list of local wines. Closed late November through March. 1 Bd. Clemenceau, Beaune (phone: 80-22-08-11). Expensive.

En Route from Beaune – Although the Côte d'Or ends at Chagny, 9 miles (14 km) south, this is not the end of Burgundy's wine country. Between Chagny and Chalon-sur-Saône is the area known as the Côte Chalonnais, which has four more wine villages — Rully, Mercurey, Givry, and Montagny. And, about 35 miles (54 km) south of Chalon, is the town of Mâcon and the surrounding Mâconnais wine country. Still farther south is that area known as the Beaujolais.

EATING OUT: *Lameloise* – At this atmospheric, 15th-century country mansion, which has been given three Michelin stars, Burgundian cooking is raised to a high art. The prices are pretty high, too, but the gustatory experience is worth it, and there are 24 rooms in case you need to sleep it off. Closed Wednesdays, Thursday lunch, and most of January. 36 Pl. d'Armes, Chagny (phone: 85-87-08-85). Expensive.

Moulin d'Hauterive – A bit more off the beaten track is this restaurant in a restored mill on the edge of a sleepy stream. The isolated setting and tranquil surroundings only enhance the kitchen's fine renditions of nouvelle cuisine. Closed Sunday evenings and Mondays off-season and from November to February. Take D62 from Chagny to Chaublanc and follow signs to the tiny hamlet of St.-Gervais-en-Vallière (phone: 85-91-55-56). Moderate.

TOURNUS: At the northern edge of the Mâconnais is the city of Tournus, the home of an ancient abbey and church, Eglise St.-Philibert. The abbey was built on the spot where Valerian, an early Christian, was martyred in the 2nd century AD. Begun in the 10th and continued over the next several centuries, the church is a marvel of Romanesque architecture as exemplified by its plain façade and simple, heavy narthex. Its nave, though devoid of decoration, is nonetheless handsome and uplifting, suffused with light from high windows toward which reach tall, slender columns made of beautiful rosy stone quarried in Préty, near Tournus.

CHECKING IN/EATING OUT: *Greuze* – Fine Burgundian food and beaujolais wines are offered at this charming country inn named for Jean-Baptiste Greuze, an 18th-century artist born in Tournus. Chef Jean Ducloux's efforts have earned him two Michelin stars. There are 21 rooms in the nearby *Hôtel de Greuze* (5 Pl. de l'Abbaye) which Ducloux opened in 1986. Closed the first 10 days of December. 1 Rue Thibaudet, Tournus (phone: 85-51-13-52). Expensive.

MÂCON: About 18 miles (31 km) south of Tournus and also on the Saône is the village of Mâcon. Its famous native son is Alphonse de Lamartine, a 19th-century poet and politician. Lamartine wrote several volumes of poetry, the most successful of which was *Méditations Poétiques;* his work is generally characterized as being in the romantic tradition. To learn more about his life, visit the *Musée Lamartine* or the house where he was raised (Hôtel d'Ozenay, 15 Rue Lamartine). There's also the Circuit Lamartine, a 40-mile (64-km) drive through the environs of Mâconnais. Among the high points of the circuit are the Château de Monceau, now an old age home, one of Lamartine's favorite residences, and Milly-Lamartine, the town where Lamartine lived as a child and where he wrote his first meditation, *L'Isolement.*

The vineyards of the Mâconnais region begin at Tournus and extend south past Mâcon to the northern reaches of the Beaujolais. Perhaps the best known of the Mâconnais wines is the pouilly-fuissé, produced in the villages of Solutré-Pouilly, Davayé, and Fuissé. All three are in the lovely hills west of Mâcon, in the general direction of the Rock of Solutré and the Rock of Vergisson. After a visit to these vineyards, head up to Solutré for a look at the precipice over which thousands of wild horses were stampeded 10,000 years ago.

En Route from Mâcon – The region between Mâcon and Villefranche-sur-Saône is known as the Beaujolais, and vineyards are found in many of the villages here. However, those that consistently produce first class wines are referred to as the Beaujolais-Villages and include St.-Amour, Juliénas, Chénas, Moulin-à-Vent, Fleurie, Chiroubles, Morgon, Brouilly, Côtes de Brouilly, and Regnie, the latest cru to be promoted to Villages status.

CHECKING IN/EATING OUT: *Château de Fleurville* – This quiet 15-room hotel and its restaurant are part of a group of fortified buildings that were built by the Counts of Fleurville and later belonged to the Counts of Talleyrand-Périgord. Hotel closed mid-November to mid-December, and weekdays in February; restaurant closed Monday lunches. Fleurville (phone: 85-33-12-17). Expensive.

CLUNY: Northwest of Mâcon on routes N79 and D980 is the ancient city of Cluny, home of the once very powerful Abbey of Cluny. Founded in 910, the Cluniac order was unique in that its constitution provided for freedom from secular supervision as well as from that of the local bishop. As a result, the abbey became a wellspring of spiritual influence and religious reform throughout Europe. Numerous small priories were opened, with as many as 10,000 monks in different countries under the authority of the abbot at Cluny. During the 14th century, the power of the order began to decline, and in the aftermath of the French Revolution many of the abbey's buildings at Cluny were torn down (including a magnificent cathedral, which until the construction of St. Peter's in Rome was the largest in the world). Today, only the south part of the transepts remains, and a visit to Cluny is rather like visiting many prehistoric ruins. One is forced to imagine how things must have been but are no longer. Nonetheless, the tour is stimulating, and the journey up to Cluny, through surprisingly rough hill country, is quite enjoyable. You might stop at one of the many goatherds' huts along the way to pick up some homemade *chèvre* (goat cheese).

CHECKING IN: *Bourgogne* – Near the abbey, it has 16 comfortable rooms and a dining room rating one Michelin star. Room rates include breakfast and dinner. Closed mid-November through mid-February; restaurant also closed Tuesdays and Wednesday lunch, except during July, August, and September. Pl. de l'Abbaye, Cluny (phone: 85-59-00-58). Expensive.

Moderne Bernigaud – Another small hotel with 15 rooms. Its restaurant is closed Sunday evenings and Mondays off-season, and mid-November to mid-February. Pont-de-l'Etang, Cluny (phone: 85-59-05-65). Moderate.

EATING OUT: *Café du Nord* – A friendly little bistro, with bar and terrace looking out over the abbey, it has checkered tablecloths and serves simple, hearty fare. It's delightfully unaffected considering its touristy locale. Pl. de l'Abbaye, Cluny (phone: 85-59-09-96). Inexpensive.

En Route from Cluny – About 25 miles (40 km) west on N79 is Paray-le-Monial, worth a stop for its Basilique du Sacré-Coeur. Modeled after the cathedral in Cluny, no longer extant, it is a fine example of Romanesque architecture. Simple yet elegant, the church has two square towers over the narthex and an octagonal tower over the transept. Inside, the edifice is striking for its height and, again, its simplicity. Just next door in what was formerly the priory is a museum devoted to the faïence of Charolaise, a decorative earthenware made in the region. In addition to exhibiting a collection of over 2,000 pieces, the oldest of which date from 1836, the museum contains a section devoted to pottery making tools and an archive of designs used for Charolaise faïence. Av. Jean-Paul II (phone: 85-88-83-07); open from 2 PM to 6 PM daily, except Thursdays, from March 20 to October 20.

About 35 miles (56 km) east of Cluny, in the southeasternmost corner of Burgundy, is Bourg-en-Bresse. This busy city, which does not feel totally Burgundian — traces of neighboring Savoie are already detectable — is noted for the remarkable monastic enclave of Brou. Behind it is a story of conjugal devotion and familial obligation. In the 15th century, the Count of Bresse had a hunting accident. His wife vowed that if he recovered, she would convert the priory of Brou into an abbey. He recovered, but she never fulfilled her vow. This failure haunted her all her life, and on her deathbed she expressed her regrets to her son and husband. More time passed and still nothing was done until the death of the count's son, Philibert le Beau. This event was interpreted by the daughter-in-law, Marguerite, as divine punishment; concerned that her husband's soul would suffer eternal damnation, she began work on Brou at last. The resulting church is a magnificent example of Flamboyant Gothic architecture, with a skillfully carved triangular façade and sculpted tympanum over the doorway. The vagaries of history have taken their toll on the adjacent monastery. Over the years it has been a pig farm, a prison, and a mental hospital. Today, at last, it is simply a monument to the past.

Alsace

The green strip that is Alsace lies between the Vosges Mountains and the Rhine Valley. Much of it is hilly and some parts are actually mountainous. Natives say that the mountains act as umbrellas, protecting their vine-covered hillsides from too much rain. And so much is covered with vineyards — principally the area from Marlenheim to Thann, in the valleys of the Thur and the Bruche rivers — and orchards that Louis XIV is reported to have exclaimed "What a beautiful garden!" upon seeing this verdant region. The many varieties of fruit grown here are used to make the prized Alsatian *eaux-de-vie* — some 25 different dry, colorless, fruit-flavored alcohols — and the grapes are turned into fresh, fruity, mostly white wines quite unlike those from Bordeaux and Burgundy.

Alsace comprises two *départements*, the Bas-Rhin and the Haut-Rhin, which are bordered by Germany and Switzerland as well as the Rhine River. Paradoxically, the Haut-Rhin (Upper Rhine) *département* is south of the Bas-Rhin (Lower Rhine).

Alsace has been inhabited since prehistoric days, but it was the Celts, in the 8th century BC, who really settled it. Like most of Europe, it was annexed by the Romans, who were thrown out in AD 352. In the 8th century, under Charlemagne, it was near the center of power while remaining an independent province, not actually part of France. Alsace was officially annexed to France under the terms of the Treaty of Westphalia, in 1648, but was then ceded to Germany after the Franco-Prussian War, in 1871. The desire to reclaim Alsace became part of the growing French nationalism prior to World War I, and it was a joyful day for the entire country when in 1918 the region was returned to France. Later, when France fell to Hitler, in 1940, Alsace was occupied by Germany until the Liberation, in 1945.

Today, the relationship between this very singular region and France and Germany is rightfully complex. Perhaps because of its seesaw history — Alsace was bandied between the two nations four times in 75 years — it has clung ferociously to its own, albeit mixed, culture, architecture, and traditions. Some of its villages, its wines, and its people have German names, and until a couple of years ago, most of the street names were in German. Alsatian architecture often is reminiscent of that found in northern European Rhenish villages, with Hansel and Gretel confections of white, geranium-trimmed, half-timbered houses with steeply pitched roofs. (Visitors will be delighted to happen upon villages little changed since the Renaissance.) However, in certain cultural aspects — art, music, and hospitality — Alsace is most resolutely French. This dichotomy of history and culture has given the region much of its charm and quirkiness.

To preserve its natural parks and villages while allowing for 20th-century advances, the Alsatians have organized several preservation groups. Architects are paid by the state to consult with developers, striving for harmony between new buildings and old. Entire sections of Strasbourg and Colmar, two of the three major cities, have been restored to their original condition and closed to automobile traffic.

The region boasts a first-rate opera company and a good symphony orchestra, which both travel from Strasbourg to Colmar and Mulhouse, the third major city. Cultural activity in these three centers is brisk: Each has a local theater and many visiting troupes.

Strasbourg and Mulhouse are easily reached by plane, train, and car from nearly every major European city. Alsace is very well organized for tourism, with *Syndicats d'Initiative* in most towns. There is a seemingly endless supply of maps and brochures on every aspect of tourism, from mountain climbing and camping to visiting châteaux, all conveniently published in French, English, and German.

The Bas-Rhin is appealing for its forests and national parks, which have a complex pattern of meticulously marked hiking trails, maps of which are available at most tourist offices. Short-term rentals of rustic farms and houses also are possible through an association called the *Gîte Rural de France.* The Haut-Rhin region gave birth to the idea of *fermes auberges* — working farms that give adventurous tourists an alternative to traditional hotels and inns. Travelers can dine and spend the night with families of the many *fermes auberges* scattered throughout the region, a great many located in the Vosges Mountains. To receive information about the Bas-Rhin, write to the *Relais Départemental des Gîtes Ruraux de France* (7 Place des Meuniers, Strasbourg; phone: 88-75-56-50); for the Haut-Rhin, contact the *Association Départmentale du Tourisme du Haut-Rhin* (Hôtel du Département, BP 371, Colmar 68007; phone: 89-23-21-11).

Like other French regions, Alsace has its own style of cooking, which borrows several ingredients from its German and Swiss neighbors. Its basic character is homey, simple, and lusty, although there are many refined, elegant restaurants. Basically, visitors can expect to find pork and goose variations, with potatoes and cabbage the main vegetables.

It is wise to become familiar with some specialties, such as *tarte à l'oignon* and *tarte flambée:* the former with onions and cream, the latter a type of thin pizza with cream, cheese, onion, and bacon. *Coq au Riesling* is chicken cooked in the regional white wine. *Schiefala,* smoked pork shoulder, often is served with warm potato salad. *Baeckaeoffe,* a long-simmered stew of pork, lamb, and veal with onions and potatoes, often must be ordered in advance. The best-known specialty is *choucroute,* sauerkraut cooked in wine and served with a vast variety of sausage and ham. Desserts are simple fruit tarts, light *tarte au fromage* (cheese tart), and *kugelhopf,* a sweet yeast bread studded with raisins and dusted with sugar and almonds.

Alsatian wines, primarily white, constitute 20% of French production and are a source of great pride. They take their names from the vine plants, not from the regions where they are grown, as in the rest of France. Sylvaner is a fresh and fruity dry wine; pinot blanc has more body. The best known, riesling, gets better with age and can be full-bodied and dry, an elegant wine.

Tokay d'Alsace, or pinot gris, is an excellent accompaniment to fowl or white meat. Gewürztraminer is a spicy, fruity wine, to be drunk with rich foods; it's a good choice with foie gras, the fattened goose livers that are another prized regional specialty. Pinot Noir is the Alsatian red, lightweight but fruity, and sometimes resembling a rosé. Muscat is a dry white wine usually served as an apéritif.

The suggested route is divided into two parts. The first itinerary makes a circle through the northernmost portion of Alsace; it begins in the cosmopolitan yet charming city of Strasbourg and then tours the countryside, giving the traveler a look at the several national parks and forests of the region as well as its many lovely villages. The second itinerary, the 90-mile (145-km) Route du Vin (Wine Road), extends from Marlenheim to Mulhouse, near the Swiss border, and includes a number of typical villages whose well-ordered fields produce the popular Alsatian wines. This route also includes Colmar, noted for its architectural beauty. The entire route is covered by the Michelin map No. 87.

Although this area generally has not been discovered by Americans, it does see a fair amount of tourism. Reservations are advised in high season (summer). Hotel listings include a very expensive category, over $120 for a double room with bath; expensive, from $80 to $120; moderate, $50 to $80; and inexpensive, under $50. Restaurants that charge more than $90 for two people are listed as expensive; from $50 to $90, moderate; and under $50, inexpensive. Prices do not include wine or drinks; service usually is included. Good restaurants are full even off-season, so make reservations when you can.

STRASBOURG: For a detailed report on the city, its sights, hotels, and restaurants, see *Strasbourg* in THE CITIES. To start this tour, take D41 northwest from Strasbourg to Saverne.

SAVERNE: A small town perched on a hill, Saverne has the enormous and elegant Château de Rohan, named after the powerful family of princes and bishops. Its façade of pink sandstone overlooks the Canal de la Marne au Rhin; inside is a small archaeology and history museum. In early August, the city puts on a *son et lumière* performance, which usually animates historical subjects using special sound and lighting effects. For dates and information, contact the *Services Culturels de la Ville de Saverne* (phone: 88-91-18-52). Other local attractions include a nearby outdoor market that bustles on Thursday and Sunday mornings on the Place du Général-de-Gaulle. On Grande-Rue, the main pedestrian street, is the Hôtel de Ville (Town Hall), flanked by the Maison Katz, dating from 1605, with its lovely mullioned windows. *Muller Oberling,* at 68 Grande-Rue, is a good tearoom.

CHECKING IN/EATING OUT: *Chez Jean* – Here you'll find 30 clean, rustic rooms and a restaurant that serves hearty food, including an immense *choucroute* and good steaks, and Alsatian wines by the carafe. The latest addition to this operation is a new *winstub* next door. Closed December 20 to January 15. 3 Rue Gare, Saverne (phone: 88-91-10-19). Moderate.

***Auberge de Kochersberg* –** This is actually the cafeteria for Adidas sneaker factory employees, but it's also open to the public, after 12:30 PM for lunch and after 7 PM for dinner. Closed Sundays, Mondays, and late July to mid-August. Landersheim, 8 miles (13 km) outside Saverne on D4l (phone 88-69-91-58). Inexpensive.

En Route from Saverne – Follow the signs to the Col de Saverne. Along the way is the Jardin des Roses, which has some 2,000 plants and is open from May to September. The forest here, filled with footpaths and picnic tables, is a tempting place to stop for lunch.

Take D122, D133, and D178 to La Petite-Pierre, where a fortified château dominates the mountaintop. From La Petite-Pierre, D7 leads east to Weiterswiller, a pretty Alsatian village notable for its 17th-century houses with exposed beams. Next, take D7 and D6 to Ingwiller and D28 northeast to Niederbronn-les-Bains, and enjoy the gorgeous scenery, rolling hills, and tiny villages of the Parc National des Vosges du Nord. Niederbronn is a spa, prized for its mountain waters used in the treatment of arthritis and rheumatism. The town's municipal museum also has a small collection of medieval artifacts.

From Niederbronn, follow the zigzagging roads to Wissembourg, passing the ruins of centuries-old châteaux on the way. North on D653, then left on D53, are the Châteaux de Windstein, two castles built in 1212 and 1340, right next to each other. The ruins can be reached only on foot.

Back on N62, go northwest to the Château de Falkenstein, which was founded in 1128 and destroyed in 1564; only ruins remain. They also may be reached only by foot. From the ruins one has a view of the northern Vosges. Follow the small road of N62 to Etang de Hanau; link up with D3 and travel east through Obersteinbach and on to the Château de Fleckenstein. This stretch passes a large, curious, and beautiful Alsatian farm, with crooked rooftops and windows crazily askew. The château, another ruin, overlooks the German border. Inside, the rooms are cut directly from the rock.

 CHECKING IN: *Les Trois Roses* – A fine view, an indoor pool, and a tennis court enhance this 35-room hotel. Closed January. 19 Rue Principale, La Petite-Pierre (phone: 88-70-45-02). Moderate.

Des Vosges – This hotel faces the valley and has 30 charming rooms; the restaurant serves fine Alsatian food. Closed mid-November to mid-December. 30 Rue Principale, La Petite-Pierre (phone: 88-70-45-05). Moderate.

EATING OUT: *Auberge de l'Imsthal* – In a calm setting next to a large pond, this restaurant serves several Alsatian specialties, such as ham, game, and *pot-au-feu* (a hearty meat and vegetable stew). Closed Monday evenings and Tuesdays. Rte. Forestière, La Petite-Pierre (phone: 88-70-45-21). Expensive to moderate.

Bristol – A sophisticated dining spot that is run by a young chef. Menu offerings change regularly but generally include a mouth-watering cabbage tart, tasty turbot with tomatoes and basil, and sumptuous desserts. Closed Wednesdays and during January. 4 Pl. Hôtel-de-Ville, Niederbronn (phone: 88-09-61-44). Moderate to inexpensive.

WISSEMBOURG: The doorway between France and Germany during the last two wars, this village fortunately remains beautifully preserved. On the main square, the Place du Marché-aux-Choux (Cabbage Market), an outdoor market, is held on Sunday mornings. On the Rue de la République is the Hôtel de Ville (Town Hall), built in the mid-18th century. A tiny street leads to the Lauter River, with its small bridge and view of the old houses along it.

The Eglise St.-Pierre et St.-Paul, built in the 13th century, is Alsace's largest church after the Strasbourg Cathedral. It has an ornate Gothic interior of pink stone, with the vestiges of frescoes (that of St. Christopher, near the apse, is perhaps the largest portrait in France) and 13th-century stained glass windows. Across the river, on Quai Anselman, is a richly decorated house dated 1540.

Five miles (8 km) west of Wissembourg on the D3, near Lembach, are the Maginot

Line fortifications built by the French between the world wars to protect their north-eastern border with Germany. In the town of Lembach, take D65 south to the Valley of Sauer where almost 2 miles of shops await visitors (open daily from March 15 to November 20; phone: 88-94-48-62).

Follow D263 south to Haguenau.

CHECKING IN: *L'Ange* – This 16th-century house with 8 rooms is more picturesque outside than in, but the food is good: The fixed-price menu of country meat pie, game stew, and crème caramel is a bargain. 2 Rue de la République, Wissembourg (phone 88-94-12-11). Hotel, inexpensive; restaurant, expensive to moderate.

***Au Cygne* –** Choose the pretty rooms in the annex next door to the main hotel. Closed Thursday lunch, Wednesdays, February, and 2 weeks in July. 3 Rue du Sel, Wissembourg (phone 88-94-00-16). Inexpensive.

En Route from Wissembourg – Halfway to Haguenau, on village-dotted D263, you can detour onto D243 to visit Betschdorf, known for its pretty blue and white pottery. A museum in the village at 4 Rue de Kehlendorf (phone: 88-54-48-00; closed Tuesdays, and November to May) is devoted to it, and several shops sell it.

HAGUENAU: With its modern buildings, the city itself is of little interest, but it does have a worthwhile museum and church. The *Musée Alsatien* is in a restored 15th-century building (1 Pl. Joseph Thierry; phone: 88-73-30-41; closed Tuesdays). On the first floor are beautiful furniture collections as well as pottery and metal household objects. Upstairs is a re-created potter's studio and some examples of Betschdorf pottery. There's also the *Historical Museum* (9 Rue du Maréchal Foch; phone: 88-93-79-22; closed Saturday afternoons, Sundays, and Mondays) which houses important archaeological collections including items from Bronze and Iron Age tombs in the Hanguenau Forest as well as bronze objects from the Roman period, books printed in the 15th and 16th centuries, and an exhibit devoted to the history of the town.

The Eglise St.-Nicolas boasts magnificent 18th-century woodwork on the organ and choir stalls; the chapels have several intriguing woodcarvings of religious subjects.

From here, take N63 to return to Strasbourg; then take N4 due west to Marlenheim, where the Wine Road begins.

MARLENHEIM and the ROUTE DU VIN: The Route du Vin begins at Marlenheim, about 12 miles (19 km) from Strasbourg on N4. The scenery changes as the road nears, then veers from, the mountains. The villages along the way, with similar architecture of half-timbered façades and quirky roofs, all have their charms. The road, which is very well marked, winds south, zigzagging back and forth across N422, which joins N83 north of Sélestat. The wine villages are completely hidden from these main arteries.

Alsace's vineyards bear little resemblance to France's other wine producing regions, primarily because the area is mountainous. The wineries welcome visitors, and all along the road wine stands offer free tastings and sell bottled wines to travelers. (Note that the wines of Alsace are unusual in that they are known by the name of the grape — Riesling, for example — rather than by the name of the town in which they are grown.)

Journey west, then south, from Marlenheim through Wangen and Westhoffen to Molsheim; these are typical wine villages, with old houses and winding, narrow streets that climb the hillsides.

CHECKING IN/EATING OUT: *Hostellerie du Cerf* – This comfortable hotel has a fine restaurant that has earned two Michelin stars. Imaginative adaptations of many regional favorites are served, including game, foie gras, and several stews of fish and fowl. Closed Mondays and Tuesdays. 30 Rue du Général-de-Gaulle, Marlenheim (phone 88-87-73-73). Hotel, moderate; restaurant, expensive.

MOLSHEIM: A lovely town, it clings to the left bank of the Bruche River, at the foot of the Vosges. Visit the Metzig, a Renaissance building on Place de l'Hôtel-de-Ville with typical Rhenish architecture of a steeply pitched roof with dormer windows. A double staircase leads to a central door surmounted by a fanciful clock tower; built in the 16th century by the local butchers' corporation, it now houses a museum. On Place de l'Eglise is a former Jesuit seminary, built in 1618; inside are elaborate stucco decorations and a richly sculpted pulpit. Lovely houses line the Rue de Strasbourg: One is decorated with sculpted heads representing people and animals.

Routes D422 and D35 lead to Rosheim.

 CHECKING IN/EATING OUT: *Père Benoît* – A family-run hotel on the site of an 18th-century farmhouse just east of Molsheim via A352 and only 5 minutes from the Strasbourg airport. Alsatian specialties such as *tarte flambée* are served in front of a log fire under the vaulted ceiling of the former farmhouse's cellar. Closed Mondays, and January and August. 34 Rte. de Strasbourg, Entzheim (phone: 88-68-98-00). Moderate.

ROSHEIM: This Romanesque village nestles in a verdant, sweeping valley. On Rue du Général-de-Gaulle are some of Alsace's oldest houses, made of gray stone with curious, tiny windows. The oldest house, nicknamed "House of the Heathen," dates from around 1170. The ancient gateways to the town remain, as do some of the ramparts. The town also produces rouge aottrott, one of Alsace's few red wines.

Obernai lies 4 miles (6 km) south of Rosheim.

OBERNAI: This is the most beautiful village, completely preserved, in this part of the Route du Vin. The ramparts and towers date from the Middle Ages, the Town Hall and belfry from the Renaissance. The Hôtel de Ville (Town Hall), built of the local golden stone, marks the beginning of a passageway lined with galleries. The old Wheat Market is topped by a huge stork's nest. *Urban,* a pastry shop on the Place du Marché, has windows full of *kugelhopf,* the buttery circular cake so popular in this region. Three hundred feet down Route du Général-Gouraud is *Gross,* another fine pastry shop. On Sundays, a bustling flea market is held on this main square. Every year on December 13, the *Festival of St. Odilia,* patron saint of Alsace, attracts pilgrims from all over the region.

CHECKING IN: *A La Cour d'Alsace* – An elegant addition to Obernai's accommodations, this 30-room country hotel is housed in an ensemble of 16th- and 17th-century structures. 3 Rue de Gail, Obernai (phone: 88-95-07-00). Expensive.

Le Parc – This hotel not only has roomy accommodations but saunas and a gymnasium to recommend it. Try its restaurant for a sumptuous Sunday lunch buffet or, any day, the many updated Alsatian specialties. There's an unparalleled selection of *eaux-de-vie,* the passion of the owner, Marc Wucher. Hotel closed during December; restaurant closed Sunday evenings and Mondays. 169 Rue Général-Gouraud, Obernai (phone: 88-95-50-08). Hotel, moderate; restaurant, expensive.

La Diligence – Really three hotels in a series of old, picturesque buildings in the center of town. Hotel open year-round; restaurant closed January and February. 23 Pl. Mairie, Obernai (phone 88-95-55-69). Moderate to inexpensive.

Les Vosges – This small place offers convenient but modest lodgings. The rooms are clean, and the price is right. Hotel open year-round; restaurant closed 2 weeks in January, 2 weeks in June, and Sunday evenings and Mondays off-season. 5 Pl. de la Gare, Obernai (phone: 88-95-53-78). Inexpensive.

 EATING OUT: *Halles aux Blés* – Perhaps the prettiest restaurant in town; in the old Wheat Market, it has a brasserie on the main floor and a more elegant restaurant upstairs. Pl. du Marché, Obernai (phone 88-95-56-09). Moderate to inexpensive.

L'Etoile – A simple *winstub* — a bistro serving regional food and wines, often by the glass. Closed Mondays, Tuesday lunch in autumn, and from mid-November to mid-March. 6 Pl. de l'Etoile, Obernai (phone: 88-95-50-57). Inexpensive.

En Route from Obernai – Proceed south to Sélestat, stopping off at Barr, where an annual wine fair is held in July and a harvest fair in October (for information, inquire at the *Syndicat d'Initiative,* Pl. Hôtel-de-Ville). Also stop off at Andlau, whose mostly 12th-century church is sculpted with fantastical figures.

Continue south on D35 to Châtenois, then southwest on N59 to Haut-Koenigsbourg. The road to this town climbs through two parks: Monkey Mountain and Eagle's Park. The castle in Haut-Koenigsbourg, which belonged to a family of Swiss counts, is one of the most visited in Alsace; it dates from feudal times but was completely restored in 1908, a bit heavy-handedly. As a result, some of the present architecture suggests the early 20th century rather than the Middle Ages. The castle sits high — some 2,000 feet — above the Rhine plain on a rocky outcrop and thus commands a fine view of the surrounding vineyards and neighboring Germany.

Route D159 leads back to Sélestat.

SÉLESTAT: A mostly modern town on the left bank of the Ill River, Sélestat does have two lovely churches. The 12th-century pink sandstone Eglise Ste.-Foy, in the center of town, is considered one of the best examples of Romanesque churches in Alsace. Next to it is the Eglise St.-Georges (dating from the 13th to the 15th century), which displays a mélange of styles with stained glass windows that show angels playing 16th-century musical instruments. The stained glass windows were executed by Max Ingrand. Sélestat was once the seat of a flourishing university, and the Bibliothèque Humaniste, founded in 1452, is rich in rare manuscripts, such as a 7th-century Merovingian dictionary and some 2,000 15th-century Humanist works. The name "America" was born in the Alsace town of St.-Dié. It first appeared in print in 1507, to identify the Western Hemisphere, named after Amerigo Vespucci. The historic document, *Cosmographiae Introductio,* is on view in Sélestat's Humanist Library.

The second leg of the Route du Vin begins south of Sélestat, on the way to Ribeauvillé.

En Route from Sélestat – Detour briefly off the Route du Vin (Wine Road) by crossing the Ill River on D424 and heading 9 miles (14 km) southeast to Marckolsheim, where the *Mémorial-Musée de la Ligne Maginot du Rhin* (Memorial Museum of the Maginot Line) is installed in a World War II bunker. Among the exhibits here are a Sherman tank, French and German arms, and maps of the area showing the French defense strategy. Closed mid-November to mid-March; open weekends only from mid-March to mid-June and mid-September to mid-November. (Rte. du Rhin; phone: 88-92-51-70.)

To rejoin the Route du Vin, head west on D10 and D106 to Ribeauvillé. On the way, in Illhaeusern, is the region's best (and best-known) restaurant.

 EATING OUT: *Auberge de l'Ill* – On the bank of the Ill, with a sweeping green lawn bordered by feathery willow trees, this three-star restaurant is a romantic spot indeed. The dining room is serene and filled with flowers, sparkling with old silver collected by the owners, the Haeberlin brothers, Paul and Jean-Pierre. Some specialties are flan of frogs' legs with watercress, venison in a light pepper sauce, and salmon soufflé. The wine list has the best Alsatian vintages as well as a large selection from other regions. Book well in advance. Closed Monday nights, Tuesdays, and the first week of July. (See also *Haute Gastronomie*, DIVERSIONS.) Illhaeusern (phone: 89-71-83-23). Expensive.

RIBEAUVILLÉ: This bustling wine town is filled with old houses and picturesque public buildings. Two towers of the ancient fortifications are left, now topped with storks' nests. Leave your car at the entrance to town, where there is a statue of a wine maker. Grande-Rue, the main street, is lined with old buildings. *Pfifferhüs,* a *winstub,* or bistro, from the 16th century, is in one of the oldest (see *Eating Out*). One house, inscribed "Ave Maria," has a central oriel window flanked by two caryatids, one representing an angel, the other representing the Virgin Mary, portraying the Annunciation.

The Wheat Market, a 16th-century Gothic building with two arches, leads to the tiny Rue des Tanneurs, bordered with lovely houses. The Chapelle de l'Hôpital dates from the 14th century.

At 58 Grande-Rue, *John,* a pastry shop, sells *kugelhopf* by the slice. The street widens at the Hôtel de Ville (Town Hall), a lovely 18th-century structure. Opposite is the Eglise des Augustins, with its multicolored tile roof. At the square's edge is the Tour des Bouchers, a 13th-century belfry. The street, and the town, ends at the Place de la République with a Renaissance fountain bearing the coat of arms of the town. *Pfifferday* (Pipers Day), a folklore festival, is held the first week in September. There's also a wine festival on the next to last weekend in July, and a village music festival on the last Sunday in August.

From Ribeauvillé, travel south to Riquewihr. This road, and beyond it as far as Kaysersberg, which was the scene of intense fighting during World War II, is dotted with memorials and gravesites.

CHECKING IN: *Clos St.-Vincent* – A lovely place with 8 rooms and 3 suites, and a restaurant, it is set in the vineyards above Ribeauvillé. Hotel and restaurant closed mid-November to mid-March. Restaurant closed Tuesdays and Wednesdays. Rte. de Bergheim, Ribeauvillé (phone: 89-73-67-65). Very expensive.

Le Menestrel – Alsace's gently sloping vineyards surround this modern, flower-studded inn just outside Ribeauvillé, opened in 1989 by a pastry chef and his wife. Av. du Général de Gaulle, Ribeauvillé (phone: 89-73-80-52). Moderate.

Les Signeurs de Ribeaupierre – A fine bargain, this family-run 17th-century inn offers 10 rooms — large, pretty, and spotless. Closed February to mid-March. 11 Rue du Château, Ribeauvillé (phone: 89-73-70-31). Moderate.

La Tour – This charming place is run by a wine family who has turned an old winery into a hotel. Closed January to mid-March. 1 Rue de la Mairie, Ribeauvillé (phone 89-73-72-73). Moderate to inexpensive.

EATING OUT: *Des Vosges* – Clean and modern, this restaurant (with one Michelin star) features an extensive menu with a three-course, reasonably fixed-price meal. 2 Grande-Rue, Ribeauvillé (phone 89-73-61-39). Hotel, moderate; restaurant, expensive to moderate.

Zum Pfifferhüs – An appealing *winstub* in a landmark building, this one has excellent *choucroute.* Closed Wednesdays, Thursdays, and during February. 14 Grande-Rue, Ribeauvillé (phone: 89-73-62-28). Inexpensive.

En Route from Ribeauvillé – Continuing on D3 toward Riquewihr, you'll pass a stork preserve near Hunawihr. Generally regarded as the symbol of Alsace, the stork has been threatened with extinction due to the disappearance of the marshes, its natural habitat. The preserve is part of a program to restock the area with these harbingers of good fortune. Domestic birds are mated with wild ones, and the stork couples then are returned to the wild for their annual migration.

RIQUEWIHR: It's almost too much, this picture-postcard town resembling a stage set. In fact, some of it is only façade; the Hugel winery, for example, occupies two 16th-century houses that have been gutted to make room for its equipment. The entire village is a historical monument.

The town's Société d'Archéologie publishes an excellent map showing 33 buildings of interest; ask for it in tourist offices (there's one on Place Voltaire), bookstores, and hotels. At the beginning of the cobblestoned main street, the Grande-Rue, the *Musée des Postes et Télécommunications* (formerly the castle of the Dukes of Montbéllard-Wurtemberg) has an exhibit that explains that the mail system was created by the Roman emperor Augustus to transmit his orders throughout the Roman Empire, which included Alsace. Beautiful wrought-iron signs, old wagons, telephones, and mailmen's costumes are other attractions (closed during the winter; phone: 89-47-93-80).

The Grande-Rue is lined with extraordinary houses, completely preserved; many are now restaurants and tearooms. One, 18 Grande-Rue, dating from 1535, has a courtyard surrounded by a sculpted balcony. Vaulted passageways lead to tiny streets and hidden courtyards. In the Cour des Vignerons, the old Wine Makers' Guildhall is decorated with a dazzling array of windowboxes brimming with flowers. The Rue des Cerfs, marked by a stag's head, has many signs welcoming guests to bed-and-breakfast accommodations.

The Dolder, a 13th-century guard tower set into the city walls, houses a museum of old money and arms. The walls themselves formed a double ring of protection for the town, and the old gates and iron doors are perfectly preserved (phone: 89-47-92-15).

Many wineries are open for tastings. Because Riquewihr attracts so many tourists, avoid it during the summer, except in the early morning and late afternoon, and the entire month of August.

Continue south, then west, to Kaysersberg.

CHECKING IN: *St. Nicolas* – Actually an old Alsatian house, it is now a comfortable hotel. Closed mid-January to mid-March. 2 Rue St.-Nicolas, Riquewihr (phone: 89-49-01-51). Inexpensive.

EATING OUT: *Auberge de Schoenenbourg* – Enjoy Alsatian food with nouvelle cuisine touches and gaze out at the vineyard stretching behind the restaurant. The wines served are made from grapes grown here. Closed Wednesday nights, Thursdays, and mid-January to mid-February. 2 Rue de la Piscine, Riquewihr (phone: 89-47-92-28). Expensive.

Au Tire Bouchon – Hearty local food is served amid lovely decor. 29 Rue de Général-de-Gaulle, Riquewihr (phone: 89-47-91-61). Moderate to inexpensive.

En Route from Riquewihr – The road through Beblenheim to Kaysersberg climbs into the hillier vineyards and is marked with military cemeteries and memorials to the two world wars. In Mittelwihr, the Mur des Fleurs was covered in red, white, and blue flowers during the Occupation as a symbol of Alsatian fidelity to France. The National Cemetery at Sigolsheim, which looks out over the vine-covered hills, is a burial ground for French soldiers who died in World War II.

The church in Kientzheim has a gravestone for Lazare de Schwendi, who supposedly imported the Tokay grape to Alsace from Hungary.

KAYSERSBERG: Known mainly as the birthplace of Albert Schweitzer (in 1875), the town is also a delightful wine village filled with medieval houses and bustling farm activity. The southern bank of the meandering Weiss River affords a good view of the ruins of the ancient castle perched above the town, the Hôtel de Ville (Town Hall), an elegant 16th-century building, and the Romanesque Eglise de la Ste.-Croix, hugged by tiny streets (Rues Eglise, Hôpital, Gendarmerie) bordered with ancient houses. Rue du Général-de-Gaulle, also called Grande-Rue, has its fair share of lovely old houses as well. The quirky architecture here is silhouetted against a pine forest. Cross over on the fortified bridge that dates from 1511 and has a minuscule chapel built into it.

The tourist office is immediately behind Ste.-Croix, and next door is tiny St.-Michel chapel, which dates from 1463. To visit, knock on the door of house No. 43, to the left of the chapel; once inside, make a point to see the interesting 14th-century crucifix in the choir.

Schweitzer's birthplace is now a museum in his honor (126 Rue du Général de Gaulle; phone: 89-47-36-55; closed November to *Easter*). There is also the *Historical Museum* (62 Rue du Général-de-Gaulle; phone: 89-78-22-78; open daily in July and August and weekends only from *Easter* to November), featuring some notable works of religious art, regional archaeological finds, and documents of Kayserberg's famous sons, including Jean Geiler and Mathias Zell.

Every 5 years, Kaysersberg holds a *Fêtes des Vendanges* (Grape Harvest Festival); the next one will be held in 1995.

CHECKING IN/EATING OUT: *Résidence Chambard* – A comfortable, modern 20-room hotel, it has conveniences that include direct-dial telephones. Its classic restaurant with one Michelin star offers a gracious dining room and specialties such as foie gras cooked in cabbage leaves. Hotel closed at *Christmas* and for most of March; restaurant closed Mondays and Tuesday lunch. *Résidence Chambard* is just behind the *Chambard* restaurant at 9 Rue du Général-de-Gaulle, Kayserberg (phone: 89-47-10-17). Hotel, moderate; restaurant, expensive.

Château – This simple but acceptable 10-room lodging is near the *Schweitzer Museum* and has a restaurant. Closed Wednesday evenings, Thursdays, and January. 38 Rue du Général-de-Gaulle, Kayserberg (phone: 89-78-24-33). Inexpensive.

En Route from Kayserberg – Through Ammerschwihr and Niedermorschwihr, the Wine Road overlooks the entire plain of Alsace and passes through lovely villages. At the *Caveau Morakopf,* a fine *winstub* in Niedermorschwihr, the bill comes with the handwritten message "Thank you and see you soon." Nearby, at the pastry shop *Au Relais des Trois Epis* (La Barroche; phone: 89-49-83-67), Maurice Ferber makes what is probably the best *kugelhopf* in Alsace.

In the town of Turckheim, a few miles farther south, a watchman in Renaissance costume patrols the streets in summer, sword in one hand, lantern in the other. The three ancient entries into town remain: France Gate, with its huge tower, and Munster Gate, both just off the quay beside the Fecht River, and the Brand Gate, on Rue des Vignerons.

Go west on D10 to Munster, where the famous cheese is made. From here, the well-marked Route des Crêtes, sinuous and lovely, offers some spectacular views. Scattered nearby are *fermes auberges,* farms open to the public that serve simple meals for low prices. Some also offer rooms and other amenities such as horseback riding and skiing. An excellent guide to the Vallée de Munster is available free at most tourist offices in the area.

From Munster, take D417 to Colmar.

CHECKING IN/EATING OUT: *Aux Armes de France* – Run with impressive efficiency by chef Gaertner, this restaurant's traditional French cuisine has earned it two Michelin stars. The foie gras alone is outstanding. It also offers 8 moderately priced rooms. Closed Wednesdays, Thursday lunch, and the month of January. 1 Grand-Rue, Ammerschwihr (phone: 89-47-10-12). Expensive.

COLMAR: Unquestionably Alsace's most beautiful city, now lovingly restored, Colmar was once the royal residence of Charlemagne. Since the Middle Ages, it has housed artists and artisans, and its graceful streets and often spectacular architecture still reflect this past.

Begin at La Petite Venise (Little Venice), a restored neighborhood of half-timbered houses, shops, and artist's studios perched along the banks of the Lauch River. Pont St.-Pierre overlooks the tranquil scene. Wander along any of the picturesque streets toward the Ancienne Douane (Ancient Custom House), a large, 15th-century arcaded building with a roof tiled in a colorful diamond pattern; also known as the Koifhus, its inscription ("In 1480 was the house built") is in German. This landmark now is a local conference center.

Directly north, the Quartier des Tanneurs, where leatherworkers once labored, is another neighborhood that has been restored and converted to a pedestrian zone (as has most of Old Colmar). Many distinguished buildings are crammed into the tiny streets, and all are well marked in French and German. The tourist office (4 Rue Unterlinden; phone: 89-41-02-29) and bookshops can provide excellent maps and guides in English.

Maison Pfister, built midway along lovely Rue des Marchands in 1537 and restored in 1971, displays an imaginatively painted exterior of emperors, allegorical figures, and animals. Five swooping arches grace the ground level, and a spiral staircase leads to the upper floors. An especially large oriel window looks onto the outdoor café in the plaza below, and the third-floor balcony overflows with pink, purple, and red impatiens. A jaunty green turret caps the impressive creation. Across the street is the Maison Schongauer; the house once belonged to the family of the 15th-century artist Martin Schongauer.

Maison des Têtes (19 Rue des Têtes), now a brasserie, dates from 1608 and takes its name from the dozens of tiny carved heads of people and animals that ornament its façade (see *Eating Out*).

The Eglise des Dominicains, built in the 14th century of warm, golden stone, houses a magnificent altar painting by Martin Schongauer, *The Virgin of the Rose Bush* (1473); the stained glass windows deserve special attention, as well. The 14th-century Eglise St.-Martin, recently restored, has a pink stone exterior with an intricately sculpted portal showing the Last Judgment.

Entire books have been written on France's *Musée d'Unterlinden,* the most visited museum outside of Paris, and its two major treasures, the Issenheim altarpiece by Matthias Grünewald and the 24-panel series of the Passion by Schongauer. The altar is an artistic curiosity, its paintings alternately expressionist and surrealist. Chamber pots and dirty linen are depicted next to angels and virgins. The altar's central panel is flanked by side panels that open in an intricate design. A *maquette* (model) in the gallery demonstrates how the work looks both open and closed. The museum, in a 13th-century convent with a vine-covered cloister, has a delightful collection of Alsatian folk art on the second floor: peasant scenes of old farms, folk costumes, unique musical instruments, arms, and ceramics. Ask the guard to turn on the sophisticated animated toys. The museum is at Place de la Sinn (phone: 89-41-89-23). There are plans for a new municipal museum — the *Rhine Museum of the Manuscript and the Ancient Book* — that will be located in the Convent of the Dominicans. It will house some 1,200 manuscripts and a rare collection of early printed books. For information, call 89-41-02-29.

Scattered throughout the squares in this town are statues by Auguste Bartholdi, the sculptor of the Statue of Liberty, who was born here in 1834. A museum in his family's home at 30 Rue des Marchands displays many of his works (phone: 89-41-90-60).

Every year the town holds a week-long wine festival that encompasses the *Feast of the Assumption* holiday (August 15). A newer annual tradition is the *Festival Interna-*

tional de Colmar, held in early July and featuring a week of classical concerts by *Les Virtuoses de Moscou* and other visiting groups and soloists. Colmar's first biennial *International Festival of Gastronomy,* held in March 1990, hosted chefs and participants from all over France as well as other countries. The next one will take place in late March 1992. For information about both festivals, call 89-41-02-29.

The third leg of the journey along the Wine Road begins due west of Colmar, in Wintzenheim.

CHECKING IN: *Terminus-Bristol* – A large, old-fashioned hotel that recently remodeled several of its rooms. Ask for a deluxe room to experience the best of these high-style *chambres.* Its one-star restaurant, *Rendez-vous de Chasse* (phone: 89-41-10-10), has a new and talented young chef who offers one of the town's most refined and inventive menus. (A second, less formal restaurant next door, *L'Auberge,* has traditional fare.) 7 Pl. de la Gare, Colmar (phone: 89-23-59-59). Expensive.

Le Maréchal – At the water's edge in the Little Venice quarter of Colmar, this sprawling collection of half-timbered houses with flower-strewn balconies and crooked stairways has a special, quirky charm. Rooms are named for composers — Mozart, Wagner, Beethoven — and each is decorated differently. The paneled, candlelit restaurant overlooks the water. 4-6 Pl. des Six Montagnes Noires, Colmar (phone: 89-41-60-32). Expensive to moderate.

Amiral – This former factory at the edge of town has been converted into a pleasant, modern hotel with a military theme. Adjoining it is *Le Best Bar* with piano playing nightly. 11A Bd. du Champ de Mars, Colmar (phone: 89-23-26-25). Moderate.

St. Martin – In the center of the old town of Colmar, this residence with its superb Renissance staircase has expanded across the courtyard, adding 11 modern rooms to its original simple but comfortable 12 *chambres.* Closed during January and February. 38 Grand-Rue, Colmar (phone: 89-24-11-51). Moderate.

EATING OUT: *Au Fer Rouge* – Tucked into a charming house in the center of town and run by a young chef full of inventive ideas that have won him one Michelin star, it has a good wine list and a luxurious but still cozy atmosphere. Closed Sunday evenings, Mondays, and a week in August. 52 Grande-Rue, Colmar (phone: 89-41-37-24). Expensive.

Schillinger – Enjoy caring service and regional specialties and game, such as partridge on a bed of *choucroute,* foie gras, and sumptuous desserts, which have been given two Michelin stars. Closed Sunday evenings, Mondays, and most of July. 16 Rue Stanislas, Colmar (phone: 89-41-43-17). Expensive.

Maison des Têtes – A simple brasserie in an extraordinary 17th-century landmark building, where heads of people and mythical animals adorn the façade, imploring you to enter. Closed Sunday evenings, Mondays, and mid-January to mid-February. 19 Rue des Têtes, Colmar (phone: 89-24-43-43). Expensive to moderate.

Le Boulevard – This new and trendy restaurant, with expansive sloping picture windows reminiscent of an ocean liner, is docked on the main thoroughfare. Its nouvelle cuisine is served in a club-like atmosphere. Open until midnight; closed Sundays. 15 Bd. du Champ de Mars (phone: 89-24-24-44). Moderate.

Le Petit Bouchon – Tucked away on a small square, this tiny upstairs eatery is decorated in pink tones and with flowers, and serves Lyonnais and Alsatian fare that is carefully prepared. Portions are generous and prices reasonable. Closed Wednesdays and Thursday lunch. 11 Rue d'Alspach (phone: 89-23-45-57). Moderate.

Caveau St.-Pierre – From this *winstub,* smack on the water in La Petite Venise, you can admire the scene, fill up on reasonably priced fare, and imbibe at leisure. Closed Sunday evenings and Mondays. 24 Rue de la Herse, Colmar (phone: 89-41-99-33) Moderate to inexpensive.

En Route from Colmar – Take the Wine Road from Wintzenheim and Wettolsheim to Eguisheim, another perfectly preserved wine village set into the vine-crested hills. The main square, with a lovely Renaissance fountain, is the center of a web of circular streets and alleys crammed full of old houses. The imposing pink sandstone towers, ruins of the castle built 7 centuries ago, dominate the hill. Shops line the main square. The best buys here are in cooking equipment: pottery for preparing Alsatian specialties and copper utensils. The village of Husseren-les-Châteaux, the highest point on the Wine Road, has an excellent view of the entire valley and of Eguisheim, to the north. Hattstatt, once a fortified town, has an interesting church that comprises Romanesque, Renaissance, and baroque styles.

Continue south, through Gueberschwihr and Pfaffenheim, to Rouffach.

EATING OUT: _Caveau d'Eguisheim_ – Renowned for its _choucroute,_ frogs' legs, onion tart, _kugelhopf,_ and other regional specialties, this warm, homey dining place has earned one Michelin star. It also features wines of the village, namely those from Léon Beyer. The building itself dates from 1603. Closed Wednesday evenings, Thursdays, and mid-January to March. 3 Pl. du Château-St.-Léon, Eguisheim (phone: 89-41-08-89). Expensive to moderate.

ROUFFACH: The Eglise Notre-Dame de l'Assomption, begun in the Romanesque style in the 11th century and completed a number of centuries later, was built in the same pink stone as the Strasbourg Cathedral. Plan to visit at the end of the day, when the western sunlight filters through its lovely rose window. On the square outside the church is the 16th-century Wheat Market and an old Hôtel de Ville (Town Hall) with a charming Renaissance façade. The crenelated Tour des Sorcières (Witches' Tower) dates from the 13th century and wears a stork's nest headdress.

From Rouffach, take N83 south to Guebwiller.

CHECKING IN/EATING OUT: _Château d'Isenbourg_ – This luxurious, spacious, and utterly hospitable Relais & Châteaux inn sits above the village in the midst of a vineyard and is gracefully landscaped. Its 37 rooms and 3 suites are decorated with antiques, and some offer a view of the valley. Other amenities include a swimming pool, tennis courts, and a good restaurant, _Les Tommeries,_ in a vaulted room dating from the 13th century. Closed January to March. Rouffach (phone: 89-49-63-53). Expensive.

GUEBWILLER: Many remarkable old Alsatian houses — 107 Rue Théodore-Deck with its 3-story oriel window, for instance — grace this town, the gateway to the Florival, the flower-filled Lauch River valley. The Hôtel de Ville has a lovely protruding window with geraniums cascading from it as well as a 16th-century carved Virgin. Next door, note the outstanding Art Nouveau building with winding plant motifs.

The triple-towered Eglise St.-Léger, just off Rue de la République, was built during the 12th and 13th centuries and has an elegant portal with ribbed arches and bays. The choir is carved ornately in wood.

Routes 430 and 431 lead in a roundabout fashion from Guebwiller into the mountains past the Grand Ballon peak to Cernay. Called the Route des Crêtes (roughly, the crest or ridge road), this is perhaps the loveliest trip: steep, forested, and spectacularly colored in autumn. Route N66 leads west to Thann.

En Route from Guebwiller – Due east, across N83 via D4, lies Ungershein, the site of _Ecomusée,_ an open-air museum. It includes old farms, peasant houses, and other examples of Alsatian architecture that were destined for demolition until a group of students got the idea of dismantling, moving, and carefully reassembling them here.

THANN: This village marks the southern end of the Route du Vin. The soaring, yellow stone Collégiale St.-Thiébaut (Collegiate Church of St. Theobald) dominates the town, its elegant spire piercing the sky. Nicknamed "the Cathedral," it was built in stages from 1351 to the end of the 15th century and was restored in 1989. Although the exterior is obscured by scaffolding, this remains the most beautiful Gothic structure in all of Alsace. Inside, the vaults are joined by painted keys. The extraordinary carved wooden choir stalls display sculptures of monsters and humans in minute detail. Small angels peer from the ceiling, painted at the cross of the vaults' ribs.

From Thann, take N66 east to Mulhouse (pronounced Mu-*looz*), almost at the Swiss border.

MULHOUSE: Compared with the delightful wine villages and the seductive architecture of Colmar, this is an ugly, predominantly modern city. Once the center of a prosperous textile industry, it is now mainly a border town with thriving chemical plants. Yet travelers may prefer to stay here rather than next door in pricier Switzerland. Mulhouse has several modern, comfortable, and moderately priced hotels that welcome families with children. At least five other good reasons to pay a visit are its five museums — of fine arts, history, textiles, railroad cars, and automobiles (one of the world's best collections of old cars).

The *Musée Historique,* in the beautifully restored 16th-century Hôtel de Ville, at Place de la Réunion, is a lovable blend of the past and present. The town council still meets here in a room decorated with the portraits of all the mayors since 1347. The museum is filled with costumes and musical instruments, a charming postcard collection, playing cards, dolls, toy soldiers, and *kugelhopf* molds. Several rooms depict bourgeois living in the late 19th century and are furnished with household utensils. The entrance is at ground level to the right of the stairs; admission includes access to the other parts of the Hôtel de Ville (4 Rue des Archives; phone: 89-43-98-11).

The *Musée de l'Impression des Etoffes* (closed Tuesdays; 3 Rue des Bonnes-Gens; phone: 89-45-51-20) is devoted to the art of fabric printing. Several Rube Goldberg–esque presses function during the summer, showing various printing techniques. The archives contain some 8 million samples of fabric and designs and are an important reference point for designers and couturiers. There's also an outstanding collection of handkerchiefs; the gift shop sells copies.

Nearby, at the corner of Rue du Sauvage and Rue de Sinne, *Charcutière Alsacienne* beckons museumgoers with 12 varieties of homemade sausage.

On the edge of town, the *Musée Français du Chemin de Fer* (2 Rue Alfred-de-Glehn; phone: 89-42-25-67) is in a huge train station where old locomotives rest on six tracks. All the railroad cars, some dating from the 1800s, have been beautifully restored and painted. Three kinds of steam engines are on display along with the first electric train, from 1900. One car, from the prestigious *Train Bleu,* has gleaming brass and crystal figures. Another, from 1856, was used by Napoleon's aides and was decorated by the architect Viollet-le-Duc.

Also at the edge of town, the *Musée National de l'Automobile* (closed Tuesdays; 192 Av. de Colmar; phone: 89-42-29-17) is perhaps the town's greatest attraction. Once the private collection of two Swiss industrialists and claimed by the French government in payment of taxes, this vast building is crammed with Bugattis, Mercedes-Benzes, Rolls-Royces, and Hispano Suizas. A Rolls-Royce Silver Ghost, from 1910, has silver-plated fittings. The Dion Bouton, with facing seats and no roof, gaily painted in blue and red, resembles an open stagecoach on wheels. A Bugatti T16 Garros, built for the French aviator Roland Garros, is one of only two ever made; its transparent plastic body reveals the motor.

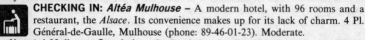

CHECKING IN: *Altéa Mulhouse* – A modern hotel, with 96 rooms and a restaurant, the *Alsace*. Its convenience makes up for its lack of charm. 4 Pl. Général-de-Gaulle, Mulhouse (phone: 89-46-01-23). Moderate.

***Novotel Mulhouse-Sausheim* –** In Sausheim, 3 miles (5 km) northeast of Mulhouse, this contemporary 77-room hotel offers a grill-type restaurant, a buffet breakfast, a bar, and an especially pleasant swimming pool. Rue de l'Ile-Napoléon, Sausheim (phone: 89-61-84-84). Moderate.

EATING OUT: *Wir* – Perfect for busy sightseers, it provides a straightforward menu, quickly served. Closed Fridays and July. 1 Porte de Bâle, Mulhouse (phone: 89-56-13-22). Expensive to moderate.

La Bucherie – A good choice for excellent grilled meats and local fruit tarts. Closed Saturday lunch, Sundays, and during February. 2 Av. du Président-Kennedy, Mulhouse (phone: 89-42-12-51). Moderate.

Auberge du Vieux Mulhouse – Well-located, this place offers a variety of prix fixe menus. Closed Sundays. Pl. de la Réunion, Mulhouse (phone: 89-45-84-18). Inexpensive.

Lorraine

Lorraine is a land of quiche, quetsch (a variety of plum), and crystal. It contains forests and farms, factories and shops, and two proud and prominent cities: Metz and Nancy. It is inextricably linked in people's minds with Alsace, its sister province with which part of it switched back and forth between French and German rule in recent centuries, but it is profoundly different in its geography, architecture, cuisine, and temperament. Indeed, the many parts of Lorraine are strikingly different from one another. Although Lorraine has a historical and artistic unity, it is a region of enormous diversity — perhaps one of its chief appeals to visitors.

Lorraine is by no means a magnet attracting tourists from abroad. The northeastern corner, with its famous and severely depressed mining (coal and iron) and steel industries, often is bleak. But Lorraine does have beauty and points of interest. French campers head for popular sites in forests and by rivers and lakes throughout the region. In the southeast, the countryside of predominantly gently rolling hills rises to the Vosges Mountains, where winter and summer resorts attract French vacationers. The health spas of its south also have a strong French following, especially the notable watering spots of Vittel and Contrexéville. Moreover, remnants of Lorraine's rich history, from Roman times through the world wars, provide some broadly appealing attractions — churches, châteaux, artworks, and war memorials — and its splendid chief cities genuinely merit attention. In short, although Lorraine lacks the reputation and the high spots of a major tourist area, it provides the traveler with a variety of richly rewarding stops.

"Traveler" is a word to bear in mind when contemplating a visit, because Lorraine is a time-established crossroads of Europe. It is bordered on the north by Belgium and Luxembourg and on the northeast by Germany; Switzerland is not far from its southeastern corner. In addition, three of France's most celebrated provinces are next to or near it: Besides Alsace to the east, Champagne is its western boundary, and Burgundy is just a short way across the tip of Champagne to the south. Its role as a major European crossroads is enhanced by an excellent highway system and by its railroad lines, which are trunk routes to the east and west of Europe.

Lorraine first came into prominence as a center of trade and communication between the Mediterranean and northern Europe after the conquest of Gaul by the Romans. Its name, however, dates from the 9th century. In 843, the Treaty of Verdun divided Charlemagne's huge empire among his three grandsons, one of whom, Lothair, received a portion consequently known as Lotharingia and in due course simply as Lorraine. Lothair's original allotment included the present Netherlands, Belgium, Luxembourg, Lorraine, Alsace, and parts of Germany, but during the Middle Ages, as the fates of the German ruling families in the area rose and fell and divisions and subdivisions took place, a much-reduced entity known as the duchy of Lorraine emerged, pockmarked by various independent fiefs — such as the duchy of Bar and the three bishoprics of Metz, Toul, and Verdun — which the dukes were unable to control.

The French domination of Lorraine dates only from the 16th century, and the formal annexation of Lorraine to France did not take place until 1766, with the death of Stanislas Leszczynski, the former Polish king who was given the duchy by his son-in-law Louis XV. A century later, as a result of the French defeat in the Franco-Prussian War in 1870–71, part of Lorraine passed to Germany with Alsace as Alsace-Lorraine but was returned to France after the German defeat in World War I; it has remained French except for 4 years of German occupation during World War II. Throughout these vicissitudes, the sympathies of the people of Lorraine have tended strictly toward Paris (it's no accident that two of the most potent symbols of French patriotism — Joan of Arc and the Cross of Lorraine — are native to the region), and the reality of German rule caused many Lorrainers to resettle in more western areas of France. In their place are new Lorrainers, i.e., the many foreign workers from Mediterranean and North African countries who came to take advantage of the post–World War II boom in Lorraine's industrial areas and settled here permanently.

The route outlined below begins just across the border of Champagne, in Verdun, and tours the World War I battlefields and war memorials surrounding the town before presenting the option of detouring to Bar-le-Duc or continuing directly east to Metz, an attractive city with a splendid cathedral. Via A4, the drive to Metz takes an hour and passes through the farmland and forests of the huge Parc Naturel Régional de Lorraine, but it is possible to take in a few towns and a few more glimpses of the inhabited countryside by skipping the fast pay road and following the slower D903. Then it's south to Nancy, an elegant commercial and intellectual center and the base for side trips to such places as the old town of Toul and the birthplace of Joan of Arc in Domrémy-la-Pucelle, or to the town famous for its small-scale version of Versailles, Lunéville, and the town synonymous with crystal, Baccarat. (Although it is Lorraine's most famous name in crystal, Baccarat is not the only place in the region where crystal is made and sold.) The final leg of the tour is farther south, to the resort-spas of Vittel and Contrexéville to sample the waters as well as their other offerings, and east, to Gérardmer, a winter-summer lake resort on the western slopes of the Vosges. In Gérardmer, you are merely a mountain's crest away from Alsace. Michelin maps No. 57 and No. 62 cover the area.

Though there are no world class restaurants in Lorraine, you'll find lots of good ones, and there will be plenty of opportunities to taste the local specialties — including quiche par excellence. The traditional and hospitable people of Lorraine especially love bacon and pork and mix them beautifully with cream and butter. For desserts there are the famous *madeleines* of Commercy, the macaroons of Boulay and Nancy, and many fresh fruits and berries, including quetsch plums and *mirabelles,* the small yellow plums that are a particular specialty of Metz. The same fruits are distilled into a potent *eau-de-vie,* the universal digestif of the region, and for those who like their fruits sweet and without alcohol, there are always the special jams of Bar-le-Duc, made of local *groseilles* (red currants).

Hotel accommodations should present no problem. For a double room (private bath and toilet are standard) without breakfast ($4 to $6 extra per person for the continental fare), expect to pay $85 or more at places we list as expensive; $60 to $85 for those in the moderate range; and $40 to $60 for inexpensive lodgings. It's about the same for meals — but depending on your eyes, stomach, and will power — your final tally could go into a category higher than the one intended. A full meal for two, excluding wine and drinks (service usually is included), will run about $90 or more in an expensive restaurant; $60 to $90 in a moderate one; and $30 to $60 in an inexpensive one.

VERDUN: Built on the banks of the Meuse River, this former fortified town has played a strategic role in French history. Approached from the west, from Paris through Champagne, it is the gateway to Lorraine, to its principal cities of Metz and Nancy, and to areas of Germany, Luxembourg, and Alsace that lie beyond. Invaders, however, historically have approached it from the east, seeing it as a gateway of a different sort. Verdun was already a fortress in Gallic and Roman times and it has a huge underground citadel from the reign of Louis XIV, but it was following a siege by the Prussians in 1870 that a string of forts was built around the town to make it France's most formidable bulwark against the Germans. In 1916, then, Verdun became the site of the longest and perhaps the bloodiest battle of the First World War.

The battle of Verdun began in February with a massive German assault along an 8-mile front to the north and east of town. The first of the outlying forts fell almost instantly, General Pétain organized the French resistance to the cry of "They shall not pass!" (which became the French slogan for the rest of the war), and fighting of the most brutal kind, characterized by the use of poison gas and flame throwers, went on for 11 months. By December, Verdun's defenders had recovered most of the territory lost and the Germans — whose aim was to "bleed France white" — had been driven back approximately to the same positions held before the attack. In the meantime, the city had been destroyed, nearly 350,000 French soldiers and an almost equal number of Germans had lost their lives, and Verdun had become a symbol of the most horrific and pointless aspects of war.

Despite further heavy damage in 1944, Verdun (pop. 24,000) is today a pleasant administrative center, busy and modern, though with more than a few architectural hints of its past. The Meuse divides it into a lower town of residential and commercial areas (the tourist office is near the river at Place de la Nation; phone: 29-84-18-85) and an upper town, which overlooks the valley and contains the restored Cathédrale Notre-Dame and the Citadelle Souterraine, both worth a visit. The cathedral, built on the highest spot in town, is an interesting blend of Romanesque and Gothic styles; it dates back largely to the 11th and 12th centuries, and its cloister dates from the 14th to the 16th century. Not far away, the Citadelle — the work of the 17th-century military engineer Sébastien Vauban — contains several miles of subterranean galleries in which troops defending the city were fed and housed (open to the public from February through mid-December). The Unknown Soldier who lies under the Arc de Triomphe in Paris was selected in a ceremony here in 1920.

The Monument de la Victoire, a war memorial with books listing the names of all who fought in Verdun's defense, is in town, but most of what makes Verdun a place of pilgrimage is in the surrounding countryside. Several circuits lead through the battlefields and commemorative monuments, but the visit to the right bank of the

Meuse is by far the most concentrated and moving; the circuit of the left bank is distinguished perhaps only by the 14,000 marble crosses of the American cemetery in Romagne-sous-Montfaucon.

For the right circuit, an approximately 20-mile (32-km) drive, take N3 out of Verdun toward Etain, passing the 5,000 graves of the Cimetière National du Faubourg-Pavé. Farther along, take the turnoff for Fort de Vaux (left onto D913, right onto D913A). The Germans laid siege to this fort on March 9, 1916, but did not overcome a heroic defense by the garrison until June 7. Five months later, the fort was recaptured. Guided tours (from *Easter* through October) take visitors through the fort, and from the top there is an impressive panorama of the surrounding landscape and war memorials. From Fort de Vaux, return to D913 and follow it toward Douaumont. The *Memorial-Musée de la Bataille de Verdun* (closed from mid-December to mid-January) is where the village of Fleury once stood. Farther along, the Ossuaire de Douaumont (open all year) is the most important French memorial to the dead of 1914–18. The remains of 100,000 unidentified soldiers lie in this long, low necropolis; in the Cimetière National in front of it, 15,000 crosses on a carpet of green mark another 15,000 graves. In the center of the ossuary is a Catholic chapel, where mass is held at 10:30 AM on Sundays (earlier on other days), and at the top of the tower rising above it, orientation tables pick out the various sectors of the battlefield. The nearby Fort de Douaumont, which fell on February 25, 1916 (only 4 days after the surprise German attack began), and was not retaken until late in October, also is open to visitors. From the heights of this multilevel fortification (guided tours take place from *Easter* through October), there is a full view of the battlefield, surrounding forest, and the ossuary. To reach the next monument of the right circuit, the Tranchée des Baïonnettes (Trench of Bayonets), where an infantry section was buried alive following violent bombing on June 10, 1916, return from Fort de Douaumont toward the ossuary and follow the signs. After the visit, the winding road down the "Ravin de la Mort" to Bras and then D964 will return you to Verdun.

CHECKING IN/EATING OUT: *Hostellerie Coq Hardi* – Near the center of town, there are 40 rooms and 3 apartments in this comfortable, Lorraine house, old-fashioned but for color television sets. Its family-run restaurant is an opulent-looking dining room. The chef turns out superb sauces and a "light" cuisine that has earned one Michelin star. It can be tasted to maximum effect in such dishes as *salade Coq Hardi,* foie gras with fresh noodles, or wild salmon with parsley and flamed *mirabelles.* Hotel closed late December through January; restaurant closed Wednesdays. 8 Av. de la Victoire, Verdun (phone: 29-86-36-36). Hotel, moderate; restaurant, expensive.

***Bellevue* –** Operated by the owners of the *Coq Hardi,* it has 75 rooms in all, with color television sets, some with lovely views of Verdun's Botanical Garden. Another garden is in back, there is a restaurant, and a garage is available. Closed November through March, except January. 1 Rond-point du Maréchal-de-Lattre-de-Tassigny, Verdun (phone: 29-84-39-41). Moderate.

En Route from Verdun – Proceed 48 miles (77 km) east on A4 to Metz, or detour southwest via N35 to the town of Bar-le-Duc. The 35-mile (56-km) stretch of road between Verdun and Bar-le-Duc is known as the Voie Sacrée (Sacred Way), so called because it was the crucial supply route for men and *matériel* coming to bolster the defense of Verdun following the surprise German attack in 1916.

BAR-LE-DUC: This busy commercial center of 20,500 people was once the capital of the important duchy of Bar, which was united to the duchy of Lorraine late in the 15th century. It occupies a picturesque spot on the Ornain River and contains a remarkable group of 16th-to-18th-century houses as well as the 15th-century Gothic

Eglise St.-Etienne, which has a famous and decidedly macabre statue by Ligier Richier, a distinguished regional artist of the 16th century. Called *Le Squelette* (The Skeleton), the statue is a likeness of René de Châlon, Prince of Orange, who is pictured, according to his wishes, as he would appear after death. Another work by Richier is a wooden statue of Christ in the town's Eglise Notre-Dame.

Bar-le-Duc is known well beyond Lorraine for its currant preserves (*confiture de groseilles*), the production of which is a flourishing cottage industry following centuries of tradition. The currant harvest begins in July, preparation is well under way by August, and though it isn't possible to visit the places where the preserves are made, if you come to town in early September, you can witness the annual *Fête de la Groseille*, an old-fashioned country fair and antiques show that celebrates the Barisien delicacy. Bar-le-Duc's tourist office is in the Hôtel de Ville (Town Hall), 5 Rue Jeanne d'Arc (phone: 29-45-16-03).

 EATING OUT: *La Meuse Gourmande* – This very popular restaurant in a former convent serves good regional cuisine — mushrooms, snails, eels, blood sausage — and good local wines, particularly the Côtes-de-Meuse. Avoid any nouvelle dishes. Closed Sunday evenings, Mondays, and holidays. 1 Rue François-de-Guise, Bar-le-Duc (phone: 29-79-28-40). Moderate to inexpensive.

METZ: Set at the confluence of the Seille and Moselle rivers, Metz (pronounced *Mess*) is a thriving regional administrative, political, commercial, and economic center, the home of some 118,500 Messins. Though it was the scene of violent fighting and much destruction in World War II, the rebuilt city is today an attractive blend of old and new architecture. Streets in the heart of town have been closed to traffic and turned into appealing pedestrian shopping malls; riverside parks and an esplanade are filled with flowers, terraces, views, and recreational facilities; sailing and other boating activities are popular along the Moselle.

Metz was an important city of Roman Gaul from the time of Caesar to the time of the Frankish King Clovis. Later, during the reign of Charlemagne (768–814), it became the intellectual cradle of the Carolingian Empire (Charlemagne favored Metz so much that he chose to bury his wife, Hildegarde, here). In the 12th century, it became a free city, a rival to the great Flemish, German, and Italian cities of the time and strong enough to repel the frequent attempts of the Dukes of Lorraine to annex it. Instead, along with the other two independent bishoprics of Verdun and Toul, it was captured by Henry II of France in 1552 and its status as part of France was confirmed in 1648 by the Treaty of Westphalia.

The city's one touristic "must" is the soaring Gothic Cathédrale St.-Etienne, built largely from the mid-13th to the early 16th century on the site of two previous, adjoining churches: an ancient oratory dedicated to St. Stephen, which miraculously escaped the devastation of Attila and the Huns in the 5th century, and a later church, Notre-Dame la Ronde. The height of St.-Etienne's nave (131 feet) and aisles (44 feet) makes it one of the loftiest cathedrals in France, and, at 372 feet, it also is one of the longest, but it is most noted for its sublime stained glass windows. The rose window above the central doorway is the work of Hermann of Munster (1384–92); the great window of the left transept in Flamboyant Gothic, that of Theobald of Lyxheim (1504); the great window of the right transept in Renaissance style, that of Valentin Bousch (1521–27). The latter two windows, said to be the largest in the world (each covers about 4,140 square feet), bathe the transept in a glorious symphony of colored light. Many of the cathedral's other stained glass windows were lost in wartime, but there are splendid modern replacements, including those done in the 1960s by Marc Chagall.

Not far away, the city's exemplary *Musée d'Art et d'Histoire* (2 Rue du Haut-Poirier; phone: 87-75-10-18) also merits a visit. Its contents, covering 1,700 years of history, are housed in ancient structural remains ranging from the marble-covered sandstone walls of Roman baths to the façade of a Renaissance mansion built in 1529. Exhibits include a collection of Merovingian artifacts excavated in Metz over the last 150 years and, particularly interesting, objects belonging to the legendary Charlemagne. Incorporated in the museum is a 5-story, 15th-century granary, the only one of its kind in Europe, which houses the extensive Gothic collection as well as ambitious programs of Gothic art and artisanship; for example, pottery, porcelain, and glassware workshops. The museum is closed Tuesdays.

Among Metz's other notable buildings is its enormous train station, built from 1905 to 1908 in the massive Roman Rhenan style; across from it, the post office, built in the same style in 1911 in red sandstone from the Vosges; the large 18th-century Hôtel de Ville (Town Hall); the Porte des Allemands, a 13th-century château-fort on the Seille River; and the Eglise St.-Pierre-aux-Nonnains. This church, which dates from the 4th century and is reportedly the oldest in France, is closed to visitors, however, and is not overly impressive from the outside. There is useful information on Metz, some in English, at the Office de Tourisme (Pl. d'Armes; phone: 87-75-65-21).

CHECKING IN: *Altéa St. Thiébault* – This modern hotel with 112 large, well-equipped rooms is on a beautiful square near the city center. 29 Pl. St.-Thiébault, Metz (phone: 87-36-17-69). Expensive.

Novotel Metz Centre – Right downtown, near the main shopping area and the heart of the St.-Jacques commercial center, this hotel has 98 comfortable, air conditioned rooms, a piano bar, and a pool. Pl. des Paraiges, Metz (phone: 87-37-38-39). Expensive.

Royal-Concorde – A turn-of-the-century choice in the residential area near the train station; the 74 rooms are large and comfortable. 23 Av. Foch, Metz (phone: 87-66-81-11). Expensive.

Cécil – Also near the train station, it's a small, sound, but undistinguished hotel with 39 modern, functional rooms in an old building. 14 Rue Pasteur, Metz (phone: 87-66-66-13). Moderate to inexpensive.

Foch – Between the town center and the train station, this pretty 1920s building now houses an old-style hostelry offering comfortable rooms with modern baths and television sets. 8 Av. P. Mondon, Metz (phone: 87-75-56-42). Inexpensive.

Ibis – In the Pontiffroy quarter on the outskirts of town, this small modern hostelry caters to French businesspeople and families. The 79 rooms are functional and well-kept. 47 Rue Chambière, Metz (phone: 87-31-01-73). Inexpensive.

EATING OUT: *La Dinanderie* – The best restaurant in the city, and overall a good one, in a contemporary and elegant setting. Expect fine produce and diverse dishes with light sauces that show off the chef's masterful touch. The fish dishes are good. Closed Sundays, Mondays, August 8–31, and *Christmas* to early January. 2 Rue de Paris, Metz (phone: 87-30-14-40). Expensive.

Le Crinouc – The latest "in" restaurant caters to the same clientele as *La Goulue* (below). The cuisine is a successful blend of tradition and innovation, and the sauces are perfection. Closed Thursdays, Saturday lunch, and the first 2 weeks of January. 79 Rue du Général-Metman, Metz (phone: 87-74-12-46). Expensive to moderate.

La Goulue – A lovely bistro with an emphasis on fish, it also has excellent produce. Closed Mondays and from *Christmas* to after *New Year's*. 24 Pl. St.-Simplice, Metz (phone: 87-75-10-69). Expensive to moderate.

A La Ville de Lyon – Where the Messins (locals) eat. The cuisine is traditional, regional, and consistently good. Closed Sunday evenings, Mondays, and during August. 7 Rue des Piques, Metz (phone: 87-36-07-01). Moderate to inexpensive.

NANCY: Thirty-five miles (56 km) south of Metz, this city of about 100,000 inhabitants is another regional hub of government and commerce, a center of finance, mining, metallurgy, and engineering, and the seat of the third largest scientific university in France. It also is a city of classic French culture and elegance, with an astonishing group of 18th-century buildings at its core to testify to a notable past.

As the capital of the duchy of Lorraine from the 12th to the 18th century, the city was the creation of its dukes, and particularly of its last duke, who was not French at all but Polish. By an arrangement that ended the War of the Polish Succession, François III, Duke of Lorraine, exchanged his duchy for that of Tuscany. In his place, Louis XV installed Stanislas Leszczynski, his own father-in-law and the deposed King of Poland, on the throne of Nancy in 1737, with the proviso that on his death (which occurred in 1766), Nancy and Lorraine would become part of France.

The last Duke of Lorraine set about beautifying and developing the city, and the huge, regal square now named Place Stanislas was his showplace. The work of architect Emmanuel Héré and ironmaster Jean Lamour, this beautifully proportioned ensemble of palaces and gilded wrought-iron grillwork — in gateways, fountains, railings, and balconies — is considered a supreme achievement of 18th-century art. The largest building on the square, now the Hôtel de Ville (Town Hall), contains a magnificent wrought-iron staircase leading to salons from which the rest of Stanislas's urban plan is visible in all its refined harmony. Four larger and two smaller buildings ornamented with imposing arcades flank the Hôtel de Ville; directly in front of it is the Arc de Triomphe in honor of Louis XV. Behind that is a second square, Place de la Carrière, which dates from the 16th and 17th centuries but was transformed by Héré. This long rectangle is surrounded by 18th-century townhouses, embellished by more fountains and grillwork and closed off, at its far end, by a colonnade and the Palais du Gouvernement, once the residence of the Governors of Lorraine.

Pass to the left of the Palais du Gouvernement and take the Grande-Rue to two more sites of merit: the Palais Ducal, the palace where the dukes and their courts once resided, and the Eglise des Cordeliers, the now deconsecrated church where most of the dukes are buried. The palace as it stands today was built principally by Duke Antoine in the 16th century (on the site of an earlier structure) but restored considerably following damage in the 18th century. Of particular interest is the famous Porterie, an elaborate doorway in the Grande-Rue façade surmounted by an equestrian statue of Duke Antoine topped with a Flamboyant Gothic gable. Adjoining the palace, the Eglise des Cordeliers was the final stop of funeral ceremonies for the dukes that were long enough (they took weeks) and showy enough to compare with the coronations of emperors at Frankfurt and the investitures of kings at Reims, according to an old French proverb. The church (open from 10 AM to noon and 2 to 5 PM except Tuesdays) contains numerous ducal tombs, including the notable 16th-century tombs of René II and his wife, Philippa de Gueldre, the tomb of the latter a work of Ligier Richier. However, Duke Stanislas and his wife, Catherine Opalinska, are buried in another church, the Eglise Notre-Dame-de-Bon-Secours, somewhat southeast of the center on Avenue de Strasbourg.

Nancy also has some museums of considerable distinction. The *Musée Historique Lorrain,* in the ducal palace, has a rich collection pertaining to the history of Nancy and the region. An archaeological garden displays Celtic, Gallo-Roman, and Frankish artifacts; there's an almost complete collection of the engravings of Jacques Callot (a native of Nancy), a sampling of paintings by Georges de la Tour (a native of Lorraine), a floor full of the furniture and folk art of the area, Judaica, and a museum of pharmacology. (64 Grande-Rue; phone: 88-32-18-74; open daily except Tuesdays from 10 AM to noon and 2 to 5 PM.) The *Musée des Beaux-Arts,* in one of the palaces off Place Stanislas, is devoted to European paintings from the 14th century to modern times, including works by Perugino, Tintoretto, Rubens, Delacroix, Manet, Bonnard, Utrillo, and Modigliani, among others. (3 Pl. Stanislas; phone: 83-37-65-01; hours as above.) Southwest of the city's center, a third museum of interest is the *Musée de l'Ecole de Nancy* (38-46 Rue Sergent-Blandan; phone: 83-40-14-86; hours as above.), with furniture, glassware, and ceramics by artists of Nancy's own school of Art Nouveau, including objects from the workshop of Emile Gallé, who was its inspiration.

Nancy is a fine city for walking, and not just in its 18th-century core. Just a short walk from Place Stanislas is the factory and showroom for Daum, a fine French crystal less well known than Baccarat, whose factory also is nearby (see *Baccarat,* below). Daum's workrooms can be visited Mondays through Saturdays from 9:30 AM to 12:30 PM and Saturday afternoons from 2:30 to 6 PM (17 Rue des Cristalleries; phone: 83-32-14-55). There are shop-lined streets and shopping arcades for browsing and buying, university areas, pleasant squares with fountains, and numerous parks for sitting and strolling, notably the large Parc de la Pépinière off Place de la Carrière.

CHECKING IN: *Grand Hôtel de la Reine* – A fine hotel in one of the landmark 18th-century buildings right on Place Stanislas. All 58 rooms have modern conveniences, including color TV sets; there's a good restaurant, the *Stanislas,* with a wonderful fixed-price menu and a very talented chef. 2 Pl. Stanislas, Nancy (phone: 83-35-03-01). Expensive.

***Albert Ier–Astoria* –** A quiet, comfortable stop with 126 rooms near the train station, it was renovated a year ago by new owners who added conference rooms and other conveniences. No restaurant. 3 Rue de l'Armée-Patton, Nancy (phone: 83-40-31-24). Moderate.

***Altéa Thiers* –** The 112 rooms of this member of the reliable chain are comfortable (with TV sets and air conditioning), effectively decorated, and in a perfect location near Place Stanislas. There's a good restaurant and bar as well. 11 Rue Raymond-Poincaré, Nancy (phone: 83-35-61-01). Moderate.

EATING OUT: *Le Capucin Gourmand* – There's delicious food here at the city's finest restaurant, which has been given one Michelin star, and the decor features some shining examples of Nancy's own Art Nouveau. Traditional cuisine is limited to a few outstanding choices (try the fresh foie gras), supplemented by a half dozen or so of the chef's varied specials (notable are the *feuilleté* of oysters and the pigeon *kefta*). The cheese tray is outstanding, and the desserts, such as apple *galette* perfumed with *bergamote* — the local bonbon — unusual. Closed Sundays, Mondays, 2 weeks in January, and August; reservations advised. 31 Rue Gambetta, Nancy (phone: 83-35-26-98). Expensive.

***Le Goëland* –** The only place in town with a really luxurious, contemporary dining room. The specialties are "products of the sea" prepared with inventiveness and subtlety, and there's a nice wine list. Closed Sunday evenings, Mondays, and holidays. 27 Rue des Ponts, Nancy (phone: 83-35-17-25). Expensive.

***Excelsior* –** A classic, Art Nouveau brasserie that boasts high, ornate ceilings, leaded stained glass, and graceful fixtures. It offers a varied choice of reasonably priced specialties. Service can be slow. Open daily, with drinks and snacks served between meal times. 50 Rue Henri Poincaré, Nancy (phone: 83-35-24-57). Moderate.

***La Gentilhommière* –** This charming provincial restaurant has excellent meats, poultry (veal, squab, duck), and refined sauces. Closed Saturdays, Sundays, most of August, and at *Christmas.* 29 Rue des Maréchaux, Nancy (phone: 83-32-26-44). Moderate.

***Le Comptoir de Gastrolatre* –** A charming bistro offering simple and delicious country food at bargain prices. Closed Sundays, Monday lunch, *Easter Week,* and the first half of September. 1 Pl. Vaudemont, Nancy (phone: 83-35-51-94). Inexpensive.

En Route from Nancy – Several points of interest south of Nancy are arranged in a manner that allows you to visit them easily in a series of excursions using Nancy as a base. Domrémy-la-Pucelle, the birthplace of Joan of Arc, is southwest of the city, via

Toul, once an important town and worth an excursion in its own right. Southeast of the city, there is a splendid 18th-century château at Lunéville; after a visit, fanciers of fine crystal often proceed to Baccarat. Directly south of Nancy, the spa towns of Vittel and Contrexéville and then the summer and winter resort of Gérardmer farther east can be the objects of a pleasant day's outing from Nancy or stops on the way to Burgundy or Alsace.

TOUL: Take A33 west from Nancy; this old town is only 14 miles 22 km) away. Toul, along with Metz and Verdun, was one of the three bishoprics that emerged as independent cities during the Middle Ages and remained free until captured for France by Henry II in the mid-16th century. Much damaged during World War II, the town is the site of the battered yet still fascinating Cathédrale St.-Etienne, built from the 13th to the 16th century. The church has a Flamboyant Gothic façade that is especially magnificent and a beautiful cloister.

DOMRÉMY-LA-PUCELLE: From Toul, it's another 24 miles (38 km; N74 south, then D19 west) to Domrémy — or Domrémy-la-Pucelle (Domrémy-the-Maid), as the village has been renamed in honor of its most famous daughter. Joan of Arc was born to two pious peasants (in 1411 or 1412) in a starkly simple house here (open daily April through mid-September; closed Tuesdays in winter) and baptized in the local church, which, though much changed, contains a few objects of her time, including the baptismal font. Next door, a small museum is devoted to her life.

LUNÉVILLE: The center of attraction in this town 22 miles (35 km) southeast of Nancy is a château known as "little Versailles." Lunéville was the favorite residence of Léopold, Duke of Lorraine, who commissioned the château as a modest replica of the great palace of Versailles in 1703. Later, Stanislas Leszczynski, the last duke and the inspired developer of Nancy, was instrumental in decorating it and in laying out the beautiful gardens of the adjoining Parc des Bosquets, now the setting for a summer *son et lumière* show. Lunéville became Stanislas's favorite residence, too, and it was here that he died, but not before contributing to the reputation of the "petit Versailles" by the quality of his guests, who included such notables as Voltaire and Diderot. Designed by architect Germain Boffrand (a student of Jules Hardouin-Mansart, the architect of Louis XIV's royal buildings), the château has a huge, majestic court on the west side, two small wings separated from the great halls by porticoes, and a chapel modeled on that at Versailles. A small museum established early in the 18th century displays furniture, engravings, historical documents, and an especially distinguished collection of Lunéville faïences.

EATING OUT: *Château d'Adoménil* – This delightful château and its well-tended park are in a lovely country setting 3 miles (5 km) outside Lunéville. The menu, rating one Michelin star, features seasonal fish and game specialties, and the service is excellent. Closed Sunday evenings, Mondays, and 2 weeks in February. South of Lunéville in Réhainviller-A-Doménil (phone: 83-74-04-81). Expensive to moderate.

BACCARAT: Southeast from Lunéville down N59, it's 15 miles (24 km) to Baccarat, a name synonymous with fine crystal since the founding of its factory in 1764. During the summer, tourists throng the small town to marvel at antique and modern crystal works in the *Musée du Crystal* (Rue de Cristalleries; for information, call the tourist office: 83-75-10-46), thence to acquire souvenirs in glass — at comparatively good prices — in any number of accommodating shops along the main street. The best is *Baccarat-Magasin de Vente* (Rue des Cristalleries; phone: 83-75-10-01), which ships all over the world. The crystal decorations in the little town church, built in 1957, also are worth a stop.

VITTEL: South of Nancy, in the woods of southern Lorraine, is an area known for its mineral and thermal springs and consequently for its spa resorts. The town of Vittel, 43 miles (69 km) from Nancy via D413, is the largest and one of the best known of these spa towns. Its cold-water springs were familiar to the Romans, then forgotten, then rediscovered in the mid-19th century. Today, Vittel water at its source is used internally and externally to treat a variety of illnesses (including liver and kidney diseases, gout, and rheumatism), and bottled Vittel water is much more likely to be found on French tables than Perrier water. Besides the thermal establishment, in a large park, the town is well equipped to attract the health-conscious visitor. Facilities for amusements — golf, tennis, swimming, and riding, among them — are in good supply, there's a good selection of hotels and restaurants, and there's a gambling casino.

CONTREXÉVILLE: Like Vittel, its neighbor 3 miles (5 km) away, Contrexéville is known for its mineral water, which also springs cold from its source and which also is bottled and popular all over France. Both resorts are low-key places, and Contrexéville, too, has a casino, but it is the smaller of the two and has the nicer accommodations.

CHECKING IN: *Cosmos* – This hotel with a restaurant and 70 beautifully furnished rooms is in a lovely and quiet park. Closed from October through April. 13 Rue de Metz, Contrexéville (phone: 29-08-15-90). Moderate.

Grand Hôtel Etablissement – A charming old hotel inside the thermal park, it has 60 rooms and a restaurant. Closed from mid-September to April. Cour d'Honneur, Contrexéville (phone: 29-08-17-30). Moderate.

EATING OUT: *L'Aubergade* – A warm welcome greets all who enter this lovely, small dining room. Specialties include salmon in puff pastry, mousse of frogs, steaks with mushrooms, and a few daring but successful experimental dishes. The homemade desserts use such local fruits as peaches and *mirabelles* (yellow plums) and are delicious. Adjoining is a 9-room hotel added 5 years ago. Closed Sunday evenings and Mondays. 265 Av. de Tilleul, Contrexéville (phone: 29-08-04-39). Expensive to moderate.

En Route from Vittel or Contrexéville – You can take a trip southeast through the lovely forest of Darney, then go on to the nearby hot water spas of Bains-les-Bains and Plombières-les-Bains, both of them in use in Roman times. From Plombières, it is 26 miles (42 km) to Gérardmer, the main resort of the Vosges Mountains, which separate Lorraine from Alsace.

GÉRARDMER: This popular resort occupies a magnificent site in the midst of evergreen forests on the western slopes (the Lorraine side) of the Vosges and at the eastern end of the largest of the range's many lakes, Lac de Gérardmer. It is an excellent spot for skiing and skating in winter and for swimming, boating, fishing, and hiking in summer. Sightseeing possibilities include a look at the local church, made of Vosges sandstone; a circuit of the lake, which can be done by motorboat or car (a 4-mile/6-km drive partly through forest that opens up to views of water and encircling mountains); and any number of excursions — to neighboring slopes, to Lac de Longemer and Lac de Retournemer, and along the road to Colmar in Alsace, which crosses the panoramic Route des Crêtes running north and south along the ridge of the Vosges 9 miles (14 km) east of Gérardmer. The town is well equipped for visitors, with the oldest tourist office in France, hotels, restaurants, and a gambling casino.

CHECKING IN/EATING OUT: *Hostellerie Bas-Rupts* – This modern, chalet-style hostelry of 18 rooms is on a quiet mountainside approximately 2½ miles (4 km) south of Gérardmer via D486. There are tennis courts and instruction is offered. Its restaurant, *Les Bas-Rupts,* is a luxurious dining room done in rustic Louis XIII decor. It boasts a chef trained by France's masters, exquisite service, and a refined menu of light, delicious dishes that merits one Michelin star. In good weather you can eat outdoors on the terrace. Bas-Rupts, just south of Gérardmer (phone: 29-63-09-25). Hotel, moderate; restaurant, expensive to moderate.

Bragard – In town, this nicely furnished hotel has 49 rooms plus a swimming pool, a sauna, and an exercise room. It's restaurant, *Au Grand Cerf*, offers fine traditional local dishes and nouvelle cuisine. Open year-round. Pl. du Tilleul, Gérardmer (phone: 29-63-06-31). Moderate.

Champagne

Champagne. The word is magical, as charged with rich associations as the bottles of sparkling wine that bear it on their labels. The world's most famous wine takes its name from the region 90 miles (145 km) east of Paris that produces it, though La Champagne, the region, is much less known outside France than *le champagne*, the celebrated bubbly product.

An elongated oval stretching 100 miles from north to south, Champagne nevertheless offers visitors a surprising wealth of sights; foremost among them are its glorious Romanesque and Gothic churches, including the incomparable Cathedral of Reims; its great champagne houses, with miles of cellars housing millions of bottles of champagne in the making; and, of course, the vineyards themselves, more than 64,000 fertile acres spread across the landscape. Yet perhaps the greatest charm of the region lies in the villages scattered throughout the countryside. An hour and a half from Paris, less than 10 minutes outside urban Reims, and beyond the often uninteresting, even bleak views afforded by the region's highways, it is possible to sample French provincial life, to step back, it seems, into the 19th century in villages crowded around medieval churches, and to drive along narrow, nearly deserted roads through fields and vineyards looking as if time had cradled them ever so gently.

This serene aspect is an illusion. The word "champagne" comes from the Latin *campania*, meaning "open, level, unforested land," and despite undulating hills, rivers, and lakes — despite, even, numerous forests — such it is. The entire area is a plateau seldom exceeding 600 feet in altitude, and this topographical fact, combined with the region's geographical location, shaped its destiny. Civilized since the neolithic era, Champagne has been a crossroads of Europe, a route of invasion, and a battlefield for 2,000 years. It has been ravaged repeatedly, and Epernay alone was destroyed close to 2 dozen times.

Julius Caesar brought his Roman legions to Champagne when he conquered Gaul between 58 and 51 BC. The region flourished under the subsequent Roman occupation, and Reims, then a city of 80,000-plus inhabitants, far exceeded Paris in size and importance. In AD 451, Attila the Hun and half a million barbarian soldiers stormed into Roman Gaul and made their camp on the plains of Champagne. What ensued was one of the fiercest and bloodiest battles in history, a monumental encounter between Orient and Occident in which 1 million soldiers fought, 200,000 died, and Attila was defeated. This saga of war and destruction continued, and before the end of the 10th century Champagne had been the scene of numerous invasions and annexations, and Reims had been razed to the ground seven times. A few centuries of peace and prosperity followed: Champagne became a center of commerce between the textile regions of the north and the Mediterranean (to this day, Troyes and Reims are textile centers), and the great Champagne fairs of the Middle

Ages attracted merchants from all over Europe six times a year. Prosperity led to a flowering of culture, which culminated in the poetry of Chrétien de Troyes and in the Gothic cathedral at Reims. This peaceful interlude was only temporary, however: Champagne was one of the principal battlegrounds of the bloody Hundred Years War (1337–1453) and the site of many other conflicts through the centuries, including some during the French Revolution, the Napoleonic Wars of the late 18th and early 19th centuries, and during the Franco-Prussian War of 1870–71.

In our century, the region was spared nothing during the two world wars. In World War I, the Champagne district was the scene of the nightmare battles of the Marne (1914 and 1918), and it was in 1914 that the Germans committed an outrage never forgotten by the people of Champagne: the shelling of Reims Cathedral at the onset of more than 1,000 days of bombardment of the city. Not for the first time, the Champenois took to the relative safety of the champagne cellars to live and work. Throughout the war, fighting took place in the vineyards, and at the war's end, the countryside was scorched and the large towns heavily damaged. The Champenois had it little better during World War II. In 1940, Nazi tanks stormed into France via Champagne, and during the next 5 years, only Normandy suffered greater devastation in France. Afterward, accounts emerged of the powerful underground resistance movement that had operated in German-occupied Champagne — accounts of walled-off champagne cellars hiding precious stocks from the Germans, of rerouted trains, of remarkable individual heroics. Today the two wars are part of the Champenois soul, and monuments, cemeteries, and rebuilt towns throughout the region are poignant reminders of its recent ordeals.

A remarkable indicator of the Champenois character is that throughout both world wars, throughout all the shelling of the vineyards and the towns, the vines were tended and harvested, and each year champagne was bottled in the cellars (albeit not in prewar quantities). When there were few men available, the women and children stepped in, and some lost their lives while working. The Champenois have been known throughout history as hardworking, sensible, thrifty, and honorable. If, after centuries of war, they also are a rather serious and reserved people, it is understandable.

Since champagne is the region's lifeblood and since a stretch of vineyards and at least one champagne cellar are sure to be on your itinerary, a brief introduction to the king of wines (and the wine of kings) is indispensable. Ever since the Romans planted vines in the 1st century, Champagne has been known for its wine. By the Middle Ages, the wine was being exported, and there are clear indications that according to the standards of the day, its quality was outstanding. But it was not sparkling wine. The techniques that gave birth to the foaming wine were developed only at the end of the 17th century, the same century that saw the wines of Champagne — still and sparkling — become the wines of aristocrats and connoisseurs. In the next century, the sparkling wine became supreme, welcomed and praised widely at all the best tables. This in turn led to the mystique of champagne, to the industry's expansion, and to the exportation of the wine in the 19th and 20th centuries. Meanwhile, a significant change in the character of the wine was occurring. At first the sparkling wine was sweet, but as tastes changed, particularly in this century, most champagne was made drier and drier. Today, 85% of the approximately 200 million bottles produced annually are *brut* champagne and can be characterized as bone dry.

Champagne is the northernmost vine-growing region in France — essentially, in Europe (exceptions are the more northerly Rheingau and Mosel vineyards of Germany). This climate is one of the factors that guarantees the uniqueness and quality of the most imitated wine in the world. Others are the chalky soil; the type, characteristics, and quality of the grapes (by law, only chardonnay, pinot noir, and pinot meunier may be used); and time-honored, meticulous, and painstaking techniques of vine cultivation and wine making. The making of champagne is the most regulated and legislated wine producing process anywhere.

Strictly speaking, champagne is a blend of many wines that have been caused to ferment a second time in a stoppered bottle. The grapes, which come from 250 villages, are pressed according to rigorous standards and are fermented in vats into still wines at the region's 110 champagne houses (only 2 dozen of which are large and widely known). The still wines are then married to wines from other vine stocks, other sources, and even other years, according to the taste of the cellar master, resulting in a harmonious blend known as the *cuvée*. Most champagnes contain wines from several years and are classified as non-vintage. If the wines are all from the same year, an exceptional year, the champagne will be vintage and will bear the year on its label.

Up to this point, the blend still is simply white wine. Now it is bottled, and special yeasts and a small quantity of sugar are added to cause the second fermentation, which takes place in the champagne house's old labyrinthine chalk cellars, where the wines are left to mature for at least a year, usually 3 to 5 years. A few steps remain. The sediment thrown off by the second fermentation is eliminated by tilting the bottle neck downward and rotating it frequently, thus collecting the sediment on the cork. This process, usually done by hand, can take 3 months and is known as riddling, or *remuage*. The *dégorgement* process follows, whereby the neck is frozen and the cork is removed, allowing the pressure in the bottle to expel the ice pellet with the sediment. The bottle is then topped off with the *dosage*, a reserve wine with cane sugar added to establish the desired sweetness, and corked. *Et voilà*, champagne.

From north to south, the Champagne region has four vine-growing areas — the Mountain of Reims, the Valley of the Marne, the Côte des Blancs (Slope of the Whites), and the Region of the Aube — and the three centers of Reims, Epernay, and Troyes. The route we suggest begins in the cathedral city and champagne center of Reims and circles south through the hilly vineyards and small villages of the Montagne de Reims before reaching Epernay. Next, it follows the Valley of the Marne, which stretches east and west of Epernay, then turns south through the villages and vineyards of the Côte des Blancs. After a visit to the historic crossroads town of Châlons-sur-

Marne, it continues south to Troyes, the former capital of Champagne as well as an art center, and from there proceeds southeast through the remaining Aube vineyard area to end at the threshold of yet another famous wine region, Burgundy. If you want detailed maps, Michelin No. 56 covers the entire Champagne Road area (and the northern leg of our route) and map No. 61 covers the remaining area beyond Châlons-sur-Marne.

Since a good deal of what you will want to see lies in and around Reims and Epernay, which are only 16 miles (26 km) apart (by the direct, not the scenic, route), doubling back to hotels, restaurants, villages, and other sites presents little inconvenience. There are many inviting restaurants in this part of France, but the hotels are not as appealing; though Reims has an ample supply of beds, there are some charming small hotels in the country, and there generally is good value for money throughout the region. If you hope to stay in a small hotel or to visit during the harvest (usually beginning the second half of September and lasting 2 to 3 weeks), reservations are a good idea. For a double room (private bath and toilet are standard) without breakfast ($6 to $10 extra per person for the continental kind), expect to pay $125 or more at places we list as expensive, $75 to $125 for those in the moderate range, and $40 to $75 for those listed as inexpensive. It's about the same for food. A full meal for two, excluding wine and drinks, will run about $125 or more in an expensive restaurant, $75 to $125 in a moderate one, and $50 to $75 in an inexpensive one. Service usually is included.

REIMS: This historic city straddles autoroute A4 (which runs between Paris and Lorraine and Germany) and is on the main train route connecting Paris and northern Europe. Hence, it is the logical starting point for a visit to Champagne. For a detailed report on the city, its sights, hotels, and restaurants, see *Reims,* in THE CITIES.

En Route from Reims – The Montagne de Reims, the first of the wine growing areas of Champagne, is a gentle, wooded rising between Reims and the valleys of the Vesle and the Ardre to the north and Epernay and the Valley of the Marne to the south. Route N51 cuts across it from north to south — between what is known as the *petite montagne* to the west and the *grande montagne* to the east — and connects the two cities somewhat as the crow flies, but the vineyards and wine villages, lying against the slopes, lead from one city to the other by a more circuitous route. To begin, take N380 from Reims toward Château-Thierry, then turn left onto D26 — the road to follow for the next 23 miles (37 km), as far as the village of Ambonnay.

On D26 you will first follow the flank of the "small" mountain whose vineyards are the most acidic in the region. Leave the road briefly to see the beautiful church with a square steeple and lovely interior in Ville-Dommange and, nearby, the small 12th-to-16th-century chapel of St. Lié, surrounded by a quiet cemetery marked with two World War I casemates (bombproof shelters with openings for the guns). Pause for the view of Reims and its cathedral, the Reims plain, and the Tardenois woods, then drive on to Sacy, which has a beautiful 12th-century church, and follow D26 through Ecueil, Chamery, and Sermiers (there's a nice statue-fountain dated 1900 near its church) until you come to Montchenot, which has a splendid view of the flatland and also of Reims.

CHECKING IN: *Hostellerie du Château* – Though slightly off the route, this Renaissance château set in a 14-acre park northwest of Reims is worth a detour — not only for its luxurious rooms, but also for its fish and other specialties served in its one-star (Michelin) dining room. Between the towns of Château-Thierry and Fismes in the village of Fère-en-Tardenois (phone: 23-82-21-13). Expensive.

EATING OUT: *Auberge du Grand Cerf* – With one Michelin star, this restaurant is rapidly becoming one of the best in the area, with a chef who tends to avoid traditional dishes in favor of more inventive nouvelle ones. For a perfect marriage with champagne, try the warm oysters or the scallops in puff pastry. Any fish dish is recommended. Also recommended are the beautiful salads made of whatever is freshest in the market, duck liver fritters, lamb with ginger and mangoes, and the pastry cart. The prix fixe menus give a good sampling. Closed Tuesday evenings, Wednesdays, late December to early January, and the last 2 weeks of August. On N51, Montchenot (phone: 26-97-60-07). Expensive to moderate.

En Route from Montchenot – After crossing N51, D26 begins to follow the flank of the "big" mountain. Villers-Allerand, which contains a church from the 13th and 14th centuries, is the first village down the road; then comes Rilly-la-Montagne, which counts a number of champagne producers among its 1,000 inhabitants. Fittingly, the town's church has sculptured stalls depicting *vignerons* (vine growers). Rilly is the starting point for walks on 900-foot-high Mt. Joli, one of the few places where the Montagne de Reims comes to a point and thus one that affords a wonderful panorama of the plain of Reims.

Next on D26 is Chigny-les-Roses, where there's an interesting Renaissance door to the sanctuary of the church, and Ludes, whose 15th-to-16th-century church has a statue of the Virgin and Child holding a bunch of grapes. Ludes also has the champagne cellars of Canard-Duchêne (phone: 26-61-10-96), which can be visited. These beautiful, long, and scrupulously clean chalk cellars with attractively arched galleries are open weekdays (10 AM to noon and 2 to 4 PM) year-round except August and holidays. Tours in English are available.

An area of first-rate vineyards begins at Mailly-Champagne, where, by appointment on weekdays, you can visit the champagne cellar of the village's cooperative Société des Producteurs (phone: 26-49-41-10). The vineyards of Verzenay, less than 2 miles (3 km) away, produce exceptional wine, but the town also is well known for its old windmill, probably the only one left in Champagne, which was used as an observation tower during World War I. In nearby Verzy, follow the road on the right (D34) into the forest, leave the car in the parking lot, and walk to the observatory of Mt. Sinaï. From this very panoramic spot, the highest point in the Montagne de Reims (928 feet), General Gouraud watched the progress of the battle of Reims in 1918. For an interesting — and unusual — sight, take the forest road to the left of the modern chapel of St. Basles on D34 to reach the Faux de Verzy, a bizarre landscape of twisted beech trees with corkscrew-like branches, some 1,000 years old.

Beyond Verzy is Villers-Marmery, where you can detour 3 miles (5 km) off D26 — crossing highways A4 and N44 and the village of Les Petites Loges — to Sept-Saulx, the site of a fine restaurant and hotel.

CHECKING IN/EATING OUT: *Cheval Blanc* – In the middle of a quiet village, this charming, vine covered inn offers views of a park and of the Vesle River. There are 2 suites and 19 well-equipped rooms (all with color TV sets and decorated with antique furniture) as well as a tennis court. The large and comfortable dining room has an elegant country look and even a fireplace for broiling meats over an open flame. The atmosphere is friendly and cordial, the service attentive, and the food rates (and earns) stars (one from Michelin). Try the fish dishes or the lamb with fresh mint. The wine list is among the area's best.

Closed from mid-January to mid-February. Rue du Moulin, Sept-Saulx (phone: 26-03-90-27). Hotel, moderate to inexpensive; restaurant, moderate.

En Route from Sept-Saulx – Continuing on D26, you come to Trépail, where the small church has columns decorated with sculptured animals, before reaching villages that are known for their fruity red wines. One of these, Ambonnay, is picturesquely set amid the vines with a church that has an elegant Romanesque steeple and a pure, well-preserved interior. Another, Bouzy — reached by switching from D26 to D19 at Ambonnay — is famous for its non-sparkling bouzy *rouge* (as well as for the particularly suggestive sound of its name to speakers of English). Louvois, with a 12th-century church, lies just northwest of Bouzy. Here, where the vineyards end, you can look through 18th-century wrought-iron gates and be rewarded with the classic prospect of an impressive château standing in the midst of a vast park. Much of Château Louvois, which belonged to a chancellor of France and the father of one of Louis XIV's ministers, was destroyed during the French Revolution, so, except for its outbuildings, most of what you see dates from post-revolutionary days.

From Louvois to Epernay on D9, you drive through farmland and woods and the villages of Tauxières, Mutry, Fontaine-sur-Ay, and Avenay-Val-d'Or. This last is worth a stop to see the Flamboyant Gothic portal and rich interior of St. Trésain, a beautiful church built in the 12th and 16th centuries. Then you'll be among lovely vineyards again, but by now belonging to the Vallée de la Marne. Following D9, D1, and D201, you will shortly be in Ay, a small town that is the home of champagne houses, then Epernay, with even more champagne houses; its importance in the production of champagne belies its size. You can stop to visit Ay at this point, but since it is an appropriate starting place for a tour of the villages and vineyards of the Marne, stretching east and west of here, you may want to visit Epernay first, returning to Ay as you take to the road later.

EPERNAY: In the heart of the vineyards, strongly provincial in character, and dotted with parks and gardens, Epernay rivals Reims as the capital of the king of wines. It is small (pop. 29,000) compared to Reims, and it lacks the other city's architectural richness — lovers of "old stones" are reminded that often during its history, Epernay was in the path of invading armies sweeping along the Marne. The great champagne firms established here are its main attractions. Miles and miles of champagne cellars (*caves*), where millions of bottles of bubbly now are aging, have been hewn out of the chalky soil under Epernay, and the major champagne houses offer tours of their facilities. The Office du Tourisme (7 Av. de Champagne; phone: 26-55-33-00) distributes a brochure giving the firms' hours; several of the most famous houses are right on the Avenue de Champagne. Remember that the cellars have a constant temperature of 45F to 50F, so bring a jacket or warm sweater. Appropriate shoes also are recommended, in part because some cellars are damp and may be slippery, in part because the tours usually involve a bit of walking underground, occasionally in rather dark surroundings. All tours are free, and it is not unusual for them to end with a taste of the product, though this is unpredictable. Tours in English are offered by all the firms, but if you are traveling in the off-season, it might be best to call ahead to make sure a guide is available.

Of the major houses open to the public in Epernay, Moët & Chandon (20 Av. de Champagne; phone: 26-54-71-11) is the largest and has the most extensive cellars — 17 miles of galleries. Although they are not the most beautiful cellars, Moët's explanation of the making of champagne is extremely good, hence it is one of the most popular tourist spots in all of France. The cellars are open weekdays (9:30 AM to 12:30 PM and 2 to 5:30 PM) year-round, and also on Saturdays (9:30 AM to noon and 2 to 5:30 PM) and Sundays (9:30 AM to noon and 2 to 4 PM) between March 29 and October

31. Nearby, Mercier (73 Av. de Champagne; phone: 26-54-75-26) conducts the tour of its 11 miles of cellars aboard an electric train. The cellars are open from March 1 to October 1 daily, from 9:30 AM to noon and 2 to 5:30 PM except Sundays and holidays, when closing is at 4:30 PM; they also are open from November 1 to December 12. Neither Moët & Chandon nor Mercier requires an appointment, but at Perrier-Jouët (26 Av. de Champagne; phone: 26-55-20-53), which has 6 miles of brick, chalk, and stone cellars, an appointment is requested. It is open from May 1 to September 15, weekdays from 9 AM to noon and 2 to 5 PM only. The 6 miles of cellars at De Castellane (57 Rue de Verdun; phone: 26-55-15-33) can be seen by appointment only, weekdays except holidays and August; and the dark and spacious cellars of Pol Roger (1 Rue Henri-Lelarge; phone: 26-55-41-95) also are open weekdays, except August, by appointment only.

Other points of interest in Epernay include the colorful *Musée du Champagne et de Préhistoire* (13 Av. de Champagne; phone: 26-51-90-31; closed November 30 to March 1). Set up in the 19th-century Château Perrier, it contains maps of the region, agricultural tools, wine presses, and a collection of labels and old bottles. (Open from 9 AM to noon and from 2 to 6 PM except on Sundays, when the hours are 10 AM to noon and 2 to 5 PM; closed Tuesdays and from December through February.) The Hôtel de Ville (Town Hall), at the Place de la République end of Avenue de Champagne, is an imposing building in the center of a 19th-century garden. The Renaissance stained glass windows in the Eglise St.-Martin are worth a look, too. Finally, the governing body of the champagne industry, Comité Interprofessionnel du Vin de Champagne, is headquartered in Epernay (5 Rue Henri-Martin; phone: 26-54-47-20), the place for anyone with a serious interest in champagne to ask unanswered questions.

CHECKING IN: *Champagne* – This small hotel near the center of town has 33 functional rooms. The management has taken over a neighboring restaurant with two separate dining rooms: *La Manoir* and *L'Etiquette* (19 Av. Champagne; phone: 26-55-04-45; moderate to inexpensive). Parking is available. 30 Rue Eugène-Mercier, Epernay (phone: 26-55-30-22). Inexpensive.

EATING OUT: There is no temple of haute cuisine in Epernay, but a number of small, unpretentious restaurants offer good meals at reasonable prices.

Les Berceaux – The cooking is good, the atmosphere that of a country dining room. Try the turbot in champagne sauce or thin veal with *chanterelles* (wild mushrooms). Closed Sunday evenings, also Mondays from November to March. 13 Rue des Berceaux, Epernay (phone: 26-55-28-84). Inexpensive.

Le Chapon Fin – It can't claim the most elegant dining room, but it's a nice place to try a few local dishes such as *andouillette* (small sausages made with chitterlings) *au champagne.* Closed Wednesdays and the last 2 weeks in August. 2 Pl. Mendès-France, Epernay (phone: 26-55-40-03). Inexpensive.

Le Palmier – If you feel like eating a fine couscous, this is the place; try it with a local red wine. The restaurant is run by native Moroccans. Closed Mondays. 2 Pl. Carnot, Epernay (phone: 26-54-54-71). Inexpensive.

La Terrasse – The menu is limited, but it represents good value. Closed Sunday evenings and Mondays. 7 Quai de la Marne, Epernay (phone: 26-55-26-05). Inexpensive.

En Route from Epernay – You can tour the vine-laden slopes and graceful landscapes of the winding Marne Valley by taking D201 directly into Ay, crossing the Marne and the canal that runs along it. Or, for a more comprehensive trip, take N3 east, crossing the Marne some miles down the road via D19 into Tours-sur-Marne, and return west toward Ay via D1. If you opt for the detour you will see several towns: Tours-sur-Marne, a town with an old priory and, near the tree-lined canal, the headquarters of Laurent-Perrier, whose ancient cellars and collection of rare, large champagne bottles are open weekdays, except August, by appointment only (phone: 26-58-91-22); Bisseuil, famous for its red wines and with a church worth visiting for the beauty of its vaults and fine columns (ask for the key at the house next door); and Mareuil-sur-Ay, which offers a good view of the vineyards, a 12th-century church, and the headquarters of Philipponnat, whose cellars also can be visited weekdays, except August, by appointment (phone: 26-50-60-43).

AY: This quiet town of 5,000 stands on the banks of the canal across the Marne almost 2 miles (3 km) north of Epernay. Because the vineyards of the area are on slopes of undulating ground in a particularly felicitous position, its wine has been renowned for centuries and was supplied in earlier days to the Kings of France and England and to a Renaissance pope. Ay (pronounced Ah-*ee*) suffered serious damage during the war, but it still has some preserved 15th- and 16th-century churches and several half-timbered houses, including a wood paneled one on Rue St.-Vincent that is described as once having been the press house of Henri IV. The champagne cellars of Bollinger (4 Bd. Maréchal de Lattre; phone: 26-55-21-31), Deutz (16 Rue Jeanson; phone: 26-55-15-11), and Ayala (2 Bd. du Nord; phone: 26-55-15-44) can be visited by appointment on weekdays only. There also is a museum containing a collection of tools relating to the cultivation of the vine.

En Route from Ay – As you head west on D1, celebrated vineyards are on your right; the left is dominated by a developing suburb of Epernay. In Dizy, turn right onto N51 (the main road to Reims) and drive up the rising road to Champillon. Here, amid hilly landscape, is a splendid, not-to-be-missed panorama of the Marne Valley vineyards. Nearby Hautvillers can be reached directly from D1 back at Dizy via N386 or through the tiniest of back roads from Champillon.

CHECKING IN/EATING OUT: *Royal Champagne* – Set high in the countryside, this outstanding small hotel looks down on the vineyards, the Marne Valley, and Epernay. Its 22 small rooms, set off from the main building — formerly an 18th-century coaching house — are furnished beautifully, and most of them have a terrace with a vineyard view. Apart from *Boyer "Les Crayères"* in Reims, the *Royal Champagne* is probably the region's best hotel, so book ahead, especially during the summer and around harvest time. Its celebrated restaurant, with one Michelin star, still offers a mix of traditional and nouvelle dishes, particularly fish dishes that go splendidly with champagne as well as such specialties as veal *grenadin* and chicken fricassee. There is a nice selection of local cheeses and an extensive wine list from which a competent and friendly sommelier will help you select a champagne or local still wine not normally found outside France. Expect to see producers entertaining their guests in the comfortable and tastefully decorated dining room with a lovely view of the vine-covered hills. Restaurant closed for 3 weeks in January. On N51, Champillon (phone: 26-52-87-11). Expensive.

HAUTVILLERS: This tiny hilltop village has old houses with arched doorways and interesting wrought-iron signs depicting the various tasks of the *vigneron* (vine grower), but it is the Abbaye de St.-Pierre d'Hautvillers that always has been the focus for travelers. Of all the medieval abbeys in Champagne — and the abbeys of the Middle Ages were powerful, both as intellectual centers and as the owners of vast properties, including vineyards — none was better known than Hautvillers, which for nearly 12 centuries from the time of its founding in 660 was one of the most famous in France. The continuing fame of the abbey (though not much of it remains) is due to the Benedictine monk Pierre Pérignon, its cellar master from the late 1660s to the end of his life, in 1715. Dom Pérignon revolutionized local wine making by developing the technique of the second fermentation in the bottle that gives champagne its sparkle, by creating the *cuvée* (blend) that in part is champagne's guarantee of quality and consistency, and by making other innovations. Dom Pérignon is said to have exclaimed to his fellow monks, "Come quickly! I am drinking stars!" on the occasion of the world's first champagne tasting.

The abbey site, above the village, is now owned by Moët & Chandon, whose attractive *Musée Dom Pérignon,* filled with historical documents and artifacts relating to champagne making, is open only to guests of the company. Open to the general public and not to be missed is the spectacular view from the abbey's broad stone terrace — the same spot is sometimes used for celebrations and *fêtes* relating to champagne. Then visit the little church, with its fine woodcarvings and organ, where Dom Pérignon and his uncle and friend, Dom Thierry Ruinart, are buried.

En Route from Hautvillers – Return to D1 and turn right to reach Cumières, a village known for its delicate red wine. The picturesque road continues along the right bank of the Marne through Damery, which has a fine 12th-to-16th-century church, and then through Venteuil, Reuil, and Binson, which has an old priory with a restored 12th-century chapel. A little farther west and just off D1 is Châtillon-sur-Marne, with a large statue of Pope Urban II, the remains of a castle, and a good view of the Marne. Go through Verneuil and Vincelles — the limit of the Marne *département* — and cross the river to Dormans, a picturesque old town considerably damaged by the war but still endowed with a beautiful church dating from the 13th century and a 17th-century château. From the Chapelle de la Reconnaissance (Chapel of Gratitude), built in the middle of a large park to commemorate the battles of the Marne (1914 and 1918), there is a fine view over the valley.

Dormans is the turnaround point for the stretch of the Champagne route leading through the vineyards of the Marne Valley. You can return to Epernay along the southern side of the river by staying on N3 the whole way or, for a better view from a higher road, by going part of the way on D222 (reached by taking D226 uphill out of Port-à-Binson) and passing through Oeuilly, Boursault, and Vauciennes before dropping down again to N3.

The vineyards of the Côte des Blancs, where the aristocratic white chardonnay grapes grow, are traversed by D10 and D9 south of Epernay. The excursion — as far as Bergères-les-Vertus — is a peaceful and leisurely morning or afternoon drive begun by leaving Epernay on N51 and turning left onto D10 at Pierry.

CHECKING IN/EATING OUT: *La Briqueterie* – A quiet place surrounded by gardens and vineyards, this hotel is in one of the area's nicest spots. Since it is only about 4 miles (6 km) from Epernay (off N51 beyond Pierry), it can be a convenient base for touring. Its 42 rooms and public areas recently underwent extensive renovation, and brought the comfort level in line with the French government's four-star rating. A swimming pool, sauna, workout room, conference facilities, and a new restaurant were added. Pleasant and inviting, the one-star (Michelin) restaurant is the sort of place where French families take their midday meal on Sundays. The continental breakfast is wonderful. During the summer, have a drink outside on the lovely terrace. 4 Rte. de Sézanne, Vinay (phone: 26-54-11-22). Expensive to moderate.

En Route from Vinay – Heading south on D10, you come to the boundary of the black grape area at Cuis, where a 12th-century Romanesque church built on a terrace dominating the village affords a pretty view. The next town, Cramant, is one of the most renowned in the region for the quality of its grapes, which are white only. Cramant is a charming village, and if you detour up through its vineyards you'll see the elegant and finely maintained Château Saran set imposingly on the hillside. South of Cramant,

Avize, in the heart of the Côte des Blancs, has an interesting church, mostly 12th-century Romanesque but with a 15th-century Gothic transept and choir. Next comes Oger, also with an early church, and then Le Mesnil-sur-Oger, another village producing famous *blanc de blancs* with another interesting church. Note particularly the 17th-century paneling inside and the Renaissance door.

Vertus lies on D9 after it merges with D10. This quiet little town with irregular streets and charming squares was once a fortified city. A medieval gate remains as does the church of St. Martin, a remarkable example of the transition from Romanesque to Gothic style. Walk around the church to see "the wells of St. Martin," where springs form a mirrorlike pond.

CHECKING IN/EATING OUT: *Le Commerce* – This bar-tabac-PMU (bar, tobacco shop, and offtrack betting parlor) and hotel (11 basic rooms) provide a chance to meet the people and try the local food — veal kidney and fish in champagne sauce are good choices. Three very inexpensive prix fixe menus are offered. 4 Rue de Châlons, Vertus (phone: 26-52-12-20). Inexpensive.

Hostellerie de la Reine Blanche – Looking something like a streamlined Alpine ski lodge, this 23-room hotel is well equipped and comfortable and includes a restaurant. Closed 2 weeks in February. 18 Av. Louis-Lenoir, Vertus (phone: 26-52-20-76). Hotel, inexpensive; restaurant, moderate to inexpensive.

En Route from Vertus – Between Vertus and Bergères-les-Vertus, the Côte des Blancs ends and black grapes are seen again. Beyond Bergères, Mont-Aimé, the site of prehistoric, Roman, and feudal remains, offers a splendid view back over the Côte des Blancs vineyards and forward toward Châlons-sur-Marne, 18 miles (29 km) north-east on N33.

CHÂLONS-SUR-MARNE: Built on both sides of the Marne, this ancient crossroads town of 54,300 is an administrative center for the Marne *département.* Attila the Hun was defeated on the plain of Châlons in AD 451, and the town has played a significant role in military history ever since, especially under Napoleon III and during the two world wars. It is still the home of an important military school. Châlons has, in part, a bourgeois look, with 17th- and 18th-century townhouses, tree-lined riverbanks, and 16th-century bridges (Pont de l'Arche-Mauvillan, Pont des Viviers, Pont des Marini-ers) crossing canals formed by Marne tributaries. A tourist office is at 3 Quai des Arts (phone: 26-65-17-89).

Two of Châlons's many churches stand out. The Cathédrale St.-Etienne is known for the pure Gothic style of its northern façade and for its beautiful stained glass windows, which span the 12th to the 16th century — a veritable survey of the develop-ment of the art. Its 17th-century western portal is massive and impressive, and there also is superb artwork in various other sections — in chapels, the northern transept, and in the treasury. The Eglise Notre-Dame en Vaux shows characteristics of the Romanesque-Gothic transition period and is a masterpiece of 12th-century *cham-penoise* architecture. The interior is harmoniously proportioned and illuminated by beautiful 16th-century stained glass windows, and its carillon of 56 bells chimes out ancient melodies. Just north is the *Musée du Cloître* (Rue Nicola Durand; phone: 26-44-03-87) which contains some 50 recently excavated carved columns, marvels of 12th-century art. (Open daily except Tuesdays from 10 AM to noon and from 2 to 6 PM.)

Two other medieval churches in Châlons — St. Jean and St. Alpin — also are note-worthy, particularly for their stained glass windows. The 18th-century Préfecture (County Hall) is of architectural interest, and the *Musée Municipal,* containing artifacts from the Stone Age to the Gallo-Roman era, is of archaeological interest (Rue Carnot; phone: 26-64-38-42; open from 2 to 6 PM daily except Tuesdays and holidays). The

Bibliothèque Municipale (Town Library), in an 18th-century residence (Passage Vendel; phone: 26-68-54-44), has a rich collection of antiquarian books and illuminated manuscripts, including *The Confessions of St. Augustine,* the *Romance of the Rose,* and the *Book of Hours.* (Open from 9 AM to noon and 2 to 6 PM except Sundays, Mondays, and holidays.)

Before driving the 48 miles (77 km) via N77 directly to Troyes, a short detour on N3 to L'Epine, 6 miles (10 km) east, is well worth the time.

CHECKING IN/EATING OUT: *Angleterre* – In the center of town, this charming hotel has 18 rooms and a garden where you may lunch or dine. Named after its chef, *Jacky Michel,* the restaurant offers three attractive prix fixe menus, a wine list that changes monthly, and good values — especially on champagne. It now is considered by many to be the best in town. Closed Saturdays at lunch, Sundays, and with the hotel from late December to early January and the first half of July. 19 Pl. Monseigneur-Tissier, Châlons-sur-Marne (phone: 26-68-21-51). Moderate.

L'EPINE: This village is famous for the Basilique Notre-Dame-de-l'Epine, built in the 15th and early 16th centuries and one of the special sights of the region. As you drive toward L'Epine, the large church suddenly rises majestically in the midst of the flatlands of Champagne and calls to mind the Cathedral of Reims, though on a reduced scale. The Flamboyant Gothic façade, graced with three sculptured doorways depicting Christ's birth, passion, and resurrection, is its glory, but note also the realistic, sometimes racy, gargoyles found all around the exterior (they symbolize the vices and evil spirits chased from the sanctuary by divine power). From the beginning and continuing to this day, each May pilgrims make their way to Notre-Dame-de-l'Epine to venerate its statue of the Virgin. In the summer of 1988, the group that brought laser, light, and music spectacles to Reims and Troyes cathedrals brought *Cathédral de Lumière* to L'Epine. The show is offered on Friday and Saturday nights at about 10:30 PM from mid-June to mid-September. For information, contact the *Mairie* (Town Hall); phone: 26-66-96-99.

CHECKING IN/EATING OUT: *Aux Armes de Champagne* – You can see the basilica from the neo-rustic dining room of this charming 40-room hotel. The rooms are lovely, as is the garden, which has a miniature golf course. The cuisine, which already has earned one Michelin star and is getting better every year, includes both nouvelle dishes and regional specialties (pigeon with bouzy wine, gratin of fresh pasta with seafood, snails with champagne). The cheese tray is a must if you want to try the local products; sample the native red wine, too. If you are stopping for lunch only, the prix fixe menus are a good idea. Pl. de la Basilique, L'Epine (phone: 26-66-96-79). Moderate.

TROYES: The southern part of Champagne is all too often ignored by visitors, especially Troyes, the region's former capital. This was not so in the Middle Ages, when the city was a center of international commerce and one of the sites of the annual champagne trade fairs (troy weight, one of the standards of measurement set by the fairs, persists today). Troyes was an equally famous center of the arts in medieval times and remained so even after its commercial importance had begun to decline. As the Renaissance replaced the Gothic age, the influence of a uniquely Troyen school of architecture spread over the entire region and into Burgundy, Troyen sculptors approached their finest hour, and Troyen stained glass craftsmen were well on their way to filling the city's churches with kaleidoscopic light. Today, Troyes remains at once one of the great art towns of France, with a delightful old section of narrow streets and half-timbered houses, and a modern, bustling, prosperous town of 64,800 inhabitants, many employed in the manufacture of textiles — as their ancestors were since the 16th century. There's an Office de Tourisme near the station (16 Bd. Carnot; phone: 25-73-00-36) and another one near the cathedral (24 Quai Dampierre; phone: 25-72-34-30).

Troyes's churches were the main beneficiaries of its artists' outpouring of sculpture and stained glass, and the Cathédrale St.-Pierre-et-St.-Paul is endowed with a wealth of it. Built from the 13th to the 17th century, the church has a richly decorated 16th-century Flamboyant Gothic façade with a rose window above the central portal (carvings and statues missing from the tympana of the doors were destroyed during the French Revolution). Walk around to the doorway of the north transept — the 13th-century "Beau Portail" — for another rose window and four rosettes. Inside, the stained glass is stunning, from the earlier, 13th-century windows of the choir to the mainly 16th-century windows of the nave, including the Tree of Jesse window. The treasury of the church has a collection of beautiful 16th-century enamels, and the church tower provides a fine view of the town. Friday and Saturday evenings from early June through September, a spectacular *Cathédral de Lumière* show featuring laser images and sound is performed here, as in the cathedrals of nearby Reims and L'Epine. For information, call the tourist office (phone numbers listed above).

The Basilique St.-Urbain, built in the 13th century by Pope Urban IV on the spot where his father had a cobbler's shop, also is known for its splendid stained glass windows — which here occupy so much wall space, you'll wonder how the edifice stays upright. It also is known for its many noteworthy statues, especially the "Vierge au raisin," a beautiful example of local 16th-century sculpture. A third church, Eglise Ste.-Madeleine, dates from the 12th century. Though it is Troyes's oldest church, the marvelous stained glass in its choir is from the 16th century, as are its sculptured masterpieces: the intricately Flamboyant rood screen and the statue of St. Martha.

You'll see the picturesque old section of town, full of restored 16th-century houses, if you wander around in the vicinity of the Eglise St.-Jean. Do walk along Rue Champeaux, and don't miss Rue des Chats, where the cantilevered gables of the houses almost touch each other across the narrow street. Troyes also has several interesting small museums. The *Musée des Beaux-Arts et d'Histoire Naturelle* (1 Rue Chrétien de Troyes), in the 18th-century Abbaye St.-Loup, has a varied collection of art and artifacts including a nice collection of 15th-to-16th-century paintings. (Open from 10 AM to noon and 2 to 6 PM daily except Tuesdays.) The *Musée Historique de Troyes et de Champagne,* with good sculptures, drawings, and paintings from the region, and the *Musée de la Bonneterie,* which traces the history of the region's textile industry, are both in the Hôtel de Vauluisant (4 Rue de Vauluisant), a 16th-century building with an interesting façade. (Its hours are the same as those of the *Musée des Beaux-Arts,* with which there is a reciprocal entry arrangement.) There also is the Maison de l'Outil et de la Pensée Ouvrière (7 Rue de la Trinité), which has tools and craftsmen's implements. (Open daily except Tuesdays from 9 AM to noon and 2 to 7 PM, closing an hour earlier in winter.) The *Musée de Pharmacie* (Hôtel Dieu le Comte, Quai des Comtes de Champagne) is a beautiful old pharmacy that remains as it was at the beginning of the 18th century. It include collections of tools, faïences, and other objects used in the original pharmacy. For information about this and other museums in Troyes, call 25-73-49-49. But to many, the city's most interesting museum is the *Musée d'Art Moderne* (Pl. St.-Pierre; phone: 25-80-57-30). Located to the right of the cathedral in the former episcopal palace, this collection featuring some 1,500 works by Braque, Bonnard, Cézanne, Gauguin, Matisse, Picasso, and other artists is one of Europe's most important gatherings of contemporary art. (Open from 11 AM to 6 PM, except Tuesdays and holidays.)

 CHECKING IN: *Grand Hôtel* – This traditional establishment near the train station has 100 pleasant rooms, the majority with color TV sets. Two restaurants — moderately priced *Le Champagne* and inexpensive *Le Croco* —

make it convenient for meals, too. 4 Av. Maréchal-Joffre, Troyes (phone: 25-79-90-90). Moderate to inexpensive.

La Poste – Its 34 rooms, also with television sets, are within striking distance of the old quarter of St.-Jean, Basilique St.-Urbain, and other sights. The elegant restaurant is in the moderate range with some agreeable prix fixe menus and a wine list offering many great *crus* at reasonable rates. 35 Rue Emile-Zola, Troyes (phone: 25-73-05-05). Inexpensive.

EATING OUT: *Bourgogne* – This is a safe address in Troyes, meaning that the dishes are well prepared (one Michelin star) but not very innovative, and that the wine list is nice but limited. The service, however, is impeccable. Closed Sundays, Monday evenings, and August. 40 Rue Général-de-Gaulle, Troyes (phone: 25-73-02-67). Moderate.

Valentino – The city's finest place to eat, and its prettiest, is in the old part of town. The emphasis is on fish, and although all the dishes are commendable, the sea bass preparations are remarkable. And don't skip dessert. Closed Sunday evenings, Mondays, mid-August to September 6, and early January. Cour de la Rencontre, Troyes (phone: 25-73-14-14). Moderate.

En Route from Troyes – Because the fourth vine growing area of Champagne — the region of the Aube — actually is less esteemed in the making of champagne than the three areas described above, many visitors take N71 southeast directly into Burgundy. Our route, however, traces a final loop eastward to encompass the Aube vineyards and picks N71 farther along, at Bar-sur-Seine.

Leaving Troyes on N19, you'll soon come (13 miles/21 km) to the Lac et Forêt d'Orient, part of a large regional park and recreation area that includes reserves for birds and animals as well as water sports facilities for Troyens on weekend outings. Mesnil-St.-Père, on the south side of the lake just off N19, and Géraudot, on the north side on D1, are tiny villages with sand beaches. From Géraudot, it is 15 miles (24 km; via D1 and D11) northeast to Brienne-le-Château, the birthplace of Jean de Brienne, who made a name for himself in the Crusades; but it is better known through Napoleon Bonaparte, who went to the military academy here from 1779 to 1784. A small museum, *Musée Napoléon Premier* (phone: 25-92-82-41), contains souvenirs of the young Napoleon as well as mementos of his nearby battles during the campaign of 1814. (Open from 9 AM to noon and 2 to 5:30 PM, except Tuesdays and holidays, and December 1 to March 1.)

Another 15 miles (24 km), this time to the southeast (via D396 and N19), and you'll be in Bar-sur-Aube, in the center of one section of the Aube vineyards. On the right bank of the river, this little town of 7,000 people already was famous in the Middle Ages, at the time of the great fairs of Champagne, and it is now bordered by boulevards instead of ramparts. See the churches of St.-Pierre and St.-Maclou, the former built in the 12th, 14th, and 16th centuries and surrounded by picturesque wooden galleries, the latter built in the 13th and 15th centuries.

EATING OUT: *Commerce* – This good restaurant is halfway between the town's two historic churches. Try the salmon with herbs, langoustine with whiskey, or duck with a type of cranberry — and with them drink one of the local still wines. Closed during January. Also available are 16 guestrooms. 38 Rue Nationale, Bar-sur-Aube (phone: 25-27-08-76). Moderate to inexpensive.

En Route from Bar-sur-Aube – A detour 9 miles (14 km) east via N19 will take you to the quiet village of Colombey-les-Deux-Eglises. Charles de Gaulle is buried here, and part of his private residence, La Boisserie, which he maintained from 1933 to his death in 1970, is open to visitors. From Bar, you also can take a brief excursion south to Bayel, well known for its Cristalleries de Champagne glassworks (you'll see lots of crystal for sale) and of interest for several beautiful sculptures in the village church, including a 14th-century Virgin and Child and a 16th-century Pietà attributed to the same hand as the St. Martha in the Eglise Ste.-Madeleine in Troyes.

From Bar-sur-Aube, head southwest, winding 23 miles (37 km) on D4 across the region to pick up N71 at Bar-sur-Seine, the central town of the remaining section of the Aube vineyards and the end of the Champagne route. Besides some interesting 15th- and 16th-century houses, Bar-sur-Seine has the Eglise St.-Etienne, whose stained glass windows and paintings representing the life of the Virgin are noteworthy. There also are a number of interesting, typical villages to the south of Bar-sur-Aube. Chaource, well known for its cheese, has some old houses on wooden stilts and a 16th-century Entombment, possibly from the *atelier* (studio) of the St. Martha master, in its church. Les Riceys, a holiday resort, turns out a tasty rosé wine and has several 16th-century churches. Essoyes is associated with Renoir, who used to live here, and Mussy-sur-Seine, finally, is a nice town with numerous historical buildings. At Mussy, you are back on N71, a main route into the heart of Burgundy.

Corsica

Corsica, France's largest island and the third largest in the Mediterranean, lies southeast of the Côte d'Azur some 100 miles from Nice, a 6-hour boat trip or 35 minutes by air. But there the promixity ends; in just about every other way, Corsica and the Côte d'Azur are worlds apart. While the chic, opulent Côte is where the beautiful people go to see and be seen, Corsica, with its wild, rugged terrain and vast, uninhabited stretches, is where people come to get away from it all. And on Corsica, wealth and good looks are not a prerequisite for fitting in; the only beauty that's seriously worshiped here is that of the landscape.

Corsica has been described as a mountain growing out of the sea. Except for the eastern coast, with its 190-mile stretch of white and gold sand beaches, the island is covered with mountains, from its coastal hills to the towering peaks of the central range (Monte Cinto is the highest, at 8,900 feet). Much of the mountainous center and northwest is deeply forested, though there are treeless, barren stretches as well, including the Agriates Desert in the north. Some of the most dramatic scenery anywhere can be found on the rocky western coast between Calvi and Ajaccio, with deep wooded gorges, sparkling gulf waters, and jagged mountain precipices diving straight into the sea. Equally beautiful, though not quite so dramatic, are the mountains and seascapes of Cap Corse, a 30-mile peninsula projecting fingerlike from St.-Florent and Bastia in the northwest.

The sun shines year-round in Corsica and in the summer can be unrelentingly hot. Spring is the gentler season, when the island becomes green and vivid with flowers: mostly wild roses and, everywhere, acres of *maquis* — the wild, white heather that covers the island with a thick underbrush.

Abundant in natural beauty, Corsica in many other ways is quite barren. There is very little culture or nightlife, and the island's 300 Romanesque churches from the 11th and 12th centuries constitute the only architecture of any significance. Even the population has dwindled over the years — it's just under 300,000 today — making this 3,369-square-mile island the least densely populated in the Mediterranean. Part of the reason for this widespread emigration is the mechanization of farming on an island where tobacco growing supports roughly one-fourth of the economy. Another factor was the arrival of the French from Algeria after it gained its independence in 1962. Many of the Corsicans, claiming that the outsiders obtained land unjustly, fled the island in anger.

But this is a minor incident in Corsica's long, embattled history. Over the centuries it has absorbed countless invasions; nearly every major city was once a fortress. Occupied by Greece in 560 BC, Corsica later became a colony of Rome, then Pisa. The Genoese came in the 13th century and held the island until 1768 (a year before Napoleon's birth here), when it was sold to France.

And except for a brief British takeover — quashed by Napoleon and his troops in 1796 — it has been under French rule ever since.

The centuries of political occupation as well as the hard and isolated life imposed by the terrain have had a powerful influence on the character of Corsica's inhabitants. Generally speaking, they are an insular and fiercely independent people, despite the numerous outside attempts to crush that independence. More recently, during the past few decades, the issue of French separatism has reared its head, with Corsica demanding — sometimes violently — cultural recognition and greater autonomy. For years the French government tried to suppress the Corsican language (a form of Italian) by banning it in the schools; however, it always was spoken in the home, and though most residents do speak French, Corsican remains the preferred tongue.

Many Corsicans, particularly those who live in the isolated valleys of the central region, still practice what's known as "a politics of the clan," with loyalties to leaders that often go back centuries. The island's past, perhaps even its present, is filled with feuds between families and regions. It's no accident that the word "vendetta" is Corsica's sole contribution to the English language.

 TOURIST INFORMATION: Although prices generally are higher between June and September, tourist services on the island also are more plentiful then, so plan your trip accordingly. Here is a list of major tourist offices in Corsica:

Ajaccio: 38 Cours Napoléon (phone: 95-21-55-31); Hôtel de Ville, 1 Pl. Foch, by the harbor (phone: 95-21-40-87)
Bastia: 3 Pl. St. Nicolas (phone: 95-31-00-89)
Bonifacio: Rue Longue (phone: 95-73-11-88)
Calvi: Port de Plaisance (phone: 95-65-16-67)
Corte: Hôtel de la Paix (phone: 95-46-24-20)
Ile-Rousse: Rue J.-Galizi (phone: 95-60-04-35)
Porto: 9 Rte. de la Marine (phone: 95-26-10-55)
Porto Vecchio: 2 Rue Maréchal-Juin (phone: 95-70-09-58)
Propriano: 17 Rue du Général-de-Gaulle (phone: 95-76-01-49)
Sartène: Cours Saranelli (phone: 95-77-15-40)

Numerous free guides are available in English from the local tourist offices. An excellent one is *Guide to Corsica,* an illustrated index of hotels, restaurants, camping sites, and bungalows and apartments to rent. Supplement this with the *Guide to Hotels,* published by the Corsican Tourist Office, which lists hotels by region, including prices and amenities. For information before visiting, write the *C.R.T. de Corse* (22 Cours Grandval, BP 19 Ajaccio-Cedex 20-176; phone: 95-51-00-22). The best map of Corsica is the Michelin yellow map No. 90, available at any newsstand.

Telephone – The area code for Corsica is 95, which is incorporated into all local 8-digits numbers. When calling a number in Corsica from the Paris region (including Ile-de-France), dial 16, then the 8-digit number. When calling a number from outside Paris, dial only the 8-digit number. When calling from the US, dial 33 (which is the country code), followed by the 8-digit number.

 FOOD AND WINE: While Corsican cuisine can't compete with the gastronomic wonders of a city like Paris, there are still some delicious specialties. The good *charcuterie* here includes *prisuttu,* smoked raw ham, and *figatellus,*

smoked liver sausage. *Brocciu* is a soft cheese used in all sorts of dishes; often it's served with *fiandonu,* pastries made of chestnut flour. Main dishes include *aziminu,* Corsica's version of the Provençal fish stew bouillabaisse, and lamb kebabs in which the meat is skewered on myrtle twigs and barbecued over an aromatic wood fire. The island offers a wide variety of game in season and fresh fish year-round.

Corsican wines are greatly underestimated by the French. The best come from the vineyards of Patrimonio and Sartenais — robust reds and dry, aromatic whites and rosés.

 GETTING AROUND: *Air France* offers daily flights to Ajaccio and Bastia from Paris, Nice, and Marseilles, and there are weekly flights from Amsterdam and Brussels. *Air France*'s domestic carrier, *Air Inter,* also flies from Paris, Nice, and Marseilles to Ajaccio, Bastia, and Calvi. From May through October, *Air Alpes* flies from Nice and Hyères to Ajaccio, Bastia, Propriano, and Figari.

Once you're here, car is by far the most practical way to explore the island. But be extra careful; though roads generally are well paved, they're also tortuous. Allow plenty of time to reach your destination — 100 miles (160 km) through the mountains is a hard day's drive. Since some villages have neither garage nor gas station, it's not a bad idea to carry a spare steel container (safer than plastic) of gas in the trunk.

Car Rental – Ajaccio: *Avis* (4 Av. de Paris; phone: 95-21-01-86) and at the airport (phone: 95-23-25-14); *Europcar* (16 Cours Grandval; phone: 95-21-05-49) and airport (phone: 95-23-18-73); *Hertz* (8 Cours Grandval; phone: 95-21-70-94) and airport (phone: 95-23-24-17); and *Inter-Rent* (5 Montée St.-Jean; phone: 95-22-61-79) and airport (phone: 95-23-19-42). Bastia: *Avis* (9 Av. M. Sebastiani; phone: 95-32-57-30) and airport (phone: 95-36-03-56); *Europcar* (1 Rue du Nouveau Port; phone: 95-31-59-29) and airport (phone: 95-36-03-55); *Hertz* (Sq. St.-Victor; phone: 95-31-14-84) and airport (phone: 95-36-02-46); and *Inter-Rent* (2 Rue Notre Dame de Lourdes; phone: 95-31-03-11). Calvi: *Avis* (6 Av. de la République; phone: 95-65-06-74); *Europcar* (Av. de la République; phone: 95-65-10-35) and airport (phone: 95-65-10-19); *Hertz* (2 Rue Mal-Joffre; phone: 95-65-06-64) and airport (phone: 95-65-02-98); and *Inter-Rent* (Pl. Christophe-Colomb; phone: 95-65-02-13).

Train – A scenic railway links Ajaccio, Corte, Bastia, Ile-Rousse, and Calvi, a distance of 145 miles (233 km). And a special tramway-train service runs 30 shuttles a day between the ports of Calvi and Ile-Rousse — a good way to visit the many beaches along this part of the coast. Ajaccio station (Pl. de la Gare; phone: 95-23-11-03 or 95-21-03-09); Bastia station (Av. Mal-Sebastiani; phone: 95-32-60-06 or 95-31-20-09); Calvi station (Av. de la Gare; phone: 95-65-00-61); Corte station (Pl. de la Gare; phone: 95-46-00-97). For general train information on Corsica, call 95-23-11-03.

Bus – There is regular and inexpensive bus service to most villages, generally once a day. Numerous bus tours of the island, ranging from ½ day to 7 days, are organized by the *Service d'Autocars de la SNCF* (phone: 95-21-14-08) and by local firms in Ajaccio, Bastia, Ile-Rousse, and Calvi. Contact the Gare Routière (phone: 95-21-28-04) or the local tourist office for details.

Ferry – *SNCM* (*Société Nationale Corse Maritime*) serves the following ports: *Ajaccio:* Quai l'Herminier (phone: 95-21-90-70); *Bastia:* Nouveau Port, BP 40 (phone: 95-313663); *Calvi:* Quai Landry (phone: 95-65-01-38); *Ile-Rousse:* Av. J.-Calizi (phone: 95-60-09-56); *Propriano:* Quai Commandant-l'Herminier (phone: 95-76-04-36). You also can make a ferry connection from Marseilles (61 Bd. des Dames; phone: 91-56-32-00), Nice (3 Av. Gustave-V; and Gare Maritime, Quai du Commerce; phone: 93-89-89-89), and Toulon (21 and 49 Av. de l'Infantène-de-Marine; phone: 94-41-25-76 and 94-41-01-76). The crossing takes from 5 to 12 hours, depending on the route you choose.

Tours – In addition to bus tours of the island organized by the *Service d'Autocars* *de la SNCF* (phone: 95-21-14-08), the following agencies offer tours: *SAIB Bus Tours* (2 Rue Maréchal Ornano, Ajaccio; phone: 95-21-53-74); *Autocars Bastiais* (40 Bd. Paoli, Basita; phone: 95-31-01-79); *Autocars Balesi* (Rte. De Bastia, Porto Vecchio; phone: 95-70-15-55); and *Corsc Voyage Autocars Mariani* (Quai Landry, Calvi; phone: 95-46-00-35). Daily boat excursions run from Ajaccio, Bonifacio, Calvi, Ile-Rousse, Porto, and Propriano, ranging from 1-hour to day trips. One of the most popular is a 3-hour cruise from Ajaccio to the Iles-Sanguinaires (literally "the bloody islands," so named because at sunset they're suffused with the blood red glow of the sun). The cruise leaves from Ajaccio Harbor (phone: 95-21-41-31 or 95-21-06-95).

 SPECIAL EVENTS: One of the best-known religious ceremonies on Corsica is the *Catenacciu* procession, held on *Good Friday.* Penitents dressed in red hoods and shackled with heavy chains bear a large wooden cross through the cobbled streets of Sartène. A more festive occasion, blending religion and folklore, is the *Santa di u Niulu,* held on September 8 in Casamaccioli to celebrate the birth of the Virgin. After a procession, in which a painted, wooden statue of the Virgin is carried through the street, the celebrants — largely mountain folk and shepherds — recite poetry and improvise songs.

Perhaps the biggest cultural event on the island is the *Milleli,* a festival of music, theater, and poetry held during July and August in Ajaccio. For more information, contact the local tourist office.

 SPORTS: Boating – Sailors insist that the best way to see Corsica is from the sea. Certainly, some of the most beautiful parts of the coast as well as certain beaches are accessible only by boat. The following are some of the places where you can rent vessels ranging from sailboats to windsurfers: *Balagne Sport,* Ile-Rousse (phone: 95-60-05-17); *Cap Corse Voile,* Macinaggio, on the northeast of Cap Corse (phone: 95-35-41-47); *Europe Yachting,* Ajaccio (phone: 95-21-00-57), Porto-Vecchio (phone: 95-70-18-69); *Scim Corse,* Bonifacio (phone: 95-73-03-13).

To find out about the island's many sailing schools and clubs, contact *Ligue Corse de Voile* (Corsican Sailing League), Villa Suspirata, Bastelicaccia CP, Ajaccio 20000 (phone: 95-21-90-33).

Fishing – The waters of Corsica teem with some 200 species of fish. Trout can be caught in the fast-running mountain streams. Some rivers and parts of the coast are restricted, however. For more fishing information, contact *Fédération Départementale de Pêche et de Pisciculture* (7 Bd. Paoli, Bastia; phone: 95-31-47-31). If you find yourself in a port town and speak some French, you probably can find a fisherman who will be a guide by inquiring in the port cafés.

Hiking, Climbing, and Skiing – Corsica is a hiker's dream. The Regional National Park (phone: 95-21-56-54) is a fine place to start, and is accessible to pedestrians via GR20. In the park and its environs, you can explore the Col de Vergio (Vergio Pass), Gorges de Resontica (Resontica Gorges), Forêt de Bavella (Bavella Forest), and Scala di Santa Regina (St. Regina's "Staircase"). On the west coast, good hiking can be found around the gulfs of Girolata and Valinco and along the stunning Calanques of Piana, natural rock formations that resemble immense Henry Moore sculptures.

If you're serious about mountaineering or cross-country skiing, the island has 50 peaks above 6,500 feet, snow-covered from November through May. For information, contact the *Comité Corse de Ski* (1 Bd. Auguste Gandin, Bastia 20200). Local clubs for climbing and cross-country skiing include the ones in Ajaccio (phone: 95-22-09-86) and Bastia (phone: 95-31-17-32). The main resorts for downhill skiing are at Asco (phone: 95-31-02-04), Ghisoni (phone: 95-57-61-28, 95-56-02-72, or 95-56-12-12), and Col de Vergio (phone: 95-48-00-01). For cross-country skiing, the main resorts are at Val d'Ese (phone: 95-28-71-73) and the region of Coscione (Quenza, phone: 95-78-60-97 or 95-78-62-85); Zicavo, phone: 95-24-40-05 or 95-24-42-13).

Scuba Diving – The average sea temperature ranges from 55F in March to 74F in August, and the clear water abounds with grouper, multicolored rockfish, and red coral. Two diving schools on the island are the *Harpoon Club* at Ajaccio (phone: 95-22-23-78, 95-22-04-83, or 95-21-64-80) and the *Neptune Club* at Bastia (phone: 95-31-69-02). There also are a number of diving clubs in most of the main port cities. For more information contact *Centre d'Etudes Sous-Marines* (28 Rue du Four, Paris 75006; phone: 42-22-52-66), *La Fédération Française d'Etude et des Sports Sous-Marins* (50 Ter. Av. Général-Graziani, Bastia; phone: 95-31-03-32), or the *Comité Corse de Plonger* (phone: 95-20-26-79).

Swimming – The island has countless beaches and the choice is yours. The east coast offers long stretches of golden sand. On the west there's more variety: large bays and small creeks; beaches that are half rock, half sand; and some spots where you can be alone even at the height of the season.

AJACCIO-BONIFACIO-CALVI

The route outlined below begins on the western coast in Ajaccio, then dips south through coastal resorts and mountains to Bonifacio, at the island's southern tip. From there it runs along the eastern coast, with its miles and miles of beaches, then travels inland to the ancient capital, Corte. After a swing west to the port of Calvi, the route ends back in Ajaccio — a distance of some 340 miles (547 km). Allow yourself at least 3 or 4 days to make the trip.

Prices on Corsica generally are lower than those on the mainland of France. Expect to pay $75 to $90 for a double room in hotels listed as expensive; $50 to $70 in those listed as moderate; and under $50 in the inexpensive ones. Booking ahead isn't essential, even during the height of vacation season. A meal for two in an expensive restaurant costs $80 and up; $45 to $80 in a moderate establishment; and less than $45 at one that's inexpensive. These prices include tax, service charge, and in some cases, wine. Fresh seafood, which usually is delicious on Corsica, is by far the best bargain when dining out.

AJACCIO: Founded in the 15th century by the Genoese, Ajaccio is the capital of Corsica's southern district (Corse du Sud); it and Bastia are the island's two largest cities. Ajaccio perhaps is best known as the birthplace of Napoleon Bonaparte. The 3-story Maison Bonaparte, where Napoleon entered the world on August 15, 1769, can be seen in a guided tour starting from the Hôtel de Ville (Town Hall; Pl. Maréchal-Foch; phone: 95-21-40-87). A gold mine of Napoleona, the tour encompasses the 16th-century baroque cathedral where Napoleon was baptized; the Chapelle Impériale, which served as a mausoleum for members of the Bonaparte family; and the *Musée Fesch,* housing some of France's best Italian primitive and Renaissance paintings found outside the *Louvre,* and bequeathed to the town by Cardinal Fesch, Napoleon's uncle. The tour also takes you through the picturesque alleys of Ajaccio's old town, near the fishing port with its splendid bay. If you prefer to just take it easy, there's a pleasant beach along Boulevard Lantivy.

CHECKING IN: *Cala di Sole* – On the beach, with a superb view of the Gulf of Ajaccio, this small, 30-room, air conditioned luxury hotel is 4 miles (6 km) out of town on D111. There is a pool, water sports, and tennis. Closed October to April. Rte. de Sanguinaires, Ajaccio (phone: 95-52-01-36). Expensive.

Campo dell'Oro – A comfortable, modern hostelry in a garden setting, 2 minutes from the airport and the beach. Ajaccio (phone: 95-22-32-41). Expensive.

Eden Roc – Sleek, modern elegance and comfort characterize this resort hotel with 45 balconied rooms and suites, all overlooking the sea. A state-of-the-art saltwater spa facility, a sheltered beach, tennis courts, and a restaurant and piano bar with a panoramic view make this garden paradise complete. Rte. des Iles-Sanguinaires, Ajaccio (phone: 95-52-01-47). Expensive.

Sofitel – Another modern luxury hotel, this one has 100 rooms, a heated pool, fine sandy beaches, and a very good restaurant serving French and Corsican fare. A few miles south of town on the D55, close to the Thalassa baths and spa. Porticcio (phone: 95-25-00-33). Expensive.

Albion – Quiet and relaxed, with air conditioned rooms. In the residential area. 15 Av. Général-Leclerc, Ajaccio (phone: 95-21-66-70). Moderate.

Fesch – This traditional hotel is in the heart of the Old Town. 7 Rue Fesch, Ajaccio (phone: 95-21-50-52). Moderate.

 EATING OUT: *Le Bec Fin* – A very good fish restaurant by the harbor. Closed October to April. 3 bis Bd. Roi-Jérôme, Ajaccio (phone: 95-21-30-52). Expensive.

Côte d'Azur – Traditional French cuisine. Closed Sundays and from June 21 through July 20. 12 Cours Napoléon, Ajaccio (phone: 95-21-50-24). Moderate.

En Route from Ajaccio – Route N196 heads east before dipping south, through the ubiquitous mountains and charming villages like Petreto-Bicchisano and Olmeto. The road is winding, and at nearly every turn there are views of deep, forested gorges. For a more panoramic view, stop at the Col de Celaccia, a mountain pass 38 miles (61 km) from Ajaccio. From there you can take D57 6 miles (10 km) to the archaeological site of Filitosa (phone: 95-74-00-91), where recently unearthed stone monoliths carved with human faces stare out to sea. Back on the main road, it's a short drive to Propriano, a family resort with fine sand beaches. If you're inclined to stay overnight, the best hotel in town is the *Miramar,* with rooms facing the sea and a pool (phone: 95-76-06-13).

Leaving Propriano, stay on N196 inland to Sartène. The writer Prosper Mérimée, who was a government official in Corsica in the 1860s, called Sartène "the most Corsican of Corsican towns." He considered it severe and somber; perhaps he also was thinking of the town's 19th-century history of bloody vendettas among the feudal barons who controlled it. Today, however, Sartène is neither severe nor embattled; in fact, it would be difficult to find a more peaceful city. The oldest part of town is especially picturesque, with its narrow steps and alleyways, and the surrounding region is rich in prehistoric finds. While you're here, sample the regional specialties at *La Chaumière* (39 Rue Capitaine-Benedetti; phone: 95-77-07-13).

As you drive from Roccapina to Bonifacio, the terrain becomes flatter and more rugged, with rocky creeks and sandy beaches off to the right, private enough for nude swimming and sunbathing.

BONIFACIO: Set on a peninsula of sheer limestone cliffs overlooking the port, this town at the southern tip of Corsica boasts one of the most dramatic sites in the Mediterranean. Bonafacio, founded as a fortress, is actually a town of two levels. Atop the cliffs, rising more than 200 feet above the sea, are the houses and churches of the *haute ville,* or upper town, as well as the citadel, the ancient fortress that is now garrisoned by the French Foreign Legion. The Marine (port) below can be reached from the *haute ville* by descending the Aragonese Steps, a long stairway carved from the rocky cliffs; most of Bonifacio's hotels, restaurants, and other tourist facilities are on this level.

The cliffs are full of caves and grottoes, and boat excursions can be arranged through a boat owners' association (phone: 95-73-05-43 or 95-73-03-76). The same group offers excursions to the nearby islands of Cavallo and Lavezzi, with their excellent beaches. *Tirrenia* (phone: 95-73-00-96) runs boats to the island of Sardinia, 8 miles away, another good spot for a day trip.

If you turn right on D58 out of Bonifacio, you'll soon reach the Sémaphore Phare de Pertusato, a lighthouse that provides a sweeping coastal view.

 CHECKING IN: *Nautique* – A charming hotel, with deluxe studio apartments. Open year-round. Reservations necessary. On the port, Bonifacio (phone: 95-73-02-11). Moderate.

 EATING OUT: *L'Albatros* – Excellent fish is served at this portside restaurant. Open year-round. Quai du Port, Bonifacio (phone: 95-73-01-97). Moderate.

En Route from Bonifacio – Driving north, the road (N198) becomes straighter. Take it 17 miles (27 km) to Porto-Vecchio, a popular resort with great beaches along the gulf. In summer, the water is crammed with sailboats and other pleasure craft.

Continue north until you reach the town of Ghisonaccia. Perhaps you'll want to stop for lunch and a swim at the *Taverne des Naufrageurs* (phone: 95-73-21-32) on the beach to your right, just before the town of Tarco, or for pizza at *Veniqui,* a restaurant in Favone, 1½ miles (2 km) farther on N198. From Ghisonaccia, head inland 4 miles (6 km) on D344, approaching the gorges of Inzecca and Strette, and their striking overhangs of rock. At nearby Ghisoni, pick up D69, which winds through some glorious mountain scenery to join the main Ajaccio-Bastia road (N193). Turn right to reach Corte, 12 miles (19 km) north.

 CHECKING IN/EATING OUT: *Grand Hôtel de Cala Rossa* – In a pine wood on a beach, this luxury establishment is 6 miles (10 km) north of Porto-Vecchio. Open from mid-May through October. On D468 via D568 and N198, Porto-Vecchio (phone: 95-71-61-51). Expensive.

Ziglione – An attractive hotel with rooms overlooking a garden and the beach, and a good restaurant. Closed from October through May 15. 3 miles (5 km) east of Porto-Vecchio on Rte. de Picovaggia (phone: 95-70-09-83). Moderate.

CORTE: The stillness of this hilltop town in the heart of the central mountains belies its somewhat rocky history. Occupied intermittently since ancient times, Corte became the capital of Corsica during the island's 18th-century War of Independence, fought against the ruling Genoese. No longer the capital, it's now quiet and slumberous, with little to do save excellent hiking in the gorges and forests of Tavignano and Restonica, just southwest of the city on D623.

 CHECKING IN: *Paix* – A pleasantly located place, on a tree-lined square. Open from *Easter* through October. Pl. du Général-de-Gaulle, Corte (phone: 95-46-06-72). Moderate to inexpensive.

Poste – The proprietors are friendly and the rooms large. Closed during December. 2 Pl. Padove, Corte (phone: 95-46-01-37). Inexpensive.

 EATING OUT: *Pascal Paoli* – Named for the great 18th-century Corsican leader who established Corte as the capital, this is a relaxed, friendly place on the main square. Weather permitting (almost always), you can sit at a sidewalk table and watch the world pass slowly by. Open from *Easter* through October 15. Pl. Paoli, Corte (phone: 95-46-13-48). Inexpensive.

En Route from Corte – Follow N193 north for 15 miles (24 km) to Ponte Leccia, where you pick up N197 headed northwest. As you get closer to the sea, the mountains become more rounded and wooded. At Lozari, head south on the coastal road, N197, for 16 miles (26 km) — through Ile-Rousse, a yachting port with good beaches — to Calvi.

CALVI: Corsica's chic-est and most popular resort, Calvi is also a fortress town with a military history that goes back centuries. Occupied through the Roman era and the Middle Ages, it was settled in the 15th century by the Genoese, who built the town's

Citadel on an immense rock towering above the sea. During the Napoleonic wars, Calvi was taken by the British after 2 months of incessant combat in which Admiral Nelson lost his eye.

At the Citadel you can see the ruins of the house where Christopher Columbus was born in 1441. Also worth a visit is the *Oratoire St.-Antoine,* within the walls of the fortified part of town. Built in the 15th century, it's now a museum of ancient and medieval religious art.

History aside, Calvi boasts some enticing long, white beaches. You also can take a boat trip on the *Colombo* line (phone: 95-65-03-40 or 95-65-15-52) to Grotte des Veaux Marins, the well-known caves on nearby Peninsula de la Revelata (phone: 95-65-28-16 or 95-65-29-65). South of Calvi lies some of the island's most magnificent coastline, best appreciated when viewed from the sea, so the boat ride is a treat in itself.

 CHECKING IN: *Caravelle* – A pleasant beach hotel. Open from May through September. On N197, just north of Calvi (phone: 95-65-01-21). Moderate.

Clos des Amandiers – A charming place with guest bungalows in a garden setting and a pool and tennis facilities. Closed from November through April. A mile (1.6 km) south of Calvi on Rte. Pietra-Major, via N197 (phone: 95-65-08-32). Moderate.

 EATING OUT: *Comme Chez Soi* – On the lively waterfront strip, this place serves delicious fish. Closed February. Quai Landry, Calvi (phone: 95-65-00-59). Expensive.

Ile de Beauté – Also on the waterfront, this excellent spot specializes in lobster dishes; the oysters with lime are popular, too. Closed Wednesdays and October to May. Reservations necessary. Quai Landry, Calvi (phone: 95-65-00-46). Expensive.

En Route from Calvi – Heading south on D81, the road soon ascends to 400 feet above the sea, providing a final panoramic view of the Peninsula de la Revelata, its caves, and its lighthouse. Driving by the peninsula, on the left is the belvedere of Notre-Dame-de-la-Serra, a tiny chapel that's the site of Santa di u Niuli, Calvi's annual pilgrimage celebrating the birth of the Virgin.

The next 40-mile (64-km) stretch is, quite simply, breathtaking, even for an island where spectacular scenery is abundant. Driving along the rugged cliff road you see mountains and rocky headlands on your left, the sea on the right, visible from almost every bend. From atop the Col de Bassa, 850 feet high and 17 miles (27 km) from Calvi, you can see the long, isolated beach at Galeria; or climb the nearby Col de Palmarella for a look at the Gulf of Girolata.

Porto, 10 miles (16 km) on, is a small beach resort where you can take a boat excursion to Girolata or, to the south, visit the famous Calanques of Piana. These are red-brown rock formations, the texture of giant coral, molded by nature into phantasmagorical shapes, that plunge into bays of sparkling green and black water. From the road out of Porto, rising to 870 feet, the Calanques can be seen in all their glory. The village of Piana, 8 miles (13 km) from Porto, has a fine beach, Ficajola; it's a 2-mile (3-km) descent down D624 — well paved but with a wicked hairpin turn.

From Piana, D81 strikes inland to rejoin the coast at Cargèse, a small Greek Orthodox community north of the Gulf of Sagone, 70 miles (113 km) from Calvi. The road from Cargèse back to Ajaccio is 32 miles (54 km); for half the distance it hugs the Gulf coast before plunging you into the mountains.

 CHECKING IN: *Auberge de Ferayola* – Midway between Calvi and Porto; a quite comfortable hotel. The view from every room is splendid, the restaurant is good, and there's a beach a mile (1.6 km) away at Argentella. Closed October to June. D81, Ferayola (phone: 95-65-25-25). Expensive to moderate.

Capo Rosso – A luxury hotel overlooking the Calanques and the gulf. Sunning yourself by the pool, you feel as though you're part of this glorious landscape. A good restaurant serves fresh fish from the gulf. Closed from mid-October through March. Rte. des Calanches, Piana (phone: 95-27-82-40). Expensive to moderate.

Dolce Vita – Also between Calvi and Porto, this is a fine hostelry on a hilltop, 2 miles (3 km) from a good sand beach. Open from April through October. Col de la Croix, Osani (phone: 95-27-31-86). Moderate.

Hélios – Comfortable and modern and right by the beach. Closed from November through March. Just outside Cargèse on D81 (phone: 95-26-41-24). Inexpensive.

Marina – A modern hotel with a pool, a sun deck, and a fine view of the sea and mountains. Open from May through September. Porto-Marine, Porto (phone: 95-26-10-34). Inexpensive.

 EATING OUT: ***V Campinale*** – Crayfish and other specialties from the gulf are served on a terrace overlooking the village square. Open from April through September. Pl. de l'Eglise, Piana (phone: 95-27-81-71). Moderate to inexpensive.

CAP CORSE

A much shorter alternate route covers the Cap Corse, a narrow peninsula on the northeast that offers some of the island's most beautiful coastal and mountain scenery. It's an 80-mile (129-km) round trip from Bastia, on the eastern heel of the cape.

A Genoese fortress from the 15th to the 18th century, Bastia today is the capital of Corsica's northern district (Haute-Corse) and the island's industrial center. In Terra-Vecchia, the 17th-century neighborhood north of the old port, is Bastia's landmark, the 17th-century Eglise St.-Jean-Baptiste, with its simple, pretty façade. From here you can climb from the Quai du Sud up to Terra-Nova, the Genoese citadel in Bastia's Vieux Port. Just inside the citadel's main gate is the *Musée d'Ethnographie Corse.* It's an excellent introduction to Corsica, with artifacts spanning the island's history from prehistoric to medieval times. Several exhibitions portray Corsican customs, handicrafts, and folklore as well as 19th-century photographs and collections of Napoleona. More artifacts, including the emperor's death mask, are displayed on the second floor.

Drive inland on D81, a mountain road that twists and curls its way across the base of the peninsula. At the midpoint is the Col de Teghime, the site of a major battle during Corsica's liberation in World War II. Eventually you will reach the port of St.-Florent, now a beach resort. Just to the east, and worth a look, is a 13th-century Pisan cathedral, practically all that remains of the medieval city of Nebbio. Some very good fish restaurants can be found in the port's Old Town, among them *Gaffe* (phone: 95-37-00-12; closed Mondays and from November to mid-December). In St.-Florent, you can take a motorboat across the gulf to explore the solitary beaches of the Agriates Desert and the salt lakes of Mortella.

Heading north, D81 swings inland to the vineyards of Patrimonio and then back to the coast. Twelve miles (19 km) from St.-Florent is the village of Nonza, with its sand beach and medieval fortress on a cliff. At the northwest corner of the cape is tiny Centuri-Port, where you can get decent food and lodging. From Centuri take D80 across the cape to the marina at Macinaggio. Driving the eastern length of the cape back to Bastia, the beaches aren't as attractive as those on the west, but the sight of the sea will sustain you.

 CHECKING IN: ***Pietracap*** – A modern hotel set in a park of olive trees; its heated pool offers a view of the sea. Closed December through February. Rte. de San Martino, 2 miles (3 km) north of Bastia on the coast at Pietranera (phone: 95-31-64-63). Expensive to moderate.

Thalassa – This small, quiet, 30-room hotel on the beach has an excellent restaurant serving regional specialties. Closed December through February. Rte. du Cap, Pietranera (phone: 95-31-56-63). Moderate.

 EATING OUT: *Le Bistrot du Port* – Small and friendly, this restaurant is in an alley off the quai. Try the gratin of mussels with spinach. Closed Sundays and October. Right off the Quai Martyrs de la Libération, Bastia (phone: 95-32-19-83). Expensive to moderate.

Le Vieux Moulin – A dining spot where you also can spend the night. Closed from November to February. On the port, Centuri-Port (phone: 95-35-60-15). Moderate.

INDEX

Index